T0140450

Lecture Notes in Computer Science 13663

More information about this series at https://link.springer.com/bookseries/558

Shai Avidan · Gabriel Brostow ·
Moustapha Cissé · Giovanni Maria Farinella ·
Tal Hassner (Eds.)

Computer Vision – ECCV 2022

17th European Conference
Tel Aviv, Israel, October 23–27, 2022
Proceedings, Part III

 Springer

Editors
Shai Avidan
Tel Aviv University
Tel Aviv, Israel

Gabriel Brostow ⓘ
University College London
London, UK

Moustapha Cissé
Google AI
Accra, Ghana

Giovanni Maria Farinella ⓘ
University of Catania
Catania, Italy

Tal Hassner ⓘ
Facebook (United States)
Menlo Park, CA, USA

ISSN 0302-9743   ISSN 1611-3349 (electronic)
Lecture Notes in Computer Science
ISBN 978-3-031-20061-8   ISBN 978-3-031-20062-5 (eBook)
https://doi.org/10.1007/978-3-031-20062-5

This Springer imprint is published by the registered company Springer Nature Switzerland AG
The registered company address is: Gewerbestrasse 11, 6330 Cham, Switzerland

Foreword

Organizing the European Conference on Computer Vision (ECCV 2022) in Tel-Aviv during a global pandemic was no easy feat. The uncertainty level was extremely high, and decisions had to be postponed to the last minute. Still, we managed to plan things just in time for ECCV 2022 to be held in person. Participation in physical events is crucial to stimulating collaborations and nurturing the culture of the Computer Vision community.

There were many people who worked hard to ensure attendees enjoyed the best science at the 16th edition of ECCV. We are grateful to the Program Chairs Gabriel Brostow and Tal Hassner, who went above and beyond to ensure the ECCV reviewing process ran smoothly. The scientific program includes dozens of workshops and tutorials in addition to the main conference and we would like to thank Leonid Karlinsky and Tomer Michaeli for their hard work. Finally, special thanks to the web chairs Lorenzo Baraldi and Kosta Derpanis, who put in extra hours to transfer information fast and efficiently to the ECCV community.

We would like to express gratitude to our generous sponsors and the Industry Chairs, Dimosthenis Karatzas and Chen Sagiv, who oversaw industry relations and proposed new ways for academia-industry collaboration and technology transfer. It's great to see so much industrial interest in what we're doing!

Authors' draft versions of the papers appeared online with open access on both the Computer Vision Foundation (CVF) and the European Computer Vision Association (ECVA) websites as with previous ECCVs. Springer, the publisher of the proceedings, has arranged for archival publication. The final version of the papers is hosted by SpringerLink, with active references and supplementary materials. It benefits all potential readers that we offer both a free and citeable version for all researchers, as well as an authoritative, citeable version for SpringerLink readers. Our thanks go to Ronan Nugent from Springer, who helped us negotiate this agreement. Last but not least, we wish to thank Eric Mortensen, our publication chair, whose expertise made the process smooth.

October 2022

Rita Cucchiara
Jiří Matas
Amnon Shashua
Lihi Zelnik-Manor

Preface

Welcome to the proceedings of the European Conference on Computer Vision (ECCV 2022). This was a hybrid edition of ECCV as we made our way out of the COVID-19 pandemic. The conference received 5804 valid paper submissions, compared to 5150 submissions to ECCV 2020 (a 12.7% increase) and 2439 in ECCV 2018. 1645 submissions were accepted for publication (28%) and, of those, 157 (2.7% overall) as orals.

846 of the submissions were desk-rejected for various reasons. Many of them because they revealed author identity, thus violating the double-blind policy. This violation came in many forms: some had author names with the title, others added acknowledgments to specific grants, yet others had links to their github account where their name was visible. Tampering with the LaTeX template was another reason for automatic desk rejection.

ECCV 2022 used the traditional CMT system to manage the entire double-blind reviewing process. Authors did not know the names of the reviewers and vice versa. Each paper received at least 3 reviews (except 6 papers that received only 2 reviews), totalling more than 15,000 reviews.

Handling the review process at this scale was a significant challenge. To ensure that each submission received as fair and high-quality reviews as possible, we recruited more than 4719 reviewers (in the end, 4719 reviewers did at least one review). Similarly we recruited more than 276 area chairs (eventually, only 276 area chairs handled a batch of papers). The area chairs were selected based on their technical expertise and reputation, largely among people who served as area chairs in previous top computer vision and machine learning conferences (ECCV, ICCV, CVPR, NeurIPS, etc.).

Reviewers were similarly invited from previous conferences, and also from the pool of authors. We also encouraged experienced area chairs to suggest additional chairs and reviewers in the initial phase of recruiting. The median reviewer load was five papers per reviewer, while the average load was about four papers, because of the emergency reviewers. The area chair load was 35 papers, on average.

Conflicts of interest between authors, area chairs, and reviewers were handled largely automatically by the CMT platform, with some manual help from the Program Chairs. Reviewers were allowed to describe themselves as senior reviewer (load of 8 papers to review) or junior reviewers (load of 4 papers). Papers were matched to area chairs based on a subject-area affinity score computed in CMT and an affinity score computed by the Toronto Paper Matching System (TPMS). TPMS is based on the paper's full text. An area chair handling each submission would bid for preferred expert reviewers, and we balanced load and prevented conflicts.

The assignment of submissions to area chairs was relatively smooth, as was the assignment of submissions to reviewers. A small percentage of reviewers were not happy with their assignments in terms of subjects and self-reported expertise. This is an area for improvement, although it's interesting that many of these cases were reviewers hand-picked by AC's. We made a later round of reviewer recruiting, targeted at the list of authors of papers submitted to the conference, and had an excellent response which helped provide enough emergency reviewers. In the end, all but six papers received at least 3 reviews.

The challenges of the reviewing process are in line with past experiences at ECCV 2020. As the community grows, and the number of submissions increases, it becomes ever more challenging to recruit enough reviewers and ensure a high enough quality of reviews. Enlisting authors by default as reviewers might be one step to address this challenge.

Authors were given a week to rebut the initial reviews, and address reviewers' concerns. Each rebuttal was limited to a single pdf page with a fixed template.

The Area Chairs then led discussions with the reviewers on the merits of each submission. The goal was to reach consensus, but, ultimately, it was up to the Area Chair to make a decision. The decision was then discussed with a buddy Area Chair to make sure decisions were fair and informative. The entire process was conducted virtually with no in-person meetings taking place.

The Program Chairs were informed in cases where the Area Chairs overturned a decisive consensus reached by the reviewers, and pushed for the meta-reviews to contain details that explained the reasoning for such decisions. Obviously these were the most contentious cases, where reviewer inexperience was the most common reported factor.

Once the list of accepted papers was finalized and released, we went through the laborious process of plagiarism (including self-plagiarism) detection. A total of 4 accepted papers were rejected because of that.

Finally, we would like to thank our Technical Program Chair, Pavel Lifshits, who did tremendous work behind the scenes, and we thank the tireless CMT team.

October 2022

Gabriel Brostow
Giovanni Maria Farinella
Moustapha Cissé
Shai Avidan
Tal Hassner

Organization

General Chairs

Rita Cucchiara	University of Modena and Reggio Emilia, Italy
Jiří Matas	Czech Technical University in Prague, Czech Republic
Amnon Shashua	Hebrew University of Jerusalem, Israel
Lihi Zelnik-Manor	Technion – Israel Institute of Technology, Israel

Program Chairs

Shai Avidan	Tel-Aviv University, Israel
Gabriel Brostow	University College London, UK
Moustapha Cissé	Google AI, Ghana
Giovanni Maria Farinella	University of Catania, Italy
Tal Hassner	Facebook AI, USA

Program Technical Chair

Pavel Lifshits	Technion – Israel Institute of Technology, Israel

Workshops Chairs

Leonid Karlinsky	IBM Research, Israel
Tomer Michaeli	Technion – Israel Institute of Technology, Israel
Ko Nishino	Kyoto University, Japan

Tutorial Chairs

Thomas Pock	Graz University of Technology, Austria
Natalia Neverova	Facebook AI Research, UK

Demo Chair

Bohyung Han	Seoul National University, Korea

Social and Student Activities Chairs

Tatiana Tommasi   Italian Institute of Technology, Italy
Sagie Benaim   University of Copenhagen, Denmark

Diversity and Inclusion Chairs

Xi Yin   Facebook AI Research, USA
Bryan Russell   Adobe, USA

Communications Chairs

Lorenzo Baraldi   University of Modena and Reggio Emilia, Italy
Kosta Derpanis   York University & Samsung AI Centre Toronto, Canada

Industrial Liaison Chairs

Dimosthenis Karatzas   Universitat Autònoma de Barcelona, Spain
Chen Sagiv   SagivTech, Israel

Finance Chair

Gerard Medioni   University of Southern California & Amazon, USA

Publication Chair

Eric Mortensen   MiCROTEC, USA

Area Chairs

Lourdes Agapito   University College London, UK
Zeynep Akata   University of Tübingen, Germany
Naveed Akhtar   University of Western Australia, Australia
Karteek Alahari   Inria Grenoble Rhône-Alpes, France
Alexandre Alahi   École polytechnique fédérale de Lausanne, Switzerland
Pablo Arbelaez   Universidad de Los Andes, Columbia
Antonis A. Argyros   University of Crete & Foundation for Research and Technology-Hellas, Crete
Yuki M. Asano   University of Amsterdam, The Netherlands
Kalle Åström   Lund University, Sweden
Hadar Averbuch-Elor   Cornell University, USA

Matthijs Douze	Facebook AI Research, USA
Mohamed Elhoseiny	King Abdullah University of Science and Technology, Saudi Arabia
Sergio Escalera	University of Barcelona, Spain
Yi Fang	New York University, USA
Ryan Farrell	Brigham Young University, USA
Alireza Fathi	Google, USA
Christoph Feichtenhofer	Facebook AI Research, USA
Basura Fernando	Agency for Science, Technology and Research (A*STAR), Singapore
Vittorio Ferrari	Google Research, Switzerland
Andrew W. Fitzgibbon	Graphcore, UK
David J. Fleet	University of Toronto, Canada
David Forsyth	University of Illinois at Urbana-Champaign, USA
David Fouhey	University of Michigan, USA
Katerina Fragkiadaki	Carnegie Mellon University, USA
Friedrich Fraundorfer	Graz University of Technology, Austria
Oren Freifeld	Ben-Gurion University, Israel
Thomas Funkhouser	Google Research & Princeton University, USA
Yasutaka Furukawa	Simon Fraser University, Canada
Fabio Galasso	Sapienza University of Rome, Italy
Jürgen Gall	University of Bonn, Germany
Chuang Gan	Massachusetts Institute of Technology, USA
Zhe Gan	Microsoft, USA
Animesh Garg	University of Toronto, Vector Institute, Nvidia, Canada
Efstratios Gavves	University of Amsterdam, The Netherlands
Peter Gehler	Amazon, Germany
Theo Gevers	University of Amsterdam, The Netherlands
Bernard Ghanem	King Abdullah University of Science and Technology, Saudi Arabia
Ross B. Girshick	Facebook AI Research, USA
Georgia Gkioxari	Facebook AI Research, USA
Albert Gordo	Facebook, USA
Stephen Gould	Australian National University, Australia
Venu Madhav Govindu	Indian Institute of Science, India
Kristen Grauman	Facebook AI Research & UT Austin, USA
Abhinav Gupta	Carnegie Mellon University & Facebook AI Research, USA
Mohit Gupta	University of Wisconsin-Madison, USA
Hu Han	Institute of Computing Technology, Chinese Academy of Sciences, China

Bohyung Han	Seoul National University, Korea
Tian Han	Stevens Institute of Technology, USA
Emily Hand	University of Nevada, Reno, USA
Bharath Hariharan	Cornell University, USA
Ran He	Institute of Automation, Chinese Academy of Sciences, China
Otmar Hilliges	ETH Zurich, Switzerland
Adrian Hilton	University of Surrey, UK
Minh Hoai	Stony Brook University, USA
Yedid Hoshen	Hebrew University of Jerusalem, Israel
Timothy Hospedales	University of Edinburgh, UK
Gang Hua	Wormpex AI Research, USA
Di Huang	Beihang University, China
Jing Huang	Facebook, USA
Jia-Bin Huang	Facebook, USA
Nathan Jacobs	Washington University in St. Louis, USA
C. V. Jawahar	International Institute of Information Technology, Hyderabad, India
Herve Jegou	Facebook AI Research, France
Neel Joshi	Microsoft Research, USA
Armand Joulin	Facebook AI Research, France
Frederic Jurie	University of Caen Normandie, France
Fredrik Kahl	Chalmers University of Technology, Sweden
Yannis Kalantidis	NAVER LABS Europe, France
Evangelos Kalogerakis	University of Massachusetts, Amherst, USA
Sing Bing Kang	Zillow Group, USA
Yosi Keller	Bar Ilan University, Israel
Margret Keuper	University of Mannheim, Germany
Tae-Kyun Kim	Imperial College London, UK
Benjamin Kimia	Brown University, USA
Alexander Kirillov	Facebook AI Research, USA
Kris Kitani	Carnegie Mellon University, USA
Iasonas Kokkinos	Snap Inc. & University College London, UK
Vladlen Koltun	Apple, USA
Nikos Komodakis	University of Crete, Crete
Piotr Koniusz	Australian National University, Australia
Philipp Kraehenbuehl	University of Texas at Austin, USA
Dilip Krishnan	Google, USA
Ajay Kumar	Hong Kong Polytechnic University, Hong Kong, China
Junseok Kwon	Chung-Ang University, Korea
Jean-Francois Lalonde	Université Laval, Canada

Ivan Laptev	Inria Paris, France
Laura Leal-Taixé	Technical University of Munich, Germany
Erik Learned-Miller	University of Massachusetts, Amherst, USA
Gim Hee Lee	National University of Singapore, Singapore
Seungyong Lee	Pohang University of Science and Technology, Korea
Zhen Lei	Institute of Automation, Chinese Academy of Sciences, China
Bastian Leibe	RWTH Aachen University, Germany
Hongdong Li	Australian National University, Australia
Fuxin Li	Oregon State University, USA
Bo Li	University of Illinois at Urbana-Champaign, USA
Yin Li	University of Wisconsin-Madison, USA
Ser-Nam Lim	Meta AI Research, USA
Joseph Lim	University of Southern California, USA
Stephen Lin	Microsoft Research Asia, China
Dahua Lin	The Chinese University of Hong Kong, Hong Kong, China
Si Liu	Beihang University, China
Xiaoming Liu	Michigan State University, USA
Ce Liu	Microsoft, USA
Zicheng Liu	Microsoft, USA
Yanxi Liu	Pennsylvania State University, USA
Feng Liu	Portland State University, USA
Yebin Liu	Tsinghua University, China
Chen Change Loy	Nanyang Technological University, Singapore
Huchuan Lu	Dalian University of Technology, China
Cewu Lu	Shanghai Jiao Tong University, China
Oisin Mac Aodha	University of Edinburgh, UK
Dhruv Mahajan	Facebook, USA
Subhransu Maji	University of Massachusetts, Amherst, USA
Atsuto Maki	KTH Royal Institute of Technology, Sweden
Arun Mallya	NVIDIA, USA
R. Manmatha	Amazon, USA
Iacopo Masi	Sapienza University of Rome, Italy
Dimitris N. Metaxas	Rutgers University, USA
Ajmal Mian	University of Western Australia, Australia
Christian Micheloni	University of Udine, Italy
Krystian Mikolajczyk	Imperial College London, UK
Anurag Mittal	Indian Institute of Technology, Madras, India
Philippos Mordohai	Stevens Institute of Technology, USA
Greg Mori	Simon Fraser University & Borealis AI, Canada

Mathieu Salzmann   École polytechnique fédérale de Lausanne,
                                     Switzerland
Dimitris Samaras   Stony Brook University, USA
Aswin Sankaranarayanan   Carnegie Mellon University, USA
Imari Sato   National Institute of Informatics, Japan
Yoichi Sato   University of Tokyo, Japan
Shin'ichi Satoh   National Institute of Informatics, Japan
Walter Scheirer   University of Notre Dame, USA
Bernt Schiele   Max Planck Institute for Informatics, Germany
Konrad Schindler   ETH Zurich, Switzerland
Cordelia Schmid   Inria & Google, France
Alexander Schwing   University of Illinois at Urbana-Champaign, USA
Nicu Sebe   University of Trento, Italy
Greg Shakhnarovich   Toyota Technological Institute at Chicago, USA
Eli Shechtman   Adobe Research, USA
Humphrey Shi   University of Oregon & University of Illinois at
                                     Urbana-Champaign & Picsart AI Research,
                                     USA
Jianbo Shi   University of Pennsylvania, USA
Roy Shilkrot   Massachusetts Institute of Technology, USA
Mike Zheng Shou   National University of Singapore, Singapore
Kaleem Siddiqi   McGill University, Canada
Richa Singh   Indian Institute of Technology Jodhpur, India
Greg Slabaugh   Queen Mary University of London, UK
Cees Snoek   University of Amsterdam, The Netherlands
Yale Song   Facebook AI Research, USA
Yi-Zhe Song   University of Surrey, UK
Bjorn Stenger   Rakuten Institute of Technology
Abby Stylianou   Saint Louis University, USA
Akihiro Sugimoto   National Institute of Informatics, Japan
Chen Sun   Brown University, USA
Deqing Sun   Google, USA
Kalyan Sunkavalli   Adobe Research, USA
Ying Tai   Tencent YouTu Lab, China
Ayellet Tal   Technion – Israel Institute of Technology, Israel
Ping Tan   Simon Fraser University, Canada
Siyu Tang   ETH Zurich, Switzerland
Chi-Keung Tang   Hong Kong University of Science and
                                     Technology, Hong Kong, China
Radu Timofte   University of Würzburg, Germany & ETH Zurich,
                                     Switzerland
Federico Tombari   Google, Switzerland & Technical University of
                                     Munich, Germany

Todd Zickler   Harvard University, USA
Wangmeng Zuo   Harbin Institute of Technology, China

Technical Program Committee

Davide Abati
Soroush Abbasi
  Koohpayegani
Amos L. Abbott
Rameen Abdal
Rabab Abdelfattah
Sahar Abdelnabi
Hassan Abu Alhaija
Abulikemu Abuduweili
Ron Abutbul
Hanno Ackermann
Aikaterini Adam
Kamil Adamczewski
Ehsan Adeli
Vida Adeli
Donald Adjeroh
Arman Afrasiyabi
Akshay Agarwal
Sameer Agarwal
Abhinav Agarwalla
Vaibhav Aggarwal
Sara Aghajanzadeh
Susmit Agrawal
Antonio Agudo
Touqeer Ahmad
Sk Miraj Ahmed
Chaitanya Ahuja
Nilesh A. Ahuja
Abhishek Aich
Shubhra Aich
Noam Aigerman
Arash Akbarinia
Peri Akiva
Derya Akkaynak
Emre Aksan
Arjun R. Akula
Yuval Alaluf
Stephan Alaniz
Paul Albert
Cenek Albl

Filippo Aleotti
Konstantinos P.
  Alexandridis
Motasem Alfarra
Mohsen Ali
Thiemo Alldieck
Hadi Alzayer
Liang An
Shan An
Yi An
Zhulin An
Dongsheng An
Jie An
Xiang An
Saket Anand
Cosmin Ancuti
Juan Andrade-Cetto
Alexander Andreopoulos
Bjoern Andres
Jerone T. A. Andrews
Shivangi Aneja
Anelia Angelova
Dragomir Anguelov
Rushil Anirudh
Oron Anschel
Rao Muhammad Anwer
Djamila Aouada
Evlampios Apostolidis
Srikar Appalaraju
Nikita Araslanov
Andre Araujo
Eric Arazo
Dawit Mureja Argaw
Anurag Arnab
Aditya Arora
Chetan Arora
Sunpreet S. Arora
Alexey Artemov
Muhammad Asad
Kumar Ashutosh

Sinem Aslan
Vishal Asnani
Mahmoud Assran
Amir Atapour-Abarghouei
Nikos Athanasiou
Ali Athar
ShahRukh Athar
Sara Atito
Souhaib Attaiki
Matan Atzmon
Mathieu Aubry
Nicolas Audebert
Tristan T.
  Aumentado-Armstrong
Melinos Averkiou
Yannis Avrithis
Stephane Ayache
Mehmet Aygün
Seyed Mehdi
  Ayyoubzadeh
Hossein Azizpour
George Azzopardi
Mallikarjun B. R.
Yunhao Ba
Abhishek Badki
Seung-Hwan Bae
Seung-Hwan Baek
Seungryul Baek
Piyush Nitin Bagad
Shai Bagon
Gaetan Bahl
Shikhar Bahl
Sherwin Bahmani
Haoran Bai
Lei Bai
Jiawang Bai
Haoyue Bai
Jinbin Bai
Xiang Bai
Xuyang Bai

Yang Bai
Yuanchao Bai
Ziqian Bai
Sungyong Baik
Kevin Bailly
Max Bain
Federico Baldassarre
Wele Gedara Chaminda
    Bandara
Biplab Banerjee
Pratyay Banerjee
Sandipan Banerjee
Jihwan Bang
Antyanta Bangunharcana
Aayush Bansal
Ankan Bansal
Siddhant Bansal
Wentao Bao
Zhipeng Bao
Amir Bar
Manel Baradad Jurjo
Lorenzo Baraldi
Danny Barash
Daniel Barath
Connelly Barnes
Ioan Andrei Bârsan
Steven Basart
Dina Bashkirova
Chaim Baskin
Peyman Bateni
Anil Batra
Sebastiano Battiato
Ardhendu Behera
Harkirat Behl
Jens Behley
Vasileios Belagiannis
Boulbaba Ben Amor
Emanuel Ben Baruch
Abdessamad Ben Hamza
Gil Ben-Artzi
Assia Benbihi
Fabian Benitez-Quiroz
Guy Ben-Yosef
Philipp Benz
Alexander W. Bergman

Urs Bergmann
Jesus Bermudez-Cameo
Stefano Berretti
Gedas Bertasius
Zachary Bessinger
Petra Bevandić
Matthew Beveridge
Lucas Beyer
Yash Bhalgat
Suvaansh Bhambri
Samarth Bharadwaj
Gaurav Bharaj
Aparna Bharati
Bharat Lal Bhatnagar
Uttaran Bhattacharya
Apratim Bhattacharyya
Brojeshwar Bhowmick
Ankan Kumar Bhunia
Ayan Kumar Bhunia
Qi Bi
Sai Bi
Michael Bi Mi
Gui-Bin Bian
Jia-Wang Bian
Shaojun Bian
Pia Bideau
Mario Bijelic
Hakan Bilen
Guillaume-Alexandre
    Bilodeau
Alexander Binder
Tolga Birdal
Vighnesh N. Birodkar
Sandika Biswas
Andreas Blattmann
Janusz Bobulski
Giuseppe Boccignone
Vishnu Boddeti
Navaneeth Bodla
Moritz Böhle
Aleksei Bokhovkin
Sam Bond-Taylor
Vivek Boominathan
Shubhankar Borse
Mark Boss

Andrea Bottino
Adnane Boukhayma
Fadi Boutros
Nicolas C. Boutry
Richard S. Bowen
Ivaylo Boyadzhiev
Aidan Boyd
Yuri Boykov
Aljaz Bozic
Behzad Bozorgtabar
Eric Brachmann
Samarth Brahmbhatt
Gustav Bredell
Francois Bremond
Joel Brogan
Andrew Brown
Thomas Brox
Marcus A. Brubaker
Robert-Jan Bruintjes
Yuqi Bu
Anders G. Buch
Himanshu Buckchash
Mateusz Buda
Ignas Budvytis
José M. Buenaposada
Marcel C. Bühler
Tu Bui
Adrian Bulat
Hannah Bull
Evgeny Burnaev
Andrei Bursuc
Benjamin Busam
Sergey N. Buzykanov
Wonmin Byeon
Fabian Caba
Martin Cadik
Guanyu Cai
Minjie Cai
Qing Cai
Zhongang Cai
Qi Cai
Yancheng Cai
Shen Cai
Han Cai
Jiarui Cai

Bowen Cai
Mu Cai
Qin Cai
Ruojin Cai
Weidong Cai
Weiwei Cai
Yi Cai
Yujun Cai
Zhiping Cai
Akin Caliskan
Lilian Calvet
Baris Can Cam
Necati Cihan Camgoz
Tommaso Campari
Dylan Campbell
Ziang Cao
Ang Cao
Xu Cao
Zhiwen Cao
Shengcao Cao
Song Cao
Weipeng Cao
Xiangyong Cao
Xiaochun Cao
Yue Cao
Yunhao Cao
Zhangjie Cao
Jiale Cao
Yang Cao
Jiajiong Cao
Jie Cao
Jinkun Cao
Lele Cao
Yulong Cao
Zhiguo Cao
Chen Cao
Razvan Caramalau
Marlène Careil
Gustavo Carneiro
Joao Carreira
Dan Casas
Paola Cascante-Bonilla
Angela Castillo
Francisco M. Castro
Pedro Castro

Luca Cavalli
George J. Cazenavette
Oya Celiktutan
Hakan Cevikalp
Sri Harsha C. H.
Sungmin Cha
Geonho Cha
Menglei Chai
Lucy Chai
Yuning Chai
Zenghao Chai
Anirban Chakraborty
Deep Chakraborty
Rudrasis Chakraborty
Souradeep Chakraborty
Kelvin C. K. Chan
Chee Seng Chan
Paramanand Chandramouli
Arjun Chandrasekaran
Kenneth Chaney
Dongliang Chang
Huiwen Chang
Peng Chang
Xiaojun Chang
Jia-Ren Chang
Hyung Jin Chang
Hyun Sung Chang
Ju Yong Chang
Li-Jen Chang
Qi Chang
Wei-Yi Chang
Yi Chang
Nadine Chang
Hanqing Chao
Pradyumna Chari
Dibyadip Chatterjee
Chiranjoy Chattopadhyay
Siddhartha Chaudhuri
Zhengping Che
Gal Chechik
Lianggangxu Chen
Qi Alfred Chen
Brian Chen
Bor-Chun Chen
Bo-Hao Chen

Bohong Chen
Bin Chen
Ziliang Chen
Cheng Chen
Chen Chen
Chaofeng Chen
Xi Chen
Haoyu Chen
Xuanhong Chen
Wei Chen
Qiang Chen
Shi Chen
Xianyu Chen
Chang Chen
Changhuai Chen
Hao Chen
Jie Chen
Jianbo Chen
Jingjing Chen
Jun Chen
Kejiang Chen
Mingcai Chen
Nenglun Chen
Qifeng Chen
Ruoyu Chen
Shu-Yu Chen
Weidong Chen
Weijie Chen
Weikai Chen
Xiang Chen
Xiuyi Chen
Xingyu Chen
Yaofo Chen
Yueting Chen
Yu Chen
Yunjin Chen
Yuntao Chen
Yun Chen
Zhenfang Chen
Zhuangzhuang Chen
Chu-Song Chen
Xiangyu Chen
Zhuo Chen
Chaoqi Chen
Shizhe Chen

Xiaotong Chen
Xiaozhi Chen
Dian Chen
Defang Chen
Dingfan Chen
Ding-Jie Chen
Ee Heng Chen
Tao Chen
Yixin Chen
Wei-Ting Chen
Lin Chen
Guang Chen
Guangyi Chen
Guanying Chen
Guangyao Chen
Hwann-Tzong Chen
Junwen Chen
Jiacheng Chen
Jianxu Chen
Hui Chen
Kai Chen
Kan Chen
Kevin Chen
Kuan-Wen Chen
Weihua Chen
Zhang Chen
Liang-Chieh Chen
Lele Chen
Liang Chen
Fanglin Chen
Zehui Chen
Minghui Chen
Minghao Chen
Xiaokang Chen
Qian Chen
Jun-Cheng Chen
Qi Chen
Qingcai Chen
Richard J. Chen
Runnan Chen
Rui Chen
Shuo Chen
Sentao Chen
Shaoyu Chen
Shixing Chen

Shuai Chen
Shuya Chen
Sizhe Chen
Simin Chen
Shaoxiang Chen
Zitian Chen
Tianlong Chen
Tianshui Chen
Min-Hung Chen
Xiangning Chen
Xin Chen
Xinghao Chen
Xuejin Chen
Xu Chen
Xuxi Chen
Yunlu Chen
Yanbei Chen
Yuxiao Chen
Yun-Chun Chen
Yi-Ting Chen
Yi-Wen Chen
Yinbo Chen
Yiran Chen
Yuanhong Chen
Yubei Chen
Yuefeng Chen
Yuhua Chen
Yukang Chen
Zerui Chen
Zhaoyu Chen
Zhen Chen
Zhenyu Chen
Zhi Chen
Zhiwei Chen
Zhixiang Chen
Long Chen
Bowen Cheng
Jun Cheng
Yi Cheng
Jingchun Cheng
Lechao Cheng
Xi Cheng
Yuan Cheng
Ho Kei Cheng
Kevin Ho Man Cheng

Jiacheng Cheng
Kelvin B. Cheng
Li Cheng
Mengjun Cheng
Zhen Cheng
Qingrong Cheng
Tianheng Cheng
Harry Cheng
Yihua Cheng
Yu Cheng
Ziheng Cheng
Soon Yau Cheong
Anoop Cherian
Manuela Chessa
Zhixiang Chi
Naoki Chiba
Julian Chibane
Kashyap Chitta
Tai-Yin Chiu
Hsu-kuang Chiu
Wei-Chen Chiu
Sungmin Cho
Donghyeon Cho
Hyeon Cho
Yooshin Cho
Gyusang Cho
Jang Hyun Cho
Seungju Cho
Nam Ik Cho
Sunghyun Cho
Hanbyel Cho
Jaesung Choe
Jooyoung Choi
Chiho Choi
Changwoon Choi
Jongwon Choi
Myungsub Choi
Dooseop Choi
Jonghyun Choi
Jinwoo Choi
Jun Won Choi
Min-Kook Choi
Hongsuk Choi
Janghoon Choi
Yoon-Ho Choi

Yukyung Choi
Jaegul Choo
Ayush Chopra
Siddharth Choudhary
Subhabrata Choudhury
Vasileios Choutas
Ka-Ho Chow
Pinaki Nath Chowdhury
Sammy Christen
Anders Christensen
Grigorios Chrysos
Hang Chu
Wen-Hsuan Chu
Peng Chu
Qi Chu
Ruihang Chu
Wei-Ta Chu
Yung-Yu Chuang
Sanghyuk Chun
Se Young Chun
Antonio Cinà
Ramazan Gokberk Cinbis
Javier Civera
Albert Clapés
Ronald Clark
Brian S. Clipp
Felipe Codevilla
Daniel Coelho de Castro
Niv Cohen
Forrester Cole
Maxwell D. Collins
Robert T. Collins
Marc Comino Trinidad
Runmin Cong
Wenyan Cong
Maxime Cordy
Marcella Cornia
Enric Corona
Huseyin Coskun
Luca Cosmo
Dragos Costea
Davide Cozzolino
Arun C. S. Kumar
Aiyu Cui
Qiongjie Cui

Quan Cui
Shuhao Cui
Yiming Cui
Ying Cui
Zijun Cui
Jiali Cui
Jiequan Cui
Yawen Cui
Zhen Cui
Zhaopeng Cui
Jack Culpepper
Xiaodong Cun
Ross Cutler
Adam Czajka
Ali Dabouei
Konstantinos M. Dafnis
Manuel Dahnert
Tao Dai
Yuchao Dai
Bo Dai
Mengyu Dai
Hang Dai
Haixing Dai
Peng Dai
Pingyang Dai
Qi Dai
Qiyu Dai
Yutong Dai
Naser Damer
Zhiyuan Dang
Mohamed Daoudi
Ayan Das
Abir Das
Debasmit Das
Deepayan Das
Partha Das
Sagnik Das
Soumi Das
Srijan Das
Swagatam Das
Avijit Dasgupta
Jim Davis
Adrian K. Davison
Homa Davoudi
Laura Daza

Matthias De Lange
Shalini De Mello
Marco De Nadai
Christophe De
    Vleeschouwer
Alp Dener
Boyang Deng
Congyue Deng
Bailin Deng
Yong Deng
Ye Deng
Zhuo Deng
Zhijie Deng
Xiaoming Deng
Jiankang Deng
Jinhong Deng
Jingjing Deng
Liang-Jian Deng
Siqi Deng
Xiang Deng
Xueqing Deng
Zhongying Deng
Karan Desai
Jean-Emmanuel Deschaud
Aniket Anand Deshmukh
Neel Dey
Helisa Dhamo
Prithviraj Dhar
Amaya Dharmasiri
Yan Di
Xing Di
Ousmane A. Dia
Haiwen Diao
Xiaolei Diao
Gonçalo José Dias Pais
Abdallah Dib
Anastasios Dimou
Changxing Ding
Henghui Ding
Guodong Ding
Yaqing Ding
Shuangrui Ding
Yuhang Ding
Yikang Ding
Shouhong Ding

Haisong Ding
Hui Ding
Jiahao Ding
Jian Ding
Jian-Jiun Ding
Shuxiao Ding
Tianyu Ding
Wenhao Ding
Yuqi Ding
Yi Ding
Yuzhen Ding
Zhengming Ding
Tan Minh Dinh
Vu Dinh
Christos Diou
Mandar Dixit
Bao Gia Doan
Khoa D. Doan
Dzung Anh Doan
Debi Prosad Dogra
Nehal Doiphode
Chengdong Dong
Bowen Dong
Zhenxing Dong
Hang Dong
Xiaoyi Dong
Haoye Dong
Jiangxin Dong
Shichao Dong
Xuan Dong
Zhen Dong
Shuting Dong
Jing Dong
Li Dong
Ming Dong
Nanqing Dong
Qiulei Dong
Runpei Dong
Siyan Dong
Tian Dong
Wei Dong
Xiaomeng Dong
Xin Dong
Xingbo Dong
Yuan Dong

Samuel Dooley
Gianfranco Doretto
Michael Dorkenwald
Keval Doshi
Zhaopeng Dou
Xiaotian Dou
Hazel Doughty
Ahmad Droby
Iddo Drori
Jie Du
Yong Du
Dawei Du
Dong Du
Ruoyi Du
Yuntao Du
Xuefeng Du
Yilun Du
Yuming Du
Radhika Dua
Haodong Duan
Jiafei Duan
Kaiwen Duan
Peiqi Duan
Ye Duan
Haoran Duan
Jiali Duan
Amanda Duarte
Abhimanyu Dubey
Shiv Ram Dubey
Florian Dubost
Lukasz Dudziak
Shivam Duggal
Justin M. Dulay
Matteo Dunnhofer
Chi Nhan Duong
Thibaut Durand
Mihai Dusmanu
Ujjal Kr Dutta
Debidatta Dwibedi
Isht Dwivedi
Sai Kumar Dwivedi
Takeharu Eda
Mark Edmonds
Alexei A. Efros
Thibaud Ehret

Max Ehrlich
Mahsa Ehsanpour
Iván Eichhardt
Farshad Einabadi
Marvin Eisenberger
Hazim Kemal Ekenel
Mohamed El Banani
Ismail Elezi
Moshe Eliasof
Alaa El-Nouby
Ian Endres
Francis Engelmann
Deniz Engin
Chanho Eom
Dave Epstein
Maria C. Escobar
Victor A. Escorcia
Carlos Esteves
Sungmin Eum
Bernard J. E. Evans
Ivan Evtimov
Fevziye Irem Eyiokur
    Yaman
Matteo Fabbri
Sébastien Fabbro
Gabriele Facciolo
Masud Fahim
Bin Fan
Hehe Fan
Deng-Ping Fan
Aoxiang Fan
Chen-Chen Fan
Qi Fan
Zhaoxin Fan
Haoqi Fan
Heng Fan
Hongyi Fan
Linxi Fan
Baojie Fan
Jiayuan Fan
Lei Fan
Quanfu Fan
Yonghui Fan
Yingruo Fan
Zhiwen Fan

Zicong Fan
Sean Fanello
Jiansheng Fang
Chaowei Fang
Yuming Fang
Jianwu Fang
Jin Fang
Qi Fang
Shancheng Fang
Tian Fang
Xianyong Fang
Gongfan Fang
Zhen Fang
Hui Fang
Jiemin Fang
Le Fang
Pengfei Fang
Xiaolin Fang
Yuxin Fang
Zhaoyuan Fang
Ammarah Farooq
Azade Farshad
Zhengcong Fei
Michael Felsberg
Wei Feng
Chen Feng
Fan Feng
Andrew Feng
Xin Feng
Zheyun Feng
Ruicheng Feng
Mingtao Feng
Qianyu Feng
Shangbin Feng
Chun-Mei Feng
Zunlei Feng
Zhiyong Feng
Martin Fergie
Mustansar Fiaz
Marco Fiorucci
Michael Firman
Hamed Firooz
Volker Fischer
Corneliu O. Florea
Georgios Floros

Wolfgang Foerstner
Gianni Franchi
Jean-Sebastien Franco
Simone Frintrop
Anna Fruehstueck
Changhong Fu
Chaoyou Fu
Cheng-Yang Fu
Chi-Wing Fu
Deqing Fu
Huan Fu
Jun Fu
Kexue Fu
Ying Fu
Jianlong Fu
Jingjing Fu
Qichen Fu
Tsu-Jui Fu
Xueyang Fu
Yang Fu
Yanwei Fu
Yonggan Fu
Wolfgang Fuhl
Yasuhisa Fujii
Kent Fujiwara
Marco Fumero
Takuya Funatomi
Isabel Funke
Dario Fuoli
Antonino Furnari
Matheus A. Gadelha
Akshay Gadi Patil
Adrian Galdran
Guillermo Gallego
Silvano Galliani
Orazio Gallo
Leonardo Galteri
Matteo Gamba
Yiming Gan
Sujoy Ganguly
Harald Ganster
Boyan Gao
Changxin Gao
Daiheng Gao
Difei Gao

Chen Gao
Fei Gao
Lin Gao
Wei Gao
Yiming Gao
Junyu Gao
Guangyu Ryan Gao
Haichang Gao
Hongchang Gao
Jialin Gao
Jin Gao
Jun Gao
Katelyn Gao
Mingchen Gao
Mingfei Gao
Pan Gao
Shangqian Gao
Shanghua Gao
Xitong Gao
Yunhe Gao
Zhanning Gao
Elena Garces
Nuno Cruz Garcia
Noa Garcia
Guillermo
    Garcia-Hernando
Isha Garg
Rahul Garg
Sourav Garg
Quentin Garrido
Stefano Gasperini
Kent Gauen
Chandan Gautam
Shivam Gautam
Paul Gay
Chunjiang Ge
Shiming Ge
Wenhang Ge
Yanhao Ge
Zheng Ge
Songwei Ge
Weifeng Ge
Yixiao Ge
Yuying Ge
Shijie Geng

Zhengyang Geng
Kyle A. Genova
Georgios Georgakis
Markos Georgopoulos
Marcel Geppert
Shabnam Ghadar
Mina Ghadimi Atigh
Deepti Ghadiyaram
Maani Ghaffari Jadidi
Sedigh Ghamari
Zahra Gharaee
Michaël Gharbi
Golnaz Ghiasi
Reza Ghoddoosian
Soumya Suvra Ghosal
Adhiraj Ghosh
Arthita Ghosh
Pallabi Ghosh
Soumyadeep Ghosh
Andrew Gilbert
Igor Gilitschenski
Jhony H. Giraldo
Andreu Girbau Xalabarder
Rohit Girdhar
Sharath Girish
Xavier Giro-i-Nieto
Raja Giryes
Thomas Gittings
Nikolaos Gkanatsios
Ioannis Gkioulekas
Abhiram
    Gnanasambandam
Aurele T. Gnanha
Clement L. J. C. Godard
Arushi Goel
Vidit Goel
Shubham Goel
Zan Gojcic
Aaron K. Gokaslan
Tejas Gokhale
S. Alireza Golestaneh
Thiago L. Gomes
Nuno Goncalves
Boqing Gong
Chen Gong

Yuanhao Gong
Guoqiang Gong
Jingyu Gong
Rui Gong
Yu Gong
Mingming Gong
Neil Zhenqiang Gong
Xun Gong
Yunye Gong
Yihong Gong
Cristina I. González
Nithin Gopalakrishnan
    Nair
Gaurav Goswami
Jianping Gou
Shreyank N. Gowda
Ankit Goyal
Helmut Grabner
Patrick L. Grady
Ben Graham
Eric Granger
Douglas R. Gray
Matej Grcić
David Griffiths
Jinjin Gu
Yun Gu
Shuyang Gu
Jianyang Gu
Fuqiang Gu
Jiatao Gu
Jindong Gu
Jiaqi Gu
Jinwei Gu
Jiaxin Gu
Geonmo Gu
Xiao Gu
Xinqian Gu
Xiuye Gu
Yuming Gu
Zhangxuan Gu
Dayan Guan
Junfeng Guan
Qingji Guan
Tianrui Guan
Shanyan Guan

Denis A. Gudovskiy
Ricardo Guerrero
Pierre-Louis Guhur
Jie Gui
Liangyan Gui
Liangke Gui
Benoit Guillard
Erhan Gundogdu
Manuel Günther
Jingcai Guo
Yuanfang Guo
Junfeng Guo
Chenqi Guo
Dan Guo
Hongji Guo
Jia Guo
Jie Guo
Minghao Guo
Shi Guo
Yanhui Guo
Yangyang Guo
Yuan-Chen Guo
Yilu Guo
Yiluan Guo
Yong Guo
Guangyu Guo
Haiyun Guo
Jinyang Guo
Jianyuan Guo
Pengsheng Guo
Pengfei Guo
Shuxuan Guo
Song Guo
Tianyu Guo
Qing Guo
Qiushan Guo
Wen Guo
Xiefan Guo
Xiaohu Guo
Xiaoqing Guo
Yufei Guo
Yuhui Guo
Yuliang Guo
Yunhui Guo
Yanwen Guo

Akshita Gupta
Ankush Gupta
Kamal Gupta
Kartik Gupta
Ritwik Gupta
Rohit Gupta
Siddharth Gururani
Fredrik K. Gustafsson
Abner Guzman Rivera
Vladimir Guzov
Matthew A. Gwilliam
Jung-Woo Ha
Marc Habermann
Isma Hadji
Christian Haene
Martin Hahner
Levente Hajder
Alexandros Haliassos
Emanuela Haller
Bumsub Ham
Abdullah J. Hamdi
Shreyas Hampali
Dongyoon Han
Chunrui Han
Dong-Jun Han
Dong-Sig Han
Guangxing Han
Zhizhong Han
Ruize Han
Jiaming Han
Jin Han
Ligong Han
Xian-Hua Han
Xiaoguang Han
Yizeng Han
Zhi Han
Zhenjun Han
Zhongyi Han
Jungong Han
Junlin Han
Kai Han
Kun Han
Sungwon Han
Songfang Han
Wei Han

Xiao Han
Xintong Han
Xinzhe Han
Yahong Han
Yan Han
Zongbo Han
Nicolai Hani
Rana Hanocka
Niklas Hanselmann
Nicklas A. Hansen
Hong Hanyu
Fusheng Hao
Yanbin Hao
Shijie Hao
Udith Haputhanthri
Mehrtash Harandi
Josh Harguess
Adam Harley
David M. Hart
Atsushi Hashimoto
Ali Hassani
Mohammed Hassanin
Yana Hasson
Joakim Bruslund Haurum
Bo He
Kun He
Chen He
Xin He
Fazhi He
Gaoqi He
Hao He
Haoyu He
Jiangpeng He
Hongliang He
Qian He
Xiangteng He
Xuming He
Yannan He
Yuhang He
Yang He
Xiangyu He
Nanjun He
Pan He
Sen He
Shengfeng He

Songtao He
Tao He
Tong He
Wei He
Xuehai He
Xiaoxiao He
Ying He
Yisheng He
Ziwen He
Peter Hedman
Felix Heide
Yacov Hel-Or
Paul Henderson
Philipp Henzler
Byeongho Heo
Jae-Pil Heo
Miran Heo
Sachini A. Herath
Stephane Herbin
Pedro Hermosilla Casajus
Monica Hernandez
Charles Herrmann
Roei Herzig
Mauricio Hess-Flores
Carlos Hinojosa
Tobias Hinz
Tsubasa Hirakawa
Chih-Hui Ho
Lam Si Tung Ho
Jennifer Hobbs
Derek Hoiem
Yannick Hold-Geoffroy
Aleksander Holynski
Cheeun Hong
Fa-Ting Hong
Hanbin Hong
Guan Zhe Hong
Danfeng Hong
Lanqing Hong
Xiaopeng Hong
Xin Hong
Jie Hong
Seungbum Hong
Cheng-Yao Hong
Seunghoon Hong

Yi Hong
Yuan Hong
Yuchen Hong
Anthony Hoogs
Maxwell C. Horton
Kazuhiro Hotta
Qibin Hou
Tingbo Hou
Junhui Hou
Ji Hou
Qiqi Hou
Rui Hou
Ruibing Hou
Zhi Hou
Henry Howard-Jenkins
Lukas Hoyer
Wei-Lin Hsiao
Chiou-Ting Hsu
Anthony Hu
Brian Hu
Yusong Hu
Hexiang Hu
Haoji Hu
Di Hu
Hengtong Hu
Haigen Hu
Lianyu Hu
Hanzhe Hu
Jie Hu
Junlin Hu
Shizhe Hu
Jian Hu
Zhiming Hu
Juhua Hu
Peng Hu
Ping Hu
Ronghang Hu
MengShun Hu
Tao Hu
Vincent Tao Hu
Xiaoling Hu
Xinting Hu
Xiaolin Hu
Xuefeng Hu
Xiaowei Hu

Yang Hu
Yueyu Hu
Zeyu Hu
Zhongyun Hu
Binh-Son Hua
Guoliang Hua
Yi Hua
Linzhi Huang
Qiusheng Huang
Bo Huang
Chen Huang
Hsin-Ping Huang
Ye Huang
Shuangping Huang
Zeng Huang
Buzhen Huang
Cong Huang
Heng Huang
Hao Huang
Qidong Huang
Huaibo Huang
Chaoqin Huang
Feihu Huang
Jiahui Huang
Jingjia Huang
Kun Huang
Lei Huang
Sheng Huang
Shuaiyi Huang
Siyu Huang
Xiaoshui Huang
Xiaoyang Huang
Yan Huang
Yihao Huang
Ying Huang
Ziling Huang
Xiaoke Huang
Yifei Huang
Haiyang Huang
Zhewei Huang
Jin Huang
Haibin Huang
Jiaxing Huang
Junjie Huang
Keli Huang

Lang Huang
Lin Huang
Luojie Huang
Mingzhen Huang
Shijia Huang
Shengyu Huang
Siyuan Huang
He Huang
Xiuyu Huang
Lianghua Huang
Yue Huang
Yaping Huang
Yuge Huang
Zehao Huang
Zeyi Huang
Zhiqi Huang
Zhongzhan Huang
Zilong Huang
Ziyuan Huang
Tianrui Hui
Zhuo Hui
Le Hui
Jing Huo
Junhwa Hur
Shehzeen S. Hussain
Chuong Minh Huynh
Seunghyun Hwang
Jaehui Hwang
Jyh-Jing Hwang
Sukjun Hwang
Soonmin Hwang
Wonjun Hwang
Rakib Hyder
Sangeek Hyun
Sarah Ibrahimi
Tomoki Ichikawa
Yerlan Idelbayev
A. S. M. Iftekhar
Masaaki Iiyama
Satoshi Ikehata
Sunghoon Im
Atul N. Ingle
Eldar Insafutdinov
Yani A. Ioannou
Radu Tudor Ionescu

Umar Iqbal
Go Irie
Muhammad Zubair Irshad
Ahmet Iscen
Berivan Isik
Ashraful Islam
Md Amirul Islam
Syed Islam
Mariko Isogawa
Vamsi Krishna K. Ithapu
Boris Ivanovic
Darshan Iyer
Sarah Jabbour
Ayush Jain
Nishant Jain
Samyak Jain
Vidit Jain
Vineet Jain
Priyank Jaini
Tomas Jakab
Mohammad A. A. K.
  Jalwana
Muhammad Abdullah
  Jamal
Hadi Jamali-Rad
Stuart James
Varun Jampani
Young Kyun Jang
YeongJun Jang
Yunseok Jang
Ronnachai Jaroensri
Bhavan Jasani
Krishna Murthy
  Jatavallabhula
Mojan Javaheripi
Syed A. Javed
Guillaume Jeanneret
Pranav Jeevan
Herve Jegou
Rohit Jena
Tomas Jenicek
Porter Jenkins
Simon Jenni
Hae-Gon Jeon
Sangryul Jeon

Boseung Jeong
Yoonwoo Jeong
Seong-Gyun Jeong
Jisoo Jeong
Allan D. Jepson
Ankit Jha
Sumit K. Jha
I-Hong Jhuo
Ge-Peng Ji
Chaonan Ji
Deyi Ji
Jingwei Ji
Wei Ji
Zhong Ji
Jiayi Ji
Pengliang Ji
Hui Ji
Mingi Ji
Xiaopeng Ji
Yuzhu Ji
Baoxiong Jia
Songhao Jia
Dan Jia
Shan Jia
Xiaojun Jia
Xiuyi Jia
Xu Jia
Menglin Jia
Wenqi Jia
Boyuan Jiang
Wenhao Jiang
Huaizu Jiang
Hanwen Jiang
Haiyong Jiang
Hao Jiang
Huajie Jiang
Huiqin Jiang
Haojun Jiang
Haobo Jiang
Junjun Jiang
Xingyu Jiang
Yangbangyan Jiang
Yu Jiang
Jianmin Jiang
Jiaxi Jiang

Jing Jiang
Kui Jiang
Li Jiang
Liming Jiang
Chiyu Jiang
Meirui Jiang
Chen Jiang
Peng Jiang
Tai-Xiang Jiang
Wen Jiang
Xinyang Jiang
Yifan Jiang
Yuming Jiang
Yingying Jiang
Zeren Jiang
ZhengKai Jiang
Zhenyu Jiang
Shuming Jiao
Jianbo Jiao
Licheng Jiao
Dongkwon Jin
Yeying Jin
Cheng Jin
Linyi Jin
Qing Jin
Taisong Jin
Xiao Jin
Xin Jin
Sheng Jin
Kyong Hwan Jin
Ruibing Jin
SouYoung Jin
Yueming Jin
Chenchen Jing
Longlong Jing
Taotao Jing
Yongcheng Jing
Younghyun Jo
Joakim Johnander
Jeff Johnson
Michael J. Jones
R. Kenny Jones
Rico Jonschkowski
Ameya Joshi
Sunghun Joung

Felix Juefei-Xu
Claudio R. Jung
Steffen Jung
Hari Chandana K.
Rahul Vigneswaran K.
Prajwal K. R.
Abhishek Kadian
Jhony Kaesemodel Pontes
Kumara Kahatapitiya
Anmol Kalia
Sinan Kalkan
Tarun Kalluri
Jaewon Kam
Sandesh Kamath
Meina Kan
Menelaos Kanakis
Takuhiro Kaneko
Di Kang
Guoliang Kang
Hao Kang
Jaeyeon Kang
Kyoungkook Kang
Li-Wei Kang
MinGuk Kang
Suk-Ju Kang
Zhao Kang
Yash Mukund Kant
Yueying Kao
Aupendu Kar
Konstantinos Karantzalos
Sezer Karaoglu
Navid Kardan
Sanjay Kariyappa
Leonid Karlinsky
Animesh Karnewar
Shyamgopal Karthik
Hirak J. Kashyap
Marc A. Kastner
Hirokatsu Kataoka
Angelos Katharopoulos
Hiroharu Kato
Kai Katsumata
Manuel Kaufmann
Chaitanya Kaul
Prakhar Kaushik

Yuki Kawana
Lei Ke
Lipeng Ke
Tsung-Wei Ke
Wei Ke
Petr Kellnhofer
Aniruddha Kembhavi
John Kender
Corentin Kervadec
Leonid Keselman
Daniel Keysers
Nima Khademi Kalantari
Taras Khakhulin
Samir Khaki
Muhammad Haris Khan
Qadeer Khan
Salman Khan
Subash Khanal
Vaishnavi M. Khindkar
Rawal Khirodkar
Saeed Khorram
Pirazh Khorramshahi
Kourosh Khoshelham
Ansh Khurana
Benjamin Kiefer
Jae Myung Kim
Junho Kim
Boah Kim
Hyeonseong Kim
Dong-Jin Kim
Dongwan Kim
Donghyun Kim
Doyeon Kim
Yonghyun Kim
Hyung-Il Kim
Hyunwoo Kim
Hyeongwoo Kim
Hyo Jin Kim
Hyunwoo J. Kim
Taehoon Kim
Jaeha Kim
Jiwon Kim
Jung Uk Kim
Kangyeol Kim
Eunji Kim

Daeha Kim
Dongwon Kim
Kunhee Kim
Kyungmin Kim
Junsik Kim
Min H. Kim
Namil Kim
Kookhoi Kim
Sanghyun Kim
Seongyeop Kim
Seungryong Kim
Saehoon Kim
Euyoung Kim
Guisik Kim
Sungyeon Kim
Sunnie S. Y. Kim
Taehun Kim
Tae Oh Kim
Won Hwa Kim
Seungwook Kim
YoungBin Kim
Youngeun Kim
Akisato Kimura
Furkan Osman Kınlı
Zsolt Kira
Hedvig Kjellström
Florian Kleber
Jan P. Klopp
Florian Kluger
Laurent Kneip
Byungsoo Ko
Muhammed Kocabas
A. Sophia Koepke
Kevin Koeser
Nick Kolkin
Nikos Kolotouros
Wai-Kin Adams Kong
Deying Kong
Caihua Kong
Youyong Kong
Shuyu Kong
Shu Kong
Tao Kong
Yajing Kong
Yu Kong

Zishang Kong
Theodora Kontogianni
Anton S. Konushin
Julian F. P. Kooij
Bruno Korbar
Giorgos Kordopatis-Zilos
Jari Korhonen
Adam Kortylewski
Denis Korzhenkov
Divya Kothandaraman
Suraj Kothawade
Iuliia Kotseruba
Satwik Kottur
Shashank Kotyan
Alexandros Kouris
Petros Koutras
Anna Kreshuk
Ranjay Krishna
Dilip Krishnan
Andrey Kuehlkamp
Hilde Kuehne
Jason Kuen
David Kügler
Arjan Kuijper
Anna Kukleva
Sumith Kulal
Viveka Kulharia
Akshay R. Kulkarni
Nilesh Kulkarni
Dominik Kulon
Abhinav Kumar
Akash Kumar
Suryansh Kumar
B. V. K. Vijaya Kumar
Pulkit Kumar
Ratnesh Kumar
Sateesh Kumar
Satish Kumar
Vijay Kumar B. G.
Nupur Kumari
Sudhakar Kumawat
Jogendra Nath Kundu
Hsien-Kai Kuo
Meng-Yu Jennifer Kuo
Vinod Kumar Kurmi

Yusuke Kurose
Keerthy Kusumam
Alina Kuznetsova
Henry Kvinge
Ho Man Kwan
Hyeokjun Kweon
Heeseung Kwon
Gihyun Kwon
Myung-Joon Kwon
Taesung Kwon
YoungJoong Kwon
Christos Kyrkou
Jorma Laaksonen
Yann Labbe
Zorah Laehner
Florent Lafarge
Hamid Laga
Manuel Lagunas
Shenqi Lai
Jian-Huang Lai
Zihang Lai
Mohamed I. Lakhal
Mohit Lamba
Meng Lan
Loic Landrieu
Zhiqiang Lang
Natalie Lang
Dong Lao
Yizhen Lao
Yingjie Lao
Issam Hadj Laradji
Gustav Larsson
Viktor Larsson
Zakaria Laskar
Stéphane Lathuilière
Chun Pong Lau
Rynson W. H. Lau
Hei Law
Justin Lazarow
Verica Lazova
Eric-Tuan Le
Hieu Le
Trung-Nghia Le
Mathias Lechner
Byeong-Uk Lee

Chen-Yu Lee
Che-Rung Lee
Chul Lee
Hong Joo Lee
Dongsoo Lee
Jiyoung Lee
Eugene Eu Tzuan Lee
Daeun Lee
Saehyung Lee
Jewook Lee
Hyungtae Lee
Hyunmin Lee
Jungbeom Lee
Joon-Young Lee
Jong-Seok Lee
Joonseok Lee
Junha Lee
Kibok Lee
Byung-Kwan Lee
Jangwon Lee
Jinho Lee
Jongmin Lee
Seunghyun Lee
Sohyun Lee
Minsik Lee
Dogyoon Lee
Seungmin Lee
Min Jun Lee
Sangho Lee
Sangmin Lee
Seungeun Lee
Seon-Ho Lee
Sungmin Lee
Sungho Lee
Sangyoun Lee
Vincent C. S. S. Lee
Jaeseong Lee
Yong Jae Lee
Chenyang Lei
Chenyi Lei
Jiahui Lei
Xinyu Lei
Yinjie Lei
Jiaxu Leng
Luziwei Leng

Jan E. Lenssen
Vincent Lepetit
Thomas Leung
María Leyva-Vallina
Xin Li
Yikang Li
Baoxin Li
Bin Li
Bing Li
Bowen Li
Changlin Li
Chao Li
Chongyi Li
Guanyue Li
Shuai Li
Jin Li
Dingquan Li
Dongxu Li
Yiting Li
Gang Li
Dian Li
Guohao Li
Haoang Li
Haoliang Li
Haoran Li
Hengduo Li
Huafeng Li
Xiaoming Li
Hanao Li
Hongwei Li
Ziqiang Li
Jisheng Li
Jiacheng Li
Jia Li
Jiachen Li
Jiahao Li
Jianwei Li
Jiazhi Li
Jie Li
Jing Li
Jingjing Li
Jingtao Li
Jun Li
Junxuan Li
Kai Li

Kailin Li
Kenneth Li
Kun Li
Kunpeng Li
Aoxue Li
Chenglong Li
Chenglin Li
Changsheng Li
Zhichao Li
Qiang Li
Yanyu Li
Zuoyue Li
Xiang Li
Xuelong Li
Fangda Li
Ailin Li
Liang Li
Chun-Guang Li
Daiqing Li
Dong Li
Guanbin Li
Guorong Li
Haifeng Li
Jianan Li
Jianing Li
Jiaxin Li
Ke Li
Lei Li
Lincheng Li
Liulei Li
Lujun Li
Linjie Li
Lin Li
Pengyu Li
Ping Li
Qiufu Li
Qingyong Li
Rui Li
Siyuan Li
Wei Li
Wenbin Li
Xiangyang Li
Xinyu Li
Xiujun Li
Xiu Li

Xu Li
Ya-Li Li
Yao Li
Yongjie Li
Yijun Li
Yiming Li
Yuezun Li
Yu Li
Yunheng Li
Yuqi Li
Zhe Li
Zeming Li
Zhen Li
Zhengqin Li
Zhimin Li
Jiefeng Li
Jinpeng Li
Chengze Li
Jianwu Li
Lerenhan Li
Shan Li
Suichan Li
Xiangtai Li
Yanjie Li
Yandong Li
Zhuoling Li
Zhenqiang Li
Manyi Li
Maosen Li
Ji Li
Minjun Li
Mingrui Li
Mengtian Li
Junyi Li
Nianyi Li
Bo Li
Xiao Li
Peihua Li
Peike Li
Peizhao Li
Peiliang Li
Qi Li
Ren Li
Runze Li
Shile Li

Sheng Li
Shigang Li
Shiyu Li
Shuang Li
Shasha Li
Shichao Li
Tianye Li
Yuexiang Li
Wei-Hong Li
Wanhua Li
Weihao Li
Weiming Li
Weixin Li
Wenbo Li
Wenshuo Li
Weijian Li
Yunan Li
Xirong Li
Xianhang Li
Xiaoyu Li
Xueqian Li
Xuanlin Li
Xianzhi Li
Yunqiang Li
Yanjing Li
Yansheng Li
Yawei Li
Yi Li
Yong Li
Yong-Lu Li
Yuhang Li
Yu-Jhe Li
Yuxi Li
Yunsheng Li
Yanwei Li
Zechao Li
Zejian Li
Zeju Li
Zekun Li
Zhaowen Li
Zheng Li
Zhenyu Li
Zhiheng Li
Zhi Li
Zhong Li

Zhuowei Li
Zhuowan Li
Zhuohang Li
Zizhang Li
Chen Li
Yuan-Fang Li
Dongze Lian
Xiaochen Lian
Zhouhui Lian
Long Lian
Qing Lian
Jin Lianbao
Jinxiu S. Liang
Dingkang Liang
Jiahao Liang
Jianming Liang
Jingyun Liang
Kevin J. Liang
Kaizhao Liang
Chen Liang
Jie Liang
Senwei Liang
Ding Liang
Jiajun Liang
Jian Liang
Kongming Liang
Siyuan Liang
Yuanzhi Liang
Zhengfa Liang
Mingfu Liang
Xiaodan Liang
Xuefeng Liang
Yuxuan Liang
Kang Liao
Liang Liao
Hong-Yuan Mark Liao
Wentong Liao
Haofu Liao
Yue Liao
Minghui Liao
Shengcai Liao
Ting-Hsuan Liao
Xin Liao
Yinghong Liao
Teck Yian Lim

Che-Tsung Lin
Chung-Ching Lin
Chen-Hsuan Lin
Cheng Lin
Chuming Lin
Chunyu Lin
Dahua Lin
Wei Lin
Zheng Lin
Huaijia Lin
Jason Lin
Jierui Lin
Jiaying Lin
Jie Lin
Kai-En Lin
Kevin Lin
Guangfeng Lin
Jiehong Lin
Feng Lin
Hang Lin
Kwan-Yee Lin
Ke Lin
Luojun Lin
Qinghong Lin
Xiangbo Lin
Yi Lin
Zudi Lin
Shijie Lin
Yiqun Lin
Tzu-Heng Lin
Ming Lin
Shaohui Lin
SongNan Lin
Ji Lin
Tsung-Yu Lin
Xudong Lin
Yancong Lin
Yen-Chen Lin
Yiming Lin
Yuewei Lin
Zhiqiu Lin
Zinan Lin
Zhe Lin
David B. Lindell
Zhixin Ling

Zhan Ling
Alexander Liniger
Venice Erin B. Liong
Joey Litalien
Or Litany
Roee Litman
Ron Litman
Jim Little
Dor Litvak
Shaoteng Liu
Shuaicheng Liu
Andrew Liu
Xian Liu
Shaohui Liu
Bei Liu
Bo Liu
Yong Liu
Ming Liu
Yanbin Liu
Chenxi Liu
Daqi Liu
Di Liu
Difan Liu
Dong Liu
Dongfang Liu
Daizong Liu
Xiao Liu
Fangyi Liu
Fengbei Liu
Fenglin Liu
Bin Liu
Yuang Liu
Ao Liu
Hong Liu
Hongfu Liu
Huidong Liu
Ziyi Liu
Feng Liu
Hao Liu
Jie Liu
Jialun Liu
Jiang Liu
Jing Liu
Jingya Liu
Jiaming Liu

Jun Liu
Juncheng Liu
Jiawei Liu
Hongyu Liu
Chuanbin Liu
Haotian Liu
Lingqiao Liu
Chang Liu
Han Liu
Liu Liu
Min Liu
Yingqi Liu
Aishan Liu
Bingyu Liu
Benlin Liu
Boxiao Liu
Chenchen Liu
Chuanjian Liu
Daqing Liu
Huan Liu
Haozhe Liu
Jiaheng Liu
Wei Liu
Jingzhou Liu
Jiyuan Liu
Lingbo Liu
Nian Liu
Peiye Liu
Qiankun Liu
Shenglan Liu
Shilong Liu
Wen Liu
Wenyu Liu
Weifeng Liu
Wu Liu
Xiaolong Liu
Yang Liu
Yanwei Liu
Yingcheng Liu
Yongfei Liu
Yihao Liu
Yu Liu
Yunze Liu
Ze Liu
Zhenhua Liu

Zhenguang Liu
Lin Liu
Lihao Liu
Pengju Liu
Xinhai Liu
Yunfei Liu
Meng Liu
Minghua Liu
Mingyuan Liu
Miao Liu
Peirong Liu
Ping Liu
Qingjie Liu
Ruoshi Liu
Risheng Liu
Songtao Liu
Xing Liu
Shikun Liu
Shuming Liu
Sheng Liu
Songhua Liu
Tongliang Liu
Weibo Liu
Weide Liu
Weizhe Liu
Wenxi Liu
Weiyang Liu
Xin Liu
Xiaobin Liu
Xudong Liu
Xiaoyi Liu
Xihui Liu
Xinchen Liu
Xingtong Liu
Xinpeng Liu
Xinyu Liu
Xianpeng Liu
Xu Liu
Xingyu Liu
Yongtuo Liu
Yahui Liu
Yangxin Liu
Yaoyao Liu
Yaojie Liu
Yuliang Liu

Yongcheng Liu
Yuan Liu
Yufan Liu
Yu-Lun Liu
Yun Liu
Yunfan Liu
Yuanzhong Liu
Zhuoran Liu
Zhen Liu
Zheng Liu
Zhijian Liu
Zhisong Liu
Ziquan Liu
Ziyu Liu
Zhihua Liu
Zechun Liu
Zhaoyang Liu
Zhengzhe Liu
Stephan Liwicki
Shao-Yuan Lo
Sylvain Lobry
Suhas Lohit
Vishnu Suresh Lokhande
Vincenzo Lomonaco
Chengjiang Long
Guodong Long
Fuchen Long
Shangbang Long
Yang Long
Zijun Long
Vasco Lopes
Antonio M. Lopez
Roberto Javier
   Lopez-Sastre
Tobias Lorenz
Javier Lorenzo-Navarro
Yujing Lou
Qian Lou
Xiankai Lu
Changsheng Lu
Huimin Lu
Yongxi Lu
Hao Lu
Hong Lu
Jiasen Lu

Juwei Lu
Fan Lu
Guangming Lu
Jiwen Lu
Shun Lu
Tao Lu
Xiaonan Lu
Yang Lu
Yao Lu
Yongchun Lu
Zhiwu Lu
Cheng Lu
Liying Lu
Guo Lu
Xuequan Lu
Yanye Lu
Yantao Lu
Yuhang Lu
Fujun Luan
Jonathon Luiten
Jovita Lukasik
Alan Lukezic
Jonathan Samuel Lumentut
Mayank Lunayach
Ao Luo
Canjie Luo
Chong Luo
Xu Luo
Grace Luo
Jun Luo
Katie Z. Luo
Tao Luo
Cheng Luo
Fangzhou Luo
Gen Luo
Lei Luo
Sihui Luo
Weixin Luo
Yan Luo
Xiaoyan Luo
Yong Luo
Yadan Luo
Hao Luo
Ruotian Luo
Mi Luo

Tiange Luo
Wenjie Luo
Wenhan Luo
Xiao Luo
Zhiming Luo
Zhipeng Luo
Zhengyi Luo
Diogo C. Luvizon
Zhaoyang Lv
Gengyu Lyu
Lingjuan Lyu
Jun Lyu
Yuanyuan Lyu
Youwei Lyu
Yueming Lyu
Bingpeng Ma
Chao Ma
Chongyang Ma
Congbo Ma
Chih-Yao Ma
Fan Ma
Lin Ma
Haoyu Ma
Hengbo Ma
Jianqi Ma
Jiawei Ma
Jiayi Ma
Kede Ma
Kai Ma
Lingni Ma
Lei Ma
Xu Ma
Ning Ma
Benteng Ma
Cheng Ma
Andy J. Ma
Long Ma
Zhanyu Ma
Zhiheng Ma
Qianli Ma
Shiqiang Ma
Sizhuo Ma
Shiqing Ma
Xiaolong Ma
Xinzhu Ma

Gautam B. Machiraju
Spandan Madan
Mathew Magimai-Doss
Luca Magri
Behrooz Mahasseni
Upal Mahbub
Siddharth Mahendran
Paridhi Maheshwari
Rishabh Maheshwary
Mohammed Mahmoud
Shishira R. R. Maiya
Sylwia Majchrowska
Arjun Majumdar
Puspita Majumdar
Orchid Majumder
Sagnik Majumder
Ilya Makarov
Farkhod F.
   Makhmudkhujaev
Yasushi Makihara
Ankur Mali
Mateusz Malinowski
Utkarsh Mall
Srikanth Malla
Clement Mallet
Dimitrios Mallis
Yunze Man
Dipu Manandhar
Massimiliano Mancini
Murari Mandal
Raunak Manekar
Karttikeya Mangalam
Puneet Mangla
Fabian Manhardt
Sivabalan Manivasagam
Fahim Mannan
Chengzhi Mao
Hanzi Mao
Jiayuan Mao
Junhua Mao
Zhiyuan Mao
Jiageng Mao
Yunyao Mao
Zhendong Mao
Alberto Marchisio

Diego Marcos
Riccardo Marin
Aram Markosyan
Renaud Marlet
Ricardo Marques
Miquel Martí i Rabadán
Diego Martin Arroyo
Niki Martinel
Brais Martinez
Julieta Martinez
Marc Masana
Tomohiro Mashita
Timothée Masquelier
Minesh Mathew
Tetsu Matsukawa
Marwan Mattar
Bruce A. Maxwell
Christoph Mayer
Mantas Mazeika
Pratik Mazumder
Scott McCloskey
Steven McDonagh
Ishit Mehta
Jie Mei
Kangfu Mei
Jieru Mei
Xiaoguang Mei
Givi Meishvili
Luke Melas-Kyriazi
Iaroslav Melekhov
Andres Mendez-Vazquez
Heydi Mendez-Vazquez
Matias Mendieta
Ricardo A. Mendoza-León
Chenlin Meng
Depu Meng
Rang Meng
Zibo Meng
Qingjie Meng
Qier Meng
Yanda Meng
Zihang Meng
Thomas Mensink
Fabian Mentzer
Christopher Metzler

Gregory P. Meyer
Vasileios Mezaris
Liang Mi
Lu Mi
Bo Miao
Changtao Miao
Zichen Miao
Qiguang Miao
Xin Miao
Zhongqi Miao
Frank Michel
Simone Milani
Ben Mildenhall
Roy V. Miles
Juhong Min
Kyle Min
Hyun-Seok Min
Weiqing Min
Yuecong Min
Zhixiang Min
Qi Ming
David Minnen
Aymen Mir
Deepak Mishra
Anand Mishra
Shlok K. Mishra
Niluthpol Mithun
Gaurav Mittal
Trisha Mittal
Daisuke Miyazaki
Kaichun Mo
Hong Mo
Zhipeng Mo
Davide Modolo
Abduallah A. Mohamed
Mohamed Afham
   Mohamed Aflal
Ron Mokady
Pavlo Molchanov
Davide Moltisanti
Liliane Momeni
Gianluca Monaci
Pascal Monasse
Ajoy Mondal
Tom Monnier

Aron Monszpart
Gyeongsik Moon
Suhong Moon
Taesup Moon
Sean Moran
Daniel Moreira
Pietro Morerio
Alexandre Morgand
Lia Morra
Ali Mosleh
Inbar Mosseri
Sayed Mohammad
    Mostafavi Isfahani
Saman Motamed
Ramy A. Mounir
Fangzhou Mu
Jiteng Mu
Norman Mu
Yasuhiro Mukaigawa
Ryan Mukherjee
Tanmoy Mukherjee
Yusuke Mukuta
Ravi Teja Mullapudi
Lea Müller
Matthias Müller
Martin Mundt
Nils Murrugarra-Llerena
Damien Muselet
Armin Mustafa
Muhammad Ferjad Naeem
Sauradip Nag
Hajime Nagahara
Pravin Nagar
Rajendra Nagar
Naveen Shankar Nagaraja
Varun Nagaraja
Tushar Nagarajan
Seungjun Nah
Gaku Nakano
Yuta Nakashima
Giljoo Nam
Seonghyeon Nam
Liangliang Nan
Yuesong Nan
Yeshwanth Napolean

Dinesh Reddy
    Narapureddy
Medhini Narasimhan
Supreeth
    Narasimhaswamy
Sriram Narayanan
Erickson R. Nascimento
Varun Nasery
K. L. Navaneet
Pablo Navarrete Michelini
Shant Navasardyan
Shah Nawaz
Nihal Nayak
Farhood Negin
Lukáš Neumann
Alejandro Newell
Evonne Ng
Kam Woh Ng
Tony Ng
Anh Nguyen
Tuan Anh Nguyen
Cuong Cao Nguyen
Ngoc Cuong Nguyen
Thanh Nguyen
Khoi Nguyen
Phi Le Nguyen
Phong Ha Nguyen
Tam Nguyen
Truong Nguyen
Anh Tuan Nguyen
Rang Nguyen
Thao Thi Phuong Nguyen
Van Nguyen Nguyen
Zhen-Liang Ni
Yao Ni
Shijie Nie
Xuecheng Nie
Yongwei Nie
Weizhi Nie
Ying Nie
Yinyu Nie
Kshitij N. Nikhal
Simon Niklaus
Xuefei Ning
Jifeng Ning

Yotam Nitzan
Di Niu
Shuaicheng Niu
Li Niu
Wei Niu
Yulei Niu
Zhenxing Niu
Albert No
Shohei Nobuhara
Nicoletta Noceti
Junhyug Noh
Sotiris Nousias
Slawomir Nowaczyk
Ewa M. Nowara
Valsamis Ntouskos
Gilberto Ochoa-Ruiz
Ferda Ofli
Jihyong Oh
Sangyun Oh
Youngtaek Oh
Hiroki Ohashi
Takahiro Okabe
Kemal Oksuz
Fumio Okura
Daniel Olmeda Reino
Matthew Olson
Carl Olsson
Roy Or-El
Alessandro Ortis
Guillermo Ortiz-Jimenez
Magnus Oskarsson
Ahmed A. A. Osman
Martin R. Oswald
Mayu Otani
Naima Otberdout
Cheng Ouyang
Jiahong Ouyang
Wanli Ouyang
Andrew Owens
Poojan B. Oza
Mete Ozay
A. Cengiz Oztireli
Gautam Pai
Tomas Pajdla
Umapada Pal

Simone Palazzo
Luca Palmieri
Bowen Pan
Hao Pan
Lili Pan
Tai-Yu Pan
Liang Pan
Chengwei Pan
Yingwei Pan
Xuran Pan
Jinshan Pan
Xinyu Pan
Liyuan Pan
Xingang Pan
Xingjia Pan
Zhihong Pan
Zizheng Pan
Priyadarshini Panda
Rameswar Panda
Rohit Pandey
Kaiyue Pang
Bo Pang
Guansong Pang
Jiangmiao Pang
Meng Pang
Tianyu Pang
Ziqi Pang
Omiros Pantazis
Andreas Panteli
Maja Pantic
Marina Paolanti
Joao P. Papa
Samuele Papa
Mike Papadakis
Dim P. Papadopoulos
George Papandreou
Constantin Pape
Toufiq Parag
Chethan Parameshwara
Shaifali Parashar
Alejandro Pardo
Rishubh Parihar
Sarah Parisot
JaeYoo Park
Gyeong-Moon Park

Hyojin Park
Hyoungseob Park
Jongchan Park
Jae Sung Park
Kiru Park
Chunghyun Park
Kwanyong Park
Sunghyun Park
Sungrae Park
Seongsik Park
Sanghyun Park
Sungjune Park
Taesung Park
Gaurav Parmar
Paritosh Parmar
Alvaro Parra
Despoina Paschalidou
Or Patashnik
Shivansh Patel
Pushpak Pati
Prashant W. Patil
Vaishakh Patil
Suvam Patra
Jay Patravali
Badri Narayana Patro
Angshuman Paul
Sudipta Paul
Rémi Pautrat
Nick E. Pears
Adithya Pediredla
Wenjie Pei
Shmuel Peleg
Latha Pemula
Bo Peng
Houwen Peng
Yue Peng
Liangzu Peng
Baoyun Peng
Jun Peng
Pai Peng
Sida Peng
Xi Peng
Yuxin Peng
Songyou Peng
Wei Peng

Weiqi Peng
Wen-Hsiao Peng
Pramuditha Perera
Juan C. Perez
Eduardo Pérez Pellitero
Juan-Manuel Perez-Rua
Federico Pernici
Marco Pesavento
Stavros Petridis
Ilya A. Petrov
Vladan Petrovic
Mathis Petrovich
Suzanne Petryk
Hieu Pham
Quang Pham
Khoi Pham
Tung Pham
Huy Phan
Stephen Phillips
Cheng Perng Phoo
David Picard
Marco Piccirilli
Georg Pichler
A. J. Piergiovanni
Vipin Pillai
Silvia L. Pintea
Giovanni Pintore
Robinson Piramuthu
Fiora Pirri
Theodoros Pissas
Fabio Pizzati
Benjamin Planche
Bryan Plummer
Matteo Poggi
Ashwini Pokle
Georgy E. Ponimatkin
Adrian Popescu
Stefan Popov
Nikola Popović
Ronald Poppe
Angelo Porrello
Michael Potter
Charalambos Poullis
Hadi Pouransari
Omid Poursaeed

Shraman Pramanick
Mantini Pranav
Dilip K. Prasad
Meghshyam Prasad
B. H. Pawan Prasad
Shitala Prasad
Prateek Prasanna
Ekta Prashnani
Derek S. Prijatelj
Luke Y. Prince
Véronique Prinet
Victor Adrian Prisacariu
James Pritts
Thomas Probst
Sergey Prokudin
Rita Pucci
Chi-Man Pun
Matthew Purri
Haozhi Qi
Lu Qi
Lei Qi
Xianbiao Qi
Yonggang Qi
Yuankai Qi
Siyuan Qi
Guocheng Qian
Hangwei Qian
Qi Qian
Deheng Qian
Shengsheng Qian
Wen Qian
Rui Qian
Yiming Qian
Shengju Qian
Shengyi Qian
Xuelin Qian
Zhenxing Qian
Nan Qiao
Xiaotian Qiao
Jing Qin
Can Qin
Siyang Qin
Hongwei Qin
Jie Qin
Minghai Qin

Yipeng Qin
Yongqiang Qin
Wenda Qin
Xuebin Qin
Yuzhe Qin
Yao Qin
Zhenyue Qin
Zhiwu Qing
Heqian Qiu
Jiayan Qiu
Jielin Qiu
Yue Qiu
Jiaxiong Qiu
Zhongxi Qiu
Shi Qiu
Zhaofan Qiu
Zhongnan Qu
Yanyun Qu
Kha Gia Quach
Yuhui Quan
Ruijie Quan
Mike Rabbat
Rahul Shekhar Rade
Filip Radenovic
Gorjan Radevski
Bogdan Raducanu
Francesco Ragusa
Shafin Rahman
Md Mahfuzur Rahman
  Siddiquee
Hossein Rahmani
Kiran Raja
Sivaramakrishnan
  Rajaraman
Jathushan Rajasegaran
Adnan Siraj Rakin
Michaël Ramamonjisoa
Chirag A. Raman
Shanmuganathan Raman
Vignesh Ramanathan
Vasili Ramanishka
Vikram V. Ramaswamy
Merey Ramazanova
Jason Rambach
Sai Saketh Rambhatla

Clément Rambour
Ashwin Ramesh Babu
Adín Ramírez Rivera
Arianna Rampini
Haoxi Ran
Aakanksha Rana
Aayush Jung Bahadur
  Rana
Kanchana N. Ranasinghe
Aneesh Rangnekar
Samrudhdhi B. Rangrej
Harsh Rangwani
Viresh Ranjan
Anyi Rao
Yongming Rao
Carolina Raposo
Michalis Raptis
Amir Rasouli
Vivek Rathod
Adepu Ravi Sankar
Avinash Ravichandran
Bharadwaj Ravichandran
Dripta S. Raychaudhuri
Adria Recasens
Simon Reiß
Davis Rempe
Daxuan Ren
Jiawei Ren
Jimmy Ren
Sucheng Ren
Dayong Ren
Zhile Ren
Dongwei Ren
Qibing Ren
Pengfei Ren
Zhenwen Ren
Xuqian Ren
Yixuan Ren
Zhongzheng Ren
Ambareesh Revanur
Hamed Rezazadegan
  Tavakoli
Rafael S. Rezende
Wonjong Rhee
Alexander Richard

Christian Richardt
Stephan R. Richter
Benjamin Riggan
Dominik Rivoir
Mamshad Nayeem Rizve
Joshua D. Robinson
Joseph Robinson
Chris Rockwell
Ranga Rodrigo
Andres C. Rodriguez
Carlos Rodriguez-Pardo
Marcus Rohrbach
Gemma Roig
Yu Rong
David A. Ross
Mohammad Rostami
Edward Rosten
Karsten Roth
Anirban Roy
Debaditya Roy
Shuvendu Roy
Ahana Roy Choudhury
Aruni Roy Chowdhury
Denys Rozumnyi
Shulan Ruan
Wenjie Ruan
Patrick Ruhkamp
Danila Rukhovich
Anian Ruoss
Chris Russell
Dan Ruta
Dawid Damian Rymarczyk
DongHun Ryu
Hyeonggon Ryu
Kwonyoung Ryu
Balasubramanian S.
Alexandre Sablayrolles
Mohammad Sabokrou
Arka Sadhu
Aniruddha Saha
Oindrila Saha
Pritish Sahu
Aneeshan Sain
Nirat Saini
Saurabh Saini

Takeshi Saitoh
Christos Sakaridis
Fumihiko Sakaue
Dimitrios Sakkos
Ken Sakurada
Parikshit V. Sakurikar
Rohit Saluja
Nermin Samet
Leo Sampaio Ferraz
    Ribeiro
Jorge Sanchez
Enrique Sanchez
Shengtian Sang
Anush Sankaran
Soubhik Sanyal
Nikolaos Sarafianos
Vishwanath Saragadam
István Sárándi
Saquib Sarfraz
Mert Bulent Sariyildiz
Anindya Sarkar
Pritam Sarkar
Paul-Edouard Sarlin
Hiroshi Sasaki
Takami Sato
Torsten Sattler
Ravi Kumar Satzoda
Axel Sauer
Stefano Savian
Artem Savkin
Manolis Savva
Gerald Schaefer
Simone Schaub-Meyer
Yoni Schirris
Samuel Schulter
Katja Schwarz
Jesse Scott
Sinisa Segvic
Constantin Marc Seibold
Lorenzo Seidenari
Matan Sela
Fadime Sener
Paul Hongsuck Seo
Kwanggyoon Seo
Hongje Seong

Dario Serez
Francesco Setti
Bryan Seybold
Mohamad Shahbazi
Shima Shahfar
Xinxin Shan
Caifeng Shan
Dandan Shan
Shawn Shan
Wei Shang
Jinghuan Shang
Jiaxiang Shang
Lei Shang
Sukrit Shankar
Ken Shao
Rui Shao
Jie Shao
Mingwen Shao
Aashish Sharma
Gaurav Sharma
Vivek Sharma
Abhishek Sharma
Yoli Shavit
Shashank Shekhar
Sumit Shekhar
Zhijie Shen
Fengyi Shen
Furao Shen
Jialie Shen
Jingjing Shen
Ziyi Shen
Linlin Shen
Guangyu Shen
Biluo Shen
Falong Shen
Jiajun Shen
Qiu Shen
Qiuhong Shen
Shuai Shen
Wang Shen
Yiqing Shen
Yunhang Shen
Siqi Shen
Bin Shen
Tianwei Shen

Xi Shen
Yilin Shen
Yuming Shen
Yucong Shen
Zhiqiang Shen
Lu Sheng
Yichen Sheng
Shivanand Venkanna
  Sheshappanavar
Shelly Sheynin
Baifeng Shi
Ruoxi Shi
Botian Shi
Hailin Shi
Jia Shi
Jing Shi
Shaoshuai Shi
Baoguang Shi
Boxin Shi
Hengcan Shi
Tianyang Shi
Xiaodan Shi
Yongjie Shi
Zhensheng Shi
Yinghuan Shi
Weiqi Shi
Wu Shi
Xuepeng Shi
Xiaoshuang Shi
Yujiao Shi
Zenglin Shi
Zhenmei Shi
Takashi Shibata
Meng-Li Shih
Yichang Shih
Hyunjung Shim
Dongseok Shim
Soshi Shimada
Inkyu Shin
Jinwoo Shin
Seungjoo Shin
Seungjae Shin
Koichi Shinoda
Suprosanna Shit

Palaiahnakote
  Shivakumara
Eli Shlizerman
Gaurav Shrivastava
Xiao Shu
Xiangbo Shu
Xiujun Shu
Yang Shu
Tianmin Shu
Jun Shu
Zhixin Shu
Bing Shuai
Maria Shugrina
Ivan Shugurov
Satya Narayan Shukla
Pranjay Shyam
Jianlou Si
Yawar Siddiqui
Alberto Signoroni
Pedro Silva
Jae-Young Sim
Oriane Siméoni
Martin Simon
Andrea Simonelli
Abhishek Singh
Ashish Singh
Dinesh Singh
Gurkirt Singh
Krishna Kumar Singh
Mannat Singh
Pravendra Singh
Rajat Vikram Singh
Utkarsh Singhal
Dipika Singhania
Vasu Singla
Harsh Sinha
Sudipta Sinha
Josef Sivic
Elena Sizikova
Geri Skenderi
Ivan Skorokhodov
Dmitriy Smirnov
Cameron Y. Smith
James S. Smith
Patrick Snape

Mattia Soldan
Hyeongseok Son
Sanghyun Son
Chuanbiao Song
Chen Song
Chunfeng Song
Dan Song
Dongjin Song
Hwanjun Song
Guoxian Song
Jiaming Song
Jie Song
Liangchen Song
Ran Song
Luchuan Song
Xibin Song
Li Song
Fenglong Song
Guoli Song
Guanglu Song
Zhenbo Song
Lin Song
Xinhang Song
Yang Song
Yibing Song
Rajiv Soundararajan
Hossein Souri
Cristovao Sousa
Riccardo Spezialetti
Leonidas Spinoulas
Michael W. Spratling
Deepak Sridhar
Srinath Sridhar
Gaurang Sriramanan
Vinkle Kumar Srivastav
Themos Stafylakis
Serban Stan
Anastasis Stathopoulos
Markus Steinberger
Jan Steinbrener
Sinisa Stekovic
Alexandros Stergiou
Gleb Sterkin
Rainer Stiefelhagen
Pierre Stock

Ombretta Strafforello
Julian Straub
Yannick Strümpler
Joerg Stueckler
Hang Su
Weijie Su
Jong-Chyi Su
Bing Su
Haisheng Su
Jinming Su
Yiyang Su
Yukun Su
Yuxin Su
Zhuo Su
Zhaoqi Su
Xiu Su
Yu-Chuan Su
Zhixun Su
Arulkumar Subramaniam
Akshayvarun Subramanya
A. Subramanyam
Swathikiran Sudhakaran
Yusuke Sugano
Masanori Suganuma
Yumin Suh
Yang Sui
Baochen Sun
Cheng Sun
Long Sun
Guolei Sun
Haoliang Sun
Haomiao Sun
He Sun
Hanqing Sun
Hao Sun
Lichao Sun
Jiachen Sun
Jiaming Sun
Jian Sun
Jin Sun
Jennifer J. Sun
Tiancheng Sun
Libo Sun
Peize Sun
Qianru Sun

Shanlin Sun
Yu Sun
Zhun Sun
Che Sun
Lin Sun
Tao Sun
Yiyou Sun
Chunyi Sun
Chong Sun
Weiwei Sun
Weixuan Sun
Xiuyu Sun
Yanan Sun
Zeren Sun
Zhaodong Sun
Zhiqing Sun
Minhyuk Sung
Jinli Suo
Simon Suo
Abhijit Suprem
Anshuman Suri
Saksham Suri
Joshua M. Susskind
Roman Suvorov
Gurumurthy Swaminathan
Robin Swanson
Paul Swoboda
Tabish A. Syed
Richard Szeliski
Fariborz Taherkhani
Yu-Wing Tai
Keita Takahashi
Walter Talbott
Gary Tam
Masato Tamura
Feitong Tan
Fuwen Tan
Shuhan Tan
Andong Tan
Bin Tan
Cheng Tan
Jianchao Tan
Lei Tan
Mingxing Tan
Xin Tan

Zichang Tan
Zhentao Tan
Kenichiro Tanaka
Masayuki Tanaka
Yushun Tang
Hao Tang
Jingqun Tang
Jinhui Tang
Kaihua Tang
Luming Tang
Lv Tang
Sheyang Tang
Shitao Tang
Siliang Tang
Shixiang Tang
Yansong Tang
Keke Tang
Chang Tang
Chenwei Tang
Jie Tang
Junshu Tang
Ming Tang
Peng Tang
Xu Tang
Yao Tang
Chen Tang
Fan Tang
Haoran Tang
Shengeng Tang
Yehui Tang
Zhipeng Tang
Ugo Tanielian
Chaofan Tao
Jiale Tao
Junli Tao
Renshuai Tao
An Tao
Guanhong Tao
Zhiqiang Tao
Makarand Tapaswi
Jean-Philippe G. Tarel
Juan J. Tarrio
Enzo Tartaglione
Keisuke Tateno
Zachary Teed

Ajinkya B. Tejankar
Bugra Tekin
Purva Tendulkar
Damien Teney
Minggui Teng
Chris Tensmeyer
Andrew Beng Jin Teoh
Philipp Terhörst
Kartik Thakral
Nupur Thakur
Kevin Thandiackal
Spyridon Thermos
Diego Thomas
William Thong
Yuesong Tian
Guanzhong Tian
Lin Tian
Shiqi Tian
Kai Tian
Meng Tian
Tai-Peng Tian
Zhuotao Tian
Shangxuan Tian
Tian Tian
Yapeng Tian
Yu Tian
Yuxin Tian
Leslie Ching Ow Tiong
Praveen Tirupattur
Garvita Tiwari
George Toderici
Antoine Toisoul
Aysim Toker
Tatiana Tommasi
Zhan Tong
Alessio Tonioni
Alessandro Torcinovich
Fabio Tosi
Matteo Toso
Hugo Touvron
Quan Hung Tran
Son Tran
Hung Tran
Ngoc-Trung Tran
Vinh Tran

Phong Tran
Giovanni Trappolini
Edith Tretschk
Subarna Tripathi
Shubhendu Trivedi
Eduard Trulls
Prune Truong
Thanh-Dat Truong
Tomasz Trzcinski
Sam Tsai
Yi-Hsuan Tsai
Ethan Tseng
Yu-Chee Tseng
Shahar Tsiper
Stavros Tsogkas
Shikui Tu
Zhigang Tu
Zhengzhong Tu
Richard Tucker
Sergey Tulyakov
Cigdem Turan
Daniyar Turmukhambetov
Victor G. Turrisi da Costa
Bartlomiej Twardowski
Christopher D. Twigg
Radim Tylecek
Mostofa Rafid Uddin
Md. Zasim Uddin
Kohei Uehara
Nicolas Ugrinovic
Youngjung Uh
Norimichi Ukita
Anwaar Ulhaq
Devesh Upadhyay
Paul Upchurch
Yoshitaka Ushiku
Yuzuko Utsumi
Mikaela Angelina Uy
Mohit Vaishnav
Pratik Vaishnavi
Jeya Maria Jose Valanarasu
Matias A. Valdenegro Toro
Diego Valsesia
Wouter Van Gansbeke
Nanne van Noord

Simon Vandenhende
Farshid Varno
Cristina Vasconcelos
Francisco Vasconcelos
Alex Vasilescu
Subeesh Vasu
Arun Balajee Vasudevan
Kanav Vats
Vaibhav S. Vavilala
Sagar Vaze
Javier Vazquez-Corral
Andrea Vedaldi
Olga Veksler
Andreas Velten
Sai H. Vemprala
Raviteja Vemulapalli
Shashanka
    Venkataramanan
Dor Verbin
Luisa Verdoliva
Manisha Verma
Yashaswi Verma
Constantin Vertan
Eli Verwimp
Deepak Vijaykeerthy
Pablo Villanueva
Ruben Villegas
Markus Vincze
Vibhav Vineet
Minh P. Vo
Huy V. Vo
Duc Minh Vo
Tomas Vojir
Igor Vozniak
Nicholas Vretos
Vibashan VS
Tuan-Anh Vu
Thang Vu
Mårten Wadenbäck
Neal Wadhwa
Aaron T. Walsman
Steven Walton
Jin Wan
Alvin Wan
Jia Wan

Jun Wan
Xiaoyue Wan
Fang Wan
Guowei Wan
Renjie Wan
Zhiqiang Wan
Ziyu Wan
Bastian Wandt
Dongdong Wang
Limin Wang
Haiyang Wang
Xiaobing Wang
Angtian Wang
Angelina Wang
Bing Wang
Bo Wang
Boyu Wang
Binghui Wang
Chen Wang
Chien-Yi Wang
Congli Wang
Qi Wang
Chengrui Wang
Rui Wang
Yiqun Wang
Cong Wang
Wenjing Wang
Dongkai Wang
Di Wang
Xiaogang Wang
Kai Wang
Zhizhong Wang
Fangjinhua Wang
Feng Wang
Hang Wang
Gaoang Wang
Guoqing Wang
Guangcong Wang
Guangzhi Wang
Hanqing Wang
Hao Wang
Haohan Wang
Haoran Wang
Hong Wang
Haotao Wang

Hu Wang
Huan Wang
Hua Wang
Hui-Po Wang
Hengli Wang
Hanyu Wang
Hongxing Wang
Jingwen Wang
Jialiang Wang
Jian Wang
Jianyi Wang
Jiashun Wang
Jiahao Wang
Tsun-Hsuan Wang
Xiaoqian Wang
Jinqiao Wang
Jun Wang
Jianzong Wang
Kaihong Wang
Ke Wang
Lei Wang
Lingjing Wang
Linnan Wang
Lin Wang
Liansheng Wang
Mengjiao Wang
Manning Wang
Nannan Wang
Peihao Wang
Jiayun Wang
Pu Wang
Qiang Wang
Qiufeng Wang
Qilong Wang
Qiangchang Wang
Qin Wang
Qing Wang
Ruocheng Wang
Ruibin Wang
Ruisheng Wang
Ruizhe Wang
Runqi Wang
Runzhong Wang
Wenxuan Wang
Sen Wang

Shangfei Wang
Shaofei Wang
Shijie Wang
Shiqi Wang
Zhibo Wang
Song Wang
Xinjiang Wang
Tai Wang
Tao Wang
Teng Wang
Xiang Wang
Tianren Wang
Tiantian Wang
Tianyi Wang
Fengjiao Wang
Wei Wang
Miaohui Wang
Suchen Wang
Siyue Wang
Yaoming Wang
Xiao Wang
Ze Wang
Biao Wang
Chaofei Wang
Dong Wang
Gu Wang
Guangrun Wang
Guangming Wang
Guo-Hua Wang
Haoqing Wang
Hesheng Wang
Huafeng Wang
Jinghua Wang
Jingdong Wang
Jingjing Wang
Jingya Wang
Jingkang Wang
Jiakai Wang
Junke Wang
Kuo Wang
Lichen Wang
Lizhi Wang
Longguang Wang
Mang Wang
Mei Wang

Min Wang
Peng-Shuai Wang
Run Wang
Shaoru Wang
Shuhui Wang
Tan Wang
Tiancai Wang
Tianqi Wang
Wenhai Wang
Wenzhe Wang
Xiaobo Wang
Xiudong Wang
Xu Wang
Yajie Wang
Yan Wang
Yuan-Gen Wang
Yingqian Wang
Yizhi Wang
Yulin Wang
Yu Wang
Yujie Wang
Yunhe Wang
Yuxi Wang
Yaowei Wang
Yiwei Wang
Zezheng Wang
Hongzhi Wang
Zhiqiang Wang
Ziteng Wang
Ziwei Wang
Zheng Wang
Zhenyu Wang
Binglu Wang
Zhongdao Wang
Ce Wang
Weining Wang
Weiyao Wang
Wenbin Wang
Wenguan Wang
Guangting Wang
Haolin Wang
Haiyan Wang
Huiyu Wang
Naiyan Wang
Jingbo Wang

Jinpeng Wang
Jiaqi Wang
Liyuan Wang
Lizhen Wang
Ning Wang
Wenqian Wang
Sheng-Yu Wang
Weimin Wang
Xiaohan Wang
Yifan Wang
Yi Wang
Yongtao Wang
Yizhou Wang
Zhuo Wang
Zhe Wang
Xudong Wang
Xiaofang Wang
Xinggang Wang
Xiaosen Wang
Xiaosong Wang
Xiaoyang Wang
Lijun Wang
Xinlong Wang
Xuan Wang
Xue Wang
Yangang Wang
Yaohui Wang
Yu-Chiang Frank Wang
Yida Wang
Yilin Wang
Yi Ru Wang
Yali Wang
Yinglong Wang
Yufu Wang
Yujiang Wang
Yuwang Wang
Yuting Wang
Yang Wang
Yu-Xiong Wang
Yixu Wang
Ziqi Wang
Zhicheng Wang
Zeyu Wang
Zhaowen Wang
Zhenyi Wang

Zhenzhi Wang
Zhijie Wang
Zhiyong Wang
Zhongling Wang
Zhuowei Wang
Zian Wang
Zifu Wang
Zihao Wang
Zirui Wang
Ziyan Wang
Wenxiao Wang
Zhen Wang
Zhepeng Wang
Zi Wang
Zihao W. Wang
Steven L. Waslander
Olivia Watkins
Daniel Watson
Silvan Weder
Dongyoon Wee
Dongming Wei
Tianyi Wei
Jia Wei
Dong Wei
Fangyun Wei
Longhui Wei
Mingqiang Wei
Xinyue Wei
Chen Wei
Donglai Wei
Pengxu Wei
Xing Wei
Xiu-Shen Wei
Wenqi Wei
Guoqiang Wei
Wei Wei
XingKui Wei
Xian Wei
Xingxing Wei
Yake Wei
Yuxiang Wei
Yi Wei
Luca Weihs
Michael Weinmann
Martin Weinmann

Congcong Wen
Chuan Wen
Jie Wen
Sijia Wen
Song Wen
Chao Wen
Xiang Wen
Zeyi Wen
Xin Wen
Yilin Wen
Yijia Weng
Shuchen Weng
Junwu Weng
Wenming Weng
Renliang Weng
Zhenyu Weng
Xinshuo Weng
Nicholas J. Westlake
Gordon Wetzstein
Lena M. Widin Klasén
Rick Wildes
Bryan M. Williams
Williem Williem
Ole Winther
Scott Wisdom
Alex Wong
Chau-Wai Wong
Kwan-Yee K. Wong
Yongkang Wong
Scott Workman
Marcel Worring
Michael Wray
Safwan Wshah
Xiang Wu
Aming Wu
Chongruo Wu
Cho-Ying Wu
Chunpeng Wu
Chenyan Wu
Ziyi Wu
Fuxiang Wu
Gang Wu
Haiping Wu
Huisi Wu
Jane Wu

Jialian Wu
Jing Wu
Jinjian Wu
Jianlong Wu
Xian Wu
Lifang Wu
Lifan Wu
Minye Wu
Qianyi Wu
Rongliang Wu
Rui Wu
Shiqian Wu
Shuzhe Wu
Shangzhe Wu
Tsung-Han Wu
Tz-Ying Wu
Ting-Wei Wu
Jiannan Wu
Zhiliang Wu
Yu Wu
Chenyun Wu
Dayan Wu
Dongxian Wu
Fei Wu
Hefeng Wu
Jianxin Wu
Weibin Wu
Wenxuan Wu
Wenhao Wu
Xiao Wu
Yicheng Wu
Yuanwei Wu
Yu-Huan Wu
Zhenxin Wu
Zhenyu Wu
Wei Wu
Peng Wu
Xiaohe Wu
Xindi Wu
Xinxing Wu
Xinyi Wu
Xingjiao Wu
Xiongwei Wu
Yangzheng Wu
Yanzhao Wu

Yawen Wu
Yong Wu
Yi Wu
Ying Nian Wu
Zhenyao Wu
Zhonghua Wu
Zongze Wu
Zuxuan Wu
Stefanie Wuhrer
Teng Xi
Jianing Xi
Fei Xia
Haifeng Xia
Menghan Xia
Yuanqing Xia
Zhihua Xia
Xiaobo Xia
Weihao Xia
Shihong Xia
Yan Xia
Yong Xia
Zhaoyang Xia
Zhihao Xia
Chuhua Xian
Yongqin Xian
Wangmeng Xiang
Fanbo Xiang
Tiange Xiang
Tao Xiang
Liuyu Xiang
Xiaoyu Xiang
Zhiyu Xiang
Aoran Xiao
Chunxia Xiao
Fanyi Xiao
Jimin Xiao
Jun Xiao
Taihong Xiao
Anqi Xiao
Junfei Xiao
Jing Xiao
Liang Xiao
Yang Xiao
Yuting Xiao
Yijun Xiao

Yao Xiao
Zeyu Xiao
Zhisheng Xiao
Zihao Xiao
Binhui Xie
Christopher Xie
Haozhe Xie
Jin Xie
Guo-Sen Xie
Hongtao Xie
Ming-Kun Xie
Tingting Xie
Chaohao Xie
Weicheng Xie
Xudong Xie
Jiyang Xie
Xiaohua Xie
Yuan Xie
Zhenyu Xie
Ning Xie
Xianghui Xie
Xiufeng Xie
You Xie
Yutong Xie
Fuyong Xing
Yifan Xing
Zhen Xing
Yuanjun Xiong
Jinhui Xiong
Weihua Xiong
Hongkai Xiong
Zhitong Xiong
Yuanhao Xiong
Yunyang Xiong
Yuwen Xiong
Zhiwei Xiong
Yuliang Xiu
An Xu
Chang Xu
Chenliang Xu
Chengming Xu
Chenshu Xu
Xiang Xu
Huijuan Xu
Zhe Xu

Jie Xu
Jingyi Xu
Jiarui Xu
Yinghao Xu
Kele Xu
Ke Xu
Li Xu
Linchuan Xu
Linning Xu
Mengde Xu
Mengmeng Frost Xu
Min Xu
Mingye Xu
Jun Xu
Ning Xu
Peng Xu
Runsheng Xu
Sheng Xu
Wenqiang Xu
Xiaogang Xu
Renzhe Xu
Kaidi Xu
Yi Xu
Chi Xu
Qiuling Xu
Baobei Xu
Feng Xu
Haohang Xu
Haofei Xu
Lan Xu
Mingze Xu
Songcen Xu
Weipeng Xu
Wenjia Xu
Wenju Xu
Xiangyu Xu
Xin Xu
Yinshuang Xu
Yixing Xu
Yuting Xu
Yanyu Xu
Zhenbo Xu
Zhiliang Xu
Zhiyuan Xu
Xiaohao Xu

Yanwu Xu
Yan Xu
Yiran Xu
Yifan Xu
Yufei Xu
Yong Xu
Zichuan Xu
Zenglin Xu
Zexiang Xu
Zhan Xu
Zheng Xu
Zhiwei Xu
Ziyue Xu
Shiyu Xuan
Hanyu Xuan
Fei Xue
Jianru Xue
Mingfu Xue
Qinghan Xue
Tianfan Xue
Chao Xue
Chuhui Xue
Nan Xue
Zhou Xue
Xiangyang Xue
Yuan Xue
Abhay Yadav
Ravindra Yadav
Kota Yamaguchi
Toshihiko Yamasaki
Kohei Yamashita
Chaochao Yan
Feng Yan
Kun Yan
Qingsen Yan
Qixin Yan
Rui Yan
Siming Yan
Xinchen Yan
Yaping Yan
Bin Yan
Qingan Yan
Shen Yan
Shipeng Yan
Xu Yan

Yan Yan
Yichao Yan
Zhaoyi Yan
Zike Yan
Zhiqiang Yan
Hongliang Yan
Zizheng Yan
Jiewen Yang
Anqi Joyce Yang
Shan Yang
Anqi Yang
Antoine Yang
Bo Yang
Baoyao Yang
Chenhongyi Yang
Dingkang Yang
De-Nian Yang
Dong Yang
David Yang
Fan Yang
Fengyu Yang
Fengting Yang
Fei Yang
Gengshan Yang
Heng Yang
Han Yang
Huan Yang
Yibo Yang
Jiancheng Yang
Jihan Yang
Jiawei Yang
Jiayu Yang
Jie Yang
Jinfa Yang
Jingkang Yang
Jinyu Yang
Cheng-Fu Yang
Ji Yang
Jianyu Yang
Kailun Yang
Tian Yang
Luyu Yang
Liang Yang
Li Yang
Michael Ying Yang

Yang Yang
Muli Yang
Le Yang
Qiushi Yang
Ren Yang
Ruihan Yang
Shuang Yang
Siyuan Yang
Su Yang
Shiqi Yang
Taojiannan Yang
Tianyu Yang
Lei Yang
Wanzhao Yang
Shuai Yang
William Yang
Wei Yang
Xiaofeng Yang
Xiaoshan Yang
Xin Yang
Xuan Yang
Xu Yang
Xingyi Yang
Xitong Yang
Jing Yang
Yanchao Yang
Wenming Yang
Yujiu Yang
Herb Yang
Jianfei Yang
Jinhui Yang
Chuanguang Yang
Guanglei Yang
Haitao Yang
Kewei Yang
Linlin Yang
Lijin Yang
Longrong Yang
Meng Yang
MingKun Yang
Sibei Yang
Shicai Yang
Tong Yang
Wen Yang
Xi Yang

Xiaolong Yang
Xue Yang
Yubin Yang
Ze Yang
Ziyi Yang
Yi Yang
Linjie Yang
Yuzhe Yang
Yiding Yang
Zhenpei Yang
Zhaohui Yang
Zhengyuan Yang
Zhibo Yang
Zongxin Yang
Hantao Yao
Mingde Yao
Rui Yao
Taiping Yao
Ting Yao
Cong Yao
Qingsong Yao
Quanming Yao
Xu Yao
Yuan Yao
Yao Yao
Yazhou Yao
Jiawen Yao
Shunyu Yao
Pew-Thian Yap
Sudhir Yarram
Rajeev Yasarla
Peng Ye
Botao Ye
Mao Ye
Fei Ye
Hanrong Ye
Jingwen Ye
Jinwei Ye
Jiarong Ye
Mang Ye
Meng Ye
Qi Ye
Qian Ye
Qixiang Ye
Junjie Ye

Sheng Ye
Nanyang Ye
Yufei Ye
Xiaoqing Ye
Ruolin Ye
Yousef Yeganeh
Chun-Hsiao Yeh
Raymond A. Yeh
Yu-Ying Yeh
Kai Yi
Chang Yi
Renjiao Yi
Xinping Yi
Peng Yi
Alper Yilmaz
Junho Yim
Hui Yin
Bangjie Yin
Jia-Li Yin
Miao Yin
Wenzhe Yin
Xuwang Yin
Ming Yin
Yu Yin
Aoxiong Yin
Kangxue Yin
Tianwei Yin
Wei Yin
Xianghua Ying
Rio Yokota
Tatsuya Yokota
Naoto Yokoya
Ryo Yonetani
Ki Yoon Yoo
Jinsu Yoo
Sunjae Yoon
Jae Shin Yoon
Jihun Yoon
Sung-Hoon Yoon
Ryota Yoshihashi
Yusuke Yoshiyasu
Chenyu You
Haoran You
Haoxuan You
Yang You

Quanzeng You
Tackgeun You
Kaichao You
Shan You
Xinge You
Yurong You
Baosheng Yu
Bei Yu
Haichao Yu
Hao Yu
Chaohui Yu
Fisher Yu
Jin-Gang Yu
Jiyang Yu
Jason J. Yu
Jiashuo Yu
Hong-Xing Yu
Lei Yu
Mulin Yu
Ning Yu
Peilin Yu
Qi Yu
Qian Yu
Rui Yu
Shuzhi Yu
Gang Yu
Tan Yu
Weijiang Yu
Xin Yu
Bingyao Yu
Ye Yu
Hanchao Yu
Yingchen Yu
Tao Yu
Xiaotian Yu
Qing Yu
Houjian Yu
Changqian Yu
Jing Yu
Jun Yu
Shujian Yu
Xiang Yu
Zhaofei Yu
Zhenbo Yu
Yinfeng Yu

Zhuoran Yu
Zitong Yu
Bo Yuan
Jiangbo Yuan
Liangzhe Yuan
Weihao Yuan
Jianbo Yuan
Xiaoyun Yuan
Ye Yuan
Li Yuan
Geng Yuan
Jialin Yuan
Maoxun Yuan
Peng Yuan
Xin Yuan
Yuan Yuan
Yuhui Yuan
Yixuan Yuan
Zheng Yuan
Mehmet Kerim Yücel
Kaiyu Yue
Haixiao Yue
Heeseung Yun
Sangdoo Yun
Tian Yun
Mahmut Yurt
Ekim Yurtsever
Ahmet Yüzügüler
Edouard Yvinec
Eloi Zablocki
Christopher Zach
Muhammad Zaigham
    Zaheer
Pierluigi Zama Ramirez
Yuhang Zang
Pietro Zanuttigh
Alexey Zaytsev
Bernhard Zeisl
Haitian Zeng
Pengpeng Zeng
Jiabei Zeng
Runhao Zeng
Wei Zeng
Yawen Zeng
Yi Zeng

Yiming Zeng
Tieyong Zeng
Huanqiang Zeng
Dan Zeng
Yu Zeng
Wei Zhai
Yuanhao Zhai
Fangneng Zhan
Kun Zhan
Xiong Zhang
Jingdong Zhang
Jiangning Zhang
Zhilu Zhang
Gengwei Zhang
Dongsu Zhang
Hui Zhang
Binjie Zhang
Bo Zhang
Tianhao Zhang
Cecilia Zhang
Jing Zhang
Chaoning Zhang
Chenxu Zhang
Chi Zhang
Chris Zhang
Yabin Zhang
Zhao Zhang
Rufeng Zhang
Chaoyi Zhang
Zheng Zhang
Da Zhang
Yi Zhang
Edward Zhang
Xin Zhang
Feifei Zhang
Feilong Zhang
Yuqi Zhang
GuiXuan Zhang
Hanlin Zhang
Hanwang Zhang
Hanzhen Zhang
Haotian Zhang
He Zhang
Haokui Zhang
Hongyuan Zhang

Hengrui Zhang
Hongming Zhang
Mingfang Zhang
Jianpeng Zhang
Jiaming Zhang
Jichao Zhang
Jie Zhang
Jingfeng Zhang
Jingyi Zhang
Jinnian Zhang
David Junhao Zhang
Junjie Zhang
Junzhe Zhang
Jiawan Zhang
Jingyang Zhang
Kai Zhang
Lei Zhang
Lihua Zhang
Lu Zhang
Miao Zhang
Minjia Zhang
Mingjin Zhang
Qi Zhang
Qian Zhang
Qilong Zhang
Qiming Zhang
Qiang Zhang
Richard Zhang
Ruimao Zhang
Ruisi Zhang
Ruixin Zhang
Runze Zhang
Qilin Zhang
Shan Zhang
Shanshan Zhang
Xi Sheryl Zhang
Song-Hai Zhang
Chongyang Zhang
Kaihao Zhang
Songyang Zhang
Shu Zhang
Siwei Zhang
Shujian Zhang
Tianyun Zhang
Tong Zhang

Tao Zhang
Wenwei Zhang
Wenqiang Zhang
Wen Zhang
Xiaolin Zhang
Xingchen Zhang
Xingxuan Zhang
Xiuming Zhang
Xiaoshuai Zhang
Xuanmeng Zhang
Xuanyang Zhang
Xucong Zhang
Xingxing Zhang
Xikun Zhang
Xiaohan Zhang
Yahui Zhang
Yunhua Zhang
Yan Zhang
Yanghao Zhang
Yifei Zhang
Yifan Zhang
Yi-Fan Zhang
Yihao Zhang
Yingliang Zhang
Youshan Zhang
Yulun Zhang
Yushu Zhang
Yixiao Zhang
Yide Zhang
Zhongwen Zhang
Bowen Zhang
Chen-Lin Zhang
Zehua Zhang
Zekun Zhang
Zeyu Zhang
Xiaowei Zhang
Yifeng Zhang
Cheng Zhang
Hongguang Zhang
Yuexi Zhang
Fa Zhang
Guofeng Zhang
Hao Zhang
Haofeng Zhang
Hongwen Zhang

Hua Zhang
Jiaxin Zhang
Zhenyu Zhang
Jian Zhang
Jianfeng Zhang
Jiao Zhang
Jiakai Zhang
Lefei Zhang
Le Zhang
Mi Zhang
Min Zhang
Ning Zhang
Pan Zhang
Pu Zhang
Qing Zhang
Renrui Zhang
Shifeng Zhang
Shuo Zhang
Shaoxiong Zhang
Weizhong Zhang
Xi Zhang
Xiaomei Zhang
Xinyu Zhang
Yin Zhang
Zicheng Zhang
Zihao Zhang
Ziqi Zhang
Zhaoxiang Zhang
Zhen Zhang
Zhipeng Zhang
Zhixing Zhang
Zhizheng Zhang
Jiawei Zhang
Zhong Zhang
Pingping Zhang
Yixin Zhang
Kui Zhang
Lingzhi Zhang
Huaiwen Zhang
Quanshi Zhang
Zhoutong Zhang
Yuhang Zhang
Yuting Zhang
Zhang Zhang
Ziming Zhang

Zhizhong Zhang
Qilong Zhangli
Bingyin Zhao
Bin Zhao
Chenglong Zhao
Lei Zhao
Feng Zhao
Gangming Zhao
Haiyan Zhao
Hao Zhao
Handong Zhao
Hengshuang Zhao
Yinan Zhao
Jiaojiao Zhao
Jiaqi Zhao
Jing Zhao
Kaili Zhao
Haojie Zhao
Yucheng Zhao
Longjiao Zhao
Long Zhao
Qingsong Zhao
Qingyu Zhao
Rui Zhao
Rui-Wei Zhao
Sicheng Zhao
Shuang Zhao
Siyan Zhao
Zelin Zhao
Shiyu Zhao
Wang Zhao
Tiesong Zhao
Qian Zhao
Wangbo Zhao
Xi-Le Zhao
Xu Zhao
Yajie Zhao
Yang Zhao
Ying Zhao
Yin Zhao
Yizhou Zhao
Yunhan Zhao
Yuyang Zhao
Yue Zhao
Yuzhi Zhao

Bowen Zhao
Pu Zhao
Bingchen Zhao
Borui Zhao
Fuqiang Zhao
Hanbin Zhao
Jian Zhao
Mingyang Zhao
Na Zhao
Rongchang Zhao
Ruiqi Zhao
Shuai Zhao
Wenda Zhao
Wenliang Zhao
Xiangyun Zhao
Yifan Zhao
Yaping Zhao
Zhou Zhao
He Zhao
Jie Zhao
Xibin Zhao
Xiaoqi Zhao
Zhengyu Zhao
Jin Zhe
Chuanxia Zheng
Huan Zheng
Hao Zheng
Jia Zheng
Jian-Qing Zheng
Shuai Zheng
Meng Zheng
Mingkai Zheng
Qian Zheng
Qi Zheng
Wu Zheng
Yinqiang Zheng
Yufeng Zheng
Yutong Zheng
Yalin Zheng
Yu Zheng
Feng Zheng
Zhaoheng Zheng
Haitian Zheng
Kang Zheng
Bolun Zheng

Haiyong Zheng
Mingwu Zheng
Sipeng Zheng
Tu Zheng
Wenzhao Zheng
Xiawu Zheng
Yinglin Zheng
Zhuo Zheng
Zilong Zheng
Kecheng Zheng
Zerong Zheng
Shuaifeng Zhi
Tiancheng Zhi
Jia-Xing Zhong
Yiwu Zhong
Fangwei Zhong
Zhihang Zhong
Yaoyao Zhong
Yiran Zhong
Zhun Zhong
Zichun Zhong
Bo Zhou
Boyao Zhou
Brady Zhou
Mo Zhou
Chunluan Zhou
Dingfu Zhou
Fan Zhou
Jingkai Zhou
Honglu Zhou
Jiaming Zhou
Jiahuan Zhou
Jun Zhou
Kaiyang Zhou
Keyang Zhou
Kuangqi Zhou
Lei Zhou
Lihua Zhou
Man Zhou
Mingyi Zhou
Mingyuan Zhou
Ning Zhou
Peng Zhou
Penghao Zhou
Qianyi Zhou

Shuigeng Zhou
Shangchen Zhou
Huayi Zhou
Zhize Zhou
Sanping Zhou
Qin Zhou
Tao Zhou
Wenbo Zhou
Xiangdong Zhou
Xiao-Yun Zhou
Xiao Zhou
Yang Zhou
Yipin Zhou
Zhenyu Zhou
Hao Zhou
Chu Zhou
Daquan Zhou
Da-Wei Zhou
Hang Zhou
Kang Zhou
Qianyu Zhou
Sheng Zhou
Wenhui Zhou
Xingyi Zhou
Yan-Jie Zhou
Yiyi Zhou
Yu Zhou
Yuan Zhou
Yuqian Zhou
Yuxuan Zhou
Zixiang Zhou
Wengang Zhou
Shuchang Zhou
Tianfei Zhou
Yichao Zhou
Alex Zhu
Chenchen Zhu
Deyao Zhu
Xiatian Zhu
Guibo Zhu
Haidong Zhu
Hao Zhu
Hongzi Zhu
Rui Zhu
Jing Zhu

Jianke Zhu
Junchen Zhu
Lei Zhu
Lingyu Zhu
Luyang Zhu
Menglong Zhu
Peihao Zhu
Hui Zhu
Xiaofeng Zhu
Tyler (Lixuan) Zhu
Wentao Zhu
Xiangyu Zhu
Xinqi Zhu
Xinxin Zhu
Xinliang Zhu
Yangguang Zhu
Yichen Zhu
Yixin Zhu
Yanjun Zhu
Yousong Zhu
Yuhao Zhu
Ye Zhu
Feng Zhu
Zhen Zhu
Fangrui Zhu
Jinjing Zhu
Linchao Zhu
Pengfei Zhu
Sijie Zhu
Xiaobin Zhu
Xiaoguang Zhu
Zezhou Zhu
Zhenyao Zhu
Kai Zhu
Pengkai Zhu
Bingbing Zhuang
Chengyuan Zhuang
Liansheng Zhuang
Peiye Zhuang
Yixin Zhuang
Yihong Zhuang
Junbao Zhuo
Andrea Ziani
Bartosz Zieliński
Primo Zingaretti

Nikolaos Zioulis
Andrew Zisserman
Yael Ziv
Liu Ziyin
Xingxing Zou
Danping Zou
Qi Zou

Shihao Zou
Xueyan Zou
Yang Zou
Yuliang Zou
Zihang Zou
Chuhang Zou
Dongqing Zou

Xu Zou
Zhiming Zou
Maria A. Zuluaga
Xinxin Zuo
Zhiwen Zuo
Reyer Zwiggelaar

Contents – Part III

TOCH: Spatio-Temporal Object-to-Hand Correspondence for Motion Refinement

Keyang Zhou[1,2]($\boxtimes$), Bharat Lal Bhatnagar[1,2], Jan Eric Lenssen[2], and Gerard Pons-Moll[1,2]

[1] University of Tübingen, Tübingen, Germany
{keyang.zhou,gerard.pons-moll}@uni-tuebingen.de
[2] Max Planck Institute for Informatics, Saarland Informatics Campus, Munich, Germany
{bbhatnag,jlenssen}@mpi-inf.mpg.de

Abstract. We present TOCH, a method for refining incorrect 3D hand-object interaction sequences using a correspondence based prior learnt directly from data. Existing hand trackers, especially those that rely on very few cameras, often produce visually unrealistic results with hand-object intersection or missing contacts. Although correcting such errors requires reasoning about temporal aspects of interaction, most previous works focus on static grasps and contacts. The core of our method are TOCH fields, a novel spatio-temporal representation for modeling correspondences between hands and objects during interaction. TOCH fields are a point-wise, object-centric representation, which encode the hand position relative to the object. Leveraging this novel representation, we learn a latent manifold of plausible TOCH fields with a temporal denoising auto-encoder. Experiments demonstrate that TOCH outperforms state-of-the-art 3D hand-object interaction models, which are limited to static grasps and contacts. More importantly, our method produces smooth interactions even before and after contact. Using a single trained TOCH model, we quantitatively and qualitatively demonstrate its usefulness for correcting erroneous sequences from off-the-shelf RGB/RGB-D hand-object reconstruction methods and transferring grasps across objects. Our code and model are available at [1].

Keywords: Hand-object interaction · Motion refinement · Hand prior

1 Introduction

Tracking hands that are in interaction with objects is an important part of many applications in Virtual and Augmented Reality, such as modeling digital

Supplementary Information The online version contains supplementary material available at https://doi.org/10.1007/978-3-031-20062-5_1.

humans capable of manipulation tasks [6,23,59,70,77]. Although there exists a vast amount of literature about tracking hands in isolation, much less work has focused on joint tracking of objects and hands. The high degrees of freedom in possible hand configurations, frequent occlusions, noisy or incomplete observations (*e.g* lack of depth channel in RGB images) make the problem heavily ill-posed. We argue that tracking interacting hands requires a powerful prior learned from a set of clean interaction sequences, which is the core principle of our method.

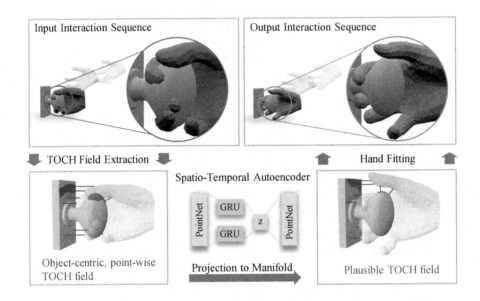

Fig. 1. We propose TOCH, a model for correcting erroneous hand-object interaction sequences. TOCH takes as input a tracking sequence produced by any existing tracker. We extract TOCH fields, a novel object-centric correspondence representation, from a noisy hand-object mesh sequence. The extracted noisy TOCH fields are fed into an auto-encoder, which projects it onto a learned hand motion manifold. Lastly, we obtain the corrected tracking sequence by fitting hands to the reconstructed TOCH fields. TOCH is applicable to interaction sequences even before and after contact happens.

Beyond the aforementioned challenges, subtle errors in hand estimation have a huge impact on perceived realism. For example, if the 3D object is floating in the air, is grasped in a non-physically plausible way, or hand and object intersect, the perceived quality will be poor. Unfortunately, such artifacts are common in pure hand-tracking methods. Researchers have used different heuristics to improve plausibility, such as inter-penetration constraints [28] and smoothness priors [26]. A recent line of work predicts likely static hand poses and grasps for a given object [24,35] but those methods can not directly be used as a prior to fix common capturing and tracking errors. Although there exists work to refine hand-object interactions [22,60], it is only concerned with static grasps.

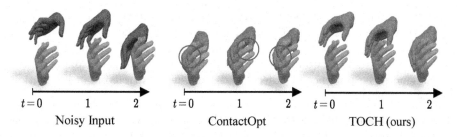

Fig. 2. Example refinement of an interaction sequence. Left: a noisy sequence of a hand approaching and grasping another static hand. Middle: ContactOpt [22] always snaps the hand into grasping posture regardless of its position relative to the object, as it is not designed for sequences. Right: TOCH preserves the relative hand-object arrangement during interaction while refining the final grasp.

In this work, we propose TOCH, a data-driven method for refining noisy 3D hand-object interaction sequences. In contrast to previous work in interaction modeling, TOCH not only considers static interactions but can also be applied to sequences without introducing snapping artifacts. The whole approach is outlined in Fig. 1. Our key insight is that estimating point-wise, spatio-temporal object-hand correspondences are crucial for realism, and sufficient to constrain the high-dimensional hand poses. Thus, the point-wise corresponcendes between object and hand are encoded in a novel spatio-temporal representation called *TOCH field*, which takes the object geometry and the configuration of the hand with respect to the object into account. We then learn the manifold of plausible TOCH fields from the recently released MoCap dataset of hand-object interactions [60] using an auto-encoder and apply it to correcting noisy observations. In contrast to conventional binary contacts [11,22,67], TOCH fields also encode the position of hand parts that are not directly in contact with the object, making TOCH applicable to whole interaction sequences, see Fig. 2. TOCH has further useful properties for practical application:

- TOCH can effectively project implausible hand motions to the learned object-centric hand motion manifold and produces visually correct interaction sequences that outperform previous static approaches.
- TOCH does not depend on specific sensor data (RGB image, depth map *etc.*) and can be used with any tracker.
- TOCH can be used to transfer grasp sequences across objects sharing similar geometry, even though it is not designed for this task.

2 Related Work

2.1 Hand and Object Reconstruction

Hand Reconstruction and Tracking. Reconstructing 3D hand surfaces from RGB or depth observations is a well-studied problem [31]. Existing work can generally be classified into two paradigms: discriminative approaches [9,14,20,44,80] directly estimate hand shape and pose parameters from the observation, while generative approaches [58,61,63] iteratively optimize a parametric hand model so that its projection matches the observation. Recently, more challenging settings such as reconstructing two interacting hands [47,56,72] are also explored. These works ignore the presence of objects and are hence less reliable in interaction-intensive scenarios.

Joint Hand and Object Reconstruction. Jointly reconstructing hand and object in interaction [4,49,51,57,66,73,74] has received much attention. Owing to the increasing amount of hand-object interaction datasets with annotations [11,19,25,29,39,82], deep neural networks are often used to estimate an initial hypothesis for hand and object poses, which are then jointly optimized to meet certain interaction constraints [13,15,26,27,29]. Most works in this direction improve contact realism by encouraging a small hand-to-object distance and penalizing inter-penetrating vertices [4,33]. However, these simple approaches often yield implausible interaction and do not take the whole motion sequence into account. In contrast, our method alleviates both shortcomings through a object-centric, temporal representation that also considers frames in which hand and object are not in direct contact.

2.2   Hand Contact and Grasp

Grasp Synthesis. Synthesizing novel hand grasp given an object has been widely studied in robotics [55]. Traditional approaches either optimize for force-closure condition [17] or sample and rank grasp candidates based on learned features [8]. There are also hybrid approaches that combine the merits of both [40,45]. Recently, a number of neural network-based models have been proposed for this task [16,28,32,60,81]. In particular, [34,35] represent the hand-object proximity as an implicit function. We took a similar approach and represent the hand relative to the object by signed distance values distributed on the object.

Object Manipulation Synthesis. In comparison with static grasp synthesis, generating dexterous manipulation of objects is a more difficult problem since it additionally requires dynamic hand and object interaction to be modeled. This task is usually approached by optimizing hand poses to satisfy a range of contact force constraints [42,46,69,79]. Hand motions generated by these works are physically plausible but lack natural variations. Zhang *et al.* [75] utilized various hand-object spatial representations to learn object manipulation from data. An IK solver is used to avoid inter-penetration. We took a different approach and solely use an object-centric spatio-temporal representation, which is shown to be less prone to interaction artifacts.

Contact Refinement. Recently, some works focus on refining hand and object contact [22,60,68]. Both [68] and [22] propose to first estimate the potential contact region on the object and then fit the hand to match the predicted contact. However, limited by the proposed contact representation, they can only model hand and object *in stable grasp*. While we share a similar goal, our work can also deal with the case where the hand is *close to* but not in contact with the object, as a result of our novel hand-object correspondence representation. Hence our method can be used to refine a tracking sequence.

2.3 Pose and Motion Prior

It has been observed that most human activities lie on low-dimensional manifolds [18,65]. Therefore natural motion patterns can be found by applying learned data priors. A pose or motion prior can facilitate a range of tasks including pose estimation from images or videos [3,7,43,71], motion interpolation [41], motion capture [64,76], and motion synthesis [2,12,30]. Early attempts in capturing pose and motion priors mostly use simple statistical models such as PCA [50], Gaussian Mixture Models [7] or Gaussian Process Dynamical Models [65]. With the advent of deep generative models [21,36], recent works rely on auto-encoders [37,52] and adversarial discriminators [38,78] to more faithfully capture the motion distribution.

Compared to body motion prior, there is less work devoted to hand motion priors. Ng et al. [48] learned a prior of conversational hand gestures conditioned on body motion. Our work bears the most similarity to [24], where an object-dependent hand pose prior was learned to foster tracking. Hamer et al. [24] proposed to map hand parts into local object coordinates and learn the object-dependent distribution with a Parzen density estimator. The prior is learned on a few objects and subsequently transferred to objects from the same class by geometric warping. Hence it cannot truly capture the complex correlation between hand gesture and object geometry.

3 Method

In this section, we describe our method for refining hand pose sequences during interaction with an object. We begin by introducing the problem setting and outlining our approach. Let $\boldsymbol{H} = (\boldsymbol{H}^i)_{1 \leq i \leq T}$ with $\boldsymbol{H}^i \in \mathbb{R}^{K \times 3}$ denote a sequence of vertices that describe hand meshes over the course of an interaction over T frames. We only deal with sequences containing a single hand and a single rigid object mesh, whose vertices we denote as $\boldsymbol{O} \in \mathbb{R}^{L \times 3}$. We assume the object shape to be known. Since we care about hand motion relative to the object, we express the hands in local object space, and the object coordinates remain fixed over the sequence. The per-frame hand vertices $\boldsymbol{H}^i$ in object space are produced by a parametric hand model MANO [54] using linear blend skinning:

$$\boldsymbol{H}^i = \text{LBS}\left(\boldsymbol{Y}; \beta, \boldsymbol{\theta}^i\right) + \boldsymbol{t}^i_H. \tag{1}$$

where the parameters $\{\beta^i, \boldsymbol{\theta}^i, \boldsymbol{t}^i\}$ denote shape, pose and translation w.r.t. template hand mesh $\boldsymbol{Y}$ respectively.

Observing the hand-object motion through RGB or depth sensors, a hand tracker yields an estimated hand motion sequence $\tilde{\boldsymbol{H}} = (\tilde{\boldsymbol{H}}^i)_{1 \leq i \leq T}$. The goal of our method is to improve the perceptual realism of this potentially noisy estimate using prior information learned from training data.

Concept. We observe that during hand-object interactions, the hand motion is heavily constrained by the object shape. Therefore, noisy hand-object interaction is a deviation from a low-dimensional manifold of realistic hand motions, conditioned on the object. We formulate our goal as learning a mapping to maximize the posterior $p(\boldsymbol{H}|\tilde{\boldsymbol{H}}, \boldsymbol{O})$ of the real motion $\boldsymbol{H}$ given the noisy observation $\tilde{\boldsymbol{H}}$ and the object with which the hand interacts. This amounts to finding an appropriate sequence of MANO parameters, which is done in three steps (see Fig. 1): **1)** The initial estimate of a hand motion sequence is encoded with a TOCH field, our object-centric, point-wise correspondence representation (Sect. 3.1). **2)** The TOCH fields are projected to a learned low-dimensional manifold using a temporal denoising auto-encoder (Sect. 3.2). **3)** A sequence of corrected hand meshes is obtained from the processed TOCH fields (Sect. 3.3).

3.1   TOCH Fields

Naively training an auto-encoder on hand meshes is problematic, because the model could ignore the conditioning object and learn a plain hand motion prior (Sect. 4.5). Moreover, if we include the object into the formulation, the model would need to learn manifolds for all joint rigid transformation of hand and object, which leads to high problem complexity [35]. Thus, we represent the hand as a TOCH field $\boldsymbol{F}$, which is a spatio-temporal object-centric representation that makes our approach invariant to joint hand and object rotation and translation.

TOCH Field Representation. For an initial estimation $\tilde{\boldsymbol{H}}$ of the hand mesh and the given object mesh $\boldsymbol{O}$, we define the TOCH field as a collection of point-wise vectors on a set $\{\boldsymbol{o}_i\}_{i=1}^N$ of N points, sampled from the object surface:

$$\boldsymbol{F}(\tilde{\boldsymbol{H}}, \boldsymbol{O}) = \{(c_i, d_i, \boldsymbol{y_i})\}_{i=1}^N, \tag{2}$$

where $c_i \in \{0, 1\}$ is a binary flag indicating whether the i-th sampled object point has a corresponding point on the hand surface, $d_i \in \mathbb{R}$ is the signed distance between the object point and its corresponding hand point, and $\boldsymbol{y}_i \in \mathbb{R}^3$ are the coordinates of the corresponding hand point on the un-posed canonical MANO template mesh. Note that $\boldsymbol{y}_i$ is a 3D location on the hand surface embedded in $\mathbb{R}^3$, encoding the correspondence similar to [5, 62].

Finding Correspondences. As we model whole interaction sequences, including frames in which the hand and the object are not in contact, we cannot simply define the correspondences as points that lie within a certain distance to each other. Instead, we generalize the notion of contact by diffusing the object mesh into $\mathbb{R}^3$. We cast rays from the object surface along its normal directions, as outlined in Fig. 1. The object normal vectors are obtained from the given object mesh. The correspondence of an object point is obtained as the first intersection with the hand mesh. If there is no intersection, or the first intersection is not the hand, this object point has no correspondence. If the object point is inside the hand, which might happen in case of noisy observations, we search for correspondences along the negative normal direction. The detailed procedure for determining correspondences is listed in Algorithm 1.

Algorithm 1: Finding object-hand correspondences

Input: Hand mesh H, object mesh O, uniformly sampled object points and normals $\{o_i, n_i\}_{i=1}^N$

Output: Binary correspondence indicators $\{c_i\}_{i=1}^N$

for $i = 1$ to N do
> $c_i \leftarrow 0$;
> if o_i inside H $s \leftarrow -1$ else $s \leftarrow 1$ $r_1 \leftarrow \text{ray}(o_i, sn_i)$;
> $p_1 \leftarrow \text{ray\_mesh\_intersection}(r_1, H)$;
> if $p_1 \neq \varnothing$
>> $r_2 \leftarrow \text{ray}(o_i + \epsilon sn_i, sn_i)$;
>> $p_2 \leftarrow \text{ray\_mesh\_intersection}(r_2, O)$;
>> if $p_2 = \varnothing$ or $\|o_i - p_1\| < \|o_i - p_2\|$
>>> $c_i \leftarrow 1$;

Representation Properties. The described TOCH field representation has the following advantages. **1)** It is naturally invariant to joint rotation and translation of object and hand, which reduces required model complexity. **2)** By specifying the distance between corresponding points, TOCH fields enable a subsequent auto-encoder to reason about point-wise proximity of hand and object. This helps to correct various artifacts, *e.g.* inter-penetration can be simply detected by finding object vertices with a negative correspondence distance. **3)** From surface normal directions of object points and the corresponding distances, a TOCH field can be seen as an encoding of the partial hand point cloud from the perspective of the object surface. We can explicitly derive that point cloud from the TOCH field and use it to infer hand pose and shape by fitting the hand model to the point cloud (c.f. Sect. 3.3).

3.2 Temporal Denoising Auto-Encoder

To project a noisy TOCH field to the correct manifold, we use a temporal denoising auto-encoder, consisting of an encoder $g_{\text{enc}} : (\tilde{F}_i)_{1 \leq i \leq T} \mapsto (z_i)_{1 \leq i \leq T}$, which maps a sequence of noisy TOCH fields (concatenated with the coordinates and normals of each object point) to latent representation, and a decoder $g_{\text{dec}} : (z_i)_{1 \leq i \leq T} \mapsto (\hat{F}_i)_{1 \leq i \leq T}$, which computes the corrected TOCH fields $\hat{F}$ from the latent codes. As TOCH fields consist of feature vectors attached to points, we use a PointNet-like [53] architecture. The point features in each frame are first processed by consecutive PointNet blocks to extract frame-wise features. These features are then fed into a bidirectional GRU layer to capture temporal motion patterns. The decoder network again concatenates the encoded frame-wise features with coordinates and normals of the object points and produces denoised TOCH fields $(\hat{F}_i)_{1 \leq i \leq T}$. The network is trained by minimizing

$$\mathcal{L}(\hat{F}, F) = \sum_{i=1}^{T} \sum_{j=1}^{N} c_j^i \left(\|\hat{y}_j^i - y_j^i\|_2^2 + w_{ij}(\hat{d}_j^i - d_j^i)^2 \right) - \text{BCE}(\hat{c}_j^i, c_j^i), \qquad (3)$$

where $\boldsymbol{F}$ denotes the groundtruth TOCH fields and $\text{BCE}(\hat{c}_j^i, c_j^i)$ is the binary cross entropy between output and target correspondence indicators. Note that we only compute the first two parts of the loss on TOCH field elements with $c_j^i = 1$, i.e. object points that have a corresponding hand point. We use a weighted loss on the distances $\hat{d}_j^i$. The weights are defined as

$$w_{ij} = \frac{\exp\left(-\left\|d_j^i\right\|\right)}{\sum_{k=1}^{N_i} \exp\left(-\left\|d_k^i\right\|\right)} N_i, \tag{4}$$

where $N_i = \sum_{j=1}^{N} c_j^i$. This weighting scheme encourages the network to focus on regions of close interaction, where a slight error could have huge impact on contact realism. Multiplying by the sum of correspondence ensures equal influence of all points in the sequence instead of equal influence of all frames.

3.3   Hand Motion Reconstruction

After projecting the noisy TOCH fields of input tracking sequence to the manifold learned by the auto-encoder, we need to recover the hand motion from the processed TOCH fields. The TOCH field is not fully differentiable w.r.t. the hand parameters, as changing correspondences would involve discontinuous function steps. Thus, we cannot directly optimize the hand pose parameters to produce the target TOCH field. Instead, we decompose the optimization into two steps. We first use the denoised TOCH fields to locate hand points corresponding to the object points. We then optimize the MANO model to find hands that best fit these points, which is a differentiable formulation.

Formally, given denoised TOCH fields $\boldsymbol{F}^i(\boldsymbol{H}, \boldsymbol{O}) = \{(c_j^i, d_j^i, \boldsymbol{y}_j^i)\}_{j=1}^{N}$ for frames $i \in \{1, ..., T\}$ on object points $\{\boldsymbol{o}_j\}_{j=1}^{N}$, we first produce the partial point clouds $\hat{\boldsymbol{Y}}^i$ of the hand as seen from the object's perspective:

$$\hat{\boldsymbol{y}}_j^i = \boldsymbol{o}_j + d_j^i \boldsymbol{n}_j^i. \tag{5}$$

Then, we fit MANO to those partial point clouds by minimizing:

$$\mathcal{L}(\boldsymbol{\beta}, \boldsymbol{\theta}, \boldsymbol{t}_H) = \sum_{i=1}^{T} \mathcal{L}_{\text{corr}}(\boldsymbol{\beta}, \boldsymbol{\theta}^i, \boldsymbol{t}_H) + \mathcal{L}_{\text{reg}}(\boldsymbol{\beta}, \boldsymbol{\theta}). \tag{6}$$

The first term of Eq. 6 is the hand-object correspondence loss

$$\mathcal{L}_{\text{corr}}(\boldsymbol{\beta}, \boldsymbol{\theta}^i, \boldsymbol{t}_H) = \sum_{j=1}^{N} c_j^i \left\| \hat{\boldsymbol{y}}_j^i - \left(\text{LBS} \left(\text{Proj}_{\boldsymbol{Y}}\left(\boldsymbol{y}_j^i\right); \boldsymbol{\beta}, \boldsymbol{\theta}^i\right) + \boldsymbol{t}_H \right) \right\|^2, \tag{7}$$

where LBS is the linear blend skinning function in Eq. 1 and $\text{Proj}_{\boldsymbol{Y}}(\cdot)$ projects a point to the nearest point on the template hand surface. This loss term ensures that the deformed template hand point corresponding to $\boldsymbol{o}_i$ is at a predetermined position derived from the TOCH field.

The last term of (6) regularizes shape and pose parameters of MANO,

$$\mathcal{L}_{\text{reg}}(\boldsymbol{\beta}, \boldsymbol{\theta}) = w_1 \|\boldsymbol{\beta}\|^2 + w_2 \sum_{i=1}^{T} \|\boldsymbol{\theta}^i\|^2 + w_3 \sum_{i=1}^{T-1} \|\boldsymbol{\theta}^{i+1} - \boldsymbol{\theta}^i\|^2 + w_4 \sum_{i=2}^{T-1} \sum_{k=1}^{J} \|\ddot{\boldsymbol{p}}_k^i\|$$

(8)

where $\ddot{\boldsymbol{p}}_k^i$ is the acceleration of hand joint k in frame i. Besides regularizing the norm of MANO parameters, we additionally enforce temporal smoothness of hand poses. This is necessary because (7) only constrains those parts of a hand with object correspondences. Per-frame fitting of TOCH fields leads to multiple plausible solutions, which can only be disambiguated by considering neighbouring frames. Since (6) is highly nonconvex, we optimize it in two stages. In the first stage, we freeze shape and pose, and only optimize hand orientation and translation. We then jointly optimize all the variables in the second stage.

4 Experiments

In this section, we evaluate the presented method on synthetic and real datasets of hand/object interaction. Our goal is to verify that TOCH produces *realistic interaction sequences* (Sect. 4.3), *outperforms previous static approaches* in several metrics (Sect. 4.4), and derives a *meaningful representation* for hand object interaction (Sect. 4.5). Before presenting the results, we introduce the used datasets in Sect. 4.1 and the evaluated metrics in Sect. 4.2.

4.1 Datasets

GRAB. We train TOCH on GRAB [60], a MoCap dataset for whole-body grasping of objects. GRAB contains interaction sequences with 51 objects from [10]. We pre-select 10 objects for validation and testing, and train with the rest sequences. Since we are only interested in frames where interaction is about to take place, we filter out frames where the hand wrist is more than 15 cm away from the object. Due to symmetry of the two hands, we anchor correspondences to the right hand and flip left hands to increase the amount of training data.

HO-3D. HO-3D is a dataset of hand-object video sequences captured by RGB-D cameras. It provides frame-wise annotations for 3D hand poses and 6D object poses, which are obtained from a novel joint optimization procedure. To ensure fair comparison with baselines which are not designed for sequences without contact, we compare on a selected subset of static frames with hand-object contact.

4.2 Metrics

Mean Per-Joint Position Error (MPJPE). We report the average Euclidean distance between refined and groundtruth 3D hand joints. Since pose annotation quality varies across datasets, this metric should be jointly assessed with other perceptual metrics.

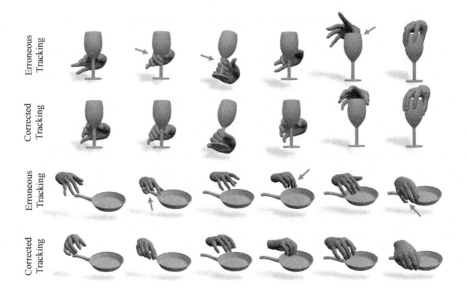

Fig. 3. Qualitative results on two synthetic hand-object interaction sequences that suffer from inter-penetration and non-smooth hand motion. The results after TOCH refinement show correct contact and are much more visually plausible. Note that TOCH only applies minor changes in hand poses but the perceived realism is largely enhanced. Check the supplemental video for animated results.

Mean Per-Vertex Position Error (MPVPE). This metric represents the average Euclidean distance between refined and groundtruth 3D meshes. It assesses the reconstruction accuracy of both hand shape and pose.

Solid Intersection Volume (IV). We measure hand-object inter-penetration by voxelizing hand and object meshes and reporting the volume of voxels occupied by both. Solely considering this metric can be misleading since it does not account for the case where the object is not in effective contact with the hand.

Contact IoU (C-IoU). This metric assesses the Intersection-over-Union between the groundtruth contact map and the predicted contact map. The contact map is obtained from the binary hand-object correspondence by thresholding the correspondence distance within ± 2 mm. We only report this metric on GRAB since the groundtruth annotations in HO-3D are not accurate enough [22].

4.3   Refining Synthetic Tracking Error

In order to use TOCH in real settings, it would be ideal to train the model on the predictions of existing hand trackers. However, this requires large amount of images/depth sequences paired with accurate hand and object annotations, which is currently not available. Moreover, targeting a specific tracker might lead to overfitting to tracker-specific errors, which is undesirable for generalization.

Table 1. We quantitatively evaluate TOCH on multiple perturbed GRAB test sets with different types and magnitude of noise. The numbers inside the parentheses indicate standard deviation of the sampled Gaussian noise. Although pose accuracy is not always improved, TOCH significantly boosts interaction realism for all noise levels, which is demonstrated by the increase in contact IoU and reduction in hand-object inter-penetration.

GRAB-Type → Noise →	GRAB-T (0.01)	GRAB-T (0.02)	GRAB-R (0.3)	GRAB-R (0.5)	GRAB-B (0.01 & 0.3)
MPJPE (mm) ↓	16.0 → **9.93**	31.9 → **12.3**	**4.58** → 9.58	**7.53** → 9.12	17.3 → **10.3**
MPVPE (mm) ↓	16.0 → **11.8**	31.9 → **13.9**	**6.30** → 11.5	**10.3** → 11.0	18.3 → **12.1**
IV (cm³) ↓	2.48 → **1.79**	**2.40** → 2.50	1.88 → **1.52**	1.78 → **1.35**	2.20 → **1.78**
C-IoU (%) ↑	3.56 → **29.2**	2.15 → **16.7**	11.4 → **26.6**	5.06 → **24.4**	1.76 → **26.6**

Table 2. Quantitative evaluation on HO-3D compared to Hasson *et al.* [26], RefineNet [60] and ContactOpt [22]. We follow the evaluation protocol of HO-3D and report hand joint and mesh errors after Procrustes alignment. TOCH outperforms all the baselines in terms of pose error and interaction quality.

Method	HO-3D		
	MPJPE (mm) ↓	MPVPE (mm) ↓	IV (cm³) ↓
Hasson *et al.*	11.4	11.4	9.26
RefineNet	11.6	11.5	8.11
ContactOpt	9.47	9.45	5.71
TOCH (ours)	**9.32**	**9.28**	**4.66**

We observe that hand errors can be decomposed into inaccurate global translation and inaccurate joint rotations, and the inaccuracies produced by most state-of-the-art trackers are small. Therefore, we propose to synthesize tracking errors by manually perturbing the groundtruth hand poses of the GRAB dataset. To this end, we apply three different types of perturbation to GRAB: translation-dominant perturbation (abbreviated GRAB-T in the table) applies an additive noise to hand translation t_H only, pose-dominant perturbation (abbreviated GRAB-R) applies an additive noise to hand pose θ only, and balanced perturbation (abbreviated GRAB-B) uses a combination of both. We only train on the last type while evaluate on all three. The quantitative results are shown in Table 1 and qualitative results are presented in Fig. 3.

We can make the following observations. First, TOCH is most effective for correcting translation-dominant perturbations of the hand. For pose-dominant perturbations where the vertex and joint errors are already very small, the resulting hands after TOCH refinement exhibit larger errors. This is because TOCH aims to improve interaction quality of a tracking sequence, which can hardly be reflected by distance based metrics such as MPJPE and MPVPE. We argue that more important metrics for interaction are intersection volume and contact IoU. As an example, the perturbation of GRAB-R (0.3) only induces a tiny joint position error of 4.6 mm, while it results in a significant 88.6% drop in

Input Image   HOnnotate   ContactOpt   TOCH (ours)

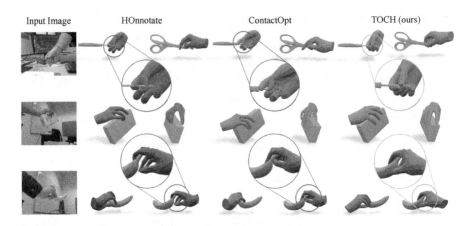

Fig. 4. Qualitative comparison with HOnnotate and ContactOpt. Each sample reconstruction is visualized in two views, the image-aligned view and a side view. We can clearly see hand-object inter-penetrations for HOnnotate and ContactOpt, while our reconstructions are more visually realistic.

contact IoU. This validates our observation that any slight change in pose has a notable impact on physical plausibility of interaction. TOCH effectively reduces hand-object intersection as well as boosts the contact IoU even when the noise of testing data is higher than that of training data.

4.4   Refining RGB(D)-Based Hand Estimators

To evaluate how well TOCH generalizes to real tracking errors, we test TOCH on state-of-the-art models for joint hand-object estimation from image or depth sequences. We first report comparisons with the RGB-based hand pose estimator [26], and two grasp refinement methods RefineNet [60] and ContactOpt [22] in Table 2. Hasson *et al.* [26] predict hand meshes from images, while RefineNet and ContactOpt have no knowledge about visual observations and directly refine hands based on 3D inputs. Groundtruth object meshes are assumed to be given for all the methods. TOCH achieves the best score for all three metrics on HO-3D. In particular, it reduces the mesh intersection volume, indicating an improved interaction quality. We additionally evaluate TOCH on HOnnotate [25], a state-of-the-art RGB-D tracker which annotates the groundtruth for HO-3D. Figure 4 shows some of its failure cases and how they are corrected by TOCH.

4.5   Analysis and Ablation Studies

Grasp Transfer. In order to demonstrate the wide-applicability of our learned features, we utilize the pre-trained TOCH auto-encoder for grasp transfer although it was not trained for this task. The goal is to transfer grasping

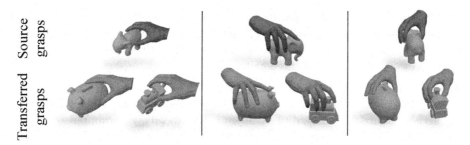

Fig. 5. Transferring grasping poses across objects of different geometry. The top row shows three different source grasps which are subsequently transferred to two target objects in the bottom row. The hand poses are adjusted according to shape of target objects while preserving overall contact.

Table 3. Comparison with various baselines on GRAB-B (0.01 & 0.3). We show that TOCH achieves the lowest hand joint error and intersection volume while recovers the highest percentage of contact regions among all the baselines.

Method	MPJPE (mm) ↓	IV (cm^3) ↓	C-IoU (%) ↑
Hand-centric baseline	11.2	2.03	18.9
TOCH (w/o corr.)	12.2	2.10	18.6
TOCH (w/o GRU)	10.8	1.87	20.4
TOCH (same obj.)	11.7	1.95	23.1
TOCH (full model)	**10.3**	**1.78**	**26.6**

sequences from one object to another object while maintaining plausible contacts. Specifically, given a source hand motion sequence and a source object, we extract the TOCH fields and encode them with our learned encoder network. We then simply decode using the target object – we perform a point-wise concatenation of the latent vectors with point clouds of the target object, and reconstruct TOCH fields with the decoder. This way we can transfer the TOCH fields from the source object to the target object. Qualitative examples are shown in Fig. 5.

Object-Centric Representation. To show the importance of the object-centric representation, we train a baseline model which directly takes noisy hand joint sequences $\{\tilde{\boldsymbol{j}}^i\}_{i=1}^T$ as input and naively condition it on the object motion sequence $\{\boldsymbol{O}^i\}_{i=1}^T$. See Table 3 for a quantitative comparison with TOCH. We can observe that although the hand-centric baseline makes small errors in joint positions, the resulting motion is less physically plausible, as reflected by its higher interpenetration and lower contact IoU.

Semantic Correspondence. We argue that explicitly reasoning about dense correspondence plays a key role in modeling hand-object interaction. To show this, we train another baseline model in the same manner as in Sect. 3, except that we adopt a simpler representation $\boldsymbol{F}(\boldsymbol{H}, \boldsymbol{O}) = \{(c_i, d_i)\}_{i=1}^N$, where we keep the binary indicator and signed distance without specifying which hand point is in correspondence. The loss term (7) accordingly changes from mean squared error to Chamfer distance. We can see from Table 3 that this baseline model gives the worst results in all three metrics.

Train and Test on the Same Objects. We test the scenario where objects in test sequences are also seen at training time. We split the dataset based on the action intent label instead of by objects. Specifically, we train on sequences labelled as 'use', 'pass' and 'lift', and evaluate on the remaining. Results from Table 3 show that generalization to different objects works slightly better than generalizing to different actions. Note that the worse results are also partly attributed to the smaller training set under this new split.

Temporal Modeling. We verify the effect of temporal modeling by replacing the GRU layer with global feature aggregation. We concatenate the global average latent code with per-frame latent codes and feed the concatenated feature of each frame to a fully connected layer. As seen in Table 3, temporal modeling with GRU largely improves interaction quality in terms of recovered contact.

Complexity and Running Time. The main overhead incurred by TOCH field is in computing ray-triangle intersections, the complexity of which depends on the object geometry and the specific hand-object configuration. As an illustration, it takes around 2s per frame to compute the TOCH field on 2000 sampled object points for an object mesh with 48k vertices and 96k triangles on Intel Xeon CPU. In hand-fitting stage, TOCH is significantly faster than ContactOpt since the hand-object distance can be minimized with mean squared error loss once correspondences are known. Fitting TOCH to a sequence runs at approximately 1 fps on average while it takes ContactOpt over a minute to fit a single frame.

5   Conclusion

In this paper, we introduced TOCH, a spatio-temporal model of hand-object interactions. Our method encodes the hand with TOCH fields, an effective novel object-centric correspondence representation which captures the spatio-temporal configurations of hand and object even before and after contact occurs. TOCH reasons about hand-object configurations beyond plain contacts, and is naturally invariant to rotation and translation. Experiments demonstrate that TOCH outperforms previous methods on the task of 3D hand-object refinement. In future work, we plan to extend TOCH to model more general human-scene interactions.

Acknowledgements. This work is supported by the German Federal Ministry of Education and Research (BMBF): Tübingen AI Center, FKZ: 01IS18039A. This work is funded by the Deutsche Forschungsgemeinschaft (DFG, German Research Foundation) - 409792180 (Emmy Noether Programme, project: Real Virtual Humans). Gerard Pons-Moll is a member of the Machine Learning Cluster of Excellence, EXC number 2064/1 - Project number 390727645.

References

1. https://virtualhumans.mpi-inf.mpg.de/toch/
2. Aliakbarian, S., Saleh, F.S., Salzmann, M., Petersson, L., Gould, S.: A stochastic conditioning scheme for diverse human motion prediction. In: Proceedings of the IEEE/CVF Conference on Computer Vision and Pattern Recognition, pp. 5223–5232 (2020)
3. Arnab, A., Doersch, C., Zisserman, A.: Exploiting temporal context for 3d human pose estimation in the wild. In: Proceedings of the IEEE/CVF Conference on Computer Vision and Pattern Recognition, pp. 3395–3404 (2019)
4. Ballan, L., Taneja, A., Gall, J., Van Gool, L., Pollefeys, M.: Motion capture of hands in action using discriminative salient points. In: Fitzgibbon, A., Lazebnik, S., Perona, P., Sato, Y., Schmid, C. (eds.) ECCV 2012. LNCS, vol. 7577, pp. 640–653. Springer, Heidelberg (2012). https://doi.org/10.1007/978-3-642-33783-3_46
5. Bhatnagar, B.L., Sminchisescu, C., Theobalt, C., Pons-Moll, G.: Loopreg: self-supervised learning of implicit surface correspondences, pose and shape for 3d human mesh registration. Adv. Neural Inf. Process. Syst. **33**, 12909–12922 (2020)
6. Bhatnagar, B.L., Xie, X., Petrov, I., Sminchisescu, C., Theobalt, C., Pons-Moll, G.: Behave: dataset and method for tracking human object interactions. In: IEEE Conference on Computer Vision and Pattern Recognition (CVPR), June 2022
7. Bogo, F., Kanazawa, A., Lassner, C., Gehler, P., Romero, J., Black, M.J.: Keep It SMPL: automatic estimation of 3d human pose and shape from a single image. In: Leibe, B., Matas, J., Sebe, N., Welling, M. (eds.) ECCV 2016. LNCS, vol. 9909, pp. 561–578. Springer, Cham (2016). https://doi.org/10.1007/978-3-319-46454-1_34
8. Bohg, J., Morales, A., Asfour, T., Kragic, D.: Data-driven grasp synthesis-a survey. IEEE Trans. Robot. **30**(2), 289–309 (2013)
9. Boukhayma, A., Bem, R.D., Torr, P.H.: 3d hand shape and pose from images in the wild. In: Proceedings of the IEEE/CVF Conference on Computer Vision and Pattern Recognition, pp. 10843–10852 (2019)
10. Brahmbhatt, S., Ham, C., Kemp, C.C., Hays, J.: ContactDB: analyzing and predicting grasp contact via thermal imaging. In: Proceedings of the IEEE/CVF Conference on Computer Vision and Pattern Recognition, pp. 8709–8719 (2019)
11. Brahmbhatt, S., Tang, C., Twigg, C.D., Kemp, C.C., Hays, J.: ContactPose: a dataset of grasps with object contact and hand pose. In: Vedaldi, A., Bischof, H., Brox, T., Frahm, J.-M. (eds.) ECCV 2020. LNCS, vol. 12358, pp. 361–378. Springer, Cham (2020). https://doi.org/10.1007/978-3-030-58601-0_22
12. Cai, Y., et al.: A unified 3d human motion synthesis model via conditional variational auto-encoder. In: Proceedings of the IEEE/CVF International Conference on Computer Vision, pp. 11645–11655 (2021)
13. Cao, Z., Radosavovic, I., Kanazawa, A., Malik, J.: Reconstructing hand-object interactions in the wild. In: Proceedings of the IEEE/CVF International Conference on Computer Vision, pp. 12417–12426 (2021)
14. Chen, L., Lin, S.Y., Xie, Y., Lin, Y.Y., Xie, X.: MVHM: a large-scale multi-view hand mesh benchmark for accurate 3d hand pose estimation. In: Proceedings of the IEEE/CVF Winter Conference on Applications of Computer Vision, pp. 836–845 (2021)
15. Chen, Y., et al.: Joint hand-object 3d reconstruction from a single image with cross-branch feature fusion. IEEE Trans. Image Process. **30**, 4008–4021 (2021)
16. Corona, E., Pumarola, A., Alenya, G., Moreno-Noguer, F., Rogez, G.: GanHand: predicting human grasp affordances in multi-object scenes. In: Proceedings of the

IEEE/CVF Conference on Computer Vision and Pattern Recognition, pp. 5031–5041 (2020)

17. El-Khoury, S., Sahbani, A., Bidaud, P.: 3d objects grasps synthesis: a survey. In: 13th World Congress in Mechanism and Machine Science, pp. 573–583 (2011)

18. Elgammal, A., Lee, C.S.: The Role of Manifold Learning in Human Motion Analysis. In: Rosenhahn, B., Klette, R., Metaxas, D. (eds.) Human Motion. Computational Imaging and Vision, vol. 36, pp. 25–56. Springer, Dordrecht (2008). https://doi.org/10.1007/978-1-4020-6693-1_2

19. Garcia-Hernando, G., Yuan, S., Baek, S., Kim, T.K.: First-person hand action benchmark with RGB-D videos and 3d hand pose annotations. In: Proceedings of the IEEE Conference on Computer Vision and Pattern Recognition, pp. 409–419 (2018)

20. Ge, L., et al.: 3d hand shape and pose estimation from a single RGB image. In: Proceedings of the IEEE/CVF Conference on Computer Vision and Pattern Recognition, pp. 10833–10842 (2019)

21. Goodfellow, I., et al.: Generative adversarial nets. Adv. Neural Inf. Process. Syst. **27** (2014)

22. Grady, P., Tang, C., Twigg, C.D., Vo, M., Brahmbhatt, S., Kemp, C.C.: ContactOpt: optimizing contact to improve grasps. In: Proceedings of the IEEE/CVF Conference on Computer Vision and Pattern Recognition, pp. 1471–1481 (2021)

23. Guzov, V., Sattler, T., Pons-Moll, G.: Visually plausible human-object interaction capture from wearable sensors. In: arXiv (May 2022)

24. Hamer, H., Gall, J., Weise, T., Van Gool, L.: An object-dependent hand pose prior from sparse training data. In: 2010 IEEE Computer Society Conference on Computer Vision and Pattern Recognition, pp. 671–678. IEEE (2010)

25. Hampali, S., Rad, M., Oberweger, M., Lepetit, V.: HOnnotate: a method for 3d annotation of hand and object poses. In: Proceedings of the IEEE/CVF Conference on Computer Vision and Pattern Recognition, pp. 3196–3206 (2020)

26. Hasson, Y., Tekin, B., Bogo, F., Laptev, I., Pollefeys, M., Schmid, C.: Leveraging photometric consistency over time for sparsely supervised hand-object reconstruction. In: Proceedings of the IEEE/CVF Conference on Computer Vision and Pattern Recognition, pp. 571–580 (2020)

27. Hasson, Y., Varol, G., Laptev, I., Schmid, C.: Towards unconstrained joint hand-object reconstruction from RGB videos. arXiv preprint arXiv:2108.07044 (2021)

28. Hasson, Y., et al.: Learning joint reconstruction of hands and manipulated objects. In: CVPR (2019)

29. Hasson, Y., et al.: Learning joint reconstruction of hands and manipulated objects. In: Proceedings of the IEEE/CVF Conference on Computer Vision and Pattern Recognition, pp. 11807–11816 (2019)

30. Henter, G.E., Alexanderson, S., Beskow, J.: MoGlow: probabilistic and controllable motion synthesis using normalising flows. ACM Trans. Graph. (TOG) **39**(6), 1–14 (2020)

31. Huang, L., Zhang, B., Guo, Z., Xiao, Y., Cao, Z., Yuan, J.: Survey on depth and RGB image-based 3d hand shape and pose estimation. Virtual Reality Intell. Hardware **3**(3), 207–234 (2021)

32. Jiang, H., Liu, S., Wang, J., Wang, X.: Hand-object contact consistency reasoning for human grasps generation. arXiv preprint arXiv:2104.03304 (2021)

33. Jiang, W., Kolotouros, N., Pavlakos, G., Zhou, X., Daniilidis, K.: Coherent reconstruction of multiple humans from a single image. In: Proceedings of the IEEE/CVF Conference on Computer Vision and Pattern Recognition, pp. 5579–5588 (2020)

34. Jiang, Z., Zhu, Y., Svetlik, M., Fang, K., Zhu, Y.: Synergies between affordance and geometry: 6-DoF grasp detection via implicit representations. Robot. Sci. Syst. (2021)
35. Karunratanakul, K., Yang, J., Zhang, Y., Black, M.J., Muandet, K., Tang, S.: Grasping field: Learning implicit representations for human grasps. In: 2020 International Conference on 3D Vision (3DV), pp. 333–344. IEEE (2020)
36. Kingma, D.P., Welling, M.: Auto-encoding variational bayes. In: Bengio, Y., LeCun, Y. (eds.) 2nd International Conference on Learning Representations, ICLR 2014, Banff, AB, Canada, 14–16 April 2014, Conference Track Proceedings (2014). http://arxiv.org/abs/1312.6114
37. Kocabas, M., Athanasiou, N., Black, M.J.: Vibe: video inference for human body pose and shape estimation. In: Proceedings of the IEEE/CVF Conference on Computer Vision and Pattern Recognition, pp. 5253–5263 (2020)
38. Kundu, J.N., Gor, M., Babu, R.V.: BiHMP-GAN: bidirectional 3d human motion prediction GAN. In: Proceedings of the AAAI Conference on Artificial Intelligence, vol. 33, pp. 8553–8560 (2019)
39. Kwon, T., Tekin, B., Stuhmer, J., Bogo, F., Pollefeys, M.: H2o: two hands manipulating objects for first person interaction recognition. arXiv preprint arXiv:2104.11181 (2021)
40. León, B., et al.: OpenGRASP: a toolkit for robot grasping simulation. In: Ando, N., Balakirsky, S., Hemker, T., Reggiani, M., von Stryk, O. (eds.) SIMPAR 2010. LNCS (LNAI), vol. 6472, pp. 109–120. Springer, Heidelberg (2010). https://doi.org/10.1007/978-3-642-17319-6_13
41. Li, J., et al.: Task-generic hierarchical human motion prior using vaes. arXiv preprint arXiv:2106.04004 (2021)
42. Liu, C.K.: Dextrous manipulation from a grasping pose. In: ACM SIGGRAPH 2009 papers, pp. 1–6 (2009)
43. Luo, Z., Golestaneh, S.A., Kitani, K.M.: 3d human motion estimation via motion compression and refinement. In: Proceedings of the Asian Conference on Computer Vision (2020)
44. Malik, J., et al.: HandVoxNet: deep voxel-based network for 3d hand shape and pose estimation from a single depth map. In: Proceedings of the IEEE/CVF Conference on Computer Vision and Pattern Recognition, pp. 7113–7122 (2020)
45. Miller, A.T., Allen, P.K.: Graspit! a versatile simulator for robotic grasping. IEEE Robot. Autom. Mag. **11**(4), 110–122 (2004)
46. Mordatch, I., Popović, Z., Todorov, E.: Contact-invariant optimization for hand manipulation. In: Proceedings of the ACM SIGGRAPH/Eurographics Symposium on Computer Animation, pp. 137–144 (2012)
47. Mueller, F., et al.: Real-time pose and shape reconstruction of two interacting hands with a single depth camera. ACM Trans. Graph. (TOG) **38**(4), 1–13 (2019)
48. Ng, E., Ginosar, S., Darrell, T., Joo, H.: Body2hands: learning to infer 3d hands from conversational gesture body dynamics. In: Proceedings of the IEEE/CVF Conference on Computer Vision and Pattern Recognition, pp. 11865–11874 (2021)
49. Oikonomidis, I., Kyriazis, N., Argyros, A.A.: Full DOF tracking of a hand interacting with an object by modeling occlusions and physical constraints. In: 2011 International Conference on Computer Vision, pp. 2088–2095. IEEE (2011)
50. Ormoneit, D., Sidenbladh, H., Black, M.J., Hastie, T.: Learning and tracking cyclic human motion. Adv. Neural Inf. Process. Syst. 894–900 (2001)
51. Panteleris, P., Argyros, A.: Back to RGB: 3d tracking of hands and hand-object interactions based on short-baseline stereo. In: Proceedings of the IEEE International Conference on Computer Vision Workshops, pp. 575–584 (2017)

52. Pavlakos, G., et al.: Expressive body capture: 3d hands, face, and body from a single image. In: Proceedings of the IEEE/CVF Conference on Computer Vision and Pattern Recognition, pp. 10975–10985 (2019)

53. Qi, C.R., Su, H., Mo, K., Guibas, L.J.: Pointnet: Deep learning on point sets for 3d classification and segmentation. In: Proceedings of the IEEE Conference on Computer Vision and Pattern Recognition, pp. 652–660 (2017)

54. Romero, J., Tzionas, D., Black, M.J.: Embodied hands: modeling and capturing hands and bodies together. ACM Trans. Graph. (Proc. SIGGRAPH Asia) **36**(6) (2017)

55. Sahbani, A., El-Khoury, S., Bidaud, P.: An overview of 3d object grasp synthesis algorithms. Robot. Auton. Syst. **60**(3), 326–336 (2012)

56. Smith, B., et al.: Constraining dense hand surface tracking with elasticity. ACM Trans. Graph. (TOG) **39**(6), 1–14 (2020)

57. Sridhar, S., et al.: Real-time joint tracking of a hand manipulating an object from RGB-D input. In: Leibe, B., Matas, J., Sebe, N., Welling, M. (eds.) ECCV 2016. LNCS, vol. 9906, pp. 294–310. Springer, Cham (2016). https://doi.org/10.1007/978-3-319-46475-6_19

58. Sridhar, S., Rhodin, H., Seidel, H.P., Oulasvirta, A., Theobalt, C.: Real-time hand tracking using a sum of anisotropic gaussians model. In: 2014 2nd International Conference on 3D Vision, vol. 1, pp. 319–326. IEEE (2014)

59. Starke, S., Zhang, H., Komura, T., Saito, J.: Neural state machine for character-scene interactions. ACM Trans. Graph. **38**(6), 209–210 (2019)

60. Taheri, O., Ghorbani, N., Black, M.J., Tzionas, D.: GRAB: a dataset of whole-body human grasping of objects. In: Vedaldi, A., Bischof, H., Brox, T., Frahm, J.-M. (eds.) ECCV 2020. LNCS, vol. 12349, pp. 581–600. Springer, Cham (2020). https://doi.org/10.1007/978-3-030-58548-8_34

61. Taylor, J., et al.: Efficient and precise interactive hand tracking through joint, continuous optimization of pose and correspondences. ACM Trans. Graph. (TOG) **35**(4), 1–12 (2016)

62. Taylor, J., Shotton, J., Sharp, T., Fitzgibbon, A.: The vitruvian manifold: Inferring dense correspondences for one-shot human pose estimation. In: 2012 IEEE Conference on Computer Vision and Pattern Recognition, pp. 103–110. IEEE (2012)

63. Taylor, J., et al.: Articulated distance fields for ultra-fast tracking of hands interacting. ACM Trans. Graph. (TOG) **36**(6), 1–12 (2017)

64. Tiwari, G., Antic, D., Lenssen, J.E., Sarafianos, N., Tung, T., Pons-Moll, G.: Pose-NDF: modeling human pose manifolds with neural distance fields. In: European Conference on Computer Vision (ECCV), Springer, Cham October 2022

65. Urtasun, R., Fleet, D.J., Fua, P.: 3d people tracking with gaussian process dynamical models. In: 2006 IEEE Computer Society Conference on Computer Vision and Pattern Recognition (CVPR 2006), vol. 1, pp. 238–245. IEEE (2006)

66. Wang, Y., et al.: Video-based hand manipulation capture through composite motion control. ACM Trans. Graph. (TOG) **32**(4), 1–14 (2013)

67. Xie, X., Bhatnagar, B.L., Pons-Moll, G.: Chore: contact, human and object reconstruction from a single RGB image. In: European Conference on Computer Vision (ECCV). Springer, Cham, (October 2022

68. Yang, L., Zhan, X., Li, K., Xu, W., Li, J., Lu, C.: CPF: learning a contact potential field to model the hand-object interaction. In: Proceedings of the IEEE/CVF International Conference on Computer Vision, pp. 11097–11106 (2021)

69. Ye, Y., Liu, C.K.: Synthesis of detailed hand manipulations using contact sampling. ACM Trans. Graph. (TOG) **31**(4), 1–10 (2012)

70. Yi, H., et al.: Human-aware object placement for visual environment reconstruction. In: Computer Vision and Pattern Recognition (CVPR), pp. 3959–3970 (Jun 2022)

71. Zeng, A., Yang, L., Ju, X., Li, J., Wang, J., Xu, Q.: SmoothNet: a plug-and-play network for refining human poses in videos. In: European Conference on Computer Vision. Springer, Cham (2022)

72. Zhang, B., et al.: Interacting two-hand 3d pose and shape reconstruction from single color image. In: Proceedings of the IEEE/CVF International Conference on Computer Vision, pp. 11354–11363 (2021)

73. Zhang, H., Bo, Z.H., Yong, J.H., Xu, F.: InteractionFusion: real-time reconstruction of hand poses and deformable objects in hand-object interactions. ACM Trans. Graph. (TOG) **38**(4), 1–11 (2019)

74. Zhang, H., Zhou, Y., Tian, Y., Yong, J.H., Xu, F.: Single depth view based real-time reconstruction of hand-object interactions. ACM Trans. Graph. (TOG) **40**(3), 1–12 (2021)

75. Zhang, H., Ye, Y., Shiratori, T., Komura, T.: ManipNet: neural manipulation synthesis with a hand-object spatial representation. ACM Trans. Graph. (TOG) **40**(4), 1–14 (2021)

76. Zhang, S., Zhang, Y., Bogo, F., Pollefeys, M., Tang, S.: Learning motion priors for 4d human body capture in 3d scenes. In: Proceedings of the IEEE/CVF International Conference on Computer Vision, pp. 11343–11353 (2021)

77. Zhang, X., Bhatnagar, B.L., Guzov, V., Starke, S., Pons-Moll, G.: Couch: towards controllable human-chair interactions. In: European Conference on Computer Vision (ECCV). Springer, Cham, October 2022

78. Zhao, R., Su, H., Ji, Q.: Bayesian adversarial human motion synthesis. In: Proceedings of the IEEE/CVF Conference on Computer Vision and Pattern Recognition, pp. 6225–6234 (2020)

79. Zhao, W., Zhang, J., Min, J., Chai, J.: Robust realtime physics-based motion control for human grasping. ACM Trans. Graph. (TOG) **32**(6), 1–12 (2013)

80. Zhao, Z., Wang, T., Xia, S., Wang, Y.: Hand-3d-studio: a new multi-view system for 3d hand reconstruction. In: ICASSP 2020–2020 IEEE International Conference on Acoustics, Speech and Signal Processing (ICASSP), pp. 2478–2482. IEEE (2020)

81. Zhu, T., Wu, R., Lin, X., Sun, Y.: Toward human-like grasp: dexterous grasping via semantic representation of object-hand. In: Proceedings of the IEEE/CVF International Conference on Computer Vision, pp. 15741–15751 (2021)

82. Zimmermann, C., Ceylan, D., Yang, J., Russell, B., Argus, M., Brox, T.: Frei-HAND: a dataset for markerless capture of hand pose and shape from single RGB images. In: Proceedings of the IEEE/CVF International Conference on Computer Vision, pp. 813–822 (2019)

LaTeRF: Label and Text Driven Object Radiance Fields

Ashkan Mirzaei$^{(\boxtimes)}$, Yash Kant, Jonathan Kelly, and Igor Gilitschenski

University of Toronto, Toronto, Canada
ashkan@cs.toronto.edu

Abstract. Obtaining 3D object representations is important for creating photo-realistic simulations and for collecting AR and VR assets. Neural fields have shown their effectiveness in learning a continuous volumetric representation of a scene from 2D images, but acquiring object representations from these models with weak supervision remains an open challenge. In this paper we introduce LaTeRF, a method for extracting an object of interest from a scene given 2D images of the entire scene, known camera poses, a natural language description of the object, and a set of point-labels of object and non-object points in the input images. To faithfully extract the object from the scene, LaTeRF extends the NeRF formulation with an additional 'objectness' probability at each 3D point. Additionally, we leverage the rich latent space of a pre-trained CLIP model combined with our differentiable object renderer, to inpaint the occluded parts of the object. We demonstrate high-fidelity object extraction on both synthetic and real-world datasets and justify our design choices through an extensive ablation study.

Keywords: Image-based rendering · Neural radiance fields · 3d reconstruction · 3d computer vision · Novel view synthesis

1 Introduction

Extracting a partially-occluded object of interest (OOI) from a 3D scene remains an important problem with numerous applications in computer vision and elsewhere. For example, OOI extraction enables the creation of faithful photo-realistic simulators for robotics, supports the creation of digital content (*e.g.* animated movies), and facilitates the building of AR and VR tools. Although 3D scene reconstruction from 2D images has been extensively explored [14,18,23,35,46], the ability to extract semantically consistent and meaningful objects from complex scenes remains an open challenge.

Early approaches [34,56] attempted to segment objects from real images, but could not extract their 3D geometry and did not consider the underlying image formation process. Recent work has attempted to disentangle object-centric representations from a scene by learning to decompose the scene into a

---

Supplementary Information The online version contains supplementary material available at https://doi.org/10.1007/978-3-031-20062-5_2.

S. Avidan et al. (Eds.): ECCV 2022, LNCS 13663, pp. 20–36, 2022.
https://doi.org/10.1007/978-3-031-20062-5_2

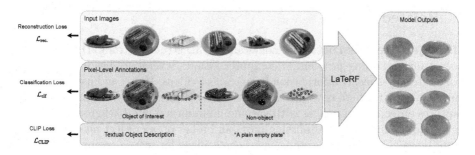

Fig. 1. An overview of LaTeRF showing the extraction of a plate. The method takes as input 2D images with camera parameters and poses, a few manually annotated pixel labels corresponding to the object, and labels pointing to the places in the images that do not belong to the object (foreground or background parts). LaTeRF is able to extract the object from the scene while also filling the missing details of the object that are not visible in the input views.

graph and train object representations at the leaf nodes [27], or via the use of joint 3D semantic segmentation and neural volumetric rendering [55]. The approach described in [27] is specifically designed for automotive data and is not applicable to object instances from other categories, whereas [55] leads to non-photorealistic object extraction due to training constraints required for real-time deployment. Moreover, none of these works allow for reasoning about occlusions of the OOI in the scene. Approaches that rely on unsupervised discovery of 3D objects from a single image [38,51] typically require optimizing a non-trivial loss function and do not work well with high-resolution real-world scenes. Other approaches [47] require large-scale prior category-level videos that are expensive to collect and might not generalize well to novel categories.

We propose LaTeRF, a novel object extraction method that requires a set of 2D images (with known camera parameters) containing the OOI mixed with other clutter, a textual description of the OOI, and a minimal set of pixel annotations distinguishing the object and non-object boundaries. We assign an objectness probability to each point in the 3D space and use this to guide the disentanglement of the OOI and non-object parts in the scene during training. Once trained, we use an *objectness threshold* to filter points belonging to the OOI while ignoring non-object points. Moreover, we find that reasoning about occlusion is an important aspect of extracting objects without artifacts (such as holes, or clutter). Thus, we leverage CLIP [31], a large cross-modal vision-language model, for formulating a loss to fill in the occluded parts using supervision derived from a textual prompt. Combining these two loss functions we can perform high-fidelity object extraction from real-world. An overview of our approach is visualized in Fig. 1. We evaluate LaTeRF on real and synthetic data and study the effects of individual design choices in extensive ablation studies. We find that, in challenging settings with significant occlusions, LaTeRF leads to 11.19 and 0.63 gains in PSNR and SSIM metrics respectively compared to *Mask+NeRF*.

2 Related Work

3D Object Reconstruction: Understanding 3D structure from 2D images has been a long-standing problem in computer vision. Several studies have tried to learn category-specific information from a set of videos [10,47] and use this information to generalize to new instances within the same category. Recent work [17] captures objects from images with varying illumination and backgrounds, but is unable to inpaint potential missing parts and relies on an object mask for every input image. Neural scene graphs have been utilized for scene decomposition into background and object instances for automotive applications [27]. Another line of work involves recovering the 3D structure of a scene from a single image only and in an unsupervised manner [38,51], but is limited to simple scenarios and performs poorly in complex scenes. Although these methods can recover the 3D shape and appearance of an object with a few 2D images, most rely on training on a large set of either category-specific or general objects; collecting such data can be expensive for certain categories. We aim to overcome the need for prior training and instead employ a minimal set of test-time clues given by a human annotator to extract a photo-realistic object radiance field from the scene.

Representing Scenes with Neural Fields: Volumetric rendering of 3D objects and scenes via neural fields has attracted significant attention recently [41]. In the past few years and based on differentiable volume rendering [9,42], NeRF-style methods [23,25,28,33,49,50,53] have achieved impressive results in reconstructing high-quality 3D models and novel views learned from 2D inputs of bounded static scenes. The success of NeRF in capturing the details of scenes is due in part to the use of positional encoding [7,43] and periodic activations [5,36,37] that help to increase the model's capacity. The backbone of our method is a neural field [23,48] that we use to learn the density and view-dependent color of the scene and the object simultaneously based on the camera parameters and input images of the scene containing the object of interest. It is worthwhile to mention that our method is not limited to a specific neural field method and can be extended easily to faster [15,19,40] and better-quality NeRFs [2,24].

Semantic Segmentation in 3D: Semantic segmentation in 3D has been studied using multi-view fusion-based representations [1,11,20–22,39,44,52] that require only 2D supervision when training, and a separate 3D mesh at testing time, unlike implicit methods like ours. Recently, there have been promising attempts to recover 3D semantic maps from 2D inputs using NeRFs. NeSF [45] recovers the 3D geometry as density fields from posed RGB images and uses 2D semantic maps to train a semantic field to assign a probability of belonging to each of the semantic classes to every point in the space. Another proposed approach is to extend the NeRF MLP and add a view-independent semantic head to it to get the logits for each of the semantic classes [54,55]. Our idea is conceptually similar to these, and we propose using binary partitioning of 3D points into two categories (object of interest vs. non-object). In contrast to the previous works, we introduce a differentiable rendering scheme to only render the object of interest using these objectness probabilities, which enables us to fill the visual gaps in the object.

Language-Guided NeRFs: In the representation learning [3] literature, self-supervised approaches [6,8,12,26] are some of the most compelling settings due to the rather cheap availability of unlabelled data. CLIP [31] is a contrastive-based representation learning method that learns visual and textual feature extraction by looking at a massive set of diverse image-caption pairs scraped from the internet. Following the success of CLIP in finding the similarity of image and text samples, recent works have used it for image generation guided by language [32]. More recently, fusing CLIP with NeRF has been explored. In [14], CLIP similarity of the rendered scene from different views is utilized to reduce the amount of data needed to train the model. This is based on CLIP's ability to assign similar features to different views of a single object. CLIP-NeRF [46] makes use of the joint image-text latent space of CLIP and provides a framework to manipulate neural radiance fields using multi-modal inputs. Dream field [13] uses the potential of CLIP in finding the similarity between a text and an image and optimizes a NeRF to increase the similarity of its different renders to a text prompt. This way, starting from a phrase, a 3D object closely representing the text is created.

Motivated by these results, which demonstrate the possibility and benefits of using CLIP alongside neural radiance fields. We leverage the rich multi-modal feature space of the pre-trained CLIP model to give our object extractor semantic information as text. It helps to inpaint the points of the object of interest that are invisible and obscured by other elements in the scene. Notably, we only use CLIP as a good, recent instance of a joint image-language model, and our results can be improved with richer joint embedding functions in the future. The language module of our method is closely related to dream field [13] but we use it to generate 3D objects that are consistent with the ones provided in a scene.

3   Background

Neural radiance fields (NeRFs) [23] use a multi-layer perceptron (MLP) to implicitly capture the geometry and visual appearance of a 3D scene. A scene is encoded as a mapping between the 3D coordinates x and view direction d, to a view-dependent color c and view-independent density σ using an MLP $f : (x, d) \rightarrow (c, \sigma)$. For simplicity, for every point x and view direction d, we write the outputs of the MLP as $c(x, d)$ and $\sigma(x)$, respectively.

Consider a ray r with origin o and direction d characterized by $r(t) = o + td$ with near and far bounds t_n and t_f respectively. Similar to the original NeRF formulation [23], the rendering equation to calculate the expected color for the ray $C(r)$ is

$$C(r) = \int_{t_n}^{t_f} T(t)\sigma\big(r(t)\big)c\big(r(t), d\big) \, \mathrm{d}t, \tag{1}$$

where $T(t) = \exp\big(-\int_{t_n}^{t} \sigma(r(s)) \, \mathrm{d}s\big)$ is the transmittance. This integral is numerically estimated via quadrature. The interval between t_n and t_f is partitioned into N equal sections, and t_i is uniformly sampled from the i-th section. In this way, the continuous ray from t_n to t_f is discretized and the estimated rendering integral can be obtained as

$$\hat{C}(r) = \sum_{i=1}^{N} T_i \big(1 - \exp(-\sigma_i \delta_i)\big) c_i, \tag{2}$$

where $T_i = \exp\big(-\sum_{j=1}^{i-1} \sigma_j \delta_j\big)$ is the discretized estimate of the transmittance and $\delta_i = t_{i+1} - t_i$ is the distance between two adjacent sample points along the ray. Note that for the sake of simplicity, $\sigma\big(r(t_i)\big)$ and $c\big(r(t_i), d\big)$ are shown as σ_i and c_i, respectively. The rendering scheme given by Eq. 2 is differentiable, allowing us to train our MLP by minimizing the L2 reconstruction loss between the estimated color $C(r)$ and the ground-truth color $C_{\mathrm{GT}}(r)$. We use a variant of stochastic gradient descent [16], and minimize the following loss term:

$$\mathcal{L}_{\mathrm{rec.}} = \sum_{r \in \mathcal{R}} \big\| C(r) - C_{\mathrm{GT}}(r) \big\|^2, \tag{3}$$

where $\mathcal{R}$ is a batch of rays sampled from the set of rays where the corresponding pixels are available in the training data. In this paper, we use the reconstruction loss $\mathcal{L}_{\mathrm{rec.}}$ to ensure the consistency of the extracted object radiance field with respect to that of the original scene. The goal is to make the resulting object look similar to the one represented in the 2D input images of the scene, and not just to generate an object within the same category.

4   Method

In this paper, we propose a simple framework to extract 3D objects as radiance fields from a set of 2D input images. Built on top of the recent advances in scene representation via neural fields [23,41], our method aims to softly partition the space into the object and the foreground/background by adding an object probability output to the original NeRF MLP. We leverage pixel-level annotations pointing to the object or the foreground/background and a text prompt expressing the visual features and semantics of the object.

4.1   Objectness Probability

We wish to extract an OOI from a neural radiance field guided by a minimal set of human instructions. Our approach is to reason about the probability of each point in the space being part of the object. Recent work proposed to append a view-independent semantic classifier output [54] to the original NeRF architecture. Inspired by this, we extend the NeRF MLP to return an additional objectness score $s(x)$ for every point x in the space. The objectness probability $p(x)$ is obtained from the MLP as

$$p(x) = \mathrm{Sigmoid}\big(s(x)\big). \tag{4}$$

For an overview of the architecture of the MLP used in LaTeRF please refer to our supplementary material.

4.2 Differentiable Object Volume Renderer

The most straightforward approach to render the object using the NeRF model with the objectness probabilities is to apply a threshold on the probability values and to zero out the density of all points in the space that have an objectness probability less than 0.5. In other words, for every point x, the new density function would be $\sigma'(x) = \sigma(x)\mathbb{1}\big(p(x) \geq 0.5\big)$ and the naive object rendering integral would be

$$C_{\mathrm{obj}}(r) = \int_{t_n}^{t_f} T_{\mathrm{obj}}(t)\sigma\big(r(t)\big)\mathbb{1}\Big(p\big(r(t)\big) \geq 0.5\Big)c\big(r(t),d\big)\, \mathrm{d}t, \qquad (5)$$

where the object transmittance T_{obj} is defined as

$$T_{\mathrm{obj}}(t) = \exp\left(-\int_{t_n}^{t} \sigma\big(r(s)\big)\mathbb{1}\Big(p\big(r(s)\big) \geq 0.5\Big)\, \mathrm{d}s\right). \qquad (6)$$

This approach leads to a hard-partitioning of the scene into two categories: 1) The extracted object, 2) background and foreground. Although this method works in practice and gives a rough outline of the object, if we apply numerical quadrature to Eq. 5 to evaluate the pixel values for the object, the gradients of the resulting pixel colors with respect to the weights of the MLP become zero in most of the domain due to the use of the indicator function. As a result, it is not possible to define a loss function that enforces properties on the rendered images of the object (more on this loss function later).

We fix the aforementioned issue with a minor tweak. The transmittance (density) $\sigma(x)$ can be interpreted as the differential probability of an arbitrary ray passing through x being terminated at the particle at point x in the space. Let T_x represent the event that a ray terminates at point x, that is, we have $\sigma(x) = \mathbb{P}(T_x)$. In addition, denote the event that location x contains a particle belonging to the OOI as O_x $(p(x) = \mathbb{P}(O_x))$. With this change, the object can be rendered with a new density function $\sigma_{\mathrm{obj}}(x)$ defined as the joint probability of T_x and O_x by $\sigma_{\mathrm{obj}}(x) = \mathbb{P}(T_x, O_x)$. With the assumption that T_x and O_x are independent, the object density function is:

$$\sigma_{\mathrm{obj}}(x) = \mathbb{P}(T_x, O_x) = \mathbb{P}(T_x)\mathbb{P}(O_x) = \sigma(x)p(x). \qquad (7)$$

Given the above equation, the object rendering integral in Eq. 5 can be changed to

$$C_{\mathrm{obj}}(r) = \int_{t_n}^{t_f} T_{\mathrm{obj}}(t)\sigma\big(r(t)\big)p\big(r(t)\big)c\big(r(t),d\big)\, \mathrm{d}t, \qquad (8)$$

and the object transmittance T_{obj} in Eq. 6 becomes

$$T_{\mathrm{obj}}(t) = \exp\left(-\int_{t_n}^{t} \sigma\big(r(s)\big)p\big(r(s)\big)\, \mathrm{d}s\right). \qquad (9)$$

Now, similar to the previous quadrature formulation, the integral in Eq. 8 is approximated as follows,

$$\hat{C}_{\text{obj}}(r) = \sum_{i=1}^{N} T_i^{\text{obj}} \big(1 - \exp(-\sigma_i p_i \delta_i)\big) c_i, \tag{10}$$

where the discretized object transmittance is $T_i^{\text{obj}} = \exp\big(-\sum_{j=1}^{i-1} \sigma_j p_j \delta_j\big)$ and $p_i = p\big(r(t_i)\big)$. Note that with this new object rendering method, the gradients are smoother and it is possible to use iterative optimization to minimize common loss functions defined over the rendered views of the object. Compared to the previous rendering equation with the indicator function, the new equation can be interpreted as a soft-partitioning of the space where every point belongs to one of the two classes (the object or the foreground/background) and the partitioning is stochastic.

4.3   Object Classification Using Pixel Annotations

The first source of 'clues' obtained from a human annotator to extract the object is pixel-level annotation information. The user selects a few of the 2D input images of the scene and, for each of them, chooses a few pixels on the OOI and a few pixels corresponding to the background or the foreground. After collecting these data, for a ray r corresponding to one of the annotated pixels, the label $t(r)$ is defined as 1 if the pixel is labelled as the object, and $t(r) = 0$ if it is labelled as either foreground or background. The objectness score $S(r)$ is calculated using the classical volume rendering principles:

$$S(r) = \int_{t_n}^{t_f} T(t)\sigma\big(r(t)\big)s\big(r(t)\big)\,dt. \tag{11}$$

The objectness probability for a ray r is obtained as $P(r) = \text{Sigmoid}\big(S(r)\big)$. In our implementation, the numerical estimate of the integral above is determined as

$$\hat{S}(r) = \sum_{i=1}^{N} T_i\big(1 - \exp(-\sigma_i \delta_i)\big)s_i, \tag{12}$$

where $s_i = s\big(r(t_i)\big)$. Consequently, the approximated objectness probability is $\hat{P}(r) = \text{Sigmoid}\big(\hat{S}(r)\big)$ and following [54], the classification loss $\mathcal{L}_{\text{clf}}$ is defined as

$$\mathcal{L}_{\text{clf}} = -t(r)\log\hat{P}(r) - \big(1 - t(r)\big)\log\big(1 - \hat{P}(r)\big). \tag{13}$$

This loss function guides the model to tune $s(x)$ to be large for points that belong to the object, and to decrease the value for the rest of the points. The MLP is able to propagate the sparse pixel-level data over the OOI and the background/foreground [54], resulting in a binary classification of points in the space. However, this loss function alone is not able to reason about the occluded parts of the object, which results in an extracted object with holes and other possible artifacts in areas that are not visible in any of the input images or that are visible in only a small number of the inputs.

4.4 CLIP Loss

To mitigate the shortcomings of the classification loss in inpainting the unseen parts of the object, we propose the use of a phrase describing the object as the additional input signal. This signal helps to train the MLP to extract the OOI from the scene with any holes being filled in. The user is asked to describe the object in a few words by pointing out its semantics and appearance. Let t_{text} represent this user input. Subsequently, the CLIP loss is used to make sure that the object, when rendered from random views, is similar to the textual clue.

The contrastive language-image pre-training (CLIP) [31] model is a multimodal feature extractor trained on a large dataset of image and caption pairs collected from the Internet. It includes two encoders with a shared normalized latent (output) space. For an image I and the text t (typically a sentence or phrase), the similarity of their features is proportional to the probability of the text t being associated with I. CLIP has a massive and diverse training dataset and has been shown to be useful in zero-shot transfer applications for visual and textual data, for example, object recognition and image synthesis. Recent results suggest that it is applicable to and beneficial for novel view synthesis tasks [13,14,46].

The object can be rendered from a random view v pixel-by-pixel using the differentiable object rendering scheme in Eq. 10, resulting in an image $I_{\text{obj}}(v)$ based on the current estimate of the object by the model. In order to maximize the similarity between the rendered object $I_{\text{obj}}(v)$ and the clue phrase t_{text}, the CLIP loss function $\mathcal{L}_{\text{CLIP}}$ is defined as

$$\mathcal{L}_{\text{CLIP}} = -\text{Sim}_{\text{CLIP}}(I_{\text{obj}}(v), t_{\text{text}}), \tag{14}$$

where $\text{Sim}_{\text{CLIP}}(I, t)$ is the similarity of the features of the image I and the text t extracted by the pre-trained CLIP model. This loss is influenced by the recent work [13] that utilizes the CLIP model to generate 3D shapes from text descriptions. Our proposed method begins with a complete scene as a starting point and already has a template of the object, and so uses the CLIP loss to fix the obscured regions and surfaces and to reason about the shape and color of the missing parts.

4.5 Training Details

In summary, the reconstruction loss $\mathcal{L}_{\text{rec.}}$ is applied to make sure that the final object shape and appearance are consistent with the training images of the scene, while the classification loss $\mathcal{L}_{\text{clf}}$ is used to guide the model to find the OOI in the scene and to resolve any potential ambiguities and redundancies that may occur when only using the text query. Meanwhile, the CLIP loss $\mathcal{L}_{\text{CLIP}}$ facilitates the inpainting of potential holes and occluded parts of the object through a high-level description of semantics and appearance. The final loss function $\mathcal{L}$ used to train the model is

$$\mathcal{L} = \mathcal{L}_{\text{rec.}} + \lambda_{\text{clf}}\mathcal{L}_{\text{clf}} + \lambda_{\text{CLIP}}\mathcal{L}_{\text{CLIP}}, \tag{15}$$

where the constants λ_{clf} and λ_{CLIP} are the hyperparameters of the model. Having both λ_{clf} and λ_{CLIP} set to zero (or close to zero) yields a reproduction of the whole scene without any object extraction.

5   Experiments

Training an object radiance field using LaTeRF can be done with either 360° inward-facing posed 2D images or forward-facing posed views of the scene, in addition to the visual and textual cues for OOI selection. Besides qualitative results, we study the consequences of applying the different loss terms, the number of visual cues, and the underlying NeRF representation quality on the quality of the resulting object asset on our synthetic dataset that includes challenging scenes with object occlusions.

Datasets. In our experiments, we use a subset of real-world scenes borrowed from NeRD [4], scenes that we collected ourselves of real-world objects, and a collection of synthetic scenes full of occlusions that we specifically designed to conduct our quantitative studies. Our synthetic data are rendered using Blender and consists of views of the scene, ground-truth object masks, and ideal extracted objects, as illustrated in Fig. 2. The lighting between different views of most of the scenes provided by NeRD [4] (scenes which are partly from the British Museum's photogrammetry dataset [30]) is inconsistent because NeRD was designed for the task of decomposing a scene into the underlying shape,

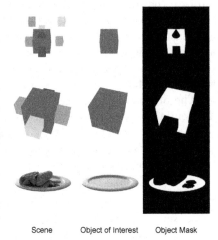

Scene   Object of Interest   Object Mask

Fig. 2. Sample data from 3 of our synthetic scenes.

illumination, and reflectance components. As a result, we manually select a subset of the images in these datasets that are roughly similar in terms of lighting and train LaTeRF on them.

Baseline. To the best of our knowledge, LaTeRF is the only method that is able to extract and inpaint a 3D object from 2D views of a scene, without having a huge category-specific multi-view or video data prior to extraction. As a baseline, we use a NeRF [23,48] model (implemented in PyTorch [29]) trained on the images of each scene after applying object masks, which we call *Mask+NeRF*. In Mask+NeRF, prior to training, we substitute every pixel marked as non-object in the ground-truth mask with a black pixel and then train a NeRF on the new masked images.

Metrics. For quantitative comparison of the synthetic dataset, we report the peak signal-to-noise ratio (PSNR) and the structural similarity index measure (SSIM); in both cases, higher is better.

5.1   Real-World Scenes

Qualitative results that demonstrate LaTeRF extracting objects from real-world scenes are shown in Fig. 3 (the text queries used in these examples are "A dark green book", "A mug", and "A wooden ukulele", respectively). In the real-world scenes with textured and complex backgrounds, we observed that small particles (points with small densities) emerge throughout the scene that are almost invisible from the training views. These particles blend into the background or the OOI and disappear,

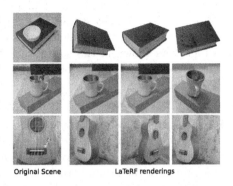

Original Scene   LaTeRF renderings

Fig. 3. Extracting occluded objects.

but when filtering the object, they become visible. This leads to object renderings full of noise in the background (see the soft threshold results in Fig. 4). In order to remove this noise, we first make the sampled densities along each ray smoother by substituting the density of each point with the average of its density and the density of its direct neighbors; we do this for five steps. After smoothing the densities, most of the small particles, which are abrupt peaks in the value of density, become close to zero. As a result, they can be filtered by applying a hard threshold based on the density and filtering all the points with a value below this threshold. Later, the object mask is rendered by substituting the objectness score instead of the color in Eq. 10 and applying the sigmoid function to the result, while assuming that, along each ray and at an infinitely far point, there is a particle with high density and low objectness score. As a result of this process, the denoised object renderings can be obtained by applying object masks to the noisy images (the result of each step of this denoising pipeline is shown in Fig. 4). Please refer to the supplementary material for more details on the denoising process.

5.2   Synthetic Scene Evaluations

In order to be able to quantitatively evaluate our proposed method in different scenarios, we generate synthetic scenes using Blender, each containing the following information: 1) Multi-view 400×400 pixel images of the scene that contains different

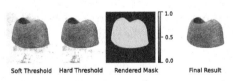

Soft Threshold   Hard Threshold   Rendered Mask   Final Result

Fig. 4. The denoising pipeline.

objects including an OOI, 2) the ground-truth images of the OOI so that we can evaluate the reconstruction quality of our object selection method, 3) the mask for the OOI in each of the 100 training images of the scene, used instead of manual pixel-level annotations for evaluations, 4) and the ground-truth camera intrinsic and extrinsic parameters for each of the input images.

Having ground-truth object masks in the dataset makes it easy to automatically sample a certain number of pixels from the object and from the foreground/background to study the effects of pixel labels on the results. Sample data from some of the challenging cases of our synthetic dataset can be found in Fig. 2. As shown in the figure, the synthetic scenes have been designed such that parts of the OOI are obscured with other objects, making the extraction more challenging.

Pixel Label Count. We ablate along the number of pixel labels used during training to demonstrate the effect on reconstruction quality. Since we have the ground-truth object masks in the synthetic dataset, at each step, we simply sample a different number of pixel labels from the mask, based on a uniform distribution, while making sure that the number of positive labels (labels on the OOI) and negative ones (non-objects) are the same. Using the sampled subset of the pixel labels, we extract the OOI from the scene. In order to calculate the reconstruction

Table 1. The effect of the label count on reconstruction quality of the OOI

Pixel Labels #	PSNR↑	SSIM↑
16,000,000	**26.93**	**0.95**
1,600,000	26.90	0.94
160,000	26.48	0.90
16,000	26.36	0.90
1,600	26.10	0.94
160	26.00	0.85
16	20.81	0.86

probability, we compare the results of our method to the ground-truth renderings of the OOI in the dataset from 30 different viewpoints and report the average PSNR and SSIM. Table 1 shows the results of this experiment with different numbers of pixel labels. Since each of the 100 training images has 400×400 pixels and the ground-truth object mask includes labels for each of these pixels, there are overall $16,000,000$ labels for each of the scenes. As is evident in Table 1, the reconstruction quality of the OOI stays within the same range when reducing the number of labels from $16,000,000$ to only 160 labels (an overall of 80 positive labels and 80 negative labels that are uniformly distributed across 100 training images). Note that a total of 160 labels can easily be obtained within a few minutes by a human annotator and that this is much easier than having someone mask out the entire object for every single training image.

Importance of Boundary Pixel Labels. Intuitively, it is clear that not all pixel labels have the same importance. Pixels close to the boundary of the object and non-object portions of each view can help the model to extract the OOI with sharper and more accurate edges. In this experiment, we show that selecting labels close to the boundaries of the object helps to improve the reconstruction quality. This way, the human annotator can be asked to spend most of their time labelling pixels around the edges. Moreover, we can increase the annotator's brush size (allow the user to label a larger area at a time instead of a single pixel) to allow them quickly annotate the points further from the boundaries and then to focus on the more important boundary labels.

Table 2. The effect of the number of boundary labels on the reconstruction quality

Boundary Labels #	PSNR↑	SSIM↑
16,000	**26.78**	**0.93**
1,600	26.50	0.91
160	26.36	0.92
16	24.82	0.90

Table 3. The effect of the loss terms against Mask+NeRF

Model	PSNR↑	SSIM↑
Mask+NeRF	15.74	0.32
$\mathcal{L}_{\text{rec.}}$	12.91	0.79
$\mathcal{L}_{\text{rec.}} + \lambda_{\text{clf}}\mathcal{L}_{\text{clf}}$	14.10	0.82
$\mathcal{L}_{\text{rec.}} + \lambda_{\text{CLIP}}\mathcal{L}_{\text{CLIP}}$	21.95	0.84
LaTeRF (ours)	**26.93**	**0.95**

The boundary labels are computed by applying minimum and maximum filters with a kernel size of 3 on the object masks, reducing the number of labels from $16,000,000$ to less than $500,000$ for our scenes. The pixel labels for this experiment are then uniformly sampled among these boundary pixels. Table 2 contains the results with different numbers of boundary labels. As is shown in the table, the reconstruction quality of the model is less affected than the experiment with uniform labels all around the images when reducing the number of boundary labels. The results show an improvement of up to 4.81 in the PSNR compared to the previous experiment, and this happens when using only 16 pixel labels. It is worth mentioning that this case has 16 labels total across all of the input images and not 16 labels per image.

Effects of Different Loss Functions. As shown in Eq. 15, the loss function used to train the main model contains three different parts: 1) The reconstruction loss $\mathcal{L}_{\text{rec.}}$, which is the same loss function used in NeRF [23], to let the model learn the whole scene, 2) the classification loss $\mathcal{L}_{\text{clf}}$, which is defined over the pixel-level annotations to detect the OOI, 3) and the CLIP loss $\mathcal{L}_{\text{CLIP}}$ that guides the model to fill in occluded portions of the OOI. In this section, the effect of each of these loss terms on the final reconstruction quality of the model is studied.

The reconstruction loss is the main loss enforcing the 3D consistency of the learned scene and OOI. Thus, it can not be removed and must be present in all of the baselines. Our experiment scenarios involve four cases including: 1) $\mathcal{L}_{\text{rec.}}$, where the classification loss and the CLIP loss are not used. This is similar to the original NeRF [23] in that there are no clues guiding the model to find the OOI. 2) $\mathcal{L}_{\text{rec.}} + \lambda_{\text{clf}}\mathcal{L}_{\text{clf}}$, where the CLIP loss is ignored and the object is extracted using the pixel labels only. The model has no clue to help reason about missing parts in this case. 3) $\mathcal{L}_{\text{rec.}} + \lambda_{\text{CLIP}}\mathcal{L}_{\text{CLIP}}$, where only the text clue is used to 'push' the model towards finding the OOI in the scene. 4) $\mathcal{L}_{\text{rec.}} + \lambda_{\text{clf}}\mathcal{L}_{\text{clf}} + \lambda_{\text{CLIP}}\mathcal{L}_{\text{CLIP}}$, which is our complete proposed method. We compare the results with the baseline, which is Mask+NeRF.

Table 3 compares the results of this experiment with the aforementioned baselines. When only the reconstruction loss is used, the semantic head of the MLP can not be trained and the results are unsatisfactory, as expected. The model

Original Scene $\mathcal{L}_{\text{rec.}} + \lambda_{\text{clf}}\mathcal{L}_{\text{clf}}$ $\mathcal{L}_{\text{rec.}} + \lambda_{\text{clf}}\mathcal{L}_{\text{clf}} + \lambda_{\text{CLIP}}\mathcal{L}_{\text{CLIP}}$

Fig. 5. A qualitative representation of the effectiveness of the CLIP loss in filling in object parts that are invisible in the input images. The OOI is the empty plate. The text prompt used here is *"A plain empty plate"*.

with the classification loss only is unable to produce results on par with our proposed method, since the synthetic dataset includes objects of interest that are partly covered by other objects (by design), while the CLIP loss is the only semantic clue that is used to fill in the occluded regions. The best result is obtained when using all of the loss terms together; each of them contributes to extracting high-quality objects.

Figure 5 visually compares the effect of the presence or absence of the CLIP loss on the rendered object produced. The scene used in this example is a challenging scenario where the goal is to extract the empty plate and remove the contents of the plate. There are various parts of the plate's surface for which no visual information is available in the 2D input images. This example demonstrates that the CLIP loss, making use of a text phrase like *"A plain empty plate"*, is able to reason about the missing area on the surface of the plate and render a plausible empty plate. In addition, the CLIP loss is able to remove the reflectance of the hotdogs on the plate to some extent. However, there are still are limited artifacts on the plate even after applying the CLIP loss. This result is due to the challenging nature of the task, since a large portion of the plate's surface is covered in the input images. As another example, the model has difficulty removing the shadow of the hotdogs from the original plate and tries to complete the shadow instead of removing it. This issue can be mitigated by increasing the CLIP loss, but the result is a plate that is less consistent with the one in the original scene, as shown in Fig. 6. Notice that not only the depth of the plate is reduced compared to the one in the original scene when the CLIP weight λ_{CLIP} is increased to 0.02; the lighting highlight on the plate surface is also rotated and differs from the original radiance of the plate. For the case without the CLIP loss (the middle row in Fig. 5), the background has been set to black to better visualize the holes in the plate.

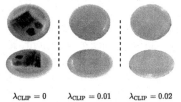

$\lambda_{\text{CLIP}} = 0$ $\lambda_{\text{CLIP}} = 0.01$ $\lambda_{\text{CLIP}} = 0.02$

Fig. 6. The effect of the weight of the CLIP loss on the extracted plate.

Importance of the Number of Input Views. The neural volumetric rendering method that is used in LaTeRF is not limited to a certain implementation of NeRF. We argue that with better quality and faster neural rendering approaches, the reconstruction quality and the speed of LaTeRF can be increased. In this experiment, the effect of the quality of the base neural renderer on final object reconstruction quality is studied. In order to mimic the behavior of a lower-quality neural rendering model, we limit the number of training input views fed when calculating the reconstruction loss $\mathcal{L}_{rec.}$. The results in Table 4 indicate that the detail and quality of the rendered object produced by LaTeRF is closely related to the reconstruction quality of the base NeRF model used to ensure the consistency of the extracted object with the one present in the scene. Consequently, as better volumetric rendering approaches for 3D reconstruction are introduced, LaTeRF will be able to take advantage of them to enable the creation of better object extractors.

Table 4. The effect of the number of training views for the calculation of $\mathcal{L}_{rec.}$.

# Views	PSNR↑	SSIM↑
100	**26.93**	**0.96**
80	26.62	0.95
60	26.50	0.92
40	26.20	0.95
20	25.35	0.94

6 Conclusion

We have presented LaTeRF, a method to extract digital objects via neural fields from 2D input images of a scene, and a minimal set of visual and natural language clues that guide the model to the object of interest. The geometry and color of different points are captured via NeRF, while the objectness probability of scene points is mainly determined via pixel labels provided by the user that identify whether some of the input pixels belong to the object of interest or not. Additionally, a CLIP loss is defined to ensure high similarity between the rendered images of the object and a text prompt that expresses the appearance and semantics of the object, enabling the model to reason about any missing parts of the object. The effectiveness of each of the components of the training scheme is shown through our experiments. However, we observed a need for per-scene fine-tuning of the hyper-parameters λ_{clf} and λ_{CLIP}. An additional challenge for LaTeRF is to extract transparent objects or objects with shiny surfaces that reflect other objects. Moreover, LaTeRF naturally comes with the general limitations associated with NeRFs, including the need for per-scene training and data intensity. Additionally, the rendered images used to calculate the CLIP loss had to be downsized to avoid memory shortages. Applying the CLIP loss to higher-resolution images will result in better inpainting.

References

1. Armeni, I., et al.: 3d scene graph: a structure for unified semantics, 3d space, and camera. In: ICCV (2019)
2. Barron, J.T., Mildenhall, B., Tancik, M., Hedman, P., Martin-Brualla, R., Srinivasan, P.P.: Mip-nerf: a multiscale representation for anti-aliasing neural radiance fields. arXiv (2021)
3. Bengio, Y., Courville, A., Vincent, P.: Representation learning: a review and new perspectives. In: IEEE Transactions on Pattern Analysis and Machine Intelligence (2013)
4. Boss, M., Braun, R., Jampani, V., Barron, J.T., Liu, C., Lensch, H.: Nerd: neural reflectance decomposition from image collections. In: ICCV (2021)
5. Candès, E.J.: Harmonic analysis of neural networks. Appl. Comput. Harmonic Anal. **6**(2), 197–218 (1999)
6. Chen, T., Kornblith, S., Norouzi, M., Hinton, G.: A simple framework for contrastive learning of visual representations. In: ICML (2020)
7. Gehring, J., Auli, M., Grangier, D., Yarats, D., Dauphin, Y.N.: Convolutional sequence to sequence learning. In: ICML (2017)
8. He, K., Fan, H., Wu, Y., Xie, S., Girshick, R.: Momentum contrast for unsupervised visual representation learning. In: CVPR (2020)
9. Henzler, P., Mitra, N.J., Ritschel, T.: Escaping plato's cave: 3d shape from adversarial rendering. In: ICCV (2019)
10. Henzler, P., et al.: Unsupervised learning of 3d object categories from videos in the wild. In: CVPR (2021)
11. Hermans, A., Floros, G., Leibe, B.: Dense 3d semantic mapping of indoor scenes from RGB-D images. In: ICRA (2014)
12. Hénaff, O.J., et al.: Data-efficient image recognition with contrastive predictive coding. In: ICML (2020)
13. Jain, A., Mildenhall, B., Barron, J.T., Abbeel, P., Poole, B.: Zero-shot text-guided object generation with dream fields. arXiv (2021)
14. Jain, A., Tancik, M., Abbeel, P.: Putting nerf on a diet: semantically consistent few-shot view synthesis. In: ICCV (2021)
15. Jiang, G., Kainz, B.: Deep radiance caching: Convolutional autoencoders deeper in ray tracing. Comput. Graph. **94**, 22–31 (2021)
16. Kingma, D.P., Ba, J.: Adam: a method for stochastic optimization. In: ICLR (2015)
17. Kuang, Z., Olszewski, K., Chai, M., Huang, Z., Achlioptas, P., Tulyakov, S.: NeROIC: Neural object capture and rendering from online image collections. arXiv (2022)
18. Lin, C.H., Ma, W.C., Torralba, A., Lucey, S.: Barf: bundle-adjusting neural radiance fields. In: ICCV (2021)
19. Liu, L., Gu, J., Lin, K.Z., Chua, T.S., Theobalt, C.: Neural sparse voxel fields. In: NeurIPS (2020)
20. Ma, L., Stückler, J., Kerl, C., Cremers, D.: Multi-view deep learning for consistent semantic mapping with RGB-D cameras. In: IROS (2017)
21. Mascaro, R., Teixeira, L., Chli, M.: Diffuser: multi-view 2d-to-3d label diffusion for semantic scene segmentation. In: ICRA (2021)
22. McCormac, J., Handa, A., Davison, A., Leutenegger, S.: Semanticfusion: dense 3d semantic mapping with convolutional neural networks. In: ICRA (2017)
23. Mildenhall, B., Srinivasan, P.P., Tancik, M., Barron, J.T., Ramamoorthi, R., Ng, R.: Nerf: representing scenes as neural radiance fields for view synthesis. In: ECCV (2020)

24. Müller, T., Evans, A., Schied, C., Keller, A.: Instant neural graphics primitives with a multiresolution hash encoding. arXiv (2022)
25. Niemeyer, M., Geiger, A.: Giraffe: representing scenes as compositional generative neural feature fields. In: CVPR (2021)
26. van den Oord, A., Li, Y., Vinyals, O.: Representation learning with contrastive predictive coding. arXiv (2019)
27. Ost, J., Mannan, F., Thuerey, N., Knodt, J., Heide, F.: Neural scene graphs for dynamic scenes. In: CVPR (2021)
28. Park, K., et al.: Nerfies: deformable neural radiance fields. In: ICCV (2021)
29. Paszke, A., et al.: PyTorch: an imperative style, high-performance deep learning library. In: Wallach, H., Larochelle, H., Beygelzimer, A., d'Alché-Buc, F., Fox, E., Garnett, R. (eds.) NeurIPS (2019)
30. Pett, D.: BritishMuseumDH/moldGoldCape: first release of the cape in 3D (2017). https://doi.org/10.5281/zenodo.344914
31. Radford, A., et al.: Learning transferable visual models from natural language supervision. In: Meila, M., Zhang, T. (eds.) ICML (2021)
32. Ramesh, A., et al.: Zero-shot text-to-image generation. arXiv (2021)
33. Rebain, D., Jiang, W., Yazdani, S., Li, K., Yi, K.M., Tagliasacchi, A.: Derf: decomposed radiance fields. In: CVPR (2020)
34. Rubinstein, M., Joulin, A., Kopf, J., Liu, C.: Unsupervised joint object discovery and segmentation in internet images. In: CVPR (2013)
35. Fridovich-Keil, S., Yu, A., Tancik, M., Chen, Q., Recht, B., Kanazawa, A.: Plenoxels: radiance fields without neural networks. In: CVPR (2022)
36. Sitzmann, V., Martel, J.N., Bergman, A.W., Lindell, D.B., Wetzstein, G.: Implicit neural representations with periodic activation functions. In: NeurIPS (2020)
37. Sonoda, S., Murata, N.: Neural network with unbounded activation functions is universal approximator. Appl. Comput. Harmonic Anal. **3**(2), 233–268 (2017)
38. Stelzner, K., Kersting, K., Kosiorek, A.R.: Decomposing 3d scenes into objects via unsupervised volume segmentation. arXiv (2021)
39. Su, H., Maji, S., Kalogerakis, E., Learned-Miller, E.: Multi-view convolutional neural networks for 3d shape recognition. In: ICCV (2015)
40. Takikawa, T., et al.: Neural geometric level of detail: real-time rendering with implicit 3D shapes. In: CVPR (2021)
41. Tewari, A., et al.: Advances in neural rendering. In: SIGGRAPH (2021)
42. Tulsiani, S., Zhou, T., Efros, A.A., Malik, J.: Multi-view supervision for single-view reconstruction via differentiable ray consistency. In: CVPR (2017)
43. Vaswani, A., et al.: Attention is all you need. In: NeurIPS (2017)
44. Vineet, V., et al.: Incremental dense semantic stereo fusion for large-scale semantic scene reconstruction. In: ICRA (2015)
45. Vora, S., et al.: Nesf: neural semantic fields for generalizable semantic segmentation of 3d scenes. arXiv (2021)
46. Wang, C., Chai, M., He, M., Chen, D., Liao, J.: Clip-nerf: text-and-image driven manipulation of neural radiance fields. arXiv (2021)
47. Wu, S., Jakab, T., Rupprecht, C., Vedaldi, A.: Dove: learning deformable 3d objects by watching videos. arXiv (2021)
48. Yen-Chen, L.: Nerf-pytorch. https://github.com/yenchenlin/nerf-pytorch/ (2020)
49. Yen-Chen, L., Florence, P., Barron, J.T., Rodriguez, A., Isola, P., Lin, T.Y.: iNeRF: inverting neural radiance fields for pose estimation. In: IROS (2021)
50. Yu, A., Ye, V., Tancik, M., Kanazawa, A.: pixelNeRF: neural radiance fields from one or few images. In: CVPR (2021)

51. Yu, H.X., Guibas, L.J., Wu, J.: Unsupervised discovery of object radiance fields. In: ICLR (2022)
52. Zhang, C., Liu, Z., Liu, G., Huang, D.: Large-scale 3d semantic mapping using monocular vision. In: ICIVC (2019)
53. Zhang, K., Riegler, G., Snavely, N., Koltun, V.: Nerf++: analyzing and improving neural radiance fields. arXiv (2020)
54. Zhi, S., Laidlow, T., Leutenegger, S., Davison, A.: In-place scene labelling and understanding with implicit scene representation. In: ICCV (2021)
55. Zhi, S., Sucar, E., Mouton, A., Haughton, I., Laidlow, T., Davison, A.J.: iLabel: interactive neural scene labelling (2021)
56. Zhu, J.Y., Wu, J., Xu, Y., Chang, E., Tu, Z.: Unsupervised object class discovery via saliency-guided multiple class learning. IEEE Trans. Pattern Anal. Mach. Intell. **37**(4), 862–875 (2015)

MeshMAE: Masked Autoencoders for 3D Mesh Data Analysis

Yaqian Liang[1], Shanshan Zhao[2], Baosheng Yu[3], Jing Zhang[3],
and Fazhi He[1(✉)]

[1] School of Computer Science, Wuhan University, Wuhan, China
{yqliang,fzhe}@whu.edu.cn
[2] JD Explore Academy, Beijing, China
sshan.zhao00@gmail.com
[3] School of Computer Science, The University of Sydney, Sydney, Australia
{baosheng.yu,jing.zhang1}@sydney.edu.au

Abstract. Recently, self-supervised pre-training has advanced Vision Transformers on various tasks *w.r.t.* different data modalities, *e.g.*, image and 3D point cloud data. In this paper, we explore this learning paradigm for 3D mesh data analysis based on Transformers. Since applying Transformer architectures to new modalities is usually non-trivial, we first adapt Vision Transformer to 3D mesh data processing, *i.e.*, Mesh Transformer. In specific, we divide a mesh into several non-overlapping local patches with each containing the same number of faces and use the 3D position of each patch's center point to form positional embeddings. Inspired by MAE, we explore how pre-training on 3D mesh data with the Transformer-based structure benefits downstream 3D mesh analysis tasks. We first randomly mask some patches of the mesh and feed the corrupted mesh into Mesh Transformers. Then, through reconstructing the information of masked patches, the network is capable of learning discriminative representations for mesh data. Therefore, we name our method MeshMAE, which can yield state-of-the-art or comparable performance on mesh analysis tasks, *i.e.*, classification and segmentation. In addition, we also conduct comprehensive ablation studies to show the effectiveness of key designs in our method.

Keywords: Transformer · Masked autoencoding · 3D mesh analysis · Self-supervised pre-training

1 Introduction

In recent years, Transformers [55] have been the technological dominant architecture in NLP community [7,16,31]. With autoregressive language modeling [46,47] or masked autoencoding [16], Transformer architectures can be

---

Y. Liang—This work was done during Y. Liang's internship at JD Explore Academy.

Supplementary Information The online version contains supplementary material available at https://doi.org/10.1007/978-3-031-20062-5_3.

© The Author(s), under exclusive license to Springer Nature Switzerland AG 2022
S. Avidan et al. (Eds.): ECCV 2022, LNCS 13663, pp. 37–54, 2022.
https://doi.org/10.1007/978-3-031-20062-5_3

trained on a very large unlabeled corpus of text. In computer vision, to pre-train a generalizable vision model, many strategies have been intensively studied, such as contrastive learning [27], egomotion prediction [2], and geometric transformation recognition [20]. Recently, inspired by the success of the masked autoencoding strategy in NLP, some works [5,64] also apply such a strategy to images or point clouds by reconstructing the masked tokens. Instead of predicting the tokens, a latest work, MAE [26], proposes to directly reconstruct raw pixels with a very impressive performance achieved, which provides a new self-supervised pre-training paradigm. Inspired by this, in this paper, we further explore the masked autoencoding strategy on 3D mesh data, whose structure is different from either 2D images or 3D point clouds.

As an effective 3D representation, 3D mesh has been widely exploited in computer graphics, such as 3D rendering, model reconstruction, and animation [22,28,51]. Along with the development of deep learning, remarkable achievements have been made in various mesh analysis tasks by adopting deep neural networks, such as 3D mesh classification [19], segmentation [29], and 3D human reconstruction [36]. In comparison with a image, the 3D mesh is composed of vertices and faces, which have not the specific order. While the connection between vertices makes 3D mesh not completely discrete data as point cloud. In light of the distinct structure of mesh data, there are some key challenges that need to be solved before applying the masked autoencoding strategy to the 3D mesh.

In this paper, we start from adapting the vanilla Vision Transformer [18] to process mesh data, which remains unexplored. As there are lots of faces in a mesh, e.g., from 10^3 to 10^5 in the original ModelNet40 (or ShapeNet), it is almost infeasible to apply the self-attention mechanism in Transformers over all faces. Inspired by [18], we split the original mesh into a set of non-overlapping mesh patches, which are regarded as the basic unit processed by the Transformer block. In addition, we calculate the positional embeddings in a naive manner since 3D mesh data inherently contains positional information. Specifically, the 3D coordinate of the center point of each mesh patch is used as the positional embedding. Finally, built upon the vanilla Vision Transformers, our Mesh Transformer processes these mesh embeddings via the multi-head self-attention layer and feedforward network sequentially. Basically, exploiting these operations, we can apply the Transformer architecture for 3D mesh data, i.e., Mesh Transformer.

Inspired by MAE [26], we wonder whether performing masked autoencoding on the unlabeled 3D mesh data could also promote the ability of the network. To arrive at this, we are required to design an efficient reconstruction objective first. Unlike MAE [26], which reconstructs the raw pixels naturally, we choose to recover the geometric information of the masked patches. In detail, we achieve the reconstruction at two levels, i.e., point-level and face-level. For point-level, we aim to predict the position of all points belonging to the masked patch, while for face-level, we regress the features for each face. Taking advantage of the two reconstruction objectives, the model can learn discriminative mesh representation in a self-supervised manner from large-scale unlabeled 3D mesh data.

On the basis of the above analysis, we present MeshMAE, a masked autoencoder network for Transformer-based 3D mesh pre-training. To show the effectiveness of the proposed pre-text task, we visualize the reconstructed meshes. We observe that our MeshMAE model correctly predicts the shape of masked mesh patches and infers diverse, holistic reconstructions through our decoder. We conduct the pre-training on ModelNet40 and ShapeNet respectively and conduct the fine-tuning and linear probing experiments for mesh classification. In addition, we also finetune the pre-trained network for the part segmentation task. The experimental results and comprehensive ablations demonstrate the effectiveness of our method. The main contributions of our method are as follows:

- We explore adapting the masked-autoencoding-based pre-training strategy to 3D mesh analysis. To achieve this, we design a feasible Transformer-based network, Mesh Transformer, and reconstruction objectives in light of the distinctive structure of 3D mesh data.
- Our method achieves new state-of-the-art or comparable performance on the mesh classification and segmentation tasks. We also conduct intensive ablations to better understand the proposed MeshMAE.

2   Related Works

2.1   Transformer

Transformers [55] were first introduced as an attention-based framework in NLP and currently have become the dominant framework in NLP [16,47] due to its salient benefits, including massively parallel computing, long-distance characteristics, and minimal inductive bias. Along with its remarkable success in NLP, the trend towards leveraging Transformer architecture into the computer vision community has also emerged. The Vision Transformer (ViT) [18] makes a significant attempt to exploit the self-attention mechanism, and has obtained many state-of-the-art (SOTA) records. So far, Transformers have already been extensively studied in various computer tasks, especially 2D image analysis tasks, such as image classification [9,18,52,61,65], object detection [8,14,42,68], semantic segmentation [11,17,58,67], pose estimation [30,34,36], and depth estimation [35,62]. However, the application of ViT in 3D data still remains limited.

Almost simultaneously, [23,53,63,66] proposes to extend Transformer architectures into the disordered and discrete 3D point cloud. Among them, [23] proposes an offset attention (OA) module to sharpen the attention weights and reduce the influence of noise. To save the computational costs, [66] proposes a local vector self-attention mechanism to construct a point Transformer layer. In comparison, to facilitate Transformer to better leverage the inductive bias of point clouds, [63] devises a geometry-aware block to model the local geometric relationships. Nevertheless, those prior efforts all involve more or less inductive biases, making them out of line with standard Transformers. As for meshes, to the best of our knowledge, there are no existing papers that directly apply Transformers to process the irregular mesh data. Instead, some works only use images as the input of the Transformer and output mesh data. For example, Mesh-Graphormer [37] combines the graph convolutions and self-attentions to model both local and global interactions, METRO [36] proposes to utilize Transformer to learn the correlation among long-range joints and vertices in images. PolyGen [44] proposes to generate the vertices and faces in sequence with Transformer. In this work, we would explore how to apply the standard Transformer to 3D mesh data.

2.2 Self-supervised Learning

Self-supervised learning could learn the meaningful feature representations via pretext tasks that do not require extra annotations. For example, contrastive learning learns feature representations by increasing intra-class distance and decreasing extra-class distance [45,59]. In comparison, autoencoding pursues a conceptually different direction by mapping an input to a latent representation in an encoder and reconstructing the input using a decoder. In NLP, BERT [16] first attempts to pre-train bidirectional representations from the unlabeled text in a self-supervised scheme. Since then, the pretext of Masked Language Modeling (MLM) has arisen significant interest in NLP [7,46,47]. Motivated by the success of BERT in NLP, there are many attempts in the computer vision area [5,10,12,31,39,54]. Among them, iGPT [10] proposes to operate on sequences of pixels and predict the unknown pixels, while ViT [18] proposes to reshape the images into patches, and then adapts the standard Transformer to process images. Recently, BEiT [5] proposes a pretext task that tokenizes the input images into discrete visual tokens firstly and then recovers the masked discrete tokens, while MAE [26] encourages the model to reconstruct those missing pixels directly without the tokenization. For 3D data analysis, PointBERT [64] generalizes the concept of BERT into 3D point clouds by devising a masked point reconstruction task to pre-train the Transformers. Variation autoencoder (VAE) has been applied to implement 3D mesh deformation and pose transfer [4,13]. Our work is greatly inspired by MAE and PointBERT. However, the distinctive characteristics of 3D meshes hinder the straightforward use of BERT on 3D mesh analysis. In this paper, we aim to explore how to adapt mask autoencoding pre-training to 3D meshes with minimal modification.

2.3 Mesh Analysis

The polygon mesh is an effective 3D representation, which can depict the geometric context of a 3D object preciously. However, the vertices in 3D meshes do not have the same number of adjacent vertices, leading to the general convolution and pooling operations cannot be applied to the mesh data directly. Accompanied by the development of deep learning methods on 3D data, how to adapt the neural network to 3D mesh processing is always the highlight. Initially, Masci *et al.* [15] makes the first effort to generalize convolutional neural networks to 3D mesh based on localized frequency analysis. More recently, researchers extensively study how to implement feature aggregation and downsampling operations

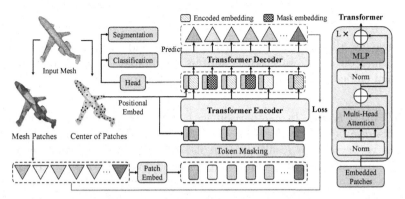

Fig. 1. The overall architecture of the proposed MeshMAE framework. The input mesh is divided into several non-overlapping patches, which would be embedded by the MLP. During pre-training, patch embeddings will be randomly masked, and only the visible embeddings will be fed into the Transformers. Then, the mask embeddings are introduced and sent to the decoder together with the combination of encoded embeddings. The targets of the decoder are to reconstruct the vertices and face features of masked patches. After pre-training, the decoder is discarded and the encoder is applied to downstream tasks.

on irregular structures. For example, MeshCNN [25] explores classical methods of Graphics, which defines an ordering invariant convolution operation for edges and utilizes the edge collapse operation to implement pooling. To overcome the problem that the unfixed number of vertex neighborhoods in the mesh, some methods introduce graph neural networks (GNNs) [41,43,49,56] to implement the convolution on vertices, where the feature aggregation is conducted on the vertices and their 1-ring neighbors. While each face must have three adjacent faces in the manifold mesh, this kind of stable structure makes feature aggregation of faces easier. MeshNet learns the spatial and structural features of a face by aggregating its three adjacent faces. SubdivNet [29] processes the meshes to obtain the fine-to-coarse hierarchical structure, which could be processed by the convolution-like operation. Actually, the attention-based Transformer does not require convolution or pooling operation and would not be affected by the data structure. Therefore, it may be more suitable for irregular mesh data.

3   Method

In this paper, we aim to extend the Vision Transformer into mesh analysis, Mesh Transformer, and apply the masked-autoencoding-based self-supervised pre-training strategy to Mesh Transformer. Here, we introduce the details of our Transformer-based mesh analysis framework, Mesh Transformer, and the MAE-based pre-training strategy. Figure 1 shows the framework of MeshMAE.

3.1   Mesh Transformer

A triangle mesh $M = (V, F)$ is defined by vertices and triangular faces. To apply Transformer on mesh, we need to address patch split, patch embedding, and positional embedding, which are introduced in the following parts.

Mesh Patch Split. In comparison with 3D point cloud data containing a set of discrete points, the faces of 3D mesh provide the connection relationship between vertices. As a result, we can use the geometric information of each face to represent the feature. In detail, as SubdivNet [29] does, for face f_i, we define its feature as a 10-dimensional vector, consisting of the face area (1-dim), three interior angles of the triangle (3-dim), face normal (3-dim), and three inner products between the face normal and three vertex normals (3-dim).

The self-attention-based architectures of Transformers ease the pains of designing especial feature aggregation operations for 3D meshes. However, if we apply the self-attention mechanism over all faces, the huge computational cost of quadratic complexity would be unbearable. Therefore, before applying Transformers to mesh, we first group the faces of a mesh into a set of non-overlapping patches. However, unlike image data, which is regular and could be divided into a grid of square patches, mesh data is irregular and the faces are usually unordered, which makes the patch split challenging. To address this issue, we propose to first 'remesh' the original mesh to make the structure regular and hierarchical. Specifically, we adopt MAPS algorithm [33] to implement the remeshing operation, which simplifies the mesh to a base mesh with N faces ($96 \leq N \leq 256$ in our experiments). After the remeshing process, the base mesh, *simplified mesh*, is coarser than the original mesh and is incapable of representing the shape accurately. Therefore, we further subdivide all faces in the base mesh t times in a 1-to-4 manner and get a refined mesh called $t-$mesh. We can divide $t-$mesh into non-overlapping patches by grouping the faces corresponding to the same face in the base mesh into a patch. In practice, we subdivide 3 times and thus each patch contains 64 faces. The process is illustrated in Fig. 2.

Transformer Backbone. In this paper, we adopt the standard Transformer as the backbone network, consisting of a series of multi-headed self-attention layers and feedforward network (FFN) blocks.

To represent each patch, for image data, we can concatenate the RGB values of raw pixels located in the same patch in a natural order. For mesh data, thanks to remeshing operation which subdivides the face orderly, we can also use the concatenation of the 10-dim feature vectors of all faces belonging to the same patch as the patch's feature. As shown in Fig. 2, we can find that the face in the base mesh is always divided in a fixed order starting from a selected vertex. Although the selected vertex might impact the order, we experimentally find that the impact is very slight (Sect. 4.3). Therefore, we can concatenate the faces' features according to the order generated by the remeshing process as the patch's representation (as shown in Fig. 5). Then, we adopt an MLP to project

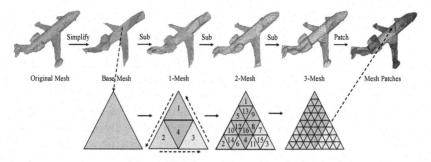

Fig. 2. The process of remeshing operation. The input mesh is simplified first, and a bijection is constructed between the original mesh and the base mesh. Then the base mesh is subdivided 3 times and new vertices are projected back onto the input.

the feature vector of those patches into representations $\{e_i\}_{i=1}^{g}$, where g denotes the number of patches. The representations are thus regarded as the input into the Transformer. The input features only describe the shape information of faces. Generally, Transformer-based methods utilize the positional embedding to provide the position information of patches. In comparison against natural language or image where the serial number is taken as the position, the mesh data contains 3D space position of each face. In this paper, we adopt the center 3D coordinates of faces to compute the positional embeddings, which would be more suitable for the geometric data and unordered patches. In practical, we first calculate the center point coordinates $\{c_i\}_{i=1}^{g}$ of each patch, and then apply an MLP to $\{c_i\}_{i=1}^{g}$ to obtain the positional embedding $\{p_i\}_{i=1}^{g}$ for patches.

Formally, we define the input embeddings $X = \{x_i\}_{i=1}^{g}$ as the combination of patch embeddings $E = \{e_i\}_{i=1}^{g}$ and positional embeddings $P = \{p_i\}_{i=1}^{g}$. In this way, the overall input sequence is defined as $H^0 = \{x_1, x_2, ..., x_g\}$. There are L layers of Transformer block in the encoder network, and the output of the last layer $H^L = \{h_1^L, ..., h_g^L\}$ represents the encoded representation of the input patches.

3.2   Mesh Pre-training Task

Motivated by BERT [16] and MAE [26], we study the masked modeling strategy for mesh representation learning based on the introduced Mesh Transformer. Specifically, we devise a masked mesh modeling task that aims at reconstructing the geometric structure of the masked patches from partially visible sub-meshes. Our method is based on autoencoders, where an encoder is utilized to map the visible sub-meshes into latent representations and the decoder reconstructs the geometric structure from the latent representations. By modeling the masked parts, the model attains the geometric understanding of the mesh. Below, we provide more details.

Encoder and Decoder. In the pre-training task, the encoder and decoder networks are both composed of several Transformer blocks. We set the encoder, *i.e.,* our Mesh Transformer, as 12 layers and a lightweight decoder with 6 layers. In our method, according to a pre-defined masking ratio, some patches of the input mesh are masked, and the remaining visible patches are fed into the encoder. Before feeding into the decoder, we utilize a shared mask embedding to replace all the masked embeddings, which indicates the presence of the missing patches that need to be predicted. Then, the input to the decoder is composed of encoded visible embeddings and mask embeddings. Here, we add the positional embeddings to all embeddings once again, which provide the location information for both masked and visible patches. It is noted that the decoder is only used during pre-training to perform mesh reconstruction tasks, while only the encoder is used in the downstream tasks.

Masked Sequence Generation. The complete mesh embeddings are denoted by $E = \{e_1, ..., e_g\}$ and their indices are denoted by $I = \{1, ..., g\}$. Following MAE, we first randomly mask a subset of patches, where the indices I_m of masked embeddings are sampled from I randomly with the ratio r. In this way, we denote the masked embeddings as $E_m = E[I_m]$ and the unmasked embeddings as $E_{um} = E[I - I_m]$. Next, we replace the masked embeddings E_m with a shared learnable mask embedding E_{mask} while keeping their positional embedding unchanged. Finally, the corrupted mesh embeddings $E_c = E_{um} \cup \{E_{mask} + p_i : i \in I_m\}$ are fed into the encoder. When the masking ratio is high, the redundancy can be eliminated largely and the masked parts would not be solved easily by extrapolation from visible neighboring patches. Therefore, the reconstruction task is relatively challenging.

Reconstruction Targets. The targets of the pre-training task are also crucial. In NLP, BERT [16] proposes the pretext of Masked Language Modeling (MLM), which first masks the input randomly and then recovers a sequence of input tokens. Following it, there are also similar works on images, *e.g.,* BEiT [5], and on point clouds, *e.g.,* PointBert [64], both of which train the models by recovering the tokens learned via dVAE [48]. However, these kinds of dVAE tokenizer reconstruction require one more pre-training stage. Recently, MAE [26] skips the dVAE training process and proposes to reconstruct the pixel values directly, which is simpler and saves much computation overhead.

Inspired by MAE [26], our method directly recovers the input patches. Specifically, we define a reconstruction target as the shape of the masked patches. As shown in Fig. 2, there are only 45 unique vertices in the 64 faces of a mesh patch. To recover the shape of patches, these 45 vertices are required to be located in the corresponding ground truth positions. Therefore, we propose to predict the 3D relative coordinate (x, y, z) of them directly (relative to the center point of the patch), and the output of the decoder can be written as $P_r = \{p_{r_i}\}_{i=1}^{45}$. During the training phase, we adopt the l_2-form Chamfer distance to calculate the reconstruction loss between the relative coordinates of predicted vertices and that of ground truth vertices, which is shown as follows:

$$\mathcal{L}_{CD}(P_r, G_r) = \frac{1}{|P_r|} \sum_{p \in P_r} \min_{g \in G_r} ||p - g|| + \frac{1}{|G_r|} \sum_{g \in G_r} \min_{p \in P_r} ||g - p||, \qquad (1)$$

where G_r denotes the relative coordinates of the 45 ground truth vertices in a patch.

In the real mesh, the vertices are connected with edges to compose the faces, which are the important unit of the mesh data. However, due to the disorder of the vertices, it is intractable to recover the faces' information if we only predict the vertices' position, which might degrade the network's capability of recovering the geometric structure. In order to enhance the restraint and predict the local details, we propose to additionally predict the face-wise features, *i.e.*, the input representation of the face. To achieve this, we add another linear layer behind the decoder to predict all faces' features for each patch. We denote the predicted features by $J \in \mathcal{R}^{64 \times 10}$. Here, we organize the faces' features in the order generated by the remeshing operation. We adopt the face-wise MSE loss $\mathcal{L}_{MSE}$ to evaluate the reconstruction effect of features. The overall optimization object is combined by both $\mathcal{L}_{CD}$ and $\mathcal{L}_{MSE}$, as follows,

$$\mathcal{L} = \mathcal{L}_{MSE} + \lambda \cdot \mathcal{L}_{CD}, \qquad (2)$$

where λ is the loss weight.

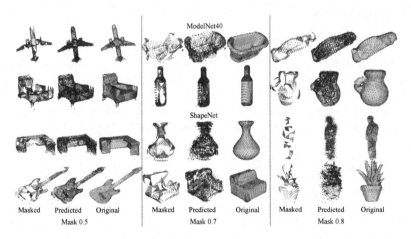

Fig. 3. Reconstruction results on ModelNet40 test set. Top two lines are the results of model trained on ModelNet40, and bottom two lines are the results of model trained on ShapeNet. Here, we show the effects when the mask ratio is 0.5, 0.7 and 0.8 respectively. More results will be demonstrated in the Supplementary.

It is noted that the input features do not contain coordinates of the three vertices of each face, while we propose to predict the vertices coordinates of the masked patches. Here, we illustrate the shape reconstruction effect on the ModelNet40 in Fig. 3, where the models are pre-trained on ModelNet40 and

Table 1. Classification accuracy on ModelNet40. The first row is a point cloud method.

Method	Acc (%)
PCT [23]	92.4
MeshWalker [32]	90.5
MeshNet [19]	88.4
SubdivNet [29]	91.4
Transformer (w/o PT)	91.5
MeshMAE (PT M)	91.7
MeshMAE (PT S)	92.5

ShapeNet, respectively. We directly show the vertices in mesh instead of faces, because the vertices are disordered and it is difficult to define the edge connection between them, which has also no impact on the pre-training task. It can be seen that our model can recover the shape of original meshes precisely by predicting vertices, and the performance of our model is still well even if the mask ratio is 80%, suggesting that the proposed model has indeed learned the geometric information of 3D meshes.

4   Experiments

Here, we first describe the data pre-processing methods and introduce the settings of the proposed pre-training scheme. The learned representation would be evaluated through doing supervised training under two settings: end-to-end fine-tuning and linear probing. The experiments are conducted on two downstream tasks, including object classification and part segmentation. We provide more experimental results, analyses, and visualizations in the Supplementary.

4.1   Implementation Details

Data Pre-processing. In the original mesh datasets, *e.g.*, ShapeNet and ModelNet40, the number of faces varies dramatically among meshes and most 3D meshes are not watertight or 2-manifold, that is, there are holes or boundaries on the surface. In order to facilitate the subsequent mesh preprocessing, we first reconstruct the shapes to build the corresponding manifold meshes and simplify the manifold meshes into 500 faces uniformly. Then, we remesh all meshes in the datasets using MAPS algorithm [33,38] to obtain the meshes with regular structures. In this process, the input mesh (500 faces) would be simplified to a base mesh with a smaller resolution (96–256 faces), and the base mesh would be further subdivided 3 times. After pre-processing, the remeshed meshes contain $n \times 64$ faces, where n denotes the face number in the base mesh. To improve the data diversity, we generate 10-times remeshed meshes for each input mesh by collapsing random edges in the remeshing process.

Data Augmentation. We apply random anisotropic scaling with a normal distribution $\mu = 1$ and $\sigma = 0.1$ to reduce network sensitivity to the size of meshes. According to the geometrical characteristics of 3D meshes, we additionally utilize shape deformation. The shape deformation is based on the free form deformation (FFD) [50], driven by moving the position of external lattice control points.

Training Details. For pre-training, we utilize ShapeNet and ModelNet40 as the dataset respectively to explore the difference between small datasets and large datasets. Among them, ShapeNet covers about 51, 000 3D meshes from 55 common object categories and ModelNet40 contains 12, 311 3D meshes from 40 categories. We utilize ViT-Base [18] as the encoder network with very slight modification, *e.g.,* the number of input features' channels. And following [26], we set a lightweight decoder, which has 6 layers. We employ an AdamW optimizer, using an initial learning rate of 1e-4 with a cosine learning schedule. The weight decay is set as 0.05 and the batch size is set as 32. We set the same encoder network that of pre-training in downstream tasks. For the classification task, we exploit the max-pooling operation behind the encoder and append a linear classifier. While for the segmentation task, we utilize two segmentation heads to provide a two-level feature aggregation, which would be introduced in the following part. We set the batch size as 32, and employ AdamW optimizer with an initial learning rate of 1e-4. The learning rate is decayed by a factor of 0.1 at 30 and 60 epochs in classification (80 and 160 epochs in segmentation).

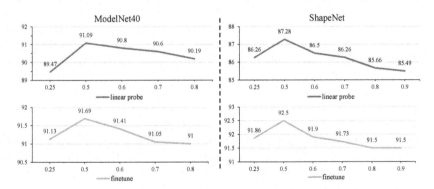

Fig. 4. The experimental results under different masking ratios, where the pre-trained models are obtained on ModelNet40 in the left two figures while that are obtained on ShapeNet in the right two figures. The x-axes denotes the masking ratio and y-axes denotes the classification accuracy.

4.2   Downstream Tasks

In this subsection, we present the experimental results of classification and segmentation tasks. Here, we demonstrate the results of Mesh Transformer without pre-training ('w/o PT'), the results of MeshMAE with pre-training on ModelNet ('PT M') and ShapeNet ('PT S').

Object Classification. For the classification task, we utilize the Manifold40 [29] (generated from ModelNet40) as the dataset. To demonstrate the effectiveness of the proposed method, we compare it with several recent mesh classification methods and a recent point cloud-based method. Experimental results are reported in Table 1. In this part, we denote the results of mesh Transformer as 'Transformer'. Here, we list the fine-tuning results of models pre-trained on ModelNet40 and ShapeNet, respectively. The results of them both outperform the baseline, demonstrating that the proposed mask autoencoding strategy is also effective in the mesh analysis task. Compared with the result of 'ModelNet40', the result of 'ShapeNet' is higher and obtains the state-of-the-art performance, which shows that larger data sets can promote to learn a better feature representation in the proposed pre-training task. This is consistent with the conclusion in the CV.

Figure 4 shows the linear probing and fine-tuning results under different masking ratios on ModelNet40. Though the number of meshes in ShapeNet is almost 5 times that in ModelNet40, the linear probing results of ShapeNet are always lower than that of ModelNet40. We think this is due to the domain gaps between ShapeNet and ModelNet40. And the fine-tuning results of ShapeNet are much higher than that of ModelNet40, demonstrating a larger pre-training dataset could indeed bring better results. From Fig. 4, we find that masking 50% patches works well for both fine-tuning and linear probing settings.

Part Segmentation. In this part, we utilize two datasets to conduct segmentation experiments, Human Body [40] and COSEG-aliens [60]. Specifically, the Human Body dataset consists of 381 training meshes from SCAPE [3], FAUST [6], MIT [57], and Adobe Fuse [1], and 18 test meshes from SHREC07 [21]. Each mesh sample is segmented into 8 parts. We also evaluate our method on the COSEG-aliens dataset with 200 meshes labeled with 4 parts. Both two datasets are processed by the remeshing operation, and the face labels are obtained from the mapping between the remeshed data and the raw meshes using the nearest-face strategy. Compared with classification, the segmentation task is more challenging, since it needs to predict dense labels for each face while faces within a patch might belong to different categories. In practice, we utilize two segmentation heads to provide a two-level feature aggregation. Specifically, we concatenate the output of the encoder with the feature embedding of each face to provide a fine-grained embedding. Besides, we do not design any other network structure specific for segmentation. Tables 2 and 3 show the segmentation results on Human and COSEG-aliens datasets. Our method achieves comparable performance with recent state-of-the-art methods in segmentation tasks. Considering that the proposed method only uses patch embeddings, it might be difficult for the network to learn detailed structure information. Therefore, the performance improvement on the segmentation task is very limited compared with it on the classification task. Despite this, pre-training can still bring improvements.

Table 2. Mesh segmentation accuracy on the COSEG-aliens dataset.

Method	Acc (%)
MeshCNN [25]	94.4
PD-MeshNet [41]	89.0
SubdivNet [29]	98.5
Transformer (w/o PT)	97.6
MeshMAE (PT M)	97.9
MeshMAE (PT S)	98.0

Table 3. Mesh segmentation accuracy on Human Body dataset.

Method	Acc (%)
Toric Cover [40]	88.0
MeshCNN [25]	87.7
SNGC [24]	91.3
SubdivNet [29]	90.8
Transformer (w/o PT)	90.1
MeshMAE (PT M)	90.1
MeshMAE (PT S)	90.3

4.3 Ablation Studies

Here, we present several ablation studies to further analyze the components in our method. To facilitate the analysis, we only conduct pre-training on Model-Net40 in this subsection.

Reconstruction Target. In the proposed masked autoencoding task, we propose to recover the input feature and predict the vertices of masked patches simultaneously. In this part, we would verify their effectiveness separately and find an appropriate loss weight between them. In Table 4, we list the classification performance under several loss settings when the mask ratio is set as 0.5. It is found that the best classification performance can be obtained when $\mathcal{L}_{MSE}/\mathcal{L}_{CD} = 1 : 0.5$.

Table 4. Comparison of reconstruction targets. The values of $\mathcal{L}_{MSE}$ and $\mathcal{L}_{CD}$ denote the weights of them, respectively. 'Fine' indicates the results of fine-tuning, while 'Line' indicates the results of linear probing.

$\mathcal{L}_{MSE}$	$\mathcal{L}_{CD}$	Fine (%)	Line (%)
1	0	91.2	89.8
0	1	90.6	89.7
1	0.1	90.8	90.4
1	0.25	90.8	90.7
1	0.5	91.7	91.1
1	1	91.5	90.3
1	2	91.5	89.7

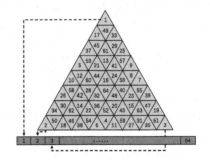

Fig. 5. The order of face features, where the serial number of the face denotes the location of its feature vector in the concatenated feature vector.

Face Order. In comparison with images with regular structure, the faces in patches are triangular and they cannot be arranged by row and column. In this paper, we set the order of face features in a patch as shown in Fig. 5, which is defined according to the remeshing process. Here, we conduct several test experiments to verify whether the other orders of faces would lower the performance. In Table 5, 'Original' denotes the faces order in our method, 'Rotate' denotes the structure of faces remains unchanged while starting from another two angles, *e.g.*, starting from face 2 (Rotate-l) or face 3 (Rotate-r), and 'Random' denotes the face features are arranged randomly. In Table 5, we repeat the experiments 5 times for each setting. According to the results, we find that even if the order of faces is randomly disturbed, the performance decreases very slightly and remains basically stable, which demonstrates the our selection of the order works well for patch representation.

Table 5. The effect of different orders of face features in the patches.

Sorting Method	Acc (%)	Std.
Original	91.7	4e-2
Rotate-l	91.7	5e-2
Rotate-r	91.6	2e-2
Random	91.6	4e-2

Table 6. Comparison of different positional embedding strategies.

Strategy	Mask	Acc (%)	Mask	Acc (%)
a)	0.25	42.6	0.5	46.1
b)	0.25	88.2	0.5	89.3
c)	0.25	75.0	0.5	77.5
d)	0.25	83.7	0.5	89.7

Positional Embedding. Each patch contains 64 faces, and how to embed positional information of 64 faces is a problem worth exploring. Here, we propose several positional embedding strategies: a) utilizing learnable parameters as MAE [26] does; b) first embedding the center coordinates of each face, then applying max-pooling; c) first reshaping the center coordinates of 64 faces (64, 3) into a one-dimension vector (64×3), then embedding this vector directly; d) first calculating the center coordinates of the whole patches, then embedding the center of the patch directly (ours). Table 6 lists the classification results of the above strategies, which are all obtained by linear probing. We find that embedding the center of the patch directly could obtain the best results.

5   Conclusions

In this paper, we introduce Transformer-based architecture (Mesh Transformer) into mesh analysis and investigate the masked-autoencoding-based pre-training method for Mesh Transformer pre-training. By recovering the features and shape of the masked patches, the model could learn the geometric information of 3D meshes. And the comprehensive experimental results and ablations prove that the proposed MeshMAE could learn a more effective feature representation. The study shows the feasibility of the Transformer-based method on mesh analysis. In future, we would like to explore its applications in other mesh-related tasks.

Acknowledgements. This work is supported by the National Natural Science Foundation of China under Grant No. 62072348. Dr. Baosheng Yu and Dr. Jing Zhang are supported by ARC Project FL-170100117.

References

1. Adobe.com: animate 3d characters for games, film, and more. Accessed 24 2021. https://www.mixamo.com (2021)
2. Agrawal, P., Carreira, J., Malik, J.: Learning to see by moving. In: ICCV, pp. 37–45 (2015)
3. Anguelov, D., Srinivasan, P., Koller, D., Thrun, S., Rodgers, J., Davis, J.: Scape: shape completion and animation of people. In: ACM Transactions on Graphics (TOG), pp. 408–416 (2005)
4. Aumentado-Armstrong, T., Tsogkas, S., Jepson, A., Dickinson, S.: Geometric disentanglement for generative latent shape models. In: CVPR, pp. 8181–8190 (2019)
5. Bao, H., Dong, L., Wei, F.: Beit: bert pre-training of image transformers. arXiv preprint arXiv:2106.08254 (2021)
6. Bogo, F., Romero, J., Loper, M., Black, M.J.: Faust: dataset and evaluation for 3d mesh registration. In: CVPR, pp. 3794–3801 (2014)
7. Brown, T., et al.: Language models are few-shot learners. NeurIPS **33**, 1877–1901 (2020)
8. Carion, N., Massa, F., Synnaeve, G., Usunier, N., Kirillov, A., Zagoruyko, S.: End-to-end object detection with transformers. In: Vedaldi, A., Bischof, H., Brox, T., Frahm, J.-M. (eds.) ECCV 2020. LNCS, vol. 12346, pp. 213–229. Springer, Cham (2020). https://doi.org/10.1007/978-3-030-58452-8_13
9. Chen, C.F., Fan, Q., Panda, R.: CrossViT: cross-attention multi-scale vision transformer for image classification. arXiv preprint arXiv:2103.14899 (2021)
10. Chen, M., et al.: Generative pretraining from pixels. In: ICML, pp. 1691–1703. PMLR (2020)
11. Cheng, B., Schwing, A., Kirillov, A.: Per-pixel classification is not all you need for semantic segmentation. In: NeurIPS, pp. 17864–17875 (2021)
12. Conneau, A., Lample, G.: Cross-lingual language model pretraining. In: NeurIPS, pp. 7059–7069 (2019)
13. Cosmo, L., Norelli, A., Halimi, O., Kimmel, R., Rodolà, E.: LIMP: learning latent shape representations with metric preservation priors. In: Vedaldi, A., Bischof, H., Brox, T., Frahm, J.-M. (eds.) ECCV 2020. LNCS, vol. 12348, pp. 19–35. Springer, Cham (2020). https://doi.org/10.1007/978-3-030-58580-8_2
14. Dai, Z., Cai, B., Lin, Y., Chen, J.: UP-DETR: unsupervised pre-training for object detection with transformers. In: CVPR, pp. 1601–1610 (2021)
15. Davide, B., Jonathan, M., Simone, M., Michael, M.B., Umberto, C., Pierre, V.: Learning class-specific descriptors for deformable shapes using localized spectral convolutional networks. Comput. Graph. Forum **34**(5), 13–23 (2015)
16. Devlin, J., Chang, M.W., Lee, K., Toutanova, K.: Bert: pre-training of deep bidirectional transformers for language understanding. arXiv preprint arXiv:1810.04805 (2018)
17. Ding, L., et al.: Looking outside the window: wide-context transformer for the semantic segmentation of high-resolution remote sensing images. arXiv preprint arXiv:2106.15754 (2021)
18. Dosovitskiy, A., et al.: An image is worth 16 x 16 words: transformers for image recognition at scale. In: ICLR (2020)

19. Feng, Y., Feng, Y., You, H., Zhao, X., Gao, Y.: MeshNet: mesh neural network for 3d shape representation. In: AAAI, pp. 8279–8286 (2019)
20. Gidaris, S., Singh, P., Komodakis, N.: Unsupervised representation learning by predicting image rotations. In: ICLR (2018)
21. Giorgi, D., Biasotti, S., Paraboschi, L.: Shape retrieval contest 2007: watertight models track. SHREC Compet. **8**(7) (2007)
22. Guan, S., Xu, J., Wang, Y., Ni, B., Yang, X.: Bilevel online adaptation for out-of-domain human mesh reconstruction. In: CVPR, pp. 10472–10481 (2021)
23. Guo, M.H., Cai, J.X., Liu, Z.N., Mu, T.J., Martin, R.R., Hu, S.M.: PCT: point cloud transformer. Comput. Visual Media **7**(2), 187–199 (2021)
24. Haim, N., Segol, N., Ben-Hamu, H., Maron, H., Lipman, Y.: Surface networks via general covers. In: ICCV, pp. 632–641 (2019)
25. Hanocka, R., Hertz, A., Fish, N., Giryes, R., Fleishman, S., Cohenor, D.: MeshCNN: a network with an edge. ACM Trans. Graph. (TOG) **38**(4), 90 (2019)
26. He, K., Chen, X., Xie, S., Li, Y., Dollár, P., Girshick, R.: Masked autoencoders are scalable vision learners. In: CVPR, pp. 16000–16009 (2022)
27. Hjelm, R.D., et al.: Learning deep representations by mutual information estimation and maximization. In: ICLR (2018)
28. Hu, S.-M., Liang, D., Yang, G.-Y., Yang, G.-W., Zhou, W.-Y.: Jittor: a novel deep learning framework with meta-operators and unified graph execution. Sci. China Inf. Sci. **63**(12), 1–21 (2020). https://doi.org/10.1007/s11432-020-3097-4
29. Hu, S.M., et al.: Subdivision-based mesh convolution networks. ACM Trans. Graph. (TOG) (2021)
30. Huang, L., Tan, J., Liu, J., Yuan, J.: Hand-transformer: non-autoregressive structured modeling for 3d hand pose estimation. In: Vedaldi, A., Bischof, H., Brox, T., Frahm, J.-M. (eds.) ECCV 2020. LNCS, vol. 12370, pp. 17–33. Springer, Cham (2020). https://doi.org/10.1007/978-3-030-58595-2_2
31. Joshi, M., Chen, D., Liu, Y., Weld, D.S., Zettlemoyer, L., Levy, O.: SpanBERT: improving pre-training by representing and predicting spans. Trans. Assoc. Comput. Linguist. **8**, 64–77 (2020)
32. Lahav, A., Tal, A.: MeshWalker: deep mesh understanding by random walks. ACM Trans. Graph. (TOG) **39**(6), 1–13 (2020)
33. Lee, A.W., Sweldens, W., Schröder, P., Cowsar, L., Dobkin, D.: Maps: multiresolution adaptive parameterization of surfaces. In: ACM SIGGRAPH, pp. 95–104 (1998)
34. Li, W., Liu, H., Tang, H., Wang, P., Van Gool, L.: MHFormer: multi-hypothesis transformer for 3d human pose estimation. arXiv preprint arXiv:2111.12707 (2021)
35. Li, Z., Liu, X., Drenkow, N., Ding, A., Creighton, F.X., Taylor, R.H., Unberath, M.: Revisiting stereo depth estimation from a sequence-to-sequence perspective with transformers. In: CVPR, pp. 6197–6206 (2021)
36. Lin, K., Wang, L., Liu, Z.: End-to-end human pose and mesh reconstruction with transformers. In: CVPR, pp. 1954–1963 (2021)
37. Lin, K., Wang, L., Liu, Z.: Mesh graphormer. arXiv preprint arXiv:2104.00272 (2021)
38. Liu, H.T.D., Kim, V.G., Chaudhuri, S., Aigerman, N., Jacobson, A.: Neural subdivision. arXiv preprint arXiv:2005.01819 (2020)
39. Liu, Y., et al.: Roberta: a robustly optimized bert pretraining approach. arXiv preprint arXiv:1907.11692 (2019)
40. Maron, H., et al.: Convolutional neural networks on surfaces via seamless toric covers. ACM Trans. Graph. (TOG) **36**(4), 71–1 (2017)

41. Milano, F., Loquercio, A., Rosinol, A., Scaramuzza, D., Carlone, L.: Primal-dual mesh convolutional neural networks. NeurIPS **33**, 952–963 (2020)
42. Misra, I., Girdhar, R., Joulin, A.: An end-to-end transformer model for 3d object detection. In: CVPR, pp. 2906–2917 (2021)
43. Monti, F., Shchur, O., Bojchevski, A., Litany, O., Günnemann, S., Bronstein, M.M.: Dual-primal graph convolutional networks. arXiv preprint arXiv:1806.00770 (2018)
44. Nash, C., Ganin, Y., Eslami, S.A., Battaglia, P.: PolyGen: an autoregressive generative model of 3d meshes. In: PMLR, pp. 7220–7229. PMLR (2020)
45. Pathak, D., Girshick, R., Dollár, P., Darrell, T., Hariharan, B.: Learning features by watching objects move. In: CVPR, pp. 2701–2710 (2017)
46. Radford, A., Narasimhan, K., Salimans, T., Sutskever, I.: Improving language understanding by generative pre-training (2018)
47. Radford, A., et al.: Language models are unsupervised multitask learners. OpenAI blog **1**(8), 9 (2019)
48. Rolfe, J.T.: Discrete variational autoencoders. arXiv preprint arXiv:1609.02200 (2016)
49. Saleh, M., Wu, S.C., Cosmo, L., Navab, N., Busam, B., Tombari, F.: Bending graphs: Hierarchical shape matching using gated optimal transport. In: CVPR (2022)
50. Sederberg, T.W., Parry, S.R.: Free-form deformation of solid geometric models. In: ACM SIGGRAPH Computer Graphics, pp. 151–160 (1986)
51. Tianyu, L., Yali, W., Junhao, Z., Zhe, W., Zhipeng, Z., Yu, Q.: PC-HMR: pose calibration for 3d human mesh recovery from 2d images/videos. In: AAAI, pp. 2269–2276. AAAI Press (2021)
52. Touvron, H., Cord, M., Douze, M., Massa, F., Sablayrolles, A., Jégou, H.: Training data-efficient image transformers & distillation through attention. In: ICLR, pp. 10347–10357 (2021)
53. Trappolini, G., Cosmo, L., Moschella, L., Marin, R., Melzi, S., Rodolà, E.: Shape registration in the time of transformers. In: NeurIPS, pp. 5731–5744 (2021)
54. Trinh, T.H., Luong, M.T., Le, Q.V.: Selfie: self-supervised pretraining for image embedding. arXiv preprint arXiv:1906.02940 (2019)
55. Vaswani, A., et al.: Attention is all you need. In: NeurIPS, pp. 5998–6008 (2017)
56. Verma, N., Boyer, E., Verbeek, J.: FeaStNet: feature-steered graph convolutions for 3d shape analysis. In: CVPR, pp. 2598–2606 (2018)
57. Vlasic, D., Baran, I., Matusik, W., Popović, J.: Articulated mesh animation from multi-view silhouettes. In: ACM SIGGRAPH, pp. 1–9 (2008)
58. Wang, H., Zhu, Y., Adam, H., Yuille, A., Chen, L.C.: MaX-DeepLab: end-to-end panoptic segmentation with mask transformers. In: CVPR, pp. 5463–5474 (2021)
59. Wang, X., Gupta, A.: Unsupervised learning of visual representations using videos. In: ICCV, pp. 2794–2802 (2015)
60. Wang, Y., Asafi, S., Van Kaick, O., Zhang, H., Cohen-Or, D., Chen, B.: Active co-analysis of a set of shapes. ACM Trans. Graph. (TOG) **31**(6), 1–10 (2012)
61. Xu, Y., Zhang, Q., Zhang, J., Tao, D.: Vitae: vision transformer advanced by exploring intrinsic inductive bias. In: NeurIPS, pp. 28522–28535 (2021)
62. Yang, G., Tang, H., Ding, M., Sebe, N., Ricci, E.: Transformer-based attention networks for continuous pixel-wise prediction. In: CVPR, pp. 16269–16279 (2021)
63. Yu, X., Rao, Y., Wang, Z., Liu, Z., Lu, J., Zhou, J.: PoinTr: diverse point cloud completion with geometry-aware transformers. In: ICCV, pp. 12498–12507 (2021)

64. Yu, X., Tang, L., Rao, Y., Huang, T., Zhou, J., Lu, J.: Point-BERT: pre-training 3d point cloud transformers with masked point modeling. arXiv preprint arXiv:2111.14819 (2021)
65. Zhang, Q., Xu, Y., Zhang, J., Tao, D.: Vitaev2: vision transformer advanced by exploring inductive bias for image recognition and beyond. arXiv preprint arXiv:2202.10108 (2022)
66. Zhao, H., Jiang, L., Jia, J., Torr, P.H., Koltun, V.: Point transformer. In: ICCV, pp. 16259–16268 (2021)
67. Zheng, S., et al.: Rethinking semantic segmentation from a sequence-to-sequence perspective with transformers. In: CVPR, pp. 6881–6890 (2021)
68. Zhu, X., Su, W., Lu, L., Li, B., Wang, X., Dai, J.: Deformable detr: deformable transformers for end-to-end object detection. arXiv preprint arXiv:2010.04159 (2020)

Unsupervised Deep Multi-shape Matching

Dongliang Cao[1,2(✉)] and Florian Bernard[1]

[1] University of Bonn, Bonn, Germany
`dcao@uni-bonn.de`
[2] Technical University of Munich, Munich, Germany

Abstract. 3D shape matching is a long-standing problem in computer vision and computer graphics. While deep neural networks were shown to lead to state-of-the-art results in shape matching, existing learning-based approaches are limited in the context of multi-shape matching: (i) either they focus on matching pairs of shapes only and thus suffer from cycle-inconsistent multi-matchings, or (ii) they require an explicit template shape to address the matching of a collection of shapes. In this paper, we present a novel approach for deep multi-shape matching that ensures cycle-consistent multi-matchings while not depending on an explicit template shape. To this end, we utilise a shape-to-universe multi-matching representation that we combine with powerful functional map regularisation, so that our multi-shape matching neural network can be trained in a fully unsupervised manner. While the functional map regularisation is only considered during training time, functional maps are not computed for predicting correspondences, thereby allowing for fast inference. We demonstrate that our method achieves state-of-the-art results on several challenging benchmark datasets, and, most remarkably, that our unsupervised method even outperforms recent supervised methods.

Keywords: 3D shape matching · Multi-shape matching · Functional maps · 3D deep learning

1 Introduction

The matching of 3D shapes is a long-standing problem in computer vision and computer graphics. Due to its wide range of applications, numerous approaches that address diverse variants of shape matching problems have been proposed over the past decades [44,46]. In recent years, with the success of deep learning, many learning-based methods were introduced for shape matching. One common way to address shape matching is to formulate it as classification problem [6,13,23,26,29,49]. The advantage of such methods is that after training the classifier, shape correspondences can efficiently and directly be predicted. A major downside is that for training such a classifier typically a large amount of

---

Supplementary Information The online version contains supplementary material available at https://doi.org/10.1007/978-3-031-20062-5_4.

S. Avidan et al. (Eds.): ECCV 2022, LNCS 13663, pp. 55–71, 2022.
https://doi.org/10.1007/978-3-031-20062-5_4

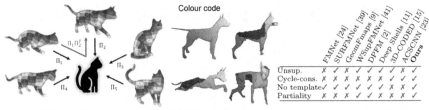

Our multi-matching representation   Partial multi-matching   Comparison of methods

Fig. 1. Left: We present a novel unsupervised learning approach for cycle-consistent multi-shape matching based on matching each shape to a (virtual) universe shape. **Middle**: Our approach can successfully solve challenging *partial* multi-shape matching problems. **Right**: Our method is the first learning-based multi-shape matching approach that combines several favourable properties, i.e. it can be trained in an unsupervised manner, obtains cycle-consistent multi-matchings, does not require a template, and allows for partial matchings.

data that is annotated with ground truth correspondences is required. However, specifically in the domain of 3D shapes, annotated data is scarce, since data annotation is particularly time-consuming and tedious. Thus, in practice, the above methods are often trained with small datasets, so that in turn they are prone to overfitting and lack the ability to generalise across datasets.

Another line of learning-based shape matching solutions build upon the functional map framework [9,16,24,39,41]. Functional maps can serve as a powerful regularisation, so that respective methods were even trained successfully in an unsupervised manner, i.e. without the availability of ground truth correspondences [2,39,41]. However, a downside of such approaches is that the conversion of the obtained functional map to a point-wise correspondence map is typically non-trivial. On the one hand, this may limit the matching accuracy, while on the other hand this may have a negative impact on inference speed (see Sect. 5.1).

In this work we aim to alleviate the shortcomings of both paradigms, while combining their advantages. To this end, we present a novel unsupervised learning approach for obtaining cycle-consistent multi-shape matchings, see Fig. 1. Our approach predicts shape-to-universe matchings based on a *universe classifier*, so that cycle-consistency of so-obtained pairwise matchings is guaranteed by construction. Unlike previous classification methods that rely on supervision based on ground truth correspondences, the training of our universe classifier purely relies on functional map regularisation, thereby allowing for a fully unsupervised training. Yet, at inference time, our method does not require to compute functional maps, and directly predicts shape-to-universe matchings via our classifier. We summarise our main contributions as follows:

- For the first time we enable the *unsupervised training* of a classification-based neural network for *cycle-consistent 3D multi-shape matching*.
- To this end, our method uses *functional maps as strong regularisation during training* but does *not require the computation of functional maps during inference*.

- Our method achieves *state-of-the-art results* on several challenging 3D shape matching benchmark datasets, even in comparison to most recent supervised methods.

2   Related Work

Shape matching is a well-studied problem in computer vision and graphics [44,46]. Rather than providing an exhaustive literature survey, in the following we will focus on reviewing those methods that we consider most relevant to our work. First, we will provide an overview of works that rely on the functional map framework for 3D shape matching. Subsequently, we will focus on recent learning-based approaches that utilise functional maps. Afterwards, we will briefly discuss other learning-based methods. Eventually, we will discuss methods that are specifically tailored for the case of multi-shape matching, as opposed to the more commonly studied case of two-shape matching.

Functional Maps. The functional map framework [31] enables to formulate the correspondence problem in the functional domain by computing functional maps instead of point-wise maps. The key advantage of functional maps is that they allow for a low-dimensional representation of shape correspondences, i.e. small matrices that encode how functions can be transferred between two domains (3D shapes). Unlike finding point-to-point correspondences, which can for example be phrased as the NP-hard quadratic assignment problem [22], functional maps can efficiently be obtained by solving a linear least-squares problem. The functional map framework has been extensively studied and was extended in numerous works, e.g. in terms of improving the accuracy or robustness [36], as well as extending its application to partial shape matching [38], non-isometric shape matching [30,37] and multi-shape matching [18,19]. Nevertheless, in these approaches functional maps are typically utilised in an axiomatic manner, meaning that they heavily rely on handcrafted feature descriptors, such as HKS [7], WKS [3] or SHOT [40], which potentially limits their performance.

Learning Methods Based on Functional Maps. In contrast to axiomatic approaches that use handcrafted features, a variety of methods have been proposed to learn the feature descriptors directly from data. Starting from [24], the (supervised) FMNet was proposed to learn a non-linear transformation of SHOT descriptors [40]. Later work [16] modified the loss to enable FMNet training in an unsupervised manner. However, both methods compute a loss that relies on geodesic distances, which is computationally expensive, particularly for high-resolution shapes. SURFMNet [39] proposed an unsupervised loss based on functional map regularisation, which, however, does not directly obtain point-to-point correspondences. More recently, several works [9,41] replaced FMNet with point-based networks [35,45] to achieve better performance. However, such point-based networks cannot utilise the connectivity information that exists in triangle meshes. To make use of it, DiffusionNet [42] introduced a diffusion layer, which was shown to achieve state-of-the-art performance for 3D shape matching.

Most recently, DPFM [2] extended DiffusionNet with a cross-attention refinement mechanism [47] for partial shape matching. DPFM addresses two variants of partial matching problems: for partial-to-partial matching it relies on a supervised training strategy, and for partial-to-complete matching it can be trained in an unsupervised manner based on functional map regularisation [25,38]. While DPFM predicts functional maps and thereby requires a post-processing to obtain point-wise maps, our proposed approach directly predicts point-wise maps without the need of computing functional maps during inference.

Other Learning-Based Methods. Despite the success of functional maps for diverse learning-based shape matching approaches, there is a wide variety of other learning-based methods. Many of the recent works formulate shape matching as a classification problem [6,13,23,26,29,49]. In these methods, special network architectures were proposed to extend and generalise convolutions from Euclidean grids to surfaces. However, these methods require ground truth correspondences as supervision for training the classifier. 3D-CODED [15] factorised a given input shape into a template shape and a learned global feature vector that encodes the deformation from the template shape to the input shape. In this way, it finds correspondences between input shapes and the template shape. In contrast, our method does not require to choose a template shape for matching. Deep shells [11] proposed a coarse-to-fine matching pipeline that utilises an iterative alignment of smooth shells [10]. While this iterative process may be time-consuming, our method directly predicts shape correspondences in one shot.

Multi-shape Matching. There are several works that explicitly consider the matching of a collection of shapes, i.e. the so-called *multi-shape matching problem*. The key aspect in which multi-shape matching differs from the more commonly studied two-shape matching problem is that in the former one needs to ensure cycle-consistency between pairwise matchings across a collection of data. This is often achieved by first solving a quadratic number of pairwise matching problems (e.g. between all pairs of shapes), and subsequently establishing cycle consistency as a post-processing, e.g. based on permutation synchronisation [17,32]. The higher-order projected power iteration (HiPPI) method [4] circumvented this two-stage approach by generalising permutation synchronisation to explicitly consider geometric relations. In the context of functional maps, Consistent ZoomOut [19] extended ZoomOut [27] by adding functional map consistency constraints. IsoMuSh [14] simultaneously optimises for functional maps and point-wise maps that are both multi-shape consistent. In contrast to these axiomatic methods, which usually downsample the original shape for matching, our method can be directly applied on shapes up to 10,000 vertices. Several learning-based approaches, such as 3D-CODED [15], HSN [49] or ACSCNN [23], utilised an explicit template shape in order to ensure cycle-consistent multi-matchings. However, the use of an explicit template shape poses severe limitations in practice, since a suitable template shape needs to be available, and the specific choice of template also induces a bias. In stark contrast, our method does not rely on an explicit template shape, thereby effectively alleviating such a bias while at the same time providing substantially more flexibility.

3   Background

Our approach is based on the functional map framework and aims for a cycle-consistent multi-shape matching. For completeness, we first recap the basic pipeline for functional map computation and the desirable properties of functional maps. Then, we introduce the notion of cycle consistency for multi-shape matching.

3.1   Functional Maps

Basic Pipeline. Given is a pair of 3D shapes $\mathcal{X}$ and $\mathcal{Y}$ that are represented as triangle meshes with n_x and n_y vertices, respectively. The basic pipeline for computing a functional map between both shapes mainly consists of the following steps:

- Compute the first k eigenfunctions $\Phi_x \in \mathbb{R}^{n_x \times k}, \Phi_y \in \mathbb{R}^{n_y \times k}$ of the respective Laplacian matrix [34] as the basis functions.
- Compute feature descriptors $\mathcal{F}_x \in \mathbb{R}^{n_x \times c}, \mathcal{F}_y \in \mathbb{R}^{n_y \times c}$ on each shape, and (approximately) represent them in the (reduced) basis of the respective eigenfunctions, i.e. $A_x = \Phi_x^\dagger \mathcal{F}_x, A_y = \Phi_y^\dagger \mathcal{F}_y$.
- Compute the optimal functional map $C_{xy} \in \mathbb{R}^{k \times k}$ by solving the optimisation problem

$$C_{xy} = \arg \min_C \mathcal{L}_{\text{data}}(C) + \lambda \mathcal{L}_{\text{reg}}(C), \tag{1}$$

where the data term $\mathcal{L}_{\text{data}}$ ensures that C maps between the feature descriptors represented in the reduced basis, and the regularisation term $\mathcal{L}_{\text{reg}}$ penalises the map by its structural properties (as explained below).
- Convert the functional map C_{xy} to a point map $\Pi_{yx} \in \{0, 1\}^{n_y \times n_x}$, e.g. using nearest neighbour search or other post-processing techniques [27,33,48] based on the relationship

$$\Phi_y C_{xy} \approx \Pi_{yx} \Phi_x. \tag{2}$$

Structural Properties. In the context of near-isometric shape pairs, functional maps have the following properties [39,41]:

- **Bijectivity.** Given functional maps in both directions C_{xy}, C_{yx}, bijectivity requires the map from $\mathcal{X}$ through $\mathcal{Y}$ to $\mathcal{X}$ to be the identity. The requirement can be formulated as the difference between their composition and the identity map [12]. Thus, the bijectivity regularisation for functional maps can be expressed in the form

$$\mathcal{L}_{\text{bij}} = \|C_{xy}C_{yx} - I\|_F^2 + \|C_{yx}C_{xy} - I\|_F^2. \tag{3}$$

- **Orthogonality.** A point map is locally area-preserving if and only if the associated functional map is an orthogonal matrix [31]. The orthogonality regularisation for functional maps can be expressed in the form

$$\mathcal{L}_{\text{orth}} = \left\|C_{xy}^{\top}C_{xy} - I\right\|_F^2 + \left\|C_{yx}^{\top}C_{yx} - I\right\|_F^2. \tag{4}$$

- **Laplacian commutativity.** A point map is an intrinsic isometry if and only if the associated functional map commutes with the Laplace-Beltrami operator [31]. The Laplacian commutativity regularisation for functional maps can expressed in the form

$$\mathcal{L}_{\text{lap}} = \left\|C_{xy}\Lambda_x - \Lambda_y C_{xy}\right\|_F^2 + \left\|C_{yx}\Lambda_y - \Lambda_x C_{yx}\right\|_F^2, \tag{5}$$

where Λ_x and Λ_y are diagonal matrices of the Laplace-Beltrami eigenvalues on the respective shapes.

3.2 Multi-shape Matching

Given is a collection 3D shapes $\mathcal{S}$. For any pair $\mathcal{X}, \mathcal{Y} \in \mathcal{S}$ with n_x, n_y vertices, respectively, the point map Π_{xy} between them can be expressed in the form

$$\Pi_{xy} \in \left\{ \Pi \in \{0,1\}^{n_x \times n_y} : \Pi\mathbf{1}_{n_y} \leq \mathbf{1}_{n_x}, \mathbf{1}_{n_x}^{\top}\Pi \leq \mathbf{1}_{n_y}^{\top} \right\}, \tag{6}$$

where $\Pi_{xy}(i,j) = 1$ can be interpreted as the i-th vertex in shape $\mathcal{X}$ corresponding to the j-th vertex in shape $\mathcal{Y}$.

Cycle-consistency is a desirable property between pairwise matchings in a collection, as it must hold for the true matchings. Cycle consistency means that for any given triplet $\mathcal{X}, \mathcal{Y}, \mathcal{Z} \in \mathcal{S}$, the matching composition from $\mathcal{X}$ through $\mathcal{Y}$ to $\mathcal{Z}$ should be identical to the direct matching from $\mathcal{X}$ to $\mathcal{Z}$, i.e.

$$\Pi_{xz} = \Pi_{xy}\Pi_{yz}. \tag{7}$$

We note that if cycle consistency holds for all triplets in $\mathcal{S}$, it also holds for any higher-order tuples of matching compositions, since the latter can be constructed by composing triplet matching compositions.

Alternatively, one can use a shape-to-universe matching representation [17, 32] to avoid explicitly modelling the (non-convex) cycle-consistency constraint in Eq. (7). This idea builds upon a *virtual* universe shape, which can be thought of a shape that is never explicitly instantiated, i.e. as opposed to a template shape we do not require a 3D mesh of the universe shape. Instead, we merely assume that there is such a shape, so that for all points of the shapes in $\mathcal{S}$ there exists a corresponding (virtual) universe point. We denote the number of universe points as d. For $\Pi_x \in \{0,1\}^{n_x \times d}$ being the matching from shape $\mathcal{X}$ to the universe shape, and $\Pi_y^{\top} \in \{0,1\}^{d \times n_y}$ being the matching from the universe shape to shape $\mathcal{Y}$, this shape-to-universe representation allows to compute pairwise matchings as

$$\Pi_{xy} = \Pi_x\Pi_y^{\top}. \tag{8}$$

4   Our Unsupervised Multi-shape Matching Method

Our novel unsupervised learning approach for cycle-consistent multi-shape matching is illustrated in Fig. 2. Conceptually, our pipeline comprises of two main components that are trained in an end-to-end manner.

Analogous to other learning-based approaches [39, 41], the first main component (blue in Fig. 2) performs feature extraction. Given the source and target shapes $\mathcal{X}$ and $\mathcal{Y}$, a Siamese feature extraction network with (shared) trainable weights Θ extracts features $\mathcal{F}_x$ and $\mathcal{F}_y$ from the input shapes, respectively. Then, a (non-trainable but differentiable) FM solver (yellow in Fig. 2) is applied to compute the bidirectional functional maps C_{xy} and C_{yx}. The second main component (red in Fig. 2) is a Siamese universe classifier with shared weights Φ. It takes features from the first part as input to predict the shape-to-universe matchings Π_x and Π_y for each shape. The pairwise matching Π_{xy} is based on their composition, see Eq. (8). To allow for an unsupervised end-to-end training of our architecture, we build upon functional map regularisation (green in Fig. 2) described in Sect. 3.1. In the following we explain the individual parts in detail.

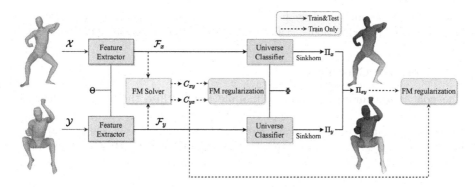

Fig. 2. Overview of our unsupervised learning approach for cycle-consistent multi-shape matching. First, features $\mathcal{F}_x$ and $\mathcal{F}_y$ are extracted from the input shapes $\mathcal{X}$ and $\mathcal{Y}$. The feature descriptors are then used to compute the bidirectional functional maps C_{xy} and C_{yx} based on the FM solver. Subsequently, our novel universe classifier takes the feature descriptors as input and predicts a shape-to-universe matching (Π_x and Π_y) for each shape. The pairwise matching Π_{xy} is obtained by the composition of shape-to-universe point maps $\Pi_x \Pi_y^\top$. During training (solid and dashed lines) we utilise functional maps (FM) as regularisation, whereas at inference time no FM have to be computed (solid lines). (Color figure online)

4.1   Feature Extractor

The goal of the feature extraction module is to compute feature descriptors of 3D shapes that are suitable both for functional map computation and shape-to-universe matching prediction. Our feature extraction is applied in a Siamese manner, i.e. the identical network is used for both $\mathcal{X}$ and $\mathcal{Y}$. The outputs of this module are point-wise feature descriptors for each shape, which we denote as $\mathcal{F}_x$ and $\mathcal{F}_y$ respectively.

4.2   Functional Map Solver

The FM solver aims to compute the bidirectional functional maps C_{xy} and C_{yx} based on the extracted feature descriptors $\mathcal{F}_x$ and $\mathcal{F}_y$ (see Sect. 3.1). We use a regularised formulation to improve the robustness when computing the optimal functional map [2], i.e. we consider

$$C_{xy} = \arg\min_C \|CA_x - A_y\|_F^2 + \lambda \sum_{ij} C_{ij}^2 M_{ij}, \tag{9}$$

where

$$M_{ij} = \left(\frac{\Lambda_y(i)^\gamma}{\Lambda_y(i)^{2\gamma} + 1} - \frac{\Lambda_x(j)^\gamma}{\Lambda_x(j)^{2\gamma} + 1} \right)^2 + \left(\frac{1}{\Lambda_y(i)^{2\gamma} + 1} - \frac{1}{\Lambda_x(j)^{2\gamma} + 1} \right)^2. \tag{10}$$

The regulariser can be viewed as an extension of Laplacian commutativity defined in Eq. (5) with well-justified theoretical foundation, see [36] for details.

4.3   Universe Classifier

The goal of the universe classifier module is to utilise the extracted feature descriptors $\mathcal{F}_x$ and $\mathcal{F}_y$ in order to predict the point-to-universe maps Π_x and Π_y, respectively. Similarly to our feature extractor, the universe classifier is applied in a Siamese way. The output dimension of our universe classifier is equal to the number of points d in the universe shape (see supp. mat. for details how it is chosen).

For our shape-to-universe matching representation, each point of a shape needs to be classified into exactly one universe class, and a universe class cannot be chosen multiple times (per shape). Mathematically, this means that the point-to-universe map Π_x must be a partial permutation matrix as defined in Eq. (6), where in addition the rows of Π_x sum up to one, i.e.

$$\Pi_x \in \left\{ \Pi \in \{0,1\}^{n_x \times d} : \Pi\mathbf{1}_d = \mathbf{1}_{n_x}, \mathbf{1}_{n_x}^\top \Pi \leq \mathbf{1}_d^\top \right\}. \tag{11}$$

We approximate these combinatorial constraints in terms of Sinkhorn normalisation [28,43] to make the prediction differentiable. Sinkhorn normalisation iteratively normalises rows and columns of a matrix based on the softmax operator and a temperature parameter τ (see [28]).

4.4   Unsupervised Loss

Our unsupervised loss is composed of two main parts:

FM Regularisation for Feature Extractor. Following [39,41], we use functional map regularisation to compute unsupervised losses for optimised bidirectional functional maps C_{xy} and C_{yx}. Specifically, we use the bijectivity loss $\mathcal{L}_{\text{bij}}$ in Eq. (3), the orthogonality loss $\mathcal{L}_{\text{orth}}$ in Eq. (4), and the Laplacian commutativity loss $\mathcal{L}_{\text{lap}}$ in Eq. (5) to regularise the functional maps. As such, the total loss for training the feature extractor can be expressed in the form

$$\mathcal{L}_{\text{ft}} = w_{\text{bij}}\mathcal{L}_{\text{bij}} + w_{\text{orth}}\mathcal{L}_{\text{orth}} + w_{\text{lap}}\mathcal{L}_{\text{lap}}. \tag{12}$$

In case of partial shape matching, the functional map from the complete shape to the partial shape becomes a slanted diagonal matrix [38]. We follow DPFM [2] to regularise the predicted functional maps based on this observation. For $\mathcal{X}$ being the complete shape and $\mathcal{Y}$ being the partial shape, in the partial matching case the loss terms can be expressed as

$$\mathcal{L}_{\text{bij}} = \|C_{xy}C_{yx} - \mathbf{I}_r\|_F^2, \text{ and } \mathcal{L}_{\text{orth}} = \|C_{xy}C_{xy}^\top - \mathbf{I}_r\|_F^2, \tag{13}$$

where $\mathbf{I}_r$ is a diagonal matrix in which the first r elements on the diagonal are equal to 1, and r is the slope of the functional map estimated by the area ratio between two shapes, i.e. $r = \max\left\{i \mid \Lambda_y^i < \max(\Lambda_x)\right\}$.

FM Regularisation for Universe Classifier. To train our universe classifier in an unsupervised manner, we build upon the relationship $\Phi_x C_{yx} \approx \Pi_{xy}\Phi_y$ between the functional map C_{yx} and the point-wise map Π_{xy}, as explained in Eq. (2). In our case, the pairwise point map Π_{xy} is obtained from the composition of the shape-to-universe point maps $\Pi_{xy} = \Pi_x\Pi_y^\top$. With that, the unsupervised loss for training the universe classifier can be expressed in the form

$$\mathcal{L}_{\text{cls}} = \|\Phi_x C_{yx} - \Pi_{xy}\Phi_y\|_F^2. \tag{14}$$

This loss is differentiable with respect to both the functional map C_{yx} and the point map Π_{xy}, so that we can train our network in an end-to-end manner. By doing so, the predicted functional map and the predicted point map are improved during training. Overall, we demonstrate that we are able to achieve better matching results even in comparison a network trained with ground truth correspondences (see Sect. 5.3).

The total loss combines the loss terms of the feature extractor and the universe classifier and has the form

$$\mathcal{L}_{\text{total}} = \mathcal{L}_{\text{ft}} + \lambda_{\text{cls}}\mathcal{L}_{\text{cls}}. \tag{15}$$

4.5 Implementation Details

We implemented our method in PyTorch. Our feature extractor takes SHOT descriptors [40] as inputs. We use DiffusionNet [42] as the network architecture for both our feature extractor and universe classifier. In terms of training, we use the Adam optimiser [21] with learning rate $1e^{-3}$ in all experiments. More details are provided in the supp. mat.

5   Experimental Results

For our experimental evaluation, we consider complete shape matching, partial shape matching, as well as an ablation study that analyses the importance of individual components of our method. We note that in all experiments we train a single network for all shapes in a dataset (as opposed to a per-shape category network).

Geodesic error (×100)	FAUST	SCAPE	F on S	S on F	△
Axiomatic Methods					
BCICP [37]	6.4	11	-	-	✗
ZOOMOUT [27]	6.1	7.5	-	-	✗
Smooth Shells [10]	2.5	4.7	-	-	✗
Supervised Methods					
FMNet [24]	11	17	30	33	✗
+ *pmf*	5.9	6.3	11	14	✗
3D-CODED [15]	2.5	31	31	33	✓
GeomFmaps-KPC [9]	3.1	4.4	11	6.0	✗
+ *zo*	1.9	3.0	9.2	4.3	✗
GeomFmaps-DFN [42]	2.6	3.0	3.3	3.0	✗
+ *zo*	1.9	2.4	2.4	1.9	✗
HSN [49]	3.3	3.5	25.4	16.7	✓
ACSCNN [23]	2.7	3.2	8.4	6.0	✓
Unsupervised Methods					
SURFMNet [39]	15	12	32	32	✗
+ *icp*	7.4	6.1	19	23	✗
Unsup FMNet [16]	10	16	29	22	✗
+ *pmf*	5.7	10	12	9.3	✗
WSupFMNet [41]	3.3	7.3	11.7	6.2	✗
+ *zo*	1.9	4.9	8.0	4.3	✗
Deep Shells [11]	1.7	2.5	5.4	**2.7**	✗
Ours (*fine-tune*)	**1.5**	**2.0**	7.3 (**3.2**)	8.6 (3.2)	✓

FAUST (Ours)   FAUST (Deep Shells)

SCAPE (Ours)   SCAPE (Deep Shells)

Fig. 3. Left: Quantitative results on the FAUST and SCAPE datasets in terms of mean geodesic errors (×100). 'F on S' stands for training on FAUST and testing on SCAPE datasets ('S on F' analogously). The rows in grey show refined results using the indicated post-processing procedure. Ours is the only unsupervised method that obtains cycle-consistent (△) multi-matchings. **Right:** Qualitative multi-matching results using our method and Deep Shells. Although qualitatively both methods perform similarly, ours directly predicts shape correspondences without iterative refinement, thereby leading to a faster inference, cf. Fig. 5.

5.1   Complete Shape Matching

Datasets. To be consistent and comparable with prior works, we evaluate our method on two standard benchmarks, FAUST [5] and SCAPE [1] (for both, we use the more challenging remeshed versions from [37]). The FAUST dataset contains 100 shapes consisting of 10 people, each in 10 poses. The SCAPE dataset comprises 71 different poses of the same person. Consistent with previous works, we split both datasets into training sets with 80 and 51 shapes, respectively, and test sets with 20 shapes.

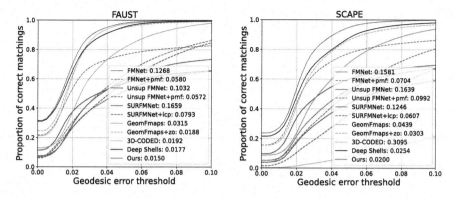

Fig. 4. PCK curves for the FAUST and SCAPE dataset. Dashed lines indicate methods with refinement. Our method achieves the best scores on both datasets.

Quantitative Results. For the evaluation we use the mean geodesic error defined in the Princeton benchmark protocol [20]. We compare our method with state-of-the-art axiomatic, supervised and unsupervised methods, as shown in Fig. 3. Our method outperforms the previous state-of-the-art in most settings, even in comparison to the supervised methods. The last two columns in the table shown in Fig. 3 (left) show generalisation results. Our method generalises better compared to previous unsupervised methods based on functional map regularisation [16,39,41]. In comparison to Deep Shells [11], our method shows comparative results after fine-tuning our pipeline with the loss in Eq. (15) for each shape pair individually (see details on fine-tuning in supp. mat.). We plot the percentage of correct keypoints (PCK) curves for both datasets in Fig. 4, where it can be seen that our method achieves the best results in comparison to a wide range of methods. Moreover, our method does not require post-processing techniques, such as ZOOMOUT [27] or PMF [48], which are often time-consuming, see Fig. 5 for runtime comparisons.

5.2   Partial Shape Matching

Datasets. We evaluate our method in the setting of partial shape matching on the challenging SHREC'16 Partial Correspondence Benchmark [8]. This dataset consists of 200 shapes with 8 categories (humans and animals). The dataset is divided into two subsets, namely CUTS (removal of a large part) with 120 pairs and HOLES (removal of many small parts) with 80 pairs. We follow the training procedure as in WSupFMNet [41].

Quantitative Results. We compare our method with two axiomatic methods FPS [25], PFM [38] and two unsupervised methods WSupFMNet [41], unsupervised DPFM [2]. In Fig. 6 we show quantitative results (in terms of the mean geodesic error) and qualitative results. Our method outperforms previous axiomatic and unsupervised methods. The major difference in comparison

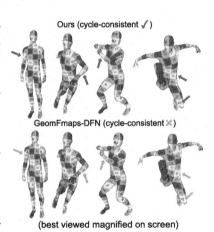

Runtime (s)	Inference	Refine	Total
Axiomatic Methods			
BCICP [37]	881.	-	881.
ZoomOut [27]	43.	-	43.
Smooth Shells [10]	125.	-	125.
Supervised Methods			
FMNet [24]	5.1	223.	228.
3D-CODED [15]	725.	-	725.
GeomFmaps-KPC [9]	1.9	35.	37.
GeomFmaps-DFN [42]	1.5	35.	37.
Unsupervised Methods			
SURFMNet [39]	5.7	43.	49.
Unsup FMNet [16]	5.1	216.	221.
WSupFMNet [41]	2.1	35.	37.
Deep Shells [11]	14.	-	14.
Ours (*fine-tune*)	**0.6** (5.0)	-	**0.6** (5.0)

Fig. 5. Left: Runtimes for the matchings in the experiments of Fig. 3. **Right:** Texture transfer using our method and the supervised GeomFmaps-DFN (erroneous matchings indicated by red arrows). Cycle consistency ensures that our method consistently transfers textures. (Color figure online)

to the unsupervised DPFM that predicts partial-to-complete functional maps, is that our method directly predicts shape-to-universe correspondences based on our universe classifier, so that ours leads to cycle-consistent multi-matchings.

Geo. error (×100)	CUTS	HOLES	△
Axiomatic Methods			
FSP [25]	13.0	16.0	✗
PFM [38]	9.2	12.6	✗
Unsupervised Methods			
WSupFMNet [41]	15.0	13.0	✗
DPFM [2]	6.6	10.4	✗
Ours	**5.5**	**8.9**	✓

Fig. 6. Left: Quantitative results on the CUTS and HOLES subsets of the SHREC'16 Partial Correspondence Benchmark. Reported are mean geodesic errors (×100). Ours is the only method that obtains cycle-consistent (△) multi-matchings. **Right:** Qualitative multi-matching results using our method and DPFM on the HOLES subset (erroneous matchings indicated by red arrows). (Color figure online)

5.3   Ablation Study

The goal of this section is to evaluate the importance of the individual components of our approach, including the universe classifier and our unsupervised loss. For all ablation experiments, we consider the same experimental protocol as in Sect. 5.1. We summarise the results for all ablative experiments and our full method in Fig. 7. We study a total of three different ablative settings that consider the removal of the universe classifier, or the modification of the loss. In the following we explain these in detail.

Classifier-Free. We remove the universe classifier in our pipeline and only train the feature extractor with the unsupervised loss $\mathcal{L}_{ft}$ defined in Eq. (12). At test time, we convert the optimised functional maps to point maps using nearest neighbour search. In comparison to our complete method, the matching performance drops substantially, especially in the last two columns of Fig. 7, indicating that this results in poor generalisation ability across datasets. Overall, this implies that our universe classifier is able to predict more accurate point maps compared to point maps converted from functional maps.

Feature Similarity. In the previous ablative experiment, we modify our network architecture by removing the classifier and change our unsupervised loss at the same time. Here, we focus on the universe classifier only, i.e. we remove it from our pipeline, while keeping our unsupervised loss. To this end, we construct a soft pairwise point map based on the feature similarity between two shapes with the help of Sinkhorn normalisation, similar to Deep Shells [11]. By doing so, the pairwise point map can be expressed in the form $\Pi_{xy}(i,j) \propto \exp\left(-\frac{1}{\lambda}\|\mathcal{F}_x(i) - \mathcal{F}_y(j)\|_2^2\right)$. In comparison to classifier-free experiment, we observe that point maps based on such a feature similarity have similar performance on the intra-dataset experiments, while it significantly improves the generalisation ability across datasets. However, there is still a performance gap compared with our complete method.

Supervised Training. The goal of this ablative experiment is to show the superiority of our unsupervised loss based on functional map regularisation compared to a supervised classification loss. In this experiment, we use the same network architecture as for our complete method. However, we replace our unsupervised loss defined in Eq. (15) by a cross entropy loss between the predicted correspondences and the ground truth correspondences. In comparison to our complete method, we observe that the supervised alternative achieves better performance on FAUST dataset, but leads to a worse performance on other datasets, especially for the generalisation cases. We believe that the main reason is that the supervised approach is overfitting to the training data, but lacks the ability to generalise across datasets.

Geo. error (×100)	FAUST	SCAPE	F on S	S on F
Classifier-free	2.1	3.8	17.4	22.9
Feat. similarity	2.1	3.7	10.6	13.9
Supervised	**1.4**	2.8	9.8	18.5
Ours	1.5	**2.0**	**7.3**	**8.6**

Fig. 7. Left: Quantitative results of our ablation study on the FAUST and SCAPE datasets. **Right:** Qualitative results for the considered ablative experiments on the SCAPE dataset (erroneous matchings indicated by red arrows). (Color figure online)

6   Limitations and Future Work

Our work is the first unsupervised learning-based approach for finding cycle-consistent matchings between multiple 3D shapes, and additionally pushes the current state of the art in multi-shape matching. Yet, there are also some limitations that give rise to interesting future research questions.

For our approach it is not necessary that the universe shape is explicitly instantiated (e.g. in the form of 3D mesh). However, we require to fix the maximum number of points d of this (virtual) universe shape for training, since d corresponds to the number of output classes that are predicted by our classifier. With that, a universe classifier trained with a fixed number of d classes is not able to predict (unique) correspondences of shapes with more than d vertices. The exploration of alternative formalisms that do not require to fix d as a-priori is an interesting future direction.

Our universe classifier can be trained in an unsupervised manner both with datasets comprising of complete shapes only, as well as with mixed datasets (comprising of partial shapes and at least a single complete shape of the same category). As such, our current neural network does not allow for the unsupervised training with datasets that contain only partially observed shapes. This is due to limitations for partial-to-partial matchings that our approach inherits from the functional map framework. We note that DPFM [2] also shares this limitation – in their case, the authors utilise a *supervised* training strategy when considering the partial-to-partial matching case. Since DPFM uses different network architectures for partial-to-complete and partial-to-partial settings, it cannot be applied to different settings during training and inference. For example, it cannot be trained using partial-to-complete shape pairs and then be applied to predict partial-to-partial correspondences. In contrast, our method is more flexible, as we use a single neural network architecture based on our universe classifier, where the shape-to-universe matching formalism naturally allows to represent complete, partial-to-complete as well as partial-to-partial matchings.

7   Conclusion

We introduce the first approach for the unsupervised training of a deep neural network for predicting cycle-consistent matchings across a collection of 3D shapes. Our approach builds upon the powerful functional map framework in order to allow for an unsupervised training. Yet, during inference we directly predict point-wise matchings and do not require to compute functional maps, which has a positive impact on the runtime. The major strength of our approach is that it combines a unique set of favourable properties: our approach can be trained in an unsupervised manner, obtains cycle-consistent multi-matchings, does not rely on a template shape, and can handle partial matchings. Overall, due to the conceptual novelties and the demonstrated state-of-the-art performance on diverse shape matching benchmarks, we believe that our work advances the field of 3D shape matching.

References

1. Anguelov, D., Srinivasan, P., Koller, D., Thrun, S., Rodgers, J., Davis, J.: Scape: shape completion and animation of people. In: ACM SIGGRAPH (2005)
2. Attaiki, S., Pai, G., Ovsjanikov, M.: DPFM: deep partial functional maps. In: International Conference on 3D Vision (3DV) (2021)
3. Aubry, M., Schlickewei, U., Cremers, D.: The wave kernel signature: a quantum mechanical approach to shape analysis. In: ICCV (2011)
4. Bernard, F., Thunberg, J., Swoboda, P., Theobalt, C.: HiPPI: higher-order projected power iterations for scalable multi-matching. In: ICCV (2019)
5. Bogo, F., Romero, J., Loper, M., Black, M.J.: Faust: dataset and evaluation for 3d mesh registration. In: CVPR (2014)
6. Boscaini, D., Masci, J., Rodolà, E., Bronstein, M.: Learning shape correspondence with anisotropic convolutional neural networks. In: NIPS (2016)
7. Bronstein, M.M., Kokkinos, I.: Scale-invariant heat kernel signatures for non-rigid shape recognition. In: CVPR (2010)
8. Cosmo, L., Rodola, E., Bronstein, M.M., Torsello, A., Cremers, D., Sahillioglu, Y.: Shrec 2016: partial matching of deformable shapes. Proc. 3DOR 2(9), 12 (2016)
9. Donati, N., Sharma, A., Ovsjanikov, M.: Deep geometric functional maps: robust feature learning for shape correspondence. In: CVPR (2020)
10. Eisenberger, M., Lahner, Z., Cremers, D.: Smooth shells: multi-scale shape registration with functional maps. In: CVPR (2020)
11. Eisenberger, M., Toker, A., Leal-Taixé, L., Cremers, D.: Deep shells: unsupervised shape correspondence with optimal transport. In: NIPS (2020)
12. Eynard, D., Rodola, E., Glashoff, K., Bronstein, M.M.: Coupled functional maps. In: International Conference on 3D Vision (3DV) (2016)
13. Fey, M., Lenssen, J.E., Weichert, F., Müller, H.: SplineCNN: fast geometric deep learning with continuous b-spline kernels. In: CVPR (2018)
14. Gao, M., Lahner, Z., Thunberg, J., Cremers, D., Bernard, F.: Isometric multi-shape matching. In: CVPR (2021)
15. Groueix, T., Fisher, M., Kim, V.G., Russell, B.C., Aubry, M.: 3d-coded: 3d correspondences by deep deformation. In: ECCV (2018)
16. Halimi, O., Litany, O., Rodola, E., Bronstein, A.M., Kimmel, R.: Unsupervised learning of dense shape correspondence. In: CVPR (2019)
17. Huang, Q.X., Guibas, L.: Consistent shape maps via semidefinite programming. In: Computer Graphics Forum, vol. 32, pp. 177–186 (2013)
18. Huang, Q., Wang, F., Guibas, L.: Functional map networks for analyzing and exploring large shape collections. ACM Trans. Graph. (ToG) 33(4), 1–11 (2014)
19. Huang, R., Ren, J., Wonka, P., Ovsjanikov, M.: Consistent ZoomOut: efficient spectral map synchronization. In: Computer Graphics Forum, vol. 39, pp. 265–278. Wiley Online Library (2020)
20. Kim, V.G., Lipman, Y., Funkhouser, T.: Blended intrinsic maps. ACM Trans. Graph. (TOG) 30(4), 1–12 (2011)
21. Kingma, D.P., Ba, J.: Adam: a method for stochastic optimization. In: ICLR (2015)
22. Lawler, E.L.: The quadratic assignment problem. Manage. Sci. 9(4), 586–599 (1963)
23. Li, Q., Liu, S., Hu, L., Liu, X.: Shape correspondence using anisotropic chebyshev spectral CNNs. In: CVPR (2020)
24. Litany, O., Remez, T., Rodola, E., Bronstein, A., Bronstein, M.: Deep functional maps: structured prediction for dense shape correspondence. In: ICCV (2017)

25. Litany, O., Rodolà, E., Bronstein, A.M., Bronstein, M.M.: Fully spectral partial shape matching. In: Computer Graphics Forum, vol. 36, pp. 247–258. Wiley Online Library (2017)
26. Masci, J., Boscaini, D., Bronstein, M., Vandergheynst, P.: Geodesic convolutional neural networks on riemannian manifolds. In: ICCV (2015)
27. Melzi, S., Ren, J., Rodola, E., Sharma, A., Wonka, P., Ovsjanikov, M.: Zoomout: spectral upsampling for efficient shape correspondence. arXiv preprint arXiv:1904.07865 (2019)
28. Mena, G., Belanger, D., Linderman, S., Snoek, J.: Learning latent permutations with gumbel-sinkhorn networks. In: ICLR (2018)
29. Monti, F., Boscaini, D., Masci, J., Rodola, E., Svoboda, J., Bronstein, M.M.: Geometric deep learning on graphs and manifolds using mixture model CNNs. In: CVPR (2017)
30. Nogneng, D., Ovsjanikov, M.: Informative descriptor preservation via commutativity for shape matching. In: Computer Graphics Forum, vol. 36, pp. 259–267. Wiley Online Library (2017)
31. Ovsjanikov, M., Ben-Chen, M., Solomon, J., Butscher, A., Guibas, L.: Functional maps: a flexible representation of maps between shapes. ACM Trans. Graph. (ToG) 31(4), 1–11 (2012)
32. Pachauri, D., Kondor, R., Singh, V.: Solving the multi-way matching problem by permutation synchronization. In: NIPS (2013)
33. Pai, G., Ren, J., Melzi, S., Wonka, P., Ovsjanikov, M.: Fast sinkhorn filters: using matrix scaling for non-rigid shape correspondence with functional maps. In: CVPR (2021)
34. Pinkall, U., Polthier, K.: Computing discrete minimal surfaces and their conjugates. Exp. Math. 2(1), 15–36 (1993)
35. Qi, C.R., Yi, L., Su, H., Guibas, L.J.: Pointnet++: deep hierarchical feature learning on point sets in a metric space. In: NIPS (2017)
36. Ren, J., Panine, M., Wonka, P., Ovsjanikov, M.: Structured regularization of functional map computations. In: Computer Graphics Forum, vol. 38, pp. 39–53. Wiley Online Library (2019)
37. Ren, J., Poulenard, A., Wonka, P., Ovsjanikov, M.: Continuous and orientation-preserving correspondences via functional maps. ACM Trans. Graph. (ToG) 37, 1–16 (2018)
38. Rodolà, E., Cosmo, L., Bronstein, M.M., Torsello, A., Cremers, D.: Partial functional correspondence. In: Computer Graphics Forum, vol. 36, pp. 222–236. Wiley Online Library (2017)
39. Roufosse, J.M., Sharma, A., Ovsjanikov, M.: Unsupervised deep learning for structured shape matching. In: ICCV (2019)
40. Salti, S., Tombari, F., Di Stefano, L.: Shot: Unique signatures of histograms for surface and texture description. Comput. Vis. Image Underst. 125, 251–264 (2014)
41. Sharma, A., Ovsjanikov, M.: Weakly supervised deep functional maps for shape matching. In: NIPS (2020)
42. Sharp, N., Attaiki, S., Crane, K., Ovsjanikov, M.: DiffusionNet: discretization agnostic learning on surfaces. arXiv preprint arXiv:2012.00888 (2020)
43. Sinkhorn, R., Knopp, P.: Concerning nonnegative matrices and doubly stochastic matrices. Pac. J. Math. 21(2), 343–348 (1967)
44. Tam, G.K., et al.: Registration of 3d point clouds and meshes: a survey from rigid to nonrigid. IEEE Trans. Vis. Comput. Graph. 19(7), 1199–1217 (2012)
45. Thomas, H., Qi, C.R., Deschaud, J.E., Marcotegui, B., Goulette, F., Guibas, L.J.: KPConv: flexible and deformable convolution for point clouds. In: ICCV (2019)

46. Van Kaick, O., Zhang, H., Hamarneh, G., Cohen-Or, D.: A survey on shape correspondence. In: Computer Graphics Forum, vol. 30, pp. 1681–1707 (2011)
47. Vaswani, A., et al.: Attention is all you need. In: NIPS (2017)
48. Vestner, M., Litman, R., Rodola, E., Bronstein, A., Cremers, D.: Product manifold filter: non-rigid shape correspondence via kernel density estimation in the product space. In: CVPR (2017)
49. Wiersma, R., Eisemann, E., Hildebrandt, K.: CNNs on surfaces using rotation-equivariant features. ACM Trans. Graph. (TOG) **39**(4), 1–92 (2020)

Texturify: Generating Textures on 3D Shape Surfaces

Yawar Siddiqui[1]($\boxtimes$), Justus Thies[2], Fangchang Ma[3], Qi Shan[3],
Matthias Nießner[1], and Angela Dai[1]

[1] Technical University of Munich, Munich, Germany
yawar.siddiqui@tum.de
[2] Max Planck Institute for Intelligent Systems, Stuttgart, Germany
[3] Apple, Cupertino, USA

Abstract. Texture cues on 3D objects are key to compelling visual representations, with the possibility to create high visual fidelity with inherent spatial consistency across different views. Since the availability of textured 3D shapes remains very limited, learning a 3D-supervised data-driven method that predicts a texture based on the 3D input is very challenging. We thus propose *Texturify*, a GAN-based method that leverages a 3D shape dataset of an object class and learns to reproduce the distribution of appearances observed in real images by generating high-quality textures. In particular, our method does not require any 3D color supervision or correspondence between shape geometry and images to learn the texturing of 3D objects. *Texturify* operates directly on the surface of the 3D objects by introducing face convolutional operators on a hierarchical 4-RoSy parameterization to generate plausible object-specific textures. Employing differentiable rendering and adversarial losses that critique individual views and consistency across views, we effectively learn the high-quality surface texturing distribution from real-world images. Experiments on car and chair shape collections show that our approach outperforms state of the art by an average of 22% in *FID* score.

1 Introduction

3D content is central to many application areas, including content creation for visual consumption in films, games, and mixed reality scenarios. Recent years have seen remarkable progress in modeling 3D geometry [1,7,9,28,36,39,42], achieving significant improvements on geometric fidelity, driven by new generative learning approaches on large-scale 3D shape datasets [6,11,43]. While strong promise has been shown in modeling geometry, generating fully textured 3D objects remains a challenge that is less explored. As such, textured 3D content generation still demands tedious manual efforts. A notable challenge in learning to automatically generate textured 3D content is the lack of high-quality textured

Supplementary Information The online version contains supplementary material available at https://doi.org/10.1007/978-3-031-20062-5_5.

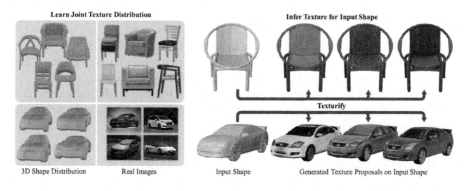

Fig. 1. *Texturify* learns to generate geometry-aware textures for untextured collections of 3D objects. Our method produces textures that when rendered to various 2D image views, match the distribution of real image observations. *Texturify* enables training from only a collection of images and a collection of untextured shapes, which are both often available, without requiring any explicit 3D color supervision or shape-image correspondence. Textures are created directly on the surface of a given 3D shape, enabling generation of high-quality, compelling textured 3D shapes.

3D data. Large-scale shape datasets such as ShapeNet [6] have helped to drive the success of 3D geometric shape modeling, but tend to contain simplistic and often uniform textures associated with the objects. Furthermore, existing texture generation approaches primarily follow popular generative geometric representations that define surfaces implicitly over a volume in space [10,33,44], which results in inefficient learning and tends to produce blurry results, since textures are only well-defined on geometric surfaces (Fig. 1).

We propose *Texturify* to address these challenges in the task of automatic texture generation for 3D shape collections. That is, for a given shape geometry, *Texturify* learns to automatically generate a variety of different textures on the shape when sampling from a latent texture space. Instead of relying on supervision from 3D textured objects, we utilize only a set of images along with a collection of 3D shape geometry from the same class category, without requiring any correspondence between image and geometry nor any semantic part information of the shapes. We employ differentiable rendering with an adversarial loss to ensure that generated textures on the 3D shapes produce realistic imagery from a variety of views during training. Rather than generating textures for 3D shapes defined over a volume in space as has been done with implicit representations [3,5,35,41] or volumetric representations [10,44], we instead propose to tie texture generation directly to the surface of the 3D shape. We formulate a generative adversarial network, conditioned on the 3D shape geometry and a latent texture code, to operate on the faces of a 4-way rotationally symmetric quad mesh by defining face convolutional operators for texture generation. In contrast to the common 2D texture parameterization with UV maps, our method enables generating possible shape textures with awareness of 3D structural neighborhood relations and minimal distortion. We show the effectiveness of Texturify in texturing ShapeNet chairs and cars, trained with real-world imagery; our approach outperforms the state of the art by an average of 22% FID scores.

In summary, our contributions are:

– A generative formulation for texture generation on a 3D shape that learns to create realistic, high-fidelity textures from 2D images and a collection of 3D shape geometry, without requiring any 3D texture supervision.
– A surface-based texture generation network that reasons on 3D surface neighborhoods to synthesize textures directly on a mesh surface following the input shape geometry and a latent texture code.

2   Related Works

Texturify aims at generating high-quality textures for 3D objects. Our generative method is trained on distinct sets of 3D shape and real 2D image data. Related approaches either require aligned 2D/3D datasets to optimize for textures, meshes with surface color, or learn a joint distribution of shape and appearance directly from 2D images. In contrast, our method predicts textures for existing 3D shapes using a parameterization that operates directly on the surface and convolutions on the 3D meshes.

Texturing via Optimization. Texture optimization methods address instance-specific texture generation by iteratively optimizing over certain objective functions requiring aligned 2D/3D data. Traditional methods [52] employ global optimization for mapping color images onto geometric reconstructions. To improve robustness against pose misalignments, Adversarial Texture Optimization [19] reconstructs high-quality textures from RGBD scans with a patch-based, misalignment-tolerant conditional discriminator, resulting in sharper textures. Note that these methods are not able to complete missing texture regions and heavily rely on the provided input images. Recently, Text2Mesh [29] proposes to optimize for both color and geometric details of an input mesh to conform to a target text using a CLIP-based [40] multi-view loss.

Texture Completion. IF-Net-Texture [8] focuses on texture completion from partial textured scans and completed 3D geometry using IF-Nets [7], with a convolutional encoder and an implicit decoder. This method learns locally-implicit representations and requires 3D supervision for training. SPSG [10] proposes a self-supervised approach for training a fully convolutional network to first predict the geometry and then the color, both of which are represented as 3D volumetric grids. In comparison to these completion methods, our proposed method only requires an uncoupled collection of 3D shapes and 2D images as supervision.

Retrieval-Based Texturing. PhotoShape [37] proposes retrieval-based texturing using a dictionary of high-quality material assets. Specifically, it classifies the part material of an object in a 2D image and applies the corresponding material to the respective parts of a 3D object. While this approach is able to generate high-quality renderings, it requires detailed segmentations in the 2D image as well as for the 3D object, and is unable to produce material that is not present in the synthetic material dataset.

Generative Texturing. TextureFields [33] learns a continuous representation for representing texture information in 3D, parameterized by a fully connected residual network. While this approach can be trained in an uncoupled setting, it tends to produce blurry or uniform textures (see Sect. 4). The work closest to ours in terms of problem formulation is Learning Texture Generators From Internet Photos (LTG) [50], where the texture generation task is formulated as a shape-conditioned StyleGAN [23] generator. This approach requires several different training sets, each containing images and silhouettes from similar viewpoints, and multiple discriminators are employed to enforce correct rendering onto these corresponding viewing angles. In comparison, our method makes no explicit assumptions on the partitioning of viewpoints. LTG also makes use of UV parameterization, where the texture atlases come from fixed views around the object, which inevitably results in seams and could struggle for non-convex shapes, whereas our method operates directly on mesh faces and is thus free from these two issues. Additionally, LTG utilizes only the silhouettes but not surface features for training, but our approach is geometry-aware.

Generative Models for Geometry and Appearance. 3D-aware image synthesis and automatic generation of 3D models have gained attention recently. Early approaches use discretized spatial representations such as a 3D voxel grid [12,17,30,31,47,48,53], with the downside of high memory footprint that grows cubically with resolution. Scaling up to high-resolution image generation with 3D voxel grids can be challenging, even with sparse volumetric representations [16]. To further alleviate memory consumption, upsampling of synthesized images with 2D convolutional networks has been proposed [32]. An alternative approach is neural implicit representations [5,13,35,41] which encode both the geometry and texture into a single multi-layer perceptron (MLP) network. Seminal work along this line of research includes HoloGAN [30], GIRAFFE [32], GRAF [41], and PiGAN [3]. Several concurrent works focus on the generation of high-resolution images with implicit representations, for example, EG3D [4], StyleNeRF [14], CIPS-3D [51], and StyleSDF [34]. These approaches generate high-quality 2D views rather than the textures for given input meshes, which is the focus of this paper. Additionally, these works generate both the pseudo-geometry and colors in a coupled fashion, resulting in tangled geometry and texture that are difficult to be separated for downstream applications. More recent work [38] generates textured triangle meshes from either random noise latent or 3D semantic layouts, which is also different from our problem formulation which conditions on untextured geometry.

Convolutions on 3D Meshes. Several approaches have been proposed for applying convolutions on meshes [15,20,27,45,46]. For instance, MeshCNN [15] proposes a trimesh-based edge convolution operator, demonstrating part segmentation on relatively small or decimated 3D shape meshes, while our approach aims to generate high-fidelity textures on the faces of high-resolution shape meshes. TangentConv [45] proposes tangent convolution, which projects local surface geometry on a tangent plane around every point and applies 2D planar convolutions within these tangent images. TextureConv [20] defines a smooth, consistently oriented domain for surface convolutions based on four-way rotationally symmetric (4-RoSy) fields and demonstrate superior performance compared to TangentConvs for semantic segmentation. Our approach builds on this TextureConv 4-RoSy parameterization to generate textures on mesh faces.

3   Method

Given a collection of untextured meshes of a class of objects, our method aims to learn a texture generator using only 2D image collections as supervision. We do not assume any correspondence between the shapes and the image collection, except that they should represent the same class category of objects.

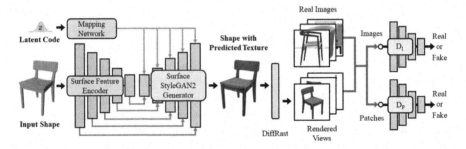

Fig. 2. *Texturify* Overview. Surface features from an input 3D mesh are encoded through a face convolution-based encoder and decoded through a StyleGAN2-inspired decoder to generate textures directly on the surface of the mesh. To ensure that generated textures are realistic, the textured mesh is differentiably rendered from different view points and is critiqued by two discriminators. An image discriminator D_I operates on full image views from the real or rendered views, while a patch-consistency discriminator D_P encourages consistency between views by operating on patches coming from a single real view or patches from different views of rendered images.

We propose a generative adversarial framework to tackle this problem (see Fig. 2). Given a 3D mesh of an object, and latent texture code, our generator produces textures directly on the mesh surface. To this end, we parameterize the mesh with a hierarchy of 4-way rotationally symmetric (4-RoSy) fields from QuadriFlow [21] of different resolutions. This parameterization enables minimal distortion without seams and preserving geodesic neighborhoods. Thus we define convolution, pooling and unpooling operations that enable processing features on the mesh surface and aggregate features across resolution hierarchy levels. Using these operators, we design the generator as a U-Net encoder-decoder network, with the encoder as a ResNet-style feature extractor and the decoder inspired by StyleGAN2 [24], both modified to work on object surfaces. We use differentiable rendering to render the 3D meshes with the generated textures and enforce losses to match the appearance distribution of real image observations. Specifically, we apply two discriminators against the real image distribution for supervision: the

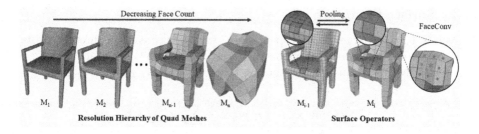

Fig. 3. Texturify generates textures on 4-RoSy parameterized quad meshes, where we define face convolutions with pooling and unpooling operations to operate on a hierarchy of the quad meshes. This enables reasoning about local surface neighborhoods across multiple resolutions to obtain effective global structures as well as fine details.

first discriminator is inspired by StyleGAN2 on individual rendered images to match the real distribution, while the other encourages global texture consistency on an object through patch discrimination across multiple views. The pipeline is trained end-to-end using a non-saturating GAN loss with gradient penalty and path length regularization.

3.1 Parameterization

Since textures are naturally a surface attribute, parameterizing them in 3D space is inefficient and can result in blurry textures. Therefore, we aim to generate textures directly on the surface using a surface parameterization. One popular way of representing textures on the surface of a mesh is through UV mapping. However, generating a consistent UV parameterization for a set of shapes of varying topology is very challenging. Furthermore, it can introduce distortions due to flattening as well as seams at surface cuts. Seams in particular make learning using neighborhood-dependent operators (e.g., convolutions) difficult, since neighboring features in UV space might not necessarily be neighbors in the geodesic space. To avoid these issues, we instead generate surface texture on the four-fold rotationally symmetric (4-RoSy) field parameterization from Quadriflow [21], a method to remesh triangle meshes as quad meshes. A 4-RoSy field is a set of tangent directions associated with a vertex where the neighboring directions are parallel to each other by rotating one of them around their surface normals by a multiple of 90°. This can be realized as a quad-mesh, without seams and with minimal distortions, near-regular faces, and preservation of geodesic neighborhoods, making it very suitable for convolutional feature extraction (as shown in Fig. 3). To facilitate a hierarchical processing of features on the surface of the mesh, we precompute this 4-RoSy field representation of the mesh $\mathcal{M}$ at multiple resolution levels to obtain quad meshes $M_1, M_2, .., M_n$ with face count $\frac{|M_1|}{4^{l-1}}$, with $|M_1|$ being the face count at the finest level (leftmost in Fig. 3).

3.2   Surface Operators

Given a 4-RoSy parameterized quad-mesh, we process features directly on its surface by defining convolutions on the faces. A face convolution operates on a face with feature $\mathbf{x}_i$ and its neighboring faces' features $\mathcal{N}_i = [\mathbf{y}_1, \mathbf{y}_2, ...]$ by:

$$\text{FaceConv}(\mathbf{x}_i, \mathcal{N}_i) = \mathbf{w}_0^T \mathbf{x}_i + \sum_{j=1}^{|\mathcal{N}_i|} \mathbf{w}_j^T \mathbf{y}_j + \mathbf{b} \tag{1}$$

with $\mathbf{x}_i \in \mathbb{R}^{C_0}$, $\mathbf{y}_j \in \mathbb{R}^{C_0}$, learnable parameters $\mathbf{w} \in \mathbb{R}^{C_0 \times C_1}$, $\mathbf{b} \in \mathbb{R}^{C_1}$, where C_0 and C_1 are input and output feature channels respectively. We use a fixed face neighborhood size $|\mathcal{N}_i| = 8$, since the vast majority of the faces in the quad mesh have a neighborhood of 8 faces, with very few singularities from Quadriflow remeshing. In the rare case of singularities (see suppl. doc.), we zero-pad the faces so that the number of neighbors is always 8. Additionally, neighbors are ordered anticlockwise around the face normal, with the face having the smallest Cartesian coordinates (based on x, then y, then z) as the first face.

For aggregating features across mesh resolution hierarchy levels, we define inter-hierarchy pooling and unpooling operators. The pooled features $\mathbf{x}_{l+1}^j$ are given as $\mathbf{x}_{l+1}^j = \text{agg}\left(\left\{\mathbf{x}_l^i : i \in \mathrm{F}_{l+1}^j\right\}\right)$, where F_{l+1}^j defines the set of face indices of the finer layer l which are nearest to the j-th face of the coarser layer $l+1$ in terms of a chamfer distance and with 'agg' as an aggregation operator. The unpooled features are computed as: $\mathbf{x}_l^j = \mathbf{x}_{l+1}^{\hat{\mathrm{F}}_l^j}$, where $\hat{\mathrm{F}}_l^j$ defines correspondence of the j-th face of the fine layer to the coarse layer (in terms of minimal chamfer distance).

3.3   Surface Texture GAN Framework

With our hierarchical surface parameterization and surface features operators, we design a GAN framework that generates colors on the mesh surface that can be trained using only a collection of images and untextured shapes without any explicit 3D texture supervision.

Our generator takes a U-shaped encoder-decoder architecture. Face normals and mean curvature are used as input features to the network. The encoder is then designed to extract features from the mesh surface at different resolution levels. These features are processed through a series of FaceResNet blocks (ResNet blocks with FaceConv instead of Conv2D) and inter-hierarchy pooling layers as defined above. Features extracted at each level of the hierarchy are then passed to the appropriate level of the decoder through U-Net skip connections. This multi-resolution understanding is essential towards generating compelling textures on a 3D shape, as the deeper features at coarse hierarchy levels enable reasoning about global shape and textural structure, with finer hierarchy levels allowing for generation of coherent local detail.

The decoder is inspired by the StyleGAN2 [24] generator, which has proven to be a stable and efficient generative model in 2D domain. We thus use a

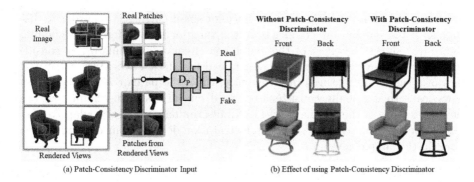

(a) Patch-Consistency Discriminator Input   (b) Effect of using Patch-Consistency Discriminator

Fig. 4. The patch-consistency discriminator encourages global consistency in generated shape textures across multiple views. (a) While for real image data we are only considering patches from the same view (since the 2D image dataset does not contain multi-view data), we use patches from multiple views in the scenario of generated images. (b) Without patch-consistency discriminator rendered texture can end up having inconsistent styles across viewpoints. Using the patch consistency discriminator prevents this issue.

mapping network to map a latent code to a style code. Additionally, we upsample (via inter-hierarchy unpooling) and sum up RGB contributions at different mesh hierarchy levels, analogous to StyleGAN2 upsampling and summation at different image resolutions. Instead of the style-modulated Conv2D operators of StyleGAN2 style blocks, we use style-modulated FaceConvs. In contrast to the StyleGAN2 setting, where the generated image has a fixed structure, we aim to generate textures on varying input 3D shape geometries. Therefore, we further condition the style blocks on surface features extracted by the mesh encoder. This is achieved by concatenating the features generated by the decoder at each hierarchy level with the encoder features from the same level. The decoder outputs face colors for the highest resolution mesh ($l = 1$) representing the texture.

To enable training using only 2D image collections for texture supervision, the resulting textured mesh is rendered as an image from multiple viewpoints using a rasterization-based differentiable renderer, Nvdiffrast [26]. Note that we do not assume a known pose for the individual images in the real distribution; however, we assume a distribution on the poses from which viewpoints are sampled. Images of the generated textured mesh are then rendered from views sampled from the distribution, which are then critiqued by 2D convolutional discriminators. We use two discriminators: the first, like conventional discriminators, considers whether a single image comes from the real or generated distributions; the second considers whether a set of rendered views from a generated textured shape is consistent across the shape. Since we do not have access to multiple views of the same sample from the real distribution, we consider multiple patches from a single real image sample. For generated images, we then consider multiple patches from different views as input to the patch-consistency discriminator. As patches coming from the same view have a consistent style, the generated patches across views are also encouraged to have a matching style.

Operating at patch level is important since for small patches it is harder to distinguish if the patches are coming from the same or from different viewpoints. Figure 4(b) shows the effect of this patch-consistency discriminator, as considering only single views independently can lead to artifacts where the front and back of a shape are textured inconsistently, while the patch consistency across views leads to a globally consistent textured output. Both discriminators use the architecture of the original StyleGAN2 discriminators and use adaptive discriminator augmentation [22]. The implementation details of our method can be found in the supplementary.

4 Experiments

Data. We evaluate our method on 3D shape geometry from the 'chair' and 'car' categories of the ShapeNet dataset [6]. For chairs, we use 5,097 object meshes split into 4,097 train and 1,000 test shapes, and 15,586 images from the

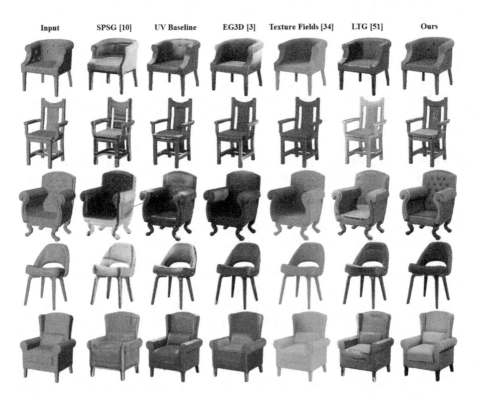

Fig. 5. Qualitative results on ShapeNet chairs dataset trained with real images from the Photoshape dataset. While methods producing textures in 3D space like SPSG [10], EG3D [4] and TextureFields [33] produce blurry textures, UV based methods like LTG [50] show artifacts at UV seams, specially for non-convex shapes like chairs. By operating on the surface, our method can generate realistic and detailed textures.

| Input | SPSG [10] | UV Baseline | EG3D [3] | Texture Fields [34] | LTG [51] | Ours |

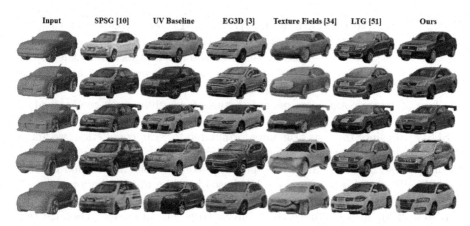

Fig. 6. Qualitative results on ShapeNet cars trained with real images from the Comp-Cars dataset. Our method can generate realistic and diverse cars textures on varying shape geometries like sedans, sportscars, SUVs and hatchbacks.

Photoshape dataset [37] which were collected from image search engines. For cars, we use 1,256 cars split into 956 train and 300 test shapes. We use 18,991 real images from the CompCars dataset [49] and use an off-the-shelf segmentation model [25] to obtain foreground-background segmentations.

Evaluation Metrics. Our evaluation is based on common GAN image quality and diversity metrics. Specifically, we use the Frechet Inception Distance (FID) [18] and Kernel Inception Distance (KID) [2] for evaluating the generative models. For each mesh, we render images of the textured shapes produced by each method at a resolution of 256×256 from 4 random view points using 4 random latent codes, and evaluate these metrics against all available real images segmented from their background. Note that we do not have ground truth textures available for the 3D shapes and specific style codes, thus, a classical reconstruction metric (e.g., an ℓ_1 distance) is not applicable.

Table 1. Comparison against state-of-the-art texture generation approaches on ShapeNet chairs and cars learned on real-world 2D images.

Method	Parameterization	Chairs		Cars	
		KID $\times 10^{-2}\downarrow$	FID$\downarrow$	KID $\times 10^{-2}\downarrow$	FID$\downarrow$
Texture fields [33]	Global implicit	6.06	85.01	17.14	177.15
SPSG [10]	Sparse 3D Grid	5.13	65.36	9.59	110.65
UV baseline	UV	2.46	38.98	5.77	73.63
LTG [50]	UV	2.39	37.50	5.72	70.06
EG3D [4]	Tri-plane Implicit	2.15	36.45	5.95	83.11
Ours	4-RoSy Field	**1.54**	**26.17**	**4.97**	**59.55**

Comparison Against State of the Art. Table 1 shows a comparison to state-of-the-art methods for texture generation on 3D shape meshes. We compare with Texture Fields [33], which generates textures as implicit fields around the object, Yu et al. [50] which learns texture generation in the UV parameterization space, and a modified version of EG3D [4] such that it uses a hybrid explicit-implicit tri-plane 3D representation to predict textures for a given mesh conditioned on its geometry. Additionally, we compare with the voxel-based 3D color generation of SPSG [10]; since this was originally formulated for scan completion, we adopt its differentiable rendering to our encoder-decoder architecture using 3D convolutions instead of FaceConvs, with sparse 3D convolutions in the final decoder layer. Finally, we also compare to a UV-based baseline which takes our network architecture with 2D convolutions to learn directly in UV space rather than on a 4-RoSy field. In contrast to these alternatives, our approach generates textures directly on the mesh surface, maintaining local geometric reasoning which leads to more compelling appearance generation for both chair and car meshes (see Fig. 5 and 6). The network architectures for our method and baselines are detailed in the supplementary.

Which Surface Features are the Most Informative for Texture Generation? We evaluate a variety of different local surface features used as input to the encoder network, see Table 2. In particular, we consider a case *'None'*, where we do not use a surface feature encoder, thus, the surface StyleGAN generator is reasoning only via the mesh neighborhood structure, a case where we input the 3D *position* of the face centroid, and the cases with local geometric neighborhood characterizations using *Laplacian, curvature, discrete fundamental forms*, and *normals* as input features. We find that using surface features help significantly over using no features (*'None'*). Further, features dependent on surface geometry like curvature, fundamental forms perform better than positional features like absolute 3D position and Laplacian, with a combination of normals and curvature providing the most informative surface descriptor for our texture generation (see Fig. 7).

What is the Impact of the Patch-Consistency Discriminator? When a patch consistency discriminator is not used (see Fig. 4), our method can end up generating textures that might look valid from distinct view points, but as a whole incorporate different styles. Using a discriminator that considers patch consistency across multiple different views enables more globally coherent texture generation (Fig. 4, right), also reflected in improved KID and FID scores (Table 2, last two lines).

What is the Effect of the Mesh Resolution on the Quality? We compare our base method with 6 hierarchy levels with number of faces as (24576, 6144, 1536, 384, 96, 24) against our method with 5 hierarchy levels with number of faces as (6144, 1536, 384, 96, 24). As seen in Table 2 and Fig. 8(a), the increased mesh resolution helps to produce higher-quality fine-scale details, resulting in notably improved performance. Even higher resolutions on our setup were prohibitive in memory consumption.

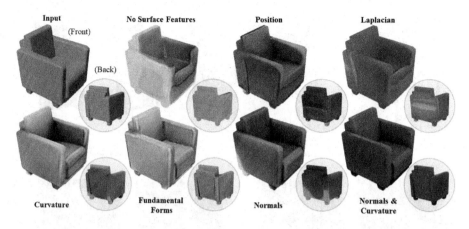

Fig. 7. Effect of different input surface features. Using no surface features (i.e. no surface encoder, only the decoder) produces poor textures since the decoder has limited understanding of the shape. 3D location based features such as position and Laplacian suffer from the inability to effectively align texture patterns with geometric ones. Curvature and fundamental forms introduce spurious line effects due to strong correlation with curvature. Surface normal are quite effective, and are further stabilised when used along with curvature.

How does the Rendered View Resolution Affect Results? Table 2 and Fig. 8(b) show the effect of several different rendering resolutions during training: 64, 128, 256, and 512. Increasing the rendering resolution results in improved quality enabling more effective generation of details.

Does Rendering from Multiple Viewpoints During Training Help? We consider a varying number of viewpoints rendered per object during each optimization step while training in Table 2, using 1, 2, and 4 views. We see that using more views continues to help when increasing from 1 to 2 to 4. Specifically, we see that using multiple views helps avoid artifacts that appear in the mesh across vastly different viewpoints as shown in Fig. 8(c). Note that the multi-view setting also allows patch consistency discriminator to generate consistent textures. We use 4 views during training since increasing the number of views has a decreasing marginal benefit as views will become more redundant.

Learned Texture Latent Space Behavior. The learned latent space is consistent in style across different shapes, i.e. the same code represents a similar style across shapes (Fig. 9), and can be used, for example, in style transfer applications. Furthermore, for a fixed shape, our learned latent space is well behaved with a smooth interpolation yielding valid textures (see supplementary).

Limitations. While our approach takes a promising step towards texture generation on shape collections, some limitations remain. Since our method uses a real image distribution that comes with lighting effects, and our method does not factor out lighting, the textures learned by our method can have lighting

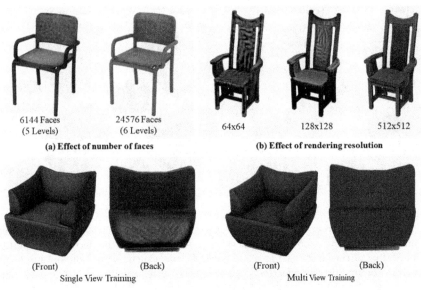

(a) **Effect of number of faces**   (b) **Effect of rendering resolution**

(c) **Effect of using multiple views while training**

Fig. 8. (a) Increased mesh resolution enables synthesis of higher quality texture. (b) Higher rendering resolution during training helps synthesize more details. (c) Using a single viewpoint per mesh for discrimination can introduce artifacts in the texture across different regions of the mesh. In contrast, using multiple views instead encourages more coherent textures across views.

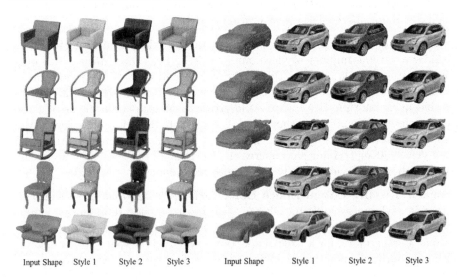

Fig. 9. The latent texture space is consistent across different shape geometry, such that the same latent code gives a similar texture style for different geometries.

Table 2. Ablations on geometric input features, mesh and image resolution, number of views, and the patch-consistency discriminator for our method on ShapeNet chairs.

Input Feature	Mesh-Res	Render-Res	# views	Patch D	KID×10⁻²↓	FID↓
None	24K	512	4	✓	2.53	37.95
Position	24K	512	4	✓	2.10	34.45
Laplacian	24K	512	4	✓	2.05	34.18
Curvatures	24K	512	4	✓	1.79	29.86
Fundamental Forms	24K	512	4	✓	1.80	30.91
Normals	24K	512	4	✓	1.68	27.73
Normals + Curvature	6K	512	4	✓	2.01	33.95
Normals + Curvature	24K	64	4	✓	2.35	39.32
Normals + Curvature	24K	128	4	✓	1.93	32.22
Normals + Curvature	24K	256	4	✓	1.54	26.99
Normals + Curvature	24K	512	1	✓	1.67	27.83
Normals + Curvature	24K	512	2	✓	1.56	26.95
Normals + Curvature	24K	512	4	X	1.64	27.22
Normals + Curvature	24K	512	4	✓	**1.54**	**26.17**

effects baked in. Further, the resolution of the texture generated by our method is limited by the number of faces used at the highest level of the 4-RoSy parameterization, whereas learned implicit functions or explicit subdivison at these highest-level faces could potentially capture even higher texture resolutions.

5 Conclusion

We have introduced *Texturify*, a new approach to generate textures on mesh surfaces from distinct collections of 3D shape geometry and 2D image collections, i.e., without requiring any correspondences between 2D and 3D or any explicit 3D color supervision. Our texture generation approach operates directly on a given mesh surface and synthesizes high-quality, coherent textures. In our experiments we show that the 4-RoSy parameterization in combination with face convolutions using geometric features as input outperforms the state-of-the-art methods both quantitatively, as well qualitatively. We believe that *Texturify* is an important step in 3D content creation through automatic texture generation of 3D objects which can be used in standard computer graphics pipelines.

Acknowledgements. This work was supported by the Bavarian State Ministry of Science and the Arts coordinated by the Bavarian Research Institute for Digital Transformation (bidt), a TUM-IAS Rudolf Mößbauer Fellowship, an NVidia Professorship Award, the ERC Starting Grant Scan2CAD (804724), and the German Research Foundation (DFG) Grant Making Machine Learning on Static and Dynamic 3D Data Practical. Apple was not involved in the evaluations and implementation of the code. Further, we thank the authors of LTG [50] for assistance with their code and data.

References

1. Azinović, D., Martin-Brualla, R., Goldman, D.B., Nießner, M., Thies, J.: Neural RGB-D surface reconstruction. arXiv preprint arXiv:2104.04532 (2021)
2. Bińkowski, M., Sutherland, D.J., Arbel, M., Gretton, A.: Demystifying mmd GANs. arXiv preprint arXiv:1801.01401 (2018)
3. Chan, E., Monteiro, M., Kellnhofer, P., Wu, J., Wetzstein, G.: pi-GAN: Periodic implicit generative adversarial networks for 3d-aware image synthesis. In: arXiv (2020)
4. Chan, E.R., et al.: Efficient geometry-aware 3d generative adversarial networks. ArXiv (2021)
5. Chan, E.R., Monteiro, M., Kellnhofer, P., Wu, J., Wetzstein, G.: pi-GAN: periodic implicit generative adversarial networks for 3D-aware image synthesis. In: CVPR (2021)
6. Chang, A.X., et al.: ShapeNet: an information-rich 3d model Repository. Technical Report arXiv:1512.03012 [cs.GR], Stanford University – Princeton University – Toyota Technological Institute at Chicago (2015)
7. Chibane, J., Alldieck, T., Pons-Moll, G.: Implicit functions in feature space for 3d shape reconstruction and completion. In: Proceedings of the IEEE/CVF Conference on Computer Vision and Pattern Recognition, pp. 6970–6981 (2020)
8. Chibane, J., Pons-Moll, G.: Implicit feature networks for texture completion from partial 3d data. In: Bartoli, A., Fusiello, A. (eds.) ECCV 2020. LNCS, vol. 12536, pp. 717–725. Springer, Cham (2020). https://doi.org/10.1007/978-3-030-66096-3_48
9. Dai, A., Diller, C., Nießner, M.: SG-NN: sparse generative neural networks for self-supervised scene completion of RGB-D scans. In: CVPR, pp. 849–858 (2020)
10. Dai, A., Siddiqui, Y., Thies, J., Valentin, J., Nießner, M.: SPSG: self-supervised photometric scene generation from RGB-D scans. In: Proceedings of the IEEE/CVF Conference on Computer Vision and Pattern Recognition, pp. 1747–1756 (2021)
11. Fu, H., et al.: 3D-FUTURE: 3d furniture shape with TextURE. Int. J. Comput. Vision **129**(12), 3313–3337 (2021). https://doi.org/10.1007/s11263-021-01534-z
12. Gadelha, M., Maji, S., Wang, R.: 3D shape induction from 2D views of multiple objects. In: 3DV (2017)
13. Gafni, G., Thies, J., Zollhofer, M., Nießner, M.: Dynamic neural radiance fields for monocular 4d facial avatar reconstruction. In: Proceedings of the IEEE/CVF Conference on Computer Vision and Pattern Recognition, pp. 8649–8658 (2021)
14. Gu, J., Liu, L., Wang, P., Theobalt, C.: StyleNeRF: A style-based 3D-aware generator for high-resolution image synthesis. ArXiv (2021)
15. Hanocka, R., Hertz, A., Fish, N., Giryes, R., Fleishman, S., Cohen-Or, D.: Meshcnn: a network with an edge. ACM Trans. Graph. (TOG) **38**(4), 1–12 (2019)
16. Hao, Z., Mallya, A., Belongie, S., Liu, M.Y.: GANcraft: unsupervised 3d neural rendering of minecraft worlds. In: ICCV (2021)
17. Henzler, P., Mitra, N.J., Ritschel, T.: Escaping plato's cave: 3D shape from adversarial rendering. In: ICCV (2019)
18. Heusel, M., Ramsauer, H., Unterthiner, T., Nessler, B., Hochreiter, S.: GANs trained by a two time-scale update rule converge to a local nash equilibrium. Adv. Neural Inf. Process. Syst. **30** (2017)
19. Huang, J., et al.: Adversarial texture optimization from RGB-d scans. In: Proceedings of the IEEE/CVF Conference on Computer Vision and Pattern Recognition, pp. 1559–1568 (2020)

20. Huang, J., Zhang, H., Yi, L., Funkhouser, T., Nießner, M., Guibas, L.J.: TextureNet: consistent local parametrizations for learning from high-resolution signals on meshes. In: Proceedings of the IEEE/CVF Conference on Computer Vision and Pattern Recognition, pp. 4440–4449 (2019)
21. Huang, J., Zhou, Y., Niessner, M., Shewchuk, J.R., Guibas, L.J.: QuadriFlow: a scalable and robust method for quadrangulation. Comput. Graph. Forum (2018). https://doi.org/10.1111/cgf.13498
22. Karras, T., Aittala, M., Hellsten, J., Laine, S., Lehtinen, J., Aila, T.: Training generative adversarial networks with limited data. Adv. Neural Inf. Process. Syst. **33**, 12104–12114 (2020)
23. Karras, T., Laine, S., Aila, T.: A style-based generator architecture for generative adversarial networks. In: CVPR (2019)
24. Karras, T., Laine, S., Aittala, M., Hellsten, J., Lehtinen, J., Aila, T.: Analyzing and improving the image quality of stylegan. In: CVPR (2020)
25. Kirillov, A., Wu, Y., He, K., Girshick, R.: PointRend: image segmentation as rendering. In: Proceedings of the IEEE/CVF Conference on Computer Vision and Pattern Recognition, pp. 9799–9808 (2020)
26. Laine, S., Hellsten, J., Karras, T., Seol, Y., Lehtinen, J., Aila, T.: Modular primitives for high-performance differentiable rendering. In: TOG (2020)
27. Masci, J., Boscaini, D., Bronstein, M., Vandergheynst, P.: Geodesic convolutional neural networks on riemannian manifolds. In: Proceedings of the IEEE International Conference on Computer Vision Workshops, pp. 37–45 (2015)
28. Mescheder, L., Oechsle, M., Niemeyer, M., Nowozin, S., Geiger, A.: Occupancy networks: Learning 3d reconstruction in function space. In: Proceedings of the IEEE/CVF Conference on Computer Vision and Pattern Recognition, pp. 4460–4470 (2019)
29. Michel, O., Bar-On, R., Liu, R., Benaim, S., Hanocka, R.: Text2mesh: text-driven neural stylization for meshes. arXiv preprint arXiv:2112.03221 (2021)
30. Nguyen-Phuoc, T., Li, C., Theis, L., Richardt, C., Yang, Y.L.: HoloGAN: unsupervised learning of 3D representations from natural images. In: ICCV (2019)
31. Nguyen-Phuoc, T., Richardt, C., Mai, L., Yang, Y.L., Mitra, N.J.: BlockGAN: learning 3d object-aware scene representations from unlabelled images. In: NeurIPS (2020)
32. Niemeyer, M., Geiger, A.: GIRAFFE: representing scenes as compositional generative neural feature fields. In: CVPR (2021)
33. Oechsle, M., Mescheder, L., Niemeyer, M., Strauss, T., Geiger, A.: Texture fields: learning texture representations in function space. In: Proceedings of the IEEE/CVF International Conference on Computer Vision, pp. 4531–4540 (2019)
34. Or-El, R., Luo, X., Shan, M., Shechtman, E., Park, J.J., Kemelmacher-Shlizerman, I.: Stylesdf: high-resolution 3d-consistent image and geometry generation. ArXiv (2021)
35. Pan, X., Xu, X., Loy, C.C., Theobalt, C., Dai, B.: A shading-guided generative implicit model for shape-accurate 3d-aware image synthesis. In: NeurIPS (2021)
36. Park, J.J., Florence, P., Straub, J., Newcombe, R., Lovegrove, S.: Deepsdf: Learning continuous signed distance functions for shape representation. In: CVPR (2019)
37. Park, K., Rematas, K., Farhadi, A., Seitz, S.M.: Photoshape: photorealistic materials for large-scale shape collections. arXiv preprint arXiv:1809.09761 (2018)
38. Pavllo, D., Kohler, J., Hofmann, T., Lucchi, A.: Learning generative models of textured 3d meshes from real-world images. In: Proceedings of the IEEE/CVF International Conference on Computer Vision, pp. 13879–13889 (2021)

39. Peng, S., Niemeyer, M., Mescheder, L., Pollefeys, M., Geiger, A.: Convolutional occupancy networks. arXiv preprint arXiv:2003.04618 2 (2020)
40. Radford, A., et al.: Learning transferable visual models from natural language supervision. In: International Conference on Machine Learning, pp. 8748–8763. PMLR (2021)
41. Schwarz, K., Liao, Y., Niemeyer, M., Geiger, A.: GRAF: generative radiance fields for 3D-aware image synthesis. In: NeurIPS (2020)
42. Siddiqui, Y., Thies, J., Ma, F., Shan, Q., Nießner, M., Dai, A.: RetrievalFuse: neural 3d scene reconstruction with a database. In: Proceedings of the IEEE/CVF International Conference on Computer Vision, pp. 12568–12577 (2021)
43. Sun, X., et al.: Pix3d: dataset and methods for single-image 3d shape modeling. In: IEEE Conference on Computer Vision and Pattern Recognition (CVPR) (2018)
44. Sun, Y., Liu, Z., Wang, Y., Sarma, S.E.: Im2avatar: colorful 3d reconstruction from a single image. arXiv preprint arXiv:1804.06375 (2018)
45. Tatarchenko, M., Park, J., Koltun, V., Zhou, Q.Y.: Tangent convolutions for dense prediction in 3d. In: Proceedings of the IEEE Conference on Computer Vision and Pattern Recognition, pp. 3887–3896 (2018)
46. Verma, N., Boyer, E., Verbeek, J.: Feastnet: feature-steered graph convolutions for 3d shape analysis. In: Proceedings of the IEEE Conference on Computer Vision and Pattern Recognition, pp. 2598–2606 (2018)
47. Wu, J., Zhang, C., Xue, T., Freeman, W.T., Tenenbaum, J.B.: Learning a probabilistic latent space of object shapes via 3D generative-adversarial modeling. In: NIPS (2016)
48. Xu, Q., et al.: Point-nerf: Point-based neural radiance fields. arXiv preprint arXiv:2201.08845 (2022)
49. Yang, L., Luo, P., Change Loy, C., Tang, X.: A large-scale car dataset for fine-grained categorization and verification. In: Proceedings of the IEEE Conference on Computer Vision and Pattern Recognition, pp. 3973–3981 (2015)
50. Yu, R., Dong, Y., Peers, P., Tong, X.: Learning texture generators for 3d shape collections from internet photo sets (2021)
51. Zhou, P., Xie, L., Ni, B., Tian, Q.: CIPS-3D: a 3d-aware generator of GANs based on conditionally-independent pixel synthesis. ArXiv (2021)
52. Zhou, Q.Y., Koltun, V.: Color map optimization for 3d reconstruction with consumer depth cameras. ACM Trans. Graph. (ToG) 33(4), 1–10 (2014)
53. Zhu, J.Y., et al.: Visual object networks: image generation with disentangled 3D representations. In: NeurIPS (2018)

Autoregressive 3D Shape Generation via Canonical Mapping

An-Chieh Cheng[1(✉)], Xueting Li[2], Sifei Liu[2], Min Sun[1,3],
and Ming-Hsuan Yang[4,5,6]

[1] National Tsing-Hua University, Hsinchu, Taiwan
ac.cheng.tw@gmail.com
[2] NVIDIA, Santa Clara, USA
[3] Joint Research Center for AI Technology and All Vista Healthcare,
Taipei City, Taiwan
[4] Yonsei University, Seoul, Korea
[5] Google Research, Mountain View, USA
[6] UC Merced, Merced, USA

Abstract. With the capacity of modeling long-range dependencies in sequential data, transformers have shown remarkable performances in a variety of generative tasks such as image, audio, and text generation. Yet, taming them in generating less structured and voluminous data formats such as high-resolution point clouds have seldom been explored due to ambiguous sequentialization processes and infeasible computation burden. In this paper, we aim to further exploit the power of transformers and employ them for the task of 3D point cloud generation. The key idea is to decompose point clouds of one category into semantically aligned sequences of shape compositions, via a learned canonical space. These shape compositions can then be quantized and used to learn a context-rich composition codebook for point cloud generation. Experimental results on point cloud reconstruction and unconditional generation show that our model performs favorably against state-of-the-art approaches. Furthermore, our model can be easily extended to multimodal shape completion as an application for conditional shape generation. The source code and trained models can be found at https://github.com/AnjieCheng/CanonicalVAE.

Keywords: 3D shape generation · Autoregressive models

1 Introduction

In the past few years, transformers not only dominate the natural language processing area [2,9,27], but also consistently show remarkable performance in a

---

A.-C. Cheng, X. Li and S. Liu—Equal contribution.

Supplementary Information The online version contains supplementary material available at https://doi.org/10.1007/978-3-031-20062-5_6.

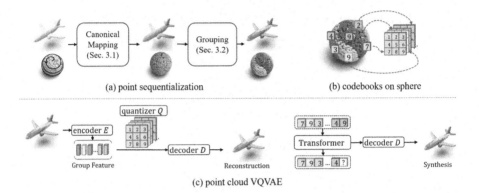

(a) point sequentialization   (b) codebooks on sphere

(c) point cloud VQVAE

Fig. 1. Given a point cloud, we first decompose it into a sequence of perceptually meaningful shape compositions via a canonical auto-encoder in (a). A group of codebooks is then learned on the sequentialized shape compositions in (b). Finally, we introduce an autoregressive model for point cloud generation in (c).

variety of vision tasks such as image classification [10], semantic and instance segmentation [20,24] and image generation [12]. Compared to convolutional neural networks, transformers learn dependencies between visual elements from scratch without making any prior assumptions about data structure. As a result, they are more flexible and capable of capturing long-range dependencies in sequential data. Such property is especially desirable in the autoregressive generation of globally coherent long-range sequential data, such as high-resolution images. Indeed, promising performance of autoregressive generation via transformers has been demonstrated in [12] for image generation.

However, employing transformers for autoregression generation on less structured data, such as raw point clouds, has seldom been explored hitherto. The main challenge is that the sequentialization of such data is non-trivial. Naively arranging a point cloud as a sequence of points will break shape structural information and is computationally infeasible. To resolve the limitation, similar to the grid-like patches applied to 2D images [12,23], one can uniformly divide a point cloud into several groups and lay them out as a sequence. However, learning the sequential shape representation can be difficult since such shape compositions are entirely random.

In this paper, we resolve these issues and take the first step to employ transformers in 3D point cloud generation. The key idea is to decompose a point cloud into a sequence of semantically meaningful shape compositions, which are further encoded by an autoregressive model for point cloud generation. Specifically, we first learn a mapping function that maps each point cloud onto a shared canonical sphere primitive. Through a canonical auto-encoder with a few self-supervised objectives, the mapping function ensures that corresponding parts (e.g., tails of two airplanes) from different instances overlap when mapped onto the canonical sphere, i.e., dense correspondences of different instances are established and are explicitly represented via a canonical sphere (see Fig. 1(a) middle).

Grouping is carried out on the canonical sphere to obtain the shape compositions (see Fig. 1(a) right). Thanks to the correspondence constraint, each group on the canonical sphere essentially corresponds to the same semantic part on all point cloud instances. As a result, each point cloud can be sequentialized into a set of shape compositions that are semantically aligned across different instances. Finally, we train a vector-quantized autoencoder (VQVAE) using these sequentialized point cloud sequences, followed by learning a transformer that resolves the point cloud generation task.

The main contributions of this work include:

- We propose a novel transformer-based autoregressive model for point cloud generation.
- We introduce a canonical autoencoder and a self-supervised point grouping network to sequentialize point clouds into semantically aligned sequences of shape compositions.
- We train a VQVAE with group-specific codebooks, followed by learning a transformer model using the sequentialized point clouds to resolve the task of point cloud generation.
- Qualitative and quantitative comparisons demonstrate that our model can achieve state-of-the-art performance for point cloud auto-encoding and generation. We also extend our model to multi-modal shape completion as an application for conditional shape generation.

2   Related Work

2.1   3D Shape Generation

3D shape generation targets at learning generative models on 3D shapes including but not limited to point clouds [33], voxels [29], implicit surfaces [5], etc. Some early works generate point clouds with a fixed-dimensional matrix [1,13]. Although these models can be easily applied with existing generative models (e.g., [13] a variational auto-encoder or [1] a generative adversarial network), they are restricted to generating a fixed number of points and are not permutation invariant. Several works [14,18,34] mitigate this issue by mapping a primitive to a point cloud. Specifically, they attach a global latent code to each sampled point on the primitive and then apply the transformation to the concatenation. In this work, we also generate point clouds from a shared primitive. Different from existing works, we decompose the primitive into different compositions and represent each group as a local latent code. Thanks to the local latent code representation, our model can generate point clouds with more fine-grained details.

Several recent works consider point clouds as samples from a distribution and propose different probabilistic models to capture the distribution. For example, PointFlow (PF) [33] applies normalizing flow to 3D point clouds. ShapeGF [3] models the gradient of the log-density field of shapes and generates point clouds using Langevin dynamics. DFM [21] and PVD [38] are both diffusion models that learn a probabilistic model over a denoising process on inputs.

Most related to our work, PointGrow [25], AutoSDF [22] and ShapeFormer [32] also use autoregressive models to generate 3D shapes. Specifically, the PointGrow discretizes point coordinates of a point cloud to fixed values and generates a shape in a point-wise manner following the spatial order. However, due to the large number of points in each point cloud, the size of generated point clouds is limited. Instead, our model decomposes a point cloud into compact shape compositions that are both semantically meaningful and more efficient to process. The AutoSDF learns an autoregressive model on volumetric Truncated-Signed Distance Field (T-SDF), where a 3D shape is represented as a randomly permuted sequence of latent variables, while the proposed method takes raw point clouds as inputs and decomposes them into ordered sequences of shape compositions. The ShapeFormer represents 3D shapes as voxel grids that have limited capacity to encode details. Moreover, the ShapeFormer uses row-major order to turn voxels into sequences, which can be sensitive to object rotation and missing parts.

2.2   Transformers for Point Clouds

Recently, several works have started to apply transformers for point clouds due to their impressive representation ability. For example, Zhao et al. [37] design self-attention layers for point clouds and show improvement in point cloud classification and segmentation. Guo et al. [15] use a transformer to enhance local information within the point cloud. Nico et al. [11] propose to extract local and global features from point clouds and relate two features with the attention mechanism. Xiang et al. [31] leverage a transformer to extract local features with a focus on shape completion. Kim et al. [17] work on the shape generation task, in which they propose to encode a hierarchy of latent codes for flexible subset structures using a transformer. However, these works only employ transformer architectures on the encoding side. In contrast, we use transformer architectures as the decoder and focus on the autoregressive generation process.

3   Method

We propose a framework that employs transformers in the task of point cloud generation. The overview of our framework is illustrated in Fig. 1. Given a point cloud, our method first maps it onto a canonical sphere in Sect. 3.1. By adopting self-supervised training objectives (e.g., Chamfer distance loss, Earth Mover distance loss), we ensure that the semantically corresponding points from different instances overlap on the canonical sphere. Thus, by grouping points on the canonical sphere and serializing them as a sequence, we equivalently decompose each point cloud into an ordered sequence of shape compositions. This process is described in Sect. 3.2. We then learn a vector-quantized variational auto-encoder (VQVAE) using the sequentialized point clouds in Sect. 3.3, with codebooks as a library of the shape compositions in the point clouds. Finally, a transformer is trained for point cloud generation in Sect. 3.4.

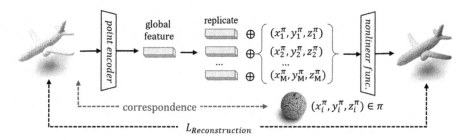

Fig. 2. Our Canonical Auto-encoder contains two parts: a point encoder that produces the shape feature of an input point cloud; a nonlinear function that decodes the canonical sphere, along with the shape feature, back to the input shape.

3.1 Point Cloud Sequentialization

Different from convolutional neural networks, transformer models require sequential data as inputs. Taking the transformer in [12] as an example, an image is first sequentialized by starting from the top left patch and sequentially moving to the bottom right patch in a zigzag order. The underline key is that all images are sequentialized by the same "zigzag" order, allowing the transformer to learn to predict patches based on their surrounding context. However, when it comes to an orderless data structure such as point clouds, it remains challenging to sequentialize the unordered points similarly to images.

To resolve this issue, two key questions need to be answered: a) what forms a unit in a sequentialized point cloud? b) how to sort these units in a consistent order for different point clouds? In this section, for ease of understanding, we consider a single point as a unit in each point cloud and demonstrate how to sort these points in a consistent order for different point clouds. We then discuss how to learn more semantically meaningful and memory-friendly units (i.e., shape compositions) in the next section.

To sequentialize all point clouds in a consistent order, we first map them onto a shared canonical sphere. Each point on the sphere is from semantically corresponding points on different point clouds. Thus, by finding an order for points on the sphere, all the point clouds can be sequentialized accordingly. For instance, if a point on the canonical sphere is labeled as the kth point in a sequence, then all its corresponding points in different point clouds are also labeled as the kth point in the sequentialized point cloud. In the following, we first discuss how to map point clouds to a canonical sphere and then describe the order we choose to sort all points.

Mapping Point Clouds to a Canonical Sphere. We learn a nonlinear function to associate all point clouds with a canonical sphere π and thus obtain their correspondences, as inspired by [8]. As shown in Fig. 2, given an input point cloud $x \in \mathcal{R}^{M \times 3}$ including M points, we first encode it as a 256-dimensional global latent code by an encoder, e.g., DGCNN [28]. We then replicate the global code and concatenate it with points sampled from a canonical unit sphere as the input

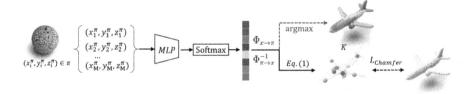

Fig. 3. We learn a self-supervised network to decompose the canonical sphere into non-overlapping groups. With canonical mapping, point clouds are simultaneously decomposed into semantically aligned shape compositions. See Sect. 3.2.

to the nonlinear function. At the output end of the function, we reconstruct the input point cloud via a Chamfer loss and an Earth Mover distance loss. The function thus performs a nonlinear transformation between the sphere and an individual instance, conditioned on its latent shape feature. We follow [8], in which the nonlinear function is a parameterized model implemented as a neural network. We name the combination of the shape encoder and the nonlinear function as *Canonical Auto-encoder*. For any point x_i from an input point cloud x, to locate its corresponding point on the sphere, we can (1) search its nearest neighbor $\hat{x}_i$ on the reconstructed point cloud $\hat{x}$, then (2) trace the point π_i on the sphere where $\hat{x}_i$ is mapped from.

As proved by Cheng et al. [8], points of all the reconstructed shapes are "re-ordered" according to the point indices of the canonical sphere (see Fig. 2). We note that as the key difference, we remove the "point cloud-to-sphere mapping network" designed in [8] to avoid processing the points that are inaccurately mapped to locations far away from the sphere surface. Our design also simplifies the following process in Sect. 3.2, i.e., the grouping and sequentialization can be conducted on a complete sphere instead of a subset of it [8]. For brevity, in the following, we denote the canonical mapping process as Φ, the corresponding point of $x_i \in x$ on the sphere π as $\Phi_{x \to \pi}(x_i)$, and the corresponding point of $\pi_i \in \pi$ on x as $\Phi_{\pi \to x}^{-1}(\pi_i)$.

Canonical Sphere Serialization. Since all point clouds are aligned with the canonical sphere by the Canonical Auto-encoder, any order defined on the canonical sphere can be easily transferred to any point cloud. In this paper, we traverse the canonical sphere from the pole with a Fibonacci spiral (see Fig. 1(a)) and serialize the points in the spiral order along the way. As a result, the index of a point in a point cloud can be easily determined as the index of its corresponding point on the canonical sphere.

3.2   Shape Composition Learning

Though the re-ordered point clouds in Sect. 3.1 can be readily represented as sequences of points, such sequences usually include thousands of points and are intractable to be modeled by autoregressive models. In this section, we introduce a more semantically meaningful and memory-efficient unit for point cloud sequentialization.

Specifically, we decompose the points of each point cloud instance into G groups ($G = 128$ throughout all experiments). We call each group a shape composition, which is analogous to an image patch in the 2D domain. As discussed above, since each point cloud is aligned to the canonical sphere, decomposing the point clouds is thus equivalent to decomposing the canonical sphere. A straightforward way is to uniformly divide the sphere by randomly sampling G points as center points and assigning each point to the nearest center point. However, this approach does not take the semantic prior into consideration and often produces discontinuous shape compositions.

Instead, we introduce a self-supervised grouping network as shown in Fig. 3. For each point on the sphere, we predict its group assignment by a multi-layer perceptron (MLP), followed by a SoftMax activation function. Both are shared by all the points on the sphere. This results in an assignment probability map P for all points $q \in \pi$, where P_i^j indicates the probability of assigning point π_i to the jth group.

To train this network and produce reasonable shape compositions, at the output end, we transfer the grouping assignment probability from each point $\pi_i \in \pi$ on the canonical sphere to its corresponding point $\Phi_{\pi \to x}^{-1}(\pi_i)$ on the input point cloud. As a result, we obtain an assignment probability map for each point cloud instance. To ensure the learned grouping captures the structure of a point cloud and formulates a decent abstraction of it, we compute G structure points $K \in \mathcal{R}^{G \times 3}$ [7], where each K_j is computed as:

$$K_j = \sum_{i=1}^{m} \Phi_{\pi \to x}^{-1}(\pi_i)P_i^j \quad \text{with} \quad \sum_{i=1}^{m} P_i^j = 1 \quad \text{for} \quad j = 1, 2, ..., G \qquad (1)$$

Finally, a Chamfer distance is applied between the predicted structure points K and the input point cloud x, as $\mathcal{L}_{CD}(K, x)$.

After training, we assign each point on π to the group with the highest probability. To assign each point $x_i \in x$ to a group, we simply let it take the group label of its corresponding point $\Phi_{x \to \pi}(x_i)$ on the sphere. In different point clouds, points on corresponding semantic parts share the same grouping assignment through the canonical sphere. As a result, any point cloud instance is decomposed into a set of shape compositions, each of which includes the points assigned to this group.

These shape compositions form the basic shape units and are further sorted into a sequence following the Fibonacci spiral order described in Sect. 3.1. In the following sections, we still denote each point cloud as x for brevity, but we assume that all point clouds have been processed into sequences of shape compositions using the method described above.

3.3 Point Cloud Reconstruction Through VQVAE

Now we introduce how to utilize the sequentialized point clouds to learn a VQVAE. Our VQVAE includes three components, an encoder E, a decoder D, and a vector quantizer Q, as shown in Fig. 1(c). We discuss each component in detail in the following.

Point Cloud Encoding. Given a sequentialized instance x, we first compute the point-wise feature by the encoder E. To compute the feature of each shape composition, we apply max-pooling to aggregate features of all points belonging to this shape composition. We denote the feature of the jth group as z^j.

Point Cloud Sequence Quantization. Next, we quantize the group feature vectors z by a group of jointly learned codebooks. In conventional VQVAEs, a single codebook is learned and shared by all the compositions (e.g., image patches in 2D VQVAEs [26]). However, we found that this strategy often leads to low code utilization. The model struggles to capture the diverse feature of all groups via only a few codes while leaving all the others unused. Such design leads to the usage of an unnecessarily large codebook and inferior reconstruction results.

To resolve this issue, we learn an independent codebook for each group where at least one code from each codebook will be utilized. Since each codebook is only responsible for representing one particular shape composition, we can safely reduce the number of codes and the dimension of each code without degrading the performance. Specifically, given z^j for group j, we first reduce its dimension from 256 to 4 to obtain a low dimensional feature $\hat{z}^j$ by learning a linear projection. We then quantize $\hat{z}^j$ into z_q^{low} by finding its nearest neighbor token from the corresponding group codebook Z^j. Note that each group codebook Z^j contains 50 4-dimensional latent codes. Finally, we project the matched codebook token back to the high-dimension embedding space and denote the quantized group feature as z_q. We note that the recent work [35] also shows that this dimension reduction process improves the reconstruction quality. We show in Sect. 4.4 that our design choices for codebook significantly increase codebook usage.

Point Cloud Sequence Decoding. To recover the input point cloud from z_q, we concatenate each point in the canonical sphere π with the corresponding quantized group feature and feed the concatenation to the decoder D.

VQVAE Training. We use the same network architecture as in Sect. 3.1 for both E and D. We train them together with the codebooks by applying the Chamfer and Earth Mover Distance between the reconstructed point cloud $\hat{x}$ and the input point cloud x:

$$\mathcal{L}_{Quantization} = \mathcal{L}_{CD}(x, \hat{x}) + \mathcal{L}_{EMD}(x, \hat{x}) + \left\| sg[z_q^{low}] - \hat{z} \right\|_2^2 \qquad (2)$$

where $sg[\cdot]$ is the stop-gradient operation. We use exponential moving average (EMA) [4] to maintain the embeddings in each of the group codebooks Z^j.

3.4 Point Cloud Generation Through Transformers

Given the learned codebooks, we can represent a point cloud sequence as a sequence of codebook token indices in order to learn an auto-regressive model.

Specifically, we represent the codebook token indices as $s_1, s_2, ..., s_G$, where G is the total group number. Given indices $s_{<i}$, we train a transformer model to predict the distribution of possible next indices s_i based on its preceeding codebook tokens as:

Table 1. Shape auto-encoding on the ShapeNet dataset. The best results are highlighted in bold. CD is multiplied by 10^4 and EMD is multiplied by 10^2.

Dataset	Metric	AtlasNet		PF	ShapeGF	DPM	Ours	Oracle
		Sphere	Patches					
Airplane	CD	1.002	0.969	1.208	0.966	0.997	**0.889**	0.837
	EMD	2.672	2.612	2.757	2.562	2.227	**2.122**	2.062
Chair	CD	6.564	6.693	10.120	**5.599**	7.305	6.177	3.201
	EMD	5.790	5.509	6.434	4.917	4.509	**4.218**	3.297
Car	CD	5.392	5.441	6.531	5.328	5.749	**5.050**	3.904
	EMD	4.587	4.570	5.138	4.409	4.141	**3.614**	3.251

PF   ShapeGF   DPM   Ours   Input

Fig. 4. Auto-encoding (reconstruction) results. We also shown results from PF (Point-Flow) [33], ShapeGF [3], and DPM [21] on the left for comparison.

$$\prod_{i=1}^{G} p(s_i | s_1, s_2, ..., s_{i-1}) \tag{3}$$

The training objective is to minimize the negative log-likelihood by

$$\mathcal{L}_{Transformer} = \mathbb{E}_{x \sim p(x))} \left[-\log p(s) \right] \tag{4}$$

The architecture of our transformer model is similar to as [12], where the indices are projected into the embedding space at each position together with an additive positional embedding. However, since each of our groups owns its own codebook, we do not use a shared embedding space for all codebook token indices. Instead, each index s_i is mapped to the embedding space using a separate linear layer.

Unconditional Generation. With the learned transformer model, unconditional shape generation is carried out by sampling token-by-token from the output distribution. The sampled tokens are then fed into the decoder D in the VQVAE to decode output shapes.

Conditional Generation. Going beyond unconditional generation, we further incorporate our transformer with a conditional input. Specifically, given a condition c (e.g., a depth image), we use our transformer to generate a shape that matches the semantic meaning of c. For instance, if c is a depth image, then the transformer is expected to generate a 3D shape that renders the depth image from the given viewpoint. To this end, we first encode the condition c into a feature vector in the same dimension of token embedding, then prepend the feature vector before the first token embedding.

4   Experiments

Datasets. Following previous works [3,17,33], we conduct our auto-encoding and generation experiments on the airplane, chair, and car category from the ShapeNet [6] dataset. For the multi-modal shape completion task, we follow [38] which uses the ShapeNet rendering data from Genre [36]. For baselines that take additional partial point clouds as inputs, we use the data provided by [38].

Evaluation Metrics. For a fair comparison, we follow prior works [3,33,34] and use the symmetric Chamfer Distance (CD) as well as the Earth Mover's Distance (EMD) to evaluate the quality of the reconstructed point clouds. To evaluate the quality of the unconditionally generated point clouds, we use the Minimum Matching Distance (MMD) [1], the Coverage Score (COV) [1], and the 1-NN classifier accuracy (1-NNA) [33]. To evaluate the multi-modal shape completion performance for the conditional generation task, we follow Wu et al. [30] that uses a) the Total Mutual Difference (TMD) to measure the generation diversity and b) the Minimal Matching Distance (MMD) to measure the completion quality with Chamfer Distance (CD). We normalize each point cloud for all generation experiments to a unit sphere before measuring the metrics.

4.1   Shape Auto-Encoding

We first evaluate how well our model can approximate a shape with quantized features. We quantitatively compare our results against the following state-of-the-art point cloud auto-encoders: AtlasNet [14] variants that deform from patches and from sphere, respectively, PointFlow (PF) [33], ShapeGF [3], and DPM [21]. Following [3], we also report the lower bound of the reconstruction errors in the "Oracle" column. As shown in Table 1, our method consistently outperforms other methods when measured by EMD. Note that EMD is usually considered a better metric to measure a shape's visual quality [38] as it requires the outputs to have the same density as the ground-truth shapes [19]. This suggests that our reconstructed point clouds have more uniformly distributed points on the surface. We also provide qualitative results compared to baselines in Fig. 4 to validate the effectiveness of our model.

4.2   Unconditional Generation

We quantitatively compare our method with the following state-of-the-art generative models: PointGrow [25], ShapeGF [3], SP-GAN [18], PointFlow (PF) [33], SetVAEF [17], DPM [21], and PVD [38]. We summarize the quantitative results in Table 2. For most of the metrics, our model has comparable, if not better, performance than other baselines. This suggests that our model is capable of generating diverse and realistic samples. We provide qualitative results comparing to baselines in Fig. 5.

Among these baselines, PointGrow is most relevant to our work that generates point clouds in an autoregressive manner. Our model significantly

Table 2. Shape generation results. ↑ means the higher the better, ↓ means the lower the better. MMD-CD is multiplied by 10^3 and MMD-EMD is multiplied by 10^2.

Category	Model	MMD (↓)		COV (%, ↑)		1-NNA (%, ↓)	
		CD	EMD	CD	EMD	CD	EMD
Airplane	PointGrow	3.07	11.64	10.62	10.62	99.38	99.38
	ShapeGF	**1.02**	6.53	**41.48**	32.84	80.62	88.02
	SP-GAN	1.49	8.03	30.12	23.21	96.79	98.40
	PF	1.15	6.31	36.30	38.02	85.80	83.09
	SetVAE	1.04	**6.16**	39.51	38.77	89.51	87.65
	DPM	1.10	7.11	36.79	25.19	86.67	90.49
	PVD	1.12	6.17	40.49	<u>45.68</u>	80.25	**77.65**
	Ours	**<u>0.83</u>**	**<u>5.50</u>**	<u>45.67</u>	44.19	**<u>63.45</u>**	**<u>71.60</u>**
Chair	PointGrow	16.23	18.83	12.08	13.75	98.05	99.10
	ShapeGF	**7.17**	**11.85**	**45.62**	44.71	61.78	64.27
	SP-GAN	8.51	13.09	34.74	26.28	77.87	84.29
	PF	7.26	12.12	42.60	**45.47**	65.56	65.79
	SetVAE	7.60	12.10	42.75	40.48	65.79	70.39
	DPM	**<u>6.81</u>**	11.91	43.35	42.75	64.65	69.26
	PVD	7.65	11.87	<u>45.77</u>	45.02	**<u>60.05</u>**	**<u>59.52</u>**
	Ours	7.37	**<u>11.75</u>**	<u>45.77</u>	<u>46.07</u>	60.12	61.93
Car	PointGrow	14.12	18.33	6.82	11.65	99.86	98.01
	ShapeGF	**3.63**	9.11	<u>48.30</u>	44.03	**60.09**	61.36
	PF	3.69	**9.03**	44.32	45.17	63.78	**<u>57.67</u>**
	SetVAE	**3.63**	9.05	39.77	37.22	65.91	67.61
	DPM	3.70	9.39	38.07	30.40	74.01	73.15
	PVD	3.74	9.31	43.47	39.49	65.62	63.35
	Ours	**<u>3.31</u>**	**<u>8.89</u>**	41.76	<u>47.72</u>	**<u>55.68</u>**	57.81

outperforms PointGrow in all metrics because PointGrow scales poorly [25] when generating large point sets. In contrast, our method can generate shapes in an arbitrary resolution ranging from low to high with sharp details within a single model. We show point clouds generated with different resolutions compared to PointGrow in Fig. 6.

4.3   Conditional Generation

During inference, our transformer model generates a sequence by a probabilistic sampling of each token, which naturally allows multi-modal generation. On the other hand, the shape completion problem is multi-modal in nature since the incompleteness introduces significant ambiguity [30]. Motivated by this property, we extend our approach to shape completion as an application for conditional shape generation. Specifically, we use a depth map as the input condition to the transformer model. We employ a ResNet50 [16] encoder to extract global features from the depth map and prepend the feature vector to the transformer as discussed in follow Sect. 3.4.

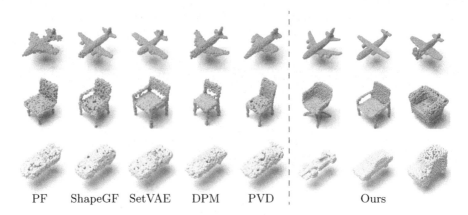

PF   ShapeGF   SetVAE   DPM   PVD   Ours

Fig. 5. Shape generation results. We shown results from PF (PointFlow) [33], ShapeGF [3], SetVAE [17], DPM [21], and PVD [38].

$n = 1024$ $n = 2048$ | $n = 1024$ $n = 2048$ $n = 4096$ $n = 8194$
        PointGrow   Ours

Fig. 6. High-resolution generation results comparing to PointGrow [25]. n refers to the number of output points.

We compare with two state-of-the-art approaches on multi-modal shape completion: MSC [30] and PVD [38]. Note that both MSC [30] and PVD [38] take aligned point clouds as inputs. Therefore, they require additional camera parameters to obtain partial scans from the depth map. We present quantitative comparison results in Table 3 and show that our approach can achieve comparable or even better performance without requiring additional camera parameters. We also report results using different temperatures, which suggests that our model can provide controllable diversity by scaling the temperature parameter.

We visualize qualitative results in Fig. 7. In general, our model produces shapes with better visual quality. However, due to the inherent ambiguity in single-view reconstruction, it is difficult to infer the real scale of objects without knowing the camera parameters, especially for depth maps rendered from the side views. For instance, given a depth map of a chair from side viewpoints, our model generates plausible but wider chairs than the ground truth 3D shapes, as shown in the first row of Fig. 7.

4.4 Ablation Study

Effectiveness of the Canonical Mapping Function. Table 4 shows ablations on the effectiveness of our canonical mapping function, with empirical

Table 3. Multi-modal completion on the Chair dataset. t denotes the temperature scaling factor. ↑ means the higher the better, ↓ means the lower the better. MMD and TMD are both multiplied by 10^3.

Category	Metric	Input	MMD (↓)	TMD (↑)
Airplane	MSC	Depth+Camera	1.475	0.925
	PVD	Depth+Camera	1.012	2.108
	Ours (t = 1)	Depth	0.663	1.449
	Ours (t = 2)	Depth	0.673	2.406
	Ours (t = 3)	Depth	0.684	2.352
Chair	MSC	Depth+Camera	6.372	5.924
	PVD	Depth+Camera	5.042	7.524
	Ours (t = 1)	Depth	5.142	6.553
	Ours (t = 2)	Depth	5.261	8.174
	Ours (t = 3)	Depth	6.427	13.341

Table 4. Ablation study on the effectiveness of primitive grouping on the Chair dataset. CD is multiplied by 10^4 and EMD is multiplied by 10^2.

	Canonical grouping			Uniform grouping		
#groups	16	128	256	16	128	256
CD (↓)	7.542	6.177	7.933	8.646	7.676	7.278
EMD (↓)	4.466	4.218	4.645	4.772	4.541	4.627

results on CD and EMD metrics using the ShapeNet Chair dataset. We report variants of our model using a different number of groups G and an alternative way to segment the canonical sphere (in the "Uniform Grouping" column). Specifically, we uniformly sample G points on the sphere as centers and use the nearest neighbor search to assign all points on the sphere to its nearest center point. Though straightforward, this approach does not provide any semantic correspondence across shape instances; thereby, our model consistently performs better than this baseline in different G settings. For the uniform setting, the auto-encoding results directly relate to the G because a larger G results in a finer segmentation. However, our model performs the best with a moderate $G = 128$. Since the size of each group is automatically determined in our model (i.e. rather than an equal size), therefore, some groups may include only a few points when G is large. This tends to hurt the encoding performance and results in over-fitting.

Effectiveness of Group-Wise Codebooks. Table 5 demonstrates the effectiveness of the latent reduction and group-wise codebook (see Sect. 3.3) in our vector quantizer Q. In addition to CD and EMD, we also report the codebook usage for each model. The usage is computed as the percentage of codes that have been utilized at least once over the entire test set. For a fair comparison

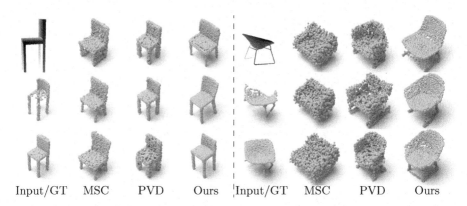

Input/GT   MSC   PVD   Ours   Input/GT   MSC   PVD   Ours

Fig. 7. Multi-modal shape completion results. We shown 4 samples comparing to MSC and PVD. The input depth-map, partial point cloud, and reference ground-truth shape for each sample is shown in the first column, respectively (from top to bottom).

Table 5. Ablation study on using different vector quantization on the Chair dataset. CD is multiplied by 10^4 and EMD is multiplied by 10^2.

Dimension reduction	✗	256→64	256→4	256→64	256→4
Grouped Codebook	✗	✗	✗	✓	✓
CD (↓)	7.139	6.561	6.298	6.442	6.177
EMD (↓)	4.376	4.272	4.283	4.228	4.218
Codebook usage (%, ↑)	11.72	21.04	35.72	70.22	79.28

with our full model that uses 128 group codebooks in size 50, we use a global codebook in size 5000 ($\approx$ 128×50) for each variant that does not use group-wise codebooks. Our full model performs the best with dimension reduction from 256 to 4 together with a group-wise codebook. Reducing the lookup dimension in the codebook and using a group-wise codebook significantly boost the codebook usage, thereby achieving better auto-encoding quality.

5   Conclusions

We propose a transformer-based autoregressive model for point cloud generation. The key idea is to decompose a point cloud into a sequence of semantically aligned shape compositions in a learned canonical space. We show that these compositions can be further used to learn a group of context-rich codebooks for point cloud generation. Experimental results demonstrate that the proposed method can achieve state-of-the-art performance for point cloud auto-encoding and generation. Finally, we show that our model can be easily extended to multi-modal shape completion as an application for conditional shape generation.

Acknowledgments. The MOST, Taiwan under Grants 110-2634-F-002-051, MOST Joint Research Center for AI Technology, All Vista Healthcare, and NSF CAREER grant 1149783. We thank National Center for High-performance Computing (NCHC) for providing computational and storage resources.

References

1. Achlioptas, P., Diamanti, O., Mitliagkas, I., Guibas, L.: Learning representations and generative models for 3D point clouds. In: ICML, pp. 40–49 (2018)
2. Brown, T., et al.: Language models are few-shot learners. In: NeurIPS (2020)
3. Cai, R., et al.: Learning gradient fields for shape generation. In: Vedaldi, A., Bischof, H., Brox, T., Frahm, J.-M. (eds.) ECCV 2020. LNCS, vol. 12348, pp. 364–381. Springer, Cham (2020). https://doi.org/10.1007/978-3-030-58580-8_22
4. Cai, Z., Ravichandran, A., Maji, S., Fowlkes, C., Tu, Z., Soatto, S.: Exponential moving average normalization for self-supervised and semi-supervised learning. In: CVPR (2021)
5. Chan, E.R., et al.: Efficient geometry-aware 3D generative adversarial networks. In: CVPR (2022)
6. Chang, A.X., et al.: Shapenet: An information-rich 3D model repository. arXiv preprint arXiv:1512.03012 (2015)
7. Chen, N., et al.: Unsupervised learning of intrinsic structural representation points. In: CVPR (2020)
8. Cheng, A.C., Li, X., Sun, M., Yang, M.H., Liu, S.: Learning 3D dense correspondence via canonical point autoencoder. In: NeurIPS (2021)
9. Devlin, J., Chang, M.W., Lee, K., Toutanova, K.: BERT: pre-training of deep bidirectional transformers for language understanding. arXiv preprint arXiv:1810.04805 (2018)
10. Dosovitskiy, A., et al.: An image is worth 16x16 words: transformers for image recognition at scale. arXiv preprint arXiv:2010.11929 (2020)
11. Engel, N., Belagiannis, V., Dietmayer, K.: Point transformer. IEEE. Access **9**, 134826–134840 (2021)
12. Esser, P., Rombach, R., Ommer, B.: Taming transformers for high-resolution image synthesis. In: CVPR (2021)
13. Gadelha, M., Wang, R., Maji, S.: Multiresolution tree networks for 3d point cloud processing. In: Ferrari, V., Hebert, M., Sminchisescu, C., Weiss, Y. (eds.) ECCV 2018. LNCS, vol. 11211, pp. 105–122. Springer, Cham (2018). https://doi.org/10.1007/978-3-030-01234-2_7
14. Groueix, T., Fisher, M., Kim, V.G., Russell, B.C., Aubry, M.: A papier-mâché approach to learning 3D surface generation. In: CVPR, pp. 216–224 (2018)
15. Guo, M.H., PCT: Point cloud transformer. Comput. Vis. Media **7**, 187–199 (2021)
16. He, K., Zhang, X., Ren, S., Sun, J.: Deep residual learning for image recognition. In: CVPR, pp. 770–778 (2016)
17. Kim, J., Yoo, J., Lee, J., Hong, S.: SetVAE: learning hierarchical composition for generative modeling of set-structured data. In: CVPR, pp. 15059–15068 (2021)
18. Li, R., Li, X., Hui, K.H., Fu, C.W.: SP-GAN: sphere-guided 3D shape generation and manipulation. Trans. Graph. **40**(4), 1–12 (2021)
19. Liu, M., Sheng, L., Yang, S., Shao, J., Hu, S.M.: Morphing and sampling network for dense point cloud completion. In: AAAI, pp. 11596–11603 (2020)
20. Liu, Z., et al.: Swin transformer: Hierarchical vision transformer using shifted windows. In: ICCV (2021)

21. Luo, S., Hu, W.: Diffusion probabilistic models for 3D point cloud generation. In: Proceedings of the IEEE/CVF Conference on Computer Vision and Pattern Recognition, pp. 2837–2845 (2021)

22. Mittal, P., Cheng, Y.C., Singh, M., Tulsiani, S.: AutoSDF: shape priors for 3D completion, reconstruction and generation. arXiv preprint arXiv:2203.09516 (2022)

23. Razavi, A., Van den Oord, A., Vinyals, O.: Generating diverse high-fidelity images with VQ-VAE-2. In: NeurIPS, vol. 32 (2019)

24. Strudel, R., Garcia, R., Laptev, I., Schmid, C.: Segmenter: transformer for semantic segmentation. In: ICCV (2021)

25. Sun, Y., Wang, Y., Liu, Z., Siegel, J., Sarma, S.: PointGrow: autoregressively learned point cloud generation with self-attention. In: Proceedings of the IEEE/CVF Winter Conference on Applications of Computer Vision, pp. 61–70 (2020)

26. Van Den Oord, A., et al.: Neural discrete representation learning. In: NeurIPS, vol. 30 (2017)

27. Vaswani, A., et al.: Attention is all you need. In: NeurIPS (2017)

28. Wang, Y., Sun, Y., Liu, Z., Sarma, S.E., Bronstein, M.M., Solomon, J.M.: Dynamic graph cnn for learning on point clouds. Trans. Graph. 38(5), 1–12 (2019)

29. Wu, J., Zhang, C., Xue, T., Freeman, B., Tenenbaum, J.: Learning a probabilistic latent space of object shapes via 3D generative-adversarial modeling. In: NeurIPS (2016)

30. Wu, R., Chen, X., Zhuang, Y., Chen, B.: Multimodal Shape completion via conditional generative adversarial networks. In: Vedaldi, A., Bischof, H., Brox, T., Frahm, J.-M. (eds.) ECCV 2020. LNCS, vol. 12349, pp. 281–296. Springer, Cham (2020). https://doi.org/10.1007/978-3-030-58548-8_17

31. Xiang, P., e al.: nowflakeNet: point cloud completion by snowflake point deconvolution with skip-transformer. In: Proceedings of the IEEE International Conference on Computer Vision (ICCV), (2021)

32. Yan, X., Lin, L., Mitra, N.J., Lischinski, D., Cohen-Or, D., Huang, H.: ShapeFormer: Transformer-based shape completion via sparse representation. In: CVPR, pp. 6239–6249 (2022)

33. Yang, G., Huang, X., Hao, Z., Liu, M.Y., Belongie, S., Hariharan, B.: PointFlow: 3D point cloud generation with continuous normalizing flows. In: CVPR, pp. 4541–4550 (2019)

34. Yang, Y., Feng, C., Shen, Y., Tian, D.: FoldingNet: point cloud auto-encoder via deep grid deformation. In: CVPR, pp. 206–215 (2018)

35. Yu, J., et al.: Vector-quantized image modeling with improved VQGAN. In: ICLR (202)

36. Zhang, X., Zhang, Z., Zhang, C., Tenenbaum, J.B., Freeman, W.T., Wu, J.: Learning to Reconstruct Shapes From Unseen Classes. In: NeurIPS (2018)

37. Zhao, H., Jiang, L., Jia, J., Torr, P.H., Koltun, V.: Point transformer. In: Proceedings of the IEEE/CVF International Conference on Computer Vision, pp. 16259–16268 (2021)

38. Zhou, L., Du, Y., Wu, J.: 3D shape generation and completion through point-voxel diffusion. In: Proceedings of the IEEE/CVF International Conference on Computer Vision, pp. 5826–5835 (2021)

PointTree: Transformation-Robust Point Cloud Encoder with Relaxed K-D Trees

Jun-Kun Chen$^{(\boxtimes)}$ and Yu-Xiong Wang

University of Illinois at Urbana-Champaign, Champaign, USA
{junkun3,yxw}@illinois.edu

Abstract. Being able to learn an effective semantic representation directly on raw point clouds has become a central topic in 3D understanding. Despite rapid progress, state-of-the-art encoders are restrictive to canonicalized point clouds, and have weaker than necessary performance when encountering geometric transformation distortions. To overcome this challenge, we propose *PointTree*, a general-purpose point cloud encoder that is *robust to transformations* based on *relaxed* K-D trees. Key to our approach is the design of the division rule in K-D trees by using principal component analysis (PCA). We use the structure of the relaxed K-D tree as our computational graph, and model the features as border descriptors which are merged with pointwise-maximum operation. In addition to this novel architecture design, we further improve the robustness by introducing *pre-alignment* – a simple yet effective PCA-based normalization scheme. Our PointTree encoder combined with pre-alignment consistently outperforms state-of-the-art methods by large margins, for applications from object classification to semantic segmentation on various transformed versions of the widely-benchmarked datasets. Code and pre-trained models are available at https://github.com/immortalCO/PointTree.

1 Introduction

3D sensing technology has advanced rapidly over the past few years, playing a significant role in many applications such as augmented reality, autonomous driving, and geographic information systems [1,6,9]. As one of the most commonly-used output formats of 3D sensors, 3D point clouds flexibly describe the surface information of the sensed objects or scenes with collection of points. Therefore, being able to learn an effective semantic representation directly on raw point clouds, which is useful for high-level tasks such as object recognition, has become a central topic in 3D understanding, with various powerful deep learning architecture based encoders emerging like PointNet [18] and PointMLP [17]. In real-world applications, a desired encoder is supposed to cope with a wide range of *geometric transformations* – point clouds of the same object category

Supplementary Information The online version contains supplementary material available at https://doi.org/10.1007/978-3-031-20062-5_7.

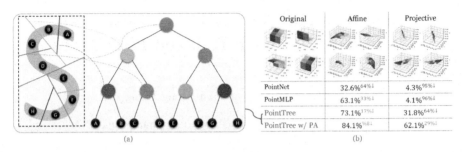

	Original	Affine	Projective
PointNet		$32.6\%^{64\%\downarrow}$	$4.3\%^{95\%\downarrow}$
PointMLP		$63.1\%^{33\%\downarrow}$	$4.1\%^{96\%\downarrow}$
PointTree		$73.1\%^{17\%\downarrow}$	$31.8\%^{64\%\downarrow}$
PointTree w/ PA		$84.1\%^{8\%\downarrow}$	$62.1\%^{29\%\downarrow}$

(a) (b)

Fig. 1. Our **robust** PointTree vs. **non-robust** existing point cloud encoders under geometric transformations. **(a)** PointTree is based on *relaxed* K-D trees, and its robustness is mainly achieved by designing the division plane of each node to be robust against transformations: An example of a relaxed K-D tree operated on an 8-point S-shaped point cloud. Each node is related to the division line with the same color, and each point is related to a leaf node. **(b)** Affine and projective transformations can highly deform the point clouds, dramatically decreasing the object classification accuracy of existing point cloud encoders like the widely-used PointNet [18] and more recent PointMLP [17] ('↓' indicates the relative performance drop compared with their accuracy on the canonicalized point clouds which is 90.6% and 94.5%, respectively). We illustrate an example point cloud in ModelNet40 [27]. For the original (canonicalized), affine, and projective versions, we show 4 different point of views of the same point cloud, and use different colors to represent different octants. PointTree significantly outperforms its counterparts in challenging transformation scenarios. With the additionally proposed pre-alignment ('PA'), PointTree further improves the accuracy

may undergo different similarity/affine/projective transformations, leading to large intra-class variations. This paper demonstrates that existing state-of-the-art point cloud encoders have weaker than necessary performance when encountering geometric transformation distortions, and proposes *PointTree*, a new type of encoder based on *relaxed* K-D trees that is *robust to transformations* and thus offers substantial improvements in performance.

Such investigation on transformation robustness for point cloud encoders is under-explored in existing work, partially because most of the commonly-used benchmark datasets, like ModelNet [27] and ShapeNet [3], make a simplifying assumption – the point clouds are in precise shapes and aligned in a canonical coordinate system. For example, a point cloud of a table in such a dataset always has its tabletop parallel to the xOy plane, and all its legs vertical to the top. However, such an assumption is restrictive and hardly satisfied *in the wild* – e.g., an object scanned by a 3D sensor is often not aligned with the sensor, leading to unaligned point clouds. Due to noise, perturbation, viewpoint change, miscalibration, or precision limitation of the sensor itself [16, 24, 34], the scanned point cloud may have a different shape from the object, and the shape might be deformed by a 3D affine or projective transformation. On the other hand, most of existing encoders developed on these benchmarks highly rely on this assumption and are thus sensitive to input point cloud deformations, leading to dramatically degenerated recognition performance as shown in Fig. 1-b. Notably, while effective for simple input corruptions, the common strategy (e.g., the T-Net [18] used in PointNet) that adopts a transformer network to explicitly predict a transformation for canonicalization of input data cannot deal with more general deformations here.

To overcome this challenge, we propose PointTree, a transformation-robust, general-purpose point cloud encoder architecture. Key to our approach is the use of *relaxed* K-D trees [4]. While there have been some existing approaches [10, 33] that utilize K-D trees, they are based on the *conventional* K-D tree that only divides the point set along an axis at each node, which implicitly uses the aligned assumption and thus still performs poorly on transformed point clouds. By contrast, our use of the relaxed K-D tree removes the restriction of division rules, allowing more flexible designs. Particularly, in PointTree, we design the division rule by using principal component analysis (PCA) as illustrated in Fig. 1-a. By doing so, theoretically, we show that our division of the point set and construction of the whole K-D tree are *invariant to similarity transformations*; and empirically, we observe that our PointTree exhibits strong *robustness against more complicated affine and projective transformations* (Fig. 1-b).

In addition to the proposed division rule, the robustness of our approach further stems from other properties of K-D trees and additional design strategies. As a tree structure containing multiple layers, PointTree natively divides a point cloud into components at bottom layers. This facilitates the recognition of multi-component objects (e.g., an airplane), as PointTree may still capture useful local features from lower layers even if the whole point cloud undergoes severe deformation. Also, the similarity transformation-invariant division induced by relaxed K-D trees prevents cutting two components with the same shape (e.g., two engines of the airplane) in different directions, so that the symmetricity can still be leveraged. Moreover, following PointNet [18] and PointNet++ [19], we model the features in PointTree as border descriptors which can be merged with pointwise-maximum operation. We use the structure of the relaxed K-D tree as our computational graph, which contains a native locality clustering and down-sampling scheme. Finally, not only from this novel architecture design, but we also improve the robustness by introducing a simple PCA-based normalization scheme (called "pre-alignment") on input point clouds to PointTree. This is shown as a general normalization scheme that consistently and effectively improves the performance of other encoders under transformations as well.

Our contributions are three-folds. (1) We propose PointTree, a general-purpose point cloud encoder architecture based on relaxed K-D trees, which is robust against geometric (affine and projective) transformations. (2) We introduce pre-alignment, a simple yet general PCA-based normalization scheme, which can consistently improve the performance of a variety of point cloud encoders under geometric transformations. (3) We show that our PointTree encoder combined with pre-alignment consistently outperforms state-of-the-art methods by large margins, on various transformed versions of ModelNet40 [27], ShapeNetPart [3], and S3DIS [2] benchmarks.

2   Related Work

Deep Learning on Point Clouds. There are mainly four directions to build a deep learning model to process and analyze point clouds [7]: (i) multi-layer perceptron (MLP) methods [17–19] that use pointwise MLPs along with some multi-stage locality clustering and down-sampling; (ii) convolution methods [14,15] that perform convolutions on voxels, grids, or directly in continuous 3D space; (iii) graph methods [26,35] that construct graphs with points as vertices and with neighborhood relations as edges, and apply graph models; and (iv) data structure methods [10,21,22,33] that use a hierarchical data structure like an OCTree or a K-D tree as the computational graph. Our PointTree belongs to a data structure method, since it uses a relaxed K-D tree as the computational graph. Intuitively, pure MLP methods (without locality clustering) are not robust against transformations, since they only rely on coordinate values; by exploiting locality, locality clustering and neighborhood graph may improve the robustness.

Point Cloud Encoders Based on K-D Trees. To the best of our knowledge, mainly four methods in the literature use K-D trees to build point cloud encoders: KD-Net [10], 3DContextNet [33], PD-Net [31], and MRT-Net [5], while more approaches exist based on OCTrees [11,21,22,28]. KD-Net is a simple version of the K-D tree-based point cloud encoder – it uses MLP to merge the information of two children nodes for each node. As an advanced version, 3DContextNet uses the border descriptor features from PointNet [18] which can be merged by pointwise-maximum; it further proposes multi-stage training to exploit local and global context. PD-Net [31] is a variant of KD-Net that replaces the vanilla K-D tree with a PCA-based K-D tree, but its feature aggregation still highly relies on coordinates. MRT-Net [5] uses the K-D tree only for preprocessing and uses convolutional layers for further modeling.

Relation Between Our PointTree and Previous Models. Instead of using conventional K-D trees, PointTree leverages relaxed K-D trees with a proposed division plane selection method, making it different from all existing K-D tree-based models. Similar to PointNet [18] and 3DContextNet [33], PointTree models the features as border descriptors. While the model design of PointTree is inspired by and similar to that of 3DContextNet in the "feature learning stage," PointTree is simpler *without* relying on multi-stage training and local and global cues. Furthermore, PointTree has an extra alignment network as in PointNet.

Investigation on Transformation Robustness. While there has been interest in addressing robustness against geometric transformations of input point clouds, existing work mainly focuses on specific transformations like rotation and similarity. IT-Net [32] proposes a learnable normalization component (or "alignment network") which learns to recover the original point cloud. Other work [12,13,23,36] proposes $SO(3)$ (similarity transformation) robust, invariant, or equivariant architectures that maintain stable results when training on rotated point clouds. Shear transformation is also studied [25], which is a special type of affine transformation with deformation only performed on two of the three axes.

None of the existing methods are able to cope with robustness against general affine or projective transformations as our work.

3   Methodology

Problem Setting. We design a deep learning model as a general-purpose point cloud encoder. A **point cloud** is an unordered set of points $P = \{p_i\}_{i=1}^n$. Each point p_i is a 3-D vector (x_i, y_i, z_i) representing the three coordinates. Our model directly takes P as input, and outputs a set of vectors O. For a downstream task, another model takes O as input, and outputs task-specific predictions.

3.1   Point Cloud Encoder Based on Relaxed K-D Trees

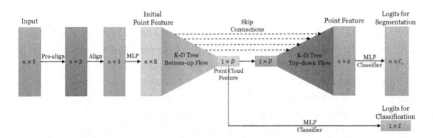

Fig. 2. Architecture of PointTree. The input point cloud passes through a pre-alignment process, followed by an alignment network, and is then fed to our Point-Tree model. A K-D tree bottom-up flow is applied on such input, obtaining the point cloud feature which can be used for classification. For segmentation tasks, another K-D tree top-down flow is applied on the output of the bottom-up flow with some skip connections, obtaining point features which can be used for segmentation

K-D Trees and Relaxed K-D Trees. Our proposed point cloud encoder *PointTree* is based on relaxed K-D trees, as illustrated in Fig. 2. K-D trees are a classical data structure designed to solve K-dimensional range counting problems. It is a special decision tree built on n K-dimensional input points, in two specific ways: (i) each node has an axis-parallel criterion; and (ii) such a criterion strictly divides the input points that go through this node to two equal-size parts. Each leaf node is related to exactly one input point.

A K-D tree of depth d is a full binary tree with 2^d points. The root is at layer 0; the leaves are at layer d. Each non-leaf node o has two unordered children nodes o_l and o_r, while each leaf node has a corresponding point $p(o)$. Each non-root node has a unique parent node **par**(o). At each non-leaf node, a linear criterion $W_o p + b_o \leq 0$ divides the point set into two subsets, which is recursively processed at the left and right nodes. Hence, the subtree of each node contains the points in a continuous 3-D space, leading to a native locality clustering.

Existing K-D tree-based methods [10,33] use the conventional definition of K-D trees that only divides along one axis, i.e., $W_o \in \{(0, 0, 1), (0, 1, 0), (1, 0, 0)\}$.

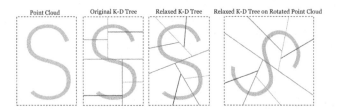

Fig. 3. Relaxed K-D tree's **division and similarity equivariance**. For the S-shape point cloud, the original K-D tree divides it into a large number of *imbalanced* segments (one of the parts even contains two disconnected segments of S), while the relaxed K-D tree can cut it into a small number of *balanced* segments. Also, when rotating the S-shape with an angle, each division plane and pieces of the point cloud divided by the relaxed K-D tree rotate with the same angle and each divided segment keeps unchanged. This shows that relaxed K-D trees are equivariant to similarity transformations

However, such methods are not exploiting the expressiveness of K-D trees. By contrast, we adopt **relaxed K-D trees** [4] – a generalization of K-D trees by removing the restriction of division plane, so that the point set can be divided with any criterion. Here, to improve the transformation robustness, we consider an arbitrary linear criterion, i.e., W_o can be an arbitrary vector.

Concretely, PointTree uses the first principle component (obtained by a PCA algorithm) as the division plane, and chooses the medium value as the division boundary. As PCA is similarity-transformation equivariant, this K-D tree construction has the invariance against similarity transformations, as shown in Fig. 3. Importantly, this property also brings in strong robustness against affine and projective transformations, as empirically validated in Sect. 4. In addition, if the point cloud contains multiple similar components due to repeating or symmetricity, e.g., airplane engines, table legs, and desk drawers, our similarity-transformation invariant K-D tree construction can divide these components in the same way, further improving the model robustness and facilitating feature extraction from these components.

Bottom-Up Information Flow. In a traditional K-D tree algorithm, there is a scheme to upload information in a bottom-up way, called **bottom-up information flow**. In such information flow, each node o takes some information as a vector info(o). The information at each leaf node is derived from the corresponding point, and the information at each non-leaf node is the aggregated information of its children nodes, as the formula below:

$$\text{info}(o) = \begin{cases} \textbf{point-info}_o(p(o)), & o \in L_d, \\ \textbf{merge-info}_o(\text{info}(o_l), \text{info}(o_r)), & o \in L_i. \end{cases} \quad (1)$$

The uploading process of the information flow is a natural down-sampling scheme. In the layer-by-layer bottom-up uploading process, the number of nodes in layer i (which is 2^i) is decreasing, and the size of the subtree of each node (which contains information of 2^{d-i} points) is increasing. Thus, we can regard

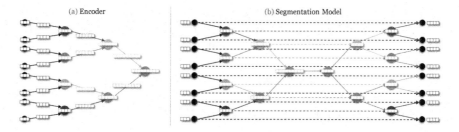

Fig. 4. (a) **Our PointTree encoder**. The encoder has a multi-stage down-sampling and dimension increasing scheme, where each layer in the K-D tree is a stage. The points are down-sampled through layers via a bottom-up information flow. The grids on the nodes and edges show the dimension of features. For each node, the features from its two children nodes are first fed to a dimension-increasing MLP, and then merged with pointwise-maximum operation. (b) **The segmentation model**. The two symmetric K-D trees represent two stages: a bottom-up information flow (**left, the same as (a) with simplified notation**) and a top-down information flow (**right**), on the same K-D tree. The information is first uploaded from leaves to root to obtain global features, and then downloaded from root to leaves, obtaining the relationship between each leaf/point and the whole point cloud which is used for segmentation classification. For the top-down information flow (**right**), each node has a carried feature that represents the information of the relationship between its subtree and the whole point cloud. Such feature is obtained by merging its parent nodes' carried information and with a skip connection (dotted lines) from the same node in the bottom-up feature

each layer as a stage of down-sampling with down-sampled points. Such down-sampling process starts with the information of original points P and ends with a single point info(R), where R is the root of the K-D tree.

Our Encoder. We design the encoder of PointTree (see Fig. 4-a) by leveraging the idea of PointNet [18] and its improved version PointNet++ [19], but in the information flow of a relaxed K-D tree. Specifically, we model the information as the border descriptor or "global shape descriptor" defined in PointNet [18], which can be aggregated with pointwise-maximum operation (a.k.a. maximum pooling). For each node o, the information or feature info(o) is the coarse shape descriptor of the points in its subtree.

We compute the information of each node layer-by-layer in a bottom-up order. For leaf nodes, the information is obtained by applying an MLP on the coordinates. For non-leaf nodes, the information is obtained by processing their left and right children nodes with a dimension-increasing linear transformation (defined on each layer), followed by aggregation with a pointwise-maximum operation, as the formula below:

$$\text{info}(o) = \begin{cases} \mathbf{MLP}(p(o)), & o \in L_d, \\ \mathbf{pointwise\text{-}max}(W_i\text{info}(o_l), W_i\text{info}(o_r)), & \text{otherwise.} \end{cases} \quad (2)$$

The encoder of PointTree can be regarded as a K-D tree-guided version of PointNet++, where at each stage of down-sampling, the points are clustered under some rule, and each cluster is down-sampled to one point with higher dimension. In PointTree, instead of some ad hoc clustering strategies used by PointNet++, K-D trees provide a native and principled way to cluster according to the spatial and neighborhood information, making it more powerful, general, and reliable. The output of the PointTree encoder is defined as $O = \{\text{info}(o) \mid o\}$.

3.2   Robustness Against Transformations

The robustness of PointTree against transformations mainly stems from our design of the division rule. Here, we discuss the robustness in more detail, introduce additional strategies that further improve the robustness, and propose a metric that quantifies the transformation intensity.

Similarity Transformation. PointTree uses relaxed K-D trees as its base tree, which holds the following lemma (the proof is in the supplementary material):

Lemma. If the rule to choose the division plane at each node is equivariant to similarity transformation σ, or more formally,

$$\textbf{choose-division-plane}(\sigma(P)) = \sigma(\textbf{choose-division-plane}(P)), \quad (3)$$

where **choose-division-plane**(P) is the procedure to choose the division plane on point set P, then the construction of the relaxed K-D tree is invariant to such a similarity transformation.

PointTree uses PCA to implement **choose-division-plane**(P), which is equivariant under any similarity transformation. As a result, our model is natively invariant to similarity transformations.

Affine (and Projective) Transformations. Interestingly, as empirically validated in Sect. 4, this invariance against similarity transformations enables Point-Tree also highly robust against affine and even more complicated projective transformations. To further improve the robustness to affine transformations, we introduce two additional strategies: pre-alignment and alignment network. Correspondingly, an input point cloud is fed forward the pre-alignment process and then the alignment network, before passing to our PointTree encoder (Fig. 2).

Pre-alignment: A Normalization for Affine Transformations. We design a PCA-based pre-alignment scheme as "normalization" of affine transformed point clouds. For a centered point cloud $P \in \mathbb{R}^{n \times 3}$, applying PCA obtains $P = U\textbf{diag}(\Sigma)V^T$, where U is a 3×3 matrix, Σ is a length-3 vector which can be regarded as scalings of each axis, and V is an orthogonal 3×3 matrix which can be regarded as a rotation. When we apply an affine transformation to a point cloud, the scaling and rotation can be arbitrary, and thus the normalization should not take these two pieces of information. So we disregard them in Σ and V, and take U as the normalized or pre-aligned point cloud (equivalent to normalizing P by applying another affine transformation $V\textbf{diag}(\Sigma^{-1})$). *Notably*, this pre-alignment scheme does not rely on the properties of K-D trees. As shown in Sect. 4, it is a general approach and can be used for a variety of existing point cloud encoders to improve their robustness. In our implementation, we found that applying pre-alignment *iteratively* further improves the performance, especially for part segmentation. Also, we have proven empirically that such a pre-alignment method is invariant to affine transformations. See the supplementary material for more details.

Alignment Network: A Learnable Component for Alignment. The pre-alignment is simply unlearnable. We also propose a *learnable* alignment network, inspired by PointNet [18]. This network takes a feature vector of a point cloud as input, feeds it into an MLP, and outputs a length-9 vector, which is reshaped to a 3×3 affine matrix to align the points. The encoder to generate the feature vector and the MLP are the learnable components of the alignment network.

The alignment network supports any encoder that outputs a feature vector, like a PointNet, another PointTree encoder, etc. Our default model uses the same architecture as "T-Net" in PointNet [18]. Note that such an alignment network is *not* designed for restoring the original point cloud (as a registration task). Instead, we only expect that it can learn to convert the input point cloud into an easier form for the following PointTree encoder. In Sect. 3.4, we also consider other variants of the alignment network that adopt different architectures.

Transformation Intensity Metric: Expected Angle Difference (EAD). To evaluate the intensity of a transformation, we propose a metric called expected angle difference (EAD). It is defined on two point clouds P and P' as follows: if we uniformly sample three different point indices $a, b, c \in [\|P\|]$, then the EAD is defined as the expected difference of $\angle P_b P_a P_c$ and $\angle P'_b P'_a P'_c$. Or,

$$\mathbf{EAD}(P, P') = \mathbb{E}_{a,b,c \in [\|P\|]} \left[\mathbf{angle\text{-}diff}(\angle P_b P_a P_c, \angle P'_b P'_a P'_c) \right]. \tag{4}$$

EAD is a metric for measuring the deformation of the transformed point cloud. By definition, similarity transformations hold $\mathbf{EAD}(P, P') = 0$, representing the minimum deformation – no deformation. Also, for the affine transformation which we randomly generated, the EAD is approximately $\frac{\pi}{8}$ (supplementary material). Meanwhile, the experiment shows that our pre-alignment scheme yields

$$\mathbf{EAD}(\mathbf{pre\text{-}align}(\mathbf{affine}_1(P)), \mathbf{pre\text{-}align}(\mathbf{affine}_2(P))) < 10^{-4}, \tag{5}$$

for any two affine transformations $\mathbf{affine}_1$ and $\mathbf{affine}_2$. This indicates that our pre-alignment is effective, which can normalize different affine transformations on a same point cloud to similar point clouds. More analysis about the EAD of transformations and pre-alignment methods are in the supplementary material.

3.3 Downstream Components

Classification: Point Cloud Features. In a classification task, each point cloud belongs to one class. Given a point cloud, the model should predict its class within all class candidates. For PointTree, the root node's information accounts for the whole point cloud, and we treat it as a global feature. We then build an MLP classifier that takes the root information $\text{info}(R)$ as input. The output will be the log-likelihood scores for C candidate classes (Fig. 2).

General Segmentation: Point Features with Top-Down Information Flow. In a general segmentation (e.g., part or semantic segmentation) task, for a given point cloud, each point belongs to one of C_S candidate classes. The model should classify all points in the given point cloud. We design a segmentation decoder following KD-Net [10], as shown in Fig. 4-b. The decoder is a K-D tree symmetric to the encoder. It follows a top-down flow, as opposite to the bottom-up flow in the encoder. Every node in the decoder has a feature called "carried information," representing the global-local relationship between inside and outside its subtree. Therefore, we can model the "role" of the subtree in the global shape. And when the node is leaf, it is exactly the "role" of the corresponding point in the global shape, which can be viewed as point feature.

Each node takes two inputs: the carried information from its ancestor, and the skip connection from the symmetric node in the encoder. The node merges these two inputs with one MLP, obtaining the carried information of itself. The top-down flow ends at leaf nodes and outputs the carried information of leaves. Such information is the feature of each point and is used for segmentation.

3.4 PointTree Variants

We introduce three variants of PointTree with different design of alignment networks and encoders. Note that, as mentioned in Sect. 3.2, the alignment network supports any encoder that outputs a point cloud feature. (1) **Default encoder ('Def')** uses T-Net in PointNet [18] as the alignment network. (2) **Encoder with K-D tree alignment ('KA')** introduces the default encoder as a stronger alignment network. (3) **ResNet-style encoder ('RNS')** is a ResNet-Style variant of PointTree with increased model capacity, by stacking more layers in a ResNet's style [8]. By connecting a default encoder and a general segmentation component, we can convert the $N \times 3$ input features to $N \times d$ intermediate features. We define such a connected structure as a "ResNet block," and stack a block followed by a default encoder to build a ResNet-style encoder. The output of each block is linked with the output of the previous block through a skip connection as in ResNet. For this variant, we can also treat the last encoder as the main encoder, and all previous encoders as part of the alignment network (since they mostly affect the input of the last encoder). The detailed architectures are shown and explained in the supplementary material.

4 Experiments

Transformations. We evaluate our model on affine and projective transformed versions of existing datasets, including ModelNet40 [27], ShapeNetPart [3], and S3DIS [2]. For a dataset $D = \{P\}$ and a random distribution T of transformations, we construct the T-transformed dataset as follows: for each $P \in D$, we sample a fixed number ("augment time") of transformations $\{t\}$, and add all $t(P)$ in the dataset. Different point clouds will be applied to different transformations. We perform such process for D_{train}, D_{val}, and D_{test} separately with some specific "augment time," obtaining a full transformed dataset.

Table 1. PointTree significantly outperforms state-of-the-art point cloud encoders under affine transformations for object classification (instance-level overall accuracy (%)) on the affine transformed ModelNet40 dataset. With the proposed pre-alignment ('PA'), the performance of all methods consistently improves, and PointTree still achieves the best result. The results of baselines are obtained by running publicly released code on the transformed dataset. In addition, PointTree's accuracy has a lower standard deviation on different affine transformed datasets (supplementary material)

Type	Method	Affine w/PA	Affine w/o PA
PointNet related	PointNet [18]	51.1	32.6
	PointNet++ [19]	72.7	47.8
K-D Tree-based	KD-Net [10]	65.3	23.1
	3DContextNet [33]	76.7	37.1
	PD-Net [31]	62.0	25.7
State-of-the-art	DGCNN [26]	79.4	57.4
	GBNet [20]	69.4	18.7
	GDANet [30]	72.8	15.6
	CurveNet [29]	82.1	59.3
	PointMLP [17]	82.3	63.1
	IT-Net [32] + DGCNN [26]	80.6	64.2
SO(3) Invariant/Equivariant	CloserLook [12]	82.4	64.9
	LGR-Net [36]	80.1	62.7
Ours	PointTree RNS	**84.1**	**73.1**

Baselines and PointTree Variants. For baseline models, we run the experiments with their official code by injecting the transformations into their data loaders. We keep their original optimal hyper-parameters, and train the models until convergence. We focus on four types of baselines: (i) PointNet related models (PointNet [18] and PointNet++ [19]), (ii) K-D tree-based models (KD-Net [10], 3DContextNet [33], and PD-Net [31]), (iii) recent state-of-the-art models (DGCNN [26], GBNet [20], GDANet [30], CurveNet [29], and PointMLP [17]), and (iv) SO(3) robust models (CloserLook [12] and LGR-Net [36]). As some baselines do not release their code on segmentation tasks, we only evaluate them on the classification task. We evaluate all three PointTree variants (Sect. 3.4).

Classification on ModelNet40. For the classification task, we evaluate our model on ModelNet40 [27]. ModelNet40 contains 9,843 point clouds for training and 2,468 point clouds for testing, and each of them belongs to one of 40 categories. We run the experiment on affine and projective transformations, and report the overall accuracy as our metric.

Affine Transformations. As shown in Table 1, our robust PointTree consistently outperforms all other point cloud models. Notably, PointTree significantly outperforms other models in the setting of affine without pre-alignment by at least 8.2%. This clearly shows that PointTree has much higher robustness against affine transformations. Our accuracy is also 8% and 36% higher than 3DContextNet [33], the previous best K-D tree-based model, in settings of affine with

Table 2. PointTree is robust even on the highly-challenging projective transformed ModelNet40 dataset, with and without pre-alignment ('PA'). It significantly outperforms all other models with a huge gap of 25% at instance-level accuracy (%) in the setting without pre-alignment

Method	Projective w/PA	Projective w/o PA
PointNet	15.4	4.3
DGCNN	47.3	6.2
PointMLP	49.9	4.1
CurveNet	37.6	5.6
PointTree RNS	**62.1**	**31.8**

Table 3. Ablation study results show that both pre-alignment ('PA') and alignment network improve our accuracy on ModelNet. Among the three variants, RNS achieves the best performance, but all of them outperform baselines in Table 1. Also, relaxed K-D tree is crucial for the transformation robustness in PointTree

Method			ModelNet40 Affine
PointTree RNS	w/ PA		84.1
PointTree KA	w/ PA		83.4
PointTree Def	w/ PA		82.7
PointTree RNS	w/o PA		73.1
PointTree KA	w/o PA		71.7
PointTree Def	w/o PA		70.2
PointTree Def	w/ PA	w/o Alignment Network	82.4
PointTree Def	w/ PA	w/ Original K-D Tree	68.8
PointTree RNS	w/ PA	w/ Concatenate-MLP	79.3

and without pre-alignment, respectively. This validates that the relaxed K-D tree is crucial to achieving the robustness that the original K-D tree is unable to. In addition, PD-Net [31] uses a similar PCA-based relaxed K-D tree as ours, but its design of feature aggregation highly relies on coordinates (by using the normal vector of children nodes' division plane), which wastes and nullifies the affine robustness of the tree structure, yielding a 22.1% worse accuracy than ours. Our method also consistently outperforms the SO(3) robust baselines, showing that the SO(3) robustness is not sufficient for coping with affine transformations.

Finally, by comparing the settings of affine with and without pre-alignment, we observe an at least 10% improvement in accuracy when applying pre-alignment in each baseline. This shows that pre-alignment is a general and effective approach to normalizing affine transformed point clouds.

Projective Transformations. Table 2 shows the accuracy of our model and top baselines on the projective transformed ModelNet40 dataset. In this experiment, PointTree significantly outperforms all baselines by at least 12% in the setting with pre-alignment, and more than 25% in the setting without pre-alignment. For the most challenging setting, projective ModelNet40 without pre-alignment,

Table 4. PointTree significantly outperforms baselines for part segmentation on affine transformed ShapeNetPart with pre-alignment, increasing class-level mIoU (%) by 7%

Method	airplane	bag	cap	car	chair	earphone	guitar	knife	lamp	laptop	motorbike	mug	pistol	rocket	skateboard	table	mIoU
PointNet [18]	69.7	53.5	57.8	59.2	84.1	44.9	62.9	41.7	61.9	64.5	31.8	71.0	50.3	35.4	46.1	76.6	56.9
PointNet++ [19]	66.5	73.7	58.6	37.6	72.0	71.5	85.9	74.4	72.5	51.0	29.1	74.9	54.1	41.6	57.1	71.9	62.1
DGCNN [26]	**89.0**	71.3	**91.2**	33.7	11.7	**94.3**	84.6	67.5	72.6	**92.9**	10.3	84.1	**83.7**	35.1	62.9	**97.3**	67.6
GDANet [30]	76.4	74.3	78.3	59.1	84.4	72.7	86.7	75.9	74.0	70.0	31.1	89.5	65.7	53.8	**75.6**	79.5	71.7
CurveNet [29]	75.8	64.7	79.3	60.7	86.9	59.5	86.2	72.4	74.8	69.3	24.6	89.5	63.5	39.2	60.1	78.4	67.8
PointTree RNS	83.6	**74.7**	82.5	**80.4**	**90.6**	66.5	**92.1**	**84.0**	**82.0**	88.3	**56.0**	**95.4**	78.0	**55.4**	68.9	81.2	**78.7**

Table 5. PointTree consistently outperforms state of the art for large-scale semantic segmentation on S3DIS, with notable margins of 2.2% and 6.7% on affine and projective transformed datasets, respectively, in overall accuracy (%) of Area5

Method	Affine w/PA	Affine w/o PA	Projective w/PA	Projective w/o PA
PointNet [18]	64.9	69.1	49.3	31.1
DGCNN [26]	80.0	70.8	67.1	57.8
PointTree Def	**82.2**	**74.9**	**73.8**	**61.2**

PointTree still achieves a reasonable accuracy, while all other baselines can only obtain an accuracy that is a little higher than random guess.

Ablation Study. From the ablation study results in Table 3, we have the following observations. (1) By comparing the accuracy of the three PointTree variants in settings with and without pre-alignment, we observe that pre-alignment is helpful for our already-robust PointTree. (2) The three variants – Def, KA, and RNS – can be also interpreted as different types of the "alignment network" component in PointTree, from simplest to the most sophisticated. By comparing their accuracy, along with the variant "PointTree Def w/o Alignment Network," we can find that the improvement in alignment networks leads to higher accuracy. (3) RNS is the most powerful variant, due to its multiple layers and intermediate features. *Notably,* even the other variants have lower accuracy than RNS, they still outperform all the baselines in Table 1. (4) When we replace the relaxed K-D tree with the original K-D tree in PointTree, the performance experiences a dramatical drop by more than 10%. This indicates that the relaxed K-D tree is crucial for the robustness against transformations. (5) When we replace the implementation of **merge-info** from pointwise-maximum in Formula (2) to concatenate-MLP (concatenate o_l and o_r and apply an MLP), the accuracy clearly drops, showing that pointwise-maximum is a critical design choice.

Part Segmentation on ShapeNetPart. We test PointTree for the point cloud part segmentation task on ShapeNetPart [3]. It contains 16,881 point clouds in 16 classes. Each point belongs to one of 50 parts, where different classes have different sets of parts. We report the class-level mean intersection over union (mIoU) as the accuracy. Figure 5 visualizes two point clouds with PointTree and PointNet [18] as baseline. In both cases, the pre-alignment successfully normalizes the very flat affine transformed point cloud into a reasonable shape. For the

| Original (GT) | Affine (GT) | Affine w/ PA (GT) | Baseline (PointNet) | PointTree |

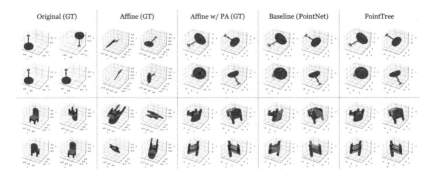

Fig. 5. Visualization of two point clouds in ShapeNetPart, showing that pre-alignment can successfully normalize the highly-deformed point clouds under affine transformations into reasonable shapes, and that PointTree works almost perfectly in this setting. Each grid of the table contains 4 point of views of a same point cloud. The third column shows the pre-aligned point clouds of the second column. The point clouds in first 3 columns are colored according to ground truth ('GT') segmentation, while last 2 columns are colored according to the segmentation outputs of PointNet and PointTree

lamp case, both PointNet and PointTree make a small mistake at the center of the lamp top (which is marked blue but should be green), while PointTree is more accurate at the bottom of the light pole. For the chair case, PointNet is performing badly, while our PointTree's accuracy is almost perfect.

Table 4 shows the segmentation results on affine transformed ShapeNetPart with pre-alignment. Our PointTree achieves a top mIoU over all baselines with an increase of more than 7%, and achieves best IoUs for more than half of the classes. This shows that PointTree is a general-purpose encoder that can work in both classification and segmentation tasks, being significantly more robust than other models. The results on projective transformed ShapeNetPart in the supplementary material demonstrate similar observations.

Semantic Segmentation on S3DIS. Table 5 shows the semantic segmentation results on affine and projective transformed S3DIS [2] in settings with and without pre-alignment. Our PointTree achieves a top Area 5 overall accuracy over all baselines by large margins of at least 2.2%. PointTree is thus not only robust in simple single-object point cloud tasks like ModelNet40 and ShapeNetPart, but is also robust in complicated multi-object point cloud tasks like S3DIS.

5   Conclusion

In this paper, we proposed PointTree, a general-purpose point cloud encoder that is highly robust against affine and projective transformations. The key insight of PointTree is the use of relaxed K-D trees with PCA-induced similarity transformation-invariant construction. We further introduced pre-alignment, an effective and model-agnostic normalization scheme. Empirical evaluation shows that PointTree significantly outperforms state-of-the-art methods on various transformed datasets for classification and segmentation tasks. Notably, under affine transformations, the combination of PointTree with pre-alignment even achieves an accuracy that is close to the accuracy on the canonicalized point clouds. We hope our work could inspire more efforts on developing robust point cloud analysis models, and promote better exploitation of powerful K-D trees.

Acknowledgement. This work was supported in part by NSF Grant 2106825, the Jump ARCHES endowment through the Health Care Engineering Systems Center, the New Frontiers Initiative, the National Center for Supercomputing Applications (NCSA) at the University of Illinois at Urbana-Champaign through the NCSA Fellows program, and the IBM-Illinois Discovery Accelerator Institute.

References

1. Agarwal, P.K., Arge, L., Danner, A.: From point cloud to grid DEM: A scalable approach. In: International Symposium on Spatial Data Handling (2006)
2. Armeni, I., Sax, A., Zamir, A.R., Savarese, S.: Joint 2D-3D-semantic data for indoor scene understanding. arXiv: 1702.01105 (2017)
3. Chang, A.X., et al.: ShapeNet: An information-rich 3D model repository. arXiv: 1512.03012 (2015)
4. Duch, A., Estivill-Castro, V., Martinez, C.: Randomized K-dimensional binary search trees. In: International Symposium on Algorithms and Computation (1998)
5. Gadelha, M., Wang, R., Maji, S.: Multiresolution tree networks for 3D point cloud processing. arxiv: 1807.03520 (2018)
6. Geiger, A., Lenz, P., Urtasun, R.: Are we ready for autonomous driving? The KITTI vision benchmark suite. In: CVPR (2012)
7. Guo, Y., Wang, H., Hu, Q., Liu, H., Liu, L.: Bennamoun: Deep learning for 3D point clouds: A survey. IEEE Trans. Pattern Anal. Mach. Intell. **43**(12), 4338–4364 (2021)
8. He, K., Zhang, X., Ren, S., Sun, J.: Deep residual learning for image recognition. In: CVPR (2016)
9. Klein, G., Murray, D.: Parallel tracking and mapping for small AR workspaces. In: IEEE and ACM International Symposium on Mixed and Augmented Reality (2007)
10. Klokov, R., Lempitsky, V.: Escape from cells: Deep Kd-Networks for the recognition of 3D point cloud models. In: ICCV (2017)
11. Lei, H., Akhtar, N., Mian, A.S.: Octree guided CNN with spherical kernels for 3D point clouds. In: CVPR (2019)
12. Li, F., Fujiwara, K., Okura, F., Matsushita, Y.: A closer look at rotation-invariant deep point cloud analysis. In: ICCV (2021)
13. Li, X., Li, R., Chen, G., Fu, C.W., Cohen-Or, D., Heng, P.A.: A rotation-invariant framework for deep point cloud analysis. IEEE Trans. Vis. Comput. Graph. 4503–4514 (2021)
14. Li, Y., Bu, R., Sun, M., Wu, W., Di, X., Chen, B.: PointCNN: Convolution on X-transformed points. In: NeurIPS (2018)
15. Liu, Y., Fan, B., Meng, G., Lu, J., Xiang, S., Pan, C.: DensePoint: Learning densely contextual representation for efficient point cloud processing. In: ICCV (2019)

16. Lv, X., Wang, B., Dou, Z., Ye, D., Wang, S.: LCCNet: LiDAR and camera self-calibration using cost volume network. In: CVPRW (2021)
17. Ma, X., Qin, C., You, H., Ran, H., Fu, Y.: Rethinking network design and local geometry in point cloud: A simple residual MLP framework. In: ICLR (2022)
18. Qi, C.R., Su, H., Kaichun, M., Guibas, L.J.: PointNet: Deep learning on point sets for 3D classification and segmentation. In: CVPR (2017)
19. Qi, C.R., Yi, L., Su, H., Guibas, L.J.: PointNet++: Deep hierarchical feature learning on point sets in a metric space. In: NeurIPS (2017)
20. Qiu, S., Anwar, S., Barnes, N.: Geometric feedback network for point cloud classification. arXiv: 1911.12885 (2019)
21. Que, Z., Lu, G., Xu, D.: VoxelContext-Net: An octree based framework for point cloud compression. arXiv: 2105.02158 (2021)
22. Riegler, G., Ulusoy, A., Geiger, A.: OctNet: Learning deep 3D representations at high resolutions. In: CVPR (2017)
23. Shen, W., Zhang, B., Huang, S., Wei, Z., Zhang, Q.: 3D-rotation-equivariant quaternion neural networks. In: Vedaldi, A., Bischof, H., Brox, T., Frahm, J.-M. (eds.) ECCV 2020. LNCS, vol. 12365, pp. 531–547. Springer, Cham (2020). https://doi.org/10.1007/978-3-030-58565-5_32
24. Siekański, P., Paśko, S., Malowany, K., Malesa, M.: Online correction of the mutual miscalibration of multimodal VIS-IR sensors and 3D data on a UAV platform for surveillance applications. Remote Sensing 11(21) (2019)
25. Sun, J., Zhang, Q., Kailkhura, B., Yu, Z., Xiao, C., Mao, Z.M.: Benchmarking robustness of 3D point cloud recognition against common corruptions. arXiv: 2201.12296 (2022)
26. Wang, Y., Sun, Y., Liu, Z., Sarma, S.E., Bronstein, M.M., Solomon, J.M.: Dynamic graph CNN for learning on point clouds. ACM Trans. Graph. 38(5) (2019)
27. Wu, Z., Song, S., Khosla, A., Tang, X., Xiao, J.: 3D shapenets for 2.5D object recognition and next-best-view prediction. arXiv: 1406.5670 (2014)
28. Xiang, B., Tu, J., Yao, J., Li, L.: A novel octree-based 3-D fully convolutional neural network for point cloud classification in road environment. IEEE Trans. Geosci. Remote Sens. 57(10), 7799–7818 (2019)
29. Xiang, T., Zhang, C., Song, Y., Yu, J., Cai, W.: Walk in the cloud: Learning curves for point clouds shape analysis. In: ICCV (2021)
30. Xu, M., Zhang, J., Zhou, Z., Xu, M., Qi, X., Qiao, Y.: Learning geometry-disentangled representation for complementary understanding of 3D object point cloud. In: AAAI (2021)
31. Yi, L., et al.: Large-scale 3D shape reconstruction and segmentation from ShapeNet Core55. arXiv: 1710.06104 (2017)
32. Yuan, W., Held, D., Mertz, C., Hebert, M.: Iterative transformer network for 3D point cloud. arXiv: 1811.11209 (2018)
33. Zeng, W., Gevers, T.: 3DContextNet: K-d tree guided hierarchical learning of point clouds using local and global contextual cues. In: Leal-Taixé, L., Roth, S. (eds.) ECCV 2018. LNCS, vol. 11131, pp. 314–330. Springer, Cham (2019). https://doi.org/10.1007/978-3-030-11015-4_24
34. Zhang, X., Zhu, S., Guo, S., Li, J., Liu, H.: Line-based automatic extrinsic calibration of lidar and camera. In: ICRA (2021)
35. Zhang, Y., Rabbat, M.G.: A graph-CNN for 3D point cloud classification. In: ICASSP (2018)
36. Zhao, C., Yang, J., Xiong, X., Zhu, A., Cao, Z., Li, X.: Rotation invariant point cloud classification: Where local geometry meets global topology. Pattern Recogn. 127(C) (2019)

UNIF: United Neural Implicit Functions for Clothed Human Reconstruction and Animation

Shenhan Qian[1,2], Jiale Xu[2], Ziwei Liu[3], Liqian Ma[1(✉)],
and Shenghua Gao[2,4,5]

[1] ZMO AI Inc., Guangzhou, China
[2] ShanghaiTech University, Shanghai, China
{qianshh,xujl1,gaoshh}@shanghaitech.edu.cn
[3] S-Lab, Nanyang Technological University, Singapore, Singapore
[4] Shanghai Engineering Research Center of Intelligent Vision and Imaging,
Shanghai, China
[5] Shanghai Engineering Research Center of Energy Efficient and Custom AI IC,
Shanghai, China

Abstract. We propose united implicit functions (UNIF), a part-based method for clothed human reconstruction and animation with raw scans and skeletons as the input. Previous part-based methods for human reconstruction rely on ground-truth part labels from SMPL and thus are limited to minimal-clothed humans. In contrast, our method learns to separate parts from body motions instead of part supervision, thus can be extended to clothed humans and other articulated objects. Our Partition-from-Motion is achieved by a bone-centered initialization, a bone limit loss, and a section normal loss that ensure stable part division even when the training poses are limited. We also present a minimal perimeter loss for SDF to suppress extra surfaces and part overlapping. Another core of our method is an adjacent part seaming algorithm that produces non-rigid deformations to maintain the connection between parts which significantly relieves the part-based artifacts. Under this algorithm, we further propose "Competing Parts", a method that defines blending weights by the relative position of a point to bones instead of the absolute position, avoiding the generalization problem of neural implicit functions with inverse LBS (linear blend skinning). We demonstrate the effectiveness of our method by clothed human body reconstruction and animation on the CAPE and the ClothSeq datasets. Our code is available at https://github.com/ShenhanQian/UNIF.git.

Keywords: Clothed human reconstruction · Neural implicit functions · Shape representation · Non-rigid deformation

S. Qian—Work conducted during an internship at ZMO AI Inc.

Supplementary Information The online version contains supplementary material available at https://doi.org/10.1007/978-3-031-20062-5_8.

S. Avidan et al. (Eds.): ECCV 2022, LNCS 13663, pp. 121–137, 2022.
https://doi.org/10.1007/978-3-031-20062-5_8

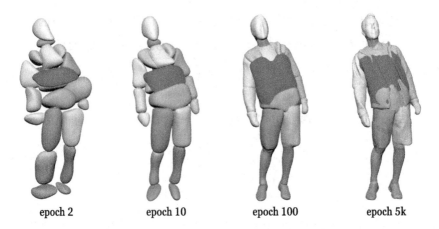

Fig. 1. The evolution of the learned parts of our model.

1   Introduction

As residents of the 21st century, we are embracing a new life in the virtual world, digitizing everything around us. Recent research interest in human body reconstruction and animation increases dramatically. A popular human body model is SMPL [16], which models minimal-clothed human bodies across genders and figures. Later methods extend SMPL [16] to the clothed human body by overlying vertex offsets [14,18] or attaching template clothing meshes [25]. However, for complex clothes, the fixed topology of SMPL [16] mesh and the predefined template clothing limit the expressiveness. Recently, the rise of neural implicit representations [5,19,24] indicates a higher modeling fidelity and flexibility. These models take in a point position and output an indicator of the geometry such as occupancy and SDF (signed distance function), theoretically supporting an infinitely high resolution. The infinity of resolution is perfect for fidelity but a disaster for skinning since we can no longer store the LBS (linear blend skinning) weights for every point. Although recent methods use another neural implicit function to learn the weights [20,27,30,31], they generalize poorly under unseen poses because the LBS weights of a point vary along with the pose.

Besides learning a whole shape and deforming it with LBS, we can also model an object with separate parts. NASA [6] models the human body with several occupancy networks, each of which is bound to a joint. Therefore, when the skeleton moves, the learned shape is articulated. However, a key limitation of NASA [6] and later part-based methods [1,15] is that they rely on SMPL's LBS weights for part division, therefore still limited to minimal-clothed human reconstruction. Another shortage of previous part-based methods is that they model the non-rigid deformation crudely by simply feeding the positions of posed joints or similar pose descriptors into the networks. This results in an overfitted model that produces artifacts under novel poses especially when the training poses are limited.

To push the boundary of part-based methods, we propose UNIF (united neural implicit functions), a method that learns the shape of an object with multiple neural implicit functions. Our method features two novelties: 1) UNIF learns to decouple parts from a whole shape with no need for ground-truth partition labels; 2) UNIF models non-rigid deformations by considering the interaction between parts.

To illustrate the basic idea of automatic part division, let us consider an arm moving relative to the body. For a part-based method, we expect the arm and the body to be modeled by two separate networks. In case they are captured by one network, they will always move as a rigid one, then the model will not be able to reconstruct the same shape when the arm moves. Therefore, when minimizing the surface reconstruction loss with changing poses, we are pushing the networks to converge into separate rigid parts. We call this process *Partition-from-Motion*. However, when the training poses are limited, *e.g.*, the subject in the raw scans never moves the arms, then there will be no driving force to decouple the arm from the body. This is not a big issue for reconstruction but unacceptable for novel-pose animation since the arms can never move. To ensure a good body partition when the training poses are limited, we propose a bone limit loss and a section normal loss that constrain the boundary and the normal of each part by its neighboring joints. These terms significantly enhance the stability of our Partition-from-Motion. Furthermore, motivated by PHASE [12], we derive a minimal perimeter loss on SDF to suppress extra parts and hidden surfaces, which also contributes to a high-quality reconstruction.

Partition-from-Motion helps us separate rigid parts, but this is insufficient because non-rigid deformations are not negligible for human bodies and clothes. We propose an APS (adjacent part seaming) algorithm that deforms points to maintain the connection between parts. APS greatly relieves artifacts such as cracks and exposure of hidden surfaces. Alike other non-rigid deformation algorithms, APS also needs to define the blending weights of a point. Differently, we define blending weights not by the absolute position but by the relative position of a point to each bone and the competition between bones. Such a local definition of blending weights avoids overfitting of absolute positions, generalizing better to unseen poses.

Overall, our contributions can be summarized as:

- We propose united neural implicit functions (UNIF) for clothed human reconstruction and animation from raw scan sequences.
- We decouple rigid parts without partition labels and enhance the robustness with carefully designed initialization and regularization strategies.
- We design an adjacent part seaming (APS) algorithm for non-rigid deformation based on a localized definition of blending weights (Competing Parts).
- We show the effectiveness of our method by clothed human reconstruction and animation on the CAPE [18] and the ClothSeq [31] dataset.

2   Related Work

Our method adopts compound neural implicit functions for human body reconstruction and animation with special attention to part division and non-rigid deformation.

2.1   Neural Implicit Functions

Compared to classic geometry representations such as meshes, point clouds, and voxels that are stored as discrete elements, neural implicit functions [2,5,9,19,21,24] are stored with neural networks. They take in the coordinate of a point and output an indicator of geometry, appearance, or other properties. Early methods need dense supervision of occupancy or SDF [5,19,24]. Later works make it possible to learn smooth surfaces with sparse supervision [2,9,12]. SAL [2] proposes a geometric initialization to realize signed distance learning with unsigned ground-truth data. Benefitting from the Eikonal loss to maintain a valid SDF field, IGR [9] only takes raw scans or triangle soups as the input. Lipman *et al.* [12] unifies SDF and occupancy and proposes a minimal perimeter loss to encourage tight surfaces. Our method follows this line of methods for its lower requirement for the data. It is also possible to model a scene or an object from 2D images without explicitly decoupling the geometry, appearance, and lighting condition [21,22,32–34]. For the usage of compound implicit functions, existing trials mainly lie in template-based shape learning [7,8].

2.2   Human Body Reconstruction and Animation

As the most popular mesh-based human body model, SMPL [16] and its variations [11,26,29] dominate the area of human body reconstruction for its expressiveness and flexibility, supporting innumerable downstream task [2,9,13,14,25, 27,28]. Since the new trend of neural implicit functions for shape learning, several papers [1,4,6,15,20] have attempted to substitute SMPL with an implicit counterpart for higher fidelity and flexibility. Besides the minimal-clothed human body, later works also use neural implicit functions to model clothed humans [23,27,28,30,31].

For body animation, there exist two types of pose representation - latent vector and skeleton. SAL [2], IGR [9], and NPMs [23] model body poses with a latent space, which is especially useful when no skeleton is available. But they only support interpolation between poses instead of direct animation. As to pose interpolation in the latent space, Atzmon et al. [3] regularize the deformation field concerning the latent vector to maintain the as-rigid-as-possible property.

Among the skeleton-based methods, the mainstream practice is to learn a canonical shape and animate it with LBS (linear blend skinning). However, since a neural implicit function lacks point-wise correspondences, a forward and a backward skinning network are introduced [20,27,30,31] to save LBS weights for the bidirectional mapping between a posed shape and the canonical shape. The main limitation here is the poor generalization ability of inverse LBS since the LBS weights vary when the pose changes. SCANimate [30] and LEAP [20] use the cycle consistency to regularize the learned neural skinning weights. In contrast, SNARF [4] only learns the stable forward skinning weights and solves backward skinning by iteratively minimizing the cycle consistency error.

Aside from LBS-based methods, another series of methods model the human body with separate parts. NASA [6] merges the output of a group of occupancy

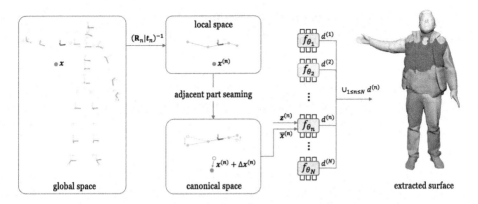

Fig. 2. The pipeline of our method. Given a point x, we first transform it into the local space of each bone and then apply our adjacent part seaming algorithm to obtain its position $\bar{x}^{(n)}$ in the canonical space of the n-th bone. Each neural implicit function takes the position $\bar{x}^{(n)}$ and a pose condition vector $z^{(n)}$ to predict the SDF value of a part $d^{(n)}$. The final output of our method is the union of all output.

networks, each anchored on a joint of the body. Both LatentHuman [15] and imGHUM [1] train combinational signed distance functions on muti-subject data. LatentHuman [15] pays special attention to relieve part based artifacts, while imGHUM [1] provides additional controllability on hands and expressions. A common feature of the above part-based methods is that they all rely on the LBS weights of SMPL to partite the body. In contrast, we learn part division from body motion. As to the non-rigid deformation, previous part-based methods [6,15] simply feed skeleton states as an input of networks, leading to limited pose generalization ability.

3   United Neural Implicit Functions

The input of our method is a sequence of point clouds, which captures the shapes of a person in varying poses. For each frame, we fit the body skeleton (*e.g.*, the skeleton of SMPL [16]) represented by the orientations and translations of body joints. Then, we set up local coordinate systems based on the skeleton and learn a neural implicit function in each local space.

We illustrate the pipeline of our method in Fig. 2. For a point x in the global space, we first transform it to the local space of each bone and get $x^{(n)}$. Then we deform the point by an offset $\Delta x^{(n)}$ with an adjacent part seaming (APS) algorithm and get its position $\bar{x}^{(n)}$ in the canonical space of the n-th bone. Finally, we feed the position $\bar{x}^{(n)}$ and a pose condition vector $z^{(n)}$ to each neural implicit function and take the union of their output.

3.1   Shape Representation and Learning

Our united neural implicit functions are based on IGR [9], which adopts a single neural network to model the surface of an object. Given a point cloud $\mathcal{X} = \{\boldsymbol{x}_i\}_{i \in I} \subset \mathbb{R}^3$ and corresponding surface normals $\mathcal{N} = \{\boldsymbol{n}_i\}_{i \in I} \subset \mathbb{R}^3$, IGR [9] optimizes the parameters θ of an MLP $f_\theta(\boldsymbol{x})$ to approximate the signed distance function of the surface behind the point cloud $\mathcal{X}$ with the loss

$$\mathcal{L} = \mathcal{L}_{\mathrm{recon}} + \lambda_{\mathrm{unit}} \mathcal{L}_{\mathrm{unit}}, \tag{1}$$

where

$$\mathcal{L}_{\mathrm{recon}} = \frac{1}{|I|} \sum_{i \in I} \left(|f_\theta(\boldsymbol{x}_i)| + \lambda_{\mathrm{normal}} \left\| \nabla_{\boldsymbol{x}} f_\theta(\boldsymbol{x}_i) - \boldsymbol{n}_i \right\|_2 \right), \tag{2}$$

$$\mathcal{L}_{\mathrm{unit}} = \mathbb{E}_{\boldsymbol{x}} \left(\left\| \nabla_{\boldsymbol{x}} f_\theta(\boldsymbol{x}) \right\|_2 - 1 \right)^2. \tag{3}$$

$\mathcal{L}_{\mathrm{recon}}$ supervises the zero-level set of f to go across $\mathcal{X}$ with the given normals $\mathcal{N}$. $\mathcal{L}_{\mathrm{unit}}$ encourages the gradient of f to be unit-norm, which is necessary for a signed distance function.

For our UNIF model, we use N ($N = 20$) separate MLPs $(f_{\theta_1}, \ldots, f_{\theta_N})$, each learns the SDF of a body part. Given a point $\boldsymbol{x}$ from the input point cloud $\mathcal{X}$, the output of UNIF is

$$d = \cup_{1 \leq n \leq N} d^{(n)}, \quad \text{with } d^{(n)} = f_{\theta_n} \left(\boldsymbol{x}^{(n)} \right). \tag{4}$$

$\cup$ is an union operation on the output of all networks. Geometrically, the union of multiple signed distance functions is the minimum of all:

$$d = \min_{1 \leq n \leq N} d^{(n)}. \tag{5}$$

To ease learning and enhance robustness, we use an improved union operation, which is presented in the supplementary material. $\boldsymbol{x}^{(n)}$ is the local point position for the n-th part with

$$\boldsymbol{x}^{(n)} = \mathbf{R}_n^T (\boldsymbol{x} - \boldsymbol{t}_n), \tag{6}$$

where $\mathbf{R}_n$ and $\boldsymbol{t}_n$ are the global orientation and translation of the n-th coordinate system.

Finally, the supervision on our UNIF model becomes

$$\mathcal{L} = \mathcal{L}_{\mathrm{recon}} + \lambda_{\mathrm{unit}} \mathcal{L}_{\mathrm{unit}}, \tag{7}$$

where

$$\mathcal{L}_{\mathrm{recon}} = \frac{1}{|I|} \sum_{i \in I} \left(|d| + \lambda_{\mathrm{normal}} \left\| \nabla_{\boldsymbol{x}} d - \boldsymbol{n}_i \right\|_2 \right) \quad (\lambda_{\mathrm{normal}} = 0.01), \tag{8}$$

$$\mathcal{L}_{\mathrm{unit}} = \mathbb{E}_{\boldsymbol{x}} \left(\left\| \nabla_{\boldsymbol{x}} d \right\|_2 - 1 \right)^2 + \frac{1}{N} \sum_{n=1}^{N} \mathbb{E}_{\boldsymbol{x}} \left(\left\| \nabla_{\boldsymbol{x}} d^{(n)} \right\|_2 - 1 \right)^2. \tag{9}$$

The unit-gradient-norm loss $\mathcal{L}_{\mathrm{unit}}$ has two terms. The first term is applied on the SDF after the union operation (d), and the second term is applied on the output of each part ($d^{(n)}$). Both are necessary according to our experiments.

(a) Bone-centered initialization. Each neural implicit function is initialized to a small sphere at the center of a bone.

(b) Bone limit loss and section normal loss. The boundary (in red) and section normals (in blue) of a part are constrained by its neighboring joints.

Fig. 3. Improving Partition-from-Motion with skeleton-based priors.

3.2   Partition-from-Motion

Unlike previous methods [1,6,15] that use ground-truth partition labels from SMPL [16], we exploit separating parts automatically while learning the entire shape. The key to achieving this is using SDF instead of occupancy because occupancy is constantly zero for locations away from the surface, while SDF provides distance information so that we can determine which part is closer to the query point and then optimize that part to go across the point. This reveals an implicit hypothesis of our method: a point should be assigned to the closest part to it. However, the SDF of a part is randomly initialized and thus may not provide correct distance information at the beginning of training. Therefore, we propose a bone-centered initialization.

Bone-Centered Initialization. We set up local coordinate systems at the center of bones and use the geometric initialization [2] to turn each part into a small sphere ($r = 0.01$) at the bone center (Fig. 3a). Then, parts are not intersected, and the SDF of a part approximately equals the distance to the bone center. This ensures that most points are assigned to the right part when training begins.

Bone Limit Loss and Section Normal Loss. With a proper initialization, we can already separate parts, but the quality and stability of body partition highly depend on the variance of training poses. For example, when two parts barely have relative motions in the training set, they are at high risk of overlapping. This leads to artifacts when the model is animated under novel poses. Therefore, we propose a bone limit loss

$$\mathcal{L}_{\text{lim}} = \frac{1}{N \cdot |J^{(n)}|} \sum_{n=1}^{N} \sum_{j \in J^{(n)}} \left| d_j^{(n)} \right|, \tag{10}$$

and a section normal loss

$$\mathcal{L}_{\text{sec}} = \frac{1}{N \cdot |J^{(n)}|} \sum_{n=1}^{N} \sum_{j \in J^{(n)}} \left\| \nabla_x d_j^{(n)} - n_j^{(n)} \right\|_2, \tag{11}$$

where $J^{(n)}$ is the n-th bone's adjacent joints and $\left|J^{(n)}\right|$ is the number of its adjacent joints; $d_j^{(n)}$ is the predicted SDF at joint j; $\boldsymbol{n}_j^{(n)}$ is the section normal at joint j derived from the angle between adjacent bones. As illustrated by Fig. 3b, these two terms utilize the positions of joints as a prior to limit the range of a part along the axis of its bone and the normal of the sections.

Minimal Perimeter Loss. In experiments, our method often produces artifacts like extra surfaces, which are due to the insufficiency of the IGR [9] loss. Considering Eq. (1), the reconstruction term $\mathcal{L}_{\text{recon}}$ ensures a zero value at the positions of raw scans and the unit-norm term $\mathcal{L}_{\text{unit}}$ regularize the gradient of the neural field, but neither punish extra surfaces where no scan points lie. Inspired by PHASE [12], we propose a minimal perimeter loss specifically for SDF:

$$\mathcal{L}_{\text{perim}} = \mathbb{E}_{\boldsymbol{x}} \left\| \nabla_{\boldsymbol{x}} \sigma(d) \right\|^2 + \frac{1}{N} \sum_{n=1}^{N} \mathbb{E}_{\boldsymbol{x}} \left\| \nabla_{\boldsymbol{x}} \sigma(d^{(n)}) \right\|^2, \tag{12}$$

where $\sigma(x) = \frac{1}{1+e^{-\beta x}}$ (we use $\beta = 10$). This minimal perimeter loss $\mathcal{L}_{\text{perim}}$ is applied both globally and locally, similar to $\mathcal{L}_{\text{unit}}$. The global term ensures the tightness of the overall shape, while the local term suppresses the extra surfaces hidden behind the overall shape. We leave further discussion of this loss in the supplementary material.

3.3   Adjacent Part Seaming

Now, we are able to learn separate parts automatically with proper initialization and regularization. But be aware that the entire model is moving as rigid parts, obviously insufficient for either human bodies or clothes. To support non-rigid deformation, previous part-based methods [1,6,15] feed a descriptor of joints into networks. We construct a similar descriptor by first transforming the orientation matrices and translation vectors of all joints into each part's local space, then flattening and concatenating them into a pose condition vector

$$\boldsymbol{z}^{(n)} = \oplus_{1 \leq j \leq N} \left(\mathbf{R}_n^T \mathbf{R}_j \oplus \mathbf{R}_n^T \left(\boldsymbol{t}_j - \boldsymbol{t}_n \right) \right), \tag{13}$$

where $\mathbf{R}_n$ and $\boldsymbol{t}_n$ are the orientation and translation of the n-th bone; $\mathbf{R}_j$ and $\boldsymbol{t}_j$ are the orientation and translation of the j-th joint; N is the number of parts and $\oplus$ refers to vector concatenation. Then, our neural implicit functions become

$$d^{(n)} = f_{\theta_n} \left(\boldsymbol{x}^{(n)}, \boldsymbol{z}^{(n)} \right), 1 \leq n \leq N. \tag{14}$$

The above pose descriptor does help the network fit the training sequence but generalizes poorly to unseen poses. As demonstrated in recent comparisons [4, 31], part-based models always produce broken parts in unseen poses.

Then, can we make non-rigid deformations of part-based models generalizable to unseen poses? Here is an observation: when two linked parts have a relative rotation ((Fig. 4a), some regions are squeezed while others are stretched. We believe that explicitly modeling the phenomenon is the key to relieving part-based artifacts. Therefore, we propose the adjacent part seaming (APS) algorithm.

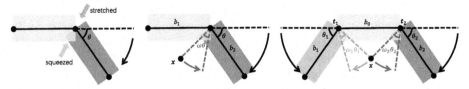

(a) Relative rotation of two linked parts. (b) Part seaming for two bones. (c) Part seaming for three and more bones

Fig. 4. 2D examples to illustrate the process of part seaming.

Adjacent Part Seaming by Local Rotations. Considering a point x on the bone b_1 (Fig. 4b), the adjacent bone b_2 has rotated for an angle θ from the rest pose. What we pursue is the original position of x in the rest pose. If the bone b_1 is infinitely rigid, then the point x on b_1 would not have moved no matter the rotation angle of b_2. Otherwise, x should have rotated for an angle of $w\theta$, where $0 < w < 1$ (we assume the blending weight w known at the moment and will discuss it later). Then, we can obtain the original position of x under the rest pose by

$$\bar{x} = \mathbf{R}_{w\theta}^T x, \tag{15}$$

where $\mathbf{R}_{w\theta}$ is the corresponding rotation matrix for $w\theta$. While we use a 2D example for illustration, the same process can be directly generalized to 3D cases with axis-angles.

For the skeleton of SMPL [16], a bone can be connected to up to four neighbors. We then consider the case of three connected bones, which also applies to more connections. As shown in Fig. 4c, when trying to recover a point x on the bone b_0 to its original position, the point x is expected to go through two different rotations. Since the axes of the two rotations are not the same, we cannot simply blend the angles. Instead, we blend the offset vectors:

$$\Delta x = \left(\mathbf{R}_{w_1\theta_1}^T (x - t_1) + t_1 - x\right) + \left(\mathbf{R}_{w_2\theta_2}^T (x - t_2) + t_2 - x\right), \tag{16}$$

where t_1 and t_2 are the center points of the two rotations. Then we obtain the original position of x by

$$\bar{x} = x + \Delta x. \tag{17}$$

Finally, our neural implicit functions are formulated as

$$d^{(n)} = f_{\theta_n}\left(\bar{x}^{(n)}, z^{(n)}\right), 1 \le n \le N, \tag{18}$$

with

$$\bar{x}^{(n)} = x^{(n)} + \Delta x^{(n)} = x^{(n)} + \sum_{b \in B^{(n)}} \left(\mathbf{R}_{w_b\theta_b}^T (x^{(n)} - t_b) + t_b - x^{(n)}\right), \tag{19}$$

where $B^{(n)}$ is the indices of joints connected to the n-th part.

Taking a step back, you may feel the above APS algorithm is quite like inverse LBS since it cancels deformations by reversing transformations as well. But there is a contradiction for inverse LBS: it needs the LBS weights defined in the canonical space before reverting the deformation; but if we already know where to take the LBS weights in the canonical space, we do not need this inverse deformation. To evade this problem, we should avoid saving blending weights by the absolute position. Therefore, we present "Competing Parts", a method that defines the blending weights of a point by its relative position to bones so that the blending weights can generalize to arbitrary poses.

Blending Weights from "Competing Parts".
The basic idea here is that the deformation of a point on a part is the result of the interaction between this part and its adjacent parts. We define the tendency of a point to stay static on the part as the rigidness at this point. Then, we can construct a rigidness field for a part with respect to each of its adjacent part. Taking Fig. 5 as an example, we connect the end points of both bones and split the connecting line with point Q by the ratio of bone lengths, then the rigidness of bone b_1 and bone b_2 at the point X are defined as

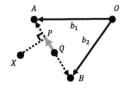

Fig. 5. A 2D example to illustrate the definition of rigidness.

$$r_1 = \exp(\alpha_1 \frac{\overrightarrow{QP} \cdot \overrightarrow{QA}}{\|\overrightarrow{QA}\|^2} + \beta_1), \quad r_2 = \exp(\alpha_2 \frac{\overrightarrow{QP} \cdot \overrightarrow{QB}}{\|\overrightarrow{QB}\|^2} + \beta_2), \quad (20)$$

where P is the projection of X onto the connecting line; α_1 and β_1 are learnable parameters to adjust the rigidness of bone b_1; α_2 and β_2 adjust the rigidness of bone b_2. When the point X moves closer to bone b_1, its rigidness about bone b_1 increases while its rigidness about bone b_2 decreases.

Based on the defined rigidness, we define the blending weights of a point with respect to bone b_1 and b_2 as

$$w_1 = \frac{r_1}{r_1 + r_2}, \quad w_2 = \frac{r_2}{r_1 + r_2}. \quad (21)$$

Given Eq. (21), $w_1 + w_2 = 1$, which is crucial for perfect part seaming. As an explanation, when two parts undergo a relative rotation for angle θ, their sections will have an angle gap of θ. To maintain the connection, the sum of relative rotations $w_1\theta + w_2\theta$ must equals to θ. Therefore, $w_1 + w_2 = 1$ is required.

3.4   Optimization

The complete supervision of our UNIF model is

$$\mathcal{L} = \mathcal{L}_{\text{recon}} + \lambda_{\text{unit}}\mathcal{L}_{\text{unit}} + \lambda_{\text{lim}}\mathcal{L}_{\text{lim}} + \lambda_{\text{sec}}\mathcal{L}_{\text{sec}} + \lambda_{\text{perim}}\mathcal{L}_{\text{perim}}, \quad (22)$$

where $\lambda_{\text{unit}} = 0.1$, $\lambda_{\text{lim}} = 1.0$, $\lambda_{\text{sec}} = 0.01$, $\lambda_{\text{perim}} = 0.001$.

We follow the same network architecture of IGR [9] except that we lower the largest width of each MLP from 256 to 64 for a comparable number of parameters. For each frame of the raw scan sequence, we sample 5k points as surface points for the reconstruction term $\mathcal{L}_{\text{recon}}$; we also sample 5k points near the surface points with local disturbances ($\sigma_{\text{local}} \sim \mathcal{N}(0, 0.1)$) and another 5k points in the enlarged bounding box ($\sigma_{\text{global}} = 1.5$) of the point cloud for the regularization terms $\mathcal{L}_{\text{unit}}$ and $\mathcal{L}_{\text{perim}}$. We use an NVIDIA A40 GPU for each experiment with 4 scans in a batch. We train our model on each subject for 5k epochs using the Adam optimizer [10] with a learning rate of 1e-3 and scale it down with a coefficient of 0.3 three times every 1k epochs. To extract surfaces from our learned neural implicit functions, we use the Marching Cubes algorithm [17] with the help of MISE [19] under a resolution of 256.

4   Experiments

4.1   Settings

Datasets. We test our method on two datasets with raw scan sequences of clothed humans. The CAPE [18] dataset contains 15 subjects registered by SMPL [16] with additional vertex offsets to model the clothes. Only four of the subjects have their raw scans released. Each of the four subjects has 4 to 6 sequences with 2 clothing types. We learn a model for each clothing type of a subject with one sequence left out for the extrapolation test. The length of each sequence ranges from about 200 to 550. For the training sequences, we use the first frame of every 10 frames for training and the fifth frame of every 10 frames for the interpolation test. The ClothSeq [31] dataset contains three subjects wearing loose clothes, therefore is more challenging. Each subject has one sequence, the length of which ranges from about 500 to 750. We use the first 80% frames with a stride of 10 for training, the last 20% frames for extrapolation test also with a stride of 10. For the interpolation test, we use frames from the first 80% with an offset of 5.

Baselines. NASA [6] is a typical part-based method that learns a group of occupancy networks anchored on joints. SCANimate [30] learns a forward and a backward skinning network with cycle consistency. SNARF [4] conducts backward skinning with iterative root finding to improve generalizing to novel poses.

Metrics. For quantitative evaluation, we sample 100k points from each raw scan and our extracted surface, respectively. We report four metrics during our experiments including the point-to-surface distance (p2s), the recall rate, the Chamfer distance (CD), and the F-score. The point-to-surface distance is computed by the mean distance from a point in the raw scan to its closet point on our extracted surface. The recall rate counts the ratio of points with a point-to-surface distance lower than a threshold (1 mm). The Chamfer distance is the mean of the point-to-surface and the surface-to-point distance, and the F-score is the harmonic mean of recall and precision.

Table 1. Comparison with baselines on the CAPE [18] dataset. In the upper half rows are the results of the extrapolation test, which shows the generalization ability of a model, and the lower half are from the interpolation test, which shows the expressiveness of a model.

	seq.	SCANimate				SNARF				NASA				Ours			
		CD↓	F1↑	p2s↓	Rec.↑	CD↓	F1↑	p2s↓	Rec.↑	CD↓	F1↑	p2s↓	Rec.↑	CD↓	F1↑	p2s↓	Rec.↑
E	0032-SL	10.19	66.16	10.19	67.31	10.71	65.40	10.68	66.96	98.23	15.78	103.35	15.16	**8.06**	**75.09**	**7.87**	**75.93**
	0032-SS	9.89	65.56	9.45	66.54	15.49	49.58	15.55	48.58	131.79	9.01	74.52	11.81	**8.37**	**72.55**	**8.18**	**72.86**
	0096-SL	14.53	56.97	16.89	57.25	12.19	63.70	14.35	63.93	92.74	10.69	93.72	10.53	**10.40**	**64.36**	**10.04**	**65.54**
	0096-SS	11.25	64.89	11.51	65.50	23.57	**72.47**	24.68	**73.42**	101.51	14.37	86.82	14.77	**8.74**	71.57	**8.50**	72.87
	0159-SL	7.93	75.24	7.49	76.96	29.34	68.65	33.26	67.22	118.10	8.08	153.04	7.47	**6.64**	**82.42**	**6.28**	**83.05**
	0159-SS	6.52	84.34	6.15	85.71	20.76	78.39	26.82	77.42	85.46	11.73	81.09	12.37	**5.91**	**86.20**	**5.66**	**87.61**
	3223-SL	8.12	77.95	8.60	78.28	25.29	68.29	30.17	67.20	66.91	21.31	73.49	20.06	**6.24**	**86.77**	**5.47**	**88.99**
	3223-SS	9.45	75.08	10.93	74.24	13.90	83.83	16.32	84.41	70.15	22.78	67.47	23.04	**5.61**	**87.88**	**5.31**	**89.61**
I	0032-SL	6.86	85.81	6.80	88.76	4.93	**95.51**	5.06	**97.93**	10.00	74.16	10.01	75.38	**4.14**	95.46	**3.72**	97.60
	0032-SS	5.70	90.45	5.23	93.39	**4.07**	**96.79**	3.99	**98.23**	10.28	68.45	10.38	69.26	4.17	95.30	**3.83**	97.01
	0096-SL	8.48	89.50	10.69	91.94	6.48	**96.93**	8.92	98.07	15.47	61.22	18.34	62.08	**4.69**	96.05	**4.47**	**98.33**
	0096-SS	7.08	82.76	6.47	85.05	4.05	96.41	3.84	97.84	12.73	67.40	11.29	69.12	**3.74**	**97.08**	**3.42**	**98.94**
	0159-SL	5.18	91.79	4.35	96.01	3.77	96.35	3.18	99.27	11.82	66.37	11.39	69.81	**3.39**	**96.80**	**2.72**	**99.91**
	0159-SS	4.77	93.75	4.20	96.71	3.42	97.74	3.18	99.19	12.28	65.86	12.04	67.05	**2.94**	**98.00**	**2.69**	**99.81**
	3223-SL	5.31	93.40	5.26	96.81	5.06	95.70	5.86	95.84	8.17	84.47	7.92	85.61	**3.89**	**96.55**	**3.07**	**99.58**
	3223-SS	4.89	94.09	4.74	97.15	3.76	97.68	3.88	99.24	7.80	86.61	6.95	87.93	**3.09**	**97.81**	**2.84**	**99.68**

Table 2. Comparison with baselines on the ClothSeq [31] dataset. In the upper half rows are the results of the extrapolation test, and the lower half are from the interpolation test.

	seq.	SCANimate				SNARF				NASA				Ours			
		CD↓	F1↑	p2s↓	Rec.↑	CD↓	F1↑	p2s↓	Rec.↑	CD↓	F1↑	p2s↓	Rec.↑	CD↓	F1↑	p2s↓	Rec.↑
E	JP	14.33	56.25	14.29	58.02	17.72	58.49	21.58	59.16	69.76	16.88	68.24	16.59	**13.04**	**58.60**	**11.24**	**62.06**
	JS	**11.05**	61.26	10.85	62.58	13.40	57.48	13.91	57.72	116.14	8.51	97.25	9.61	11.84	**65.94**	**9.00**	**70.03**
	SP	14.32	54.06	14.19	54.80	15.06	60.22	16.47	60.19	65.73	19.93	39.26	21.29	**12.10**	**65.90**	**9.81**	**69.46**
I	JP	10.05	71.78	7.38	79.40	8.43	80.82	8.67	83.92	22.37	44.95	21.97	45.42	**7.87**	**84.66**	**5.47**	**90.01**
	JS	8.84	74.84	7.77	78.33	**8.81**	80.20	7.86	81.80	33.66	31.61	34.35	31.34	8.89	**81.48**	**5.96**	**86.72**
	SP	13.20	57.74	12.52	59.28	11.21	73.04	11.08	74.40	48.69	38.02	33.54	40.06	**10.18**	**75.49**	**7.42**	**80.31**

4.2   Comparisons

We show quantitative results in Table 1 and Table 2 and qualitative results in Fig. 6. Our method shows clear superiority over NASA [6] (also a part-based method) and outperforms SCANimate [30] and SNARF [4] in most cases.

The extrapolation test is extremely challenging, especially on CAPE [18] because the test poses differ a lot from the limited training poses. Therefore, NASA [6] completely collapses; SCANimate [30] and SNARF [4] produce distortions due to bad neural skinning weights. Our method shows higher robustness under novel poses, benefiting from the proper part division and the generalizable non-rigid deformation modeling.

In the interpolation test, NASA [6] exhibits reasonable results on CAPE [18] but has difficulty in partitioning and reconstructing the subjects in ClothSeq [31]. Our method produces visually comparable results with SCANimate [30] and SNARF [4] on CAPE [18]. However, on the ClothSeq [31] dataset, where clothes are much more complex, our method makes less body distortion or extra surfaces and reconstructs the pose of the subjects more precisely.

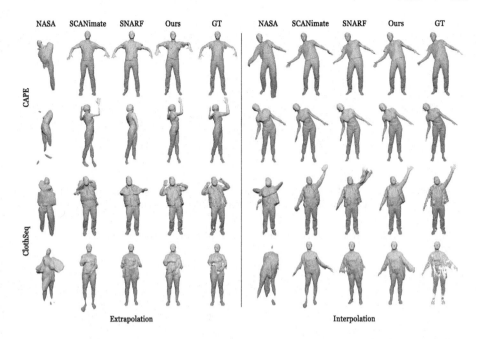

Fig. 6. Qualitative comparison with baselines.

4.3   Visualization and Analysis

Ablation Study. To validate the effectiveness of our main components, we run experiments with each of them disabled and visualize parts in an unseen pose at the early stage of training in Fig. 7. Compared to our full model, dropping the adjacent part seaming algorithm leaves the model almost rigid (*e.g.*, the sections near the knees are exposed and the neck is not completely connected to the body). When disabling the bone limit loss, we lose the restriction on the boundary of a part. Then we see the left foot and leg of the man falsely included in the same part. However, merely using the bone limit loss is not sufficient. If we drop the section normal loss, the model converges to a bad partition where the surface does go across the joint but the main body of the part lies somewhere else. Finally, the minimal perimeter loss is also necessary to suppress extra surfaces such as the one on the right leg.

Limitations. Since the #13 and #14 joints of SMPL [16] are too close to the spine, our method learns a small chest and large shoulders. When shoulders move drastically, our model converges to overlapped parts to reconstruct the shape. Therefore, we can observe inconsistent part division around the chest during animation (Fig. 8). The current framework does not model the dynamics of loose clothes. Seams between parts are still visible due to the generalization problem caused by the pose condition vector.

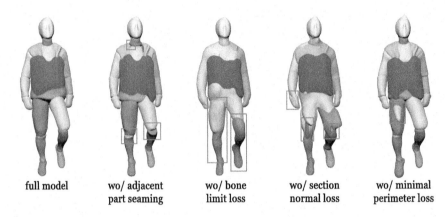

| full model | wo/ adjacent part seaming | wo/ bone limit loss | wo/ section normal loss | wo/ minimal perimeter loss |

Fig. 7. Ablation study on main components of our method.

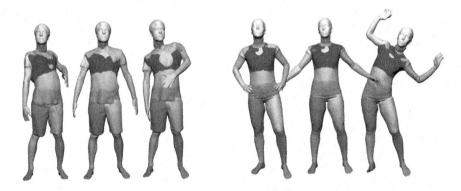

Fig. 8. Visualization of learned parts during animation.

5   Conclusions

We present a novel method for clothed human reconstruction and animation. We explore initialization and regularization strategies to learn body parts without ground-truth part labels. Towards a higher generalization ability to novel poses, we propose an adjacent part seaming algorithm to model non-rigid deformations by explicitly modeling the interaction between parts. Experiments on two datasets validate the effectiveness of our method.

Acknowledgments. The work is supported by National Key R&D Program of China (2018AAA0100704), NSFC #61932020, #62172279, Science and Technology Commission of Shanghai Municipality (Grant No. 20ZR1436000), and "huguang Program" supported by Shanghai Education Development Foundation and Shanghai Municipal Education Commission. This work is supported by NTU NAP, MOE AcRF Tier 2 (T2EP20221-0033), and under the RIE2020 Industry Alignment Fund - Industry Collaboration Projects (IAF-ICP) Funding Initiative, as well as cash and in-kind contribution from the industry partner(s).

References

1. Alldieck, T., Xu, H., Sminchisescu, C.: imghum: Implicit generative models of 3d human shape and articulated pose. In: Proceedings of the IEEE/CVF International Conference on Computer Vision, pp. 5461–5470 (2021)
2. Atzmon, M., Lipman, Y.: Sal: Sign agnostic learning of shapes from raw data. In: Proceedings of the IEEE/CVF Conference on Computer Vision and Pattern Recognition, pp. 2565–2574 (2020)
3. Atzmon, M., Novotny, D., Vedaldi, A., Lipman, Y.: Augmenting implicit neural shape representations with explicit deformation fields. arXiv preprint arXiv:2108.08931 (2021)
4. Chen, X., Zheng, Y., Black, M.J., Hilliges, O., Geiger, A.: Snarf: Differentiable forward skinning for animating non-rigid neural implicit shapes. In: Proceedings of the IEEE/CVF International Conference on Computer Vision, pp. 11594–11604 (2021)
5. Chen, Z., Zhang, H.: Learning implicit fields for generative shape modeling. In: Proceedings of the IEEE/CVF Conference on Computer Vision and Pattern Recognition, pp. 5939–5948 (2019)
6. Deng, B., et al.: NASA neural articulated shape approximation. In: Vedaldi, A., Bischof, H., Brox, T., Frahm, J.-M. (eds.) ECCV 2020. LNCS, vol. 12352, pp. 612–628. Springer, Cham (2020). https://doi.org/10.1007/978-3-030-58571-6_36
7. Genova, K., Cole, F., Sud, A., Sarna, A., Funkhouser, T.: Local deep implicit functions for 3d shape. In: Proceedings of the IEEE/CVF Conference on Computer Vision and Pattern Recognition, pp. 4857–4866 (2020)
8. Genova, K., Cole, F., Vlasic, D., Sarna, A., Freeman, W.T., Funkhouser, T.: Learning shape templates with structured implicit functions. In: Proceedings of the IEEE/CVF International Conference on Computer Vision, pp. 7154–7164 (2019)
9. Gropp, A., Yariv, L., Haim, N., Atzmon, M., Lipman, Y.: Implicit geometric regularization for learning shapes. In: ICML (2020)
10. Kingma, D.P., Ba, J.: Adam: A method for stochastic optimization. In: Proceedings of the 3rd International Conference on Learning Representations (ICLR) (2014)
11. Li, T., Bolkart, T., Black, M.J., Li, H., Romero, J.: Learning a model of facial shape and expression from 4d scans. ACM Trans. Graph. 36(6), 1–194 (2017)
12. Lipman, Y.: Phase transitions, distance functions, and implicit neural representations. arXiv preprint arXiv:2106.07689 (2021)
13. Liu, L., Habermann, M., Rudnev, V., Sarkar, K., Gu, J., Theobalt, C.: Neural actor: Neural free-view synthesis of human actors with pose control. ACM Trans. Graph. (TOG) 40(6), 1–16 (2021)
14. Liu, W., Piao, Z., Min, J., Luo, W., Ma, L., Gao, S.: Liquid warping gan: A unified framework for human motion imitation, appearance transfer and novel view synthesis. In: Proceedings of the IEEE/CVF International Conference on Computer Vision, pp. 5904–5913 (2019)
15. Lombardi, S., et al.: Latenthuman: Shape-and-pose disentangled latent representation for human bodies. In: 2021 International Conference on 3D Vision (3DV), pp. 278–288. IEEE (2021)
16. Loper, M., Mahmood, N., Romero, J., Pons-Moll, G., Black, M.J.: Smpl: A skinned multi-person linear model. ACM Trans. Graph. (TOG) 34(6), 1–16 (2015)
17. Lorensen, W.E., Cline, H.E.: Marching cubes: A high resolution 3d surface construction algorithm. ACM Siggraph Comput. Graph. 21(4), 163–169 (1987)

18. Ma, Q., et al.: Learning to dress 3d people in generative clothing. In: Proceedings of the IEEE/CVF Conference on Computer Vision and Pattern Recognition, pp. 6469–6478 (2020)

19. Mescheder, L., Oechsle, M., Niemeyer, M., Nowozin, S., Geiger, A.: Occupancy networks: Learning 3d reconstruction in function space. In: Proceedings of the IEEE/CVF Conference on Computer Vision and Pattern Recognition, pp. 4460–4470 (2019)

20. Mihajlovic, M., Zhang, Y., Black, M.J., Tang, S.: Leap: Learning articulated occupancy of people. In: Proceedings of the IEEE/CVF Conference on Computer Vision and Pattern Recognition, pp. 10461–10471 (2021)

21. Mildenhall, B., Srinivasan, P.P., Tancik, M., Barron, J.T., Ramamoorthi, R., Ng, R.: NeRF: Representing scenes as neural radiance fields for view synthesis. In: Vedaldi, A., Bischof, H., Brox, T., Frahm, J.-M. (eds.) ECCV 2020. LNCS, vol. 12346, pp. 405–421. Springer, Cham (2020). https://doi.org/10.1007/978-3-030-58452-8_24

22. Oechsle, M., Peng, S., Geiger, A.: Unisurf: Unifying neural implicit surfaces and radiance fields for multi-view reconstruction. In: Proceedings of the IEEE/CVF International Conference on Computer Vision, pp. 5589–5599 (2021)

23. Palafox, P., Božič, A., Thies, J., Nießner, M., Dai, A.: Npms: Neural parametric models for 3d deformable shapes. In: Proceedings of the IEEE/CVF International Conference on Computer Vision, pp. 12695–12705 (2021)

24. Park, J.J., Florence, P., Straub, J., Newcombe, R., Lovegrove, S.: Deepsdf: Learning continuous signed distance functions for shape representation. In: Proceedings of the IEEE/CVF Conference on Computer Vision and Pattern Recognition, pp. 165–174 (2019)

25. Patel, C., Liao, Z., Pons-Moll, G.: Tailornet: Predicting clothing in 3d as a function of human pose, shape and garment style. In: Proceedings of the IEEE/CVF Conference on Computer Vision and Pattern Recognition, pp. 7365–7375 (2020)

26. Pavlakos, G., et al.: Expressive body capture: 3d hands, face, and body from a single image. In: Proceedings of the IEEE/CVF Conference on Computer Vision and Pattern Recognition, pp. 10975–10985 (2019)

27. Peng, S., et al.: Animatable neural radiance fields for modeling dynamic human bodies. In: Proceedings of the IEEE/CVF International Conference on Computer Vision, pp. 14314–14323 (2021)

28. Peng, S., et al.: Neural body: Implicit neural representations with structured latent codes for novel view synthesis of dynamic humans. In: Proceedings of the IEEE/CVF Conference on Computer Vision and Pattern Recognition, pp. 9054–9063 (2021)

29. Romero, J., Tzionas, D., Black, M.J.: Embodied hands: Modeling and capturing hands and bodies together. ACM Trans. Graph. (Proc. SIGGRAPH Asia) **36**(6) (2017)

30. Saito, S., Yang, J., Ma, Q., Black, M.J.: Scanimate: Weakly supervised learning of skinned clothed avatar networks. In: Proceedings of the IEEE/CVF Conference on Computer Vision and Pattern Recognition, pp. 2886–2897 (2021)

31. Tiwari, G., Sarafianos, N., Tung, T., Pons-Moll, G.: Neural-gif: Neural generalized implicit functions for animating people in clothing. In: Proceedings of the IEEE/CVF International Conference on Computer Vision, pp. 11708–11718 (2021)

32. Wang, P., Liu, L., Liu, Y., Theobalt, C., Komura, T., Wang, W.: Neus: Learning neural implicit surfaces by volume rendering for multi-view reconstruction. In: NeurIPS (2021)
33. Yariv, L., Gu, J., Kasten, Y., Lipman, Y.: Volume rendering of neural implicit surfaces. In: Advances in Neural Information Processing Systems, vol. 34 (2021)
34. Yariv, L., et al.: Multiview neural surface reconstruction by disentangling geometry and appearance. Adv. Neural. Inf. Process. Syst. **33**, 2492–2502 (2020)

PRIF: Primary Ray-Based Implicit Function

Brandon Y. Feng[1(✉)], Yinda Zhang[2], Danhang Tang[2], Ruofei Du[2], and Amitabh Varshney[1]

[1] University of Maryland, College Park, USA
yfeng97@umd.edu
[2] Google Research, Mountain View, USA

Abstract. We introduce a new implicit shape representation called Primary Ray-based Implicit Function (PRIF). In contrast to most existing approaches based on the signed distance function (SDF) which handles spatial locations, our representation operates on oriented rays. Specifically, PRIF is formulated to directly produce the surface hit point of a given input ray, without the expensive sphere-tracing operations, hence enabling efficient shape extraction and differentiable rendering. We demonstrate that neural networks trained to encode PRIF achieve successes in various tasks including single shape representation, category-wise shape generation, shape completion from sparse or noisy observations, inverse rendering for camera pose estimation, and neural rendering with color.

1 Introduction

Learning an accurate and efficient geometric representation of a 3D object is an important problem for computer graphics, computer vision, and robotics. Recent advances in machine learning have inspired a growing trend of implicit neural shape representations, where a neural network learns to predict the signed distance function (SDF) for an arbitrary location in the 3D space. Moreover, in addition to the 3D location (x, y, z), the neural SDF network may take in a latent vector that describes the object identity, thus enabling the generative modeling of multiple objects. Such an implicit neural representation (INR) not only produces fine-grained geometry, but also enables a plethora of applications [28], *e.g.*, shape completion, pose estimation, via a differentiable rendering based optimization.

However, rendering and extracting the shape from a trained neural SDF network are computationally expensive and often limited to watertight shapes. The direct approach to rendering from SDF requires sphere tracing, which needs access to the SDF values at multiple locations along each pixel ray [21]. The indirect approach computes and stores the SDF values at predefined 3D grid points, from which the shape can be rendered with sphere-tracing or extracted as

---

Supplementary Information The online version contains supplementary material available at https://doi.org/10.1007/978-3-031-20062-5_9.

S. Avidan et al. (Eds.): ECCV 2022, LNCS 13663, pp. 138–155, 2022.
https://doi.org/10.1007/978-3-031-20062-5_9

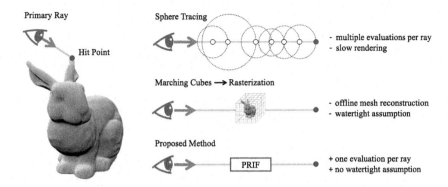

Fig. 1. Overview. Common neural shape representation methods learn the level-set functions implicitly describing the object geometry, such as SDF and OF. Rendering from these implicit networks requires either sphere tracing or rasterizing a separately extracted mesh. Sphere tracing is inefficient due to multiple network evaluations for a single ray. Rasterization induces a separate meshing step (often through Marching Cubes), which hinders end-to-end gradient propagation in differentiable applications, and the shape quality is ultimately restricted by the meshing algorithm's limitation, such as grid resolutions and shape watertightness. Our new representation, PRIF, directly maps each primary ray to its hit point. A network encoding PRIF is more efficient and convenient for rendering, since it requires only one evaluation for each ray, avoids the watertight constraint in conventional methods, and easily enables differentiable rendering.

a polygon mesh through Marching Cubes [30]. Both cases demand a large number of network evaluations since they require sampling SDF values at locations far away from the surface. Moreover, the shape quality is ultimately constrained by the converging criteria of sphere tracing or the resolution of the 3D grid.

In this work, we present a novel geometric representation that is efficient, accurate, and innately compatible for downstream tasks involving reconstruction and rendering. We break away from the conventional point-wise implicit functions and propose to encode 3D geometry into a novel ray-based implicit function. Specifically, our representation operates on the realm of oriented rays $r = (\mathbf{p}_r, \mathbf{d}_r)$, where $\mathbf{p}_r \in \mathbb{R}^3$ is the ray origin and $\mathbf{d}_r \in \mathbb{S}^2$ is the normalized ray direction. Unlike SDF that only outputs the distance to the nearest but undetermined surface point, we formulate our representation such that its output directly reveals the surface hit point of the input ray. The rays whose surface intersection we care about are specifically known in computer graphics as *primary* rays, whose origins are the rendering viewpoint, as opposed to *secondary* rays that originate from the object surface [1]. Therefore, we name our representation as Primary Ray-based Implicit Function (PRIF). In effect, a neural network trained to encode PRIF represents the manifestation of the object's geometry at any viewpoint that it is observed.

Modeling the object from the ray-based perspective, rather than 3D-point-based, has huge implications for efficient application in any task that involves rendering the object from a viewpoint. In Sect. 4, we show that PRIF outperforms common functions such as SDF and OF, and we further demonstrate successful applications of PRIF to various tasks using neural networks.

Properly formulating the rays is nontrivial. While it may be intuitive to let PRIF output the distance from the ray origin $\mathbf{p}_r$ to the hit point $\mathbf{h}_r$, this formulation leads to ray aliasing - *i.e.*, if we move $\mathbf{p}_r$ along the ray direction $\mathbf{d}_r$, the distance to the hit point $\mathbf{h}_r$ needs to change. However, the actual surface intersection point would not change to translation along the view direction. Therefore, it is undesirable to have such a potential variance as it adds unnecessary complexity to the network output.

To avoid the aliasing, we reparametrize the ray r by replacing the view position $\mathbf{p}_r$ with perpendicular foot $\mathbf{f}_r$ from the coordinate origin O to r. Wherever we move $\mathbf{p}_r$ along the ray direction $\mathbf{d}_r$, the perpendicular foot $\mathbf{f}_r$ stays the same. Furthermore, we can easily define the surface hit point $\mathbf{h}_r$ by a single scalar value: its distance from $\mathbf{f}_r$. Thus, we formulate PRIF so that it outputs this distance for an input ray. More details are in Sect. 3.

In summary, our main contributions are the followings:

- We present PRIF, a novel formulation for geometric representation using ray-based neural networks.
- We show that PRIF outperforms common level-set-based methods in shape representation accuracy and extraction speed.
- We demonstrate that PRIF enables generative modeling, shape completion, and camera pose estimation.

2   Related Work

We discuss prior art on neural representations for 3D shapes and scene rays.

2.1   3D Shape Representations

Functional Representations. Traditional 3D shape representations include polygon meshes, point clouds, and voxels. In recent years, as deep neural networks achieve remarkable success on various vision-related tasks, there has been a growing interest in developing implicit neural representations (INRs) of 3D shapes. Following seminal works [9,32,36] showing successful applications of neural network to encode 3D shapes, many methods have been introduced to solve various vision and graphics tasks using INRs of 3D shapes [3,4,7,10,11,15,17, 24,28,29,35,38,40,42,43,49,52,53,56].

INRs usually use the multilayer perceptron (MLP) architecture to encode geometric information of a 3D shape by learning the mapping from a given 3D spatial point and a scalar value. Typically, the output scalar value denotes either the occupancy at the given point, or the signed distance from the given point to the nearest point on the shape. On one hand, networks that are trained to encode the occupancy function [32] (OF) essentially learns the binary classification problem, where the output equals 0 if the point is empty, and equals 1 if occupied. Therefore, the decision boundary where the network predictions equal to 0.5 represents the surface of the encoded shape. On the other hand, for networks trained to encode the signed distance function [9,36] (SDF), the surface is represented by the decision boundary where the network predictions equal to 0. A 3D surface determined in such fashions is also known as an isosurface, which is a level set of a continuous 3D function. In practice, however, obtaining 3D meshes from these isosurfaces extracted from INRs still requires an additional meshing step often through the Marching Cubes algorithm.

In this paper, we introduce a new shape representation which is not determined by an isosurface. Instead, our representation encodes a 3D shape by learning the PRIF associated with the shape. Outputs of such a function directly correspond to points on the surface, and the shape can be extracted without an additional meshing step that could inject inaccuracies to the final representation.

Global *v.s.* Local Representations. The initial works of INRs for 3D shapes inspire many techniques to improve its the rendering efficiency [28,55] and representation quality [44,48]. Among many techniques, a common thread is the idea of spatial partitions which manifest in two main approaches. One approach divides the surfaces of shapes into different local patches, reducing the difficulty of globally fitting a complex surface with a single network [5,19,20,23,37,50]. Another approach divides the 3D volume into small local regions (often based on the spatial octree structure), and then train INRs to encode the geometric information within each local region [8,14,27,31,34,41,47,54].

In this paper, we only focus on global representations, where a shape is represented by a single network without any spatial partitions. While the aforementioned works largely focus on improving the performance of INRs based on SDF, our main contribution is a new functional representation in place of isosurface-based representations like SDF. Nonetheless, the idea of spatial partitions explored in previous works has the potential to improve the performance of our currently global representation, and we see local specializations as a promising future direction to explore.

2.2 Ray-Based Neural Networks

Our method is closely related to an emerging concept called Ray-based Neural Networks. Rays are a common construct from computer graphics, and can be denoted by a tuple consisting of a 3D point (ray origin) and a 3D direction (ray direction). Due to their closeness to rendering 3D scenes, rays have become a central component in the problem formulation of many recent works using neural networks to model 3D scenes [33,46]. Feng *et al.* [18] and Attal *et al.* [2] have further demonstrated that for front-facing light field scenes, MLPs can be trained to accurately map camera rays to their observed colors in highly detailed real-world scenes, but their networks only consider rays restricted within two parallel planes. Most recently, Sitzmann *et al.* [45] successfully train a MLP to encode the observed color of unrestricted rays with arbitrary origins and directions, and the key is to parametrize rays using the Plucker coordinates [22].

We similarly adopt rays as input to the neural network. However, instead of the Plucker parametrization which replaces the ray position by its moment vector about the origin, we replace the moment vector by the perpendicular foot between the ray and the origin. As discussed in Sect. 3, our formulation allows the network to simply produce an affine transformation to its input.

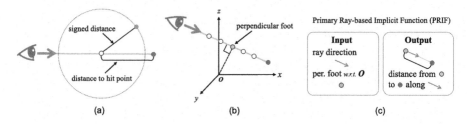

Fig. 2. Representation. (a) Signed distance at a sampling position (white) reveals the sphere (blue dots) where its nearest surface point (blue) exists, but that may be irrelevant when we really want to know the hit point (red) *along a specific direction.* Thus, multiple samples are often required. (b) Our new representation uses only one sample (yellow) along the ray to obtain its surface hit point. The sampling position is the perpendicular foot between the given ray and the coordinate system's origin O. (c) The proposed function takes in the ray's direction and its sampling point, and returns the distance from that point to the actual surface hit point. We train neural networks to encode geometry by learning this new function, and we demonstrate the capability of our trained networks in various tasks involving shape representation and rendering.

3   Method

In this section, we introduce our new representation for 3D shapes. We first discuss the motivation behind ray parametrization used in prior works, and then we present our new formulation specifically designed for shape representations.

3.1   Background

Sitzmann *et al.* [45] encode light fields by training an MLP Φ_ϕ with parameters ϕ on a set of observed rays to learn the mapping of $r = (\mathbf{p}_r, \mathbf{d}_r) \rightarrow c_r$, where c_r denotes the color of the observed radiance. However, naively concatenating $\mathbf{p}_r$ and $\mathbf{d}_r$ as input to the network is not ideal due to ray aliasing. If we move the position of a ray r along the ray direction $\mathbf{d}_r$, we would obtain a ray $r' = (\mathbf{p}_{r'}, \mathbf{d}_r)$ that is really an aliased version of r. There is no guarantee that the trained network would produce the same output for different aliases r' of the ray r.

To resolve ray aliasing, Sitzmann *et al.* [45] reparametrize the ray $r = (\mathbf{p}_r, \mathbf{d}_r)$ into Plucker coordinates as $r = (\mathbf{m}_r, \mathbf{d}_r)$, where $\mathbf{m}_r = \mathbf{p}_r \times \mathbf{d}_r$ is also known as the moment vector of $\mathbf{p}_r$ about the origin O. Plucker coordinates represent all oriented rays in space without singularity or special cases, and they are invariant to changes in the ray position along the ray direction. To better understand this property, consider moving the ray position to some other point $\mathbf{p}'_r$ at a fixed ray direction $\mathbf{d}_r$. Then, for a certain $\lambda \in \mathbb{R}$, $\mathbf{p}'_r = \mathbf{p}_r - \lambda \mathbf{d}_r$, and

$$
\begin{aligned}
\mathbf{p}'_r \times \mathbf{d}_r &= (\mathbf{p}_r - \lambda \mathbf{d}_r) \times \mathbf{d}_r \\
&= \mathbf{p}_r \times \mathbf{d}_r - \lambda \mathbf{0} \\
&= \mathbf{p}_r \times \mathbf{d}_r.
\end{aligned}
\tag{1}
$$

Therefore, $\mathbf{m}_r = \mathbf{p}_r \times \mathbf{d}_r$ is invariant to any change of λ along $\mathbf{d}_r$.

3.2 Describing Geometry with Perpendicular Foot

Our goal is to train a neural network to encode the mapping from a ray to its hit point on the 3D shape's surface. Although replacing ray position with the moment vector $\mathbf{m}_r$ allows Sitzmann et al. [45] to train networks to encode light fields, it is hard to geometrically relate a ray's moment vector to its surface hit point. We propose an alternative way to parameterize a ray as input to the network. which has an intuitive and intrinsic relationship to its hit point.

Specifically, we consider the perpendicular foot $\mathbf{f}_r$ between the ray r and the coordinate system's origin O, which may be computed by

$$\mathbf{f}_r = \mathbf{d}_r \times (\mathbf{p}_r \times \mathbf{d}_r). \tag{2}$$

Similar to $\mathbf{m}_r$ in Plucker coordinates, $\mathbf{f}_r$ is also invariant to changing the ray position along the ray direction. Specifically, let $\mathbf{p}'_r$ be the translated ray position defined as before, we can then write $\mathbf{p}_{r'} = \mathbf{p}_r - \lambda\mathbf{d}_r$, and

$$\begin{aligned}
\mathbf{f}_{r'} &= \mathbf{d}_r \times (\mathbf{p}_{r'} \times \mathbf{d}_r) \\
&= \mathbf{d}_r \times ((\mathbf{p}_r - \lambda\mathbf{d}_r) \times \mathbf{d}_r) \\
&= \mathbf{d}_r \times (\mathbf{p}_r \times \mathbf{d}_r - \lambda\mathbf{0}) \\
&= \mathbf{d}_r \times (\mathbf{p}_r \times \mathbf{d}_r) \\
&= \mathbf{f}_r
\end{aligned} \tag{3}$$

In other words, $\mathbf{f}_r$ is invariant to moving $\mathbf{p}_r$ along the direction $\mathbf{d}_r$.

As a result, we can represent any ray $r = (\mathbf{f}_r, \mathbf{d}_r)$, and we can further establish the following relationship for each ray r:

$$\mathbf{h}_r = s_r \cdot \mathbf{d}_r + \mathbf{f}_r, \tag{4}$$

where $s_r \in \mathbb{R}$ denotes the signed displacement between the ray's hit point $\mathbf{h}_r$ and its perpendicular foot $\mathbf{f}_r$ *w.r.t.* the world origin O.

To encode a 3D shape, we propose the mapping function $(\mathbf{f}_r, \mathbf{d}_r) \rightarrow s_r$, which we call Primary Ray-based Implicit Function (PRIF). Different than SDF or OF, which implicitly encodes the geometry through the distance from any given point to its nearest surface point *in any direction*, PRIF operates on oriented points with *a specific ray direction*.

In practice, we train an MLP to learn

$$\Phi(\mathbf{f}_r, \mathbf{d}_r) = s_r. \tag{5}$$

With this new representation, we are able to represent the surface hit point of a ray with a single value. In effect, our objective is equivalent to finding a simple affine transformation $f(\mathbf{x}) = \mathbf{A}\mathbf{x} + \mathbf{b}$, with the input $\mathbf{x} = \mathbf{d}_r$, $\mathbf{A} = s_r I_3$, and $\mathbf{b} = \mathbf{f}_r$.

We also avoid a major limitation in previous sphere-tracing-based methods, which is having to sample multiple points and perform multiple network evaluations to obtain a hit point.

3.3 Background Mask

For 3D functions like SDF or OF, every 3D point has a well-established scalar value denoting the distance to surface or the occupancy at that point. In contrast, our function would take in rays that never intersect with the shape and therefore do not even have a hit point.

To address this issue, we let the network additionally produce

$$\Phi(\mathbf{f}_r, \mathbf{d}_r) = a_r, \tag{6}$$

where $a_r \in [0, 1]$ denotes the probability in which the ray r hits the foreground. We compute the cross-entropy loss

$$\mathcal{L}_a = \sum_r -a_r^{gt} \log(a_r) - \left(1 - a_r^{gt}\right) \log(1 - a_r), \tag{7}$$

where $a_r^{gt} = 0$ for background rays and $a_r^{gt} = 1$ for foreground rays.

For the signed displacement s_r, we supervise the learning by computing its absolute difference to the ground truth as $\mathcal{L}_s = \sum_{r \in \mathcal{F}} \|s_r - s_r^{gt}\|$, given the set of foreground rays $\mathcal{F}$. As a result, the total loss function to train our network is $\mathcal{L} = \mathcal{L}_a + \mathcal{L}_s$ and is averaged among all rays in a training batch

3.4 Outlier Points Removal

In rare cases where sharp surface discontinuities exist between two neighboring rays, the network would likely produce continuous predictions when interpolating between those two rays, resulting in undesirable outlier points. Fortunately, since our network is fully differentiable, for each prediction s_r we can compute its gradient with respect to the changes in ray position. We discard all predictions that satisfy the threshold: $\left\| \frac{\partial s_r}{\partial \mathbf{p}_r} \right\| \geq \delta$. In our experiments, δ is set equal to 5.

4 Experiments

In this section, we first verify the efficacy of neural PRIF for shape representation. Then, we show verious applications achieved by using PRIF as the underlying neural shape representation. Note that the scope of our experiments is to compare these functional shape representations *encoded by neural networks*.

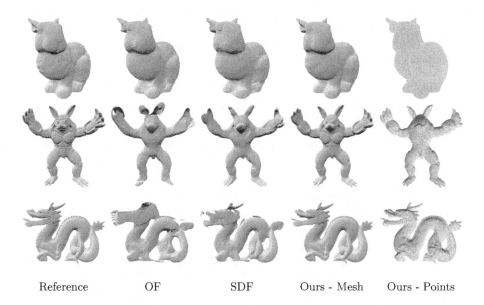

Reference   OF   SDF   Ours - Mesh   Ours - Points

Fig. 3. Single Shape. To examine the representation capability of PRIF, we train networks with the same architecture to encode the occupancy function (OF), signed distance function (SDF), and our proposed function (PRIF). Here, we visualize the extracted shapes from the trained neural representations. For OF and SDF, we follow the convention and extract the shapes by Marching Cubes. Our method directly outputs hit points, and we also apply the point-based Screened Poisson algorithm and present the resulting mesh for comparison.

4.1   Single Shape Representation

We select five models (*Armadillo, Bunny, Buddha, Dragon, Lucy*) from the Stanford 3D Scanning Repository [13,51] and train a neural network to fit the PRIF for each 3D model. We also fit the signed distance function (SDF) and the 3D occupancy function (OF) for these models. For a fair comparison between these functions, we adopt the same network architecture as Park et al. [36], containing eight layers with 512 hidden dimensions and ReLU activation.

Compared to SDF and OF which are trained on individual spatial points (x, y, z), PRIF requires an inherently different strategy to generate the training data since it takes in individual rays. In our experiments, for each 3D model, we select 50 virtual camera locations oriented towards the origin, and we capture 200×200 rays at each location. For SDF and OF, we follow Park et al. [36] and sample $500,000$ points with more aggressive sampling near the object surface.

For all three functions, we train the neural representation for 100 epochs with the learning rate initialized as 10^{-4} and decayed to 10^{-7} with a cosine annealing strategy. After training, the SDF- and OF-based shape representation are obtained by evaluating the neural network at uniform 256^3 volume grid and extracted using Marching Cubes. On the other hand, with our PRIF-based

Table 1. Quantitative results on single shape representation on 3D models from the Stanford 3D Scanning Repository. The left and right numbers represent the mean and median CD (multiplied by 10^{-4}). After extracting shapes from each representation, 30,000 points are sampled for evaluation.

Method	Armadillo	Bunny	Buddha	Dragon	Lucy
SDF	1.905|1.260	1.717|1.147	6.119|2.258	5.184|1.946	3.387|1.417
OF	4.805|1.624	1.704|1.133	17.279|3.113	19.577|3.014	3.396|1.427
PRIF	**0.978|0.706**	**1.169|0.835**	**1.443|0.821**	**1.586|0.913**	**0.846|0.519**

representation, we can evaluate the neural network at those virtual camera rays in the training set and directly obtain a dense set of surface points.

To evaluate the representation quality, for SDF- and OF-based representations, we first follow conventions [36] and sample 8,192 points on the mesh extracted with Marching Cubes. For the point set produced by the PRIF-based representation, we apply the point-based meshing algorithm Screened Poisson [25] in MeshLab [12] and then sample 8,192 points from the reconstructed mesh. Then, we obtain 8,192 Poisson-disk samples of the ground truth surface points from the original 3D model. Finally, we compute the mean and median Chamfer Distance (CD) between the ground truth point set and point sets sampled from those three representations. In Table 1 and Fig. 3, we provide quantitative and qualitative comparisons among the three representations. PRIF significantly outperform SDF and OF in accurately preserving the fine details of the 3D shapes.

Table 2. Quantitative results on generative representation on unseen 3D shapes of six categories from ShapeNetCore. The left and right numbers represent the mean and median CD ($\times 10^{-3}$) averaged over the test set. After extracting shapes from each representation, 30,000 points are sampled for evaluation.

Method	Car	Chair	Table	Plane	Lamp	Sofa
SDF	2.315|0.495	2.649|0.407	7.213|0.441	2.728|0.170	32.571|3.475	6.427|0.218
OF	2.820|0.587	4.589|0.835	6.427|1.296	2.999|0.169	143.377|145.753	12.672|0.184
PRIF	**1.961|0.347**	**0.982|0.267**	**4.532|0.315**	**0.389|0.125**	**3.276|0.534**	**1.236|0.222**

4.2   Shape Generation

Having established the representation power of PRIF for single shapes, we now examine its capability for generative shape modeling. We adopt the strategy from Park *et al.* [36] and enable multi-shape generation from a single network by concatenating a latent code for each object with the original network input.

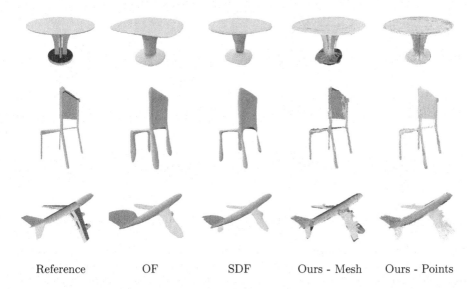

Reference   OF   SDF   Ours - Mesh   Ours - Points

Fig. 4. Shape Generation. We further examine the representation power on generative modeling over multiple shapes. After training the neural networks to learn shapes from a category, we use auto-decoding to find latent vectors that best represents novel shapes within this category. Here, we visualize the extracted shapes from networks trained to encode the three different functions. Note that *Points* are the immediate output of the PRIF networks.

In line with Park *et al.* [36], we select five categories of 3D objects from ShapeNetCore [6]. Within each category, we select the first 180 objects as the training set and the next 20 as the testing set. We maintain the same network architecture and training schedule when training neural networks to fit OF, SDF, and PRIF. We evaluate the trained networks on unseen shapes from the test set using auto-decoding [36] and provide quantitative and qualitative comparisons in Table 2 and Fig. 4. The PRIF-based representation extends its success from representing single shapes and remains effective in the generative task.

4.3   Shape Denoising and Completion

As depth sensors have become available on mobile and AR/VR devices, there are an array of applications for persistent geometric reconstructions [16]. Given real-world data of sparse and noisy observations, the capability of generative modeling could enable shape recovery from noisy and incomplete point clouds.

In Fig. 5, we demonstrate the denoising and completion ability of a trained generative PRIF network. Specifically, after training a PRIF network on an object category as described before, we provide the network with an unseen object's point cloud observations, which are either incomplete or contain noise.

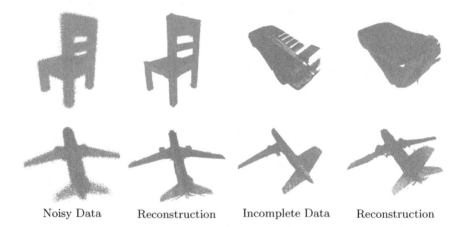

Noisy Data   Reconstruction   Incomplete Data   Reconstruction

Fig. 5. Noisy and Incomplete Observations. Networks trained for shape generation can reconstruct unseen shapes in challenging scenarios where only noisy or incomplete observations are available. Here we visualize the observations and reconstructions as raw point cloud data.

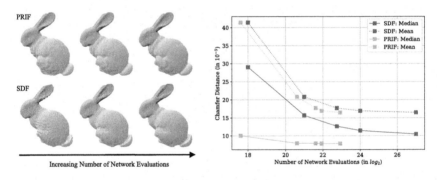

Fig. 6. Complexity Analysis. We evaluate the trained SDF network at grid resolutions of 64^3, 128^3, 192^3, 256^3, 512^3 and obtain final meshes by Marching Cubes. We evaluate the trained PRIF network at resolutions of 5×200^2, 10×400^2, 20×400^2, 25×400^2, 50×400^2 (# of Cameras $\times$ Resolution), and we apply Screened Poisson [25] to the output hit points to obtain the final mesh. The reconstructed mesh quality is measured by mean and median CD ($\times 10^{-5}$). The PRIF network achieves better quality with fewer evaluations.

4.4 Analysis and Ablations

Complexity Analysis. Shapes are commonly extracted from networks encoding SDF or OF using meshing algorithms like Marching Cubes. This meshing step requires evaluating the network at many 3D grid sampling points, and the grid resolution affects the final quality of the mesh. In our case, we can extract the shapes by rendering the scene from multiple positions and change the number of evaluations by varying the number and resolution of virtual cameras. For

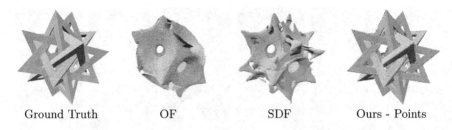

Ground Truth   OF   SDF   Ours - Points

Fig. 7. Stress Testing. We test on a Tetrahedron grid that is self-intersecting and non-watertight. We obtain the SDF and OF values with the scanning method [26], and extract the mesh by Marching Cubes. While the level-set representations fail as expected, our method reliably preserves the shape.

Fig. 8. Ablations. Impact of outlier removal described in Sect. 3. While the outliers have little impact on the quantitative metrics since they are scant, removing them improves visual consistency.

Table 3. Mean and median CD ($\times 10^{-5}$) of network prediction on trained rays and novel rays under different setup. Notice that changing $\mathbf{f}_r \Rightarrow \mathbf{p}_r$ causes ray aliasing discussed in Sect. 3, leading the network to overfit on trained rays and collapse on novel rays.

Setup	Trained	Novel
Proposed	**12.07|7.95**	**20.81|12.05**
$\mathbf{f}_r \Rightarrow \mathbf{m}_r$	12.15|8.05	28.38|13.53
$\mathbf{f}_r \Rightarrow \mathbf{p}_r$	1.16|0.77	1924.4|1067.7
w/ Outliers	12.14|8.06	21.32|12.05

a more objective comparison against prior arts that require meshing, we further apply Screened Poisson to mesh our output hit points. In Fig. 6, we analyze the trade-off between the number of network evaluations and the reconstructed mesh quality measured in mean and median CD. Evidently, PRIF produces reconstruction with a better quality with fewer network evaluations.

Stress Testing. Figure 7 shows an example of encoding a self-intersecting and non-watertight shape, which is expected to be challenging for neural networks trained to encode conventional functional representations like SDF and OF. In contrast, the shape is well preserved by the network trained to encode our proposed functional representation PRIF.

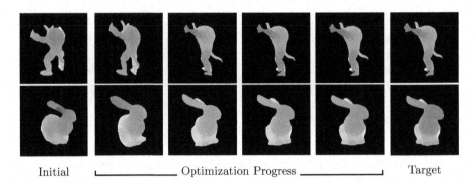

Initial ┕――――――― Optimization Progress ―――――――┙ Target

Fig. 9. Learning Camera Poses. Starting from the *Initial* camera pose, we optimize the learnable pose parameters based on the difference between PRIF output rendered at the current pose and the PRIF output rendered at an unknown *Target* pose. Here, we render the PRIF output as depth images. PRIF-based rendering successfully facilitates the differentiable optimization progress as the camera pose gradually converges to the correct *Target* pose.

Ablations. We present ablation studies validating the effectiveness of our proposed techniques in Fig. 8 and Table 3. The results verify that: 1) not reparametrizing $r = (\mathbf{p}_r, \mathbf{d}_r)$ leads to severe overfitting on the training data, and 2) replacing the Plucker moment vector $\mathbf{m}_r$ with our proposed $\mathbf{f}_r$ improves the encoding quality, possibly because the network only has to learn a simple affine transform matrix as mentioned in Sect. 3.2.

4.5   Further Applications

Learning Camera Poses. Evaluating the PRIF network on some input camera rays is essentially performing differentiable rendering of the underlying scene represented by the network. With a PRIF network trained on a 3D shape, given a silhouette image at an unknown camera pose, our task is to recover that camera pose based on the silhouette image. In this task, the weights of the PRIF network are frozen, and the only learnable parameters are the camera pose matrix. At each iteration, we render the scene through the PRIF network with camera rays defined by the current estimate of the camera pose, and we adjust the estimate based on the silhouette difference between the observed and rendered images. In Fig. 9, we present the rendered image during the optimization steps. The estimated camera pose gradually converges to the correct solution as the rendered image becomes more similar to the observed image.

Neural Rendering with Color. The PRIF network behaves as a geometry renderer since it effectively returns the surface hit point given a viewing ray. Here we show that the PRIF network can be further extended to rendering color at the surface. We select a 3D model of human from the Renderpeople

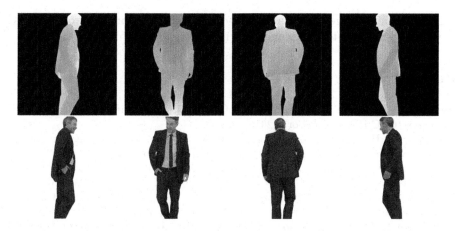

Fig. 10. Incorporating Color Rendering. After training the PRIF network to encode the geometry (rendered as depth images in the first row), we can further train a second-stage network that takes in the hit point produced by PRIF and produces its corresponding color (rendered in the second row).

dataset [39] and virtually capture the hit points and RGB colors at 25 locations surrounding the model. We then train the PRIF network to fit the geometric shape, similar to the single shape experiments. Finally, we extend the network to produce the observed RGB color given the input ray while fixing its hit point prediction. Figure 10 shows the rendered results of geometry and appearance of the 3D model.

Limitation. This paper is focused on 3D shape encoding and decoding through hit points of rays from known views. PRIF can render at novel views by sampling new rays, but to guarantee consistent novel view results would likely require further modifications such as multi-view consistency loss or denser training views.

5   Conclusion

We propose PRIF, a new 3D shape representation based on the relationship between a ray and its perpendicular foot with the origin. We demonstrate that neural networks can successfully encode PRIF to achieve accurate shape representations. With this new representation, we avoid multi-sample sphere tracing and obtain the hit point with a single network evaluation. Neural networks trained to encode PRIF inherit such advantages and can represent shapes more accurately than common neural shape representations using the same network architecture. We further extend the neural PRIF networks to enable various downstream tasks including generative shape modeling, shape denoising and completion, camera pose optimization, and color rendering. Promising future directions include using spatial partitions to improve the network accuracy, jointly learning the geometry and view-dependent color directly from images, speeding up network training, and real-time inference for robotic applications.

References

1. Akenine-Moller, T., Haines, E., Hoffman, N.: Real-Time Rendering. AK Peters/CRC Press, New York (2019)
2. Attal, B., Huang, J.B., Zollhoefer, M., Kopf, J., Kim, C.: Learning neural light fields with ray-space embedding networks. arXiv Preprint arXiv:2112.01523 (2021)
3. Atzmon, M., Lipman, Y.: SAL: Sign agnostic learning of shapes from raw data. In: Proceedings of the IEEE/CVF Conference on Computer Vision and Pattern Recognition, pp. 2565–2574 (2020). https://doi.org/10.1109/CVPR42600.2020.00264
4. Bhatnagar, B.L., Sminchisescu, C., Theobalt, C., Pons-Moll, G.: Combining implicit function learning and parametric models for 3D human reconstruction. In: Vedaldi, A., Bischof, H., Brox, T., Frahm, J.-M. (eds.) ECCV 2020. LNCS, vol. 12347, pp. 311–329. Springer, Cham (2020). https://doi.org/10.1007/978-3-030-58536-5_19
5. Chabra, R., et al.: Deep local shapes: learning local SDF priors for detailed 3D reconstruction. In: Vedaldi, A., Bischof, H., Brox, T., Frahm, J.-M. (eds.) ECCV 2020. LNCS, vol. 12374, pp. 608–625. Springer, Cham (2020). https://doi.org/10.1007/978-3-030-58526-6_36
6. Chang, A.X., et al.: ShapeNet: an Information-Rich 3D Model Repository. Technical Report. arXiv:1512.03012, Stanford University – Princeton University – Toyota Technological Institute at Chicago (2015)
7. Chen, Z., et al.: Multiresolution deep implicit functions for 3D shape representation. In: Proceedings of the IEEE/CVF International Conference on Computer Vision, pp. 13087–13096 (2021). https://doi.org/10.1109/ICCV48922.2021.01284
8. Chen, Z., Tagliasacchi, A., Zhang, H.: BSP-Net: generating compact meshes via binary space partitioning. In: Proceedings of the IEEE/CVF Conference on Computer Vision and Pattern Recognition, pp. 45–54 (2020). https://doi.org/10.1109/CVPR42600.2020.00012
9. Chen, Z., Zhang, H.: Learning implicit fields for generative shape modeling. In: Proceedings of the IEEE/CVF Conference on Computer Vision and Pattern Recognition, pp. 5939–5948 (2019). https://doi.org/10.1109/CVPR.2019.00609
10. Chibane, J., Alldieck, T., Pons-Moll, G.: Implicit functions in feature space for 3D shape reconstruction and completion. In: 2020 IEEE/CVF Conference on Computer Vision and Pattern Recognition (CVPR), pp. 6968–6979 (2020). https://doi.org/10.1109/CVPR42600.2020.00700
11. Chibane, J., Alldieck, T., Pons-Moll, G.: Implicit functions in feature space for 3D shape reconstruction and completion. In: Proceedings of the IEEE/CVF Conference on Computer Vision and Pattern Recognition, pp. 6970–6981 (2020)
12. Cignoni, P., Callieri, M., Corsini, M., Dellepiane, M., Ganovelli, F., Ranzuglia, G.: MeshLab: an open-source mesh processing tool. In: Eurographics Italian Chapter Conference, vol. 2008, pp. 129–136. Salerno, Italy (2008)
13. Curless, B., Levoy, M.: A volumetric method for building complex models from range images. In: Proceedings of the 23rd Annual Conference on Computer Graphics and Interactive Techniques, pp. 303–312 (1996). https://doi.org/10.1145/237170.237269

14. Deng, B., Genova, K., Yazdani, S., Bouaziz, S., Hinton, G., Tagliasacchi, A.: CvxNet: learnable convex decomposition. In: Proceedings of the IEEE/CVF Conference on Computer Vision and Pattern Recognition, pp. 31–44 (2020). https://doi.org/10.1109/CVPR42600.2020.00011

15. Driess, D., Ha, J.S., Toussaint, M., Tedrake, R.: Learning models as functionals of signed-distance fields for manipulation planning. In: Conference on Robot Learning, pp. 245–255. PMLR (2022). 10.48550/arXiv.2110.00792

16. Du, R., et al.: DepthLab: real-time 3D interaction with depth maps for mobile augmented reality. In: Proceedings of the 33rd Annual ACM Symposium on User Interface Software and Technology, pp. 829–843. UIST, ACM (2020). https://doi.org/10.1145/3379337.3415881

17. Duan, Y., Zhu, H., Wang, H., Yi, L., Nevatia, R., Guibas, L.J.: Curriculum DeepSDF. In: Vedaldi, A., Bischof, H., Brox, T., Frahm, J.-M. (eds.) ECCV 2020. LNCS, vol. 12353, pp. 51–67. Springer, Cham (2020). https://doi.org/10.1007/978-3-030-58598-3_4

18. Feng, B.Y., Varshney, A.: SIGNET: efficient neural representation for light fields. In: Proceedings of the IEEE/CVF International Conference on Computer Vision, pp. 14224–14233 (2021). https://doi.org/10.1109/ICCV48922.2021.01396

19. Genova, K., Cole, F., Sud, A., Sarna, A., Funkhouser, T.: Local deep implicit functions for 3D shape. In: Proceedings of the IEEE/CVF Conference on Computer Vision and Pattern Recognition, pp. 4857–4866 (2020). https://doi.org/10.1109/CVPR42600.2020.00491

20. Genova, K., Cole, F., Vlasic, D., Sarna, A., Freeman, W.T., Funkhouser, T.: Learning shape templates with structured implicit functions. In: Proceedings of the IEEE/CVF International Conference on Computer Vision, pp. 7154–7164 (2019). https://doi.org/10.1109/ICCV.2019.00725

21. Hart, J.C.: Sphere tracing: a geometric method for the antialiased ray tracing of implicit surfaces. Vis. Comput. **12**(10), 527–545 (1996)

22. Jia, Y.B.: Plucker coordinates for lines in the space. https://faculty.sites.iastate.edu/jia/files/inline-files/plucker-coordinates.pdf (2020)

23. Jiang, C., et al.: Local implicit grid representations for 3D scenes. In: Proceedings of the IEEE/CVF Conference on Computer Vision and Pattern Recognition, pp. 6001–6010 (2020). https://doi.org/10.1109/CVPR42600.2020.00604

24. Jiang, Y., Ji, D., Han, Z., Zwicker, M.: SDFDiff: differentiable rendering of signed distance fields for 3D shape optimization. In: Proceedings of the IEEE/CVF Conference on Computer Vision and Pattern Recognition, pp. 1251–1261 (2020). https://doi.org/10.1109/CVPR42600.2020.00133

25. Kazhdan, M., Hoppe, H.: Screened poisson surface reconstruction. ACM Trans. Graph. (ToG) **32**(3), 1–13 (2013). https://doi.org/10.1145/2487228.2487237

26. Kleineberg, M., Fey, M., Weichert, F.: Adversarial generation of continuous implicit shape representations. In: Wilkie, A., Banterle, F. (eds.) 41st Annual Conference of the European Association for Computer Graphics, Eurographics 2020 - Short Papers, Norrköping, Sweden, May 25–29, 2020, pp. 41–44. Eurographics Association (2020). https://doi.org/10.2312/egs.20201013

27. Lindell, D.B., Van Veen, D., Park, J.J., Wetzstein, G.: BACON: band-limited coordinate networks for multiscale scene representation. arXiv Preprint arXiv:2112.04645 (2021)

28. Liu, S., Zhang, Y., Peng, S., Shi, B., Pollefeys, M., Cui, Z.: DIST: rendering deep implicit signed distance function with differentiable sphere Tracing. In: 2020 IEEE/CVF Conference on Computer Vision and Pattern Recognition (CVPR). IEEE (2020). https://doi.org/10.1109/CVPR42600.2020.00209

29. Liu, S., Saito, S., Chen, W., Li, H.: Learning to infer implicit surfaces without 3D supervision. In: Advances in Neural Information Processing Systems 32 (2019)
30. Lorensen, W.E., Cline, H.E.: Marching cubes: a high resolution 3D surface construction algorithm. ACM SIGGRAPH Comput. Graph. **21**(4), 163–169 (1987). https://doi.org/10.1007/978-3-030-58452-8_24
31. Martel, J.N., Lindell, D.B., Lin, C.Z., Chan, E.R., Monteiro, M., Wetzstein, G.: ACORN: adaptive coordinate networks for neural scene representation. arXiv Preprint arXiv:2105.02788 (2021)
32. Mescheder, L., Oechsle, M., Niemeyer, M., Nowozin, S., Geiger, A.: Occupancy Networks: learning 3D reconstruction in function space. In: Proceedings of the IEEE/CVF Conference on Computer Vision and Pattern Recognitionm, pp. 4460–4470 (2019). https://doi.org/10.1109/CVPR.2019.00459
33. Mildenhall, B., Srinivasan, P.P., Tancik, M., Barron, J.T., Ramamoorthi, R., Ng, R.: NeRF: representing scenes as neural radiance fields for view synthesis. In: Vedaldi, A., Bischof, H., Brox, T., Frahm, J.-M. (eds.) ECCV 2020. LNCS, vol. 12346, pp. 405–421. Springer, Cham (2020). https://doi.org/10.1007/978-3-030-58452-8_24
34. Müller, T., Evans, A., Schied, C., Keller, A.: Instant neural graphics primitives with a multiresolution hash encoding. arXiv Preprint arXiv:2201.05989 (2022)
35. Niemeyer, M., Mescheder, L., Oechsle, M., Geiger, A.: Differentiable volumetric rendering: learning implicit 3D representations without 3D supervision. In: Proceedings of the IEEE/CVF Conference on Computer Vision and Pattern Recognition, pp. 3504–3515 (2020). https://doi.org/10.1109/CVPR42600.2020.00356
36. Park, J.J., Florence, P., Straub, J., Newcombe, R., Lovegrove, S.: DeepSDF: learning continuous signed distance functions for shape representation. In: 2019 IEEE/CVF Conference on Computer Vision and Pattern Recognition (CVPR) (2019). https://doi.org/10.1109/CVPR.2019.00025
37. Paschalidou, D., Katharopoulos, A., Geiger, A., Fidler, S.: Neural Parts: learning expressive 3D shape abstractions with invertible neural networks. 2021 IEEE/CVF Conference on Computer Vision and Pattern Recognition (CVPR), pp. 3203–3214 (2021). https://doi.org/10.1109/CVPR46437.2021.00322
38. Peng, S., Niemeyer, M., Mescheder, L., Pollefeys, M., Geiger, A.: Convolutional occupancy networks. In: Vedaldi, A., Bischof, H., Brox, T., Frahm, J.-M. (eds.) ECCV 2020. LNCS, vol. 12348, pp. 523–540. Springer, Cham (2020). https://doi.org/10.1007/978-3-030-58580-8_31
39. Renderpeople: renderpeople.com (2022)
40. Saito, S., Huang, Z., Natsume, R., Morishima, S., Kanazawa, A., Li, H.: PIFu: pixel-aligned implicit function for high-resolution clothed human digitization. In: Proceedings of the IEEE/CVF International Conference on Computer Vision, pp. 2304–2314 (2019). https://doi.org/10.1109/ICCV.2019.00239
41. Saragadam, V., Tan, J., Balakrishnan, G., Baraniuk, R.G., Veeraraghavan, A.: MINER: multiscale implicit neural representations (2022). https://doi.org/10.48550/arXiv.2202.03532
42. Simeonov, A., et al.: Neural Descriptor Fields: SE(3)-equivariant object representations for manipulation. arXiv Preprint arXiv:2112.05124 (2021)
43. Sitzmann, V., Chan, E., Tucker, R., Snavely, N., Wetzstein, G.: MetaSDF: meta-learning signed distance functions. Adv. Neural. Inf. Process. Syst. **33**, 10136–10147 (2020). https://doi.org/10.5555/3495724.3496574
44. Sitzmann, V., Martel, J., Bergman, A., Lindell, D., Wetzstein, G.: Implicit neural representations with periodic activation functions. Adv. Neural. Inf. Process. Syst. **33**, 7462–7473 (2020). https://doi.org/10.1109/WACV51458.2022.00234

45. Sitzmann, V., Rezchikov, S., Freeman, B., Tenenbaum, J., Durand, F.: Light Field Networks: neural scene representations with single-evaluation rendering. In: Advances in Neural Information Processing Systems 34 (2021). https://doi.org/10.48550/arXiv.2106.02634

46. Sitzmann, V., Zollhöfer, M., Wetzstein, G.: Scene representation networks: continuous 3D-structure-aware neural scene representations. In: Advances in Neural Information Processing Systems 32 (2019). https://doi.org/10.48550/arXiv.1906.01618

47. Takikawa, T., et al.: Neural geometric level of detail: real-time rendering with implicit 3D shapes. In: Proceedings of the IEEE/CVF Conference on Computer Vision and Pattern Recognition, pp. 11358–11367 (2021). https://doi.org/10.1109/CVPR46437.2021.01120

48. Tancik, M., et al.: Fourier features let networks learn high frequency functions in low dimensional domains. Adv. Neural. Inf. Process. Syst. **33**, 7537–7547 (2020). https://doi.org/10.48550/arXiv.2006.10739

49. Tang, D., et al.: Deep implicit volume compression. In: Proceedings of the IEEE/CVF Conference on Computer Vision and Pattern Recognition, pp. 1293–1303 (2020). https://doi.org/10.1109/CVPR42600.2020.00137

50. Tretschk, E., Tewari, A., Golyanik, V., Zollhöfer, M., Stoll, C., Theobalt, C.: PatchNets: patch-based generalizable deep implicit 3D shape representations. In: Vedaldi, A., Bischof, H., Brox, T., Frahm, J.-M. (eds.) ECCV 2020. LNCS, vol. 12361, pp. 293–309. Springer, Cham (2020). https://doi.org/10.1007/978-3-030-58517-4_18

51. Turk, G., Levoy, M.: Zippered polygon meshes from range images. In: Proceedings of the 21st Annual Conference on Computer Graphics and Interactive Techniques, pp. 311–318 (1994). https://doi.org/10.1145/192161.192241

52. Xu, Q., Wang, W., Ceylan, D., Mech, R., Neumann, U.: DISN: Deep implicit surface network for high-quality single-view 3D reconstruction. In: Advances in Neural Information Processing Systems 32 (2019). https://doi.org/10.5555/3454287.3454332

53. Yang, G., Belongie, S., Hariharan, B., Koltun, V.: Geometry processing with neural fields. In: Thirty-Fifth Conference on Neural Information Processing Systems (2021). https://papers.nips.cc/paper/2021/file/bd686fd640be98efaae0091fa301e613-Paper.pdf

54. Yao, S., Yang, F., Cheng, Y., Mozerov, M.G.: 3D shapes local geometry codes learning with SDF. In: Proceedings of the IEEE/CVF International Conference on Computer Vision, pp. 2110–2117 (2021). https://doi.org/10.1109/ICCVW54120.2021.00239

55. Yariv, L., Gu, J., Kasten, Y., Lipman, Y.: Volume rendering of neural implicit surfaces. In: Advances in Neural Information Processing Systems 34 (2021). https://doi.org/10.1109/CVPR46437.2021.01120

56. Zakharov, S., Kehl, W., Bhargava, A., Gaidon, A.: Autolabeling 3D objects with differentiable rendering of SDF shape priors. In: Proceedings of the IEEE/CVF Conference on Computer Vision and Pattern Recognition, pp. 12224–12233 (2020). https://doi.org/10.1109/CVPR42600.2020.01224

Point Cloud Domain Adaptation via Masked Local 3D Structure Prediction

Hanxue Liang[1(✉)], Hehe Fan[2], Zhiwen Fan[1], Yi Wang[1], Tianlong Chen[1], Yu Cheng[3], and Zhangyang Wang[1]

[1] The University of Texas, Austin, USA
haliang@utexas.edu
[2] National University of Singapore, Singapore, Singapore
[3] Microsoft Research Redmond, Redmond, USA

Abstract. The superiority of deep learning based point cloud representations relies on large-scale labeled datasets, while the annotation of point clouds is notoriously expensive. One of the most effective solutions is to transfer the knowledge from existing labeled source data to unlabeled target data. However, domain bias typically hinders knowledge transfer and leads to accuracy degradation. In this paper, we propose a Masked Local Structure Prediction (MLSP) method to encode target data. Along with the supervised learning on the source domain, our method enables models to embed source and target data in a shared feature space. Specifically, we predict masked local structure via estimating point cardinality, position and normal. Our design philosophies lie in: 1) Point cardinality reflects basic structures (*e.g.*, line, edge and plane) that are invariant to specific domains. 2) Predicting point positions in masked areas generalizes learned representations so that they are robust to incompletion-caused domain bias. 3) Point normal is generated by neighbors and thus robust to noise across domains. We conduct experiments on shape classification and semantic segmentation with different transfer permutations and the results demonstrate the effectiveness of our method. Code is available at https://github.com/VITA-Group/MLSP.

Keywords: Point cloud representation learning · Unsupervised domain adaptation · Shape classification · Semantic segmentation

1 Introduction

Point cloud representation learning based on deep neural networks constitute the recent achievements in 3D vision [19,28,29,42]. However, most of them are conducted under supervised learning and therefore require a large amount of annotated data. The expensive labeling cost limits the scalability to more

---

Supplementary Information The online version contains supplementary material available at https://doi.org/10.1007/978-3-031-20062-5_10.

S. Avidan et al. (Eds.): ECCV 2022, LNCS 13663, pp. 156–172, 2022.
https://doi.org/10.1007/978-3-031-20062-5_10

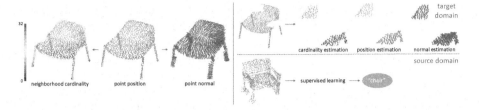

Fig. 1. Illustration of the proposed method. To encode unlabeled target data, we predict masked local structure via estimating point cardinality, position and normal. Point cardinality reflects basic structures such as line, edge and plane, which are invariant to specific domains. Predicting the positions of missing points enables the network to infer structure from partial observation, thus learning a robust representation for incompletion-caused domain bias. Point normal is generated by a few neighbors and thus robust to different individual noisy points across domains. Along with the supervised learning on the source domain, source and target data are embedded into a shared feature space.

unseen environments. To alleviate this problem, we can transfer the knowledge from existing labeled source data to unseen unlabeled target data. However, due to different point scales, object styles, LiDAR viewpoints, incompletion, sensor noise, *etc*, models often suffer the problem of domain bias, leading to poor accuracy. Although part of the biases can be addressed by data preprocessing, *e.g.*, unifying point scales and normalizing object sizes, the other biases have to be reduced via well-designed learning approaches.

To alleviate the problem of domain bias, the first solution is to employ adversarial learning [12,41] to directly learn unbiased representations. Specifically, a discriminator is trained to judge whether the learned representations are from the target domain or the source domain, whereas the model is trained to confuse the discriminator [30]. The second solution is to directly align source and target representations in a shared feature space via assigning pseudo labels to target data [10]. The key to this solution is how to achieve pseudo labels and avoid adding noise [7,47]. The third solution is to design self-supervised learning tasks to learn the internal structure of unlabeled target data [1,7,36,47]. Along with the supervised learning on labeled source data, self-supervised tasks enable models to embed source and target data in a shared feature space. Note that, the adversarial learning and pseudo label solutions are independent of point cloud modality and can be borrowed from general learning methods. Therefore, in this work we emphasize exploiting point cloud characters for self-supervised learning tasks design, and make a minor effort in the pseudo label solution.

In this paper, we propose a Masked Local Structure Prediction (MLSP) method for point cloud domain adaptation. Different from most existing methods [1,47], which mainly focus on designing multiple effective SSL tasks (*e.g.*, predicting the angle between two point clouds and the location of distorted area [47]), our method focuses on exploiting domain-invariant features or attributes. Specifically, we mask a random local area of the input point cloud and then ask models to predict the area structure by estimating the neighborhood cardinalities (the number of neighboring points within a predefined radius), positions and normals of the missing points, respectively. First, we find that point cardinality can reflect basic structures of local areas, *e.g.*, line, edge and plane. As shown in Fig. 1, points at the chair seat have larger cardinalities than points at the legs. Predicting neighborhood cardinality enables models to learn the primitive structure of target objects, which is invariant to different domains. Second, incomplete point clouds are usually encountered in sim-to-real adaptation. Therefore, we follow [1] to predict the positions of missing points to generalize learned representations so that they are invariant to different region missing scenarios between source and target domains. Third, different from image pixels, point clouds are usually not smooth with noisy points, to different degrees in different domains. This hinders models to learn accurate features across different domains [31]. To mitigate this problem, we integrate a normal prediction task in our framework, because point normal is generated by a few neighbors and can be robust to noise. In addition to MLSP, we develop a self-paced learning [10,14,17] variant that leverages prediction probability entropy to select reliable pseudo-labeled samples. The motivation is that a target sample with small entropy of prediction probability is discriminative and its pseudo label is most probably correct.

We conduct extensive experiments including shape classification on the PointDA dataset [30] and semantic segmentation on the PointSegDA dataset [1]. Results demonstrate the effectiveness of our method. Our main contributions are threefold:

⋆ We propose a novel Masked Local Structure Prediction (MLSP) method for point cloud domain adaption, which exploits three types of local attributes to encode unlabeled target data.
⋆ We propose a new point cloud attribute, *i.e.*, neighborhood cardinality, which is able to reflect the basic or primitive structure of point clouds.
⋆ We achieve the new state-of-the-art accuracy of unsupervised domain adaption on shape classification and segmentation benchmarks.

2   Related Work

Point Cloud Representation Learning. Point clouds, which use a set of points with 3D coordinates to specify object positions, are the most straightforward way to preserve 3D spatial information and are very closed to a number of 3D environment understanding applications (*e.g.*, autonomous driving, indoor scene parsing). Point cloud object-level classification and point-level segmentation are two of the fundamental tasks for point cloud processing. Recently, a number of deep neural networks have been proposed to address the two problems [9,19,28,29,39,42,46]. For example, PointNet [28] pioneeringly proposes the first deep neural networks to directly deal with raw point clouds. The successor PointNet++ [29] is based on PointNet and is enhanced to extract both local and global geometric information in a hierarchical way. PointCNN [19] proposes a novel convolution on point cloud to aggregate features in local and equipped with a bottom-up network structure. Recently, PointTransformer [46] adopts the self-attention mechanism to point cloud processing alone with an encoder-decoder structure and achieves state-of-the-art performance in several point cloud benchmarks. Although straightforward to use, point clouds are difficult to be annotated because it requires a huge amount of labor work, especially for point-level labeling. Therefore, it is necessary and urgent for us to develop an effective method for point cloud-based unsupervised domain adaptation to mitigate the domain gap between labeled data in the source domain and unlabeled data in another domain.

Unsupervised Domain Adaptation. Unsupervised domain adaptation (UDA) methods for 2D tasks mainly focus on reducing the discrepancy across different domains. For example, UDA for image classification can be roughly classified into two categories: 1) Minimize the domain discrepancy of a proxy. Methods in [5,15,20,23,26,32,44] measure such discrepancy using the domain distribution statistics. 2) Align feature distributions in an adversarial manner. Works in [3,11,11,12,18,27,33,34,41] either play minimax games at domain level or category level. UDA has also been applied to point cloud processing in works [1,30], which also faces the challenge of gaps in semantic level and domain-agostic feature encoding from local geometries of the point cloud. In the above works, [30] proposes a node module with an adaptive receptive field to model the discriminative local structures and minimize MMD loss to align features in different domains. [1] adopts a self-supervised manner to learn an informative representation with local geometries. The work [24] proposes a multi-level consistency network for 3D detection domain adaptation and enjoys the benefits of the detector-agnostic feature. GAST [47] aims to learn a domain-shared representation of semantic categories by proposing two self-supervised geometric learning tasks as feature regularization.

Self-supervised Learning on Point Clouds. Self-supervised learning (SSL) aims to leverage the raw input as supervision signals by a pre-defined rule or task. SSL is able to learn the representation which benefits downstream tasks. A comprehensive summary of existing methods in SSL can be found in [22]. Several recent works [13,21,35,38,45] studied using SSL framework for learning rich representations of point cloud. [1] studied point cloud reconstruction for DA on point clouds. [13] adopted three tasks including clustering, prediction and reconstruction from noisy input. The work [35] proposed to generate new point cloud by splitting a shape into voxels and then shuffling them. The task is defined as finding the voxel assignment to reconstruct the original point cloud. [38] proposed a task to predict the next point in a space-filling sequence which further boosts the performance. [37] proposed normal prediction for point cloud and aims at multi-task geometric learning network to improve semantic analysis. [45] splitted the point cloud into two parts and proposed to learn a classifier to determine which part it comes from.

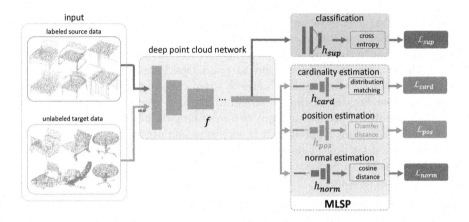

Fig. 2. Overview of the proposed framework for unsupervised domain adaptation on point clouds. The supervised pathway takes as input the point clouds from the source domain and calculates the cross-entropy loss with ground-truth labels. The self-supervised pathway takes point clouds from target domain and calculates the self-supervised loss with the proposed masked local structure prediction, including cardinality, position and normal.

3   Method

In this section, we present our proposed Masked Local Structure Prediction (MLSP) for point cloud domain adaptation. We first formulate the general setup of unsupervised point cloud domain adaptation in Sect. 3.1. Then, we introduce our solution to domain adaptation and describe the proposed MLSP scheme in Sect. 3.2. In Sect. 3.3, we design entropy-based self-paced learning to select reliable pseudo-labeled target data for global representation alignment. We conclude our framework with the overall loss function during our training process in Sect. 3.4. For clarity, we describe MLSP in the context of a classification task, but the same principle applies to the segmentation task as well.

3.1   Overview

We follow the conventional unsupervised domain adaptation (UDA) framework [30] for point cloud representation learning, which aims at transferring the knowledge from a labeled source domain $\mathcal{S} = \{(\boldsymbol{P}_i^{(s)}, y_i^{(s)})\}_{i=1}^{n^{(s)}}$ to an unlabeled target domain $\mathcal{T} = \{\boldsymbol{P}_i^{(t)}\}_{i=1}^{n^{(t)}}$, where $n^{(s)}$ and $n^{(t)}$ denote the numbers of source and target point clouds, respectively. $\boldsymbol{P}_i^{(s)}$ and $\boldsymbol{P}_i^{(t)}$ denote two point clouds from source and target domain, respectively. $y_i^{(s)} \in \mathcal{Y} = \{1, \cdots, L\}$ is the label for source point cloud $\boldsymbol{P}_i^{(s)}$.

We employ a common approach to tackle this learning setup for UDA, which is to learn a shared feature encoder f and trained on two tasks: (1) a supervised task over source domain $\mathcal{S}$, and (2) a self-supervised task that can be trained over both source domain $\mathcal{S}$ and target domain $\mathcal{T}$. In this work, we propose the MLSP method which includes three distinct components: cardinality, position and normal prediction. An overall pipeline is illustrated in Fig. 2. During training, the supervised task and MLSP task will be trained in an alternating fashion. Specifically, in the supervised task flow, the labeled source samples will be processed by shared encoder f and a classification head h_{sup} to produce the prediction result. A supervision loss will be applied to it. In MLSP flow, after the shared encoder, the unlabeled source/target samples will be passed separately through h_{card}, h_{pos} and h_{norm} to predict the cardinality, position and normal of missing points. Different losses are applied to each prediction.

3.2 Masked Local Structure Prediction

The main idea of the proposed domain adaptation scheme is to learn an unbiased feature across both source and target domains. To this end, we enforce models to predict **cardinality**, **position** and **normal** of masked points so that they can encode the internal structure of unlabed target data. To be more specific, point cardinality reflects the primitive structure of local areas, *e.g.*, line, edge and plane, which is invariant to different domains. Missing position prediction enables models to infer point cloud structure from partial observation. In this way, models can learn robust representation against incompletion-caused domain bias. Point normal is generated from a few neighboring points and thus robust to noisy points. By predicting point normal, our models can learn features mitigating the noisy point distortion across different domains.

We refer to $p \in \mathbb{R}^3$ as an individual point and denote $P_{\mathcal{M}}$ as the point

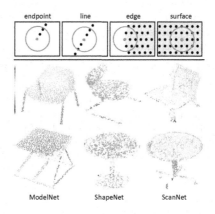

Fig. 3. **Top**: Visualization of point cardinality. It reflects the basis geometry structure, *e.g.*, the cardinalities of points on lines are smaller than that of those on edges and larger than those on endpoints. **Bottom**: Cardinality visualization in three point cloud domains. Cardinalities of different regions or parts show a strong pattern. Therefore, we can use the cardinality attribute to reflect basic local structures, *e.g.*, endpoint, line, edge and surface. This representation is invariant across different domains and classes.

cloud after masking P. For each masked point $p \in P \backslash P_{\mathcal{M}}$, we denote prediction of cardinality as $f_{card}(p) = h_{card} \circ f(P_{\mathcal{M}})$, position as $f_{pos}(p) = h_{pos} \circ f(P_{\mathcal{M}})$, and normal vector as $f_{norm}(p) = h_{norm} \circ f(P_{\mathcal{M}})$, respectively. Following [1], we employ the voxel partition-based method to generate masked point set $P_{\mathcal{M}}$, which uniformly samples one of the spatial partition of $3 \times 3 \times 3$ cubes and remove all the points in the sampled cube. The masked points are replaced with new points sampled from a Gaussian distribution around the mask center.

Neighborhood Cardinality Prediction. Given a sampled point cloud, neighborhood cardinality indicates the basis geometry structures (*e.g.*, line, edge and plane) around each point. As shown in Fig. 3, for points lie on lines (*e.g.*, chair legs), the number of neighbors within a given radius is generally smaller than that of points on planes (*e.g.*, tabletop). The basic geometry structures are shared across different domains and object categories. This observation motivates us to predict point cardinalities to learn domain-invariant features across different domains. More formally, we define neighborhood cardinality as follows:

$$\mathcal{N}(\boldsymbol{p}, r) = \{\boldsymbol{q} \in P \mid \|\boldsymbol{p} - \boldsymbol{q}\| \leq r, \ \boldsymbol{q} \neq \boldsymbol{p}\}, \quad \mathcal{C}(\boldsymbol{p}, r) = |\mathcal{N}(\boldsymbol{p}, r)|, \qquad (1)$$

where r is the radius of the neighborhood. As point cardinality only reflects a few basic structures, representing these discrete values in a regression manner is not necessary. Therefore, we formulate the cardinalty prediction task as a classification problem. Specifically, we first experimentally choose the maximum cardinality value of a dataset, denoted by C_{max}. Then we choose the number of cardinality bins K and obtain cardinality interval $c_0 = C_{max}/K$. We consider K as a hyperparameter in our method. From here, we can convert $C(\boldsymbol{p}, r)$ into a groudtruth class label $c = \left\lfloor \frac{C(\boldsymbol{p}, r)}{c_0} \right\rfloor$. For each point $\boldsymbol{p}$, the cardinality head will predict its cardinality class. To calculate the cardinality classification loss, we convert the one-hot classification labels into a two-points probability vector representation which is justified in Fig. 4. Specifically, for each point $\boldsymbol{p}$, we convert its cardinality $C(\boldsymbol{p}, r)$ into a probability vector $\boldsymbol{\lambda}$ with two non-zero values:

$$\lambda_i = \begin{cases} 1 - \frac{C(\boldsymbol{p}, r) - c*c_0}{c_0} & i = c, \\ \frac{C(\boldsymbol{p}, r) - c*c_0}{c_0} & i = c+1, \\ 0 & \text{otherwise.} \end{cases} \qquad (2)$$

Such a representation includes richer distribution information than a one-hot vector. Cardinality prediction for point $\boldsymbol{p}$ will be $\hat{\boldsymbol{\lambda}} = h_{card} \circ f(\boldsymbol{P_M})$ and we employ KL divergence as the measurement to minimize the gap between prediction weights $\hat{\boldsymbol{\lambda}}$ and "ground-truth" weights $\boldsymbol{\lambda}$, leading to the following cardinality loss:

$$\mathcal{L}_{card}(\boldsymbol{P_M}, f_{card}) = \sum_{\boldsymbol{p} \in P \backslash \boldsymbol{P_M}} \sum_{i=1}^{K} \lambda_i \log(\hat{\lambda}_i). \qquad (3)$$

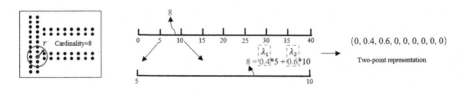

Fig. 4. The proposed two-point representations for the neighborhood cardinality. It is represented by two adjacent bins instead of one-hot vectors

Point Position Prediction. To recover the missing or masked region, point coordinate information is necessary. Even though non-smoothness and noisiness appear in point cloud input, reconstructed points can not deviate too much from the given ground-truth points. Similar to [1], we utilize the Chamfer distance [6] between the predicted point cloud coordinates and ground-truth point coordinates at the masked region. The loss of position prediction has the following form:

$$\mathcal{L}_{pos}(\boldsymbol{P}_{\mathcal{M}}, f_{pos}) = \sum_{p \in P \backslash P_{\mathcal{M}}} \min_{q \in f_{pos}(P_{\mathcal{M}})} \|\boldsymbol{p} - \boldsymbol{q}\|^2 + \sum_{q \in f_{pos}(P_{\mathcal{M}})} \min_{p \in P \backslash P_{\mathcal{M}}} \|\boldsymbol{q} - \boldsymbol{p}\|^2. \quad (4)$$

Point Normal Prediction. Normal vector estimation of a point cloud is relevant to maintaining local geometric features. It is generated from a few neighboring points and thus robust to noisy points. Motivated by this observation, we integrate normal estimation as a self-supervised task into our method and expect that models can learn features mitigating the noisy point distortion across different domains. The ground-truth normal vector at the point $\boldsymbol{p}$ is obtained via least-square fit based on all the points in the original point cloud in the neighboring region:

$$n(p) = \operatorname*{argmin}_{n \in \mathbb{R}^3} \sum_{q \in \mathcal{N}(p)} (\boldsymbol{n} \cdot (\boldsymbol{q} - \boldsymbol{p}))^2, \quad (5)$$

where $\hat{n}(\boldsymbol{p}) = f_{norm}(\boldsymbol{p})$ is the predicted normal vector of masked point $\boldsymbol{p}$. As shown in Fig 5, the normal is robust against instrumental noise from the point cloud data acquisition. To obtain the appropriate neighbouring point set $\mathcal{N}(\boldsymbol{p})$ of $\boldsymbol{p}$, we test with using both neighbouring points defined with a radius r of point $\boldsymbol{p}$ as $\mathcal{N}(\boldsymbol{p}) = \mathcal{N}(\boldsymbol{p}, r)$ in Eq. 1 and nearest neighbors search, where $\mathcal{N}(\boldsymbol{p}) = kNN(\boldsymbol{p}, k)$. The orientation of normal vector is defined towards the center of the object. We use the cosine-similarity metric to measure the distance between predicted normal and the estimated "true" normal, leading to the following self-supervised loss:

$$\mathcal{L}_{norm}(\boldsymbol{P}_{\mathcal{M}}, f_{norm}) = \sum_{p \in P \backslash P_{\mathcal{M}}} \frac{\boldsymbol{n}(p) \cdot \hat{\boldsymbol{n}}(p)}{\|\boldsymbol{n}(p)\| \|\hat{\boldsymbol{n}}(p)\|}. \quad (6)$$

At last, we define the total loss of MLSP for a given masked point cloud $\boldsymbol{P}_{\mathcal{M}}$ as:

$$\mathcal{L}_{pred}(\boldsymbol{P}_{\mathcal{M}}) = \alpha_1 \mathcal{L}_{card}(\boldsymbol{P}_{\mathcal{M}}, f_{card}) + \alpha_2 \mathcal{L}_{pos}(\boldsymbol{P}_{\mathcal{M}}, f_{pos}) + \alpha_3 \mathcal{L}_{norm}(\boldsymbol{P}_{\mathcal{M}}, f_{norm}) \quad (7)$$

where $\alpha_1, \alpha_2, \alpha_3$ are hyperparemters that control the weights of masked point cloud attribute predictions.

3.3 Entropy-Guided Self-paced Global Representation Alignment

In addition to the MLSP, we also exploit pseudo labels to boost the domain adaptation accuracy by aligning source and target global representations. The key to

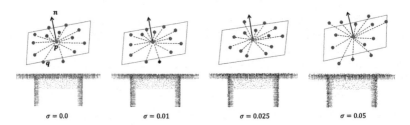

Fig. 5. Normal regression visualization under different scales of Gaussian noise. Top row: our normal regression scheme fits a least-square plane using neighboring points to obtain the pseudo label of "true" normal n at target domain $\mathcal{T}$. As the noise increases, even though the point coordinates are shifting, the estimation of normal shall be consistent. Bottom row: An example point cloud in the PointDA-10 dataset. The estimated normals (blue arrows) are mostly robust even when point position are shifted under large-scale noise ($\sigma = 0.05$). Value of standard derivations σ shown below are set under the normalized point cloud scaling.

this approach is how to assign correct pseudo labels and avoid introducing noise. To this end, we follow [47] to employ self-paced learning [8,10,14,17] to select reliable pseudo-labeled target samples. We first assign the corresponding class of the maximum prediction probability as the pseudo label of each target sample. Then, we only use the target samples whose prediction probability entropies are small enough to train the model with their pseudo labels. We denote $\boldsymbol{y}_i^{(t)}$ as the prediction probability vector of the i-th target sample. We first predict the pseudo label as $\hat{y}_i^{(t)} = \arg\max_l \boldsymbol{y}_{i,l}^{(t)}$. Then, we select the target samples as follows,

$$v_i = \begin{cases} 1, & \sum_{l=1}^{L} -\boldsymbol{y}_{i,l}^{(t)} \log \boldsymbol{y}_{i,l}^{(t)} \leq \gamma, \\ 0, & \text{otherwise,} \end{cases} \tag{8}$$

where $v_i = 1$ indicates the i-th target sample is selected.

The value of the threshold γ controls how confident the predicted class labeling is. Our motivation is that small entropy means the sample is discriminative and can be easily recognized. Therefore, pseudo labels with small prediction probability entropies are more likely correct. Compared to [47], which selects pseudo labels whose probabilities are large enough, entropy is robust and reflects the "entire discriminativeness" of target samples. Note that, although with a fixed γ, as models become stronger and domain bias reduces during training, more and more target samples are selected. As the number of selected target samples increases, models are improved in return. In this way, the accuracy progressively increases.

3.4   Overall Loss

The overall loss function is the sum of supervision loss under $\mathcal{S}$ and linear combination of three estimation tasks as well as the self-paced learning loss under $\mathcal{T}$:

$$\mathcal{L}(\mathcal{S},\mathcal{T},\mathcal{M}) = \sum_{i=1}^{n^{(s)}} \mathcal{L}_{sup}(\boldsymbol{P}_i^{(s)}, y_i^{(s)}) + \sum_{i=1}^{n^{(t)}} \mathcal{L}_{pred}(\boldsymbol{P}_{i,\mathcal{M}}^{(t)}) + \beta \sum_{i=1}^{n^{(t)}} v_i \mathcal{L}_{sup}(\boldsymbol{P}_i^{(t)}, \hat{y}_i^{(t)}), \quad (9)$$

where β controls the importance of the self-paced loss. Both β and $\alpha_1, \alpha_2, \alpha_3$ in Equ. 7 are selected empirically and more details can be found in supplementary. The classification loss $\mathcal{L}_{sup}(\boldsymbol{P}_i^{(t)}, \tilde{y}_i^{(t)})$ under the target is the sum of all the samples that are selected and assigned pseudo labels.

4   Experiments

We evaluate the proposed method under the standard protocol of unsupervised domain adaptation on the task of point cloud data classification and segmentation. We conduct experiments on PointDA-10 and PointSegDA datasets.

4.1   Datasets

PointDA-10 [30] contains three widely-used datasets: ModelNet [43], ShapeNet [2] and ScanNet [4]. All three datasets share the same ten categories (bed, table, sofa, chair, etc.). ModelNet(**M**) contains 4183 train samples and 856 test samples and ShapeNet(**S**) contains 17,378 train samples and 2492 test samples. Both ModelNet and ShapeNet are sampled from 3D CAD models. ScanNet(**S***) is a more challenging dataset, which contains 6110 train and 1769 test samples. Samples from this dataset are scanned and reconstructed from real-world indoor scenes. The objects often lose some parts and get occluded by surroundings. We follow the data preparation procedure used in [1]. Specifically, all object point clouds in all datasets are aligned along the direction of gravity, while arbitrary rotations along the z-axis are allowed. Each sample is down-sampled to 1024 points and normalized within a unit ball. A typical 80%/20% data split for training and validation on both source and target domains is employed.

PointSegDA is based on a dataset of meshes of human models proposed by [1] and consists of four subsets: ADOBE, FAUST, MIT, and SCAPE. They share eight classes of human body parts (hand, head, feet, etc.) with difference in point distribution, pose and human shapes. PointSegDA differs from PointDA-10 in the type of the domain shifts and the actual shapes representing deformable objects. Thus, PointSegDA allows us to evaluate the proposed method in a fundamentally different setup. For data processing, we follow the data processing in [1] and aligned the shapes with the positive Z-axis and scaled them to the unit cube. Each sample contains 2048 points sampled from mesh vertices and downsampled by farthest point sampling.

4.2   Implementation Details

Network Architecture. We adopt DGCNN [42] with the same configurations as in the official implementation for feature extractor backbone and supervised task head. As for SSL heads, they share the same input as global feature vector concatenated to point-wise feature from the backbone network. Please refer to the supplement for more details about network architecture.

Training Procedure. During training, we alternate between a batch of source samples and a batch of target samples in all methods. We run each configuration with 3 different random seeds for 150 epochs and use source-validation-based early stopping. We use a fixed batch size of 32 for PointDA-10 and a batch size of 16 for PointSegDA. We adopt ADAM [16] optimizer with learning rate 0.001 and weight decay 0.00005. A cosine annealing learning rate scheduler implemented via PyTorch is assigned in training. β is selected to be 1 and γ is selected over $\{1.516, 1.549, 1.551, 1.628\}$ and we empirically set it to be 1.549. Please refer to the supplement for more details about training.

4.3   Classification Results on PointDA-10 Dataset

We compare our proposed method with a list of recent state-of-the-art point-based DA methods including Domain Adversarial Neural Network (DANN) [11], Point Domain Adaptation Network (PointDAN) [30], Reconstruction Space Network (RS) [35] , Deformation Reconstruction Network with Point Cloud Mixup (DefRec+PCM) [1] and Geometry-aware self-training (GAST) [47]. [1] demonstrates the effectiveness of Mixup training on source domain and we adopt this setup in our PointDA-10 experiments. The supervised model is trained on labeled target data and the baseline model is trained only with labeled source samples. All comparative methods take the same training protocol and the best models are selected according to source-validation based early stopping. Results are presented in Table 1.

By only adopting a self-supervised learning strategy, our approach outperforms all competing domain adaptation methods by a significant margin. Particularly, it improves the average accuracy by relative 2.2% and 3.5% over the state-of-the-art DefRec+PCM [1] and Geometry-aware self-training (GAST) [47]. Considering that our model uses the same backbone DGCNN as the baseline, this performance gain should be attributed to the design of the local feature prediction algorithm, which helps to learn a more adaptive representation across domains. More importantly, in comparison with [1], MLSP achieves superior performance on almost all six adaptation tasks. This demonstrates the effectiveness of our designed local point structure. Particularly, we improve with a large margin on M $\rightarrow$ S* (55.4% *vs.* 51.8%), S*$\rightarrow$M (78.2% *vs.* 73.7%) and S* $\rightarrow$ S (76.1% *vs.* 71.1%) tasks.

After adopting the pseudo label strategy, MLSP can outperform all previous domain adaptation methods. Using entropy-based global alignment(EGA) strategy, we further boost our model's performance to a high level of average accuracy

74.0%. The superior of MLSP+EGA over MLSP+SPST demonstrates the effectiveness of our entropy-guided pseudo label selection design. It is noteworthy that we are able to reach a remarkable performance on two synthetic-to-real M $\rightarrow$ S* and S $\rightarrow$ S* tasks, with mean accuracy 59.1% and 57.6% respectively.

Table 1. Comparative evaluation in classification accuracy (%) averaged over 3 seeds ($\pm$ SEM) on the PointDA-10 dataset. *BS* indicate baseline method, *PS* means Pseudo Label.

Methods	SSL	PS	M$\rightarrow$S	M$\rightarrow$S*	S$\rightarrow$M	S$\rightarrow$S*	S* $\rightarrow$M	S* $\rightarrow$S	Avg.
Supervised			93.9 $\pm$ 0.2	78.4 $\pm$ 0.6	96.2 $\pm$ 0.1	78.4 $\pm$ 0.6	96.2 $\pm$ 0.1	93.9 $\pm$ 0.2	89.5 $\pm$ 0.3
BS (w/o adap.)			83.3 $\pm$ 0.7	43.8 $\pm$ 2.3	75.5 $\pm$ 1.8	42.5 $\pm$ 1.4	63.8 $\pm$ 3.9	64.2 $\pm$ 0.8	62.2 $\pm$ 1.8
DANN [11]			74.8 $\pm$ 2.8	42.1 $\pm$ 0.6	57.5 $\pm$ 0.4	50.9 $\pm$ 1.0	43.7 $\pm$ 2.9	71.6 $\pm$ 1.0	56.8 $\pm$ 1.5
PointDAN [30]			83.9 $\pm$ 0.3	44.8 $\pm$ 1.4	63.3 $\pm$ 1.1	45.7 $\pm$ 0.7	43.6 $\pm$ 2.0	56.4 $\pm$ 1.5	56.3 $\pm$ 1.2
RS [35]	✓		79.9 $\pm$ 0.8	46.7 $\pm$ 4.8	75.2 $\pm$ 2.0	51.4 $\pm$ 3.9	71.8 $\pm$ 2.3	71.2 $\pm$ 2.8	66.0 $\pm$ 1.6
DefRec+PCM [1]	✓		81.7 $\pm$ 0.6	51.8 $\pm$ 0.3	78.6 $\pm$ 0.7	54.5 $\pm$ 0.3	73.7 $\pm$ 1.6	71.1 $\pm$ 1.4	68.6 $\pm$ 0.8
GAST [47]	✓		83.9 $\pm$ 0.2	56.7 $\pm$ 0.3	76.4 $\pm$ 0.2	55.0 $\pm$ 0.2	73.4 $\pm$ 0.3	72.2 $\pm$ 0.2	69.5 $\pm$ 0.2
Ours	✓		83.7 $\pm$ 0.4	55.4 $\pm$ 1.8	77.1 $\pm$ 0.9	55.6 $\pm$ 0.7	78.2 $\pm$ 1.5	76.1 $\pm$ 0.5	71.0 $\pm$ 0.8
GAST+SPST [47]	✓	✓	74.8 $\pm$ 0.1	**59.8 $\pm$ 0.2**	80.8 $\pm$ 0.6	56.7 $\pm$ 0.2	81.1 $\pm$ 0.8	74.9 $\pm$ 0.5	73.0 $\pm$ 0.4
Ours+SPST	✓	✓	85.7 $\pm$ 0.6	59.4 $\pm$ 1.3	82.3 $\pm$ 0.9	57.3 $\pm$ 0.7	**82.2 $\pm$ 0.5**	76.4 $\pm$ 0.5	73.8 $\pm$ 1.0
Ours+EGA	✓	✓	**86.2 $\pm$ 0.8**	59.1 $\pm$ 0.9	**83.5 $\pm$ 0.4**	**57.6 $\pm$ 0.6**	81.2 $\pm$ 0.4	**76.4 $\pm$ 0.3**	**74.0 $\pm$ 0.5**

4.4 Segmentation Results on PointSegDA Dataset

We evaluate the generalization ability of MLSP beyond classification tasks on PointSegDA dataset. We compare against several methods including unsupervised baseline, RS [35], Adapt-SegMap [40] and DefRec+PCM [1] on the mean Intersection over Union (IoU). As is shown in Table 2, our model achieves the highest accuracy compared with all previous adaptation methods, which demonstrates that MLSP can generalize well on segmentation task. Particularly, it demonstrates the best performance on most adaptations.

4.5 Ablation Study and Analysis

In this section, we conduct ablation study experiments to analyze the effectiveness of different components of the model. Experiments are conducted on PointDA-10 dataset.

Effect of Neighborhood Cardinality, Position and Normal Prediction.
In this part, we separately evaluate the performance of neighborhood cardinality, position and normal prediction. To get a unified measure of performance, we tuned the loss weight between SSL loss and source domain supervised loss, so that the best performance can be reached for each prediction component. More details can be found in supplementary and the result is shown in Table 3. Evidently, all three prediction components can improve the domain adaptation performance by a good margin. Among them, cardinality prediction can provide

Table 2. Point Cloud Segmentation Performance(mean IoU.) on PointSegDA dataset, averaged over three runs (± SEM).

Methods	FAUST to ADOBE	FAUST to MIT	FAUST to SCAPE	MIT to ADOBE	MIT to FAUST	MIT to SCAPE	ADOBE to FAUST	ADOBE to MIT	ADOBE to SCAPE	SCAPE to ADOBE	SCAPE to FAUST	SCAPE to MIT	Avg.
Supervised-T	84.0 ± 1.8	84.0 ± 1.8	84.0 ± 1.8	81.8 ± 0.3	81.8 ± 0.3	81.8 ± 0.3	80.9 ± 7.2	80.9 ± 7.2	80.9 ± 7.2	82.4 ± 1.2	82.4 ± 1.2	82.4 ± 1.2	82.3 ± 2.6
Unsupervised	78.5 ± 0.4	60.9 ± 0.6	66.5 ± 0.6	26.6 ± 3.8	53.6 ± 1.3	69.9 ± 1.2	38.5 ± 2.2	31.2 ± 1.4	30.0 ± 3.6	74.1 ± 1.0	68.4 ± 2.4	65.5 ± 0.5	53.6 ± 1.6
Adapt-SegMap [49]	70.5 ± 3.4	60.1 ± 0.6	65.3 ± 1.3	49.1 ± 9.7	54.0 ± 0.5	62.8 ± 7.6	44.3 ± 1.7	35.4 ± 0.3	35.1 ± 1.4	70.1 ± 2.5	67.7 ± 1.4	63.8 ± 1.2	56.5 ± 2.6
RS [35]	76.7 ± 0.5	60.7 ± 0.4	66.9 ± 0.4	59.6 ± 5.0	38.4 ± 2.1	70.4 ± 1.0	44.0 ± 0.6	30.4 ± 0.5	36.6 ± 0.8	70.7 ± 0.8	73.0 ± 1.5	65.3 ± 0.1	57.9 ± 1.1
DefRec [1]	79.7 ± 0.3	81.6 ± 0.1	67.4 ± 1.0	67.1 ± 1.0	40.1 ± 1.4	72.6 ± 0.5	42.5 ± 0.3	28.9 ± 1.5	32.2 ± 1.2	66.4 ± 0.9	72.2 ± 1.2	66.2 ± 0.9	58.1 ± 0.9
Ours	80.9 ± 0.4	80.0 ± 0.2	65.5 ± 0.5	67.3 ± 0.3	40.4 ± 0.6	70.8 ± 1.0	45.4 ± 1.0	31.1 ± 0.8	38.4 ± 0.5	74.8 ± 1.0	72.5 ± 0.5	66.6 ± 0.9	59.5 ± 0.6

Table 3. Ablation study of MLSP prediction tasks on PointDA-10 dataset

Cardinality	Position	Normal	M→S	M→S*	S→M	S→S*	S* →M	S* →S	Avg.
✓			83.0	54.3	74.0	53.5	71.9	75.6	68.7
	✓		82.1	52.3	76.2	53.7	75.1	72.4	68.6
		✓	83.5	49.4	74.9	53.4	75.5	72.4	68.2
✓		✓	83.6	52.6	74.8	52.7	74.5	75.6	69.0
	✓	✓	83.1	56.0	77.8	55.7	76.4	72.2	70.2
✓	✓		82.5	54.9	76.6	55.5	76.8	77.3	70.6
✓	✓	✓	83.7	55.4	77.1	55.6	78.2	76.1	71.0

the highest average accuracy of 68.7%. By combining these three components together, we are able to further improve the performance, which demonstrates the compatibility between these components. The combination of position estimation and normal estimation provides the best accuracy in the sim-to-real scenario.

Effect of Class Number of Cardinality. For cardinality estimation, we consider the number of cardinality classes as a hyper-parameter and analyze its influence on the domain adaptation performance. As is shown in Table 3 in supplement, 8-class reaches the highest performance accuracy on PointDA-10. When we further increase the class number, we notice a performance drop. This might be explained that when we over-classify the cardinality, features of some similar geometric structure with different cardinalities will be encourage to be separative.

Effect of Loss for Cardinality Estimation. In this part, we compare our proposed cardinality estimation loss with cross-entropy loss. Experiments demonstrate the superiority of our proposed loss over directly using cross-entropy loss. And the former achieves better accuracy on four tasks and reaches a higher average accuracy.

Effect of Number of Neighboring Points for Normal Estimation. To validate that point normal attribute can help mitigate the distortion caused by noisy points, we change the number of neighboring points to calculate each point's ground truth normal, and compare their performance in PointDA-10 benchmark. As shown in Fig. 1 in supplement, we notice that improving the number of neighboring points considered for normal estimation will help the transfer learning process. While when we further increase it after 15 points, we

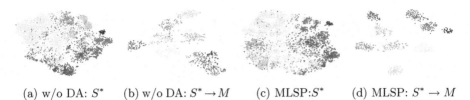

(a) w/o DA: S^* (b) w/o DA: $S^* \to M$ (c) MLSP:S^* (d) MLSP: $S^* \to M$

Fig. 6. The t-SNE visualization of learnt feature vectors from model f under source (Scannet) and target (ModelNet) domain. First two images are generated without domain adaptation. Different colors reveals different classes.

Table 4. Cardinality prediction on PointDA-10 dataset with different loss.

Loss Function	M→S	M→S^*	S→M	S→S^*	S^* →M	S^* →S	Average
CE	83.4	55.6	73.6	52.6	69.9	71.9	67.8
Ours	83.0	54.3	74.0	53.5	71.9	75.6	68.7

witness a small performance drop. This can be explained that if we use too many neighboring points, the smoothing effect is too strong which can affect learning detail structure.

Feature Visualization. We utilize t-SNE [25] to visualize the feature distribution of the 1024-dimension latent codes in Fig. 6. Without domain adaptation, features of different classes in the target domain are mixed up. After adaptation. the distribution of the features in the target domain demonstrates clear clusters.

5   Conclusions

Our work focuses on designing an algorithm to solve the object point cloud domain adaptation problems. Starting from a self-supervised framework, we propose MLSP method that is beneficial to point cloud DA goal, which includes cardinally, position and normal estimation. We validate the effectiveness of these three point features in mitigating the domain bias problems. And our method achieves state-of-art performance on point cloud shape classification and semantic segmentation benchmarks.

References

1. Achituve, I., Maron, H., Chechik, G.: Self-supervised learning for domain adaptation on point clouds. In: Proceedings of the IEEE/CVF Winter Conference on Applications of Computer Vision, pp. 123–133 (2021)
2. Chang, A.X., et al.: ShapeNet: an information-rich 3D model repository. arXiv preprint arXiv:1512.03012 (2015)

3. Chen, X., Wang, S., Long, M., Wang, J.: Transferability vs. Discriminability: batch spectral penalization for adversarial domain adaptation. In: International Conference on Machine Learning, pp. 1081–1090. PMLR (2019)
4. Dai, A., Chang, A.X., Savva, M., Halber, M., Funkhouser, T., Nießner, M.: ScanNet: richly-annotated 3D reconstructions of indoor scenes. In: Proceedings of the IEEE Conference on Computer Vision and Pattern Recognition, pp. 5828–5839 (2017)
5. Deng, Z., Luo, Y., Zhu, J.: Cluster alignment with a teacher for unsupervised domain adaptation. In: Proceedings of the IEEE/CVF International Conference on Computer Vision, pp. 9944–9953 (2019)
6. Fan, H., Su, H., Guibas, L.J.: A point set generation network for 3D object reconstruction from a single image. In: Proceedings of the IEEE Conference on Computer Vision and Pattern Recognition, pp. 605–613 (2017)
7. Fan, H., Chang, X., Zhang, W., Cheng, Y., Sun, Y., Kankanhalli, M.: Self-supervised global-local structure modeling for point cloud domain adaptation with reliable voted pseudo labels. In: Proceedings of the IEEE/CVF Conference on Computer Vision and Pattern Recognition, pp. 6377–6386 (2022)
8. Fan, H., Liu, P., Xu, M., Yang, Y.: Unsupervised visual representation learning via dual-level progressive similar instance selection. IEEE Trans. Cybern. (2021). https://doi.org/10.1109/TCYB.2021.3054978
9. Fan, H., Yu, X., Ding, Y., Yang, Y., Kankanhalli, M.: PSTNet: point spatio-temporal convolution on point cloud sequences. In: International Conference on Learning Representations (2020)
10. Fan, H., Zheng, L., Yan, C., Yang, Y.: Unsupervised person re-identification: clustering and fine-tuning. ACM Trans. Multim. Comput. Commun. Appl. 14(4), 83:1-83:18 (2018). https://doi.org/10.1145/3243316
11. Ganin, Y., et al.: Domain-adversarial training of neural networks. J. Mach. Learn. Res. 17(59), 1–35 (2016)
12. Goodfellow, I., et al.: Generative adversarial nets. In: Advances in Neural Information Processing Systems 27 (2014)
13. Hassani, K., Haley, M.: Unsupervised multi-task feature learning on point clouds. In: Proceedings of the IEEE/CVF International Conference on Computer Vision, pp. 8160–8171 (2019)
14. Jiang, L., Meng, D., Yu, S., Lan, Z., Shan, S., Hauptmann, A.G.: Self-paced learning with diversity. In: Advances in Neural Information Processing Systems, pp. 2078–2086 (2014)
15. Kang, G., Jiang, L., Yang, Y., Hauptmann, A.G.: Contrastive adaptation network for unsupervised domain adaptation. In: Proceedings of the IEEE/CVF Conference on Computer Vision and Pattern Recognition, pp. 4893–4902 (2019)
16. Kingma, D.P., Ba, J.: Adam: a method for stochastic optimization. arXiv preprint arXiv:1412.6980 (2014)
17. Kumar, M.P., Packer, B., Koller, D.: Self-paced learning for latent variable models. In: Advances in Neural Information Processing Systems, pp. 1189–1197 (2010)
18. Lee, C.Y., Batra, T., Baig, M.H., Ulbricht, D.: Sliced wasserstein discrepancy for unsupervised domain adaptation. In: Proceedings of the IEEE/CVF Conference on Computer Vision and Pattern Recognition, pp. 10285–10295 (2019)
19. Li, Y., Bu, R., Sun, M., Wu, W., Di, X., Chen, B.: PointCNN: convolution on X-transformed points. In: Advances in Neural Information Processing Systems 31 (2018)

20. Liang, H., Zhang, Q., Dai, P., Lu, J.: Boosting the generalization capability in cross-domain few-shot learning via noise-enhanced supervised autoencoder. In: Proceedings of the IEEE/CVF International Conference on Computer Vision, pp. 9424–9434 (2021)
21. Liang, H., et al.: Exploring geometry-aware contrast and clustering harmonization for self-supervised 3D object detection. In: Proceedings of the IEEE/CVF International Conference on Computer Vision, pp. 3293–3302 (2021)
22. Liu, X., et al.: Self-supervised learning: generative or contrastive. IEEE Trans. Knowl. Data Eng. (2021)
23. Long, M., Cao, Y., Cao, Z., Wang, J., Jordan, M.I.: Transferable representation learning with deep adaptation networks. IEEE Trans. Pattern Anal. Mach. Intell. **41**(12), 3071–3085 (2018)
24. Luo, Z., et al.: Unsupervised domain adaptive 3D detection with multi-level consistency. In: Proceedings of the IEEE/CVF International Conference on Computer Vision, pp. 8866–8875 (2021)
25. Van der Maaten, L., Hinton, G.: Visualizing data using t-SNE. J. Mach. Learn. Res. **9**(86), 2579–2605 (2008)
26. Pan, Y., Yao, T., Li, Y., Wang, Y., Ngo, C.W., Mei, T.: Transferrable prototypical networks for unsupervised domain adaptation. In: Proceedings of the IEEE/CVF Conference on Computer Vision and Pattern Recognition, pp. 2239–2247 (2019)
27. Pinheiro, P.O.: Unsupervised domain adaptation with similarity learning. In: Proceedings of the IEEE Conference on Computer Vision and Pattern Recognition, pp. 8004–8013 (2018)
28. Qi, C.R., Su, H., Mo, K., Guibas, L.J.: PointNet: deep learning on point sets for 3D classification and segmentation. In: Proceedings of the IEEE Conference on Computer Vision and Pattern Recognition, pp. 652–660 (2017)
29. Qi, C.R., Yi, L., Su, H., Guibas, L.J.: PointNet++: deep hierarchical feature learning on point sets in a metric space. In: Advances in Neural Information Processing Systems 30 (2017)
30. Qin, C., You, H., Wang, L., Kuo, C.C.J., Fu, Y.: PointDAN: a multi-scale 3D domain adaption network for point cloud representation. In: Advances in Neural Information Processing Systems 32 (2019)
31. Rakotosaona, M.J., La Barbera, V., Guerrero, P., Mitra, N.J., Ovsjanikov, M.: PointCleanNet: learning to denoise and remove outliers from dense point clouds. In: Computer Graphics Forum, vol. 39, pp. 185–203. Wiley Online Library (2020)
32. Rozantsev, A., Salzmann, M., Fua, P.: Beyond sharing weights for deep domain adaptation. IEEE Trans. Pattern Anal. Mach. Intell. **41**(4), 801–814 (2018)
33. Saito, K., Ushiku, Y., Harada, T., Saenko, K.: Adversarial dropout regularization. arXiv preprint arXiv:1711.01575 (2017)
34. Saito, K., Watanabe, K., Ushiku, Y., Harada, T.: Maximum classifier discrepancy for unsupervised domain adaptation. In: Proceedings of the IEEE Conference on Computer Vision and Pattern Recognition, pp. 3723–3732 (2018)
35. Sauder, J., Sievers, B.: Self-supervised deep learning on point clouds by reconstructing space. In: Advances in Neural Information Processing Systems 32 (2019)
36. Shen, Y., Yang, Y., Yan, M., Wang, H., Zheng, Y., Guibas, L.J.: Domain adaptation on point clouds via geometry-aware implicits. In: Proceedings of the IEEE/CVF Conference on Computer Vision and Pattern Recognition, pp. 7223–7232 (2022)
37. Tang, L., Chen, K., Wu, C., Hong, Y., Jia, K., Yang, Z.X.: Improving semantic analysis on point clouds via auxiliary supervision of local geometric priors. IEEE Trans. Cybern. (2020)

38. Thabet, A., Alwassel, H., Ghanem, B.: MortonNet: self-supervised learning of local features in 3D point clouds. arXiv preprint arXiv:1904.00230 (2019)
39. Thomas, H., Qi, C.R., Deschaud, J.E., Marcotegui, B., Goulette, F., Guibas, L.J.: KPConv: flexible and deformable convolution for point clouds. In: Proceedings of the IEEE/CVF International Conference on Computer Vision, pp. 6411–6420 (2019)
40. Tsai, Y.H., Hung, W.C., Schulter, S., Sohn, K., Yang, M.H., Chandraker, M.: Learning to adapt structured output space for semantic segmentation. In: Proceedings of the IEEE Conference on Computer Vision and Pattern Recognition, pp. 7472–7481 (2018)
41. Tzeng, E., Hoffman, J., Saenko, K., Darrell, T.: Adversarial discriminative domain adaptation. In: Proceedings of the IEEE Conference on Computer Vision and Pattern Recognition, pp. 7167–7176 (2017)
42. Wang, Y., Sun, Y., Liu, Z., Sarma, S.E., Bronstein, M.M., Solomon, J.M.: Dynamic graph CNN for learning on point clouds. ACM Trans. Graph. (ToG) **38**(5), 1–12 (2019)
43. Wu, Z., et al.: 3D ShapeNets: a deep representation for volumetric shapes. In: Proceedings of the IEEE Conference on Computer Vision and Pattern Recognition, pp. 1912–1920 (2015)
44. Xie, S., Zheng, Z., Chen, L., Chen, C.: Learning semantic representations for unsupervised domain adaptation. In: International Conference on Machine Learning, pp. 5423–5432. PMLR (2018)
45. Zhang, L., Zhu, Z.: Unsupervised feature learning for point cloud by contrasting and clustering with graph convolutional neural network. arXiv preprint arXiv:1904.12359 (2019)
46. Zhao, H., Jiang, L., Jia, J., Torr, P.H., Koltun, V.: Point transformer. In: Proceedings of the IEEE/CVF International Conference on Computer Vision, pp. 16259–16268 (2021)
47. Zou, L., Tang, H., Chen, K., Jia, K.: Geometry-aware self-training for unsupervised domain adaptation on object point clouds. In: Proceedings of the IEEE/CVF International Conference on Computer Vision, pp. 6403–6412 (2021)

CLIP-Actor: Text-Driven Recommendation and Stylization for Animating Human Meshes

Kim Youwang[1(✉)] , Kim Ji-Yeon[2] , and Tae-Hyun Oh[1,2]

[1] Department of EE, POSTECH, Pohang, Korea
{youwang.kim,taehyun}@postech.ac.kr
[2] Department of CiTE, POSTECH, Pohang, Korea
jiyeon.kim@postech.ac.kr
https://clip-actor.github.io

Abstract. We propose CLIP-Actor, a text-driven motion recommendation and neural mesh stylization system for human mesh animation. CLIP-Actor animates a 3D human mesh to conform to a text prompt by recommending a motion sequence and optimizing mesh style attributes. We build a text-driven human motion recommendation system by leveraging a large-scale human motion dataset with language labels. Given a natural language prompt, CLIP-Actor suggests a text-conforming human motion in a coarse-to-fine manner. Then, our novel zero-shot neural style optimization detailizes and texturizes the recommended mesh sequence to conform to the prompt in a temporally-consistent and pose-agnostic manner. This is distinctive in that prior work fails to generate plausible results when the pose of an artist-designed mesh does not conform to the text from the beginning. We further propose the spatio-temporal view augmentation and mask-weighted embedding attention, which stabilize the optimization process by leveraging multi-frame human motion and rejecting poorly rendered views. We demonstrate that CLIP-Actor produces plausible and human-recognizable style 3D human mesh in motion with detailed geometry and texture solely from a natural language prompt.

Keywords: Mesh animation · Mesh stylization · Text-driven editing

1 Introduction

Manual generation of animatable and detailed 3D avatars is cumbersome and requires time-consuming efforts with intensive labor and pain of creation. To reduce such burdens, many attempts have been introduced to automate such processes [5,9,10,12,16,21,29,38,50]. Furthermore, highly deformable human bodies make it more challenging to design temporally-consistent detailed geometries

---

K. Youwang and K. Ji-Yeon—Authors contributed equally to this work.
T.-H. Oh—Joint affiliated with Yonsei University, Korea.

Supplementary Information The online version contains supplementary material available at https://doi.org/10.1007/978-3-031-20062-5_11.

ⓒ The Author(s), under exclusive license to Springer Nature Switzerland AG 2022
S. Avidan et al. (Eds.): ECCV 2022, LNCS 13663, pp. 173–191, 2022.
https://doi.org/10.1007/978-3-031-20062-5_11

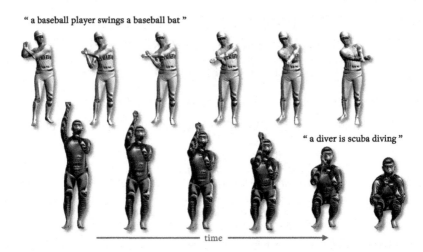

Fig. 1. CLIP-Actor. Given an input text prompt, CLIP-Actor recommends the best matching human meshes in motion and iteratively stylizes them by synthesis-through-optimization. CLIP-Actor can detail and texturize not just a single mesh frame but a short action clip by optimizing temporal-consistent and pose-agnostic style attributes.

and textures. This process may be fully automated by text-guided 3D avatar generation, *i.e.*, making a machine understand the human text prompt to create a 3D avatar amenable to the prompt. Text-guided 3D avatar generation can be widely applied to machine-created media, such as virtual human animation [50], language-driven robot task planning [52,59], and movie script visualization [22].

Our key intuition is from the text-visual coupled understanding of humans. For example, when an actor reads a script for a play, the actor brings up an image of gestures, tone of speech, and clothes to her/his mind following the context described in the script. We believe such text-visual coupled imagination can be a breakthrough for accelerating machine-created media, *e.g.*, stylized 3D humans in motion. We can embody it to the machine by leveraging the text-image joint embedding space of CLIP [45]. With the representational power of the CLIP embedding space, the similarity measure between text and image provides concrete signals in building text-to-3D human meshes in motion.

In this work, we propose **CLIP-Actor**, an automated framework of text-driven recommendation and stylization of animating 3D human meshes. Given a text prompt describing human action and style, CLIP-Actor crafts a short clip of animated human meshes conforming to the prompt (see Fig. 1). Our method is free from extra artist-designed 3D mesh inputs since it searches meshes in motion from a database that strongly correlates with the given query text. The CLIP-Actor then detailizes and texturizes the mesh sequence by optimizing our proposed Decoupled Neural Style Fields (DNSF) in a pose-agnostic manner. The objective of the optimization is to maximize the correlation between the input text prompt and 2D rendered images of the stylized 3D mesh. We optimize DNSF with spatio-temporally augmented rendered images and provide an initial content mesh with a multi-modal sampling strategy. Moreover, we propose mask-weighted embedding attention for stable neural optimization. We demonstrate that CLIP-Actor can stylize visually and physically plausible 3D human meshes in motion with various text descriptions in zero-shot.

We summarize our main contributions as follows:

- We propose CLIP-Actor, a text-driven animated human mesh synthesis system.
- We propose a hierarchical text-driven human motion recommendation module that utilizes fine-grained textual semantic matching to capture visual and textual cues within the text prompt.
- Our novel decoupled neural style field (DNSF) learns style attributes of the human meshes in motion in a temporally consistent and pose-agnostic manner.
- We further develop novel methods to improve the convergence of the text-driven neural DNSF optimization: multi-modal content mesh sampling, spatio-temporal view augmentation, and mask-weighted embedding attention.

2   Related Work

Our work is closely related to text-driven 3D object contents and style manipulation. Multi-modal object stylization has been mainly studied using learned multi-modal embedding space, such as CLIP [45] and 3D content/style manipulation methods. We briefly review these lines of research.

Text-driven Visual Data Manipulation. Recent advances in learned text and image joint embedding space [13,45] have lit a fire in research about the style manipulation of images and 3D objects. CLIP embedding space is learned with abundant natural images and texts and was originally developed for zero-shot image and language analysis tasks. Interestingly, its representation turns out powerful enough to manipulate visual data with intuitive text guides. For images, text conditional image generation [15,17,27,28,36] has been notably advanced by CLIP. A representative work, StyleCLIP [39], manipulates an input image by optimizing over its latent code of a pre-trained generative model given a natural language text-prompt. CLIPDraw [15] synthesizes images with text guidance by optimizing the parameters of a set of curves via gradient descent.

Analogous to the image domain, several works [23,34] extend the manipulation target domain to 3D objects by leveraging the advances in differentiable rendering [3,26,35,37,46]. The differentiable rendering technique enables seamless gradient flow from 2D rendered images to their 3D objects, allowing CLIP to bridge between language and 3D modalities through 2D images. Dream Fields [23] generates a 3D structure using implicit representation in free space, given a text prompt. It exploits no structural prior knowledge to learn or manipulate 3D contents. This allows flexible content exploration with novel styles but often results in abstract visual contents. As another concurrent work, Michel *et al.* [34] propose Text2Mesh, a CLIP-guided optimization method to manipulate the given fixed source mesh styles to conform to the target text condition prompt. In contrast to Dream Fields, since Text2Mesh stylizes a 3D object over the displacement and its texture map defined on a fixed, T-posed template human mesh, it imposes strong structural prior. It demonstrates plausible and interesting styles and textures of meshes given a text prompt. However, we observed that when the given template mesh is hard to conform to the given text prompt, it produces undesirable stylization; *e.g.*, the text containing detailed human action produces a failure of stylization when the pose of the given human template mesh and the action are not conformed to each other.

We focus on animating human meshes with details and styles according to the input text prompt. We exploit the parametric human mesh model to disentangle style from geometric contents, *i.e.*, pose. Such disentanglement enables the pose, detail, and style of human mesh to conform to the input text sequentially. This enables to stably manipulate 3D human objects, better conforming to the input text prompt from action to style.

Text-Driven Human Motion Manipulation. Many recent approaches have been studied to generate human body motion with given natural language descriptions. One line of work [1,2,18,30,43] guides the machine to translate natural language descriptions in a sequential manner and generate human skeletal motions using recurrent neural models. Another line of work [19,20,41] generates human motion conditioned on the limited number of closed-set action categories. CLIP-Actor focuses on textual and visual semantics in a whole sentence and can tackle various natural language descriptions.

Recently, MotionCLIP [55] and TEMOS [42] propose to learn the natural language conditioned mesh motion generation. MotionCLIP learns the human motion autoencoder and makes its latent space compatible with CLIP text and image space using semantic similarity. Similarly, TEMOS learns generative human mesh motion latent space with transformer-VAE [14,25,41] and aligns it with natural language latent space via DistilBERT [51], thus composing the cross-modal motion latent space. While both methods focus on the latent space to capture textual and visual semantics of natural language descriptions, CLIP-Actor directly maps the descriptions to realistic motion using a recommendation system. Moreover, our detailed volumetric meshes are stylized with appearance attributes much more expressive than those of the aforementioned methods.

Texture and Geometric Stylization of Human Mesh in Motion. Aside from 3D mesh pose, recent work has added different levels of details to bare human meshes, *e.g.*, cloth modeling or texture color. The separate modeling of human and cloth meshes [5,21,29], the neural extension of the parametric human mesh model [4,11,32], the neural parametric approach [9,10,38], and the neural implicit approach [48,49,58] show promising clothed human mesh results from the given human scans, but without surface colors. Those works deal with texture and geometric styles separately. Recently, Saito *et al.* [50] propose a weakly-supervised way to recover both texture and geometric styles.

None of these methods can generate diverse color and cloth details of human motion in zero-shot, *e.g.*, with only a text guide. We present a novel text-driven recommendation, detailization, and texturization of animating human meshes in zero-shot, where human meshes in motion with texture and geometric details are generated from the machine's imagination without the task dataset.

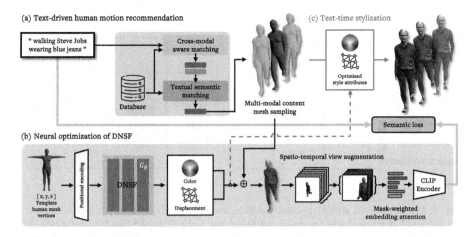

Fig. 2. Overall architecture. Given a text description of the human action, the text-driven human motion recommendation module finds the best semantically matched motion sequence from the motion database [44]. Content meshes are then sampled in a multi-modal context. Decoupled Neural Style Field takes a T-posed human mesh and learns text-driven style attributes, which are then applied to the content meshes. We apply spatio-temporal view augmentation and weight rendered images to guide the neural optimization with similarity among rendered images and the text.

3   CLIP-Actor: An Overview

Our goal is to visualize 3D motion that conforms to the input description by styl-izing mesh with the color and displacement of its vertices. For example, consider a natural language prompt, "walking Steve Jobs wearing blue jeans." Instead of preparing extra fixed 3D mesh inputs, our model obtains a sequence of 3D meshes that conforms to the input prompt, *i.e.*, walking, by retrieving a motion sequence from a dataset, *e.g.*, BABEL [44]. The retrieved mesh sequence becomes the *"content"* of our mesh stylization. We then grant the characteristics, *e.g.*, cloth, hair, to the meshes by optimizing the neural model to learn the color and displacement of the mesh vertices. Finally, our model generates a short clip of walking Steve jobs wearing blue jeans (see Fig. 2).

Formally, given a text prompt y, we retrieve a sequence of pose param-eters $\mathbf{R}_{1:T} = [\mathbf{R}_1, \ldots, \mathbf{R}_T]$ of SMPL [31,40,47] for duration T. In a single frame t, mesh vertices $\mathbf{M}_t$ can be acquired with a linear mapping as: $\mathbf{M}_t = \mathcal{M}(\mathbf{R}_t, \boldsymbol{\beta}_t)$, $\forall t \in \{1, \ldots, T\}$, where $\mathbf{R}_t$ denotes the pose parameters, and $\boldsymbol{\beta}_t$ the shape parameters for a human mesh. Then, a single mesh at frame t is rep-resented by the faces F, and the 3D mesh vertices $\mathbf{M}_t \in \mathbb{R}^{V \times 3}$, where V is the number of vertices. Since SMPL mesh faces F for every frame are identical with given triangulation, we represent a single mesh using the mesh vertices, $\mathbf{M}_t$. Hence, $\mathbf{M}_{1:T} = [\mathbf{M}_1, \ldots, \mathbf{M}_T]$ denotes a full sequence of human meshes and is taken to our decoupled neural style field (DNSF) as *"content."* The DNSF then learns *"style,"* *i.e.*, color and displacement, of mesh vertices and produces a sequence of textured mesh $\mathbf{M}_{1:T}^*$.

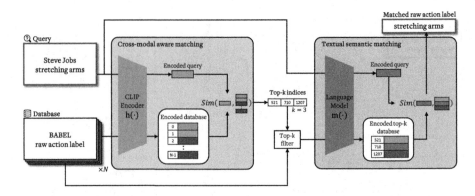

Fig. 3. Hierarchical multi-modal motion retrieval. Given text prompt as a query, our retrieval module finds the most relevant raw action label from the database [44]. First, the query and all of the raw action labels are encoded by CLIP text encoder $\mathbf{h}(\cdot)$, and we measure similarity between them. Top-k indices of raw action labels are selected, and corresponding raw action labels are retrieved by the `top−k` filter. The language model encoder $\mathbf{m}(\cdot)$ vectorizes the query and top-k action labels. The highest-scored raw action label is retrieved as the final matched result for the input text prompt.

4   Text-driven Human Motion Recommendation

In this section, we propose a motion recommendation module to obtain a motion sequence that conforms to the text prompt. We recommend the motion by retrieving visually and textually relevant action labels from the dataset.

Hierarchical Multi-modal Motion Retrieval. We propose a hierarchical multi-modal motion retrieval module to obtain a motion sequence corresponding to the given prompt (see Fig. 3). We utilize a large scale human motion dataset with language labels, BABEL [44], containing frame-level aligned SMPL pose parameters and raw action labels. Given the text prompt as a query, the raw action label that is visually and linguistically associated with the query is matched through our motion recommendation system. We design a two-stage retrieval; cross-modal aware matching and textual semantic matching. The hierarchical matching enables CLIP-Actor to catch visual-language (cross-modal) aware contexts and linguistic semantics. These comprehensive matching modules hand over good initial content to the subsequent neural mesh stylization.

Cross-Modal Aware Matching. Cross-modal aware matching finds the action labels similar to the input text prompt on the joint image-text space. We prepare the database, *i.e.*, a set of raw action labels $\mathcal{A}$, gathered from BABEL [44]. We retrieve a set $\mathcal{A}_\mathbf{k} \subset \mathcal{A}$ of the raw action label $a_i \in \mathcal{A}$, given a text prompt y as:

$$\mathcal{A}_k = \texttt{top-k}[\mathcal{S}(\mathbf{h}(a_i), \mathbf{h}(y))], \quad \text{where } \mathcal{S}(\mathbf{x}, \mathbf{y}) = \frac{\mathbf{x}^\top \mathbf{y}}{\|\mathbf{x}\|_2 \|\mathbf{y}\|_2}, \tag{1}$$

$\mathbf{h}(\cdot)$ is the pre-trained CLIP text encoder, and $\texttt{top-k}[\cdot]$ denotes a function that returns $\mathbf{k}$ best matches. The similarity is measured by the cosine similarity.

Specifically, consider an input prompt "a man walking backwards." The cross-modal aware matching vectorizes the input prompt and the action labels using the CLIP text encoder and computes the similarity between them. The set of matched action labels $\mathcal{A}_k$ is determined as {"walking in place," "walking backward," "walking laterally"} and the top-1 matched label is "walking in place." Since the CLIP text encoder is learned to focus on words that appear visually, it catches visual semantics (*i.e.*, walking), and all the elements in $\mathcal{A}_k$ are closely related to the input prompt in visual space. However, the text encoder of CLIP is trained with still images instead of videos so that it cannot distinguish fine-grained action (*i.e.*, "walking in place" vs. "walking backwards"; because both appear to be the same in a still image). Thus, we propose textual semantic matching as the following step to compensate for the single-stage retrieval.

Textual Semantic Matching. The textual semantic matching finds the most relevant action label with the input prompt by capturing textual semantics in the sentence. We utilize the language expert, MPNet [53], so that our two-stage module can distinguish textual semantics and grammatical structures. The best matching label a_* is retrieved as:

$$a_* = \text{argmax}_{a_j \in \mathcal{A}_k} \mathcal{S}(\mathbf{m}(a_j), \mathbf{m}(y)), \tag{2}$$

where $\mathbf{m}(\cdot)$ denotes the pre-trained MPNet encoder. Again, consider our above example of "a man walking backwards." The top-k action labels are re-ranked, and the most similar action label "walking backward" is retrieved as a final result. The sequence of meshes $\mathbf{M}_{1:T}$ associated with the retrieved action label is passed to the following neural mesh stylization pipeline as the content mesh sequence.

5   Decoupled Stylization of Human Meshes in Motion

We represent a stylized human mesh with the content mesh and the style attributes. In practice, we denote the content mesh as $\mathbf{M}_i \in \mathbb{R}^{V \times 3}$ sampled from the retrieved human motion sequence of T frames, $\mathbf{M}_{1:T}$. The mesh's surface style attributes $(\mathbf{c}, \mathbf{d}) \in \mathbb{R}^{V \times 3} \times \mathbb{R}^V$ are interpreted as the per-vertex RGB color and per-vertex displacement, which are applied over surfaces via given triangulation. The Neural Style Field [34] takes a fixed static mesh as input and learns the style attributes with a multi-layer perceptron (MLP). Michel *et al.* [34] claim that this implicit formulation tightly couples the style field to the source mesh. However, since Neural Style Field takes a single posed mesh at a time, a significant number of MLPs are required to stylize a sequence of human meshes.

Decoupled Neural Style Field. Instead, we introduce *Decoupled Neural Style Field* (DNSF). We propose to rather decouple the style field from the content mesh so that we need only one neural network to learn style attributes for the meshes in motion. Specifically, we first map the style attributes from the template human mesh $\mathbf{M}_c$ and merge it with the content meshes $\mathbf{M}_i, \forall i \in \{1, \ldots, T\}$, right before rendering (refer to Fig. 2). DNSF can achieve the same mesh stylization as the basic Neural Style Field while effectively decoupling the style from the content mesh. In practice, parameterized as an MLP G_θ, DNSF maps the vertices on the template human mesh, $i.e.$, T-posed SMPL $\mathbf{M}_c$, to style attributes $\mathbf{c}$ and $\mathbf{d}$, in a pose-agnostic manner as:

$$\text{DNSF:} \quad G_\theta(\mathbf{M}_c) \mapsto \{\mathbf{c}, \mathbf{d}\}. \tag{3}$$

We also employ the Fourier feature-based positional encoding to the mesh vertices, which helps the style field to cover higher frequency details [54]. In detail, the MLP G_θ gets the positional encoded feature as input and outputs per-vertex RGB value, $\mathbf{c} \in [0,1]^{V \times 3}$, and per-vertex displacement value, $\mathbf{d} \in [-0.1, 0.1]^V$, along the per-vertex normal direction. The predicted style attributes are then applied to the content posed mesh $\mathbf{M}_i$ to produce the stylized human mesh $\mathbf{M}_i^*$.

Text-Driven DNSF Optimization. The core of the text-driven DNSF optimization is to maximize the semantic correlation between the visual mesh observation and the input text prompt. However, we cannot directly utilize CLIP to measure the semantic correlation with the created 3D mesh itself because the CLIP visual encoder is designed and trained only for 2D images.

We leverage an intuitive idea that the observations of a 3D object can be described similarly from any viewpoint [23,24,57]. To utilize the representation power of CLIP as a supervision signal, we first render images of the 3D meshes for input compatibility. With randomly sampled N camera poses, $\mathbf{p} = [\mathbf{p}_1, \ldots, \mathbf{p}_N]$, we differentiably render the stylized mesh $\mathbf{M}_i^*$ to get N-view rendered images $\mathbf{I}_{ij}^*$, $\forall j \in \{1, 2, \ldots, N\}$ [56]. Thereby, our main optimization objective, $semantic\ loss$, is defined with the pre-trained CLIP image and text encoders, $\mathbf{g}(\cdot)$ and $\mathbf{h}(\cdot)$, as:

$$\mathcal{L}_s = 1 - \frac{\bar{\mathbf{g}}(\mathbf{I}_i^*)^\top \mathbf{h}(y)}{\|\bar{\mathbf{g}}(\mathbf{I}_i^*)\|_2 \|\mathbf{h}(y)\|_2}, \quad \bar{\mathbf{g}}(\mathbf{I}_i^*) = \frac{1}{N} \sum_{j=1}^{N} \mathbf{g}(\mathbf{I}_{ij}^*), \tag{4}$$

where y denotes the input text prompt, and $\mathbf{g}(\mathbf{I}_i^*) \in \mathbb{R}^{512}$ and $\mathbf{h}(y) \in \mathbb{R}^{512}$ the unnormalized CLIP embedding vectors for the image and the text prompt, respectively. The semantic loss is basically a cosine similarity between the normalized mean embedding vectors for N rendered images of the stylized mesh $\mathbf{M}_i^*$ and the normalized embedding for the input text prompt y.

Spatio-Temporal View Augmentation. Prior works show that $spatial$ augmentations, such as 3D viewpoint or 2D image augmentations, improve the quality of content generation [15,23,24,34]. We extend it to $spatio\text{-}temporal\ view\ augmentation$, where we propose to leverage both multi-view property and human motion originating from the temporal movement. This naturally diversifies views in a combinatorial way by the spatio-temporal context of human motion.

The strength of DNSF is amplified with the spatio-temporal view augmentation. Recall that DNSF G_θ takes a template SMPL mesh as an input, which is pose-agnostic. Therefore, the semantic loss $\mathcal{L}_s$ can be measured with any content mesh $\mathbf{M}_{i \in \{1,...,T\}}$ in the motion sequence for learning DNSF. One can sample and use the center frame or the frame that conforms best with the text prompt. This increases the chance to measure the loss with a view favorable to DNSF learning. Considering that the naïve selection of the content mesh fails to generate plausible color and geometric details when it does not conform with the text prompt, the content mesh sampling strategy is a crucial design choice.

Multi-modal Content Mesh Sampling. One naïve way to choose the content mesh to stylize with is to randomly select a single mesh within a mesh sequence. However, as careful text prompt and its semantic alignment with the mesh's rendered image are crucial for the optimization [34,62], we design *multi-modal content mesh sampling* that finds the best text-conforming meshes within the motion. Specifically, we render the images of the content mesh sequence, $\mathbf{I}(\mathbf{M}_{1:T})$, and compute each image's CLIP similarity score with y. For example, when the text prompt is given as "a man jumping kick", we render each mesh in retrieved motion into an image and find the semantically matching frames with the jumping kick action (refer to Fig. 4).

Text prompt: "a man jumping kick"

Top-k

← time

0.2522 0.2710 **0.2952** 0.2825 0.2771

Fig. 4. We choose the top-k best matching mesh frames that conform with a given text prompt. We show the CLIP scores.

Mask-Weighted Embedding Attention. Before the pre-trained CLIP encoder $\mathbf{g}(\cdot)$ encodes the rendered images, we apply differentiable 2D image augmentations, including random crop and perspective transformations [46]. Such 2D augmentations help DNSF learn style attributes from diverse perspective images, thus can achieve better generalization in 3D contents [23,34].

However, the problem occurs when careless random crops are applied. The prior work [34] applies extreme close-ups to crop the rendered images, which severely samples the empty renders (see Fig. 5). Such redundant images do not conform to the text prompt even for the properly stylized meshes and distract the stable DNSF optimization.

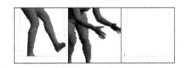

Fig. 5. Naïve mean embedding of the random-cropped renders may distract the optimization of DNSF.

We mitigate this issue by weighting the CLIP embedded vectors $\mathbf{g}(\mathbf{I}_{ij}^*)$ from N different camera poses $\{\mathbf{p}_j\}_{j=1}^N$ according to each image's foreground pixel ratio. In other words, we reject the embedding vector $\mathbf{g}(\mathbf{I}_{ij}^*)$, if $\mathbf{I}_{ij}^*$ has an extremely small portion of mesh foreground pixels in it. We call this *mask-weighted embedding attention*, and implement it by simply adding the weight w_{ij} to Eq. (4) as:

$$\bar{\mathbf{g}}(\mathbf{I}_i^*) = \sum_{j=1}^N \frac{w_{ij}}{\sum_{k=1}^N w_{ik}} \mathbf{g}(\mathbf{I}_{ij}^*), \quad w_{ij} = \frac{1}{HW} \sum_{H,W} \mathbb{1}[\mathbf{m}_{ij}(h,w) = 1], \quad (5)$$

"jumping Spiderman"   "Messi jumping over object"   "Freddie Mercury dancing"   "walking Gandhi"

"Alan Turing walking forwards"   "Bruno Mars dance stepping"   "Daft Punk turning music on"   "Steve Jobs stretching arms"

Fig. 6. Qualitative results of CLIP-Actor. Each image shows the representative frame from the recommended motion sequence, with detailed surface geometries and textures, along with the input text prompt. CLIP-Actor shows good action and style consistency, vivid and attractive texture results.

where H and W denote the height and width of the rendered image $\mathbf{I}^*_{ij}$ and its foreground mask $\mathbf{m}_{ij}$.

6   Experiments

In this section, we evaluate CLIP-Actor in several aspects. Since our model is in an over-fitting regime and the first approach that addresses the stylization of 3D human meshes in "motion" conditioned on the natural language, we mainly ablate our technical components and the design choices qualitatively.

Specifically, we describe the models for our evaluation and ablation study in Sect. 6.1. We then show our qualitative and quantitative results compared with competing methods in Sects. 6.2 and 6.3. In Sect. 6.4, we empirically support our choice of the hierarchical motion retrieval. In Sect. 6.5, we show how our decoupled style representation, mesh sampling, view augmentation, and attention mechanism help us achieve better qualitative results.

6.1   Model Description

We define our full model, **CLIP-Actor**, as the one that uses the top-3 best matching mesh frames conforming with a given text prompt, *i.e.*, using multimodal content mesh sampling and spatio-temporal view augmentations along with the mask-weighted embedding attention. Also, the CLIP-Actor (base) is the model that utilizes only the center frame of the retrieved motion sequence and

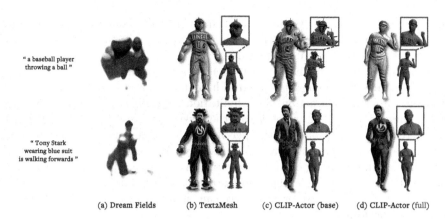

"a baseball player throwing a ball"

"Tony Stark wearing blue suit is walking forwards"

(a) Dream Fields   (b) Text2Mesh   (c) CLIP-Actor (base)   (d) CLIP-Actor (full)

Fig. 7. Qualitative comparison. We compare CLIP-Actor with other competing methods [23,34] and our strong baseline, CLIP-Actor (base). Given the same text prompts as input, (a) Dream Fields shows abstract generations, which are blurry and hard to recognize, (b) Text2Mesh shows a better generation than Dream Fields but suffers from substantial defects on the surfaces. (c) CLIP-Actor (base) shows more text-conforming meshes with human-recognizable style attributes but still suffers from surface defects. (d) CLIP-Actor shows human-recognizable and semantically conforming action, while presenting detailed color and geometry, such as hairstyle and face identities.

does not utilize DNSF, *i.e.*, using posed mesh to learn the style field. Still, CLIP-Actor (base) is a strong baseline model since it at least mitigates the limitation of Text2Mesh [34] by suggesting the initial mesh to the neural optimization.

6.2   Qualitative Results

In Fig. 6, we visualize CLIP-Actor's recommendation and mesh stylization results for a given text prompt. With only a single text prompt, CLIP-Actor can retrieve visually conforming motion sequences containing representative poses. Moreover, CLIP-Actor can capture the subject's representative identities. For example, the geometric and texture details such as Spiderman's webbed costume, the iconic color of Lionel Messi's uniform, Freddie Mercury's hairstyle, and the robe that Gandhi wears are well-illustrated in Fig. 6.

We also evaluate CLIP-Actor with other recent competing methods, Dream Fields [23] and Text2Mesh [34], and our strong baseline model, CLIP-Actor (base). Figure 7 illustrates the visual comparison of the methods.

Given the same text prompts, Dream Fields shows blurry and non-human-recognizable renderings of the generated 3D content. We postulate that such performance degradation is due to the lack of structural prior when training the Dream Fields. Dream Fields learns the occupancy and the color of 3D points in virtual space without any structural guidance. For example, we cannot impose the human body's physical constraints on Dream Fields when performing specific actions (refer to Fig. 7a). We found that applying only semantic supervision to such a highly unrestrained content generation process fails to handle physically constrained human motion and textures.

Text2Mesh shows enhanced texture generation than Dream Fields. However, it still fails since the given artist-designed human mesh is absolutely uncorrelated with the target human action. Such limitation is originated from Text2Mesh's highly coupled style field, which learns the style field from the "posed" content mesh. Text2Mesh also clamps the per-vertex displacement to lie in a limited range, preventing style attributes from largely changing the content [34]. On the other hand, by adding our novel text-driven human motion recommendation module before Text2Mesh, and providing the text-conforming content mesh as an initial point, *i.e.*, CLIP-Actor (base), we can significantly enhance Text2Mesh's qualitative performance.

Finally, our full CLIP-Actor further enhances the qualitative result by capturing semantically meaningful details such as a cap on a baseball player and the hairstyle of Tony Stark (see Fig. 7d) while reducing the messy spikes. Our novel DNSF, multi-modal content mesh sampling, and spatio-temporal view augmentation enable CLIP-Actor to leverage multi-view renderings originating from multi-frame human motion; thus, results are much smoother and text-conforming. More importantly, note that all the other methods except CLIP-Actor cannot handle human motion. CLIP-Actor recommends text-conforming human motion and synthesizes temporally consistent and pose-agnostic mesh style attributes.

6.3   Quantitative Results

Since there are no benchmarks for our task, we conduct a user study to evaluate CLIP-Actor quantitatively. We ask 46 non-expert users to score (1–5) five random text-avatar paired results regarding motion-text consistency, stylization quality, and overall consistency with the given text. Figure 8 shows that our CLIP-Actor outperforms other competing methods in all aspects, while none of the competing

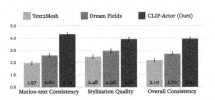

Fig. 8. User study results. CLIP-Actor outperforms other competing methods in various aspects.

methods scored higher than a neutral point (*i.e.*, <3). The differences are significantly noticeable in the motion-text consistency, which validates our good action consistency.

6.4   Evaluation on Retrieval Module

We validate the performance of our retrieval module design choice by comparing it with other variants. We use the SICK dataset [33] that contains contextually similar sentence pairs generated from image descriptions. We build module variants to simulate various retrieval scenarios. Details about the dataset and the experiment settings can be found in the supplementary material.

Table 1. Evaluation results on the retrieval module. (a) The precision is measured as the percentage of matched sentence pairs among all pairs. (b) The samples of each range of the SICK dataset. Our hierarchical retrieval outperforms all the other variants.

<table>
<tr><td colspan="4" align="center">(a)</td><td colspan="2" align="center">(b)</td></tr>
<tr><td></td><td colspan="3" align="center">**Retrieval Precision [%]**</td><td rowspan="2">SICK4.9</td><td>A: A man is slicing an onion</td></tr>
<tr><td>Retrieval Module</td><td>SICK4.8</td><td>SICK4.4</td><td>SICK[4.4,4.8]</td><td>B: An onion is being sliced by a man</td></tr>
<tr><td></td><td></td><td></td><td></td><td rowspan="2">SICK4.8</td><td>A: A skateboarder is jumping off a ramp</td></tr>
<tr><td>CLIP</td><td>91.94</td><td>85.21</td><td>81.62</td><td>B: A skateboarder is making a jump off a ramp</td></tr>
<tr><td>MPNet</td><td>91.94</td><td>83.56</td><td>80.55</td><td rowspan="2">SICK4.4</td><td>A: A man is performing with a guitar</td></tr>
<tr><td>MPNet+CLIP</td><td>91.34</td><td>85.48</td><td>80.41</td><td>B: A man is playing a guitar</td></tr>
<tr><td></td><td></td><td></td><td></td><td rowspan="2">SICK4.3</td><td>A: A man is cutting a paper</td></tr>
<tr><td>CLIP+MPNet (Ours)</td><td>**92.24**</td><td>**85.75**</td><td>**81.90**</td><td>B: There is no man cutting a paper</td></tr>
</table>

Retrieval Module Variants. We consider two hierarchical modules and two single-stage baselines for the design variants. Our full hierarchical retrieval module utilizes pre-trained CLIP and MPNet sequentially (see CLIP+MPNet in Sect. 4). We also design the reverse ordered hierarchical module, MPNet+CLIP. For hierarchical models, top-k candidates are matched at the first stage, and the best-matched item is selected after re-ranking. Finally, our single-stage baselines are the modules that only use either pre-trained CLIP or MPNet encoder.

Quantitative Results. We empirically show the performance of our hierarchical motion retrieval module by comparing it with the different design variants. As shown in Table 1a, the single-stage baselines show comparable results with our hierarchical model in the SICK4.8 setting, where the sentence pairs are more related to each other (refer to Table 1b). However, CLIP shows higher precision than MPNet in SICK4.4. We postulate that CLIP catches the visual semantics, *e.g.*, similar context can be imagined from "performing with a guitar" and "playing a guitar". On the other hand, the language expert, MPNet, focuses on the textual difference of description, *e.g.*, "performing with" and "playing". Thus, it is sensitive to the textual structure. In the setting with the increased number of samples, *i.e.*, SICK[4.4,4.8], CLIP shows comparable results with ours but is still insufficient without the help of the language expert. Moreover, the MPNet+CLIP shows unstable performances over settings. In contrast, our full retrieval module consistently outperforms over all settings. We demonstrate that a coarse-to-fine matching system achieves favorable retrieval performance on natural language.

6.5 Ablation on Decoupled Neural Style Fields (DNSF)

We analyze CLIP-Actor by ablating each of the components of DNSF. Figure 9 shows the qualitative ablation results for our major technical components.

Effects of Temporal Augmentation. First, we remove temporal view augmentation so that DNSF utilizes only a single mesh frame (top-1). Removing the multi-frame renderings significantly degrades the visual quality, where it

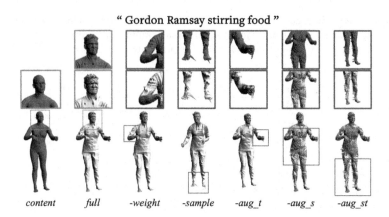

"Gordon Ramsay stirring food"

content   full   -weight   -sample   -aug_t   -aug_s   -aug_st

Fig. 9. Ablation results. We remove each of CLIP-Actor's components to validate corresponding effects. Our *full* model shows the most smooth geometry and vivid color.

presents noticeable spikes on the surface and unrealistic colors ($-aug\_t$ in Fig. 9). Since our full model utilizes top-3 relevant frames and 2D, 3D augmentations, it leverages multi-view of stylized mesh, which regularizes the model from overfitting [23,34].

Effects of Multi-modal Content Mesh Sampling. We also compare the full CLIP-Actor with the model without *multi-modal content mesh sampling*. Multi-modal content mesh sampling enables DNSF to begin its optimization with better initialization that conforms with the text prompt. Naïve sampling of the content mesh yields unrecognizable face identities, degraded texture, and geometric details (see $-sample$ in Fig. 9).

Effects of Mask-Weighted Embedding Attention. The *mask-weighted embedding attention* adds detailed touches to the stylized meshes. By preventing empty renderings from guiding the optimization, it enables learning fine geometric and texture details via focused gradient flow in back-propagation. When the augmented rendered images contain extreme close-ups of distal body regions, such as tiptoe or fingertips, our embedding attention method draws the DNSF's attention to the mesh foreground pixels rather than empty space with focused gradient flow. In Fig. 9, *-weight* shows the result when we train DNSF without our attention mechanism. Our full CLIP-Actor shows much smooth, fine-grained geometric details. We believe our novel attention mechanism can be applied to not only text-driven 3D object manipulation pipelines [23,34,62] but also differentiable rendering applications [24,35,61].

7   Conclusion

We present CLIP-Actor, a text-driven animated human mesh synthesis system. Leveraging multi-modal aware and semantic textual matching, CLIP-Actor recommends the best semantically matching human motion sequence with the input text prompt in a hierarchical manner. Our CLIP-Actor then stylizes the meshes of recommended motion by synthesis-through-optimization in a pose-agnostic manner via decoupled neural style fields. We further develop novel neural optimization techniques to utilize multi-modal sampling and embedding weighting, which stabilize and enhance the detailization and texturization quality.

CLIP-Actor can be extended to other parametric mesh models, such as hands and animals [6–8,47,60,63,64], enabling diverse animation of 3D objects. One promising future application of CLIP-Actor would be a dataset generation of stylized meshes in motion, paired with natural language description. We believe such multi-modal datasets can boost exciting future applications.

Acknowledgment. This work was supported by Institute of Information & communications Technology Planning & Evaluation (IITP) grant funded by the Korea government(MSIT) (No.2022-00164860, Development of Human Digital Twin Technology Based on Dynamic Behavior Modeling and Human-Object-Space Interaction; and No.2021-0-02068, Artificial Intelligence Innovation Hub).

References

1. Ahn, H., Ha, T., Choi, Y., Yoo, H., Oh, S.: Text2action: generative adversarial synthesis from language to action. In: IEEE International Conference on Robotics and Automation (ICRA) (2018)
2. Ahuja, C., Morency, L.P.: Language2pose: natural language grounded pose forecasting. In: International Conference on 3D Vision (3DV) (2019)
3. Barron, J.T., Mildenhall, B., Verbin, D., Srinivasan, P.P., Hedman, P.: MIP-NERF 360: unbounded anti-aliased neural radiance fields. In: IEEE Conference on Computer Vision and Pattern Recognition (CVPR) (2021)
4. Bhatnagar, B.L., Sminchisescu, C., Theobalt, C., Pons-Moll, G.: Combining implicit function learning and parametric models for 3d human reconstruction. In: Vedaldi, A., Bischof, H., Brox, T., Frahm, J.-M. (eds.) ECCV 2020. LNCS, vol. 12347, pp. 311–329. Springer, Cham (2020). https://doi.org/10.1007/978-3-030-58536-5_19
5. Bhatnagar, B.L., Tiwari, G., Theobalt, C., Pons-Moll, G.: Multi-garment net: Learning to dress 3d people from images. In: IEEE International Conference on Computer Vision (ICCV) (2019)
6. Biggs, B., Boyne, O., Charles, J., Fitzgibbon, A., Cipolla, R.: Who left the dogs out? 3D animal reconstruction with expectation maximization in the loop. In: Vedaldi, A., Bischof, H., Brox, T., Frahm, J.-M. (eds.) ECCV 2020. LNCS, vol. 12356, pp. 195–211. Springer, Cham (2020). https://doi.org/10.1007/978-3-030-58621-8_12
7. Biggs, B., Roddick, T., Fitzgibbon, A., Cipolla, R.: Creatures great and SMAL: recovering the shape and motion of animals from video. In: Asia Conference on Computer Vision (ACCV) (2018)
8. Blanz, V., Vetter, T.: A morphable model for the synthesis of 3d faces. In: SIGGRAPH (1999)
9. Božič, A., Palafox, P., Zollhöfer, M., Thies, J., Dai, A., Nießner, M.: Neural deformation graphs for globally-consistent non-rigid reconstruction. In: Advances in Neural Information Processing Systems (NeurIPS) (2021)

10. Bozic, A., Palafox, P., Zollöfer, M., Dai, A., Thies, J., Nießner, M.: Neural non-rigid tracking. In: Advances in Neural Information Processing Systems (NeurIPS) (2020)
11. Burov, A., Nießner, M., Thies, J.: Dynamic surface function networks for clothed human bodies. In: IEEE International Conference on Computer Vision (ICCV) (2021)
12. Canfes, Z., Atasoy, M.F., Dirik, A., Yanardag, P.: Text and image guided 3d avatar generation and manipulation. arXiv:2202.06079 (2022)
13. Du, Y., Collins, M.K., Tenenbaum, B.J., Sitzmann, V.: Learning signal-agnostic manifolds of neural fields. In: Advances in Neural Information Processing Systems (NeurIPS) (2021)
14. Fragkiadaki, K., Levine, S., Felsen, P., Malik, J.: Recurrent network models for human dynamics. In: IEEE International Conference on Computer Vision (ICCV) (2015)
15. Frans, K., Soros, L.B., Witkowski, O.: ClipDraw: exploring text-to-drawing synthesis through language-image encoders. arXiv:2106.14843 (2021)
16. Gafni, G., Thies, J., Zollhöfer, M., Nießner, M.: Dynamic neural radiance fields for monocular 4d facial avatar reconstruction. In: IEEE Conference on Computer Vision and Pattern Recognition (CVPR) (2021)
17. Gal, R., Patashnik, O., Maron, H., Chechik, G., Cohen-Or, D.: StyleGAN-NADA: clip-guided domain adaptation of image generators. In: ACM Transactions on Graphics (SIGGRAPH) (2022)
18. Ghosh, A., Cheema, N., Oguz, C., Theobalt, C., Slusallek, P.: Synthesis of compositional animations from textual descriptions. In: IEEE International Conference on Computer Vision (ICCV) (2021)
19. Guo, C., Zuo, X., Wang, S., Liu, X., Zou, S., Gong, M., Cheng, L.: Action2video: generating videos of human 3d actions. In: International Journal of Computer Vision (IJCV), pp. 1–31 (2022)
20. Guo, C., et al.: Action2motion: conditioned generation of 3d human motions. In: ACM International Conference on Multimedia (MM) (2020)
21. Guo, J., Li, J., Narain, R., Park, H.: Inverse simulation: Reconstructing dynamic geometry of clothed humans via optimal control. In: IEEE Conference on Computer Vision and Pattern Recognition (CVPR) (2021)
22. Hanser, E., Kevitt, P.M., Lunney, T.F., Condell, J.: SceneMaker: intelligent multimodal visualisation of natural language scripts. In: Proceedings of the 20th Irish Conference on Artificial Intelligence and Cognitive Science (2009)
23. Jain, A., Mildenhall, B., Barron, J.T., Abbeel, P., Poole, B.: Zero-shot text-guided object generation with dream fields. In: IEEE Conference on Computer Vision and Pattern Recognition (CVPR) (2022)
24. Jain, A., Tancik, M., Abbeel, P.: Putting nerf on a diet: semantically consistent few-shot view synthesis. In: IEEE International Conference on Computer Vision (ICCV) (2021)
25. Jiang, J., Xia, G.G., Carlton, D.B., Anderson, C.N., Miyakawa, R.H.: Transformer VAE: a hierarchical model for structure-aware and interpretable music representation learning. In: IEEE International Conference on Acoustics, Speech, and Signal Processing (ICASSP) (2020)
26. Kato, H., et al.: Differentiable rendering: a survey. arXiv:2006.12057 (2020)
27. Kim, G., Ye, J.C.: DiffusionClip: text-guided diffusion models for robust image manipulation. In: IEEE Conference on Computer Vision and Pattern Recognition (CVPR) (2022)

28. Kwon, G., Ye, J.C.: ClipStyler: image style transfer with a single text condition. In: IEEE Conference on Computer Vision and Pattern Recognition (CVPR) (2022)
29. Li, Y., et al.: N-Cloth: predicting 3D cloth deformation with mesh-based networks. In: Computer Graphics Forum (Proceedings of Eurographics), pp. 547–558 (2022)
30. Lin, A.S., Wu, L., Corona, R., Tai, K.W.H., Huang, Q., Mooney, R.J.: Generating animated videos of human activities from natural language descriptions. In: Proceedings of the Visually Grounded Interaction and Language Workshop at NeurIPS 2018 (2018)
31. Loper, M., Mahmood, N., Romero, J., Pons-Moll, G., Black, M.J.: SMPL: a skinned multi-person linear model. ACM Trans. Graph. (SIGGRAPH Asia) **34**(6), 248 (2015)
32. Ma, Q., et al.: Learning to dress 3d people in generative clothing. In: IEEE Conference on Computer Vision and Pattern Recognition (CVPR) (2020)
33. Marelli, M., Menini, S., Baroni, M., Bentivogli, L., Bernardi, R., Zamparelli, R.: A sick cure for the evaluation of compositional distributional semantic models. In: International Conference on Language Resources and Evaluation (LREC) (2014)
34. Michel, O., Bar-On, R., Liu, R., Benaim, S., Hanocka, R.: Text2mesh: text-driven neural stylization for meshes. In: IEEE Conference on Computer Vision and Pattern Recognition (CVPR) (2022)
35. Mildenhall, B., Srinivasan, P.P., Tancik, M., Barron, J.T., Ramamoorthi, R., Ng, R.: NeRF: representing scenes as neural radiance fields for view synthesis. In: Vedaldi, A., Bischof, H., Brox, T., Frahm, J.-M. (eds.) ECCV 2020. LNCS, vol. 12346, pp. 405–421. Springer, Cham (2020). https://doi.org/10.1007/978-3-030-58452-8_24
36. Nichol, A., et al.: Glide: towards photorealistic image generation and editing with text-guided diffusion models. In: International Conference on Machine Learning (ICML) (2022)
37. Niemeyer, M., Mescheder, L., Oechsle, M., Geiger, A.: Differentiable volumetric rendering: learning implicit 3d representations without 3d supervision. In: IEEE Conference on Computer Vision and Pattern Recognition (CVPR) (2020)
38. Palafox, P., Bozic, A., Thies, J., Nießner, M., Dai, A.: Neural parametric models for 3d deformable shapes. In: IEEE International Conference on Computer Vision (ICCV) (2021)
39. Patashnik, O., Wu, Z., Shechtman, E., Cohen-Or, D., Lischinski, D.: StyleClip: text-driven manipulation of StyleGAN imagery. In: IEEE International Conference on Computer Vision (ICCV) (2021)
40. Pavlakos, G., et al.: Expressive body capture: 3D hands, face, and body from a single image. In: IEEE Conference on Computer Vision and Pattern Recognition (CVPR) (2019)
41. Petrovich, M., Black, M.J., Varol, G.: Action-conditioned 3D human motion synthesis with transformer VAE. In: IEEE International Conference on Computer Vision (ICCV) (2021)
42. Petrovich, M., Black, M.J., Varol, G.: TEMOS: generating diverse human motions from textual descriptions. In: Avidan, S., Brostow, G., Cissé, M., Farinella, G.M., Hassner, T. (eds.) Computer Vision–ECCV 2022. LNCS vol. 13682, pp. 480–497. Springer, Cham (2022). https://doi.org/10.1007/978-3-031-20047-2_28
43. Plappert, M., Mandery, C., Asfour, T.: Learning a bidirectional mapping between human whole-body motion and natural language using deep recurrent neural networks. Robot. Auton. Syst. **109**, 13–26 (2018)

44. Punnakkal, A.R., Chandrasekaran, A., Athanasiou, N., Quiros-Ramirez, A., Black, M.J.: BABEL: bodies, action and behavior with English labels. In: IEEE Conference on Computer Vision and Pattern Recognition (CVPR) (2021)

45. Radford, A., et al.: Learning transferable visual models from natural language supervision. In: International Conference on Machine Learning (ICML) (2021)

46. Ravi, N., et al.: Accelerating 3d deep learning with pytorch3d. arXiv:2007.08501 (2020)

47. Romero, J., Tzionas, D., Black, M.J.: Embodied hands: modeling and capturing hands and bodies together. ACM Trans. Graph. (SIGGRAPH Asia). **36**(6), 1–6 (2017)

48. Saito, S., Huang, Z., Natsume, R., Morishima, S., Kanazawa, A., Li, H.: PiFU: pixel-aligned implicit function for high-resolution clothed human digitization. In: IEEE International Conference on Computer Vision (ICCV) (2019)

49. Saito, S., Simon, T., Saragih, J., Joo, H.: PiFUHD: multi-level pixel-aligned implicit function for high-resolution 3d human digitization. In: IEEE Conference on Computer Vision and Pattern Recognition (CVPR) (2020)

50. Saito, S., Yang, J., Ma, Q., Black, M.J.: SCANimate: weakly supervised learning of skinned clothed avatar networks. In: IEEE Conference on Computer Vision and Pattern Recognition (CVPR) (2021)

51. Sanh, V., Debut, L., Chaumond, J., Wolf, T.: Distilbert, a distilled version of BERT: smaller, faster, cheaper and lighter. arXiv:1910.01108 (2019)

52. Shree, V., Asfora, B., Zheng, R., Hong, S., Banfi, J., Campbell, M.: Exploiting natural language for efficient risk-aware multi-robot SAR planning. IEEE Robot. Autom. Lett. **6**(2), 3152–3159 (2021)

53. Song, K., Tan, X., Qin, T., Lu, J., Liu, T.Y.: MPNet: masked and permuted pre-training for language understanding. In: Advances in Neural Information Processing Systems (NeurIPS) (2020)

54. Tancik, M., et al.: Fourier features let networks learn high frequency functions in low dimensional domains. In: Advances in Neural Information Processing Systems (NeurIPS) (2020)

55. Tevet, G., Gordon, B., Hertz, A., Bermano, A.H., Cohen-Or, D.: MotionCLIP: exposing human motion generation to CLIP space. In: Avidan, S., Brostow, G., Cissé, M., Farinella, G.M., Hassner, T. (eds.) Computer Vision–ECCV 2022. LNCS, vol. 13682. Springer, Cham (2022). https://doi.org/10.1007/978-3-031-20047-2_21

56. Tsang, C.F., et al.: Kaolin (2019)

57. Wang, C., Chai, M., He, M., Chen, D., Liao, J.: Clip-NeRF: text-and-image driven manipulation of neural radiance fields. In: IEEE Conference on Computer Vision and Pattern Recognition (CVPR) (2022)

58. Wang, S., Mihajlovic, M., Ma, Q., Geiger, A., Tang, S.: MetaAvatar: learning animatable clothed human models from few depth images. In: Advances in Neural Information Processing Systems (NeurIPS) (2021)

59. Yoon, Y., Ko, W.R., Jang, M., Lee, J., Kim, J., Lee, G.: Robots learn social skills: end-to-end learning of co-speech gesture generation for humanoid robots. In: IEEE International Conference on Robotics and Automation (ICRA) (2019)

60. Youwang, K., Ji-Yeon, K., Joo, K., Oh, T.H.: Unified 3d mesh recovery of humans and animals by learning animal exercise. In: British Machine Vision Conference (BMVC) (2021)

61. Yu, A., Ye, V., Tancik, M., Kanazawa, A.: pixelNeRF: neural radiance fields from one or few images. In: IEEE Conference on Computer Vision and Pattern Recognition (CVPR) (2021)

62. Zhang, R., et al.: PointClip: point cloud understanding by clip. In: IEEE Conference on Computer Vision and Pattern Recognition (CVPR) (2021)
63. Zuffi, S., Kanazawa, A., Berger-Wolf, T., Black, M.J.: Three-d safari: learning to estimate zebra pose, shape, and texture from images "in the wild". In: IEEE International Conference on Computer Vision (ICCV) (2019)
64. Zuffi, S., Kanazawa, A., Jacobs, D., Black, M.J.: 3D menagerie: modeling the 3D shape and pose of animals. In: IEEE Conference on Computer Vision and Pattern Recognition (CVPR) (2017)

PlaneFormers: From Sparse View Planes to 3D Reconstruction

Samir Agarwala$^{(\boxtimes)}$, Linyi Jin, Chris Rockwell, and David F. Fouhey

University of Michigan, Ann Arbor, USA
{samirag,jinlinyi,cnris,fouhey}@umich.edu

Abstract. We present an approach for the planar surface reconstruction of a scene from images with limited overlap. This reconstruction task is challenging since it requires jointly reasoning about single image 3D reconstruction, correspondence between images, and the relative camera pose between images. Past work has proposed optimization-based approaches. We introduce a simpler approach, the PlaneFormer, that uses a transformer applied to 3D-aware plane tokens to perform 3D reasoning. Our experiments show that our approach is substantially more effective than prior work, and that several 3D-specific design decisions are crucial for its success. Code is available at https://github.com/samiragarwala/PlaneFormers.

1 Introduction

Consider the two images shown in Fig. 1. Even though you are not provided with the relative pose between the cameras that took the pictures you see, and even though you have never been to this particular location, you can form a single coherent explanation of the scene. You may notice, for instance, the doors and closet that are visible in both pictures. From here, you can deduce the relative positioning of the cameras and join your 3D perception of each image. The goal of this paper is to further the ability of computers to solve this problem.

The *sparse view* (wide and unknown baseline, few image) setting is challenging for existing systems because it falls between two main strands of 3D reconstruction in contemporary computer vision: multiview 3D reconstruction (usually by correspondence) and learned single view 3D reconstruction (usually by statistical models). In particular, traditional multiview tools [17,25,41,46,47] depend heavily on triangulation as a cue. Thus, in addition to struggling when view overlap is small, their cues usually entirely fail with no overlap. While single-view tools [12,19,34] can reconstruct single views via learning, merging the overlap between the views to produce one coherent reconstruction is challenging: identifying whether one extracted wall goes with another requires understanding appearance, the local geometry, as well as the relationship between the cameras.

Supplementary Information The online version contains supplementary material available at https://doi.org/10.1007/978-3-031-20062-5_12.

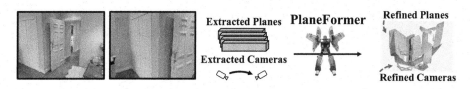

Fig. 1. Given a sparse set of images, our method detects planes and cameras, and produces plane correspondences and refined cameras using a Plane Transformer (Plane-Former [60]), from which it can reconstruct the scene in 3D.

Existing approaches in this multiview area have key limitations in either input requirements or approach. Many approaches assume known camera poses [26,39], which fundamentally changes the problem by restricting a search for correspondence for a pixel in one image to a single line in another [17]. While some works relax the assumption [30] or avoid it via many images [21], these have not been demonstrated in the few-image, wide baseline case. Most work in the sparse view setting (e.g., [4,8]) does pose estimation but not reconstruction and works that produce reconstructions from sparse views [24,42] come with substantial limitations. Qian et al. [42] require multiple networks, watertight synthetic ground-truth, and use a heuristic RANSAC-like search. Jin et al. [24] apply a complex hand-designed discrete/continuous optimization applied to plane segments found by an extended PlaneRCNN [34] output. This optimization includes bundle-adjustment on SIFT [36] on viewpoint-normalized texture like VIP [61].

We propose an approach (Sect. 3), named the PlaneFormer, that overcomes these limitations. Following existing work in this area [24,42], we construct a scene reconstruction by merging scene elements that are visible in multiple views and estimating relative camera transformations. We build on [24] and construct a piecewise planar reconstruction from the images. However, rather than perform an optimization, we directly train a transformer that ingests the scene components as tokens. These tokens integrate 3D knowledge and a working hypothesis about the relative pose between input views. As output, this transformer estimates plane correspondence, predicts the accuracy of the working hypothesis for the relative poses, as well as a correction to the poses. By casting the problem via transformers, we eliminate manual design and tuning of an optimization. Moreover, once planes are predicted, our reconstruction operations are performed via transformer forward passes that test out hypothesized relative camera poses.

Our experiments (Sect. 4) on Matterport3D [6] demonstrate the effectiveness of our approach compared to other approaches. We evaluate with set of image pairs with limited overlap (mean rotation: 53°; translation: 2.3 m; overlap: 21%). Our approach substantially surpasses the state of the art [24] before its post-processing bundle adjustment step: the number of pairs registered within 1m increases from 56.5% to 66.8%, and pairs with 90% correspondences correct increases from 28.1% to 40.6%. Even when [24] uses the additional bundle adjustment step, the our approach matches or exceeds the method. We next show that our approach can be used on multiple views, and that several 3D design decisions in the construction of the PlaneFormer are critical to its success.

2   Related Work

Our approach to 3D reconstruction from sparse views draws upon the well-studied tasks of correspondence estimation, i.e., 3D from many images; and learning strong 3D priors, i.e., 3D from a single image.

Correspondence and Camera Pose Estimation. The tasks of estimating correspondences and relative camera pose [10,13,45,63,66,67] across images are central to predicting 3D structure from multiple images [3,20,46,50]. Some methods jointly refine camera and depth across many images [30,33,40,51,68] in a process classically approached via Bundle Adjustment [1,52]. We also refine both camera and reconstruction; however, we do not have the requirement of many views. Additionally, we use self-attention, a powerful concept that has been successfully used in several vision tasks [3,31,45,49,69]. Our approach of using self-attention through transformers [54] is similar to SuperGlue [45] and LoFTR [49] in that it permits joint reasoning over the set of potential correspondences. We apply it to the task of planes, and also show that the learned networks can also predict relative camera pose directly (via residuals to a working hypothesis).

3D from a Single Image. Learned methods have enabled 3D inference given only a single viewpoint. These methods cannot rely on correspondences, and therefore use image cues along with learned priors and a variety of representations. Their 3D structure representations include voxels [11,48], meshes [16,55], point clouds [14,59], implicit functions [23,38], depth [29,43], surface normals [9,58], and planes [35,62,65]. We use planes to reconstruct 3D as they are often good approximations [15] and have strong baselines for detection such as PlaneRCNN [34]; we build off this architecture. In contrast with PlaneRCNN and single-image methods, we incorporate information across multiple views and therefore can also use correspondences.

3D from Sparse Views. Recent approaches enable learned reasoning with multiple views. Several works perform novel view synthesis using radiance fields [7,22,56,64]. Learned methods also estimate pose [4,57] and depth [27,53] given few views, but do not create a unified scene reconstruction. Our focus is also on wide-baseline views [41], further separating us from monocular stereo methods [27,53]. Two recent works approach this task. Qian et al. [42] reconstruct objects from two views but use heuristic stitching across views, and struggle on realistic data [24]. Jin et al. [24] jointly optimize plane correspondences and camera pose from two views with a hand-designed optimization. In contrast, we use a transformer to directly predict plane correspondence and camera pose. Our experiments (Sect. 4) show our approach outperforms these methods.

3   Approach

Our approach aims to jointly reason about a pair of images with an unknown relationship and reconstruct a single, coherent, global planar reconstruction of the scene depicted by the images. This process entails extracting three key related pieces of information: the position of the planes that constitute the scene; the correspondence between the planes in each view so that each real piece of the scene is reconstructed once and only once; and finally, the previously unknown relationship between the cameras that took each image.

At the heart of our approach is a plane transformer that accepts an initial independent reconstruction of each view and hypothesized global coordinate frame for the cameras. In a single forward pass, the plane transformer identifies which planes correspond with each other, predicts whether the cameras have correct relative pose, and estimates an updated relative camera pose as a residual. Inference for the scene consists of running one forward pass of the PlaneFormer network per camera hypothesis.

3.1   Backbone Plane Predictor

The PlaneFormer is built on top of a single-view plane estimation backbone from [24], which is an extended version of PlaneRCNN [34]. We refer the reader to [24] for training details, but summarize the key properties here. This plane backbone produces two outputs: per-image planes and a probability distribution over relative camera poses.

Plane Branch. The per-image planes are extracted from an image I_i via a Mask-RCNN [18]-like architecture. This architecture detects a set of plane segments, yielding M_i detections. Each detected segment in the ith image is indexed by j and has a mask segment $\mathcal{S}_{i,j}$, plane parameters $\boldsymbol{\pi}_{i,j} \in \mathbb{R}^4$, and appearance embedding $\mathbf{e}_{i,j} \in \mathbb{R}^{128}$. The plane parameter $\boldsymbol{\pi}_{i,j}$ can further be factored into a normal $\mathbf{n}_{i,j}$ and offset $o_{i,j}$ (defining a plane equation $\mathbf{n}_{i,j}^T[x, y, z] - o_{i,j} = 0$). The appearance embedding can be used to match between images i and i': the distance in embedding space $||\mathbf{e}_{i,j} - \mathbf{e}_{i',j'}||$ ought to be small whenever plane j' corresponds to the plane j.

Camera Branch. The backbone also produces a probability distribution over a predefined codebook of relative camera transformations $\{\hat{\mathbf{R}}_k, \hat{\mathbf{t}}_k\}$. To predict this distribution, it uses a CNN applied to cross-attention features between early layers of the network backbone (specifically, the P3 layers of the ResNet-50-FPN [32]). This camera branch combines cross-attention features [4,24] and pose via regression-by-classification [4,8,24,42], both of which have been shown to lead to strong performance. While a strong baseline, past work [24,42] has shown that the predictions of such networks need to be coupled with reasoning. For instance, [24] uses the probability for each camera pose as a term in its optimization problem. In our case, we use it to generate a set of initial hypotheses about the relative camera poses.

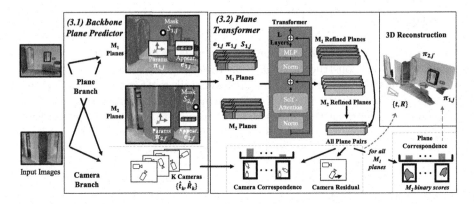

Fig. 2. Approach. Given two input images, the backbone network detects planes and predicts camera pose across images. The plane transformer refines these planes by predicting correspondence and refined camera pose, producing a final 3D reconstruction.

3.2 The PlaneFormer

The core of our method is a transformer [2,54] that jointly processes the planes detected in the 2 images given a hypothesized global coordinate system for the images. Since transformers operate on sets of inputs using a self-attention mechanism, they are able to consider context from all inputs while making predictions. This makes them effective in tasks such as ours where we want to collectively reason about multiple planes across the images to generate a coherent reconstruction. In our case, the transformer takes in a set of feature vectors representing plane detections as the input and maps them to an equal number of outputs which are then further processed and passed through MLP heads to predict our outputs. This function can take in a variable number of feature vectors as an input and is learned end-to-end. The plane transformer aims to identify: correspondence between the planes (i.e., whether they represent the same plane in 3D and can be merged), whether the hypothesized relative camera pose is correct, and how to improve the relative camera pose (Fig. 2).

As input, the plane transformer takes $M = M_1 + M_2$ tokens. These tokens contain features that integrate the hypothesized coordinate frame to help the transformer. The hypothesized coordinate frame consists of rotations and translations $\{\mathbf{R}_i, \mathbf{t}_i\}$ that are hypothesized to bring the two camera views into a common coordinate frame. For convenience, we assume that the common coordinate frame is centered at image 2 (i.e., $\mathbf{R}_2 = \mathbf{I}_{3\times3}$, $\mathbf{t}_2 = \mathbf{0}$), but note that the transformer never has explicit access to these rotation and translations.

Input Features. We concatenate three inputs to the network from the plane backbone to represent each of the M plane tokens. Each token is 899D.

Appearance Features (128D). The first token part is the appearance feature from [24]'s extended PlaneRCNN.

Plane Features (3D). The second part of the token is the plane equation $\pi_{i,j}$ comprising a normal that is scaled by the plane offset. This equation is transformed to the hypothesized canonical space by $\mathbf{R}_i, \mathbf{t}_i$. This feature functions like a positional encoding, and enables logic such as: if two planes have a similar appearance and plane parameters, then they are likely the same plane.

Mask Features (768D). We directly provide information about the plane segments via mask features. These features complement the plane features since they represent a plane segment rather than an infinite plane. We use the hypothesized relative camera pose and 3D to produce mask features. The mapping from image i to the common coordinate frame's view for plane j is given by a homography $\mathbf{H} = \mathbf{R}_i + (\mathbf{t}_i^T \mathbf{n}_{i,j})/o_{i,j}$ [37]. This lets us warp each mask $\mathcal{S}_{i,j}$ to a common reference frame. Once the mask is warped to the common reference frame, we downsample it to a 24×32 image. We hypothesize that the explicit representation facilitates reasoning such as: these two planes look the same, but they are on opposite sides so the provided transformation may be wrong; or these planes are the same and roughly in the right location but one is bigger, so the translation ought to be adjusted.

Outputs. As output, we produce a set of tensors that represent plane correspondence, whether cameras have the correct relative transformation, and updated camera transformations. Specifically, the outputs are:

Plane Correspondence. $\boldsymbol{\Pi} \in \mathbb{R}^{M_1 \times M_2}$ that gives the correspondence score between two planes across the input images. If $\boldsymbol{\Pi}_{j,j'}$ is large, then the planes j and j' likely are the same plane in a different view. We minimize a binary cross-entropy loss between the predicted $\boldsymbol{\Pi}$ and ground-truth.

Camera Correspondence. $C \in \mathbb{R}$ that indicates whether the two cameras have the correct relative transformation. If C has a high score, then it is likely that the hypothesized relative pose between the input cameras is correct. We minimize a binary cross-entropy loss between the predicted C and ground-truth.

Camera Residual. $\boldsymbol{\Delta} \in \mathbb{R}^7$ giving a residual for the hypothesized relative pose. This residual is expressed as the concatenation of a 4D quaternion for rotation and 3D translation vector for translation. Updating the relative transformation between the cameras is likely to improve the transformation. We minimize an L_1 loss between the predicted camera rotation and translation residual and the ground-truth camera rotation and translation residual with relative weight λ_t to translation. During training, hypothesized camera poses come from the codebook from the Camera Branch; thus there is a residual that needs to be corrected.

PlaneFormer Model. A full description of the method appears in the supplement, but our PlaneFormer consists of a standard transformer followed by the construction of pairwise features between planes. The transformer maps the M plane input tokens to M output tokens using a standard Transformer [54] with 5 layers and a feature size equal to plane tokens of 899. We use only a single head to facilitate joint modeling of all plane features.

After the transformer produces M per-plane output tokens, the M outputs are expanded to $M \times M$ pairwise features in an outer-product-like fashion. To assist in prediction, we also produce a per-image token: given M output tokens, where $\mathbf{o}_{i,j}$ denotes the output token for the jth plane in image i, we compute the per-image average token $\boldsymbol{\mu}_i = (1/M_i) \sum_{j=1}^{M_i} \mathbf{o}_{i,j}$. The pairwise feature for planes (i,j) and (i',j') is the concatenation of the plane output tokens $\mathbf{o}_{i,j}$, $\mathbf{o}_{i',j'}$, and their per-image tokens $\boldsymbol{\mu}_i$, and $\boldsymbol{\mu}_{i'}$. This 3596 (4×899) feature is passed into separate 4-hidden-layer MLP heads that estimate $\boldsymbol{\Pi}$, C, and $\boldsymbol{\Delta}$ per-pair of planes. At each hidden layer, we halve the input feature dimension. We average pool the MLP output over plane pairs across the images to produce the final estimate for C and $\boldsymbol{\Delta}$. $\boldsymbol{\Pi}$ can be used after masking to $M_1 \times M_2$. Finally, we apply a sigmoid function to C and $\boldsymbol{\Pi}$ to generate the model output.

3.3 Inference

Once the PlaneFormer has been trained, we can apply it to solve reconstruction tasks. Given a set of planes and hypothesized poses of cameras, the Planeformer can estimate correspondence, identify whether the hypothesized poses are correct, and estimate a correction to the camera poses.

Two View Inference. Given two images, one takes the top h hypotheses for the relative camera pose from the Camera Branch (Sect. 3.1) and evaluates them with the PlaneFormer. The pose hypothesis with highest camera correspondence score is selected, and the predicted residual is added. We note that these camera pose hypotheses can be explored in parallel, since they only change the token features. After the plane correspondences have been predicted, we match using the Hungarian Algorithm [28] with thresholding. Sample outputs of PlaneFormer appear in Fig. 3 and throughout the paper.

Multiview Inference. In order to extend the method to multiple views, we can apply it pairwise to the images. We apply the above approach pairwise to edges in an acyclic view graph that connects the images. The graph is generated greedily on a visibility score for a pair of images (i, i') that represents the number of planes with close matches. For the appearance embedding $\mathbf{e}_{i,j}$ of plane j in image i, we compute the minimum distance to the appearance embeddings of the planes in image i', or $d_j = \min_{j'} \|\mathbf{e}_{i,j} - \mathbf{e}_{i',j'}\|$. Rather than threshold the distance, we softly count the numbers of close correspondence via a score $\sum_j \exp(-d_j^2/\sigma^2)$. We repeat the process from i' to i and then sum for symmetry.

3.4 Training and Implementation Details

Training procedure. During training, each sample must assume a set of camera transformations (i.e., $\{\mathbf{R}_i, \mathbf{t}_i\}$). We train on a mix of correct camera transformations (using the nearest rotation and translation in the sparse codebook) and incorrect camera transformations (using a randomly selected non-nearest rotation and translation in the sparse codebook). Given a correct camera hypothesis, we backpropagate losses on all outputs; given an incorrect hypothesis, we

Input Views	Plane Correspondence	Reconstruction

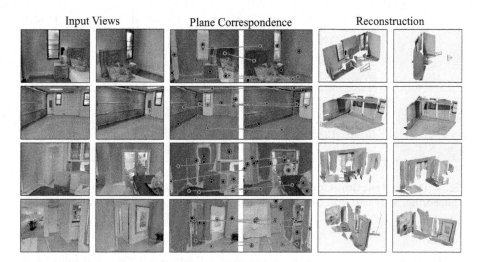

Fig. 3. Sample Outputs on the Test Set. PlaneFormer produces jointly refined plane correspondences and cameras, from which it reconstructs the input scene. It can produce high-quality reconstructions in cases of moderate view change (top two rows), and coherent reconstructions in cases of large view change (bottom two rows).

backpropagate losses only on the camera correspondence C. Thus, the camera correspondence output is trained to discriminate between correct and incorrect cameras, and the other outputs do not have their training contaminated (e.g., by having to predict residuals even if the camera hypothesis is completely incorrect). The correct and incorrect cameras are sampled equally during training.

Implementation Details. We train for 40k iterations using a batch size of 40 and the same Matterport3D [6] setup as Jin *et al.* [24] We use SGD with momentum of 0.9 and a learning rate of 1e-2, and follow a one-cycle cosine annealing schedule. We weight all losses equally, with the exception of $\lambda_t = 0.5$ for the residual translation loss. Training takes about 36 h using 4 RTX 2080 Tis. At inference, we select from $h = 9$ camera hypotheses.

4   Experiments

We now evaluate the proposed approach in multiple settings. We first introduce our experimental setup, including metrics and datasets. We then introduce experiments for the wide baseline two view case in Sect. 4.1. The two view setting has an abundance of baselines that we compare with. Next, we introduce experiments for more views, specifically 3 and 5 views, in Sect. 4.2. Finally, we analyze which parts of our method are most important in Sect. 4.3.

Metrics. The sparse view reconstruction problem integrates several challenging, complex problems: detecting 3D planes from a 2D image, establishing correspondence across images, and estimating relative camera pose. We therefore evaluate the problem in multiple parts.

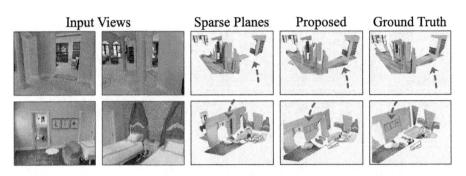

Fig. 4. Reconstruction Comparison. Sparse Plane reconstructions are a good, but PlaneFormer's are better in terms of stitched planes (top), and camera poses (bottom).

Plane Correspondence. We evaluate correspondence separately. We follow Cai et al. [5] and use IPAA-X, or the fraction of image pairs with no less than X% of planes associated correctly. We use ground-truth plane boxes in this setting since otherwise this metric measures both plane detection and plane correspondence.

Relative Camera Pose. We next evaluate camera relative pose estimation. We follow [24,42] and report the mean error, the median error, and the fraction of image pairs with error below a threshold of $30°$ and $1\,\mathrm{m}$ following [42].

Full Scene Results. Finally, we report results using the full scene metric from [24]. This metric counts detected planes as true positives if their mask IoU is ≥ 0.5, surface normal distance is $\leq 30°$; and offset distance is less than $1\,\mathrm{m}$. This metric integrates all three components: to get the planes correct, one needs to reconstruct them in 3D, estimate the relative camera configuration to map the second view's planes into the first view, and identify duplicated planes to suppress false positives. While this metric is important, any component can limit performance, including components we do not alter, like plane detection.

Datasets. We evaluate on three datasets: two-, three-, and five-view. *Two view dataset:* We use the exact dataset used in [24] for fair comparison. This consists of 31392 training image pairs, 4707 validation image pairs, and 7996 test image pairs. These views are widely spearated. On average: view overlap is 21% of pixels; relative rotation is $53°$; and relative translation is $2.3\,\mathrm{m}$. *Multiview datasets:* We generate a set of 3- and 5- view pairs using the same procedure as [24]. We evaluate on a total of 258 3-view and 76 5-view samples.

Baselines. The full problem of reconstructing the scene from a set of sparse views requires solving the three separate problems of correspondence, relative camera pose estimation, and 3D reconstruction. We compare with full systems as well as approaches that solve each problem independently.

All Settings. In all cases, we compare with *Sparse Planes* [24]. For fair comparison, we use an identical backbone to [24] so that any performance gain stems from the PlaneFormer rather than improved systems tuning. The full version is our strongest baseline. It uses the same plane information and follows it with a discrete-continuous optimization. The continuous optimization requires extracting view-normalized texture maps, performing SIFT matching, and then bundle adjustment and is expensive and a complementary contribution. Since our method does not do an additional step of extracting feature correspondences and optimizing, a more comparable system to the contribution of our paper is the discrete-optimization only version, or *Sparse Planes* [24] *(No Continuous)*, which performs all the steps except bundle adjustment on point correspondences.

Plane Correspondence. We additionally compare with (*Appearance Only*), or the Hungarian algorithm with thresholding on the appearance embedding distances. This approach outperformed other methods like [5] and [42] in [24].

Relative Camera Pose Estimation. We also compare with a number of other methods. The most important is the (*Sparse Planes* [24] Camera Branch) which is the top prediction from the Camera Branch network that our system uses for hypotheses. Gain over this is attributable to the PlaneFormer camera correspondence and residual branch, since these produce different relative camera poses. Other methods include: (Odometry [44] + GT/ [43]), which combines a RGBD odometry with ground-truth or estimated depth; (*Assoc. 3D* [42]), a previous approach for camera pose estimation; (*Dense Correlation Volumes* [4]) which uses correlation volumes to predict rotation; *SuperGlue* [45] and *LoFTR* [49], which are learned feature matching system. Since [45] and [49] solve for an essential matrix, their estimate of translation is intrinsically scale-free [17].

Full Scene Reconstruction. For full-evaluation, we report some of the top performing baselines from [24] along with [49]. These are constructed by joining the outputs of [24]'s extended PlaneRCNN [34] with a relative camera pose estimation method that gives a joint coordinate frame. These are as described in the relative camera pose estimation, except *SuperGlue GT Scale* and *LoFTR GT Scale* are also given the ground-truth translation scale. This extra information is needed since the method intrinsically cannot provide a translation scale.

Table 1. Two View Plane Correspondence. IPAA-X [5] measures the fraction of pairs with no less than X% of planes associated correctly. Ground truth bounding boxes are used. Since the Sparse Planes continuous optimization does not update correspondence, there is not a separate entry for Sparse Planes without continuous optimization.

	IPAA-100	IPAA-90	IPAA-80
Appearance only	6.8	23.5	55.7
Sparse Planes [24]	16.2	28.1	55.3
Proposed	**19.6**	**40.6**	**71.0**

Table 2. Two View Relative Camera Pose. We report median, mean error and % error ≤ 1 m or 30° for translation and rotation.

Method	Translation			Rotation		
	Med	Mean	(≤1 m)	Med	Mean	(≤30°)
Odometry [44] + GT Depth	3.20	3.87	16.0	50.43	55.10	40.9
Odometry [44] + [43]	3.34	4.00	8.3	50.98	57.92	29.9
Assoc. 3D [42]	2.17	2.50	14.8	42.09	52.97	38.1
Dense Correlation Volumes [4]	-	-	-	28.01	41.56	52.45
Camera Branch [24]	0.90	1.40	55.5	7.65	24.57	81.9
Sparse Planes [24] (No Continuous)	0.88	1.36	56.5	7.58	22.84	83.7
Proposed	0.66	**1.19**	**66.8**	5.96	22.20	83.8
Sparse Planes [24] (Full)	**0.63**	1.25	66.6	7.33	22.78	83.4
SuperGlue [45]	-	-	-	3.88	24.17	77.8
LoFTR-DS [49]	-	-	-	**0.71**	**11.11**	**90.47**

Table 3. Two View Evaluation. Average Precision, treating reconstruction as a 3D plane detection problem. We use three definitions of true positive. (*All*) requires Mask IoU ≥ 0.5, Normal error ≤ 30°, and Offset error ≤ 1 m. (*-Offset*) removes the offset condition; (*-Normal*) removes the normal condition.

Methods	All	-Offset	-Normal
Odometry [44] + PlaneRCNN [34]	21.33	27.08	24.99
SuperGlue-GT Scale [45] + PlaneRCNN [34]	30.06	33.24	33.52
LoFTR-DS-GT Scale [49]	33.31	36.17	35.72
Camera Branch [24] + PlaneRCNN [34]	29.44	35.25	31.67
Sparse Planes [24] (No Continuous)	35.87	42.13	38.8
Proposed	**37.62**	**43.19**	**40.36**
Sparse Planes [24] (Full)	36.02	42.01	39.04

4.1   Wide Baseline Two-View Case

Our primary point of comparison is the wide baseline two view case. This two-view case has been extensively studied and benchmarked in [24]. We have shown qualitative results of the full system in Fig. 3 by itself and show a comparison with Sparse Planes in Fig. 4. We now discuss each aspect of performance.

Plane Correspondence Results. As reported in Table 1, the PlaneFormer substantially increases IPAA across multiple metrics compared to Sparse Planes [24]. We show qualitative results on Fig. 5, including one of the images that Jin *et al.* [24] reported as a representative failure mode of their system. This particular case is challenging for geometry-based optimization since the bed footboards are co-planar and similar in appearance. These have similar appearance and plane parameter features; our mask token, however, can separate them out.

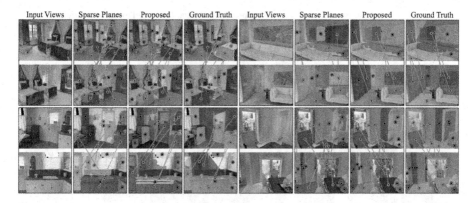

Fig. 5. Plane Comparison. Matching surfaces across large view changes is challenging. Multiple surfaces may be similar in appearance, causing correspondence mixups like bed footboards (top left) or paintings (top right). By jointly refining planes across images via a transformer, the proposed method better associates across images. It can also reduce inconsistent outlier detections (bottom).

Relative Camera Pose Results. We next evaluate relative camera pose. Our results in Table 2 show that the PlaneFormer outperforms most other approaches that do not do bundle adjustment on feature correspondence: by integrating plane information, the proposed system improves over the camera branch by over 10% in translation accuracy and reduces rotation error by 22% (relative). The approach outperforms the Sparse Planes system before continuous optimization. Even when Sparse Planes performs this step, our approach outperforms it in all but one metric. Our approach is competitive with SuperGlue [45] while LoFTR [49] outperforms competing systems in rotation estimation. Since these point-feature based approaches do not provide translation scale, we see them as complementary. Future systems might benefit from both points and planes.

Full Scene Evaluation Results. We finally report full scene evaluation results (AP) in Table 3. Our approach outperforms alternate methods, including the full version of Sparse Planes. The relative performance gains of our method are smaller than compared to those for plane correspondence. However, it is important to note that the full scene evaluations is limited by every component. We hypothesize that one of the current key limiting factors is the accuracy of single-view reconstruction, or the initial PlaneRCNN [34].

4.2 Wide Baseline Multiview Case

We next report the multiview case. The multiview case is substantially more challenging than performing pairwise reconstruction since the output must be a single coherent reconstruction. For instance, in relative camera pose, the composition of the rotation from image 1 to image 2 and the rotation from image 2 to image 3 must be the rotation from image 1 to image 3.

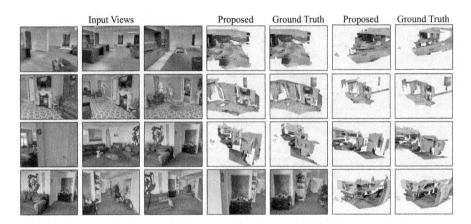

Input Views   Proposed   Ground Truth   Proposed   Ground Truth

Fig. 6. Multiview Test Results. With 3 views, our approach model can often construct extensive reconstruction of rooms (top 3 rows). With 5 views, the model continues to stitch larger sets of planes together effectively (bottom row).

Baselines. We extend the top baselines from the two view case to the multiview case. For fair comparison, we apply each baseline to the same view graph that is used for our method (defined in Sect. 3.3). We report both the full version of [24] and the version without the continuous optimization (*No Cont.* [24]). For correspondence, we additionally report the appearance feature only baseline, which outperforms [5,42]. For camera pose estimation, we report the Camera Branch (Camera) of [24], which outperforms multiple other baselines such as [42, 44].

Quantitative Results. We report correspondence results in Table 4. As was the case in the 2-view setting, our approach substantially outperforms the baselines. Overall performance reduces as the number of views increases; this is because the space covered often spreads out as the number of images increase, raising the difficulty of reconstruction. We next report relative camera pose estimation results in Table 5. Trends are similar to the 2-view case: our method is competitive with the full pipeline of Jin et al. [24] in camera estimation, and often surpasses it. Our approach also substantially outperforms the top prediction from the Camera Branch and the discrete optimization version of [24].

Qualitative Results. We show qualitative results on 3- and 5-view inputs in Fig. 6. Our method can often generate high quality scenes.

4.3   Ablations

We finally analyze ablations of the method in Table 6. We report the IPAA-90 and average camera pose translation and rotation errors. In all cases, ablations follow the same training procedure and are trained until validation accuracy plateaus. Full details and comparisons appear in supplement.

Table 4. Multiview Evaluation: Plane Correspondence We report IPAA-X for 3- and 5-view datasets. Our approach continues to substantially outperform baseline methods (but overall performance drops due to the increasing difficulty of the task).

	3-view IPAA-X			5-view IPAA-X		
	IPAA-100	IPAA-90	IPAA-80	IPAA-100	IPAA-90	IPAA-80
Appearance	5.94	20.28	52.97	1.45	13.68	52.37
SparsePlanes [24]	9.95	23.77	51.16	4.87	16.58	41.45
Proposed	**14.60**	**32.69**	**66.15**	**5.92**	**20.66**	**55.92**

Table 5. Multiview Evaluation: Relative Camera Pose Estimation We report the same metrics as the two view case, while running on the 3- and 5-view dataset.

	3-view						5-view					
	Transl. Error (m)			Rot. Error (deg)			Transl. Error (m)			Rot. Error (deg)		
	Med.	Mean	$\leq 1\,m$	Med.	Mean	$\leq 30°$	Med.	Mean	$\leq 1\,m$	Med.	Mean	$\leq 30°$
Camera [24]	1.25	2.21	41.47	9.40	37.08	71.71	1.69	2.80	29.61	13.72	48.07	63.55
No Cont. [24]	1.15	2.02	43.67	8.97	30.89	**75.97**	1.62	2.73	31.58	12.08	44.99	64.08
Proposed	**0.83**	1.81	**56.69**	**7.88**	32.22	74.94	**1.10**	2.33	47.24	**9.52**	**43.22**	**67.5**
Full [24]	0.84	**1.74**	54.91	8.83	**30.19**	75.58	1.13	**2.29**	**47.37**	11.35	44.16	64.21

Feature Ablations. To test feature importance, we report results when each feature has been removed from the token. For fair comparison, we keep transformer feature size equal to the full model by mapping inputs through an MLP. Table 6 (left) shows all three sets of features are important for performance. Removing appearance features causes the largest drop in plane correspondence, likely due to the importance of appearance when matching many planes across images. In contrast, removing plane parameters is most damaging to camera accuracy. As plane parameters represent position and orientation, this comparison indicates the position and orientation of planes are a powerful signal for inferring relative camera pose across images. Mask features have little impact on camera performance, but are still important for plane correspondence.

Network Ablations. We next test the importance of the transformer and camera residual (Table 6, right). Our no transformer model simply applies the MLP heads for plane correspondence, camera correctness, and residuals. The plane features do not interact in this model, but it outperforms all prior baselines for plane correspondence and is competitive in camera pose, which illustrates the value of discriminatively learned correspondence rather than optimization. However, adding a transformer to enable inter-plane interaction substantially improve performance, with IPAA-90 increasing by nearly 8%. The camera residual is also an important design decision, enabling refinement on predicted cameras. Note even without the residual, camera performance is similar to or better than all baselines. The camera residual does not impact plane predictions.

Table 6. Ablations. We perform ablations of input features (left) and network design (right). We report IPAA-90 and relative camera pose translation and rotation error.

Feature Ablation	Plane IPAA-90 ↑	Trans. Mean ↓	Rot. Mean ↓	Network Ablation	Plane IPAA-90 ↑	Trans. Mean ↓	Rot. Mean ↓
Proposed	**40.6**	**1.19**	22.20	Proposed	**40.6**	**1.19**	**22.20**
- Appearance	26.9	1.23	22.78	- Transformer	32.7	1.48	26.43
- Plane	35.2	1.32	25.92	- Residual	40.6	1.34	22.38
- Mask	34.5	1.26	**21.21**				

5   Conclusion

We have introduced a new model for performing reconstructions between images separated by wide baselines. Our approach replaces hand-designed optimization with a discriminatively learned transformer and shows substantial improvements over the state of the art across multiple metrics and settings.

Acknowledgements. This work was supported by the DARPA Machine Common Sense Program. We would like to thank Richard Higgins and members of the Fouhey lab for helpful discussions and feedback.

References

1. Agarwal, S., Snavely, N., Seitz, S.M., Szeliski, R.: Bundle adjustment in the large. In: Daniilidis, K., Maragos, P., Paragios, N. (eds.) ECCV 2010. LNCS, vol. 6312, pp. 29–42. Springer, Heidelberg (2010). https://doi.org/10.1007/978-3-642-15552-9_3
2. Bloem, P.: August 2019. http://peterbloem.nl/blog/transformers
3. Bozic, A., Palafox, P., Thies, J., Dai, A., Nießner, M.: Transformerfusion: monocular RGB scene reconstruction using transformers. In: NeurIPS, vol. 34 (2021)
4. Cai, R., Hariharan, B., Snavely, N., Averbuch-Elor, H.: Extreme rotation estimation using dense correlation volumes. In: IEEE/CVF Conference on Computer Vision and Pattern Recognition (CVPR) (2021)
5. Cai, Z., et al.: MessyTable: instance association in multiple camera views. In: Vedaldi, A., Bischof, H., Brox, T., Frahm, J.-M. (eds.) ECCV 2020. LNCS, vol. 12356, pp. 1–16. Springer, Cham (2020). https://doi.org/10.1007/978-3-030-58621-8_1
6. Chang, A., et al.: Matterport3D: learning from RGB-D data in indoor environments. In: 3DV (2017)
7. Chen, A., et al.: MVSNeRF: fast generalizable radiance field reconstruction from multi-view stereo. In: ICCV, pp. 14124–14133 (2021)
8. Chen, K., Snavely, N., Makadia, A.: Wide-baseline relative camera pose estimation with directional learning. In: CVPR, pp. 3258–3268, June 2021
9. Chen, W., Qian, S., Fan, D., Kojima, N., Hamilton, M., Deng, J.: Oasis: a large-scale dataset for single image 3D in the wild. In: CVPR (2020)

10. Choy, C., Dong, W., Koltun, V.: Deep global registration. In: CVPR, pp. 2514–2523 (2020)
11. Choy, C.B., Xu, D., Gwak, J.Y., Chen, K., Savarese, S.: 3D-R2N2: a unified approach for single and multi-view 3D object reconstruction. In: Leibe, B., Matas, J., Sebe, N., Welling, M. (eds.) ECCV 2016. LNCS, vol. 9912, pp. 628–644. Springer, Cham (2016). https://doi.org/10.1007/978-3-319-46484-8_38
12. Eigen, D., Fergus, R.: Predicting depth, surface normals and semantic labels with a common multi-scale convolutional architecture. In: ICCV (2015)
13. El Banani, M., Gao, L., Johnson, J.: Unsupervised R&R: unsupervised point cloud registration via differentiable rendering. In: CVPR (2021)
14. Fan, H., Su, H., Guibas, L.J.: A point set generation network for 3D object reconstruction from a single image. In: CVPR (2017)
15. Furukawa, Y., Curless, B., Seitz, S.M., Szeliski, R.: Manhattan-world stereo. In: CVPR (2009)
16. Gkioxari, G., Malik, J., Johnson, J.: Mesh R-CNN. In: ICCV (2019)
17. Hartley, R.I., Zisserman, A.: Multiple View Geometry in Computer Vision. Cambridge University Press, Cambridge (2004). ISBN 0521540518
18. He, K., Gkioxari, G., Dollár, P., Girshick, R.: Mask R-CNN. In: ICCV (2017)
19. Hoiem, D., Efros, A.A., Hebert, M.: Geometric context from a single image. In: ICCV, vol. 1, pp. 654–661. IEEE (2005)
20. Huang, P.H., Matzen, K., Kopf, J., Ahuja, N., Huang, J.B.: DeepMVS: learning multi-view stereopsis. In: CVPR (2018)
21. Huang, Z., et al.: Deep volumetric video from very sparse multi-view performance capture. In: Ferrari, V., Hebert, M., Sminchisescu, C., Weiss, Y. (eds.) ECCV 2018. LNCS, vol. 11220, pp. 351–369. Springer, Cham (2018). https://doi.org/10.1007/978-3-030-01270-0_21
22. Jain, A., Tancik, M., Abbeel, P.: Putting nerf on a diet: semantically consistent few-shot view synthesis. In: ICCV, pp. 5885–5894 (2021)
23. Jiang, C., Sud, A., Makadia, A., Huang, J., Nießner, M., Funkhouser, T., et al.: Local implicit grid representations for 3D scenes. In: CVPR, pp. 6001–6010 (2020)
24. Jin, L., Qian, S., Owens, A., Fouhey, D.F.: Planar surface reconstruction from sparse views. In: ICCV (2021)
25. Jin, Y., et al.: Image matching across wide baselines: from paper to practice. IJCV 129(2), 517–547 (2020)
26. Kar, A., Häne, C., Malik, J.: Learning a multi-view stereo machine. In: NeurIPS (2017)
27. Kopf, J., Rong, X., Huang, J.B.: Robust consistent video depth estimation. In: CVPR, pp. 1611–1621 (2021)
28. Kuhn, H.W.: The Hungarian method for the assignment problem. Nav. Res. Logist. Q. 2(1–2), 83–97 (1955)
29. Li, Z., Snavely, N.: Megadepth: learning single-view depth prediction from internet photos. In: CVPR, pp. 2041–2050 (2018)
30. Lin, C.H., Ma, W.C., Torralba, A., Lucey, S.: Barf: bundle-adjusting neural radiance fields. In: ICCV (2021)
31. Lin, K., Wang, L., Liu, Z.: End-to-end human pose and mesh reconstruction with transformers. In: CVPR (2021)
32. Lin, T.Y., Dollár, P., Girshick, R., He, K., Hariharan, B., Belongie, S.: Feature pyramid networks for object detection. In: CVPR (2017)
33. Lindenberger, P., Sarlin, P.E., Larsson, V., Pollefeys, M.: Pixel-perfect structure-from-motion with featuremetric refinement. In: ICCV, pp. 5987–5997 (2021)

34. Liu, C., Kim, K., Gu, J., Furukawa, Y., Kautz, J.: Planercnn: 3D plane detection and reconstruction from a single image. In: CVPR (2019)
35. Liu, C., Yang, J., Ceylan, D., Yumer, E., Furukawa, Y.: Planenet: piece-wise planar reconstruction from a single RGB image. In: CVPR, pp. 2579–2588 (2018)
36. Lowe, D.G.: Distinctive image features from scale-invariant keypoints. IJCV **60**(2), 91–110 (2004)
37. Ma, Y., Soatto, S., Košecká, J., Sastry, S.: An Invitation to 3-D Vision: From Images to Geometric Models, vol. 26. Springer, New York (2004). https://doi.org/10.1007/978-0-387-21779-6
38. Mescheder, L., Oechsle, M., Niemeyer, M., Nowozin, S., Geiger, A.: Occupancy networks: learning 3D reconstruction in function space. In: CVPR, pp. 4460–4470 (2019)
39. Mildenhall, B., Srinivasan, P.P., Tancik, M., Barron, J.T., Ramamoorthi, R., Ng, R.: NeRF: representing scenes as neural radiance fields for view synthesis. In: Vedaldi, A., Bischof, H., Brox, T., Frahm, J.-M. (eds.) ECCV 2020. LNCS, vol. 12346, pp. 405–421. Springer, Cham (2020). https://doi.org/10.1007/978-3-030-58452-8_24
40. Mur-Artal, R., Montiel, J.M.M., Tardos, J.D.: Orb-slam: a versatile and accurate monocular slam system. TOG **31**(5), 1147–1163 (2015)
41. Pritchett, P., Zisserman, A.: Wide baseline stereo matching. In: ICCV (1998)
42. Qian, S., Jin, L., Fouhey, D.F.: Associative3D: volumetric reconstruction from sparse views. In: Vedaldi, A., Bischof, H., Brox, T., Frahm, J.-M. (eds.) ECCV 2020. LNCS, vol. 12360, pp. 140–157. Springer, Cham (2020). https://doi.org/10.1007/978-3-030-58555-6_9
43. Ranftl, R., Lasinger, K., Hafner, D., Schindler, K., Koltun, V.: Towards robust monocular depth estimation: mixing datasets for zero-shot cross-dataset transfer. TPAMI (2020)
44. Raposo, C., Lourenço, M., Antunes, M., Barreto, J.P.: Plane-based odometry using an RGB-D camera. In: BMVC (2013)
45. Sarlin, P.E., DeTone, D., Malisiewicz, T., Rabinovich, A.: Superglue: learning feature matching with graph neural networks. In: CVPR (2020)
46. Schonberger, J.L., Frahm, J.M.: Structure-from-motion revisited. In: CVPR (2016)
47. Schönberger, J.L., Zheng, E., Frahm, J.-M., Pollefeys, M.: Pixelwise view selection for unstructured multi-view stereo. In: Leibe, B., Matas, J., Sebe, N., Welling, M. (eds.) ECCV 2016. LNCS, vol. 9907, pp. 501–518. Springer, Cham (2016). https://doi.org/10.1007/978-3-319-46487-9_31
48. Song, S., Yu, F., Zeng, A., Chang, A.X., Savva, M., Funkhouser, T.: Semantic scene completion from a single depth image. In: CVPR (2017)
49. Sun, J., Shen, Z., Wang, Y., Bao, H., Zhou, X.: LoFTR: detector-free local feature matching with transformers. In: CVPR (2021)
50. Sun, J., Xie, Y., Chen, L., Zhou, X., Bao, H.: Neuralrecon: real-time coherent 3D reconstruction from monocular video. In: CVPR, pp. 15598–15607 (2021)
51. Teed, Z., Deng, J.: Droid-slam: deep visual slam for monocular, stereo, and RGB-D cameras. In: NeurIPS, vol. 34 (2021)
52. Triggs, B., McLauchlan, P.F., Hartley, R.I., Fitzgibbon, A.W.: Bundle adjustment — a modern synthesis. In: Triggs, B., Zisserman, A., Szeliski, R. (eds.) IWVA 1999. LNCS, vol. 1883, pp. 298–372. Springer, Heidelberg (2000). https://doi.org/10.1007/3-540-44480-7_21
53. Ummenhofer, B., et al.: Demon: depth and motion network for learning monocular stereo. In: CVPR (2017)

54. Vaswani, A., et al.: Attention is all you need. In: NeurIPS (2017)
55. Wang, N., Zhang, Y., Li, Z., Fu, Y., Liu, W., Jiang, Y.G.: Pixel2mesh: generating 3D mesh models from single RGB images. In: ECCV, pp. 52–67 (2018)
56. Wang, Q., et al.: IBRNet: learning multi-view image-based rendering. In: CVPR (2021)
57. Wang, W., Hu, Y., Scherer, S.: TartanVO: a generalizable learning-based VO. In: CoRL (2020)
58. Wang, X., Fouhey, D.F., Gupta, A.: Designing deep networks for surface normal estimation. In: CVPR (2015)
59. Wiles, O., Gkioxari, G., Szeliski, R., Johnson, J.: Synsin: end-to-end view synthesis from a single image. In: CVPR, pp. 7467–7477 (2020)
60. Wong, S.: Takaratomy transformers henkei octane. https://live.staticflickr.com/3166/2970928056_c3b59be5ca_b.jpg
61. Wu, C., Clipp, B., Li, X., Frahm, J.M., Pollefeys, M.: 3D model matching with viewpoint-invariant patches (VIP). In: CVPR (2008)
62. Yang, F., Zhou, Z.: Recovering 3D planes from a single image via convolutional neural networks. In: ECCV (2018)
63. Yi, K.M., Trulls, E., Ono, Y., Lepetit, V., Salzmann, M., Fua, P.: Learning to find good correspondences. In: CVPR, pp. 2666–2674 (2018)
64. Yu, A., Ye, V., Tancik, M., Kanazawa, A.: pixelNeRF: neural radiance fields from one or few images. In: CVPR (2021)
65. Yu, Z., Zheng, J., Lian, D., Zhou, Z., Gao, S.: Single-image piece-wise planar 3D reconstruction via associative embedding. In: CVPR, pp. 1029–1037 (2019)
66. Zhang, J., et al.: Learning two-view correspondences and geometry using order-aware network. In: ICCV, pp. 5845–5854 (2019)
67. Zhang, Z.: Iterative point matching for registration of free-form curves and surfaces. IJCV **13**(2), 119–152 (1994)
68. Zhang, Z., Cole, F., Tucker, R., Freeman, W.T., Dekel, T.: Consistent depth of moving objects in video. TOG **40**(4), 1–12 (2021)
69. Zhao, H., Jiang, L., Jia, J., Torr, P.H., Koltun, V.: Point transformer. In: Proceedings of the IEEE/CVF International Conference on Computer Vision, pp. 16259–16268 (2021)

Learning Implicit Templates for Point-Based Clothed Human Modeling

Siyou Lin$^{(\boxtimes)}$, Hongwen Zhang , Zerong Zheng , Ruizhi Shao,
and Yebin Liu

Tsinghua University, Beijing, China
linsy21@mails.tsinghua.edu.cn

Abstract. We present FITE, a First-Implicit-Then-Explicit framework
for modeling human avatars in clothing. Our framework first learns
implicit surface templates representing the coarse clothing topology, and
then employs the templates to guide the generation of point sets which
further capture pose-dependent clothing deformations such as wrinkles.
Our pipeline incorporates the merits of both implicit and explicit representations, namely, the ability to handle varying topology and the ability
to efficiently capture fine details. We also propose diffused skinning to
facilitate template training especially for loose clothing, and projection-
based pose-encoding to extract pose information from mesh templates
without predefined UV map or connectivity. Our code is publicly available at https://github.com/jsnln/fite.

Keywords: 3D modeling · Clothed humans · Implicit surfaces · Point
set surfaces

1 Introduction

The modeling of clothed human avatars is an important topic in many graphics-
related fields, such as animation, video games, virtual reality, etc. Traditional
solutions [5,20,34,35] are mostly based on rigging and skinning artist-designed
avatars, and thus lack realism in representing clothed humans. Another possibility is to apply physics-based simulation [15,24,25,45] which is in general computationally heavy and requires manually designed outfits. Recent work explores
learning realistic pose-dependent deformations (e.g. wrinkles) of clothes from
posed scan data. From the data-driven perspective, we identify two major challenges in this task: (i) learning the clothing topology; (ii) learning fine details and
pose-dependent clothing deformations. In fact, most methods are limited by the

---

Supplementary Information The online version contains supplementary material
available at https://doi.org/10.1007/978-3-031-20062-5_13.

representation they choose and cannot fully tackle the challenges above. In particular, mesh-based methods [2, 3, 8, 9, 13, 14, 24, 25, 27, 32, 38, 43, 45, 55, 58, 59, 64] are essentially limited by the fixed topology and typically require registered scans for training. On the other hand, implicit surfaces [11, 12, 16, 22, 40, 41, 44, 52–54, 60] can represent varying topology, but are computationally heavy and struggle to represent details. Point sets, on the other hand, enjoys efficiency as well as flexibility. However, generating point sets with details is difficult. Most methods generate sparse points [1, 19, 33] or points grouped into patches [6, 17, 18, 23, 37]. Although some methods achieve higher quality, they typically require dozens of iterations for a single output [31, 36, 62].

Recently, the state-of-the-art (SOTA) point-based method, POP [39] demonstrates the power of points for cross-outfit modeling and for capturing pose-dependent clothing details. The success of POP lies in its robust body-template-plus-offsets formulation, the flexibility of point sets, and its fine-grained UV-space features. However, POP applies the same minimal body [35, 46] for all outfits, which suffers from artifacts such as overly sparse points and discontinuity in clothing, negatively affecting the overall visual quality.

The analysis above suggests implicit surfaces and point sets are complementary in a way that: (i) implicit surfaces can handle varying topology but do not efficiently converge to details; (ii) point sets are efficient and can represent fine details, but even the SOTA point-based scheme [39] is limited to an underlying template with fixed topology, leading to topology-related artifacts. This makes us wonder: Can we incorporate the merits of both types of representations to simultaneously capture the overall topology and final details? With this as motivation, we propose a **First-Implicit-Then-Explicit** framework, abbreviated **FITE**, where the implicit representation and the point set representation are tasked to do what they excel at. Our proposal is a two-stage pipeline: In stage one we train implicit templates that capture the coarse clothing topology for each outfit, and in stage two we predict pose-dependent offsets from the template to generate fine details and pose-dependent clothing deformations. To avoid any conceptual confusion with related work [21, 67], we define an *implicit template* as a canonically posed clothed body associated with linear blend skinning weights. Since the templates already capture the coarse topology of given outfits, the second stage can focus on pose-dependent deformations. Compared with POP [39] which directly employs a fixed body template for all outfits, our divide-and-conquer scheme leads to better topology as well as better details. Note that our templates resemble the canonical-space shapes in [11, 54], but pose-dependent deformation for the templates is not required in our setting.

Two problems naturally arise with the formulation above. First, in stage one, the training of implicit templates from posed scans requires known correspondences between the canonical space and the posed spaces. Existing approaches [11, 54] learn such correspondences by predicting 3D skinning fields. However, they are less accurate in regions far away from the skeleton. To tackle this problem, we precompute a 3D skinning field by smoothly diffusing the skinning weights of SMPL [35] into the whole space, and fix it for subsequent training.

This approach effectively reduces the number of learnable parameters and induces more stable correspondences, especially in the case of limited data. Additionally, since the skinning is diffused smoothly, it can handle loose clothing as well. Another problem lies in stage two: How do we encode pose information for learned templates, which do not come with predefined UV or mesh connectivity? We propose to render the canonically posed template to multi-view images whose pixels are the coordinates of the corresponding posed vertices (following [39], we refer to them as *position maps*), and feed them to U-Nets [51] to encode pose information. Compared with UV-space position maps [37,39], our solution introduces a more continuous feature space for the templates and exhibits less topological artifacts.

We summarize our contributions as follows.

- We propose a **First-Implicit-Then-Explicit** framework for clothed human modeling which incorporates the merits of both implicit and explicit representations, and exhibits better topology properties than current methods.
- For coarse template training, we propose **diffused skinning** which induces stable correspondences from the canonical space to posed spaces, even for limited data or loose clothing.
- For extracting pose information, we propose **projection-based pose encoding** which introduces a continuous feature space on trained templates without predefined UV map or connectivity.

2   Related Work

Modeling clothed human avatars is a task involving various techniques. An ideal approach should at least (i) adopt a suitable 3D representation; (ii) be compatible with existing animation pipelines; (iii) model fine details and pose-dependent clothing deformations. We mainly focus on these three aspects in this review.

2.1   Representations for Clothed Humans

Mesh surfaces are to-date the predominant choice for representing 3D shapes for their compactness and efficiency. For human modeling, most methods represent clothing as deformations [3,8,9,38,43,56,58,64] from minimal bodies [4,26,35,46], or as separate layers [24,25,32,45,55]. Meshes are essentially limited their fixed topology. On the other hand, neural implicit human representations are not subject to a fixed topology [11,12,16,22,40,41,44,52–54,60]. Despite the obvious advantages, the low computational efficiency often forbids high-fidelity outputs by implicit methods. Articulating implicitly represented humans is also challenging. Recent methods [11,16,41,54] learn volumetric linear blend skinning to achieve articulation. However, extending linear blend skinning to 3D can be tricky, especially with limited data or loose clothing. Point sets enjoy efficiency as well as flexibility. Nonetheless, producing points with fine details is difficult. Pioneer work [1,19,33] only generates sparse points. Later approaches [6,17,18,23,37] achieve denser generation by grouping points into patches, with notable inter-patch discontinuity as a side-effect. POP [39] conditions the generation on fine-grained UV features to produce dense structured points, but its performance it still limited by the underlying topology of SMPL/SMPL-X [35,46]. Recently, based on neural radiance fields (NeRF) [42], attempts have been made to bypass the underlying geometry and synthesize rendered images of clothed humans directly [48,49,61,66]. However, the lack of an explicit geometry limits their application in downstream tasks such as editing and animation.

2.2   Animating Humans with Linear Blend Skinning

Linear blend skinning (LBS) is a widely used technique for animating human avatars among other articulatable objects. With LBS, a surface is associated with an underlying skeleton, and when the skeleton is articulated, each point on the surface is also transformed by linearly combining the transformations of the bones in the skeleton, according to a set of predefined skinning weights.

LBS is traditionally only applied to 2D mesh surfaces [5,35,46]. Recently, motivated by the need to articulate implicit representations, LBS has also been extended to 3D (called skinning fields) [7,11,16,41,54]. However, there is no direct supervision on the skinning weights for locations far away from the skeleton. LoopReg [7] uses the nearest point on SMPL to extend skinning to 3D, leading to clearly observable spatial discontinuity. SNARF [11] trains a forward skinning field jointly with a canonical-space implicit occupancy field. SCANimate [54] predicts both forward and backward skinning fields and enforce cycle consistency. Despite these efforts, such skinning fields are still limited to tight clothing.

2.3   Modeling Pose-Dependent Clothing Deformations

Clothing deformations are in general non-rigid and pose-dependent, e.g., wrinkles, sliding motions and bulging. Generating realistic pose-dependent deformations requires effectively encoding pose information. Going beyond prior methods that apply a single global feature [16,32,38,45,63], recent work has demonstrated utilizing local information leads to better details and better generalization [37,39,54,56], e.g. UV maps [37,39,56] and attention mechanisms [54].

In our framework, we propose projection-based pose encoding to introduce a continuous pose feature space on templates without predefined UV map or mesh connectivity. Although similar ideas have also appeared elsewhere [10,50,52,53], to the best of our knowledge, we are the first to apply such architectures to encode pose information for animating clothed humans.

3   Method

3.1   Task Formulation and Notations

Our task is to learn animatable clothed human avatars with realistic pose-dependent clothing deformations from a set of posed scans, under a multi-outfit setting. Figure 1 shows our overall pipeline, where implicit templates are trained in stage one and pose-dependent offsets are predicted in stage two. For simplicity in notations let us for now assume a single outfit worn by the same person. We will introduce how the formulation can be easily extended to the multi-outfit setting at the end of Sect. 3.3.

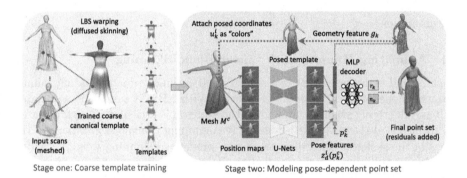

Fig. 1. Overall pipeline of our first-implicit-then-explicit framework. Left: In stage one we learn implicit templates of different outfits with diffused skinning. Right: In stage two we predict pose-dependent offset from features extracted by projection-based encoders.

We assume input scans are presented in the form of point sets with normals that cover most of the body so that watertight meshes can be extracted for obtaining ground truth occupancy labels (0 for outside and 1 for inside). We denote the point set of the i-th posed scan as $\{p_k^i\}_{k=1}^{N_i} \subset \mathbb{R}^3$, where N_i is the number of points in the i-th scan. The normal at p_k^i is denoted n_k^i. We also assume each scan has a fitted SMPL model [35]. This assumption is reasonable since there are a number of existing techniques that can tractably obtain parametric body models [28,47,57,65]. Note that SMPL is needed only for its skeletal structure and skinning weights for reposing, and that for point set generation our learned implicit templates will be used instead. Let T denote the canonical-pose SMPL body template of the subject and let $\theta^i \in \mathbb{R}^{72}$ denote the SMPL pose parameter corresponding to the i-th scan. T, together with θ^i, determines a set of rigid transformations R_j^i associated to each joint of the SMPL skeleton ($j = 1, \cdots, 24$ is the index for different joints).

Given T and θ^i, if a point $p \in \mathbb{R}^3$ in the canonical space has skinning weights $w(p) = (w_1(p), \cdots, w_{24}(p)) \in \mathbb{R}^{24}$ associated to each joint, we can warp p to its corresponding position q^i in the i-th scan via LBS. We denote this warping as $W(\,\cdot\,,\,\cdot\,;T,\theta^i) : \mathbb{R}^3 \times \mathbb{R}^{24} \to \mathbb{R}^3$. More specifically:

$$q^i = W(p, w(p), T, \theta^i) = \sum_{j=1}^{24} w_j(p)R_j^i(p). \tag{1}$$

Note that $w(p)$ is for now only defined on the SMPL surface T. We introduce how to extend w to the 3D space in Sect. 3.2.

3.2 Stage One: Coarse Template Training with Diffused Skinning

In this stage, we seek to obtain a template T^c representing the coarse clothing topology. We follow SNARF [11] to learn the template as the 1/2-level-set of a 0-1 occupancy field $F^c : \mathbb{R}^3 \to [0,1]$ in the canonical space:

$$T^c = \{p \in \mathbb{R}^3 : F^c(p) = 1/2\}. \tag{2}$$

As a quick recap, SNARF [11] jointly optimizes the pose-dependent canonical-space occupancy field $f_{\sigma_f}(\,\cdot\,, \theta^i) : \mathbb{R}^3 \to [0,1]$ and the forward skinning field $w_{\sigma_w}(\,\cdot\,) : \mathbb{R}^3 \to \mathbb{R}^{24}$, both represented by neural networks with σ_f and σ_w as the parameters, by minimizing the binary cross entropy (BCE) loss on the predicted occupancy $f_{\sigma_f}(p, \theta_i)$ and the ground truth occupancy label $o(q^i)$ at the warped location $q^i = W(p, w_{\sigma_w}(p), T, \theta^i)$, i.e.,

$$\min_{\sigma_f, \sigma_w} \mathcal{L}_{\text{BCE}}(f_{\sigma_f}(p, \theta^i), o(q^i)). \tag{3}$$

However, we empirically found that jointly optimizing σ_f and σ_w leads to local minima due to the non-uniqueness of solution of (3). More specifically, an incorrect canonical shape with an incorrect skinning field can accidentally be warped to a correct posed shape (see Fig. 2).

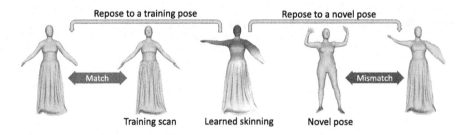

Fig. 2. Illustration of the ill-posedness of jointly optimizing the canonical shape and the skinning fields. An incorrect canonical shape with incorrect skinning can be accidentally warped to a correct pose, but generalization to new poses can be problematic.

To address this ambiguity, we propose to fix the skinning weights in (3) and let the optimization focus on the occupancy only. This effectively reduces learnable parameters and generates more stable results, which is essential for stage two. A good forward skinning weight field $w : \mathbb{R}^3 \to \mathbb{R}^{24}$ should satisfy the following constraints: (i) $w(p)$ should be identical to the SMPL skinning weights $w^s(p)$ for p lying on the SMPL body surface T; (ii) w should naturally diffuse from the SMPL surface, in the sense that its rate of change along the normal direction should be zero. These lead to the following constraints (equations below should be regarded as component-wise):

$$w(p) = w^s(p), \quad \nabla_p w(p) \cdot n^s(p) = 0, \quad \text{for } p \in T, \tag{4}$$

where $w^s(p)$ denotes the SMPL skinning weights at p, and $n^s(p)$ denotes the normal direction of T at p. We remark that the gradient of a scalar function on a curved surface is a defined concept and is in fact a tangent field of the surface. Considering each component of w^s as a scalar function on T, we compute their gradients along T as $\nabla_T w^s$. Note that Eq. (4) says $\nabla_p w$ is tangential to T, and that $w = w^s$ on T. Hence, we can equivalently rewrite Eq. (4) as

$$w(p) = w^s(p), \quad \nabla_p w(p) = \nabla_T w^s(p), \quad \text{for } p \in T, \tag{5}$$

which can be reformulated as minimizing the following energy (with smoothness regularization term $\left\| \nabla^2 w \right\|^2$):

$$\lambda_p^s \int_{p \in T} \left\| w(p) - w^s(p) \right\|^2 + \lambda_g^s \int_{p \in T} \left\| \nabla_p w(p) - \nabla_T w^s(p) \right\|^2 + \lambda_{reg}^s \int_{\mathbb{R}^3} \left\| \nabla^2 w \right\|^2, \tag{6}$$

where the λ's are weights to ensure numerical stability. We apply an off-the-shelf solver [29] to obtain w. Note that each component of w is solved separately, clamped to the range of $[0, 1]$ and finally re-normalized to sum up to 1 (Fig. 3). Please refer to the supplementary material for more details.

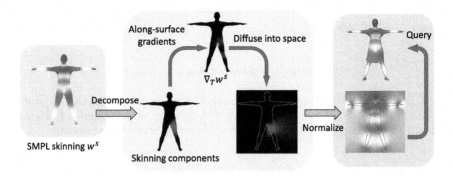

Fig. 3. Diffused skinning visualized. Each component of the skinning weights on SMPL [35] is diffused independently and re-normalized to form a skinning field.

Having solved w from Eq. (6), we fix it in SNARF [11] and train F_{σ_f} in (3). Techniques such as multiple correspondences in are still employed (see the supplementary material for details). Stage one terminates as soon as a coarse shape is available, which is much shorter than the original setup which strives for fine details. After training, we set F^c as:

$$F^c(p) = F_{\sigma_f}(p, \theta^{i_0}), \quad \text{where } \theta^{i_0} = \arg\min\{\left\|\theta^i\right\|_1 : \theta_i \text{ in the training poses}\}.$$
(7)

In other words, we pick the canonical shape closest to the zero-pose in L_1-norm out of all training poses. Note that although F^c is not pose-dependent, it is enough for our purpose. Finally, we extract the $1/2$-level-set T^c of $F^c(p)$ as our canonical template, which can be posed via LBS with skinning weights queried from w. This concludes stage one.

3.3 Stage Two: Modeling Pose-Dependent Clothing Deformations

After obtaining the canonical template T^c representing the coarse clothing topology in stage one, we further predict pose-dependent offsets from its surface. First, we uniformly sample a point set $\{p_k^c\}_{k=1}^{N_c}$ on the learned canonical template surface T^c and query their skinning weights in the diffused skinning field: $w(p_k^c)$. Moreover, we follow [39] to assign a geometric feature vector $g_k \in \mathbb{R}^{C_{\text{geom}}}$ to each p_k^c, learned in an auto-decoding fashion [44]. For a specific pose θ, the final output point set $\{q_k\}_{k=1}^{N_c}$ representing pose-dependent deformations is obtained by offsetting the canonical point set after applying LBS warping. In addition, we take into consideration the possible inaccuracy in T^c and add a template correction offset c_k, leading to the formulation

$$q_k = W(p_k^c + c_k, w(p_k^c), T, \theta) + r_k.$$
(8)

Since c_k are corrections made to the template itself, they are designed to be pose-agnostic. In the rest of this section, we introduce how to obtain c_k and r_k.

Pose-Agnostic Template Correction. Since T^c is only coarsely trained, it may have not fully converged to align with training scans. For example, T^c may lack facial details, which is generally pose-*in*dependent, but requiring only r_k in Eq. (8) to account for both pose-dependent deformation and pose-independent correction leads to sub-optimal performance. We propose a template correction offset c_k that is pose-agnostic, obtained by feeding the geometric feature g_k to a 4-layer MLP $C(\,\cdot\,)$. The offset c_k is added to p_k^c before LBS warping.

Projection-Based Pose Encoding. To generate pose-dependent offsets r_k in Eq. (8), we need to encode pose-dependent features for r_k to condition on. POP [39], which greatly inspired our work, render the coordinates of posed vertices to the UV-space, and encode them with U-Nets [51]. This scheme provides a continuous feature space over the SMPL body surface. However, the continuity of UV-space features only extends up to the boundaries of the UV islands. Moreover, in our case there is no predefined UV mapping for our templates.

To adapt such pose encoding to a more general setting where templates do not have predefined UV, and to make the feature space more continuous, we propose to directly render the posed coordinates to images instead of UV maps. First, we extract the template surface T^c as a triangle mesh M^c, with vertices $\{v_k^c\}$ and associated skinning weights $\{w(v_k^c)\}$. We then warp v_k^c to the i-th pose: $u_k^i = W(v_k^c, w(v_k^c), T, \theta_i)$. Next, we color the mesh M^c by attaching the coordinates of u_k^i to the vertex v_k^c as its "color". Finally we render the "colored" mesh M^c to images with orthographic projections. Each pixel of the rendered images contains the coordinates of the corresponding *posed* vertices. We also adopt a multi-view setup for better coverage of the surface. We choose $N_v = 4$ views, looking at the template from its left-front side, left-back side, right-front side and right-back side. Moreover, each view is slightly tilted to provide coverage for the top of the head and the bottom of the feet. Following [39], we refer to these rendered images as position maps.

Let the position maps for the i-th pose be denoted as $I_d^i \in \mathbb{R}^{H \times W \times 3}$, where $d = 1, 2, 3, 4$ is the index for 4 viewing directions. We feed them to U-Net [51] encoders U_d (one for each view, but shared across all poses) to extract pose-dependent features $z_d^i = U_d(I_d^i) \in \mathbb{R}^{H \times W \times C_{\text{pose}}}$, where C_{pose} is the number of channels of feature maps. With encoded position maps, we are able to extract pixel-aligned features for an arbitrary point p on T^c by first projecting it to each image and then querying the pixel feature via bilinear interpolation. The sampled pixel-aligned feature is denoted as $z_d^i(p) \in \mathbb{R}^{C_{\text{pose}}}$. We concatenate the sampled features from all views as the final pose feature for p, denoted as $z^i(p) = [z_1^i(p), z_2^i(p), z_3^i(p), z_4^i(p)] \in \mathbb{R}^{N_v \cdot C_{\text{pose}}}$, where $[\cdots]$ denotes concatenation.

Decoding Pose-Dependent Deformations. The final step is to generate r_k in Eq. (8) and associated normals n_k conditioned on projection-based pose features to represent fine details and pose-dependent clothing deformations. Following [39], we decode the r_k and n_k with an 8-layer MLP $D(\,\cdot\,)$:

$$[r_k^c, n_k^c] = D([z^i(p_k^c), g_k]), \quad r_k^c, n_k^c \in \mathbb{R}^3. \tag{9}$$

In addition, we also employ local transformations as in [39]. Recall that R_j^i in Eq. (1) are rigid transformations determined by θ^i. Let $\hat{R}_j^i$ be the rotation part of R_j^i. Then we apply the weighted combination of $\hat{R}_j^i$ to the output of the decoder $D(\,\cdot\,)$, i.e., $r_k = \sum_{j=1}^{24} w_j(p_k^c)\hat{R}_j^i(r_k^c)$ and $n_k = n_k' / \|n_k'\|$, where $n_k' = \sum_{j=1}^{24} w_j(p_k^c)\hat{R}_j^i(n_k^c)$. Plugging r_k into (8), together with normals n_k, gives the final point cloud (with normals) $\{(q_k, n_k)\}_{k=1}^{N_c}$ of our method.

When multiple outfits are present in the input data, the templates for different outfits are trained separately in stage one, but share the template corrector C, the pose encoders U_d, and the deformation decoder D. By sharing the neural networks in stage two for all outfits, they can learn clothing deformation patterns in common for different outfit styles.

3.4   Training Losses

For stage one, we did not modify the training loss and training procedure of SNARF [11]. Interested readers are referred to the original paper for more details. For stage two, we define the following loss terms in the spirit of [39]:

$$\mathcal{L}_{\text{total}} = \lambda_{\text{p}}\mathcal{L}_{\text{p}} + \lambda_{\text{n}}\mathcal{L}_{\text{n}} + \lambda_{\text{c,reg}}\mathcal{L}_{\text{c,reg}} + \lambda_{\text{r,reg}}\mathcal{L}_{\text{r,reg}} + \lambda_{\text{g,reg}}\mathcal{L}_{\text{g,reg}}, \qquad (10)$$

where the λ's are the weighting coefficient for different loss terms. The first two terms $\mathcal{L}_{\text{p}}$ and $\mathcal{L}_{\text{n}}$ are losses on the point cloud and the normals, respectively. More specifically, let $P^{\text{gt}} = \{(p_k^{\text{gt}}, n_k^{\text{gt}})\}_{k=1}^{N_{\text{gt}}}$ be the ground truth point cloud and let $P^{\text{pd}} = \{(q_k^{\text{pd}}, n_k^{\text{pd}})\}_{k=1}^{N_{\text{pd}}}$ be the predicted point cloud (with normals). Then

$$\mathcal{L}_{\text{p}} = \frac{1}{N_{\text{pd}}} \sum_{k=1}^{N_{\text{pd}}} \min_{k'} \left((q_k^{\text{pd}} - p_{k'}^{\text{gt}}) \cdot n_{k'}^{\text{gt}} \right)^2 + \frac{1}{N_{\text{gt}}} \sum_{k'=1}^{N_{\text{gt}}} \min_{k} \left\| p_{k'}^{\text{gt}} - q_k^{\text{pd}} \right\|_2^2, \quad (11)$$

$$\mathcal{L}_{\text{n}} = \frac{1}{N_{\text{pd}}} \sum_{k=1}^{N_{\text{pd}}} \left\| n_k^{\text{pd}} - n_{k'}^{\text{gt}} \right\|_1, \text{ where } k' = \text{argmin}_{k'} \left\| q_k^{\text{pd}} - p_{k'}^{\text{gt}} \right\|. \quad (12)$$

The other three terms are regularization terms on the template correction offsets, the pose-dependent offsets, and the per-point geometric features, respectively:

$$\mathcal{L}_{\text{c,reg}} = \frac{1}{N_{\text{pd}}} \sum_{k=1}^{N_{\text{pd}}} \|c_k\|_2^2, \ \mathcal{L}_{\text{r,reg}} = \frac{1}{N_{\text{pd}}} \sum_{k=1}^{N_{\text{pd}}} \|r_k\|_2^2, \ \mathcal{L}_{\text{g,reg}} = \frac{1}{N_{\text{pd}}} \sum_{k=1}^{N_{\text{pd}}} \|g_k\|_2^2. \quad (13)$$

Please refer to the supplementary material for details of model architectures, hyper-parameter settings and the training procedure.

4   Experiments

In this section we evaluate the representation ability of our method. Due to space limits, we report the results for interpolation, extrapolation and novel scan animation here, and provide extended evaluations, ablation studies and failure cases in the supplementary material.

4.1   Evaluation Details

Baselines. We compare our method with the SOTA clothed human modeling methods: POP [39], SNARF [11], and SCANimate [54]. POP [39] also adopts a point cloud representation which is conditioned on SMPL/SMPL-X [35,46] templates. SNARF [11] and SCANimate [54] are currently the SOTA implicit methods with learned volumetric skinning fields.

Datasets. We evaluate our method on two large-scale datasets with multiple outfits: ReSynth [39] and CAPE [38]. We follow POP [39] to use 12 outfits and 14 outfits from ReSynth and CAPE, respectively, for cross-outfit training. Note that ReSynth is much more diverse in outfit types than CAPE, and serves as a more convincible test for modeling outfits with different topologies. Moreover, since the implicit baselines do not output point clouds, and the generated point sets from FITE and POP have different densities, we use Screened Poisson Reconstruction [30] to obtain closed meshes for evaluation. Please refer to the supplementary material for more details on dataset preprocessing.

Metrics. Following the common evaluation pipeline [39], we use the Chamfer-L_2 distance $d_{\mathrm{cham.}}$ (lower is better) and cosine similarity S_{cos} [44] (higher is better) to measure the error of generated clothed humans. Due to the stochastic nature of clothing, error measurement with the ground truth scans in extrapolated poses does not faithfully reflect the modeling quality. Thus, following previous work [39,54], we conduct a large-scale user study to evaluate the visual quality of different methods for extrapolation experiments. During the user study, each viewer is given either a pair of point clouds or a pair of meshes placed side-by-side, and is asked to vote on the one with higher **overall** visual quality after considering factors such as realism, details and artifacts. The left-right order is randomly shuffled to prevent the preference for a certain side. The choice of presented outfit and pose is also random with equal probability.

4.2 Interpolation Experiments

We evaluate the representation ability of our method with interpolation experiments on the ReSynth dataset and the CAPE dataset. Considering dataset sizes, for training, we choose every 2nd frame for ReSynth and choose every 4th frame for CAPE, both from their official training splits. The rest of the training sequences are used for evaluation.

Table 1 shows the quantitative results of the interpolation evaluation. Note that the modeling difficulty, as well as the error distribution, varies drastically from outfit to outfit. We thus report the quantitative results for each outfit separately. Due to page limits, we report three outfits from CAPE and three from ReSynth and present more in the supplementary material. The results in Table 1 shows that both point-based methods, FITE and POP, outperform implicit methods by a large margin. Between FITE and POP, our method performs notably better for outfits that greatly differ from the minimal body (long dress). Note that the benefit of cross-outfit training for FITE can be more clearly observed from the long dress example. This is due to the fact that projection-based encoding is harder to train than UV encoding and can thus benefit more from the regularization effect brought by cross-outfit training. We will discuss this more closely in the supplementary material.

The improvement can be more obviously observed in Fig. 4. For a long dress, FITE generates densely distributed points for the loose part and is able to represent more details, while the output of POP becomes sparse and can only model

Table 1. Quantitative results of interpolation experiments. Since SNARF [11] and SCANimate [54] do not support cross-outfit modeling, we evaluate the outfit-specific versions of POP and FITE for fairness (denoted as POP-OS and FITE-OS). Note that d_{cham} reported below have been multiplied by 10^5.

Method	CAPE data						ReSynth data					
	00096 jerseyshort		00215 poloshort		03375 blazerlong		Carla 004 long pants		Christine 027 short dress		Felice 004 long dress	
	d_{cham}	S_{cos}	d_{cham}	S_{cos}	d_{cham}	S_{cos}	d_{cham}	S_{cos}	d_{cham}	S_{cos}	d_{cham}	S_{cos}
SCANimate [54]	0.632	0.942	0.730	0.927	0.957	0.914	0.721	0.943	1.750	0.940	17.578	0.803
SNARF [11]	0.155	0.964	0.191	0.941	0.624	0.929	0.340	0.949	0.621	0.953	2.426	0.906
POP-OS [39]	**0.036**	**0.987**	0.084	0.980	**0.249**	**0.967**	0.507	0.940	0.437	**0.964**	1.591	0.925
POP [39]	0.044	0.986	0.091	0.978	0.252	0.966	0.485	0.939	**0.421**	0.960	1.718	0.920
FITE-OS	0.041	**0.987**	**0.074**	**0.981**	0.271	0.966	0.300	**0.957**	0.462	**0.964**	1.805	0.918
FITE	0.042	**0.987**	0.076	0.980	0.274	0.964	**0.299**	0.956	0.455	0.963	**1.355**	**0.933**
	Tight clothing $\Longrightarrow$										Loose clothing	

a coarse shape. For implicit methods, the modeling of details is less faithful to the ground truth and perceptually less realistic.

4.3   Extrapolation Experiments

For extrapolation experiments, we use the official training sequences (full data, multi-outfit) and test sequences. Figure 5 shows qualitative comparisons of our method and POP, with seen outfits in unseen poses. For long dresses, POP produces overly sparse points and fail to represent the surface. For short dresses, POP must deform points from the legs of the SMPL-X template [46] to form the dresses. This incoherency leads to the discontinuity on the dresses. Even for tight clothing, the discontinuity in the UV space also leaves visible seams on the clothing. On the other hand, FITE utilizes templates that already capture the clothing topology and encode pose information in a multi-view projection scheme, producing outputs topologically coherent with given data.

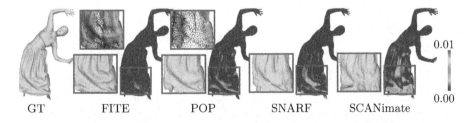

GT   FITE   POP   SNARF   SCANimate

0.01

0.00

Fig. 4. Qualitative results of the interpolation experiment. Error maps are visualized w.r.t. the largest error in this comparison.

We also conduct a large-scale user study to evaluate quantitatively the extrapolation performance (421 participants, each with 20 votes; 8420 votes in total). Among all votes we received, in terms of generated point clouds (4690 votes), 75.42% prefer FITE over POP (24.58%); in terms of reconstructed meshes

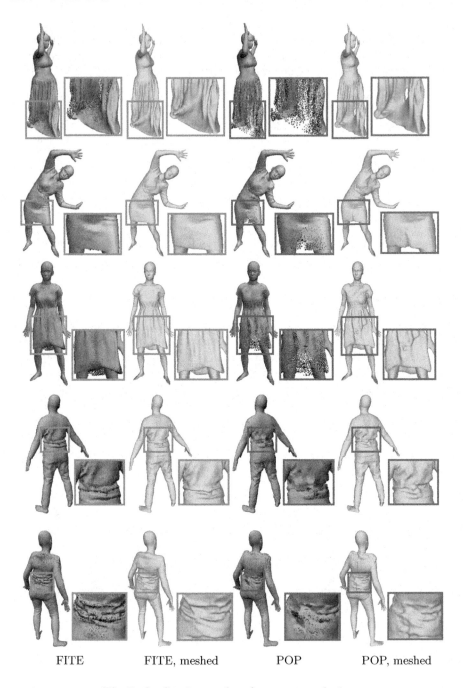

FITE   FITE, meshed   POP   POP, meshed

Fig. 5. Qualitative results of pose extrapolation.

(3730 votes), 59.37% prefer FITE over POP (40.63%). Although surface reconstruction partly compensates the drawbacks of POP, the perceptual advantage of our method is still clearly observable. As a final remark, the artifacts of POP in Fig. 5 are not clearly observable in the training set, but they appear frequently in the test set. We believe this reveals that the generalizability of POP is essentially limited by the fixed underlying body template. Please refer to the supplementary material for more details on how the user study is conducted.

4.4 Novel Scan Animation

In stage two, the networks C, U_d and D are shared across outfits and learn the common deformation pattern for different outfits. Thus, they can be used to fit novel scans by optimizing the geometric features only w.r.t. a new scan. Figure 6 shows the generalization to novel scans. Our method adds pose-dependent to LBS warped templates and produces less noise than POP [39]. Please refer to the supplementary material for more details.

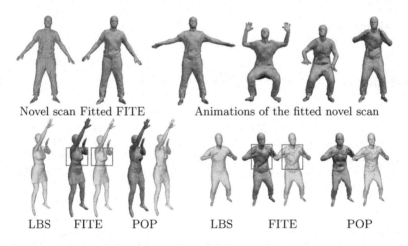

Fig. 6. Novel scan animation results (pose-dependent offsets highlighted).

5 Conclusion

We present FITE, a first-implicit-then-explicit framework for modeling clothed humans with realistic pose-dependent deformations. Evaluated on outfits with different topologies, our method is shown to outperform previous methods by incorporating the merits of both the implicit representation and the point set representation. Moreover, we believe several individual modules in this framework can also inspire related search, namely, diffused skinning as a smooth interpolation of the learned SMPL skinning weights, and projection-based pose encoding for introducing a continuous feature space on arbitrary mesh surfaces. However, as is currently formulated, several aspects still require further exploration.

Unifying Canonical Templates. In the current framework, stage one learns the coarse templates for each outfit separately. It is worthwhile to explore unifying different outfits with a single shape network, i.e., learning not only a prior for deformations, but also a prior for the outfits, which can lead to faster and more stable outfit generalization.

Driving the Underlying Templates. After obtaining coarse templates in stage one, LBS is applied for reposing. However, LBS does not always reflect true clothing motions, especially for loose clothing in extreme poses. Replacing LBS in stage one with coarse-level physics-based simulation can possibly improve the performance for certain outfits.

Disentanglement of Clothing and Pose. In the second stage of FITE, the projection-based encoders are used to extract pose information from rendered position maps. However, these position maps already contain the clothing information, and thus clothing and pose are not fully disentangled. Future work should explore a representation that further disentangles these factors.

Acknowledgements. This paper is supported by National Key R&D Program of China (2021ZD0113501) and the NSFC project No. 62125107 and No. 61827805.

References

1. Achlioptas, P., Diamanti, O., Mitliagkas, I., Guibas, L.: Learning representations and generative models for 3D point clouds. In: Proceedings of the International Conference on International Conference on Machine Learning (ICML), pp. 40–49. PMLR (2018)
2. Alldieck, T., Magnor, M., Bhatnagar, B.L., Theobalt, C., Pons-Moll, G.: Learning to reconstruct people in clothing from a single RGB camera. In: Proceedings of the IEEE Conference on Computer Vision and Pattern Recognition (CVPR), pp. 1175–1186 (2019)
3. Alldieck, T., Pons-Moll, G., Theobalt, C., Magnor, M.: Tex2shape: detailed full human body geometry from a single image. In: Proceedings of the IEEE International Conference on Computer Vision (ICCV), pp. 2293–2303 (2019)
4. Anguelov, D., Srinivasan, P., Koller, D., Thrun, S., Rodgers, J., Davis, J.: Scape: shape completion and animation of people. In: ACM Transactions on Graphics (TOG), vol. 24, pp. 408–416. ACM (2005)
5. Baran, I., Popović, J.: Automatic rigging and animation of 3D characters. ACM Trans. Graph. (TOG) **26**(3), 72–es (2007)
6. Bednařík, J., Parashar, S., Gundogdu, E., Salzmann, M., Fua, P.: Shape reconstruction by learning differentiable surface representations. In: Proceedings of the IEEE/CVF Conference on Computer Vision and Pattern Recognition (CVPR), pp. 4715–4724 (2020)
7. Bhatnagar, B.L., Sminchisescu, C., Theobalt, C., Pons-Moll, G.: LoopReg: self-supervised learning of implicit surface correspondences, pose and shape for 3D human mesh registration. In: Advances in Neural Information Processing Systems (NIPS) (2020)

8. Bhatnagar, B.L., Tiwari, G., Theobalt, C., Pons-Moll, G.: Multi-garment net: learning to dress 3D people from images. In: Proceedings of the IEEE International Conference on Computer Vision (ICCV), pp. 5420–5430 (2019)

9. Burov, A., Nießner, M., Thies, J.: Dynamic surface function networks for clothed human bodies. In: Proceedings of the IEEE International Conference on Computer Vision (ICCV), pp. 10754–10764 (2021)

10. Chan, E.R., et al.: Efficient geometry-aware 3D generative adversarial networks. In: arXiv (2021)

11. Chen, X., Zheng, Y., Black, M.J., Hilliges, O., Geiger, A.: SNARF: differentiable forward skinning for animating non-rigid neural implicit shapes. In: Proceedings of the IEEE International Conference on Computer Vision (ICCV), pp. 11594–11604 (2021)

12. Chibane, J., Mir, A., Pons-Moll, G.: Neural unsigned distance fields for implicit function learning. In: Advances in Neural Information Processing Systems (NIPS), pp. 21638–21652 (2020)

13. Corona, E., Pumarola, A., Alenya, G., Pons-Moll, G., Moreno-Noguer, F.: SMPLicit: topology-aware generative model for clothed people. In: Proceedings of the IEEE Conference on Computer Vision and Pattern Recognition (CVPR), pp. 11875–11885 (2021)

14. De Aguiar, E., Sigal, L., Treuille, A., Hodgins, J.K.: Stable spaces for real-time clothing. In: ACM Transactions on Graphics (TOG), vol. 29, pp. 106. ACM (2010)

15. Deform Dynamics. https://deformdynamics.com/

16. Deng, B., et al.: NASA neural articulated shape approximation. In: Vedaldi, A., Bischof, H., Brox, T., Frahm, J.-M. (eds.) ECCV 2020. LNCS, vol. 12352, pp. 612–628. Springer, Cham (2020). https://doi.org/10.1007/978-3-030-58571-6_36

17. Deng, Z., Bednařík, J., Salzmann, M., Fua, P.: Better patch stitching for parametric surface reconstruction. In: ThreeDV, pp. 593–602 (2020)

18. Deprelle, T., Groueix, T., Fisher, M., Kim, V., Russell, B., Aubry, M.: Learning elementary structures for 3D shape generation and matching. In: Advances in Neural Information Processing Systems (NIPS), pp. 7433–7443 (2019)

19. Fan, H., Su, H., Guibas, L.J.: A point set generation network for 3D object reconstruction from a single image. In: Proceedings of the IEEE/CVF Conference on Computer Vision and Pattern Recognition (CVPR), pp. 2463–2471 (2017)

20. Feng, A., Casas, D., Shapiro, A.: Avatar reshaping and automatic rigging using a deformable model. In: Proceedings of the ACM SIGGRAPH Conference on Motion in Games, pp. 57–64 (2015)

21. Genova, K., Cole, F., Vlasic, D., Sarna, A., Freeman, W.T., Funkhouser, T.: Learning shape templates with structured implicit functions. In: Proceedings of the IEEE/CVF International Conference on Computer Vision (ICCV) (2019)

22. Gropp, A., Yariv, L., Haim, N., Atzmon, M., Lipman, Y.: Implicit geometric regularization for learning shapes. In: Proceedings of the International Conference on International Conference on Machine Learning (ICML), pp. 3569–3579 (2020)

23. Groueix, T., Fisher, M., Kim, V.G., Russell, B., Aubry, M.: AtlasNet: a papier-Mâché approach to learning 3D surface generation. In: Proceedings IEEE Conference on Computer Vision and Pattern Recognition (CVPR) (2018)

24. Guan, P., Reiss, L., Hirshberg, D.A., Weiss, A., Black, M.J.: DRAPE: DRessing Any PErson. ACM Trans. Graph. (TOG) 31(4), 1–10 (2012)

25. Gundogdu, E., Constantin, V., Seifoddini, A., Dang, M., Salzmann, M., Fua, P.: GarNet: a two-stream network for fast and accurate 3D cloth draping. In: Proceedings of the IEEE/CVF Conference on Computer Vision and Pattern Recognition (CVPR), pp. 8739–8748 (2019)

26. Hirshberg, D.A., Loper, M., Rachlin, E., Black, M.J.: Coregistration: simultaneous alignment and modeling of articulated 3D shape. In: Fitzgibbon, A., Lazebnik, S., Perona, P., Sato, Y., Schmid, C. (eds.) ECCV 2012. LNCS, vol. 7577, pp. 242–255. Springer, Heidelberg (2012). https://doi.org/10.1007/978-3-642-33783-3_18

27. Jiang, B., Zhang, J., Hong, Y., Luo, J., Liu, L., Bao, H.: BCNet: learning body and cloth shape from a single image. In: Vedaldi, A., Bischof, H., Brox, T., Frahm, J.-M. (eds.) ECCV 2020. LNCS, vol. 12365, pp. 18–35. Springer, Cham (2020). https://doi.org/10.1007/978-3-030-58565-5_2

28. Kanazawa, A., Black, M.J., Jacobs, D.W., Malik, J.: End-to-end recovery of human shape and pose. In: Proceedings of the IEEE/CVF Conference on Computer Vision and Pattern Recognition (CVPR) (2018)

29. Kazhdan, M.: Pointinterpolant (2021). https://github.com/mkazhdan/PoissonRecon

30. Kazhdan, M., Hoppe, H.: Screened poisson surface reconstruction. ACM Trans. Graph. **32**(3), 1–13 (2013). https://doi.org/10.1145/2487228.2487237

31. Klokov, R., Boyer, E., Verbeek, J.: Discrete point flow networks for efficient point cloud generation. In: Vedaldi, A., Bischof, H., Brox, T., Frahm, J.-M. (eds.) ECCV 2020. LNCS, vol. 12368, pp. 694–710. Springer, Cham (2020). https://doi.org/10.1007/978-3-030-58592-1_41

32. Lähner, Z., Cremers, D., Tung, T.: DeepWrinkles: accurate and realistic clothing modeling. In: Ferrari, V., Hebert, M., Sminchisescu, C., Weiss, Y. (eds.) ECCV 2018. LNCS, vol. 11208, pp. 698–715. Springer, Cham (2018). https://doi.org/10.1007/978-3-030-01225-0_41

33. Lin, C.H., Kong, C., Lucey, S.: Learning efficient point cloud generation for dense 3D object reconstruction. In: Proceedings of the AAAI Conference on Artificial Intelligence, pp. 7114–7121 (2018)

34. Liu, L., Zheng, Y., Tang, D., Yuan, Y., Fan, C., Zhou, K.: NeuroSkinning: automatic skin binding for production characters with deep graph networks. ACM Trans. Graph. (TOG) **38**(4), 1–12 (2019)

35. Loper, M., Mahmood, N., Romero, J., Pons-Moll, G., Black, M.J.: SMPL: a skinned multi-person linear model. ACM Trans. Graph. (TOG) **34**(6), 248 (2015)

36. Luo, S., Hu, W.: Diffusion probabilistic models for 3D point cloud generation. In: Proceedings of the IEEE/CVF Conference on Computer Vision and Pattern Recognition (CVPR) (2021)

37. Ma, Q., Saito, S., Yang, J., Tang, S., Black, M.J.: Scale: modeling clothed humans with a surface codec of articulated local elements. In: Proceedings of the IEEE Conference on Computer Vision and Pattern Recognition (CVPR), pp. 16082–16093 (2021)

38. Ma, Q., et al.: Learning to dress 3D people in generative clothing. In: Proceedings of the IEEE Conference on Computer Vision and Pattern Recognition (CVPR), pp. 6469–6478 (2020)

39. Ma, Q., Yang, J., Tang, S., Black, M.J.: The power of points for modeling humans in clothing. In: Proceedings of the IEEE/CVF International Conference on Computer Vision (ICCV) (2021)

40. Mescheder, L., Oechsle, M., Niemeyer, M., Nowozin, S., Geiger, A.: Occupancy networks: learning 3D reconstruction in function space. In: Proceedings of the IEEE/CVF Conference on Computer Vision and Pattern Recognition (CVPR), pp. 4460–4470 (2019)

41. Mihajlovic, M., Zhang, Y., Black, M.J., Tang, S.: LEAP: learning articulated occupancy of people. In: Proceedings of the IEEE Conference on Computer Vision and Pattern Recognition (CVPR), pp. 10461–10471 (2021)

42. Mildenhall, B., Srinivasan, P.P., Tancik, M., Barron, J.T., Ramamoorthi, R., Ng, R.: NeRF: representing scenes as neural radiance fields for view synthesis. Commun. ACM **65**(1), 99–106 (2021). https://doi.org/10.1145/3503250
43. Neophytou, A., Hilton, A.: A layered model of human body and garment deformation. In: ThreeDV, pp. 171–178 (2014)
44. Park, J.J., Florence, P., Straub, J., Newcombe, R., Lovegrove, S.: DeepSDF: learning continuous signed distance functions for shape representation. In: Proceedings of the IEEE/CVF Conference on Computer Vision and Pattern Recognition (CVPR), pp. 165–174 (2019)
45. Patel, C., Liao, Z., Pons-Moll, G.: TailorNet: predicting clothing in 3D as a function of human pose, shape and garment style. In: Proceedings of the IEEE/CVF Conference on Computer Vision and Pattern Recognition (CVPR), pp. 7363–7373 (2020)
46. Pavlakos, G., et al.: Expressive body capture: 3D hands, face, and body from a single image. In: Proceedings of the IEEE Conference on Computer Vision and Pattern Recognition (CVPR), pp. 10975–10985 (2019)
47. Pavlakos, G., Malik, J., Kanazawa, A.: Human mesh recovery from multiple shots. In: Proceedings of the IEEE/CVF Conference on Computer Vision and Pattern Recognition (CVPR) (2022)
48. Peng, S., et al.: Animatable neural radiance fields for modeling dynamic human bodies. In: Proceedings of the IEEE International Conference on Computer Vision (ICCV) (2021)
49. Peng, S., et al.: Neural body: implicit neural representations with structured latent codes for novel view synthesis of dynamic humans. In: Proceedings of the IEEE/CVF Conference on Computer Vision and Pattern Recognition (CVPR) (2021)
50. Peng, S., Niemeyer, M., Mescheder, L., Pollefeys, M., Geiger, A.: Convolutional occupancy networks. In: Vedaldi, A., Bischof, H., Brox, T., Frahm, J.-M. (eds.) ECCV 2020. LNCS, vol. 12348, pp. 523–540. Springer, Cham (2020). https://doi.org/10.1007/978-3-030-58580-8_31
51. Ronneberger, O., Fischer, P., Brox, T.: U-Net: convolutional networks for biomedical image segmentation. In: Navab, N., Hornegger, J., Wells, W.M., Frangi, A.F. (eds.) MICCAI 2015. LNCS, vol. 9351, pp. 234–241. Springer, Cham (2015). https://doi.org/10.1007/978-3-319-24574-4_28
52. Saito, S., Huang, Z., Natsume, R., Morishima, S., Kanazawa, A., Li, H.: PIFu: pixel-aligned implicit function for high-resolution clothed human digitization. In: Proceedings of the IEEE International Conference on Computer Vision (ICCV), pp. 2304–2314 (2019)
53. Saito, S., Simon, T., Saragih, J., Joo, H.: PIFuHD: multi-level pixel-aligned implicit function for high-resolution 3D human digitization. In: Proceedings of the IEEE/CVF Conference on Computer Vision and Pattern Recognition (CVPR), pp. 84–93 (2020)
54. Saito, S., Yang, J., Ma, Q., Black, M.J.: SCANimate: weakly supervised learning of skinned clothed avatar networks. In: Proceedings of the IEEE Conference on Computer Vision and Pattern Recognition (CVPR), pp. 2886–2897 (2021)
55. Santesteban, I., Otaduy, M.A., Casas, D.: Learning-based animation of clothing for virtual try-on. Comput. Graph. Forum **38**(2), 355–366 (2019)
56. Su, Z., Yu, T., Wang, Y., Liu, Y.: DeepCloth: neural garment representation for shape and style editing. IEEE Trans. Pattern Anal. Mach. Intell. (2022). https://doi.org/10.1109/TPAMI.2022.3168569

57. Tian, Y., Zhang, H., Liu, Y., Wang, L.: Recovering 3D human mesh from monocular images: a survey. arXiv preprint arXiv:2203.01923 (2022)

58. Tiwari, G., Bhatnagar, B.L., Tung, T., Pons-Moll, G.: SIZER: a dataset and model for parsing 3D clothing and learning size sensitive 3D clothing. In: Vedaldi, A., Bischof, H., Brox, T., Frahm, J.-M. (eds.) ECCV 2020. LNCS, vol. 12348, pp. 1–18. Springer, Cham (2020). https://doi.org/10.1007/978-3-030-58580-8_1

59. Vidaurre, R., Santesteban, I., Garces, E., Casas, D.: Fully convolutional graph neural networks for parametric virtual try-on. In: Computer Graphics Forum, vol. 39, pp. 145–156. Wiley Online Library (2020)

60. Wang, S., Mihajlovic, M., Ma, Q., Geiger, A., Tang, S.: MetaAvatar: learning animatable clothed human models from few depth images. In: Advances in Neural Information Processing Systems (NIPS) (2021)

61. Weng, C.Y., Curless, B., Srinivasan, P.P., Barron, J.T., Kemelmacher-Shlizerman, I.: HumanNeRF: free-viewpoint rendering of moving people from monocular video. In: Proceedings of the IEEE/CVF Conference on Computer Vision and Pattern Recognition (CVPR) (2022)

62. Yang, G., Huang, X., Hao, Z., Liu, M.Y., Belongie, S., Hariharan, B.: PointFlow: 3D point cloud generation with continuous normalizing flows. In: Proceedings of the IEEE International Conference on Computer Vision (ICCV) (2019)

63. Yang, J., Franco, J.-S., Hétroy-Wheeler, F., Wuhrer, S.: Analyzing clothing layer deformation statistics of 3D human motions. In: Ferrari, V., Hebert, M., Sminchisescu, C., Weiss, Y. (eds.) ECCV 2018. LNCS, vol. 11211, pp. 245–261. Springer, Cham (2018). https://doi.org/10.1007/978-3-030-01234-2_15

64. Yang, S., et al.: Physics-inspired garment recovery from a single-view image. ACM Trans. Graph. (TOG) **37**(5), 1–14 (2018)

65. Zhang, Y., Li, Z., An, L., Li, M., Yu, T., Liu, Y.: Lightweight multi-person total motion capture using sparse multi-view cameras. In: Proceedings of the IEEE/CVF International Conference on Computer Vision (ICCV), pp. 5560–5569 (2021)

66. Zheng, Z., Huang, H., Yu, T., Zhang, H., Guo, Y., Liu, Y.: Structured local radiance fields for human avatar modeling. In: Proceedings of the IEEE/CVF Conference on Computer Vision and Pattern Recognition (CVPR) (2022)

67. Zheng, Z., Yu, T., Dai, Q., Liu, Y.: Deep implicit templates for 3D shape representation. In: Proceedings of the IEEE/CVF Conference on Computer Vision and Pattern Recognition (CVPR), pp. 1429–1439 (2021)

Exploring the Devil in Graph Spectral Domain for 3D Point Cloud Attacks

Qianjiang Hu, Daizong Liu, and Wei Hu[(✉)]

Wangxuan Institute of Computer Technology, Peking University, No. 128,
Zhongguancun North Street, Beijing, China
{hqjpku,forhuwei}@pku.edu.cn, dzliu@stu.pku.edu.cn

Abstract. With the maturity of depth sensors, point clouds have received increasing attention in various applications such as autonomous driving, robotics, surveillance, *etc.*, while deep point cloud learning models have shown to be vulnerable to adversarial attacks. Existing attack methods generally add/delete points or perform point-wise perturbation over point clouds to generate adversarial examples in the data space, which may neglect the geometric characteristics of point clouds. Instead, we propose point cloud attacks from a new perspective—Graph Spectral Domain Attack (GSDA), aiming to perturb transform coefficients in the graph spectral domain that corresponds to varying certain geometric structure. In particular, we naturally represent a point cloud over a graph, and adaptively transform the coordinates of points into the graph spectral domain via graph Fourier transform (GFT) for compact representation. We then analyze the influence of different spectral bands on the geometric structure of the point cloud, based on which we propose to perturb the GFT coefficients in a learnable manner guided by an energy constraint loss function. Finally, the adversarial point cloud is generated by transforming the perturbed spectral representation back to the data domain via the inverse GFT (IGFT). Experimental results demonstrate the effectiveness of the proposed GSDA in terms of both imperceptibility and attack success rates under a variety of defense strategies. The code is available at https://github.com/WoodwindHu/GSDA.

Keywords: Point cloud · Adversarial attack · Graph spectral domain

1 Introduction

Deep Neural Networks (DNNs) are known to be vulnerable to adversarial examples [12,43], which are indistinguishable from legitimate ones by adding trivial perturbations, but lead to incorrect model prediction. Many efforts have been made into the attacks on the 2D image field [8,22,30,46], which often add

---

Q. Hu and D. Liu—Contributed equally to this work.
This work was supported by National Natural Science Foundation of China under Contract No. 61972009.

S. Avidan et al. (Eds.): ECCV 2022, LNCS 13663, pp. 229–248, 2022.
https://doi.org/10.1007/978-3-031-20062-5_14

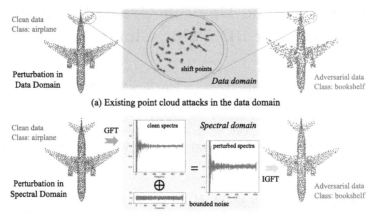

(a) Existing point cloud attacks in the data domain

(b) The proposed Graph Spectral Domain Attack

Fig. 1. (a) Existing point cloud attacks generally perturb point coordinates by shifting points in the data domain. (b) We explore perturbation in the graph spectral domain, leading to more imperceptible and effective adversarial examples. This is enlightened by spectral characteristics: most energies are concentrated in low-frequency components that represent the rough shape of point clouds while high-frequency components encode fine-grained details. When attacked with bounded spectral noise, spectra of the point cloud keeps similar patterns with the clean one, thus preserving geometric structures.

imperceptible pixel-wise noise onto images to deceive the DNNs. Nevertheless, adversarial attacks on 3D point clouds—discrete representations of 3D scenes or objects that consist of a set of points residing on irregular domains—are still relatively under-explored, which are however crucial in various safety-critical applications such as autonomous driving [4] and medical data analysis [41].

Existing 3D point cloud attacks [14,45,50,53,61,64–66] are all developed in the *data space*. Some of them [50,53,61,65] employ the gradient search method to identify critical points from point clouds and modify (add or delete) them to distort the most representative features for misclassification. Recently, more works [2,14,26,29,45,49,63] follow the C&W framework [12] to learn to perturb xyz coordinates of each point by gradient optimization in an end-to-end manner. Although the above two types of works achieve high attack success rates, the perturbed point clouds are often easily perceivable to humans, such as outliers and uneven distribution. This is because preserving geometric characteristics of point clouds is generally not considered yet in these methods.

To this end, we propose point cloud attacks from a new perspective—Graph Spectral Domain Attack (GSDA), aiming to exploit the elegant characterization of geometric structures in the graph spectral domain and thereby perturb graph transform coefficients that explicitly varies certain geometric structure. On the one hand, we provide graph spectral analysis of point clouds, which shows that the rough shape of point clouds is represented by low-frequency components while the fine details of objects are encoded in high-frequency components in general. With trivial perturbation in the spectral domain, the point cloud could retain the original rough shape with similar local details, as shown in Fig. 1.

On the other hand, the spectral characteristics of point clouds represent higher-level and global information than point-to-point relations leveraged in previous works. That is, the spectral representation encodes more abstract and essential contexts for recognizing the point cloud.

Based on the above analysis, we develop a novel paradigm of Graph Spectral Domain Attack (GSDA) for point cloud attacks. In particular, different from images that are sampled on regular grids and typically transformed in the Discrete Cosine Transform (DCT) domain, point clouds reside on irregular domains with no ordering of points. Hence, we represent a point cloud over a graph naturally and adaptively, where each point is treated as a vertex and connected to its K nearest neighbors, and the coordinates of each point serve as the graph signal. Then, we compute the graph Laplacian matrix [39] that encodes the edge connectivity and vertex degree of the graph, whose eigenvectors form the basis of the Graph Fourier Transform (GFT) [15]. Because of the compact representation of point clouds in the GFT domain [19], we transform the coordinate signal of point clouds onto the spectral domain via the GFT, leading to transform coefficients corresponding to each spectral component. Next, we develop a learnable spectrum-aware perturbation approach to perturb the spectral domain with adversarial noise. In order to keep the energy balance among the whole frequency bands, we design an energy constraint function to restrict the perturbation size. Finally, we transform the perturbed GFT coefficients back to the data domain via the inverse GFT (IGFT) to produce the crafted point cloud. We iteratively optimize the adversarial loss function, and perform back-propagation to retrieve the gradient in the spectral domain for generating and updating the desired spectrum-aware perturbations. The point clouds reconstructed by the IGFT are taken as the adversarial examples.

Our main contributions are summarized as follows:

- We propose a novel paradigm of point cloud attacks—Graph Spectral Domain Attack (GSDA), which perturbs point clouds in the graph spectral domain to exploit the high-level spectral characterization of geometric structures. Such spectral approach marks the first significant departure from the current practice of point cloud attacks.
- We provide in-depth graph spectral analysis of point clouds, which enlightens our formulation of exploring destructive perturbation on appropriate frequency components. Based on this, we develop a learnable spectrum-aware perturbation approach to attack 3D models in an end-to-end manner.
- Extensive experiments show that the proposed GSDA achieves 100% of attack success rates in both targeted and untargeted settings with the least required perturbation size. We also demonstrate the imperceptibility of the GSDA compared to state-of-the-arts, as well as the robustness of the GSDA by attacking existing defense methods and implementing transfer-based attacks.

2   Related Works

3D Point Cloud Classification. Deep 3D point cloud learning has emerged in recent years, which has diverse applications in many fields, such as 3D object classification [42,58], 3D scene segmentation [13,47,54], and 3D object detection in autonomous driving [4,56]. Among them, 3D object classification is the most fundamental yet important task, which learns representative information including both local details and global context of point clouds. Early works attempt to classify point clouds by adapting deep learning models in the 2D space [42,58]. In order to directly learn the 3D structure and address the unorderness problem of point clouds, pioneering methods DeepSets [59] and PointNet [33] propose to achieve end-to-end learning on point cloud classification by formulating a general specification. PointNet++ [34] and other extensive works [9,27,57] are built upon PointNet to further capture the fine local structural information from the neighborhood of each point. Recently, some works focus on either designing special convolutions on the 3D domain [1,24,28,44] or developing graph neural networks [11,38,40,48,54] to improve point cloud learning. In this paper, we focus on PointNet [33], PointNet++ [34] and DGCNN [48] since these 3D models are extensively involved with practical 3D applications.

Adversarial Attack on 3D Point Clouds. Deep neural networks are vulnerable to adversarial examples, which has been extensively explored in the 2D image domain [31,32]. Recently, many works [14,25,45,50,53,61,64–66] adapt adversarial attacks into the 3D vision community, which can be divided into two categories: 1) point adding/dropping attack: Xiang *et al.* [53] proposed point generation attacks by adding a limited number of synthesized points/clusters/objects to a point cloud. Recently, more works [50,61,65] utilize gradient-guided attack methods to identify critical points from point clouds for deletion. 2) point perturbation attack: Previous point-wise perturbation attacks [45,49] learn to perturb xyz coordinates of each point by adopting the C&W framework [2] based on the Chamfer and Hausdorff distance with additional consideration of the benign distribution of points. Later works [14,26,29,63] further apply the iterative gradient method to achieve more fine-grained adversarial perturbation.

Spectral Methods for Point Clouds. In the graph spectral domain, the rough shape of a point cloud will be encoded into low-frequency components, which is suitable for denoising point clouds. Rosman *et al.* proposed spectral point cloud denoising based on the non-local framework [36]. They group similar surface patches into a collaborative patch and perform shrinkage in the GFT domain by a low-pass filter, which leads to denoising of the 3D shape. Zhang *et al* proposed a tensor-based method to estimate hypergraph spectral components and frequency coefficients of point clouds, which can be used to denoise 3D shapes [62]. On the contrary, high-frequency components often represent fine details of point clouds, which can be used to detect contours or process redundant information. Chen *et al.* proposed a high-pass filtering-based resampling method to highlight contours for large-scale point cloud visualization and extract key points for accurate 3D registration [3]. Sameera *et al.* proposed Spectral-GANs to generate high-resolution 3D point clouds, which takes the advantage of spectral representations for compact representation [35].

3   Graph Spectral Analysis for Point Clouds

In this section, we provide graph spectral analysis for point clouds, which lays the foundation for the proposed graph spectral domain attack in Sect. 4. We first discuss the benefit of graph spectral representations of point clouds and introduce how to transform point clouds onto the spectral domain in Sect. 3.1. Then, we analyze the roles of different spectral components with respect to geometric structures in Sect. 3.2.

3.1   Spectral Representations of Point Clouds

Signals can be compactly represented in the spectral domain, provided that the transformation basis characterizes principle components of the signals. For instance, images are often transformed onto the Discrete Cosine Transform (DCT) domain for compression and processing [5, 23]. Different from images supported on regular grids, point clouds reside on irregular domains with no ordering of points, which hinders the deployment of traditional transformations such as the DCT. Though we may quantize point clouds onto regular voxel grids or project onto a set of depth images from multiple viewpoints, this would inevitably introduce quantization loss. Instead, graphs serve as a natural representation for irregular point clouds, which is accurate and structure-adaptive [19]. With an appropriately constructed graph that well captures the underlying structure, the Graph Fourier Transform (GFT) will lead to a compact representation of geometric data including point clouds in the spectral domain [16–18,37,55,60], which inspires new insights and understanding of point cloud attacks.

Formally, we represent a point cloud $\boldsymbol{P} = \{\boldsymbol{p}_i\}_{i=1}^n \in \mathbb{R}^{n \times 3}$ consisting of n points over a graph $\mathcal{G} = \{\mathcal{V}, \mathcal{E}, \boldsymbol{A}\}$, which is composed of a vertex set $\mathcal{V}$ of cardinality $|\mathcal{V}| = n$ representing points, an edge set $\mathcal{E}$ connecting vertices, and an adjacency matrix $\boldsymbol{A}$. Each entry $a_{i,j}$ in $\boldsymbol{A}$ represents the weight of the edge between vertices i and j, which often captures the similarity between adjacent vertices. Here, we construct an unweighted K-nearest-neighbor graph (K-NN graph), where each vertex is connected to its K nearest neighbors in terms of the Euclidean distance with weight 1. The coordinates of points in $\boldsymbol{P}$ are treated as graph signals.

Prior to the introduction of the GFT, we first define the combinatorial graph Laplacian matrix [39] as $\boldsymbol{L} := \boldsymbol{D} - \boldsymbol{A}$, where $\boldsymbol{D}$ is the *degree matrix*—a diagonal matrix where $d_{i,i} = \sum_{j=1}^n a_{i,j}$. Given real and non-negative edge weights in an undirected graph, $\boldsymbol{L}$ is real, symmetric, and positive semi-definite [6]. Hence, it admits an eigen-decomposition $\boldsymbol{L} = \boldsymbol{U} \boldsymbol{\Lambda} \boldsymbol{U}^\top$, where $\boldsymbol{U} = [\boldsymbol{u}_1, ..., \boldsymbol{u}_n]$ is an orthonormal matrix containing the eigenvectors $\boldsymbol{u}_i$, and $\boldsymbol{\Lambda} = \mathrm{diag}(\lambda_1, ..., \lambda_n)$ consists of eigenvalues $\{\lambda_1 = 0 \leq \lambda_2 \leq ... \leq \lambda_n\}$. We refer to the eigenvalues as the *graph frequency/spectrum*, with a smaller eigenvalue corresponding to a lower graph frequency.

For any graph signal $\boldsymbol{x} \in \mathbb{R}^n$ residing on the vertices of $\mathcal{G}$, its GFT coefficient vector $\hat{\boldsymbol{x}} \in \mathbb{R}^n$ is defined as [15]:

$$\hat{\boldsymbol{x}} = \phi_{\mathrm{GFT}}(\boldsymbol{x}) = \boldsymbol{U}^\top \boldsymbol{x}. \tag{1}$$

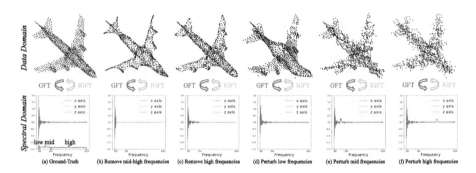

Fig. 2. Graph spectral analysis for 3D point clouds. We take an example from the *airplane* object to investigate the roles of difference frequency bands in the graph spectral domain. (a) Ground-Truth; (b) Remove mid-high frequencies; (c) Remove high frequencies; (d) Perturb low frequencies; (e) Perturb mid frequencies; (f) Perturb high frequencies.

The inverse GFT (IGFT) follows as:

$$x = \phi_{\text{IGFT}}(\hat{x}) = U\hat{x}. \tag{2}$$

Since U is an orthonormal matrix, both GFT and IGFT operations are lossless.

3.2   Analysis in Graph Spectral Domain

When an appropriate graph is constructed that captures the geometric structure of point clouds well, the low-frequency components of the corresponding GFT characterize the *rough shape* of point clouds, while the high-frequency components represent *fine details or noise* (*i.e.*, large variations such as geometric contours) in general.

To analyze such characteristics, we provide a toy experiment to investigate the roles of difference frequency bands in the graph spectral domain. We randomly take a clean point cloud *airplane* from the ModelNet40 dataset [51], and sample it into 1024 points as an example point cloud P. We construct a K-NN graph with $K = 10$ over the point cloud, and perform the GFT on the three coordinate signals of each point in P. The resulting transform coefficient vectors $\phi_{\text{GFT}}(P)$ are presented in Fig. 2(a). We see that, $\phi_{\text{GFT}}(P)$ has larger amplitudes at lower-frequency components and much smaller amplitudes at higher-frequency components, demonstrating that most information is concentrated in low-frequency components.

To further investigate how each frequency band contributes to the geometric structure of the point cloud in the data domain, we first divide the whole spectral domain into three bands: low-frequency band $B_l \in [0, \lambda_l)$, mid-frequency band $B_m \in [\lambda_l, \lambda_h)$, and high-frequency band $B_h \in [\lambda_h, \lambda_{\text{max}}]$, where $\lambda_l, \lambda_h, \lambda_{\text{max}}$ bound the three bands. While the division of frequency bands is not established, we propose an appropriate division by the distribution of energy—squared sum of transform coefficients. In this example, we compute that the lowest 32 frequencies account for almost 90% of energy, while the lowest 256 frequencies account for almost 97% of energy. Based on this observation, we set $\lambda_l = \lambda_{32} = 1.19$ and $\lambda_h = \lambda_{256} = 13.93$ in this instance.

Next, we study the influence of each frequency band on the geometric structure by removing different bands. As shown in Fig. 2(b), when GFT coefficients in both mid- and high-frequency bands are assigned 0, the point cloud reconstructed with only low-frequency components exhibits the rough shape of the original object. By adding more information from the mid-frequency band, the reconstructed point cloud has richer local contexts in Fig. 2(c), but still lacks fine-grained details such as the engines of the airplane. To summarize, each frequency band is crucial to represent different aspects of the geometric structure of a point cloud.

Then here is a key question: what are the results of attacking different frequency bands? We investigate into this by separately perturbing each frequency band with a large perturbation size, $i.e.$, we perturb consecutive 32 frequencies in each frequency band by adding noise of 0.2 on each frequency. As shown in Fig. 2(d–f), attacking low-frequency components introduces deformation in the coarse shape but remains smoothness of the surface. When attacking mid-frequency components, the shape of the object becomes much rougher. In comparison, perturbing high-frequency components loses local details and induces noise and outliers, though the silhouette of the shape is preserved to some degree thanks to the clean lower-frequency components.

Inspired by the above properties of point clouds in the graph spectral domain, we summarize several insights for developing effective spectral domain attacks:

- Each frequency band represents the geometric structure of the point cloud from different perspectives ($e.g.$, low-frequency components represent the basic shape while high-frequency components encode find-grained details). Perturbing only one frequency band may result in the corresponding distortion in the data domain.
- Although a large perturbation size can ensure a high success attack rate, it may severely change the spectral characteristics, thus leading to perceptible deformations in the data domain.

Based on the above insights, a desirable spectral domain attack for point clouds need to not only perform the perturbation among appropriate frequencies for striking a balance, but also restrict the perturbation size for preserving the original spectral characteristics.

4   Graph Spectral Domain Attack

4.1   The Formulation

Given a clean point cloud $\boldsymbol{P} = \{\boldsymbol{p}_i\}_{i=1}^{n} \in \mathbb{R}^{n \times 3}$ where each point $\boldsymbol{p}_i \in \mathbb{R}^3$ is a vector that contains the (x, y, z) coordinates, a well-trained classifier $f(\cdot)$ can

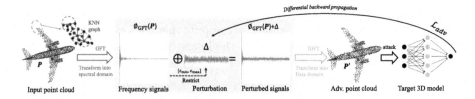

Fig. 3. The overall pipeline of the proposed GSDA. Given a clean point cloud, we first construct a K-NN graph and transform the point cloud into the spectral domain via the GFT. Then, we perturb the GFT coefficients in a learnable manner with a specifically designed restrictive function over the spectral energy. Subsequently, we transform the perturbed spectral signals back to the data domain via the IGFT. Finally, we take the reconstructed point cloud as the adversarial example and feed it into the target 3D model for attack.

predict its accurate label $y = f(\boldsymbol{P}) \in \mathbb{Y}, \mathbb{Y} = \{1, 2, 3, ..., c\}$ that represents its object class best, where c is the number of classes. The goal of point cloud attacks on classification is to perturb point cloud $\boldsymbol{P}$ into an adversarial one $\boldsymbol{P}'$, so that $f(\boldsymbol{P}') = y'$ (targeted attack) or $f(\boldsymbol{P}') \neq y$ (untargeted attack), where $y' \in \mathbb{Y}$ but $y' \neq y$.

We propose a novel GSDA attack that aims to learn destructive yet imperceptible perturbations in the spectral domain for generating adversarial point clouds. Formally, we formulate the proposed GSDA as the following optimization problem:

$$\min_{\boldsymbol{\Delta}} \mathcal{L}_{adv}(\boldsymbol{P}', \boldsymbol{P}, y), \text{s.t.} ||\phi_{\mathrm{GFT}}(\boldsymbol{P}') - \phi_{\mathrm{GFT}}(\boldsymbol{P})||_p < \epsilon,$$
$$\text{where } \boldsymbol{P}' = \phi_{\mathrm{IGFT}}(\phi_{\mathrm{GFT}}(\boldsymbol{P}) + \boldsymbol{\Delta}),$$
(3)

where $\mathcal{L}_{adv}(\boldsymbol{P}', \boldsymbol{P}, y)$ is the adversarial loss and $\boldsymbol{\Delta}$ is the perturbation. In the imposed constraint, ϵ aims to restrict the perturbation size in the spectral domain, which preserves the original spectral characteristics so that the resultant adversarial point cloud $\boldsymbol{P}'$ is visually indistinguishable from its clean version $\boldsymbol{P}$. We adopt the l_2-norm in this equation.

To back-propagate the gradient in a desired direction for optimizing the perturbation learning, we define our adversarial loss $\mathcal{L}_{adv}(\boldsymbol{P}', \boldsymbol{P}, y)$ as follows:

$$\mathcal{L}_{adv}(\boldsymbol{P}', \boldsymbol{P}, y) = \mathcal{L}_{class}(\boldsymbol{P}', y) + \beta \cdot \mathcal{L}_{reg}(\boldsymbol{P}', \boldsymbol{P}),$$
(4)

where $\mathcal{L}_{class}(\boldsymbol{P}', y)$ is to promote the misclassification of point cloud $\boldsymbol{P}'$. $\mathcal{L}_{reg}(\boldsymbol{P}', \boldsymbol{P})$ is a regularization term that minimizes the distance between $\boldsymbol{P}'$ and $\boldsymbol{P}$ to guide perturbation in appropriate frequencies. β is a penalty parameter controlling the regularization term.

Specifically, $\mathcal{L}_{class}(\boldsymbol{P}', y)$ is formulated as a cross-entropy loss as follows:

$$\mathcal{L}_{class}(\boldsymbol{P}', y) = \begin{cases} -\log(p_{y'}(\boldsymbol{P}')), & \text{for targeted attack,} \\ \log(p_y(\boldsymbol{P}')), & \text{for untargeted attack,} \end{cases}$$
(5)

where $p(\cdot)$ is the softmax functioned on the output of the target model, *i.e.*, the probability with respect to adversarial class y' or clean class y. By minimizing this loss function, our GSDA optimizes the spectral perturbation $\boldsymbol{\Delta}$ to mislead the target model $f(\cdot)$.

Besides, to strike a balance of perturbing different frequency bands, we utilize both Chamfer distance loss [10] and Hausdorff distance loss [20] as the $\mathcal{L}_{reg}(\boldsymbol{P'}, \boldsymbol{P})$ function. This reflects the imperceptibility in the data domain for updating the frequency perturbation $\boldsymbol{\Delta}$.

4.2 The Algorithm

Based on the problem formulation, we develop an efficient and effective algorithm for the GSDA model. As shown in Fig. 3, the proposed GSDA attack is composed of four steps: Firstly, the GSDA transforms the clean point cloud $\boldsymbol{P}$ from the data domain to the graph spectral domain via the GFT operation ϕ_{GFT}. Then, the GSDA perturbs the GFT coefficients through our designed perturbation strategy imposed with an energy constraint function as in Eq. (3). Next, we convert the perturbed spectral signals back to the data domain via the IGFT operation ϕ_{IGFT} for constructing the adversarial point cloud $\boldsymbol{P'}$. Finally, we optimize the adversarial loss function to iteratively update the desired perturbations added in the spectral domain. In the following, we elaborate on each module in order.

Transform onto Spectral Domain. Given a clean point cloud $\boldsymbol{P}$, we employ the GFT to transform $\boldsymbol{P}$ onto the graph spectral domain. Specifically, we first construct a K-NN graph on the whole point cloud, and then compute the graph Laplacian matrix $\mathbf{L}$. Next, we perform eigen-decomposition to acquire the orthonormal eigenvector matrix $\boldsymbol{U}$, which serves as the GFT basis. The GFT coefficients $\phi_{\mathrm{GFT}}(\boldsymbol{P})$ is then obtained by:

$$\phi_{\mathrm{GFT}}(\boldsymbol{P}) = \boldsymbol{U}^{\top}\boldsymbol{P}, \tag{6}$$

where $\phi_{\mathrm{GFT}}(\boldsymbol{P}) \in \mathbb{R}^{n \times 3}$ corresponds to the transform coefficients of the x-, y-, z-coordinate signals.

Perturbation in the Graph Spectral Domain. We deploy a trainable perturbation $\boldsymbol{\Delta}$ to perturb the spectral representation of $\boldsymbol{P}$: $\phi_{\mathrm{GFT}}(\boldsymbol{P}) + \boldsymbol{\Delta}$. Further, to restrict the perturbation size among appropriate frequencies for enhancing the imperceptibility, instead of the constraint of the entire energy in Eq. (3), we constrain the perturbation $\boldsymbol{\Delta}$ on each frequency in a valid range $[\epsilon_{min}, \epsilon_{max}]$ in order to keep the trend of spectral characteristics, *i.e.*, low-frequency components with large magnitudes and high-frequency components with small magnitudes. In particular, we define the perturbation size of each frequency as:

$$\boldsymbol{\Delta}/\phi_{\mathrm{GFT}}(\boldsymbol{P}) \in [\epsilon_{min}, \epsilon_{max}], \tag{7}$$

which maintains a certain ratio to each frequency with $\epsilon_{max} = -\epsilon_{min}$. In order to adjust the perturbation $\boldsymbol{\Delta}$ adaptively and further improve the success rate of the proposed spectral attack, we formulate the attack process as an optimization problem by leveraging the gradients of the target 3D model $f(\cdot)$ via backward-propagation. We update the perturbation $\boldsymbol{\Delta}$ with the gradients, and learn the perturbation $\boldsymbol{\Delta}$ as:

$$\boldsymbol{\Delta}' \leftarrow \boldsymbol{\Delta} - lr \cdot \partial_{\boldsymbol{\Delta}}(\mathcal{L}_{adv}(\boldsymbol{P}', \boldsymbol{P}, y)),$$
$$\text{s.t.} \quad \boldsymbol{\Delta}/\phi_{\text{GFT}}(\boldsymbol{P}) \in [\epsilon_{min}, \epsilon_{max}], \tag{8}$$

where lr is the learning rate.

Inverse Transform onto Data Domain. After obtaining the perturbed spectral representations, we apply the IGFT to convert the perturbed signals from the spectral domain back to the data domain as:

$$\boldsymbol{P}' = \phi_{\text{IGFT}}(\phi_{\text{GFT}}(\boldsymbol{P}) + \boldsymbol{\Delta}) = \boldsymbol{U}(\phi_{\text{GFT}}(\boldsymbol{P}) + \boldsymbol{\Delta}), \tag{9}$$

where $\boldsymbol{P}'$ is the crafted adversarial point cloud.

5   Experiments

5.1   Dataset and 3D Models

Dataset. We adopt the point cloud benchmark ModelNet40 [51] dataset in all the experiments. This dataset contains 12,311 CAD models from 40 most common object categories in the world. Among them, 9,843 objects are used for training and the other 2,468 for testing. As in previous works [33], we uniformly sample $n = 1,024$ points from the surface of each object, and re-scale them into a unit ball. For adversarial point cloud attacks, we follow [49,53] and randomly select 25 instances for each of 10 object categories in the ModelNet40 testing set, which can be well classified by the classifiers of interest.

3D Models. We select three commonly used networks in 3D computer vision community as the victim models, *i.e.*, PointNet [33], PointNet++ [34], and DGCNN [48]. We train them from scratch, and the test accuracy of each trained model is within 0.1% of the best reported accuracy in their original papers. We generate the adversarial point clouds on each of them, and further explore their transferability among these three models.

5.2   Implementation Details

Experimental Settings. For generating the adversarial examples, we update the frequency perturbation Δ with 500 iterations. We use Adam optimizer [21] to optimize the objective of our proposed GSDA attack in Eq. (3) with a fixed learning rate $lr = 0.01$, and the momentum is set as 0.9. We set $K = 10$ to build a K-NN graph. The penalty β in Eq. (4) is initialized as 10 and adjusted by 10 runs of binary search [30]. The weights of Chamfer distance loss [10] and Hausdorff distance loss [20] in the regularization term are set to 5.0 and 0.5, respectively. Since the targeted attack is more challenging than the untargeted attack, we focus on the targeted attack in the experiments. All experiments are implemented on a single NVIDIA RTX 2080Ti GPU.

Evaluation Metrics. To quantitatively evaluate the effectiveness of our proposed GSDA attack, we measure by the attack success rate, which is the ratio of successfully fooling a 3D model. Besides, to measure the perturbation size of different attackers, we adopt four evaluation metrics: (1) Data domain: l_2-norm distance $\mathcal{D}_{norm}$ [7] which measures the square root of the sum of squared shifting distance, Chamfer distance $\mathcal{D}_c$ [10] which measures the average squared distance between each adversarial point and its nearest original point, Hausdorff distance $\mathcal{D}_h$ [20] which measures the maximum squared distance between each adversarial point and its nearest original point and is thus sensitive to outliers; (2) Spectral domain: perturbed energy $\mathcal{E}_\Delta = ||\phi_{\mathrm{GFT}}(\boldsymbol{P}') - \phi_{\mathrm{GFT}}(\boldsymbol{P})||_2$.

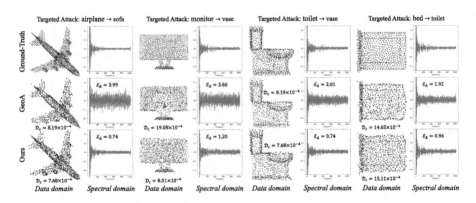

Fig. 4. Visualization of the generated adversarial examples in both the data and spectral domains. Specifically, we compare our GSDA with GeoA via evaluation metrics of the perturbation budget $\mathcal{D}_c$ in the data domain and the perturbed energy $\mathcal{E}_\Delta$ in the spectral domain.

5.3   Evaluation on Our GSDA Attack

Table 1. Comparative results on the perturbation sizes of different methods in the data domain for adversarial point clouds. The results of 3D-ADV are borrowed from its original paper. $^{p},^{c},^{o}$ denote the variant of adversarial point, adversarial cluster and adversarial object, respectively.

Attack model	Methods	Success rate	Perturbation size		
			$\mathcal{D}_{norm}$	$\mathcal{D}_c$	$\mathcal{D}_h$
PointNet	FGSM	100%	0.7936	0.1326	0.1853
	3D-ADV^p	100%	0.3032	**0.0003**	0.0105
	3D-ADV^c	92.1%	–	0.1652	–
	3D-ADV^o	81.9%	–	0.1321	–
	GeoA	100%	0.4385	0.0064	0.0175
	Ours	100%	**0.1741**	0.0007	**0.0031**
PointNet++	FGSM	100%	0.8357	0.1682	0.2275
	3D-ADV^p	100%	0.3248	**0.0005**	0.0381
	GeoA	100%	0.4772	0.0198	0.0357
	Ours	100%	**0.2072**	0.0081	**0.0248**
DGCNN	FGSM	100%	0.8549	0.189	0.2506
	3D-ADV^p	100%	0.3326	**0.0005**	0.0475
	GeoA	100%	0.4933	0.0176	**0.0402**
	Ours	100%	**0.2160**	0.0104	0.1401

Quantitative Results. In order to fairly compare our GSDA attack with existing methods, we perform four adversarial attacks, namely FGSM [61], 3D-ADV [53], GeoA [49] and ours, and measure the perturbation in the data domain with three evaluation metrics when these methods reach 100% of attack success rate. Specifically, we implement these attacks on three 3D models PointNet, Point-Net++ and DGCNN. Corresponding results are shown in Table 1. We see that, our GSDA generates adversarial point clouds with almost the lowest perturbation sizes in all evaluation metrics on three attack models.

Note that, as $\mathcal{D}_c$ measures the average squared distance between each adversarial point and its nearest original point, attacking by adding a few points in 3D-ADV^p has a natural advantage in terms of $\mathcal{D}_c$ because most of the distance is equal to 0. However, it induces much larger distortions than ours on the other two metrics.

Table 2. Defense by dropping different ratios of points via SOR.

Method	Attack success rate (%) defense via SOR						
	0%	1%	2%	5%	10%	15%	20%
GeoA	100	83.47	70.56	52.61	31.58	18.62	11.71
Ours	100	**91.87**	**89.91**	**85.38**	**72.53**	**50.00**	**27.78**

Table 3. The attack success rate (%) on PointNet model by various attacks under defense.

Attack	No defense	SRS	DUP-Net	IF-Defense
FGSM	100%	9.68%	4.38%	4.80%
3D-ADV	100%	22.53%	15.44%	13.70%
GeoA	100%	67.61%	59.15%	38.72%
Ours	100%	**81.03%**	**68.98%**	**50.26%**

Overall, this demonstrates that our generated point clouds are less distorted quantitatively. Besides, for each attack method, it takes larger perturbation sizes to successfully attack PointNet++ and DGCNN than to attack PointNet, which indicates that PointNet++ and DGCNN are harder to attack.

Visualization Results. We also provide some visualization results of generated adversarial point clouds and corresponding spectral coefficients for comparison. As shown in Fig. 4, we compare the visualization of both GeoA and ours on four examples under the setting of targeted attacks. Since GeoA implements perturbation in the data domain while we conduct it in the spectral domain, we provide the perturbation budgets in both two domains for fair comparison. Figure 4 shows that our GSDA attack has less perturbation $\mathcal{E}_\Delta$ than GeoA in the spectral domain as we develop an energy constraint function for optimization. By reflecting the perturbation in the data domain, our adversarial examples are more imperceptible than those of GeoA in both local details and distributions. Quantitatively, we achieve smaller perturbation budget $\mathcal{D}_c$ in the data domain. To conclude, our GSDA attack is more effective and imperceptible.

5.4 Analysis on Robustness of Our GSDA Attack

Attacking the Defenses. To further examine the robustness of our proposed GSDA attack, we employ several 3D defenses to investigate whether our attack is still effective. Specifically, we employ the PointNet model with the following defense methods: Statistical Outlier Removal (SOR) [67], Simple Random Sampling (SRS) [61], DUP-Net defense [67] and IF-Defense [52]. Table 2 shows that across a range of dropping ratios via the defense SOR, the attack success rates drop a lot. However, the performance of our GSDA attack decays much slower than that of GeoA, validating that our attack is much more robust. We also report the results with other defenses in Table 3. We observe that FGSM and 3D-ADV attacks have low success rates under all the defenses, which is because they often lead to uneven local distribution and outliers. Besides, GeoA achieves relatively higher attack success rates, since it utilizes a geometry-aware loss function to constrain the similarity in curvature and thus has fewer outliers. In comparison, our attack achieves the highest success rates than all other attacks under all defenses since the trivial perturbation in the spectral domain reflects less noise in the data domain, thus enhancing the robustness.

Transferability of Adversarial Point Clouds. To investigate the transferability of our proposed GSDA attack, we craft adversarial point clouds on normally trained models and test them on all the three 3D models we consider. The success rates, which are the misclassification rates of the corresponding models on adversarial examples, are shown in Table 4. The left, middle and right parts present the three models we attack: PointNet, PointNet++ and DGCNN; the columns of the table present the models we test. We observe that although our GSDA attack is not tailored for transferability, it has relatively higher success rates of transfer-based attacks than others. This is because our perturbation in

Table 4. The attack success rate (%) of transfer-based attacks.

Attacks	PointNet	PointNet++	DGCNN	PointNet	PointNet++	DGCNN	PointNet	PointNet++	DGCNN
FGSM	100%	3.99%	0.63%	3.16%	100%	5.57%	3.59%	7.21%	100%
3D-ADV	100%	8.45%	1.28%	6.63%	100%	10.98%	6.82%	13.53%	100%
GeoA	100%	11.59%	2.59%	9.47%	100%	19.77%	12.46%	24.24%	100%
Ours	100%	11.51%	8.39%	10.89%	100%	30.84%	32.31%	84.49%	100%

the spectral domain not only keeps spectral characteristics but also reflects trivial noise in the data domain, which is thus more robust. A further improvement of the transferability could be developed by employing an additional adversarial learning mechanism with the Auto-Encoder reconstruction as in [14] (left as the future works). The comparatively slightly lower transferability of our GSDA in this table may be related with special properties of certain 3D models. To summarize, this intrinsic property makes it possible to design black-box defense against such adversarial instances.

5.5   Ablation Study

Table 5. Sensitivity analysis on the number K.

Number K	Success rate	$\mathcal{D}_c$	$\mathcal{D}_h$	$\mathcal{E}_\Delta$
$K=5$	100%	**0.0007**	0.0031	3.4679
$K=10$	100%	**0.0007**	0.0031	**3.4510**
$K=20$	100%	**0.0007**	**0.0030**	3.4617
$K=40$	100%	**0.0007**	**0.0030**	3.4688

Table 6. Comparison of different spectral representations.

Method	Attack success rate (%) defense via SOR				$\mathcal{D}_c$	$\mathcal{D}_h$	$\mathcal{E}_\Delta$
	0%	5%	10%	20%			
Ours-1DDCT	**100.00**	6.84	3.24	0.62	**0.0006**	0.0037	28.7834
Ours-3DDCT	93.06	37.48	25.17	19.60	0.0029	0.0415	19.4804
Ours-GFT	**100.00**	**85.38**	**72.53**	**27.78**	0.0007	**0.0031**	**3.4510**

Choice of Spectral Representation. We first evaluate the benefit of spectral representation in the GFT domain. Since the DCT is widely used in the 2D field to transform images onto the spectral domain, we compare the spectral domain attack performances on different spectral representations of the DCT and GFT. We implement 1D DCT and 3D DCT for comparison. For 1D DCT, we regard coordinates as the signal and perform 1D DCT on it. As to 3D DCT, we voxelize the pointcloud and perform 3D DCT on coordinates signal. As shown in Table 6, we see that our attack with the GFT is more robust to SOR defense and has much lower perturbation size in the spectral domain than the attack with the DCT. The main reason is that point clouds are unordered, which makes it challenging to capture the correlations among points by the DCT. In contrast, the GFT well captures the underlying structure of point clouds via the appropriate graph construction.

Sensitivity on the Number K. As shown in Table 5, we investigate whether the adversarial effects vary with respect to different settings of the number K in the K-NN graph. Specifically, we implement $K = 5, 10, 20, 40$ to perform the proposed GSDA attack on PointNet model and report the corresponding perturbation budgets when achieving 100% of attack success rate. We see that the attack performance is insensitive to the number K since our attack with different K's requires similar perturbation budgets $\mathcal{D}_c, \mathcal{D}_h$ in the data domain, as well as in the spectral domain measured by $\mathcal{E}_\Delta$.

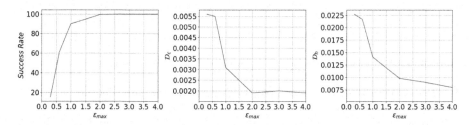

Fig. 5. Attacking performance when applying different ϵ_{max} restrict, in terms of success rate, Chamfer distance and Hausdorff distance results between adversarial point clouds and the originals.

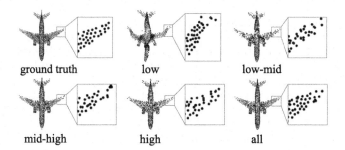

Fig. 6. Visualization of attacks on specific frequency bands.

Sensitivity on the Perturbation Size $[\epsilon_{min}, \epsilon_{max}]$. As shown in Fig. 5, when we relax the perturbation constraint $[\epsilon_{min}, \epsilon_{max}]$ in the spectral domain, the success rates of our GSDA increase and achieve almost 100% of success rate when $\epsilon_{max} = -\epsilon_{min} = 3.0$, meanwhile $\mathcal{D}_c$ and $\mathcal{D}_h$ achieve an good performance.

Attacks on Specific Frequency Bands. We also perform an ablation study on how attacking specific frequency bands (*i.e.*, low, low-mid, mid-high, high) affects point clouds in the data domain. As shown in Fig. 6, only attacking low or high frequency band results in distortion of the rough shape or local details, which is consistent with our analysis in Sect. 3. Instead, attacking appropriate positions among the entire spectra achieves the most imperceptible results.

6   Conclusion

We propose a novel paradigm of point cloud attacks—Graph Spectral Domain Attack (GSDA), which explores insightful spectral characteristics and performs perturbation in the spectral domain to generate adversarial examples with geometric structures well preserved. Extensive experiments show the vulnerability of popular 3D models to the proposed GSDA and demonstrate the robustness of our adversarial point clouds. Such spectral methodology blazes a new path of developing attacks in 3D deep learning. Future promising directions include developing effective defense methods against such spectral domain attacks.

References

1. Atzmon, M., Maron, H., Lipman, Y.: Point convolutional neural networks by extension operators. arXiv preprint arXiv:1803.10091 (2018)
2. Carlini, N., Wagner, D.: Towards evaluating the robustness of neural networks. In: 2017 IEEE Symposium on Security and Privacy (SP), pp. 39–57 (2017)
3. Chen, S., Tian, D., Feng, C., Vetro, A., Kovačević, J.: Fast resampling of three-dimensional point clouds via graphs. IEEE Trans. Sig. Process. **66**(3), 666–681 (2017)
4. Chen, X., Ma, H., Wan, J., Li, B., Xia, T.: Multi-view 3D object detection network for autonomous driving. In: Proceedings of the IEEE Conference on Computer Vision and Pattern Recognition (CVPR), pp. 1907–1915 (2017)
5. Choi, J., Han, B.: Task-aware quantization network for JPEG image compression. In: Vedaldi, A., Bischof, H., Brox, T., Frahm, J.-M. (eds.) ECCV 2020. LNCS, vol. 12365, pp. 309–324. Springer, Cham (2020). https://doi.org/10.1007/978-3-030-58565-5_19
6. Chung, F.R., Graham, F.C.: Spectral Graph Theory, vol. 92. American Mathematical Society (1997)
7. Cortes, C., Mohri, M., Rostamizadeh, A.: L2 regularization for learning kernels. arXiv preprint arXiv:1205.2653 (2012)
8. Dong, Y., et al.: Boosting adversarial attacks with momentum. In: Proceedings of the IEEE Conference on Computer Vision and Pattern Recognition (CVPR), pp. 9185–9193 (2018)
9. Duan, Y., Zheng, Y., Lu, J., Zhou, J., Tian, Q.: Structural relational reasoning of point clouds. In: Proceedings of the IEEE Conference on Computer Vision and Pattern Recognition (CVPR), pp. 949–958 (2019)
10. Fan, H., Su, H., Guibas, L.J.: A point set generation network for 3D object reconstruction from a single image. In: Proceedings of the IEEE Conference on Computer Vision and Pattern Recognition (CVPR), pp. 605–613 (2017)

11. Gao, X., Hu, W., Qi, G.J.: GraphTER: unsupervised learning of graph transformation equivariant representations via auto-encoding node-wise transformations. In: Proceedings of the IEEE/CVF Conference on Computer Vision and Pattern Recognition, pp. 7163–7172 (2020)
12. Goodfellow, I.J., Shlens, J., Szegedy, C.: Explaining and harnessing adversarial examples. arXiv preprint arXiv:1412.6572 (2014)
13. Graham, B., Engelcke, M., Van Der Maaten, L.: 3D semantic segmentation with submanifold sparse convolutional networks. In: Proceedings of the IEEE Conference on Computer Vision and Pattern Recognition (CVPR), pp. 9224–9232 (2018)
14. Hamdi, A., Rojas, S., Thabet, A., Ghanem, B.: AdvPC: transferable adversarial perturbations on 3D point clouds. In: Vedaldi, A., Bischof, H., Brox, T., Frahm, J.-M. (eds.) ECCV 2020. LNCS, vol. 12357, pp. 241–257. Springer, Cham (2020). https://doi.org/10.1007/978-3-030-58610-2_15
15. Hammond, D.K., Vandergheynst, P., Gribonval, R.: Wavelets on graphs via spectral graph theory. Appl. Comput. Harmonic Anal. **30**(2), 129–150 (2011)
16. Hu, W., Cheung, G., Li, X., Au, O.: Depth map compression using multi-resolution graph-based transform for depth-image-based rendering. In: Proceedings of the IEEE International Conference on Image Processing, pp. 1297–1300 (2012)
17. Hu, W., Cheung, G., Ortega, A.: Intra-prediction and generalized graph Fourier transform for image coding. IEEE Sig. Process. Lett. **22**(11), 1913–1917 (2015)
18. Hu, W., Cheung, G., Ortega, A., Au, O.C.: Multiresolution graph Fourier transform for compression of piecewise smooth images. IEEE Trans. Image Process. **24**(1), 419–433 (2015)
19. Hu, W., Pang, J., Liu, X., Tian, D., Lin, C.W., Vetro, A.: Graph signal processing for geometric data and beyond: theory and applications. IEEE Trans. Multimedia (2021)
20. Huttenlocher, D.P., Klanderman, G.A., Rucklidge, W.J.: Comparing images using the hausdorff distance. IEEE Trans. Pattern Anal. Mach. Intell. **15**(9), 850–863 (1993)
21. Kingma, D.P., Ba, J.: Adam: a method for stochastic optimization. arXiv preprint arXiv:1412.6980 (2014)
22. Kurakin, A., Goodfellow, I., Bengio, S.: Adversarial machine learning at scale. arXiv preprint arXiv:1611.01236 (2016)
23. Li, M., Zuo, W., Gu, S., Zhao, D., Zhang, D.: Learning convolutional networks for content-weighted image compression. In: Proceedings of the IEEE Conference on Computer Vision and Pattern Recognition (CVPR), pp. 3214–3223 (2018)
24. Li, Y., Bu, R., Sun, M., Wu, W., Di, X., Chen, B.: PointCNN: convolution on x-transformed points. In: Advances in Neural Information Processing Systems (NIPS), vol. 31, pp. 820–830 (2018)
25. Liu, D., Hu, W.: Imperceptible transfer attack and defense on 3D point cloud classification. arXiv preprint arXiv:2111.10990 (2021)
26. Liu, D., Yu, R., Su, H.: Extending adversarial attacks and defenses to deep 3D point cloud classifiers. In: 2019 IEEE International Conference on Image Processing (ICIP), pp. 2279–2283 (2019)
27. Liu, Y., Fan, B., Meng, G., Lu, J., Xiang, S., Pan, C.: DensePoint: learning densely contextual representation for efficient point cloud processing. In: Proceedings of the IEEE International Conference on Computer Vision (ICCV), pp. 5239–5248 (2019)
28. Liu, Y., Fan, B., Xiang, S., Pan, C.: Relation-shape convolutional neural network for point cloud analysis. In: Proceedings of the IEEE Conference on Computer Vision and Pattern Recognition (CVPR), pp. 8895–8904 (2019)

29. Ma, C., Meng, W., Wu, B., Xu, S., Zhang, X.: Efficient joint gradient based attack against SOR defense for 3D point cloud classification. In: Proceedings of the 28th ACM International Conference on Multimedia, pp. 1819–1827 (2020)
30. Madry, A., Makelov, A., Schmidt, L., Tsipras, D., Vladu, A.: Towards deep learning models resistant to adversarial attacks. arXiv preprint arXiv:1706.06083 (2017)
31. Moosavi-Dezfooli, S.M., Fawzi, A., Fawzi, O., Frossard, P.: Universal adversarial perturbations. In: Proceedings of the IEEE Conference on Computer Vision and Pattern Recognition (CVPR), pp. 1765–1773 (2017)
32. Moosavi-Dezfooli, S.M., Fawzi, A., Frossard, P.: DeepFool: a simple and accurate method to fool deep neural networks. In: Proceedings of the IEEE Conference on Computer Vision and Pattern Recognition (CVPR), pp. 2574–2582 (2016)
33. Qi, C.R., Su, H., Mo, K., Guibas, L.J.: PointNet: deep learning on point sets for 3D classification and segmentation. In: Proceedings of the IEEE Conference on Computer Vision and Pattern Recognition (CVPR), pp. 652–660 (2017)
34. Qi, C.R., Yi, L., Su, H., Guibas, L.J.: PointNet++: deep hierarchical feature learning on point sets in a metric space. In: Advances in Neural Information Processing Systems (NIPS) (2017)
35. Ramasinghe, S., Khan, S., Barnes, N., Gould, S.: Spectral-GANs for high-resolution 3D point-cloud generation. In: 2020 IEEE/RSJ International Conference on Intelligent Robots and Systems (IROS), pp. 8169–8176. IEEE (2020)
36. Rosman, G., Dubrovina, A., Kimmel, R.: Patch-collaborative spectral point-cloud denoising. In: Computer Graphics Forum, vol. 32, pp. 1–12. Wiley (2013)
37. Shen, G., Kim, W.S., Narang, S.K., Ortega, A., Lee, J., Wey, H.: Edge-adaptive transforms for efficient depth map coding. In: Proceedings of the Picture Coding Symposium, pp. 566–569 (2010)
38. Shen, Y., Feng, C., Yang, Y., Tian, D.: Mining point cloud local structures by kernel correlation and graph pooling. In: Proceedings of the IEEE Conference on Computer Vision and Pattern Recognition (CVPR), pp. 4548–4557 (2018)
39. Shuman, D.I., Narang, S.K., Frossard, P., Ortega, A., Vandergheynst, P.: The emerging field of signal processing on graphs: extending high-dimensional data analysis to networks and other irregular domains. IEEE Sig. Process. Mag. 30(3), 83–98 (2013)
40. Simonovsky, M., Komodakis, N.: Dynamic edge-conditioned filters in convolutional neural networks on graphs. In: Proceedings of the IEEE Conference on Computer Vision and Pattern Recognition (CVPR), pp. 3693–3702 (2017)
41. Singh, S.P., Wang, L., Gupta, S., Goli, H., Padmanabhan, P., Gulyás, B.: 3D deep learning on medical images: a review. Sensors 20(18), 5097 (2020)
42. Su, H., Maji, S., Kalogerakis, E., Learned-Miller, E.: Multi-view convolutional neural networks for 3D shape recognition. In: Proceedings of the IEEE International Conference on Computer Vision (ICCV), pp. 945–953 (2015)
43. Szegedy, C., et al.: Intriguing properties of neural networks. arXiv preprint arXiv:1312.6199 (2013)
44. Thomas, H., Qi, C.R., Deschaud, J.E., Marcotegui, B., Goulette, F., Guibas, L.J.: KPConv: flexible and deformable convolution for point clouds. In: Proceedings of the IEEE International Conference on Computer Vision (ICCV), pp. 6411–6420 (2019)
45. Tsai, T., Yang, K., Ho, T.Y., Jin, Y.: Robust adversarial objects against deep learning models. In: Proceedings of the AAAI Conference on Artificial Intelligence, vol. 34, pp. 954–962 (2020)

46. Tu, C.C., et al.: AutoZOOM: autoencoder-based zeroth order optimization method for attacking black-box neural networks. In: Proceedings of the AAAI Conference on Artificial Intelligence, vol. 33, pp. 742–749 (2019)
47. Wang, W., Yu, R., Huang, Q., Neumann, U.: SGPN: similarity group proposal network for 3D point cloud instance segmentation. In: Proceedings of the IEEE Conference on Computer Vision and Pattern Recognition (CVPR), pp. 2569–2578 (2018)
48. Wang, Y., Sun, Y., Liu, Z., Sarma, S.E., Bronstein, M.M., Solomon, J.M.: Dynamic graph CNN for learning on point clouds. ACM Trans. Graph. (TOG) **38**(5), 1–12 (2019)
49. Wen, Y., Lin, J., Chen, K., Chen, C.P., Jia, K.: Geometry-aware generation of adversarial point clouds. IEEE Trans. Pattern Anal. Mach. Intell. (TPAMI) (2020)
50. Wicker, M., Kwiatkowska, M.: Robustness of 3D deep learning in an adversarial setting. In: Proceedings of the IEEE Conference on Computer Vision and Pattern Recognition (CVPR), pp. 11767–11775 (2019)
51. Wu, Z., et al.: 3D ShapeNets: a deep representation for volumetric shapes. In: Proceedings of the IEEE Conference on Computer Vision and Pattern Recognition (CVPR), pp. 1912–1920 (2015)
52. Wu, Z., Duan, Y., Wang, H., Fan, Q., Guibas, L.J.: IF-defense: 3D adversarial point cloud defense via implicit function based restoration. arXiv preprint arXiv:2010.05272 (2020)
53. Xiang, C., Qi, C.R., Li, B.: Generating 3D adversarial point clouds. In: Proceedings of the IEEE Conference on Computer Vision and Pattern Recognition (CVPR), pp. 9136–9144 (2019)
54. Xu, Q., Sun, X., Wu, C.Y., Wang, P., Neumann, U.: Grid-GCN for fast and scalable point cloud learning. In: Proceedings of the IEEE Conference on Computer Vision and Pattern Recognition (CVPR), pp. 5661–5670 (2020)
55. Xu, Y., et al.: Predictive generalized graph Fourier transform for attribute compression of dynamic point clouds. arXiv preprint arXiv:1908.01970 (2019)
56. Yang, B., et al.: Learning object bounding boxes for 3D instance segmentation on point clouds. arXiv preprint arXiv:1906.01140 (2019)
57. Yang, J., et al.: Modeling point clouds with self-attention and Gumbel subset sampling. In: Proceedings of the IEEE Conference on Computer Vision and Pattern Recognition (CVPR), pp. 3323–3332 (2019)
58. Yu, T., Meng, J., Yuan, J.: Multi-view harmonized bilinear network for 3D object recognition. In: Proceedings of the IEEE Conference on Computer Vision and Pattern Recognition (CVPR), pp. 186–194 (2018)
59. Zaheer, M., Kottur, S., Ravanbakhsh, S., Poczos, B., Salakhutdinov, R.R., Smola, A.J.: Deep sets. In: Advances in Neural Information Processing Systems (NIPS), vol. 30 (2017)
60. Zhang, C., Florencio, D., Loop, C.: Point cloud attribute compression with graph transform. In: Proceedings of the IEEE International Conference on Image Processing, pp. 2066–2070 (2014)
61. Zhang, Q., Yang, J., Fang, R., Ni, B., Liu, J., Tian, Q.: Adversarial attack and defense on point sets. arXiv preprint arXiv:1902.10899 (2019)
62. Zhang, S., Cui, S., Ding, Z.: Hypergraph spectral analysis and processing in 3D point cloud. IEEE Trans. Image Process. **30**, 1193–1206 (2020)
63. Zhang, Y., Liang, G., Salem, T., Jacobs, N.: Defense-PointNet: protecting PointNet against adversarial attacks. In: 2019 IEEE International Conference on Big Data (Big Data), pp. 5654–5660 (2019)

64. Zhao, Y., Wu, Y., Chen, C., Lim, A.: On isometry robustness of deep 3D point cloud models under adversarial attacks. In: Proceedings of the IEEE Conference on Computer Vision and Pattern Recognition (CVPR), pp. 1201–1210 (2020)
65. Zheng, T., Chen, C., Yuan, J., Li, B., Ren, K.: PointCloud saliency maps. In: Proceedings of the IEEE International Conference on Computer Vision (ICCV), pp. 1598–1606 (2019)
66. Zhou, H., et al.: LG-GAN: label guided adversarial network for flexible targeted attack of point cloud based deep networks. In: Proceedings of the IEEE Conference on Computer Vision and Pattern Recognition (CVPR), pp. 10356–10365 (2020)
67. Zhou, H., Chen, K., Zhang, W., Fang, H., Zhou, W., Yu, N.: DUP-Net: denoiser and Upsampler network for 3D adversarial point clouds defense. In: Proceedings of the IEEE International Conference on Computer Vision (ICCV), pp. 1961–1970 (2019)

Structure-Aware Editable Morphable Model for 3D Facial Detail Animation and Manipulation

Jingwang Ling[1], Zhibo Wang[1], Ming Lu[2], Quan Wang[3],
Chen Qian[3], and Feng Xu[1(✉)]

[1] BNRist and School of Software, Tsinghua University, Beijing, China
xufeng2003@gmail.com
[2] Intel Labs, Beijing, China
[3] Sensetime Research, Shanghai, China

Abstract. Morphable models are essential for the statistical modeling of 3D faces. Previous works on morphable models mostly focus on large-scale facial geometry but ignore facial details. This paper augments morphable models in representing facial details by learning a Structure-aware Editable Morphable Model (SEMM). SEMM introduces a detail structure representation based on the distance field of wrinkle lines, jointly modeled with detail displacements to establish better correspondences and enable intuitive manipulation of wrinkle structure. Besides, SEMM introduces two transformation modules to translate expression blendshape weights and age values into changes in latent space, allowing effective semantic detail editing while maintaining identity. Extensive experiments demonstrate that the proposed model compactly represents facial details, outperforms previous methods in expression animation qualitatively and quantitatively, and achieves effective age editing and wrinkle line editing of facial details. Code and model are available at https://github.com/gerwang/facial-detail-manipulation.

1 Introduction

Morphable face models [24] capture the statistical distribution of human faces, which provides them with capabilities to generate and edit 3D faces. Therefore, they are widely used in face reconstruction [8], expression animation [15], and interactive editing [39]. In these applications, facial details play a vital role in conveying the perception of expression and age and enhancing the realism of the generated face. For example, during animation, facial details appear or disappear as muscles contract or relax, vividly reflecting the subtle expression. During interactive editing, animators may wish to manipulate wrinkles at specific positions. However, current morphable models usually only represent the large-scale facial geometry, making the results of the above applications over-smooth and

---

Supplementary Information The online version contains supplementary material available at https://doi.org/10.1007/978-3-031-20062-5_15.

unrealistic, with details absent. A morphable model for facial details is still missing to the best of our knowledge.

In this work, we augment classic 3D morphable models (3DMMs) in representing facial details by proposing a Structure-aware Editable Morphable Model (SEMM). Specifically, a detail model synthesizes a displacement map that encodes detail geometric information, which is then applied to a mesh generated by a 3DMM to get a high-fidelity 3D face. We design a separate detail model because mixing low and high frequencies hinders the learning of high frequencies [31], and the effectiveness of learning high-frequency facial details separated from large-scale geometry is verified in [14,18,29]. With careful design choices, our model is compatible with widely used large-scale face models, and can be seamlessly integrated into the animation pipeline to produce detail animation consistent with the large scale, despite modeling details separately.

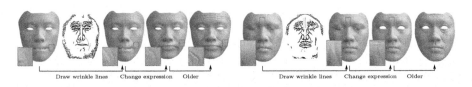

Fig. 1. SEMM allows the user to manipulate facial details by (i) drawing/erasing wrinkle lines and changing (ii) expression and (iii) age. Realistic wrinkles can be generated by drawing lines (shown in green) on the face. Generated details can be animated when changing expression and transform properly during aging. (Color figure online)

Morphable models often assume that faces can be aligned to a fixed template, which holds for the large-scale shape but cannot account for wrinkle details. For example, forehead wrinkles exhibit thin line structure and may vary in branch numbers on different subjects, making it challenging to define and compute the alignment. As observed in [57], wrinkle lines are almost always imperfectly aligned in the training data, resulting in averaged details and oversmooth generated shape. We also find missing wrinkles when directly modeling displacement maps in training an autoencoder, as the used reconstruction loss abruptly increases when wrinkles misalign even slightly. To tackle this issue, we first extract wrinkle lines that encode the structure of details on the facial surface. Inspired by [21,54,80] that use distance functions in implicit shape modeling, we develop a distance field representation of the wrinkle lines. The reconstruction loss on distance fields gradually descends as wrinkles start to align, providing meaningful gradients for autoencoder learning. Therefore, we propose to combine displacement maps and distance fields to construct implicit correspondences of facial details and more accurately model the wrinkle structure.

We instruct the model to generate accurate wrinkle structure on the displacement map, by first ensuring the consistency between the generated displacements and distance field, and then supervising the distance field to preserve the structure of wrinkle lines. Specifically, we propose an autoencoder that reconstructs a pair of displacement map and distance field map from a latent code, and train the autoencoder adversarially with a discriminator to enforce consistency. The consistency can lead to more precise wrinkle structure during autoencoding and enable a user to manipulate the details by editing the wrinkle lines.

The latent space of morphable models is often divided into identity and expression. Additionally, our detail model allows age control, another key semantic factor that provides finer granularity of facial detail editing. To allow effective expression and age control while preserving identity, we propose two transformation modules to regress direction vectors of changes in the latent space, and supervise them with expression- and age-specific discriminator outputs. The direction vectors, as suggested by [34,84], permit semantic editing while better maintaining identity. To meaningfully control the latent space, we adopt expression blendshape weights and age values as control parameters, which are intuitive and compatible with the facial animation pipeline. Our method achieves qualitatively and quantitatively better expression editing than previous methods and enables the effective control of detail aging, which is not shown in previous methods.

To summarize, our contributions are: (i) the first attempt to propose an editable morphable model that can animate details by editing wrinkle lines, changing expression weights and age values, (ii) a distance field-based autoencoder network to better model detail structure and give intuitive control over the wrinkles, and (iii) two transformation modules to model expression and age changes, which achieve both accurate representation and effective editing of these two semantic factors. Code and model will be released.

2 Related Work

Morphable Face Models. Since the pioneering work of [8], morphable face models have been widely investigated in the literature. [8,11,28] analyze the identity variation in neutral facial shape by principal component analysis. [40,53,56,76] construct person-specific linear models to describe expression variations. Furthermore, [13,16,72,79] model the joint distribution of identity and expression by constructing a multilinear model. After statistical analysis of the facial geometry, morphable models can generate 3D faces from a compact latent space and perform expression editing [3,17,36,39] through latent space editing.

To improve the representation ability of morphable models, which are often linear, several extensions are made to add nonlinearity. Some methods combine linear models with nonlinear jaw and neck articulation [46] or a physical model [32]. [2,4,12,59] propose to learn nonlinear morphable models using autoencoder architectures. Generative adversarial networks are also explored to perform 3D face modelling [1,20,64,68]. Please refer to [24] for a comprehensive survey. All the above models focus on large-scale geometry only. Our nonlinear detail model can be used on top of those morphable models to jointly fit the distribution in a complete frequency domain of both large-scale and details.

It is challenging to model details by current morphable models, as facial details are difficult to align in registration, which is a required process to establish dense scan correspondences. In practice, [57] observes that details are often averaged out during morphable model construction. To mitigate this issue, [10] proposes a method to iteratively construct a morphable model and improve

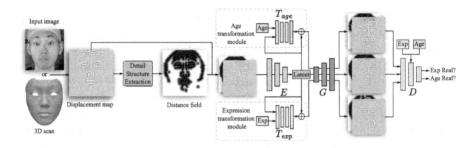

Fig. 2. Overview of our method.

registration correspondences. [80] represents facial geometry as a deep implicit function and builds a morphable model which automatically establishes correspondences between scans. Our model builds better semantic correspondences of facial details by a novel method to model the distance field of wrinkle lines.

3D Facial Detail Animation and Manipulation. Wrinkle formation is strongly correlated with physical facial layers such as elastic fibers and muscles [33,63], which share the same topology among people [58]. This fact enables modeling details either physically or in a data-driven manner. Several methods model the facial skin through physics to simulate wrinkle effects [9,44,77]. However, those methods require a lot of computation time and hand-tuned physical parameters, therefore we focus on data-driven modeling. To acquire details from the image data, plenty of methods use either shape from shading [27,51,65,69] or deep neural networks [19,25,30,35,48,60–62,71,81], but they cannot animate the reconstructed details. [25] uses an encoder-decoder to reconstruct an animatable detailed face from a single image. However, it solely relies on shading constraints from images and generates less realistic details than captured 3D scans. To leverage the scan data, [6,7,26,66,78] transfer details from a source face to a target face. They can obtain realistic details, but the details are not specific to the target face. Multi-identity local models [14,18,29,43] can be built from high-resolution scan datasets. However, they only model patch-based local detail displacements, effective for detail reconstruction but cannot synthesize detail animation. [23,45] can synthesize plausible details from large-scale shape or texture, but aging wrinkles are hard to synthesize as they cannot be fully reflected from large-scale. [42,79] can synthesize high-fidelity animatable faces given an image or scan. However, they assume that all the details in input faces are static, thus cannot handle dynamic details in inputs. Several methods allow users to intuitively create new wrinkles using sketches [5,38,47,78], but they cannot animate the generated wrinkles. Our model first represents facial details and their changes caused by structure, expression, and age in a unified latent space. Thus, it provides easier ways to animate and manipulate facial details.

3   Overview

SEMM serves as a detail model that extends a large-scale 3D morphable model in [79] to represent shape details. Recall that the large-scale model generates

Fig. 3. We extract a distance field from a displacement map by (a) removing low-frequency components, (b) extracting detail lines, and (c) applying distance transform.

a face mesh, whose expression is controlled by blendshape weights [40]. The detail model is designed to be compatible with the large-scale model both in shape representation and control parameters. For shape representation, the detail model synthesizes a displacement map that encodes surface details. It is then combined with the mesh to get a high-fidelity 3D face. The process is natively supported by modern graphics hardware [14]. The same blendshape weights are used to control the latent code of the detail model to generate expression animation. Therefore, the generated facial animation is consistent with large scale and details.

Figure 2 illustrates the pipeline of our method. To manipulate facial details, we first get original details from an input image or scan and represent them on a displacement map, from which we then extract a distance field encoding the detail structure (Sect. 4). The original details only represent a static input, thus we find their latent code for manipulation. E and G are used to encode and generate (middle path through G) both the displacement map and distance field, and are adversarially trained with discriminator D to model the joint displacement-distance distribution (Sect. 5). We add T_{exp} and T_{age} to transform the latent code to enable expression and age editing (upper and lower paths through G), and modify D to supervise expression and age (Sect. 6). Finally, Sect. 7 shows experiments of expression, age and structure editing of facial details.

4   Detail Shape Processing

We represent facial details as a displacement map for its efficiency and common use in 3D mesh animation pipelines. Each pixel is parameterized in the mesh's UV space and encodes a signed displacement from the mesh along the surface normal direction.

Either a face image or a 3D scan can be used to obtain a displacement map of input details, which enables further manipulation. Specifically, we first fit the large-scale morphable model to the image or scan. For an image input, we then extract a texture map from it and use a Pix2PixHD [73] network trained on [79] to reconstruct a displacement map. For a scan input, it is smoothed via Laplacian smoothing [70], and the difference between the original and smoothed scan is baked into UV space as a displacement map. We use the scan dataset from [79] for training, and the scans are similarly processed into displacement maps. Before modeling, we filter out low-frequency components in the displacement maps, which do not affect detail rendering (see Fig. 3(a)), but may hinder the learning of high frequencies [31].

We propose to extract the spatial location of wrinkle lines to describe detail structure. Inspired by, but different from [14] which extract wrinkle patches on the lines, we incorporate the lines into the model to supervise it to generate accurate structure. On the filtered displacement maps, wrinkles are shaped as lines because of how they are formed. We perform denoising and use a sketch simplification network [67] to extract the lines (Fig. 3(b)). The extracted lines depict the occupancy of facial details in the UV space.

However, the wrinkle lines are imperfectly aligned, which we find unsuitable for modeling. As wrinkle lines can be viewed as 2D shapes, we seek a solution from recent progress in shape modeling [54,80], which has shown improved correspondences using a signed distance function. We adopt the unsigned distance [21] to model thin lines. Specifically, we convert the line map to a distance field by Euclid distance transform [49] to obtain each pixel's distance to the nearest detail line. Following [21,75], we truncate the distance value to 5% of the map width to concentrate on the neighborhood of lines, producing the final distance field maps (Fig. 3(c)).

5   Modeling Displacements and Distance Fields

Autoencoding the Joint Distribution. For the displacement map $\mathbf{x}^d$ and its distance field map $\mathbf{x}^s$, we model their *joint* distribution $p(\mathbf{x}^d, \mathbf{x}^s)$. The joint distribution is obtained by mapping a latent code $\mathbf{z} \sim p(\mathbf{z})$ to a pair $(\widehat{\mathbf{x}}^d, \widehat{\mathbf{x}}^s)$ via a generator network, for which we use StyleGAN2 [37] to leverage its high synthesis quality. As the latent code explains variations both in the displacement map and distance field, we input $(\mathbf{x}^d, \mathbf{x}^s)$ to an encoder following the design in [55] for fast inference. The autoencoding process can be formulated as:

$$\mathbf{z} = E(\mathbf{x}) = E(\mathbf{x}^d, \mathbf{x}^s), \qquad \widehat{\mathbf{x}}_{rec} = G(\mathbf{z}) \tag{1}$$

where $\mathbf{z}$ is a compact latent code of 576 dimensions, E is the encoder, G is the generator, $\mathbf{x} = (\mathbf{x}^d, \mathbf{x}^s)$ and $\widehat{\mathbf{x}}_{rec} = (\widehat{\mathbf{x}}^d_{rec}, \widehat{\mathbf{x}}^s_{rec})$ are the input and reconstructed samples respectively.

Consistency via the Discriminator. To both enable realistic synthesis and ensure the consistency between synthesized $\widehat{\mathbf{x}}^d$ and $\widehat{\mathbf{x}}^s$, we add a discriminator which inputs $(\widehat{\mathbf{x}}^d, \widehat{\mathbf{x}}^s)$ in training. The consistency, as a benefit from joint distribution modeling, was previously exploited in [41,83] to generate segmentation labels for unannotated images. While they model a joint image-label distribution for semi-supervised learning, here we consider the consistency between displacement maps and distance fields for structure-aware generation and editing. The consistency can guide the detail structure in the generated displacements to follow the distance field. This fact allows us to add supervision on the distance field during training to more accurately reconstruct the detail structure. Compared with modeling displacements only, modeling the joint distribution can

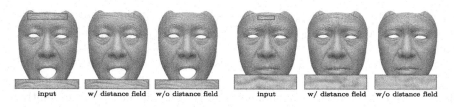

| input | w/ distance field | w/o distance field | input | w/ distance field | w/o distance field |

Fig. 4. Autoencoding results of jointly modeling displacements and distance fields (middle) and modeling displacements only (right).

better preserve wrinkles during autoencoding, as shown in Fig. 4. Additionally, the consistency allows a user to manipulate the detail structure intuitively by editing the input distance field, as shown in Sect. 7.3.

Structure-Aware Reconstruction and Editing. For a generated output $\widehat{\mathbf{x}}_* = (\widehat{\mathbf{x}}_*^d, \widehat{\mathbf{x}}_*^s)$, the above discriminator ensures consistency between $\widehat{\mathbf{x}}_*^d$ and $\widehat{\mathbf{x}}_*^s$. Additionally, to enforce $\widehat{\mathbf{x}}_*$ is consistent with a target $\mathbf{x}_* = (\mathbf{x}_*^d, \mathbf{x}_*^s)$ in Eq. 12, we design a reconstruction loss ℓ_{rec} that can be decomposed into two terms:

$$\ell_{rec}(\widehat{\mathbf{x}}_*, \mathbf{x}_*) = \ell_{FM}(\widehat{\mathbf{x}}_*, \mathbf{x}_*) + \lambda_{df}\ell_{df}(\widehat{\mathbf{x}}_*, \mathbf{x}_*) \tag{2}$$

First, we use the feature matching loss ℓ_{FM} to formulate a multi-scale reconstruction loss:

$$\ell_{FM}(\widehat{\mathbf{x}}_*, \mathbf{x}_*) = \sum_{i=1}^{T} \frac{1}{N_i} \left\| D^{(i)}(\widehat{\mathbf{x}}_*) - D^{(i)}(\mathbf{x}_*) \right\|_1 \tag{3}$$

This loss follows [73], but on a StyleGAN2 discriminator D with T layers and N_i components in the ith layer. Second, we use a distance field loss ℓ_{df} to help reconstruct the detail structure:

$$\ell_{df}(\widehat{\mathbf{x}}_*, \mathbf{x}_*) = \left\| \min(\widehat{\mathbf{x}}_*^s, \delta) - \min(\mathbf{x}_*^s, \delta) \right\|_1 \tag{4}$$

where $\mathbf{x}_* = (\mathbf{x}_*^d, \mathbf{x}_*^s)$ corresponds to the target displacement map and its distance field, $\widehat{\mathbf{x}}_* = (\widehat{\mathbf{x}}_*^d, \widehat{\mathbf{x}}_*^s)$ corresponds to the generated pair, and δ is set to 5% of the map width as a threshold to concentrate the loss to areas near details. Note that ℓ_{df} is not related to displacement maps.

To explain our design of ℓ_{rec}: First, we use feature matching loss (Eq. 3) instead of L1 loss because L1 focuses on per pixel reconstruction and tends to ignore structure similarity, as it strongly penalizes structure-similar details with merely slight misalignment. Second, by supervising the distance field instead of wrinkle lines (Fig. 3(c)), misaligned wrinkles start to have some overlap, which leads to a gradually descending loss value as wrinkles start to align. Both of the two tend to encourage structure similarity and tolerate slight misalignment of wrinkles, which we believe can lead to a more compact and well-behaved detail representation.

Supervising the distance field also enables a user to perform wrinkle line editing. Specifically, after the wrinkle line map is extracted from the displacement map (Fig. 3(b)), the user draws or erases lines on the line map, before it is converted to a distance field. The original displacement map and the edited distance field are then passed through E and G to get the edited displacement map that is consistent with user edits. This behavior is achieved via a training objective $\mathcal{L}_{struct}$. In training, we sample a displacement map $\mathbf{x}^d_{sty}$ and a distance field $\mathbf{x}^s$ from different faces to simulate user editing, and encode them jointly to synthesize the result as

$$\widehat{\mathbf{x}}_{mix} = G(E(\mathbf{x}^d_{sty}, \mathbf{x}^s)). \tag{5}$$

We use the distance field loss to enforce the model to preserve the input distance field $\mathbf{x}^s$

$$\mathcal{L}_{struct} = \mathbb{E}_{\mathbf{x}, \mathbf{x}_{sty}}[\lambda_{df} \ell_{df}(\widehat{\mathbf{x}}_{mix}, \mathbf{x})] \tag{6}$$

Notice that because the ground truth edited displacement map is unknown, here we can not use ℓ_{FM} as Eq. 2 did. However, an adversarial objective in Eq. 11 supervises the generated displacement map to be realistic. In the supplementary material, we provide more discussion on wrinkle line editing.

6   Expression and Age Editing

As a deep generative model, the detail model acquires a semantic understanding of the modeled data in its latent space [34], thus enabling expression and age semantic editing. To be compatible with the facial animation pipeline and intuitive to control, instead of exposing the latent space to the user, we adopt blendshape weights and age values as control parameters. Blendshape weights [40] are commonly used in expression animation, where each dimension corresponds to the activation strength of a predefined basic expression. This definition makes it both compatible with the large-scale mesh animation and easy to tune by hand. When a user edits the expression or age of facial details, first, she specifies the target blendshape weights or age. Then, the detail model generates edited details from transformed latent codes. For training, we get each sample's blendshape weights and age, which are usually available in a scan dataset. Note that these annotations are *not* used in testing. As detailed below, we design the training to achieve effective expression and age editing while maintaining the identity.

Edit-Guided Transformation Modules. We add two networks that output latent direction vectors, which permit semantic editing while better maintaining identity [34,84]. Specifically, given a latent code $\mathbf{z}$ of original details and target blendshape weights $\widetilde{\mathbf{e}}$, the expression transformation module regresses a direction vector. It is then added to the latent code to decode a sample that exhibits desired expression changes. Age editing is done similarly, and they can be formulated as

$$\widehat{\mathbf{x}}_{exp} = G(\mathbf{z} + T_{exp}(\mathbf{z}, \widetilde{\mathbf{e}})) \tag{7}$$

$$\widehat{\mathbf{x}}_{age} = G(\mathbf{z} + T_{age}(\mathbf{z}, \widetilde{a})) \tag{8}$$

where $\widetilde{\mathbf{e}}$ and $\widetilde{a}$ are the target expression and age, T_{exp} and T_{age} are the two transformation modules to model the difference between the target and the current latent codes, $\widehat{\mathbf{x}}_{exp}$ and $\widehat{\mathbf{x}}_{age}$ are the decoded samples that exhibit specified expression and age changes. Experiments in Sect. 7.2 demonstrate that by using transformation modules, we can achieve both accurate representation and effective editing of details.

Expression- and Age-Specific Discriminator Outputs. To supervise the editing using expression and age annotations, we modify the discriminator to separately output expression and age information in a multi-task manner [22,50]. It assumes the dataset is divided into n_{exp} key expressions and n_{age} evenly spaced age groups, and outputs a vector of length $n_{exp}+n_{age}$. Each element in the vector describes whether the sample exhibits its corresponding expression or stays in its age group. Specifically, if we want the sample to exhibit the ith expression $\mathbf{e}_*$ and in the jth age group a_*, the ith and $n_{exp}+j$th output $D_{\mathbf{e}_*}$ and D_{a_*} will be used to formulate the adversarial loss as

$$\ell_{GAN}^{Fake}(\mathbf{x}_*, \mathbf{e}_*, a_*) = \log(1 - D_{\mathbf{e}_*}(\mathbf{x}_*)) + \log(1 - D_{a_*}(\mathbf{x}_*)) \tag{9}$$

$$\ell_{GAN}^{Real}(\mathbf{x}_*, \mathbf{e}_*, a_*) = \log(D_{\mathbf{e}_*}(\mathbf{x}_*)) + \log(D_{a_*}(\mathbf{x}_*)) \tag{10}$$

where the first term of both Eq. 9 and 10 enforces sample $\mathbf{x}_*$ to exhibit expression $\mathbf{e}_*$, and the second is to constrain age a_*.

We want the reconstructed sample $\widehat{\mathbf{x}}_{rec}$ (Eq. 1) and the mix-generated sample $\widehat{\mathbf{x}}_{mix}$ (Eq. 5) to preserve the original expression $\mathbf{e}$ and age a, and the edited samples (Eq. 7 and 8) to reach target expression or age while keeping the other attribute fixed. The total adversarial objective can be formulated as

$$\mathcal{L}_{GAN} = \mathbb{E}_{\mathbf{x}, \mathbf{x}_{exp}, \widetilde{a}, \mathbf{x}_{sty}}[\ell_{GAN}^{Real}(\mathbf{x}, \mathbf{e}, a) + \ell_{GAN}^{Fake}(\widehat{\mathbf{x}}_{rec}, \mathbf{e}, a)$$
$$+\ell_{GAN}^{Fake}(\widehat{\mathbf{x}}_{exp}, \widetilde{\mathbf{e}}, a) + \ell_{GAN}^{Fake}(\widehat{\mathbf{x}}_{age}, \mathbf{e}, \widetilde{a}) + \ell_{GAN}^{Fake}(\widehat{\mathbf{x}}_{mix}, \mathbf{e}, a)] \tag{11}$$

Maintaining the Identity. To learn a meaningful latent space and maintain the identity when no editing or expression editing is performed, during training, we sample a pair of samples $\mathbf{x}, \mathbf{x}_{exp} \sim \mathcal{X}$ of the same person, with different expressions $\mathbf{e} = e(\mathbf{x})$ and $\widetilde{\mathbf{e}} = e(\mathbf{x}_{exp})$ respectively. We enforce the encoded latent code can reconstruct the input $\mathbf{x}$, and the expression-edited latent code obtained in Eq. 7 can reconstruct $\mathbf{x}_{exp}$ using the reconstruction loss ℓ_{rec} defined in Eq. 2:

$$\mathcal{L}_{rec} = \mathbb{E}_{\mathbf{x}, \mathbf{x}_{exp}}[\ell_{rec}(\widehat{\mathbf{x}}_{rec}, \mathbf{x}) + \ell_{rec}(\widehat{\mathbf{x}}_{exp}, \mathbf{x}_{exp})]. \tag{12}$$

Notice that we do not have the data of the same subject at different ages. Thus, we use a cycle consistency objective to maintain original identity during age editing. During training, we randomly sample a target age $\widetilde{a} \sim \mathcal{U}(16, 70)$, and perform age transformation according to Eq. 8. Then we enforce the reconstruction of original details when transforming the edited sample back to the original age a as

$$\mathcal{L}_{cyc} = \mathbb{E}_{\mathbf{x}, \widetilde{a}} \left[\ell_{rec} \Big(G(E(\widehat{x}_{age}) + T_{age}(E(\widehat{x}_{age}), a)), \mathbf{x} \Big) \right] \tag{13}$$

Full Objective. The total training objective can be formulated as

$$\min_{E,T_{age},T_{exp},G} \max_{D_*} \mathcal{L}_{rec} + \lambda_{GAN}\mathcal{L}_{GAN}$$
$$+\mathcal{L}_{struct} + \lambda_{cyc}\mathcal{L}_{cyc} \tag{14}$$

7   Experiments

Implementation Details. We use the publicly available dataset from [79] for training, which is randomly divided into 14,930 training and 1,623 test samples. We model the displacement map at 256×256 resolution, which we find is enough to encode wrinkle-level details. Displacement maps and distance fields are normalized to approximately the same standard deviation to balance the discriminator's attention and improve adversarial training. From the training dataset, we obtain 51-dimensional blendshape weights from the known expression and one-dimensional age from the demographic information. The expression and age transformation modules are parameterized by 4-layer MLPs. We use the network architecture of G and D in [37] and E in [55]. Following [37], our model uses a non-saturating adversarial loss with R1 regularization [52] to stabilize training. As we use a multi-task discriminator, $\mathbf{x}_{sty}^d$ and $\mathbf{x}^s$ in Eq. 5 are drawn from the same expression and the same age group. We set $\lambda_{df} = 2.5$, $\lambda_{GAN} = 0.05$ and $\lambda_{cyc} = 1$ to balance the loss terms. The loss terms can be categorized into groups, and each group shares the same weight, leading to only three above weights. We set $n_{exp} = 20$ and $n_{age} = 7$ during the training. Our model is trained on two RTX 3090 s s with a batch size of 16 for 17,700k iterations and takes 21 ms to encode-decode a displacement map at test time.

Detail Quantitative Metrics. Previous methods often conduct qualitative studies alone to evaluate facial details. In addition, we propose to use LPIPS [82] as a quantitative metric to measure the similarity between two displacement maps. While LPIPS is originally for measuring natural RGB images, we find it effective to measure the similarity of facial details because it mainly measures the visual similarity and semantic accuracy of wrinkles instead of requiring per-pixel alignment. In the supplementary material, we also investigate the behavior difference between LPIPS and L1.

7.1   Comparisons

We compare our method with FaceScape [79] and DECA [25], which are SOTAs that can both represent facial details and their changes with expressions. During the comparison, all the methods first obtain a detail representation from an input image, and then use the representation and input target expression parameters to generate details with a different expression. We use images captured in the dataset from [74] as test inputs, as it has images of various facial details caused by expressions. A reference image with the same expression as the target expression parameters is shown for visualization, and is not inputted to any method. When animating to other expressions, both the large-scale mesh and details deform according to the expression parameters. We conduct the comparison via (1) qualitative study, (2) user study and (3) quantitative study using LPIPS. Please see the supplementary material for the user study and quantitative comparison.

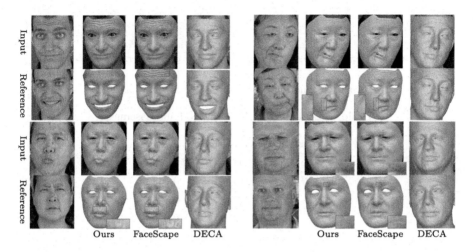

Fig. 5. Comparison with previous methods on expression editing.

Qualitative Study. For each test case in Fig. 5, the first row shows the details generated from the original representation, and the second row shows the generated details with the target expression. FaceScape can generate plausible dynamic details of the target expression, but it assumes all the details in the input images are static. Here, dynamic details refer to the details that change with expressions, while static details mean the ones invariant to expressions. Therefore, it cannot correctly animate the dynamic details presented in the input image, causing artifacts (denoted by red boxes). DECA can properly animate the facial details in arbitrary input expressions. However, its details are less person-specific, and some age-related wrinkles are absent. Our method can both generate more diverse dynamic details than other methods (top right, bottom right) and properly animate the input dynamic details. Specifically, in the bottom-left sample, our model is shown to learn to activate dynamic details according to facial muscles, by deactivating the lip region wrinkles while keeping wrinkles between eyebrows.

7.2   Ablation Studies

We evaluate three key components of our proposed method by comparing our model with three baselines with ablated components: (1) **Feature matching loss** is evaluated by the w/o ℓ_{FM} setting where we replace the feature matching loss with L1 loss. (2) **Distance field** is evaluated by the w/o df setting where use detail lines instead of distance fields for joint modeling. (3) **Transformation modules** are evaluated by the w/o $T_{exp,age}$ setting where we directly concatenate the expression and age parameters to the latent code before decoding.

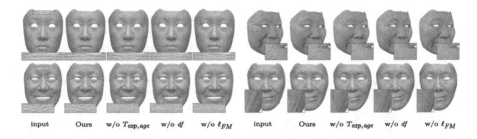

Fig. 6. Reconstruction results of our model and baselines.

Table 1. LPIPS error of our method and baselines.

Method	Reconstruction	Editing
w/o ℓ_{FM}	0.1604	0.1755
w/o df	0.1214	0.1481
w/o $T_{exp,age}$	0.1263	0.1456
Ours	**0.1134**	**0.1455**

We use the reconstruction LPIPS and the editing LPIPS to measure the ability to represent input details and make suitable expression changes of facial details. Specifically, we first encode the input displacement map to a latent code. We then decode a displacement map using the encoded latent code and calculate the reconstruction error using LPIPS. We also transform each sample to other expressions and evaluate the LPIPS between the generated details and the ground truth. The test split of the dataset from [79] is used, because it provides ground truth details of the same person with different expressions.

The average LPIPS errors are shown in Table 1, and some reconstruction samples are shown in Fig. 6. From the results, w/o ℓ_{FM} and w/o df give higher errors in both reconstruction and expression editing. They result in missing or less pronounced wrinkle details than the full model. This is because in training, they give a stronger penalization on the reconstructed wrinkles that are not pixel-aligned with the input. W/o $T_{exp,age}$ generates some details that are related to the expression, but not in the input (top left, bottom right). Some individual-specific wrinkles are also absent in its results (bottom left, top right). These lead to a larger reconstruction error.

7.3   Applications

Our model supports meaningful and intuitive ways to animate and manipulate facial details, by changing two semantic factors, expression and age, that often cause facial detail changes. Besides, by allowing directly editing wrinkle lines, we give users more flexibility to edit facial details. More application results are shown in our supplementary video.

Age Progression. Our method supports continuous age editing by specifying target age values, as shown in Fig. 7. We can both rejuvenate the input (left column) and make the input older (right column). Diverse types of wrinkles, including forehead wrinkles (top right), eye bags (middle right), and crow's feet (bottom right), can be generated by our model. Our model works with various non-neutral expressions, and can synthesize and remove details while being compatible with the person's expression and identity. One interesting phenomenon is that we find our model learns to generate nasolabial folds at an earlier age than other details like forehead wrinkles (top right), which is consistent with the biological aging process [58].

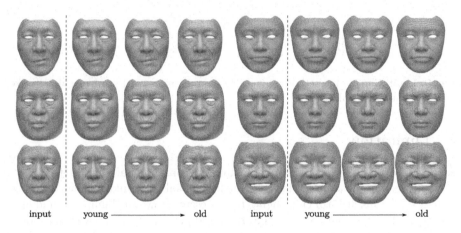

Fig. 7. Age progression synthesized by our SEMM.

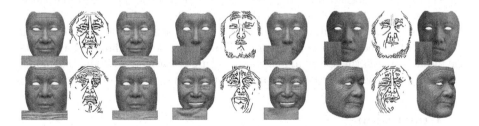

Fig. 8. Users can add or remove details by editing detail lines. Drawn lines are shown in green and erased lines are shown in red. (Color figure online)

Wrinkle Line Editing. Our model allows users to edit facial details intuitively by modifying wrinkle lines. Specifically, users directly edit the detail lines extracted from the original displacement map, then the edited lines are converted to a distance field to generate edited details together with the original displacement map. We can effectively synthesize new wrinkles and remove existing ones by drawing and erasing lines, as shown in Fig. 8. As the edited facial details are still within the representation space of our latent code, they can be further edited using expression and age editing, as shown in Fig. 1.

Blendshape Animation. Our model supports expression animation using blendshape weights. The expression editing results shown in Fig. 5 are also obtained by manipulating the blendshape weights. It has already indicated that our method can remove the dynamic details of the original expression, generate dynamic details of the new expression and keep the static details. For animation results, please refer to our supplementary video.

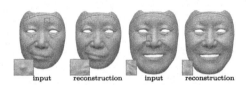

input   reconstruction   input   reconstruction

Fig. 9. Limitation of our method. Our model cannot reconstruct some rare details like moles and subtle wrinkles.

8 Limitation

As a data-driven method, our model cannot reconstruct rare details that have not been seen in the training data, like moles and subtle wrinkles shown in Fig. 9. Pore-level details are still challenging to represent. However, bumps around eyebrows and hairs, which are from the training data, are represented in our model because of its data-driven nature.

As a detail model, we only modify details during age editing. Because there does not exist a method to change the age of a large-scale mesh automatically, we fix the mesh when evaluating the detail aging effects in Fig. 7. This can often generate satisfactory results, but sometimes large nasolabial folds are located in the mesh. If in need, our model is compatible with an artist who manually edits the mesh to match the specified age value. Future research can extend our model by simultaneously editing facial details and the mesh.

9 Conclusion

In this work, we augment morphable face models in representing detail shape by proposing a detail model. We propose a detail structure representation based on the distance field of wrinkle lines. It is then combined with displacement maps in an autoencoder to represent and edit wrinkle structure. Two transformation modules enable expression and age editing while maintaining identity. Our model produces detail animation compatible with the large scale, achieves better expression control than previous methods qualitatively and quantitatively, and enables unprecedented age and wrinkle line editing. These properties make the model useful in the production pipeline of high-fidelity facial animation.

Acknowledgements. This work was supported by Beijing Natural Science Foundation (JQ19015), the NSFC (No. 62021002, 61727808), the National Key R&D Program of China 2018YFA0704000, the Key Research and Development Project of Tibet Autonomous Region (XZ202101ZY0019G). This work was supported by THUIBCS, Tsinghua University and BLBCI, Beijing Municipal Education Commission. Feng Xu is the corresponding author.

References

1. Abrevaya, V.F., Boukhayma, A., Wuhrer, S., Boyer, E.: A decoupled 3D facial shape model by adversarial training. In: Proceedings of the IEEE/CVF International Conference on Computer Vision, pp. 9419–9428 (2019)
2. Abrevaya, V.F., Wuhrer, S., Boyer, E.: Multilinear autoencoder for 3D face model learning. In: 2018 IEEE Winter Conference on Applications of Computer Vision (WACV), pp. 1–9. IEEE (2018)
3. Amberg, B., Paysan, P., Vetter, T.: Weight, sex, and facial expressions: on the manipulation of attributes in generative 3D face models. In: Bebis, G., et al. (eds.) ISVC 2009. LNCS, vol. 5875, pp. 875–885. Springer, Heidelberg (2009). https://doi.org/10.1007/978-3-642-10331-5_81
4. Bagautdinov, T., Wu, C., Saragih, J., Fua, P., Sheikh, Y.: Modeling facial geometry using compositional VAEs. In: Proceedings of the IEEE Conference on Computer Vision and Pattern Recognition, pp. 3877–3886 (2018)
5. Bando, Y., Kuratate, T., Nishita, T.: A simple method for modeling wrinkles on human skin. In: Proceedings of 10th Pacific Conference on Computer Graphics and Applications, pp. 166–175. IEEE (2002)
6. Bermano, A.H., et al.: Facial performance enhancement using dynamic shape space analysis. ACM Trans. Graph. (TOG) **33**(2), 1–12 (2014)
7. Bickel, B., Lang, M., Botsch, M., Otaduy, M.A., Gross, M.H.: Pose-space animation and transfer of facial details. In: Symposium on Computer Animation, pp. 57–66 (2008)
8. Blanz, V., Vetter, T.: A morphable model for the synthesis of 3D faces. In: Proceedings of the 26th Annual Conference on Computer Graphics and Interactive Techniques, pp. 187–194 (1999)
9. Boissieux, L., Kiss, G., Thalmann, N.M., Kalra, P.: Simulation of skin aging and wrinkles with cosmetics insight. In: Magnenat-Thalmann, N., Thalmann, D., Arnaldi, B. (eds.) Computer Animation and Simulation 2000, pp. 15–27. Springer, Vienna (2000). https://doi.org/10.1007/978-3-7091-6344-3_2
10. Bolkart, T., Wuhrer, S.: A groupwise multilinear correspondence optimization for 3D faces. In: Proceedings of the IEEE International Conference on Computer Vision, pp. 3604–3612 (2015)
11. Booth, J., Roussos, A., Zafeiriou, S., Ponniah, A., Dunaway, D.: A 3D morphable model learnt from 10,000 faces. In: Proceedings of the IEEE Conference on Computer Vision and Pattern Recognition, pp. 5543–5552 (2016)
12. Bouritsas, G., Bokhnyak, S., Ploumpis, S., Bronstein, M., Zafeiriou, S.: Neural 3D morphable models: spiral convolutional networks for 3D shape representation learning and generation. In: Proceedings of the IEEE/CVF International Conference on Computer Vision, pp. 7213–7222 (2019)

13. Brunton, A., Bolkart, T., Wuhrer, S.: Multilinear wavelets: a statistical shape space for human faces. In: Fleet, D., Pajdla, T., Schiele, B., Tuytelaars, T. (eds.) ECCV 2014. LNCS, vol. 8689, pp. 297–312. Springer, Cham (2014). https://doi.org/10.1007/978-3-319-10590-1_20

14. Cao, C., Bradley, D., Zhou, K., Beeler, T.: Real-time high-fidelity facial performance capture. ACM Trans. Graph. (ToG) **34**(4), 1–9 (2015)

15. Cao, C., Hou, Q., Zhou, K.: Displaced dynamic expression regression for real-time facial tracking and animation. ACM Trans. Graph. (TOG) **33**(4), 1–10 (2014)

16. Cao, C., Weng, Y., Zhou, S., Tong, Y., Zhou, K.: Facewarehouse: a 3D facial expression database for visual computing. IEEE Trans. Visual Comput. Graphics **20**(3), 413–425 (2013)

17. Chandran, P., Bradley, D., Gross, M., Beeler, T.: Semantic deep face models. In: 2020 International Conference on 3D Vision (3DV), pp. 345–354. IEEE (2020)

18. Chen, A., Chen, Z., Zhang, G., Mitchell, K., Yu, J.: Photo-realistic facial details synthesis from single image. In: Proceedings of the IEEE/CVF International Conference on Computer Vision, pp. 9429–9439 (2019)

19. Chen, Y., Wu, F., Wang, Z., Song, Y., Ling, Y., Bao, L.: Self-supervised learning of detailed 3D face reconstruction. IEEE Trans. Image Process. **29**, 8696–8705 (2020)

20. Cheng, S., Bronstein, M., Zhou, Y., Kotsia, I., Pantic, M., Zafeiriou, S.: MeshGAN: non-linear 3D morphable models of faces. arXiv preprint arXiv:1903.10384 (2019)

21. Chibane, J., Mir, A., Pons-Moll, G.: Neural unsigned distance fields for implicit function learning. In: Advances in Neural Information Processing Systems (NeurIPS), December 2020

22. Choi, Y., Uh, Y., Yoo, J., Ha, J.W.: StarGAN V2: diverse image synthesis for multiple domains. In: Proceedings of the IEEE/CVF Conference on Computer Vision and Pattern Recognition, pp. 8188–8197 (2020)

23. Deng, Q., Ma, L., Jin, A., Bi, H., Le, B.H., Deng, Z.: Plausible 3D face wrinkle generation using variational autoencoders. IEEE Trans. Vis. Comput. Graph. **01**, 1–1 (2021)

24. Egger, B., et al.: 3D morphable face models-past, present, and future. ACM Trans. Graph. (TOG) **39**(5), 1–38 (2020)

25. Feng, Y., Feng, H., Black, M.J., Bolkart, T.: Learning an animatable detailed 3D face model from in-the-wild images. ACM Trans. Graph. (TOG) **40**(4), 1–13 (2021)

26. Fyffe, G., Jones, A., Alexander, O., Ichikari, R., Debevec, P.: Driving high-resolution facial scans with video performance capture. ACM Trans. Graph. (TOG) **34**(1), 1–14 (2014)

27. Garrido, P., Valgaerts, L., Wu, C., Theobalt, C.: Reconstructing detailed dynamic face geometry from monocular video. ACM Trans. Graph. **32**(6), 158–1 (2013)

28. Gerig, T., et al.: Morphable face models-an open framework. In: 2018 13th IEEE International Conference on Automatic Face & Gesture Recognition (FG 2018), pp. 75–82. IEEE (2018)

29. Golovinskiy, A., Matusik, W., Pfister, H., Rusinkiewicz, S., Funkhouser, T.: A statistical model for synthesis of detailed facial geometry. ACM Trans. Graph. (TOG) **25**(3), 1025–1034 (2006)

30. Guo, Y., Cai, J., Jiang, B., Zheng, J., et al.: CNN-based real-time dense face reconstruction with inverse-rendered photo-realistic face images. IEEE Trans. Pattern Anal. Mach. Intell. **41**(6), 1294–1307 (2018)

31. Huynh, L., et al.: Mesoscopic facial geometry inference using deep neural networks. In: Proceedings of the IEEE Conference on Computer Vision and Pattern Recognition, pp. 8407–8416 (2018)

32. Ichim, A.E., Kadleček, P., Kavan, L., Pauly, M.: Phace: physics-based face modeling and animation. ACM Trans. Graph. (TOG) **36**(4), 1–14 (2017)
33. Igarashi, T., Nishino, K., Nayar, S.K.: The Appearance of Human Skin: A Survey. Now Publishers Inc. (2007)
34. Jahanian, A., Chai, L., Isola, P.: On the "steerability" of generative adversarial networks. In: International Conference on Learning Representations (2020)
35. Jiang, L., Zhang, J., Deng, B., Li, H., Liu, L.: 3D face reconstruction with geometry details from a single image. IEEE Trans. Image Process. **27**(10), 4756–4770 (2018)
36. Jiang, Z.H., Wu, Q., Chen, K., Zhang, J.: Disentangled representation learning for 3d face shape. In: Proceedings of the IEEE/CVF Conference on Computer Vision and Pattern Recognition, pp. 11957–11966 (2019)
37. Karras, T., Laine, S., Aittala, M., Hellsten, J., Lehtinen, J., Aila, T.: Analyzing and improving the image quality of StyleGAN. In: Proceedings of the IEEE/CVF Conference on Computer Vision and Pattern Recognition, pp. 8110–8119 (2020)
38. Kim, H.J., Oeztireli, A.C., Shin, I.K., Gross, M., Choi, S.M.: Interactive generation of realistic facial wrinkles from sketchy drawings. In: Computer Graphics Forum, vol. 34, pp. 179–191. Wiley Online Library (2015)
39. Lau, M., Chai, J., Xu, Y.Q., Shum, H.Y.: Face poser: interactive modeling of 3D facial expressions using facial priors. ACM Trans. Graph. (TOG) **29**(1), 1–17 (2009)
40. Lewis, J.P., Anjyo, K., Rhee, T., Zhang, M., Pighin, F.H., Deng, Z.: Practice and theory of blendshape facial models. Eurographics (State Art Rep.) **1**(8), 2 (2014)
41. Li, D., Yang, J., Kreis, K., Torralba, A., Fidler, S.: Semantic segmentation with generative models: semi-supervised learning and strong out-of-domain generalization. In: Proceedings of the IEEE/CVF Conference on Computer Vision and Pattern Recognition, pp. 8300–8311 (2021)
42. Li, J., Kuang, Z., Zhao, Y., He, M., Bladin, K., Li, H.: Dynamic facial asset and rig generation from a single scan. ACM Trans. Graph. **39**(6), 215–1 (2020)
43. Li, J., Xu, W., Cheng, Z., Xu, K., Klein, R.: Lightweight wrinkle synthesis for 3D facial modeling and animation. Comput. Aided Des. **58**, 117–122 (2015)
44. Li, M., Yin, B., Kong, D., Luo, X.: Modeling expressive wrinkles of face for animation. In: Fourth International Conference on Image and Graphics (ICIG 2007), pp. 874–879. IEEE (2007)
45. Li, R., et al.: Learning formation of physically-based face attributes. In: Proceedings of the IEEE/CVF Conference on Computer Vision and Pattern Recognition, pp. 3410–3419 (2020)
46. Li, T., Bolkart, T., Black, M.J., Li, H., Romero, J.: Learning a model of facial shape and expression from 4D scans. ACM Trans. Graph. **36**(6) (2017)
47. Li, Y.B., Xiao, H., Zhang, S.Y.: The wrinkle generation method for facial reconstruction based on extraction of partition wrinkle line features and fractal interpolation. In: Fourth International Conference on Image and Graphics (ICIG 2007), pp. 933–937. IEEE (2007)
48. Li, Y., Ma, L., Fan, H., Mitchell, K.: Feature-preserving detailed 3D face reconstruction from a single image. In: Proceedings of the 15th ACM SIGGRAPH European Conference on Visual Media Production, pp. 1–9 (2018)
49. Li, Y., Chen, X., Wu, F., Zha, Z.J.: Linestofacephoto: face photo generation from lines with conditional self-attention generative adversarial networks. In: Proceedings of the 27th ACM International Conference on Multimedia, pp. 2323–2331 (2019)

50. Liu, M.Y., et al.: Few-shot unsupervised image-to-image translation. In: Proceedings of the IEEE/CVF International Conference on Computer Vision, pp. 10551–10560 (2019)
51. Ma, L., Deng, Z.: Real-time hierarchical facial performance capture. In: Proceedings of the ACM SIGGRAPH Symposium on Interactive 3D Graphics and Games, pp. 1–10 (2019)
52. Mescheder, L., Geiger, A., Nowozin, S.: Which training methods for GANs do actually converge? In: International Conference on Machine Learning, pp. 3481–3490. PMLR (2018)
53. Neumann, T., Varanasi, K., Wenger, S., Wacker, M., Magnor, M., Theobalt, C.: Sparse localized deformation components. ACM Trans. Graph. (TOG) 32(6), 1–10 (2013)
54. Park, J.J., Florence, P., Straub, J., Newcombe, R., Lovegrove, S.: DeepSDF: learning continuous signed distance functions for shape representation. In: The IEEE Conference on Computer Vision and Pattern Recognition (CVPR), June 2019
55. Park, T., et al.: Swapping autoencoder for deep image manipulation. Adv. Neural. Inf. Process. Syst. 33, 7198–7211 (2020)
56. Parke, F.I.: A parametric model for human faces. The University of Utah (1974)
57. Paysan, P.: Statistical modeling of facial aging based on 3D scans. Ph.D. thesis, University of Basel (2010)
58. Radlanski, R.J., Wesker, K.: The Face: Pictorial Atlas of Clinical Anatomy. Quintessence Publishing (2012)
59. Ranjan, A., Bolkart, T., Sanyal, S., Black, M.J.: Generating 3D faces using convolutional mesh autoencoders. In: Proceedings of the European Conference on Computer Vision (ECCV), pp. 704–720 (2018)
60. Richardson, E., Sela, M., Or-El, R., Kimmel, R.: Learning detailed face reconstruction from a single image. In: Proceedings of the IEEE Conference on Computer Vision and Pattern Recognition, pp. 1259–1268 (2017)
61. Sela, M., Richardson, E., Kimmel, R.: Unrestricted facial geometry reconstruction using image-to-image translation. In: Proceedings of the IEEE International Conference on Computer Vision, pp. 1576–1585 (2017)
62. Sengupta, S., Kanazawa, A., Castillo, C.D., Jacobs, D.W.: SfSNet: learning shape, reflectance and illuminance of faces in the wild. In: Proceedings of the IEEE Conference on Computer Vision and Pattern Recognition, pp. 6296–6305 (2018)
63. Serup, J., Jemec, G.B., Grove, G.L.: Handbook of Non-Invasive Methods and the Skin. CRC Press, Boca Raton (2006)
64. Shamai, G., Slossberg, R., Kimmel, R.: Synthesizing facial photometries and corresponding geometries using generative adversarial networks. ACM Trans. Multimedia Comput. Commun. Appl. (TOMM) 15(3s), 1–24 (2019)
65. Shi, F., Wu, H.T., Tong, X., Chai, J.: Automatic acquisition of high-fidelity facial performances using monocular videos. ACM Trans. Graph. (TOG) 33(6), 1–13 (2014)
66. Shin, I.K., Öztireli, A.C., Kim, H.J., Beeler, T., Gross, M., Choi, S.M.: Extraction and transfer of facial expression wrinkles for facial performance enhancement. In: PG (Short Papers) (2014)
67. Simo-Serra, E., Iizuka, S., Sasaki, K., Ishikawa, H.: Learning to simplify: fully convolutional networks for rough sketch cleanup. ACM Trans. Graph. (TOG) 35(4), 1–11 (2016)
68. Slossberg, R., Shamai, G., Kimmel, R.: High quality facial surface and texture synthesis via generative adversarial networks. In: Proceedings of the European Conference on Computer Vision (ECCV) Workshops (2018)

69. Suwajanakorn, S., Kemelmacher-Shlizerman, I., Seitz, S.M.: Total moving face reconstruction. In: Fleet, D., Pajdla, T., Schiele, B., Tuytelaars, T. (eds.) ECCV 2014. LNCS, vol. 8692, pp. 796–812. Springer, Cham (2014). https://doi.org/10.1007/978-3-319-10593-2_52

70. Taubin, G.: A signal processing approach to fair surface design. In: Proceedings of the 22nd Annual Conference on Computer Graphics and Interactive Techniques, SIGGRAPH 1995, pp. 351–358. Association for Computing Machinery, New York (1995). https://doi.org/10.1145/218380.218473

71. Tran, L., Liu, F., Liu, X.: Towards high-fidelity nonlinear 3D face morphable model. In: Proceedings of the IEEE/CVF Conference on Computer Vision and Pattern Recognition, pp. 1126–1135 (2019)

72. Vlasic, D., Brand, M., Pfister, H., Popovic, J.: Face transfer with multilinear models. In: ACM SIGGRAPH 2006 Courses, pp. 24-es (2006)

73. Wang, T.C., Liu, M.Y., Zhu, J.Y., Tao, A., Kautz, J., Catanzaro, B.: High-resolution image synthesis and semantic manipulation with conditional GANs. In: Proceedings of the IEEE Conference on Computer Vision and Pattern Recognition, pp. 8798–8807 (2018)

74. Wang, Z., Yu, X., Lu, M., Wang, Q., Qian, C., Xu, F.: Single image portrait relighting via explicit multiple reflectance channel modeling. ACM Trans. Graph. (TOG) 39(6), 1–13 (2020)

75. Werner, D., Al-Hamadi, A., Werner, P.: Truncated signed distance function: experiments on voxel size. In: Campilho, A., Kamel, M. (eds.) ICIAR 2014. LNCS, vol. 8815, pp. 357–364. Springer, Cham (2014). https://doi.org/10.1007/978-3-319-11755-3_40

76. Wu, C., Bradley, D., Gross, M., Beeler, T.: An anatomically-constrained local deformation model for monocular face capture. ACM Trans. Graph. (TOG) 35(4), 1–12 (2016)

77. Wu, Y., Kalra, P., Moccozet, L., Magnenat-Thalmann, N.: Simulating wrinkles and skin aging. Vis. Comput. 15(4), 183–198 (1999)

78. Xu, F., Chai, J., Liu, Y., Tong, X.: Controllable high-fidelity facial performance transfer. ACM Trans. Graph. (TOG) 33(4), 1–11 (2014)

79. Yang, H., et al.: FaceScape: a large-scale high quality 3D face dataset and detailed riggable 3D face prediction. In: Proceedings of the IEEE/CVF Conference on Computer Vision and Pattern Recognition, pp. 601–610 (2020)

80. Yenamandra, T., et al.: i3DMM: deep implicit 3D morphable model of human heads. In: Proceedings of the IEEE/CVF Conference on Computer Vision and Pattern Recognition, pp. 12803–12813 (2021)

81. Zeng, X., Peng, X., Qiao, Y.: DF2Net: a dense-fine-finer network for detailed 3D face reconstruction. In: Proceedings of the IEEE/CVF International Conference on Computer Vision, pp. 2315–2324 (2019)

82. Zhang, R., Isola, P., Efros, A.A., Shechtman, E., Wang, O.: The unreasonable effectiveness of deep features as a perceptual metric. In: Proceedings of the IEEE Conference on Computer Vision and Pattern Recognition, pp. 586–595 (2018)

83. Zhang, Y., et al.: Datasetgan: efficient labeled data factory with minimal human effort. In: Proceedings of the IEEE/CVF Conference on Computer Vision and Pattern Recognition, pp. 10145–10155 (2021)

84. Zhuang, P., Koyejo, O.O., Schwing, A.: Enjoy your editing: controllable GANs for image editing via latent space navigation. In: International Conference on Learning Representations (2020)

MoFaNeRF: Morphable Facial Neural Radiance Field

Yiyu Zhuang, Hao Zhu, Xusen Sun, and Xun Cao$^{(\boxtimes)}$

Nanjing University, Nanjing, China
{yiyu.zhuang,xusensun}@smail.nju.edu.cn, {zhuhaoese,caoxun}@nju.edu.cn

Abstract. We propose a parametric model that maps free-view images into a vector space of coded facial shape, expression and appearance with a neural radiance field, namely Morphable Facial NeRF. Specifically, MoFaNeRF takes the coded facial shape, expression and appearance along with space coordinate and view direction as input to an MLP, and outputs the radiance of the space point for photo-realistic image synthesis. Compared with conventional 3D morphable models (3DMM), MoFaNeRF shows superiority in directly synthesizing photo-realistic facial details even for eyes, mouths, and beards. Also, continuous face morphing can be easily achieved by interpolating the input shape, expression and appearance codes. By introducing identity-specific modulation and texture encoder, our model synthesizes accurate photometric details and shows strong representation ability. Our model shows strong ability on multiple applications including image-based fitting, random generation, face rigging, face editing, and novel view synthesis. Experiments show that our method achieves higher representation ability than previous parametric models, and achieves competitive performance in several applications. To the best of our knowledge, our work is the first facial parametric model built upon a neural radiance field that can be used in fitting, generation and manipulation. The code and data is available at https://github.com/zhuhao-nju/mofanerf.

Keywords: Neural radiance field · 3D morphable models · Face synthesis

1 Introduction

Modeling 3D face is a key problem to solve face-related vision tasks such as 3D face reconstruction, reenactment, parsing, and digital human. The 3D morphable model (3DMM) [2] has long been the key solution to this problem, which is a parametric model transforming the shape and texture of the faces into a vector

---

Y. Zhuang and H. Zhu—These authors contributed equally to this work.

Supplementary Information The online version contains supplementary material available at https://doi.org/10.1007/978-3-031-20062-5_16.

S. Avidan et al. (Eds.): ECCV 2022, LNCS 13663, pp. 268–285, 2022.
https://doi.org/10.1007/978-3-031-20062-5_16

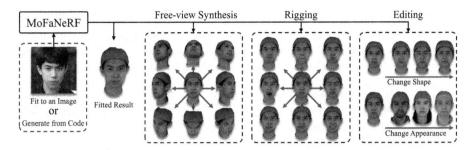

Fig. 1. We propose MoFaNeRF, which is a parametric model that can synthesize free-view images by fitting to a single image or generating from a random code. The synthesized face is *morphable* that can be rigged to a certain expression and be edited to a certain shape and appearance.

space representation. 3DMMs are powerful in representing various shapes and appearances, but require a sophisticated rendering pipeline to produce photo-realistic images. Besides, 3DMMs struggled to model non-Lambertian objects like pupils and beards. Recently, the neural radiance field (NeRF) [30] was proposed to represent the shapes and appearances of a static scene using an implicit function, which shows superiority in the task of photo-realistic free-view synthesis. The most recent progress shows that the modified NeRF can model a dynamic face [10,33,34,51], or generate diversified 3D-aware images [4,14,41]. However, there is still no method to enable NeRF with the abilities of single-view fitting, controllable generation, face rigging and editing at the same time. In summary, conventional 3DMMs are powerful in representing large-scale editable 3D faces but lack the ability of photo-realistic rendering, while NeRFs are the opposite.

To combine the best of 3DMM and NeRF, we aim at creating a facial parametric model based on the neural radiance field to have the powerful representation ability as well as excellent free-view rendering performance. However, achieving such a goal is non-trivial. The challenges come from two aspects: firstly, how to memorize and parse the very large-scale face database using a neural radiance field; secondly, how to effectively disentangle the parameters (e.g. shape, appearance, expression), which are important to support very valuable applications like face rigging and editing.

To address these challenges, we propose the Morphable Facial NeRF (MoFaNeRF) that maps free-view images into a vector space of coded facial identity, expression, and appearance using a neural radiance field. Our model is trained on two large-scale 3D face datasets, FaceScape [54,60] and HeadSpcae [7] separately. FaceScape contains 359 available faces with 20 expressions each, and HeadSpace contains 1004 faces in the neutral expression. The training strategy is elaborately designed to disentangle the shape, appearance and expression in the parametric space. The identity-specific modulation and texture encoder are proposed to maximize the representation ability of the neural network. Compared to traditional 3DMMs, MoFaNeRF shows superiority in synthesizing photo-realistic images even for pupils, mouth, and beards which can not be modeled well by 3D mesh models. Furthermore, we also propose the methods to use our model to achieve image-based fitting, random face generation, face rigging, face editing, and view extrapolation. Our contributions can be summarized as follows:

- To the best of our knowledge, we propose the first parametric model that maps free-view facial images into a vector space using a neural radiance field and is free from the traditional 3D morphable model.
- The neural network for parametric mapping is elaborately designed to maximize the solution space to represent diverse identities and expressions. The disentangled parameters of shape, appearance and expression can be interpolated to achieve a continuous and morphable facial synthesis.
- We present to use our model for multiple applications like image-based fitting, view extrapolation, face editing, and face rigging. Our model achieves competitive performance compared to state-of-the-art methods.

2   Related Work

As our work is a parametric model based on neural radiance field, we will review the related work of 3D morphable model and neural radiance field respectively.

3D Morphable Model. 3DMM is a statistical model which transforms the shape and texture of the faces into a vector space representation [2]. By optimizing and editing parameters, 3DMMs can be used in multiple applications like 3D face reconstruction [53], alignment [19], animation [58], etc. We recommend referring to the recent survey [9] for a comprehensive review of 3DMM. To build a 3DMM, traditional approaches first capture a large number of 3D facial meshes, then align them into a uniform topology representation, and finally process them with principal component analysis algorithm [3,17,25,47,54,60]. The parameter of the 3DMM can be further disengaged into multiple dimensions like identity, expression, appearance, and poses. In recent years, several works tried to enhance the representation power of 3DMM by using a non-linear mapping [1,6,42–45], which is more powerful in representing detailed shape and appearance than transitional linear mapping. However, they still suffer from the mesh representation which is hard to model fine geometry of pupils, eyelashes and hairs. Besides, traditional 3DMMs require sophisticated rendering pipelines to render photo-realistic images. By contrast, our model doesn't explicitly generate shape but directly synthesizes photo-realistic free-view images even for pupils, inner-mouth and beards.

Very recently, Yenamandra *et al.* [55] proposed to build the 3DMM with an implicit function representing facial shape and appearance. They used a neural network to learn a signed distance field(SDF) of 64 faces, which can model the whole head with hair. Similarly, our model is also formulated as an implicit function but very different from SDF. SDF still models shape while our method focuses on view synthesis and releases constraints of the shape, outperforming SDF in rendering performance by a large margin.

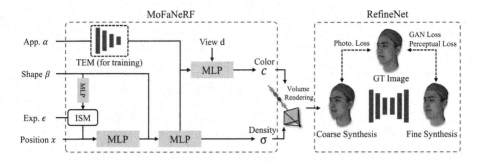

Fig. 2. MoFaNeRF takes appearance code α, shape code β, expression code ϵ, position code $\mathbf{x}$ and view direction $\mathbf{d}$ as input, synthesizing a coarse result which is then refined by a RefineNet. As shown in the right bottom corner, MoFaNeRF can be used in generating (synthesize free-view images given parameters) or fitting (optimize for parameters given a single image).

Neural Radiance Field. NeRF [30] was proposed to model the object or scene with an impressive performance in free-view synthesis. NeRF synthesizes novel views by optimizing an underlying continuous volumetric scene function that is learned from multi-view images.

As the original NeRF is designed only for a static scene, many efforts have been devoted to reconstructing deformable objects. Aiming at the human face many methods [10, 34, 51] modeled the motion of a single human head with a designed conditional neural radiance field, extending NeRF to handle dynamic scenes from monocular or multi-view videos. Aiming at human body, several methods have been proposed by introducing human parametric model (e.g. SMPL) [5, 28, 32, 36] or skeleton [35] as prior to build NeRF for human body. For a wide range of dynamic scenarios, Park *et al.* [33] proposed to augment NeRF by optimizing an additional continuous volumetric deformation field, while Pumarola *et al.* [38] optimized an underlying deformable volumetric function. Another group of works [4, 14, 41] turned NeRF into a generative model that is trained or conditioned on certain priors, which achieves 3D-aware images synthesis from a collection of unposed 2D images. To reduce the image amount for training, many works [11, 39, 48, 56] trained the model across multiple scenes to learn a scene prior, which achieved reasonable novel view synthesis from a sparse set of views.

Different from previous NeRFs, our method is the first parametric model for facial neural radiance field trained on a large-scale multi-view face dataset. Our model supports multiple applications including random face generation, image-based fitting and facial editing, which is unavailable for previous NeRFs.

3   Morphable Facial NeRF

Morphable facial NeRF is a parametric model that maps free-view facial portraits into a continuous morphable parametric space, which is formulated as:

$$\mathcal{M} : (\mathbf{x}, \mathbf{d}, \beta, \alpha, \epsilon) \rightarrow \{\mathbf{c}, \sigma\}, \tag{1}$$

where $\mathbf{x}$ is the 3D position of a sample point; $\mathbf{d}$ is the viewing direction consisting of pitch and yaw angles; β, α, ϵ are the parameters denoting facial shape, appearance, and expression respectively; $\mathbf{c}$ and σ are the RGB color and the density used to represent the neural radiance field. In the next, we will explain $\mathbf{x}, \mathbf{d}, \mathbf{c}, \sigma$ that are referred from NeRF in Sect. 3.1, then introduce β, α, ϵ in Sect. 3.2. The network design is illustrated in Sect. 3.3 and the training details are explained in Sect. 3.4.

3.1   Neural Radiance Field

As defined in NeRF [30], the radiance field is represented as volumetric density σ and color $\mathbf{c} = (R, G, B)$. An MLP is used to predict σ and $\mathbf{c}$ from a 3D point $\mathbf{x} = (x, y, z)$ and viewing direction $\mathbf{d} = (\theta, \phi)$. Position encoding is introduced to transform the continuous inputs $\mathbf{x}$ and $\mathbf{d}$ into a high-dimensional space, which is also used in our model. The field of σ and $\mathbf{c}$ can be rendered to images using a differentiable volume rendering module. For a pixel in the posed image, a ray $\mathbf{r}$ is cast through the neural volume field from the ray origin $\mathbf{o}$ along the ray direction $\mathbf{d}$ according to the camera parameters, which is formulated as $\mathbf{r}(z) = \mathbf{o} + z\mathbf{d}$. Through sampling points along this ray, and accumulating the sampled density $\sigma(\cdot)$ and RGB values $\mathbf{c}(\cdot)$ computed by $\mathcal{F}$, the final output color $\mathbf{C}(\mathbf{r})$ of this pixel can be evaluated by:

$$\mathbf{C}(\mathbf{r}) = \int_{z_n}^{z_f} T(z)\sigma(\mathbf{r}(z))\mathbf{c}(\mathbf{r}(z), \mathbf{d})dz, \text{ where } T(z) = \exp\left(-\int_{z_n}^{z} \sigma(\mathbf{r}(s))ds\right). \tag{2}$$

$T(t)$ is defined as the accumulated transmittance along the ray from z_n to z, where z_n and z_f are near and far bounds. Through the rendered color, a photometric loss can be applied to supervise the training of the MLP.

3.2   Parametric Mapping

Our model is conditioned on the parameters to represent the identity and facial expression ϵ, and the identity is further divided into shape β and appearance α. Initially, we consider integrating β and α into a single identity code, however, we find it is hard for an MLP to memorize the huge amount of appearance information. Therefore, we propose to decouple the identity into shape and appearance. These parameters need to be disentangled to support valuable applications like face rigging and editing.

Shape parameter β represents the 3D shape of the face that is only related to the identity of the subject, like the geometry and position of the nose, eyes, mouth and overall face. A straightforward idea is to use one-hot encoding to parameterize β, while we find it suffers from redundant parameters because the similarity of large-amount faces is repeatedly expressed in one-hot code. Instead, we adopt the identity parameters of the bilinear model of FaceScape [54] as shape parameter, which is the PCA factors of the 3D mesh for each subject. The numerical variation of the identity parameter reflects the similarity between face shapes, which makes the solution space of facial shapes more efficient.

Appearance parameter α reflects photometric features like the colors of skin, lips, and pupils. Some fine-grained features are also reflected by appearance parameters, such as beard and eyelashes. Considering that the UV texture provided by FaceScape dataset is the ideal carrier to convey the appearance in a spatial-aligned UV space, we propose to encode the UV texture maps into α for training. The texture encoding module (TEM) is proposed to transfer the coded appearance information into the MLP, which is a CNN based encoder network. TEM is only used in the training phase, and we find it significantly improves the quality of synthesized images. We consider the reason is that the appearance details are well disentangled from shape and spatial-aligned, which relieves the burden of memorizing appearances for the MLP.

Expression parameter ϵ is corresponding to the motions caused by facial expressions. Previous methods [34,46] try to model the dynamic face by adding a warping vector to the position code $\mathbf{x}$, namely deformable volume. However, our experiments show that the deformable volume doesn't work in our task where too many subjects are involved in a single model. More importantly, our training data are not videos but images with discrete 20 expressions, which makes it even harder to learn a continuous warping field. By contrast, we find directly concatenating expression parameters with the position code as [10,26] causes fewer artifacts, and our identity-specific modulation (detailed in Sect. 3.3) further enhances the representation ability of expression. We are surprised to find that MLP without a warping module can still synthesize continuous and plausible interpolation for large-scale motions. We believe this is the inherent advantage of the neural radiance field over 2D-based synthesis methods.

3.3   Network Design

As shown in Fig. 2, the backbone of MoFaNeRF mainly consists of MLPs, identity-specific modulation (ISM) module and texture encoding module(TEM). These networks transform the parameters α, β, ϵ, position code $\mathbf{x}$ and viewing direction $\mathbf{d}$ into the color $\mathbf{c}$ and density σ. The predicted colors are then synthesized from $\mathbf{c}$ and σ through volume rendering. Considering that the appearance code α is only related to the color c, it is only fed into the color decoder. The expression code ϵ is concatenated to the position code after the identity-specific modulation, as it mainly reflects the motions that are intuitively modulated by shape β. The RefineNet takes the coarse image predicted by MoFaNeRF as input and synthesizes a refined face. The results presented in this paper are the refined results by default. The additional texture encoding module (TEM) is used only in the training phase, which consists of 7 convolution layers and 5 full connected layers. The detailed parameters of our network are shown in the supplementary.

To represent a large-scale multi-view face database, the capacity of the network needs to be improved by increasing the number of layers in MLP and the number of nodes in each hidden layer. The generated images indeed gets improved after enlarging the model size, but is still blurry and contains artifacts in the expressions with large motions. To further improve the performance, we present the identity-specific modulation and RefineNet.

Identity-Specific modulation (ISM). Intuitively, facial expressions of different individuals differ from each other as individuals have their unique expression idiosyncrasies. However, we observed that the MLPs erase most of these unique characteristics after the disentanglement, homogenizing the expressions from different subjects. Motivated by AdaIN [20,21], we consider the unique expression of individuals as a modulation relationship between β and ϵ, which can be formulated as:

$$\epsilon' = M_s(\beta) \cdot \epsilon + M_b(\beta), \tag{3}$$

where ϵ' is the updated value to the expression code, M_s and M_b are the shallow MLPs to transform β into an identity-specific code to adjust ϵ. Both M_s and M_b output tensors with the same length as ϵ. Our experiments show that ISM improves the representation ability of the network especially for various expressions.

RefineNet. We propose to take advantage generative adversarial networks to further improve the synthesis of the facial details. We use Pix2PixHD [49] as the backbone of RefineNet, which refine the results of MoFaNeRF with GAN loss [13] and perceptual loss [18]. The input of RefineNet is the coarse image rendered by MoFaNeRF, and the output is a refined image with high-frequency details. We find that RefineNet significantly improves details and realism with less impact on identity-consistency. The influence of RefineNet on identity-consistency are validated in the ablation study in Sect. 4.2.

3.4   Training

Data Preparation. We use 7180 models released by FaceScape [54] and 1004 models released by HeadSpace [7] to train two models respectively. In FaceScape, the models are captured from 359 different subjects with 20 expressions each. For FaceScape, we randomly select 300 subjects (6000 scans) as training data, leaving 59 subjects (1180 scans) for testing. For HeadSpace, we randomly select 904 subjects as training data, leaving 100 subjects for testing. As HeadSpace only consists of a single expression for each subjects, the expression input part of the network to train HeadSpace data is removed. All these models are aligned in a canonical space, and the area below the shoulder is removed. We render 120 images in different views for each subjects. The details about the rendering setting are shown in the supplementary.

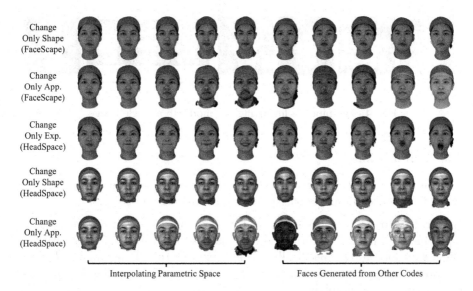

Change
Only Shape
(FaceScape)

Change
Only App.
(FaceScape)

Change
Only Exp.
(HeadSpace)

Change
Only Shape
(HeadSpace)

Change
Only App.
(HeadSpace)

Interpolating Parametric Space   Faces Generated from Other Codes

Fig. 3. Our model is able to synthesize diverse appearance, shape and expressions, while these three dimensions are well disentangled. The interpolation in the parametric space shows that the face can morph smoothly between two parameters.

Landmark-Based Sampling. In the training phase, the frequency of ray-sampling is modified besides the uniform sampling to make the network focus on the facial region. Specifically, we dectect 64 2D key-points of the mouth, nose, eyes, and eyebrows, and the inverse-projecting rays are sampled around each key-point based on a Gaussian distribution. The standard deviation of the Gaussian distribution is set to 0.025 of the image size all our experiments. The uniform sampling and the landmark-based sampling are combined with the ratio of 2:3.

Loss Function. The loss function to train MoFaNeRF is formulated as:

$$L = \sum_{\mathbf{r} \in \mathcal{R}} \left[\left\| \hat{C}_c(\mathbf{r}) - C(\mathbf{r}) \right\|_2^2 + \left\| \hat{C}_f(\mathbf{r}) - C(\mathbf{r}) \right\|_2^2 \right], \tag{4}$$

where $\mathcal{R}$ is the set of rays in each batch, $C(\mathbf{r})$ is the ground-truth color, $\hat{C}_c(\mathbf{r})$ and $\hat{C}_f(\mathbf{r})$ are the colors predicted by coarse volume and fine volume along ray $\mathbf{r}$ respectively. It is worth noting that the expression and appearance parameters are updated according to the back-propagated gradient in the training, while the shape parameters remain unchanged. We firstly train the network of MoFaNeRF, then keep the model fixed and train the RefineNet. The RefineNet is trained with the loss function following Pix2PixHD [49], which is the combination of GAN loss [13] and perceptual loss [8,12,18]. The implementation details can be found in the supplementary material.

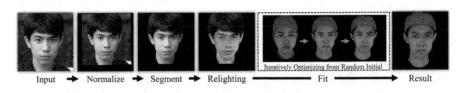

Input ➡ Normalize ➡ Segment ➡ Relighting ——————— Fit ——————————➡ Result

Fig. 4. The pipeline for fitting our model to a single image.

3.5   Application

In addition to directly generating faces from a certain or random vector, MoFaN-eRF can also used in image-based fitting, face rigging and editing.

Image-Based Fitting. As shown in Fig. 4, we propose to fit our model to an input image. Firstly, we normalize the image to the canonical image with an affine transformation. Specifically, we first extract the 2D landmarks L_t from the target image with [22], then align L_t to the predefined 3D landmarks L_c of the canonical face by solving:

$$\mathbf{d}, \mathbf{s} = \arg\min \left\| (\Pi(L_c, \mathbf{d})) \cdot \mathbf{s} - L_t \right\|_2, \tag{5}$$

where $\mathbf{d}$ is the view direction, $\mathbf{s}$ is the scale. $\Pi(L_c, \mathbf{d})$ is the function to project 3D points to the 2D image plane according to the view direction $\mathbf{d}$. The scale $\mathbf{s}$ is applied to the target image, and $\mathbf{d}$ is used in the fitting and remains constant. Then we use EHANet [23,29] to segment the background out, and normalize the lighting with the relighting method [59]. In practice, we find it important to eliminate the influence of light because our model cannot model complex lighting well.

After the pre-processing, we can optimize for β, α, ϵ through the network. Specifically, β and α are randomly initialized by Gaussian distribution, and ϵ is initialized with the learned value from the training. Then we freeze the pre-trained network weights and optimize α, β, ϵ through the network by minimizing only the MSE loss function between the predicted color and the target color. Only points around landmarks are sampled in fitting.

Face Rigging and Editing. The generated or fitted face can be rigged by interpolating in expression dimension with controllable view-point. The expression vector can be obtained by fitting to a video or manually set. Currently, we only use the basic 20 expressions provided by FaceScape to generate simple expression-changing animation. By improving the rigging of the face to higher dimensions [24], our model has the potential to perform more complex expressions. The rigged results are shown in Fig. 1, Fig. 3 and the supplementary materials.

The generated or fitted face can be edited by manipulating the shape and appearance code. As explained in Sect. 3.2, shape coder refers to the shape of the face, the geometry and position of the nose, eyes, and mouth; while appearance refers to the color of skin, lips, pupils, and fine-grained features like beard

Table 1. Quantitative evaluation of representation ability.

Model	PSNR(dB)↑	SSIM*↑	LPIPS*↓
FaceScape [54]	27.96 ± 1.34	0.932 ± 0.012	0.069 ± 0.009
FaceScape* [54]	27.07 ± 1.46	0.933 ± 0.011	0.080 ± 0.014
i3DMM [55]	24.45 ± 1.58	0.904 ± 0.014	0.112 ± 0.015
MoFaNeRF	$\mathbf{31.49 \pm 1.75}$	$\mathbf{0.951 \pm 0.010}$	0.061 ± 0.011
MoFaNeRF-fine	30.17 ± 1.71	0.935 ± 0.013	$\mathbf{0.034 \pm 0.007}$

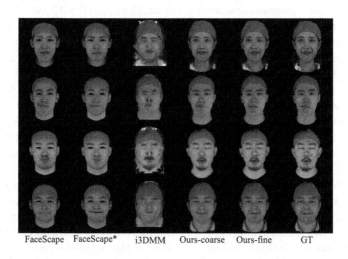

FaceScape   FaceScape*   i3DMM   Ours-coarse   Ours-fine   GT

Fig. 5. Visual comparison of representation ability. Facescape* is the smaller version with comparable model size to our model ($\approx$ 120M).

and eyelashes. These features can be replaced from face A to face B by simply replacing the shape or appearance code, as shown in Fig. 1. Our model supports manually editing by painting texture map, then using TEM to generate appearance code for a generation. However, we find only large-scale features of the edited content in the texture map will take effect, like skin color and beard, while small-scale features like moles won't be transferred to the synthesized face. We also demonstrate that the face can morph smoothly by interpolating in the vector space, as shown in Fig. 3.

4 Experiment

We firstly compare our model with previous parametric models in representation ability, then show the effectiveness of the parameter disentanglement and the network design in the ablation study. Finally, we evaluate the performance of MoFaNeRF in single-view image-based fitting, view extrapolation, and face manipulation.

Table 2. Validation of identity consistency.

Setting	Before RefineNet	After RefineNet	Ground-truth
Changing view	0.687 ± 0.027	0.707 ± 0.028	0.569 ± 0.048
Changing exp, view	0.703 ± 0.023	0.720 ± 0.025	0.633 ± 0.029

4.1 Comparison of Representation Ability

We compare the representation ability of our MoFaNeRF with two SOTA facial parametric models - FaceScape bilinear model [54] and i3DMM [55]. FaceScape is the traditional 3DMM that applies PCA to 3D triangle mesh, while i3DMM is the learning-based 3DMM that represents shape via SDF. Both models are trained on FaceScape dataset as described in Sect. 3.4. The default generated number of parameters for FaceScape is very large ($\approx$ 630M), so to be fair, we also generated a model with a similar number of parameters to our model ($\approx$120M), labeled as FaceScape*. PSNR [16], SSIM [50] and LPIPS [57] are used to measure the objective, structural, and perceptual similarity respectively. The better performance in similarity between the generated face image and ground truth indicates better representation ability.

From the visual comparison in Fig. 5, we can see that the FaceScape bilinear model doesn't model pupils and inner mouth, as it is hard to capture accurate 3D geometry for these regions. The rendered texture is blurry due to the misalignment in the registration phase and the limited representation ability of the linear PCA model. i3DMM is able to synthesize the complete head, but the rendering result is also blurry. We observed that the performance of i3DMM trained on our training set has degraded to some extent, and we think it is because our data amount is much larger than theirs (10 times larger), which makes the task more challenging. By contrast, our model yields the clearest rendering result, which is also verified in quantitative comparison shown in Table 1. The refinement improves the LPIPS but decrease PSNR and SSIM, we believe this it is because the GAN loss and perceptual loss focus on hallucinate plausible details but is less faithful to the original image.

4.2 Disentanglement Evaluation

We show the synthesis results of different parameters in the right side of Fig. 3 to demonstrate that shape, appearance and expression are well disentangled, and shown the interpolation of different attributes in the left side of Fig. 3 to demonstrate that the face can morph continuously.

We further validate identity-consistency among different views and different expressions. The distance in facial identity feature space (DFID) defined in FaceNet [40] is used to measure how well the identity is preserved. Following the standard in FaceNet, two facial images with DFID ≤ 1.1 are judged to be the same person. We use a subset of our training set for this experiment, containing 10 subjects with 10 expressions each. We evaluate DFID between the ground

Table 3. Ablation study.

Label	PSNR(dB)↑	SSIM↑	LPIPS↓
(a.1)One-hot expression code ϵ	25.59 ± 2.25	0.888 ± 0.025	0.184 ± 0.039
(a.2)PCA expression code ϵ	25.79 ± 2.25	0.886 ± 0.025	0.187 ± 0.039
(a.3)One-hot shape code β	26.27 ± 2.25	0.895 ± 0.024	0.174 ± 0.039
(a.4)Leanable shape code β	25.24 ± 2.13	0.883 ± 0.024	0.200 ± 0.041
(a.5)w/o appearance code α & TEM	25.73 ± 2.03	0.889 ± 0.025	0.184 ± 0.039
(b.1)Deformation	24.22 ± 2.33	0.863 ± 0.027	0.231+0.041
(b.2)Modulation	25.69 ± 2.22	0.886 ± 0.025	0.187 ± 0.039
(b.3)Hybrid	24.42 ± 2.13	0.857 ± 0.027	0.241+0.039
(c)Uniform Sampling	25.67 ± 2.09	0.888 ± 0.024	0.185 ± 0.037
(d)Ours with on changes	**26.57 ± 2.08**	**0.897 ± 0.025**	**0.166 ± 0.037**

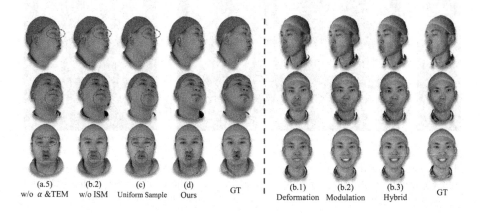

(a.5)	(b.2)	(c)	(d)	GT	(b.1)	(b.2)	(b.3)	GT
w/o α &TEM	w/o ISM	Uniform Sample	Ours		Deformation	Modulation	Hybrid	

Fig. 6. Visual comparison of ablation study.

truth and the fitted face rendered in 50 views with heading angle in $0 \sim 90°$. As reported in Table 2, the DFID scores after RefineNet are slightly increased, but are still comparable to the DFID scores of the ground-truth images. The DFID scores of both changing view and changing view and expression are much lower than 1.1, which demonstrates that the RefineNet doesn't cause severe identity inconstancy across rendering view-points.

4.3 Ablation Study

We provide ablation studies on coding strategy, morphable NeRF architecture, and sampling strategy:

- (a) Ablation Study for different coding strategy: one-hot code, PCA code, learnable code. PCA code is the PCA weights generated by the bilinear

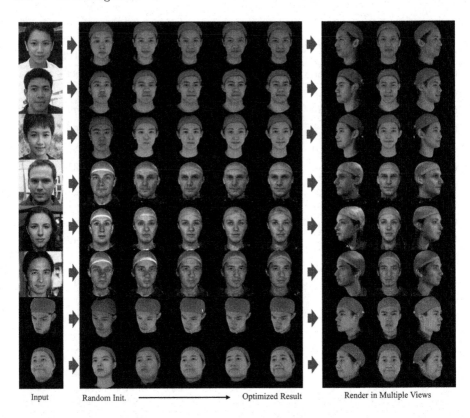

Input   Random Init.   ——————————→   Optimized Result   Render in Multiple Views

Fig. 7. The fitting results to a single-view image of MoFaNeRF. The testing image are from FaceScape testing set and in-the-wild images. The comparison with single-view face reconstruction and failure cases is shown in the supplementary material.

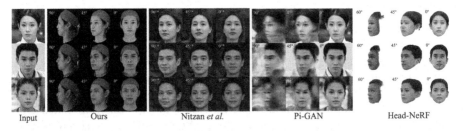

Input   Ours   Nitzan *et al.*   Pi-GAN   Head-NeRF

Fig. 8. The fitting and facial rotating results compared with previous methods.

models [3,54]; Learnable code is optimized in the training of our MoFaN-eRF model, which is initialized by a normal distribution. Our method adopts learnable expression code and PCA shape code, so the other 2 choices for expression and shape code are compared. Considering the appearance cannot be coded as one-hot or PCA code, we only compare with and without TEM module and coded appearance in the ablation study. The coding strategy and the TEM module are described in Sect. 3.2 and Sect. 3.3 respectively.

- (b) Ablation study for morphable NeRF architecture. Previous NeRF variants that support morphable or dynamic objects can be divided into three distinct categories: deformation-based approaches [33,37,46], modulation-based approaches [26,27,52], and a hybrid of both [34]. All of these methods were only tested for a single or a small collections, and our ablation study aims to verify their representative ability for a large-scale face dataset. We select NR-NeRF [46], Dy-NeRF [26], Hyper-NeRF [34] to represent deformation-based, modulation-based, and hybird architecture respectively.
- (c) Ablation study to verify our sampling strategy (Sect. 3.4). We replace our landmark-based sampling strategy with uniform sampling strategy in the training phase.
- (d) Ours with no changes.

We reconstruct 300 images of the first 15 subjects in our training set for evaluation, with random view directions and expressions. The results are reported quantitatively in Table 3 and qualitatively in Fig. 6.

Discussion. As reported in Table 3, comparing (d) to (a.1) and (a.2), we find the PCA identity code most suitable for encoding shape, which reflects the shape similarity in the parameters space. Comparing (d) to (a.3) and (a.4), we can see that learnable code is most suitable for encoding expressions. We think the reason is that the categories of the expression are only 20, which is quite easy for the network to memorize and parse, while PCA code doesn't help for the few categories. By comparing items (b.1)–(b.3), we can see that modulation-based method (Dy-NeRF) shows better representative ability in modeling large-scale morphable faces, which explain the reason why our final model is based on modulation-based structure. By comparing (b.2) and (d), the positive effect of ISM module explained in Sect. 3.3 is verified. By comparing (c) and (d), we can see our sampling method further boost the performance. Comparing (a.5), (b.2), (c) to (d), we can see that our proposed TEM, ISM, and landmark-based sampling all have positive effects on model representation ability, and synthesize more faithful results in the visual comparison.

4.4 Application Results

Image-Based Fitting. The fitted result to the testing set and in-the-wild images are shown in Fig. 7. More results, comparison with single-view reconstruction methods, and failure cases can be found in the supplementary material.

Facial Rotating. We fit our model to a single image and rotate the fitted face by rendering it from a side view, as shown in Fig. 8. The facial rotating results is compared with Nitzan et al. [31], Pi-GAN [4] and HeadNeRF [15]. We can see that our method synthesizes a plausible result even at a large angle (close to ±90°) while the facial appearance and shape are maintained. Nitzan et al.and Pi-GAN are GAN-based networks, while HeadNeRF is a parametric NeRF trained with the help of traditional 3DMM. The results of all these three methods contain obvious artifacts when the face is rotated at a large angle.

Face Rigging and Editing. As shown in Fig. 1 and Fig. 3, after the model is fitted or generated, we can rig the face by driving the expression code ϵ, and edit the face by changing shape code β and appearance code α. Please watch our results in the video and supplementary materials.

5   Conclusion

In this paper, we propose MoFaNeRF that is the first facial parametric model based on neural radiance field. Different to the previous NeRF variants that focuses on a single or a small collection of objects, our model disentangles the shape, appearance, and expression of human faces to make the face morphable in a large-scale solution space. MoFaNeRF can be used in multiple applications and achieves competitive performance comparing to SOTA methods.

Limitation. Our model doesn't explicitly generate 3D shapes and focuses on free-view rendering performance. This prevents our model from being directly used in traditional blendshapes-based driving and rendering pipelines. Besides, the single-view fitting of MoFaNeRF only works well for relatively diffused lighting, while the performance will degrade for extreme lighting conditions. In the future work, we believe that introducing illumination model with MoFaNeRF will improve the generalization and further boost the performance.

Acknowledgement. This work was supported by the NSFC grant 62025108, 62001213, and Tencent Rhino-Bird Joint Research Program. We thank Dr. Yao Yao for his valuable suggestions and Dr. Yuanxun Lu for proofreading the paper.

References

1. Bagautdinov, T., Wu, C., Saragih, J., Fua, P., Sheikh, Y.: Modeling facial geometry using compositional VAEs. In: CVPR, pp. 3877–3886 (2018)
2. Blanz, V., Vetter, T., et al.: A morphable model for the synthesis of 3D faces. In: SIGGRAPH, vol. 99, pp. 187–194 (1999)
3. Cao, C., Weng, Y., Zhou, S., Tong, Y., Zhou, K.: Facewarehouse: a 3D facial expression database for visual computing. TVCG **20**(3), 413–425 (2013)
4. Chan, E.R., Monteiro, M., Kellnhofer, P., Wu, J., Wetzstein, G.: pi-GAN: periodic implicit generative adversarial networks for 3D-aware image synthesis. In: CVPR, pp. 5799–5809 (2021)
5. Chen, J., et al.: Animatable neural radiance fields from monocular RGB videos. arXiv preprint arXiv:2106.13629 (2021)
6. Cheng, S., Bronstein, M., Zhou, Y., Kotsia, I., Pantic, M., Zafeiriou, S.: MeshGAN: non-linear 3D morphable models of faces. arXiv preprint arXiv:1903.10384 (2019)
7. Dai, H., Pears, N., Smith, W., Duncan, C.: Statistical modeling of craniofacial shape and texture. IJCV **128**(2), 547–571 (2019)
8. Dosovitskiy, A., Brox, T.: Generating images with perceptual similarity metrics based on deep networks. NIPS **29**, 658–666 (2016)

9. Egger, B., et al.: 3D morphable face models-past, present, and future. ToG **39**(5), 1–38 (2020)
10. Gafni, G., Thies, J., Zollhofer, M., Nießner, M.: Dynamic neural radiance fields for monocular 4D facial avatar reconstruction. In: CVPR, pp. 8649–8658 (2021)
11. Gao, C., Shih, Y., Lai, W.S., Liang, C.K., Huang, J.B.: Portrait neural radiance fields from a single image. https://arxiv.org/abs/2012.05903 (2020)
12. Gatys, L.A., Ecker, A.S., Bethge, M.: Image style transfer using convolutional neural networks. In: CVPR, pp. 2414–2423 (2016)
13. Goodfellow, I., et al.: Generative adversarial nets. In: NIPS, vol. 27 (2014)
14. Gu, J., Liu, L., Wang, P., Theobalt, C.: Stylenerf: a style-based 3D-aware generator for high-resolution image synthesis (2021)
15. Hong, Y., Peng, B., Xiao, H., Liu, L., Zhang, J.: Headnerf: a real-time nerf-based parametric head model. In: CVPR, pp. 20374–20384 (2022)
16. Horé, A., Ziou, D.: Image quality metrics: PSNR vs. SSIM. In: ICPR, pp. 2366–2369 (2010)
17. Jiang, Z.H., Wu, Q., Chen, K., Zhang, J.: Disentangled representation learning for 3D face shape. In: CVPR, pp. 11957–11966 (2019)
18. Johnson, J., Alahi, A., Fei-Fei, L.: Perceptual losses for real-time style transfer and super-resolution. In: Leibe, B., Matas, J., Sebe, N., Welling, M. (eds.) ECCV 2016. LNCS, vol. 9906, pp. 694–711. Springer, Cham (2016). https://doi.org/10.1007/978-3-319-46475-6_43
19. Jourabloo, A., Liu, X.: Large-pose face alignment via CNN-based dense 3D model fitting. In: CVPR, pp. 4188–4196 (2016)
20. Karras, T., Laine, S., Aila, T.: A style-based generator architecture for generative adversarial networks. In: CVPR, pp. 4401–4410 (2019)
21. Karras, T., Laine, S., Aittala, M., Hellsten, J., Lehtinen, J., Aila, T.: Analyzing and improving the image quality of StyleGAN. In: CVPR, pp. 8110–8119 (2020)
22. Kazemi, V., Sullivan, J.: One millisecond face alignment with an ensemble of regression trees. In: Proceedings of the IEEE Conference on Computer Vision and Pattern Recognition, pp. 1867–1874 (2014)
23. Lee, C.H., Liu, Z., Wu, L., Luo, P.: MaskGAN: towards diverse and interactive facial image manipulation. arXiv preprint arXiv:1907.11922 (2019)
24. Li, H., Weise, T., Pauly, M.: Example-based facial rigging. ToG **29**, 32 (2010)
25. Li, T., Bolkart, T., Black, M.J., Li, H., Romero, J.: Learning a model of facial shape and expression from 4D scans. ToG **36**(6), 194 (2017)
26. Li, T., et al.: Neural 3D video synthesis. arXiv preprint arXiv:2103.02597 (2021)
27. Li, Z., Niklaus, S., Snavely, N., Wang, O.: Neural scene flow fields for space-time view synthesis of dynamic scenes (2020). https://arxiv.org/abs/2011.13084
28. Liu, L., Habermann, M., Rudnev, V., Sarkar, K., Gu, J., Theobalt, C.: Neural actor: neural free-view synthesis of human actors with pose control. arXiv preprint arXiv:2106.02019 (2021)
29. Luo, L., Xue, D., Feng, X.: Ehanet: an effective hierarchical aggregation network for face parsing. Appl. Sci. **10**(9), 3135 (2020)
30. Mildenhall, B., Srinivasan, P.P., Tancik, M., Barron, J.T., Ramamoorthi, R., Ng, R.: NeRF: representing scenes as neural radiance fields for view synthesis. In: ECCV, pp. 405–421 (2020)
31. Nitzan, Y., Bermano, A., Li, Y., Cohen-Or, D.: Face identity disentanglement via latent space mapping. ToG **39**, 1–14 (2020)
32. Noguchi, A., Sun, X., Lin, S., Harada, T.: Neural articulated radiance field. arXiv preprint arXiv:2104.03110 (2021)

33. Park, K., et al.: Nerfies: deformable neural radiance fields. arXiv preprint arXiv:2011.12948 (2020)
34. Park, K., et al.: Hypernerf: a higher-dimensional representation for topologically varying neural radiance fields. arXiv preprint arXiv:2106.13228 (2021)
35. Peng, S., et al.: Animatable neural radiance fields for human body modeling. arXiv preprint arXiv:2105.02872 (2021)
36. Peng, S., et al.: Neural body: implicit neural representations with structured latent codes for novel view synthesis of dynamic humans. In: CVPR (2021)
37. Pumarola, A., Corona, E., Pons-Moll, G., Moreno-Noguer, F.: D-NeRF: neural radiance fields for dynamic scenes (2020). https://arxiv.org/abs/2011.13961
38. Pumarola, A., Corona, E., Pons-Moll, G., Moreno-Noguer, F.: D-nerf: neural radiance fields for dynamic scenes. In: CVPR, pp. 10318–10327 (2021)
39. Raj, A., et al.: Pixel-aligned volumetric avatars. In: CVPR, pp. 11733–11742 (2021)
40. Schroff, F., Kalenichenko, D., Philbin, J.: Facenet: a unified embedding for face recognition and clustering. In: CVPR, pp. 815–823 (2015)
41. Schwarz, K., Liao, Y., Niemeyer, M., Geiger, A.: Graf: generative radiance fields for 3D-aware image synthesis. In: CVPR (2021)
42. Tewari, A., et al.: Self-supervised multi-level face model learning for monocular reconstruction at over 250 HZ. In: CVPR, pp. 2549–2559 (2018)
43. Tran, L., Liu, F., Liu, X.: Towards high-fidelity nonlinear 3D face morphable model. In: CVPR, pp. 1126–1135 (2019)
44. Tran, L., Liu, X.: Nonlinear 3D face morphable model. In: CVPR, pp. 7346–7355 (2018)
45. Tran, L., Liu, X.: On learning 3D face morphable model from in-the-wild images. PAMI **43**(1), 157–171 (2019)
46. Tretschk, E., Tewari, A., Golyanik, V., Zollhöfer, M., Lassner, C., Theobalt, C.: Non-rigid neural radiance fields: reconstruction and novel view synthesis of a deforming scene from monocular video. https://arxiv.org/abs/2012.12247 (2020)
47. Vlasic, D., Brand, M., Pfister, H., Popović, J.: Face transfer with multilinear models. ToG **24**(3), 426–433 (2005)
48. Wang, Q., et al.: IBRNet: learning multi-view image-based rendering. In: CVPR, pp. 4690–4699 (2021)
49. Wang, T.C., Liu, M.Y., Zhu, J.Y., Tao, A., Kautz, J., Catanzaro, B.: High-resolution image synthesis and semantic manipulation with conditional GANs. In: CVPR, pp. 8798–8807 (2018)
50. Wang, Z., Bovik, A.C., Sheikh, H.R., Simoncelli, E.P.: Image quality assessment: from error visibility to structural similarity. TIP **13**(4), 600–612 (2004)
51. Wang, Z., et al.: Learning compositional radiance fields of dynamic human heads. In: CVPR, pp. 5704–5713 (2021)
52. Xian, W., Huang, J.B., Kopf, J., Kim, C.: Space-time neural irradiance fields for free-viewpoint video. In: CVPR, pp. 9421–9431 (2021)
53. Xiao, Y., Zhu, H., Yang, H., Diao, Z., Lu, X., Cao, X.: Detailed facial geometry recovery from multi-view images by learning an implicit function. In: AAAI (2022)
54. Yang, H., et al.: Facescape: a large-scale high quality 3d face dataset and detailed riggable 3D face prediction. In: CVPR (2020)
55. Yenamandra, T., et al.: i3DMM: deep implicit 3D morphable model of human heads. In: CVPR, pp. 12803–12813 (2021)
56. Yu, A., Ye, V., Tancik, M., Kanazawa, A.: pixelNeRF: neural radiance fields from one or few images. In: CVPR, pp. 4578–4587 (2021)
57. Zhang, R., Isola, P., Efros, A.A., Shechtman, E., Wang, O.: The unreasonable effectiveness of deep features as a perceptual metric. In: CVPR, pp. 586–595 (2018)

58. Zhang, Z., Li, L., Ding, Y., Fan, C.: Flow-guided one-shot talking face generation with a high-resolution audio-visual dataset. In: CVPR, pp. 3661–3670 (2021)
59. Zhou, H., Hadap, S., Sunkavalli, K., Jacobs, D.W.: Deep single-image portrait relighting. In: CVPR, pp. 7194–7202 (2019)
60. Zhu, H., et al.: FaceScape: 3D facial dataset and benchmark for single-view 3D face reconstruction. arXiv preprint arXiv:2111.01082 (2021)

PointInst3D: Segmenting 3D Instances by Points

Tong He[1(✉)], Wei Yin[1], Chunhua Shen[2], and Anton van den Hengel[1]

[1] The University of Adelaide, Adelaide, Australia
tonghe90@gmail.com
[2] Zhejiang University, Hangzhou, China

Abstract. The current state-of-the-art methods in 3D instance segmentation typically involve a clustering step, despite the tendency towards heuristics, greedy algorithms, and a lack of robustness to the changes in data statistics. In contrast, we propose a fully-convolutional 3D point cloud instance segmentation method that works in a per-point prediction fashion. In doing so it avoids the challenges that clustering-based methods face: introducing dependencies among different tasks of the model. We find the key to its success is assigning a suitable target to each sampled point. Instead of the commonly used static or distance-based assignment strategies, we propose to use an Optimal Transport approach to optimally assign target masks to the sampled points according to the dynamic matching costs. Our approach achieves promising results on both ScanNet and S3DIS benchmarks. The proposed approach removes inter-task dependencies and thus represents a simpler and more flexible 3D instance segmentation framework than other competing methods, while achieving improved segmentation accuracy.

Keywords: Clustering-free · Dependency-free · 3D instance segmentation · Dynamic target assignment · Optimal transport

1 Introduction

3D instance segmentation describes the problem of identifying a set of instances that explain the locations of a set of sampled 3D points. It is an important step in a host of 3D scene-understanding challenges, including autonomous driving, robotics, remote sensing, and augmented reality. Despite this fact, the performance of 3D instance segmentation lags that of 2D instance segmentation, not least due to the additional challenges of 3D representation, and variable density of points.

Most of the top-performing 3D instance segmentation approaches [4,7,10, 14,17,21] involve a clustering step. Despite their great success, clustering-based methods have their drawbacks: they are susceptible to the performance of the clustering approach itself, and its integration, due to either (1) error accumulation caused by the inter-task dependencies [4,14,17] or (2) non-differentiable

S. Avidan et al. (Eds.): ECCV 2022, LNCS 13663, pp. 286–302, 2022.
https://doi.org/10.1007/978-3-031-20062-5_17

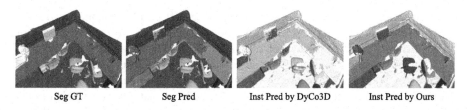

| Seg GT | Seg Pred | Inst Pred by DyCo3D | Inst Pred by Ours |

Fig. 1. A comparison of the instance segmentation results achieved by DyCo3D [14] and our method. The subpar performance of instance segmentation for DyCo3D [14] is caused by the dependency on semantic segmentation. Our method addresses the task in a per-point prediction fashion and removes the dependencies between different tasks of the model. Thus, it is free from the error accumulation introduced by the intermediate tasks. Best viewed in colors.

processing steps [10,21]. For example, in PointGroup [17], instance proposals are generated by searching homogenous clusters that have identical semantic predictions and close centroid predictions. However, the introduced dependencies on both tasks make the results sensitive to the heuristics values chosen. DyCo3D [14] addressed the issue by encoding instances as continuous functions. But the accuracy is still constrained by the semantic-conditioned convolution. As a result, it can be impossible to recover from errors in intermediate stages, particularly given that many methods greedily associate points with objects (which leaves them particularly susceptible to early clustering errors). Even with careful design, because of the diversity in the scales of instances, and the unbalanced distribution of semantic categories, the performance of these intermediate tasks is often far from satisfactory. This typically leads to fragmentation and merging of instances, as shown in Fig. 1.

In this paper, we remove the clustering step and the dependencies within the model and propose a much simpler pipeline working in a per-point prediction fashion. Every sampled point will generate a set of instance-related convolutional parameters, which are further applied for decoding the binary masks of the corresponding instances. However, building such a clustering-free and dependency-free pipeline is non-trivial. For example, removing the clustering step and conditional convolution in DyCo3D causes mAP to drop by more than 8% and 6%, respectively. We conduct comprehensive experiments and find the reason for the huge drop in performance is the ambiguity of the targets for the sampled points. In 2D instance segmentation and object detection, the center prior, which assumes the predictions from the central areas of an instance are more likely to provide accurate results, offers a guideline to select well-behaved samples [8,31,32]. This distance-based prior is hard to apply in 3D, however, as the distribution of high-quality samples in 3D point clouds is irregular and unpredictable. The fact that objects can be arbitrarily close together in real 3D scenes adds additional complexity. Thus, the resulting ambiguity in point-instance associations can contaminate the training process and impact final performance. Instead of applying a static or widely used distance-based strategy, we propose to optimally assign instances to samples via an Optimal Transport (OT) solution. It is defined in terms of a set of suppliers and demanders, and the costs of transportation between them. We thus associated a demander with each instance prediction of the sampled point, and a supplier with each potential instance ground truth. The cost of transport reflects the affinity between each pair thereof. The OT algorithm identifies the optimal strategy by which to supply the needs of each demander, given the cost of transport from each supplier. The points will then be associated with the target corresponding to the demander to which it has allocated the greatest proportion of its supply. The costs of transporting are determined by the Dice Coefficient, which is updated dynamically based on the per-point predictions. The OT solution not only minimizes the labor for heuristics tuning but allows it to make use of the sophisticated tools that have been developed for solving such problems. In particular, it can be efficiently solved by the off-the-shelf Sinkhorn-Knopp Iteration algorithm [5] with limited computation in training.

To summarise, our contributions are listed as follows.

– We propose a clustering-free framework for 3D instance segmentation, working in a per-point prediction fashion. In doing so it removes the dependencies among different tasks and thus avoids error accumulation from the intermediate tasks.
– For the first time, we address the target assignment problem for 3D instance segmentation, which has been overlooked in the 3D community. Our proposed Optimal Transport solution is free from heuristics with improved accuracy.
– We achieve promising results on both ScanNet and S3DIS, with a much simpler pipeline.

2   Related Work

Target Assignment in 2D Images. The problem of associating candidates to targets arises commonly in 2D object detection. Anchor-based detectors [22, 23, 30] apply a hard threshold to an intersection-over-union measure to divide positive and negative samples. This approach can also be found in many other methods [3, 11]. Anchor-free detectors [18, 32, 42] have drawn increasing attention due to their simplicity. These methods observe that samples around the center of objects are more likely to provide accurate predictions. Inspired by this center prior, some methods [18, 31, 33, 38] introduce a classifier by treating these central regions as positive samples. ATSS [39], in contrast, is adaptive in that it sets a dynamic threshold according to the statistics of the set of closest anchors. Free-Anchor [40] frames detector training as a maximum likelihood estimation (MLE) procedure and proposes a learning-based matching mechanism. Notably, OTA [8] formulates the task of label assigning as Optimal Transport problem.

Instance Segmentation on 3D Point Cloud. The task of instance segmentation in the 3D domain is complicated by the irregularity and sparsity of the

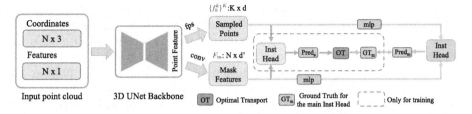

Fig. 2. The framework of our proposed method. The 'inst head' is designed to generate instance masks by applying dynamic convolution. K points are sampled via the farthest point sampling strategy. Each sampled point is responsible for one specific instance mask or background. The targets are calibrated dynamically via an Optimal Transport solution, which takes as input the mask prediction from the auxiliary head and outputs the calibrated ground truth for the main instance head. The targets for the auxiliary instance prediction 'pred$_a$' are consistent with the instance label of the sampled points.

point cloud. Unlike instance segmentation of images, in which top-down methods are the state-of-the-art, the leader board in instance segmentation of 3D point clouds has been dominated by bottom-up approaches due to unsatisfactory 3D detection results. SGPN [34], for instance, predicts an $N \times N$ matrix to measure the probability of each pair of points coming from the same instance, where N is the number of total points. ASIS [35] applies a discriminative loss function from [2] to learn point-wise embeddings. The mean-shift algorithm is used to cluster points into instances. Many works (*e.g.* [12,13,27,41]) follow this metric-based pipeline. However, these methods often suffer from low accuracy and poor generalization ability due to their reliance on pre-defined hyper-parameters and complex post-processing steps. Interestingly, PointGroup [17] exploits the voids between instances for segmentation. Both original and center-shifted coordinates are applied to search nearby points that have identical semantic categories. The authors of DyCo3D [14,15] addressed the sensitivity of clustering methods to the grouping radius using dynamic convolution. Instead of treating clusters as individual instance proposals, DyCo3D utilized them to generate instance-related convolutional parameters for decoding masks of instances. Chen *et al.* proposed HAIS [4], which is also a clustering-based architecture. It addressed the problem of the over- and under-segmentation of PointGroup [17] by deploying an intra-instance filtering sub-network and adapting the grouping radius according to the size of clusters. SSTN [21] builds a semantic tree with superpoints [20] being the leaves of the tree. The instance proposals can be obtained when a non-splitting decision is made at the intermediate tree node. A scoring module is introduced to refine the instance masks.

3   Methods

The pipeline of the proposed method is illustrated in Fig. 2, which is built upon a sparse convolution backbone [9]. It maintains a UNet-like structure and takes as input the coordinates and features, which have a shape of $N \times 3$ and $N \times I$, respectively. N is the total number of input points and I is the dimension of input features. There is one output branch of mask features, which is used to decode binary masks of instances. It is denoted as $F_m \in \mathbb{R}^{N \times d'}$, where d' is the dimension of the mask features. Inspired by DyCo3D [14], we propose to encode instance-related knowledge into a set of convolutional parameters and decode the corresponding masks with several 1×1 convolutions. Different from DyCo3D, which requires a greedy clustering algorithm and a conditioned decoding step, our proposed method, on the other hand, removes the clustering step and the dependencies among different tasks, simplifying the network in a point-wise prediction pipeline.

3.1 Preliminary on DyCo3D

DyCo3D [14] has three output branches: semantic segmentation, centroid offset prediction, and mask features. The breadth-first-searching algorithm is used to find out the homogenous points that have identical semantic labels and close centroid predictions. Each cluster is sent to the instance head and generates a set of convolution parameters for decoding the mask of the corresponding instance. Formally, the mask $\hat{M}_k$ predicted by the k-th cluster can be formulated as:

$$
\begin{aligned}
\hat{M}_k &= Conv_{1x1}(feature, weight) \\
&= Conv_{1x1}(F_m \oplus C_{\text{rel}}^k, mlp(G(P_s, P_c)_k)) \odot \mathbb{1}(P_s = s_k)
\end{aligned}
\tag{1}
$$

The input features to convolution contains two parts: F_m and C_{rel}^k. F_m is the mask features shared by all instances. $C_{\text{rel}}^k \in \mathbb{R}^{N \times 3}$ is the instance-specific relative coordinates, which are obtained by computing the difference between the center of the k-th cluster and all input points. F_m and C_{rel}^k are concatenated ('$\oplus$') along the feature dimension. The convolutional weights are dynamically generated by an mlp layer, whose input is the feature of the k-th cluster. The clustering algorithm $G(\cdot)$ takes the semantic prediction $P_s \in \mathbb{R}^N$ and centroid prediction $P_c \in \mathbb{R}^N$ as input and finds out a set of homogenous clusters. The k-th cluster is denoted as $G(\cdot)_k$. Besides, the dynamic convolution in DyCo3D is conditioned on the results of semantic segmentation. For example, DyCo3D can only discriminate one specific 'Chair' instance from all points that are semantically categorized as 'Chair', instead of the whole point set. It is implemented by an element-wise production ('$\odot$') with a binary mask ('$\mathbb{1}(\cdot)$'). s_k is the semantic label of the k-th cluster. Finally, the target mask for $\hat{M}_k$ is decided by the instance label of the k-th cluster. More details can be found in [14].

3.2 Proposed Method

Although promising, DyCo3D [14] involves a grouping step to get the instance-related clusters, depending on the accuracy of semantic segmentation and offset

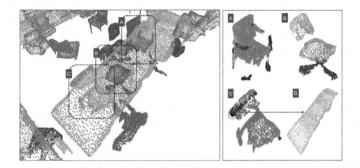

Fig. 3. The left image is an indoor scene with three instances of 'Chair'. The right image is the quality of instance predictions by each point. The brighter the color, the more accurate the mask predicted by the point. Different from the 2D image, the distribution of the positive samples in 3D point cloud is irregular, making it hard to learn a criterion to select informative samples for each instance. In addition, the ambiguity of target assignment is widespread in the 3D scenes. Some samples in instance 'C' show high-quality predictions of the instance 'D'. Best viewed in color.

prediction. Besides, the conditional convolution also forces the instance decoding to rely on the results of semantic segmentation. These inter-task dependencies cause error accumulation and lead to sub-par performance (See Fig. 1). In this paper, we propose a clustering-free and dependency-free framework in a per-point prediction fashion. Total K points are selected via the farthest point sampling strategy. The instance head takes as input both the mask feature F_m and point-wise feature f_b^k. The k-th mask $\hat{M}_k$ predicted by the instance head can be formulated as:

$$\begin{aligned}
\hat{M}_k &= Conv_{1x1}(feature, weight) \\
&= Conv_{1x1}(F_m \oplus C_{\text{rel}}^k, mlp(f_b^k))
\end{aligned} \quad (2)$$

where f_b^k is the feature of the k-th sampled point from output of the backbone. $C_{\text{rel}}^k \in \mathbb{R}^{N \times 3}$ is the relative position embedding, obtained by computing the difference between the coordinate of the k-th point and all other points.

However, building such a simplified pipeline is non-trivial. Removing the clustering step and conditional convolution causes the mAP of DyCo3D to drop dramatically.

Observation. To find out the reasons that cause the failure of this point-wise prediction pipeline, we visualize the quality of masks predicted by each point (according to Eq. 2). For training, the target mask for each point is consistent with its instance label. As shown in Fig. 3, the distribution of high-quality samples is irregular and can be influenced by many factors: (1) disconnection, (2) distance to the instance center, and (3) spatial relationships with other objects. Besides, the fact that objects can be arbitrarily close together in real 3D scenes adds additional complexity. As illustrated in Fig. 3(c,d), the poorly behaved samples in 'chair c' can accurately predict the mask of the 'desk'. Such ambiguity introduced by the static assigning strategy contaminates the training process, leading to inferior performance.

Target Assignment. Although the task of target assignment has shown its significance in 2D object detection and instance segmentation [8,39,40], to the best of our knowledge, there is very little research in the 3D domain. One of the most straightforward ways is to define a criterion to select a set of informative samples for each instance. For example, thanks to the center prior [32], many approaches [18,31,38,42] in the 2D domain treat the central areas of the instance as positive candidates. However, such regularity is hard to define for the 3D point cloud, as shown in Fig. 3. Quantitative results can be found in Table 1.

Instead of applying a static strategy or learning an indicative metric, we propose to assign a suitable target for each sample based on its prediction. A background mask (*i.e.* all zeros) is added to the target set to address the poorly-behaved points.

Optimal Transport Solution. Given K sampled points (via farthest point sampling) and their corresponding mask predictions $\{\hat{M}_k\}^K$ (using Eq. 2), the goal of target assignment is to find a suitable target for each prediction in training. There are T+1 targets in total, including T instance masks $\{M_t\}^T$ and one background mask M_{T+1} (zero mask). Inspired by [8], we formulate the task as an Optimal Transport problem, which seeks a plan by transporting the 'goods' from suppliers (*i.e.* Ground Truth and Background Mask) to demanders (*i.e.* predictions of the sampled points) at a minimal transportation cost.

Supposing the t-th target has μ_t unit of goods and each prediction needs one unit of goods, we denote the cost for transporting one unit of goods from the t-th target to the k-th prediction as C_{tk}. By applying Optimal Transport, the task of the target assignment can be written as:

$$U^* = \underset{U \in \mathbb{R}_+^{(T+1) \times K}}{\arg\min} \sum_{t,k} C_{tk} U_{tk} \tag{3}$$
$$\text{s.t.} \quad U \mathbf{1}_K = \mu_{T+1}, \quad U^\top \mathbf{1}_{T+1} = \mathbf{1}_K,$$

where U^* is the optimal assignment plan, U_{tk} is the amount of labels transported from the t-th target to the k-th prediction. μ_{T+1} is the label vector for all $T+1$ targets. The transportation cost C_{tk} is defined as:

$$C_{tk} = \begin{cases} \mathcal{L}_{\text{dice}}(M_t, \hat{M}_k) & t \leq T \\ \mathcal{L}_{\text{dice}}(1 - M_t, 1 - \hat{M}_k) & t = T+1 \end{cases} \tag{4}$$

where $\mathcal{L}_{\text{dice}}$ denotes the dice loss. To calculate the cost between the background target and the prediction, we use $1 - M_t$ and $1 - \hat{M}_k$ for a numerically stable training. The restriction in Eq. 3 describes that (1) the total supply must be equal to the total demand and (2) the goods demand for each prediction is 1 (*i.e.* each prediction needs one target mask). Besides, the label vector $\boldsymbol{\mu}_{T+1}$, indicating the total amount of goods held by each target, is updated by:

$$\mu_t = \begin{cases} int(\sum_k IoU(\hat{M}_k, M_t)) & t \leq T \\ K - \sum_{i=1}^{T} \mu_i & t = T+1 \end{cases} \tag{5}$$

where μ_{T+1} refers to the target amount maintained in the background target and $int(\cdot)$ is the rounding operation. According to Eq. 5, the amount of supplied goods for each target is dynamically decided, depending on its IoU with each prediction. Due to the restriction in Eq. 3, we set μ_{T+1} equal to $K - \sum_{t=1}^{T}$. The efficient Sinkhorn-Knopp algorithm [5] allows it to obtain $\boldsymbol{U}^*$ with limited computation overhead. After getting the optimal assignment $\boldsymbol{U}^*$, the calibrated targets for the K sampled points can be determined by assigning each point with the target that transports the largest amount of goods to it.

Compared with [8], the number of the demanders is much fewer. Thus, the minimum supply of each target can be zero in training. Doing so may make the model fall into a trivial solution when K is small: all predictions are zero masks and assigned to the background target due to the lowest transportation cost in Eq. 4. To this end, we propose a simple yet effective way by introducing an auxiliary instance head, whose targets are consistent with the instance labels of the sampled points. We use the predictions from this auxiliary head to calculate the cost matrix in Eq. 4. The dynamically calibrated targets are used for the main instance head. To alleviate the impact of the wrongly assigned samples in the auxiliary head, the loss weight for this auxiliary task is decreasing in training.

3.3   Training

To summarize, the loss function includes two terms for training, including the auxiliary loss term $\mathcal{L}_a$ and the main task loss term $\mathcal{L}_m$:

$$\mathcal{L} = w_a \sum_{k=1}^{K} \mathcal{L}_a(M_k^a, \hat{M}_k^a) + \sum_{k=1}^{K} \mathcal{L}_m(M_k^m, \hat{M}_k^m) \tag{6}$$

where $\{M_k^a\}^K \in \{0,1\}^{K \times N}$ is the ground truth masks for the K predictions. These targets are static and decided by the instance labels of the K sampled points. $\{M_k^m\}^K \in \{0,1\}^{K \times N}$ is the set of the calibrated targets for the main instance head. $\{\hat{M}_k^a\}^K$ and $\{\hat{M}_k^m\}^K$ are the predictions from auxiliary and main instance heads, respectively. w_a is the loss weight for the auxiliary task. We set w_a to 1.0 with a decaying rate of 0.99. Early in the training phase, the static targets for the auxiliary task play a significant role in stabilizing the learning process. The loss of the main task is involved until the end of a warming-up period, which is set to 6k steps. So far, we have obtained a set of binary masks. There are many ways to obtain the corresponding categories, for example, adding a classification head for each mask proposal. In our paper, we implement it by simply introducing a semantic branch. The category c_k of the k-th instance is the majority of the semantic predictions within the foreground mask of $\hat{M}_k^m$. Instances with a number of points less than 50 are ignored.

Table 1. Component-wise analysis on ScanNetV2 validation set. **CP**: the center prior tailored for 3D point cloud. **DT**: dynamic targets assignment using Optimal Transportation. **AUX**: the auxiliary loss used in Eq. 6.

Method	CP	DT	AUX	mAP	AP@50	AP@25
Baseline				33.7	52.4	65.0
	✓			34.1	53.2	65.4
Ours		✓		36.8	54.8	65.9
			✓	36.5	54.3	65.7
		✓	✓	39.6	59.2	70.4

4   Experiments

We conduct comprehensive experiments on two standard benchmarks to validate the effectiveness of our proposed method: ScanNet [6] and Stanford 3D Indoor Semantic Dataset (S3DIS) [1].

4.1   Datasets

ScanNet has 1613 scans in total, which are divided into training, validation, and testing with a size of 1201, 312, and 100, respectively. The task of instance segmentation is evaluated on 18 classes. Following [14], we report the results on the validation set for ablation study and submit the results on the testing set to the official evaluation server. The evaluation metrics are mAP (mean average precision) and AP@50.

S3DIS contains more than 270 scans, which are collected on 6 large indoor areas. It has 13 categories for instance segmentation. Following the previous method [35], the evaluation metrics include: mean coverage (mCov), mean weighed coverage (mWCov), mean precision (mPrec), and mean recall (mRec).

4.2   Implementation Details

The backbone model we use is from [9], which maintains a symmetrical UNet structure. It has 7 blocks in total and the scalability of the model is controlled by the channels of the block. To prove the generalization capability of our proposed method, we report the performance with both small and large backbones, denoted as **Ours-S** and **Ours-L**, respectively. The small model has a channel unit of 16, while the large model is 32. The default dimension of the mask features is 16 and 32, respectively.

For each input scan, we concatenate the coordinates and RGB values as the input features. All experiments are trained for 60K iteration with 4 GPUS. The batch size for each GPU is 3. The learning rate is set to 1e–3 and follows a polynomial decay policy. In testing, the computation related to the auxiliary head is ignored. Only Non-Maximum-Suppression (NMS) is required to remove the redundant mask predictions for inference, with a threshold of 0.3.

4.3   Ablation Studies

In this section, we verify the effectiveness of the key components in our proposed method. For a fair comparison, all experiments are conducted on the validation set of ScanNet [6] with the smaller model.

Baseline. We build a strong baseline by tailoring CondInst [31] for the 3D point cloud. It works in a per-point prediction fashion and each sampled point has a static target, which is consistent with the corresponding instance label. As shown in Table 1, our method achieves 33.7% 52.4%, and 65.0% in terms of mAP, AP@50, and AP@25, respectively. With a larger number of sampled points and longer iterations, our baseline model surpasses the implementation of DyCo3D [14] by a large margin.

Center Prior in 3D. To demonstrate the difficulty of selecting informative samples in 3D, we tailor the center prior [32] to 3D point cloud. As points are collected from the surface of the objects, centers of 3D instances are likely to be in empty space. To this end, we first predict the offset between each point and the center of the corresponding object. If the distance between the center-shifted point and the ground truth is close (≤ 0.3 m), the point is regarded as positive and responsible for the instance. If the distance is larger than 0.6 m, the point is defined as negative. Other points are ignored for training. As presented in Table 1, selecting positive samples based on the 3D center prior only boosts 0.4% and 0.8% in terms of mAP and mAP@50, respectively. The incremental improvement demonstrates the difficulty of selecting informative samples in 3D. In contrast, we propose to apply a dynamic strategy, by which the target for each candidate is determined based on its prediction.

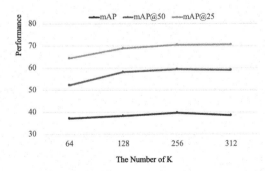

Fig. 4. Ablation study on the number of the sampling point.

Dynamic Targets. To show the effectiveness of the dynamic strategy, we implement an experiment by removing the auxiliary head. As the predictions are basically random guesses in the early stage of the training, we first warm up the model for 12k iterations with a static assignment to avoid the trivial solution. In the remaining steps, targets are calibrated by the Optimal Solution. As shown in Table 1, our approach boosts the performance of the baseline model by 3.1%, 2.4%, and 0.9%, in terms of mAP, AP@50, and AP@25, respectively.

Table 2. The performance of 3D object detection, tested on ScanNet validation set. AP@50 is reported.

3D object detection	
ScanNetV2	AP@50%
MRCNN 2D-3D [11]	10.5
F-PointNet [29]	10.8
GSPN [37]	17.7
3D-SIS [16]	22.5
VoteNet [28]	33.5
PointGroup [17]	42.3
DyCo3D [14]	45.3
3D-MPA [7]	49.2
Ours	**51.0**

Auxiliary Supervision. As illustrated in Fig. 2, we propose to regularize the intermediate layers by introducing an auxiliary instance head for decoding the instance masks. The targets for this task are static and consistent with the instance labels. Besides, as the generated parameters are convolving with the whole point set, large context and instance-related knowledge are encoded in the point-wise features. To remove the influence of the dynamic assignment, both auxiliary and the main task are applying a static assignment strategy. As shown in Table 1, the auxiliary supervision brings 2.8%, 1.9%, and 0.7% improvement in terms of mAP, mAP@50, and mAP@25, respectively. In addition to the encoded large context, the predicted instance masks are also applied to the Optimal Solution to obtain calibrated targets. Combining with the proposed dynamic assignment strategy, it further boosts mAP, AP@50, and AP@25 for 3.1%, 4.4%, and 4.5%, respectively, achieving 39.6% in terms of mAP with a small backbone.

Analysis on Efficiency. Our method takes the whole scan as input, without complex pre-processing steps. Similar to DyCo3D [14], the instance head is implemented in parallel. To make a fair comparison, we set K equal to the average number of clusters in DyCo3D. Using the same GPU, the mAP of our proposed method is 1.8% higher than DyCo3D and the inference time is 26% faster than DyCo3D.

Number of Random Selected Samples. We randomly select K points, each of which is responsible for one specific instance or the background (all zeros). In this part, we study the influence of the value of K. The performance is shown in Fig. 4. We set K to 256 for its highest mAP.

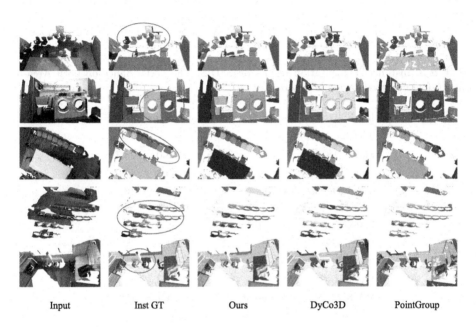

| Input | Inst GT | Ours | DyCo3D | PointGroup |

Fig. 5. Comparison with the results of DyCo3D [14] and PointGroup [17]. The ellipses highlight specific over-segmentation/joint regions. Instances are presented with different colors. Best viewed in color.

The Dimension of the Mask Feature. The mask feature contains the knowledge of instances. We conduct experiments to show the influence of different dimensions of the mask feature. We find the fluctuation of the performance is relatively small when the dimension is greater than 8, showing the strong robustness of our method to the variation of d'. We set d' to 16 in our experiments.

4.4   Comparison with State-of-the-Art Methods

We compare our method with other state-of-the-art methods on both S3DIS and ScanNet datasets.

3D Detection. Following [7,14], we evaluate the performance of 3D detection on the ScanNet dataset. The results are obtained by fitting axis-aligned bounding boxes for predicted masks, as presented in Table 2. Our method surpasses DyCo3D [14] and 3D-MPA [7] by 4.8% and 1.8% in terms of mAP, respectively. The promising performance demonstrates the compactness of the segmentation results.

Instance Segmentation on S3DIS. Following the evaluation protocols that are widely applied in the previous approaches, experiments are carried out on both Area-5 and 6-Fold cross-validation. As shown in Table 3, our proposed

Table 3. Instance segmentation results on S3DIS. The performance on both Area-5 and 6-fold cross-validation is reported.

Method	mCov	mWCov	mPrec	mRec
Test on Area 5				
SGPN'18 [34]	32.7	35.5	36.0	28.7
ASIS'19 [35]	44.6	47.8	55.3	42.4
3D-BoNet'19 [36]	–	–	57.5	40.2
3D-MPA'20 [7]	–	–	63.1	58.0
MPNet'20 [12]	50.1	53.2	62.5	49.0
InsEmb'20 [13]	49.9	53.2	61.3	48.5
PointGroup'20 [17]	–	–	61.9	62.1
DyCo3D'21 [14]	63.5	64.6	64.3	64.2
HAIS'21 [4]	**64.3**	**66.0**	71.1	65.0
SSTNet'21 [21]	–	–	65.5	64.2
Ours	**64.3**	65.3	**73.1**	**65.2**
Test on 6-fold				
SGPN'18 [34]	37.9	40.8	31.2	38.2
MT-PNet'19 [27]	–	–	24.9	–
MV-CRF'19 [27]	–	–	36.3	–
ASIS'19 [35]	51.2	55.1	63.6	47.5
3D-BoNet'19 [36]	–	–	65.6	47.6
PartNet'19 [25]	–	–	56.4	43.4
InsEmb'20 [13]	54.5	58.0	67.2	51.8
MPNet'20 [12]	55.8	59.7	68.4	53.7
PointGroup'20 [17]	–	–	69.6	69.2
3D-MPA'20 [7]	–	–	66.7	64.1
HAIS'21 [4]	67.0	70.4	73.2	69.4
SSTNet'21 [21]	–	–	73.5	73.4
Ours	**71.5**	**74.1**	**76.4**	**74.0**

method achieves the highest performance and surpasses previous methods with a much simpler pipeline. With 6-fold validation, our method improves HAIS [4] by 4.5%, 3.7%, 3.2%, and 4.6% in terms of mConv, mWConv, mPrec, and mRec, respectively. The proposed approach works in a fully end-to-end fashion, removing the error accumulation caused by the inter-task dependencies.

Instance Segmentation on ScanNet. The performance of instance segmentation on the validation and testing sets of ScanNet [6] is reported in Table 4 and Table 5, respectively. On the validation set, we report the performance with both small and large backbones, denoted as Ours-S and Ours-L, respectively. It surpasses previous top-performing methods on both architectures in terms of mAP, demonstrating strong generalization capability. Compared with DyCo3D [14], our approach exceeds it by 4.2% in terms of mAP. The qualitative result is illustrated in Fig. 5. We also make a fair comparison with HAIS [4], the highest mAP is achieved on the validation set.

Table 4. Quantitative comparison on the validation set of ScanNetV2. To make a fair comparison, we report the performance with different model scalability. The performance of HAIS-S is obtained by using the official training code.

	AP@50	mAP	Cabinet	Bed	Chair	Sofa	Table	Door	Window	Bookshe.	Picture	Counter	Desk	Curtain	Fridge	S.curtain	Toilet	Sink	Bath	Otherfu.
SGPN [34]	11.3	–	10.1	16.4	20.2	20.7	14.7	11.1	11.1	0.0	0.0	10.0	10.3	12.8	0.0	0.0	48.7	16.5	0.0	0.0
3D-SIS [16]	18.7	–	19.7	37.7	40.5	31.9	15.9	18.1	0.0	11.0	0.0	0.0	10.5	11.1	18.5	24.0	45.8	15.8	23.5	12.9
3D-MPA [7]	59.1	35.3	51.9	72.2	83.8	66.8	63.0	43.0	44.5	58.4	38.8	31.1	43.2	47.7	61.4	80.6	99.2	50.6	87.1	40.3
PointGroup [17]	56.9	34.8	48.1	69.6	87.7	71.5	62.9	42.0	46.2	54.9	37.7	22.4	41.6	44.9	37.2	62.7	98.3	61.1	80.5	53.0
DyCo3D-S [14]	57.6	35.4	50.6	73.8	84.4	72.1	69.9	40.8	44.5	62.4	34.8	21.2	42.2	37.0	41.6	62.7	92.9	61.6	82.6	47.5
HAIS-S [4]	59.1	38.0	54.4	76.0	87.7	69.4	66.5	47.5	48.5	53.1	43.6	24.0	50.9	**55.8**	45.1	58.5	94.7	53.6	80.8	53.0
Ours-S	59.2	39.6	51.1	75.9	86.5	**72.8**	67.3	45.2	**52.3**	57.2	43.8	25.7	40.5	53.7	37.2	59.4	98.2	58.9	87.0	52.9
DyCo3D-L [14]	61.0	40.6	52.3	70.4	90.2	65.8	69.6	40.5	47.2	48.4	44.7	34.9	52.3	47.5	51.5	70.3	94.8	**74.3**	77.4	56.4
HAIS-L [4]	**64.0**	43.5	55.4	70.2	82.5	67.7	75.3	48.1	51.5	49.4	**48.7**	**47.8**	**58.5**	55.7	**53.0**	76.1	**100.0**	69.2	**87.1**	56.3
Ous-L	63.7	**45.6**	**58.5**	**78.5**	**93.6**	63.2	**76.5**	**55.6**	48.5	59.4	38.3	36.9	54.2	50.7	46.2	72.3	98.3	68.8	**87.1**	**59.5**

Table 5. Quantitative results on ScanNetV2 testing set.

	mAP	Bathtub	Bed	Bookshe.	Cabinet	Chair	Counter	Curtain	Desk	Door	Otherfu.	Picture	Refrige.	S.curtain	Sink	Sofa	Table	Toilet	Window
R-PointNet [37]	15.8	35.6	17.3	11.3	14.0	35.9	1.2	2.3	3.9	13.4	12.3	0.8	6.9	14.9	11.7	22.1	12.8	56.3	9.4
3D-SIS [16]	16.1	40.7	15.5	6.8	4.3	34.6	0.1	13.4	0.5	8.8	10.6	3.7	13.5	32.1	2.8	33.9	11.6	46.6	9.3
MASC [24]	25.4	46.3	24.9	11.3	16.7	41.2	0.0	37.4	7.3	17.3	24.3	13.0	22.8	36.8	16.0	35.6	20.8	71.1	13.6
PanopticFusion [26]	21.4	25.0	33.0	27.5	10.3	22.8	0.0	34.5	2.4	8.8	20.3	18.6	16.7	36.7	12.5	22.1	11.2	66.6	16.2
3D-BoNet [36]	25.3	51.9	32.4	25.1	13.7	34.5	3.1	41.9	6.9	16.2	13.1	5.2	20.2	33.8	14.7	30.1	30.3	65.1	17.8
MTML [19]	28.2	57.7	38.0	18.2	10.7	43.0	0.1	42.2	5.7	17.9	16.2	7.0	22.9	51.1	16.1	49.1	31.3	65.0	16.2
3D-MPA [7]	35.5	45.7	48.4	29.9	27.7	59.1	4.7	33.2	21.2	21.7	27.8	19.3	41.3	41.0	19.5	57.4	35.2	84.9	21.3
DyCo3D [14]	39.5	64.2	51.8	44.7	25.9	66.6	5.0	25.1	16.6	23.1	36.2	323.2	33.1	53.5	22.9	58.7	43.8	85.0	31.7
PointGroup [17]	40.7	63.9	49.6	41.5	24.3	64.5	2.1	**57.0**	11.4	21.1	35.9	21.7	42.8	66.0	25.6	56.2	34.1	86.0	29.1
HAIS [4]	45.7	70.4	**56.1**	45.7	**36.4**	67.3	4.6	54.7	19.4	30.8	42.6	28.8	45.4	71.1	26.2	56.3	43.4	88.9	**34.4**
Ours	43.8	81.5	50.7	33.8	35.5	70.3	8.9	39.0	20.8	31.3	37.3	28.8	40.1	66.6	24.2	55.3	44.2	91.3	29.3
OccuSeg* [10]	44.3	**85.2**	56.0	38.0	24.9	67.9	9.7	34.5	18.6	29.8	33.9	23.1	41.3	80.7	34.5	50.6	42.4	**97.2**	29.1
SSTN* [21]	**50.6**	73.8	54.9	**49.7**	31.6	69.3	**17.8**	37.7	19.8	**33.0**	**46.3**	**57.6**	51.5	**85.7**	49.4	**63.7**	45.7	94.3	29.0

5   Conclusion and Future Works

In this paper, we propose a novel pipeline for 3D instance segmentation, which works in a per-point prediction fashion and thus removes the inter-task dependencies. We show that the key to its success is the target assignment, which is addressed by an Optimal Transport solution. Without bells and whistles, our method achieves promising results on two commonly used datasets.

The sampling strategy used in our method is fps, which is slightly better than random sampling. We believe there exist other informative strategies that can further improve the performance. In addition, due to the continuity representation capability, our method offers a simple solution to achieve instance-level reconstruction with the sparse point cloud. We leave these for future works.

References

1. Armeni, I., et al.: 3D semantic parsing of large-scale indoor spaces. In: Proceedings of the IEEE Conference on Computer Vision and Pattern Recognition, pp. 1534–1543 (2016)
2. Brabandere, B.D., Neven, D., Gool, L.V.: Semantic instance segmentation with a discriminative loss function. arXiv preprint arXiv:1708.02551 (2017)
3. Cai, Z., Vasconcelos, N.: Cascade R-CNN: delving into high quality object detection. In: Proceedings of the IEEE Conference on Computer Vision and Pattern Recognition, pp. 6154–6162 (2018)
4. Chen, S., Fang, J., Zhang, Q., Liu, W., Wang, X.: Hierarchical aggregation for 3D instance segmentation. In: Proceedings of the IEEE/CVF International Conference on Computer Vision, pp. 15467–15476 (2021)
5. Cuturi, M.: Sinkhorn distances: lightspeed computation of optimal transport. In: NeurIPS (2013)
6. Dai, A., Chang, A.X., Savva, M., Halber, M., Funkhouser, T., Nießner, M.: Scannet: richly-annotated 3D reconstructions of indoor scenes. In: CVPR (2017)
7. Engelmann, F., Bokeloh, M., Fathi, A., Leibe, B., Nießner, M.: 3D-MPA: multi proposal aggregation for 3D semantic instance segmentation. In: CVPR (2020)
8. Ge, Z., Liu, S., Li, Z., Yoshie, O., Sun, J.: Ota: optimal transport assignment for object detection. In: CVPR (2021)
9. Graham, B., Engelcke, M., van der Maaten, L.: 3D semantic segmentation with submanifold sparse convolutional networks. In: CVPR (2018)
10. Han, L., Zheng, T., Xu, L., Fang, L.: Occuseg: occupancy-aware 3D instance segmentation. In: CVPR (2020)
11. He, K., Gkioxari, G., Dollár, P., Girshick, R.: Mask R-CNN. In: ICCV (2017)
12. He, T., Gong, D., Tian, Z., Shen, C.: Learning and memorizing representative prototypes for 3D point cloud semantic and instance segmentation. In: Vedaldi, A., Bischof, H., Brox, T., Frahm, J.-M. (eds.) ECCV 2020. LNCS, vol. 12363, pp. 564–580. Springer, Cham (2020). https://doi.org/10.1007/978-3-030-58523-5_33
13. He, T., Liu, Y., Shen, C., Wang, X., Sun, C.: Instance-aware embedding for point cloud instance segmentation. In: Vedaldi, A., Bischof, H., Brox, T., Frahm, J.-M. (eds.) ECCV 2020. LNCS, vol. 12375, pp. 255–270. Springer, Cham (2020). https://doi.org/10.1007/978-3-030-58577-8_16

14. He, T., Shen, C., van den Hengel, A.: DyCo3d: robust instance segmentation of 3D point clouds through dynamic convolution. In: CVPR (2021)
15. He, T., Shen, C., van den Hengel, A.: Dynamic convolution for 3D point cloud instance segmentation. arXiv preprint arXiv:2107.08392 (2021)
16. Hou, J., Dai, A., Nießner, M.: 3D-SIS: 3D semantic instance segmentation of rgb-d scans. In: CVPR (2019)
17. Jiang, L., Zhao, H., Shi, S., Liu, S., Fu, C.W., Jia, J.: Pointgroup: dual-set point grouping for 3d instance segmentation. In: CVPR (2020)
18. Kong, T., Sun, F., Liu, H., Jiang, Y., Li, L., Shi, J.: Foveabox: beyond anchor-based object detector. IEEE TIP **29**, 7389–7398 (2020)
19. Lahoud, J., Ghanem, B., Pollefeys, M., Oswald, M.R.: 3D instance segmentation via multi-task metric learning. In: ICCV (2019)
20. Landrieu, L., Simonovski, M.: Large-scale point cloud semantic segmentation with superpoint graphs. In: CVPR (2018)
21. Liang, Z., Li, Z., Xu, S., Tan, M., Jia, K.: Instance segmentation in 3D scenes using semantic superpoint tree networks. In: ICCV (2021)
22. Lin, T.Y., Dollár, P., Girshick, R., He, K., Hariharan, B., Belongie, S.: Feature pyramid networks for object detection. In: CVPR (2017)
23. Lin, T.Y., Goyal, P., Girshick, R., He, K., Dollár, P.: Focal loss for dense object detection. In: ICCV (2017)
24. Liu, C., Furukawa, Y.: MASC: multi-scale affinity with sparse convolution for 3D instance segmentation. arXiv preprint arXiv:1902.04478 (2019)
25. Mo, K., et al.: PartNet: a large-scale benchmark for fine-grained and hierarchical part-level 3D object understanding. In: CVPR (2019)
26. Narita, G., Seno, T., Ishikawa, T., Kaji, Y.: Panopticfusion: online volumetric semantic mapping at the level of stuff and things. In: IROS (2019)
27. Pham, Q.H., Nguyen, D.T., Hua, B.S., Roig, G., Yeung, S.K.: JSIS3D: joint semantic-instance segmentation of 3D point clouds with multi-task pointwise networks and multi-value conditional random fields. In: CVPR (2019)
28. Qi, C.R., Litany, O., He, K., Guibas, L.J.: Deep hough voting for 3D object detection in point clouds. In: ICCV (2019)
29. Qi, C.R., Liu, W., Wu, C., Su, H., Guibas, L.J.: Frustum pointnets for 3D object detection from rgb-d data. In: CVPR (2018)
30. Ren, S., He, K., Girshick, R., Sun, J.: Faster R-CNN: towards real-time object detection with region proposal networks. In: NeurIPS (2015)
31. Tian, Z., Shen, C., Chen, H.: Conditional convolutions for instance segmentation. In: Vedaldi, A., Bischof, H., Brox, T., Frahm, J.-M. (eds.) ECCV 2020. LNCS, vol. 12346, pp. 282–298. Springer, Cham (2020). https://doi.org/10.1007/978-3-030-58452-8_17
32. Tian, Z., Shen, C., Chen, H., He, T.: FCOS: fully convolutional one-stage object detection. In: ICCV (2019)
33. Tian, Z., Shen, C., Chen, H., He, T.: FCOS: a simple and strong anchor-free object detector. IEEE TPAMI (2021)
34. Wang, W., Yu, R., Huang, Q., Neumann, U.: SGPN: similarity group proposal network for 3D point cloud instance segmentation. In: CVPR (2018)
35. Wang, X., Liu, S., Shen, X., Shen, C., Jia, J.: Associatively segmenting instances and semantics in point clouds. In: CVPR (2019)
36. Yang, B., et al.: Learning object bounding boxes for 3D instance segmentation on point clouds. In: NeurIPS (2019)
37. Yi, L., Zhao, W., Wang, H., Sung, M., Guibas, L.J.: GSPN: generative shape proposal network for 3D instance segmentation in point cloud. In: CVPR (2018)

38. Yu, J., Jiang, Y., Wang, Z., Cao, Z., Huang, T.: Unitbox: an advanced object detection network. In: ACM MM (2016)
39. Zhang, S., Chi, C., Yao, Y., Lei, Z., Li, S.Z.: Bridging the gap between anchor-based and anchor-free detection via adaptive training sample selection. In: CVPR (2020)
40. Zhang, X., Wan, F., Liu, C., Ji, R., Ye, Q.: FreeAnchor: learning to match anchors for visual object detection. In: NeurIPS (2019)
41. Zhao, L., Tao, W.: JSNet: joint instance and semantic segmentation of 3D point clouds. In: AAAI (2020)
42. Zhou, X., Wang, D., Krähenbühl, P.: Objects as points. In: arXiv preprint arXiv:1904.07850 (2019)

Cross-modal 3D Shape Generation and Manipulation

Zezhou Cheng[1], Menglei Chai[2(✉)], Jian Ren[2], Hsin-Ying Lee[2],
Kyle Olszewski[2], Zeng Huang[2], Subhransu Maji[1], and Sergey Tulyakov[2]

[1] University of Massachusetts, Amherst, USA
[2] Snap Inc., Santa Monica, USA
cmlatsim@gmail.com

Abstract. Creating and editing the shape and color of 3D objects require tremendous human effort and expertise. Compared to direct manipulation in 3D interfaces, 2D interactions such as sketches and scribbles are usually much more natural and intuitive for the users. In this paper, we propose a generic multi-modal generative model that couples the 2D modalities and implicit 3D representations through shared latent spaces. With the proposed model, versatile 3D generation and manipulation are enabled by simply propagating the editing from a specific 2D controlling modality through the latent spaces. For example, editing the 3D shape by drawing a sketch, re-colorizing the 3D surface via painting color scribbles on the 2D rendering, or generating 3D shapes of a certain category given one or a few reference images. Unlike prior works, our model does not require re-training or fine-tuning per editing task and is also conceptually simple, easy to implement, robust to input domain shifts, and flexible to diverse reconstruction on partial 2D inputs. We evaluate our framework on two representative 2D modalities of grayscale line sketches and rendered color images, and demonstrate that our method enables various shape manipulation and generation tasks with these 2D modalities.

1 Introduction

With the growth in 3D acquisition and visualization technology, there is an increasing need of tools for 3D content creation and editing tasks such as deforming the shape of an object, changing the color of a part, or inserting or removing a component. The graphics and vision community has proposed a number of tools for these tasks [2,13,39,43]. Yet, manipulating 3D still requires tremendous human labor and expertise, prohibiting wide-scale adoption by non-professionals. Compared to the traditional 3D user interfaces, 2D interactions on view-dependent image planes

---

This work was mainly done while the first author was an intern at Snap Inc. Code and data are available at https://people.cs.umass.edu/~zezhoucheng/edit3d/.

Supplementary Information The online version contains supplementary material available at https://doi.org/10.1007/978-3-031-20062-5_18.

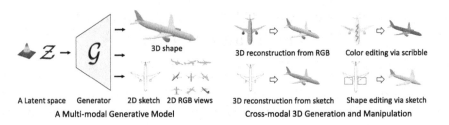

Fig. 1. We propose a multi-modal generative model that bridges multiple 2D (*e.g.*, sketch, color views) and 3D modalities via shared latent spaces (*left*). Versatile 3D shape generation and manipulation tasks can be tackled via simple latent optimization method (*right*).

can be a more intuitive way to edit the shape. This has motivated the community to leverage advances in shape representations using deep networks [9,35,38,47] for 3D shape manipulation with 2D controls, such as mesh reconstruction from sketches [20] and color editing with scribbles [34]. However, most prior works on 2D-to-3D shape manipulation are tailored to a particular editing task and interaction format, which makes generalization to new editing tasks or controls challenging, or even infeasible. This is important because there is often no single interaction that fits every use case – the preferred 2D user control depends on the editing goals, scenarios, devices, or targeted users.

Motivated by this, we propose a 2D-to-3D framework that not only works on a single control modality but also enjoys the flexibility of handling various types of 2D interactions without the need for changing the architecture or even re-training (Fig. 1 left). Our framework bridges various 2D interaction modalities and the target 3D shape through a uniform editing propagation mechanism. The key is to construct a shared latent representation across generative models of each of the 2D and 3D modalities. The shared latent representation enforces that an arbitrary latent code corresponds to a 3D model that is consistent with every modality, in terms of both shape and color. With our model, any editing can be achieved by an objective that aims to match the corresponding editing modality and backpropagating the error to estimate the latent code. Moreover, different editing operations and modalities can be combined and interleaved leading to a versatile tool for editing the shape (Fig. 1 right). The approach can be extended to a new user control by simply adding a generator for the corresponding modality in the framework.

We evaluate our framework on two representative 2D modalities, *i.e.*, grayscale line sketches, and rendered color images. We provide extensive quantitative and qualitative results in shape and color editing with sketches and scribbles, as well as single-view, few-shot, or even partial-view cross-modal shape generation. The proposed method is conceptually simple, easy to implement, robust to input domain shifts, and generalizable to new modalities with no special requirement on the network architecture.

2 Related Work

Multi-Modal Generative Models. There has been much work on learning a joint distribution of multiple modalities $p(x_0, \ldots, x_n)$ where each modality x_i represents one representation (*e.g.*, images, text) of underlying signals. Multi-modal VAEs [27,46,49,53,54] learn a joint distribution $p_\theta(x_0, \ldots, x_n \mid z)$ conditioned on common latent variables $z \in \mathcal{Z}$. Without the assumption of paired multi-modal data, multi-modal GANs [10,17,31] learn the joint distribution by sharing a latent space and model parameters across modalities. These multi-modal generative models have enabled versatile applications such as cross-modal image translation [10,31] and domain adaptation [31]. Similar to these works, we build a multi-modal generative model that bridges multiple modalities via a shared latent space. However, we generate and edit 3D shapes with sparse 2D inputs (*e.g.*, scribbles, sketches) and build a 2D-3D generative model based on variational auto-decoders (VADs) [22,57]. Prior work [57] has shown that VADs excel at generative modeling from incomplete data. In this work, we demonstrate that the multi-modal VADs (MM-VADs) are ideally suited for the task of 3D generation and manipulation from sparse 2D inputs (*e.g.*, color scribble or partial inputs).

Table 1. Comparisons to cross-modal 3D editing and generation works.

Methods	*Manipulation*		*Generation*		
	Shape	Color	Single view	Partial view	Few shot
Sketch2Mesh [20]	✓	✗	✓	✗	✗
DualSDF [22]	✓	✗	✗	✗	✗
EditNeRF [34]	✓	✓	✗	✗	✗
Ours	✓	✓	✓	✓	✓

Shape and Appearance Reconstruction. Extensive works have explored the problem of 3D reconstruction from different modalities, such as RGB images [11, 25], videos [56], sketches [20,24,60,61], or even text [8]. This problem has also been explored under diverse representations [9,11,14,15,33,35,38,47,51,55] and different levels of supervision [11,15,16,25,56]. Despite the diverse settings of this problem, the encoder-decoder network, which maps the source modalities to 3D shape directly in a feed-forward manner, remains the most popular 3D reconstruction model [11,25,38,51]. However, such feed-forward networks are not robust to input domain shift (*e.g.*, incomplete data). In this work, we demonstrate that the proposed MM-VADs perform more robustly and could provide multiple 3D reconstructions that fit the given input (*e.g.*, partial 2D views).

Shape and Appearance Manipulation. Numerous interactive tools have been developed for image editing [18,28–30,41,59] and 3D shape manipulations [2,13,39,43]. More recently, generative modeling of natural images [17,48] has became a "Swiss knife" for image editing problems [1,4,5,19,37,42,44,45,62]. Similar to these works, we build a multi-modal generative model that is able to tackle versatile 3D shape generation and editing tasks with 2D inputs. Novel interactive tools have also been proposed recently to edit implicit 3D representations [36,38]. For example, DualSDF [22] edits the SDFs [38] via shape primitives (e.g., spheres). Sketch2Mesh [20] reconstructs shapes from sketch with an encoder-decoder network and refines 3D shapes via differentiable rendering. Edit-NeRF [34] edits the radiance field [36] by fine-tuning the network weights based on user's scribbles.

Table 1 summarizes the commons and differences between our work and recent efforts [20,22,34] on 3D manipulation and generation. Similar to Sketch2Mesh [20], we edit and reconstruct 3D shape from 2D sketch. However, we tackle this problem via a novel multi-modal *generative* model that performs more robust to input domain shift (e.g., partial input, sparse color scribble). Furthermore, the shape and color edits can be combined and interleaved with our model; Like EditNeRF, we edit the appearance of 3D shapes via 2D color scribbles. However, we conduct the 3D editing via a simple latent optimization, instead of finetuning the network weights per edit; Akin to DualSDF [22], we build a generative model for 3D manipulation, yet we generate and edit shapes from 2D modalities which is more intuitive to edit the shape than using 3D primitives. Moreover, our generative model can be adapted to generate 3D shapes of a certain category (e.g., armchairs) given a few 2D examples, namely, *few-shot cross-modal shape generation*.

3   Method

We describe the Variational Auto-Decoders (VADs) [57] in Sect. 3.1, introduce the proposed VAD-based multi-modal generative model (dubbed MM-VADs) in Sect. 3.2, and illustrate the application of MM-VADs in cross-modal 3D shape generation and manipulation tasks in Sect. 3.3.

3.1   Background: Variational Auto-decoder

Given observation variables $x \sim p(x)$ and latent variables $z \sim p(z)$, a variational auto-decoder (VAD) approximates the data distribution $p(x)$ via a parametric family of distributions $p_\theta(x \mid z)$ with parameters θ. Similar to variational auto-encoders (VAEs) [27], VADs are trained by maximizing the marginal distribution $p(x) = \int p_\theta(x \mid z)p(z)dz$. In practice this integral is expensive or intractable, so the model parameters θ are learned instead by maximizing the Evidence Lower Bound (ELBO):

$$\mathcal{V}(\phi, \theta \mid x) = -\operatorname{KL}\big(q_\phi(z \mid x) \parallel p(z)\big) + \mathbb{E}_{q_\phi(z \mid x)}\big[\log p_\theta(x \mid z)\big], \qquad (1)$$

where $\operatorname{KL}(\cdot \parallel \cdot)$ is the Kullback-Leibler divergence that encourages the posterior distribution to follow the latent prior $p(z)$, and $q_\phi(z \mid x)$ is an approximation of the posterior $p(z \mid x)$. In VAEs, $q_\phi(z \mid x)$ is parametrized by a neural network and ϕ are the parameters of the encoder. In VADs, ϕ are instead learnable similar to the parameters θ in the decoder $p_\theta(x \mid z)$. For example, the multivariate Gaussian approximate posterior for a data instance x_i is defined as:

$$q_\phi(z \mid x_i) := \mathcal{N}(z; \mu_i, \Sigma_i), \tag{2}$$

where $\phi = \{\mu_i, \Sigma_i\}$. The reparametrization trick is applied in order to back-propagate the gradients to the mean μ_i and variance Σ_i in VADs. In comparison, VAEs back-propagate the gradients through the mean μ_i and variance Σ_i to learn the parameters of the encoder. At inference time, the parameters ϕ of the approximate posterior distribution can be estimated by maximizing the ELBO in Eq. 1 while the parameters θ of the decoder are frozen:

$$\phi^* = \arg\max_\phi \ \mathcal{V}(\phi \mid \theta, x_i). \tag{3}$$

Despite the similarity between VAEs and VADs, prior works [57] demonstrate that VADs perform approximate posterior inference more robustly on *incomplete data* and *input domain shifts* than VAEs.

3.2 Multi-modal Variational Auto-decoder

We consider two modalities x, w and an *i.i.d.* dataset with paired instances $(X, W) = \{(x_0, w_0), \dots, (x_N, w_N)\}$. We target at learning a joint distribution of both modalities $p(x, w)$. Like VADs [57], the multi-modal VADs (MM-VADs) are trained by maximizing the ELBO:

$$\mathcal{V}(\phi, \theta \mid x, w) = -\operatorname{KL}\big(q_\phi(z \mid x, w) \parallel p(z)\big) + \mathbb{E}_{q_\phi(z \mid x, w)}\big[\log p_\theta(x, w \mid z)\big], \tag{4}$$

where z is the latent variable shared by the two modalities x and w, $p_\theta(x, w \mid z) = p_{\theta_x}(x \mid z)p_{\theta_w}(w \mid z)$ under the assumption that the two modalities x and w are independent conditioned on the latent variable z (*i.e.*, $x \perp\!\!\!\perp w \mid z$). In practice, $p_{\theta_x}(x \mid z)$ or $p_{\theta_w}(w \mid z)$ can be parameterized by different networks for the two modalities x and w respectively. The parameters ϕ of the approximate posterior distribution $q_\phi(z \mid x, w)$ are learnable parameters where $\phi = \{\mu, \Sigma\}$ under the assumption of multivariate Gaussian posterior distribution. At inference time, the parameters ϕ are estimated via maximizing the ELBO with frozen decoder parameters θ:

$$\phi^* = \arg\max_\phi \ \mathcal{V}(\phi \mid \theta, x_i, w_i). \tag{5}$$

When one of the modalities is missing during inference, the inputs of the missing modalities are simply set to zero. This is the case when we want to infer one modality from the other (*e.g.*, 3D reconstruction from 2D sketch). This framework can be trivially extended to learn a joint distribution of more than two modalities.

3.3   Learning a Joint 2D-3D Prior with MM-VADs

Here we introduce the application of MM-VADs in cross-modal 3D shape generation and manipulation. Specifically, we learn a joint distribution of 2D and 3D modalities with MM-VADs. Once trained, MM-VADs can be applied to versatile shape generation and editing tasks via a simple posterior inference (or latent optimization). We explore three representative modalities, including 3D shape with colorful surface, 2D sketch in grayscale, and 2D rendered image in RGB color, donated as C, S, R respectively. Given a dataset $\{(C_i, S_i, R_i)\}$, we target at learning a joint distribution of the three modalities $p(C, S, R)$. Figure 2 presents the overview of the MM-VADs framework. We provide more details in the following sections.

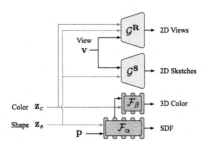

Fig. 2. Network architecture. We propose a multi-modal variational auto-decoder consisting of compact shape and color latent spaces shared across multiple 2D (*e.g.*, sketch, RGB views) or 3D modalities (*e.g.*, signed distance function and 3D surface color). (Color figure online)

Joint Latent Space. The MM-VADs share a common latent space $\mathcal{Z}$ across different modalities (Eq. 4). Targeting at editing 3D shape and surface color independently, we further disentangle the shared latent space into the shape and color subspaces, denoted as $\mathcal{Z}_s$ and $\mathcal{Z}_c$ respectively. Therefore, each latent code $z = z_s \oplus z_c$, where $z_s \in \mathcal{Z}_s$, $z_c \in \mathcal{Z}_c$, and $\oplus$ denotes the concatenation operator.

3D Colorful Shape. Targeting at generating and editing 3D shapes and their appearance, we use the 3D colorful shape as one of our modalities. Among various representations of 3D shapes (*e.g.*, voxel, mesh, point clouds), the implicit representations [35,38,47] model 3D shapes as isosurfaces of functions and are capable of capturing high-level details. We adopt the DeepSDF [38] to regress the signed distance functions (SDFs) from point samples directly using a MLP-based *3D shape network* $\mathcal{F}_\alpha(z_s \oplus p)$, whose input is a shape latent code $z_s \in \mathcal{Z}_s$ and 3D coordinates $p \in \mathbb{R}^3$. We predict the surface color with another feed-forward *3D color network* $\mathcal{F}_\beta(z_c \oplus z_s^k)$, whose input is a color latent code $z_c \in \mathcal{Z}_c$ and the intermediate features from the k-th layer of 3D shape network $\mathcal{F}_\alpha$. The generator of the 3D modality $\mathcal{G}^C$ is the combination of the 3D shape and color network:

$$\mathcal{G}^C(z_s \oplus z_c \oplus p) = \{\mathcal{F}_\alpha(z_s \oplus p), \mathcal{F}_\beta(z_c \oplus z_s^k)\}. \tag{6}$$

Both networks are trained using the same set of spatial points. The objective function $\mathcal{L}^C$ for $\mathcal{G}^C$ is the $\mathcal{L}_1$ loss defined between the prediction and the ground-truth SDF values and surface colors on the sampled points.

2D Sketch. The 2D sketch depicts the 3D structures and provides a natural way for the user to manipulate the 3D shapes. For the purpose of generalization, we adopt a simple and standard fully convolutional network [40] as our sketch generator $\mathcal{G}^S(\boldsymbol{z}_s \oplus \boldsymbol{v})$ with the shape code $\boldsymbol{z}_s \in \mathcal{Z}_s$ and the viewpoint $\boldsymbol{v}$ as input. The objective function $\mathcal{L}^S$ is defined as a cross-entropy loss between the reconstructed and ground-truth sketches.

2D Rendering. The 2D color rendering reflects a view-dependent appearance of the 3D surface. Drawing 2D scribbles on the renderings provides an efficient and straightforward interactive tool for the user to edit the 3D surface color. Similar to the 2D sketch modality, we use the standard fully convolutional architecture [40] as our 2D rendering generator $\mathcal{G}^R(\boldsymbol{z}_s \oplus \boldsymbol{z}_c \oplus \boldsymbol{v})$, which takes the concatenation of the shape code $\boldsymbol{z}_s \in \mathcal{Z}_s$, the color code $\boldsymbol{z}_c \in \mathcal{Z}_c$ and the viewpoint $\boldsymbol{v}$. We adopt Laplacian-$\mathcal{L}_1$ loss [3] to train $\mathcal{G}^R$:

$$\mathcal{L}^R(\boldsymbol{z}_i \oplus \boldsymbol{v}, \boldsymbol{R}_i) = \frac{1}{N} \sum_j^J 4^{-j} \big\| \mathrm{L}^j(\mathcal{G}^R(\boldsymbol{z}_i \oplus \boldsymbol{v})) - \mathrm{L}^j(\boldsymbol{R}_i) \big\|_1, \qquad (7)$$

where $\boldsymbol{z}_i$ is the concatenation of the shape and color codes for the target image $\boldsymbol{R}_i$, N is the total number of pixels in the image $\boldsymbol{R}_i$, J is the total number of levels of the Laplacian pyramid (e.g., 3 by default), and $\mathrm{L}^j(x)$ is the j-th level in the pyramid of image x [6]. This loss encourages sharper output [3] compared to the standard $\mathcal{L}_1$ or MSE loss.

Summary. The proposed MM-VAD framework for learning the joint distribution of the three modalities can be learned with the following objective:

$$\begin{aligned} \mathcal{V}(\phi, \theta \mid \boldsymbol{C}, \boldsymbol{S}, \boldsymbol{R}) = {} & -\mathrm{KL}\big(q_\phi(\boldsymbol{z} \mid \boldsymbol{C}, \boldsymbol{S}, \boldsymbol{R}) \,\|\, p(\boldsymbol{z})\big) \\ & + \mathbb{E}_{q_\phi(\boldsymbol{z} \mid \boldsymbol{C}, \boldsymbol{S}, \boldsymbol{R})} \big[\log p_\theta(\boldsymbol{C}, \boldsymbol{S}, \boldsymbol{R} \mid \boldsymbol{z}) \big], \end{aligned} \qquad (8)$$

where the first term regularizes the posterior distribution to a latent prior (e.g., $\mathcal{N}(\boldsymbol{0}, \boldsymbol{I})$), and the second term can be factorized into three components under the assumption that modalities are independent conditioned on the shared latent variable $\boldsymbol{z}$:

$$\begin{aligned} \mathbb{E}_{q_\phi(\boldsymbol{z} \mid \boldsymbol{C}, \boldsymbol{S}, \boldsymbol{R})} \big[\log p_\theta(\boldsymbol{C}, \boldsymbol{S}, \boldsymbol{R} \mid \boldsymbol{z}) \big] = {} & \mathbb{E}_{q_\phi(\boldsymbol{z} \mid \boldsymbol{C})} \big[\log p_\theta(\boldsymbol{C} \mid \boldsymbol{z}) \big] \\ & + \mathbb{E}_{q_\phi(\boldsymbol{z} \mid \boldsymbol{C})} \big[\log p_\theta(\boldsymbol{S} \mid \boldsymbol{z}) \big] \\ & + \mathbb{E}_{q_\phi(\boldsymbol{z} \mid \boldsymbol{C})} \big[\log p_\theta(\boldsymbol{R} \mid \boldsymbol{z}) \big] \\ = {} & \mathcal{L}^C + \mathcal{L}^S + \mathcal{L}^R, \end{aligned} \qquad (9)$$

where each term corresponds to the reconstruction loss per modality as described above. Notice that the 3D shape modality $\boldsymbol{C}$ contains all the information in the latent variable $\boldsymbol{z}$, therefore $q_\phi(\boldsymbol{z} \mid \boldsymbol{C}, \boldsymbol{S}, \boldsymbol{R}) = q_\phi(\boldsymbol{z} \mid \boldsymbol{C})$.

3.4   Cross-modal Shape Manipulation with MM-VADs

Given an initial latent code z_0 that corresponds to the initial 3D shape $\mathcal{G}^C(z_0)$ and any 2D control $\mathcal{G}^M(z_0)$ of the 2D modality $M \in \{S, R\}$, the shape manipulation is conducted by optimizing within the latent space to get the updated code $\hat{z}$ such that $\mathcal{G}(\hat{z})^M$ matches the 2D edits e^M:

$$\hat{z} = \arg\min_z \; \mathcal{L}_{\text{edit}}(\mathcal{G}^M(z), e^M) + \mathcal{L}_{\text{reg}}(z), \tag{10}$$

where $\mathcal{L}_{\text{edit}}$ could be any loss (e.g., $\mathcal{L}_1$ loss) that encourages the 2D modalities $\mathcal{G}(\hat{z})^M$ to match the 2D edits e^M, and $\mathcal{L}_{\text{reg}}(z)$ encourages the latent code to stay in the latent prior of MM-VADs. We apply the regularization loss proposed in DualSDF [22]:

$$\mathcal{L}_{\text{reg}} = \gamma \max(\|z\|_2^2, \beta), \tag{11}$$

where γ and β controls the strength of the regularization loss. The latent optimization is closely related to the posterior inference (Eq. 5) of MM-VADs.

MM-VADs allows free-form edits e^M. For example, the edits e^M could be local modifications on the sketch or sparse color scribbles on 2D renderings. This makes the MM-VADs ideally suited for the interactive 3D manipulation tasks. In comparison, the encoder-decoder networks [20] are not robust to the input domain shift (e.g., incomplete data [57]) and require re-training per type of user interactions (e.g., sketch, color scribble).

3.5   Cross-modal Shape Generation with MM-VADs

Single-View Reconstruction. Given a single input x^M of the 2D modality $M \in \{C, R\}$, the task of single-view cross-modal shape generation is to reconstruct the corresponding 3D shape satisfying the 2D constraint. Without the need of training one model per pair of 2D and 3D modalities [20,50] or designing differentiable renderers [32] for each 2D modalities [20], like shape manipulation (Sect. 3.4), this task can be tackled via the latent optimization:

$$\hat{z} = \arg\min_z \; \mathcal{L}_{\text{recon}}(\mathcal{G}^M(z), x^M) + \mathcal{L}_{\text{reg}}(z), \tag{12}$$

Partial-View Reconstruction. The MM-VADs are flexible to reconstruct 3D shapes from partially visible inputs. More interestingly, when the input is ambiguous, it provides diverse 3D reconstructions by performing the latent optimization with different initialization of the latent code z. This property has practical applications. For example, the MM-VAD could provide multiple 3D shape suggestions interactively while the user is drawing sketches.

Few-Shot Generation. Given a few 2D images spanning a subspace in the 3D distribution that represents a certain semantic attribute (e.g., armchairs, red chairs), the task of few-shot shape generation is to learn a 3D shape generative model that conceptually aligns with the provided 2D images. Given our pre-trained MM-VAD, we tackle this task by steering the latent space with adversarial loss, borrowing the idea from MineGAN [52]. Specifically, we learn a mapping function $h_\omega(z)$ that maps the prior distribution of the latent space $z \sim \hat{p}(z)$ (*i.e.*, $\mathcal{N}(\mathbf{0}, \mathbf{I})$) to a new distribution such that samples from the 2D generators $\mathcal{G}^M(h_\omega(z))$ aligns the target data distribution $x \sim \hat{p}(x)$ depicted by the provided 2D images. We apply the WGAN-GP loss [21] with frozen generators to learn the mapping function $h_\omega(z)$:

$$\min_\omega \max_\mathcal{D} \ \mathbb{E}_{x \sim \hat{p}(x)}\big[\mathcal{D}(x)\big] - \mathbb{E}_{z \sim p(z)}\big[\mathcal{D}(\mathcal{G}^M(h_\omega(z)))\big], \tag{13}$$

where both the mapping function h_ω and the discriminator $\mathcal{D}$ are trained from scratch.

4   Experiments

This section provides qualitative and quantitative results of the proposed MM-VADs in versatile tasks of 3D shape manipulation (Sect. 4.1) and generation (Sect. 4.2).

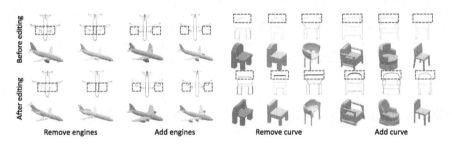

Fig. 3. Editing shape via sketch. The proposed method enables fine-grained editing of shape geometry, *e.g.*, removing the engine of an airplane or reshaping the back of a chair. Interestingly, new engines often appears at the tail of airplane after removing the engines on the wing. This is because airplanes without any engines rarely exist in the domain of our generative model. The edited local regions are highlighted in red bounding boxes.

Dataset. We conduct evaluations and comparisons mainly on 3D ShapeNet dataset [7]. For 3D shapes, We follow DeepSDF [38] to sample 3D points and their signed distances to the object surface. The points that are far from the surface (*i.e.*, with the absolute distance higher than a threshold) are assigned with a pre-defined background color (*e.g.*, white) while points surrounding the surface are assigned with the color of the nearest surface point. For 2D sketches, we use suggestive contours [12] to generate the synthetic sketches. For 2D renderings, we randomize the surface color of 3D shapes per semantic part. We use ShapeNet chairs and airplanes with the same training and test splits as DeepSDF [38].

Implementation Details. We use an 8-layer MLP as the 3D shape network which outputs SDF and a 3-layer MLP as the 3D color network which predicts RGB. We concatenate the features from the 6-th hidden layer of the 3D shape network with the color code as the input to the 3D color network. We train our MM-VADs using Adam [26]. We present more implementation details in the supplementary material.

Baselines. We use the following state-of-the-arts as our baselines:

- **Encoder-Decoder Networks** [20]. This model is trained per task of 3D generation from 2D modalities (sketches or RGB images). We do not use the differentiable rendering proposed in [20] which requires auxiliary information (*e.g.*, segmentation mask, depth) and is applicable to MM-VADs.
- **EditNeRF** [34]. This model edits 3D neural radiance field (including shape and color) by updating the neural network weights based on the user's scribbles. We make comparisons with the pre-trained EditNeRF models.

4.1 Cross-modal Shape Manipulation

Sketch-Based Shape Manipulation. The proposed MM-VADs allow users to edit the fine geometric structures via 2D sketches, as described in Sect. 3.4. We provide users with an interactive interface where users can edit the initial sketch by adding or removing a certain part or even deforming a contour line. Figure 3 presents some qualitative results of sketch-based shape manipulation. Interestingly, we find that our manipulation is semantics-aware. For example, removing

Table 2. Editing shape via sketch. We report the Chamfer distance (CD) between the manually edited shapes and our editing results (*lower* is *better*).

	Airplane		Chair	
	− engine	+ engine	− curve	+ curve
Initial shape	0.096	**0.123**	0.066	**0.085**
Edited shape	**0.059**	0.134	**0.054**	0.124

Fig. 4. Comparison with DualSDF. Left: DualSDF [22] edits 3D shapes via 3D primitives. Editing different primitives on the same part may lead to dramatically different editing results (2nd - 4th columns). **Right:** our sketch-based interactions is more intuitive for the user.

the airplane engines on the wings will automatically add new engines to the tail. Such shape priors are absent in non-generative models (*e.g.*, EditNeRF [34]).

It is challenging to quantitatively evaluate the sketch-based shape editing due to the lack of ground-truth paired 3D shapes before and after editing. For this reason, prior works [20] report the quantitative results of 3D reconstruction from sketches as a proxy. We follow prior works and report the same quantitative evaluations in Sect. 4.2. Furthermore, we manually edit the 3D shapes presented in Fig. 3 such that their sketches align with the human edits. Table 2 reports the Chamfer distance (CD) between the manually edited shapes and our editing results. We see that CD improves when removing a part, but adding parts unfortunately increases the CD as it induces more changes to the overall shape. This is often desirable, but the CD metric does not reflect that.

Figure 4 provides a comparison with DualSDF [22]. A fair comparison is not possible, as DualSDF edits shapes via 3D primitives instead of 2D views. We find that DualSDF requires users to select *right* primitives to achieve certain edits (*e.g.*, adding a curve to the chair back). In comparison, our sketch-based shape editing is more intuitive.

Scribble-Based Color Manipulation. MM-VADs allow users to edit the appearance of 3D shapes via color scribbles. Figure 5 shows that MM-VADs propagate the sparse color scribbles into desired regions (*e.g.*, from the left wing of the airplanes to the right, from the left leg of chairs to the right). We provide more color editing results with diverse color scribbles in the supplementary

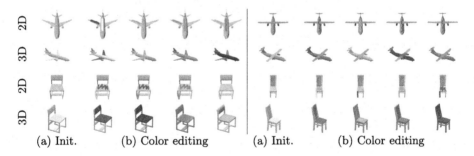

(a) Init.   (b) Color editing   (a) Init.   (b) Color editing

Fig. 5. Editing shape via color scribble. (**a**) presents the initial 2D and 3D view of the object. (**b**) shows the 2D color scribbles and 3D color editing results.

Fig. 6. Comparison with EditNeRF. Our model (**bottom**) achieves comparable editing performance with EditNeRF [34] (**top**). We provide three color edits on 2D views (**odd columns**), each followed by the 3D editing result (**even columns**).

material. As a quantitative evaluation, we select 10 shapes per category (including airplanes and chairs) and edit the surface color to make it visually similar to reference shapes with same geometry yet different surface color. The editing quality is measured by the similarity between the renderings of the edited 3D shapes and the reference shapes. Table 3 reports the PSNR and LPIPS [58] metrics of the evaluation. The surface color of 3D shapes is much closer to the reference after editing, compared to the initial shapes, suggesting the effectiveness of our MM-VAD model in editing color via scribbles.

A similar task has recently been explored in EditNeRF [34]. However, an apple-to-apple comparison with EditNeRF is not possible due to the intrinsically different 3D representations (NeRF [36] vs SDFs [38]). Moreover, the proposed MM-VADs are generative models while EditNeRF is non-generative; The MM-VADs bridge 2D and 3D via shared latent spaces while EditNeRF relies on differentiable rendering. We present more detailed comparisons in the supplementary material. We provide qualitative comparisons with EditNeRF on chairs with similar structures using their pre-trained models. Figure 6 shows that the

Table 3. Quantitative results of editing 3D via 2D scribbles. We edit the surface color of 3D shape based on reference shapes, and report the similarity between the editing results and the target (bottom row). As a reference, we also report the metrics before editing (top row).

Methods	Airplane		Chair	
	PSNR ↑	LPIPS ↓	PSNR ↑	LPIPS ↓
Initial	19.84	0.23	16.20	0.33
Edited	**26.41**	**0.13**	**22.08**	**0.20**

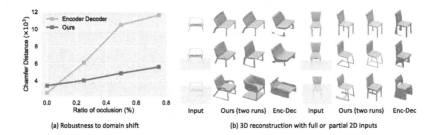

(a) Robustness to domain shift

(b) 3D reconstruction with full or partial 2D inputs

Fig. 7. (a) Robustness to domain shift. We report the Chamfer distance (*lower is better*) between 3D reconstructions and the groundtruth under different ratios of image occlusion. **(b) 3D reconstruction with full or partial 2D inputs.** When the full views are available, our model produces consistent 3D reconstruction in different trials. When only partial views are given, our model produces multiple different 3D reconstructions. In comparison, the encoder-decoder networks [20] trained on full-view sketches are not robust to the domain shift induced by occlusion and unable to provide multiple 3D shapes given partial views. Notice that the predictions of surface color is not available in the encoder-decoder networks from the prior work [20].

color editing from MM-VADs is on par with EditNeRF. The MM-VADs achieve the editing via simple latent optimization (Eq. 12), while EditNeRF requires updating the network weights per instance and fails to generate meaningful color editing results via optimizing the color code alone. Furthermore, MM-VADs take 0.06 seconds per edit and 6.78 seconds to render our 3D shapes into 256×256 RGB images, while EditNeRF takes over a minute per edit including rendering.

4.2 Cross-modal Shape Generation

Single-View and Partial-View Shape Reconstruction. Figure 7 compares the performance of our model and the encoder-decoder networks [20] under different occlusion ratios in the lower part of the objects in 2D views. The proposed model only has a slight performance drop as the occluded parts increase (Fig. 7a), mainly because of the ambiguity of 3D reconstruction given partial views. In fact, our reconstructions results fit the partial views quite well. Even though our model performs slightly worse than the encoder-decoder networks on full-view inputs, the proposed model is more robust to the input domain shift. This is because compared to task-specific training, our model achieves a better trade-off between reconstruction accuracy and domain generalization. More interestingly, our model can achieve diverse and reasonable 3D reconstruction by sampling different initialization for latent optimization (Fig. 7b).

Few-Shot Shape Generation. The proposed method is able to adapt the pre-trained multi-modal generative model with as few as 10 training samples of a specific 2D modality. Figure 8 presents some of the few-shot cross-modal shape generation results. To quantitatively evaluate the few-shot shape generation performance, we render the 3D shapes into 2D RGB images and report the Frechet Inception Distance (FID) scores [23] between the rendered images and the ground-truth samples. Since the FID score is not sensitive to the semantic difference between two image sets, we also report the classification error on the random samples from the model before and after the adaptation. Specifically, we train a binary image classifier to identify the target image categories (*e.g.*, armchairs vs. other chairs), and we run the trained classifier on the 2D

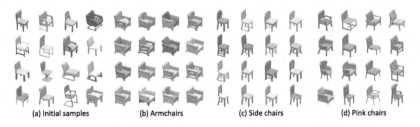

(a) Initial samples   (b) Armchairs   (c) Side chairs   (d) Pink chairs

Fig. 8. Few-shot cross-modal shape generation. (a) presents random 3D samples from our model before the adaptation. Given a few 2D exemplars of a certain category (*e.g.*, armchair), our model can be adapted to generate corresponding 3D shapes (b-d).

Table 4. Quantitative results of few-shot cross-modal shape generation. We report Frechet Inception Distance (FID) (*lower is better*) and classification error (Cls. Err) (*lower is better*). We effectively adapt the pretrained multi-modal VAD model using a few 2D images to a desired 3D shape generator. As a reference, we report the metrics before the few-shot adaptation (top row).

Stage	Metrics	Arm	Side	Red	Avg.
Init.	FID ↓	138.1	95.2	93.7	109.0
	Cls.Err. ↓	0.79	0.64	0.82	0.75
Adapt.	FID ↓	**130.4**	**92.4**	**93.0**	**105.3**
	Cls.Err. ↓	**0.01**	**0.10**	**0.00**	**0.04**

renderings of the 3D samples before and after the adaptation. As presented in Table 4, our pre-trained generative model can be effectively adapted to a certain shape subspace given as few as 10 2D examples. This capability allows us to agilely adapt our generative model to a subspace defined by a few unlabelled samples, so that users can easily narrow down the target shape during the manipulation by providing a few samples of a common attribute, such as a specific category, style, or color. We are unaware of any prior works that can tackle this task in the literature. The 2D examples used to adapt the pre-trained generative model are provided in our supplementary materials.

Shape and Color Transfer. Transferring shape and color across different 3D instances can be achieved by simply swapping the latent codes. Figure 9 shows that the shape and color are well disentangled in the proposed generative model. The transfer results also are semantically meaningful, *i.e.*, the color is only transferred across the same semantic parts (*e.g.*, seats for the chair, wings for the airplane) even though the geometry of the source and target instances are quite different.

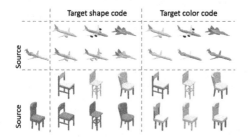

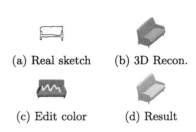

(a) Real sketch   (b) 3D Recon.

(c) Edit color   (d) Result

Fig. 9. Shape and color transfer. The reference 3D shapes (top row) provide the shape codes or color codes for each source instances (first column).

Fig. 10. Our model enables consecutive 3D reconstruction and manipulation given a hand-drawn sketch.

4.3   Case Study on Real Images

The workflow of 3D designers usually starts by drawing a 2D sketch to portray the coarse 3D geometry and then colorizes the sketch to depict the 3D appearance. These 2D arts are used as a reference to build 3D objects. Undoubtedly this procedure requires extensive human efforts and expertise. Such tasks can be automated with our MM-VADs. As shown in Fig. 10, we first reconstruct the 3D shape from a hand-drawn sketch. We then assign a surface color by randomly sampling a color code from the latent space of the MM-VADs, which can be easily edited by drawing color scribbles on the surface. Our model does not require any re-training on each of these steps and provides a tool to conduct shape generation and color editing consecutively. Such a task is infeasible with the existing works that train an encoder-decoder network to predict 3D shape from sketch [20].

5   Discussion

We propose a multi-modal generative model which bridges multiple 2D and 3D modalities through a shared latent space. One limitation of the proposed method is that we are only able to provide editing results in the prior distribution of our generative model (see supplementary material for more details). Despite this limitation, our model has enabled versatile cross-modal 3D generation and manipulation tasks without the need of re-training per task and demonstrates strong robustness to input domain shift.

Acknowledgements. Subhransu Maji acknowledges support from NSF grants #1749833 and #1908669. Our experiments were partially performed on the University of Massachusetts GPU cluster funded by the Mass. Technology Collaborative.

References

1. Abdal, R., Qin, Y., Wonka, P.: Image2stylegan: how to embed images into the stylegan latent space? In: Proceedings of the IEEE/CVF International Conference on Computer Vision, pp. 4432–4441 (2019)
2. An, X., Tong, X., Denning, J.D., Pellacini, F.: AppWarp: retargeting measured materials by appearance-space warping. In: Proceedings of the 2011 SIGGRAPH Asia Conference, pp. 1–10 (2011)
3. Athar, S., Burnaev, E., Lempitsky, V.: Latent convolutional models. In: ICLR (2018)
4. Bau, D., Liu, S., Wang, T., Zhu, J.-Y., Torralba, A.: Rewriting a deep generative model. In: Vedaldi, A., Bischof, H., Brox, T., Frahm, J.-M. (eds.) ECCV 2020. LNCS, vol. 12346, pp. 351–369. Springer, Cham (2020). https://doi.org/10.1007/978-3-030-58452-8_21
5. Bau, D., Strobelt, H., Peebles, W., Zhou, B., Zhu, J.Y., Torralba, A., et al.: Semantic photo manipulation with a generative image prior. arXiv preprint arXiv:2005.07727 (2020)

6. Burt, P.J., Adelson, E.H.: The Laplacian pyramid as a compact image code. In: Readings in computer vision, pp. 671–679. Elsevier (1987)
7. Chang, A.X., et al.: ShapeNet: an information-rich 3D model repository. arXiv preprint arXiv:1512.03012 (2015)
8. Chen, K., Choy, C.B., Savva, M., Chang, A.X., Funkhouser, T., Savarese, S.: Text2Shape: generating shapes from natural language by learning joint embeddings. In: Jawahar, C.V., Li, H., Mori, G., Schindler, K. (eds.) ACCV 2018. LNCS, vol. 11363, pp. 100–116. Springer, Cham (2019). https://doi.org/10.1007/978-3-030-20893-6_7
9. Chen, Z., Zhang, H.: Learning implicit fields for generative shape modeling. In: Proceedings of the IEEE/CVF Conference on Computer Vision and Pattern Recognition, pp. 5939–5948 (2019)
10. Choi, Y., Choi, M., Kim, M., Ha, J.W., Kim, S., Choo, J.: StarGAN: unified generative adversarial networks for multi-domain image-to-image translation. In: Proceedings of the IEEE Conference on Computer Vision and Pattern Recognition, pp. 8789–8797 (2018)
11. Choy, C.B., Xu, D., Gwak, J.Y., Chen, K., Savarese, S.: 3D-R2N2: a unified approach for single and multi-view 3D object reconstruction. In: Leibe, B., Matas, J., Sebe, N., Welling, M. (eds.) ECCV 2016. LNCS, vol. 9912, pp. 628–644. Springer, Cham (2016). https://doi.org/10.1007/978-3-319-46484-8_38
12. DeCarlo, D., Finkelstein, A., Rusinkiewicz, S., Santella, A.: Suggestive contours for conveying shape. In: ACM SIGGRAPH 2003 Papers, pp. 848–855 (2003)
13. Delanoy, J., Aubry, M., Isola, P., Efros, A.A., Bousseau, A.: 3D sketching using multi-view deep volumetric prediction. Proc. ACM Comput. Graph. Interact. Tech. 1(1), 1–22 (2018)
14. Fan, H., Su, H., Guibas, L.J.: A point set generation network for 3d object reconstruction from a single image. In: Proceedings of the IEEE Conference on Computer Vision and Pattern Recognition, pp. 605–613 (2017)
15. Gkioxari, G., Malik, J., Johnson, J.: Mesh R-CNN. In: Proceedings of the IEEE/CVF International Conference on Computer Vision, pp. 9785–9795 (2019)
16. Goel, S., Kanazawa, A., Malik, J.: Shape and viewpoint without keypoints. In: Vedaldi, A., Bischof, H., Brox, T., Frahm, J.-M. (eds.) ECCV 2020. LNCS, vol. 12360, pp. 88–104. Springer, Cham (2020). https://doi.org/10.1007/978-3-030-58555-6_6
17. Goodfellow, I., et al.: Generative adversarial nets. In: Advances in Neural Information Processing Systems, vol. 27 (2014)
18. Grady, L.: Random walks for image segmentation. IEEE Trans. Pattern Anal. Mach. Intell. 28(11), 1768–1783 (2006)
19. Gu, J., Shen, Y., Zhou, B.: Image processing using multi-code GAN prior. In: Proceedings of the IEEE/CVF Conference on Computer Vision and Pattern Recognition, pp. 3012–3021 (2020)
20. Guillard, B., Remelli, E., Yvernay, P., Fua, P.: Sketch2Mesh: reconstructing and editing 3D shapes from sketches. In: ICCV (2021)
21. Gulrajani, I., Ahmed, F., Arjovsky, M., Dumoulin, V., Courville, A.: Improved training of wasserstein GANs. In: NeurIPS (2017)
22. Hao, Z., Averbuch-Elor, H., Snavely, N., Belongie, S.: Dualsdf: semantic shape manipulation using a two-level representation. In: CVPR, pp. 7631–7641 (2020)
23. Heusel, M., Ramsauer, H., Unterthiner, T., Nessler, B., Hochreiter, S.: GANs trained by a two time-scale update rule converge to a local NASH equilibrium. In: Advances in Neural Information Processing Systems, vol. 30 (2017)

24. Jin, A., Fu, Q., Deng, Z.: Contour-based 3D modeling through joint embedding of shapes and contours. In: Symposium on Interactive 3D Graphics and Games, pp. 1–10 (2020)
25. Kanazawa, A., Tulsiani, S., Efros, A.A., Malik, J.: Learning category-specific mesh reconstruction from image collections. In: Proceedings of the European Conference on Computer Vision (ECCV), pp. 371–386 (2018)
26. Kingma, D.P., Ba, J.: Adam: a method for stochastic optimization. arXiv preprint arXiv:1412.6980 (2014)
27. Kingma, D.P., Welling, M.: Auto-encoding variational Bayes. arXiv preprint arXiv:1312.6114 (2013)
28. Lempitsky, V., Kohli, P., Rother, C., Sharp, T.: Image segmentation with a bounding box prior. In: 2009 IEEE 12th International Conference on Computer Vision, pp. 277–284. IEEE (2009)
29. Levin, A., Lischinski, D., Weiss, Y.: Colorization using optimization. In: ACM SIGGRAPH 2004 Papers, pp. 689–694 (2004)
30. Li, Y., Sun, J., Tang, C.K., Shum, H.Y.: Lazy snapping. ACM Trans. Graph. (ToG) **23**(3), 303–308 (2004)
31. Liu, M.Y., Tuzel, O.: Coupled generative adversarial networks. Adv. Neural. Inf. Process. Syst. **29**, 469–477 (2016)
32. Liu, S., Zhang, Y., Peng, S., Shi, B., Pollefeys, M., Cui, Z.: DIST: rendering deep implicit signed distance function with differentiable sphere tracing. In: CVPR, pp. 2019–2028 (2020)
33. Liu, S., Li, T., Chen, W., Li, H.: Soft rasterizer: a differentiable renderer for image-based 3D reasoning. In: Proceedings of the IEEE/CVF International Conference on Computer Vision, pp. 7708–7717 (2019)
34. Liu, S., Zhang, X., Zhang, Z., Zhang, R., Zhu, J.Y., Russell, B.: Editing conditional radiance fields. In: ICCV (2021)
35. Mescheder, L., Oechsle, M., Niemeyer, M., Nowozin, S., Geiger, A.: Occupancy networks: Learning 3d reconstruction in function space. In: Proceedings of the IEEE/CVF Conference on Computer Vision and Pattern Recognition, pp. 4460–4470 (2019)
36. Mildenhall, B., Srinivasan, P.P., Tancik, M., Barron, J.T., Ramamoorthi, R., Ng, R.: NeRF: representing scenes as neural radiance fields for view synthesis. In: Vedaldi, A., Bischof, H., Brox, T., Frahm, J.-M. (eds.) ECCV 2020. LNCS, vol. 12346, pp. 405–421. Springer, Cham (2020). https://doi.org/10.1007/978-3-030-58452-8_24
37. Pan, X., Zhan, X., Dai, B., Lin, D., Loy, C.C., Luo, P.: Exploiting deep generative prior for versatile image restoration and manipulation. In: Vedaldi, A., Bischof, H., Brox, T., Frahm, J.-M. (eds.) ECCV 2020. LNCS, vol. 12347, pp. 262–277. Springer, Cham (2020). https://doi.org/10.1007/978-3-030-58536-5_16
38. Park, J.J., Florence, P., Straub, J., Newcombe, R., Lovegrove, S.: Deepsdf: learning continuous signed distance functions for shape representation. In: CVPR, pp. 165–174 (2019)
39. Pellacini, F., Battaglia, F., Morley, R.K., Finkelstein, A.: Lighting with paint. ACM Trans. Graph. (TOG) **26**(2), 9-es (2007)
40. Radford, A., Metz, L., Chintala, S.: Unsupervised representation learning with deep convolutional generative adversarial networks. arXiv preprint arXiv:1511.06434 (2015)
41. Rother, C., Kolmogorov, V., Blake, A.: " grabcut" interactive foreground extraction using iterated graph cuts. ACM Trans. Graph. (TOG) **23**(3), 309–314 (2004)

42. Saharia, C., et al.: Palette: Image-to-image diffusion models. arXiv preprint arXiv:2111.05826 (2021)
43. Schmidt, T.W., Pellacini, F., Nowrouzezahrai, D., Jarosz, W., Dachsbacher, C.: State of the art in artistic editing of appearance, lighting and material. In: Computer Graphics Forum, vol. 35, pp. 216–233. Wiley Online Library (2016)
44. Shen, Y., Gu, J., Tang, X., Zhou, B.: Interpreting the latent space of GANs for semantic face editing. In: Proceedings of the IEEE/CVF Conference on Computer Vision and Pattern Recognition, pp. 9243–9252 (2020)
45. Shen, Y., Yang, C., Tang, X., Zhou, B.: InterfaceGAN: interpreting the disentangled face representation learned by GANs. IEEE Transactions on Pattern Analysis and Machine Intelligence (2020)
46. Shi, Y., Siddharth, N., Paige, B., Torr, P.H.: Variational mixture-of-experts autoencoders for multi-modal deep generative models. arXiv preprint arXiv:1911.03393 (2019)
47. Sitzmann, V., Zollhöfer, M., Wetzstein, G.: Scene representation networks: continuous 3D-structure-aware neural scene representations. arXiv preprint arXiv:1906.01618 (2019)
48. Sohl-Dickstein, J., Weiss, E., Maheswaranathan, N., Ganguli, S.: Deep unsupervised learning using nonequilibrium thermodynamics. In: ICML, pp. 2256–2265. PMLR (2015)
49. Suzuki, M., Nakayama, K., Matsuo, Y.: Joint multimodal learning with deep generative models. arXiv preprint arXiv:1611.01891 (2016)
50. Tatarchenko, M., Richter, S.R., Ranftl, R., Li, Z., Koltun, V., Brox, T.: What do single-view 3d reconstruction networks learn? In: CVPR, pp. 3405–3414 (2019)
51. Wang, N., Zhang, Y., Li, Z., Fu, Y., Liu, W., Jiang, Y.G.: Pixel2mesh: generating 3D mesh models from single RGB images. In: ECCV, pp. 52–67 (2018)
52. Wang, Y., Gonzalez-Garcia, A., Berga, D., Herranz, L., Khan, F.S., Weijer, J.V.D.: MineGAN: effective knowledge transfer from GANs to target domains with few images. In: CVPR, pp. 9332–9341 (2020)
53. Wu, M., Goodman, N.: Multimodal generative models for scalable weakly-supervised learning. In: Advances in Neural Information Processing Systems, vol. 31 (2018)
54. Wu, M., Goodman, N.: Multimodal generative models for compositional representation learning. arXiv preprint arXiv:1912.05075 (2019)
55. Xu, Q., Wang, W., Ceylan, D., Mech, R., Neumann, U.: Disn: deep implicit surface network for high-quality single-view 3D reconstruction. arXiv preprint arXiv:1905.10711 (2019)
56. Yang, G., et al.: LASR: learning articulated shape reconstruction from a monocular video. In: Proceedings of the IEEE/CVF Conference on Computer Vision and Pattern Recognition, pp. 15980–15989 (2021)
57. Zadeh, A., Lim, Y.C., Liang, P.P., Morency, L.P.: Variational auto-decoder: a method for neural generative modeling from incomplete data. arXiv preprint arXiv:1903.00840 (2019)
58. Zhang, R., Isola, P., Efros, A.A., Shechtman, E., Wang, O.: The unreasonable effectiveness of deep features as a perceptual metric. In: CVPR (2018)
59. Zhang, R., et al.: Real-time user-guided image colorization with learned deep priors. ACM Trans. Graph. (TOG) 9(4) (2017)
60. Zhang, S.H., Guo, Y.C., Gu, Q.W.: Sketch2model: view-aware 3D modeling from single free-hand sketches. In: Proceedings of the IEEE/CVF Conference on Computer Vision and Pattern Recognition, pp. 6012–6021 (2021)

61. Zhong, Y., Gryaditskaya, Y., Zhang, H., Song, Y.Z.: Deep sketch-based modeling: tips and tricks. In: 2020 International Conference on 3D Vision (3DV), pp. 543–552. IEEE (2020)

62. Zhu, J., Shen, Y., Zhao, D., Zhou, B.: In-domain GAN inversion for real image editing. In: Vedaldi, A., Bischof, H., Brox, T., Frahm, J.-M. (eds.) ECCV 2020. LNCS, vol. 12362, pp. 592–608. Springer, Cham (2020). https://doi.org/10.1007/978-3-030-58520-4_35

Latent Partition Implicit with Surface Codes for 3D Representation

Chao Chen[1], Yu-Shen Liu[1($\boxtimes$)], and Zhizhong Han[2]

[1] School of Software, BNRist, Tsinghua University, Beijing, China
`chenchao19@mails.tsinghua.edu.cn`, `liuyushen@tsinghua.edu.cn`
[2] Department of Computer Science, Wayne State University, Detroit, USA
`h312h@wayne.edu`

Abstract. Deep implicit functions have shown remarkable shape modeling ability in various 3D computer vision tasks. One drawback is that it is hard for them to represent a 3D shape as multiple parts. Current solutions learn various primitives and blend the primitives directly in the spatial space, which still struggle to approximate the 3D shape accurately. To resolve this problem, we introduce a novel implicit representation to represent a single 3D shape as a set of parts in the latent space, towards both highly accurate and plausibly interpretable shape modeling. Our insight here is that both the part learning and the part blending can be conducted much easier in the latent space than in the spatial space. We name our method *Latent Partition Implicit (LPI)*, because of its ability of casting the global shape modeling into multiple local part modeling, which partitions the global shape unity. LPI represents a shape as Signed Distance Functions (SDFs) using surface codes. Each surface code is a latent code representing a part whose center is on the surface, which enables us to flexibly employ intrinsic attributes of shapes or additional surface properties. Eventually, LPI can reconstruct both the shape and the parts on the shape, both of which are plausible meshes. LPI is a multilevel representation, which can partition a shape into different numbers of parts after training. LPI can be learned without ground truth signed distances, point normals or any supervision for part partition. LPI outperforms the latest methods under the widely used benchmarks in terms of reconstruction accuracy and modeling interpretability. Our code, data and models are available at https://github.com/chenchao15/LPI.

Keywords: Neural implicit representation · Surface codes · Shape reconstruction

This work was supported by National Key R&D Program of China (2022YFC3800600, 2020YFF0304100), the National Natural Science Foundation of China (62272263, 62072268), and in part by Tsinghua-Kuaishou Institute of Future Media Data.

Supplementary Information The online version contains supplementary material available at https://doi.org/10.1007/978-3-031-20062-5_19.

S. Avidan et al. (Eds.): ECCV 2022, LNCS 13663, pp. 322–343, 2022.
https://doi.org/10.1007/978-3-031-20062-5_19

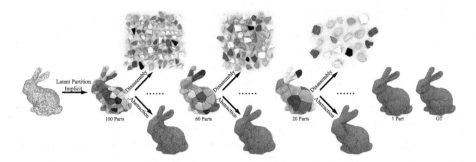

Fig. 1. We introduce *Latent Partition Implicit (LPI)* to represent 3D shapes. We learn LPI from 3D point clouds without requiring ground truth signed distances and point normals. We leverage a surface code to represent a part, and blend all parts with optional surface attributes, such as geodesic distance or segmentation, to reconstruct a surface, both of which are in the latent space. We can represent a shape (mesh) at different levels using different numbers of surface codes, which leads to different numbers of parts (meshes).

1   Introduction

Implicit functions have been a popular representation for 3D objects or scenes. They are able to describe the 3D geometry using the occupancy informa- tion [11,54] or signed distances [56,66] at arbitrary query locations. We can leverage deep neural networks to learn implicit functions, which we call deep implicit functions. Deep implicit functions usually regard input images or point clouds as conditions to discriminate different object identities in different appli- cations, such as single image reconstruction [12,22,29,43,73,83] or surface recon- struction [22,44,55,89]. Although deep implicit functions have the remarkable ability of geometry modeling, it is difficult for them to decompose shapes into parts. This significantly limits the part-based modeling or editing and makes geometry modeling not interpretable.

Recent methods [16,21,22,82] tried to resolve this problem in 3D spatial space. The key idea behind these methods is to learn to approximate a shape using var- ious primitives, such as convex polytopes [16], 3D Gaussian functions [21,22,82], superquadrics [67] and homeomorphic mappings [69]. However, it is very hard to approximate shapes well by combining primitives together in the spatial space, even a large number of primitives can be used, since both primitive learning and primitive blending in the spatial space are still challenging.

To resolve this issue, we introduce a novel implicit representation to rep- resent a single 3D shape as a set of parts in the latent space, towards both highly accurate and plausibly interpretable shape modeling. Our idea comes from the observation that we can not only learn part geometry but also blend parts together in the latent space, both of which are much easier to be imple- mented in the latent space than in the spatial space. For a 3D shape, we learn its Signed Distance Functions (SDFs) via blending a set of learnable latent codes in a geometry-aware way. Each latent code represents a part with a center on the surface, which we call *surface codes*. Our insight of surface codes is that they enable us to flexibly leverage intrinsic attributes of shapes or additional properties of surfaces. Eventually, our learned SDFs can reconstruct not only the shape but also each part on the shape, both of which are plausible meshes. Our method partitions the global shape unity by casting the global shape modeling into multiple local part modeling, as demonstrated in Fig. 1, which achieves important properties such as the reconstruction accuracy and convergence order inherited from the local part modeling. Therefore, we name our method *Latent Partition Implicit (LPI)*. LPI is a multi-level representation for both rigid and non-rigid shapes, which can partition a shape into different numbers of parts after training. LPI can be learned without ground truth signed distances, point normals or any supervision for part partition. Our numerical and visual evaluation shows that LPI outperforms the state-of-the-art methods in terms of reconstruction accuracy and modeling interpretability. Our contributions are listed as follows.

i) We introduce LPI as a novel implicit representation for 3D shapes. It enables shape modeling and decomposition at the same time, which leads to highly accurate and plausibly interpretable shape modeling.
ii) We justify the feasibility of learning part geometry and blending parts together in the latent space, which achieves more semantic and efficient parts representation.
iii) Our method significantly outperforms the state-of-the-art methods in terms of reconstruction accuracy and modeling interpretability.

2   Related Work

Deep learning-based 3D shape understanding [26–32,54,58,66,72,85,99] has achieved very promising results in different tasks [10,33,35,36,38,48,57,63,84,86,87,91].

Learning Global Implicit Functions. Implicit functions have achieved remarkable results in geometry modeling. SDFs or occupancy fields can be learned using ground truth signed distances [7,40,56,66] and binary occupancy labels [11,54]. The learned implicit functions leverage conditions to distinguish shape or scene identities. In different applications, conditions are latent codes obtained from different modalities, such as images for single image reconstruction [12,22,29,43,73,83], learnable latent codes for shape fitting [66], or point clouds for surface reconstruction [17,22,37,44,46,51,52,55,70,89].

With differentiable renderers [3,15,34,38,42,45,47,60,62,64,74,76,77,90,96, 97], we can also learn implicit functions with 2D supervision. This is achieved by minimizing the difference between the images rendered from the learned implicit functions and the ground truth images. Implicit functions achieve great results in geometry and color modeling for complex scenes with neural rendering [58].

Recent methods tried to learn implicit functions from 3D point clouds without ground truth signed distances or binary occupancy labels. Their contributions lied in additional constraints [1,2,4,24,95,98] or the way of leveraging gradients to perceive the surroundings [13,50] to learn signed [1,2,24,50,80,98] or unsigned distance fields [13].

Learning Local Implicit Functions. We can also learn implicit functions in local regions to capture more detailed geometry. The widely used strategy is to split the space occupied by the shape into a voxel grid [8,37,46,53,78,79]. Learnable latent codes located in voxels [8,37,53,78] or vertices of voxels [46,79]. The feature of each query is obtained using bilinear interpolation from these latent codes. Some other methods also used 3D Gaussian functions [21,82] to cover the local regions.

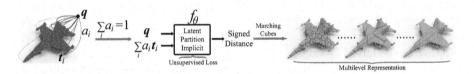

Fig. 2. Demonstration of LPI. We can learn LPI from single point clouds without ground truth signed distances or point normals. LPI can represent shapes using different numbers of parts after training.

The aforementioned methods can approximate the global implicit functions with [7,21,23,40,82,93] or without blending local implicit functions [8,18,37]. Our method shares the idea of approximating global implicit functions by blending local ones, but our novelty lies in that we allow the neural network to adaptively split shapes so that we can blend parts with spatial surface properties or intrinsic attributes in the latent space well.

Shape Decomposition. Decomposing shapes into parts with specific attributes have been extensively studied in computer graphics [19,61,75,92,94]. Recent deep learning based methods tried to resolve this problem by learning primitives using a data-driven strategy [16,20,59,68,69,75,88]. The primitives could be convex polytopes [16,68], 3D Gaussian functions or spheres [22,71]. Instead of primitives learned by these methods, we can learn parts, and blend parts in the latent space rather than spatial space. This results in more accurate approximation and better interpretability for geometry modeling.

3   Method

Problem Statement. We aim to learn LPI as SDFs f_θ for a 3D shape M using a deep neural network parameterized by θ. We can use f_θ to describe multiple shapes with conditions represented as images or point clouds, but we only use single shapes without conditions to simplify the technical details. Besides this, we also aim to decompose shape M into I parts p_i, each of which is also represented as an SDF, where $i \in [1, I]$. To achieve this, we aim to learn f_θ using the following equation,

$$f_\theta(\boldsymbol{q}, \boldsymbol{a}) = s, \tag{1}$$

where f_θ provides a signed distance s for a query $\boldsymbol{q}$ according to an affinity vector $\boldsymbol{a}$. Each element a_i in $\boldsymbol{a}$ represents its similarity to each part p_i in terms of some metrics, and $\sum_{i \in [1, I]} a_i = 1$. The affinity vector $\boldsymbol{a}$ determines how we can blend local SDFs in the latent space into a global SDF at the query location $\boldsymbol{q}$.

Overview. We demonstrate LPI in Fig. 2. Given a 3D point cloud representing shape M, we first sample I region centers $\boldsymbol{r}_i$ on the point cloud using farthest point sampling (FPS). Each center $\boldsymbol{r}_i$ localizes a part p_i. We represent each part p_i using a latent code $\boldsymbol{t}_i \in \mathbb{R}^{1 \times T}$ in the latent space. The latent codes $\boldsymbol{t}_i$ associated with part centers on the surface are called surface codes. $\boldsymbol{t}_i$ can be used to produce a local SDF to describe the surface of part p_i. We blend all parts together in the latent space by weighting latent codes $\boldsymbol{t}_i$ using an affinity vector $\boldsymbol{a}$ at each query location $\boldsymbol{q}$, which results in a global SDF. We will introduce how to obtain the affinity vector for different kinds of shapes in different applications later. Eventually, we learn the SDFs f_θ which can be further used to reconstruct the surface and decompose the shape into parts at multiple levels.

Surface Codes. It is not new to cast the learning of global SDFs into the learning of multiple local SDFs. The rationale behind this is that local regions are simpler than global shapes, which is easier to learn. A widely used strategy is to regard the space holding 3D shapes as a voxel grid [8,37,78] or a 3D Gaussian mixture model [22,71], and use a latent code to cover each split region, such as voxels or ellipsoids shown in Fig. 3(a) and (b). Different from these methods, we uniformly distribute region centers on the input point cloud, and use latent codes $\boldsymbol{t}_i$ to cover each split region as a Voronoi cell in Fig. 3(c). The benefits we can get are three-folds, which leads our method to be geometry-aware. One benefit is that these centers enable us to perceive the intrinsic attributes of surface, such as geodesic distances, especially for non-rigid shapes, such as humans. This would be helpful to plausibly decompose non-rigid shapes. Another benefit is that Voronoi cells could decompose shapes in a more compact way than voxel grids, especially with the same number of latent codes, which results in more uniformly decomposed parts. This is very helpful to achieve highly accurate shape abstraction without losing too much structure information when abstracting decomposed parts into convex polytopes. Moreover, we can also flexibly leverage additional properties of the surface, such as segmentation, to produce more semantic parts in surface reconstruction. Surface codes $\boldsymbol{t}_i$ are learnable parameters for each shape. They are learned with other network parameters θ.

Blending Regions in the Latent Space. However, the outputs of neighboring local functions are inconsistent. This problem significantly slows down the convergence during training, and also affects the final reconstruction accuracy. Current methods resolve this problem

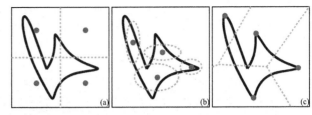

Fig. 3. Regions covered by voxels and ellipsoids in (a) and (b). Our regions are covered by Voronoi cells in (c). Red points are region centers. (Color figure online)

by blending regions into a global shape in the spatial space [65,82]. They mainly leverage a weight function with a local support to blend the output of multiple local functions, such as local SDFs. This will also bring another issue, that is, the blending requires all neighboring local functions to produce the prediction, which is not affordable when there are lots of local functions. Therefore, DeepLS [8] does not blend local functions but increases the receptive field of each local region to keep region borders consistent.

We resolve this problem by blending local functions in the latent space. Rather than blending outputs in the spatial space, we blend latent codes t_i corresponding to all local SDFs at each query q into a weighted latent code w. w is further concatenated with query q to produce its signed distance. We leverage an affinity vector a at each query q to weight latent codes t_i linearly into w below,

$$w = \sum_{i \in [1,I]} a_i t_i, \tag{2}$$

where a_i represents the affinity between query q and part p_i in terms of some metrics, and we are very flexible to define the affinity metrics, such as Euclidean distance, intrinsic distance, or semantic distance, which achieves different shape decompositions. This flexibility brought by surface codes also differentiates our method with other ones that use bilinear interpolation to blend latent codes on voxel grids [53,79], especially for non-rigid shapes like humans.

Affinity Vector a. One benefit that we can have with surface codes is to obtain geometry aware-ness. We can encode the geometry by flexibly leveraging different similarity metrics to form the affinity vector a for each query q. We will introduce three metrics

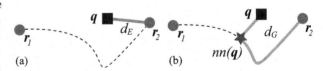

Fig. 4. (a) Euclidean distance d_E between query q and region centers r_i. (b) Intrinsic distance d_G between query q and region centers r_i.

including Euclidean distance d_E, intrinsic distance d_G, and semantic distance d_S to evaluate the distance between query q and each part p_i.

1. Euclidean distance d_E. The most intuitive metric is Euclidean distance, the distance between query q and part p_i can be evaluated using the equation below,

$$d_E(q, p_i) = ||q - r_i||_2, \qquad (3)$$

where r_i is the center of region p_i. This metric indicates that query q is more related to a region p_i if q is nearer to its center r_i, as demonstrated in Fig. 4 (a). However, Euclidean distance does not care about the intrinsic property of shapes, especially on non-rigid shapes.

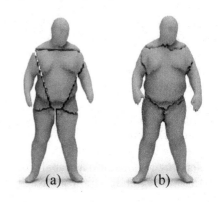

Fig. 5. The effect of Euclidean distance d_E and intrinsic distance d_G

2. Intrinsic distance d_G. To resolve this issue, we also introduce intrinsic distance d_G as a distance metric. The intrinsic distance is formed by Euclidean distance and geodesic distance. The geodesic distance is the distance of the shortest path connecting two points on the surface. So, the intrinsic distance between query q and part p_i can be evaluated using the equation below,

$$d_G(q, p_i) = ||q - nn(q, M)||_2 + G(nn(q, M)), r_i), \qquad (4)$$

where G represents all pair-wise geodesic distances on surface M, $nn(q, M) = \text{argmin}_{q' \in M} ||q - q'||_2$ is the nearest point on M of query q. We demonstrate d_G in Fig. 4 (b). We first project query q to surface M by finding the nearest point $nn(q, M)$ of q, then we calculate the geodesic distance between $nn(q, M)$ and region center r_i. In experiments, we calculate the geodesic distance between each two points on M using heat method [14] in advance.

We highlight the difference between Euclidean distance d_E and intrinsic distance d_G on a non-rigid shape in Fig. 5. Using the same set of six region centers r_i, LPI with d_E splits the human body without considering the intrinsic structures in Fig. 5 (a), while LPI with d_G can produce more reasonable splitting using geodesic distances.

For both d_E and d_G, we use the Gaussian function to obtain the similarity a_i between query q and part p_i, and the similarity is normalized by the sum of all similarities to all parts,

$$a_i = e^{-d(q,p_i)/\sigma} / \sum_{i' \in [1,I]} e^{-d(q,p_{i'})/\sigma}, \tag{5}$$

where σ is a decay parameter that determines the range in which surface codes get involved, and d could be either d_E or d_G.

3. Semantic distance d_S. With additional properties of the surface, such as segmentation information, we can also obtain the affinity vector using semantic distance d_S. In this case, d_S is an indicator which indicates the segment that query q belongs to. In this way, the affinity vector indicates the semantic similarity between a query and each predefined segment rather than region centers. Assume we were given a sparse point cloud E containing 4 segments in Fig. 6 (a), we find the nearest point $nn(q, E)$ on E for query q, and label q using the same segment label of $nn(q, E)$. Then, we set the affinity between q and its segment label to 0.8 while set the affinities to other 3 segments uniformly to keep $\sum_{i \in [1,T]} a_i = 1$. With the segmentation as guidance, LPI can reconstruct the surface of the point cloud in Fig. 2 (a) using 4 semantic parts shown in Fig. 6 (b).

Loss Function. We learn LPI as SDFs $f_\theta(q, a)$ without ground truth signed distances or point normals by optimizing network parameters θ and all surface codes $\{t_i\}$. We leverage a loss function that is modified from the pulling loss introduced in [50] to resist the sparseness of input point clouds. The loss function is defined below,

Fig. 6. LPI can reconstruct surfaces and semantic parts in (b) according to segmentation.

$$\min_{\theta, \{t_i\}} \left(\sum_{x \in M} \min_{y \in \{q'\}} ||x - y||_2^2 + \sum_{y \in \{q'\}} \min_{x \in M} ||x - y||_2^2 \right), \tag{6}$$

where we obtain the points $\{q'\}$ by projecting each query q using the predicted signed distance $s = f_\theta(q, a)$ and the gradient $\nabla f_\theta(q, a)$, such that $q' = q - s\nabla f_\theta(q, a)/||\nabla f_\theta(q, a)||_2$.

Shape and Part Reconstruction. With the learned SDFs f_θ, we reconstruct the shape surface by evaluating f_θ at points on a regular grid and running the marching cubes [49]. To reconstruct each part centered at r_i, we evaluate f_θ at points on the regular grid whose nearest region center is r_i while leveraging an unseen weighted latent code w to predict signed distances at the rest points on the regular grid, and we also leverage marching cubes to reconstruct the surface of each part. After training, we can down sample region centers $\{r_i\}$ to reconstruct the shape with fewer parts in the same way.

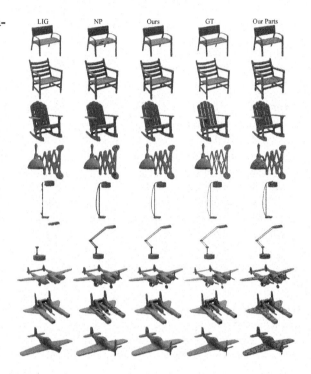

Fig. 7. Visual comparison with LIG [37] and NP [50] in surface reconstruction under ShapeNet.

4 Experiments

4.1 Setup

Details. For fair comparisons, we leverage the same neural network as NeuralPull (NP) [50] to learn the SDFs f_θ. Moreover, we overfit single shapes in an unsupervised scenario using Eq. (6) without requiring signed distances or point normals, or in a supervised scenario using an MSE loss with signed distance supervision for fair comparisons with others. In an unsupervised scenario, we leverage point clouds as input and sample queries around the point clouds using the same method as NP [50]. In a supervised scenario, we establish a training set containing queries and their ground truth signed distances for each shape. We sample queries and calculate the ground truth signed distances around the shape using the same method as DSDF [66]. All compared methods use the same training set. In both scenarios, we leverage the marching cubes algorithm [49] to reconstruct surfaces using the learned SDFs. We set $\sigma = 1$ in Eq. (5) and the dimension of t_i is $T = 100$.

Table 1. L2CD ($\times 100$) comparison under ShapeNet.

Class	PSR	DMC	BPA	ATLAS	DMC	DSDF	DGP	MeshP	NUD	SALD	NP	Ours
Display	0.273	0.269	0.093	1.094	0.662	0.317	0.293	0.069	0.077	–	0.039	**0.0080**
Lamp	0.227	0.244	0.060	1.988	3.377	0.955	0.167	0.053	0.075	0.071	0.080	**0.0172**
Airplane	0.217	0.171	0.059	1.011	2.205	1.043	0.200	0.049	0.076	0.054	0.008	**0.0060**
Cabinet	0.363	0.373	0.292	1.661	0.766	0.921	0.237	0.112	0.041	–	0.026	**0.0179**
Vessel	0.254	0.228	0.078	0.997	2.487	1.254	0.199	0.061	0.079	–	0.022	**0.0092**
Table	0.383	0.375	0.120	1.311	1.128	0.660	0.333	0.076	0.067	0.066	0.060	**0.0436**
Chair	0.293	0.283	0.099	1.575	1.047	0.483	0.219	0.071	0.063	0.061	0.054	**0.0187**
Sofa	0.276	0.266	0.124	1.307	0.763	0.496	0.174	0.080	0.071	0.058	0.012	**0.0164**
Mean	0.286	0.276	0.116	1.368	1.554	0.766	0.228	0.071	0.069	0.062	0.038	**0.0171**

Datasets. We evaluate our method in three datasets including ShapeNet [9], FAMOUS [17] and D-FAUST [6]. We leverage the same subset of ShapeNet with the same train/test splitting as [44,50]. The subset of ShapeNet contains 8 shape classes. FAMOUS is a dataset released by Points2Surf [17], it contains 22 well-known 3D shapes. D-FAUST is a large-scale dataset containing human meshes. We randomly select 10 shapes and 100 shapes representing different human identities and poses as two sets.

Metrics. We follow MeshingPoint [44] to leverage L2 Chamfer Distance (L2CD), Normal Consistency (NC) [54] and F-score [81] to evaluate our surface reconstruction accuracy under ShapeNet. We sample $100K$ points on the reconstructed and the ground truth surfaces to calculate the L2CD. Following Points2Surf [17], we leverage L2CD to evaluate the reconstruction error between our reconstructed surfaces and the ground truth meshes under FAMOUS dataset. We sample $10K$ points on both reconstructed surfaces and the ground truth meshes to calculate the L2CD. Under D-FAUST dataset, we leverage L1 Chamfer Distance (L1CD), L2CD, NC and IoU to evaluate the reconstruction accuracy. We also sample $10K$ points to calculate CD.

4.2 Surface Reconstruction

ShapeNet. We first evaluate our method in surface reconstruction under ShapeNet. We train our method to reconstruct the surface from each point cloud without using the signed distance supervision. We leverage Euclidean distance d_E to evaluate the distance between a query and each one of $I = 100$ regions to obtain the affinity vector $\boldsymbol{a}$. We use FPS to randomly sample the $I = 100$ region centers on the input point clouds.

We compare our method with the classic surface reconstruction methods and the state-of-the-art data-driven based methods. The compared methods include PSR [39], Ball-Pivoting algorithm (BPA) [5], ATLAS [25], Deep Geometric Prior (DGP) [89], Deep Marching Cube (DMC) [41], DeepSDF (DSDF) [66], MeshP [44], Neural Unsigned Distance (NUD) [13], SALD [2], Local SDF (GRID) [37], IMNET [11] and NeuralPull (NP) [50].

Table 2. Normal consistency comparison under ShapeNet.

Class	PSR	DMC	BPA	ATLAS	DMC	DSDF	MeshP	LIG	IMNET	NP	Ours
Display	0.889	0.842	0.952	0.828	0.882	0.932	0.974	0.926	0.574	0.964	**0.9780**
Lamp	0.876	0.872	0.951	0.593	0.725	0.864	**0.963**	0.882	0.592	0.930	0.9503
Airplane	0.848	0.835	0.926	0.737	0.716	0.872	0.955	0.817	0.550	0.947	**0.9560**
Cabinet	0.880	0.827	0.836	0.682	0.845	0.872	0.957	0.948	0.700	0.930	**0.9576**
Vessel	0.861	0.831	0.917	0.671	0.706	0.841	0.953	0.847	0.574	0.941	**0.9564**
Table	0.833	0.809	0.919	0.783	0.831	0.901	**0.962**	0.936	0.702	0.908	0.9527
Chair	0.850	0.818	0.938	0.638	0.794	0.886	**0.962**	0.920	0.820	0.937	0.9545
Sofa	0.892	0.851	0.940	0.633	0.850	0.906	**0.971**	0.944	0.818	0.951	**0.9713**
Mean	0.866	0.836	0.923	0.695	0.794	0.884	**0.962**	0.903	0.666	0.939	0.9596

Table 3. F-score(μ) comparison under ShapeNet. $\mu = 0.002$.

Class	PSR	DMC	BPA	ATLAS	DMC	DSDF	DGP	MeshP	NUD	LIG	IMNET	NP	Ours
Display	0.468	0.495	0.834	0.071	0.108	0.632	0.417	0.903	0.903	0.551	0.601	0.989	**0.9978**
Lamp	0.455	0.518	0.826	0.029	0.047	0.268	0.405	0.855	0.888	0.624	0.836	0.891	**0.9889**
Airplane	0.415	0.442	0.788	0.070	0.050	0.350	0.249	0.844	0.872	0.564	0.698	0.996	**0.9989**
Cabinet	0.392	0.392	0.553	0.077	0.154	0.573	0.513	0.860	0.950	0.733	0.343	0.980	**0.9849**
Vessel	0.415	0.466	0.789	0.058	0.055	0.323	0.387	0.862	0.883	0.467	0.147	0.985	**0.9955**
Table	0.233	0.287	0.772	0.080	0.095	0.577	0.307	0.880	0.908	0.844	0.425	0.922	**0.9789**
Chair	0.382	0.433	0.802	0.050	0.088	0.447	0.481	0.875	0.913	0.710	0.181	0.954	**0.9897**
Sofa	0.499	0.535	0.786	0.058	0.129	0.577	0.638	0.895	0.945	0.822	0.199	0.968	**0.9946**
Mean	0.407	0.446	0.769	0.062	0.091	0.468	0.425	0.872	0.908	0.664	0.429	0.961	**0.9912**

We report the numerical comparison in terms of L2CD in Table 1, NC in Table 2, F-score with μ in Table 3, F-score with 2μ in Table 4. Our method achieves the best in terms of L2CD and F-score, while obtains the state-of-the-art in terms of NC. We further highlight our advantage in the visual comparison with LIG and NP in Fig. 7. The comparison shows that our method can recon-

Table 4. F-score(2μ) comparison under ShapeNet. $\mu = 0.002$.

Class	PSR	DMC	BPA	ATLAS	DMC	DSDF	DGP	MeshP	NUD	NP	Ours
Display	0.666	0.669	0.929	0.179	0.246	0.787	0.607	0.975	0.944	0.991	**0.9993**
Lamp	0.648	0.681	0.934	0.077	0.113	0.478	0.662	0.951	0.945	0.924	**0.9954**
Airplane	0.619	0.639	0.914	0.179	0.289	0.566	0.515	0.946	0.944	0.997	**0.9998**
Cabinet	0.598	0.591	0.706	0.195	0.128	0.694	0.738	0.946	0.980	0.989	**0.9938**
Vessel	0.633	0.647	0.906	0.153	0.120	0.509	0.648	0.956	0.945	0.990	**0.9985**
Table	0.442	0.462	0.886	0.195	0.221	0.743	0.494	0.963	0.922	0.973	**0.9866**
Chair	0.617	0.615	0.913	0.134	0.345	0.665	0.693	0.964	0.954	0.969	**0.9940**
Sofa	0.725	0.708	0.895	0.153	0.208	0.734	0.834	0.972	0.968	0.974	**0.9982**
Mean	0.618	0.626	0.885	0.158	0.209	0.647	0.649	0.959	0.950	0.976	**0.9957**

struct surfaces with complex geometry in higher accuracy. We also visualize the parts that each surface code covers on the shape, which demonstrates that our method can reconstruct both plausible shapes and parts as meshes.

FAMOUS. We further evaluate our method using non-rigid shapes under FAMOUS dataset. Besides evaluating our surface reconstruction accuracy, we also evaluate our part representation ability. Therefore, we compare our method which also have the ability of representing parts, such as CVX [16] and

Table 5. L2CD, L1CD, and NC comparison under Famous.

Method	L2CD×100	L1CD×100	NC
CVX	0.020	**1.038**	0.906
SIF	0.050	1.600	0.913
Nglod	0.019	1.111	0.934
Ours	**0.018**	**1.038**	**0.950**

SIF [22]. Moreover, we also highlight the advantage of surface codes over the method leveraging voxel grids to cover local regions, such as Nglod [79].

Table 6. L2CD, L1CD, NC and IoU comparison under 10 models of D-FAUST.

Class	L2CD×100	L1CD×100	NC	IoU
NeuralParts	0.008	0.667	0.906	0.695
Ours(Parts)	0.007	0.649	0.886	0.828
Ours(Shape)	**0.004**	**0.555**	**0.952**	**0.837**

For fair comparisons, we train all compared methods to overfit each point cloud in the dataset using the same signed distance supervision. We train our method to regress signed distances by minimizing an MSE loss. We also keep the part number the same in all compared numbers, where we leverage $I = 100$ regions to reconstruct surfaces. We employ 125 latent codes in the 5^3 voxel grid to produce the results of Nglod. We leverage Euclidean distance d_E to calculate the affinity vector to $I = 100$ region centers that are randomly sampled on each point cloud.

We report our numerical comparison in Tab. 5. We achieve the best performance in terms of all metrics. We further highlight our advantage in visual comparison in Fig. 9 (a). We found that our method can reconstruct smoother surfaces with more geometry details than other methods. We also compare the parts that our method reconstructs in Fig. 9 (b). Our parts are more meaningful and expressive than others.

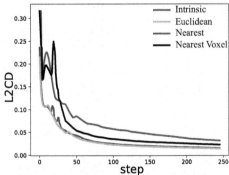

Fig. 8. Effect of surface codes on training.

D-FAUST. Finally, we evaluate our method in surface reconstruction for non-rigid shapes. To evaluate our ability of representing articulated parts, we leverage intrinsic distance d_G to calculate the affinity vector. We compare our method with NeuralParts [69] which is the latest method for representing articulated shapes. Both of our method and NeuralParts represent a human using 6 parts. We annotate $I = 6$ region centers on the input point cloud. For fair comparisons, we leverage the same signed distance supervision to overfit a shape using our method and NeuralParts.

Table 6 reports numerical comparison with NeuralParts. We report our results of global reconstruction and local part approximation, both of which outperform the results of NeuralParts. We further demonstrate our performance in visual comparison in Fig. 10, where our method can reconstruct parts with more geometry details.

Table 7. L2CD, L1CD and NC comparison under 100 models of D-FAUST.

Class	L2CD×100	L1CD×100	NC
DeepLS	0.0065	0.704	0.955
SIF	0.0067	0.681	0.945
Nglod	0.0062	0.718	**0.958**
Ours(Euclidean)	0.0064	0.698	0.955
Ours(Intrinsic)	**0.0059**	**0.611**	0.953

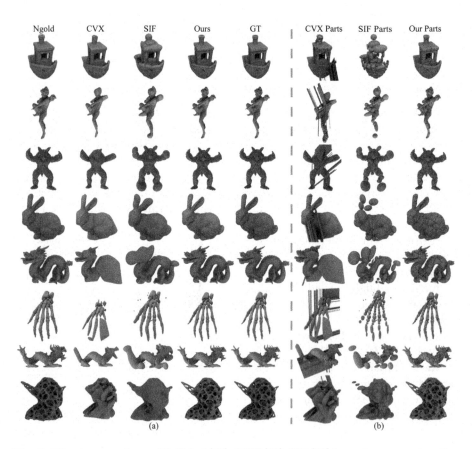

Fig. 9. Visual comparison with Nglod [79], CVX [16], SIF [22] in surface reconstruction under FAMOUS in (a). The part comparison is in (b).

We further highlight the advantages of our surface codes in surface reconstruction for humans. We compare our results obtained with Euclidean distances d_E and intrinsic distances d_G with the methods leveraging latent codes on voxel grids or 3D Gaussian functions, including DeepLS [8], Nglod [79] and SIF [22]. Similarly, we also produce the result of each method using the same set of signed distance supervision. The set contains 100 humans, and we train each method to overfit these humans. We leverage $I = 100$ latent codes to report our results and the results of SIF, while leveraging 125 latent codes to report the results of DeepLS and Nglod.

The numerical comparison is shown in Table 7. Our method achieves the best in terms of CD, and the intrinsic distances d_G work better than Euclidean distances d_E. We visualize our reconstruction in Fig. 11, and our results reveal much smoother surfaces.

4.3   Shape Abstraction

Our method can also represent a shape as an abstraction. We remove the geometry details on a shape by representing each one of its parts as a convex hull.

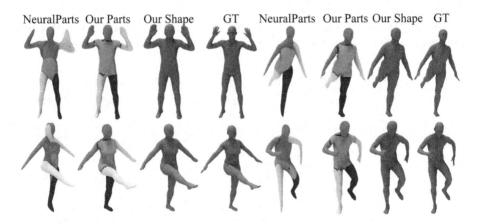

Fig. 10. Visual comparison with NeuralParts [69] under D-FAUST. Color in the same column indicates the same part label.

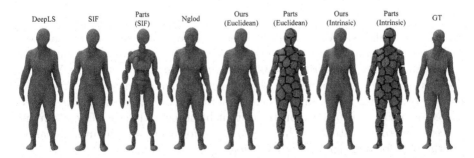

Fig. 11. Visual comparison with DeepLS [8], SIF [22] and Nglod [79] under D-FAUST.

We leverage our learned model in Table 5 to produce the abstractions for shapes in FAMOUS dataset. CVX and SIF also produced results in an overfitting way as ours. Visual comparison in Fig. 13 demonstrates that our method can reveal more complex structures on shapes with the same number of parts.

With semantic distance d_S to obtain affinity vector, our method can also produce shape abstraction with more meaningful parts. Besides the ability of encoding semantic segmentation in Fig. 6, we report our results learned by Eq. (6) with instance segmentation (100 points) in Fig. 12. We first reconstruct the shape and the parts, and abstract the shape using convex hulls of its parts. Due to our ability of using the surface attributes, our method not

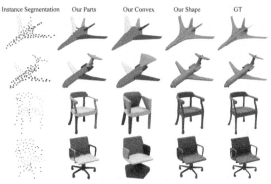

Fig. 12. Shape abstraction with instance segmentation. Color in the same row indicates the same part label.

only reconstructs smooth surfaces but also reveals plausible parts. More abstraction results are in our supplemental materials.

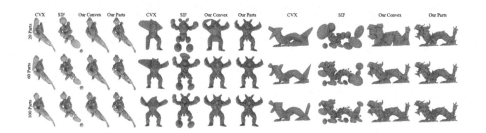

Fig. 13. Visual comparison with CVX [16] and SIF [22] in shape abstraction with different numbers of parts.

4.4   Ablation Study

Distance Metrics. We compare the effect of distance metrics on the performance under the 10 humans from D-FAUST. We compare the results with Euclidean distance d_E, intrinsic distance d_G, and no distance encoding. Without distance encoding, we produce the affinity vector as a uniform vector ("Average") or a one-hot vector indicating the nearest surface code ("Nearest"). The numerical comparison in Tab. 8 demonstrates that blending with either Euclidean distances or intrinsic distances achieves better performance and intrinsic distances are the best for non-rigid shape modeling.

Convergence. We compare the effect of surface codes on convergence under the 10 humans from D-FAUST. We compare the average L2CD obtained with Euclidean distance d_E, intrinsic distance d_G, one-hot affinity vector ("Nearest") and latent codes on voxel vertices ("Nearest Voxel"). The comparison in Fig. 8 indicates that blending parts with d_E or d_G makes the training converge faster and better than only using the nearest code on both surface or voxel grids.

Table 8. Ablation studies under 10 models of D-FAUST.

Affinity	L2CD×100	L1CD×100	NC
Average	0.0058	0.671	**0.952**
Nearest	0.0060	0.671	0.950
Euclidean	0.0057	0.661	**0.952**
Intrinsic	**0.0039**	**0.555**	**0.952**

Surface Code Number. Another advantage of surface codes is that we can represent shapes at multilevel without significant geometry details loss. We reconstruct the Stanford bunny using different numbers of surface codes. Figure 14 indicates that our method still achieves high accuracy even with few surface codes, while CVX [16] requires more parts to approximate the shape well. The reason is that our method represents parts and blends parts in the latent space, which achieves better representation ability.

5 Conclusion

We introduce latent partition implicit to represent 3D shapes. LPI is a multilevel representation, which efficiently represents a shape using different numbers of parts. Our method successfully represents parts using surface codes, and blend parts by weighting surface codes in

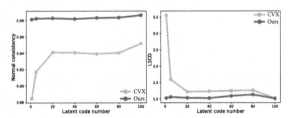

Fig. 14. Effect of surface code number.

the latent space to reconstruct surfaces. This leads to highly accurate shape and part modeling. With surface codes, latent partition implicit also enables to flexibly combine additional surface attributes, such as geodesic distance or segmentation. We can learn latent partition implicit from point clouds without requiring ground truth signed distances or point normals. Our method outperforms the state-of-the-art under widely used benchmarks.

References

1. Atzmon, M., Lipman, Y.: Sal: sign agnostic learning of shapes from raw data. In: IEEE Conference on Computer Vision and Pattern Recognition (2020)
2. Atzmon, M., Lipman, Y.: SALD: sign agnostic learning with derivatives. In: International Conference on Learning Representations (2021)

3. Azinović, D., Martin-Brualla, R., Goldman, D.B., Nießner, M., Thies, J.: Neural rgb-d surface reconstruction. In: IEEE Conference on Computer Vision and Pattern Recognition, pp. 6290–6301 (2022)
4. Ben-Shabat, Y., Koneputugodage, C.H., Gould, S.: Digs : divergence guided shape implicit neural representation for unoriented point clouds. CoRR abs/2106.10811 (2021)
5. Bernardini, F., Mittleman, J., Rushmeier, H., Silva, C., Taubin, G.: The ball-pivoting algorithm for surface reconstruction. IEEE Trans. Visual Comput. Graph. 5(4), 349–359 (1999)
6. Bogo, F., Romero, J., Pons-Moll, G., Black, M.J.: Dynamic FAUST: registering human bodies in motion. In: IEEE Computer Vision and Pattern Recognition (2017)
7. Boulch, A., Marlet, R.: Poco: Point convolution for surface reconstruction. In: IEEE Conference on Computer Vision and Pattern Recognition (2022)
8. Chabra, R., et al.: Deep local shapes: learning local sdf priors for detailed 3d reconstruction. In: Vedaldi, A., Bischof, H., Brox, T., Frahm, J.-M. (eds.) ECCV 2020. LNCS, vol. 12374, pp. 608–625. Springer, Cham (2020). https://doi.org/10.1007/978-3-030-58526-6_36
9. Chang, A.X., et al.: ShapeNet: an Information-Rich 3D Model Repository. Technical reports. arXiv:1512.03012 [cs.GR], Stanford University – Princeton University – Toyota Technological Institute at Chicago (2015)
10. Chen, C., Han, Z., Liu, Y.S., Zwicker, M.: Unsupervised learning of fine structure generation for 3D point clouds by 2D projection matching. In: IEEE International Conference on Computer Vision (2021)
11. Chen, Z., Zhang, H.: Learning implicit fields for generative shape modeling. In: IEEE Conference on Computer Vision and Pattern Recognition (2019)
12. Chibane, J., Alldieck, T., Pons-Moll, G.: Implicit functions in feature space for 3d shape reconstruction and completion. In: IEEE Conference on Computer Vision and Pattern Recognition, pp. 6968–6979 (2020)
13. Chibane, J., Mir, A., Pons-Moll, G.: Neural unsigned distance fields for implicit function learning. arXiv 2010.13938 (2020)
14. Crane, K., Weischedel, C., Wardetzky, M.: The heat method for distance computation. Commun. ACM 60(11), 90–99 (2017)
15. Darmon, F., Bascle, B., Devaux, J.C., Monasse, P., Aubry, M.: Improving neural implicit surfaces geometry with patch warping. In: IEEE Conference on Computer Vision and Pattern Recognition, pp. 6260–6269 (2022)
16. Deng, B., Genova, K., Yazdani, S., Bouaziz, S., Hinton, G.E., Tagliasacchi, A.: Cvxnet: learnable convex decomposition. In: IEEE Conference on Computer Vision and Pattern Recognition, pp. 31–41 (2020)
17. Erler, P., Guerrero, P., Ohrhallinger, S., Mitra, N.J., Wimmer, M.: POINTS2SURF learning implicit surfaces from point clouds. In: Vedaldi, A., Bischof, H., Brox, T., Frahm, J.-M. (eds.) ECCV 2020. LNCS, vol. 12350, pp. 108–124. Springer, Cham (2020). https://doi.org/10.1007/978-3-030-58558-7_7
18. Feng, W., Li, J., Cai, H., Luo, X., Zhang, J.: Neural points: point cloud representation with neural fields for arbitrary upsampling. In: IEEE Conference on Computer Vision and Pattern Recognition (2022)
19. Filoscia, I., Alderighi, T., Giorgi, D., Malomo, L., Callieri, M., Cignoni, P.: Optimizing object decomposition to reduce visual artifacts in 3d printing. Comput. Graph. Forum 39(2), 423–434 (2020)
20. Gal, R., Bermano, A., Zhang, H., Cohen-Or, D.: MRGAN: multi-rooted 3d shape generation with unsupervised part disentanglement. CoRR abs/2007.11944 (2020)

21. Genova, K., Cole, F., Sud, A., Sarna, A., Funkhouser, T.: Local deep implicit functions for 3d shape. In: IEEE Conference on Computer Vision and Pattern Recognition (2020)
22. Genova, K., Cole, F., Vlasic, D., Sarna, A., Freeman, W.T., Funkhouser, T.: Learning shape templates with structured implicit functions. In: International Conference on Computer Vision (2019)
23. Giebenhain, S., Goldluecke, B.: Air-nets: an attention-based framework for locally conditioned implicit representations. In: 2021 International Conference on 3D Vision. IEEE (2021)
24. Gropp, A., Yariv, L., Haim, N., Atzmon, M., Lipman, Y.: Implicit geometric regularization for learning shapes. arXiv 2002.10099 (2020)
25. Groueix, T., Fisher, M., Kim, V.G., Russell, B.C., Aubry, M.: A papier-mâché approach to learning 3D surface generation. In: IEEE Conference on Computer Vision and Pattern Recognition (2018)
26. Han, Z., Chen, C., Liu, Y.S., Zwicker, M.: Drwr: a differentiable renderer without rendering for unsupervised 3D structure learning from silhouette images. In: International Conference on Machine Learning (2020)
27. Han, Z., Chen, C., Liu, Y.S., Zwicker, M.: ShapeCaptioner: generative caption network for 3D shapes by learning a mapping from parts detected in multiple views to sentences. In: ACM International Conference on Multimedia (2020)
28. Han, Z., et al.: 3D2SeqViews: aggregating sequential views for 3D global feature learning by cnn with hierarchical attention aggregation. IEEE Trans. Image Process. **28**(8), 3986–3999 (2019)
29. Han, Z., Qiao, G., Liu, Y.-S., Zwicker, M.: SeqXY2SeqZ: structure learning for 3d shapes by sequentially predicting 1d occupancy segments from 2d coordinates. In: Vedaldi, A., Bischof, H., Brox, T., Frahm, J.-M. (eds.) ECCV 2020. LNCS, vol. 12369, pp. 607–625. Springer, Cham (2020). https://doi.org/10.1007/978-3-030-58586-0_36
30. Han, Z., Shang, M., Liu, Y.S., Zwicker, M.: View inter-prediction GAN: unsupervised representation learning for 3D shapes by learning global shape memories to support local view predictions. In: AAAI, pp. 8376–8384 (2019)
31. Han, Z., et al.: SeqViews2SeqLabels: learning 3D global features via aggregating sequential views by rnn with attention. IEEE Trans. Image Process. **28**(2), 672–685 (2019)
32. Han, Z., Shang, M., Wang, X., Liu, Y.S., Zwicker, M.: Y2Seq2Seq: cross-modal representation learning for 3D shape and text by joint reconstruction and prediction of view and word sequences. In: AAAI, pp. 126–133 (2019)
33. Han, Z., Wang, X., Liu, Y.S., Zwicker, M.: Multi-angle point cloud-vae:unsupervised feature learning for 3D point clouds from multiple angles by joint self-reconstruction and half-to-half prediction. In: IEEE International Conference on Computer Vision (2019)
34. Hasselgren, J., Hofmann, N., Munkberg, J.: Shape, light and material decomposition from images using monte carlo rendering and denoising. arXiv abs/2206.03380 (2022)
35. Hu, T., Han, Z., Zwicker, M.: 3D shape completion with multi-view consistent inference. In: AAAI (2020)
36. Jain, A., Mildenhall, B., Barron, J.T., Abbeel, P., Poole, B.: Zero-shot text-guided object generation with dream fields (2022)
37. Jiang, C., Sud, A., Makadia, A., Huang, J., Nießner, M., Funkhouser, T.: Local implicit grid representations for 3D scenes. In: IEEE Conference on Computer Vision and Pattern Recognition (2020)

38. Jiang, Y., Ji, D., Han, Z., Zwicker, M.: SDFDiff: differentiable rendering of signed distance fields for 3D shape optimization. In: IEEE Conference on Computer Vision and Pattern Recognition (2020)
39. Kazhdan, M.M., Hoppe, H.: Screened poisson surface reconstruction. ACM Trans. Graph. **32**(3), 29:1-29:13 (2013)
40. Li, T., Wen, X., Liu, Y.S., Su, H., Han, Z.: Learning deep implicit functions for 3D shapes with dynamic code clouds. In: IEEE Conference on Computer Vision and Pattern Recognition (2022)
41. Liao, Y., Donné, S., Geiger, A.: Deep marching cubes: learning explicit surface representations. In: Conference on Computer Vision and Pattern Recognition (2018)
42. Lin, C.H., Wang, C., Lucey, S.: Sdf-srn: learning signed distance 3d object reconstruction from static images. In: Advances in Neural Information Processing Systems (2020)
43. Littwin, G., Wolf, L.: Deep meta functionals for shape representation. In: IEEE International Conference on Computer Vision (2019)
44. Liu, M., Zhang, X., Su, H.: Meshing point clouds with predicted intrinsic-extrinsic ratio guidance. In: Vedaldi, A., Bischof, H., Brox, T., Frahm, J.-M. (eds.) ECCV 2020. LNCS, vol. 12353, pp. 68–84. Springer, Cham (2020). https://doi.org/10.1007/978-3-030-58598-3_5
45. Liu, S., Zhang, Y., Peng, S., Shi, B., Pollefeys, M., Cui, Z.: DIST: rendering deep implicit signed distance function with differentiable sphere tracing. In: IEEE Conference on Computer Vision and Pattern Recognition (2020)
46. Liu, S.L., Guo, H.X., Pan, H., Wang, P., Tong, X., Liu, Y.: Deep implicit moving least-squares functions for 3D reconstruction. In: IEEE Conference on Computer Vision and Pattern Recognition (2021)
47. Liu, S., Saito, S., Chen, W., Li, H.: Learning to infer implicit surfaces without 3D supervision. In: Advances in Neural Information Processing Systems (2019)
48. Liu, X., Han, Z., Liu, Y.S., Zwicker, M.: Point2Sequence: learning the shape representation of 3D point clouds with an attention-based sequence to sequence network. In: AAAI, pp. 8778–8785 (2019)
49. Lorensen, W.E., Cline, H.E.: Marching cubes: a high resolution 3D surface construction algorithm. Comput. Graph. **21**(4), 163–169 (1987)
50. Ma, B., Han, Z., Liu, Y.S., Zwicker, M.: Neural-pull: learning signed distance functions from point clouds by learning to pull space onto surfaces. In: International Conference on Machine Learning (2021)
51. Ma, B., Liu, Y.S., Zwicker, M., Han, Z.: Reconstructing surfaces for sparse point clouds with on-surface priors. In: IEEE Conference on Computer Vision and Pattern Recognition (2022)
52. Ma, B., Liu, Y.S., Zwicker, M., Han, Z.: Surface reconstruction from point clouds by learning predictive context priors. In: IEEE Conference on Computer Vision and Pattern Recognition (2022)
53. Martel, J.N.P., Lindell, D.B., Lin, C.Z., Chan, E.R., Monteiro, M., Wetzstein, G.: ACORN: adaptive coordinate networks for neural scene representation. CoRR abs/2105.02788 (2021)
54. Mescheder, L., Oechsle, M., Niemeyer, M., Nowozin, S., Geiger, A.: Occupancy networks: Learning 3D reconstruction in function space. In: IEEE Conference on Computer Vision and Pattern Recognition (2019)
55. Mi, Z., Luo, Y., Tao, W.: Ssrnet: scalable 3D surface reconstruction network. In: IEEE Conference on Computer Vision and Pattern Recognition (2020)

56. Michalkiewicz, M., Pontes, J.K., Jack, D., Baktashmotlagh, M., Eriksson, A.P.: Deep level sets: implicit surface representations for 3D shape inference. CoRR abs/1901.06802 (2019)

57. Michel, O., Bar-On, R., Liu, R., Benaim, S., Hanocka, R.: Text2mesh: text-driven neural stylization for meshes. In: IEEE Conference on Computer Vision and Pattern Recognition (2022)

58. Mildenhall, B., Srinivasan, P.P., Tancik, M., Barron, J.T., Ramamoorthi, R., Ng, R.: NeRF: representing scenes as neural radiance fields for view synthesis. In: Vedaldi, A., Bischof, H., Brox, T., Frahm, J.-M. (eds.) ECCV 2020. LNCS, vol. 12346, pp. 405–421. Springer, Cham (2020). https://doi.org/10.1007/978-3-030-58452-8_24

59. Yavartanoo, M., Chung, J., Neshatavar, R., Lee, K.M.: 3dias: 3d shape reconstruction with implicit algebraic surfaces. In: International Conference on Computer Vision (2021)

60. Müller, T., Evans, A., Schied, C., Keller, A.: Instant neural graphics primitives with a multiresolution hash encoding. arXiv:2201.05989 (2022)

61. Muntoni, A., Livesu, M., Scateni, R., Sheffer, A., Panozzo, D.: Axis-aligned height-field block decomposition of 3d shapes. ACM Trans. Graph. 37(5), 169:1-169:15 (2018)

62. Niemeyer, M., Mescheder, L., Oechsle, M., Geiger, A.: Differentiable volumetric rendering: Learning implicit 3D representations without 3D supervision. In: IEEE Conference on Computer Vision and Pattern Recognition (2020)

63. Novotny, D., et al.: Keytr: keypoint transporter for 3d reconstruction of deformable objects in videos. In: Proceedings of the IEEE/CVF Conference on Computer Vision and Pattern Recognition (CVPR), pp. 5595–5604 (2022)

64. Oechsle, M., Peng, S., Geiger, A.: UNISURF: unifying neural implicit surfaces and radiance fields for multi-view reconstruction. CoRR abs/2104.10078 (2021)

65. Ohtake, Y., Belyaev, A.G., Alexa, M., Turk, G., Seidel, H.: Multi-level partition of unity implicits. ACM Trans. Graph. 22(3), 463–470 (2003)

66. Park, J.J., Florence, P., Straub, J., Newcombe, R., Lovegrove, S.: DeepSDF: learning continuous signed distance functions for shape representation. In: IEEE Conference on Computer Vision and Pattern Recognition (2019)

67. Paschalidou, D., van Gool, L., Geiger, A.: Learning unsupervised hierarchical part decomposition of 3d objects from a single rgb image. In: Proceedings IEEE Conference on Computer Vision and Pattern Recognition (CVPR) (2020)

68. Paschalidou, D., Gool, L.V., Geiger, A.: Learning unsupervised hierarchical part decomposition of 3d objects from a single RGB image. In: IEEE Conference on Computer Vision and Pattern Recognition, pp. 1057–1067 (2020)

69. Paschalidou, D., Katharopoulos, A., Geiger, A., Fidler, S.: Neural parts: learning expressive 3d shape abstractions with invertible neural networks. In: IEEE Conference on Computer Vision and Pattern Recognition, pp. 3204–3215 (2021)

70. Peng, S., Jiang, C.M., Liao, Y., Niemeyer, M., Pollefeys, M., Geiger, A.: Shape as points: a differentiable poisson solver. In: Advances in Neural Information Processing Systems (2021)

71. Rebain, D., Li, K., Sitzmann, V., Yazdani, S., Yi, K.M., Tagliasacchi, A.: Deep medial fields. CoRR abs/2106.03804 (2021)

72. Rückert, D., Franke, L., Stamminger, M.: Adop: approximate differentiable one-pixel point rendering. arXiv:2110.06635 (2021)

73. Saito, S., Huang, Z., Natsume, R., Morishima, S., Kanazawa, A., Li, H.: PIFu: pixel-aligned implicit function for high-resolution clothed human digitization (2019)

74. Fridovich-Keil, S., Yu, A., Tancik, M., Chen, Q., Recht, B., Kanazawa, A.: Plenoxels: radiance fields without neural networks. In: IEEE Conference on Computer Vision and Pattern Recognition (2022)
75. Sharma, G., et al.: Surfit: learning to fit surfaces improves few shot learning on point clouds. CoRR abs/2112.13942 (2021)
76. Sitzmann, V., Martel, J.N., Bergman, A.W., Lindell, D.B., Wetzstein, G.: Implicit neural representations with periodic activation functions. In: Advances in Neural Information Processing Systems (2020)
77. Sitzmann, V., Zollhöfer, M., Wetzstein, G.: Scene representation networks: continuous 3D-structure-aware neural scene representations. In: Advances in Neural Information Processing Systems (2019)
78. Peng, S., Niemeyer, M., Mescheder, L., Pollefeys, M., Geiger, A.: Convolutional occupancy networks. In: Vedaldi, A., Bischof, H., Brox, T., Frahm, J.-M. (eds.) ECCV 2020. LNCS, vol. 12348, pp. 523–540. Springer, Cham (2020). https://doi.org/10.1007/978-3-030-58580-8_31
79. Takikawa, T., et al.: Neural geometric level of detail: Real-time rendering with implicit 3D shapes. In: IEEE Conference on Computer Vision and Pattern Recognition (2021)
80. Tang, J., Lei, J., Xu, D., Ma, F., Jia, K., Zhang, L.: Sa-convonet: sign-agnostic optimization of convolutional occupancy networks. In: Proceedings of the IEEE/CVF International Conference on Computer Vision (2021)
81. Tatarchenko, M., Richter, S.R., Ranftl, R., Li, Z., Koltun, V., Brox, T.: What do single-view 3D reconstruction networks learn? In: The IEEE Conference on Computer Vision and Pattern Recognition (2019)
82. Tretschk, E., Tewari, A., Golyanik, V., Zollhöfer, M., Stoll, C., Theobalt, C.: PatchNets: patch-based generalizable deep implicit 3d shape representations. In: Vedaldi, A., Bischof, H., Brox, T., Frahm, J.-M. (eds.) ECCV 2020. LNCS, vol. 12361, pp. 293–309. Springer, Cham (2020). https://doi.org/10.1007/978-3-030-58517-4_18
83. Wang, W., Xu, Q., Ceylan, D., Mech, R., Neumann, U.: DISN: deep implicit surface network for high-quality single-view 3D reconstruction. In: Advances In Neural Information Processing Systems (2019)
84. Wen, X., Han, Z., Cao, Y.P., Wan, P., Zheng, W., Liu, Y.S.: Cycle4completion: unpaired point cloud completion using cycle transformation with missing region coding. In: IEEE Conference on Computer Vision and Pattern Recognition (2021)
85. Wen, X., Li, T., Han, Z., Liu, Y.S.: Point cloud completion by skip-attention network with hierarchical folding. In: IEEE Conference on Computer Vision and Pattern Recognition (2020)
86. Wen, X., et al.: Pmp-net: point cloud completion by learning multi-step point moving paths. In: IEEE Conference on Computer Vision and Pattern Recognition (2021)
87. Wen, X., Zhou, J., Liu, Y.S., Su, H., Dong, Z., Han, Z.: 3D shape reconstruction from 2D images with disentangled attribute flow. In: IEEE Conference on Computer Vision and Pattern Recognition (2022)
88. Williams, F., Parent-Lévesque, J., Nowrouzezahrai, D., Panozzo, D., Yi, K.M., Tagliasacchi, A.: Voronoinet : general functional approximators with local support. In: IEEE Conference on Computer Vision and Pattern Recognition Workshops, pp. 1069–1073 (2020)
89. Williams, F., Schneider, T., Silva, C., Zorin, D., Bruna, J., Panozzo, D.: Deep geometric prior for surface reconstruction. In: IEEE Conference on Computer Vision and Pattern Recognition (2019)

90. Wu, Y., Sun, Z.: DFR: differentiable function rendering for learning 3D generation from images. Comput. Graph. Forum **39**(5), 241–252 (2020)
91. Xiang, P., et al.: Snowflakenet: point cloud completion by snowflake point deconvolution with skip-transformer. In: IEEE International Conference on Computer Vision (2021)
92. Yao, C.H., Hung, W.C., Jampani, V., Yang, M.H.: Discovering 3d parts from image collections. In: IEEE International Conference on Computer Vision (2021)
93. Yao, S., Yang, F., Cheng, Y., Mozerov, M.G.: 3d shapes local geometry codes learning with sdf. In: IEEE International Conference on Computer Vision Workshops, pp. 2110–2117 (2021)
94. Yavartanoo, M., Chung, J., Neshatavar, R., Lee, K.M.: 3dias: 3d shape reconstruction with implicit algebraic surfaces. In: Proceedings of the IEEE/CVF International Conference on Computer Vision (ICCV), pp. 12446–12455 (2021)
95. Yifan, W., Wu, S., Oztireli, C., Sorkine-Hornung, O.: Iso-points: optimizing neural implicit surfaces with hybrid representations. CoRR abs/2012.06434 (2020)
96. Yu, Z., Peng, S., Niemeyer, M., Sattler, T., Geiger, A.: Monosdf: exploring monocular geometric cues for neural implicit surface reconstruction. arXiv abs/2022.00665 (2022)
97. Zakharov, S., Kehl, W., Bhargava, A., Gaidon, A.: Autolabeling 3D objects with differentiable rendering of sdf shape priors. In: IEEE Conference on Computer Vision and Pattern Recognition (2020)
98. Zhao, W., Lei, J., Wen, Y., Zhang, J., Jia, K.: Sign-agnostic implicit learning of surface self-similarities for shape modeling and reconstruction from raw point clouds. CoRR abs/2012.07498 (2020)
99. Zhu, Z., Peng, S., et al.: Nice-slam: neural implicit scalable encoding for slam. In: IEEE Conference on Computer Vision and Pattern Recognition (2022)

Implicit Field Supervision for Robust Non-rigid Shape Matching

Ramana Sundararaman$^{(\boxtimes)}$, Gautam Pai, and Maks Ovsjanikov

LIX, École Polytechnique, Paris, IP, France
{sundararaman,pai,maks}@lix.polytechnique.fr

Abstract. Establishing a correspondence between two non-rigidly deforming shapes is one of the most fundamental problems in visual computing. Existing methods often show weak resilience when presented with challenges innate to real-world data such as noise, outliers, self-occlusion etc. On the other hand, auto-decoders have demonstrated strong expressive power in learning geometrically meaningful latent embeddings. However, their use in *shape analysis* has been limited. In this paper, we introduce an approach based on an auto-decoder framework, that learns a continuous shape-wise deformation field over a fixed template. By supervising the deformation field for points on-surface and regularizing for points off-surface through a novel *Signed Distance Regularization* (SDR), we learn an alignment between the template and shape *volumes*. Trained on clean water-tight meshes, *without* any data-augmentation, we demonstrate compelling performance on compromised data and real-world scans (Our code is available at https://github.com/Sentient07/IFMatch).

Keywords: Non-rigid 3D shape correspondence · Neural fields

1 Introduction

Understanding the relations between non-rigid 3D shapes through dense correspondences is a fundamental problem in computer vision and graphics. A common strategy is to leverage the underlying surfaces of shapes represented as triangle meshes. While recent advancements [21,65] demonstrate near-perfect correspondence accuracies, they strongly rely on idealistic settings of clean input data, which unfortunately is far from typical 3D acquisition setups. The question of generalizability of non-rigid shape correspondence to artifacts such as noise, outliers, self-occlusions, clutters, partiality, etc. which are innate to general 3D scans, is largely unanswered.

On the other hand, 3D shape representations through neural fields [80] or learned implicit functions have been shown to achieve remarkable accuracy, flexibility and generative power for a wide range of shape and scene modeling tasks

---

Supplementary Information The online version contains supplementary material available at https://doi.org/10.1007/978-3-031-20062-5_20.

S. Avidan et al. (Eds.): ECCV 2022, LNCS 13663, pp. 344–362, 2022.
https://doi.org/10.1007/978-3-031-20062-5_20

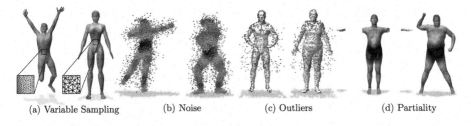

(a) Variable Sampling   (b) Noise   (c) Outliers   (d) Partiality

Fig. 1. Key advantages of our non-rigid shape correspondence pipeline: Our approach is extremely robust to common artifacts in 3D shapes like: (a) variations in sampling density, (b) significant noise, (c) cluttered outliers and (d) partiality.

[14,46,54,67]. Unlike standard shape representations, learning implicit functions through a neural network allows one to capture continuous surfaces, while seamlessly adapting to changes in topology. Indeed, implicit surface representations not only allow to introduce an adaptive level of detail, but can also benefit from strong network regularization to control the desired resolution [66,71]. As a result, although initial efforts have focused on using implicit representations primarily for generative modeling and shape recovery, several recent works have shown their utility in other tasks including differentiable rendering for image synthesis [40,68], part-level shape decomposition [55], modeling dynamic geometry [51] and novel view synthesis [48,50] among many others.

This flexibility of implicit surface representations, however, comes at a cost, especially in applications that involve multiple shapes, such as shape correspondence or comparison. Since the surface is defined as the zero-level set of a function, individual points are no longer easily identifiable. As a result, recent methods based on implicit surface representations that have aimed at shape alignment, try to model a warping field over an underlying template [17,33,84], or between shape pairs [7]. All of these works, however, primarily focus on deformations across nearby, sufficiently similar 3D shapes.

In this paper, we introduce an efficient method for establishing correspondences across *arbitrary* non-rigid shapes, using neural field representations. To this end, we develop a new architecture based on the auto-decoder framework [54], that aims to recover a 3D deformation field between a fixed template and a target shape *volume*. The key ingredient of our architecture is defining the shape-wise deformation field from the latent embedding, augmented with two effective regularizations. First, we regularize the deformation field for arbitrary points in space through a novel *Signed Distance Regularization* (SDR). Second, we simultaneously condition the latent embedding to be compact and geometrically meaningful by learning a continuous Signed Distance Function (SDF) representation of the target shape. The resulting method is able to compute dense point-to-point correspondences between shapes while being extremely robust in the presence of varying sampling density, noise, cluttered outliers and missing parts as shown in Fig. 1. To the best of our knowledge, ours is the first non-rigid correspondence method, based on neural field representation, that can be generalized to arbitrary shape categories such as articulated humans and animals.

Training on clean watertight meshes without any data-augmentation, we evaluate on a wide range of challenges across multiple benchmarks as well as real data captured by a 3D-scanner. Our approach shows compelling resilience to challenging artifacts and is more robust than existing point-based, mesh-based and spectral methods. In summary, our main contributions are: **(1)** We introduce an efficient approach based on the auto-decoder framework, capable of recovering a *volumetric* deformation field to align a source and a target shape *volumes*, even for significant non-rigid deformations. **(2)** We propose a novel way of regularizing the deformation of arbitrary points in space through the Signed Distance Regularization (SDR). **(3)** We perform rigorous evaluations by introducing challenges to existing benchmarks and on real-world data acquired by a 3D-scanner.

2 Related Work

2.1 Mesh-based Shape Correspondence

There is a large body of literature on shape matching, for shapes represented as triangle meshes. We refer interested readers to recent surveys [9,63,70,73] for a more comprehensive overview. Notable axiomatic approaches in this category are based on the functional maps paradigm [2,13,23,37,53,61]. Typically, these methods solve for near isometric shape correspondence by estimating linear transformations between spaces of real-valued functions, represented in a reduced functional basis. The conceptual framework of functional maps was further improved by learning-based formulations [19,22,30,39,62] that predict and penalize the map as a whole. Concurrently, recent advances in geometric deep learning have also tackled the correspondence problem by designing novel architectures for mesh and point cloud representation [12,21,38,43,49,58,78,83]. Such methods typically treat the correspondence learning problem as vertex labelling, which is learned efficiently using the respective architectures.

However, these methods that are predominantly based on mesh based representation of shapes are prone to sub-par performance when exposed to artifacts like sensitivity to variations in mesh discretization [65], sampling, missing or occluded parts, noise and other challenges that are common in typical 3D acquisition setups.

2.2 Template Based Shape Correspondence

Deforming a template to fit any given shape is a well-established technique in non-rigid shape registration [3,4]. The advent of learning-based skinning techniques [41,85,86] enabled deformation of a fixed template to an arbitrary shape and pose by calibrating a fixed set of SMPL model parameters. The introduction of parametric models has opened the avenue for generating copious amounts of training data [26,74,75] for data-driven methods. Such data-driven techniques have led to some seminal works in: 3D pose estimation [28,35,52], digitizing humans [16,81] and even model-based 3D shape registration for articulated humans [8,10,11,56,57]. Most relevant to our work is LoopReg [8], which proposes to diffuse SMPL parameters in space to learn correspondence. In contrast, our approach does not require any parametric models as priors and can be generalized across arbitrary categories.

On the other hand, there are techniques that learn a model-free deformation to align a fixed template to a target shape [18,26,27,77]. Most notable among them is 3D-CODED [26], which learns to deform a fixed template mesh to a target shape. While this approach is succinct and well-founded, it requires significant amounts of training data to achieve optimal performance. Moreover, the deformation space is confined only to the surface of a mesh and can suffer from deformation artifacts. To ameliorate this, recent methods [17,84] have chosen to "implicitly define the template". However, their application in non-rigid shape matching is limited.

2.3 Neural Field Shape Representations

Coordinate-based neural networks are emerging methods for efficient, differentiable and high-fidelity shape representations [6,15,25,31,51,54,66,79,82] whose fundamental objective is to represent zero level-sets using parameters of neural network. In its most general form [54,66,67], these methods share two principal common goals - to perform differentiable surface reconstruction and to learn a latent shape embedding. This has given rise to numerous applications especially in the field of generative 3D modelling [72], such as shape editing [31,69,76], shape optimization [24,47] and novel view synthesis [48,50,64,71] to name a few. Most relevant to our work are DIF-Net [17] and SIREN [66] which achieve shape-specific surface reconstruction through Hyper-Networks [29]. However, leveraging the power of this representations in the domain of dense correspondence learning has so far been limited to nearly rigid objects [17,25,33,84].

3 Method

Notation: Throughout this manuscript, we use $\mathcal{S}$ to denote the target shape whose latent embedding is denoted by $\alpha_{\mathcal{S}} \in \mathbb{R}^{512}$ and $\mathcal{T}$ as the fixed template. $\mathcal{X}$ and $\mathcal{Y}$ denote an arbitrary pair of shapes between which we aim to find a correspondence. We let $\tilde{x} \in \partial\mathcal{S}$ be a point on the surface of the target shape $\mathcal{S}$, $x \in \mathbb{R}^3$ denotes a point in space and σ_x be its signed distance, $\sigma_x := \mathrm{d}(x, \partial\mathcal{S})$. We define $[\mathcal{S}] := \{x \in \mathbb{R}^3 | \sigma_x < \zeta\}$ to be the shape volume, which is the set of points sampled in space, in the vicinity of the shape surface $\partial\mathcal{S}$, with ζ being a constant. Analogously, $[\mathcal{T}] := \{t_i \in \mathbb{R}^3 | \sigma_{t_i} < \zeta\}$ denotes the template volume.

3.1 Overview

Given a pair of shapes $\mathcal{X}$ and $\mathcal{Y}$, represented either as triangle meshes or point clouds, our goal is to estimate a point-wise map $\Pi : \mathcal{X} \to \mathcal{Y}$. To this end, we

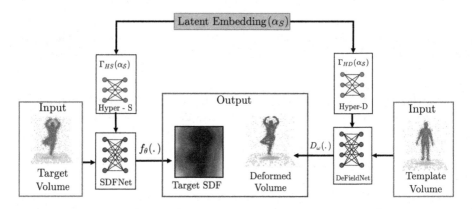

Fig. 2. Given a target shape volume (left) and a template volume (right) as input, DeFieldNet (Sect. 3.2) aligns the template to target volume regularized by SDFNet (Sect. 3.3). Shape-specific network weights are modeled by latent code (Sect. 3.1). Points sampled within volumes (input) are shown only for visualization purposes to emphasize that our network operates over the 3D domain.

learn a *shape-specific* deformation field $D_\omega(.) : \mathbb{R}^3 \to \mathbb{R}^3$ which when applied to a fixed template volume $[\mathcal{T}]$, yields the target shape volume $[\mathcal{S}]$. Then, by using $D_\omega(.)$ to independently align $[\mathcal{T}]$ to $[\mathcal{X}]$ and $[\mathcal{Y}]$, we obtain correspondence between $\mathcal{X}$ and $\mathcal{Y}$ through nearest neighbor search. We stress that differently from previous data-driven works [18,26] that align a template mesh to a target mesh, our approach aligns two *volumes*. This is because, we observe that learning a volumetric alignment between arbitrary points in space naturally leads to a more robust map estimation as the deformation field is not constrained to an underlying surface defined by a mesh or a point cloud. While aligning on-surface points is straightforward in the supervised setting, aligning off-surface points is ill-posed. To this end, we propose a novel *Signed Distance Regularization (SDR)* for constraining the change in the SDF brought about by the deformation field. Learning a continuous deformation field also allows us to impose useful smoothness and volume preservation constraints, for enhancing the regularity of the map.

To make the deformation shape-specific, we learn a latent embedding $\alpha_\mathcal{S}$, which governs the parameters $\omega_\mathcal{S}$ of $D_{\omega_\mathcal{S}}(\cdot)$. We drop the subscript of ω for the sake of brevity. This latent embedding is learned following the auto-decoder framework [54]. However, constructing an embedding based on the deformation field alone leads to topological inconsistencies as we discuss in the ablation studies (refer to Suppl). Therefore, we introduce a geometric prior to $\alpha_\mathcal{S}$ by learning a continuous Signed Distance Function (SDF) representation of the shape, resulting in two concurrent auto-decoder networks as shown in Fig. 2. On one side (left), we learn the continuous Signed Distance Function (SDF) of the target shape, which we refer to as *SDFNet*. Simultaneously (right of Fig. 2), we learn a deformation field D_ω over $[\mathcal{T}]$ through *DeFieldNet*. The parameters of our SDFNet $\theta := \Gamma_{HS}(\alpha_\mathcal{S})$ and DeFieldNet $\omega := \Gamma_{HD}(\alpha_\mathcal{S})$ are defined as two functions of the latent embedding, through Hyper-S and Hyper-D respectively. We perform an end-to-end training, to jointly learn the latent embedding α_S, through the gradients of SDFNet and DeFieldNet, similar to [29,66]. In summary, we learn a latent embedding by concurrently learning a deformation field over the template volume and the target shape's SDF. We stress that our main objective is to learn a plausible deformation field (via DeFieldNet) and the role of learning an implicit surface (via SDFNet) is to act as a geometric regularizer.

3.2 DeFieldNet

The main objective of DeFieldNet is to learn a smooth continuous shape-specific deformation field over the fixed template volume. We apply on surface supervision and off-surface regularization in order to deform the template volume $[\mathcal{T}]$ to the target shape volume $[\mathcal{S}]$.

On Surface Supervision: For two corresponding points $\tilde{x}_i \in \partial\mathcal{S}$ and $\tilde{t}_i \in \partial\mathcal{T}$, where $\Pi(\tilde{x}_i) = \tilde{t}_i$, our goal is to find a deformation $D_\omega : \tilde{t}_i \in \mathbb{R}^3 \to v \in \mathbb{R}^3$, $s.t.$ $\tilde{t}_i + v \approx \tilde{x}_i$. Thus, solving for the desirable deformation field amounts to optimising the following loss:

$$\mathcal{L}_{\text{surf}} = \sum_{\tilde{x}_i \in \partial\mathcal{S}} ||\tilde{x}_i - \hat{\tilde{x}}_i||_2 \tag{1}$$

$$\text{where,}\, \hat{\tilde{x}}_i = D_\omega(\tilde{t}_i) + \tilde{t}_i$$

Signed Distance Regularization (SDR): In addition to supervising the deformation of points on the surface, we also regularize the deformation field applied to arbitrary points in the template volume $t \in [\mathcal{T}] \in \mathbb{R}^3$. For this, we propose a *Signed Distance Regularization* which *preserves* the Signed Distance Function under deformation for points sampled close to the surface. More specifically, given signed distances: $\sigma_{t_i}, \sigma_{\hat{x}_i}$ of points $t_i, \hat{x}_i$ respectively where $\hat{x}_i = D_\omega(t_i) + t_i$, we require $\sigma_{t_i} \approx \sigma_{\hat{x}_i}$, for all points sampled closed to the surface.

While σ_{t_i} is available as a result of pre-processing, computing $\sigma_{\hat{x}_i}$ requires a continuous signed distance estimator as the SDF is measured w.r.t deformed shape. Therefore we perform *discrete approximation* of the signed distance at any predicted point using Radial Basis Function (RBF) interpolation [32]. For any $\hat{x}_i \in \mathbb{R}^3$, we first construct the RBF kernel matrix Φ as a function of its neighbors in the target shape volume $\mathcal{N}(\hat{x}_i) \in [\mathcal{S}]$.

$$\Phi_{ij} := \varphi(p_i, p_j) = \sqrt{\varepsilon_0 + ||p_i - p_j||^2} \tag{2}$$

where, φ is the radial basis function and $p_{i,j} \in \mathcal{N}(\hat{x}_i)$. Assuming $\Delta = [\sigma_1 \ldots \sigma_K]^T$ to be the vectorized representation of the SDF values of neighbors, the estimated SDF $\hat{\sigma}_{\hat{x}_i}$ of $\hat{x}_i$ w.r.t deformed template $\tilde{\mathcal{T}}$ is given as:

$$\hat{\sigma}_{\hat{x}_i} = \varphi(\hat{x}_i)\,\Phi^{-1}\Delta \tag{3}$$

We use shifted multiquadric functions as our RBF interpolant to avoid a singular interpolant matrix (refer to Suppl for more details). Therefore, our final SDF Regularization constraint can be written as:

$$\mathcal{L}_{SDR} = \sum_{t_i \in [\mathcal{T}]} \| \operatorname{clamp}(\sigma_{t_i}, \eta) - \operatorname{clamp}(\hat{\sigma}_{\hat{x}_i}, \eta) \|_2 \tag{4}$$

where $\operatorname{clamp}(x, \eta) := \min(\eta, \max(-\eta, x))$ is applied to make sure that the penalty is enforced only to points close to the surface. We highlight that this clamping is necessary, since the change in SDF under a considerable non-rigid deformation may differ significantly for points far from the surface.

Smooth Deformation: For the deformation field to be locally smooth, we ideally expect the flow vectors at neighboring points to be in "agreement" with each other. We enforce this constraint by encouraging the spatial derivatives to have minimal norm:

$$\mathcal{L}_{\text{Smooth}} = \sum_{t_i \in [\mathcal{T}]} \| \nabla D_\omega(t_i) \|_2 \tag{5}$$

Volume Preserving Flow: Since a volume-preserving deformation field must be divergence-free, it must have a Jacobian with unit determinant [1].

$$\mathcal{L}_{\text{vol}} = \sum_{t_i \in [\mathcal{T}]} | \det(\nabla D_\omega(t_i)) - 1 | \tag{6}$$

We use autograd to compute the Jacobian.

3.3   SDFNet

Given a set of N target shapes $\{\mathcal{S}_0 \ldots \mathcal{S}_N\}$, our goal is to *regularize* their latent embedding $\{\alpha_{\mathcal{S}_0} \ldots \alpha_{\mathcal{S}_N}\}$ through implicit surface reconstruction. We adopt the modified auto-decoder [66] framework with sinusoidal $\mathcal{C}^\infty$ activation function as our SDFNet. Given $f_\theta(\cdot) : x \in \mathbb{R}^3 \to \sigma_x \in \mathbb{R}$ to be the function that predicts the Signed Distance for a point $x \in [\mathcal{S}]$, SDFNet's learning objective is given by,

$$\mathcal{L}_{\mathcal{SDF}} = \sum_{x \in [\mathcal{S}]} \left(| \, \|\nabla_x f_\theta(x)\|_2 - 1 | + |f_\theta(x) - \sigma_x| \right) + \sum_{\tilde{x} \in \partial S} (1 - \langle \nabla_x f_\theta(\tilde{x}), \hat{\mathbf{n}}(\tilde{x}) \rangle)$$
$$+ \sum_{x \setminus \partial S} \psi(f(x)) \tag{7}$$

The first term penalizes the discrepancy in the predicted signed distance and enforces the Eikonal constraint for points in the shape volume. The second term encourages the gradient along the shape boundary to be oriented with surface normals. The last term applies an exponential penalty where $\psi := \exp(-C \cdot |\sigma_x|)$, $C \gg 0$, for wrong prediction of $f_\theta(x) = 0$.

3.4   Training Objective

In summary, the energy minimized at training time can be formulated as a combination of aforementioned individual constraints:

$$\mathcal{E}_{\text{Train}} = \Lambda_1 \mathcal{L}_{\mathcal{SDF}} + \Lambda_2 \mathcal{L}_{surf} + \Lambda_3 \mathcal{L}_{\mathcal{SDR}} + \Lambda_4 \mathcal{L}_{Smooth} + \Lambda_5 \mathcal{L}_{vol} \qquad (8)$$

Here, Λ_i are scalars provided in Sect. 3.6. The first term helps to regularize the latent space, while the other terms encourage a plausible deformation field.

3.5   Inference

At inference time, given $\mathcal{X}, \mathcal{Y}$ to be a pair of unseen shapes, our approach is three-staged. First, we find the optimal deformation function D_ω associated with $\mathcal{X}, \mathcal{Y}$ to deform $[\mathcal{T}]$. We solve for optimal parameters for our deformation field ω through Maximum-a-Posterior (MAP) estimation as:

$$\begin{aligned} \alpha_i &= \underset{\alpha_i}{\text{argmin}} \ \Lambda_1 \mathcal{L}_{\mathcal{SDF}} + \Lambda_3 \mathcal{L}_{\mathcal{SDR}} \\ \omega &:= \Gamma_{HD}(\alpha_i) \end{aligned} \qquad (9)$$

Second, similar to [26] we enhance the deformation field applied by minimizing the bi-directional Chamfer's Distance

$$\alpha_{\mathbf{opt}} = \underset{\alpha_i}{\text{argmin}} \ \sum_{\tilde{\mathbf{s}} \in \partial \mathcal{S}} \min_{\tilde{\mathbf{t}}_i \in \partial \mathcal{T}} \left| D_\omega(\tilde{\mathbf{t}}_i) - \tilde{\mathbf{s}} \right|^2 + \sum_{\tilde{\mathbf{s}} \in \partial \mathcal{S}} \min_{\tilde{\mathbf{t}}_i \in \partial \mathcal{T}} \left| D_\omega(\tilde{\mathbf{t}}_i) - \tilde{\mathbf{s}} \right|^2 \qquad (10)$$

Finally, we establish the correspondence between $\mathcal{X}, \mathcal{Y}$ through their respective deformed templates using a nearest neighbor search.

3.6   Implementation Details

Our two Hyper-Networks, SDFNet and DeFieldNet all use 4-layered MLPs with 20% dropout. SDFNet uses sinusoidal activation [66] while DeFieldNet uses ReLU activation. We fix $\Lambda_1 = 1, \Lambda_2 = 500, \Lambda_3 = 50, \Lambda_4 = 5, \Lambda_5 = 20$, namely the coefficients in Eq. 8. For a shape in a batch, we use 4,000 points for on-surface supervision Eq. 1. We use 8,000 points for SDF regularization in Eq. 4 and $\eta = 0.1$ after fitting all shapes within a unit-sphere. We provide additional pre-processing details in the Suppl.

4   Experiments

Overview: In this section we demonstrate the robustness of our method in computing correspondences under challenging scenarios through extensive benchmarking. We perform our experiments across 4 datasets namely, FAUST [59], SHREC'19 [44], SMAL [86] and CMU-Panoptic dataset [34]. The first three are mesh based benchmarks and are well-studied in non-rigid shape correspondence literature. In addition, we introduce challenging point cloud variants of these benchmarks which will be detailed below. CMU-Panoptic dataset [34], on the other hand, consists of raw point clouds acquired from a 3D scanner.

For evaluation, we follow the Princeton benchmark protocol [36] to measure mean geodesic distortion of correspondence on meshes. We perform evaluation on our point cloud variants by composing the predicted map to the nearest vertex point and measure the mean geodesic distortion [36]. On the CMU-Panoptic dataset [34], we measure the error on established key-points. We stress that across all experiments, while the evaluations are performed under challenging scenarios, our model is trained on clean water-tight mesh *without any data-augmentation*. Across all tables, "*" denotes a method that requires a mesh structure and cannot be evaluated on point clouds. "**" refers to computational in-feasibility in evaluating a baseline.

Baselines: We compare our method against several shape correspondence methods which can be broadly categorized into four main classes - axiomatic, spectral learning, template based and point cloud learning (PC Learning). We use ZoomOut (ZO) [45], BCICP [59] and Smooth Shells (S-Shells) [20] as our axiomatic baselines. For spectral basis learning baselines, we use Geometric Functional Maps (GeoFM) [19] with the recent more powerful Diffusion-Net [65] feature extractor and DeepShells (D-Shells) [22]. We use 3D-CODED (3DC) [26], Deformed Implicit Fields (DIF-Net) [17] and Deep Implicit Templates (DIT-Net) [84] as template based baselines. We use Diff-FMaps (Dif-FM) [42], DPC [38] and Corrnet [83] as our point cloud learning baselines. For a fair evaluation, we identically pre-train them according to their category for different experimental settings as mentioned in the respective sections. We provide more details on the hyper-parameters used for baselines in the Supplementary.

4.1   FAUST

Dataset: FAUST [10] dataset consists of 100 shapes where evaluation is performed on the last 20 shapes. Recently, Ren. *et al.* [59] introduced a re-meshed version of this dataset and Marin *et al.* [42] proposed a non-isometric, noisy point cloud version. For our robustness discussion, we introduce two additional challenges on top of the aforementioned variants. First, complimentary to [42], we introduce a dense point cloud variant consisting of 45,000 points perturbed with Gaussian noise. Second, we introduce 10% clutter points by random sampling of points in space. In summary, we perform evaluation on (1) Re-meshed shapes [59], (2) Non-isometric noisy point cloud (NI-PC) [42], (3) Dense point clouds with noise (De-PC) and (4) Clutter.

Baselines: We train our model and all data-driven methods on the first 80 meshes of the FAUST dataset. All baseline methods are trained using the publicly available code, following the configuration stipulated by the respective authors.

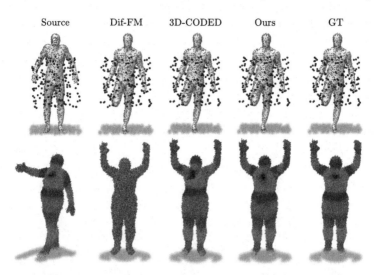

| Source | Dif-FM | 3D-CODED | Ours | GT |

Fig. 3. Correspondence quality through color transfer on challenges we introduced to FAUST [59]. 1st Row: Point clouds corrupted with 10% clutter shown in black. In contrast to baselines, our method shows strong resilience in the presence of clutter. 2nd Row: Point cloud with 45k points and noise.

Table 1. Quantitative results on FAUST-Remesh dataset and its variants reported as mean geodesic error (in cm) scaled by shape diameter.

Category	Axiomatic			PC Learning			Spectral Learning		Template Based			
Method	BCICP [59]	ZO [45]	S-Shells [20]	Dif-FM [42]	DPC [38]	CorrNet [83]	D-Shells [22]	GeoFM [19]	3DC [26]	DIF-Net [17]	DIT-Net [84]	Ours
Remesh [59]	10.5	6.0	2.5	34.0	27.1	28.1	**1.7**	2.7	2.5	21.0	20.1	2.6
NI-PC + Noise [42]	11.5	8.7	*	6.6	8.4	25.2	*	31.3	7.3	14.6	13.6	**3.1**
De-PC + Noise	*	*	*	31.8	**	27.9	*	53.7	9.1	18.1	18.0	**4.1**
Clutter	*	*	*	17.7	50.0	51.1	*	52.2	22.1	14.7	14.3	**8.1**

Discussion: Our main quantitative results are summarized in Table 1. On the re-meshed shapes [59], our method demonstrates comparable performance with existing state-of-the-art methods. However, as we decrease the perfection of data, our method shows compelling resilience towards artifacts and consistently outperforms all the other baselines by a noticeable margin. It is also worthy to remark that among all baselines that we compare with, our method is the only one that is capable of providing reasonable (less than 10cm) correspondence in the presence of clutter points. We also show two qualitative examples on our newly introduced variant in Fig. 3.

Source   3D-CODED   CorrNet   Ours   Ground Truth

Fig. 4. Correspondence quality on SHREC'19 [44] and its variants. 1st Row: Meshes. 2nd Row: Point clouds with noise and outliers. 3rd Row: Missing parts. Compared to baselines, our method exhibits strong resilience to artifacts.

4.2 SHREC'19

Dataset: SHREC'19 [44] is a challenging shape correspondence benchmark due to significant variations in mesh sampling, connectivity and presence of multiple connected components. It consists of 44 shapes and a total of 430 evaluation pairs. In addition, we introduce 3 challenging scenarios with different data imperfections. **Scenario 1:** We compare the meshes provided by Melzi et al. [44]. **Scenario 2:** We subsample the meshes to 10,000 points and introduce 20% outliers. **Scenario 3:** We further corrupt the surface information in Scenario 2 using Gaussian noise. **Scenario 4:** We introduce partiality in the form of missing parts, to a subset for a part-to-whole evaluation scheme [60].

Baseline: We pre-train all template based and point cloud learning baselines on 2,000 SURREAL shapes [75] including 10% humans in bent poses [26]. For our spectral basis learning baselines, we pre-train them on the training set of FAUST+SCAPE [5], consisting of $\binom{80}{2} + \binom{51}{2}$ shape pairs, a setting which is demonstrated to be best suited for them [19,22]. We use Partial Functional Map (PFM) [60] as an additional axiomatic baseline for Scenario 4.

Discussion: Quantitative results across 4 scenarios are summarized in Table 2. Our method demonstrates state-of-the-art performance across all variants of the SHREC'19 dataset and remains inert to imperfections in the data. While Smooth-Shells [20], is comparable to our approach in Scenario 1, it cannot be evaluated in other scenarios due to its strong dependence on spectral information. Moreover, even among template based methods, it is important to note that the supervised learning baseline 3D-CODED [26] demonstrates significant decline in performance in the presence of outliers and noise. We posit that a well defined shape embedding, obtained by learning a volumetric mapping, plays a crucial role in our method's performance. Even among methods that construct a shape space through an auto-decoder framework, DIF-Net [17] and DIT [84], are not reliable when presented with non-rigid shapes. Among point cloud learning methods, while DPC [38] shows comparable performance to our approach in Scenario 2, their performance declines in Scenario 3, when surface information is corrupted by noise. Furthermore, since DPC [38] depends on input point cloud resolution, it is infeasible to be evaluated in Scenarios 1 and 4. Finally, despite training on clean meshes with no missing components, the performance of our approach is unaffected by the partiality introduced in Scenario 4. We attribute our learning of *volumetric alignment* coupled with off-surface regularization to be the reason behind robustness to missing components. We summarize this discussion by qualitatively depicting Scenarios 1, 3 and 4 in Fig. 4, wherein, despite subsequently increasing artifacts, our method shows compelling resilience. Additional qualitative results in different poses are provided in the Supplementary.

Table 2. Quantitative results on 430 test set pairs of SHREC'19 dataset reported as mean geodesic error (in cm), scaled by shape diameter.

Category	Axiomatic		PC Learning			Spectral Learning		Template Based			
Method	S-Shells [20]	PFM [60]	CorrNet [83]	DPC [38]	Diff-FM [42]	GeoFM [19]	D-Shells [22]	3DC [26]	DIF-Net [17]	DIT-Net [84]	Ours
Scenario: 1 (Meshes) [44]	7.6	N/A	13.4	**	29.6	11.7	15.2	9.2	14.9	41.4	**6.5**
Scenario: 2 (Outliers)	*	N/A	35.9	8.5	17.1	26.1	*	12.2	12.4	12.6	**7.4**
Scenario: 3 (Outliers + Noise)	*	N/A	36.0	11.5	16.7	27.8	*	14.4	36.2	12.5	**7.7**
Scenario: 4 (Missing parts)	*	52.4	23.5	**	26.3	48.6	23.8	6.0	11.9	41.1	**4.3**

4.3 SMAL

Dataset: In this section, we show the generalization ability to *inter-class* non-rigid shape correspondence among to *non-human* shapes. To this end, we use the SMAL dataset [86], a parametric model that consists of 5 main categories of animals. We construct the training set by sampling 100 animals per each category. For correspondence evaluation, we generate 20 new shapes consisting of 4 animals per category, resulting in 180 *inter-class* evaluation pairs. We relax the degrees of freedom for selected joints while generating the test-set to introduce new poses, unseen in the training set. In addition, we introduce partiality to this dataset in the form of multiple connected components.

Baseline Settings: We train all template based methods, including ours, on the aforementioned 500 training shapes. For our method and 3D-Coded, which are supervised template based methods, we share the same animal template. Since spectral basis learning baselines learn correspondence pairwise, we train all data-driven spectral methods on $\binom{100}{2}$ shapes with 20 animals per-category.

Fig. 5. Quantitative and qualitative inter-class correspondence on SMAL [86] dataset. Our approach produces a smooth map, unaffected by partiality.

Discussion: Our main quantitative and qualitative results are summarized in Fig. 5. We observe that Geo-FM [19,65] that is a representation agnostic method and Partial Functional Maps, an approach built to tackle partial non-rigid shape correspondence methods fail to establish reasonable correspondence. Our approach on the other hand, remains agnostic to shape connectivity arising from inter-class non-isometry and introduced partiality. Finally, our method surpasses the template-based baseline method, 3D-Coded by a considerable margin.

4.4 CMU-Panoptic Dataset

Dataset: In this section, we demonstrate the generalization ability of our approach to real-world sensor data. To that end, we use the CMU Panoptic [34] dataset, which consists of 3+hrs footage of 8 subjects in frequently occurring social postures captured using the Kinect RGB+D sensor. This dataset consists of point clouds with noise, outliers, self-occlusions and clutter, allowing to evaluate correspondence methods on real-world data. We sample 200 shape pairs consisting of 3 distinct humans in 7 distinct poses. We measure non-rigid correspondence accuracy using the sparsely annotated anatomical landmark keypoints. More specifically, for each keypoint in the source, we consider 32 neighbors points and measure the disparity (as Euclidean distance, in cm) between their closest keypoint in the target and source.

Discussion: In order for a fair evaluation of generalizability, we test all approaches using the trained model elaborated in Sect. 4.2. Quantitative results of keypoint errors are summarized in Table 3. Our approach shows convincing performance in comparison to baselines, and more noticeably, it outperforms the conceptually closest supervised baseline, 3D-CODED [26] by a twofold margin. We also show a qualitative example through texture transfer in Fig. 6, highlighting the efficacy of our approach in comparison to existing approaches on real-world data.

| Source | 3D-CODED | CorrNet | Ours | Ground Truth |

Fig. 6. Qualitative comparison using texture transfer on noisy point clouds from the CMU-Panoptic [34] dataset.

Table 3. Avg. Euclidean keypoint error (cm) for 200 test pairs, scaled by shape diameter.

Method	Dif-FM [42]	GeoFM [19]	3D-CODED [26]	DIF-Net [17]	CorrNet [83]	DPC [38]	Ours
Keypoint Error	39.4	23.9	17.1	15.3	14.8	**	**8.5**

5 Conclusion, Limitations and Future Work

We presented a novel approach for robust non-rigid shape correspondence based on the auto-decoder framework. Leveraging its strong expressive power, we demonstrated the ability of our approach in exhibiting strong resilience to practical artifacts like noise, outliers, clutter, partiality and occlusion across multiple benchmarks. To the best of our knowledge, our approach is the first to successfully demonstrate the use of Neural Fields, which predominantly are used as generative models, to the field of non-rigid shape correspondence, generalizable to arbitrary shape categories.

Despite various merits, we see multiple avenues for improvement and possible future work. Firstly, our current framework of joint learning of latent spaces by continuous functions opens possibilities for local descriptor learning alongside purely extrinsic information. This can potentially lead to an unsupervised pipeline in contrast to our existing supervised method. Also, auto-decoder style learning approaches are not rotation invariant and conventional techniques like data-augmentation can prove costly in terms of training effort. Making Neural Fields rotational invariant is also an interesting future direction.

References

1. Adams, B., Ovsjanikov, M., Wand, M., Seidel, H.P., Guibas, L.J.: Meshless modeling of deformable shapes and their motion. In: Proceedings of the 2008 ACM SIGGRAPH/Eurographics Symposium on Computer Animation, pp. 77–86. SCA 2008, Eurographics Association, Goslar, DEU (2008)
2. Aflalo, Y., Kimmel, R.: Spectral multidimensional scaling. Proc. Natl. Acad. Sci. **110**(45), 18052–18057 (2013)

3. Allen, B., Curless, B., Popović, Z.: Articulated body deformation from range scan data. ACM Trans. Graph. **21**(3), 612–619 (2002). https://doi.org/10.1145/566654. 566626

4. Allen, B., Curless, B., Popović, Z.: The space of human body shapes: reconstruction and parameterization from range scans. ACM Trans. Graph. **22**(3), 587–594 (2003). https://doi.org/10.1145/882262.882311

5. Anguelov, D., Srinivasan, P., Koller, D., Thrun, S., Rodgers, J., Davis, J.: Scape: shape completion and animation of people. ACM Trans. Graph. **24**(3), 408–416 (2005). https://doi.org/10.1145/1073204.1073207

6. Atzmon, M., Lipman, Y.: Sal: sign agnostic learning of shapes from raw data. In: IEEE/CVF Conference on Computer Vision and Pattern Recognition (CVPR) (2020)

7. Atzmon, M., Novotny, D., Vedaldi, A., Lipman, Y.: Augmenting implicit neural shape representations with explicit deformation fields. arXiv preprint arXiv:2108.08931 (2021)

8. Bhatnagar, B.L., Sminchisescu, C., Theobalt, C., Pons-Moll, G.: Loopreg: self-supervised learning of implicit surface correspondences, pose and shape for 3D human mesh registration. In: Larochelle, H., Ranzato, M., Hadsell, R., Balcan, M.F., Lin, H. (eds.) Advances in Neural Information Processing Systems, vol. 33, pp. 12909–12922. Curran Associates, Inc. (2020). https://proceedings.neurips.cc/paper/2020/file/970af30e481057c48f87e101b61e6994-Paper.pdf

9. Biasotti, S., Cerri, A., Bronstein, A., Bronstein, M.: Recent trends, applications, and perspectives in 3D shape similarity assessment. Comput. Graph. Forum **35**(6), 87–119 (2016)

10. Bogo, F., Romero, J., Loper, M., Black, M.J.: FAUST: dataset and evaluation for 3D mesh registration. In: Proceedings IEEE Conference on Computer Vision and Pattern Recognition (CVPR). IEEE, Piscataway, NJ, USA (2014)

11. Bogo, F., Romero, J., Pons-Moll, G., Black, M.J.: Dynamic FAUST: registering human bodies in motion. In: 2017 IEEE Conference on Computer Vision and Pattern Recognition (CVPR), pp. 5573–5582 (2017). https://doi.org/10.1109/CVPR.2017.591

12. Boscaini, D., Masci, J., Rodolà, E., Bronstein, M.: Learning shape correspondence with anisotropic convolutional neural networks. In: Lee, D., Sugiyama, M., Luxburg, U., Guyon, I., Garnett, R. (eds.) Advances in Neural Information Processing Systems, vol. 29. Curran Associates, Inc. (2016). https://proceedings.neurips.cc/paper/2016/file/228499b55310264a8ea0e27b6e7c6ab6-Paper.pdf

13. Burghard, O., Dieckmann, A., Klein, R.: Embedding shapes with green's functions for global shape matching. Comput. Graph. **68**, 1–10 (2017)

14. Chen, Z., Zhang, H.: Learning implicit fields for generative shape modeling. In: Proceedings of the IEEE/CVF Conference on Computer Vision and Pattern Recognition, pp. 5939–5948 (2019)

15. Chen, Z., Zhang, H.: Learning implicit fields for generative shape modeling. In: 2019 IEEE/CVF Conference on Computer Vision and Pattern Recognition (CVPR), pp. 5932–5941 (2019)

16. Corona, E., Pumarola, A., Alenyà, G., Pons-Moll, G., Moreno-Noguer, F.: Smplicit: topology-aware generative model for clothed people. In: CVPR (2021)

17. Deng, Y., Yang, J., Tong, X.: Deformed implicit field: modeling 3D shapes with learned dense correspondence. In: Proceedings of the IEEE/CVF Conference on Computer Vision and Pattern Recognition, pp. 10286–10296 (2021)

18. Deprelle, T., Groueix, T., Fisher, M., Kim, V.G., Russell, B.C., Aubry, M.: Learning elementary structures for 3D shape generation and matching. In: NeurIPS (2019)
19. Donati, N., Sharma, A., Ovsjanikov, M.: Deep geometric functional maps: robust feature learning for shape correspondence. In: 2020 IEEE/CVF Conference on Computer Vision and Pattern Recognition (CVPR). IEEE (2020). https://doi.org/10.1109/cvpr42600.2020.00862
20. Eisenberger, M., Lähner, Z., Cremers, D.: Smooth shells: multi-scale shape registration with functional maps. In: 2020 IEEE/CVF Conference on Computer Vision and Pattern Recognition (CVPR), pp. 12262–12271 (2020)
21. Eisenberger, M., et al.: Neuromorph: unsupervised shape interpolation and correspondence in one go. In: Proceedings of the IEEE/CVF Conference on Computer Vision and Pattern Recognition, pp. 7473–7483 (2021)
22. Eisenberger, M., Toker, A., Leal-Taixé, L., Cremers, D.: Deep shells: unsupervised shape correspondence with optimal transport. arXiv preprint arXiv:2010.15261 (2020)
23. Ezuz, D., Ben-Chen, M.: Deblurring and denoising of maps between shapes. In: Computer Graphics Forum, vol. 36, pp. 165–174. Wiley Online Library (2017)
24. Gao, L., et al.: SDM-NET: deep generative network for structured deformable mesh. ACM Trans. Graph. **38**(6) (2019). https://doi.org/10.1145/3355089.3356488
25. Genova, K., Cole, F., Vlasic, D., Sarna, A., Freeman, W.T., Funkhouser, T.A.: Learning shape templates with structured implicit functions. In: 2019 IEEE/CVF International Conference on Computer Vision (ICCV), pp. 7153–7163 (2019)
26. Groueix, T., Fisher, M., Kim, V.G., Russell, B., Aubry, M.: 3D-coded : 3D correspondences by deep deformation. In: ECCV (2018)
27. Groueix, T., Fisher, M., Kim, V., Russell, B., Aubry, M.: Unsupervised cycle-consistent deformation for shape matching. In: Symposium on Geometry Processing (SGP) (2019)
28. Güler, R.A., Neverova, N., Kokkinos, I.: Densepose: dense human pose estimation in the wild. In: Proceedings of the IEEE Conference on Computer Vision and Pattern Recognition, pp. 7297–7306 (2018)
29. Ha, D., Dai, A., Le, Q.V.: Hypernetworks (2016)
30. Halimi, O., Litany, O., Rodola, E., Bronstein, A.M., Kimmel, R.: Unsupervised learning of dense shape correspondence. In: Proceedings of the IEEE/CVF Conference on Computer Vision and Pattern Recognition, pp. 4370–4379 (2019)
31. Hao, Z., Averbuch-Elor, H., Snavely, N., Belongie, S.: Dualsdf: semantic shape manipulation using a two-level representation. In: Proceedings of the IEEE/CVF Conference on Computer Vision and Pattern Recognition (2020)
32. Hardy, R.L.: Multiquadric equations of topography and other irregular surfaces. J. Geophys. Res. **76**(8), 1905–1915 (1971). https://doi.org/10.1029/jb076i008p01905
33. Jiang, C.M., Huang, J., Tagliasacchi, A., Guibas, L.J.: Shapeflow: learnable deformations among 3D shapes. ArXiv abs/2006.07982 (2020)
34. Joo, H., et al.: Panoptic studio: a massively multiview system for social interaction capture. TPAMI (2017)
35. Kanazawa, A., Black, M.J., Jacobs, D.W., Malik, J.: End-to-end recovery of human shape and pose. In: Computer Vision and Pattern Regognition (CVPR) (2018)
36. Kim, V.G., Lipman, Y., Funkhouser, T.: Blended intrinsic maps. ACM Trans. Graph. **30**(4), 1–12 (2011). https://doi.org/10.1145/2010324.1964974
37. Kovnatsky, A., Bronstein, M.M., Bronstein, A.M., Glashoff, K., Kimmel, R.: Coupled quasi-harmonic bases. In: Computer Graphics Forum, vol. 32, pp. 439–448. Wiley Online Library (2013)

38. Lang, I., Ginzburg, D., Avidan, S., Raviv, D.: DPC: unsupervised Deep Point Correspondence via Cross and Self Construction. In: Proceedings of the International Conference on 3D Vision (3DV), pp. 1442–1451 (2021)
39. Litany, O., Remez, T., Rodola, E., Bronstein, A., Bronstein, M.: Deep functional maps: structured prediction for dense shape correspondence. In: Proceedings of the IEEE International Conference on Computer Vision, pp. 5659–5667 (2017)
40. Liu, S., Zhang, Y., Peng, S., Shi, B., Pollefeys, M., Cui, Z.: DIST: rendering deep implicit signed distance function with differentiable sphere tracing. In: Proceedings of the IEEE/CVF Conference on Computer Vision and Pattern Recognition, pp. 2019–2028 (2020)
41. Loper, M., Mahmood, N., Romero, J., Pons-Moll, G., Black, M.J.: SMPL: a skinned multi-person linear model. ACM Trans. Graph. (Proc. SIGGRAPH Asia) **34**(6), 248:1–248:16 (2015)
42. Marin, R., Rakotosaona, M.J., Melzi, S., Ovsjanikov, M.: Correspondence learning via linearly-invariant embedding. Proc. NeurIPS (2020)
43. Masci, J., Boscaini, D., Bronstein, M., Vandergheynst, P.: Geodesic convolutional neural networks on riemannian manifolds. In: Proceedings of the IEEE International Conference on Computer Vision Workshops, pp. 37–45 (2015)
44. Melzi, S., Marin, R., Rodolà, E., Castellani, U., Ren, J., Poulenard, A., Wonka, P., Ovsjanikov, M.: Shrec 2019: matching humans with different connectivity. In: Eurographics Workshop on 3D Object Retrieval, vol. 7 (2019)
45. Melzi, S., Ren, J., Rodolà, E., Sharma, A., Wonka, P., Ovsjanikov, M.: Zoomout: spectral upsampling for efficient shape correspondence. ACM Trans. Graph. **38**(6) (2019). https://doi.org/10.1145/3355089.3356524
46. Mescheder, L., Oechsle, M., Niemeyer, M., Nowozin, S., Geiger, A.: Occupancy networks: learning 3D reconstruction in function space. In: Proceedings of the IEEE/CVF Conference on Computer Vision and Pattern Recognition, pp. 4460–4470 (2019)
47. Mezghanni, M., Boulkenafed, M., Lieutier, A., Ovsjanikov, M.: Physically-aware generative network for 3D shape modeling. In: Proceedings of the IEEE/CVF Conference on Computer Vision and Pattern Recognition (CVPR), pp. 9330–9341 (2021)
48. Mildenhall, B., Srinivasan, P.P., Tancik, M., Barron, J.T., Ramamoorthi, R., Ng, R.: Nerf: representing scenes as neural radiance fields for view synthesis. In: ECCV (2020)
49. Monti, F., Boscaini, D., Masci, J., Rodola, E., Svoboda, J., Bronstein, M.M.: Geometric deep learning on graphs and manifolds using mixture model CNNs. In: Proceedings of the IEEE conference on computer vision and pattern recognition, pp. 5115–5124 (2017)
50. Niemeyer, M., Geiger, A.: Giraffe: representing scenes as compositional generative neural feature fields. In: Proceedings IEEE Conference on Computer Vision and Pattern Recognition (CVPR) (2021)
51. Niemeyer, M., Mescheder, L., Oechsle, M., Geiger, A.: Occupancy flow: 4D reconstruction by learning particle dynamics. In: Proceedings of the IEEE/CVF International Conference on Computer Vision, pp. 5379–5389 (2019)
52. Omran, M., Lassner, C., Pons-Moll, G., Gehler, P.V., Schiele, B.: Neural body fitting: unifying deep learning and model-based human pose and shape estimation. Verona, Italy (2018)
53. Ovsjanikov, M., Ben-Chen, M., Solomon, J., Butscher, A., Guibas, L.: Functional maps: a flexible representation of maps between shapes. ACM Trans. Graph. (TOG) **31**(4), 1–11 (2012)

54. Park, J.J., Florence, P., Straub, J., Newcombe, R., Lovegrove, S.: Deepsdf: learning continuous signed distance functions for shape representation. In: Proceedings of the IEEE/CVF Conference on Computer Vision and Pattern Recognition, pp. 165–174 (2019)

55. Paschalidou, D., Gool, L.V., Geiger, A.: Learning unsupervised hierarchical part decomposition of 3D objects from a single RGB image. In: Proceedings of the IEEE/CVF Conference on Computer Vision and Pattern Recognition, pp. 1060–1070 (2020)

56. Pons-Moll, G., Pujades, S., Hu, S., Black, M.: Clothcap: seamless 4D clothing capture and retargeting. ACM Trans. Graph. (Proc. SIGGRAPH) **36**(4) (2017). https://doi.org/10.1145/3072959.3073711, two first authors contributed equally

57. Pons-Moll, G., Romero, J., Mahmood, N., Black, M.J.: Dyna: a model of dynamic human shape in motion **34**(4) (2015). https://doi.org/10.1145/2766993

58. Poulenard, A., Ovsjanikov, M.: Multi-directional geodesic neural networks via equivariant convolution. ACM Trans. Graph. (TOG) **37**(6), 1–14 (2018)

59. Ren, J., Poulenard, A., Wonka, P., Ovsjanikov, M.: Continuous and orientation-preserving correspondences via functional maps. ACM Trans. Graph. **37**(6) (2018). https://doi.org/10.1145/3272127.3275040

60. Rodolà, E., Cosmo, L., Bronstein, M.M., Torsello, A., Cremers, D.: Partial functional correspondence. Comput. Graph. Forum **36**(1), 222–236 (2016). https://doi.org/10.1111/cgf.12797

61. Rodolà, E., Cosmo, L., Bronstein, M.M., Torsello, A., Cremers, D.: Partial functional correspondence. In: Computer Graphics Forum, vol. 36, pp. 222–236. Wiley Online Library (2017)

62. Roufosse, J.M., Sharma, A., Ovsjanikov, M.: Unsupervised deep learning for structured shape matching. In: Proceedings of the IEEE/CVF International Conference on Computer Vision, pp. 1617–1627 (2019)

63. Sahillioğlu, Y.: Recent advances in shape correspondence. Vis. Comput. **36**(8), 1705–1721 (2020)

64. Schwarz, K., Liao, Y., Niemeyer, M., Geiger, A.: Graf: generative radiance fields for 3D-aware image synthesis. In: Advances in Neural Information Processing Systems (NeurIPS) (2020)

65. Sharp, N., Attaiki, S., Crane, K., Ovsjanikov, M.: Diffusionnet: discretization agnostic learning on surfaces (2021)

66. Sitzmann, V., Martel, J., Bergman, A., Lindell, D., Wetzstein, G.: Implicit neural representations with periodic activation functions. Adv. Neural Inf. Process. Syst. **33** (2020)

67. Sitzmann, V., Zollhöfer, M., Wetzstein, G.: Scene representation networks: continuous 3D-structure-aware neural scene representations. arXiv preprint arXiv:1906.01618 (2019)

68. Takikawa, T., et al.: Neural geometric level of detail: Real-time rendering with implicit 3D shapes. In: Proceedings of the IEEE/CVF Conference on Computer Vision and Pattern Recognition, pp. 11358–11367 (2021)

69. Takikawa, T., et al.: Neural geometric level of detail: real-time rendering with implicit 3D shapes (2021)

70. Tam, G.K., et al.: Registration of 3D point clouds and meshes: a survey from rigid to nonrigid. IEEE Trans. Visual Comput. Graph. **19**(7), 1199–1217 (2012)

71. Tancik, M., et al.: Fourier features let networks learn high frequency functions in low dimensional domains. NeurIPS (2020)

72. Tiwari, G., Sarafianos, N., Tung, T., Pons-Moll, G.: Neural-gif: neural generalized implicit functions for animating people in clothing. ArXiv abs/2108.08807 (2021)

73. Van Kaick, O., Zhang, H., Hamarneh, G., Cohen-Or, D.: A survey on shape correspondence. Comput. Graph. Forum **30**(6), 1681–1707 (2011)
74. Varol, G., Laptev, I., Schmid, C., Zisserman, A.: Synthetic humans for action recognition from unseen viewpoints **129**(7), 2264–2287 (2021). https://doi.org/10.1007/s11263-021-01467-7
75. Varol, G., et al.: Learning from synthetic humans. In: CVPR (2017)
76. Vasu, S., Talabot, N., Lukoianov, A., Baqué, P., Donier, J., Fua, P.: Hybridsdf: combining free form shapes and geometric primitives for effective shape manipulation. ArXiv abs/2109.10767 (2021)
77. Wang, W., Ceylan, D., Mech, R., Neumann, U.: 3DN: 3D deformation network. In: Proceedings of the IEEE/CVF Conference on Computer Vision and Pattern Recognition (CVPR) (2019)
78. Wiersma, R., Eisemann, E., Hildebrandt, K.: CNNs on surfaces using rotation-equivariant features. ACM Trans. Graph. (TOG) **39**(4), 1–92 (2020)
79. Wu, R., Zhuang, Y., Xu, K., Zhang, H., Chen, B.: PQ-NET: A generative part seq2seq network for 3D shapes. In: IEEE/CVF Conference on Computer Vision and Pattern Recognition (CVPR) (2020)
80. Xie, Y., et al.: Neural fields in visual computing and beyond (2021). https://neuralfields.cs.brown.edu/
81. Yu, T., et al.: Simulcap : single-view human performance capture with cloth simulation. In: 2019 IEEE/CVF Conference on Computer Vision and Pattern Recognition (CVPR), pp. 5499–5509 (2019)
82. Zadeh, A., Lim, Y.C., Liang, P.P., Morency, L.P.: Variational auto-decoder. ArXiv abs/1903.00840 (2019)
83. Zeng, Y., Qian, Y., Zhu, Z., Hou, J., Yuan, H., He, Y.: CorrNet3D: unsupervised end-to-end learning of dense correspondence for 3D point clouds. In: IEEE/CVF Conference on Computer Vision and Pattern Recognition (CVPR) (2021)
84. Zheng, Z., Yu, T., Dai, Q., Liu, Y.: Deep implicit templates for 3D shape representation. In: Proceedings of the IEEE/CVF Conference on Computer Vision and Pattern Recognition, pp. 1429–1439 (2021)
85. Zuffi, S., Kanazawa, A., Black, M.J.: Lions and tigers and bears: capturing non-rigid, 3D, articulated shape from images. In: IEEE Conference on Computer Vision and Pattern Recognition (CVPR). IEEE Computer Society (2018)
86. Zuffi, S., Kanazawa, A., Jacobs, D., Black, M.J.: 3D menagerie: modeling the 3D shape and pose of animals. In: IEEE Conference on Computer Vision and Pattern Recognition (CVPR) (2017)

Learning Self-prior for Mesh Denoising Using Dual Graph Convolutional Networks

Shota Hattori[✉], Tatsuya Yatagawa, Yutaka Ohtake, and Hiromasa Suzuki

School of Engineering, The University of Tokyo, Tokyo, Japan
{hattori,tatsy,ohtake,suzuki}@den.t.u-tokyo.ac.jp

Abstract. This study proposes a deep-learning framework for mesh denoising from a single noisy input, where two graph convolutional networks are trained jointly to filter vertex positions and facet normals apart. The prior obtained only from a single input is particularly referred to as a self-prior. The proposed method leverages the framework of the deep image prior (DIP), which obtains the self-prior for image restoration using a convolutional neural network (CNN). Thus, we obtain a denoised mesh without any ground-truth noise-free meshes. Compared to the original DIP that transforms a fixed random code into a noise-free image by the neural network, we reproduce vertex displacement from a fixed random code and reproduce facet normals from feature vectors that summarize local triangle arrangements. After tuning several hyperparameters with a few validation samples, our method achieved significantly higher performance than traditional approaches working with a single noisy input mesh. Moreover, its performance is better than the other methods using deep neural networks trained with a large-scale shape dataset. The independence of our method of either large-scale datasets or ground-truth noise-free mesh will allow us to easily denoise meshes whose shapes are rarely included in the shape datasets. Our code is available at: https://github.com/astaka-pe/Dual-DMP.git.

Keywords: Mesh denoising · Self-prior · Graph convolutional network

1 Introduction

The prevalence of low-cost three-dimensional (3D) scanning devices has made digitizing the shapes of real-world objects easier. However, the surface geometries captured by these 3D scanners are inevitably noisy, even when using the latest scanning devices, due to weak light reflection caused by the specularity and dark color of the object surface. Therefore, for accurate geometry processing and aesthetic reasons, denoising the surface data is essential in subsequent vision and graphics applications. A central problem of mesh denoising is the isolation of

Supplementary Information The online version contains supplementary material available at https://doi.org/10.1007/978-3-031-20062-5_21.

Fig. 1. Our method performs learning-based denoising only using a noisy input mesh, optimizing both the vertex positions and facet normals without using any training datasets. As shown, it works well for both the mechanical parts with sharp geometric features and human bodies, which are typical applications of 3D digital scanners.

geometric features from noise. To this end, a large number of studies have been conducted for mesh denoising, including filter-based [4,9,14,22,26,39,40,42,45], feature-extraction-based [1,19,34], and optimization-based [8,32,44] approaches. However, despite the long continuous efforts, the isolation of geometric features is still challenging, especially in the presence of high-level noise.

Recently, in other research areas, deep-learning techniques have raised a new trend in data-driven approaches even for mesh denoising. To our knowledge, most existing methods in this kind regress the noise-free normals from different inputs, such as handmade local geometric features [30,31,43] and learned features encoded by a neural network [15,17,24,43]. After the noise-free normals are obtained, the output vertex positions are reproduced by the standard iterative vertex updating [25], as performed by the traditional normal filtering methods [40,45]. However, this vertex updating process is not included in their network architectures because it causes a huge computation graph and can significantly slow down the backpropagation. Moreover, the vertex updating as simple postprocessing can flip faces over and obtain wrong vertex positions.

In contrast to these data-driven approaches to filtering facet normals, this study proposes the dual deep mesh prior (DDMP), which learns a self-prior for mesh denoising using graph convolutional networks (GCNs) (Fig. 1). Compared to previous approaches, our method has two advantages. First, as the name of DDMP indicates, our method trains the pair of graph convolutional networks on dual graphs that filter vertex positions and facet normals, respectively. Our method synchronously trains two GCNs for positions and normals with the position-normal consistency loss. In this way, our method does not need the iterative vertex updating and enables the network to learn the mesh denoising in an end-to-end manner. Second, our method does not use a large shape dataset and acquires a prior for mesh denoising from a single input mesh. We refer to such a prior acquired with a single input as "self-prior." To this end, our method extends the deep image prior (DIP) [29], which also acquires a self-prior for image restoration, and denoises both vertex positions and facet normals. Therefore, our method does not need time-consuming pretraining of the network using a large dataset and can obtain a specialized result for each input shape. Furthermore, our method without a training dataset has been demonstrated to achieve denoising better than other supervised learning methods.

2   Related Work

Traditional Mesh Denoising. Mesh denoising is the task of filtering 3D signals such as vertex positions and normals. Hence, the previous approaches have been inspired by the techniques for image denoising. Early approaches for mesh denoising have processed vertex positions by spatial filtering [5,9,26], energy minimization [4], and iterative error diffusion [3] but have been followed by a large number of approaches based on normal filtering. These approaches by normal filtering smooth either vertex or facet normals and reproduce noise-free meshes by iteratively updating vertex positions with the filtered normals [21,25,27]. In the past, various filters have been applied to smooth noisy normals such as Gaussian filter [22], median filter [39], bilateral filter [12,45], and other anisotropic filters [35,40,42]. When compared to filtering vertex positions, methods that used normal filtering are known to reproduce the sharp local geometries more accurately. However, these methods often cannot reproduce shape features well when they are scarcely recognized due to much noise. In contrast, optimization-based approaches solve an energy minimization problem to satisfy a set of priors imposed on the ground-truth geometry or noise patterns. They formulated the optimization problem based on techniques such as L_0-regularized minimization [8,44], compressed sensing [32], and low-rank recovery [16,33]. However, these heuristic priors cannot always be applied to shapes that do not conform to the ground-truth geometry or noise patterns to be assumed.

Learning-Based Mesh Denoising. With the increasing use of learning-based denoising for images, mesh denoising has gained increasing attention. The pioneering study by Wang et al. [31] used a simple multilayer perceptron (MLP) to regress noise-free normals from the descriptor extracted by processing input facet normals with noise. This method was followed by a two-step filtering approach [30] where the first step was equivalent to the prior one [31] and the second step enhanced geometric details of the shape obtained by the first step. Zhao et al. [43] introduced a new geometric descriptor based on the local volume around a vertex of interest and applied 3D convolution to regress noise-free normals. Li et al. [17] instead employed a non-local patch-group normal matrix [16,33] to regress the clean normals. DNF-Net [17] directly encoded the vertex positions and adjacency matrix by a neural network and regressed the clean facet normals from the encoded features. In contrast to these methods that extract geometric features using standard neural networks, GCN-Denoiser [24] scissored an input mesh into local patches and regressed the clean normals from the patch with a GCN. GeoBi-GNN [41] is akin to GCN-Denoiser, but GeoBi-GNN used two GCNs. The former filters noisy vertex positions in advance to normal regression, and the latter further filters the normals computed with filtered positions. Then, the final vertex positions are reproduced by an ordinary iterative process using both the filtered positions and normals.

Learning Deep Prior Without Ground-Truth Data. Current deep neural networks are usually composed of convolutional layers with learnable weights associated with a convolution kernel. Each set of weights is trained to extract a structural pattern commonly appearing in the input data since the weight parameters are shared over an entire data domain. Such a prior acquired by a deep neural network is referred to as a "deep prior," and it is acquired even from a single input data. DIP [29] is a seminal approach that acquires the deep prior from a single input and performs various image restoration tasks, such as denoising and inpainting, only from a corrupted input image. The DIP paper revealed that the convolutional layer can learn structural patterns more quickly than random patterns such as white noise. This nature of convolutional layers is useful to obtain the self-prior and restore images without using clean data.

For shape data, Williams et al. [37] proposed Deep Geometric Prior (DGP) for reconstructing the surface geometry from a point cloud. DGP trains several MLPs individually to reconstruct different local surface patches. In contrast, Point2Mesh [7] leverages a self-prior to reconstruct the entire surface from an input point cloud without any pretraining using a training dataset. In their method, individual MeshCNNs [6] are trained to acquire the self-priors of the shape in different triangle resolutions. The higher-dimensional information with surface geometry with colors can also be reproduced by self-priors [36]. Although these approaches require only a single point cloud to reconstruct its surface geometry, they can fail to capture global features over the entire surface or resolution because the base networks are individually trained for different patches and resolutions.

3   Dual Deep Mesh Prior

Figure 2 shows the architecture of DDMP. The input is a noisy mesh $\mathcal{M}(\mathcal{V}, \mathcal{E})$ where $\mathcal{V}$ and $\mathcal{E}$ are the sets of vertices and edges of the mesh. Based on the adjacencies of vertices and faces, we define dual graphs $\mathcal{G}_v$ and $\mathcal{G}_f$ whose nodes correspond to vertices and faces. On each graph, we define a GCN that denoises either vertex positions or facet normals. We refer to these GCNs for positions and normals as PosNet and NormNet, respectively. The denoised positions and normals are evaluated in terms of their reproducibility by E_{pos} and E_{nrm}, smoothness by E_{Lap} and E_{bnf}, and consistency by E_{con}. Specifically, our method evaluates the reproducibility with E_{pos} and E_{nrm} against the noisy input and works without the ground-truth data.

A previous method that is most similar to ours is GeoBi-GNN [41], which defines GCNs on dual graphs and filters both the vertex positions and facet normals. However, GeoBi-GNN needs the iterative vertex updating, which is not included in the network architecture. In contrast, our method is truly an end-to-end approach without requiring the iterative process [25] for recovering the final vertex positions. Furthermore, our method works well without either a large-scale shape dataset or time-consuming pretraining of the neural network.

3.1   Good Self-prior for Shape Attributes

Before explaining the proposed method, we quickly review DIP [29], by which our paper is inspired. DIP successfully removes noise from an input corrupted image

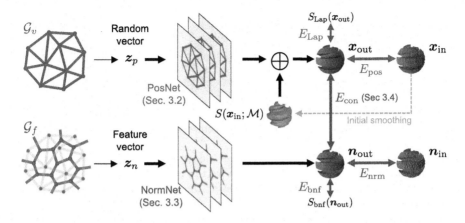

Fig. 2. DDMP builds dual graphs of the input mesh and associates two GCNs with them. The two GCNs, namely, PosNet and NormNet, are respectively in charge of filtering vertex positions and facet normals. Output positions and normals are evaluated into three groups of loss functions: (1) the first group evaluates vertex positions, (2) the second group evaluates facet normals, and (3) the last group evaluates the consistency of vertex positions and facet normals.

without using either a large-scale image dataset or a ground-truth clean image. The network of DIP transforms a static random code z to the restored image x_{out} and is trained to minimize the difference between x_{out} and the noisy input image x_{in}. Let F be the map defined by the network with a set of parameters Θ. Then, DIP trains the network to obtain the best parameter set Θ^*:

$$\Theta^* = \mathrm{argmin}_\Theta \frac{1}{|\mathcal{I}|} \sum_{i \in \mathcal{I}} \left\| x_{\mathrm{out}}^i - x_{\mathrm{in}}^i \right\|_2^2, \qquad \text{where} \quad x_{\mathrm{out}} = F(z; \Theta), \qquad (1)$$

where $\mathcal{I}$ is an index set of image pixels, $|\mathcal{I}|$ is the size of $\mathcal{I}$ (i.e., the number of image pixels), x^i is the color of the ith pixel, and $\|\cdot\|_p$ is the ℓ_p-norm of a vector.

The DIP paper [29] shows that its capability of image restoration is reasoned by the nature of neural networks, where the network learns structural patterns more quickly than random patterns. Therefore, the presence of structural patterns must be considered to apply the framework of DIP to shape attributes, such as vertex positions and facet normals. Figure 3 shows dinosaur models colorized based on vertex positions and facet normals. In Fig. 3(a), the model is fit to a unit cube $[0,1]^3$ by keeping its aspect ratio, and each vertex is colorized based on its position (i.e., $(r, g, b) = (x, y, z)$). However, the vertex colors in Fig. 3(a) are not structural, changing gradually over the surface and not corresponding to the bumps on its back. In contrast, the vertices in Fig. 3(b) are colored by the displacements from the smoothed mesh at the top left. A color pattern is repeated to follow the repetition of the bumps on the back. In light of these observations, a network will learn the displacements more easily than the positions themselves. When colorizing the faces with their normals (i.e.,

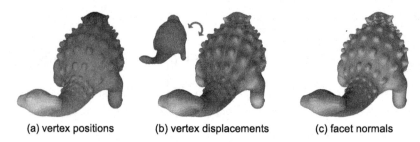

(a) vertex positions   (b) vertex displacements   (c) facet normals

Fig. 3. Colorized meshes by (a) vertex positions, (b) vertex displacements from smoothed mesh, and (c) facet normals. For vertex positions, the displacement from a smoothed mesh is more appropriate to elicit the structural pattern, whereas the facet normals form a structural pattern without any special treatment.

$(r, g, b) = (\frac{n_x+1}{2}, \frac{n_y+1}{2}, \frac{n_z+1}{2}))$, we can see the repetition of a color pattern on the bumps in Fig. 3(c). Hence, facet normals will be reconstructed due to the nature of convolutional layers without any special treatment.

The above observations suggest that PosNet and NormNet should be trained differently. We train PosNet to reproduce the displacements of vertices between a smoothed mesh and the noisy input mesh. On the other hand, we train NormNet to reproduce the facet normals as the original DIP does.

3.2   PosNet: Position Filtering Network

As previously discussed, we train PosNet to estimate the vertex displacements from the smoothed shape. PosNet consists of a stack of 12 graph convolutional layers [10] followed by 2 fully connected layers. As the original DIP does, PosNet F_p with parameters Θ_p transforms a tensor of static random codes $z_p \in \mathbb{R}^{N_p \times D_p}$ to another tensor of vertex displacement vector $F_p(z_p; \mathcal{M}, \Theta_p) \in \mathbb{R}^{N_p \times 3}$, where N_p is the number of vertices, D_p is the number of dimensions of the random codes. To avoid that a mesh scale affects the result, we normalize the size of an input mesh by the average length of edges l_e. Then, the displacement is added to a smoothed mesh $S(x_{in}; \mathcal{M}) \in \mathbb{R}^{N_p \times 3}$ to obtain a clean output, where $x_{in} \in \mathbb{R}^{N_p \times 3}$ is a tensor of input vertex positions. Specifically, the output tensor of vertex positions $x_{out} \in \mathbb{R}^{N_p \times 3}$ is expressed as

$$x_{out} = S(x_{in}; \mathcal{M}) + F_p(z_p; \mathcal{M}, \Theta_p). \tag{2}$$

The output positions were evaluated by two error functions. One is a reconstruction error defined with the root-mean-squared error (RMSE):

$$E_{pos}(x_{out}, x_{in}) = \sqrt{\frac{1}{N_p} \sum_{i=1}^{N_p} \|x_{out}^i - x_{in}^i\|_2^2}, \tag{3}$$

where x^i is an ith row of the tensor. In addition, we employed a Laplacian error for vertex positions to encourage the smoothness of the output mesh.

$$E_{\text{Lap}}(x_{\text{out}}) = \sqrt{\frac{1}{N_p} \sum_{i=1}^{N_p} \left\| x_{\text{out}}^i - S_{\text{Lap}}(x_{\text{out}}^i) \right\|_2^2}, \quad S_{\text{Lap}}(x_{\text{out}}^i) = \frac{1}{|\mathcal{V}_v(i)|} \sum_{j \in \mathcal{V}_v(i)} x_{\text{out}}^j,$$

(4)

where $\mathcal{V}_v(i)$ is an index set for neighboring vertices around the ith vertex. As shown later, this error also serves as a regularization term for PosNet that prevents overfitting to the noisy input.

3.3 NormNet: Normal Filtering Network

Discussions in Sect. 3.1 showed facet normals can represent structural patterns of local surface geometry without any special treatment. Accordingly, we train NormNet F_n to reproduce clean facet normals as in the original DIP [29]. The architecture of NormNet is the same as that of PosNet (i.e., it has 12 graph convolutional layers followed by 2 fully connected layers), but its graph convolutional layers are defined on a dual graph where each node corresponds to a face. Besides, each output is normalized to be a unit vector.

Different from PosNet, we supply a set of handmade feature vectors to Norm-Net rather than the random codes to PosNet. The feature vector summarizes the geometric features of a face. For a face indexed by k, the feature vector includes barycenter c_{in}^k, normal n_{in}^k, and area A_{in}^k, which are computed for the noisy input mesh. Refer to the supplementary document for the experimental validation of the choice of feature elements.

Let $z_n \in \mathbb{R}^{N_f \times D_n}$ be a tensor of the face features where N_f is the number of faces, and D_n is the number of dimensions of the facet features. Then, the clean output normals $n_{\text{out}} \in \mathbb{R}^{N_f \times 3}$ are represented as

$$n_{\text{out}} = F_n(z_n; \mathcal{M}, \Theta_n),$$

(5)

where Θ_n is a set of parameters of NormNet. Although the RMSE is used to train PosNet, we employ a reconstruction error using the mean absolute error (MAE) to let NormNet more sensitive to sharp geometric features.

$$E_{\text{nrm}}(n_{\text{out}}, n_{\text{in}}) = \frac{1}{N_f} \sum_{i=1}^{N_f} \left\| n_{\text{out}}^i - n_{\text{in}}^i \right\|_1.$$

(6)

Additionally, we define another error function to evaluate the smoothness of output facet normals. The smoothness error is defined based on bilateral filter [28] that has been widely used for mesh smoothing [12,45] and encourages the smoothness of the normals while preserving the local surface geometry such as sharp edges. We calculate the MAE between the output facet normals and those smoothed by the bilateral filter.

$$E_{\text{bnf}}(n_{\text{out}}) = \frac{1}{N_f} \sum_{i=1}^{N_f} \left\| n_{\text{out}}^i - S_{\text{bnf}}^{(t)}(n_{\text{out}}^i) \right\|_1,$$

(7)

where $S_{\mathrm{bnf}}^{(t)}$ means the bilateral filter S_{bnf} is applied t times. In our experiment, we empirically set $t = 5$ for CAD models that often contain sharp features and $t = 1$ for non-CAD models. As with E_{Lap} for PosNet, E_{bnf} serves as a regularization term that prevents overfitting to the noisy input.

3.4 Position and Normal Consistency

Although PosNet and NormNet filter noise on vertex positions and facet normals of the input mesh independently, these results can be inconsistent. Therefore, we may need an iterative vertex updating process [21,25,27] to make them consistent, as performed in many previous methods. However, this iterative process results in a large computation graph needed for the backpropagation and can slow down the network training significantly, which hinders the whole training process from being performed in an end-to-end manner. Furthermore, individual filters for position and normals by our PosNet and NormNet can be invalid due to the absence of the ground-truth noise-free mesh during training, resulting in flipped and self-intersected triangles.

To resolve these problems, we employ a position-normal consistency loss based on the formulation of the iterative vertex updating [25]. This approach updates the vertex positions based on the following updating rule:

$$
x_{\mathrm{new}}^{i} = x^{i} + \frac{1}{3|\mathcal{F}_v(i)|} \sum_{j \in \mathcal{F}_v(i)} n^{j}(n^{j} \cdot (c^{j} - x^{i})), \tag{8}
$$

where $\mathcal{F}_v(i)$ is a set of face indices around the ith vertex, and c^j is the centroid of the jth face. The second term of Eq. (8) represents an amount of vertex displacement during the update and is converged to zero when the update is terminated. This means that the second term can measure the consistency between given positions and normals of adjacent faces. Accordingly, we define a consistency error between the output vertex positions of PosNet and the output facet normals of NormNet by summing up the displacements.

$$
E_{\mathrm{con}}(x_{\mathrm{out}}, n_{\mathrm{out}}) = \frac{1}{N_p} \sum_{i=1}^{N_p} \sum_{j \in \mathcal{F}_v(i)} n_{\mathrm{out}}^{j} \cdot (c_{\mathrm{out}}^{j} - x_{\mathrm{out}}^{i}). \tag{9}
$$

Different from the original rule in Eq. (8), the normalizing constant $3|\mathcal{F}_v(i)|$ is omitted in the above equation for simplicity. This means that a vertex surrounded by more faces will be penalized more heavily for its displacement, but this change did not matter to the results significantly.

3.5 Loss Function

Overall, we train PosNet and NormNet synchronously using the error:

$$
E = k_1 E_{\mathrm{pos}} + k_2 E_{\mathrm{Lap}} + k_3 E_{\mathrm{nrm}} + k_4 E_{\mathrm{bnf}} + k_5 E_{\mathrm{con}}, \tag{10}
$$

Table 1. Quantitative comparison of AAD and AHD values. In each cell, AAD and AHD are written to the left and right. The AHDs are in the unit of 10^{-3} and are calculated after the size is normalized by the diagonal length of a bounding box.

Model	Type	Input	BNF [45]	GNF [40]	DNF [15]	GCN-D [24]	DDMP
block	CAD	33.72°/4.32	7.06°/1.26	4.11°/0.99	4.13°/0.99	4.19°/0.98	**2.90°/0.74**
fandisk	CAD	28.42°/3.23	3.49°/0.76	2.93°/0.68	3.33°/0.69	3.28°/0.70	**1.93°/0.49**
nut	CAD	22.23°/1.61	5.70°/0.78	4.05°/0.55	4.21°/0.52	3.64°/0.50	**3.09°/0.44**
part-lp	CAD	18.87°/2.43	2.07°/0.66	2.59°/0.69	2.84°/0.67	2.40°/0.62	**1.78°/0.46**
trim-star	CAD	29.36°/3.42	6.57°/1.16	6.95°/1.11	5.55°/0.93	4.86°/0.89	**4.71°/0.84**
ankylo.	non-CAD	14.40°/0.58	6.37°/0.44	8.05°/0.46	5.69°/0.33	**4.59°/0.31**	4.68°/0.29
fertility	non-CAD	19.39°/1.35	5.54°/0.72	5.70°/0.58	3.83°/0.44	**2.68°/0.34**	3.40°/0.45
nicolo	non-CAD	30.92°/0.92	5.48°/0.29	6.79°/0.33	5.17°/0.26	**4.73°/0.25**	5.11°/0.26
suit-man	non-CAD	13.44°/0.33	8.45°/0.42	6.57°/0.22	5.22°/0.20	**4.47°/0.17**	5.26°/0.21

where $\mathcal{K} = (k_1, k_2, k_3, k_4, k_5)$ is a set of hyperparameters (i.e., the weights for the error terms). As with the data-driven approaches using deep learning, these hyperparameters affect the denoising performance of our method. Based on the result of hyperparameter tuning by Ray Tune [18], we set $\mathcal{K} = (3, 0, 3, 4, 2)$ for CAD models, whereas $\mathcal{K} = (3, 4, 4, 4, 1)$ are set for non-CAD models. Only four meshes (i.e., sharp-sphere, twelve, carter, and grayloc), which are not used in performance comparisons, were used in the tuning process[1]. In addition, we found that the output mesh can be extremely noisy at a relatively early stage in training and that E_{bnf} can retain high-frequency noise unintentionally. Therefore, we set the weight k_4 for E_{bnf} to zero during the first 100 steps to prevent the facet normals from converging to a local minimum different from the desired ones. We show the details of this experiment in the supplementary document.

4   Experiments

Our method is implemented using PyTorch and PyTorch Geometric and is tested on a computer equipped with Intel Core i7 5930K CPU (3.5 GHz, 6 cores), NVIDIA GeForce TITAN X (12 GB graphics memory), and 64 GB of RAM. PosNet and NormNet are trained over 1000 steps by Adam optimizer with learning rate of $\gamma = 0.01$ and decay parameters $(\beta_1, \beta_2) = (0.9, 0.999)$. Following GCN-Denoiser [24], we used two metrics for evaluation, the average normal angular difference (AAD) and the average one-sided Hausdorff distance (AHD) between the ground-truth and the output. Note that AHDs are normalized by the diagonal length of a bounding box of the ground-truth mesh. A smaller value for both of them means better denoising performance. In the following figures, we visualize the denoised meshes by colorizing each face based on the normal angular difference. We also show the specific value θ of the AAD below each mesh.

---

[1] All the meshes used in this study are shown in the supplementary document.

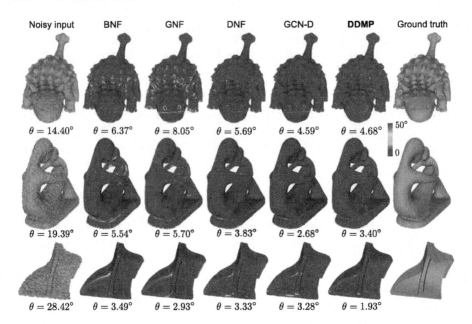

Fig. 4. Visual comparison of output meshes between our method and prior methods. AWGNs with different noise levels (i.e., $0.1l_e, 0.2l_e, 0.3l_e$) are added to three meshes from top to bottom.

Results on Artificial Noise. We demonstrate the denoising performance of our method for additive white Gaussian noise (AWGN), whose magnitude is set as a multiple of the average edge length l_e of each mesh. The results are compared with previous studies, including bilateral normal filtering (BNF) [45], guided normal filtering (GNF) [40], deep normal filtering network (DNF) [15], and mesh denoising with graph convolutional networks (GCN-D) [24]. For BNF and GNF (i.e., the traditional approaches that do not use deep learning), we tuned the hyperparameters manually. On the other hand, for DNF and GCN-D (i.e., the state-of-the-art approaches using deep learning), we used pretrained weights provided by the authors. These methods were tested with nine meshes provided by the authors of cascaded normal regression (CNR) [31] and GCN-D [24], which are classified into CAD models with many sharp features and non-CAD models with a few ones.

Table 1 shows the quantitative analysis for the meshes, and Fig. 4 shows the visual comparisons for some of them. They show that traditional approaches often oversharpen edges or oversmooth fine details, while our method removes noise while preserving both the sharp edges and fine details. Furthermore, although our method uses only a noisy input mesh, its performance is comparable with or better than the various methods using large training datasets. This tendency is more apparent in CAD models, which shows that our approach accommodates each input and keeps sharp edges and fine details.

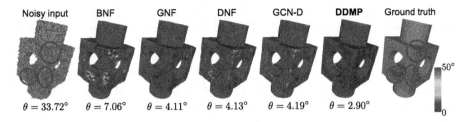

Noisy input   BNF   GNF   DNF   GCN-D   **DDMP**   Ground truth

$\theta = 33.72°$ $\theta = 7.06°$ $\theta = 4.11°$ $\theta = 4.13°$ $\theta = 4.19°$ $\theta = 2.90°$ 50° / 0

Fig. 5. Robustness to non-uniform density of triangles. The noisy input mesh and noise-free counterpart are shown to the both sides and are marked by red circles to show the densely triangulated regions. The noise level is $0.4l_e$ for this "block' example. (Color figure online)

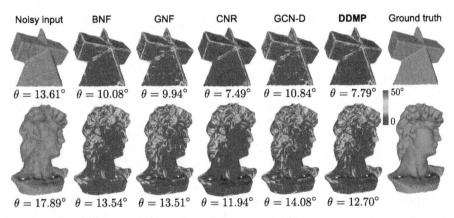

Noisy input   BNF   GNF   CNR   GCN-D   **DDMP**   Ground truth

$\theta = 13.61°$ $\theta = 10.08°$ $\theta = 9.94°$ $\theta = 7.49°$ $\theta = 10.84°$ $\theta = 7.79°$ 50° / 0

$\theta = 17.89°$ $\theta = 13.54°$ $\theta = 13.51°$ $\theta = 11.94°$ $\theta = 14.08°$ $\theta = 12.70°$

Fig. 6. Visual comparison of denoising performances for meshes obtained by real scans. The meshes are provided by the authors of the CNR paper [31].

Figure 5 shows the robustness of our method for spatially varying density of triangles, where densely triangulated regions are marked by red circles. For the "block" mesh in this figure, we added noise uniformly over the mesh surface, which means that the relative noise level is higher in the densely triangulated regions. Such regions with a high noise level are not properly denoised by most previous approaches, while GNF is robust to the triangle density but oversharpens edges. Compared to these approaches, our method obtains the lowest AAD, working more robustly to the triangle density and keeping sharp edges.

Results on Real Scans. Next, we evaluate our method using meshes obtained by real scans. The meshes used here are provided by the authors of CNR [31] that are acquired by KinectFusion [20] with Microsoft Kinect v1. For GCN-D, we used a pretrained model for artificial noise, the only one available publicly. In this experiment, our method uses the hyperparameters $\mathcal{K} = (3, 4, 4, 4, 1)$ for non-CAD models. Training only for 50 steps was sufficient for these meshes because their noise levels are comparatively less than AWGN used previously. In addition, the noise that we can see in Fig. 6 behaves differently from AWGN and

Table 2. Quantitative comparison for meshes obtained by real scans. Despite the absence of training with the ground-truth meshes, our method achieved as low AADs as CNR [31] that learns the ground-truth data.

Model	Input	BNF	GNF	CNR	GCN-D	DDMP
pyramid	13.61°/2.21	10.08°/2.18	9.94°/2.20	**7.49°/2.13**	10.84°/2.21	7.79°/2.16
david	17.89°/1.86	13.54°/**1.85**	13.51°/**1.85**	**11.94°**/1.86	14.08°/**1.85**	12.70°/1.88

Table 3. Quantitative comparison of DDMP with its variants where some of the errors have been ablated. For NormNet, NormNet w/o E_{bnf}, and DDMP w/o E_{con}, AAD and AHD are computed for output meshes recovered by posterior iterative vertex updating.

	PosNet	PosNet w/o E_{Lap}	NormNet	NormNet w/o E_{bnf}	DDMP w/o E_{con}	DDMP
E_{pos}	✓	✓			✓	✓
E_{Lap}	✓				✓	✓
E_{nrm}			✓	✓	✓	✓
E_{bnf}			✓		✓	✓
E_{con}						✓
sharp	—	15.60°/1.77	5.00°/1.43	9.55°/1.53	5.44°/1.44	**4.90°/1.40**
twelve	—	15.64°/2.14	**1.02°**/0.40	7.47°/1.36	1.04°/0.60	1.20°/**0.36**
carter	4.96°/0.31	9.27°/0.43	4.89°/0.32	**4.88°/0.32**	5.09°/0.33	4.95°/**0.31**
grayloc	9.19°/1.60	26.22°/2.03	10.50°/1.63	14.05°/1.74	8.89°/1.59	**7.25°/1.56**

consists of both the low- and high-frequency components. Hence, the denoising performances of previous approaches in Table 2 are decreased compared to those for AWGN, except for CNR learning such particular noise. Nevertheless, for such a challenging scenario, our method achieved the second best AAD next to CNR and outperformed the other approaches, including GCN-D using deep learning. These results show the dependency of previous learning-based approaches on the distribution of training datasets, as well as the advantage of our method independent of datasets. In contrast, AHDs of the input noisy meshes were not decreased significantly by all the compared approaches and ours. This is due to the non-zero average of positional displacements by real scanning, even though most compared approaches including ours implicitly assume zero-mean noise.

Effect of Error Terms. We conduct an ablation study to verify the effect of each error term in Eq. 10. Table 3 shows a list of test cases in which some of the error terms are ablated. In each test case, AAD and AHD are evaluated for sample meshes. For NormNet, NormNet w/o E_{bnf}, and DDMP w/o E_{con}, we perform the iterative vertex updating [25] to obtain output meshes. Since "sharp-sphere" and "twelve" models are categorized as non-CAD models, and k_2 for non-CAD models are set to zero, the results of PosNet and PosNet w/o E_{Lap} will be exactly the same. Hence, we drew only horizontal lines to the cells for these two models processed by PosNet. As shown by Table 3, the performance of the full DDMP is better than those of both PosNet alone and NormNet alone.

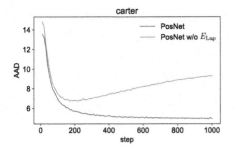
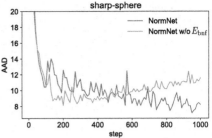

Fig. 7. Changes in AAD values during training PosNet and NormNet with and without smoothness error terms. These figures show the AAD values, which are unknown during training. Note that the AAD values of "sharp-sphere" shown in the right are computed for the direct output of NormNet before vertex updating.

This result suggests that the synchronous training of our method allows the networks to interact with each other and obtains better results than those given by only one of two networks. Moreover, the full DDMP outperforms that without E_{con} using a non-learnable process of the iterative vertex updating. This means E_{con} works not only to enable the end-to-end learning of mesh denoising but also to enhance the interaction of PosNet and NormNet.

Moreover, we ablate error terms E_{Lap} and E_{bnf} from PosNet and NormNet to verify their effects. As supposed by the lower performance of PosNet w/o E_{Lap} and NormNet w/o E_{bnf} than those with the smoothness errors, these terms regularize the shape optimization and prevent it from being stuck to an inappropriate solution. Furthermore, the lack of E_{Lap} and E_{bnf} from each network causes overfitting to noise. As shown in Fig. 7, the AADs of PosNet w/o E_{Lap} and NormNet w/o E_{bnf} get higher after hundreds of steps, which shows the networks are overfitted to noise. Therefore, these regularization terms are helpful to obtain better results almost independently of when the training is terminated.

Effect of Initial Smoothing. Our method relies on a smoothing operation on the input mesh to extract the displacements at the vertex positions. To confirm the effect of smoothing, we compare the 30-step Laplacian smoothing "without" cotangent weights (LS-no-CW) [23], which we used in the above experiments, with three other options, i.e., no smooth, bilateral normal filtering (BNF), and 3-step Laplacian smoothing "with" cotangent weights (LS-CW). The denoised results for the different smoothing operations are shown in Fig. 8, in which the meshes after initial smoothing are also shown in the top-left insets. The quantitative comparison is also shown in Table 4. The comparisons show that BNF and LS-CW obtain better results for CAD models and non-CAD models, respectively. This means an initial smoothing that gives a closer shape to the noise-free mesh may obtain a better output mesh. In contrast, LS-no-CW performs well almost equally with BNF for CAD models and better than both the BNF and LS-CW for non-CAD models. During this experiment, we found that an input smoothed shape, which is very close to the desired output, can complicate the

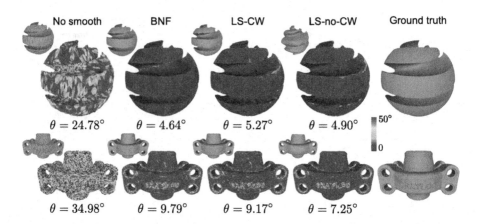

Fig. 8. Comparison of smoothed meshes obtained by different initial smoothing.

Table 4. Quantitative comparison for different initial smoothing operations.

Model	Type	Input	No smooth	BNF	LS-CW (3 itr.)	LS-no-CW (30 itr.)
Sharp	CAD	24.81°/2.24	24.78°/2.24	**4.64°/1.34**	5.27°/1.35	4.90°/1.40
Twelve	CAD	22.59°/2.74	22.42°/2.72	**0.99°/0.32**	1.47°/0.36	1.20°/0.36
Carter	non-CAD	12.87°/0.48	12.87°/0.48	5.25°/0.31	4.98°/0.31	**4.95°/0.31**
Grayloc	non-CAD	34.99°/2.32	34.98°/2.32	9.79°/1.58	9.17°/1.57	**7.25°/1.56**

network to learn structural patterns from the small difference, and the network can be just an identity mapping. In light of this, LS-no-CW that we used in the above experiments is a good choice to achieve good denoising for a wide range of meshes, although BNF may be able to achieve better results for CAD models.

5   Conclusion

This paper presented DDMP, a new mesh denoising framework using the self-prior acquired with a single input. DDMP optimizes both the vertex positions and facet normals synchronously with two GCNs (i.e., PosNet and NormNet) defined on dual graphs. These two networks can interact with each other to reduce noise while preserving sharp edges and fine details by introducing an error term to enhance position-normal consistency. Since the dual networks are trained with only a noisy input mesh, time-consuming pre-processing, such as patch generation and pretraining with large training datasets, is not required. Experimental results showed that our method achieved significantly higher performances than those of traditional approaches working only with a noisy input. Moreover, our method outperformed the state-of-the-art methods of learning many shapes.

In future work, we are interested in applying DDMP to other mesh restoration tasks, such as mesh completion and mesh simplification. To this end, we need further investigation on how an input mesh to DDMP should be obtained to share the same triangulation with an unknown desired output. We are also interested in combining DDMP with other self-supervised methods, such as Noise2Noise [13] and its variants [2,11,38], which propose their own data augmentation for noisy images and train the network without using ground-truth clean images.

Acknowledgment. This study is financially supported by a JSPS Grant-in-Aid for Early-career Scientists (22K17907).

References

1. Arvanitis, G., Lalos, A.S., Moustakas, K., Fakotakis, N.: Feature preserving mesh denoising based on graph spectral processing. IEEE Trans. Vis. Comput. Graphics **25**(3), 1513–1527 (2019). https://doi.org/10.1109/tvcg.2018.2802926
2. Calvarons, A.F.: Improved Noise2Noise denoising with limited data. In: Proceedings of the IEEE/CVF Conference on Computer Vision and Pattern Recognition (CVPR) Workshops, pp. 796–805 (2021). https://doi.org/10.1109/cvprw53098.2021.00089
3. Clarenz, U., Diewald, U., Rumpf, M.: Anisotropic geometric diffusion in surface processing (2000). https://doi.org/10.1109/VISUAL.2000.885721
4. Desbrun, M., Meyer, M., Schröder, P., Barr, A.H.: Implicit fairing of irregular meshes using diffusion and curvature flow. In: Proceedings of ACM International Conference on Computer Graphics and InteractDive Techniques (SIGGRAPH). SIGGRAPH 1999, pp. 317–324. ACM Press/Addison-Wesley Publishing Co. (1999). https://doi.org/10.1145/311535.311576
5. Fleishman, S., Drori, I., Cohen-Or, D.: Bilateral mesh denoising. ACM Trans. Graphics **22**(3), 950–953 (2003). https://doi.org/10.1145/882262.882368
6. Hanocka, R., Hertz, A., Fish, N., Giryes, R., Fleishman, S., Cohen-Or, D.: MeshCNN: a network with an edge. ACM Trans. Graphics **38**(4) (2019). https://doi.org/10.1145/3306346.3322959
7. Hanocka, R., Metzer, G., Giryes, R., Cohen-Or, D.: Point2Mesh: a self-prior for deformable meshes. ACM Trans. Graphics **39**(4) (2020). https://doi.org/10.1145/3386569.3392415
8. He, L., Schaefer, S.: Mesh denoising via L0 minimization. ACM Trans. Graphics **32**(4), 1–8 (2013). https://doi.org/10.1145/2461912.2461965
9. Jones, T.R., Durand, F., Desbrun, M.: Non-iterative, feature-preserving mesh smoothing. ACM Trans. Graphics **22**(3), 943–949 (2003). https://doi.org/10.1145/882262.882367
10. Kipf, T.N., Welling, M.: Semi-supervised classification with graph convolutional networks. In: Proceedings of International Conference on Learning Representations (ICLR) (2017)
11. Krull, A., Buchholz, T.O., Jug, F.: Noise2Void - learning denoising from single noisy images. In: Proceedings of the IEEE/CVF Conference on Computer Vision and Pattern Recognition (CVPR) 2019 (2019). https://doi.org/10.1109/cvpr.2019.00223
12. Lee, K.W., Wang, W.P.: Feature-preserving mesh denoising via bilateral normal filtering (2005). https://doi.org/10.1109/CAD-CG.2005.40

13. Lehtinen, J., et al.: Noise2Noise: learning image restoration without clean data. In: Proceedings of International Conference on Machine Learning (ICML), pp. 2965–2974. PMLR (2018)
14. Li, T., Wang, J., Liu, H., Liu, L.: Efficient mesh denoising via robust normal filtering and alternate vertex updating. Front. Inf. Technol. Electron. Eng. **18**(11), 1828–1842 (2017). https://doi.org/10.1631/FITEE.1601229
15. Li, X., Li, R., Zhu, L., Fu, C.W., Heng, P.A.: DNF-Net: a deep normal filtering network for mesh denoising. IEEE Trans. Visual Comput. Graphics (2020). https://doi.org/10.1109/TVCG.2020.3001681
16. Li, X., Zhu, L., Fu, C.W., Heng, P.A.: Non-local low-rank normal filtering for mesh denoising. Comput. Graphics Forum **37**(7), 155–166 (2018). https://doi.org/10.1111/cgf.13556
17. Li, Z., et al.: NormalF-Net: normal filtering neural network for feature-preserving mesh denoising. Comput. Aided Des. **127**, 102861 (2020). https://doi.org/10.1016/j.cad.2020.102861
18. Liaw, R., Liang, E., Nishihara, R., Moritz, P., Gonzalez, J.E., Stoica, I.: Tune: a research platform for distributed model selection and training. arXiv preprint arXiv:1807.05118 (2018)
19. Lu, X., Deng, Z., Chen, W.: A robust scheme for feature-preserving mesh denoising. IEEE Trans. Visual Comput. Graphics **22**(3), 1181–1194 (2016). https://doi.org/10.1109/TVCG.2015.2500222
20. Newcombe, R.A., et al.: KinectFusion: real-time dense surface mapping and tracking. In: Proceedings of the IEEE International Symposium on Mixed and Augmented Reality (ISMAR), pp. 127–136. IEEE (2011). https://doi.org/10.1109/ismar.2011.6092378
21. Ohtake, Y., Belyaev, A., Bogaevski, I.: Mesh regularization and adaptive smoothing. Comput.-Aided Des. **33**(11), 789–800 (2001). https://doi.org/10.1016/s0010-4485(01)00095-1
22. Ohtake, Y., Belyaev, A.G., Seidel, H.P.: Mesh smoothing by adaptive and anisotropic Gaussian filter applied to mesh normals. In: Proceeding of Vision, Modeling, and Visualization (VMV), vol. 2, pp. 203–210. Citeseer (2002)
23. Pinkall, U., Polthier, K.: Computing discrete minimal surfaces and their conjugates. Exp. Math. **2**(1), 15–36 (1993). https://doi.org/10.1080/10586458.1993.10504266
24. Shen, Y., et al.: GCN-denoiser: mesh denoising with graph convolutional networks. ACM Trans. Graphics **41**(1), 1–14 (2022). https://doi.org/10.1145/3480168
25. Sun, X., Rosin, P.L., Martin, R., Langbein, F.: Fast and effective feature-preserving mesh denoising. IEEE Trans. Visual Comput. Graphics **13**(5), 925–938 (2007). https://doi.org/10.1109/TVCG.2007.1065
26. Taubin, G.: Curve and surface smoothing without shrinkage. In: Proceedings of the IEEE International Conference on Computer Vision (ICCV) 1995, pp. 852–857. IEEE (1995)
27. Taubin, G.: Linear anisotropic mesh filtering. Research Report RC2213 (2001)
28. Tomasi, C., Manduchi, R.: Bilateral filtering for gray and color images. In: Proceedings of the IEEE International Conference on Computer Vision (ICCV) 1998, pp. 839–846. IEEE (1998)
29. Ulyanov, D., Vedaldi, A., Lempitsky, V.: Deep image prior. In: Proceedings of the IEEE Conference on Computer Vision and Pattern Recognition (CVPR) 2018, pp. 9446–9454 (2018). https://doi.org/10.1109/cvpr.2018.00984
30. Wang, J., Huang, J., Wang, F.L., Wei, M., Xie, H., Qin, J.: Data-driven geometry-recovering mesh denoising. Comput. Aided Des. **114**, 133–142 (2019). https://doi.org/10.1016/j.cad.2019.05.027

31. Wang, P.S., Liu, Y., Tong, X.: Mesh denoising via cascaded normal regression. ACM Trans. Graphics **35**(6), 1–12 (2016). https://doi.org/10.1145/2980179. 2980232

32. Wang, R., Yang, Z., Liu, L., Deng, J., Chen, F.: Decoupling noise and features via weighted $\ell 1$-analysis compressed sensing. ACM Trans. Graphics **33**(2), 1–12 (2014). https://doi.org/10.1145/2557449

33. Wei, M., Huang, J., Xie, X., Liu, L., Wang, J., Qin, J.: Mesh denoising guided by patch normal co-filtering via kernel low-rank recovery. IEEE Trans. Visual Comput. Graphics **25**(10), 2910–2926 (2019). https://doi.org/10.1109/TVCG.2018.2865363

34. Wei, M., Liang, L., Pang, W.M., Wang, J., Li, W., Wu, H.: Tensor voting guided mesh denoising. IEEE Trans. Autom. Sci. Eng. **14**(2), 931–945 (2017). https://doi.org/10.1109/TASE.2016.2553449

35. Wei, M., et al.: Bi-normal filtering for mesh denoising. IEEE Trans. Visual Comput. Graphics **21**(1), 43–55 (2015). https://doi.org/10.1109/TVCG.2014.2326872

36. Wei, X., Chen, Z., Fu, Y., Cui, Z., Zhang, Y.: Deep hybrid self-prior for full 3D mesh generation. In: Proceedings of the IEEE/CVF International Conference on Computer Vision (ICCV) 2021 (2021). https://doi.org/10.1109/iccv48922.2021.00575

37. Williams, F., Schneider, T., Silva, C., Zorin, D., Bruna, J., Panozzo, D.: Deep geometric prior for surface reconstruction. In: Proceedings of the IEEE/CVF Conference on Computer Vision and Pattern Recognition (CVPR) 2019, pp. 10122–10131 (2019). https://doi.org/10.1109/CVPR.2019.01037

38. Xu, J., et al.: Noisy-as-Clean: learning self-supervised denoising from corrupted image. IEEE Trans. Image Process. **29**, 9316–9329 (2020). https://doi.org/10.1109/tip.2020.3026622

39. Yagou, H., Ohtake, Y., Belyaev, A.: Mesh smoothing via mean and median filtering applied to face normals. In: Proceedings of Geometric Modeling and Processing. Theory and Applications. GMP. (2002). https://doi.org/10.1109/GMAP.2002.1027503

40. Zhang, W., Deng, B., Zhang, J., Bouaziz, S., Liu, L.: Guided mesh normal filtering. Comput. Graphics Forum **34**, 23–34 (2015). https://doi.org/10.1111/cgf.12742

41. Zhang, Y., Shen, G., Wang, Q., Qian, Y., Wei, M., Qin, J.: GeoBi-GNN: geometry-aware bi-domain mesh denoising via graph neural networks. Comput. Aided Des. **144**, 103154 (2022). https://doi.org/10.1016/j.cad.2021.103154

42. Zhao, W., Liu, X., Wang, S., Fan, X., Zhao, D.: Graph-based feature-preserving mesh normal filtering. IEEE Trans. Visual Comput. Graphics **27**(3), 1937–1952 (2021). https://doi.org/10.1109/TVCG.2019.2944357

43. Zhao, W., Liu, X., Zhao, Y., Fan, X., Zhao, D.: NormalNet: learning-based mesh normal denoising via local partition normalization. IEEE Trans. Circuits Syst. Video Technol. **31**(12), 4697–4710 (2021). https://doi.org/10.1109/TCSVT.2021.3099939

44. Zhao, Y., Qin, H., Zeng, X., Xu, J., Dong, J.: Robust and effective mesh denoising using L0 sparse regularization. Comput. Aided Des. **101**, 82–97 (2018). https://doi.org/10.1016/j.cad.2018.04.001

45. Zheng, Y., Fu, H., Au, O.K.C., Tai, C.L.: Bilateral normal filtering for mesh denoising. IEEE Trans. Visual Comput. Graphics **17**(10), 1521–1530 (2011). https://doi.org/10.1109/TVCG.2010.264

DiffConv: Analyzing Irregular Point Clouds with an Irregular View

Manxi Lin$^{(\boxtimes)}$ (ID) and Aasa Feragen (ID)

Technical University of Denmark, Kongens Lyngby, Denmark
{manli,afhar}@dtu.dk

Abstract. Standard spatial convolutions assume input data with a regular neighborhood structure. Existing methods typically generalize convolution to the irregular point cloud domain by fixing a regular "view" through e.g. a fixed neighborhood size, where the convolution kernel size remains the same for each point. However, since point clouds are not as structured as images, the fixed neighbor number gives an unfortunate inductive bias. We present a novel graph convolution named Difference Graph Convolution (diffConv), which does not rely on a regular view. diffConv operates on spatially-varying and density-dilated neighborhoods, which are further adapted by a learned masked attention mechanism. Experiments show that our model is very robust to the noise, obtaining state-of-the-art performance in 3D shape classification and scene understanding tasks, along with a faster inference speed. The code is publicly available at https://github.com/mmmmimic/diffConvNet.

Keywords: 3D point cloud · Local aggregation operator · Attention

1 Introduction

The availability and affordability of 3D sensors are rapidly increasing. As a result, the point cloud—one of the most widely-employed representations of 3D objects—is used extensively in computer vision applications such as autonomous driving, medical robots, and virtual reality [1,3,19]. The industrial demand has prompted a strong call for exploiting the underlying geometric information in points, fuelling deep learning models that rely on learning effective local point features [11,19,33,35].

Local feature learning schemes [19,35,38] typically consist of two main steps, namely *point grouping* and *feature aggregation*. Point grouping gathers the neighbors of key points, to be encoded and fused in the subsequent feature aggregation.

Unlike grid data, points are unordered and unstructured, posing great challenges to the processing; indeed, standard convolutional neural networks (CNNs)

Supplementary Information The online version contains supplementary material available at https://doi.org/10.1007/978-3-031-20062-5_22.

S. Avidan et al. (Eds.): ECCV 2022, LNCS 13663, pp. 380–397, 2022.
https://doi.org/10.1007/978-3-031-20062-5_22

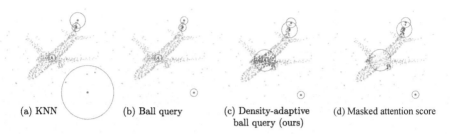

(a) KNN   (b) Ball query   (c) Density-adaptive   (d) Masked attention score
                                          ball query (ours)

Fig. 1. The blue dots refer to key points, green dots denote neighbors, orange circles indicate neighborhoods of key points. The color scale in (d) denotes the neighbor importance of the key point on the airplane body, given by masked attention score. (Color figure online)

[7,23] only work with grid data in a regular *view*, or neighborhood. Point grouping and feature aggregation are often designed to imitate the regular view, or fixed neighborhood size and structure, that we know from convolutions on images. This imitation imposes inductive biases on the point cloud structure.

Figure 1 illustrates problems associated with these inductive biases for the two most common regular point groupings, namely the k nearest neighbor (KNN) grouping [4] and ball query [19]. KNN fixes its view to the k nearest neighbors of each key point, and the resulting groupings are sensitive to noise and outliers. These are automatically grouped with far away points, sometimes belonging to the object of interest, strongly affecting their downstream features (Fig. 1a).

Ball query, conversely, constrains its view to a pre-defined constant radius ball. We see from (Fig. 1b) that using the same radius, or view, at every location also causes problems: A small radius is needed to avoid grouping noise with far away points as we saw with KNN, but this means that the less dense parts of the airplane, such as its tail, easily become disconnected and mistaken for noise.

We thus see that the inductive bias imposed by regular views leads to problems. Can we process the unstructured point cloud without regular groupings? **In this paper, we analyze the irregular point cloud with an *irregular view*.** We present a novel graph convolution operator, named Difference Graph Convolution (diffConv), which takes an irregular *view* of the point cloud. In diffConv, we improve ball query with density-dilated neighborhoods where the radius for each point depends on its kernel density. This induces asymmetric neighborhood graphs, and in Fig. 1c this e.g. helps the plane hold on to its tail.

The dilated ball query still treats all the neighbors inside the ball equally. We further adopt masked attention to introduce an additional, task-specific *learned* irregularity to the neighborhood. As illustrated in Fig. 1d, the points close to the key point get less attention than those further away, indicating that the points near the wings, where contextual differences appear, are paid more attention.

In Short, Our Key Contributions are as Follows:

- We propose diffConv, a local feature aggregator which does not rely on the regular view constraint.
- We present density-dilated ball query, which adapts its view to the local point cloud density, in particular alleviating the influence of noise and outliers.
- We are the first to introduce masked attention to local point feature aggregation. In combination with Laplacian smoothing, it allows us to learn further irregularities, e.g. focusing on contextual feature differences.
- We build a hierarchical learning architecture by stacking diffConv layers. Extensive experiments demonstrate that our model performs on par with state-of-the-art methods in noise-free settings, and outperforms state-of-the-art by far in the presence of noise.

2   Background and Related Work

Imitating the success of CNNs in local grid feature learning, most 3D point cloud models attempt to generalize CNNs to point clouds by fixing a regular view.

Local Point Feature Learning with Projection-Based Methods. Early works [21, 34,44] convert the point cloud to regular 2D or 3D grids (voxels) and leverage the well-established standard image convolutions. Su et al. [21] projected the point cloud to multiple views and utilized 2D convolutions with max-pooling to describe the global features of points. MSNet [34] partitions the point cloud into multi-scale voxels, where 3D convolutions are applied to learn discriminative local features. These methods recast the point cloud to a regular view via the convolution-friendly grid representation. Nevertheless, they suffer from the expensive computation and inevitable loss of geometric detail due to discretization.

Point-Based Methods. In contrast to the expensive projection or voxelization, point-based methods [9,10,12] process the point cloud directly and efficiently. The pioneering PointNet [18] learns point features independently with multilayer perceptrons (MLPs) and aggregates them with max-pooling. Since pointwise MLPs cannot capture local geometric structures, follow-up works obtain local point features via regular views from different types of point grouping.

Point Grouping. The KNN point grouping does not guarantee balanced density [15] and adopts different region scales at different locations of the point cloud [19]. It thus comes with an inductive bias that makes it sensitive both to noise and outliers in point clouds, as well as to different local point densities, as also shown in Fig. 1. Moreover, since KNN queries a relatively small neighborhood in the point-dense regions, the features encoded in subsequent aggregation might not contain enough semantic information to be discriminative. To keep the noise and outliers isolated, some works [14,19] adopt ball query with an upper limit of k points. Balls with less than k points are filled by repeating the first-picked point. Neighborhoods with more than k points are randomly subsampled.

The upper limit k prevents the neighborhood from having too many neighbors, but does also lead to information loss. Besides, the constant ball radius and limit k are not adaptive to the uneven density of real-world point clouds.

Local Point Feature Learning with Point-Based Methods. PointNet++ [19] suggests a hierarchical learning scheme for local point features, including point grouping and feature aggregation. Hierarchically, PointNet++ focuses on a set of subsampled *key points*, which are represented by a neighborhood defined via point grouping according to pre-defined rules. Subsequently, point aggregation encodes and fuses the features of neighboring points to represent the latent shape of the point cloud structure. These point-based local feature learning methods regularize the input point cloud in the spatial or spectral domain. The point grouping in PointNet++ is done via ball query, and PointNet++ thus also inherits the corresponding inductive biases. Although the multi-scale and multi-resolution feature learning in PointNet++ can handle the uneven density to a degree, they are too expensive for application.

Graph convolutional neural networks (GCNs) [2,8,36,45] generalize standard convolutions to graph data by considering convolutions in the spectral domain. Some methods [17,25,32] adopt GCNs for point aggregation. These methods represent the point cloud as an undirected graph for spectral analysis, where neighbors are constrained to a fixed radius ball. Thus, these methods obtain a regular view via spectral analysis, effectively using a form of ball query. It follows that the resulting algorithms also come with the inductive biases associated with ball query. Additionally, GCNs entail extra computations for signal transformation to the spectral domain.

Alternative methods find other ways to define a k-size kernel for each key point, often based on KNN. In particular, DGCNN [35] groups points by their k nearest neighbors in feature space, and then aggregates the feature difference between points and their neighbors with max-pooling. In a similar way, CurveNet [38] takes guided walks and arguments the KNN neighborhood by hypothetical curves. Other works [27,33,39,42,46] learn the importance weights of the KNN features to introduce some neighborhood irregularity, but are still confined to the fixed, and sometimes spatially limited, KNN view.

Differing from the previous generalizations of CNNs, which all rely on taking a regular view of the point clouds in order to define convolutional operators, we suggest an irregular view of point cloud analysis in this paper.

3   Method

We first revisit the general formulation of local feature learning in Sect. 3.1. Then we propose a flexible convolution operator, namely difference graph convolution in Sect. 3.2. In Sect. 3.3 and Sect. 3.4, we enrich the basic diffConv with density-dilated ball query and masked attention. We present our network architectures for 3D shape classification and segmentation in supplements.

3.1 Revisit Local Point Feature Learning

Given a point cloud consisting of N points $\mathcal{P} = \{p_i | i = 1, 2, ..., N\} \in \mathbb{R}^{N \times 3}$, and a data matrix containing their feature vectors $X = [x_1, x_2, x_3, ..., x_N]^T \in \mathbb{R}^{N \times d}$ for each point p_i, local feature extraction can be formulated as:

$$g_i = \Lambda(h(p_i, p_j, x_i, x_j) | p_j \in \mathcal{N}(p_i)) \tag{1}$$

where g_i denotes the learned local feature vector, $\mathcal{N}(p_i)$ refers to the neighbors of p_i, $h(\cdot)$ is a function encoding both the coordinates p_i of the ith point, and the coordinates p_j of its neighbors, as well as their feature vectors x_i and x_j, respectively. Moreover, Λ denotes an aggregation function such as MAX or AVG.

Most previous works focus on the design of $h(\cdot)$ [33,35,46,47]. Among them, one of the most widely applied methods is the edge convolution (edgeConv) appearing in DGCNN [35]. In edgeConv, the neighborhood of a point is defined by its KNN in the feature space. The feature difference $x_i - x_j$ is used to indicate the pair-wise local relationship between the point and its neighbor. The relationships are concatenated with the original point features. The concatenated pair is processed by a multi-layer perceptron l_θ and summarized by a MAX aggregation. The whole process can be described as

$$g_i = MAX(l_\theta(x_i - x_j \| x_i)) \tag{2}$$

where $\|$ refers to concatenation, and $p_j \in \mathcal{N}(p_i)$. In this paper, DGCNN is included as a baseline model. In edgeConv, KNN brings convenience to matrix-level operations, such as feature concatenation and linear transformation. One challenge tackled in this paper is the generalization of edgeConv to the irregular view, and in particular inclusion of feature differences into the convolution.

3.2 Difference Graph Convolution

Inspired by GCNs [8] and edgeConv [35], we propose the Difference Graph Convolution (diffConv). We present a basic version of diffConv in this subsection, with further improvements described in the following subsections. Figure 2 gives an overview of the complete diffConv, where the querying radius is pre-computed.

By treating each point as a node, we represent the aforementioned point cloud $\mathcal{P}$ as a directed graph $\mathcal{G} = \{X, A\}$, where A is the adjacency matrix, and X refers to point feature vectors. In $\mathcal{G}$, each point is connected to its neighbors. The commonly-adopted neighbor-wise feature difference in edgeConv has been proven to be very effective in capturing the local structure of point clouds [11, 35,38]. When processing graphs, the Laplacian matrix efficiently measures the difference between nodes and their neighbors. Borrowing from GCNs [8], we apply Laplacian smoothing on the point feature vector by

$$S = X - \hat{A}X \tag{3}$$

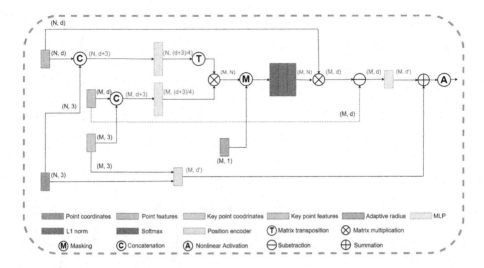

Fig. 2. Structure of our diffConv. Specifically, masking denotes the conditional statements in Eq. 9, which takes the adaptive radius r_i from density-dilated ball query. In our implementation, d_k was set to $\frac{(d+3)}{4}$. M is the number of sampled key points. The dotted line is used to avoid overlapping with the solid lines.

where $S = [s_1, s_2, ..., s_N]^T$ contains the updated feature vectors and $\hat{A}$ is the normalized adjacency matrix. Like edgeConv, our Difference Graph Convolution is an MLP l_θ on the combination of S and the original point features X

$$G = l_\theta(S || X) \tag{4}$$

where $G = [g_1, g_2, ..., g_N]^T$ includes the learned feature vectors. Here, X is concatenated to present the global shape information of the point cloud.

Relationship to edgeConv. We argue that our diffConv is a variant of edgeConv in a more flexible neighborhood. When applying diffConv on KNN grouping, it only differs in the sequence of nonlinear activation and aggregation from edge-Conv. As a demonstration, we consider a basic diffConv, with a simple binary adjacency matrix A whose entries indicate connections between points. When the neighborhood is defined by ball query (without an upper limit on the number of neighbors), the connection between p_i and p_j, A_{ij}, is given by

$$A_{ij} = \begin{cases} 1 & \text{if } \|p_i - p_j\|_2 < r \\ 0 & \text{otherwise} \end{cases} \tag{5}$$

where r is the priory-given ball query search radius. An arithmetic mean is leveraged to normalize the adjacency matrix. According to Eq. 3, for $p_j \in \mathcal{N}(p_i)$, the smoothed feature vector s_i calculated by

$$s_i = x_i - AVG(x_j) = AVG(x_i - x_j) \tag{6}$$

is the average of the neighbor-wise feature difference from Eq. 2. In line with Eq. 4, diffConv for point p_i becomes $g_i = l_\theta \left(AVG(x_i - x_j)||x_i\right)$. When l_θ is linear, diffConv can be further decribed by $g_i = AVG(l_\theta(x_i - x_j||x_i))$. Compared with Eq. 2, in the case of linear activation, the only difference between diffConv and edgeConv is in the aggregation function. When l_θ is nonlinear, the feature difference is activated before aggregation, while diffConv operates in reverse order. In contrast to edgeConv, our diffConv is more flexible with respect to the definition of neighborhood - the number of neighbors is no longer fixed.

Fig. 3. Left: Ball query in a point cloud with noise. The blue circles refer to key points, green circles denote neighbors, orange circles refer to neighborhoods, and gray circles denote other points in the point cloud. **Right:** Visualizations of the kernel density on some objects from ModelNet40 [37]. Brighter color indicates higher density. (Color figure online)

3.3   Density-Dilated Ball Query

In Eq. 5, the point cloud is constructed as an undirected graph, where $A_{ij} = A_{ji}$ for point pair p_i and p_j. The directed relations between points and their neighbors are therefore neglected, as illustrated in Fig. 1b). We relax this to a density-dilated ball query where the search radius for each point is expanded according to its kernel density.

Point density, defined as the number of neighbors of each point, reflects the spatial distribution of points. Figure 3 demonstrates a point cloud with noise. Note that under a fixed-radius ball query, contour points of the 3D object (e.g. point B) have a lower density than the points from the flat area (e.g. point A). Noise generates extreme cases (e.g. point C), which can be isolated from the object.

As illustrated in Fig. 1, in KNN, points with low density, such as noise, get a spatially larger neighborhood than others, grouping them with unrelated features far away. The adversarial effect of noise points on estimated object properties is thus negatively correlated with their density, and assigning smaller neighborhoods to low-density points therefore contributes to resisting noise.

Xiang et al. [38] claim that boundary points provide different feature differences from neighbors while points from flat areas usually have similar and unrecognizable local feature differences. To enlarge the variance of feature difference, points with a higher density (points from flat areas) thus ought to have larger local regions. The KNN grouping queries small neighborhoods for points with high density. Our ball query enlarges the neighborhood to include more contextually different neighbors, giving access to more diverse information.

Instead of counting neighbors, which is computationally expensive, we describe the spatial distribution of points using kernel density estimation [28]. For each point p_i, its kernel density d_i is estimated by a Gaussian kernel

$$d_i = \frac{1}{Nh} \sum_{j=1}^{N} \frac{1}{\sqrt{2\pi}} e^{-\frac{\|p_i - p_j\|_2^2}{2h^2}}, \qquad (7)$$

where h is a parameter controlling the bandwidth. The density d_i indicates the probability of point p_i to be located in flat areas of the object, i.e., the degree of dilation. Figure 3 shows the kernel density of various objects, where points from flat areas have a higher density. This is in accordance with our former analysis.

Based on this density, we softly dilate the searching radius from Eq. 5 to

$$r_i = \sqrt{r^2(1 + \hat{d}_i)}, \qquad (8)$$

where the square and root operations are applied to slow down the dilation speed, $\hat{d}_i$ denotes the normalized kernel density within 0 and 1 by dividing the largest density. The dilated search radius varies from point to point, resulting in a directed graph. Since the search radius is enlarged to different degrees, the message propagation on the graph is boosted, accelerating the long-range information flow. Finally, our method is intuitively robust to noise, which is also demonstrated by our experiments in Sect. 4.4.

3.4   Masked Attention

The dilated ball query still treats all the neighbors inside the ball equally. We further introduce an additional, task-specific learned irregularity to the neighborhood by attention mechanism [5,30]. Different from other attention-based methods [33,46], we employ the masking mechanism in self-attention [30] to handle the no-longer-fixed neighborhood. We call this learning scheme masked attention. In a transformer built by self-attention [30] [31], there are two kinds of masks: the padding mask in the encoder is exploited to address sequences with different lengths and the sequence mask in the decoder is used to prevent ground truth leakage in sequence prediction tasks. In contrast, we employ a neighborhood mask in our masked attention to learn the local features of points. It works in the encoder while playing a different role than the padding mask. It includes three steps, the calculation of edge weight for each pair of connected points on the graph, local normalization, and balanced renormalization.

First, we revise the adjacency matrix A in Eq. 5 to

$$A_{ij} = \begin{cases} l_\phi(x_i\|p_i) l_\psi(x_j\|p_j)^T & \text{if } \|p_i - p_j\|_2 < r_i \\ -\infty & \text{otherwise,} \end{cases} \qquad (9)$$

where l_ϕ and l_ψ are two MLPs mapping the input to a given dimension d_k. The MLPs are employed to learn the latent relationship and alignment between p_i and p_j in the feature space. The MLPs encode both point features and coordinates, as we expect them to recognize both the semantic and geometric information. In the implementation, $-\infty$ is approximated by -10^9, which is orders of magnitude smaller than the computed attention score.

The adjacency matrix is then normalized by softmax

$$\tilde{A}_{i,j} = \frac{e^{A_{i,j}}}{\sum_k^N e^{A_{i,k}}}. \tag{10}$$

Since $e^{-10^9} \approx 0$, points outside the neighborhood are automatically masked. Hence, Eq. 10 becomes the softmax normalization in neighborhoods. With the masking mechanism, we normalize the attention score locally with only matrix-wise operations instead of expensive iterations. In each local region, neighbor features are aggregated dynamically and selectively.

In self-attention [30], the dot product in Eq. 9 is scaled by $\sqrt{d_k}$ before the softmax normalization, in order to prevent the product from getting extreme values as d_k increases. Here, we refine the scaling by a balanced renormalization of the attention scores $\tilde{A}$ from Eq. 10. We apply the l_1-norm twice on the square root of the former attention score in different dimensions by

$$\overline{A}_{ij} = \frac{\sqrt{\tilde{A}_{ij}}}{\sum_k^N \sqrt{\tilde{A}_{kj}}} \quad \text{and} \quad \hat{A}_{ij} = \frac{\overline{A}_{ij}}{\sum_k^N \overline{A}_{ik}}. \tag{11}$$

Here, the square root reduces the variation in attention scores, to prevent overly attention on a few points. Considering the matrix product in Eq. 3, l_1-norm is to balance the contribution of feature channels and neighbor points respectively. The experimental results in supplemental materials illustrate the effectiveness of the proposed renormalization strategy.

Position Encoding. Local spatial information is defined as the coordinate difference between points and their neighbors. Many prior works have demonstrated the importance of local spatial information in point cloud analysis [14,33,47]. We employ the Local Point-Feature Aggregation block [38] as the position encoder in diffConv. The encoded coordinates are fused with point features by

$$G = \sigma(l_\theta(S||X) + l_\pi(P)), \tag{12}$$

where σ is a nonlinear activation function, $P = [p_1, p_2, p_3, ..., p_N]^T \in \mathbb{R}^{N \times 3}$ contains the 3D coordinates of points in $\mathcal{P}$, and l_π is the position encoder working in the dilated neighborhoods and mapping the positional difference to the same dimension as the updated point features from l_θ.

4 Experiments

We demonstrate our model performance in 3D shape classification, object shape part segmentation, and real-scene semantic segmentation tasks. Due to the limited space, we describe the training settings as well as the corresponding ablation studies on the hyperparameters in supplements.

4.1 Point Cloud Classification

ModelNet40 with the Official Split. We conducted experiments performing object shape classification on the ModelNet40 dataset [37], which contains 12,311 synthetic meshed CAD models from 40 different categories. The official split includes 9,843 models for training and 2,468 models for testing. Following most publicly available implementations [19,35,38], our validation on the official split was made by reporting the best-observed test performance over all epochs. Similar to previous works, we represented each CAD model by 1,024 points uniformly sampled from mesh faces with (x, y, z) coordinates.

We measured both the overall accuracy (OA), treating every point cloud with equal weight, and the mean accuracy (MA), where the mean was computed from

Table 1. 3D shape classification results on ModelNet40 dataset with official split as well as ModelNet40-C, and part segmentation results on ShapeNet Part dataset. Here, 'xyz' stands for coordinates of points; 'nor' stands for normals of points; '#points' means the number of input points in classification; 'OA' stands for the overall accuracy over instances on ModelNet40; and 'MA' stands for the mean accuracy within each category on ModelNet40; 'CER' denotes the corruption error rate on ModelNet40-C; 'mIOU' denotes the instance average Inter-over-Union on ShapeNetPart. Not all papers report MA and CER; these are recorded as '-' in the table.

Methods	Input	#points	OA(%)	MA(%)	CER(%)	mIOU (%)
A-CNN [10]	xyz+nor	1k	92.6	–	–	86.1
Kd-Net [9]	xyz	32k	91.8	88.5	–	82.3
SO-Net [12]	xyz+nor	5k	93.4	**90.8**	–	84.6
PointNet [18]	xyz	1k	89.2	–	28.3	83.7
PointNet++ [19]	xyz	1k	90.7	–	23.6	85.1
DGCNN [35]	xyz	1k	92.9	90.2	25.9	85.1
CurveNet [38]	xyz	1k	**93.8**	–	22.7	**86.6**
RS-CNN [14]	xyz	1k	92.9	–	26.2	86.2
Spec-GCN [32]	xyz	1k	91.5	–	–	85.4
PointASNL [41]	xyz	1k	92.9	–	–	86.1
PCT [6]	xyz	1k	93.2	–	25.5	86.4
GDANet [40]	xyz	1k	93.4	–	25.6	86.5
Ours	xyz	1k	93.6	90.6	**21.4**	85.7

the category-specific accuracies. Note that the MA up-weights the importance of small categories, giving them equal weight as the larger categories.

Our results can be found in Table 1. All results for other methods are taken from the cited papers. Note that RS-CNN, CurveNet, and GDANet adopt a voting strategy to improve the model performance. We report their classification accuracy without this trick for a fair comparison. Our model achieves the second-best overall accuracy at 93.6%. Even compared to SO-Net, which takes $5k$ points with normal as input, our model has a better performance in OA.

ModelNet40 with Resplits for Assessing Robustness. In addition to benchmarking on the official split, we also performed repeated experiments on resampled dataset splits, to obtain an evaluation that is robust to over-fitting to any specific data split. Here, we selected parameters in a more traditional fashion with the help of an independent validation set. To this end, we randomly re-split the dataset into 8,617/1,847/1,847 point clouds for training/validation/testing, respectively, and picked the model with the best validation performance for evaluation on the test. This was repeated 10 times, reporting the mean and standard deviation of the corresponding performance measures. The baseline models were trained with settings from their paper.

Table 2. Classification results on ModelNet40 with resplits and ScanObjectNN. OBJ_ONLY and OBJ_BG denote the overall accuracy in the corresponding variant.

Methods	OA(%)	MA(%)	OBJ_ONLY	OBJ_BG
PointNet [18]	90.19 ± 0.58	84.55 ± 0.81	79.2	73.3
DGCNN [35]	92.89 ± 0.43	89.62 ± 0.83	86.2	82.8
CurveNet [38]	92.86 ± 0.49	89.51 ± 0.81	84.3	84.4
Ours	$\mathbf{93.15 \pm 0.34}$	$\mathbf{89.86 \pm 0.56}$	**86.6**	**84.9**

We compare our model performance with PointNet, DGCNN, and CurveNet, where the latter has the highest performance on the official split. According to Table 2, our method outperforms all the other models in both overall and class-mean accuracy, showing a better generalization capability on the resampled data splits than other methods. Moreover, our model has the smallest standard deviation in both OA and MA, indicating a more stable performance. This supports our hypothesis that diffConv's irregular view gives discriminative local features.

ModelNet40-C with Corruptions for Assessing Robustness. To further assess the corruption robustness, we evaluated the model trained on ModelNet40 with the official split on the ModelNet40-C dataset [22], which imposes 15 common and realistic corruptions with 5 severity levels on the original ModelNet40 point clouds. We used the corruption error rate (CER) as the evaluation metric.

The corruption performance of different models is shown in Table 1. All results for other methods are taken from [22]. Our model outperforms all existing methods with at least a 1.3% difference, showing strong robustness to corruption.

ScanObjectNN. Besides the synthetic datasets, we also validated our model on the ScanObjectNN dataset [29], with 2,902 scanned real-world objects from 15 categories, with 1,024 points each. Compared to ModelNet40, ScanObjectNN is more challenging due to the presence of noise, backgrounds, and occlusion. 80% of the objects are split into the official training set and the remaining 20% are used for testing. We conducted experiments on objects with and without background respectively (the OBJ_BG and OBJ_ONLY variant of the dataset).

Table 2 summarizes the performance of our model and the baselines. The results of PointNet and DGCNN are taken from [29], while CurveNet was retrained as it is not shown in [29]. Our model gets the highest OA on both two variants, indicating that it is practical in addressing real-world problems.

Fig. 4. Example masked attention maps for ModelNet40-C. Red dots are picked key points; green dots denote neighbors; the color scale denotes the masked attention score. Zoom in for details. (Color figure online)

Visualizations of Masked Attention. Our model achieves state-of-the-art performance and shows strong robustness in 3D object classification. Figure 4 illustrates some examples of the attention maps from the second diffConv layer in our classification network on ModelNet40. We randomly picked two key points from 8 different objects of the ModelNet40-C benchmark. As shown in the figure, the noise points are isolated and the flat-area points have a larger neighborhood than the boundary points. Besides, neighbors with larger contextual differences to the query point, e.g., the edges of the airplane and the laptop, usually get more attention. More visualizations are presented in the supplements.

4.2   3D Semantic Segmentation

We performed the scene-level understanding task on Toronto3D [24]. Compared with the indoor datasets, the Toronto3D dataset, collected by LiDAR in outdoor scenarios, contains more noise and requires more from the model's robustness. Toronto3D contains 8 different classes and 78.3M points. Following TGNet [13], we divided the scene into 5mx5m blocks, and sampled 2,048 points from each block. There are 956 samples for training and 289 for testing. The mean intersection over union over categories (mean IoU) and IoU for each category are shown in Table 3, where the results of other methods are taken from [24]. Our model outperforms all other methods in mean IOU, and in many categories. Specifically, our model surpasses other methods significantly in recognizing small objects, such as road marks and poles. This demonstrates the effectiveness of our method on scene-level understanding tasks.

4.3   Shape Part Segmentation

We conducted the 3D part segmentation task on the ShapeNetPart dataset [43], which consists of 16,881 CAD models from 16 categories with up to 50 different parts. Each CAD model is represented by 2,048 uniformly-sampled points. We followed [33] and trained our model on 12,137 instances with the rest for testing. All 2,048 points in each point cloud were used.

Table 3. Segmentation results on Toronto3D. Here, mean IoU denotes the category average Inter-over-Union in Toronto3D.

Methods	mean IoU	Road	Rd. mrk	Natural	Building	Util. line	Pole	Car	Fence
PointNet++ [19]	56.55	**91.44**	7.59	89.80	74.00	68.60	59.53	52.97	7.54
PointNet++(MSG) [19]	53.12	90.67	0.00	86.68	75.78	56.20	60.89	44.51	10.19
DGCNN [35]	49.60	90.63	0.44	81.25	63.95	47.05	56.86	49.26	7.32
KPFCNN [26]	60.30	90.20	0.00	86.79	**86.83**	**81.08**	73.06	42.85	21.57
MS-PCNN [16]	58.01	91.22	3.50	90.48	77.30	62.30	68.54	52.63	17.12
TG-Net [13]	58.34	91.39	10.62	91.02	76.93	68.27	66.25	54.10	8.16
MS-TGNet [24]	60.96	90.89	18.78	**92.18**	80.62	69.36	71.22	51.05	13.59
Ours	**76.73**	83.31	**51.06**	69.04	79.55	80.48	**84.41**	**76.19**	**89.83**

We report the instance average Inter-over-Union (mIOU) in Table 1. The results for other methods are taken from the cited papers. Figure 5 shows our model predictions, which are very close to the ground truth.

4.4   Performance Analysis

Robustness Study. According to our analysis, our method is robust to noise, especially in contrast to KNN-based models. To further verify the robustness of our model, like KCNet [20], we evaluated the model on noisy points in both classification and part segmentation tasks. A certain number of randomly picked points were replaced with uniform noise ranging from −1 to 1. In segmentation, these noise points were labeled the same as the nearest original point. Figure 6 demonstrates the results. We compared our model with the baseline methods used in previous experiments. In classification, we also report the performance of KCNet and PointASNL, with the results taken from papers. As presented in the figure, our model shows clear robustness to noise. Even with 100 noise points, our method has an OA of 86.2% and an mIOU of 74.3%.

Fig. 5. Examples of ShapeNetPart segmentation. Ground truth **(top)**; ours **(bottom)**.

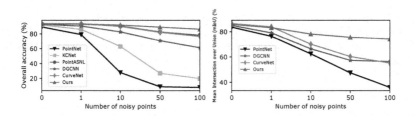

Fig. 6. Results of robustness study on ModelNet40 (left) and ShapeNetPart (right).

Computational Resources. We compare the corrupted error rate on ModelNet40-C, inference time (IT), floating-point operations (FLOPs) required, parameter number (Params), and memory cost against baselines in Table 4. FLOPs and Params are estimated by PyTorch-OpCounter[1]. The inference time per batch is recorded with a test batch size of 16. We conducted the experiments on a GTX 1080 Ti GPU. For a fair comparison in inference time and memory cost, each model is implemented in Python without CUDA programming. The table illustrates the efficiency of our method, which is twice as fast as CurveNet.

---

[1] https://github.com/Lyken17/pytorch-OpCounter.

Table 4. Computational resource requirements.

Methods	CER(%)	IT (ms)	FLOPs	Params	Memory
PointNet [18]	28.3	**19**	0.45G	3.47M	**2061M**
DGCNN [35]	25.9	88	2.43G	1.81M	8067M
CurveNet [38]	22.7	190	0.66G	2.14M	4309M
Ours	21.4	78	**0.28G**	**1.31M**	3971M

5 Conclusion

We have reviewed contemporary local point feature learning, which heavily relies on a regular inductive bias on point structure. We question the necessity of this inductive bias, and propose diffConv, which is neither a generalization of CNNs nor spectral GCNs. Instead, equipped with Laplacian smoothing, density-dilated ball query and masked attention, diffConv analyzes point clouds through an *irregular view*. Through extensive experiments we show that diffConv achieves state-of-the-art performance in 3D object classification and scene understanding, is far more robust to noise than other methods, with a faster inference speed.

Acknowledgements. This work was supported by the DIREC project EXPLAIN-ME, the Novo Nordisk Foundation through the Center for Basic Machine Learning Research in Life Science (NNF20OC0062606), and the Pioneer Centre for AI, DNRF grant nr P1.

References

1. Blanc, T., El Beheiry, M., Caporal, C., Masson, J.B., Hajj, B.: Genuage: visualize and analyze multidimensional single-molecule point cloud data in virtual reality. Nat. Methods **17**(11), 1100–1102 (2020)
2. Defferrard, M., Bresson, X., Vandergheynst, P.: Convolutional neural networks on graphs with fast localized spectral filtering. Adv. Neural. Inf. Process. Syst. **29**, 3844–3852 (2016)
3. Dometios, A.C., Papageorgiou, X.S., Arvanitakis, A., Tzafestas, C.S., Maragos, P.: Real-time end-effector motion behavior planning approach using on-line point-cloud data towards a user adaptive assistive bath robot. In: 2017 IEEE/RSJ International Conference on Intelligent Robots and Systems (IROS), pp. 5031–5036. IEEE (2017)
4. Fix, E., Hodges Jr., J.L.: Discriminatory analysis-nonparametric discrimination: small sample performance. Technical report, California Univ Berkeley (1952)
5. Gehring, J., Auli, M., Grangier, D., Dauphin, Y.: A convolutional encoder model for neural machine translation. In: Proceedings of the Annual Meeting of the Association for Computational Linguistics, pp. 123–135, July 2017
6. Guo, M.H., Cai, J.X., Liu, Z.N., Mu, T.J., Martin, R.R., Hu, S.M.: PCT: point cloud transformer. Comput. Vis. Media **7**(2), 187–199 (2021)
7. He, K., Zhang, X., Ren, S., Sun, J.: Deep residual learning for image recognition. In: Proceedings of the IEEE Conference on Computer Vision and Pattern Recognition, pp. 770–778 (2016)

8. Kipf, T.N., Welling, M.: Semi-supervised classification with graph convolutional networks. In: Proceedings of the 5th International Conference on Learning Representations (2017)
9. Klokov, R., Lempitsky, V.: Escape from cells: deep KD-networks for the recognition of 3D point cloud models. In: Proceedings of the IEEE International Conference on Computer Vision, pp. 863–872 (2017)
10. Komarichev, A., Zhong, Z., Hua, J.: A-CNN: annularly convolutional neural networks on point clouds. In: Proceedings of the IEEE/CVF Conference on Computer Vision and Pattern Recognition, pp. 7421–7430 (2019)
11. Li, G., Muller, M., Thabet, A., Ghanem, B.: DeepGCNs: can GCNs go as deep as CNNs? In: Proceedings of the IEEE/CVF International Conference on Computer Vision, pp. 9267–9276 (2019)
12. Li, J., Chen, B.M., Lee, G.H.: So-net: Self-organizing network for point cloud analysis. In: Proceedings of the IEEE Conference on Computer Vision and Pattern Recognition, pp. 9397–9406 (2018)
13. Li, Y., Ma, L., Zhong, Z., Cao, D., Li, J.: TGNet: geometric graph CNN on 3-D point cloud segmentation. IEEE Trans. Geosci. Remote Sens. **58**(5), 3588–3600 (2019)
14. Liu, Y., Fan, B., Xiang, S., Pan, C.: Relation-shape convolutional neural network for point cloud analysis. In: Proceedings of the IEEE/CVF Conference on Computer Vision and Pattern Recognition, pp. 8895–8904 (2019)
15. Liu, Z., Hu, H., Cao, Y., Zhang, Z., Tong, X.: A closer look at local aggregation operators in point cloud analysis. In: Vedaldi, A., Bischof, H., Brox, T., Frahm, J.-M. (eds.) ECCV 2020. LNCS, vol. 12368, pp. 326–342. Springer, Cham (2020). https://doi.org/10.1007/978-3-030-58592-1_20
16. Ma, L., Li, Y., Li, J., Tan, W., Yu, Y., Chapman, M.A.: Multi-scale point-wise convolutional neural networks for 3d object segmentation from lidar point clouds in large-scale environments. IEEE Trans. Intell. Transp. Syst. **22**(2), 821–836 (2019)
17. Pan, G., Wang, J., Ying, R., Liu, P.: 3dti-net: learn inner transform invariant 3D geometry features using dynamic GCN. arXiv preprint arXiv:1812.06254 (2018)
18. Qi, C.R., Su, H., Mo, K., Guibas, L.J.: Pointnet: deep learning on point sets for 3D classification and segmentation. In: Proceedings of the IEEE Conference on Computer Vision and Pattern Recognition, pp. 652–660 (2017)
19. Qi, C.R., Yi, L., Su, H., Guibas, L.J.: PointNet++: deep hierarchical feature learning on point sets in a metric space. In: Proceedings of the 31st International Conference on Neural Information Processing Systems, pp. 5105–5114 (2017)
20. Shen, Y., Feng, C., Yang, Y., Tian, D.: Mining point cloud local structures by kernel correlation and graph pooling. In: Proceedings of the IEEE Conference on Computer Vision and Pattern Recognition, pp. 4548–4557 (2018)
21. Su, H., Maji, S., Kalogerakis, E., Learned-Miller, E.: Multi-view convolutional neural networks for 3D shape recognition. In: Proceedings of the IEEE International Conference on Computer Vision, pp. 945–953 (2015)
22. Sun, J., Zhang, Q., Kailkhura, B., Yu, Z., Xiao, C., Mao, Z.M.: Benchmarking robustness of 3D point cloud recognition against common corruptions. arXiv preprint arXiv:2201.12296 (2022)
23. Tan, M., Le, Q.: Efficientnet: Rethinking model scaling for convolutional neural networks. In: International Conference on Machine Learning, pp. 6105–6114. PMLR (2019)
24. Tan, W., et al.: Toronto-3D: a large-scale mobile lidar dataset for semantic segmentation of urban roadways. In: Proceedings of the IEEE/CVF Conference on Computer Vision and Pattern Recognition Workshops, pp. 202–203 (2020)

25. Te, G., Hu, W., Zheng, A., Guo, Z.: RGCNN: regularized graph CNN for point cloud segmentation. In: Proceedings of the 26th ACM international conference on Multimedia, pp. 746–754 (2018)
26. Thomas, H., Qi, C.R., Deschaud, J.E., Marcotegui, B., Goulette, F., Guibas, L.J.: KPConv: flexible and deformable convolution for point clouds. In: Proceedings of the IEEE/CVF International Conference on Computer Vision, pp. 6411–6420 (2019)
27. Tian, F., Jiang, Z., Jiang, G.: DNet: dynamic neighborhood feature learning in point cloud. Sensors **21**(7), 2327 (2021)
28. Turlach, B.A.: Bandwidth selection in kernel density estimation: a review. In: CORE and Institut de Statistique. Citeseer (1993)
29. Uy, M.A., Pham, Q.H., Hua, B.S., Nguyen, D.T., Yeung, S.K.: Revisiting point cloud classification: a new benchmark dataset and classification model on real-world data. In: International Conference on Computer Vision (ICCV) (2019)
30. Vaswani, A., et al.: Attention is all you need. In: Advances in Neural Information Processing Systems, pp. 5998–6008 (2017)
31. Veličković, P., Cucurull, G., Casanova, A., Romero, A., Liò P., Bengio, Y.: Graph attention networks. In: 6th International Conference on Learning Representations (2017)
32. Wang, C., Samari, B., Siddiqi, K.: Local spectral graph convolution for point set feature learning. In: Ferrari, V., Hebert, M., Sminchisescu, C., Weiss, Y. (eds.) ECCV 2018. LNCS, vol. 11208, pp. 56–71. Springer, Cham (2018). https://doi.org/10.1007/978-3-030-01225-0_4
33. Wang, L., Huang, Y., Hou, Y., Zhang, S., Shan, J.: Graph attention convolution for point cloud semantic segmentation. In: Proceedings of the IEEE/CVF Conference on Computer Vision and Pattern Recognition, pp. 10296–10305 (2019)
34. Wang, L., Huang, Y., Shan, J., He, L.: MSNet: multi-scale convolutional network for point cloud classification. Remote Sensing **10**(4), 612 (2018)
35. Wang, Y., Sun, Y., Liu, Z., Sarma, S.E., Bronstein, M.M., Solomon, J.M.: Dynamic graph CNN for learning on point clouds. ACM Trans. Graphics (tog) **38**(5), 1–12 (2019)
36. Wu, F., Souza, A., Zhang, T., Fifty, C., Yu, T., Weinberger, K.: Simplifying graph convolutional networks. In: International Conference on Machine Learning, pp. 6861–6871. PMLR (2019)
37. Wu, Z., Song, S., Khosla, A., Yu, F., Zhang, L., Tang, X., Xiao, J.: 3D shapenets: a deep representation for volumetric shapes. In: Proceedings of the IEEE Conference on Computer Vision and Pattern Recognition, pp. 1912–1920 (2015)
38. Xiang, T., Zhang, C., Song, Y., Yu, J., Cai, W.: Walk in the cloud: learning curves for point clouds shape analysis. In: Proceedings of the IEEE/CVF International Conference on Computer Vision (ICCV), pp. 915–924, October 2021
39. Xu, M., Ding, R., Zhao, H., Qi, X.: PAConv: position adaptive convolution with dynamic kernel assembling on point clouds. In: Proceedings of the IEEE/CVF Conference on Computer Vision and Pattern Recognition, pp. 3173–3182 (2021)
40. Xu, M., Zhang, J., Zhou, Z., Xu, M., Qi, X., Qiao, Y.: Learning geometry-disentangled representation for complementary understanding of 3D object point cloud. arXiv preprint arXiv:2012.10921 (2020)
41. Yan, X., Zheng, C., Li, Z., Wang, S., Cui, S.: PointaSNL: robust point clouds processing using nonlocal neural networks with adaptive sampling. In: Proceedings of the IEEE/CVF Conference on Computer Vision and Pattern Recognition, pp. 5589–5598 (2020)

42. Yang, Y., Ma, Y., Zhang, J., Gao, X., Xu, M.: ATTPNet: attention-based deep neural network for 3D point set analysis. Sensors **20**(19), 5455 (2020)
43. Yi, L., et al.: A scalable active framework for region annotation in 3D shape collections. ACM Trans. Graphics (ToG) **35**(6), 1–12 (2016)
44. Zhang, L., Sun, J., Zheng, Q.: 3D point cloud recognition based on a multi-view convolutional neural network. Sensors **18**(11), 3681 (2018)
45. Zhang, M., Cui, Z., Neumann, M., Chen, Y.: An end-to-end deep learning architecture for graph classification. In: Thirty-Second AAAI Conference on Artificial Intelligence (2018)
46. Zhao, H., Jiang, L., Jia, J., Torr, P.H., Koltun, V.: Point transformer. In: Proceedings of the IEEE/CVF International Conference on Computer Vision, pp. 16259–16268 (2021)
47. Zhou, H., Feng, Y., Fang, M., Wei, M., Qin, J., Lu, T.: Adaptive graph convolution for point cloud analysis. In: Proceedings of the IEEE/CVF International Conference on Computer Vision, pp. 4965–4974 (2021)

PD-Flow: A Point Cloud Denoising Framework with Normalizing Flows

Aihua Mao[1] , Zihui Du[1] , Yu-Hui Wen[2(✉)] , Jun Xuan[1] ,
and Yong-Jin Liu[2(✉)]

[1] South China University of Technology, Guangzhou, China
ahmao@scut.edu.cn, {csusami,202020143921}@mail.scut.edu.cn
[2] Tsinghua University, Beijing, China
{wenyh1616,liuyongjin}@tsinghua.edu.cn

Abstract. Point cloud denoising aims to restore clean point clouds from raw observations corrupted by noise and outliers while preserving the fine-grained details. We present a novel deep learning-based denoising model, that incorporates normalizing flows and noise disentanglement techniques to achieve high denoising accuracy. Unlike existing works that extract features of point clouds for point-wise correction, we formulate the denoising process from the perspective of distribution learning and feature disentanglement. By considering noisy point clouds as a joint distribution of clean points and noise, the denoised results can be derived from disentangling the noise counterpart from latent point representation, and the mapping between Euclidean and latent spaces is modeled by normalizing flows. We evaluate our method on synthesized 3D models and real-world datasets with various noise settings. Qualitative and quantitative results show that our method outperforms previous state-of-the-art deep learning-based approaches. The source code is available at https://github.com/unknownue/pdflow.

Keywords: Point cloud · Denoising · Normalizing flows

1 Introduction

As one of the most widely used representations for 3D objects, point clouds have attracted considerable attention in many fields, including geometric analysis, robotic object detection, and autonomous driving. The rapid development of 3D scanning devices, such as depth cameras and LiDAR sensors, has made point cloud data increasingly popular. However, raw point clouds produced from these devices are inevitably contaminated by noise and outliers, due to inherent environment noise (e.g., lighting and background) and hardware limitation. Hence, point cloud denoising, which is a technique to restore high-quality and well-distributed points, is crucial for downstream tasks (Fig. 1).

Supplementary Information The online version contains supplementary material available at https://doi.org/10.1007/978-3-031-20062-5_23.

S. Avidan et al. (Eds.): ECCV 2022, LNCS 13663, pp. 398–415, 2022.
https://doi.org/10.1007/978-3-031-20062-5_23

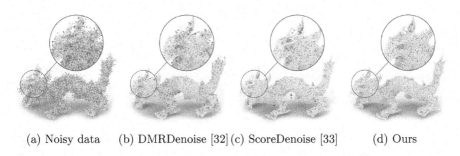

(a) Noisy data   (b) DMRDenoise [32] (c) ScoreDenoise [33]   (d) Ours

Fig. 1. The denoising results produced by (b) DMRDenoise [32], (c) ScoreDenoise [33] and (d) our method from noisy input (a). Deeper color indicates higher error. Our method preserves notably more fine details with less noise and outperforms others especially in uniformity.

Despite decades of research, point cloud denoising remains a challenging problem, because of the intrinsic complexity of the topological relationship and connectivity among points. Traditional denoising methods [2,4,8,28,30,34] perform well in some circumstances. However, they generally rely on prior knowledge on point sets or some assumptions on noise distributions, and they may compromise the denoising quality for unseen noise (e.g., distortion, non-uniformity).

Recent promising deep learning approaches [12,17,32,33,41] bring new insight to point cloud denoising in a data-driven manner and exhibit superior performance over traditional methods. These works can be classified into two categories. The first class treats existing points as approximating the underlying surface by regressing points [12], predicting displacements [41,51], or progressive movement [33]. Nonetheless, the point features are extracted from the local receptive field independently. Therefore, consistent surface properties may not be preserved between neighborhood points, resulting in artifacts, such as outliers and scatter. The second class treats downsampling noisy data as a coarse point set and resampling/upsampling points from the learned manifold with a target resolution [17,32]. However, the downsampling scheme inevitably discards geometric details, leading to distorted distribution.

In this paper, we consider the noisy point clouds as samples of the joint distribution of 3D shape and corrupted noise. Based on this setup, it is intuitive to capture the characteristics of noise and underlying surface in the form of distribution. Thus, we can formulate the point cloud denoising problem as disentangling the clean section from its latent representation. We can also interpret this idea from the perspective of signal processing [36], where clean points and noise are analogous to low- and high-frequency part of signals, respectively. We can filter out the high-frequency contents and recover the smooth signal via the low-frequency counterpart that encodes the major information of raw signal.

Our denoising technique mainly consists of three phases: 1) learning the distribution of noisy point clouds by encoding the points into a latent representation, 2) filtering out the noise section from the latent representation, and 3) decoding/restoring noise-free points from the clean latent code. To realize this

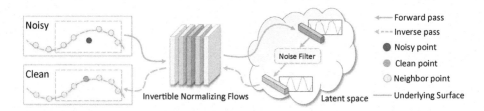

Fig. 2. Schematic illustration of the proposed method. We disentangle the noise factor from the latent representation of noisy point clouds and leverage NFs to model the transformation between Euclidean and latent spaces.

process, we require a generative model that can simultaneously learn the latent distribution and restore clean points. In this paper, we propose to exploit normalizing flows (NFs) in an invertible generative framework, to model the distribution mapping of point clouds. The whole process is illustrated in Fig. 2.

Compared with other popular deep learning models, such as generative adversarial network (GAN) and variational autoencoder, NFs provide several advantages: (i) NFs are capable of transforming complex distributions into disentangled code space, which is a desired property for point cloud denoising task, (ii) an NF is an invertible and lossless propagation process, which ensures one-to-one mapping between point clouds and their latent representations, and (iii) NFs realize the encoding and decoding process in a unified framework and share weights between forward and inverse propagations.

In summary, the main contributions of this work include:

- We propose a simple yet intuitive framework for point cloud denoising, called PD-Flow, which learns the distribution of noisy point sets and performs denoising via noise disentanglement.
- We propose to augment vanilla flows to improve the flexibility and expressiveness of the latent representation of points. We investigate various noise filtering strategies to disentangle noise from latent points.
- To validate the effectiveness of our method, extensive evaluations are conducted on synthetic and real-world datasets. Qualitative experiments show that our method outperforms the state-of-the-art works on diverse metrics.

2   Related Works

2.1   Denoising Methods

Traditional Denoising Methods. Conventional methods for point cloud denoising can be coarsely classified into three categories: 1) Statistical-based filtering methods generally apply statistical analysis theories, such as kernel density estimation [42], sparse reconstruction principle [4,34,45], principal component analysis [35], Bayesian statistics [22] and curvature extraction [24]. 2)

Projection-based filtering methods first construct a smooth surface (e.g., Moving Least Squares surface [2,3,13]) from a set of noisy points. Then, denoising is implemented by projecting points onto surfaces. According to projection strategies, this class of methods can be further divided into, e.g., locally optimal projection [19,20,28], jet fitting [5], and bilateral filtering [9]. 3) Neighborhood-based filtering methods measure the correlation and similarity between a point and its neighbor points. Nonlocal-based methods [8,21,46,52] generally detect self-similarity among nonlocal patches and consolidate them into coherent noise-free point clouds. Graph-based denoising methods [14,18,43,50] naturally represent point cloud geometry with a graph. All above methods generally require user interaction or geometric priors (e.g., normals) and still lack the ability of filtering various noise levels.

Deep-Learning-Based Denoising Methods. In recent years, several deep learning based methods [12,17,32,33,37,41] have been proposed for point cloud denoising. PointCleanNet [41] first removes outliers and then predicts inverse displacement for each point [16]. It is the first learning-based method that directly inputs noisy data without the acquisition of normals nor noise/device specifications. Hermosilla et al. proposed Total Denoising (TotalDn) [17] to regress points from the distribution of unstructured *total* noise. This allows TotalDn to approximate the underlying surface without the supervision of clean points. Pistilli et al. proposed GPDNet [37], which is a graph convolutional network, to improve denoising robustness under high noise levels. In the denoising pipeline of DMRDenoise [32], noisy input is first downsampled by a differentiable pooling layer, and then the denoised points are resampled from estimated manifolds. However, using the downsampling schema [32,41] to remove outliers may cause unnecessary detail loss. Recently, Luo and Hu developed a score-based denoising algorithm (ScoreDenoise [33]), which utilizes the gradient ascent technique and iteratively moves points to the underlying surface via estimated scores.

Our method differs from the above methods in several aspects. First, we formulate the denoising process as disentangling noise from the factorized representation of noisy input. Second, instead of applying separate modules to extract high-level features and reconstruct coordinates, we unify the point encoding/decoding process with a bijective network design.

2.2 Normalizing Flows for Point Cloud Analysis

NFs define a probability distribution transformation for data, allowing exact density evaluation and efficient sampling. In recent years, NFs have become a promising method for generative modeling and have been adopted into various applications [1,27,31,39]. Representative models include discrete normalizing flows (DNF) [10,11,25] and continuous normalizing flows (CNF) [7,15].

As the first NF-based algorithm for point cloud generation, PointFlow [48] employs CNF to learn a two-level distribution hierarchy of given shapes. Point-Flow is a flexible scheme for modeling point distribution. However, the expensive equation solvers and training instability issues still remain to be open problems.

Sharing the similar idea, Discrete PointFlow [26] proposes to use discrete flow layers as an alternative to continuous flows to reduce computation overhead. Pumarola et al. [40] introduced C-Flow, which is a parallel conditional scheme in the DNF-based architecture, to bridge data between images and point clouds domains. Postels et al. [38] recently presented mixtures of NFs to improve the representational ability of flows and show superior performance to a single NF model [26]. These works mainly focus on improving generative ability and are evaluated on toy datasets. However, there are few works concentrating on flow-based real-world point cloud applications.

In this paper, we take advantage of the invertible capacity of NFs, which enable exact latent variable inference and efficient clean point synthesis. To the best of our knowledge, no prior work has been proposed for the point cloud denoising task by developing a new framework with NFs.

3   Method

3.1   Overview

Given an input point set $\tilde{\mathcal{P}} = \{\tilde{p}_i = p_i + o_i\} \in \mathbb{R}^{N \times D_p}$ corrupted by noise $\mathcal{O} = \{o_i\}$, we aim to predict a clean point set $\hat{\mathcal{P}} = \{\hat{p}_i\} \in \mathbb{R}^{N \times D_p}$, where N is the number of points, D_p is the point coordinate dimension, and $\hat{p}_i$ is the prediction of clean point p_i. In our study, we consider the coordinate dimension with $D_p = 3$ and make no assumptions about the noise distribution of $\mathcal{O}$.

In this paper, we propose to utilize NFs to model the mapping of point distribution between Euclidean and latent spaces, thereby allowing us to formulate point cloud denoising as the problem of disentangling the noise factor from its latent representation. The overall denoising pipeline is shown in Fig. 3.

3.2   Flow-Based Denoising Method

We consider the point cloud denoising problem from the perspective of distribution learning and disentanglement. We suppose the distribution of noisy point set $\tilde{\mathcal{P}}$ is the joint distribution of clean point set $\mathcal{P} = \{p_i\}$ and noise $\mathcal{O}$. Given a dataset of observation $\tilde{\mathcal{P}}$, we aim to learn a bijective mapping f_θ, which is parameterized by θ to approximate the data distribution:

$$\tilde{z} = f_\theta(\tilde{\mathcal{P}}) = f_\theta(\mathcal{P}, \mathcal{O}), \tag{1}$$

where $\tilde{z} \sim p_\vartheta(\tilde{z})$ is a random variable with known probability density. Note that $p_\vartheta(\tilde{z})$ follows a factorized distribution [10], such that $p_\vartheta(\tilde{z}) = \prod_i p_\vartheta(\tilde{z}_i)$ (i.e. the dimensions of $\tilde{z}$ are independent of each other).

We further assume that f_θ can simultaneously learn to embed noise factor and intrinsic structure of point cloud into a disentangled latent code space (i.e. where noise is uniquely controlled by some dimensions). Based on this assumption, we approximate the clean latent representation z by

$$\hat{z} = \psi(\tilde{z}), \tag{2}$$

where $\psi : \mathbb{R}^D \to \mathbb{R}^D$ is a disentanglement function defined in latent space, and $\hat{z}$ is an estimation of z. In this way, clean point samples $\hat{\mathcal{P}}$ can be derived by taking the inverse transformation

$$\hat{\mathcal{P}} = g_\theta\left(\hat{z}\right), \tag{3}$$

where $g_\theta(\cdot) = f_\theta^{-1}(\cdot)$. The bijective mapping f_θ, which consists of a sequence of invertible transformations $f_\theta^1, \cdots, f_\theta^L$, is referred to as *normalizing flows*. Denote by h^l the output of l-th flow transformation. Then h^{l+1} can be formulated as

$$h^{l+1} = f_\theta^{l+1}\left(h^l\right), \tag{4}$$

where $h^0 = \tilde{\mathcal{P}}$, $h^L = \tilde{z}$. Applying the change-of-variables formula and chain rule [10], the output probability density of $\tilde{\mathcal{P}}$ can be obtained as

$$
\begin{aligned}
\log p(\tilde{\mathcal{P}}; \theta) &= \log p_\vartheta\left(f_\theta(\tilde{\mathcal{P}})\right) + \log\left|\det\frac{\partial f_\theta}{\partial \tilde{\mathcal{P}}}(\tilde{\mathcal{P}})\right| \\
&= \log p_\vartheta\left(f_\theta(\tilde{\mathcal{P}})\right) + \sum_{l=1}^{L}\log\left|\det\frac{\partial f_\theta^l}{\partial h^l}\left(h^l\right)\right|,
\end{aligned}
\tag{5}
$$

where $\left|\det\frac{\partial f_\theta}{\partial \tilde{\mathcal{P}}}(\tilde{\mathcal{P}})\right|$ is the log-absolute-determinant of the Jacobian of mapping f_θ, which measures the volume change [10] caused by f_θ. f_θ can be trained with the maximum likelihood principle using the gradient descent technique.

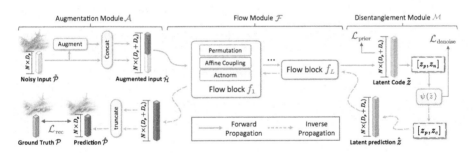

Fig. 3. The proposed flow-based denoising framework. Given a noisy point set $\tilde{\mathcal{P}} = \{\tilde{p}_i \in \mathbb{R}^{D_p}\}$, we first augment it with an additional D_a dimensional variable $\bar{p}_i \in \mathbb{R}^{D_a}$ and obtain augmented point $h_i = [\tilde{p}_i, \bar{p}_i] \in \mathbb{R}^{D_p + D_a}$. We transform the augmented points $\tilde{\mathcal{H}} = \{h_i\}$ to latent distribution $\tilde{z} \sim p_\vartheta(\tilde{z})$ by NFs. To estimate noise-free latent point $\hat{z}$, we filter out the noise factor from noisy $\tilde{z}$. We restore the noise-free point set $\hat{\mathcal{P}}$ from $\hat{z}$ by the inverse propagation of $\mathcal{F}$, which utilizes the invertible capacity of NFs. Finally, the coordinates of the clean point set are derived from truncating the first D_p dimensions and discarding the augmented D_a dimensions.

3.3   Augmentation Module

Dimensional Bottleneck. To maintain the analytical invertibility, flow models impose more constraints on the network architecture than non-invertible models. One particular constraint is that the flow components $f^1, \cdots, f^L$ must output the same dimensionality D with the input data (where $D = 3$ for raw point clouds). The network bandwidth bottleneck sacrifices the model expressiveness, as shown in Fig. 4a.

Previous works [11,25] generally use a squeezing operator to alleviate this limitation by exchanging spatial dimensions for feature channels. However, the squeezing operator is mainly designed for image manipulation. It is non-trivial to adopt squeezing to point cloud due to the unorder nature in point sets.

Dimension Augmentation. Inspired by VFlow [6], we resolve the bottleneck by increasing the dimensionality of input data. To be specific, for each input point $\tilde{p}_i \in \mathbb{R}^{D_p}$ in $\tilde{\mathcal{P}}$, we augment it with a random variable $\bar{p}_i \in \mathbb{R}^{D_a}$. This process is modeled by an augmentation module $\mathcal{A}$:

$$\bar{p}_i = \mathcal{A}\left(\tilde{p}_i, \mathcal{N}\left(\tilde{p}_i\right)\right), \bar{\mathcal{P}} = \{\bar{p}_i\}, \tag{6}$$

where $\mathcal{N}\left(\tilde{p}_i\right)$ denotes the k-nearest neighbors of $\tilde{p}_i$, and $\bar{\mathcal{P}}$ represents the set of augmented dimensions. We feed the augmented point set $\tilde{\mathcal{H}} = \{h_i = [\tilde{p}_i, \bar{p}_i]\}$ as input of flow module $\mathcal{F}$, and the underlying NFs become $\tilde{z} = f_\theta(\tilde{\mathcal{H}})$, where $\tilde{z} \in \mathbb{R}^{D_p + D_a}$, as shown in Fig. 4b.

Variational Augmentation. To model the distribution of the augmented data space, VFlow [6] resorts to optimizing the evidence lower bound observation (ELBO) on the log-likelihood of augmented data as an alternative of Eq. 5:

$$\log p(\tilde{\mathcal{P}}; \theta) \geq \mathbb{E}_{q(\bar{\mathcal{P}} | \tilde{\mathcal{P}}; \phi)} \left[\log p(\tilde{\mathcal{P}}, \bar{\mathcal{P}}; \theta) - \log q(\bar{\mathcal{P}} \mid \tilde{\mathcal{P}}; \phi)\right], \tag{7}$$

where $q(\bar{\mathcal{P}} \mid \tilde{\mathcal{P}}; \phi)$ indicates the distribution of augmented data, which is modeled by the augmentation module $\mathcal{A}$, θ and ϕ denote the parameters of $\mathcal{F}$ and $\mathcal{A}$, respectively. We briefly explain Eq. (7) in supplementary material.

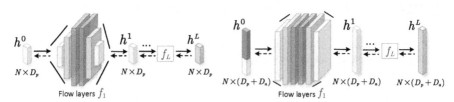

(a) Traditional flow transformation   (b) Augmented flow transformation

Fig. 4. Illustration of dimension augmentation. (a) The dimensionality of raw data limits the bandwidth of the network in vanilla flows. (b) Augmented flows can share considerable information among flow blocks, thereby improving model expressiveness.

3.4 Flow Module

The flow module $\mathcal{F}$ transforms augmented points $\tilde{\mathcal{H}} = \{h_i\} \in \mathbb{R}^{N \times (D_p + D_a)}$ from the Euclidean space to the latent space, and vice versa.

The architecture of flow module $\mathcal{F}$ comprises L blocks, where each block consists of a couple of flow components, as shown in Fig. 3. Each component is designed to satisfy the efficient invertibility and tractable Jacobian, including affine coupling layer [11], actnorm [25], and permutation layer [25]. The descriptions of each flow component are detailed in supplementary material.

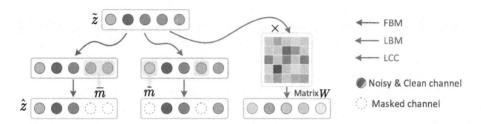

Fig. 5. Illustration of different filtering strategies.

3.5 Disentanglement Module

Let z_p and z_n be the clean point and noisy parts of the latent point $\tilde{z}$, i.e. $\tilde{z} = [z_p, z_n]$. We aim to disentangle noise z_n from $\tilde{z}$ by a smooth operator $\psi :$ $\mathbb{R}^D \to \mathbb{R}^D$

$$\hat{z} = [z_p, z_c] = \psi(\tilde{z}), \tag{8}$$

where z_c is the denoised feature and $D = D_p + D_a$. $\hat{z}$ denotes the prediction of noise-free point representation, which is fed as the input of inverse propagation of flow module $\mathcal{F}$. However, how to implement $\psi(\cdot)$ is non-trivial. In this paper, we investigate three types of noise filtering strategies (Fig. 5) to formulate $\psi(\cdot)$ as follows:

Fix Binary Mask (FBM). Similiar to a previous work [29], we explicitly divides the channels of latent code into two groups, i.e. clean and noisy channels. FBM simply sets noisy channels to 0 by

$$\psi(\tilde{z}) = \bar{m} \odot \tilde{z}, \tag{9}$$

$$\mathcal{L}_{\text{denoise}} = \mathcal{L}_{\text{FBM}} = 0, \tag{10}$$

where $\bar{m} \in \{0, 1\}^D$ is a fixed binary mask specified by the user, $\odot$ denotes element-wise product and $\mathcal{L}_{\text{FBM}}$ is the corresponding loss function of FBM.

Learnable Binary Mask (LBM). We employ a soft masking to latent $\tilde{z}$ by

$$\psi(\tilde{z}) = \tilde{m} \odot \tilde{z}, \tag{11}$$

$$\mathcal{L}_{\text{denoise}} = \mathcal{L}_{\text{LBM}} = |\tilde{m}\,(1 - \tilde{m})|\,, \tag{12}$$

where $\tilde{m} \in \mathbb{R}^D$ is a learnable parameter, $|\cdot|$ denotes L_1 norm, and $\mathcal{L}_{\text{LBM}}$ is the corresponding loss of LBM that encourages $\tilde{m}$ to approximate the binary mask.

Latent Code Consistency (LCC). We minimize the latent representation between clean points and noisy points by

$$\psi(\tilde{z}) = W\tilde{z}, \tag{13}$$

$$\mathcal{L}_{\text{denoise}} = \mathcal{L}_{\text{LCC}} = \sum_{i=1}^{N} \|W\tilde{z}^{(i)} - z^{(i)}\|, \tag{14}$$

where $W \in \mathbb{R}^{D \times D}$ is a learnable matrix to transform $\tilde{z}$, N is the number of points, $\|\cdot\|$ denotes L_2 norm, and $z = f_\theta(\mathcal{P})$ is the latent representation encoded from reference points $\mathcal{P}$ by the forward propagation of flow (similar to Eq. (1)). $\mathcal{L}_{\text{LCC}}$ is the corresponding loss of LCC that encourages the transformed $\hat{z}$ to be consistent with noise-free representation z, which is analogous to perceptual loss [23] that evaluates difference on high-level features.

3.6   Joint Loss Function

We present an objective function for training PD-Flow that combines the *reconstruction loss*, *prior loss* and *denoise loss* (Sect. 3.5) as follows:

Reconstruction loss quantifies the similarity between the generated points $\hat{\mathcal{P}} \in \mathbb{R}^{N \times D_p}$ and reference clean points $\mathcal{P} \in \mathbb{R}^{N \times D_p}$. In this paper, we use the Earth Mover's Distance (EMD) metric as $\mathcal{L}_{\text{rec}}$ by minimizing

$$\mathcal{L}_{\text{rec}} = \mathcal{L}_{\text{EMD}}(\hat{\mathcal{P}}, \mathcal{P}) = \min_{\varphi:\hat{\mathcal{P}} \to \mathcal{P}} \sum_{\hat{p} \in \hat{\mathcal{P}}} \|\hat{p} - \varphi\,(\hat{p})\|\,, \tag{15}$$

where $\varphi : \hat{\mathcal{P}} \to \mathcal{P}$ is a bijection and $\|\cdot\|$ denotes L_2 norm.

Prior loss optimizes the transformation capability of flow module $\mathcal{F}$ by maximizing the likelihood of observation $\tilde{\mathcal{P}}$. We implement the prior loss by minimizing the negative ELBO in Eq. (7):

$$\mathcal{L}_{\text{prior}}(\tilde{\mathcal{P}}) = \mathcal{L}(\tilde{\mathcal{P}}; \theta, \phi) = - \left[\log p(\tilde{\mathcal{P}}, \bar{\mathcal{P}}; \theta) - \log q(\bar{\mathcal{P}} \mid \tilde{\mathcal{P}}; \phi) \right] \tag{16}$$

where $\bar{\mathcal{P}} = \mathcal{A}(\tilde{\mathcal{P}})$ are augmented dimensions (Sect. 3.3). Intuitively, $\mathcal{L}_{\text{prior}}$ encourages the input points $\tilde{\mathcal{P}}$ to reach high probability under the predefined prior $p_\vartheta(\tilde{z})$.

Total Loss. Combining the preceding formulas, our method can be trained in an end-to-end manner by minimizing

$$\mathcal{L}\,(\theta, \phi, \sigma) = \alpha \mathcal{L}_{\text{rec}} + \beta \mathcal{L}_{\text{prior}} + \gamma \mathcal{L}_{\text{denoise}}, \tag{17}$$

where θ, ϕ and σ denotes the network parameters of $\mathcal{F}$, $\mathcal{A}$ and $\mathcal{M}$, respectively. And, α, β, γ are the hyper-parameters to balance the loss.

3.7   Discussion

Benefit of Dimension Augmentation. The dimension augmentation setting provides extra benefits to vanilla flows: (i) The augmented NFs are generalization of vanilla flows, where the extra dimensionality D_a can be freely adjusted by users, allowing it to model more complex function. (ii) The augmented dimensions afford more flexibility and expressiveness to intermediate point features (i.e. h^l in Sect. 3.2) between flow transformations, avoiding extracting high dimensional features from scratch. (iii) The augmented dimensions increase the degrees of freedom for noise filtering in the disentanglement phase, which is particularly helpful because raw point clouds contain only one dimension of $D_p = 3$. We investigate the influence of dimension augmentation in Sect. 4.3.

Table 1. Comparison of denoising algorithms on PUSet.

#Points	10K									50K								
Noise level	1%			2%			3%			1%			2%			3%		
Method	CD 10^{-4}	P2M 10^{-4}	HD 10^{-3}	CD 10^{-4}	P2M 10^{-4}	HD 10^{-3}	CD 10^{-4}	P2M 10^{-4}	HD 10^{-3}	CD 10^{-4}	P2M 10^{-4}	HD 10^{-3}	CD 10^{-4}	P2M 10^{-4}	HD 10^{-3}	CD 10^{-4}	P2M 10^{-4}	HD 10^{-3}
Jet [5]	3.47	1.20	1.58	4.83	1.89	2.97	6.15	2.86	7.00	0.82	0.19	0.90	2.38	1.35	3.36	5.64	4.16	9.05
GPF [30]	3.28	1.17	1.52	4.18	1.54	3.45	5.37	2.75	8.14	0.76	0.23	1.42	2.04	0.94	4.25	3.82	2.87	10.4
MRPCA [34]	3.14	1.01	1.77	3.87	1.26	2.59	5.13	2.03	4.84	0.70	0.12	0.79	2.11	1.06	3.21	5.64	3.97	7.65
GLR [50]	2.79	0.92	1.16	3.66	1.14	2.88	4.84	2.08	6.80	0.71	0.18	0.93	1.61	0.85	4.90	3.74	2.67	11.7
PCNet [41]	3.57	1.15	1.54	7.54	3.92	6.25	13.0	8.92	13.9	0.95	0.27	2.21	1.56	0.62	9.84	2.32	1.32	8.42
GPDNet [37]	3.75	1.33	3.03	8.00	4.50	6.08	13.4	9.33	13.5	1.97	1.09	1.94	5.08	3.84	7.56	9.65	8.14	16.7
Pointfilter [51]	2.86	0.75	2.87	3.97	1.30	6.21	4.94	2.14	9.26	0.82	0.24	2.38	1.46	0.77	4.58	2.25	1.44	8.70
DMR [32]	4.54	1.70	6.72	5.04	2.13	7.02	5.87	2.86	8.60	1.17	0.46	2.26	1.58	0.81	4.29	2.45	1.54	7.32
Score [33]	2.52	0.46	4.30	3.68	1.08	5.78	4.69	1.94	10.5	0.71	0.15	2.30	**1.28**	0.57	4.95	**1.92**	1.05	9.30
Ours	**2.12**	**0.38**	**1.36**	**3.25**	**1.02**	**3.71**	**4.45**	**2.05**	**5.31**	**0.65**	0.16	**1.71**	**1.18**	0.60	2.58	1.94	1.26	5.21

Although the augmented dimensions increase the network size of flow module $\mathcal{F}$, the overhead is only marginal. The computation overhead mainly depends on the hidden layer size D_h of the internal transformation unit of $\mathcal{F}$ instead of the output dimensionality $D_p + D_a$.

Unified Noise Disentanglement Pipeline. Considering the invertible property of NFs, raw points $\tilde{\mathcal{P}}$ and latent $\tilde{z}$ share the identical information in different domains. We only manipulate the point features in the disentanglement module throughout the whole denoising pipeline, demonstrating the feature disentanglement capability of NFs.

Additionally, we do not explicitly introduce extra network modules to predict point-wise displacement [41] or upsample to a target resolution [32] for point generation. Utilizing the flow invertibility can share parameters between forward and inverse propagations, which help us to reduce the network size and avoid the use of a decoding module.

4   Experiments

4.1   Datasets

We evaluate our method on the following datasets: (i) **PUSet.** This dataset is a subset of PUNet [49] provided by [33], which contains 40 meshes for training and 20 meshes for evaluation. (ii) **DMRSet.** This dataset collects meshes from

ModelNet40 [47] provided by [32], which contains 91 meshes for training and 60 meshes for evaluation. These point clouds are perturbed by Gaussian noise of various noise levels at resolutions ranging from 10K to 50K points.

We implement PD-Flow with the PyTorch framework. The training settings, datasets and network configurations are detailed in the supplementary material.

4.2   Comparisons with State-of-the-Art Methods

Evaluation Metrics. We use four evaluation metrics in quantitative comparison, including (i) Chamfer distance (CD), (ii) Point-to-mesh (P2M) distance, (iii) Hausdorff distance (HD), and (iv) Uniformity (Uni). The detailed description of each metric is available in the supplementary material.

Quantitative Comparison. We compare our method with traditional methods (including Jet [5], MRPCA [34], GPF [30], GLR [50]) and state-of-the-art deep learning-based methods (including PointCleanNet (PCNet) [41], Pointfilter [51], DMRDenoise (DMR) [32], GPDNet [37], ScoreDenoise (Score) [33]).

We use LCC as the default noise filter. The benchmark is based on 10K and 50K points disturbed by isotropic Gaussian noise with the standard deviation of noise ranging from 1% to 3% of the shape's bounding sphere radius.

As shown in Table 1, traditional methods can achieve good performance in some cases depending on the manual tuning parameters, but they have difficulty in extending to all metrics. PCNet [41] and DMRDenoise [32] perform less satisfactory under 10K points, while GPDNet [37] fails to handle high noise levels.

Table 2. Comparison of uniformity on 10K points under various Gaussian noise levels. This metric is estimated in the local area of different radii p. Besides, we also show the corresponding CD loss ($\times 10^{-4}$) of the full point clouds.

Noise	Methods	CD	Uniformity for different p				
			0.4%	0.6%	0.8%	1.0%	1.2%
1%	MRPCA [34]	3.14	1.89	2.30	2.42	2.59	2.83
	DMR [32]	4.54	4.02	5.06	6.02	7.03	7.95
	Score [33]	2.52	1.10	1.38	1.69	2.05	2.45
	Ours	**2.12**	**0.33**	**0.43**	**0.55**	**0.71**	**0.89**
2%	MRPCA [34]	3.87	2.21	2.56	2.85	2.97	3.14
	DMR [32]	5.04	3.45	4.04	4.68	5.35	6.03
	Score [33]	3.68	1.95	2.39	2.91	3.44	4.04
	Ours	**3.25**	**0.89**	**1.18**	**1.49**	**1.83**	**2.18**
3%	MRPCA [34]	5.13	2.28	**2.29**	**2.32**	**2.45**	**2.60**
	DMR [32]	5.87	3.81	4.53	5.16	5.85	6.55
	Score [33]	4.69	4.19	5.42	6.43	7.46	8.37
	Ours	**4.45**	**1.80**	**2.33**	2.83	3.34	3.87

In most cases, our method outperforms Pointfilter [51] and ScoreDenoise [33], especially in CD and HD metrics. The quantitative comparison on DMRSet and more results of various noise types are provided in the supplementary material.

Furthermore, we present the quantitative results on uniformity metric under various noise levels in Table 2. Although MRPCA [34] achieves the best uniformity under 3% Gaussian noise, it fails to keep good generation accuracy on CD metric. Compared with other state-of-the-art methods [32,33], our method considerably promotes the uniformity of generated points.

Qualitative Comparison. Figure 6 visualizes the qualitative denoising results between ours and competitive works. We observe that our method achieves the most robust estimation under high noise corruption. In particular, our method can keep consistent density across different regions and avoid clustering phenomenon, resulting in better uniformity.

We also compare the denoising result under the *Paris-rue-Madame* [44] dataset, which contains real-world scene data captured by laser scanner. As shown in Fig. 7, our method improves the surface smoothness and preserves better details than DMRDenoise [32] and ScoreDenoise [33].

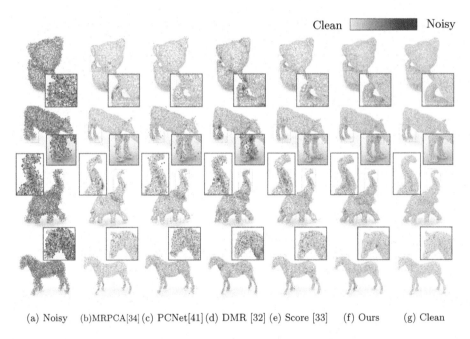

(a) Noisy   (b)MRPCA[34] (c) PCNet[41] (d) DMR [32] (e) Score [33]   (f) Ours   (g) Clean

Fig. 6. Visual comparison of state-of-the-art denoising methods under 2% isotropic Gaussian noise. The color of each point indicates its reconstruction error measured by P2M distance. See supplementary material for visual results under more noise settings.

4.3   Ablation Study

We conduct ablation studies to demonstrate the contribution of the network design of PD-Flow. The evaluation is based on 10K points with 2% Gaussian noise in PUSet.

Flow Architecture. The number of parameters mainly depends on the depth of flow module $\mathcal{F}$ (e.g., the number of flow blocks L). As shown in Table 3, the fitting capacity improve as L increases. However, when L increases to 12, the relative performance boost becomes marginal, with the cost of a large number of network parameters and training instability. We find that $L = 8$ achieves the best balance between performance and training stability.

To verify the effectiveness of inverse propagation of $\mathcal{F}$, we replace the inverse pass with MLP layers, which are commonly used in other deep-learning-based methods [32,41]. As shown in Table 3, the inverse pass achieves better generation quality without introducing extra network parameters, which demonstrates the feasibility of flow invertibility. The similar result is also verified by the "forward + mlp" curve in Fig. 8a, where using MLP as point generator leads to degraded performance.

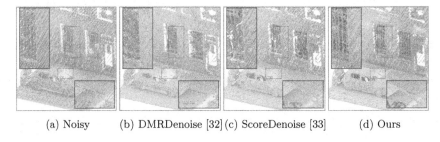

(a) Noisy   (b) DMRDenoise [32] (c) ScoreDenoise [33]   (d) Ours

Fig. 7. Visual results of our denoiser on the real-world dataset *Paris-rue-Madame* [44].

Table 3. Ablation study of flow architectures.

Pass	#Flow block	#Params	CD	P2M
Forward + Inverse	4	299K	3.55	1.22
Forward + Inverse	8	470K	**3.25**	**1.03**
Forward + Inverse	12	647K	3.57	1.23
Forward + MLP	8	578K	4.65	2.14

Dimension Augmentation. To investigate the impact of the number of augmentation channels D_a on model convergence, we show the training curve in Fig. 8a. The baseline model with $D_a = 0$ (i.e. vanilla flows) fails to converge to reasonable results. As the D_a increases, we observe faster convergence and better fitting capability. The similar trending can also be observed in quantitative evaluation under different D_a. This indicates that the dimension augmentation makes a key contribution to activate the denoising capability of NFs.

Effect on Noise Filtering Strategies. We compare the performances of various filtering strategies with $D_a = 32$. As shown in Table 4, all these strategies can achieve competitive performance, and the LCC filter achieves the best results. For LBM with $D_a = 16$ to $D_a = 64$, we observe that about 2/3 channels approximate zeros in $\tilde{m}$ after training.

We further investigate the impact of the number of masked channels D_m on FBM filter in Fig. 8b, which shows the training curve under different D_m settings. For $D_m = 0$, the flow network produces the same result as input due to the invertible nature of NFs. For $D_m = 1$ to $D_m = 16$, our method can converge to reasonable performance and presents little differences in convergence. This indicates that our method can adaptively embed noisy and clean channels to disentangled position, even if D_m is set to a low value. For $D_a = 32$ and $D_m \geq 32$, the latent code space only contains 3 or less channels to embed intrinsic information of clean points. We can observe that the insufficient channels for clean point embedding obviously lead to degrade performance, demonstrating that the dimension of latent point has great impact on model expressiveness

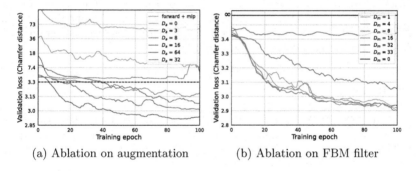

(a) Ablation on augmentation   (b) Ablation on FBM filter

Fig. 8. (a) Loss curves of training PD-Flow with augmentation channels and LCC noise filter. For better visualization, we use linear mapping below dashed line and non-linear mapping above dashed line. (b) Loss curves of training PD-Flow with FBM noise filter. All these models are augmented with $D_a = 32$ and vary in mask channels D_m.

Table 4. Ablation study of different filtering strategies.

#Points, Noise	10K,1%		10K,2%		10K,3%	
Strategy	CD	P2M	CD	P2M	CD	P2M
FBM	2.22	0.44	3.40	1.14	4.56	2.16
LBM (w/o $\mathcal{L}_{\mathrm{LBM}}$)	2.54	0.62	3.65	1.38	5.06	2.32
LBM (w/ $\mathcal{L}_{\mathrm{LBM}}$)	2.37	0.53	3.50	1.23	4.80	2.23
LCC (w/o $\mathcal{L}_{\mathrm{LCC}}$)	2.32	0.45	3.48	1.19	4.62	2.20
LCC (w/ $\mathcal{L}_{\mathrm{LCC}}$)	**2.13**	**0.38**	**3.26**	**1.03**	**4.50**	**2.09**

and denoising flexibility. In Sect. 3.5, we introduce $\mathcal{L}_{\text{denoise}}$ as a regularization term to improve noise disentanglment capability. Table 4 compares the effects of $\mathcal{L}_{\text{denoise}}$ term. The "LBM (w/o $\mathcal{L}_{\text{LBM}}$)" term means that the experiment is trained without the $\mathcal{L}_{\text{LCC}}$ loss (Eq. (12)), but still uses LBM as the filter strategy (Eq. (11)). As shown in Table 4, both $\mathcal{L}_{\text{FBM}}$ and $\mathcal{L}_{\text{LCC}}$ loss make positive contributions to model performance.

5   Conclusion

In this paper, we present PD-Flow, a point cloud denoising framework that combines NFs and distribution disentanglement techniques. It learns to transform noise perturbation and clean points into a disentangled latent code space by leveraging NFs, whereas denoising is formulated as channel masking. To alleviate the dimensional bandwidth bottleneck and improve the network expressiveness, we propose to extend additional channels to latent variables by an dimension augmentation module. Extensive experiments and ablation studies illustrate that our method outperforms existing state-of-the-art methods in terms of generation quality across various noise levels.

Acknowledgements. This work was supported by the NSF of Guangdong Province (2019A1515010833, 2022A1515011573), the Natural Science Foundation of China (61725204) and Tsinghua University Initiative Scientific Research Program, China Postdoctoral Science Foundation (2021M701891).

References

1. Abdal, R., Zhu, P., Mitra, N.J., Wonka, P.: Styleflow: attribute-conditioned exploration of stylegan-generated images using conditional continuous normalizing flows. ACM Trans. Graphics (TOG) **40**(3), 1–21 (2021)
2. Alexa, M., Behr, J., Cohen-Or, D., Fleishman, S., Levin, D., Silva, C.T.: Point set surfaces. In: Proceedings of the Conference on Visualization 2001, pp. 21–28. IEEE Computer Society, USA (2001)
3. Alexa, M., Behr, J., Cohen-Or, D., Fleishman, S., Levin, D., Silva, C.T.: Computing and rendering point set surfaces. IEEE Trans. Visual Comput. Graphics **9**(1), 3–15 (2003)
4. Avron, H., Sharf, A., Greif, C., Cohen-Or, D.: ℓ_1-sparse reconstruction of sharp point set surfaces. ACM Trans. Graphics (TOG) **29**(5), 1–12 (2010)
5. Cazals, F., Pouget, M.: Estimating differential quantities using polynomial fitting of osculating jets. Comput. Aided Geometric Des. **22**(2), 121–146 (2005)
6. Chen, J., Lu, C., Chenli, B., Zhu, J., Tian, T.: Vflow: more expressive generative flows with variational data augmentation. In: International Conference on Machine Learning, pp. 1660–1669 (2020)
7. Chen, R.T., Rubanova, Y., Bettencourt, J., Duvenaud, D.: Neural ordinary differential equations. arXiv preprint arXiv:1806.07366 (2018)
8. Deschaud, J.E., Goulette, F.: Point cloud non local denoising using local surface descriptor similarity. IAPRS **38**(3A), 109–114 (2010)

9. Digne, J., De Franchis, C.: The bilateral filter for point clouds. Image Processing On Line **7**, 278–287 (2017)

10. Dinh, L., Krueger, D., Bengio, Y.: Nice: non-linear independent components estimation. arXiv preprint arXiv:1410.8516 (2014)

11. Dinh, L., Sohl-Dickstein, J., Bengio, S.: Density estimation using real NVP. In: 5th International Conference on Learning Representations, ICLR 2017 (2017)

12. Duan, C., Chen, S., Kovacevic, J.: 3d point cloud denoising via deep neural network based local surface estimation. In: 2019 IEEE International Conference on Acoustics, Speech, and Signal Processing, ICASSP 2019 - Proceedings, pp. 8553–8557, May 2019

13. Fleishman, S., Cohen-Or, D., Silva, C.T.: Robust moving least-squares fitting with sharp features. ACM Trans. Graphics (TOG) **24**(3), 544–552 (2005)

14. Gao, X., Hu, W., Guo, Z.: Graph-based point cloud denoising. In: 2018 IEEE Fourth International Conference on Multimedia Big Data (BigMM), pp. 1–6 (2018)

15. Grathwohl, W., Chen, R.T.Q., Bettencourt, J., Sutskever, I., Duvenaud, D.: FFJORD: free-form continuous dynamics for scalable reversible generative models. In: International Conference on Learning Representations (2019)

16. Guerrero, P., Kleiman, Y., Ovsjanikov, M., Mitra, N.J.: PCPNet: learning local shape properties from raw point clouds. Comput. Graphics Forum **37**(2), 75–85 (2018). https://doi.org/10.1111/cgf.13343

17. Hermosilla, P., Ritschel, T., Ropinski, T.: Total denoising: unsupervised learning of 3D point cloud cleaning. In: Proceedings of the IEEE International Conference on Computer Vision, pp. 52–60 (2019)

18. Hu, W., Gao, X., Cheung, G., Guo, Z.: Feature graph learning for 3D point cloud denoising. IEEE Trans. Signal Process. **68**, 2841–2856 (2020)

19. Huang, H., Li, D., Zhang, H., Ascher, U., Cohen-Or, D.: Consolidation of unorganized point clouds for surface reconstruction. ACM Trans. Graphics (TOG) **28**(5), 1–7 (2009)

20. Huang, H., Wu, S., Gong, M., Cohen-Or, D., Ascher, U., Zhang, H.: Edge-aware point set resampling. ACM Trans. Graphics (TOG) **32**(1), 1–12 (2013)

21. Huhle, B., Schairer, T., Jenke, P., Straßer, W.: Robust non-local denoising of colored depth data. In: 2008 IEEE Computer Society Conference on Computer Vision and Pattern Recognition Workshops, pp. 1–7 (2008)

22. Jenke, P., Wand, M., Bokeloh, M., Schilling, A., Straßer, W.: Bayesian point cloud reconstruction. In: Computer Graphics Forum, vol. 25, pp. 379–388 (2006)

23. Johnson, Justin, Alahi, Alexandre, Fei-Fei, Li.: Perceptual losses for real-time style transfer and super-resolution. In: Leibe, Bastian, Matas, Jiri, Sebe, Nicu, Welling, Max (eds.) ECCV 2016. LNCS, vol. 9906, pp. 694–711. Springer, Cham (2016). https://doi.org/10.1007/978-3-319-46475-6_43

24. Kalogerakis, E., Nowrouzezahrai, D., Simari, P., Singh, K.: Extracting lines of curvature from noisy point clouds. Comput. Aided Des. **41**, 282–292 (2009)

25. Kingma, D.P., Dhariwal, P.: Glow: generative flow with invertible 1x1 convolutions. In: Bengio, S., Wallach, H., Larochelle, H., Grauman, K., Cesa-Bianchi, N., Garnett, R. (eds.) Advances in Neural Information Processing Systems, vol. 31. Curran Associates, Inc. (2018)

26. Klokov, Roman, Boyer, Edmond, Verbeek, Jakob: Discrete point flow networks for efficient point cloud generation. In: Vedaldi, Andrea, Bischof, Horst, Brox, Thomas, Frahm, Jan-Michael. (eds.) ECCV 2020. LNCS, vol. 12368, pp. 694–710. Springer, Cham (2020). https://doi.org/10.1007/978-3-030-58592-1_41

27. Kumar, M., et al.: Videoflow: a flow-based generative model for video. arXiv preprint arXiv:1903.01434 **2**(5) (2019)

28. Lipman, Y., Cohen-Or, D., Levin, D., Tal-Ezer, H.: Parameterization-free projection for geometry reconstruction. ACM Trans. Graphics (TOG) **26**–es(3), 22 (2007)

29. Liu, Y., Anwar, S., Qin, Z., Ji, P., Caldwell, S., Gedeon, T.: Disentangling noise from images: a flow-based image denoising neural network. arXiv preprint arXiv:2105.04746 (2021)

30. Lu, X., Wu, S., Chen, H., Yeung, S.K., Chen, W., Zwicker, M.: GPF: GMM-inspired feature-preserving point set filtering. IEEE Trans. Visual Comput. Graphics **24**(8), 2315–2326 (2017)

31. Lugmayr, Andreas, Danelljan, Martin, Van Gool, Luc, Timofte, Radu: SRFlow: learning the super-resolution space with normalizing flow. In: Vedaldi, Andrea, Bischof, Horst, Brox, Thomas, Frahm, Jan-Michael. (eds.) ECCV 2020. LNCS, vol. 12350, pp. 715–732. Springer, Cham (2020). https://doi.org/10.1007/978-3-030-58558-7_42

32. Luo, S., Hu, W.: Differentiable manifold reconstruction for point cloud denoising. In: Proceedings of the 28th ACM International Conference on Multimedia, pp. 1330–1338 (2020)

33. Luo, S., Hu, W.: Score-based point cloud denoising. In: Proceedings of the IEEE/CVF International Conference on Computer Vision (ICCV), pp. 4583–4592, October 2021

34. Mattei, E., Castrodad, A.: Point cloud denoising via moving RPCA. In: Computer Graphics Forum, vol. 36, pp. 123–137. Wiley Online Library (2017)

35. Narváez, E.A.L., Narváez, N.E.L.: Point cloud denoising using robust principal component analysis. In: Proceedings of the First International Conference on Computer Graphics Theory and Applications (GRAPP), pp. 51–58 (2006)

36. Pauly, M., Gross, M.: Spectral processing of point-sampled geometry. In: Proceedings of the 28th Annual Conference on Computer Graphics and Interactive Techniques, pp. 379–386 (2001)

37. Pistilli, Francesca, Fracastoro, Giulia, Valsesia, Diego, Magli, Enrico: Learning graph-convolutional representations for point cloud denoising. In: Vedaldi, Andrea, Bischof, Horst, Brox, Thomas, Frahm, Jan-Michael. (eds.) ECCV 2020. LNCS, vol. 12365, pp. 103–118. Springer, Cham (2020). https://doi.org/10.1007/978-3-030-58565-5_7

38. Postels, J., Liu, M., Spezialetti, R., Van Gool, L., Tombari, F.: Go with the flows: mixtures of normalizing flows for point cloud generation and reconstruction. arXiv preprint arXiv:2106.03135 (2021)

39. Prenger, R., Valle, R., Catanzaro, B.: Waveglow: a flow-based generative network for speech synthesis. In: ICASSP 2019–2019 IEEE International Conference on Acoustics, Speech and Signal Processing (ICASSP), pp. 3617–3621 (2019)

40. Pumarola, A., Popov, S., Moreno-Noguer, F., Ferrari, V.: C-flow: conditional generative flow models for images and 3D point clouds. In: Proceedings of the IEEE/CVF Conference on Computer Vision and Pattern Recognition, pp. 7949–7958 (2020)

41. Rakotosaona, M.J., La Barbera, V., Guerrero, P., Mitra, N.J., Ovsjanikov, M.: Pointcleannet: learning to denoise and remove outliers from dense point clouds. In: Computer Graphics Forum, vol. 39, pp. 185–203. Wiley Online Library (2020)

42. Schall, O., Belyaev, A., Seidel, H.P.: Robust filtering of noisy scattered point data. In: Proceedings Eurographics/IEEE VGTC Symposium Point-Based Graphics, pp. 71–144 (2005)

43. Schoenenberger, Y., Paratte, J., Vandergheynst, P.: Graph-based denoising for time-varying point clouds. In: 2015 3DTV-Conference: The True Vision-Capture, Transmission and Display of 3D Video (3DTV-CON), pp. 1–4 (2015)

44. Serna, A., Marcotegui, B., Goulette, F., Deschaud, J.E.: Paris-rue-madame database: a 3d mobile laser scanner dataset for benchmarking urban detection, segmentation and classification methods. In: 4th International Conference on Pattern Recognition, Applications and Methods ICPRAM 2014 (2014)

45. Sun, Y., Schaefer, S., Wang, W.: Denoising point sets via l0 minimization. Comput. Aided Geomet. Des. **35**, 2–15 (2015)

46. Wang, R.F., Chen, W.Z., Zhang, S.Y., Zhang, Y., Ye, X.Z.: Similarity-based denoising of point-sampled surfaces. J. Zhejiang Univ.-Sci. A **9**(6), 807–815 (2008)

47. Wu, Z., Song, S., Khosla, A., Yu, F., Zhang, L., Tang, X., Xiao, J.: 3D shapenets: a deep representation for volumetric shapes. In: Proceedings of the IEEE conference on computer vision and pattern recognition, pp. 1912–1920 (2015)

48. Yang, G., Huang, X., Hao, Z., Liu, M.Y., Belongie, S., Hariharan, B.: Pointflow: 3D point cloud generation with continuous normalizing flows. In: Proceedings of the IEEE/CVF International Conference on Computer Vision, pp. 4541–4550 (2019)

49. Yu, L., Li, X., Fu, C.W., Cohen-Or, D., Heng, P.A.: Pu-net: point cloud upsampling network. In: Proceedings of the IEEE Conference on Computer Vision and Pattern Recognition, pp. 2790–2799 (2018)

50. Zeng, J., Cheung, G., Ng, M., Pang, J., Yang, C.: 3d point cloud denoising using graph laplacian regularization of a low dimensional manifold model. IEEE Trans. Image Process. **29**, 3474–3489 (2019)

51. Zhang, D., Lu, X., Qin, H., He, Y.: Pointfilter: point cloud filtering via encoder-decoder modeling. IEEE Trans. Visual Comput. Graphics **27**, 2015–2027 (2020)

52. Zheng, Q., et al.: Non-local scan consolidation for 3D urban scenes. ACM Trans. Graphics (TOG) **29**(4), 94 (2010)

SeedFormer: Patch Seeds Based Point Cloud Completion with Upsample Transformer

Haoran Zhou[1]([✉]), Yun Cao[2], Wenqing Chu[2], Junwei Zhu[2], Tong Lu[1], Ying Tai[2], and Chengjie Wang[2]

[1] State Key Laboratory for Novel Software Technology, Nanjing University, Nanjing, China
hrzhou98@gmail.com
[2] Youtu Lab, Tencent, Shenzhen, China

Abstract. Point cloud completion has become increasingly popular among generation tasks of 3D point clouds, as it is a challenging yet indispensable problem to recover the complete shape of a 3D object from its partial observation. In this paper, we propose a novel SeedFormer to improve the ability of detail preservation and recovery in point cloud completion. Unlike previous methods based on a global feature vector, we introduce a new shape representation, namely Patch Seeds, which not only captures general structures from partial inputs but also preserves regional information of local patterns. Then, by integrating seed features into the generation process, we can recover faithful details for complete point clouds in a coarse-to-fine manner. Moreover, we devise an Upsample Transformer by extending the transformer structure into basic operations of point generators, which effectively incorporates spatial and semantic relationships between neighboring points. Qualitative and quantitative evaluations demonstrate that our method outperforms state-of-the-art completion networks on several benchmark datasets. Our code is available at https://github.com/hrzhou2/seedformer.

Keywords: Point cloud completion · Patch seeds · Upsample transformer

1 Introduction

As a commonly-used and easily-acquired data format for describing 3D objects, point clouds have boosted wider research in computer vision for understanding 3D scenes and objects. However, raw point clouds, routinely captured by LiDAR scanners or RGB-D cameras, are inevitably sparse and incomplete due to the limited sensor resolution and self-occlusion. It is an indispensable step to recover complete point clouds from partial/incomplete data in real-world scenes for various downstream applications [16,20,24].

Supplementary Information The online version contains supplementary material available at https://doi.org/10.1007/978-3-031-20062-5_24.

| (a) Input | (b) GRNet | (c) SnowflakeNet | (d) SeedFormer | (e) GT |

Fig. 1. Visual comparison of point cloud completion results. Compared with GRNet [40] and SnowflakeNet [38], SeedFormer is better at preserving existing structures (grey bounding box) and recovering missing details (green bounding box). (Color figure online)

Recent years have witnessed an increasing number of approaches applying deep neural networks on point cloud completion. The dominant architecture [1,38,43] employs a general encoder-decoder structure where a global feature (or called shape code) is extracted from partial inputs and is used to generate a complete point cloud in the decoding phase. However, this global feature structure possesses two intrinsic drawbacks in its representation ability: (i) fine-grained details are easily lost in the pooling operations in the encoding phase and can hardly be recovered from a diluted global feature in the generation, and (ii) such a global feature is captured from a partial point cloud, thus representing only the "incomplete" information of the seen part, and is contrary to the objective of generating the complete shape.

Besides the overall network architecture, another problem is derived from the designs of point cloud generators. Unlike image inpainting which predicts RGB colors of the missing pixels, the 3D point generation is designed differently to predict (x, y, z) coordinates which are unstructured yet continuously distributed in the 3D space. This suggests that the desired points, which can describe the missing parts of the target object, have close spatial and semantic relationships with surrounding points in their local neighborhoods. However, existing methods, either using folding-based generators [34,39,41–43] or following a hierarchical structure with MLP/deconvolution implementations [11,27,38], attempt to process each point independently by splitting one target point into more. These designs neglect the distribution of existing points which results in poor recovery quality of geometric details (see in Figs. 1(b) and 1(c)).

To resolve the aforementioned problems, we propose a novel point cloud completion network, namely *SeedFormer*, with better detail preservation and recovery ability as shown in Fig. 1. Based on the designed *Patch Seeds* and *Upsample Transformer*, the decoding phase of our method consists of two main steps of: (i) first generating the complete shape from incomplete features in the seed generator, and (ii) then recovering fine-grained details in a coarse-to-fine manner. In the first stage, unlike previous methods using global features, we introduce Patch Seeds as a latent representation in the point cloud completion architecture. The Patch Seeds characterize the complete shape structure with learned features stored in local seeds. This helps generate more faithful details as it preserves regional information which is highly sparse in a global feature. Secondly, a new point generator is designed for both seed generator and the subsequent layers. Following the idea discussed before, we propose to integrate useful local information into the generation operations by aggregating neighboring points in the proposed Upsample Transformer. In particular, we formulate the generation of new points as a transformer-style self-attention weighted average of point features in the local field. This leads to a better understanding of local geometric features captured by semantic relationships. Qualitative and quantitative evaluations demonstrate the clear superiority of SeedFormer over the state-of-the-art methods on several widely-used public datasets. Our main contributions can be summarized as follows:

- We propose a novel SeedFormer for point cloud completion, greatly improving the performance of generating complete point clouds in terms of both semantic understanding and detail preservation.
- We introduce Patch Seeds as a new representation in the completion architecture to preserve regional information for recovering fine details.
- We design a new point generator, *i.e.* Upsample Transformer, by extending the transformer structure into basic operations of generating points.

2   Related Work

Voxelization-Based Shape Completion. The early attempts on 3D shape completion [3,10,25] rely on intermediate representations of voxel grids to describe 3D objects. It is a simple and direct way to apply powerful CNN structures on various 3D applications [15,18,30]. However, this kind of methods inevitably suffers from information loss, and the computational cost increases heavily with regard to voxel resolution. Alternatively, Xie *et al.* [40] propose to use gridding operations and 3D CNNs for coarse completion, followed by refinement steps to generate detailed structures.

Point Cloud Completion. Recently, state-of-the-art deep networks are designed to directly manipulate raw point cloud data, instead of introducing an intermediate representation. The pioneering work PointNet [21] proposes to apply MLPs independently on each point and subsequently aggregate features through pooling operations to achieve permutation invariance. Following this architecture, PCN [43] is the first learning-based method for point cloud completion, which adopts a similar encoder-decoder design with a global feature representing the input shape. It generates a complete point cloud from the global feature using MLPs and folding operations [41]. Focusing on the decoding phase of generating point clouds with more faithful details, several works [11,27,34] extend the generation process into multiple steps in a hierarchical structure. This coarse-to-fine strategy helps produce dense point clouds with details recovered gradually on the missing parts. Furthermore, Wang *et al.* [31] propose a cascaded refinement module to refine predicted points by computing a displacement offset. Similar ideas are also explored in [35,37,39,44]. In order to utilize supervision not only from 3D points but also in the 2D image domain, some other works [39,45] use rendered single-view images to guide the completion task. Among the aforementioned methods, the global feature design is widely used due to its efficiency and simplicity, while it still represents intrinsic drawbacks as we discussed before. PoinTr [42] proposes a set-to-set translation strategy which shares similar ideas with SeedFormer. However, PoinTr designs local proxies which are used for feature translation in transformer blocks. SeedFormer introduces Patch Seeds that can be propagated to the following upsample layers, focusing on the decoding process of recovering fine details from partial inputs.

Point Cloud Generators. Generating 3D points is a fundamental step for point cloud processing and can be generalized to wider research areas. Following PointNet, early generative models [1] use fully-connected layers to produce point coordinates directly from a latent representation in auto-encoders [14,23] or GANs [8]. Then, FoldingNet [41] presents a new type of generators by adding variations from a canonical 2D grid in the point deformation. It requires lower computational cost while assuming that 3D object lies on 2D-manifold. Following this design, [39] proposes a style-based folding operator by injecting shape information into point generation using a StyleGAN [12] design. Moreover, SnowflakeNet [38] proposes to generate new points by splitting parent point features through deconvolution. More recently, with the success of transformers in natural language processing [4,5,29,36], an increasing number of research have developed such architecture for encoding 3D point clouds. In this work, we further extend the application of transformer-based structure into the basic operations of point cloud generation in the decoding phase, which also represents a new pattern of point generators with local aggregation.

3 Method

3.1 Architecture Overview

The overall architecture of SeedFormer is shown in Fig. 2. We will introduce our method in detail as follows.

Encoder. Denote the input point cloud as $\mathcal{P} = \{\mathbf{p}_i | i = 1, 2, ..., N\} \in \mathbb{R}^{N \times 3}$ where N is the total number of points and $\mathbf{p}_i$ possesses the (x, y, z) coordinates. The encoder applies point transformer [46] and set abstraction layers [22] to extract features from the incomplete shape. The number of points is reduced progressively in each layer and then we obtain patch features $\mathcal{F}_p \in \mathbb{R}^{N_p \times C_p}$ and the corresponding patch center coordinates $\mathcal{P}_p \in \mathbb{R}^{N_p \times 3}$, which represent the local structures of the partial point cloud.

Seed Generator. Seed generator aims to predict the overall structure of the complete shape. It is designed to produce a coarse yet complete point cloud (seed points) as well as seed feature of each point which can capture regional information of local patterns. Given the extracted patch features $\mathcal{F}_p$ and center coordinates $\mathcal{P}_p$, we use Upsample Transformer (Sect. 3.3) to generate a new set of seed features:

$$\mathcal{F} = \text{UpTrans}(\mathcal{F}_p, \mathcal{P}_p). \tag{1}$$

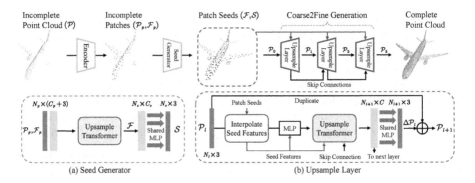

Fig. 2. The overall architecture of SeedFormer is shown in the upper part. (a) The seed generator is applied to obtain Patch Seeds which are subsequently propagated into each of the following layers by interpolating seed features. (b) Several upsample layers are used in the coarse-to-fine generation where an Upsample Transformer is applied for producing new points with skip-connection and seed feature encoding.

Then, we obtain the corresponding seed points $\mathcal{S} = \{x_i\}_{i=1}^{N_s} \in \mathbb{R}^{N_s \times 3}$ by applying MLPs on the generated seed features $\mathcal{F} = \{f_i\}_{i=1}^{N_s} \in \mathbb{R}^{N_s \times C_s}$. Grouping seed points and features together yields our Patch Seeds representation (more details are discussed in Sect. 3.2).

Coarse-to-Fine Generation. Afterwards, we follow the coarse-to-fine generation [11,38,41] to progressively recover faithful details in a hierarchical structure. This process consists of several upsample layers, each of which takes the previous point cloud and produces a dense output $\mathcal{P}_l$ ($l = 1, 2, ...$) with an upsampling rate of r_l where our Patch Seeds are closely involved. Specifically, each point in the input point cloud is upsampled into r_l points using the Upsample Transformer. The coarse point cloud $\mathcal{P}_0$ which is fed to the first layer is produced by fusing seeds $\mathcal{S}$ and the input point cloud $\mathcal{P}$ using Farthest Point Sampling (FPS) [22] to preserve partial structure of the original input [31].

3.2 Point Cloud Completion with Patch Seeds

Patch Seeds. Patch Seeds serve as a new shape representation in point cloud completion. It consists of both seed coordinates $\mathcal{S}$ and features $\mathcal{F}$ where each seed covers a small region around this point with seed feature containing semantic clues about this area. With rich information provided in seed features, SeedFormer can recover ambiguous missing details as shown in Fig. 1(d). Thus, compared with a global feature, the Patch Seeds representation possesses two advantages: (i) it can preserve *regional information of local patterns*, thus tiny details can be recovered in the complete point cloud; (ii) it represents the *complete shape structure* which is recovered from the partial input with explicit supervision (Sect. 3.4).

Usage. Throughout the following steps, Patch Seeds are incorporated into each of the upsample layers to provide regional information. Given an input point cloud $\mathcal{P}_l$, we propagate seed features to each point $p_i \in \mathcal{P}_l$ by interpolating

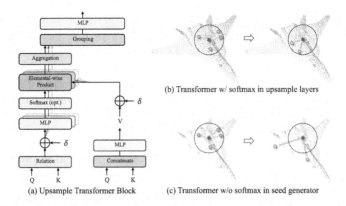

Fig. 3. (a) shows the design of our Upsample Transformer. The generation processes of new points around a target point (red) are shown: (b) an upsample layer can produce dense points within its local neighborhood; (c) the seed generator tends to generate seed points covering unseen parts of the object where the softmax function can be optionally disabled. (Color figure online)

feature values in its neighborhood $\mathcal{N}_s(i)$ (k nearest seeds of p_i). We use weighted average based on inverse distances [22] to compute the interpolated features:

$$s_i^l = \frac{\sum_{j \in \mathcal{N}_s(i)} \hat{d}_{ij} f_j}{\sum_{j \in \mathcal{N}_s(i)} \hat{d}_{ij}} \quad \text{where} \quad \hat{d}_{ij} = \frac{1}{d_{ij}}. \tag{2}$$

Here, d_{ij} denotes the distance between p_i and seed point x_j, and f_j is the corresponding seed feature. The interpolated features in this layer are $\{s_i^l\}_{i=1}^{N_l}$.

3.3 Upsample Transformer

Point Generator via Local Aggregation. The generation process in point cloud completion aims to produce a set of new points, either maintaining data fidelity by preserving geometric details or well inferring missing parts based on the existing shape structure. The commonly-used folding operations [34,39,41,43] are designed to upsample each point independently with fixed 2D variants which leads to poor detail recovery. Differently, our Upsample Transformer is designed to incorporate closely-related local information into the generation by aggregating features from neighboring points. To this end, based on the point transformer [46] structure, we propose to formulate the generation process of new points as a self-attention weighted average of point features in the local field (Fig. 3(a)). Moreover, following the idea of local aggregation, we can extend other successful encoder designs, e.g., PointNet++ [22], Transformers [29,46] or point cloud convolutions [28,32,47], into point generators in point cloud completion, to produce a new set of features with upsampled points. This is further evaluated in Sect. 4.5.

Upsample Layer. We first explain how to apply the designed Upsample Transformer in an upsample layer (Fig. 2(b)). Given the input points $\mathcal{P}_l \in \mathbb{R}^{N_l \times 3}$ and the corresponding interpolated seed features $\{s_i^l\}_{i=1}^{N_l}$, we concatenate them and apply a shared MLP to form the point-wise queries $\{q_i^l\}_{i=1}^{N_l}$. Following [38], we use the output features from the previous layer as keys $\{k_i^l\}_{i=1}^{N_l}$ in the transformer. It is used to preserve learned features of the existing points in the input. Then, the values $\{v_i^l\}_{i=1}^{N_l}$ are obtained by applying a MLP on the concatenated keys and queries. Upsample Transformer applies a channel-wise attention using the subtraction relation in a local neighborhood $\mathcal{N}(i)$ (k nearest neighbors) of each point:

$$\hat{a}_{ijm} = \alpha_m(\beta(q_i^l) - \gamma(k_j^l) + \delta), j \in \mathcal{N}(i). \tag{3}$$

Here, α_m, β and γ are feature mapping functions (*i.e.*, MLPs) to produce attention vectors. δ is a positional encoding vector to learn spatial relations. For each upsampled point relating to the centered point p_i, a specific kernel α_m is defined where $m = 1, 2, ..., r_l$ indicates one of the r_l generation processes in this layer ($r_l N_l = N_{l+1}$). Each kernel learns a certain geometric pattern of local characteristics which outputs a separate group of self-attention weights to form a new point. In addition, to normalize the computed weights into a balanced scale, $\hat{a}_{ijm}$ is applied by a softmax function:

$$a_{ijm} = \frac{\exp(\hat{a}_{ijm})}{\sum_{j \in \mathcal{N}(i)} \exp(\hat{a}_{ijm})}. \tag{4}$$

Then, we compute the generated point features by combining weights with the duplicated values:

$$h_{im} = \sum_{j \in \mathcal{N}(i)} a_{ijm} * (\psi(v_j^l) + \delta), \tag{5}$$

where ψ is also a feature mapping function and $*$ denotes the elemental-wise product. Grouping all h_{im} from each kernel yields our produced upsampled point features $\mathcal{H}_l = \{h_{im} | i = 1, 2, ... N_l; m = 1, 2, ..., r_l\} \in \mathbb{R}^{r_l N_l \times C}$. $\mathcal{H}_l$ also serves as the keys $\{k_i^{l+1}\}_{i=1}^{N_{l+1}}$ of next layer in the skip connection. Finally, we apply shared MLPs on point features to obtain a set of point displacement offsets $\Delta \mathcal{P}_l$. The output point cloud is defined as $\mathcal{P}_{l+1} = \hat{\mathcal{P}}_l + \Delta \mathcal{P}_l$, where $\hat{\mathcal{P}}_l$ is the duplicated point cloud, for both refining existing points and generating new points.

Positional Encoding with Seed Features. The basic positional encoding in the self-attention computations is designed to capture spatial relations between 3D points [46]. Besides, since the introduced seeds contain regional features with regard to the seed positions, we encode the interpolated features into *regional* encoding as follows:

$$\delta = \rho(p_i - p_j) + \theta(s_i - s_j). \tag{6}$$

Here, δ encodes both positional relation and seed feature relation between p_i and p_j. ρ and θ are encoding functions using a two-layer MLP.

Transformer Without Softmax. Similarly, Upsample Transformer is also used in the seed generator but is implemented without skip connection and seed features (Fig. 2(a)). Generating seeds involves a different objective of producing seed points which can predict missing regions and cover the complete shape structure. As shown in Fig. 3(c), when the input point cloud represents an incomplete shape, it is essential for the seed generator to produce seed points outside the local neighborhood. However, the standard transformer structure represents an intrinsic limitation that the softmax normalization explicitly produces attention weights within a specific range of $(0, 1)$. This may limit the learning ability especially in the seed generator. To solve this, we simply remove the softmax function in the transformer; that is, $a_{ijm} = \hat{a}_{ijm}$ is applied without normalization. The experiments in Sect. 4.5 show that it is easier to generate better seed points by disabling the softmax function or using other alternatives.

3.4 Loss Function

We use Chamfer Distance (CD) as our loss function to measure the distance between two unordered point sets [6]. To ensure that the generated seeds S can cover the complete shape, we down-sample the ground-truth point cloud to the same point number as S and compute the corresponding CD loss between them. The same loss function is also applied to each output $\mathcal{P}_l$ separately in the upsample layers. Then, we define the sum of all CDs as the completion loss $\mathcal{L}_{comp}$. Besides, following [33], we compute the partial matching loss $\mathcal{L}_{part}$ on the final predicted result to preserve the shape structure of the input point cloud. The total training loss is defined as:

$$\mathcal{L} = \mathcal{L}_{comp} + \mathcal{L}_{part}. \tag{7}$$

4 Evaluation

4.1 Implementation Details

The SeedFormer encoder applies two layers of set abstraction [22] and obtain $N_p = 128$ patches of the incomplete point cloud. Then, in the seed generator, we produce a set of seed features $\mathcal{F} \in \mathbb{R}^{N_s \times C_s}$ where $N_s = 256$ and $C_s = 128$. The coarse point cloud $\mathcal{P}_0$ contains $N_0 = 512$ points which is obtained by merging S and $\mathcal{P}$ using FPS. Three upsample layers are used in the following coarse-to-fine generation procedure which output dense point clouds $\{\mathcal{P}_1, \mathcal{P}_2, \mathcal{P}_3\}$ and $\mathcal{P}_3$ corresponds to the final predicted result. Channel number of generated features is set to $C = 128$ for all upsample layers.

We train our network end-to-end using pytorch [19] implementation. We use Adam [13] optimizer with $\beta_1 = 0.9$ and $\beta_2 = 0.999$. All the models are trained with a batch size of 48 on two NVIDIA TITAN Xp GPUs. The initial learning rate is set to 0.001 with continuous decay of 0.1 for every 100 epochs.

4.2 Experiments on PCN Dataset

Data. The PCN dataset [43] is one of the most widely used benchmark datasets for point cloud completion. It is a subset of ShapeNet [2] with shapes from 8

Table 1. Completion results on PCN dataset in terms of per-point L1 Chamfer Distance ×1000 (lower is better).

Methods	Average	Plane	Cabinet	Car	Chair	Lamp	Couch	Table	Boat
FoldingNet [41]	14.31	9.49	15.80	12.61	15.55	16.41	15.97	13.65	14.99
TopNet [27]	12.15	7.61	13.31	10.90	13.82	14.44	14.78	11.22	11.12
AtlasNet [9]	10.85	6.37	11.94	10.10	12.06	12.37	12.99	10.33	10.61
PCN [43]	9.64	5.50	22.70	10.63	8.70	11.00	11.34	11.68	8.59
GRNet [40]	8.83	6.45	10.37	9.45	9.41	7.96	10.51	8.44	8.04
CRN [31]	8.51	4.79	9.97	8.31	9.49	8.94	10.69	7.81	8.05
NSFA [44]	8.06	4.76	10.18	8.63	8.53	7.03	10.53	7.35	7.48
PMP-Net [35]	8.73	5.65	11.24	9.64	9.51	6.95	10.83	8.72	7.25
PoinTr [42]	8.38	4.75	10.47	8.68	9.39	7.75	10.93	7.78	7.29
SnowflakeNet [38]	7.21	4.29	9.16	8.08	7.89	6.07	9.23	6.55	6.40
SeedFormer	**6.74**	**3.85**	**9.05**	**8.06**	**7.06**	**5.21**	**8.85**	**6.05**	**5.85**

(a) Input   (b) PCN   (c) GRNet   (d) Snowflake   (e) Ours   (f) GT

Fig. 4. Visual comparisons on PCN dataset.

categories. The incomplete point clouds are generated by back-projecting 2.5D depth images from 8 viewpoints in order to simulate real-world sensor data. For each shape, 16,384 points are uniformly sampled from the mesh surfaces as complete ground-truth, and 2,048 points are sampled as partial input. We follow the same experimental setting with PCN for a fair comparison.

Results. Following previous methods, we report the Chamfer Distances with L1 norm (×1000) in Table 1. Detailed results of each category are also provided. SeedFormer achieves the best scores on all categories of this dataset, outperforming previous state-of-the-art methods by a large amount. Moreover, in Fig. 4, we show visual results of shapes from three categories (Lamp, Chair and Couch), compared with PCN [43], GRNet [40] and SnowflakeNet [38]. It shows that Seed-Former can produce clearly better results with more faithful details. As shown

Table 2. Completion results on ShapeNet-55 dataset evaluated as L2 Chamfer Distance ×1000 (lower is better) and F-Score@1% (higher is better).

Methods	Table	Chair	Plane	Car	Sofa	CD-S	CD-M	CD-H	CD-Avg	F1
FoldingNet [41]	2.53	2.81	1.43	1.98	2.48	2.67	2.66	4.05	3.12	0.082
PCN [43]	2.13	2.29	1.02	1.85	2.06	1.94	1.96	4.08	2.66	0.133
TopNet [27]	2.21	2.53	1.14	2.18	2.36	2.26	2.16	4.3	2.91	0.126
PFNet [11]	3.95	4.24	1.81	2.53	3.34	3.83	3.87	7.97	5.22	0.339
GRNet [40]	1.63	1.88	1.02	1.64	1.72	1.35	1.71	2.85	1.97	0.238
PoinTr [42]	0.81	0.95	0.44	0.91	0.79	0.58	0.88	1.79	1.09	0.464
SeedFormer	**0.72**	**0.81**	**0.40**	**0.89**	**0.71**	**0.50**	**0.77**	**1.49**	**0.92**	**0.472**

Table 3. Completion results on ShapeNet-34 dataset evaluated as L2 Chamfer Distance ×1000 (lower is better) and F-Score@1% (higher is better).

Methods	34 seen categories					21 unseen categories				
	CD-S	CD-M	CD-H	Avg	F1	CD-S	CD-M	CD-H	Avg	F1
FoldingNet [41]	1.86	1.81	3.38	2.35	0.139	2.76	2.74	5.36	3.62	0.095
PCN [43]	1.87	1.81	2.97	2.22	0.154	3.17	3.08	5.29	3.85	0.101
TopNet [27]	1.77	1.61	3.54	2.31	0.171	2.62	2.43	5.44	3.50	0.121
PFNet [11]	3.16	3.19	7.71	4.68	0.347	5.29	5.87	13.33	8.16	0.322
GRNet [40]	1.26	1.39	2.57	1.74	0.251	1.85	2.25	4.87	2.99	0.216
PoinTr [42]	0.76	1.05	1.88	1.23	0.421	1.04	1.67	3.44	2.05	0.384
SeedFormer	**0.48**	**0.70**	**1.30**	**0.83**	**0.452**	**0.61**	**1.07**	**2.35**	**1.34**	**0.402**

in the 2-nd and 3-rd rows, our network can preserve complicated details in the regions of chair arms and backs, without introducing undesired components.

4.3 Experiments on ShapeNet-55/34

Data. We further evaluate our model on ShapeNet-55 and ShapeNet-34 datasets from [42]. These two datasets are also generated from the synthetic ShapeNet [2] dataset while they contain more object categories and incomplete patterns. All 55 categories in ShapeNet are included in ShapeNet-55 with 41,952 shapes for training and 10,518 shapes for testing. ShapeNet-34 uses a subset of 34 categories for training and leaves 21 unseen categories for testing where 46,765 object shapes are used for training, 3,400 for testing on seen categories and 2,305 for testing on novel (unseen) categories. In both datasets, 2,048 points are sampled as input and 8,192 points as ground-truth. Following the same evaluation strategy with [42], 8 fixed viewpoints are selected and the number of points in partial point cloud is set to 2,048, 4,096 or 6,144 (25%, 50% or 75% of the complete point cloud) which corresponds to three difficulty levels of *simple*, *moderate* and *hard* in the test stage.

Table 4. Completion results on KITTI dataset evaluated as Fidelity Distance and Minimal Matching Distance (MMD). Lower is better.

	PCN [43]	FoldingNet [41]	TopNet [27]	MSN [17]	GRNet [40]	SeedFormer
Fidelity	2.235	7.467	5.354	0.434	0.816	**0.151**
MMD	1.366	0.537	0.636	2.259	0.568	**0.516**

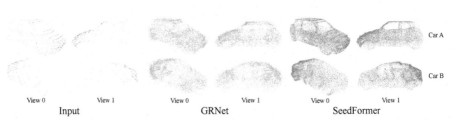

Fig. 5. Visual comparison of point cloud completion results on KITTI dataset. For a clearer comparison, we show two different views of each object.

Results. The ShapeNet-55 dataset tests the ability of dealing with more diverse objects and incompleteness levels. Table 2 reports the average L2 Chamfer Distances ($\times 1000$) on three difficulty levels and the overall CDs. Additionally, we show results from 5 categories (Table, Chair, Plane, Car and Sofa) with more than 2,500 samples in the training set. Complete results for all 55 categories are available in the supplemental material. We also provide results under the F-Score@1% metric [26]. Compared with previous methods, SeedFormer achieves the best scores on all categories and evaluation metrics. In particular, our method outperforms the SOTA model PoinTr [42] by 15.6% in terms of overall CD and 16.8% in terms of average CD on hard difficulty.

On ShapeNet-34, the networks should handle novel objects from unseen categories which do not appear in the training phase. We show results on two test sets in Table 3. Our method again achieves the best scores. Especially, when dealing with unseen objects, SeedFormer shows better generalization ability achieving an average CD of 1.34 which is 34.6% lower than PoinTr.

4.4 Experiments on KITTI

Data. In order to evaluate the proposed model on real-scanned data, we further conduct experiments on the KITTI [7] dataset for completing sparse point clouds of cars in real-world environments. This dataset consists of a sequence of LiDAR scans from outdoor scenes where car objects are extracted in each frame according to the 3D bounding boxes, resulting in a total of 2,401 partial point clouds. Unlike other datasets which are built from synthetic models, the scanned data in KITTI can be highly sparse and does not have complete point cloud as ground-truth. Thus, we follow the experimental settings of GRNet [40] and evaluate our method using two metrics: (i) Fidelity Distance, which is the average distance from each point in the input to its nearest neighbour in the

Table 5. Ablation study on shape representations. We also evaluate the density of Patch Seeds.

Methods	CD-Avg
global feature	6.97
seed number = 128	7.00
seed number = 256	6.74
seed number = 512	6.75

Table 6. Ablation study on different generator designs.

Methods	CD-Avg
folding operation	6.93
deconvolution	6.90
graph convolution	6.88
point-wise attention	6.85
Upsample Transformer	6.74

Table 7. Alternatives to softmax function in seed generator.

Methods	CD-Avg
w/ softmax	6.83
w/o softmax	6.74
w/ scaled-softmax	6.80
w/ log-softmax	6.80

Table 8. Ablation study on different positional encoding in Upsample Transformer.

Methods	CD-Avg
none	6.88
positional	6.80
positional + regional	6.74
combined	6.78

output. This measures how well the input is preserved; (ii) Minimal Matching Distance (MMD), which is the Chamfer Distance between the output and the car point cloud from ShapeNet that is closest to the output point cloud in terms of CD. This measures how much the output resembles a typical car.

Results. Following GRNet, we fine-tune our model (pretrained on PCN dataset) on ShapeNetCars (the cars from ShapeNet) for a fair comparison. Quantitative evaluation results are shown in Table 4 compared with previous methods. We also show some visual comparisons of the predicted point clouds in Fig. 5. Each of the car objects is visualized in two different views for a clearer comparison. We can see that our method performs clearly better on real-scanned data. Even with a very sparse input (see the 2-nd row in Fig. 5), SeedFormer can produce general structures of the desired object.

4.5 Ablation Studies

In this section, we demonstrate the effectiveness of several architecture designs in SeedFormer and provide some optional choices that can be applied in the network. All the networks are trained on PCN dataset with identical settings.

Patch Seeds. The Patch Seeds representation attempts to preserve geometric features locally, which shows clear superiority of detail recovery over previous global feature designs. We first ablate these two network architectures by replacing Patch Seeds with a global feature in the SeedFormer network. Specifically, in the seed generator, the global feature is obtained through max-pooling from input patch features, and is used to produce a coarse point cloud by a deconvolution layer [38]. Then, in the subsequent upsample layers, this global feature is concatenated with each input point which is fed to the Upsample Transformer similarly. All other architectures are identical. Results in Table 5 show clear improvement of our Patch Seeds design (6.74 vs 6.97). In addition, we ablate the number of seeds in the network and show that 256 seed points are suitable for covering an input 3D object with proper density.

Upsample Transformer and Other Generator Designs. We compare Upsample Transformer with other point cloud generators. Among previous methods for point cloud completion, folding-based operation [41] and deconvolution [38] are commonly-used. Unlike our generator which considers semantic relationships between points, these two designs are applied to process each point independently without using contextual information of point clouds.

The information from local areas is vital for point cloud completion, and we provide two optional choices for point generation operators. As discussed in Sect. 3.3, we adopt graph convolution [32] and vanilla Transformer (point-wise attention) to further demonstrate the effectiveness of local aggregation. In this experiment, we replace the Upsample Transformers in both seed generator and upsample layers, and keep other architectures the same. All the generators are designed to produce new features with upsampled points. Table 6 shows point generation by local aggregation performs better than previous methods, and the performance of Upsample Transformer stands out in similar designs.

Alternatives to Softmax Function. The softmax function can provide balanced weights in the self-attention mechanism. However, in the case of seed generators, it also presents intrinsic limitations on generating new points. In Table 7, we show that the standard transformer structure (w/ softmax) is not the best choice (6.83) in the seed generator. Our improvement (w/o softmax) by applying self-attention without softmax function aims to release the points from limited weights within a specific range of $(0, 1)$. Similar results can be achieved by using a log-softmax or scaled-softmax (multiplied by a scale parameter λ) function, which are also alternatives to the original softmax function.

Positional Encoding. Upsample Transformer applies both positional encoding from spatial relations and regional encoding from seed feature relations. This extends the original positional encoding in transformers by utilizing information from interpolated seed features. Table 8 shows that this design performs better which also demonstrates the effectiveness of incorporating information from Patch Seeds into the generation process of Upsample Transformer. Moreover, we design another ablation which combines both features in one encoding (6.78). We concatenate the two inputs and obtain a joint version through MLPs.

5   Visualization of Patch Seeds

In this section, we give some insights to achieve a deeper understanding of the generation process of Patch Seeds. The seed generator takes $N_p = 128$ patches

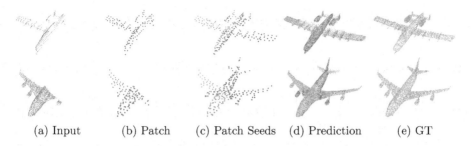

(a) Input   (b) Patch   (c) Patch Seeds   (d) Prediction   (e) GT

Fig. 6. Illustration of Patch Seeds and other intermediate results. (a) Input point cloud. (b) Extracted patch centers from partial input. (c) Generated seeds (red: seed0, blue: seed1) according to the seed generator process. (d) Our predicted results with each point colored according its nearest seed. (e) Ground truth. (Color figure online)

(Fig. 6(b)) extracted from the input point cloud and produces a new set of $N_s = 256$ seed points (Fig. 6(c)). Instead of using a global feature, adopting a patch-to-patch translation allows us to track the paths in the seed generation process. Specifically, the generated seeds can be divided into two groups, denoted as seed0 and seed1, since each patch center is split into two seeds according to different groups of self-attention weights in Upsample Transformer (see in Eq. 3). Thus, we visualize the obtained Patch Seeds in Fig. 6(c) with specific colors (red: seed0, blue: seed1). We can see that the red points (seed0) are close to the partial patches where the network tries to preserve the input structures. As for another group (blue points), if the input point cloud is symmetric to the ground-truth (the 1-st row in Fig. 6(a)), SeedFormer learns to duplicate the existing points as well as features, thus it can recover the missiles which are inferred from the seen parts. If the input is asymmetric (in the 2-nd row), our network can also predict missing parts according to the similar observations in the seen point cloud. For a clearer illustration, we also visualize the predicted complete point clouds in Fig. 6(d) where each point is colored according to its nearest seed.

6   Conclusion

In this paper, we propose a novel point cloud completion network, termed Seed-Former. As opposed to previous methods, SeedFormer introduce a new shape representation, namely Patch Seeds, in point cloud completion. The idea of Patch Seeds is to capture both global shape structure and fine-grained local details by learning regional features which are stored in several local seeds. This leads to a better performance of shape recovery and detail preservation in the generated point clouds. Furthermore, by extending the transformer structure into point generation, we propose a novel Upsample Transformer to capture useful neighborhood information. Comprehensive experiments show that our method achieves clear improvements on several challenging benchmark dataset compared to state-of-the-art competitors.

Acknowledgements. This work is supported by the National Natural Science Foundation of China (No. 61832008).

References

1. Achlioptas, P., Diamanti, O., Mitliagkas, I., Guibas, L.: Learning representations and generative models for 3d point clouds. In: International Conference on Machine Learning, pp. 40–49. PMLR (2018)
2. Chang, A.X., et al.: ShapeNet: an information-rich 3d model repository. arXiv preprint arXiv:1512.03012 (2015)
3. Dai, A., Ruizhongtai Qi, C., Nießner, M.: Shape completion using 3d-encoder-predictor CNNs and shape synthesis. In: Proceedings of the IEEE Conference on Computer Vision and Pattern Recognition, pp. 5868–5877 (2017)
4. Dai, Z., Yang, Z., Yang, Y., Carbonell, J., Le, Q.V., Salakhutdinov, R.: Transformer-xl: attentive language models beyond a fixed-length context. arXiv preprint arXiv:1901.02860 (2019)
5. Devlin, J., Chang, M.W., Lee, K., Toutanova, K.: Bert: pre-training of deep bidirectional transformers for language understanding. arXiv preprint arXiv:1810.04805 (2018)
6. Fan, H., Su, H., Guibas, L.J.: A point set generation network for 3d object reconstruction from a single image. In: Proceedings of the IEEE Conference on Computer Vision and Pattern Recognition, pp. 605–613 (2017)
7. Geiger, A., Lenz, P., Stiller, C., Urtasun, R.: Vision meets robotics: the KITTI dataset. Int. J. Robot. Res. **32**(11), 1231–1237 (2013)
8. Goodfellow, I., et al.: Generative adversarial nets. Adv. Neural Inf. Process. Syst. **27**, 1–11 (2014)
9. Groueix, T., Fisher, M., Kim, V.G., Russell, B.C., Aubry, M.: A papier-mâché approach to learning 3d surface generation. In: Proceedings of the IEEE Conference on Computer Vision and Pattern Recognition, pp. 216–224 (2018)
10. Han, X., Li, Z., Huang, H., Kalogerakis, E., Yu, Y.: High-resolution shape completion using deep neural networks for global structure and local geometry inference. In: Proceedings of the IEEE International Conference on Computer Vision, pp. 85–93 (2017)
11. Huang, Z., Yu, Y., Xu, J., Ni, F., Le, X.: PF-Net: point fractal network for 3d point cloud completion. In: Proceedings of the IEEE/CVF Conference on Computer Vision and Pattern Recognition, pp. 7662–7670 (2020)
12. Karras, T., Laine, S., Aila, T.: A style-based generator architecture for generative adversarial networks. In: Proceedings of the IEEE/CVF Conference on Computer Vision and Pattern Recognition, pp. 4401–4410 (2019)
13. Kingma, D.P., Ba, J.: Adam: a method for stochastic optimization. arXiv preprint arXiv:1412.6980 (2014)
14. Kingma, D.P., Welling, M.: Auto-encoding variational Bayes. arXiv preprint arXiv:1312.6114 (2013)
15. Le, T., Duan, Y.: PointGrid: a deep network for 3d shape understanding. In: Proceedings of the IEEE Conference on Computer Vision and Pattern Recognition, pp. 9204–9214 (2018)
16. Liang, M., Yang, B., Wang, S., Urtasun, R.: Deep continuous fusion for multi-sensor 3D object detection. In: Ferrari, V., Hebert, M., Sminchisescu, C., Weiss, Y. (eds.) ECCV 2018. LNCS, vol. 11220, pp. 663–678. Springer, Cham (2018). https://doi.org/10.1007/978-3-030-01270-0_39

17. Liu, M., Sheng, L., Yang, S., Shao, J., Hu, S.M.: Morphing and sampling network for dense point cloud completion. In: Proceedings of the AAAI Conference on Artificial Intelligence, vol. 34, pp. 11596–11603 (2020)
18. Maturana, D., Scherer, S.: Voxnet: A 3d convolutional neural network for real-time object recognition. In: 2015 IEEE/RSJ International Conference on Intelligent Robots and Systems (IROS), pp. 922–928. IEEE (2015)
19. Paszke, A., et al.: Pytorch: an imperative style, high-performance deep learning library. Adv. Neural Inf. Process. Syst. **32**, 1–12 (2019)
20. Qi, C.R., Liu, W., Wu, C., Su, H., Guibas, L.J.: Frustum pointnets for 3d object detection from RGB-D data. In: Proceedings of the IEEE Conference on Computer Vision and Pattern Recognition, pp. 918–927 (2018)
21. Qi, C.R., Su, H., Mo, K., Guibas, L.J.: PointNet: deep learning on point sets for 3d classification and segmentation. In: Proceedings of the IEEE Conference on Computer Vision and Pattern Recognition, pp. 652–660 (2017)
22. Qi, C.R., Yi, L., Su, H., Guibas, L.J.: Pointnet++: deep hierarchical feature learning on point sets in a metric space. Adv. Neural Inf. Process. Syst. **30**, 1–10 (2017)
23. Rumelhart, D.E., Hinton, G.E., Williams, R.J.: Learning representations by back-propagating errors. Nature **323**(6088), 533–536 (1986)
24. Rusu, R.B., Marton, Z.C., Blodow, N., Dolha, M., Beetz, M.: Towards 3d point cloud based object maps for household environments. Robot. Auton. Syst. **56**(11), 927–941 (2008)
25. Stutz, D., Geiger, A.: Learning 3d shape completion from laser scan data with weak supervision. In: Proceedings of the IEEE Conference on Computer Vision and Pattern Recognition, pp. 1955–1964 (2018)
26. Tatarchenko, M., Richter, S.R., Ranftl, R., Li, Z., Koltun, V., Brox, T.: What do single-view 3d reconstruction networks learn? In: Proceedings of the IEEE/CVF Conference on Computer Vision and Pattern Recognition, pp. 3405–3414 (2019)
27. Tchapmi, L.P., Kosaraju, V., Rezatofighi, H., Reid, I., Savarese, S.: TopNet: structural point cloud decoder. In: Proceedings of the IEEE/CVF Conference on Computer Vision and Pattern Recognition, pp. 383–392 (2019)
28. Thomas, H., Qi, C.R., Deschaud, J.E., Marcotegui, B., Goulette, F., Guibas, L.J.: Kpconv: Flexible and deformable convolution for point clouds. In: Proceedings of the IEEE/CVF International Conference on Computer Vision, pp. 6411–6420 (2019)
29. Vaswani, A., et al.: Attention is all you need. In: Advances in Neural Information Processing Systems, vol. 30 (2017)
30. Wang, P.S., Liu, Y., Guo, Y.X., Sun, C.Y., Tong, X.: O-CNN: octree-based convolutional neural networks for 3d shape analysis. ACM Trans. Graph. (TOG) **36**(4), 1–11 (2017)
31. Wang, X., Ang Jr, M.H., Lee, G.H.: Cascaded refinement network for point cloud completion. In: Proceedings of the IEEE/CVF Conference on Computer Vision and Pattern Recognition, pp. 790–799 (2020)
32. Wang, Y., Sun, Y., Liu, Z., Sarma, S.E., Bronstein, M.M., Solomon, J.M.: Dynamic graph CNN for learning on point clouds. ACM Trans. Graph. (TOG) **38**(5), 1–12 (2019)
33. Wen, X., Han, Z., Cao, Y.P., Wan, P., Zheng, W., Liu, Y.S.: Cycle4completion: Unpaired point cloud completion using cycle transformation with missing region coding. In: Proceedings of the IEEE/CVF Conference on Computer Vision and Pattern Recognition, pp. 13080–13089 (2021)

34. Wen, X., Li, T., Han, Z., Liu, Y.S.: Point cloud completion by skip-attention network with hierarchical folding. In: Proceedings of the IEEE/CVF Conference on Computer Vision and Pattern Recognition, pp. 1939–1948 (2020)
35. Wen, X., et al.: PMP-Net: point cloud completion by learning multi-step point moving paths. In: Proceedings of the IEEE/CVF Conference on Computer Vision and Pattern Recognition, pp. 7443–7452 (2021)
36. Wu, F., Fan, A., Baevski, A., Dauphin, Y.N., Auli, M.: Pay less attention with lightweight and dynamic convolutions. arXiv preprint arXiv:1901.10430 (2019)
37. Xia, Y., Xia, Y., Li, W., Song, R., Cao, K., Stilla, U.: ASFM-Net: asymmetrical Siamese feature matching network for point completion. In: Proceedings of the 29th ACM International Conference on Multimedia, pp. 1938–1947 (2021)
38. Xiang, P., et al.: SnowflakeNet: point cloud completion by snowflake point deconvolution with skip-transformer. In: Proceedings of the IEEE/CVF International Conference on Computer Vision, pp. 5499–5509 (2021)
39. Xie, C., Wang, C., Zhang, B., Yang, H., Chen, D., Wen, F.: Style-based point generator with adversarial rendering for point cloud completion. In: Proceedings of the IEEE/CVF Conference on Computer Vision and Pattern Recognition, pp. 4619–4628 (2021)
40. Xie, H., Yao, H., Zhou, S., Mao, J., Zhang, S., Sun, W.: GRNet: gridding residual network for dense point cloud completion. In: Vedaldi, A., Bischof, H., Brox, T., Frahm, J.-M. (eds.) ECCV 2020. LNCS, vol. 12354, pp. 365–381. Springer, Cham (2020). https://doi.org/10.1007/978-3-030-58545-7_21
41. Yang, Y., Feng, C., Shen, Y., Tian, D.: FoldingNet: point cloud auto-encoder via deep grid deformation. In: Proceedings of the IEEE Conference on Computer Vision and Pattern Recognition, pp. 206–215 (2018)
42. Yu, X., Rao, Y., Wang, Z., Liu, Z., Lu, J., Zhou, J.: PoinTR: diverse point cloud completion with geometry-aware transformers. In: Proceedings of the IEEE/CVF International Conference on Computer Vision, pp. 12498–12507 (2021)
43. Yuan, W., Khot, T., Held, D., Mertz, C., Hebert, M.: PCN: point completion network. In: 2018 International Conference on 3D Vision (3DV), pp. 728–737. IEEE (2018)
44. Zhang, W., Yan, Q., Xiao, C.: Detail preserved point cloud completion via separated feature aggregation. In: Vedaldi, A., Bischof, H., Brox, T., Frahm, J.-M. (eds.) ECCV 2020. LNCS, vol. 12370, pp. 512–528. Springer, Cham (2020). https://doi.org/10.1007/978-3-030-58595-2_31
45. Zhang, X., et al.: View-guided point cloud completion. In: Proceedings of the IEEE/CVF Conference on Computer Vision and Pattern Recognition, pp. 15890–15899 (2021)
46. Zhao, H., Jiang, L., Jia, J., Torr, P.H., Koltun, V.: Point transformer. In: Proceedings of the IEEE/CVF International Conference on Computer Vision, pp. 16259–16268 (2021)
47. Zhou, H., Feng, Y., Fang, M., Wei, M., Qin, J., Lu, T.: Adaptive graph convolution for point cloud analysis. In: Proceedings of the IEEE/CVF International Conference on Computer Vision, pp. 4965–4974 (2021)

DeepMend: Learning Occupancy Functions to Represent Shape for Repair

Nikolas Lamb$^{(\boxtimes)}$, Sean Banerjee , and Natasha Kholgade Banerjee

Clarkson University, Potsdam, NY 13699, USA
{lambne,sbanerje,nbanerje}@clarkson.edu

Abstract. We present DeepMend, a novel approach to reconstruct restorations to fractured shapes using learned occupancy functions. Existing shape repair approaches predict low-resolution voxelized restorations or smooth restorations, or require symmetries or access to a pre-existing complete oracle. We represent the occupancy of a fractured shape as the conjunction of the occupancy of an underlying complete shape and a break surface, which we model as functions of latent codes using neural networks. Given occupancy samples from a fractured shape, we estimate latent codes using an inference loss augmented with novel penalties to avoid empty or voluminous restorations. We use the estimated codes to reconstruct a restoration shape. We show results with simulated fractures on synthetic and real-world scanned objects, and with scanned real fractured mugs. Compared to existing approaches and to two baseline methods, our work shows state-of-the-art results in accuracy and avoiding restoration artifacts over non-fracture regions of the fractured shape.

Keywords: Learned occupancy · Shape representation · Repair · Fracture · Implicit surface · Neural networks

1 Introduction

Automated restoration of fractured shapes is an important area of study, with applications in consumer waste reduction, commercial recycling, cultural heritage object restoration, medical fields such as orthopedics and dentistry, and robot-driven repair. Despite its wide application, automated repair of fractured shapes has received little attention. Most current automated techniques use symmetries to complete fractured shapes [17,37]. These techniques do not generalize to objects with non-symmetrical damage. The only existing generalizable approaches for repair operate in low-resolution voxel space [22], or infer restoration shapes directly, resulting in smooth restorations with a high rate of failure [25].

In this work, we present DeepMend, a novel deep learning based approach to generate high-fidelity restoration shapes given an input fractured shape. Our

Supplementary Information The online version contains supplementary material available at https://doi.org/10.1007/978-3-031-20062-5_25.

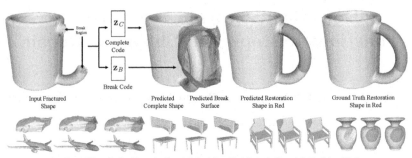

Fig. 1. Given a fractured shape, our approach infers latent codes for an underlying complete shape and a break surface. We use the codes to generate a restoration shape that repairs the input fracture shape.

approach is inspired by work that learns the signed distance function (SDF) or occupancy function to implicitly represent a shape surface over the continuous 3D domain [7,14,21,38,45,51,51,57,62]. These approaches perform partial shape completion by inferring a latent code using point samples from a partial shape, and reconstruct the complete shape from the latent code. Different from partial shape completion, DeepMend addresses the challenge that, unlike a partial shape that is a subset of a complete shape, a fractured shape contains a novel break region that is missing in the complete shape, as shown on the left of Fig. 1. DeepMend leverages the autodecoder architecture from DeepSDF [38] to estimate restorations, by addressing key challenges in the autodecoder that prevent its direct use in restoration generation. DeepSDF is geared toward single shape representation. By itself, DeepSDF cannot predict one shape, i.e., the restoration, from point samples of a different shape, i.e., the fractured shape. To solve this, our first contribution is to represent occupancies for fractured and restoration shapes as logical operations on occupancies for a shape space common to them both, i.e., complete shapes and break surfaces. We use T-norms [19] to relax the logical operations into arithmetic operations. We restructure the autodecoder loss using the fractured shape's dependence on complete/break codes, and reconstruct the restoration from codes estimated at inference.

Our approach estimates two codes (complete and break) from point samples of a single fractured shape at inference, a more complex problem than DeepSDF, that estimates one code. Using the autodecoder loss alone, trivial codes can be estimated where the break surface lies outside the complete shape or coincides with the fractured shape surface yielding empty or voluminous restorations. Our second contribution is to augment the inference loss with two penalty terms—(i) a non-empty restoration term that penalizes the mean restoration occupancy against being zero to avoid empty restorations, and (ii) a proximity term that encourages the mean distance between the complete and fractured occupancy to be low to prevent voluminous restorations. We compute the restoration occupancy as the conjunction of the complete occupancy and the negation of the break occupancy, and obtain a restoration mesh using Marching Cubes [33].

We train and test our approach on synthetically fractured meshes from 8 classes in the ShapeNet [5] dataset, and on the Google Scanned Objects dataset [42] which contains 1,032 scanned real-world objects. We use ShapeNet-trained networks to restore synthetically fractured meshes from the QP Cultural Heritage dataset [24], and to generate restorations for physically fractured and scanned real-world mugs. We compare our work to 3D-ORGAN [22] and Mend-Net [25], the only existing automated fracture restoration approaches, and to two baselines. We show state-of-the-art results in overall accuracy and avoiding inaccurate artifacts over non-fracture regions. Our code is available at: https:// github.com/Terascale-All-sensing-Research-Studio/DeepMend.

2   Related Work

Restoration of Fractured Shapes. Most existing approaches to generate restoration shapes from fractured shapes rely on shape symmetry [17,37]. They restore shapes by reflecting non-fractured regions of the shape onto fractured regions and computing the subtraction. These approaches fail to restore asymmetrical shapes or shapes that have non-symmetric fractures. Lamb et al. [26] perform repair without relying on symmetries. However, they require that a complete counterpart be provided as input alongside the fractured shape. The complete shape may not always be available, e.g., in the case of a rare object. Our work only requires the fractured shape as input. 3D-ORGAN [22] performs shape restoration in voxel space using a generative adversarial network. 3D-ORGAN operates at a resolution of $32 \times 32 \times 32$, which is insufficient to accurately represent the geometric complexity of the fracture region. Scaling 3D-ORGAN to a voxel resolution necessary to represent fracture is impractical at current dataset volumes and hardware. MendNet [25] overcomes the low resolution of 3D-ORGAN by representing shapes using the occupancy function, similar to DeepMend. However, MendNet represents overall shape structure and the high-frequency break surface using a single latent code, resulting in overly smooth restoration shapes. DeepMend overcomes the challenges of MendNet by learning separate codes for the complete shape and break surface, yielding high resolution restoration shapes that accurately reconstruct high-frequency break geometry.

Completion of Partial Shapes. Though not directly related to our work, a large body of prior work focuses on completing shapes from partial shape representations, e.g. depth maps or color images. Recent approaches hypothesize complete shapes from partial shapes using deep networks. Approaches that use point clouds as input [1,11,20,32,36,43,47,61] lack an intrinsic surface representation. Some approaches predict 3D meshes [18,60] to incorporate surfaces. These approaches are limited in the complexity of meshes reliably predicted [35], and cannot represent arbitrary topologies. Most approaches using voxels [3,44,46,53] struggle to predict high-resolution outputs while being computationally tractable. Some voxel approaches address computational inefficiency by employing hierarchical models [9,10] or sparse convolutions [9,59]. However, voxel approaches pre-discretize the domain, making it challenging to use them to represent arbitrarily fine resolutions needed for geometric detail, especially for the problem of fracture surface representation considered in this work.

A large body of recent work focuses on using neural networks to represent point samples of values that implicitly define surfaces, e.g., occupancy [7,8,15,23, 28,30,35,39,40,49,56,57], SDF [4,14,21,29,34,38,45,51,54,55,58,62], unsigned distance [50], or level sets [16]. By representing shapes as continuous functions, these approaches show high reconstruction fidelity while remaining computationally tractable. In contrast to traditional encoder-decoder architectures, approaches based on the autodecoder introduced by DeepSDF [38] use maximum *a posteriori* estimation to obtain a latent code for an input shape. The approach enables reconstruction of a complete shape using a latent code estimated from observations of an incomplete shape. Later approaches provide improvements by using meta-learning and post-training optimization [45,58], learning increasingly complex shape representations during training [12], deforming implicit shape templates [62], or reconstructing shapes at multiple resolutions [21].

A potential approach for shape restoration is to convert the fractured shape into a partial shape by removing the fracture surface, perform shape completion, and subtract the fractured shape from the complete shape to obtain a restoration. In Sect. 5 we show that subtraction approaches yield surface artifacts on the non-fracture regions of the fractured shape. Our approach mitigates artifacts by learning the interplay between the complete shape and break surface.

3   Representing Fractured Shapes

We represent the complete, fractured, and restoration shapes as point sets C, F, and R. For $S \in \{C, F, R\}$ the occupancy $o_S(\mathbf{x}) \in \{0, 1\}$ of a point $\mathbf{x}$ is 1 if $\mathbf{x}$ is inside the shape, and 0 if it is on the boundary or outside the shape. The original shapes are closed surfaces. However, we exclude boundary points from the definitions of the sets C, F, and R to ensure that a point does not simultaneously belong to two sets, e.g., F and R. Exclusion of boundary points makes the sets C, F, and R open and bounded. We define the break surface as a 2D surface that intersects the fracture region of F. Points on the side of the break surface corresponding to the fractured shape receive an occupancy of 1. Points on the side corresponding to the restoration shape have an occupancy of 0. We use the open unbounded set B, termed the 'break set' to represent the set of points with an occupancy $o_B(\mathbf{x})$ of 1. In principle, the break surface is infinite. In practice, we limit the region containing the break set to be a cube of finite length to make point sampling for network training and inference tractable[1].

As shown in Fig. 2(a), we represent the fractured shape set as the intersection of the sets for the complete shape C and the break set B, i.e., as $F = C \cap B$. The relationship implies that for a point $\mathbf{x}$, occupancy $o_F(\mathbf{x})$ of the fractured shape F is the logical conjunction of the occupancies $o_C(\mathbf{x})$ and $o_B(\mathbf{x})$ of C and B, i.e., $o_F(\mathbf{x}) = o_C(\mathbf{x}) \wedge o_B(\mathbf{x})$. We represent the restoration shape R as the intersection of C and the complement of B, i.e., as $R = C \cap B'$. The relationship

---

[1] Hereafter, we drop 'set' from references to C, F, and R, and refer to them as shapes.

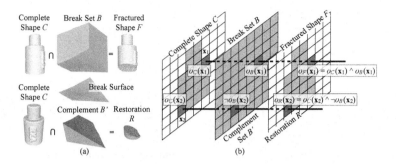

Fig. 2. (a) We represent fractured and restoration shapes F and R as intersections of the complete shape C with the break set B and its complement B'. (b) Logical expressions for occupancy at points $\mathbf{x}_1$ in F and $\mathbf{x}_2$ in R using C and B occupancies.

implies that occupancy $o_R(\mathbf{x})$ of R is expressed as the logical conjunction of $o_C(\mathbf{x})$ with the negation of $o_B(\mathbf{x})$, i.e., $o_R(\mathbf{x}) = o_C(\mathbf{x}) \wedge \neg o_B(\mathbf{x})$. We show the logical relationships in Fig. 2(b). For use in neural networks, we relax the logical relationships using the product T-norm [19], as

$$o_F(\mathbf{x}) = o_C(\mathbf{x})o_B(\mathbf{x}) \text{ and} \tag{1}$$

$$o_R(\mathbf{x}) = o_C(\mathbf{x})(1 - o_B(\mathbf{x})). \tag{2}$$

We represent the occupancy functions for the complete shape C and break set B respectively using neural networks f_Θ and g_Φ, such that $o_C(\mathbf{x}) = f_\Theta(\mathbf{z}_C, \mathbf{x})$ and $o_B(\mathbf{x}) = g_\Phi(\mathbf{z}_B, \mathbf{x})$. Θ and Φ are the network weights, $\mathbf{z}_C \in \mathbb{R}^p$ is a latent code of size p corresponding to the complete shape, and $\mathbf{z}_B \in \mathbb{R}^q$ is a latent code of size q corresponding to the break set. We use the autodecoder architecture introduced by Park et al. [38] for f_Θ and g_Φ. Figure 3(a) shows our network structure. We provide network details in the supplementary.

3.1 Network Training

During training, we optimize for network parameters Θ and Φ, and the latent codes $\mathbf{z}_B$ and $\mathbf{z}_C$ over each training sample. Each sample consists of a tuple (F, C, R, B) representing the fractured, complete, and restoration shapes F, C, and R, and the break set B for the sample. We define the training loss as

$$\mathcal{L} = \sum_{\mathbf{z}_C \in Z_C, \mathbf{z}_B \in Z_B} \mathcal{L}_F + \mathcal{L}_C + \mathcal{L}_R + \mathcal{L}_B + \lambda_{\mathrm{reg}}\mathcal{L}_{\mathrm{reg}} \tag{3}$$

where Z_C is the set of all training complete latent codes, and Z_B is the set of all training break latent codes. The term $\mathcal{L}_F$, represented as

$$\mathcal{L}_F = (1/|X|) \sum_{\mathbf{x} \in X} BCE\left(f_\Theta(\mathbf{z}_C, \mathbf{x})g_\Phi(\mathbf{z}_B, \mathbf{x}), o_F(\mathbf{x})\right), \tag{4}$$

models the reconstruction of the fractured shape occupancy values. BCE represents the binary cross-entropy loss function. The first argument to

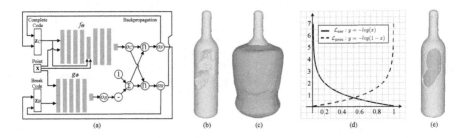

Fig. 3. (a) Networks f_Θ and g_Φ represent the complete and break occupancy in terms of an input point $\mathbf{x}$ and latent codes $\mathbf{z}_C$ and $\mathbf{z}_B$. As shown, the fractured and restoration occupancies, o_F and o_R, are obtained using the complete and break occupancies, o_C and o_B, where Π and Σ represent the product and sum respectively. (b) Predicted restoration shape with high non-empty penalty and (c) with high proximity penalty. (d) Functions used for the non-empty penalty term $\mathcal{L}_{ner}$ and the proximity penalty term $\mathcal{L}_{prox}$ during inference. (e) Predicted restoration with balanced penalties. Restoration shapes (red) shown with ground truth fractured shapes (gray). (Color figure online)

BCE represents the occupancy expression from Eq. (1), with the expressions for the complete and break occupancy values in terms of f_Θ and g_Φ substituted in. The second argument represents the fractured shape ground truth occupancy values. X represents the set of point samples used to probe the ground truth occupancy values. We include terms $\mathcal{L}_C$, $\mathcal{L}_B$, and $\mathcal{L}_R$ to improve the representation capability of the network by using ground truth occupancy values from training complete shapes, break sets, and restorations. We define $\mathcal{L}_C$ and $\mathcal{L}_B$ as

$$\mathcal{L}_C = (1/|X|) \sum_{\mathbf{x} \in X} BCE\left(f_\Theta(\mathbf{z}_C, \mathbf{x}), o_C(\mathbf{x})\right) \text{ and} \tag{5}$$

$$\mathcal{L}_B = (1/|X|) \sum_{\mathbf{x} \in X} BCE\left(g_\Phi(\mathbf{z}_B, \mathbf{x}), o_B(\mathbf{x})\right). \tag{6}$$

In Eqs. (5) and (6), the first argument to BCE represents the occupancy for the complete shape and break set respectively expressed in terms of f_Θ and g_Φ. The second argument represents the ground truth occupancy values for the complete shape C and break set B. We define $\mathcal{L}_R$ as

$$\mathcal{L}_R = (1/|X|) \sum_{\mathbf{x} \in X} BCE\left(f_\Theta(\mathbf{z}_C, \mathbf{x})(1 - g_\Phi(\mathbf{z}_B, \mathbf{x})), o_R(\mathbf{x})\right). \tag{7}$$

The first argument to BCE in Eq. (7) represents the expression for restoration shapes from Eq. (2), with expressions for complete and break occupancy in terms of f_Θ and g_Φ substituted in. The second argument represents the ground truth restoration occupancy. We train f_Θ and g_Φ together to incorporate dependency of gradient descent update of complete parameters on break parameters and vice versa, based on the product rule with terms from Eqs. (4) and (7). Joint training enables learning of fractured and restoration shapes in terms of complete shapes and break surfaces. $\mathcal{L}_{reg} = \|\mathbf{z}_C\|_2^2 + \|\mathbf{z}_B\|_2^2$ regularizes latent code estimation by imposing a zero-mean Gaussian prior on the latent codes. We set the weight λ_{reg} on $\mathcal{L}_{reg}$ to be $1e - 4$.

3.2   Inference of Latent Codes

During inference, we estimate optimal latent codes $\mathbf{z}_C$ and $\mathbf{z}_B$ for point observations of occupancy $o_F(\mathbf{x})$ from a novel input fractured shape F. With knowledge of the fractured shape occupancy, the inference loss is given as $\mathcal{L}_{\mathrm{inf}} = \mathcal{L}_F + \lambda_{\mathrm{reg}}\mathcal{L}_{\mathrm{reg}}$. By itself, the loss does not prevent the break surface from being predicted outside or on the boundary of the complete shape. This may result in an empty restoration shape as shown in Fig. 3(b). The loss also does not constrain the restoration shape from growing arbitrarily large. Gradient descent on the loss may generate a locally optimal latent code that yields a plausible complete shape, but a large restoration as shown in Fig. 3(c). We introduce two penalty terms that encourage point occupancy values for the restoration that constrain its structure. The non-empty penalty term $\mathcal{L}_{\mathrm{ner}}$, given as

$$\mathcal{L}_{\mathrm{ner}} = -\log\left((1/|X|)\sum_{\mathbf{x}\in X} f_\Theta(\mathbf{z}_C,\mathbf{x})(1-g_\Phi(\mathbf{z}_B,\mathbf{x}))\right), \tag{8}$$

penalizes the mean restoration occupancy against being zero. The term encourages the complete shape to have a non-empty intersection with the break set on the restoration side of the break surface. The proximity loss, $\mathcal{L}_{\mathrm{prox}}$, given as

$$\mathcal{L}_{\mathrm{prox}} = -\log\left(1-(1/|X|)\sum_{\mathbf{x}\in X}(f_\Theta(\mathbf{z}_C,\mathbf{x})-o_F(\mathbf{x}))^2\right), \tag{9}$$

penalizes the network from predicting complete shapes that are not in close proximity to the fractured shape. The term discourages voluminous restorations. As shown in Fig. 3(d), the negative log functions for $\mathcal{L}_{\mathrm{ner}}$ and $\mathcal{L}_{\mathrm{prox}}$ strongly penalize the mean occupancy from being too low or the mean complete-fractured occupancy distance from being too high. Using the non-empty and proximity penalties, we express the augmented inference loss $\mathcal{L}_{\mathrm{infaug}}$ as

$$\mathcal{L}_{\mathrm{infaug}} = \mathcal{L}_{\mathrm{inf}} + \lambda_{\mathrm{ner}}\mathcal{L}_{\mathrm{ner}} + \lambda_{\mathrm{prox}}\mathcal{L}_{\mathrm{prox}} + \lambda_{\mathrm{reg}}\mathcal{L}_{\mathrm{reg}} \tag{10}$$

where λ_{ner} and λ_{prox} are weights on the non-empty and proximity penalties. During code estimation, we use $\lambda_{\mathrm{ner}} = 1e-5$, $\lambda_{\mathrm{prox}} = 5e-3$, and $\lambda_{\mathrm{reg}} = 1e-4$. We optimize $\mathcal{L}_{\mathrm{infaug}}$ to estimate the complete and break codes $\mathbf{z}_C$ and $\mathbf{z}_B$. We use the estimated codes to reconstruct restoration occupancy values using Eq. (2), and obtain the restoration shape as a 3D mesh using Marching Cubes [33].

4   Datasets and Data Preparation

We evaluate our work using 3D meshes from four datasets.

1. **ShapeNet.** We use meshes from 8 classes in the ShapeNet dataset [5]: airplanes, bottles, cars, chairs, jars, mugs, sofas, and tables. The classes have 1,534 to 5,614 shapes, with an average of 3,019 shapes. We train one network per class, and use an 80%/20% train/test split within each class.
2. **Google Scanned Objects Dataset.** The dataset [42] contains 1,032 digitally scanned common objects such as cups, bowls, plates, baskets, and shoes. We train a network with an 80%/20% train/test split of the dataset.

Fig. 4. Ground truth fractured shapes shown with fitted thin-plate splines (TPS) corresponding to the break surface, and with ground truth restoration shapes. Fractured shapes and TPS are shown in gray, restoration shapes are shown in red. (Color figure online)

3. **QP Cultural Heritage Object Dataset.** The QP dataset [24] contains 317 meshes computer-modeled in the style of ancient Greek pottery. We use all models for testing using a network trained on ShapeNet jars.
4. **Real-World Fractured Mugs.** We perform in-house fractures of 4 real-world mugs, and scan the fractured mugs for testing. We use all mug models for testing using a network trained on ShapeNet mugs.

Data Preparation. We center meshes and scale them to lie within a unit cube. ShapeNet and QP models come pre-oriented to be consistent. Though meshes from the Google Scanned Objects dataset have a common ground plane, they are not oriented in a consistent direction. We augment the training set for Google Scanned Objects by randomly rotating meshes by 90° around the ground plane normal. We orient all real-world mugs to line up with ShapeNet mugs. We waterproof all meshes using the approach of Stutz and Geiger [48].

The ShapeNet, Google Scanned Objects, and QP datasets lack fractures. We synthetically fracture meshes in these datasets by repeatedly subtracting a randomized geometric primitive from each mesh. We adopt the fracture approach from Lamb et al. [27] to remove 5–20% of the mesh surface area. We show example fractured shapes, restorations, and break surfaces in Fig. 4. The mugs, jars, and bottles classes from ShapeNet have fewer than 600 meshes. We fracture meshes belonging to these classes 10, 3, and 3 times respectively. We augment the mugs set by requiring that 3 fractures for each complete mesh only remove parts of the handle. We fracture meshes in the remaining ShapeNet classes and the QP and Google Scanned Objects datasets once.

We obtain point samples for the set X by randomly sampling a unit cube around the object and sampling on the surface of the mesh, as described in the supplementary. To generate the break surface for each training sample, we fit a thin-plate spline (TPS) [13] to the fracture vertices, such that the spline domain corresponds to the closest fitting plane to the fracture region vertices. We use the spline to partition sample points in the interior of the fractured and restoration meshes into two groups. We denote the side of the spline that contains the most fractured shape sample points as belonging to the break set B.

5   Results

Metrics. For evaluation we use the chamfer distance (CD), non-empty restoration percent (NE%), and non-fracture region error (NFRE). NFRE measures

(a)   (b)

Fig. 5. (a) Predicted break surface and predicted complete shape, predicted break surface and fractured shape, predicted restoration shape and fractured shape, and ground truth fractured and restoration shape for three objects. (b) Predicted restoration shapes, shown with ground truth fractured shapes joined and opened to show the fracture surface. Restoration shapes and break surfaces in red, all other shapes in gray. (Color figure online)

the presence of incorrect geometric protrusions on the restoration near the non-fracture region of the fractured shape. Bulk metrics, e.g. precision/recall using point occupancies over the whole shape, do not model thin protrusions which contain very few points. To capture protrusions using the NFRE, we sample n points on the surfaces of the predicted restoration, ground truth restoration, and non-fractured region of the fractured shape. We count protruding points on the predicted restoration shape as points that have a nearest neighbor in the non-fracture region of the fractured shape closer than η and a nearest neighbor in the ground truth restoration farther than η. We normalize the count by n. We use $\eta = 0.02$ and $n = 30,000$.

5.1   Results Using ShapeNet

Figure 5(a) shows DeepMend-generated complete shapes and predicted break surfaces, and restoration shapes joined to input fractured shapes using shapes from ShapeNet. The break surfaces predicted by DeepMend mimic the fracture region at the join, resulting in accurate connections between fractured and restoration shapes. Figure 5(b) shows restorations joined to corresponding ground truth fractured shapes and opened to show the fracture. DeepMend restoration shapes match closely to the fracture, and avoid surface artifacts that may otherwise prevent the restoration shape from being joined to the fractured shape. DeepMend regenerates complex missing geometry, such as the tail of the plane in Fig. 5(b) and the car spoiler in Fig. 1. It also restores multi-component fractures such as the center airplane, top right mug, and armchair in Fig. 5(b). In contrast to symmetric approaches [17,37], DeepMend repairs shapes with asymmetrical fractures such as the sofa, plane with broken tail, bottle, and chairs in Fig. 5, and the car, mug, sofa, and airplane in Fig. 1.

Effect of Penalties on Restoration Shape During Inference. We evaluate the impact of our augmented inference loss $\mathcal{L}_{\text{infaug}}$ in Eq. (10) versus adding no penalty terms, adding solely the non-empty term $\mathcal{L}_{\text{ner}}$, and adding solely the proximity term $\mathcal{L}_{\text{prox}}$. We also evaluate alternate penalties given as

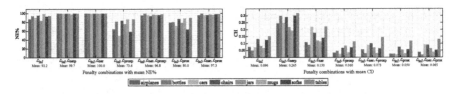

Fig. 6. Percentage of non-empty restorations (NE%, left) and chamfer distance (CD, right) for our approach with various combinations of penalties for the inference loss.

Fig. 7. Predicted restoration shapes (red) shown with ground truth fractured shapes (gray) using various combinations of penalty terms for the inference loss. (Color figure online)

$$\mathcal{L}_{\mathrm{nerp}} = -(1/|X|)\sum_{\mathbf{x}\in X}\log\left(f_{\Theta}(\mathbf{z}_C,\mathbf{x})(1 - g_{\Phi}(\mathbf{z}_B,\mathbf{x}))\right) \text{ and} \tag{11}$$

$$\mathcal{L}_{\mathrm{proxp}} = (1/|X|)\sum_{\mathbf{x}\in X} BCE(f_{\Theta}(\mathbf{z}_C,\mathbf{x}), o_F(\mathbf{x})), \tag{12}$$

that penalize individual distance rather than mean distance. $\mathcal{L}_{\mathrm{nerp}}$ penalizes 0 values for R, and is the same as the non-zero penalty used in MendNet [25] restorations. $\mathcal{L}_{\mathrm{proxp}}$ encourages individual values in C to be similar to F.

We summarize results in the bar plots in Fig. 6. Using no penalties predicts large restoration shapes, or generates multiple empty restorations as shown by the jar in Fig. 7(a). Mean NE% and CD with $\mathcal{L}_{\mathrm{inf}}$ are 92.2% and 0.096. Including $\mathcal{L}_{\mathrm{nerp}}$ raises mean NE% to 99.7%. However, since the penalty is applied to individual points, restorations appear splayed out and non-smooth as shown by the jar in Fig. 7(b). Mean CD is the highest with $\mathcal{L}_{\mathrm{nerp}}$ at 0.265. By penalizing mean occupancy, $\mathcal{L}_{\mathrm{ner}}$ remedies the splaying by keeping occupancy values concentrated, improves restoration quality, and lowers CD to a mean of 0.150. However, restorations may now appear bulkier as shown by the mug in Fig. 7(c). Mean CD is higher than when no penalty term is used.

When comparing the effect of the proximity penalties on inference, we find that including $\mathcal{L}_{\mathrm{proxp}}$ improves mean CD to 0.060. However, it drops the percentage of non-empty restorations to 73.6%. The per-point penalty induces individual points to approach the fracture surface, causing sparse and non-smooth restorations as shown in Fig. 7(d). Including the non-empty restoration term $\mathcal{L}_{\mathrm{ner}}$ improves NE% to 96.8% with minimal impact on CD. However, shapes are still non-smooth, as shown by the jar in Fig. 7(e). By using the penalty on the mean complete-fractured proximity $\mathcal{L}_{\mathrm{prox}}$, per-point distances remain concentrated and NE% is higher than with $\mathcal{L}_{\mathrm{proxp}}$. Combining it with $\mathcal{L}_{\mathrm{ner}}$ improves NE% over solely using $\mathcal{L}_{\mathrm{prox}}$ from 80.0% to 97.3%, without compromising on the mean CD at 0.065. As shown by Fig. 7(g), penalties on the mean occupancy and proximity values provides balanced, concentrated, and smooth restorations.

5.2   Comparing DeepMend to Existing Approaches and Baselines

We compare DeepMend restorations to MendNet [25] and 3D-ORGAN [22], the only existing approaches to restore fractured shapes, and to two baselines.

MendNet. MendNet takes a fractured shape as input and predicts a restoration shape directly using the occupancy function. We train MendNet on fractured shapes from ShapeNet. As recommended by the authors, we use a latent code of size 256 for bottles, jars, and mugs, and of size 400 for all other classes.

3D-ORGAN. 3D-ORGAN takes a voxelized fractured shape at a resolution of 32^3 as input and predicts a corresponding complete voxelized shape. We obtain the restoration shape for 3D-ORGAN as the element-wise difference between the predicted complete voxels and the input fractured voxels. We train 3D-ORGAN on fractured shapes from ShapeNet. During training, we generate random fractured shapes by removing voxel regions from each complete shape according to the original implementation. During testing, we input voxelized fractured shapes generated using the approach described in Sect. 4. As recommended by the authors, we use a two-step approach to predict complete shapes by feeding the output of the first iteration to 3D-ORGAN again for a second iteration.

Baselines of Performing Subtraction from Complete Shape. We adapt the partial shape completion approach of DeepSDF [38] to generate restoration shapes using subtraction. We generate a partial shape from the fractured shape by removing fracture region points detected by a fracture/non-fracture classifier. We train a PointNet [41] classifier to classify points as fracture versus non-fracture. The classifier provides a test accuracy of 81.3%. We remove detected fracture points to generate the partial shape. We train DeepSDF on complete shapes for the 8 ShapeNet classes studied in this work. We use DeepSDF to complete the partial shape using the shape completion method discussed by the authors. We use two approaches for subtraction as baselines. For the first approach, **Sub-Occ**, we convert SDF values for the input fractured shape and DeepSDF-predicted complete shape into occupancy values. We take the difference of the complete and fractured occupancy, and extract the 0-level isosurface. To remove artifacts, we discard closed surfaces with a volume less than $\eta = 0.01$. If this step removes all closed surfaces, we retain the largest surface. For the second method, **Sub-Lamb**, we use Lamb et al. [26] to perform subtraction. Lamb et al. additionally requires a complete counterpart to be provided as input. We use the complete shape from DeepSDF as the complete counterpart. We repair self-intersections at the fracture-restoration join using MeshFix [2].

Table 1 summarizes results of CD and NFRE using MendNet, 3D-ORGAN, Sub-Occ, Sub-Lamb, and DeepMend. 100% of restorations are generated by Sub-Occ and Sub-Lamb for all classes, and by 3D-ORGAN for all classes except cars and mugs. We report results over all shapes where DeepMend and MendNet return non-empty restorations. For 3D-ORGAN, we exclude metrics for cars and mugs, as 3D-ORGAN only produces restorations for 6 out of 349 or 1.7% of mugs and 159 out of 661 or 24.1% of cars. Figure 8 shows qualitative results.

Table 1. Chamfer (CD) distance and NFRE for MendNet, 3D-ORGAN, Sub-Occ, Sub-Lamb, and DeepMend. For 3D-ORGAN, we do not report results for cars and mugs, as it only restores 21.7% cars and 1.8% mugs. Overall mean values are provided over reported classes. Bold values correspond to the lowest value within a class.

	Metric	Airplanes	Bottles	Cars	Chairs	Jars	Mugs	Sofas	Tables	Mean
MendNet	CD	0.091	0.080	0.025	0.171	0.129	0.109	0.190	0.208	0.126
	NFRE	0.070	0.045	**0.017**	0.143	0.028	**0.008**	0.085	0.203	0.075
3D-ORGAN	CD	0.173	0.146	-	0.184	0.262	-	0.320	0.333	0.237
	NFRE	0.192	0.070	-	0.588	0.041	-	0.200	0.138	0.205
Sub-Occ	CD	0.050	0.041	**0.024**	0.112	0.119	**0.035**	0.066	0.122	0.071
	NFRE	0.099	0.076	0.142	0.262	0.183	0.070	0.170	0.175	0.147
Sub-lamb	CD	0.075	0.039	0.050	**0.086**	0.082	0.100	**0.053**	**0.093**	0.072
	NFRE	0.302	0.120	0.272	0.330	0.289	0.452	0.192	0.204	0.270
DeepMend (Ours)	CD	**0.037**	**0.022**	0.108	0.088	**0.065**	**0.035**	0.057	0.129	**0.068**
	NFRE	**0.009**	**0.012**	**0.017**	**0.009**	**0.007**	**0.008**	**0.012**	**0.012**	**0.011**

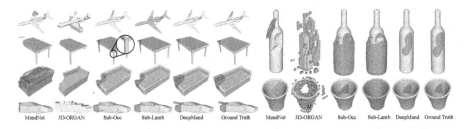

Fig. 8. Pictorial results of restorations using MendNet, 3D-ORGAN, baselines Sub-Occ and Sub-Lamb, and DeepMend, together with ground truth restorations.

DeepMend shows state-of-the-art results compared to MendNet, 3D-ORGAN, and the baselines in terms of overall CD and NFRE and per-class NFRE. DeepMend also shows lower CD for all classes compared to 3D-ORGAN, 7 out of 8 classes compared to MendNet, 5 out of 8 classes compared to to Sub-Occ, and 4 out of 8 classes compared to Sub-Lamb. MendNet predicts smooth restoration shapes that may not join completely to the fractured shape. While MendNet generates lower CD than DeepMend for cars common to both methods, MendNet only restores 57.9% cars, and fails for 42.1% cars as shown in Fig. 8. On average, MendNet generates 84.8% restorations compared to 97.3% generated by DeepMend. As shown in Fig. 8, 3D-ORGAN predicts small restoration shapes, e.g. the table, sofa, and car. The histogram on the left of Fig. 9 shows that MendNet and 3D-ORGAN predict 36.3% and 1.0% restorations with a chamfer distance less than 0.05 respectively, compared to 67.9% with DeepMend.

Restoration shapes generated using Sub-Occ exhibit artifacts on the surface of the fractured shape as shown in Fig. 8. The histogram of the NFRE values for Sub-Occ in Fig. 9 shows that 21.8% of restorations have NFRE lower than 0.025, as opposed to 87.8% by DeepMend. The fracture classifier may not reliably

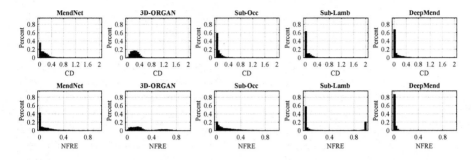

Fig. 9. Histograms of chamfer distance (CD, top) and non-fracture region error (NFRE, bottom) for MendNet, 3D-ORGAN, Sub-Occ, Sub-Lamb, and DeepMend.

(a) Google Scanned Objects   (b) QP Cultural Heritage Objects   (c) Scans of Real Fractured Mugs

Fig. 10. Results using (a) synthetic breaks on Greek pottery from QP [24], (b) synthetic fractures on 3D scans from Google Scanned Objects [42], and (c) 3D scans for real-world fractured mugs. Ground truth restoration shapes shown on right when applicable.

remove the entire fracture region to create a partial shape that is a precise subset of the complete shape. As such, Sub-Occ generates restorations that exhibit elements of the fracture, e.g., the sofa, car, and bottle in Fig. 8. As shown in Fig. 9, Sub-Lamb is effective at removing artifacts for some objects, as 58.0% of restoration shapes have NFRE lower than 0.025. However, Sub-Lamb may incorrectly mark the exterior region of the fractured shape as belonging to the fracture, causing the entirety of the fractured shape to be merged with the restoration, e.g., for the airplane and jar in Fig. 8. Figure 9 shows that for Sub-Lamb, 20.4% of restoration shapes have a high NFRE between 0.975 and 1.

5.3   Results with Google Scanned Objects, QP, and Fractured Mugs

We show results of training and testing DeepMend with the Google Scanned Objects dataset in Fig. 10(a). We obtain a chamfer distance of 0.112. DeepMend generates closely fitting restorations for objects that are prone to fracture such as the plate, the pot, and the bowls in Fig. 10(a), and reasonable restoration shapes for objects with high intra-class variety such as shoes.

We demonstrate the generalizability of our approach to novel datasets by using ShapeNet-trained jars and mugs networks to restore synthetically fractured shapes for objects from the QP dataset, shown in Fig. 10(b), and for 3D scans of 4 real-world fractured mugs, shown in Fig. 10(c). We achieve a mean chamfer distance of 0.047 for QP objects. DeepMend generates plausible restorations for shapes that resemble modern bowls, such as the effigy bowl in Fig. 10(b), and for uncommon shapes, such as the psykter vase in Fig. 10(b).

The restoration process for real-world mugs is particularly challenging. For synthetic breaks, the fractured and non-fracture regions in synthetic breaks have a clear edge. In real-world mugs, the break structure is far more complex with sharp curvature and smoothed out edges as seen in Fig. 10(c). Scanning limitations may cause the fracture surface geometry to be less precisely captured in comparison to the roughness of simulated fractures. Despite the challenges, our approach shows the capability to reconstruct the restoration by generating break surfaces that approach the fracture surface of real broken mugs.

6   Conclusion

We provide DeepMend, an approach to automatically restore fractured shapes by learning to represent complete shapes, break surfaces, and their interplay. We contribute penalty functions for inference that penalize mean occupancy values against being too high or low, thereby ensuring well-structured restorations. DeepMend does not require ground truth knowledge of the fracture region, making it amenable for rapid repair.

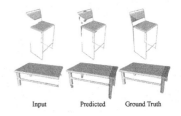

Input   Predicted   Ground Truth

Fig. 11. Restorations with multiple components.

One **limitation** of our work is that it may predict multiple unnecessary components, especially for thin structures, e.g., the chair in Fig. 11, which are often problematic for learned volumetric functions. Since the components are on the restoration side of the surface, NFRE remains lower than with the baseline methods and the components do not effect joinability. In many cases, e.g. the table in Fig. 11, multiple components yield plausible restorations. For the table class, these components together with the high intra-class variance contribute to an increased CD, as shown in Table 1. Multiple component prediction may arise as the break surface can adopt arbitrarily complex geometries during inference. As part of future work, data-driven priors can be incorporated on the structure of break surfaces. Future work can use datasets to learn prior probability distributions of occupancy of 3D objects. The learned shape representation can be strengthened with structural constraints, e.g., symmetries and planarity.

While not explored in this work, DeepMend may be combined with approaches to perform fractured object reassembly [6,31,52] to enable automatic restoration of fractured objects with multiple components. Novel scanned datasets of objects with diverse materials and diverse damage, e.g., chipping, shearing, splintering, and ductile versus brittle fractures can benefit the study of the damage process and impact on fracture surface geometry. Our work contributes a geometric foundation for the study of fractured shape repair using closed 3D surfaces. The work opens the scope for future research on automated shape repair using depth and color images to facilitate democratization of the repair process.

Acknowledgments. This work is supported by the National Science Foundation (NSF) Graduate Research Fellowship Program under Grant 1945954. We thank the Clarkson University Office of Information Technology for the use of the ACRES GPU server sponsored by NSF Grant 1925596.

References

1. Achlioptas, P., Diamanti, O., Mitliagkas, I., Guibas, L.: Learning representations and generative models for 3d point clouds. In: International Conference On Machine Learning. PMLR (2018)
2. Attene, M.: A lightweight approach to repairing digitized polygon meshes. Visual Comput. **26**(11), 1393–1406 (2010)
3. Brock, A., Lim, T., Ritchie, J.M., Weston, N.: Generative and discriminative voxel modeling with convolutional neural networks. arXiv preprint arXiv:1608.04236 1(1), 1–9 (2016)
4. Chabra, R., Lenssen, J.E., Ilg, E., Schmidt, T., Straub, J., Lovegrove, S., Newcombe, R.: Deep local shapes: learning local SDF priors for detailed 3D reconstruction. In: Vedaldi, A., Bischof, H., Brox, T., Frahm, J.-M. (eds.) ECCV 2020. LNCS, vol. 12374, pp. 608–625. Springer, Cham (2020). https://doi.org/10.1007/978-3-030-58526-6_36
5. Chang, A.X., et al.: ShapeNet: An Information-Rich 3D Model Repository. Technology Report. arXiv:1512.03012 [cs.GR], Stanford University – Princeton University – Toyota Technological Institute at Chicago (2015)
6. Chen, Y.C., Li, H., Turpin, D., Jacobson, A., Garg, A.: Neural shape mating: self-supervised object assembly with adversarial shape priors. In: Proceedings of the IEEE/CVF Conference on Computer Vision and Pattern Recognition, pp. 12724–12733 (2022)
7. Chen, Z., Zhang, H.: Learning implicit fields for generative shape modeling. In: Proceedings of CVPR, pp. 5939–5948. IEEE, Piscataway, NJ (2019)
8. Chibane, J., Alldieck, T., Pons-Moll, G.: Implicit functions in feature space for 3d shape reconstruction and completion. In: Proceedings of CVPR, pp. 6970–6981. IEEE, Piscataway, NJ (2020)
9. Dai, A., Diller, C., Nießner, M.: SG-NN: sparse generative neural networks for self-supervised scene completion of RGB-D scans. In: Proceedings of the IEEE/CVF Conference on Computer Vision and Pattern Recognition, pp. 849–858 (2020)
10. Dai, A., Ritchie, D., Bokeloh, M., Reed, S., Sturm, J., Nießner, M.: ScanComplete: large-scale scene completion and semantic segmentation for 3d scans. In: Proceedings of CVPR, pp. 4578–4587. IEEE, Piscataway, NJ (2018)
11. Dai, A., Ruizhongtai Qi, C., Nießner, M.: Shape completion using 3d-encoder-predictor CNNs and shape synthesis. In: Proceedings of the IEEE Conference on Computer Vision and Pattern Recognition, pp. 5868–5877 (2017)
12. Duan, Y., Zhu, H., Wang, H., Yi, L., Nevatia, R., Guibas, L.J.: Curriculum DeepSDF. In: Vedaldi, A., Bischof, H., Brox, T., Frahm, J.-M. (eds.) ECCV 2020. LNCS, vol. 12353, pp. 51–67. Springer, Cham (2020). https://doi.org/10.1007/978-3-030-58598-3_4

13. Duchon, J.: Splines minimizing rotation-invariant semi-norms in Sobolev spaces. In: Schempp, W., Zeller, K. (eds) Constructive Theory of Functions of Several Variables. Lecture Notes in Mathematics, vol. 571. Springer, Berlin, Heidelberg (1977). https://doi.org/10.1007/BFb0086566

14. Duggal, S., et al.: Mending neural implicit modeling for 3d vehicle reconstruction in the wild. In: Proceedings of the IEEE/CVF Winter Conference on Applications of Computer Vision, pp. 1900–1909 (2022)

15. Genova, K., Cole, F., Sud, A., Sarna, A., Funkhouser, T.: Local deep implicit functions for 3d shape. In: Proceedings of CVPR, pp. 4857–4866. IEEE, Piscataway, NJ (2020)

16. Genova, K., Cole, F., Vlasic, D., Sarna, A., Freeman, W.T., Funkhouser, T.: Learning shape templates with structured implicit functions. In: Proceedings of CVPR, pp. 7154–7164. IEEE, Piscataway, NJ (2019)

17. Gregor, R., Sipiran, I., Papaioannou, G., Schreck, T., Andreadis, A., Mavridis, P.: Towards automated 3d reconstruction of defective cultural heritage objects. In: GCH, pp. 135–144. EUROGRAPHICS, Geneva, Switzerland (2014)

18. Groueix, T., Fisher, M., Kim, V.G., Russell, B.C., Aubry, M.: A papier-mâché approach to learning 3d surface generation. In: Proceedings of CVPR, pp. 216–224. IEEE, Piscataway, NJ (2018)

19. Gupta, M.M., Qi, J.: Theory of T-norms and fuzzy inference methods. Fuzzy Sets Syst. **40**(3), 431–450 (1991)

20. Han, X., Li, Z., Huang, H., Kalogerakis, E., Yu, Y.: High-resolution shape completion using deep neural networks for global structure and local geometry inference. In: Proceedings of the IEEE International Conference on Computer Vision, pp. 85–93 (2017)

21. Hao, Z., Averbuch-Elor, H., Snavely, N., Belongie, S.: DualSDF: semantic shape manipulation using a two-level representation. In: Proceedings of the IEEE/CVF Conference on Computer Vision and Pattern Recognition, pp. 7631–7641 (2020)

22. Hermoza, R., Sipiran, I.: 3d reconstruction of incomplete archaeological objects using a generative adversarial network. In: Proceedings of Computer Graphics International, pp. 5–11. ACM, New York, NY (2018)

23. Jia, M., Kyan, M.: Learning occupancy function from point clouds for surface reconstruction. arXiv preprint arXiv:2010.11378 (2020)

24. Koutsoudis, A., Pavlidis, G., Arnaoutoglou, F., Tsiafakis, D., Chamzas, C.: QP: a tool for generating 3d models of ancient Greek pottery. J. Cult. Herit. **10**(2), 281–295 (2009)

25. Lamb, N., Banerjee, S., Banerjee, N.K.: MendNet: Restoration of Fractured Shapes Using Learned Occupancy Functions. Computer Graphics Forum (2022)

26. Lamb, N., Banerjee, S., Banerjee, N.K.: Automated reconstruction of smoothly joining 3d printed restorations to fix broken objects. In: Proceedings of SCF, pp. 1–12. ACM, New York, NY (2019)

27. Lamb, N., Wiederhold, N., Lamb, B., Banerjee, S., Banerjee, N.K.: Using learned visual and geometric features to retrieve complete 3d proxies for broken objects. In: Proceedings of SCF, pp. 1–15. ACM, New York, NY (2021)

28. Liao, Y., Donne, S., Geiger, A.: Deep marching cubes: learning explicit surface representations. In: Proceedings of CVPR, pp. 2916–2925. IEEE, Piscataway, NJ (2018)

29. Lin, C.H., Wang, C., Lucey, S.: SDF-SRN: learning signed distance 3d object reconstruction from static images. arXiv preprint arXiv:2010.10505 (2020)

30. Lionar, S., Emtsev, D., Svilarkovic, D., Peng, S.: Dynamic plane convolutional occupancy networks. In: Proceedings of WACV, pp. 1829–1838. IEEE, Piscataway, NJ (2021)
31. Liu, B., Wang, M., Niu, X., Wang, S., Zhang, S., Zhang, J.: A fragment fracture surface segmentation method based on learning of local geometric features on margins used for automatic utensil reassembly. Comput. Aid. Des. **132**, 102963 (2021)
32. Liu, M., Sheng, L., Yang, S., Shao, J., Hu, S.M.: Morphing and sampling network for dense point cloud completion. In: Proceedings of the AAAI Conference on Artificial Intelligence, vol. 34, pp. 11596–11603. AAAI, Menlo Park, CA (2020)
33. Lorensen, W.E., Cline, H.E.: Marching cubes: a high resolution 3d surface construction algorithm. ACM SIGGRAPH Comput. Graph. **21**(4), 163–169 (1987)
34. Ma, B., Han, Z., Liu, Y.S., Zwicker, M.: Neural-pull: learning signed distance functions from point clouds by learning to pull space onto surfaces. arXiv preprint arXiv:2011.13495 (2020)
35. Mescheder, L., Oechsle, M., Niemeyer, M., Nowozin, S., Geiger, A.: Occupancy networks: learning 3d reconstruction in function space. In: Proceedings of CVPR, pp. 4460–4470. IEEE, Piscataway, NJ (2019)
36. Pan, L., et al.: Variational relational point completion network. In: Proceedings of the IEEE/CVF Conference on Computer Vision and Pattern Recognition, pp. 8524–8533 (2021)
37. Papaioannou, G., et al.: From reassembly to object completion: a complete systems pipeline. J. Comput. Cult. Herit. **10**(2), 1–22 (2017)
38. Park, J.J., Florence, P., Straub, J., Newcombe, R., Lovegrove, S.: DeepSDF: learning continuous signed distance functions for shape representation. In: Proceedings of CVPR, pp. 165–174. IEEE, Piscataway, NJ (2019)
39. Peng, S., Niemeyer, M., Mescheder, L., Pollefeys, M., Geiger, A.: Convolutional occupancy networks. In: Vedaldi, A., Bischof, H., Brox, T., Frahm, J.-M. (eds.) ECCV 2020. LNCS, vol. 12348, pp. 523–540. Springer, Cham (2020). https://doi.org/10.1007/978-3-030-58580-8_31
40. Poursaeed, O., Fisher, M., Aigerman, N., Kim, V.G.: Coupling explicit and implicit surface representations for generative 3D modeling. In: Vedaldi, A., Bischof, H., Brox, T., Frahm, J.-M. (eds.) ECCV 2020. LNCS, vol. 12355, pp. 667–683. Springer, Cham (2020). https://doi.org/10.1007/978-3-030-58607-2_39
41. Qi, C.R., Su, H., Mo, K., Guibas, L.J.: Pointnet: deep learning on point sets for 3d classification and segmentation. In: Proceedings of CVPR, pp. 652–660. IEEE, Piscataway, NJ (2017)
42. Google Research: Google scanned objects, August 2021. https://fuel.ignitionrobotics.org/1.0/Google%20Research/fuel/collections/Google%20Scanned%20Objects
43. Sarmad, M., Lee, H.J., Kim, Y.M.: RL-GAN-Net: a reinforcement learning agent controlled GAN network for real-time point cloud shape completion. In: Proceedings of CVPR, pp. 5898–5907. IEEE, Piscataway, NJ (2019)
44. Sharma, A., Grau, O., Fritz, M.: VConv-DAE: deep volumetric shape learning without object labels. In: Hua, G., Jégou, H. (eds.) ECCV 2016. LNCS, vol. 9915, pp. 236–250. Springer, Cham (2016). https://doi.org/10.1007/978-3-319-49409-8_20
45. Sitzmann, V., Chan, E.R., Tucker, R., Snavely, N., Wetzstein, G.: MetaSDF: meta-learning signed distance functions. arXiv preprint arXiv:2006.09662 (2020)
46. Smith, E.J., Meger, D.: Improved adversarial systems for 3d object generation and reconstruction. In: Conference on Robot Learning, pp. 87–96. PMLR, Cambridge, UK (2017)

47. Son, H., Kim, Y.M.: SAUM: Symmetry-aware upsampling module for consistent point cloud completion. In: Ishikawa, H., Liu, C.-L., Pajdla, T., Shi, J. (eds.) ACCV 2020. LNCS, vol. 12622, pp. 158–174. Springer, Cham (2021). https://doi.org/10.1007/978-3-030-69525-5_10

48. Stutz, D., Geiger, A.: Learning 3d shape completion under weak supervision. CoRR abs/1805.07290 (2018). https://arxiv.org/abs/1805.07290

49. Sulzer, R., Landrieu, L., Boulch, A., Marlet, R., Vallet, B.: Deep surface reconstruction from point clouds with visibility information. arXiv preprint arXiv:2202.01810 (2022)

50. Tang, J., Lei, J., Xu, D., Ma, F., Jia, K., Zhang, L.: Sign-agnostic CoNet: learning implicit surface reconstructions by sign-agnostic optimization of convolutional occupancy networks. arXiv preprint arXiv:2105.03582 (2021)

51. Tretschk, E., Tewari, A., Golyanik, V., Zollhöfer, M., Stoll, C., Theobalt, C.: Patch-Nets: patch-based generalizable deep implicit 3d shape representations. In: Vedaldi, A., Bischof, H., Brox, T., Frahm, J.-M. (eds.) ECCV 2020. LNCS, vol. 12361, pp. 293–309. Springer, Cham (2020). https://doi.org/10.1007/978-3-030-58517-4_18

52. Wang, H., Zang, Y., Liang, F., Dong, Z., Fan, H., Yang, B.: A probabilistic method for fractured cultural relics automatic reassembly. J. Comput. Cult. Herit. (JOCCH) **14**(1), 1–25 (2021)

53. Wu, J., Zhang, C., Xue, T., Freeman, W.T., Tenenbaum, J.B.: Learning a probabilistic latent space of object shapes via 3d generative-adversarial modeling. In: Proceedings of NeurIPS, pp. 82–90. Neural Information Processing Systems, San Diego, CA (2016)

54. Xiao, Y., Xu, J., Gao, S.: Taylorimnet for fast 3d shape reconstruction based on implicit surface function. arXiv preprint arXiv:2201.06845 (2022)

55. Xu, Yifan, Fan, Tianqi, Yuan, Yi., Singh, Gurprit: Ladybird: quasi-monte Carlo sampling for deep implicit field based 3d reconstruction with symmetry. In: Vedaldi, Andrea, Bischof, Horst, Brox, Thomas, Frahm, Jan-Michael. (eds.) ECCV 2020. LNCS, vol. 12346, pp. 248–263. Springer, Cham (2020). https://doi.org/10.1007/978-3-030-58452-8_15

56. Yan, S., Yang, Z., Li, H., Guan, L., Kang, H., Hua, G., Huang, Q.: Implicit autoencoder for point cloud self-supervised representation learning. arXiv preprint arXiv:2201.00785 (2022)

57. Yan, X., Lin, L., Mitra, N.J., Lischinski, D., Cohen-Or, D., Huang, H.: Shape-Former: Transformer-based shape completion via sparse representation. arXiv preprint arXiv:2201.10326 (2022)

58. Yang, M., Wen, Y., Chen, W., Chen, Y., Jia, K.: Deep optimized priors for 3d shape modeling and reconstruction. In: Proceedings of CVPR, pp. 3269–3278. IEEE, Piscataway, NJ (2021)

59. Yi, L., Gong, B., Funkhouser, T.: Complete & label: a domain adaptation approach to semantic segmentation of lidar point clouds. In: Proceedings of the IEEE/CVF Conference on Computer Vision and Pattern Recognition, pp. 15363–15373 (2021)

60. Yu, Q., Yang, C., Wei, H.: Part-wise Atlasnet for 3d point cloud reconstruction from a single image. Knowledge-Based Systems, p. 108395 (2022)

61. Yuan, W., Khot, T., Held, D., Mertz, C., Hebert, M.: PCN: point completion network. In: 2018 International Conference on 3D Vision (3DV), pp. 728–737. IEEE (2018)

62. Zheng, Z., Yu, T., Dai, Q., Liu, Y.: Deep implicit templates for 3d shape representation. In: Proceedings of CVPR, pp. 1429–1439. IEEE, Piscataway, NJ (2021)

A Repulsive Force Unit for Garment Collision Handling in Neural Networks

Qingyang Tan[1]($\boxtimes$)(ID), Yi Zhou[2], Tuanfeng Wang[2], Duygu Ceylan[2], Xin Sun[2], and Dinesh Manocha[1]

[1] Department of Computer Science, University of Maryland at College Park, College Park, USA
{qytan,dmanocha}@umd.edu
[2] Adobe Research, San Jose, USA
{yizho,yangtwan,ceylan,xinsun}@adobe.com
https://gamma.umd.edu/researchdirections/mlphysics/refu/

Abstract. Despite recent success, deep learning-based methods for predicting 3D garment deformation under body motion suffer from interpenetration problems between the garment and the body. To address this problem, we propose a novel collision handling neural network layer called Repulsive Force Unit (ReFU). Based on the signed distance function (SDF) of the underlying body and the current garment vertex positions, ReFU predicts the per-vertex offsets that push any interpenetrating vertex to a collision-free configuration while preserving the fine geometric details. We show that ReFU is differentiable with trainable parameters and can be integrated into different network backbones that predict 3D garment deformations. Our experiments show that ReFU significantly reduces the number of collisions between the body and the garment and better preserves geometric details compared to prior methods based on collision loss or post-processing optimization.

1 Introduction

Predicting how a 3D garment deforms in response to the underlying 3D body motion is essential for many applications, including realistically dressed human body reconstruction [6], interactive garment design [45], virtual try-on [35], and robotics control [38]. To generate accurate cloth deformations, most techniques are based on physically-based simulation (PBS). Common physically-based models include the mass-spring system [2,9], the finite element approach [22,27], the thin-shell model [15], etc. However, these methods tend to be computationally intensive since they typically involve solving large linear systems and handling collisions. In particular, robust collision handling based on collision detection and response computation is a critical component of cloth or garment simulation. Even a single missed collision can considerably affect the accuracy of the overall simulator [7,14].

Supplementary Information The online version contains supplementary material available at https://doi.org/10.1007/978-3-031-20062-5_26.

Fig. 1. Collisions solved by applying ReFU in garment prediction neural networks. Our approach reduces the number of artifacts.

The most accurate physically-based simulators run at 0.5 seconds per frame on commodity GPUs [42], where collision handling can take 50–80% of total simulation time. As a result, these simulators are unable to provide real-time performance for interactive applications such as gaming and virtual try-on.

Machine learning methods provide a promising direction to dramatically reduce the computational cost of cloth simulators. Hence, in recent years, various neural network methods have been proposed to predict 3D cloth deformations. However, a common setback of such methods is the lack of efficient handling of collisions between the garments and the body surface as shown in the yellow garments in Fig. 1. In our experiments (Sect. 4), we observe that only 49% of garments predicted from TailorNet [32], a state-of-the-art neural network based 3D garment prediction method, are collision-free. For some tight clothes like shirts, only 12% of models are collision-free. Thus, the resulting state of the cloth mesh can collide with the body mesh, which affects the reliability and usefulness of these methods for many applications related to rendering, simulation, and animation [8,34,44]. As a result, it is important to design learning methods that can significantly reduce or eliminate such collisions.

One option to address the body-cloth collision problem is to perform post processing optimizations [17]. However, these optimization approaches can take considerable CPU time (around 0.6–0.8s per frame), which can be too expensive for interactive applications. A more common practice is to apply specialized collision loss functions during training [3–5,18,35]. However, this only provides a soft constraint to avoid collisions for network training, and the network still cannot handle the penetrated vertices when collisions happen during inference.

Main Results: To let the network learn to solve the collisions through inference, we propose a novel neural network layer called Repulsive Force Unit (ReFU). ReFU is fully differentiable and can be plugged into different garment prediction backbone networks, trained either through fine-tuning or from scratch.

Our design of ReFU is inspired by physically-based simulators [13,25,43], which use a scheme that collects repulsive forces, friction forces, and adhesion forces as part of time integration. Our goal is to design a learning scheme that can model the effects of repulsive forces and can easily cope with existing 3D garment prediction networks. We compute the force based on the implicit field of the body geometry to quickly detect the set of penetrated garment vertices and the repulsive direction. The repulsive strength is predicted by the neural network inside the ReFU layer. Instead of simply pushing the problematic garment vertices to the body surface, ReFU applies a flexible offset to move them. This improves the overall collision handling performance, avoids additional Edge-Edge (EE) collisions that normally cannot be detected by the signed distance of the vertices, and overcomes the artifacts in the estimated implicit functions of the human body. To achieve real-time performance for the whole garment prediction system, we leverage the power of neural implicit surface representation and use a neural network to quickly estimate the approximate Signed Distance Function (SDF) of the human body under different poses [16].

To evaluate ReFU with different backbones, we train it with TailorNet [32], the state-of-the-art 3D garment prediction network, and a 3D mesh convolutional neural network [47]. Our experiments show that backbone networks trained with ReFU can significantly reduce the number of body-cloth collisions while achieving real-time performance for the whole garment prediction system during testing. The ReFU layer and SDF network will only add 2 ms of inference time to the overall system. Overall, our method achieves much better results in terms of the number of interpenetrating vertices, the number of collision-free 3D garment models, and the reconstruction error of the generated garments. Compared to prior learning-based methods, the use of ReFU results in garment meshes with fewer artifacts and higher visual quality.

2 Related Work

2.1 Physically-Based Collision Handling

Many accurate techniques have been proposed for collision detection between discrete time intervals using continuous methods (CCD), which reduce to solving cubic polynomials for linear interpolating motion [8,34,41,44]. There is extensive literature on collision response computation based on constraint solvers [28], impulse responses [7], and impact zone methods [19,34]. These methods have been used to develop robust physics-based simulators that are widely used in animation and VR applications. Current learning-based methods are significantly faster than these physics-based simulators but cannot offer the same level of accuracy or robustness. Other techniques for collision handling are based on optimization-based refinement [17] but have computational overhead.

2.2 Cloth Prediction Using Machine Learning

Many fast techniques have been used to predict cloth deformation in 3D. These include simple linear models such as [11,17] and motion graph methods [21]. More recent works use neural networks [3–5,18,32,35,36]. Many of these learning methods have been designed for SMPL-based [23] parametric obstacle models, including human shapes. Other methods are designed for general triangle mesh-based obstacles [20]. The GarNet network architecture [18] can predict the cloth deformation from the target posture with DQS pre-processing. However, these learning methods do not explicitly account for cloth-obstacle collisions.

2.3   Learning-Based Collision Handling

Several techniques have been proposed to handle collisions in machine learning methods. Recently Tan et al. [39] estimated a collision-free subspace for 3D
human models, but it is not practical to compute a similar subspace for deforming garments as they have a lot of degrees of freedom. Its performance can be
improved using active learning [40], but this approach is limited by the use of
numerical optimization algorithm. These methods can't be combined with general garment prediction backbone networks. Many recent works [3–5,18] use collision loss to penalize penetrated garment-body pairs during training. However,
these methods have no component or feature in the network that can resolve
these penetrations during inference.

Recently, Santesteban et al. [36] proposed a self-supervised
collision handling method, but it requires strict additional
restrictions on the training data, i.e., that both garments in
the global space and the canonical space must be collision-
free. However, most public garment datasets cannot satisfy
this restriction. We show an example on the left from Tai-
lorNet dataset which is collision-free in canonical space, but not in the posed
space.

To solve the collision problems for the testing set, a simple approach is to
perform post-processing on the predicted cloth by detecting the vertices inside
the human body and moving them directly to the nearest point on the body
surface [20,35]. However, there are two issues with these approaches: first, computing nearest points on the body surface is time-consuming; second, simply
moving the garment vertices may generate abrupt cloth movements and lose
some properties of the original garment.

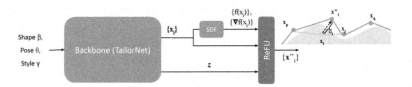

Fig. 2. A garment inference model with ReFU: Given body shape β, pose θ, and
garment style γ parameters, the backbone network is used generate a deformed garment
with potential body-cloth collisions. Our ReFU layer is attached to the backbone and
processes every point $\{x_i\}_{i=1}^{N}$ in the garment. This layer first checks whether the point
is inside the human body or not based on the SDF value $f(x_i)$. If it is outside, ReFU
directly outputs the point. Otherwise, ReFU will apply a repulsive force along the
direction of the gradient of the SDF $\nabla f(x_i)$ with a predicted amount of movement
d_i. Finally, we collect all the vertices passed through the ReFU layer and obtain a 3D
garment mesh with fewer collisions.

3   Collision Handling Using ReFU

In this section, we will first explain the formulation of the Repulsive Force Unit (ReFU) (Sect. 3.1) then describe how to apply and train it in the garment prediction backbone network as an additional network layer using the example of TailorNet [32] (Sect. 3.2). Finally, we will present how we train a neural network to quickly estimate the SDF for the human body (Sect. 3.3). Our overall learning-based pipeline is shown in Fig. 2. With a neural network-based SDF approximation, our system can achieve real-time performance for garment prediction given the body pose and shape parameters.

3.1   ReFU: Repulsive Force Unit

The goal of body-cloth collision handling is to find the penetrating garment vertices and move them to the proper positions to resolve the collision while preserving original wrinkles and other details on the garments. Let N_c be the number of vertices that need to be moved. The degrees of freedom of this set of vertices result in a large solution space of dimension $3N_c$. Our goal is to reduce the dimension of the solution space. Inspired by prior work in physically-based simulation [13,43], we design the Repulsive Force Unit (ReFU) to move the vertices only along a *repulsion* direction, which is toward the closest point on the body surface. Our formulation of ReFU can be seen as applying a virtual repulsive force to move the penetrated vertex outside the human body.

To find the repulsion direction, ReFU uses the implicit representation of the body, i.e., the signed distance function (SDF). Given a query point x, the SDF function f returns its distance to the closest point on the corresponding surface, and its sign is associated with whether the point is inside (negative) or outside (positive) the surface:

$$f(x) = s, \quad x \in \mathbb{R}^3, s \in \mathbb{R}. \tag{1}$$

The zero-level set of $f(x)$ indicates the surface.

Given the nature of SDF, we can quickly determine whether a vertex x_i on the garment mesh is inside or outside the body. For x_i with negative SDF value, the gradient of the SDF at x_i is pointing towards the nearest point on the surface along the normal direction. Thus, we formulate ReFU as

$$\text{ReFU}(x_i) = \begin{cases} x_i - d_i \widehat{\nabla_{x_i} f(x_i)}, & f(x_i) < 0; \\ x_i, & otherwise, \end{cases} \tag{2}$$

where d_i is a predicted offset scalar indicating the amount of movement, and $\widehat{\nabla_x f(\cdot)}$ is the normalized gradient of f at x, indicating the direction of movement, calculated as below:

$$\widehat{\nabla_x f(x)} = \frac{\nabla_x f(x)}{\|\nabla_x f(x)\|_2} \tag{3}$$

Although the gradient of accurate SDF should be a unit vector [10,16], the approximated SDF by neural networks [24,37] might not strictly satisfy this property. Thus, we need to normalize the gradient in practice.

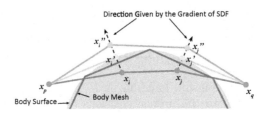

Fig. 3. We show an example of resolving vertex-face (VF) and edge-edge (EE) collisions. Assume the blue polyline is a part of the human body mesh, and the light blue region is the body represented by the SDF estimator f. We show four garment vertices $x_{i,j,p,q}$, where $x_{i,j}$ are inside the human body and $x_{p,q}$ are outside of it. The dotted arrows are the repulsive force directions given by the gradient of f. If we set $\alpha_{i,j} = 1$ and the moving offset to be $|f(x_{i,j})|$, the vertices will moved to $x'_{i,j}$. While the collision along the edges $\overline{x_p x'_i}$ and $\overline{x_q x'_j}$ are resolved, the edge $\overline{x'_i x'_j}$ will still induce a collision. By allowing $\alpha_{i,j} > =1$, we can move the vertices to $x''_{i,j}$, resolving all the VF and EE collisions. (Color figure online)

A Learned Moving Offset. A straightforward way to decide the moving offset is to use the SDF value directly. However, as pointed out in the context of physically-based simulators [42], this is only guaranteed to solve the Vertex-Face (VF) collisions, but not the Edge-Edge (EE) collisions. As shown in Fig. 3, we push the two neighboring garment vertices further outside to resolve the EE collisions. To compute this extra offset based on the mesh representation, we need to use a global optimizer in an iterative manner. However, this computation can be time consuming and the resulting configuration may not match the groundtruth. Instead, we use neural networks to predict α_i, the scale of movement, and multiply it with the SDF value to compute the final offset as:

$$d_i = \alpha_i f(x_i), \alpha \geq 0. \tag{4}$$

α_i is predicted based on the global latent feature z of the whole garment and the SDF value of vertex x_i.

$$\alpha_i = g(k(z)_i, f(x_i)), z \in \mathbb{R}^M, \tag{5}$$

where $k : \mathbb{R}^M \to \mathbb{R}^{N \times D}$ is a topology-dependent Multilayer Perception (MLP) network that infers the latent vector for every vertex from the global feature z, and $k(z)_i \in \mathbb{R}^D$ is for i-th vertex x_i. g is another MLP that outputs the movement scale for x_i. Both $g(\cdot, \cdot)$ and $k(\cdot)$ are jointly trained with the backbone network in an end-to-end manner. We choose $M = 1024$ and $D = 10$ for our experiments.

The global garment latent vector z can be obtained from the backbone network. In terms of using TailorNet as the backbone network, z is computed from the predefined body pose and shape parameters β, θ and the garment style parameter γ (as formulated in Tailornet [32] for the definition of β, θ, and γ) with an MLP function h.

$$z = h(\beta, \theta, \gamma). \tag{6}$$

When the accurate groundtruth SDF is given, the output range of g can be set as $[1, +\infty)$ so it ensures all penetrated vertices will be pushed outside. When using a neural network based approximate SDF, we relax the range to be $[0, +\infty)$ to account for inaccuracies in the SDF prediction. Implementation details of the MLPs are given in Sect. 4.2.

Using the learned offset has several benefits. First, a flexible extent can handle the collision more naturally and let the moved vertices blend more smoothly with neighboring vertices. Second, it can help resolve additional Edge-Edge (EE) collisions. Finally, the flexible offset can cope with the inaccuracies of the neural network approximated SDF. For example, when the absolute SDF value predicted by $f(x)$ is smaller than the ground truth, directly using the $f(x)$ as the offset could leave the penetrated vertex inside the human body. On the other hand, if $f(x)$ predicts larger distance than the ground truth, the resulting vertex may be pushed too far away from the human body, resulting in a "pump out" artifact, as shown in Fig. 5. However, when using ReFU during training, the backbone network and the MLPs in the ReFU layer will foresee the quality of the SDF function. As a result, it will learn to adjust the prediction of both x_i and α_i and thereby result in a more accurate final output garment with fewer collisions.

3.2   Train Backbone with ReFU

ReFU can be easily plugged into current neural network frameworks for garment prediction. Here we show how to train the backbone network with ReFU with the example of TailorNet [32]. When using ReFU, we assume that the colliding vertices are not far from the body surface so that the repulsive force can be estimated through the SDF. Thus, we train the ReFU layer with the backbone network in the fine-tuning stage. One could also train the ReFU with the garment network from scratch. We will explain the use of Graph Convolutional Neural Network (GCNN) [47] in the supplementary material.

The original TailorNet trains different frequency focused components separately to allow the different components realize the difference between low-frequency and high-frequency deformations. However, the groundtruth representation of the garment, obtained after the frequency division, may not satisfy the collision-free condition, i.e., the high-frequency pieces may have deeper penetrations inside the human body. If we plug in ReFU after computing the high-frequency output, the new vertices will all be moved outside the body, and their coordinates will be different from their high-frequency groundtruth. Thus, we propose training ReFU as a finetuning process together with all the components of TailorNet, which have the summation of all the frequencies with no collisions in the groundtruth data.

We attached a ReFU layer to the end of the pre-trained TailorNet so that it receives the raw output of $\{x_i\}_{i=1}^N$. Assuming the predicted garment vertex positions after the ReFU layer is $\{x_i'\}_{i=1}^N$ and the corresponding groundtruth is $\{\tilde{x}_i\}_{i=1}^N$, we use the following loss terms to train the backbone network and the ReFU layer:

$$\mathcal{L} = \lambda_1 \mathcal{L}_r + \lambda_2 \mathcal{L}_c, \tag{7}$$

$$\mathcal{L}_r = \sum_{i=1}^N \|x_i' - \tilde{x}_i\|_2^2, \tag{8}$$

$$\mathcal{L}_c = \sum_{i=1}^N |\max(-f(x_i'), 0)|, \tag{9}$$

where $\mathcal{L}_r$ is the reconstruction loss and $\mathcal{L}_c$ is the collision loss to cover missed penetrated vertices. $\lambda_{1,2}$ are weights to balance the loss terms.

We train the network with groundtruth collision-free garment data so the reconstruction loss will guide the prediction of the x_i and α_i to move x_i' to the position with no EE collisions. In this manner, it better preserves the local smoothness and details.

It turns out that the post-processing methods in previous works [20,35] can only move the vertex along the gradient direction of the SDF of x_i. With our method, however, although the adjustment space of each collided vertex is also one degree-of-freedom (DOF) during inference, through the training, both the backbone and the ReFU layer are fine-tuned so the adjustment space extends to 4 DOFs, i.e., the movement scale α_i and the original network output x_i. With higher adjustment capability, our method achieves performance on par with complex optimization-based post-processing such as [17]. Detailed comparisons with previous methods are described in Sect. 4.5.

3.3   Neural Network for Body SDF

In physically-based simulation methods, the SDF values are computed using analytical methods and accelerated using spatial data structures like KD-trees. Even with these acceleration data structures, the SDF computation is far from real-time as shown in the running time comparison in the supplementary material. Recent works [16,30] show that the implicit function of a 3D geometry can be approximated by a neural network. As a result, one can use the trained network to quickly estimate the SDF values of a 3D point set. We design the network to predict SDF conditioned on the SMPL [23] parameters, please see more details in the supplementary material.

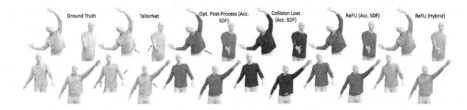

Fig. 4. Benefits of ReFU: The baseline models from TailorNet have collisions (red arrow), optimization-based post-processing results in non-smooth regions (blue arrow); collision loss cannot resolve the collisions well; our method based on ReFU resolves the collisions and preserves the original shape with plausible wrinkles in both offline (using accurate SDF) and real-time ("Hybrid") modes. The results obtained using approximated SDF ("Hybrid") are similar to those obtained using accurate SDF. (Color figure online)

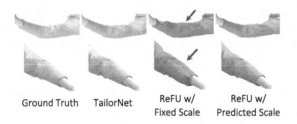

Fig. 5. We zoom in to highlight the "pump out" artifacts with fixed moving scale and approximated SDF. When $\alpha_i = 1$, the ReFU layer may wrongly push out some regions (blue arrow) with higher approximated SDF values than the ground truth. However, with predicted scale, the network learns how to cope with the inaccuracies of the approximated SDF and generates smooth results. This also reduces the number of VF and EE collisions (Table 3).

4 Experimental Results

In this section, we will quantitatively and qualitatively evaluate our method. Given our goal of achieving real-time performance for the whole garment prediction system, we use an approximated neural network predicted SDF (abbreviated as Approx. SDF) and combine it with ReFU. We also want to see the upper bound of our method, so we combine with an approach that computes accurate SDF (abbreviated as Acc. SDF).

Table 1. We highlight the details of the datasets used to evaluate our approach. We have selected collision-free subsets from the datasets in [32]. The resulting datasets include different genders and garment types.

Dataset	# of vertices	# of Training models	# of Testing models
Shirt male	9723	28360	3197
T-shirt male	7702	21097	2688
Short-pant male	2710	14555	2691
Skirt female	7130	15664	3525

4.1 Datasets, Metrics, and Settings

We utilize the datasets from TailorNet [32] to evaluate our method. We use an exact collision detection algorithm available as part of FCL [29] to select a subset of the garments from different genders and garment types that have no garment-body collisions or any self-penetrations in the 3D garment mesh. Except for this modification, we use the same train-test split as in [32] for both garment networks and SDF networks on different garment types to perform a fair comparison. The resulting dataset is summarized in Table 1. "All garments" in Table 3 correspond to the weighted-average performance for four types of datasets. We include more results on the dataset from Santesteban et al.'s [36] in the supplementary material and highlight the benefits of our approach.

We use the following metrics in our comparisons with prior methods:

MPVE [33] (Mean per-vertex error): Euclidean distance between the ground-truth and predicted garment vertices. It indicates the reconstruction error of the predicted garments. We use millimeters as the underlying unit.

VFCP [5] (Vertex-face collision percentage): The percentage of vertices on the garment that are inside the body surface.

CFMP [39] (Collision-free models percentage): The percentage of garment models that are body-cloth collision-free in both types of VF and EE collisions.

For training and testing, we have three settings:

Approx. SDF: Always use the neural network approximated SDF for training, testing and post-processing.

Acc. SDF: Always use the accurate SDF for training, testing and post-processing. For discretized 3D models such as the human body represented by the SMPL parameters, we compute the SDF value for one query point. This accurate formulation can compute closest point/face and returns the distance on the normal direction, thought it is time consuming (shown in the supplementary material.)

Hybrid: Use the accurate SDF for computing the collision loss during training but the approximate SDF for ReFU during both training and testing.

4.2   Implementation

We implement our method using PyTorch [31]. All the training and testing are performed on a server machine with a 96-core CPU, 740GB memory, and 4 NVIDIA V100 GPU with 32GB memory. To estimate the body surface SDF, we design the neural network f with nine hidden layers each with 1024 neurons. Between each layer, we use a Softplus activation layer [46] with $\beta = 100$. We include a skip connection in the fourth layer, i.e., concatenating the query point coordinate with the hidden vector. To train f, we feed a batch with 32 human body models each with SDF value of 4000 random sampled points. For the network predicting the scale α_i, we use three 1024-dimension layer for h, one $N \times 10$-dimension layers for k, and two 10-dimension layers for g. They all use ReLU as the activation layer in between. We set the weights of the loss terms as $\lambda_1 = 1.5$ and $\lambda_2 = 0.5$. For all the training, we use an Adam optimizer with a learning rate of 1×10^{-5}.

4.3   Performance

We first evaluate how ReFU performs when using the accurate body SDF during both training and testing. As listed in Table 3, only 49.09% of the garments generated by the original TailorNet are collision-free. After fine-tuning TailorNet with ReFU, the collision-free models increase significantly to 76.77%. For difficult cases like men's shirts, which have dense meshes and are tight fitting on the body, collision free models increase significantly by 5.3×, from 11.92% to 63.06%. Since we set $\alpha > =1$, all the interpenetrating vertices are pushed outside, and the VFCP drops from 0.6% to 0%. In the meantime, for MPVE, the reconstruction error also decreases from 8.89 to 8.64. However, querying the SDF values is computationally expensive, adding around 0.106 s of time cost to each garment inference (see in the supplementary material.).

Then we train and test how ReFU performs when using the neural network approximated body SDF. In other words, we train and test ReFU with imperfect but much faster SDF. The result shows that although this strategy cannot achieve the same level of collision handling as using accurate SDF, it still improves the collision and reconstruction accuracy of the original TailorNet a considerable level. The collision-free models increase to 58.52%, MPVE drops to 8.66, and VFCP decreases by half as shown in the third to last column in Table 3. The inference time for the ReFU layer with approximated SDF is 2.00 ms, and the inference time for the whole garment prediction system is 22.57 ms.

To improve the collision handling capability while maintaining the real-time performance during testing, we experiment with using accurate SDF values when computing the collision loss during training while feeding the approximate SDF into the ReFU layer during both training and testing. The network is guided with accurate collision loss during training while learning to accommodate the errors in the approximated SDF, which will be provided at test time. Now the result is much closer to the case of using accurate SDF. We call this a "hybrid" mode for simplicity. As shown in the last column in Table 3, the collision-free models achieve 68.71%, VFCP improves to 0.24%, and the reconstruction error is nearly the same.

From the last two columns in Fig. 4, we can visually observe how using ReFU improves the body-cloth collision problems in the original TailorNet. When trained and tested with Accurate SDF, the body penetrations are almost solved and the predicted garments look much more like the groundtruth. In the hybrid mode, although the network cannot achieve the same quantitative results as in the accurate SDF mode, the visual quality is quite similar. This is impressive for a real-time garment prediction system.

4.4   Ablation Study

Table 2. Ablation study on the predicted scale in ReFU. As we mentioned in Sect. 3.1, we use networks to predict the scale α_i to determine the moving offset of collided vertices. Here, we show that if we use only fixed scale (α_i always equals to 1), the performances are worse than the predicted ones with either approximated or accurate SDF. These experimental results show that our approach can also reduce the number of EE collisions.

Metric	Method					
	TailorNet	w/ Fixed Scale		w/ Predicted Scale		
		Approx. SDF	Acc. SDF	Approx. SDF	Acc. SDF	Hybrid
MPVE	11.27	10.84	10.60	10.59	10.56	10.57
VFCP	1.18%	0.58%	0.00%	0.62%	0.00%	0.51%
CFMP	11.92%	4.88%	37.22%	26.9%	63.06%	49.32%
Avg. VF	180.36	287.85	1.94	110.12	1.45	78.21
Avg. EE	11.56	19.60	8.89	8.6	6.98	7.39

In ReFU, we design a network-predicted scale α_i to determine the offset length d_i for each vertex. Theoretically it can help solve EE collisions and improve the reconstruction quality. Here we perform the ablation study to evaluate the effect of using predicted scale. We report the experimental results for male shirt in Table 2. As listed in the third and fourth columns, when only using $f(\boldsymbol{x}_i)$ without scaling, the quantitative results for all metrics are worse than with the predicted scaling. The percentage of collision-free models drops by two times in the case of using accurate SDF and over 5 times in the case of using the approximate SDF. Figure 5 further shows that when using the approximate SDF resulted in some pump out artifacts. With the fixed scale, the predicted cloth covers the pump out region of the approximate body surface (where approximated SDF values are larger than the accurate ones) in an awkward way. However, when trained with the predicted offset scale, the network learns to handle the imperfectness in the SDF and generates a smoother and more plausible result.

We also include the average number of colliding triangles on the garment, based on VF and EE contacts, denoted as "Avg. VF" and "Avg. EE". The results in Table 2 shows that our predicted α_i can further reduce the number of EE collisions, as compared with a fixed value. We also include another ablation study related to the design choices and other components of our networks, highlighted in Eq. 5, in the supplementary material.

4.5 Comparisons

Table 3. Comparison with baseline and different collision handling methods, including naïve post-processing [20,35], optimization-based post-processing [17], and soft collision loss [3–5,18]. We include an additional row called "Trend" to show the rate of change for each method compared to TailorNet, the baseline model. The report shows all methods perform better with accurate SDF than with approximate SDF. In either situation, ReFU has the best results among all the methods. Overall, ReFU with "hybrid" SDF works better than approximate SDF, and ReFU with accurate SDF achieves the best results.

Dataset	Metric	Method TailorNet	w/ Naïve Post-Process		w/ Opt. Post-Process		w/Collision Loss		w/ ReFU		
			Approx. SDF	Acc. SDF	Approx. SDF	Acc. SDF	Approx. SDF	Acc. SDF	Approx. SDF	Acc. SDF	Hybrid
Shirt Male	MPVE	11.27	11.45	11.26	11.30	11.26	10.85	10.61	10.59	**10.56**	10.57
	VFCP	1.18%	0.69%	0.00%	0.41%	0.00%	1.28%	0.68%	0.62%	**0.00%**	0.51%
	CFMP	11.92%	3.1%	27.5%	25.21%	50.36%	20.21%	39.35%	26.9%	**63.06%**	49.32%
T-Shirt Male	MPVE	10.77	10.81	10.75	10.76	10.75	10.60	10.59	10.58	**10.57**	10.56
	VFCP	0.95%	0.56%	0.00%	0.39%	0.00%	0.85%	0.86%	0.53%	**0.00%**	0.34%
	CFMP	23.96%	12.01%	38.02%	36.57%	51.60%	28.98%	28.76%	32.18%	**58.77%**	47.25%
Short-pant Male	MPVE	6.81	6.87	6.83	6.82	6.81	6.79	6.80	6.79	**6.76**	6.77
	VFCP	0.27%	0.83%	0.07%	0.11%	0.00%	0.19%	0.21%	0.13%	**0.00%**	0.13%
	CFMP	60.35%	20.07%	73.47%	68.60%	81.42%	68.38%	66.78%	73.28%	**83.05%**	76.89%
Skirt Female	MPVE	6.90	9.35	6.90	6.98	6.90	6.92	6.90	6.90	**6.87**	6.89
	VFCP	0.067%	0.04%	0.00%	0.015%	0.000%	0.059%	0.047%	0.028%	**0.00%**	0.027%
	CFMP	93.36%	78.78%	93.87%	94.01%	96.45%	93.99%	94.44%	96.03%	**98.16%**	96.43%
All Garments	MPVE	8.89	9.67	8.89	8.92	8.88	8.74	8.67	8.66	**8.64**	8.65
	VFCP	0.60%	0.50%	0.01%	0.22%	0.00%	0.58%	0.43%	0.31%	**0.00%**	0.24%
	CFMP	49.09%	30.89%	59.39%	57.42%	70.97%	54.36%	59.15%	58.52%	**76.77%**	68.71%
Trend	MPVE	-	+8.77%	0.00%	+0.34%	−0.11%	−1.69%	−2.47%	−2.59%	**−2.81%**	−2.70%
	VFCP	-	−16.67%	−99.90%	−97.72%	−100.00%	−94.00%	−95.55%	−96.79%	**−100.00%**	−97.52%
	CFMP	-	−37.07%	+20.98%	+16.97%	+44.57%	+10.74%	+20.49%	+19.21%	**+56.39%**	+39.97%

As reported in Table 3, we compared our method with other collision handling approaches. A typical approach is to employ a post-processing step. A naïve method is to move the penetrating vertices directly to the body surface along the SDF gradient direction using $f(\boldsymbol{x}_i)\widehat{\nabla_{\boldsymbol{x}_i} f(\boldsymbol{x}_i)}$ [20,35] to eliminate the VF-collision. As shown in Fig. 3, this method does not handle EE-collisions and might introduce new artifacts. Our experiments verify that this naïve approach increases the collision-free models only marginally from 49.0% to 59.39%. When tested with approximate SDF, the collision-free models drop to 30.89% and MPVE increases to 9.67, compared with 8.89 in TailorNet.

Guan et al. [17] propose a more advanced technique to post-process the collisions using optimization. While this technique is more effective than the naïve approach, it cannot beat the performance of our ReFU-based method in terms of both quantitative results and computational speed.

Given the accurate SDF value, it eliminates the VF collisions and increases the ratio of collision-free models to 70.97%. Examples are shown in the third column in Fig. 4. Although this approach attempts to preserve the original details of the garments, it still results in higher reconstruction error and the resulting garments are not smooth, as shown by the blue arrow in Fig. 4 (a close-up view of the corresponding area is shown in the inset figure). When tested with approximate SDF, the accuracy with respect to the reconstruction error and collision handling drops significantly. Furthermore, the optimization requires $0.6 - 0.8$s per frame even with approximated SDF.

Instead of performing post-processing optimization, some techniques [3–5, 18] apply the collision loss in Eq. 9 in the garment prediction models. The collision loss provides a soft constraint during network training. According to our benchmarks in Table 3, adding collision loss to TailorNet can reduce the overall collision artifacts and improve the reconstruction accuracy for garment samples close to the training set, however, it introduces even more collisions for testing samples that are farther away from the training set (see detail analysis in the supplementary material). After fine-tuning the TailorNet network with the collision loss using accurate SDF values, the collision-free garment models are around 56% for both approximate SDF and accurate SDF. Moreover, the reconstruction errors are around 8.7. The fourth column in Fig. 4 shows visible collisions in the predicted garments. Overall, our approach based on ReFU offers improved accuracy (i.e., fewer collisions), real-time performance, and higher visual quality.

5   Conclusion, Limitations, and Future Work

We propose ReFU for handling body-cloth collisions in neural networks for 3D garment prediction. Our method is inspired by the use of repulsive forces in physics-based simulators. Specifically, ReFU predicts the repulsion direction and the magnitude based on the SDF of the collided vertices and the global latent feature of the garment. ReFU can be combined with different backbone networks, and we highlight the benefits with state-of-the-art learning methods.

While our experiments show that using ReFU for training can significantly reduce the body-cloth collisions and improve the reconstruction accuracy, our approach has some limitations. To achieve live performance for the whole system, we must use a neural network approximated human body SDF for real-time computation. However, the accuracies in the SDF network prediction affects ReFU's capability of collision handling. But using more advanced neural SDF methods such as the articulated occupancy networks [1, 12, 26] can improve ReFU's overall performance. Furthermore, our computation of the moving offset may not fully resolve all collisions, especially all EE collisions.

References

1. Alldieck, T., Xu, H., Sminchisescu, C.: imghum: implicit generative models of 3d human shape and articulated pose. In: Proceedings of the IEEE/CVF International Conference on Computer Vision (ICCV), pp. 5461–5470, October 2021
2. Baraff, D., Witkin, A.: Large steps in cloth simulation. In: Proceedings of the 25th Annual Conference on Computer Graphics and Interactive Techniques, pp. 43–54 (1998)
3. Bertiche, H., Madadi, M., Escalera, S.: CLOTH3D: clothed 3D humans. In: Vedaldi, A., Bischof, H., Brox, T., Frahm, J.-M. (eds.) ECCV 2020. LNCS, vol. 12365, pp. 344–359. Springer, Cham (2020). https://doi.org/10.1007/978-3-030-58565-5_21
4. Bertiche, H., Madadi, M., Escalera, S.: PBNS: physically based neural simulator for unsupervised garment pose space deformation. arXiv preprint arXiv:2012.11310 (2020)
5. Bertiche, H., Madadi, M., Tylson, E., Escalera, S.: DeepSD: automatic deep skinning and pose space deformation for 3d garment animation. In: Proceedings of the IEEE/CVF International Conference on Computer Vision, pp. 5471–5480 (2021)
6. Bhatnagar, B.L., Tiwari, G., Theobalt, C., Pons-Moll, G.: Multi-garment net: learning to dress 3d people from images. In: Proceedings of the IEEE/CVF International Conference on Computer Vision, pp. 5420–5430 (2019)
7. Bridson, R., Fedkiw, R., Anderson, J.: Robust treatment of collisions, contact and friction for cloth animation. ACM Trans. Graph. **21**(3), 594–603 (2002)
8. Brochu, T., Edwards, E., Bridson, R.: Efficient geometrically exact continuous collision detection. ACM Trans. Graph. **31**(4), 96:1–96:7 (2012)
9. Choi, K.J., Ko, H.S.: Stable but responsive cloth. In: ACM SIGGRAPH 2005 Courses (2005)
10. Crandall, M.G., Lions, P.L.: Viscosity solutions of Hamilton-Jacobi equations. Trans. Am. Math. Soc. **277**(1), 1–42 (1983)
11. De Aguiar, E., Sigal, L., Treuille, A., Hodgins, J.K.: Stable spaces for real-time clothing. ACM Trans. Graph. (TOG) **29**(4), 1–9 (2010)
12. Bertiche, H., Madadi, M., Escalera, S.: CLOTH3D: clothed 3D humans. In: Vedaldi, A., Bischof, H., Brox, T., Frahm, J.-M. (eds.) ECCV 2020. LNCS, vol. 12365, pp. 344–359. Springer, Cham (2020). https://doi.org/10.1007/978-3-030-58565-5_21
13. Fisher, S., Lin, M.C.: Fast penetration depth estimation for elastic bodies using deformed distance fields. In: Proceedings 2001 IEEE/RSJ International Conference on Intelligent Robots and Systems. Expanding the Societal Role of Robotics in the the Next Millennium (Cat. No. 01CH37180), vol. 1, pp. 330–336. IEEE (2001)
14. Govindaraju, N.K., Lin, M.C., Manocha, D.: Quick-CULLIDE: fast inter- and intra-object collision culling using graphics hardware. In: IEEE Virtual Reality Conference 2005, VR 2005, Bonn, Germany, 12–16 March 2005, pp. 59–66 (2005)
15. Grinspun, E., Hirani, A.N., Desbrun, M., Schröder, P.: Discrete shells. In: Proceedings of the 2003 ACM SIGGRAPH/Eurographics Symposium on Computer Animation, pp. 62–67. Citeseer (2003)
16. Gropp, A., Yariv, L., Haim, N., Atzmon, M., Lipman, Y.: Implicit geometric regularization for learning shapes. arXiv preprint arXiv:2002.10099 (2020)
17. Guan, P., Reiss, L., Hirshberg, D.A., Weiss, A., Black, M.J.: Drape: dressing any person. ACM Trans. Graph. (TOG) **31**(4), 1–10 (2012)
18. Gundogdu, E., Constantin, V., Seifoddini, A., Dang, M., Salzmann, M., Fua, P.: Garnet: a two-stream network for fast and accurate 3d cloth draping. In: Proceedings of the IEEE/CVF International Conference on Computer Vision, pp. 8739–8748 (2019)

19. Harmon, D., Vouga, E., Tamstorf, R., Grinspun, E.: Robust treatment of simultaneous collisions. ACM Trans. Graph. **27**(3), 23:1–23:4 (2008)

20. Holden, D., Duong, B.C., Datta, S., Nowrouzezahrai, D.: Subspace neural physics: Fast data-driven interactive simulation. In: Proceedings of the 18th Annual ACM SIGGRAPH/Eurographics Symposium on Computer Animation, pp. 1–12 (2019)

21. Kim, D., Koh, W., Narain, R., Fatahalian, K., Treuille, A., O'Brien, J.F.: Near-exhaustive precomputation of secondary cloth effects. ACM Trans. Graph. **32**(4), 87:1–87:7 (2013)

22. Larson, M.G., Bengzon, F.: The Finite Element Method: Theory, Implementation, and Applications, vol. 10. Springer Science & Business Media, Heidelberg (2013). https://doi.org/10.1007/978-3-642-33287-6

23. Loper, M., Mahmood, N., Romero, J., Pons-Moll, G., Black, M.J.: SMPL: a skinned multi-person linear model. ACM Trans. Graph. (TOG) **34**(6), 1–16 (2015)

24. Ma, B., Han, Z., Liu, Y.S., Zwicker, M.: Neural-pull: Learning signed distance functions from point clouds by learning to pull space onto surfaces. arXiv preprint arXiv:2011.13495 (2020)

25. Macklin, M., Erleben, K., Müller, M., Chentanez, N., Jeschke, S., Corse, Z.: Local optimization for robust signed distance field collision. Proc. ACM Comput. Graph. Interact. Techn. **3**(1), 1–17 (2020)

26. Mihajlovic, M., Zhang, Y., Black, M.J., Tang, S.: LEAP: learning articulated occupancy of people. In: Proceedings IEEE Conference on Computer Vision and Pattern Recognition (CVPR), June 2021

27. Narain, R., Samii, A., O'Brien, J.F.: Adaptive anisotropic remeshing for cloth simulation. ACM Trans. Graph. 31(6), 147:1–147:10 (2012)

28. Otaduy, M.A., Tamstorf, R., Steinemann, D., Gross, M.: Implicit contact handling for deformable objects. Comput. Graph. Forum **28**(2), 559–568 (2009)

29. Pan, J., Chitta, S., Manocha, D.: FCL: a general purpose library for collision and proximity queries. In: 2012 IEEE International Conference on Robotics and Automation, pp. 3859–3866. IEEE (2012)

30. Park, J.J., Florence, P., Straub, J., Newcombe, R., Lovegrove, S.: DeepSDF: learning continuous signed distance functions for shape representation. In: Proceedings of the IEEE/CVF Conference on Computer Vision and Pattern Recognition, pp. 165–174 (2019)

31. Paszke, A., et al.: Pytorch: an imperative style, high-performance deep learning library. Adv. Neural. Inf. Process. Syst. **32**, 8026–8037 (2019)

32. Patel, C., Liao, Z., Pons-Moll, G.: TailorNet: predicting clothing in 3d as a function of human pose, shape and garment style. In: Proceedings of the IEEE/CVF Conference on Computer Vision and Pattern Recognition, pp. 7365–7375 (2020)

33. Pavlakos, G., Zhu, L., Zhou, X., Daniilidis, K.: Learning to estimate 3d human pose and shape from a single color image. In: CVPR, pp. 459–468 (2018)

34. Provot, X.: Collision and self-collision handling in cloth model dedicated to design garments. In: Thalmann, D., van de Panne, M. (eds.) Computer Animation and Simulation 1997. Eurographics, pp. 177–189. Springer, Vienna (1997). https://doi.org/10.1007/978-3-7091-6874-5_13

35. Santesteban, I., Otaduy, M.A., Casas, D.: Learning-based animation of clothing for virtual try-on. In: Computer Graphics Forum, vol. 38, pp. 355–366. Wiley Online Library (2019)

36. Santesteban, I., Thuerey, N., Otaduy, M.A., Casas, D.: Self-supervised collision handling via generative 3d garment models for virtual try-on. In: Proceedings of the IEEE/CVF Conference on Computer Vision and Pattern Recognition (2021)

37. Sitzmann, V., Chan, E.R., Tucker, R., Snavely, N., Wetzstein, G.: MetaSDF: meta-learning signed distance functions. arXiv preprint arXiv:2006.09662 (2020)
38. Tan, Q., Pan, Z., Gao, L., Manocha, D.: Realtime simulation of thin-shell deformable materials using CNN-based mesh embedding. IEEE Robot. Autom. Lett. 5(2), 2325–2332 (2020)
39. Tan, Q., Pan, Z., Manocha, D.: Lcollision: Fast generation of collision-free human poses using learned non-penetration constraints. In: Thirty-Fifth AAAI Conference on Artificial Intelligence, AAAI (2021)
40. Tan, Q., Pan, Z., Smith, B., Shiratori, T., Manocha, D.: Active learning of neural collision handler for complex 3d mesh deformations (2021)
41. Tang, M., Tong, R., Wang, Z., Manocha, D.: Fast and exact continuous collision detection with Bernstein sign classification. ACM Trans. Graph. (SIGGRAPH Asia). 33, 186:1–186:8 (2014)
42. Tang, M., Wang, T., Liu, Z., Tong, R., Manocha, D.: I-Cloth: Incremental collision handling for GPU-based interactive cloth simulation. ACM Trans. Graph. 37(6), 204:1–204:10 (2018)
43. Teng, Y., Otaduy, M.A., Kim, T.: Simulating articulated subspace self-contact. ACM Trans. Graph. (TOG) 33(4), 1–9 (2014)
44. Wang, H.: Defending continuous collision detection against errors. ACM Trans. Graph. (SIGGRAPH). 33(4), 122:1–122:10 (2014)
45. Wang, T.Y., Ceylan, D., Popovic, J., Mitra, N.J.: Learning a shared shape space for multimodal garment design. ACM Trans. Graph. 37(6), 1:1–1:14 (2018). https://doi.org/10.1145/3272127.3275074
46. Zheng, H., Yang, Z., Liu, W., Liang, J., Li, Y.: Improving deep neural networks using softplus units. In: 2015 International Joint Conference on Neural Networks (IJCNN), pp. 1–4 (2015). https://doi.org/10.1109/IJCNN.2015.7280459
47. Zhou, Y., et al.: Fully convolutional mesh autoencoder using efficient spatially varying kernels. arXiv preprint arXiv:2006.04325 (2020)

Shape-Pose Disentanglement Using SE(3)-Equivariant Vector Neurons

Oren Katzir[1]([envelope]) [ID], Dani Lischinski[2] [ID], and Daniel Cohen-Or[1] [ID]

[1] Tel-Aviv University, Tel Aviv-Yafo, Israel
orenkatzir@mail.tau.ac.il
[2] Hebrew University of Jerusalem, Jerusalem, Israel

Abstract. We introduce an unsupervised technique for encoding point clouds into a canonical shape representation, by disentangling shape and pose. Our encoder is stable and consistent, meaning that the shape encoding is purely pose-invariant, while the extracted rotation and translation are able to semantically align different input shapes of the same class to a common canonical pose. Specifically, we design an auto-encoder based on Vector Neuron Networks, a rotation-equivariant neural network, whose layers we extend to provide translation-equivariance in addition to rotation-equivariance only. The resulting encoder produces pose-invariant shape encoding by construction, enabling our approach to focus on learning a consistent canonical pose for a class of objects. Quantitative and qualitative experiments validate the superior stability and consistency of our approach.

Keywords: Point clouds · Canonical pose · Equivariance · Shape-pose disentanglement

1 Introduction

Point clouds reside at the very core of 3D geometry processing, as they are acquired at the beginning of the 3D processing pipeline and usually serve as the raw input for shape analysis or surface reconstruction. Thus, understanding the underlying geometry of a point cloud has a profound impact on the entire 3D processing chain. This task, however, is challenging since point clouds are unordered, and contain neither connectivity, nor any other global information.

In recent years, with the emergence of neural networks, various techniques have been developed to circumvent the challenges of analyzing and understanding point clouds [11,14,15,19,20,23,27,31]. However, most methods rely on *pre-aligned* datasets, where the point clouds are normalized, translated and oriented to have the same pose.

Supplementary Information The online version contains supplementary material available at https://doi.org/10.1007/978-3-031-20062-5_27.

S. Avidan et al. (Eds.): ECCV 2022, LNCS 13663, pp. 468–484, 2022.
https://doi.org/10.1007/978-3-031-20062-5_27

In this work, we present an unsupervised technique to learn a canonical shape representation by disentangling shape, translation, and rotation. Essentially, the canonical representation is required to meet two conditions: *stability* and *consistency*. The former means that the shape encoding should be invariant to any rigid transformation of the same input, while the latter means that different shapes of the same class should be semantically aligned, sharing the same canonical pose.

Canonical alignment is not a new concept. Recently, Canonical Capsules [25] and Compass [24] proposed self-supervised learning of canonical representations using augmentations with Siamese training. We discuss these methods in more detail in the next section. In contrast, our approach is to extract a *pose-invariant* shape encoding, which is explicitly disentangled from the separately extracted translation and rotation.

Specifically, we design an auto-encoder, trained on an unaligned dataset, that encodes the input point cloud into three disentangled components: (i) a pose-invariant shape encoding, (ii) a rotation matrix and (iii) a translation vector. We achieve pure $SE(3)$-invariant shape encoding and $SE(3)$-equivariant pose estimation (enabling reconstruction of the input shape), by leveraging a novel extension of the recently proposed Vector Neuron Networks (VNN) [6]. The latter is an $SO(3)$-equivariant neural network for point cloud processing, and while translation invariance could theoretically be achieved by centering the input point clouds, such approach is sensitive to noise, missing data and partial shapes. Therefore we propose an extension to VNN achieving $SE(3)$-equivariance.

It should be noted that the shape encodings produced by our network are stable (i.e., pose-invariant) *by construction*, due to the use of $SE(3)$-invariant layers. At the same time, the extracted rigid transformation is equivariant to the pose of the input. This enables the learning process to focus on the consistency across different shapes. Consistency is achieved by altering the input point cloud with a variety of simple shape augmentations, while keeping the pose fixed, allowing us to constrain the learned transformation to be invariant to the identity, (i.e., the particular shape), of the input point cloud.

Moreover, our disentangled shape and pose representation is not limited to point cloud decoding, but can be combined with any 3D data decoder, as we demonstrate by learning a canonical implicit representation of our point cloud utilizing occupancy networks [16].

We show, both qualitatively and quantitatively, that our approach leads to a stable, consistent, and purely $SE(3)$-invariant canonical representation compared to previous approaches.

2 Background and Related Work

2.1 Canonical Representation

A number of works proposed techniques to achieve learnable canonical frames, typically requiring some sort of supervision [10,17,21]. Recently, two unsupervised methods were proposed: Canonical Capsules [25] and Compass [24]. Canonical Capsules [25] is an auto-encoder network that extracts positions and pose-invariant descriptors for k capsules, from which the input shape may be reconstructed. Pose invariance and equivariance are achieved only implicitly via Siamese training, by feeding the network with pairs of rotated and translated versions of the same input point cloud.

Compass [24] builds upon spherical CNN [4], a semi-equivariant $\mathbf{SO}(3)$ network, to estimate the pose with respect to the canonical representation. It should be noted that Compass is inherently tied to spherical CNN, which is not purely equivariant [4]. Thus, similarly to Canonical Capsules, Compass augments the input point cloud with a rotated version to regularize an equivariant pose estimation. It should be noted that neither method guarantees pure equivariance.

Similarly to Canonical Capsules, we employ an auto-encoding scheme to disentangle pose from shape, i.e., the canonical representation, and similarly to Compass, we strive to employ an equivariant network, however, our network is $\mathbf{SE}(3)$-equivariant and not only $\mathbf{SO}(3)$-equivariant. More importantly, differently from these two approaches, the different branches of our network are $\mathbf{SE}(3)$-invariant or $\mathbf{SE}(3)$-equivariant *by construction*, and thus the learning process is free from the burden of enforcing these properties. Rather, the process focuses on learning a consistent shape representation in a canonical pose. Close to our work are Equi-pose [13] and a concurrent work ConDor [22]. Both methods use a relatively intricate equivariant backbone to estimate multiple proposal poses. Differently, we employ a simple equivariant network (VNN) and predict a single pose, easing the incorporation of our method with other SOTA methods for 3D shape reconstruction. We further discuss Equi-pose [13] in our suppl. material.

2.2   3D Reconstruction

Our method reconstructs an input point cloud by disentangling the input 3D geometry into shape and pose. The encoder outputs a pose encoding and a shape encoding which is pose-invariant by construction, while the decoder reconstructs the 3D geometry from the shape encoding alone. Consequently, our architecture can be easily integrated into various 3D auto-encoding pipelines. In this work, we shall demonstrate our shape-pose disentanglement for point cloud encoding and implicit representation learning.

State-of-the-art point cloud auto-encoding methods rely on a folding operation of a template (optionally learned) hyperspace point cloud to the input 3D point cloud [7,9,30]. Following this approach, we employ AtlasNetV2 [7] which uses multiple folding operations from hyperspace patches to 3D coordinates, to reconstruct point clouds in a pose-invariant frame.

Implicit 3D representation networks [16,18,29] enable learning of the input geometry with high resolution and different mesh topology. We utilize occupancy networks [16] to learn an implicit pose-invariant shape representation.

2.3   Rotation-Equivariance and Vector Neuron Network

The success of 2D convolutional neural networks (CNN) on images, which are equivariant to translation, drove a similar approach for 3D data with rotation as the symmetry group. Most works on 3D rotation-equivariance [4,8,26,28], focus on steerable CNNs [5], where each layer "steers" the output features according to the symmetry property (rotation and occasionally translation for 3D data). For example, Spherical CNNs [4,8] transform the input point cloud to a spherical signal, and use spherical harmonics filters, yielding features on $\mathbf{SO}(3)$-space.

Usually, these methods are tied with specific architecture design and data input which limit their applicability and adaptation to SOTA 3D processing.

Recently, Deng et al. [6] introduced Vector Neuron Networks (VNN), a rather light and elegant framework for $\mathbf{SO}(3)$-equivariance. Empirically, the VNN design performs on par with more complex and specific architectures. The key benefit of VNNs lies in their simplicity, accessibility and generalizability. Conceptually, any standard point cloud processing network can be elevated to $\mathbf{SO}(3)$-equivariance (and invariance) with minimal changes to its architecture. Below we briefly describe VNNs and refer the reader to [6] for further details.

In VNNs the representation of a single neuron is lifted from a sequence of scalar values to a sequence of 3D vectors. A single vector neuron feature is thus a matrix $\mathbf{V} \in \mathbb{R}^{C \times 3}$, and we denote a collection of N such features by $\mathcal{V} \in \mathbb{R}^{N \times C \times 3}$. The layers of VNNs, which map between such collections, $f : \mathbb{R}^{N \times C \times 3} \to \mathbb{R}^{N \times C' \times 3}$, are equivariant to rotations $R \in \mathbb{R}^{3 \times 3}$, that is:

$$f(\mathcal{V}R) = f(\mathcal{V})R, \tag{1}$$

where $\mathcal{V}R = \{\mathbf{V}_n R\}_{n=1}^{N}$.

Ordinary linear layers fulfill this requirement, however, other non-linear layers, such as ReLU and max-pooling, do not. For ReLU activation, VNNs apply a truncation w.r.t to a learned half-space. Let $\mathbf{V}, \mathbf{V}' \in \mathbb{R}^{C \times 3}$ be the input and output vector neuron features of a single point, respectively. Each 3D vector $\mathbf{v}' \in \mathbf{V}'$ is obtained by first applying two learned matrices $\mathbf{Q}, \mathbf{K} \in \mathbb{R}^{1 \times C}$ to project $\mathbf{V}$ to a feature $\mathbf{q} = \mathbf{Q}\mathbf{V} \in \mathbb{R}^{1 \times 3}$ and a direction $\mathbf{k} = \mathbf{K}\mathbf{V} \in \mathbb{R}^{1 \times 3}$. To achieve equivariance, $\mathbf{v}' \in \mathbf{V}'$ is then defined by truncating the part of $\mathbf{q}$ that lies in the negative half-space of $\mathbf{k}$, as follows,

$$\mathbf{v}' = \begin{cases} \mathbf{q} & \text{if } \langle \mathbf{q}, \mathbf{k} \rangle \geq 0, \\ \mathbf{q} - \left\langle \mathbf{q}, \frac{\mathbf{k}}{\|\mathbf{k}\|} \right\rangle \frac{\mathbf{k}}{\|\mathbf{k}\|} & \text{otherwise.} \end{cases} \tag{2}$$

In addition, VNNs employ rotation-equivariant pooling operations and normalization layers. We refer the reader to [6] for the complete definition.

Invariance layers can be achieved by inner product of two rotation-equivariant features. Let $\mathbf{V} \in \mathbb{R}^{C \times 3}$, and $\mathbf{V}' \in \mathbb{R}^{C' \times 3}$ be two equivariant features obtained from an input point cloud $\mathbf{X}$. Then rotating $\mathbf{X}$ by a matrix R, results in the features $\mathbf{V}R$ and $\mathbf{V}'R$, and

$$\langle \mathbf{V}R, \mathbf{V}'R \rangle = \mathbf{V}R(\mathbf{V}'R)^T = \mathbf{V}RR^T\mathbf{V}'^T = \mathbf{V}\mathbf{V}'^T = \langle \mathbf{V}, \mathbf{V}' \rangle. \tag{3}$$

Note that VNN is also reflection equivariant which may be beneficial for symmetrical objects, although we do not take advantage of this attribute directly.

In our work, we also utilize vector neurons, but we extend the different layers to be $\mathbf{SE}(3)$-equivariant, instead of $\mathbf{SO}(3)$-equivariant, as described in Sect. 3.1. This new design allow us to construct an $\mathbf{SE}(3)$-invariant encoder, which gradually disentangles the pose from the shape, first the translation and then the rotation, resulting in a pose-invariant shape encoding.

3   Method

We design an auto-encoder to disentangle shape, translation, and rotation. We wish the resulting representation to be stable, i.e., the shape encoding should be pose-invariant, and the pose $\mathbf{SE}(3)$-equivariant. At the same time, we wish multiple different shapes in the same class to have a consistent canonical pose. To achieve stability, we revisit VNNs and design new $\mathbf{SE}(3)$-equivariant and invariant layers, which we refer to as Vector Neurons with Translation (VNT). Consistency is then achieved by self-supervision, designed to preserve pose across shapes. In the following, we first describe the design of our new VNT layers. Next, we present our VNN and VNT-based auto-encoder architecture. Finally, we elaborate on our losses to encourage disentanglement of shape from pose in a consistent manner.

3.1   SE(3)-Equivariant Vector Neuron Network

As explained earlier, Vector Neuron Networks (VNN) [6] provide a framework for $\mathbf{SO}(3)$-equivariant and invariant point cloud processing. Since a pose of an object consists of translation and rotation, $\mathbf{SE}(3)$-equivariance and invariance are needed for shape-pose disentanglement. While it might seem that centering the input point cloud should suffice, note that point clouds are often captured with noise and occlusions, leading to missing data and partial shapes, which may significantly affect the global center of the input. Specifically, for canonical representation learning, a key condition is consistency across different objects, thus, such an approach assumes that the center of the point cloud is consistently semantic between similar but different objects, which is hardly the case. Equivariance to translation, on the other-hand, allows identifying local features in different locations with the same filters, without requiring global parameters.

Therefore, we revisit the Vector Neuron layers and extend them to Vector Neurons with Translation (VNT), thereby achieving $\mathbf{SE}(3)$-equivariance.

Linear Layers: While linear layers are by definition rotation-equivariant, they are not translation-equivariant. Following VNN, our linear module $f_{\text{lin}}\left(\cdot; \mathbf{W}\right)$ is defined via a weight matrix $\mathbf{W} \in \mathbb{R}^{C' \times C}$, acting on a vector-list feature $\mathbf{V} \in \mathbb{R}^{C \times 3}$. Let $R \in \mathbb{R}^{3 \times 3}$ be a rotation matrix and $T \in \mathbb{R}^{1 \times 3}$ a translation vector. For $f_{\text{lin}}\left(\cdot; \mathbf{W}\right)$ to be $\mathbf{SE}(3)$-equivariant, the following must hold:

$$f_{\text{lin}}\left(\mathbf{V}R + \mathbb{1}_C T\right) = \mathbf{W}\mathbf{V}R + \mathbb{1}_{C'}T, \tag{4}$$

where $\mathbb{1}_C = [1, 1, \ldots, 1]^T \in \mathbb{R}^{C \times 1}$ is a column vector of length C. A sufficient condition for (4) to hold is achieved by constraining each row of $\mathbf{W}$ to sum to one. Formally, $\mathbf{W} \in \mathcal{W}^{C' \times C}$, where

$$\mathcal{W}^{C' \times C} = \left\{ \mathbf{W} \in \mathbb{R}^{C' \times C} \mid \sum_{j=1}^{C} w_{i,j} = 1 \quad \forall i = 1, \ldots, C' \right\}, \tag{5}$$

See our supplementary material for a complete proof.

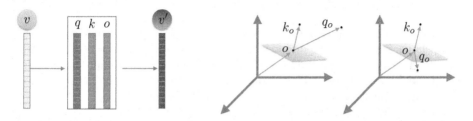

Fig. 1. Vector Neuron Translation equivariant non linear layer. We learn for each input point feature $\mathbf{v}$, three component $\mathbf{o}, \mathbf{q}, \mathbf{k}$, and interpret them as an origin $\mathbf{o}$, a feature $\mathbf{q_o} = \mathbf{q} - \mathbf{o}$ and a direction $\mathbf{k_o} = \mathbf{k} - \mathbf{o}$. Similarly to VNN operation, the feature component of $\mathbf{q_o}$ which is in the half-space defined by $-\mathbf{k_o}$ is clipped. In-addition, we translate the feature by the learned origin $\mathbf{o}$ outputting the $\mathbf{v}'$.

Non-linear Layers: We extend each non-linear VNN layer to become $\mathbf{SE}(3)$-equivariant by adding a learnable origin. More formally, for the ReLU activation layer, given an input feature list $\mathbf{V} \in \mathbb{R}^{C \times 3}$, we learn three (rather than two) linear maps, $\mathbf{Q}, \mathbf{K}, \mathbf{O} \in \mathcal{W}^{1 \times C}$ projecting the input to $\mathbf{q}, \mathbf{k}, \mathbf{o} \in \mathbb{R}^{1 \times 3}$. The feature and direction are defined w.r.t the origin $\mathbf{o}$, i.e., the feature is given by $\mathbf{q_o} = \mathbf{q} - \mathbf{o}$, while the direction is given by $\mathbf{k_o} = \mathbf{k} - \mathbf{o}$, as illustrated in Fig. 1. The ReLU is applied by clipping the part of $\mathbf{q_o}$ that resides behind the plane defined by $\mathbf{k_o}$ and $\mathbf{o}$, i.e.,

$$\mathbf{v}' = \begin{cases} \mathbf{o} + \mathbf{q_o} & \text{if } \langle \mathbf{q_o}, \mathbf{k_o} \rangle \geq 0, \\ \mathbf{o} + \mathbf{q_o} - \left\langle \mathbf{q_o}, \frac{\mathbf{k_o}}{\|\mathbf{k_o}\|} \right\rangle \frac{\mathbf{k_o}}{\|\mathbf{k_o}\|}, & \text{otherwise.} \end{cases} \tag{6}$$

Note that $\mathbf{o} + \mathbf{q_o} = \mathbf{q}$, and that $\mathbf{K}, \mathbf{O}$ may be shared across the elements of $\mathbf{V}$.

It may be easily seen that we preserve the equivariance w.r.t $\mathbf{SO}(3)$ rotations, as well as translations. In the same manner, we extend the $\mathbf{SO}(3)$-equivariant VNN maxpool layer to become $\mathbf{SE}(3)$-equivariant. We refer the reader to the supplementary material for the exact adaptation and complete proof.

Translation-Invariant Layers: Invariance to translation can be achieved by subtracting two $\mathbf{SE}(3)$-equivariant features. Let $\mathbf{V}, \mathbf{V}' \in \mathbb{R}^{C \times 3}$ be two $\mathbf{SE}(3)$-equivariant features obtained from an input point cloud $\mathbf{X}$. Then, rotating $\mathbf{X}$

by a matrix R and translating by T, results in the features $\mathbf{V}R + \mathbb{1}_C T$ and $\mathbf{V}'R + \mathbb{1}_C T$, whose difference is translation-invariant:

$$(\mathbf{V}R + \mathbb{1}_C T) - (\mathbf{V}'R + \mathbb{1}_C T) = (\mathbf{V} - \mathbf{V}')R \tag{7}$$

Note that the resulting feature is still rotation-equivariant, which enables to process it with VNN layers, further preserving $\mathbf{SO}(3)$-equivariance.

3.2 SE(3)-Equivariant Encoder-Decoder

We design an auto-encoder based on VNT and VNN layers to disentangle pose from shape. Thus, our shape representation is pose-invariant (i.e., stable), while our pose estimation is $\mathbf{SE}(3)$-pose-equivariant, by construction. The decoder, which can be an arbitrary 3D decoder network, reconstructs the 3D shape from the invariant features.

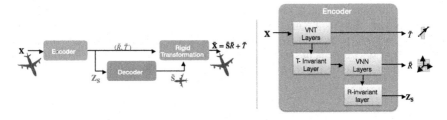

Fig. 2. The architecture of our auto-encoder for shape-pose disentanglement. The auto-encoder (left) disentangles the input point cloud $\mathbf{X}$ to rotation $\tilde{R}$, translation $\tilde{T}$ and a canonical representation $\tilde{\mathbf{S}}$. The shape encoding $\mathbf{Z_s}$ is invariant by construction to the pose, while the learned rotation and translation are equivariant to it. Our encoder (right) learns features that are initially equivariant to the pose, and gradually become invariant to it, first to translation and then to rotation, eventually yielding pose invariant features $\mathbf{Z_s}$.

The overall architecture of our AE is depicted in Fig. 2. Given an input point cloud $\mathbf{X} \in \mathbb{R}^{N \times 3}$, we can represent it as a rigid transformation of an unknown canonical representation $\mathbf{S} \in \mathbb{R}^{N \times 3}$:

$$\mathbf{X} = \mathbf{S}R + \mathbb{1}_N T, \tag{8}$$

where $\mathbb{1}_N = [1, 1, \ldots, 1]^T \in \mathbb{R}^{N \times 1}$ is a column vector of length N, $R \in \mathbb{R}^{3 \times 3}$ is a rotation matrix and $T \in \mathbb{R}^{1 \times 3}$ is a translation vector.

Our goal is to find the shape $\mathbf{S}$, which is by definition pose-invariant and should be consistently aligned across different input shapes. To achieve this goal, we use an encoder that first estimates the translation $\tilde{T}$ using translation-equivariant VNT layers, then switches to a translation-invariant representation from which the rotation $\tilde{R}$ is estimated using rotation-equivariant VNN layers.

Finally, the representation is made rotation-invariant and the shape encoding $\mathbf{Z_s}$ is generated. A reconstruction loss is computed by decoding $\mathbf{Z_s}$ into the canonically-positioned shape $\tilde{S}$ and applying the extracted rigid transformation. In the following we further explain our encoder architecture and the type of decoders used.

SE(3)-Equivariant Encoder. Our encoder is composed of rotation and translation equivariant and invariant layers as shown in Fig. 3. We start by feeding $\mathbf{X}$ through linear and non-linear VNT layers yielding $\mathbf{X_{RT}} \in \mathbb{R}^{N \times C \times 3}$, where the RT subscript indicates $\mathbf{SE}(3)$-equivariant features, as described in Sect. 3.1.

$\mathbf{X_{RT}}$ is then fed-forward through additional VNT layers resulting in a single vector neuron per point $\bar{\mathbf{X}}_{\mathbf{RT}} \in \mathbb{R}^{N \times 1 \times 3}$. We mean-pool the features to produce a 3D SE(3)-equivariant vector as our translation estimation, as shown in the upper branch of Fig. 3, yielding $\tilde{T} = f_T(\mathbf{X}) = f_T(\mathbf{S})R + T \in \mathbb{R}^{1 \times 3}$, where we denote by $f_T : \mathbb{R}^{N \times 3} \to \mathbb{R}^{1 \times 3}$ the aggregation of the VNT-layers from the input point cloud $\mathbf{X}$ to the estimated $\tilde{T}$, thus, it is a translation and rotation equivariant network. In addition, as explained in Sect. 3.1, the following creates translation invariant features, $\mathbf{Y_R} = \mathbf{X_{RT}} - \bar{\mathbf{X}}_{\mathbf{RT}} \in \mathbb{R}^{N \times C \times 3}$.

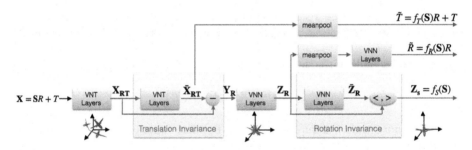

Fig. 3. The architecture of our encoder. The representation of the input point cloud $\mathbf{X}$ yields a pose-invariant (bottom branch) shape encoding $\mathbf{Z_s}$ in two steps: first, making it invariant to translation and then to rotation. At the same time, the learned rigid transformation $(\tilde{R}, \tilde{T})$ (top and middle branches) is equivariant to the input pose. The small rendered planes at the bottom, illustrate the alignment at each stage.

While $\mathbf{Y_R}$ is translation invariant, it is still rotation equivariant, thus, we can proceed to further process $\mathbf{Y_R}$ with VNN layers, resulting in (deeper) rotation equivariant features $\mathbf{Z_R} \in \mathbb{R}^{N \times C' \times 3}$.

Finally, $\mathbf{Z_R}$ is fed forward through a VNN rotation-invariant layer as explained in Sect. 2.3, resulting in a shape encoding, $\mathbf{Z_s}$, which is by construction pose invariant. Similar to the translation reconstruction, the rotation is estimated by mean pooling $\mathbf{Z_R}$ and feeding it through a single VN linear layer yielding $\tilde{R} = f_R(\mathbf{X}) = f_R(\mathbf{S})R \in \mathbb{R}^{3 \times 3}$, where $f_R : \mathbb{R}^{N \times 3} \to \mathbb{R}^{3 \times 3}$ denotes the aggregation of the layers from the input point cloud $\mathbf{X}$ to the estimated rotation

$\tilde{R}$ and, as such, it is a rotation-equivariant network. The entire encoder architecture is shown in Fig. 3 and we refer the reader to our supplementary for a detailed description of the layers.

Decoder. The decoder is applied on the shape encoding $\mathbf{Z_s}$ to reconstruct the shape $\tilde{\mathbf{S}}$. We stress again that $\tilde{\mathbf{S}}$ is invariant to the input pose, regardless of the training process. Motivated by the success of folding networks [7,9,30] for point clouds auto-encoding, we opt to use AtlasNetV2 [7] as our decoder, specifically using the point translation learning module. For implicit function reconstruction, we follow Occupancy network decoder [16]. Please note, that our method is not coupled with any decoder structure.

3.3 Optimizing for Shape-Pose Disentanglement

While our auto-encoder is pose-invariant by construction, the encoding has no explicit relation to the input geometry. In the following we detail our losses to encourage a rigid relation between $\tilde{\mathbf{S}}$ and X, and for making $\tilde{\mathbf{S}}$ consistent across different objects.

Rigidity. To train the reconstructed shape $\tilde{\mathbf{S}}$ to be isometric to the input point cloud $\mathbf{X}$, we enforce a rigid transformation between the two, namely $\mathbf{X} = \tilde{\mathbf{S}}\tilde{R} + \mathbb{1}_N\tilde{T}$.

For point clouds auto-encoding we have used the Chamfer Distance (CD):

$$\mathcal{L}_{rec} = CD\left(\mathbf{X}, \tilde{\mathbf{S}}\tilde{R} + \mathbb{1}_N\tilde{T}\right), \tag{9}$$

Please note that other tasks such as implicit function reconstruction use equivalent terms, as we detail in our supplementary files.

In addition, while $\tilde{R} = f_R(\mathbf{X})$ is rotation-equivariant we need to constrain it to SO(3), and we do so by adding an orthonormal term:

$$\mathcal{L}_{ortho} = \|I - \tilde{R}\tilde{R}^T\|_2^2 \tag{10}$$

where $\|\cdot\|_2$ is mean square error (MSE) loss.

Consistency. Now, our shape reconstruction $\tilde{\mathbf{S}}$ is isometric to $\mathbf{X}$ and it is invariant to T and R. However, there is no guarantee that the pose of $\tilde{\mathbf{S}}$ would be consistent across different instances.

Assume two different point clouds $\mathbf{X_1}, \mathbf{X_2}$ are aligned. If their canonical representations $\mathbf{S_1}, \mathbf{S_2}$ are also aligned, then they have the same rigid transformation w.r.t their canonical representation and vice versa, i.e., $\mathbf{X_i} = \mathbf{S_i}R + \mathbb{1}_NT$, $i = 1, 2$. To achieve such consistency, we require:

$$(f_T(\mathbf{X_1}), f_R(\mathbf{X_1})) = (f_T(\mathbf{X_2}), f_R(\mathbf{X_2})). \tag{11}$$

We generate such pairs of aligned point clouds, by augmenting the input point cloud $\mathbf{X}$ with several simple augmentation processes, which do not change the pose of the object. In practice, we have used Gaussian noise addition, furthest point sampling (FPS), patch removal by k-nn (we select one point randomly and remove k of its nearest neighbors) and re-sampling of the input point cloud. We then require that the estimated rotation and translation is the same for the original and augmented versions,

$$\mathcal{L}_{consist}^{aug} = \sum_{A\in\mathcal{A}} \|f_R\left(\mathbf{X}\right) - f_R\left(A(\mathbf{X})\right)\|_2^2 + \|f_T\left(\mathbf{X}\right) - f_T\left(A(\mathbf{X})\right)\|_2^2, \qquad (12)$$

where $\mathcal{A}$ is the group of pose preserving augmentations and $\|\cdot\|_2$ is MSE loss.

In addition, we can also generate a version of $\mathbf{X}$, with a known pose, by feeding again the learned canonical shape. Empirically, we found it beneficial to use the reconstructed shape, thus, we transform $\tilde{\mathbf{S}}$ by a random rotation matrix R^* and a random translation vector T^* and require the estimated pose to be consistent with this transformation.

$$\mathcal{L}_{consist}^{can} = \|f_R\left(\tilde{\mathbf{S}}R^* + T^*\right) - R^*\|_2^2 + \|f_T\left(\tilde{\mathbf{S}}R^* + T^*\right) - T^*\|_2^2, \qquad (13)$$

Our overall loss is

$$\mathcal{L} = \mathcal{L}_{rec} + \lambda_1\mathcal{L}_{ortho} + \lambda_2\mathcal{L}_{consist}^{aug} + \lambda_3\mathcal{L}_{consist}^{can}, \qquad (14)$$

where the λ_i are hyper parameters, whose values in all our experiments were set to $\lambda_1 = 0.5$, $\lambda_2 = \lambda_3 = 1$.

Fig. 4. Aligning planes and chairs. The input planes and chairs (first and third row, respectively) have different shapes and different poses, as can be seen separately and together (rightmost column). We apply the inverse learned pose, transforming the input to its canonical pose (second and fourth row).

3.4   Inference

At inference time, we feed forward point cloud $\mathbf{X} \in \mathbb{R}^{N \times 3}$ and retrieve its shape and pose. However, since our estimated rotation matrix $\tilde{R}$ is not guaranteed to be orthonormal, at inference time, we find the closest orthonormal matrix to $\tilde{R}$ (i.e., minimize the Forbenius norm), following [1], by solving:

$$\hat{R} = \tilde{R} \left(\tilde{R}^T \tilde{R} \right)^{-\frac{1}{2}}. \tag{15}$$

The inverse of the square root can be computed by singular value decomposition (SVD). While this operation is also differentiable we have found it harmful to incorporate this constraint during the training phase, thus it is only used during inference. We refer the reader to [1] for further details.

4   Results

We preform qualitative and quantitative comparison of our method for learning shape-invariant pose. Due to page limitations, more results can be found in our supplementary files.

4.1   Dataset and Implementation Details

We employ the ShapeNet dataset [2] for evaluation. For point cloud auto-encoding we follow the settings in [25] and [7], and use ShapeNet Core focusing on airplanes, chairs, tables and cars. While airplanes and cars are more semantically consistent and containing less variation, chairs exhibit less shape-consistency and may contain different semantic parts. All 3D models are randomly rotated and translated in the range of $[-0.1, 0.1]$ at train and test time.

For all experiments, unless stated otherwise, we sample random 1024 points for each point cloud. The auto-encoder is trained using Adam optimizer with learning rate of $1e^{-3}$ for 500 epochs, with drop to the learning rate at 250 and 350 by a factor of 10. We save the last iteration checkpoint and use it for our evaluation. The decoder is AtlasNetV2 [7] decoder with 10 learnable grids.

4.2   Pose Consistency

We first qualitatively evaluate the consistency of our canonical representation as shown in Fig. 4. At test time, we feed different instances at different poses through our trained network, yielding estimated pose of the input object w.r.t the pose-invariant shape. We then apply the inverse transformation learned, to transform the input to its canonical pose. As can be seen, the different instances are roughly aligned, despite having different shapes. More examples can be found in our supplementary files.

We also compare our method, both qualitatively and quantitatively, to Canonical Capsules [25] and Compass [24] by using the alignment in ShapeNet

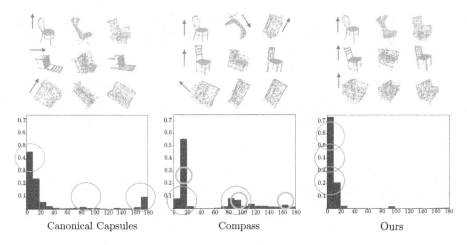

Fig. 5. Histogram of canonical pose deviation from the mean canonical pose. We estimate the canonical pose of aligned 3D point clouds from ShapeNet using our method, Canonical Capsules [25] and Compass [24]. In the bottom row, we show the normalized histogram of the deviation from the mean pose. It is clear that while our method is shape-consistent, both Compass and Canonical Capsules struggle to have a single canonical pose. In the top row, we focus on small, medium and large deviation cases of Canonical Capsules, marked by cyan, red, and orange circles on the histogram plot, respectively. The canonical pose of the same objects is shown for Compass and our method, as well as their location on the corresponding histogram plot. The arrow next to the objects is directed toward the local shape z+ direction.

(for Compass no translation is applied). First, we feed forward all of the aligned test point clouds $\{\mathbf{X}_i\}_{i=1}^{N_t}$ through all methods and estimate their canonical pose $\{\tilde{R}_i\}_{i=1}^{N_t}$. We expect to have a consistent pose for all aligned input shapes, thus, we quantify for each instance i the angular deviation $d_i^{consist}$ of its estimated pose $\tilde{R}_i$ from the Chordal L2-mean [12] pose $d_i^{consist} = \angle\left(\tilde{R}_i, \frac{1}{N_t}\sum_i \tilde{R}_i\right)$. We present an histogram of $\{d_i^{consist}\}_{i=1}^{N_t}$ in Fig. 5. As can be seen, our method results in a more aligned canonical shapes as indicated by the peak around the lower deviation values. We visualize the misalignment of Canonical Capsules by sampling objects with small, medium and large deviation, and compare them to the canonical representation achieved by Compass and our method for the same instances. The misalignment of Canonical Capsules may be attributed to the complexity of matching unsupervised semantic parts between chairs as they exhibit high variation (size, missing parts, varied structure). In Table 1 we quantify the consistency by the standard deviation of the estimated pose $\sqrt{\frac{1}{N_t}\sum_i d_i^2}$ and we present the Instance-Level Consistency (IC) and Ground Truth Consistency (GC) as defined in [22]. Evidently, Compass falls short for all object classes, while our method preforms overall in a consistent manner. Canonical Capsules preforms slightly better than our method for planes, though most of the miss-consistency is rooted in the symmetry of the object as indicated by the low GC. The table class is a unique example of a canonic pose which is not well-defined due to the rotation symmetry of tables (especially round tables). Despite the relatively low quantitative performance, in our supplementary files we show that the canonic shape of the tables is generally aligned.

Input

Canonical
Capsules

Compass

Ours

Fig. 6. Stability of the canonical representation to rigid transformation of the input. The location and orientation of the same point cloud affects its canonical representation in both Canonical Capsules [25] and Compass [24]. Our canonical representation (bottom row) is **SE**(3)-invariant to the rigid transformation of the input.

4.3 Stability

A key attribute in our approach is the network construction, which outputs a purely **SE**(3)-invariant canonical shape. Since we do not require any optimization for such invariance, our canonical shape is expected to be very stable compared with Canonical Capsules and Compass. We quantify the stability, as proposed by Canonical Capsules, in a similar manner to the consistency metric. For each instance i, we randomly rotate the object $k = 10$ times, and estimate the canonical pose for each rotated instance $\{\tilde{R}_{ij}\}_{j=1}^{k}$. We average across all N_t instances the standard deviation of the angular pose estimation as follows,

Table 1. Comparison of consistency and stability (lower is better).

	Stability/Consistency			IC/GC ($\times 10^3$)		
	Capsules	Compass	Ours	Capsules	Compass	Ours
Airplanes	7.42 /**45.76**	13.81/71.43	**0.02/49.97**	2.1/**6.4**	6.3/20.1	**1.9e−4/8.1**
Chairs	4.79/68.13	12.01/68.2	**0.04/24.31**	2.4/13.1	8.4/51.2	**2e−4/12.1**
Cars	81.9/11.1	19.2/87.5	**0.03/35.6**	34.5/3.53	5.7/10.5	**1.6e−4/1.2**
Tables	14.7/119.3	74.8/115.3	**0.02/106.3**	10.5/78.1	14/92.9	**1.2e−3/15.3**

$$d^{stability} = \frac{1}{N_t} \sum_i \sqrt{\sum_j \angle\left(\tilde{R}_{ij}, \frac{1}{k}\sum_j \tilde{R}_{ij}\right)^2}.$$

The results are reported in Table 1. As expected, Canonical Capsules and Compass exhibit non-negligible instability, as we visualize in Fig. 6.

4.4   Reconstruction Quality

We show qualitatively our point cloud reconstruction in Fig. 7. Please note that our goal is not to build a SOTA auto-encoder in terms of reconstruction, rather we learn to disentangle pose from shape via auto-encoding. Nonetheless, our auto-encoder does result in a pleasing result as shown in Fig. 7. Moreover, since we employ AtlasNetV2 [7] which utilizes a multiple patch-based decoder, we can examine which point belongs to which decoder. As our shape-encoding is both invariant to pose and consistent across different shapes, much like in the aligned scenario, each decoder assume some-what of semantic meaning, capturing for example the right wing of the airplanes. Please note that we do not enforce any structuring on the decoders.

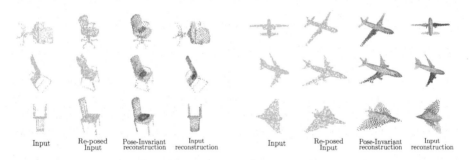

Fig. 7. Reconstruction of chairs and planes under SE(3) transformations. The input point cloud (left) is disentangled to shape (second from the right) and pose, which together reconstruct the input point cloud, as shown in the right most column. The inverse pose is applied to the input point cloud to achieve a canonical representation (second image from the left). The colors of the reconstructed point cloud indicate different decoders of AtlasNetV2 [7].

4.5   3D Implicit Reconstruction

We show that our encoder can be attached to a different reconstruction task by repeating OccNet [16] completion experiment. We replace OccNet encoder with our shape-pose disentagling encoder. The experiment is preformed with the same settings as in [16]. We use the subset of [3], and the point clouds are sub-sampled from the watertight mesh, containing only 300 points and applied with a Gaussian noise. We have trained OccNet for $600K$ iterations and report the results of the best (reconstruction wise) checkpoint. We show in Fig. 8 a few examples of rotated point clouds (left), its implicit function reconstruction (middle) and the implicit function reconstruction in the canonical pose (right).

Fig. 8. Reconstruction results of OccNet [16] via shape-pose disentanglement. An input point cloud on the left is disentangled to shape encoding and pose. OccNet decodes only the shape encoding yielding a canonical shape on the right column. The reconstruction is then transformed by the estimated pose as seen in the middle column. Meshes are extracted via Multiresolution IsoSurface Extraction (MISE) [16]

5   Conclusions

We have presented a stable and consistent canonical representation learning. To achieve a pose-invariant representation, we have devised an **SE**(3)-equivairant encoder, extending the VNN framework, to meet the requirements of canonical pose learning, i.e., learning rigid transformations. Our experiments show, both qualitatively and quantitatively, that our canonical representation is significantly more stable than recent approaches and has similar or better consistency, especially for diverse object classes. Moreover, we show that our approach is not limited to specific decoding mechanism, allowing for example to reconstruct canonical implicit neural field. In the future, we would like to explore the potential of our canonical representation for point cloud processing tasks requiring aligned settings, such as completion and unsupervised segmentation, where the canonical representation is learned on-the-fly, along with the task.

Acknowledgments. This work was supported in part by the Israel Science Foundation (grants no. 2492/20, 3441/21 and 3611/21).

References

1. Bar-Itzhack, I.Y.: Iterative optimal orthogonalization of the strapdown matrix. IEEE Trans. Aerosp. Electron. Syst. **1**, 30–37 (1975)

2. Chang, A.X., et al.: Shapenet: an information-rich 3D model repository. arXiv preprint arXiv:1512.03012 (2015)
3. Choy, C.B., Xu, D., Gwak, J.Y., Chen, K., Savarese, S.: 3D-R2N2: a unified approach for single and multi-view 3D object reconstruction. In: Leibe, B., Matas, J., Sebe, N., Welling, M. (eds.) ECCV 2016. LNCS, vol. 9912, pp. 628–644. Springer, Cham (2016). https://doi.org/10.1007/978-3-319-46484-8_38
4. Cohen, T.S., Geiger, M., Köhler, J., Welling, M.: Spherical CNNs. arXiv preprint arXiv:1801.10130 (2018)
5. Cohen, T.S., Welling, M.: Steerable CNNs. arXiv preprint arXiv:1612.08498 (2016)
6. Deng, C., Litany, O., Duan, Y., Poulenard, A., Tagliasacchi, A., Guibas, L.J.: Vector neurons: a general framework for SO(3)-equivariant networks. In: Proceedings of the IEEE/CVF International Conference on Computer Vision, pp. 12200–12209 (2021)
7. Deprelle, T., Groueix, T., Fisher, M., Kim, V., Russell, B., Aubry, M.: Learning elementary structures for 3D shape generation and matching. In: Advances in Neural Information Processing Systems, pp. 7433–7443 (2019)
8. Esteves, C., Allen-Blanchette, C., Makadia, A., Daniilidis, K.: Learning SO(3) equivariant representations with spherical CNNs. In: Proceedings of the European Conference on Computer Vision (ECCV), pp. 52–68 (2018)
9. Groueix, T., Fisher, M., Kim, V.G., Russell, B.C., Aubry, M.: A papier-mâché approach to learning 3D surface generation. In: Proceedings of the IEEE Conference on Computer Vision and Pattern Recognition, pp. 216–224 (2018)
10. Gu, J., et al.: Weakly-supervised 3D shape completion in the wild. In: Vedaldi, A., Bischof, H., Brox, T., Frahm, J.-M. (eds.) ECCV 2020. LNCS, vol. 12350, pp. 283–299. Springer, Cham (2020). https://doi.org/10.1007/978-3-030-58558-7_17
11. Hamdi, A., Giancola, S., Ghanem, B.: MVTN: multi-view transformation network for 3D shape recognition. In: Proceedings of the IEEE/CVF International Conference on Computer Vision, pp. 1–11 (2021)
12. Hartley, R., Trumpf, J., Dai, Y., Li, H.: Rotation averaging. Int. J. Comput. Vis. **103**(3), 267–305 (2013)
13. Li, X., et al.: Leveraging SE(3) equivariance for self-supervised category-level object pose estimation from point clouds. In: Advances in Neural Information Processing Systems, vol. 34, pp. 15370–15381 (2021)
14. Liu, Z., Zhao, X., Huang, T., Hu, R., Zhou, Y., Bai, X.: TANet: robust 3D object detection from point clouds with triple attention. In: Proceedings of the AAAI Conference on Artificial Intelligence, vol. 34, pp. 11677–11684 (2020)
15. Ma, X., Qin, C., You, H., Ran, H., Fu, Y.: Rethinking network design and local geometry in point cloud: a simple residual MLP framework. In: International Conference on Learning Representations (2022)
16. Mescheder, L., Oechsle, M., Niemeyer, M., Nowozin, S., Geiger, A.: Occupancy networks: learning 3D reconstruction in function space. In: Proceedings of the IEEE/CVF Conference on Computer Vision and Pattern Recognition, pp. 4460–4470 (2019)
17. Novotny, D., Ravi, N., Graham, B., Neverova, N., Vedaldi, A.: C3DPO: canonical 3D pose networks for non-rigid structure from motion. In: Proceedings of the IEEE/CVF International Conference on Computer Vision, pp. 7688–7697 (2019)
18. Park, J.J., Florence, P., Straub, J., Newcombe, R., Lovegrove, S.: DeepSDF: learning continuous signed distance functions for shape representation. In: Proceedings of the IEEE/CVF Conference on Computer Vision and Pattern Recognition, pp. 165–174 (2019)

19. Qi, C.R., Su, H., Mo, K., Guibas, L.J.: Pointnet: deep learning on point sets for 3D classification and segmentation. In: Proceedings of the IEEE Conference on Computer Vision and Pattern Recognition, pp. 652–660 (2017)
20. Qi, C.R., Yi, L., Su, H., Guibas, L.J.: PointNet++: deep hierarchical feature learning on point sets in a metric space. In: Advances in Neural Information Processing Systems, vol. 30 (2017)
21. Rempe, D., Birdal, T., Zhao, Y., Gojcic, Z., Sridhar, S., Guibas, L.J.: CaSPR: learning canonical spatiotemporal point cloud representations. In: Advances in Neural Information Processing Systems, vol. 33, pp. 13688–13701 (2020)
22. Sajnani, R., Poulenard, A., Jain, J., Dua, R., Guibas, L.J., Sridhar, S.: ConDor: self-supervised canonicalization of 3d pose for partial shapes. In: Proceedings of the IEEE/CVF Conference on Computer Vision and Pattern Recognition, pp. 16969–16979 (2022)
23. Shi, S., Wang, X., Li, H.: PointRCNN: 3D object proposal generation and detection from point cloud. In: Proceedings of the IEEE/CVF Conference on Computer Vision and Pattern Recognition, pp. 770–779 (2019)
24. Spezialetti, R., Stella, F., Marcon, M., Silva, L., Salti, S., Di Stefano, L.: Learning to orient surfaces by self-supervised spherical CNNs. arXiv preprint arXiv:2011.03298 (2020)
25. Sun, W., et al.: Canonical capsules: self-supervised capsules in canonical pose. In: Advances in Neural Information Processing Systems, vol. 34 (2021)
26. Thomas, N., et al.: Tensor field networks: rotation-and translation-equivariant neural networks for 3D point clouds. arXiv preprint arXiv:1802.08219 (2018)
27. Wang, Y., Sun, Y., Liu, Z., Sarma, S.E., Bronstein, M.M., Solomon, J.M.: Dynamic graph CNN for learning on point clouds. ACM Trans. Graph. (TOG) 38(5), 1–12 (2019)
28. Weiler, M., Geiger, M., Welling, M., Boomsma, W., Cohen, T.: 3D steerable CNNs: learning rotationally equivariant features in volumetric data. arXiv preprint arXiv:1807.02547 (2018)
29. Xu, Q., Wang, W., Ceylan, D., Mech, R., Neumann, U.: DISN: deep implicit surface network for high-quality single-view 3D reconstruction. In: Advances in Neural Information Processing Systems, vol. 32 (2019)
30. Yang, Y., Feng, C., Shen, Y., Tian, D.: FoldingNet: point cloud auto-encoder via deep grid deformation. In: Proceedings of the IEEE Conference on Computer Vision and Pattern Recognition, pp. 206–215 (2018)
31. Yang, Z., Sun, Y., Liu, S., Jia, J.: 3DSSD: point-based 3D single stage object detector. In: Proceedings of the IEEE/CVF Conference on Computer Vision and Pattern Recognition, pp. 11040–11048 (2020)

3D Equivariant Graph Implicit Functions

Yunlu Chen[1]([✉]), Basura Fernando[2], Hakan Bilen[3], Matthias Nießner[4], and Efstratios Gavves[1]

[1] University of Amsterdam, Amsterdam, The Netherlands
ychen9201@gmail.com, e.gavves@uva.nl
[2] CFAR, IHPC, A*STAR, Singapore, Singapore
fernandopbc@ihpc.a-star.edu.sg
[3] University of Edinburgh, Edinburgh, UK
hbilen@ed.ac.uk
[4] Technical University of Munich, Munich, Germany
niessner@tum.de

Abstract. In recent years, neural implicit representations have made remarkable progress in modeling of 3D shapes with arbitrary topology. In this work, we address two key limitations of such representations, in failing to capture local 3D geometric fine details, and to learn from and generalize to shapes with unseen 3D transformations. To this end, we introduce a novel family of graph implicit functions with equivariant layers that facilitates modeling fine local details and guaranteed robustness to various groups of geometric transformations, through local k-NN graph embeddings with sparse point set observations at multiple resolutions. Our method improves over the existing rotation-equivariant implicit function from 0.69 to 0.89 (IoU) on the ShapeNet reconstruction task. We also show that our equivariant implicit function can be extended to other types of similarity transformations and generalizes to unseen translations and scaling.

Keywords: Implicit neural representations · Equivariance · Graph neural networks · 3D reconstruction · Transformation

1 Introduction

Neural implicit representations are effective at encoding 3D shapes of arbitrary topology [10,30,32]. Their key idea is to represent a shape by a given latent code in the learned manifold and for each point in space, the neural implicit function checks whether a given coordinate location is occupied within the shape or not. In contrast to traditional discrete 3D representations such as triangle meshes or point clouds, this new paradigm of implicit neural representations has gained significant popularity due to the advantages such as being continuous, grid-free, and the ability to handle various topologies.

Despite their success, latent-code-conditioned implicit representations have two key limitations. First, the latent code of the shape captures coarse high-level shape details

---

Supplementary Information The online version contains supplementary material available at https://doi.org/10.1007/978-3-031-20062-5_28.

S. Avidan et al. (Eds.): ECCV 2022, LNCS 13663, pp. 485–502, 2022.
https://doi.org/10.1007/978-3-031-20062-5_28

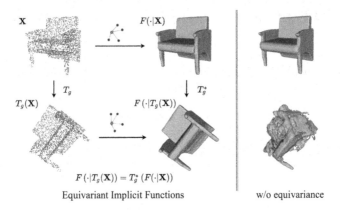

$$F(\cdot|T_g(\mathbf{X})) = T_g^*(F(\cdot|\mathbf{X}))$$

Equivariant Implicit Functions   w/o equivariance

Fig. 1. Our equivariant graph implicit function infers the implicit field $F(\cdot|\mathbf{X})$ for a 3D shape, given a sparse point cloud observation $\mathbf{X}$. When a transformation T_g (rotation, translation, or/and scaling) is applied to the observation $\mathbf{X}$, the resulting implicit field $F(\cdot|T_g(\mathbf{X}))$ is *guaranteed* to be the same as applying a corresponding transformation T_g^* to the inferred implicit field from the untransformed input (*middle*). The property of equivariance enables generalization to unseen transformations, under which existing models such as ConvONet [34] often struggle (*right*).

(i.e., the global structure) without any explicit local spatial information, hence it is not possible to learn correlations between the latent code and local 3D structural details of the shape. As a result, the surface reconstruction from latent-code-conditioned implicit functions tends to be over-smoothed and they are not good at capturing local surface detail [11,18,21,25,34]. Second, implicit representations are sensitive to various geometric transformations, in particular to rotations [16]. The performance of the implicit representations heavily relies on the assumption that shape instances in the same category are required to be in the same canonical orientation such that shape structures of planes and edges are in line with the coordinate axes. While data augmentation loosely addresses this second issue to some degree, a principled approach is to enable the representations to be inherently aware of common geometric operations such as rotations, translations, and scaling, which are found commonly in real-world 3D objects.

To address the first challenge of modeling local spatial information, recent methods [11,34] first discretize 3D space into local 2D or 3D grids and then store implicit codes locally in the respective grid cells. However, these methods are still sensitive to transformations as the grid structure is constructed in line with the chosen coordinate axes. This results in deteriorated performance under transformations as shown in Fig. 1. In addition, the grid discretization often has to trade fine details of the shape, hence the quality of shape reconstruction, for better computational efficiency through a low resolution grid. Deng *et al.* [17] propose VN-ONet to tackle the second challenge of pose-sensitivity with a novel vector neuron formulation, which enables the network architecture to have a rotation equivariant representation. Nevertheless, similar to implicit representations, the VN-ONet encodes each shape with a global representation and hence fails to capture local details. As grid discretization is not robust to transformations, this solution is not compatible with the grid-based local implicit methods. Thus, integrating VN-ONet with grid-approach is not a feasible solution.

In this work, our goal is to simultaneously address both challenges of encoding local details in latent representations and dealing with the sensitivity to geometric transformations such as rotations, translations, and scaling. To this end, we propose a novel equivariant graph-based local implicit function that unifies both of these properties. In particular, we use graph convolutions to capture local 3D information in a non-Euclidean manner, with a multi-scale sampling design in the architecture to aggregate global and local context at different sampling levels. We further integrate equivariant layers to facilitate generalization to unseen geometric transformations. Unlike the grid-based methods [11,34] that requires discretization of 3D space into local grids, our graph-based implicit function uses point features from the input point cloud observation directly without interpolation from grid features. Our graph mechanism allows the model to attend detailed information from fine areas of the shape surface points, while the regularly-spanned grid frame may place computations to less important areas. In addition, our graph structure is not biased towards the canonical axis directions of the given Cartesian coordinate frame, hence less sensitive than the grid-local representations [11,34]. Therefore, our graph representation is maximally capable of realizing an equivariant architecture for 3D shape representation. In summary, our contributions are as follows:

- We propose a novel graph-based implicit representation network that enables effective encoding of local 3D information in a multi-scale sampling architecture, and thus modeling of high-fidelity local 3D geometric detail. Our model features a non-Euclidean graph representation that naturally adapts with geometric transformations.
- We incorporate equivariant graph layers in order to facilitate inherent robustness against geometric transformations. Together with the graph embedding, our equivariant implicit model significantly improves the reconstruction quality from the existing rotation equivariant implicit method [17].
- We extend our implicit method to achieve a stronger equivariant model that handles more types of similarity transformations simultaneously with guaranteed perfect generalization, including rotation, translation and scaling.

2   Related Work

Implicit 3D Representations. Neural implicits have been shown to be highly effective for encoding continuous 3D signals of varying topology [10,30,32]. Its variants have been used in order to reconstruct shapes from a single image [38,52,53], or use weaker supervision for raw point clouds [1–3] and 2D views [26,29,31].

Local Latent Implicit Embeddings. ConvONet [34] and IF-Net [11] concurrently propose to learn multi-scale local grid features with convolution layers to improve upon global latent implicit representations. Other variants of grid methods [5,25] takes no global cues, hence restricted by requiring additional priors during inference such as normals [25] or the partial implicit field [5]. The paradigm is extended to adaptive grids or octrees [44,45,47]. Inspired by non-grid local embeddings in point cloud networks [20,28,36,48], we aim for non-grid local implicit methods, which are less explored. The existing non-grid local implicits [18,22] are limited without multi-scale hierarchical designs, and thus restricted to single objects. The pose-sensitivity problem is not addressed in all these local methods. In contrast, we use a hierarchical graph embedding that effectively encodes multi-scale context, as the first local implicit method to address the pose-sensitivity problem.

Pose-Sensitivity in Implicit Functions. As generalization becomes a concern for 3D vision [4,8,9,42], Davies *et al.* [16] first point out that the implicit 3D representations are biased towards canonical orientations. Deng *et al.* [17] introduce a rotation equivariant implicit network VN-ONet that generalises to random unseen rotations, but yet with the restrictions from the global latent. Concurrent to our work, [7,41,54] extend equivariance of implicit reconstruction to SE(3) group for reconstruction and robotic tasks, while our method further handles scaling transformation, and recovers significantly better local details with the graph local embedding design. As grid embeddings are sensitive to rotation, seeking a compatible local latent embedding is a non-trivial problem.

Rotation Equivariance with 3D Vector Features. Equivariance has drawn attention in deep learning models with inductive priors of physical symmetries, e.g., the success of ConvNets are attributed to translation equivariance. Advanced techniques are developed for equivariance to rotation [14,46,51], scale [43,56] and permutation [35,55]. Recently, a new paradigm for rotation equivariance uses 3D vectors as neural features [17,40] with improved effectiveness and efficiency upon methods based on spherical harmonics [19,46,49–51]. Shen *et al.* [40] first introduced pure quaternion features that are equivalent to 3D vectors. Deng *et al.* [17] proposed a similar design with improved nonlinear layers. Satorras *et al.* [39] proposed to aggregate vector inputs in graph message passing, but without vector nonlinearities involved. Leveraging on existing work [17,39,40], we introduce hybrid vector and scalar neural features for better performance and efficiency. We also adapt the paradigm for scale equivariance, for the first time in literature.

3   A Definition of Equivariance for Implicit Representations

While equivariance to common geometric transformations is widely studied for explicit representations of 2D and 3D data [13,46,51], the property for implicit representations that encode signals in a function space is more challenging since continuous queries are involved, yet an important problem for 3D reconstruction. We discuss standard 3D implicit functions and then define equivariance for the representation.

3D Implicit Representations. We build our model on neural 3D occupancy field functions [30], widely used as a shared implicit representation for a collection of 3D shapes. Given an observation $\mathbf{X} \in \mathcal{X}$ of a 3D shape, the conditional implicit representation of the shape, $F(\cdot|\mathbf{X}) : \mathbb{R}^3 \to [0, 1]$, is a 3D scalar field that maps the 3D Euclidean domain to occupancy probabilities, indicating whether there is a surface point at the coordinate. In this work, we consider $\mathbf{X}$ as a sparse 3D point cloud, such that the information from the observation is indifferent under an arbitrary global transformation, as required for equivariance. For each 3D query coordinate $\vec{p} \in \mathbb{R}^3$, the conditioned implicit representation is in the form of

$$F(\vec{p}|\mathbf{X}) = \Psi(\vec{p}, \vec{z}) = \Psi(\vec{p}, \Phi(\mathbf{X})), \tag{1}$$

where $\Phi(\mathbf{X}) = \vec{z} \in \mathbb{R}^{C_{\vec{z}}}$ is the latent code in the form of a $C_{\vec{z}}$-dimensional vector from the observation $\mathbf{X}$, and Φ is the *latent feature extractor* that encodes the observation data $\mathbf{X}$. Ψ is the implicit decoder implemented using a multi-layered perceptron with ReLU activations. Occupancy probabilities are obtained by the final sigmoid activation function of the implicit decoder. Following [30, 34], the model is trained with binary cross-entropy loss supervised by ground truth occupancy. The underlying shape surface is the 2-manifold $\{\vec{p'}|F(\vec{p'}|\mathbf{X}) = \tau\}$, where $\tau \in (0, 1)$ is the surface decision boundary.

Preliminary of Equivariance. Consider a set of transformations $T_g : \mathcal{X} \to \mathcal{X}$ on a vector space $\mathcal{X}$ for $g \in G$, where G is an abstract group. Formally, $T_g = T(g)$ where T is a representation of group G, such that $\forall g, g' \in G, T(gg') = T(g)T(g')$. In the case that G is the 3D rotation group SO(3), T_g instantiates a 3D rotation matrix for a rotation denoted by g. We say a function $\Xi : \mathcal{X} \to \mathcal{Y}$ is equivariant with regard to group G if there exists $T_g^* : \mathcal{Y} \to \mathcal{Y}$ such that for all $g \in G$: $T_g^* \circ \Xi = \Xi \circ T_g$. We refer to [13,46] for more detailed background theory. Next, we define equivariance for implicit representations as follows:

Definition 1 (Equivariant 3D implicit functions). *Given a group G and the 3D transformations T_g with $g \in G$, the conditioned implicit function $F(\cdot|\mathbf{X})$ is equivariant with regard to G, if*

$$F\big(\cdot|T_g(\mathbf{X})\big) = T_g^*\big(F(\cdot|\mathbf{X})\big), \quad \text{for all } g \in G, \mathbf{X} \in \mathcal{X}. \tag{2}$$

where the transformation T_g^* applied on the implicit function associated to T_g is applying the inverse coordinate transform on query coordinates $T_g^*(F(\cdot|\mathbf{X})) \equiv F(T_g^{-1}(\cdot)|\mathbf{X})$.

Remark 1. *Equation (2) can be reformulated more intuitively as:*

$$F(\cdot|\mathbf{X}) = F\big(T_g(\cdot)|T_g(\mathbf{X})\big), \quad \text{for all } g \in G, \mathbf{X} \in \mathcal{X}. \tag{3}$$

Equation (3) indicates that the equivariance is satisfied if for any observation $\mathbf{X}$ and query $\vec{p}$, the implicit output of $F(\vec{p}|\mathbf{X})$ is *locally* invariant to any T_g applied jointly to $\mathbf{X}$ and $\vec{p}$ in the implicit model.

4 Transformation-Robust Graph Local Implicit Representations

Our goal is to design an equivariant implicit function model using local feature embeddings to capture fine details of the 3D geometry. However, existing grid-based local implicit functions are sensitive to geometric transformations such as rotations, thus not suitable for equivariant implicit representations. To address this limitation, we propose a graph-based local embedding which is robust to geometric transformations.

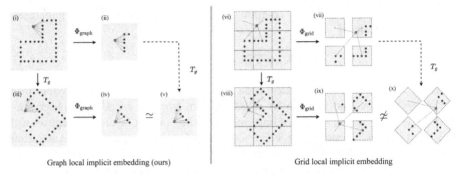

Graph local implicit embedding (ours)   Grid local implicit embedding

Fig. 2. Graph (*left*) **vs. grid** (*right*) **local implicit feature embeddings under rotation.** Φ_{graph} extracts k-NN graphs and applies graph convolutions; Φ_{grid} partitions points into regular grids and applies regular convolutions. *Left*: given a point cloud observation $\mathbf{X}$ (*navy*) (i), our method aggregates the local latent feature at any query coordinate $\mathbf{p}$ (*orange*) from a local k-NN graph connecting its neighbours in $\mathbf{X}$ (ii). Moreover, when a transformation T_g, *e.g.* rotation, is applied to the shape, (iv) the constructed local graph is in the same structure as (v) applying T_g to the graph from untransformed data. *Right*: in contrast, (vi) visualizes discretized grid features. (vii) The off-the-grid query location $\mathbf{p}$ interpolates the neighboring on-grid features. However, (viii) with T_g applied to the raw observation, often (ix) the sub-grid point patterns for the local features are different from (x) applying T_g to the untransformed local grids. This makes the grid local implicit models sensitive to transformations such as rotation.

Background: Grid Local Implicit Representations. To overcome the limitation of a global latent feature, recent methods, such as ConvONet [34] and IF-Net [11], propose to learn spatially-varying latent features $\mathbf{z_p} = \Phi_{\text{grid}}(\mathbf{p}; \mathbf{X})$. The main idea is to partition the 3D space into a grid and compute latent codes locally. Specifically, these methods formulate the local latent implicit function on the grid as $F_{\text{grid}}(\mathbf{p}|\mathbf{X}) = \Psi(\mathbf{p}, \mathbf{z_p}) = \Psi(\mathbf{p}, \Phi_{\text{grid}}(\mathbf{p}; \mathbf{X}))$, where the *grid local latent extractor* Φ_{grid} is further decomposed as $\Phi_{\text{grid}}(\mathbf{p}; \mathbf{X}) = \psi_{\text{grid}}(\mathbf{p}, \phi_{\text{grid}}(\mathbf{X}))$. The function ϕ_{grid} is the *grid feature encoder* that learns to generate a 2D or 3D grid-based feature tensor $\mathbf{M}$ from the entirety of point observations $\mathbf{X}$. For each grid location, point features are aggregated for all $\mathbf{x}_i \in \mathbf{X}$ in the corresponding bin. Convolutional layers are applied to the grid-based $\mathbf{M}$ to capture multi-scale information and maintain translation equivariance. Given the local 3D feature tensor $\mathbf{M}$, the *local latent aggregator* ψ_{grid} computes local latent feature $\mathbf{z_p}$ on any off-the-grid query coordinate $\mathbf{p}$ using a simple trilinear interpolation. We refer to [5,25] for other variants of grid-based representations using purely local information without global cues, while restricted by requiring additional priors during inference such as the normals. Overall, grid partitioning is not robust to general transformations such as rotations, especially when the sub-grid structure is considered for the resolution-free implicit reconstruction. Figure 2 (*right*) shows an illustration of this limitation, which we will address in our method.

4.1 Graph-Structured Local Implicit Feature Embeddings

We propose to use graphs as a non-regular representation, such that our local latent feature function is robust to these transformations and free from feature grid resolutions. The graph-local implicit function extends the standard form of Eq. (1) to

$$F_{\text{graph}}(\mathbf{p}|\mathbf{X}) = \Psi(\mathbf{p}, \mathbf{z_p}) = \Psi(\mathbf{p}, \Phi_{\text{graph}}(\mathbf{p}; \mathbf{X})) = \Psi(\mathbf{p}, \psi(\mathbf{p}, \phi(\mathbf{X}))). \qquad (4)$$

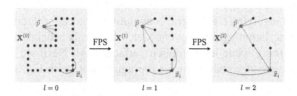

Fig. 3. Multi-scale design, with enlarged receptive fields of local k-NN graphs for the graph point encoder ϕ (*orange*) and the graph local latent aggregator ψ (*violet*).

Φ_{graph} is a deep network that extracts *local* latent features $\mathbf{z_p}$ on the graph, composed of two sub-networks ϕ and ψ. The *point feature encoder* ϕ maps the point set $\mathbf{X} = \{\mathbf{x}_i\}$ to the associated features $\{\mathbf{h}_i\}$, and is invariant to the sampled query location $\mathbf{p}$. The *graph local latent feature aggregator* ψ propagates the input point feature to the query coordinate $\mathbf{p}$. Unlike grid-based methods, we directly aggregate local information from the point cloud feature $\{(\mathbf{x}_i, \mathbf{h}_i)\}$ without an intermediate grid feature tensor. In particular, we construct a local k-nearest neighbor (k-NN) graph $(\mathcal{V}, \mathcal{E})$ for every query point $\mathbf{p}$, where the vertices $\mathcal{V} = \mathbf{X} \cup \{\mathbf{p}\}$ include the point set elements and the query coordinate. The edges $\mathcal{E} = \{(\mathbf{p}, \mathbf{x}_i)\}$ are between the query point $\mathbf{p}$ and its k-NN points from the observation point set $\mathbf{x}_{i'} \in \mathcal{N}_k(\mathbf{p}, \mathbf{X})$, with $\mathcal{N}_k(\mathbf{p}, \mathbf{X})$ denoting the set of the k-NN points of $\mathbf{p}$ from $\mathbf{X}$. Last, with graph convolutions, we aggregate into the local feature vector $\mathbf{z_p}$ the point features of the neighbors of $\mathbf{p}$. We adopt a simple spatial graph convolution design in the style of Message Passing Neural Network (MPNN) [23], which is widely used for 3D shape analysis [24,48]. For each neighboring point $\mathbf{x}_{i'}$ from the query $\mathbf{p}$, messages are passed through a function η as a shared two-layer ReLU-MLP, where the inputs are the point features $\mathbf{h}_{i'}$ and the query coordinate $\mathbf{p}$ as node feature as well as the displacement vector $\mathbf{x}_{i'}$ - $\mathbf{p}$ as the edge feature, followed by a permutation-invariant aggregation AGGRE over all neighboring nodes, e.g., max- or mean-pooling:

$$\mathbf{z_p} = \underset{i'}{\text{AGGRE}} \; \eta(\mathbf{p}, \mathbf{h}_{i'}, \mathbf{x}_{i'} - \mathbf{p}). \qquad (5)$$

For each neighboring point as a graph node, the edge function η take as inputs, the query coordinate $\mathbf{p}$, the node point feature $\mathbf{h}_{i'}$, and the relative position $\mathbf{x}_{i'} - \mathbf{p}$.

As all the graph connections are relative between vertices, the local latent feature aggregation is robust to transformations like rotations, as illustrated in Fig. 2 (*left*).

4.2 Learning Multi-scale Local Graph Latent Features

To capture the context of the 3D geometry at multiple scales, both ConvONet [34] and IF-Net [11] rely on a convolutional U-Net [37], with progressively downsampled and then upsampled feature grid resolutions to share neighboring information at different scales. Our graph model enables learning at multiple scales by farthest point sampling (FPS). That is, we downsample the point set $\mathbf{X}$ to $\mathbf{X}^{(l)}$ at sampling levels $l = 1, \ldots, L$ with a progressively smaller cardinality $|\mathbf{X}^{(l)}| < |\mathbf{X}^{(l-1)}|$, where $\mathbf{X}^{(0)} = \mathbf{X}$ is the original set.

Moreover, we use a graph encoder for the point encoder ϕ, instead of PointNet [35]. This way, without involving regular grid convolutions, we can still model local features and facilitate a translation-equivariant encoder, which is beneficial in many scenarios, especially for learning scene-level implicit surfaces [34]. Next, we sketch the multi-scale graph point encoder and latent feature aggregator, with Fig. 3 as a conceptual illustration.

The *graph point encoder* ϕ learns point features $\{\mathbf{h}_i^{(l)}\}$ for the corresponding points $x_i \in \mathbf{X}^{(l)}$ at each sampling level $l = 0 \ldots, L$. The encoder starts from the initial sampling level $l = 0$ where the input features are the raw coordinates. At each sampling level, a graph convolution is applied to each point to aggregate message from its local k-nearest neighbor point features, followed by an FPS operation to the downsampled level $l + 1$. The graph convolution is similar to that in Eq. (5), with the point features from both sides of the edge and the relative position as inputs. The graph convolutions and FPS downsampling are applied until the coarsest sampling level $l = L$. Then the point features are sequentially upsampled back from $l = L$ to $l = L - 1$, until $l = 0$. At each sampling level l, the upsampling layer is simply one linear layer followed by ReLU activation. For each point, the input of the upsampling layer is the nearest point feature from the last sampling level $l + 1$, and the skip-connected feature of the same point at the same sampling level from the downsampling stage. Thus far, we obtain multi-scale point features $\{(\mathbf{x}_i, \mathbf{h}_i^{(l)})\}$ for $\mathbf{x}_i \in \mathbf{X}^{(l)}$ at sampling levels $l = 0, \ldots, L$, as the output from the graph point encoder ϕ.

For the *graph latent feature aggregator* ψ, at each query coordinate $\mathbf{p}$, we use graph convolutions to aggregate the k-neighboring features $\{(\mathbf{x}_i, \mathbf{h}_i^{(l)})\}$ at different sampling levels l, as described in Sect. 4.1. The aggregated features from all sampling levels l are concatenated to yield the local latent vector $\mathbf{z_p}$ as output. The detailed formulations of ϕ and ψ are provided in the supplementary material.

5 Equivariant Graph Implicit Functions

The local graph structure of the proposed implicit function, with $\mathbf{X} \cup \{\mathbf{p}\}$ as the set of vertices, is in line with the requirement of equivariance in Sect. 3 and Eq. (3). As a result, the local graph implicit embedding can be used for an equivariant model to achieve theoretically guaranteed generalization to unseen transformations. To do this, we further require all the graph layers in the latent extractor Φ_{graph} to be equivariant in order to obtain equivariant local latent feature. We present the equivariant layers for 3D rotation group $G = SO(3)$, a difficult case for implicit functions [16].

To build the equivariant model from equivariant layers, we additionally remove the query coordinate input $\mathbf{p}$ to ensure the implicit decoder Ψ spatially invariant in Eq. (4), as the local spatial information is already included in the latent $\mathbf{z_p}$. See Appendix A.1 for details. We also extend the method to other similarity transformations, such as translation and scaling. See Appendix A.2.

5.1   Hybrid Feature Equivariant Layers

Our equivariant layers for the graph convolution operations is inspired by recent methods [17,40] that lift from a regular neuron feature $h \in \mathbb{R}$ to a vector $\mathbf{v} \in \mathbb{R}^3$ to encode rotation, and the list of 3D vector features $\mathbf{V} = [\mathbf{v}_1, \mathbf{v}_2, \ldots, \mathbf{v}_{C_v}]^\top \in \mathbb{R}^{C_v \times 3}$ that substitutes the regular features $\mathbf{h} \in \mathbb{R}^{C_h}$. However, using only vector features in the network is non-optimal for both effectiveness and efficiency, with highly regularized linear layers and computation-demanding nonlinearity projections (Fig. 4).

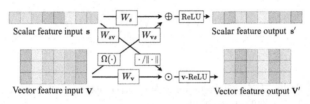

Fig. 4. Hybrid feature equivariant layers. Visualization of how vector and scalar features share information in linear and nonlinear layers. Vector features go through an invariant function Ω that is added to the scalar part. Scalar features are transformed with normalizing $\cdot / \| \cdot \|$ to scale the vector feature channels.

To this end, we extend the method and propose hybrid features $\{\mathbf{s}, \mathbf{V}\}$ to replace the regular feature $\mathbf{h}$, where vector features $\mathbf{V}$ encode rotation equivariance, and scalar features $\mathbf{s} \in \mathbb{R}^{C_s}$ are rotation-invariant. In practice, hybrid features show improved performance and computation efficiency by transferring some learning responsibility to the scalar features through more powerful and efficient standard neural layers.

Linear Layers. For input hybrid hidden feature $\{\mathbf{s}, \mathbf{V}\}$ with $\mathbf{s} \in \mathbb{R}^{C_s}$, and $\mathbf{V} = [\mathbf{v}_1, \mathbf{v}_2, \ldots, \mathbf{v}_{C_v}]^\top \in \mathbb{R}^{C_v \times 3}$, we define a set of weight matrices, $\mathbf{W}_s \in \mathbb{R}^{C'_s \times C_s}$, $\mathbf{W}_v \in \mathbb{R}^{C'_v \times C_v}$, $\mathbf{W}_{sv} \in \mathbb{R}^{C'_s \times C_s}$, and $\mathbf{W}_{vs} \in \mathbb{R}^{C'_s \times C_v}$ for the linear transformation, with information shared between scalar and vector features in the inputs. The resulting output features $\{\mathbf{s}', \mathbf{V}'\}$ become:

$$\mathbf{s}' = \mathbf{W}_s \mathbf{s} + \mathbf{W}_{vs}\, \Omega(\mathbf{V}) \tag{6}$$

$$\mathbf{V}' = \mathbf{W}_v \mathbf{V} \odot (\mathbf{W}_{sv}\, \mathbf{s}\, /\, \|\mathbf{W}_{sv}\, \mathbf{s}\|) \tag{7}$$

where $\odot$ is channel-wise multiplication between $\mathbf{W}_v \mathbf{V} \in \mathbb{R}^{C'_s \times 3}$ and $\mathbf{W}_{sv}\mathbf{h} \in \mathbb{R}^{C'_v \times 1}$, and the normalized transformed scalar feature $\mathbf{W}_{sv}\, \mathbf{s}\, /\, \|\mathbf{W}_{sv}\, \mathbf{s}\|$ learns to scale the output vectors in each channel; $\Omega(\cdot)$ is the invariance function that maps the rotation equivariant vector feature $\mathbf{V} \in \mathbb{R}^{C_v \times 3}$ to the rotation-invariant scalar feature $\Omega(\mathbf{V}) \in \mathbb{R}^{C_v}$, to be added on the output scalar feature. The design of the invariance function $\Omega(\cdot)$ is introduced later in Eq. (9).

Nonlinearities. Nonlinearities apply separately to scalar and vector features. For scalar features, it is simply a ReLU$(\cdot)$. For vector features, the nonlinearity v-ReLU$(\cdot)$ adopts the design from Vector Neurons [17]: the vector feature $\mathbf{v}_c$ at each channel c takes an inner-product with a learnt direction $\mathbf{q} = [\mathbf{W_q V}]^{\top} \in \mathbb{R}^3$ from a linear layer $\mathbf{W_q} \in \mathbb{R}^{1 \times C_{\mathbf{v}}}$. If the inner-product is negative, $\mathbf{v}_c$ is projected to the plane perpendicular to $\mathbf{q}$.

$$[\text{v-ReLU}(\mathbf{V})]_c = \begin{cases} \mathbf{v}_c & \text{if } \left\langle \mathbf{v}_c, \frac{\mathbf{q}}{\|\mathbf{q}\|} \right\rangle \geq 0, \\ \mathbf{v}_c - \left\langle \mathbf{v}_c, \frac{\mathbf{q}}{\|\mathbf{q}\|} \right\rangle \frac{\mathbf{q}}{\|\mathbf{q}\|}. & \text{otherwise.} \end{cases} \quad (8)$$

Invariance Layer. The invariance function $\Omega(\cdot)$ maps the rotation equivariant vector feature $\mathbf{V} \in \mathbb{R}^{C_{\mathbf{v}} \times 3}$ to a rotation-invariant scalar feature $\Omega(\mathbf{V}) \in \mathbb{R}^{C_{\mathbf{v}}}$ with the same channel dimension $C_{\mathbf{v}}$. At each layer $c = 1, \ldots, C_{\mathbf{v}}$, $[\Omega(\mathbf{V})]_c \in \mathbb{R}$ takes the inner product of $\mathbf{v}_c$ with the channel-averaged direction:

$$[\Omega(\mathbf{V})]_c = \left\langle \mathbf{v}_c, \frac{\overline{\mathbf{v}}}{\|\overline{\mathbf{v}}\|} \right\rangle, \quad (9)$$

Table 1. ShapeNet implicit reconstruction from sparse noisy point clouds. The grid resolutions are marked for ConvONet and IF-Net.

	SO(3) equiv.	Mean IoU ↑	Chamfer-ℓ_1 ↓	Normal consist. ↑
ONet	✗	0.736	0.098	0.878
ConvONet-2D (3×64^2)	✗	0.884	0.044	0.938
ConvONet-3D (32^3)	✗	0.870	0.048	0.937
IF-Net (128^3)	✗	0.887	0.042	0.941
GraphONet (ours)	✗	**0.904**	**0.038**	**0.946**
VN-ONet	✓	0.694	0.125	0.866
E-GraphONet-SO(3) (ours)	✓	0.890	0.041	0.936

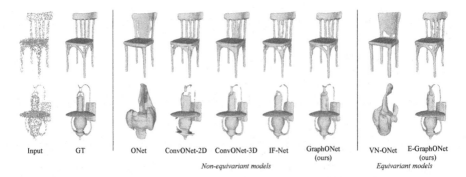

| Input | GT | ONet | ConvONet-2D | ConvONet-3D | IF-Net | GraphONet (ours) | VN-ONet | E-GraphONet (ours) |

Non-equivariant models   *Equivariant models*

Fig. 5. ShapeNet object reconstruction in canonical space. GraphONet is among the best performing non-equivariant implicit representation methods; E-GraphONet significantly improves on the existing equivariant method VN-ONet [17].

where $\overline{\mathbf{v}} = \frac{1}{C_{\mathbf{v}}} \sum_{c'=1}^{C_{\mathbf{v}}} \mathbf{v}_{c'}$ is the channel-averaged vector feature. One can verify that applying any rotation on the vector feature does not change the inner product. Our Ω adopts from [17] with modification. Ours is parameter-free using averaged direction, while [17] learns this vector.

The invariance function is applied in each linear layer in Eq. (7) to share the information between vector and scalar parts of the feature. In addition, at the end of equivariant graph feature network Φ_{graph}, $\Omega(\mathbf{V})$ is concatenated with the scalar feature as the final invariant local latent feature $\mathbf{z}_{\mathbf{p}} = \Omega(\mathbf{V})\|\mathbf{s}$, as to be locally invariant with transformed $\mathbf{p}$ and $\mathbf{X}$ in line with Eq. (3).

6   Experiments

We experiment on implicit surface reconstruction from sparse and noisy point observations. In addition, we evaluate the implicit reconstruction performance under random transformations of rotation, translation and scaling. Our method is referred to as Graph Occupancy networks, or GraphONet, while E-GraphONet is the equivariance model with 3 variants: SO(3), SE(3) and similarity transformations (Sim.).

Table 2. Implicit surface reconstruction with random rotation, IoU↑. The *left* table evaluates non-equivariant methods, and the *right* one compares the best performing model with equivariant methods. *I* denotes canonical pose and *SO(3)* random rotation. *I/SO(3)* denotes training with canonical pose and test with random rotation, and so on. *: models not re-trained with augmentation due to guaranteed equivariance.

training / test	I / I	I / SO(3)	SO(3) / SO(3)
ONet	0.742	0.271 [-0.471]	0.592 [-0.150]
ConvONet-2D	0.884	0.568 [-0.316]	0.791 [-0.093]
ConvONet-3D	0.870	0.761 [-0.109]	0.838 [-0.032]
GraphONet (ours)	**0.904**	**0.846 [-0.058]**	**0.887 [-0.017]**

training / test	equiv.	I / I	I / SO(3)	SO(3) / SO(3)
GraphONet (ours)	×	**0.904**	0.846 [-0.058]	0.887 [-0.017]
VN-ONet	SO(3)	0.694	0.694 [-0.000]	0.694* [-0.000]
E-GraphONet (ours)	SO(3)	0.890	**0.890 [-0.000]**	**0.890* [-0.000]**

Implementation Details. We implement our method using PyTorch [33]. The number of neighbours in k-NN graph is set as 20. For the multi-scale graph implicit encoder, we take $L = 2$, *i.e.*, the point set is downsampled twice with farthest point sampling (FPS) to 20% and 5% of the original cardinality respectively. The permutation invariant function $AGGRE$ adopts mean-pooling for vector features and max-pooling for scalar features. We use an Adam optimizer [27] with $\gamma = 10^{-3}$, $\beta_1 = 0.9$ and $\beta_2 = 0.999$. Main experiments are conducted on the ShapeNet [6] dataset with human designed objects, where the train/val/test splits follow prior work [12,34] with 13 categories. Following [34], we sample 3000 surface points per shape and apply Gaussian noise with 0.005 standard deviation. More details are provided in the Appendix. Code is available at https://github.com/yunlu-chen/equivariant-graph-implicit.

6.1 Canonical-Posed Object Reconstruction

We experiment on ShapeNet object reconstruction following the setups in [34]. For quantitative evaluation in Table 1, we evaluate the IoU, Chamfer-ℓ_1 distance and normal consistency, following [30,34]. The qualitative results are shown in Fig. 5. Our GraphONet outperforms the state-of-the-arts methods ConvONet [34] and IF-Net [11], as our graph-based method aggregates local feature free of spatial grid resolution and captures better local details. IF-Net is better than ConvONet but at large memory cost per batch with 128^3 resolution grid feature. For rotation equivariant models, our E-GraphONet significantly outperforms VN-ONet [17], benefiting from the graph local features.

6.2 Evaluation Under Geometric Transformations

Rotation. First, we investigate how implicit models perform under random rotations, which is challenging for neural implicits [16]. In Table 2 left, GraphONet shows the smallest performance drop among all non-equivariant methods under rotations, either with (*SO(3)/SO(3)*) or without augmentation (*I/SO(3)*) during training, since the graph structure is more robust to rotations. ConvONet [34]-2D is more sensitive than the 3D version, as 3D rotation would lead to highly distinct 2D projections. In Table 2 right, E-GraphONet, equipped with equivariant layers, achieves better performance under random rotations, even when the non-equivariant methods are trained with augmentation. It also outperforms the previous equivariant method VN-ONet [17] by a large margin.

Table 3. Implicit surface reconstruction performance under various types of seen/unseen transformations, mIoU↑.

Transformation(s)	equiv.	-	translation		scale		rot. & transl.		rot. & scale		transl. & scale		all	
Training augmentation	-	-	×	✓	×	✓	×	✓	×	✓	×	✓	×	✓
ONet	×	0.738	0.221	0.716	0.423	0.685	0.154	0.585	0.235	0.591	0.202	0.713	0.121	0.573
ConvONet-2D (3×128²)	×‡	0.882	0.791	0.878	0.812	0.850	0.532	0.771	0.542	0.789	0.723	0.838	0.481	0.728
ConvONet-3D (64³)	×‡	0.861	0.849	0.856	0.797	0.837	0.759	0.836	0.742	0.832	0.771	0.835	0.721	0.803
GraphONet (ours)	×‡	**0.901**	**0.884**	**0.898**	0.857	**0.893**	0.837	0.881	0.798	0.880	0.852	**0.888**	0.798	0.874
VN-ONet	SO(3)	0.682	0.354	0.667	0.516	0.662	0.357	0.658	0.511	0.666	0.360	0.638	0.309	0.615
E-GraphONet (ours)	SO(3)‡	0.887	0.823	0.876	0.824	0.880	0.825	0.877	0.825	**0.882**	0.726	0.872	0.729	0.870
E-GraphONet (ours)	SE(3)	0.884	**0.884**	0.884*	0.840	0.880	**0.884**	0.884*	0.838	0.880	0.841	0.878	0.840	0.878
E-GraphONet (ours)	Sim.†	0.882	0.882	0.882*	**0.882**	0.882*	0.882	0.882*	0.882	0.882*	0.882	0.882*	**0.882**	0.882*

†Similarity transformation group. ‡The (graph) convolution subnetwork is translation equivariant.
*with no augmentation due to guaranteed equivariance.

Scale, Translation and Combinations. We evaluate how implicit methods perform under various similarity transformations besides SO(3) rotation, including scale, translation and combinations. We apply random scales and rotations in a bounded unit cube $[-0.5, 0.5]^3$, as assumed by grid methods, and set the canonical scale to be half of the cube. ConvONet resolutions are doubled to keep the effective resolution. Random scaling and translation are added under the constraint of the unit bound, with the minimum scaling factor of 0.2.

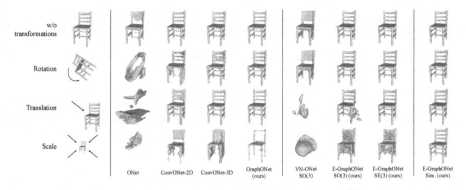

Fig. 6. Implicit surface reconstruction under *unseen* transforms. Visualizing back-transformed shapes. Shapes are scaled by a factor of 0.25, and translation is from the unit cube center to the corner. E-GraphONet-Sim is robust to all similarity transformations. See the appendix video for reconstructions under different poses and scales.

From the results in Table 3, GraphONet is more robust to transformations than other non-equivariant models. For equivariant models, VN-ONet and the SO(3) E-GraphONet models perform poorly on other types of transformations, as they are optimized towards the rotation around origin only. Similarly, the SE(3) E-GraphONet does not generalize to scaling. Our model with full equivariance performs well on all similarity transformations with numerically the same performance. Figure 6 shows qualitative examples, where our E-GraphONet-Sim handles all types of unseen similarity transformations.

Table 4. Parameter- and data-efficiency. Evaluated on the full test set with 5 runs of 130 randomly sampled training examples.

	#param	IoU↑
ConvONet-2D	2.0×10^6	0.727 ±0.009
ConvONet-3D	1.1×10^6	0.722 ±0.008
GraphONet (ours)	1.9×10^5	0.867 ±0.004
E-GraphONet (ours)	$\mathbf{6.5 \times 10^4}$	**0.873** ±0.002

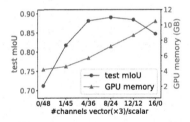

Fig. 7. Ablation on hybrid feature channels. Mixed vectors and scalars are more effective and efficient than pure vectors.

6.3 Analysis

We show some ablation experiments while more results are provided in the Appendix.

Learning from Very Few Training Examples. We show that our graph method is both parameter- and data-efficient, and the transform-robust modeling inherently benefits generalization. As reported in Table 4, we use less than 10% of the parameters of ConvONet as the graph conv kernel shares parameters for all directions. We evaluate the test set performance when training on only 130 examples - 10 per class - instead of the full training set size of 30661. While ConvONets fail to achieve good performance, GraphONets does not drop by far from the many-shot results in Table 1. The E-GraphONet demonstrates even better performance, with more parameter-sharing from the equivariance modeling, indicating better power of generalization.

Ablation on Vector and Scalar Feature Channels. We validate our design of hybrid features by experimenting different ratio of vector and scalar channels. We constrain in total 48 effective channels, with one vector channel counted as three scalars. In Fig. 7, using both vectors and scalars with a close-to-equal ratio of effective channels obtains higher performance with less memory cost than using pure vectors, i.e., in the Vector Neurons [17]. This indicates the expressive power of the scalar neuron functions. We provide additional results for non-graph-based equivariant models in the Appendix.

6.4   Scene-Level Reconstructions

In addition to the ability of handling object shape modeling under transformations, our graph implicit functions also scale to scene-level reconstruction. We experiment on two datasets: (i) *Synthetic Rooms* [34], a dataset provided by [34], with rooms constructed with walls, floors, and ShapeNet objects from five classes: chair, sofa, lamp, cabinet and table. (ii) *ScanNet* [15], a dataset of RGB-D scans of real-world rooms for testing synthetic-to-real transfer performance.

Table 5. Indoor scene reconstructions.

Dataset	Synthetic room			ScanNet
	IoU↑	Chamfer↓	Normal↑	Chamfer↓
ONet	0.514	0.135	0.856	0.546
ConvONet-2D (3×128^2)	0.802	0.038	0.934	0.162
ConvONet-3D (64^3)	0.847	0.035	0.943	0.067
GraphONet (ours)	**0.883**	**0.032**	**0.944**	**0.061**
E-GraphONet (ours)	0.851	0.035	0.934	0.069

We train and evaluate our model on Synthetic room dataset [34] using 10,000 sampled points as input. The quantitative results are shown in Table 5 and qualitative results

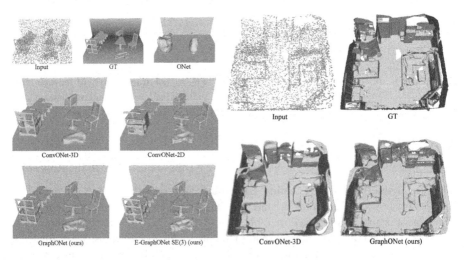

Fig. 8. Indoor scene reconstructions on Synthetic rooms (*left*) and ScanNet (*right*). Our GraphONet produces shaper edges and better finer details.

in Fig. 8 (left). Our GraphONet performs better than ConvONets [34] at recovering detailed structures. We evaluate the SE(3) variant of our equivariance model, and it performs generally well, but less smooth at flat regions. In addition, we evaluate the model transfer ability of our method on ScanNet [15] with the model trained on synthetic data, for which we report the Chamfer measure in Table 5. Our GraphONet ourperforms other methods. Figure 8 (right) shows a qualitative example of our reconstructions.

7 Conclusion

In this paper, we introduce graph implicit functions, which learn local latent features from k-NN graph on sparse point set observations, enabling reconstruction of 3D shapes and scenes in fine detail. By nature of graphs and in contrast to regular grid representations, the proposed graph representations are robust to geometric transformations. What is more, we extend the proposed graph implicit functions with hybrid feature equivariant layers, thus guarantee theoretical equivariance under various similarity transformations, including rotations, translations and scales, and obtain models that generalize to arbitrary and unseen transformations.

Acknowledgement. This research was supported in part by SAVI/MediFor project, ERC Starting Grant Scan2CAD (804724), EPSRC programme grant Visual AI EP/T028572/1, and National Research Foundation Singapore and DSO National Laboratories under its AI Singapore Programme (AISG Award No: AISG2-RP-2020-016). We thank Angela Dai for the video voice over.

References

1. Atzmon, M., Haim, N., Yariv, L., Israelov, O., Maron, H., Lipman, Y.: Controlling neural level sets. arXiv preprint arXiv:1905.11911 (2019)
2. Atzmon, M., Lipman, Y.: SAL: sign agnostic learning of shapes from raw data. In: Proceedings of the IEEE/CVF Conference on Computer Vision and Pattern Recognition, pp. 2565–2574 (2020)
3. Atzmon, M., Lipman, Y.: SAL++: sign agnostic learning with derivatives. arXiv preprint arXiv:2006.05400 (2020)
4. Bautista, M.A., Talbott, W., Zhai, S., Srivastava, N., Susskind, J.M.: On the generalization of learning-based 3D reconstruction. In: Proceedings of the IEEE/CVF Winter Conference on Applications of Computer Vision, pp. 2180–2189 (2021)
5. Chabra, R., et al.: Deep local shapes: learning local SDF priors for detailed 3D reconstruction. In: Vedaldi, A., Bischof, H., Brox, T., Frahm, J.-M. (eds.) ECCV 2020. LNCS, vol. 12374, pp. 608–625. Springer, Cham (2020). https://doi.org/10.1007/978-3-030-58526-6_36
6. Chang, A.X., et al.: ShapeNet: an information-rich 3D model repository. arXiv preprint arXiv:1512.03012 (2015)
7. Chatzipantazis, E., Pertigkiozoglou, S., Dobriban, E., Daniilidis, K.: SE(3)-equivariant attention networks for shape reconstruction in function space. arXiv preprint arXiv:2204.02394 (2022)
8. Chen, Y., Fernando, B., Bilen, H., Mensink, T., Gavves, E.: Neural feature matching in implicit 3D representations. In: International Conference on Machine Learning, pp. 1582–1593. PMLR (2021)

9. Chen, Y., et al.: PointMixup: augmentation for point clouds. arXiv preprint arXiv:2008.06374 (2020)
10. Chen, Z., Zhang, H.: Learning implicit fields for generative shape modeling. In: Proceedings of the IEEE Conference on Computer Vision and Pattern Recognition, pp. 5939–5948 (2019)
11. Chibane, J., Alldieck, T., Pons-Moll, G.: Implicit functions in feature space for 3D shape reconstruction and completion. In: Proceedings of the IEEE/CVF Conference on Computer Vision and Pattern Recognition, pp. 6970–6981 (2020)
12. Choy, C.B., Gwak, J., Savarese, S., Chandraker, M.: Universal correspondence network. arXiv preprint arXiv:1606.03558 (2016)
13. Cohen, T., Welling, M.: Group equivariant convolutional networks. In: International Conference on Machine Learning, pp. 2990–2999. PMLR (2016)
14. Cohen, T.S., Welling, M.: Steerable CNNs. arXiv preprint arXiv:1612.08498 (2016)
15. Dai, A., Chang, A.X., Savva, M., Halber, M., Funkhouser, T., Nießner, M.: ScanNet: richly-annotated 3D reconstructions of indoor scenes. In: Proceedings of the IEEE Conference on Computer Vision and Pattern Recognition, pp. 5828–5839 (2017)
16. Davies, T., Nowrouzezahrai, D., Jacobson, A.: On the effectiveness of weight-encoded neural implicit 3D shapes. arXiv preprint arXiv:2009.09808 (2020)
17. Deng, C., Litany, O., Duan, Y., Poulenard, A., Tagliasacchi, A., Guibas, L.: Vector neurons: a general framework for SO(3)-equivariant networks. arXiv preprint arXiv:2104.12229 (2021)
18. Erler, P., Guerrero, P., Ohrhallinger, S., Mitra, N.J., Wimmer, M.: POINTS2SURF learning implicit surfaces from point clouds. In: Vedaldi, A., Bischof, H., Brox, T., Frahm, J.-M. (eds.) ECCV 2020. LNCS, vol. 12350, pp. 108–124. Springer, Cham (2020). https://doi.org/10.1007/978-3-030-58558-7_7
19. Fuchs, F., Worrall, D., Fischer, V., Welling, M.: SE(3)-transformers: 3D roto-translation equivariant attention networks. In: Advances in Neural Information Processing Systems, vol. 33 (2020)
20. Fujiwara, K., Hashimoto, T.: Neural implicit embedding for point cloud analysis. In: Proceedings of the IEEE/CVF Conference on Computer Vision and Pattern Recognition, pp. 11734–11743 (2020)
21. Genova, K., Cole, F., Sud, A., Sarna, A., Funkhouser, T.: Deep structured implicit functions. arXiv preprint arXiv:1912.06126 (2019)
22. Genova, K., Cole, F., Sud, A., Sarna, A., Funkhouser, T.: Local deep implicit functions for 3D shape. In: Proceedings of the IEEE/CVF Conference on Computer Vision and Pattern Recognition, pp. 4857–4866 (2020)
23. Gilmer, J., Schoenholz, S.S., Riley, P.F., Vinyals, O., Dahl, G.E.: Neural message passing for quantum chemistry. In: International Conference on Machine Learning, pp. 1263–1272. PMLR (2017)
24. Hanocka, R., Hertz, A., Fish, N., Giryes, R., Fleishman, S., Cohen-Or, D.: MeshCNN: a network with an edge. ACM Trans. Graph. (TOG) **38**(4), 1–12 (2019)
25. Jiang, C., Sud, A., Makadia, A., Huang, J., Nießner, M., Funkhouser, T.: Local implicit grid representations for 3D scenes. In: Proceedings of the IEEE Conference on Computer Vision and Pattern Recognition (2020)
26. Jiang, Y., Ji, D., Han, Z., Zwicker, M.: SDFDiff: differentiable rendering of signed distance fields for 3D shape optimization. In: Proceedings of the IEEE/CVF Conference on Computer Vision and Pattern Recognition, pp. 1251–1261 (2020)
27. Kingma, D.P., Ba, J.: Adam: a method for stochastic optimization. arXiv preprint arXiv:1412.6980 (2014)
28. Li, J., Chen, B.M., Lee, G.H.: SO-Net: self-organizing network for point cloud analysis. In: Proceedings of the IEEE Conference on Computer Vision and Pattern Recognition, pp. 9397–9406 (2018)

29. Liu, S., Saito, S., Chen, W., Li, H.: Learning to infer implicit surfaces without 3D supervision. In: Advances in Neural Information Processing Systems, pp. 8295–8306 (2019)
30. Mescheder, L., Oechsle, M., Niemeyer, M., Nowozin, S., Geiger, A.: Occupancy networks: learning 3D reconstruction in function space. In: Proceedings of the IEEE Conference on Computer Vision and Pattern Recognition, pp. 4460–4470 (2019)
31. Niemeyer, M., Mescheder, L., Oechsle, M., Geiger, A.: Differentiable volumetric rendering: learning implicit 3D representations without 3D supervision. In: Proceedings of the IEEE/CVF Conference on Computer Vision and Pattern Recognition, pp. 3504–3515 (2020)
32. Park, J.J., Florence, P., Straub, J., Newcombe, R., Lovegrove, S.: DeepSDF: learning continuous signed distance functions for shape representation. In: Proceedings of the IEEE Conference on Computer Vision and Pattern Recognition, pp. 165–174 (2019)
33. Paszke, A., et al.: PyTorch: an imperative style, high-performance deep learning library. arXiv preprint arXiv:1912.01703 (2019)
34. Peng, S., Niemeyer, M., Mescheder, L., Pollefeys, M., Geiger, A.: Convolutional occupancy networks. In: Vedaldi, A., Bischof, H., Brox, T., Frahm, J.-M. (eds.) ECCV 2020. LNCS, vol. 12348, pp. 523–540. Springer, Cham (2020). https://doi.org/10.1007/978-3-030-58580-8_31
35. Qi, C.R., Su, H., Mo, K., Guibas, L.J.: PointNet: deep learning on point sets for 3D classification and segmentation. In: Proceedings of the IEEE Conference on Computer Vision and Pattern Recognition, pp. 652–660 (2017)
36. Qi, C.R., Yi, L., Su, H., Guibas, L.J.: PointNet++: deep hierarchical feature learning on point sets in a metric space. In: Advances in Neural Information Processing Systems, vol. 30 (2017)
37. Ronneberger, O., Fischer, P., Brox, T.: U-Net: convolutional networks for biomedical image segmentation. In: Navab, N., Hornegger, J., Wells, W.M., Frangi, A.F. (eds.) MICCAI 2015. LNCS, vol. 9351, pp. 234–241. Springer, Cham (2015). https://doi.org/10.1007/978-3-319-24574-4_28
38. Saito, S., Huang, Z., Natsume, R., Morishima, S., Kanazawa, A., Li, H.: PIFu: pixel-aligned implicit function for high-resolution clothed human digitization. In: Proceedings of the IEEE International Conference on Computer Vision, pp. 2304–2314 (2019)
39. Satorras, V.G., Hoogeboom, E., Welling, M.: E(n) equivariant graph neural networks. arXiv preprint arXiv:2102.09844 (2021)
40. Shen, W., Zhang, B., Huang, S., Wei, Z., Zhang, Q.: 3D-rotation-equivariant quaternion neural networks. In: Vedaldi, A., Bischof, H., Brox, T., Frahm, J.-M. (eds.) ECCV 2020. LNCS, vol. 12365, pp. 531–547. Springer, Cham (2020). https://doi.org/10.1007/978-3-030-58565-5_32
41. Simeonov, A., et al.: Neural descriptor fields: SE(3)-equivariant object representations for manipulation. In: 2022 International Conference on Robotics and Automation (ICRA), pp. 6394–6400. IEEE (2022)
42. Sitzmann, V., Chan, E., Tucker, R., Snavely, N., Wetzstein, G.: MetaSDF: meta-learning signed distance functions. In: Advances in Neural Information Processing Systems, vol. 33, pp. 10136–10147 (2020)
43. Sosnovik, I., Szmaja, M., Smeulders, A.: Scale-equivariant steerable networks. In: International Conference on Learning Representations (2019)
44. Takikawa, T., et al.: Neural geometric level of detail: real-time rendering with implicit 3D shapes. In: Proceedings of the IEEE/CVF Conference on Computer Vision and Pattern Recognition, pp. 11358–11367 (2021)
45. Tang, J.H., et al.: OctField: hierarchical implicit functions for 3D modeling. In: Advances in Neural Information Processing Systems, vol. 34, pp. 12648–12660 (2021)
46. Thomas, N., et al.: Tensor field networks: rotation-and translation-equivariant neural networks for 3D point clouds. arXiv preprint arXiv:1802.08219 (2018)

47. Wang, P.S., Liu, Y., Tong, X.: Dual octree graph networks for learning adaptive volumetric shape representations. arXiv preprint arXiv:2205.02825 (2022)

48. Wang, Y., Sun, Y., Liu, Z., Sarma, S.E., Bronstein, M.M., Solomon, J.M.: Dynamic graph CNN for learning on point clouds. ACM Trans. Graph. (TOG) **38**(5), 1–12 (2019)

49. Weiler, M., Geiger, M., Welling, M., Boomsma, W., Cohen, T.: 3D steerable CNNs: learning rotationally equivariant features in volumetric data. In: NeurIPS (2018)

50. Weiler, M., Hamprecht, F.A., Storath, M.: Learning steerable filters for rotation equivariant CNNs. In: Proceedings of the IEEE Conference on Computer Vision and Pattern Recognition, pp. 849–858 (2018)

51. Worrall, D.E., Garbin, S.J., Turmukhambetov, D., Brostow, G.J.: Harmonic networks: deep translation and rotation equivariance. In: Proceedings of the IEEE Conference on Computer Vision and Pattern Recognition, pp. 5028–5037 (2017)

52. Xu, Q., Wang, W., Ceylan, D., Mech, R., Neumann, U.: DISN: deep implicit surface network for high-quality single-view 3D reconstruction. In: Advances in Neural Information Processing Systems, pp. 492–502 (2019)

53. Xu, Y., Fan, T., Yuan, Y., Singh, G.: Ladybird: Quasi-Monte Carlo sampling for deep implicit field based 3D reconstruction with symmetry. In: Vedaldi, A., Bischof, H., Brox, T., Frahm, J.-M. (eds.) ECCV 2020. LNCS, vol. 12346, pp. 248–263. Springer, Cham (2020). https://doi.org/10.1007/978-3-030-58452-8_15

54. Yuan, Y., Nüchter, A.: An algorithm for the SE(3)-transformation on neural implicit maps for remapping functions. IEEE Robot. Autom. Lett. **7**, 7763–7770 (2022)

55. Zaheer, M., Kottur, S., Ravanbakhsh, S., Poczos, B., Salakhutdinov, R., Smola, A.: Deep sets. arXiv preprint arXiv:1703.06114 (2017)

56. Zhu, W., Qiu, Q., Calderbank, R., Sapiro, G., Cheng, X.: Scale-equivariant neural networks with decomposed convolutional filters. arXiv preprint arXiv:1909.11193 (2019)

PatchRD: Detail-Preserving Shape Completion by Learning Patch Retrieval and Deformation

Bo Sun[1]([✉]), Vladimir G. Kim[2], Noam Aigerman[2], Qixing Huang[1], and Siddhartha Chaudhuri[2,3]

[1] UT Austin, Austin, USA
bosun0711@gmail.com
[2] Adobe Research, San Jose, USA
[3] IIT Bombay, Mumbai, India

Abstract. This paper introduces a data-driven shape completion approach that focuses on completing geometric details of missing regions of 3D shapes. We observe that existing generative methods lack the training data and representation capacity to synthesize plausible, fine-grained details with complex geometry and topology. Our key insight is to copy and deform patches from the partial input to complete missing regions. This enables us to preserve the style of local geometric features, even if it drastically differs from the training data. Our fully automatic approach proceeds in two stages. First, we learn to retrieve candidate patches from the input shape. Second, we select and deform some of the retrieved candidates to seamlessly blend them into the complete shape. This method combines the advantages of the two most common completion methods: similarity-based single-instance completion, and completion by learning a shape space. We leverage repeating patterns by retrieving patches from the partial input, and learn global structural priors by using a neural network to guide the retrieval and deformation steps. Experimental results show our approach considerably outperforms baselines across multiple datasets and shape categories. Code and data are available at https://github.com/GitBoSun/PatchRD.

1 Introduction

Completing geometric objects is a fundamental problem in visual computing with a wide range of applications. For example, when scanning complex geometric objects, it is always difficult to scan every point of the underlying object [33]. The scanned geometry usually contains various levels of holes and missing geometries, making it critical to develop high-quality geometry completion techniques [1,10,13,18,24,61,68]. Geometry completion is also used in interactive

---

Supplementary Information The online version contains supplementary material available at https://doi.org/10.1007/978-3-031-20062-5_29.

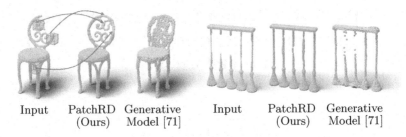

Input   PatchRD   Generative   Input   PatchRD   Generative
         (Ours)   Model [71]   (Ours)   Model [71]

Fig. 1. We propose PatchRD, a non-parametric shape completion method based on patch retrieval and deformation. Compared with the parametric generation methods, our method is able to recover complex geometric details as well as keeping the global shape smoothness.

shape modeling [7], as a way to suggest additional content to add to a partial 3D object/scene. Geometry completion is challenging, particularly when the missing regions contain non-trivial geometric content.

Early geometry completion techniques focus on hole filling [1,10,13,18,24, 61,68]. These techniques rely on the assumption that the missing regions are simple surface patches and can be filled by smoothly extending hole regions. Filling regions with complex shapes rely on data priors. Existing approaches fall into two categories. The first category extracts similar regions from the input shape. The hypothesis is that a physical 3D object naturally exhibits repeating content due to symmetries and texture. While early works use user-specified rules to retrieve and fuse similar patches, recent works have studied using a deep network to automatically complete a single image or shape [20,21,62]. The goal of these approaches is to use different layers of the neural network (e.g., a convolutional neural network) to automatically extract repeating patterns. However, these approaches are most suitable when the repeating patterns are prevalent within the partial input. They cannot infer correlations between the missing surface and the observed surface (Fig. 1).

Another category [12,17,43,46,59,71,73,78] consists of data-driven techniques, which implicitly learn a parametric shape space model. Given an incomplete shape, they find the best reconstruction using the underlying generative model to generate the complete shape. This methodology has enjoyed success for specific categories of models such as faces [4,48,74,80] and human body shapes [1,26,30,38,45], but they generally cannot recover shape details due to limited training data and difficulty in synthesizing geometric styles that exhibit large topological and geometrical variations.

This paper introduces a shape completion approach that combines the strengths of the two categories of approaches described above. Although it remains difficult to capture the space of geometric details, existing approaches can learn high-level compositional rules such as spatial correlations of geometric primitives and parts among both the observed and missing regions. We propose to leverage this property to guide similar region retrieval and fusion on a given shape for geometry completion.

Specifically, given an input incomplete shape, the proposed approach first predicts a coarse completion using an off-the-shelf method. The coarse completion does not necessarily capture the shape details but it provides guidance on locations of the missing patches. For each coarse voxel patch, we learn a shape distance function to retrieve top-k detailed shape patches in the input shape. The final stage of our approach learns a deformation for each retrieved patch and a blending function to integrate the retrieved patches into a continuous surface. The deformation prioritizes the compatibility scores between adjacent patches. The blending functions optimize the contribution of each patch and ensure surface smoothness.

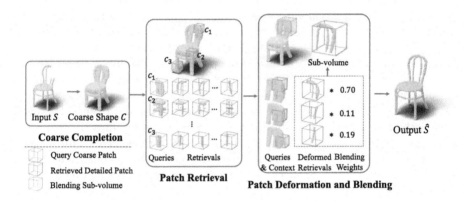

Fig. 2. Approach pipeline. Given an incomplete shape S, we first predict a coarse shape C with the rough structure and no details. For each patch on C, K detailed patch candidates are retrieved from the input shape. Then we predict deformations and blending weights for all retrieved candidates. Finally, the output shape $\hat{S}$ is computed by summing up the deformed patches and their blending weights.

Experimental results on the ShapeNet dataset [6] show that our approach outperforms existing shape completion techniques for reconstructing shape details both qualitatively and quantitatively.

In summary, our contributions are:

- We propose a non-parametric shape completion method based on patch retrieval and deformation.
- Our method preserves local shape details while enforcing global consistency.
- Our method achieves state-of-the-art shape completion results compared with various baselines.

2 Related Work

Shape Completion. Shape completion is a crucial and long-studied task in geometry processing. Non-data-driven works [27,28,40,54] address hole-filling in a purely geometric manner. Without any high-level prior on the resulting shape, they target filling holes in a "smooth-as-possible" manner with membranes. To complete more complex shapes, several works [29,34,36,44,50,55] rely on data-driven methods to get the structure priors or part references. Similarly to our method, [34,44,50] retrieve some candidate models from a database, then perform a non-rigid surface alignment to deform the retrieved shape to fit the input. However, our approach operates at the patch level and can reconstruct shapes that are topologically different from those in the training data. With the development of deep learning, neural networks can be used to learn a shape prior from a large dataset and then complete shapes. Voxel-based methods [12,69,70] are good at capturing rough structures, but are limited to low resolution by the cubic scaling of voxel counts. Our framework is especially designed to circumvent these resolution limitations. Alternatively, point cloud completion [42,59,67,71–73,77,78] has become a popular venue as well. [25,66,73] use coarse-to-fine structures to densify the output point cloud and refine local regions. NSFA [79] and HRSC [19] used a two stage method to infer global structures and refine local geometries. SnowflakeNet [71] modeled the progressive generation hierarchically and arranged the points in locally structured patterns. As point clouds are sparse and unstructured, it is difficult to recover fine-grained shape details. 3D-EPN [12] and our method both use coarse-to-fine and patch-based pipelines. However, their method only retrieves shapes from the training set and directly copies the nearest patches based on low-level concatenation of distance fields. Our method retrieves patch-level details from the input and jointly learns deformation and blending, which enables our method to handle complex details as well as maintain global coherence.

Patch-Based Image In-Painting. In the 2D domain, many works utilize detailed patches to get high-resolution image inpainting results. Traditional methods [2,14,22,32] often synthesize textures for missing areas or expanding the current images. PatchMatch [2] proposed an image editing method by efficiently searching and replacing local patches. SceneComp [22] patched up holes in images by finding similar image regions in a large database. Recently, with the power of neural networks, more methods [37,47,49,60,75,76] use patch-guided generation to get finer details. [37,47,60] modeled images to scene graphs or semantic layouts and retrieve image patches for each graph/layout component. [49,75,76] add transformers [65], pixel flow and patch blending to get better generation results respectively. Our method leverages many insights from the 2D domain, however these cannot be directly transferred to 3D, for two reasons: i) the signals are inherently different, as 2D pixels are spatially-dense and continuous, while voxels are sparse and effectively binary; ii) the number of voxels in a domain scales cubically with resolution, as opposed to the quadratic scaling of pixels. This significantly limits the performance of various algorithms. The novel pipeline proposed herein is tailor-made to address these challenges.

3D Shape Detailization. Adding or preserving details on 3D shapes is an important yet challenging problem in 3D synthesis. Details can be added to a given surface via a reference 3D texture [23,56,81]. More relevant to use various geometric representations to synthesize geometric details [5,8,9,16,35]. DLS [5] and LDIF [16] divide a shape to different local regions and reconstruct local implicit surfaces. D2IM-Net [35] disentangles shape structure and surface details. DECOR-GAN [9] trained a patch-GAN to transfer details from one shape to another. In our case, we focus on the task of partial-to-full reconstruction, and use detailization as a submodule during the process.

3D Generation by Retrieval. Instead of synthesizing shapes from scratch with a statistical model, it is often effective to simply retrieve the nearest shape from a database [15,31,57,58]. This produces high-quality results at the cost of generalization. Deformation-aware retrieval techniques [39,51,63,64] improve the representation power from a limited database. Our method also combines deformation with retrieval, but our retrieval is at the level of local patches from the input shape itself. RetrievalFuse [52] retrieves patches from a database for scene reconstruction. An attention-based mechanism is then used to regenerate the scene, guided by the patches. In contrast, we directly copy and deform retrieved patches to fit the output, preserving their original details and fidelity.

3   Overview

Our framework receives an incomplete or a partial shape S as input and completes it into a full *detailed* shape $\hat{S}$. Our main observation is that local shape details often repeat and are consistent across different regions of the shape, up to an approximately rigid deformation. Thus, our approach extracts local regions, which we call *patches*, from the given incomplete shape S, and uses them to complete and output a full complete shape. In order to analyze and synthesize topologically diverse data using convolutional architectures, we represent shapes and patches as voxel grids with occupancy values, at a resolution of s_{shape} cells.

The key challenges facing us are choosing patches from the partial input, and devising a method to deform and blend them into a seamless, complete detailed output. This naturally leads to a three-stage pipeline: (i) complete the partial input to get a coarse complete structure C to guide detail completion; (ii) for each completed coarse patch in C, retrieve candidate detailed patches from the input shape S; (iii) deform and blend the retrieved detailed patches to output the complete detailed shape $\hat{S}$ (see Fig. 2). Following is an overview of the process; we elaborate on each step in the following sections.

Coarse Completion. We generate a full coarse shape C from the partial input S using a simple 3D-CNN architecture. Our goal is to leverage advances in 3D shape completion, which can provide coarse approximations of the underlying ground truth, but does not accurately reconstruct local geometric details.

Patch Retrieval (Sect. 4). We train another neural network to retrieve k candidate detailed patches from S for each coarse patch in C. Namely, we learn geometric similarity, defined by a rigid-transformation-invariant distance d, between the coarse and detailed patches.

Deformation and Blending of Patches (Sect. 5). Given k candidate patches, we use a third neural network to predict rigid transformations and blending weights for each candidate patch, which together define a deformation and blending of patches for globally-consistent, plausible shape completion.

4   Patch Retrieval

The input to this stage is the partial detailed shape S, and a coarse and completed version of the shape, C. The goal of this step is to retrieve a set of patch candidates that can be deformed and stitched to get a fully detailed shape. A *patch* is a cube-shaped sub-region extracted from a shape, composed of s_{patch}^3 voxels. Our patch sampling process $\mathcal{P}$ takes a shape as input and outputs a collection of patches, where coarse patches $\mathcal{P}(C)$ serve as queries and detailed patches from the partial input $\mathcal{P}(S)$ as sources.

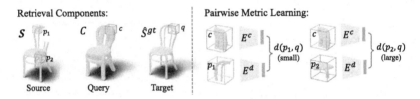

Fig. 3. Retrieval learning. We learn a feature mapping to predict geometric distances between the query coarse patches and the sampled detailed patches. We use the geometric distances between the GT detailed patches and the sampled patches as the supervision. Distances for patches that are close up to a rigid transformation are small. Otherwise, distances are large.

In order to decide whether a retrieved detailed patch could be an apt substitution for a true detailed patch, we propose a *geometric distance* metric invariant to rigid deformations (Sect. 4.1). This geometric distance will be used to supervise the neural network used during testing time, which learns similarities between coarse patches $\mathcal{P}(C)$ and their detailed counterparts $\mathcal{P}(S)$ (Sect. 4.2). Finally, we describe how to use this network at inference time to retrieve candidate patches for the full shape (Sect. 4.3).

4.1   Geometric Distance

We define a measure of geometric distance, d, between two *detailed* shape patches (p_1, p_2). This metric should be agnostic to their poses, since the pose can be fixed at the deformation stage, hence we define the distance as the minimum over all possible rigid transformations of the patch:

$$d(p_1, p_2) = \min_T \frac{\|T(p_1) - p_2\|_1}{\|T(p_1)\|_1 + \|p_2\|_1} \tag{1}$$

where T is a rigid motion composed with a possible reflection, i.e., $T = (R, \mathbf{t}, f)$, $R \in SO(3)$ is the rotation, $\mathbf{t} \in \mathbb{R}^3$ is the translation, $f \in \{0, 1\}$ denotes if a reflection is applied, and $\| \cdot \|_1$ denotes the L1 norm of positional vectors to patch centers. To practically compute this distance, we run ICP [3], initialized from two transformations (with and without reflection enabled) that align patch centers. While this geometric distance can be computed for detailed patches, at inference time we only have coarse patches. Therefore, we train a network to embed coarse patches into a latent space in which Euclidean distances match the geometric distances of the detailed patches they represent.

4.2   Metric Embedding

We train two neural networks to act as encoders, one for coarse patches and one for detailed patches, E^{c} and E^{d}, respectively. We aim to have the Euclidean distances between their generated codes reflect the distances between the true detailed patches observed during training. Given a coarse patch $c \in \mathcal{P}(C)$ with its true corresponding detailed patch $q \in \mathcal{P}(\hat{S}^{\mathrm{gt}})$, as well as a some other detailed patch $p \in \mathcal{P}(S)$, we define a metric embedding loss:

$$L_{\mathrm{r}} = \sum_{(c,p,q) \in \mathcal{T}} \| \| E^{\mathrm{c}}(c) - E^{\mathrm{d}}(p) \|_2 - d(p, q)) \|_2. \tag{2}$$

where $d(p, q)$ is the geometric distance defined in Eq. (1). Our training triplets are composed of true matches and random patches: $\mathcal{T} = \mathcal{T}_{\mathrm{true}} \cup \mathcal{T}_{\mathrm{rnd}}$. Where in both sets c is a random coarse patch, q is the corresponding true detailed patch. We either set $p = q$ for $\mathcal{T}_{\mathrm{true}}$ or randomly sample $p \in \mathcal{P}(S)$ for $\mathcal{T}_{\mathrm{rnd}}$. See Fig. 3 for an illustration.

4.3   Retrieval on a Full Shape

We can now use trained encoder networks at inference time to retrieve detailed patches for each coarse patch. First, we encode all the detailed patches in $\mathcal{P}(S)$ via E^{d}. Similarly, for each non-empty coarse patch $c \in \mathcal{P}(C)$ with lowest corner at location l, we encode it with E^{c} and find the K-nearest-neighbor detailed codes. We store the list of retrieved patches for each location, denoted as $\mathcal{R}_l$.

We sample the coarse patches using a fixed-size (s_{patch}^3) sliding window with a stride γ_{patch}. Note that in the retrieval stage we do not assume that we know which parts of the detailed shape need to be completed. Since our feature learning step observed a lot of positive coarse/fine pairs with the detailed input, we found that the input is naturally reconstructed from the retrieved detailed patches.

5   Deformation and Blending of Patches

The input to this stage is the coarse shape C, partial input S, and the retrieval candidates. The output is the full detailed shape $\hat{S}$, produced by deforming and blending the retrieved patches. As illustrated by Fig. 2 we first apply a rigid transformation to each retrieved patch and then blend these transformed patches into the final shape. Our guiding principle is the notion of partition-of-unity [41], which blends candidate patches with optimized transformations into a smooth completion. Unlike using fixed weighting functions, we propose to learn the blending weights. These weights serve the role of selecting candidate patches and stitching them smoothly.

Table 1. Shape completion results on the random-crop dataset on 8 ShapeNet categories. We show the L_2 Chamfer distance (CD) ($\times 10^3$) between the output shape and the ground truth 16384 points from PCN dataset [78] (lower is better). Our method reduces the CD drastically compared with the baselines.

	Average	Chair	Plane	Car	Table	Cabinet	Lamp	Boat	Couch
AtlasNet [17]	7.03	6.08	2.32	5.32	5.38	8.46	14.20	6.01	8.47
Conv-ONet [46]	6.42	2.91	2.29	8.60	7.94	12.6	5.82	4.03	7.21
TopNet [59]	6.30	5.94	2.18	4.85	5.63	5.13	15.32	5.60	5.73
3D-GAN [69]	6.00	6.02	1.77	3.46	5.08	7.29	12.23	7.20	4.92
PCN [78]	4.47	3.75	1.45	3.58	3.32	4.82	10.56	4.22	4.03
GRNet [73]	2.69	3.27	1.47	3.15	2.43	3.35	2.54	2.50	2.84
VRCNet [42]	2.63	2.96	1.30	3.25	2.35	2.98	2.86	2.23	3.13
SnowflakeNet [71]	2.06	2.45	**0.72**	2.55	2.15	2.76	2.17	1.33	2.35
PatchRD (Ours)	**1.22**	**1.08**	0.98	**1.01**	**1.32**	**1.45**	**1.23**	**0.99**	**1.67**

We observe that learning the blending weights requires some context (our method needs to be aware of at least a few neighboring patches), but does not require understanding the whole shape (coarse shape and retrieved patches already constrain the global structure). Thus, to maximize efficiency and generalizability, we opt to perform deformation and blending at the meso-scale of subvolumes $V \subset S$ with size s_{subv}.

Next, we provide more details on our blending operator (Sect. 5.1) and how to learn it from the data (Sect. 5.2).

5.1 The Deformation and Blending Operator

Given a subvolume V, we first identify $[r_m, m = 1...M]$ an ordered list of M best patches to be considered for blending. These patches are from the retrieved candidates $\mathcal{R}_l$ such that $l \in V$, and sorted according to two criteria: (i) retrieval index, (ii) x, y, z ordering. If more than M such patches exist, we simply take the first M. Each patch r_m is transformed with a rigid motion and possible reflection: T_m, and we have a blending weight for each patch at every point x in our volume: $\omega_m[x]$. The output at voxel x is the weighted sum of the deformed blending candidates:

$$V[x] = \frac{1}{\xi[x]} \sum_{m=1...M} \omega_m[x] \cdot T_m(r_m)[x] \tag{3}$$

where $\omega_m[x]$ is the blending weight for patch m at voxel x, and $T_m(r_m)$ is the transformed patch (placed in the volume V, and padded with 0), and $\xi[x] = \sum_{m=1..M} \omega_m[x]$ is the normalization factor. At inference time, when we need to reconstruct the entire shape, we sample V over the entire domain $\hat{S}$ (with stride γ_{subv}), and average values in the region of overlap.

5.2 Learning Deformation and Blending

Directly optimizing deformation and blending is prone to being stuck in local optimum. To address this we develop a neural network to predict deformations and blending weights and train it with reconstruction and smoothness losses.

Prediction Network. We train a neural network g to predict deformation and blending weights. The network consists of three convolutional encoders, one for each voxel grid: the coarse shape (with a binary mask for the cropped subvolume V), the partial input, and the tensor of retrieved patches (M channels at resolution of V). We use fully-connected layers to mix the output of convolutional encoders into a bottleneck, which is than decoded into deformation T and blending ω parameters.

Reconstruction Loss. The first loss L_{rec} aims to recover the target shape $\hat{S}^{\text{gt}}$:

$$L_{\text{rec}} = \|V^{\text{gt}} - V\|_2, \tag{4}$$

where $V^{\text{gt}} \subset \hat{S}^{\text{gt}}$ and $V \subset \hat{S}$ are corresponding true and predicted subvolumes (we sample V randomly for training).

Blending Smoothness Loss. The second loss L_{sm} regularizes patch pairs. Specifically, if two patches have large blending weights for a voxel, then their transformations are forced to be compatible on that voxel:

$$L_{\text{sm}} = \sum_{x \in V} \sum_{m,n} \|\omega_m[x] \cdot \omega_n[x] \cdot (T_m(r_m)[x] - T_n(r_n)[x])\|$$

where x iterates over the volume and m, n over all retrieved patches. Note that r_m and r_n are only defined on a small region based on where the patch is placed, so this sum only matters in regions where transformed patches $T_m(r_m)$ and $T_n(r_n)$ map to nearby points x accordingly.

Final Loss. The final loss term is

$$L = L_{\text{rec}} + \alpha L_{\text{sm}}. \tag{5}$$

6 Experiments

We primarily evaluate our method on the detail-preserving shape completion benchmark (Sect. 6.1), and demonstrate that our method outperforms state-of-the-art baselines (Sect. 6.2). We further demonstrate that our method can generalize beyond the benchmark setup, handling real scans, data with large missing areas, and novel categories of shapes (Sect. 6.3). Finally, we run an ablation study (Sect. 6.4) and evaluate sensitivity to the size of the missing area (Sect. 6.5).

6.1 Experimental Setup

Implementation Details. We use the following parameters for all experiments. The sizes of various voxel grids are: $s_{\text{shape}} = 128, s_{\text{patch}} = 18, s_{\text{subv}} = 40$ with strides $\gamma_{\text{patch}} = 4, \gamma_{\text{subv}} = 32$. We sample $|\mathcal{T}_{\text{rnd}}| = 800$ and $|\mathcal{T}_{\text{true}}| = 400$ triplets to train our patch similarity (Sect. 4.2). Our blending operator uses $M = 400$ best retrieved patches (Sect. 5.1). We set $\alpha = 10$ for Eq. 5. To improve performance we also define our blending weights ω_m at a coarser level than V.

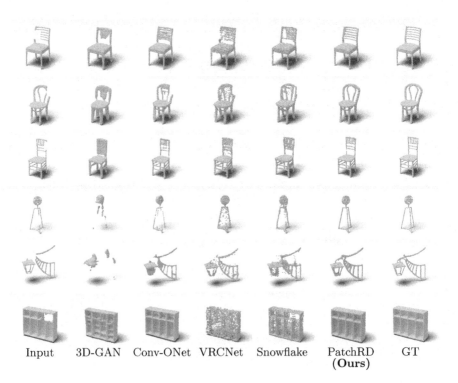

| Input | 3D-GAN | Conv-ONet | VRCNet | Snowflake | PatchRD (**Ours**) | GT |

Fig. 4. Qualitative shape completion results on the Random-Crop Dataset. Our results recover more geometric details and keep the shape smooth while other baselines often produce coarse, noisy, or discontinuous results.

Table 2. FID comparison on the chair class (note that we can only apply this metric to volumetric baselines). Our method produces more plausible shapes.

	Conv-ONet [46]	3D-GAN [69]	PatchRD(Ours)
FID	174.72	157.19	**11.89**

In particular, we use windows of size $s_{blend}^3 = 8^3$ to have constant weight, and compute the blending smoothness term at the boundary of these windows.

Dataset. We use shapes from ShapeNet [6], a public large-scale repository of 3D meshes to create the completion benchmark. We pick eight shape categories selected in prior work PCN [78]. For each category, we use the same subset of training and testing shapes with 80%/20% split as in DECOR-GAN work [9]. For voxel-based methods, we convert each mesh to a 128^3 voxel grid, and for point-based baselines, we use the existing point clouds with 16384 points per mesh [78]. We create synthetic incomplete shapes by cropping (deleting) a random cuboid with 10%–30% volume with respect to the full shape. This randomly cropped dataset is generated to simulate smaller-scale data corruption. We also show results on planar cutting and point scans in Sect. 6.3.

Metrics. To evaluate the quality of the completion, we use the L_2 Chamfer Distance (CD) with respect to the ground truth detailed shape. Since CD does not really evaluate the quality of finer details, we also use Frechet Inception Distance (FID), to evaluate plausibility. FID metric computes the distance of the layer activations from a pre-trained shape classifier. We use 3D VGG16 [53]) trained on ShapeNet and activations of the first fully connected layer.

Baseline Approaches. To the best of our knowledge, we are the first to do the 3D shape completion task on the random-cropped dataset. Considering the task similarity, we compare our method with the other shape completion and reconstruction baselines.

Our baselines span different shape representations: PCN [78], TopNet [59], GRNet [73], VRCNet [42], and SnowFlakeNet [71] are point-based scan completion baselines, 3D-GAN [69] is a voxel-based shape generation method, Conv-ONet [46] is an implicit surfaces-based shape reconstruction methods, and Atlas-Net [17] is an atlas-based shape reconstruction method. We show our method outperforms these baselines both quantitatively and qualitatively.

6.2 Shape Completion Results

Table 1 and Table 2 show quantitative comparisons between PatchRD and baselines, demonstrating that our method significantly outperforms all baselines. PatchRD achieved superior performance on all categories except airplanes, which shows that it generalizes well across different classes of shapes.

Specifically, the voxel-based baseline [69] produces coarse shapes where fine details are missing. Point-based baselines [42,71] often have noisy patterns around on fine structures while our method has clean geometry details. The implicit surface based method [46] could capture the details but the geometry is not smooth and the topology is not preserved. Our method keeps the smooth connection between geometry patches. More results can be found in the supplemental materials. Figure 4 shows qualitative comparisons. We pick four representative baselines for this visualization including point-based methods that performed the best on the benchmark [42,71] as well as voxel-based [69] and implicit-based methods [46]. Our results show better shape quality by recovering local details as well as preserving global shape smoothness.

6.3   Other Applications

Real-World Application: Scan Completion. We test our method on real-world shape completion from scans. We use shapes from ScanNet [11], 3D indoor scene dataset as input to our method. Objects in ScanNet often have some missing parts, especially thin structures, due to occlusion and incompleteness of scan viewpoints. We convert these point clouds to voxel grids and apply our completion technique trained on ShapeNet, see results in Fig. 5a. Note how our

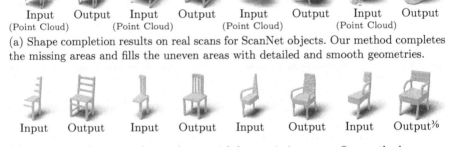

| Input | Output | Input | Output | Input | Output | Input | Output |
| (Point Cloud) | | (Point Cloud) | | (Point Cloud) | | (Point Cloud) | |

(a) Shape completion results on real scans for ScanNet objects. Our method completes the missing areas and fills the uneven areas with detailed and smooth geometries.

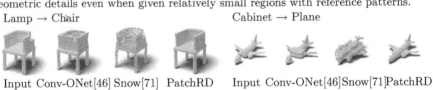

Input   Output   Input   Output   Input   Output   Input   Output‰

(b) Shape completion results on shapes with large missing areas. Our method recovers geometric details even when given relatively small regions with reference patterns.

Lamp → Chair   Cabinet → Plane

Input Conv-ONet[46] Snow[71] PatchRD   Input Conv-ONet[46]Snow[71]PatchRD

(c) Testing results on novel categories. We show results trained on lamp and cabinet categories and inferred on lamp and plane categories, respectively. Our method has better generalization ability.

Fig. 5. More applications on real scans, shapes with large missing areas and novel categories.

method completes the undersampled areas, while preserving the details of the input and smoothly blending new details to the existing content.

Shapes with Large Missing Areas. We also demonstrate that our method can handle large missing areas (Fig. 5b). In this experiment we cut the shape with a random plane, where in some cases more than half of the shape might be missing. Our method recovers the shape structure and extends the local shape details to the whole shape when only given a small region of reference details.

Completion on Novel Categories. We further evaluate the ability of our method to generalize to novel categories. Note that only the prediction of the complete coarse shape relies on any global categorical priors. Unlike other generative techniques that decode the entire shape, our method does not need to learn how to synthesize category-specific details and thus succeeds in detail-preservation as long as the coarse shape is somewhat reasonable. In Fig. 5c we demonstrate the output of different methods when tested on a novel category. Note how our method is most successful in conveying overall shape as well as matching the details of the input.

6.4   Ablation Study

We evaluate the significance of deformation learning, patch blending, and blending smoothness term via an ablation study (see Table 3).

Table 3. Ablation study. In the left figure, we visualize the effect of different components in our experiment. Patch alignment can't get good patch transformation. Results with no blending are subjective to bad retrievals. Results with no smoothing show discontinuity between neighboring patches. Results with all components contain geometric details as well as smoothness. In the right table, We show the reconstruction error CD and shape plausibility score FID on ShapeNet chair class. Results with all components get both better CD and FID.

	CD	FID
Patch Alignment	4.90	43.35
No Blending	2.03	30.25
No Smoothing	1.86	27.42
All	**1.43**	**11.89**

No Deformation Learning. We simply use ICP to align the retrieved patch to the query. Table 3 (Patch Alignment) illustrates that this leads to zigzagging artifacts due to patch misalignments.

No Patch Blending. Instead of blending several retrieved patches, we simply place the best retrieved patch at the query location. Table 3 (No Blending) shows that this single patch might not be sufficient, leading to missing regions in the output.

No Blending Smoothness. We set the blending smoothness to $L_{sm} = 0$ to remove our penalty for misalignments at patch boundaries. Doing so leads to artifacts and discontinuities at patch boundaries (Table 3, No Smoothing).

The quantitative results in Table 3 show that our method with all components performs the best with respect to reconstruction and plausibility metrics.

6.5 Sensitivity to the Size of Missing Regions

The completion task is often ill-posed, and becomes especially ambiguous as the missing region increases. We evaluate the sensitivity of our method to the size of the region by trying to increase the crop size from 10% to 50% of the volume. Table 4 demonstrates that our method can produce plausible completions even under severe crops. However, in some cases it is impossible to reconstruct details that are completely removed. We report quantitative results in Table 4. While both reconstruction and plausibility error increases for larger crops, we observe that plausibility (FID) score does not deteriorate at the same rate.

Table 4. Sensitivity to the size of missing regions. The left figure shows results with different crop ratios. Input geometries and shape contours influence the output shapes. The right table shows the reconstruction error and the shape plausibility with the increase of crop ratios. As the ratio increases, the reconstruction error keeps growing although the output shapes remain fairly plausible.

	10%	20%	40%	60%
L_2-CD	0.88	1.22	2.35	6.64
FID	9.74	10.32	13.34	15.63

Qualitative Comparison   Failure Cases

Input Snow[71] Ours Input Snow[71] Ours   Input Output GT   Input Output GT

Fig. 6. Qualitative results on the PCN Dataset [78]. On the left, we show our method is able to produce cleaner and more plausible results than the structure-based baseline. On the right, we show some failure cases where shape details are missing in the input shape.

7 Conclusions, Limitations and Future Work

Conclusions. This paper proposed a novel non-parametric shape completion method that preserves local geometric details and global shape smoothness. Our method recovers details by copying detailed patches from the incomplete shape, and achieves smoothness by a novel patch blending term. Our method obtained state-of-the-art completion results compared with various baselines with different

3D representations. It also achieved high-quality results in real-world 3D scans and shapes with large missing areas.

Limitations. Our method has two limitations: (1) It builds on the assumption that the shape details are present in the partial input shape, which might not hold if large regions are missing in the scan. For completeness, we still evaluate our method in this scenario using the PCN benchmark, which focuses on large-scale structure recovery from very sparse input. In Fig. 6 we show that our method succeeds when there are enough detail references in the input, and fails if the input is too sparse. We also provide quantitative evaluations in supplemental material. These results suggest that our method is better suited for completing denser inputs (e.g., multi-view scans).

In the future, we plan to address this issue by incorporating patches retrieved from other shapes. (2) Our method cannot guarantee to recover the global structure because the retrieval stage is performed at the local patch level. To address this issue, we need to enforce suitable structural priors and develop structure-aware representations. We leave both for future research.

Future Work. Recovering geometric details is a hard but important problem. Our method shows that reusing the detailed patches from an incomplete shape is a promising direction. In the direction of the patch-based shape completion, potential future work includes: (1) Applying patch retrieval and deformation on other 3D representations such as point cloud and implicit surfaces. This can handle the resolution limitation and computation burden caused by the volumetric representation. (2) Unifying parametric synthesis and patch-based non-parametric synthesis to augment geometric details that are not present in the partial input shape.

References

1. Anguelov, D., Srinivasan, P., Koller, D., Thrun, S., Rodgers, J., Davis, J.: SCAPE: shape completion and animation of people. ACM Trans. Graph. (TOG) **24**, 408–416 (2005). https://doi.org/10.1145/1073204.1073207
2. Barnes, C., Shechtman, E., Finkelstein, A., Goldman, D.B.: PatchMatch: a randomized correspondence algorithm for structural image editing. ACM Trans. Graph. (Proc. SIGGRAPH) **28**(3) (2009)
3. Besl, P.J., McKay, N.D.: A method for registration of 3-D shapes. IEEE Trans. Pattern Anal. Mach. Intell. **14**(2), 239–256 (1992). https://doi.org/10.1109/34.121791
4. Blanz, V., Vetter, T.: A morphable model for the synthesis of 3D faces. In: Proceedings of the 26th Annual Conference on Computer Graphics and Interactive Techniques, SIGGRAPH 1999, pp. 187–194. ACM Press/Addison-Wesley Publishing Co. (1999). https://doi.org/10.1145/311535.311556
5. Chabra, R., et al.: Deep local shapes: learning local SDF priors for detailed 3D reconstruction. In: Vedaldi, A., Bischof, H., Brox, T., Frahm, J.-M. (eds.) ECCV 2020. LNCS, vol. 12374, pp. 608–625. Springer, Cham (2020). https://doi.org/10.1007/978-3-030-58526-6_36

6. Chang, A.X., et al.: ShapeNet: an information-rich 3D model repository. Technical report. arXiv:1512.03012 [cs.GR], Stanford University—Princeton University—Toyota Technological Institute at Chicago (2015)

7. Chaudhuri, S., Koltun, V.: Data-driven suggestions for creativity support in 3D modeling. ACM Trans. Graph. **29** (2010). https://doi.org/10.1145/1866158. 1866205

8. Chen, Z., et al.: Multiresolution deep implicit functions for 3D shape representation. In: ICCV (2021)

9. Chen, Z., Kim, V.G., Fisher, M., Aigerman, N., Zhang, H., Chaudhuri, S.: DECOR-GAN: 3D shape detailization by conditional refinement. In: Proceedings of IEEE Conference on Computer Vision and Pattern Recognition (CVPR) (2021)

10. Curless, B., Levoy, M.: A volumetric method for building complex models from range images. In: Proceedings of the 23rd Annual Conference on Computer Graphics and Interactive Techniques, SIGGRAPH 1996, pp. 303–312. Association for Computing Machinery, New York (1996). https://doi.org/10.1145/237170.237269

11. Dai, A., Chang, A.X., Savva, M., Halber, M., Funkhouser, T., Nießner, M.: ScanNet: richly-annotated 3D reconstructions of indoor scenes. In: Proceedings of the Computer Vision and Pattern Recognition (CVPR). IEEE (2017)

12. Dai, A., Qi, C.R., Nießner, M.: Shape completion using 3D-encoder-predictor CNNs and shape synthesis. In: Proceedings of the Computer Vision and Pattern Recognition (CVPR). IEEE (2017)

13. Davis, J., Marschner, S., Garr, M., Levoy, M.: Filling holes in complex surfaces using volumetric diffusion. In: 3DPVT, pp. 428–441 (2002). https://doi.org/10.1109/TDPVT.2002.1024098

14. Efros, A.A., Leung, T.K.: Texture synthesis by non-parametric sampling. In: IEEE International Conference on Computer Vision (ICCV) (1999)

15. Eitz, M., Richter, R., Boubekeur, T., Hildebrand, K., Alexa, M.: Sketch-based shape retrieval. ACM Trans. Graph. **31**(4) (2012). https://doi.org/10.1145/2185520.2185527

16. Genova, K., Cole, F., Sud, A., Sarna, A., Funkhouser, T.: Local deep implicit functions for 3D shape. In: CVPR (2019)

17. Groueix, T., Fisher, M., Kim, V.G., Russell, B., Aubry, M.: AtlasNet: a Papier-Mâché approach to learning 3D surface generation. In: Proceedings IEEE Conference on Computer Vision and Pattern Recognition (CVPR) (2018)

18. Guo, X., Xiao, J., Wang, Y.: A survey on algorithms of hole filling in 3D surface reconstruction. Vis. Comput. **34**(1), 93–103 (2016). https://doi.org/10.1007/s00371-016-1316-y

19. Han, X., Li, Z., Huang, H., Kalogerakis, E., Yu, Y.: High-resolution shape completion using deep neural networks for global structure and local geometry inference. In: IEEE International Conference on Computer Vision (ICCV) (2017)

20. Hanocka, R., Hertz, A., Fish, N., Giryes, R., Fleishman, S., Cohen-Or, D.: MeshCNN: a network with an edge. ACM Trans. Graph. **38**(4) (2019). https://doi.org/10.1145/3306346.3322959

21. Hanocka, R., Metzer, G., Giryes, R., Cohen-Or, D.: Point2Mesh: a self-prior for deformable meshes. ACM Trans. Graph. **39**(4) (2020). https://doi.org/10.1145/3386569.3392415

22. Hays, J., Efros, A.A.: Scene completion using millions of photographs. ACM Trans. Graph. (SIGGRAPH 2007) **26**(3) (2007)

23. Hertz, A., Hanocka, R., Giryes, R., Cohen-Or, D.: Deep geometric texture synthesis. ACM Trans. Graph. **39**(4) (2020). https://doi.org/10.1145/3386569.3392471

24. Hu, P., Wang, C., Li, B., Liu, M.: Filling holes in triangular meshes in engineering. JSW **7**, 141–148 (2012). https://doi.org/10.4304/jsw.7.1.141-148

25. Huang, Z., Yu, Y., Xu, J., Ni, F., Le, X.: PF-Net: point fractal network for 3D point cloud completion. In: CVPR (2020)

26. Kanazawa, A., Black, M.J., Jacobs, D.W., Malik, J.: End-to-end recovery of human shape and pose. In: 2018 IEEE Conference on Computer Vision and Pattern Recognition, CVPR 2018, Salt Lake City, UT, USA, 18–22 June 2018, pp. 7122–7131. Computer Vision Foundation/IEEE Computer Society (2018). https://doi.org/10. 1109/CVPR.2018.00744. http://openaccess.thecvf.com/content_cvpr_2018/html/ Kanazawa_End-to-End_Recovery_of_CVPR_2018_paper.html

27. Kazhdan, M., Bolitho, M., Hoppe, H.: Poisson surface reconstruction. In: Proceedings of the Fourth Eurographics Symposium on Geometry Processing (2005)

28. Kazhdan, M., Hoppe, H.: Screened poisson surface reconstruction. ACM Trans. Graph. (TOG) **32**, 1–13 (2013)

29. Kim, Y.M., Mitra, N.J., Yan, D.M., Guibas, L.: Acquiring 3D indoor environments with variability and repetition. ACM Trans. Graph. (TOG) **31**, 1–11 (2012)

30. Kolotouros, N., Pavlakos, G., Black, M.J., Daniilidis, K.: Learning to reconstruct 3D human pose and shape via model-fitting in the loop. In: 2019 IEEE/CVF International Conference on Computer Vision, ICCV 2019, Seoul, Korea (South), 27 October–2 November 2019, pp. 2252–2261. IEEE (2019). https://doi.org/10. 1109/ICCV.2019.00234

31. Kuo, W., Angelova, A., Lin, T.Y., Dai, A.: Patch2CAD: patchwise embedding learning for in-the-wild shape retrieval from a single image. In: ICCV (2021)

32. Kwatra, V., Schodl, A., Essa, I., Turk, G., Bobick, A.: Graphcut textures: image and video synthesis using graph cuts. ACM Trans. Graph. SIGGRAPH 2003 **22**(3), 277–286 (2003)

33. Levoy, M., et al.: The digital Michelangelo project: 3D scanning of large statues. In: Proceedings of the 27th Annual Conference on Computer Graphics and Interactive Techniques, SIGGRAPH 2000, pp. 131–144. ACM Press/Addison-Wesley Publishing Co. (2000). https://doi.org/10.1145/344779.344849

34. Li, D., Shao, T., Wu, H., Zhou, K.: Shape completion from a single RGBD image. IEEE Trans. Vis. Comput. Graph. **23**, 1809–1822 (2016)

35. Li, M., Zhang, H.: D^2IM-Net: learning detail disentangled implicit fields from single images. In: Proceedings of the IEEE/CVF Conference on Computer Vision and Pattern Recognition (CVPR), pp. 10246–10255 (2021)

36. Li, Y., Dai, A., Guibas, L., Nießner, M.: Database-assisted object retrieval for real-time 3D reconstruction. In: Computer Graphics Forum (2015)

37. Li, Y., Ma, T., Bai, Y., Duan, N., Wei, S., Wang, X.: PasteGAN: a semi-parametric method to generate image from scene graph. In: NeurIPS (2019)

38. Loper, M., Mahmood, N., Romero, J., Pons-Moll, G., Black, M.J.: SMPL: a skinned multi-person linear model. ACM Trans. Graph. **34**(6) (2015). https://doi.org/10. 1145/2816795.2818013

39. Nan, L., Xie, K., Sharf, A.: A search-classify approach for cluttered indoor scene understanding. ACM Trans. Graph. **31**, 1–10 (2012)

40. Nealen, A., Igarashi, T., Sorkine, O., Alexa, M.: Laplacian mesh optimization. In: Proceedings of the 4th International Conference on Computer Graphics and Interactive Techniques (2006)

41. Ohtake, Y., Belyaev, A., Alexa, M., Turk, G., Seidel, H.P.: Multi-level partition of unity implicits. ACM Trans. Graph. **22**(3), 463–470 (2003). https://doi.org/10. 1145/882262.882293

42. Pan, L., et al.: Variational relational point completion network. arXiv preprint arXiv:2104.10154 (2021)
43. Park, J.J., Florence, P., Straub, J., Newcombe, R., Lovegrove, S.: DeepSDF: learning continuous signed distance functions for shape representation. In: The IEEE Conference on Computer Vision and Pattern Recognition (CVPR) (2019)
44. Pauly, M., Mitra, N.J., Giesen, J., Gross, M.H., Guibas., L.J.: Example-based 3D scan completion. In: Symposium on Geometry Processing (2005)
45. Pavlakos, G., et al.: Expressive body capture: 3D hands, face, and body from a single image. In: IEEE Conference on Computer Vision and Pattern Recognition, CVPR 2019, Long Beach, CA, USA, 16–20 June 2019, pp. 10975–10985. Computer Vision Foundation/IEEE (2019). https://doi.org/10.1109/CVPR. 2019.01123. http://openaccess.thecvf.com/content_CVPR_2019/html/Pavlakos_ Expressive_Body_Capture_3D_Hands_Face_and_Body_From_a_CVPR_2019_paper. html
46. Peng, S., Niemeyer, M., Mescheder, L., Pollefeys, M., Geiger, A.: Convolutional occupancy networks. In: Vedaldi, A., Bischof, H., Brox, T., Frahm, J.-M. (eds.) ECCV 2020. LNCS, vol. 12348, pp. 523–540. Springer, Cham (2020). https://doi. org/10.1007/978-3-030-58580-8_31
47. Qi, X., Chen, Q., Jia, J., Koltun, V.: Semi-parametric image synthesis. In: CVPR (2018)
48. Ranjan, A., Bolkart, T., Sanyal, S., Black, M.J.: Generating 3D faces using convolutional mesh autoencoders. In: Ferrari, V., Hebert, M., Sminchisescu, C., Weiss, Y. (eds.) ECCV 2018. LNCS, vol. 11207, pp. 725–741. Springer, Cham (2018). https://doi.org/10.1007/978-3-030-01219-9_43
49. Ren, Y., Yu, X., Zhang, R., Li, T.H., Liu, S., Li, G.: StructureFlow: image inpainting via structure-aware appearance flow. In: IEEE International Conference on Computer Vision (ICCV) (2019)
50. Rock, J., Gupta, T., Thorsen, J., Gwak, J., Shin, D., Hoiem, D.: Completing 3D object shape from one depth image. In: Proceedings of the IEEE Conference on Computer Vision and Pattern Recognition (CVPR) (2015)
51. Schulz, A., Shamir, A., Baran, I., Levin, D.I.W., Sitthi-Amorn, P., Matusik, W.: Retrieval on parametric shape collections. ACM Trans. Graph. 36, 1–14 (2017)
52. Siddiqui, Y., Thies, J., Ma, F., Shan, Q., Nießner, M., Dai, A.: RetrievalFuse: neural 3D scene reconstruction with a database. In: ICCV (2021)
53. Simonyan, K., Zisserman, A.: Very deep convolutional networks for large-scale image recognition. In: ICLR (2015)
54. Sorkine, O., Cohen-Or, D.: Least-squares meshes. In: Shape Modeling Applications (2004)
55. Sung, M., Kim, V.G., Angst, R., Guibas, L.: Data-driven structural priors for shape completion. ACM Trans. Graph. (TOG) 34, 1–11 (2015)
56. Takayama, K., Schmidt, R., Singh, K., Igarashi, T., Boubekeur, T., Sorkine-Hornung, O.: GeoBrush: interactive mesh geometry cloning. Comput. Graph. Forum (Proc. EUROGRAPHICS 2011) 30(2), 613–622 (2011)
57. Tangelder, J., Veltkamp, R.: A survey of content based 3D shape retrieval methods. In: Proceedings Shape Modeling Applications, pp. 145–156 (2004). https://doi.org/ 10.1109/SMI.2004.1314502
58. Tatarchenko, M., Richter, S., Ranftl, R., Li, Z., Koltun, V., Brox, T.: What do single-view 3D reconstruction networks learn? In: CVPR (2019)
59. Tchapmi, L.P., Kosaraju, V., Rezatofighi, S.H., Reid, I., Savarese, S.: TopNet: structural point cloud decoder. In: The IEEE Conference on Computer Vision and Pattern Recognition (CVPR) (2019)

60. Tseng, H.-Y., Lee, H.-Y., Jiang, L., Yang, M.-H., Yang, W.: RetrieveGAN: image synthesis via differentiable patch retrieval. In: Vedaldi, A., Bischof, H., Brox, T., Frahm, J.-M. (eds.) ECCV 2020. LNCS, vol. 12353, pp. 242–257. Springer, Cham (2020). https://doi.org/10.1007/978-3-030-58598-3_15

61. Turk, G., Levoy, M.: Zippered polygon meshes from range images. In: Proceedings of the 21st Annual Conference on Computer Graphics and Interactive Techniques, SIGGRAPH 1994, pp. 311–318. Association for Computing Machinery, New York (1994). https://doi.org/10.1145/192161.192241

62. Ulyanov, D., Vedaldi, A., Lempitsky, V.S.: Deep image prior. In: 2018 IEEE Conference on Computer Vision and Pattern Recognition, CVPR 2018, Salt Lake City, UT, USA, 18–22 June 2018, pp. 9446–9454. Computer Vision Foundation/IEEE Computer Society (2018). https://doi.org/10. 1109/CVPR.2018.00984. http://openaccess.thecvf.com/content_cvpr_2018/html/ Ulyanov_Deep_Image_Prior_CVPR_2018_paper.html

63. Uy, M.A., Huang, J., Sung, M., Birdal, T., Guibas, L.: Deformation-aware 3D model embedding and retrieval. In: Vedaldi, A., Bischof, H., Brox, T., Frahm, J.-M. (eds.) ECCV 2020. LNCS, vol. 12352, pp. 397–413. Springer, Cham (2020). https://doi.org/10.1007/978-3-030-58571-6_24

64. Uy, M.A., Kim, V.G., Sung, M., Aigerman, N., Chaudhuri, S., Guibas, L.: Joint learning of 3D shape retrieval and deformation. In: CVPR (2021)

65. Vaswani, A., et al.: Attention is all you need. In: Guyon, I., et al. (eds.) Advances in Neural Information Processing Systems, vol. 30. Curran Associates, Inc. (2017). https://proceedings.neurips.cc/paper/2017/file/ 3f5ee243547dee91fbd053c1c4a845aa-Paper.pdf

66. Wang, X., Ang, M.H., Jr., Lee, G.H.: Cascaded refinement network for point cloud completion. In: IEEE/CVF Conference on Computer Vision and Pattern Recognition (CVPR) (2020)

67. Wang, X., Ang, M.H., Jr., Lee, G.H.: Voxel-based network for shape completion by leveraging edge generation. In: ICCV (2021)

68. Wheeler, M., Sato, Y., Ikeuchi, K.: Consensus surfaces for modeling 3D objects from multiple range images. In: ICCV, pp. 917–924 (1998). https://doi.org/10. 1109/ICCV.1998.710826

69. Wu, J., Zhang, C., Xue, T., Freeman, W.T., Tenenbaum, J.B.: Learning a probabilistic latent space of object shapes via 3D generative-adversarial modeling. In: Advances in Neural Information Processing Systems, pp. 82–90 (2016)

70. Wu, Z., et al.: 3D ShapeNets: a deep representation for volumetric shape modeling. In: Proceedings of 28th IEEE Conference on Computer Vision and Pattern Recognition (CVPR) (2015)

71. Xiang, P., et al.: SnowflakeNet: point cloud completion by snowflake point deconvolution with skip-transformer. In: ICCV (2021)

72. Xie, C., Wang, C., Zhang, B., Yang, H., Chen, D., Wen, F.: Style-based point generator with adversarial rendering for point cloud completion. In: Proceedings of the IEEE/CVF Conference on Computer Vision and Pattern Recognition (CVPR), pp. 4619–4628 (2021)

73. Xie, H., Yao, H., Zhou, S., Mao, J., Zhang, S., Sun, W.: GRNet: gridding residual network for dense point cloud completion. In: Vedaldi, A., Bischof, H., Brox, T., Frahm, J.-M. (eds.) ECCV 2020. LNCS, vol. 12354, pp. 365–381. Springer, Cham (2020). https://doi.org/10.1007/978-3-030-58545-7_21

74. Xiong, X., De la Torre, F.: Supervised descent method and its applications to face alignment. In: CVPR, pp. 532–539 (2013). https://doi.org/10.1109/CVPR.2013. 75

75. Xu, R., Guo, M., Wang, J., Li, X., Zhou, B., Loy, C.C.: Texture memory-augmented deep patch-based image inpainting. IEEE Trans. Image Process. (TIP) **30**, 9112–9124 (2021)

76. Yang, F., Yang, H., Fu, J., Lu, H., Guo, B.: Learning texture transformer network for image super-resolution. In: CVPR (2020)

77. Yu, X., Rao, Y., Wang, Z., Liu, Z., Lu, J., Zhou, J.: PoinTr: diverse point cloud completion with geometry-aware transformers. In: ICCV (2021)

78. Yuan, W., Khot, T., Held, D., Mertz, C., Hebert, M.: PCN: point completion network. In: 2018 International Conference on 3D Vision (3DV) (2018)

79. Zhang, W., Yan, Q., Xiao, C.: Detail preserved point cloud completion via separated feature aggregation. In: Vedaldi, A., Bischof, H., Brox, T., Frahm, J.-M. (eds.) ECCV 2020. LNCS, vol. 12370, pp. 512–528. Springer, Cham (2020). https://doi.org/10.1007/978-3-030-58595-2_31

80. Zhao, W., Chellappa, R., Phillips, P.J., Rosenfeld, A.: Face recognition: a literature survey. ACM Comput. Surv. **35**(4), 399–458 (2003). https://doi.org/10.1145/954339.954342

81. Zhou, K., et al.: Mesh quilting for geometric texture synthesis. In: ACM SIGGRAPH 2006 Papers, SIGGRAPH 2006, pp. 690–697 (2006)

3D Shape Sequence of Human Comparison and Classification Using Current and Varifolds

Emery Pierson[1]([⊠]), Mohamed Daoudi[1,2], and Sylvain Arguillere[3]

[1] Univ. Lille, CNRS, Centrale Lille, UMR 9189 CRIStAL, F-59000 Lille, France
emery.person@univ-lille.fr, mohamed.daoudi@imt-nord-europe.fr
[2] IMT Nord Europe, Institut Mines-Télécom, Centre for Digital Systems, F-59000 Lille, France
[3] Univ. Lille, CNRS, UMR 8524 Laboratoire Paul Painlevé, 59000 Lille, France
sylvain.arguillere@univ-lille.fr

Abstract. In this paper we address the task of the comparison and the classification of 3D shape sequences of human. The non-linear dynamics of the human motion and the changing of the surface parametrization over the time make this task very challenging. To tackle this issue, we propose to embed the 3D shape sequences in an infinite dimensional space, the space of varifolds, endowed with an inner product that comes from a given positive definite kernel. More specifically, our approach involves two steps: 1) the surfaces are represented as varifolds, this representation induces metrics equivariant to rigid motions and invariant to parametrization; 2) the sequences of 3D shapes are represented by Gram matrices derived from their infinite dimensional Hankel matrices. The problem of comparison of two 3D sequences of human is formulated as a comparison of two Gram-Hankel matrices. Extensive experiments on CVSSP3D and Dyna datasets show that our method is competitive with state-of-the-art in 3D human sequence motion retrieval. Code for the experiments is available at https://github.com/CRISTAL-3DSAM/HumanComparisonVarifolds

Keywords: 3D shape sequence · Varifold · 3D shape comparison · Hankel matrix

1 Introduction

Understanding 3D human shape and motion has many important applications, such as ergonomic design of products, rapid modeling of realistic human characters for virtual worlds, and an early detection of abnormality in predictive clinical analysis. Recently, 3D human data has become highly available as a result of the

Supplementary Information The online version contains supplementary material available at https://doi.org/10.1007/978-3-031-20062-5_30.

availability of huge MoCap (Motion Capture) datasets [1,4] along with the evolution of 3D human body representation [24] leaded to the availability of huge artificial human body datasets [25,33]. In the meantime, evolutions in 4D technology for capturing moving shapes lead to paradigms with new multi-view and 4D scan acquisition systems that enable now full 4D models of human shapes that include geometric, motion and appearance information [9,15,30,35].

The first difficulty in analyzing shapes of 3D human comes from noise, variability in pose and articulation, arbitrary mesh parameterizations during data collection, and shape variability within and across shape classes. Some examples of 3D human highlighting these issues are illustrated in Fig. 1. In particular, the metrics and representations should have certain invariances or robustness to the above-mentioned variability. Recently, Kaltenmark *et al.* [21] have proposed a general framework for 2D and 3D shape similarity measures, invariant to parametrization and equivariant to rigid transformations. More recently, Bauer *et al.* [7], adopted the varifold fidelity metric as a regularizer for the problem of reparameterization in the framework of elastic shape matching using the SRNF [18] representation. Motivated by the progress of using varifolds and current in shape analysis, we propose to compare 3D surface of human shapes by comparing their varifolds.

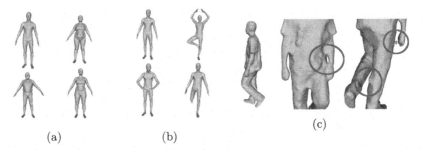

(a)   (b)   (c)

Fig. 1. Different challenges of 3D Human Sequence Comparison: (a) Shape variability within and across shape classes, (b) variability in pose and articulation, (c) noisy and arbitrary mesh parameterizations (topological noise, vertex noise and disconnected components).

As a second difficulty, it is critical to identify precise mathematical representations of underlying shapes and then impose efficient dynamical models on representation spaces that capture the essential variability in shape evolutions. In addition to the nonlinearity of shape spaces, one expects nonlinearity in temporal evolutions that makes the inference process difficult. In this paper, we propose to use Gram matrices derived from Hankels matrices to represent the dynamic of human motion.

In our approach, as illustrated in Fig. 2, we propose to embed the human shape space $\mathcal{H}$ in an infinite dimensional Hilbert space with inner product corresponding to a positive definite kernel $\langle .,. \rangle_V$ inspired by the varifold framework.

Using this kernel product we are able to compute the Gram matrix relative to a motion. Each of this Gram matrix is transformed to Gram-Hankel matrix of fixed size r.

In summary, the main contributions of this article are: *(i)* We represent 3D human surfaces as varifold. This representation is equivariant to rotation and invariant to the parametrization. This representation allows us to define an inner product between two 3D surfaces represented by varifolds. *(ii)* It is the first use of the space of varifolds in human shape analysis. The framework does not assume that the correspondences between the surfaces are given. *(iii)* We represent 4D surfaces by Hankel matrices. This key contribution enables the use of standard computational tools based on the inner product defined between two varifolds. The dynamic information of a sequence of 3D human shape is encapsulated in Hankel matrices and we propose to compare sequences by using the distance between the resulting Gram-Hankel matrices; *(iv)* The experiments results show that the proposed approach improves 3D human motion retrieval state-of-the-art and it is robust to noise.

2 Related Work

2.1 3D Human Shape Comparison

The main difficulty in comparing human shapes of such surfaces is that there is no preferred parameterization that can be used for registering and comparing features across surfaces. Since the shape of a surface is invariant to its parameterization, one would like an approach that yields the same result irrespective of the parameterization. The linear blending approaches [3,16,24] offer a good representation for human shape, along with a model of human deformations while being able to distinguish shape and pose deformations. However these methods need additional information on the raw scans such as MoCap markers [3,16], gender of the body, or additional texture information [9,24] to retrieve such representations. Recently, deep learning approaches [6,34,41] propose human bodies latent spaces that share common properties with linear blending models. However, they require training data with the same mesh parameterization and are sensitive to noise. Moreover, most current techniques treat shape and motion independently, with devoted techniques for either shape or motion in isolation.

Kurtek *et al.* [22] and Tumpach *et al.* [36] propose the quotient of the space of embeddings of a fixed surface S into $\mathbb{R}^3$ by the action of the orientation-preserving diffeomorphisms of S and the group of Euclidean transformations, and provide this quotient with the structure of an infinite-dimensional manifold. The shapes are compared using a Riemannian metric on a *pre-shape space* $\mathcal{F}$ consisting of embeddings or immersions of a model manifold into the 3D Euclidean space $\mathbb{R}^3$. Two embeddings correspond to the same shape in $\mathbb{R}^3$ if and only if they differ by an element of a shape-preserving transformation group. However the use of these approaches on human shape analysis assume a spherical parameterization of the surfaces. Pierson *et al.* [28] propose a Riemannian approach for human shape analysis. This approach provides encouraging results, but it

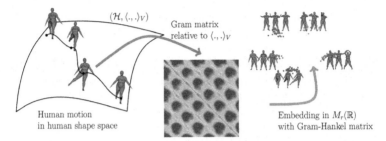

Fig. 2. Overview of our method. We embed the human shape space $\mathcal{H}$ in an infinite dimensional Hilbert space with inner product from a positive definite kernel $\langle .,.\rangle_V$ inspired by varifold framework. Using this kernel product we are able to compute Gram matrix relative to a motion. Each of this Gram matrix is transformed to Gram Hankel matrix of size r. The Frobenius distance in $M_r(\mathbb{R})$ is used to retrieve similar 3D sequences.

requires the meshes to be registered to a template. Recently, the framework of varifolds have been presented for application to shape matching. Charon *et al.* [12] generalize the framework of currents, which defines a restricted type of geometric measure on surfaces, by the varifolds framework representing surfaces as a measure on $\mathbb{R}^3 \times \mathbb{S}^2$. The proposed varifolds representation is parameterization invariant, and does not need additional information on raw scans. Inspired by these recent results, we will demonstrate the first use of this mathematical theory in 3D human shape comparison.

2.2 3D Human Sequence Comparison

A general approach adopted when comparing 3D sequences is the extension of static shape descriptors such as 3D shape distribution, Spin Image, and spherical harmonics to include temporal motion information [17,29,38]. While these approaches require the extraction of shape descriptors, our approach does not need a 3D shape feature extraction. It is based on the comparison of surface varifolds within a sequence. In addition, the comparison of 3D sequences require an alignment of the sequences. The Dynamic Time Warping (DTW) algorithm was defined to match temporally distorted time series, by finding an optimal warping path between time series. It has been used for several computer vision applications [8,20] and alignment of 3D human sequences [29,38]. However, DTW does not define a proper distance (no triangle inequality). In addition, a temporal filtering is often required for the alignment of noisy meshes [31]. Our approach enables the comparison of sequences of different temporal duration, does not need any alignment of sequences and is robust to noisy data. We model a sequence of 3D mesh as a dynamical system. The parameters of the dynamical system are embedded in our Hankel matrix-based representation. Hankel matrices have already been adopted successfully for skeleton action recognition in [40]. As we do not have finite dimensional features to build such matrix numerically, we define a novel Gram-Hankel matrix, based on the kernel product defined from surface varifold. This matrix is able to model the temporal dynamics of the 3D meshes.

3 Proposed Method

3.1 Comparing 3D Shapes Using Geometric Measures

The varifolds framework is a geometry theory used to solve famous differential geometry problems such as the Plateau's Problem. We invite the interested reader to read an introduction of the theory in [2]. We focus here on the work of Charon et al. [12], followed by Kaltenmark et al. [21] who proposed to use the varifolds framework for discretized curves and surfaces. They designed a fidelity metric using the varifold representation. This fidelity metric is proposed for 2D artificial contour retrieval, and used in 3D diffeomorphic registration in the Large deformation diffeomorphic metric mapping (LDDMM) framework. To our knowledge our work is the first use of such representation for the analysis of human shape. As far as the authors are aware, our work is the first use of such representation for the analysis of human shape. It is also the first use of the space of varifolds purely for itself, as an efficient way to perform direct computations on shapes.

A *varifold* is a measure μ on $\mathbb{R}^3 \times \mathbb{S}^2$. The integral of a function $f : \mathbb{R}^3 \times \mathbb{S}^2 \to \mathbb{R}$ with respect to such a measure is denoted $\int_{\mathbb{R}^3 \times \mathbb{S}^2} f d\mu$. Given S a smooth compact surface with outer normal unit vector field $x \mapsto n(x)$, the core idea of [12] is to represent S as a varifold. This is done in practice through the formula $\int_{\mathbb{R}^3 \times \mathbb{S}^2} f dS = \int_S f(x, n(x)) dA(x)$, with $dA(x)$ the surface area measure of S at x. Now, given a triangulated surface M of a 3D human shape with triangle faces $T_1, ..., T_m$, when the triangles are sufficiently small, each triangular face T_i is represented as an atomic measure $a_i \delta_{c_i, n_i}$ where c_i is the barycenter of the triangulated face, n_i the oriented normal of the face, a_i its area, and δ representing the dirac mass. The varifold representation of the total shape M is simply given by the sum of all these measures: $M = \sum_{i=1}^m a_i \delta_{c_i, n_i}$. To illustrate, integrating a function f on $\mathbb{R}^3 \times \mathbb{S}^2$, with respect to M yields $\int_{\mathbb{R}^3 \times \mathbb{S}^2} f dM = \sum_{i=1}^m a_i f(c_i, n_i)$.

A varifold μ can be converted into a function Φ_μ on $\mathbb{R}^3 \times \mathbb{S}^2$ using a *reproducing kernel* that comes from the product of two positive definite kernels: $k_{pos} : \mathbb{R}^3 \times \mathbb{R}^3 \to \mathbb{R}$, and $k_{or} : \mathbb{S}^2 \times \mathbb{S}^2 \to \mathbb{R}$. We just define $\Phi_\mu(x, v) = \int_{\mathbb{R}^3 \times \mathbb{S}^2} k_{pos}(y, x) k_{or}(w, v) d\mu(y, w)$. For a triangulated surface M, we get $\Phi_M(x, v) = \sum_{i=1}^m a_i k_{pos}(c_i, x) k_{or}(n_i, v)$.

One obtains a Hilbert product between any two varifolds μ, ν as follows: $\langle \mu, \nu \rangle_V = \langle \Phi_\mu, \Phi_\nu \rangle_V = \int \Phi_\mu d\nu = \int \Phi_\nu d\mu$, so that

$$\langle \mu, \nu \rangle_V = \iint k_{pos}(x, y) k_{or}(v, w) d\mu(x, v) d\nu(y, w).$$

We deduce the explicit expression for that product between two triangulated 3D shapes M and N:

$$\langle M, N \rangle_V = \langle \Phi_M, \Phi_N \rangle_V = \sum_{i=1}^{m} \sum_{j=1}^{n} a_i^M a_j^N k_{pos}(c_i^M, c_j^N) k_{or}(n_i^M, n_j^N) \qquad (1)$$

where m, n are the number of faces of M and N. The continuous version of this product presented in [12] is parametrization invariant. An important part of such a product is that it can be made equivariant to rigid transformation by carefully choosing the kernels. First we define how to apply such a deformation on a varifold. Given a rotation $R \in SO(3)$ of $\mathbb{R}^3$ and a vector $T \in \mathbb{R}^3$, the rigid transformation $\phi : x \mapsto Rx + T$ yields the push-forward transformation $\mu \mapsto \phi_{\#} \mu$ through $\int f d\phi_{\#} \mu = \int f(Rx + T, Rv) d\mu$ on the space of varifolds. For a triangulated surface M, $\phi_{\#} M$ is just $\phi(M)$, the surface obtained by applying the rigid motion ϕ to the surface M itself. We have the following important result:

Theorem 1. *If we define the positive definite kernels as following:*

$$k_{pos}(x, y) = \rho(||x - y||), \quad x, y \in \mathbb{R}^3,$$
$$k_{or}(v, w) = \gamma(v.w), \quad v, w \in \mathbb{S}^2,$$

then for any two varifolds μ, ν, and any rigid motion ϕ on $\mathbb{R}^3$, we have

$$\langle \phi_{\#} \mu, \phi_{\#} \nu \rangle_V = \langle \mu, \nu \rangle_V.$$

This result means that given a rigid motion ϕ, $\langle \phi(M), \phi(N) \rangle_V = \langle M, N \rangle_V$.

The kernel k_{pos} is usually chosen as the Gaussian kernel $k_{pos} = e^{-\frac{||x-y||^2}{\sigma^2}}$, with the scale parameter σ needed to be tuned for each application.

Kaltenmark *et al.* [21] proposed several function for the γ function of the spherical kernel. In this paper we retained the following functions: $\gamma(u) = u$ – *currents*, $\gamma(u) = e^{2u/\sigma_o^2}$ – *oriented varifolds*, and we propose $\gamma(u) = |u|$ – *absolute varifolds*. For such kernels, two surface varifolds M, N with "similar" support (for example, if M is a reparametrization of N, or if they represent two human shapes with the same pose but different body types) will have relatively small distance in the space of varifolds, so that $\langle M, N \rangle_V^2 \simeq \langle M, M \rangle_V \langle N, N \rangle_V$, that is, they are almost co-linear. On the other hand, surface varifolds with very distant support will be almost orthogonal ($\langle M, N \rangle_V \simeq 0$) because of the Gaussian term in k_{pos}. Obviously, shapes that have some parts that almost overlap while others are far away will be in-between. Combined with its rotational invariance, this leads us to believe that the kernel product can be used to differentiate between poses and motions independently of body types.

3.2 Comparing 3D Human Sequences

We need a way to compare sequences of $3D$ shapes $M_1, ..., M_T$, with T possibly differing between sequences. For this, we use the kernel product $\langle ., . \rangle_V$ as a similarity metric. Thanks to the reproducing property of positive definite kernels [5], it defines a reproducing kernel Hilbert space $\mathcal{H}$ (RKHS) which is an (infinite dimensional) Euclidean space endowed with an inner product corresponding to the kernel product, as described in the previous section. Any shape M has a corresponding representative $\Phi_M : \mathbb{R}^3 \times \mathbb{S}^2 \to \mathbb{R}$ in this space, such that $\langle \Phi_M, \Phi_N \rangle_V = \langle M, N \rangle_V$ (Fig. 3).

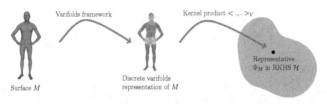

Fig. 3. An overview of varifolds framework. First, a mesh M is transformed into its corresponding varifold representation. Then, the kernel product defined in (1), transforms it into a representant Φ_M living in the Hilbert space $\mathcal{H}$ of this varifold.

Modeling Dynamics of Temporal Sequences. Thanks to the varifolds representation and the kernel product $\langle ., . \rangle$, the temporal sequence $M_1, ..., M_t$ corresponding to a motion in the human shape space can be seen as a temporal sequence $\Phi_{M_1}, ..., \Phi_{M_T}$ in the RKHS $\mathcal{H}$. Plus, since the varifold kernel is equivariant to rigid transformations, the product of two shapes within a sequence is invariant to any rigid transformation *applied to the full motion*. The Gram matrix $J_{ij} = \langle \Phi_{M_i}, \Phi_{M_j} \rangle$, which is a rigid transformation invariant matrix, would be a natural representant of the motion. However, its size vary with the length T of the sequence. Inspired by Auto-Regressive (AR) models of complexity k defined by $\Phi_{M_t} = \sum_{i=1}^{k} \alpha_i \Phi_{M_{t-i}}$, several representations [32,37] have been proposed for dynamical systems modeling. Hankel matrices [23] are one of the possible representations. The Hankel matrix of size r, s corresponding to our time series $\Phi_{M_1}, ..., \Phi_{M_T}$ is defined as:

$$\mathbf{H}_t^{r,s} = \begin{pmatrix} \Phi_{M_1} & \Phi_{M_2} & \Phi_{M_3} & \cdots & \Phi_{M_s} \\ \Phi_{M_2} & \Phi_{M_3} & \Phi_{M_4} & \cdots & \Phi_{M_{s+1}} \\ \cdots & \cdots & \cdots & \cdots & \cdots \\ \Phi_{M_r} & \Phi_{M_{r+1}} & \Phi_{M_{r+2}} & \cdots & \Phi_{M_{r+s}} \end{pmatrix} \quad (2)$$

The rank of such matrix is usually, under certain conditions, the complexity k of the dynamical system of the sequence. The comparison of two time series therefore become a comparison of high dimensional matrices.

It is not straightforward to use those matrices since our shape representatives live in infinite dimensional space. A first idea would be to think about the Nystrom reduction method [39] to build an explicit finite dimensional representation for Φ_M, but this would involve intensive computations. Another possibility is to think about the Gram matrix $\mathbf{HH}^T$ derived from the Hankel matrix $\mathbf{H}$ [23,40].

We cannot directly derive the same kind of matrices since our representatives live in an infinite dimensional space. The Gram matrix of the motion, J, however, preserves the linear relationships of the AR model. We therefore derive the following matrix:

Definition 1. *The Gram-Hankel matrix of size r, $G \in M_r(\mathbb{R})$ of the sequence $\Phi_{M_1}, ..., \Phi_{M_T}$ is defined as:*

$$\mathbf{G}_{ij} = \sum_{k=1}^{T-r} \langle \Phi_{M_{i+k}}, \Phi_{M_{j+k}} \rangle = \sum_{k=1}^{T-r} \langle M_{i+k}, M_{j+k} \rangle_V \tag{3}$$

We normalize $\mathbf{G}$ relatively to the Frobenius norm, following recommended practices [40]. This matrix is the sum of the diagonal blocks B_l^r of size r of the Gram matrix of the sequence pairwise inner products. A possible way of interpreting what encodes a single block B_l^r of size r when $r \geq k$ is to follow the idea of [20] the polar decomposition of the coordinate matrix of $\Phi_{M_l}, ...\Phi_{M_{r+l}}$. This coordinate matrix exists in the space $span(\Phi_{M_0}, ...\Phi_{M_k})$ under to the AR model hypothesis (any Φ_{M_j} is a linear combination of the first k Φ_{M_i}), and can be factorized into the product $U_l R_l$, where U_l is an orthonormal $r \times k$ matrix, and R_l an SPD matrix of size k. The matrix R_l is the covariance (multiplied by r^2) of $\Phi_{M_l}, ...\Phi_{M_{r+l}}$ in $span(\Phi_{M_0}, ...\Phi_{M_k})$, and it encodes in some way its shape in this space. An illustration of such encoding is given in Fig. 4. For three motions from CVSSP3D dataset, we compute the varifold distances Eq. (1) between all samples of the motion. We then used Multidimensional Scaling (MDS) [14] to visualize them in a 2D space. We display the ellipse associated to the covariance of each motion. We see that the one associated to jump in place (blue) motion is distinguishable from the ones associated to walk motions (red and green).

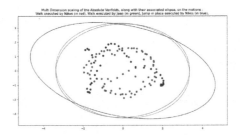

Fig. 4. MDS illustration of three motions of CVSSP3D dataset, along with ellipse associated to their covariance. (Colour figure online)

The Gram matrix block B_l^r is written as $B_l^r = U_l R_l^2 U_l^T$ and contains such information. Searching for the complexity k of the AR model would be sensitive to errors, and computing the associated R_l for comparisons with an SPD metric would be time consuming in our case. We thus preferred the rather simpler Gram-Hankel matrix, that cancels possible noise in single blocks when summing them. Finally, using the Frobenius distance $d(\mathbf{G_i}, \mathbf{G_j}) = ||\mathbf{G_i} - \mathbf{G_j}||_F$ where G_i and G_j are two Gram-Hankel matrices, to compare two motions lead us to rather good results. The blocks of size r are expressive enough when $r \geq k$, and taking their sum will ensure us to cancel possible noise added to a single block. The degenerate nature of G, does not allow for efficient use of SPD metrics such as the Log-Euclidean Riemannian Metric (LERM) on the G_i (more details are available in the supplementary material). With this approach, the comparison of two human motions is formulated as the comparison of two symmetric positive semi-definite matrices.

Proposition 1. *The Gram-Hankel matrix G associated to a motion $M_1, ..., M_T$ defined by Eq. (3) has the following properties:*

1. It is invariant to parameterization (property of the kernel product).
2. It is invariant to rigid transformation applied to a motion.

Normalizations. As the definition of the kernel shows the method is not invariant to scale, we normalize the inner products as following: $\left\langle \frac{M_i}{||M_i||_V}, \frac{M_j}{||M_j||_V} \right\rangle_V$.

While our method is translation invariant, the use of the Gaussian kernel implies that the product will be near 0 when the human shapes are at long range. To avoid this, we translate the surface M with triangles $T_1, ..., T_m$ by its centroid $c_M = \frac{\sum_{i=1}^m a_i c_i}{\sum_{i=1}^m a_i}$, where c_i and a_i correspond to the center and area of triangle T_i. We apply $M \mapsto M - c_M$ before computing the products.

4 Experiments

Computing varifold kernel products can often be time consuming, due to the quadratic cost in memory and time in terms of vertex number for computing $\langle M, N \rangle_V$. However, the recent library Keops [11], designed specifically for kernel operations proposes efficient implementations with no memory overflow, reducing time computation by two orders of magnitudes. We used those implementations with the Pytorch backend on a computer setup with Intel(R) Xeon(R) Bronze 3204 CPU @ 1.90 GHz, and a Nvidia Quadro RTX 4000 8 GB GPU.

4.1 Evaluation Setup

In order to measure the performance in motion retrieval, we use the classical performance metrics used in retrieval: Nearest neighbor (NN), First-tier (FT) and Second-tier (ST) criteria. For each experiment, we take r values ranging from 1 to T_{min} where T_{min} is the minimal sequence length in the dataset. We also take 10 σ values for the Gaussian kernel ranging from 0.001 to 10 in log scale. The score displayed is the best score among all r and σ values. For oriented varifolds, the σ_o of the gamma function is fixed to 0.5 as in [21].

4.2   Datasets

CVSSP3D Synthetic Dataset [33]. A synthetic model (1290 vertices and 2108 faces) is animated thanks to real motion skeleton data. Fourteen individuals executed 28 different motions: sneak, walk (slow, fast, turn left/right, circle left/right, cool, cowboy, elderly, tired, macho, march, mickey, sexy, dainty), run (slow, fast, turn right/left, circle left/right), sprint, vogue, faint, rock n'roll, shoot. An example of human motion from this dataset is presented in Fig. 5. The frequency of samples is set 25 Hz, with 100 samples per sequences. The maximum computation time of Gram-Hankel matrix is 0.89 s.

CVSSP3D Real Dataset [15]. This dataset contains reconstructions of multi view performances. 8 individuals performed 12 different motions: walk, run, jump, bend, hand wave (interaction between two models), jump in place, sit and stand up, run and fall, walk and sit, run then jump and walk, handshake (interaction between two models), pull. The number of vertices vary between 35000 and 70000. The frequency of samples is also set 25 Hz, and sequence length vary from 50 to 150 (average 109). We keep the 10 individual motions following [38]. An example motion of the dataset is displayed in Fig. 5(b). The maximum computation time of Gram-Hankel matrix is 6 m 30 s. The sensitivity of the reconstruction pipeline to the clothes is illustrated by the presence of noise as illustrated in Fig. 1. This noise makes this dataset challenging for 3D shape human shape comparison and for 3D human motion retrieval.

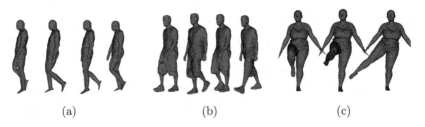

(a)   (b)   (c)

Fig. 5. Example motions from the datasets: (a) Slow walking motion from CVSSP3D synthetic dataset, (b) Walking motion from the CVSSP3D real dataset, (c) Knees motion from the Dyna dataset.

Dyna Dataset [30]. This dataset is created from 4D human scans. A human template (6890 vertices) is registered to human body scans sampled 60 Hz, and sequence length vary from 150 to 1200 (average 323). 10 individuals performed at most 14 different treadmill motions (hips, knees, light hopping stiff, light hopping loose, jiggle on toes, one leg loose, shake arms, chicken wings, punching, shake shoulders, shake hips, jumping jacks, one leg jump, running on spot), which means that the individual only move along the height axis. An example of human motion from Dyna dataset is presented in Fig. 5(c). The maximum computation time of Gram-Hankel matrix is 2 m 30 s.

4.3   Motion Retrieval on CVSSP3D Dataset

Comparison with State-of-the-Art. We compare our motion retrieval approach to the best features presented in [29, 38] and deep learning descriptors: (1) The 3D harmonics descriptor [27, 38] is a descriptor based on point cloud repartition in space, (2) Breadths spectrum Q-breadths and Q-shape invariant [29] are presented as 2 fully invariant descriptors derived from convex shape analysis, (3) Aumentado-Armstrong *et al.* [6] propose a human pose latent vector in their Geometrically Disentangled Variational AutoEncoder (GDVAE), (4) Zhou *et al.* [41] propose a human pose latent vector derived from the Neural3DMM [10] mesh autoencoder architecture, and (5) Cosmo *et al.* [13] propose a human pose latent vector in a similar approach as GDVAE, called Latent Interpolation with Metric Priors (LIMP). For the artificial dataset, the optimal σ were fixed to 0.17 for current, 0.17 for absolute varifolds, and 0.02 for oriented varifolds. The optimal r were 97.92 and 90 for current, absolute and oriented varifolds respectively.

We observe the results on the CVSSP3D artificial dataset in Table 1. Only our approach are able to get 100% in all performance metrics. We also observe that it is the only approach able to outperform the LIMP learned approach.

For the real dataset, the optimal σ were fixed to 0.06 for current, 0.17 for absolute varifolds and oriented varifolds. The optimal r were 48, 43 and 46 for current, absolute and oriented varifolds respectively.

We observe the results on the CVSSP3D real dataset in Table 1. Absolute varifolds approach outperforms by 2.5% the 3D descriptor in terms of NN metric, while being less good for FT and ST. In terms of fully invariant methods, we outperform by 10% the proposed approaches. The absolute varifolds methods is the best of our approach, but we do not observe significant sensitivity between different varifolds. We finally observe that the point cloud descriptors of GDVAE has the lowest performance.

Table 1. Full comparison of motion retrieval approaches. First two columns correspond to group invariance (Γ: reparameterization group, $SO(3)$: rotation group), telling whether or not the required invariance is fullfilled (✓: fully invariant, ≈: approximately invariant (normalization, supplementary information, ...), ✗: no invariance). Remaining columns correspond to retrieval scores, where the '/' symbol means that there is no result for the method on the given dataset for various reasons, such as unavailable implementation or the method not being adapted for the dataset (for example, in line 470, [41] is based on a given mesh with vertex correspondences and cannot be applied to CVSSP3D real dataset). The results are displayed for CVSSP3D artificial and real datasets, and Dyna datasets. Our method is competitive or better than the approach consisting of combing DTW with any descriptor, while showing all required invariances.

Representation	Γ inv.	$SO(3)$	Artificial dataset			Real dataset			Dyna dataset		
			NN	FT	ST	NN	FT	ST	NN	FT	ST
Shape Dist. [26,38]	✓	✓	92.1	88.9	97.2	77.5	51.6	65.5	/	/	/
Spin Images [19,38]	✓	✓	100	87.1	94.1	77.5	51.6	65.5	/	/	/
3D harmonics [38]	≈	≈	100	98.3	99.9	92.5	**72.7**	**86.1**	/	/	/
Breadths spectrum [29]	✓	✓	100	99.8	100	/	/	/	/	/	/
Shape invariant [29]	✓	✓	82.1	56.8	68.5	/	/	/	/	/	/
Q-Breadths spectrum [29]	≈	✓	/	/	/	80.0	44.8	59.5	/	/	/
Q-shape invariant [29]	≈	✓	/	/	/	82.5	51.3	68.8	/	/	/
Areas [29]	✓	✗	/	/	/	/	/	/	37.2	24.5	35.8
Breadths [29]	✓	✗	/	/	/	/	/	/	50.7	36.2	50.5
Areas & Breadths [29]	✓	✗	/	/	/	/	/	/	50.7	37.2	51.7
GDVAE [6]	✓	✓	100	97.6	98.8	38.7	31.6	51.6	18.7	19.6	32.2
Zhou et al. [41]	✗	✗	100	99.6	99.6	/	/	/	50.0	40.4	57.0
LIMP [13]	✓	✗	100	*99.98*	*99.98*	/	/	/	29.1	20.7	33.9
SMPL pose vector [24]	≈	✓	/	/	/	/	/	/	*58.2*	*45.7*	*63.2*
Current	✓	✓	100	100	100	92.5	66.0	78.5	59.0	34.1	50.4
Absolute varifolds	✓	✓	100	100	100	**95.0**	66.6	80.7	**60.4**	40.0	55.9
Oriented varifolds	✓	✓	100	100	100	93.8	65.4	78.2	**60.4**	40.8	55.9

4.4　Motion Retrieval on Dyna Dataset

Comparison with State-of-the-Art. No benchmark exists on this dataset, a little has been made on the registrations provided by Dyna. We applied the following methods to extract pose descriptors and made pairwise sequences comparisons using dynamic time warping, in a similar protocol as [29,38], without the temporal filtering use for clothes datasets, since the dataset is not noisy. We compare our approach to descriptor sequences of the following approaches: (1) Areas and Breadths [29] are parameterization and translation invariants derived from convex shapes analysis, (2) The pretrained GDVAE on SURREAL is applied directly on the dataset, (3) the pretrained LIMP VAE on FAUST is applied directly on the dataset, (4) Zhou et al. [41] provide pretrained weights on the AMASS dataset [25] for their approach. This dataset shares the same human body parameterization as Dyna, so we can use the pretrained network on Dyna, and (5) The Skinned Multi-Person Linear model (SMPL) body model [24] is a parameterized human body model. We use the pose vector of the body model, computed in [9] using additional information.

For the Dyna dataset, the optimal σ were fixed to 0.02 for current 0.06 for absolute varifolds, and 0.16 for oriented varifolds. The optimal r were 27, 31 and 72 for current, absolute and oriented varifolds respectively.

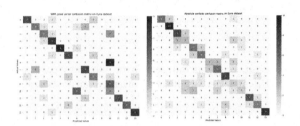

Fig. 6. Confusion matrix of SMPL (left) and Oriented Varifolds (right) on the Dyna dataset.

As shown in Table 1 the oriented and absolute varifolds is the best by 2% in terms of NN metric compare to SMPL, and by more than 10% to other approaches, including the parameterization dependant approach of [41]. The FT and ST performance are however less good than SMPL. This can be explained by its human specific design, along with the costly fitting method, that use additional information (gender, texture videos). Finally, we observe that point cloud neural networks are not suitable for high set of complex motions.

4.5 Qualitative Analysis on Dyna Dataset

We display in Fig. 6 the Nearest Neighbor score confusion matrices for both SMPL and Oriented Varifolds. The confusion matrices for the other datasets are available in the supplementary material. We observe that on Dyna, the difficult cases were *jiggle on toes, shake arms, shake hips and jumping jacks*, corresponding to l3, l6, l9 and l10 in confusion matrix. Our approach is able to classify better these motions than SMPL. In addition, SMPL was not able to retrieve as a Nearest Neighbor, a similar motion to shake arms or shake hips corresponding to l6 and l9. This Figure shows also that our approach retrieves perfectly the knees motion corresponding to l1. The Fig. 7 shows some qualitative results of our approach. It illustrates the first tier of a given query on Dyna dataset.

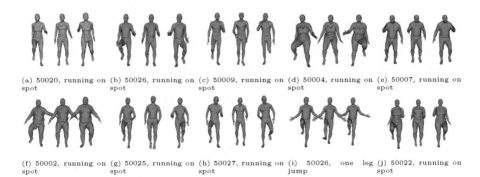

(a) 50020, running on spot (b) 50026, running on spot (c) 50009, running on spot (d) 50004, running on spot (e) 50007, running on spot

(f) 50002, running on spot (g) 50025, running on spot (h) 50027, running on spot (i) 50026, one leg jump (j) 50022, running on spot

Fig. 7. Qualitative results on Dyna dataset. Given the query corresponding to running on spot motion (a), the first tier result using oriented varifolds are given by (b)–(j).

5   Discussion

Effect of the Parameters for Oriented Varifolds on Dyna Dataset. We provide in Fig. 8, the performance relative to the parameters σ and r, for oriented varifolds on Dyna dataset. We observe that the choice of those parameters is crucial. We also display the performances of oriented varifolds with the 2 normalizations techniques, showing that they both help to obtain the best results. More discussion is provided in the supplementary material (Table 2).

Limitations. Our approach presents two main limitations: (i) To measure distance between matrices, we have used Euclidean distance, which does not exploit the geometry of the symmetric positive semi-definite matrices manifold, (ii) There is no theoretical limitation to apply this framework to the comparison of other 3D shape sequences (eg. 3D facial expressions, or 3D cortical surfaces evolutions) other than that between body shape. However, in practice one should redefine the hyperparameters (r, σ) of the Kernel (Theorem 1).

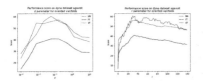

Fig. 8. NN, FT, ST metric relatively to the σ parameters (left) and to the r parameter (right) on Dyna dataset for oriented varifolds.

Table 2. Retrieval performance of the normalizations on Dyna dataset, for oriented varifolds. Both are useful.

Centroid	Inner	NN	FT	ST
✗	✗	51.5	34.6	53.4
✗	✓	52.2	33.4	50.5
✓	✗	59.7	40.7	55.8
✓	✓	**60.4**	**40.8**	**55.9**

6 Conclusion

We presented a novel framework to perform comparison of 3D human shape sequences. We propose a new representation of 3D human shape, equivariant to rotation and invariant to parameterization using the varifolds framework. We propose also a new way to represent a human motion by embedding the 3D shape sequences in infinite dimensional space using a kernel positive definite product from varifolds framework. We compared our method to the combination of dynamic time warping and static human pose descriptors. Our experiments on 3 datasets showed that our approach gives competitive or better than state-of-the-art results for 3D human motion retrieval, showing better generalization ability than popular deep learning approaches.

Acknowledgments. This work is supported by the ANR project Human4D ANR-19-CE23-0020 and partially by the Investments for the future program ANR-16-IDEX-0004 ULNE.

References

1. Carnegie Mellon University MoCap Database (2018). http://mocap.cs.cmu.edu/
2. Almgren, F.J.: Plateau's Problem: An Invitation to Varifold Geometry, vol. 13. American Mathematical Society (1966)
3. Anguelov, D., Srinivasan, P., Koller, D., Thrun, S., Rodgers, J., Davis, J.: Scape: shape completion and animation of people. In: ACM SIGGRAPH 2005 Papers, pp. 408–416 (2005)
4. Aristidou, A., Chrysanthou, Y.: Feature extraction for human motion indexing of acted dance performances. In: Proceedings of the 9th International Conference on Computer Graphics Theory and Applications, GRAPP 2014, pp. 277–287. IEEE (2014)
5. Aronszajn, N.: Theory of reproducing kernels. Trans. Am. Math. Soc. **68**(3), 337–404 (1950)
6. Aumentado-Armstrong, T., Tsogkas, S., Jepson, A., Dickinson, S.: Geometric disentanglement for generative latent shape models. In: 2019 IEEE/CVF International Conference on Computer Vision (ICCV), pp. 8180–8189 (2019)
7. Bauer, M., Charon, N., Harms, P., Hsieh, H.W.: A numerical framework for elastic surface matching, comparison, and interpolation. Int. J. Comput. Vis. **129**, 2425–2444 (2021)
8. Ben Amor, B., Su, J., Srivastava, A.: Action recognition using rate-invariant analysis of skeletal shape trajectories. IEEE Trans. Pattern Anal. Mach. Intell. **38**(1), 1–13 (2016)
9. Bogo, F., Romero, J., Pons-Moll, G., Black, M.J.: Dynamic FAUST: registering human bodies in motion. In: 2017 IEEE Conference on Computer Vision and Pattern Recognition (CVPR), Honolulu, HI, pp. 5573–5582. IEEE (2017). https://doi.org/10.1109/CVPR.2017.591. http://ieeexplore.ieee.org/document/8100074/
10. Bouritsas, G., Bokhnyak, S., Ploumpis, S., Zafeiriou, S., Bronstein, M.M.: Neural 3D morphable models: spiral convolutional networks for 3D shape representation learning and generation. In: 2019 IEEE/CVF International Conference on Computer Vision, ICCV 2019, Seoul, Korea (South), 27 October–2 November 2019, pp. 7212–7221. IEEE (2019)

11. Charlier, B., Feydy, J., Glaunès, J.A., Collin, F.D., Durif, G.: Kernel operations on the GPU, with Autodiff, without memory overflows. J. Mach. Learn. Res. **22**(74), 1–6 (2021). http://jmlr.org/papers/v22/20-275.html

12. Charon, N., Trouvé, A.: The varifold representation of nonoriented shapes for diffeomorphic registration. SIAM J. Imaging Sci. **6**(4), 2547–2580 (2013)

13. Cosmo, L., Norelli, A., Halimi, O., Kimmel, R., Rodolà, E.: LIMP: learning latent shape representations with metric preservation priors. In: Vedaldi, A., Bischof, H., Brox, T., Frahm, J.-M. (eds.) ECCV 2020. LNCS, vol. 12348, pp. 19–35. Springer, Cham (2020). https://doi.org/10.1007/978-3-030-58580-8_2

14. Cox, M., Cox, T.: Multidimensional scaling. In: Cox, M., Cox, T. (eds.) Handbook of Data Visualization. SHCS, pp. 315–347. Springer, Heidelberg (2008). https://doi.org/10.1007/978-3-540-33037-0_14

15. Gkalelis, N., Kim, H., Hilton, A., Nikolaidis, N., Pitas, I.: The i3DPost multi-view and 3D human action/interaction database. In: 2009 Conference for Visual Media Production, pp. 159–168. IEEE (2009)

16. Hasler, N., Stoll, C., Sunkel, M., Rosenhahn, B., Seidel, H.P.: A statistical model of human pose and body shape. In: Computer Graphics Forum, vol. 28, pp. 337–346. Wiley Online Library (2009)

17. Huang, P., Hilton, A., Starck, J.: Shape similarity for 3D video sequences of people. Int. J. Comput. Vis. **89**(2–3), 362–381 (2010)

18. Jermyn, I.H., Kurtek, S., Klassen, E., Srivastava, A.: Elastic shape matching of parameterized surfaces using square root normal fields. In: Fitzgibbon, A., Lazebnik, S., Perona, P., Sato, Y., Schmid, C. (eds.) ECCV 2012. LNCS, vol. 7576, pp. 804–817. Springer, Heidelberg (2012). https://doi.org/10.1007/978-3-642-33715-4_58

19. Johnson, A.E., Hebert, M.: Using spin images for efficient object recognition in cluttered 3D scenes. IEEE Trans. Pattern Anal. Mach. Intell. **21**(5), 433–449 (1999)

20. Kacem, A., Daoudi, M., Amor, B.B., Berretti, S., Alvarez-Paiva, J.C.: A novel geometric framework on gram matrix trajectories for human behavior understanding. IEEE Trans. Pattern Anal. Mach. Intell. **42**(1), 1–14 (2018)

21. Kaltenmark, I., Charlier, B., Charon, N.: A general framework for curve and surface comparison and registration with oriented varifolds. In: Proceedings of the IEEE Conference on Computer Vision and Pattern Recognition, pp. 3346–3355 (2017)

22. Kurtek, S., Klassen, E., Gore, J.C., Ding, Z., Srivastava, A.: Elastic geodesic paths in shape space of parameterized surfaces. IEEE Trans. Pattern Anal. Mach. Intell. **34**(9), 1717–1730 (2012)

23. Li, B., Camps, O.I., Sznaier, M.: Cross-view activity recognition using Hankelets. In: 2012 IEEE Conference on Computer Vision and Pattern Recognition, pp. 1362–1369. IEEE (2012)

24. Loper, M., Mahmood, N., Romero, J., Pons-Moll, G., Black, M.J.: SMPL: a skinned multi-person linear model. ACM Trans. Graphics (Proc. SIGGRAPH Asia) **34**(6), 248:1–248:16 (2015)

25. Mahmood, N., Ghorbani, N., Troje, N.F., Pons-Moll, G., Black, M.J.: AMASS: archive of motion capture as surface shapes. In: Proceedings of the IEEE International Conference on Computer Vision, pp. 5442–5451 (2019)

26. Osada, R., Funkhouser, T.A., Chazelle, B., Dobkin, D.P.: Shape distributions. ACM Trans. Graph. **21**(4), 807–832 (2002)

27. Papadakis, P., Pratikakis, I., Theoharis, T., Passalis, G., Perantonis, S.: 3D object retrieval using an efficient and compact hybrid shape descriptor. In: Eurographics Workshop on 3D Object Retrieval (2008)

28. Pierson, E., Daoudi, M., Tumpach, A.B.: A Riemannian framework for analysis of human body surface. In: Proceedings of the IEEE IEEE Winter Conference on Applications of Computer Vision (2022)
29. Pierson, E., Paiva, J.C.Á., Daoudi, M.: Projection-based classification of surfaces for 3D human mesh sequence retrieval. Comput. Graph. **102**, 45–55 (2021)
30. Pons-Moll, G., Romero, J., Mahmood, N., Black, M.J.: Dyna: a model of dynamic human shape in motion. ACM Trans. Graph. (TOG) **34**(4), 1–14 (2015)
31. Slama, R., Wannous, H., Daoudi, M.: 3D human motion analysis framework for shape similarity and retrieval. Image Vis. Comput. **32**(2), 131–154 (2014)
32. Slama, R., Wannous, H., Daoudi, M., Srivastava, A.: Accurate 3D action recognition using learning on the Grassmann manifold. Pattern Recogn. **48**(2), 556–567 (2015)
33. Starck, J., Hilton, A.: Surface capture for performance-based animation. IEEE Comput. Graph. Appl. **27**(3), 21–31 (2007)
34. Tan, Q., Gao, L., Lai, Y.K., Xia, S.: Variational autoencoders for deforming 3D mesh models. In: Proceedings of the IEEE Conference on Computer Vision and Pattern Recognition, pp. 5841–5850 (2018)
35. Tsiminaki, V., Franco, J.S., Boyer, E.: High resolution 3D shape texture from multiple videos. In: IEEE International Conference on Computer Vision and Pattern Recognition, CVPR 2014, Columbus, OH, USA, pp. 1502–1509. IEEE (2014). https://doi.org/10.1109/CVPR.2014.195. https://hal.inria.fr/hal-00977755
36. Tumpach, A.B., Drira, H., Daoudi, M., Srivastava, A.: Gauge invariant framework for shape analysis of surfaces. IEEE Trans. Pattern Anal. Mach. Intell. **38**(1), 46–59 (2016)
37. Turaga, P., Veeraraghavan, A., Chellappa, R.: Statistical analysis on Stiefel and Grassmann manifolds with applications in computer vision. In: 2008 IEEE Conference on Computer Vision and Pattern Recognition, pp. 1–8. IEEE (2008)
38. Veinidis, C., Danelakis, A., Pratikakis, I., Theoharis, T.: Effective descriptors for human action retrieval from 3D mesh sequences. Int. J. Image Graph. **19**(03), 1950018 (2019)
39. Williams, C., Seeger, M.: Using the Nyström method to speed up kernel machines. In: Proceedings of the 14th Annual Conference on Neural Information Processing Systems, pp. 682–688 (2001)
40. Zhang, X., Wang, Y., Gou, M., Sznaier, M., Camps, O.: Efficient temporal sequence comparison and classification using gram matrix embeddings on a Riemannian manifold. In: 2016 IEEE Conference on Computer Vision and Pattern Recognition (CVPR), Las Vegas, NV, USA, pp. 4498–4507. IEEE (2016). https://doi.org/10. 1109/CVPR.2016.487. http://ieeexplore.ieee.org/document/7780856/
41. Zhou, K., Bhatnagar, B.L., Pons-Moll, G.: Unsupervised shape and pose disentanglement for 3D meshes. In: Vedaldi, A., Bischof, H., Brox, T., Frahm, J.-M. (eds.) ECCV 2020. LNCS, vol. 12367, pp. 341–357. Springer, Cham (2020). https://doi. org/10.1007/978-3-030-58542-6_21

Conditional-Flow NeRF: Accurate 3D Modelling with Reliable Uncertainty Quantification

Jianxiong Shen[1]([⊠]), Antonio Agudo[1], Francesc Moreno-Noguer[1],
and Adria Ruiz[2]

[1] Institut de Robòtica i Informàtica Industrial, CSIC-UPC, Barcelona, Spain
jianxiong.shen@upc.edu
[2] Seedtag, Madrid, Spain

Abstract. A critical limitation of current methods based on Neural Radiance Fields (NeRF) is that they are unable to quantify the uncertainty associated with the learned appearance and geometry of the scene. This information is paramount in real applications such as medical diagnosis or autonomous driving where, to reduce potentially catastrophic failures, the confidence on the model outputs must be included into the decision-making process. In this context, we introduce Conditional-Flow NeRF (CF-NeRF), a novel probabilistic framework to incorporate uncertainty quantification into NeRF-based approaches. For this purpose, our method learns a distribution over all possible radiance fields modelling the scene which is used to quantify the uncertainty associated with the modelled scene. In contrast to previous approaches enforcing strong constraints over the radiance field distribution, CF-NeRF learns it in a flexible and fully data-driven manner by coupling Latent Variable Modelling and Conditional Normalizing Flows. This strategy allows to obtain reliable uncertainty estimation while preserving model expressivity. Compared to previous state-of-the-art methods proposed for uncertainty quantification in NeRF, our experiments show that the proposed method achieves significantly lower prediction errors and more reliable uncertainty values for synthetic novel view and depth-map estimation.

Keywords: 3D · Scene representation · Uncertainty quantification

1 Introduction

Neural fields [61] have recently gained a lot of attention given its ability to encode implicit representations of complex 3D scenes using deep neural networks. Additionally, they have been shown very effective in addressing multiple problems

Supplementary Information The online version contains supplementary material available at https://doi.org/10.1007/978-3-031-20062-5_31.

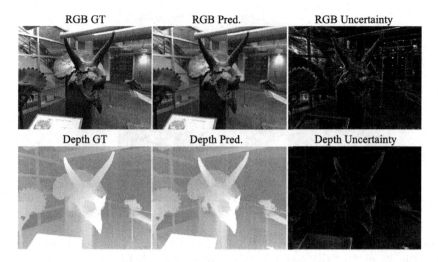

Fig. 1. Ground Truth (Left), Predictions (Center) and Uncertainty Maps (Right) obtained by our proposed CF-NeRF in novel view synthesis and depth-map estimation.

such as 3D reconstruction [31,38], scene rendering [26,30] or human body representation [37,49]. Among different methods built upon this framework [5,40,54], Neural Radiance Fields (NeRF) [32] has obtained impressive results in generating photo-realistic views of 3D scenes and solving downstream tasks such as depth estimation [60], scene editing [15,25] or pose prediction [55,64].

Despite its increasing popularity, a critical limitation of NeRF holding back its application to real-world problems has been recently pointed out by [52]. Concretely, current NeRF-based methods are not able to quantify the uncertainty associated with the model estimates. This information is crucial in several scenarios such as robotics [21,27], medical diagnosis [51] or autonomous driving [8] where, to reduce potentially catastrophic failures, the confidence on the model outputs must be included into the decision-making process.

To address this limitation, recent works [30,52] have explored different strategies to incorporate uncertainty quantification into NeRF. Remarkably, Stochastic NeRF [52] (S-NeRF) has recently obtained state-of-the-art results by employing a probabilistic model to learn a simple distribution over radiance fields. However, in order to make this problem tractable, S-NeRF makes strong assumptions over the aforementioned distribution, thus limiting model expressivity and leading to sub-optimal results for complex 3D scenes.

In this context, we propose Conditional-Flow NeRF (CF-NeRF), a novel probabilistic framework to incorporate uncertainty quantification without sacrificing model flexibility. As a result, our approach enables both effective 3D modelling and reliable uncertainty estimates (see Fig. 1). In the following, we summarise the main technical contributions of our method:

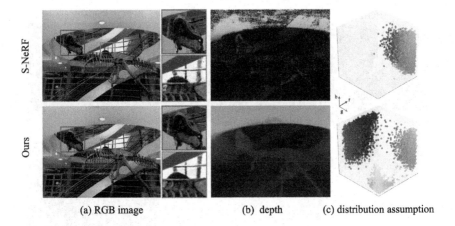

(a) RGB image   (b) depth   (c) distribution assumption

Fig. 2. Comparison between our CF-NeRF and the previous state-of-the-art method S-NeRF [52] on (a) RGB images and (b) depth-maps. S-NeRF generates noisy results due to the strong assumptions made over the radiance field distribution. In contrast, CF-NeRF renders more realistic and smooth synthetic views. (c) Illustration of the radiance distributions that can be modelled by S-NeRF and CF-NeRF. While the first is only able to represent distributions with a simple form, CF-NeRF can model arbitrary complex distributions by using Conditional Normalizing Flows. (Color figure online)

Modelling Radiance-Density Distributions with Normalizing Flows: In contrast to S-NeRF where the radiance and density in the scene are assumed to follow simple distributions (see Fig. 2(c-Top)), our method learns them in a flexible and fully data-driven manner using conditional normalizing flows [63]. This allows CF-NeRF to learn arbitrarily complex radiance and density distributions (see Fig. 2(c-Bottom)) which have the capacity to model scenes with complex geometry and appearance.

Latent Variable Modelling for Radiance Fields Distributions: Motivated by De Finetti's Theorem [17], CF-NeRF incorporates a global latent variable in order to efficiently model the joint distribution over the radiance-density variables for all the spatial locations in the scene. This contrasts with the approach followed by S-NeRF, where these variables are considered independent for different 3D coordinates. Intuitively, the independence assumption violates the fact that changes in the density and radiance between adjacent locations are usually smooth. As a consequence, S-NeRF tends to generate low-quality and noisy predictions (see Fig. 2(a, b)-Top). In contrast, the global latent variable used in CF-NeRF allows to efficiently model the complex joint distribution of these variables, leading to spatially-smooth uncertainty estimates and more realistic results (Fig. 2(a, b)-Bottom).

In our experiments, we evaluate CF-NeRF over different benchmark datasets containing scenes with increasing complexity. Our qualitative and quantitative results show that our method obtains significantly better uncertainty estimations for rendered views and predicted depth maps compared to S-NeRF and other previous methods for uncertainty quantification. Additionally, CF-NeRF provides better image quality and depth estimation precision. These results confirm that our method is able to incorporate uncertainty quantification into NeRF without sacrificing model expressivity.

2 Related Work

Neural Radiance Fields. NeRF [32] has become a popular approach for 3D scene modelling due to its simplicity and its impressive performance on several tasks. By using a sparse collection of 2D views, NeRF learns a deep neural network encoding a representation of the 3D scene. This network is composed of a set of fully-connected layers that output the volume density and emitted radiance for any input 3D spatial location and 2D viewing direction in the scene. Subsequently, novel views are generated by applying volumetric rendering [16] to the estimated density and radiance values obtained by the network. Recently, several extensions [19,35,41,50,53,57,65,67,69] over NeRF have been proposed. For instance, different works have focused on accelerating NeRF training [24,47,56] or modelling dynamic scenes [10,22,39,43,46]. Despite the advances achieved at different levels, the application of current NeRF-based methods in real scenarios is still limited since they are unable to quantify the uncertainty associated with the rendered views or estimated geometry. Our proposed CF-NeRF explicitly addresses this problem and can be easily combined with most of current NeRF-based approaches.

Uncertainty Estimation in Deep Learning. Uncertainty estimation has been extensively studied in deep learning [7,12,13,29,58] and have been applied to different computer vision tasks [3,45,62]. Early works proposed to use *Bayesian Neural Networks* (BNN) [33,34] to estimate the uncertainty of both network weights and outputs by approximating their marginal distributions. However, training BNNs is typically difficult and computationally expensive. As a consequence, their use in large deep neural networks is limited. More recently, efficient strategies have been proposed to incorporate uncertainty estimation into deep neural networks [6,48]. Among them, MC-Dropout [11] and Deep Ensembles [20] are two of the most popular approaches given that they are agnostic to the specific network architecture [1,2,14,23]. More concretely, MC-Dropout adds stochastic dropout during inference into the intermediate network layers. By doing multiple forward passes over the same input with different dropout configurations, the variance over the obtained set of outputs is used as the output uncertainty. On the other hand, Deep Ensembles applies a similar strategy by computing a set of outputs from multiple neural networks that are independently trained using different parameters initializations. In contrast to MC-Dropout and Deep Ensembles, however, we do not train independent networks to generate the samples. Instead, CF-NeRF explicitly encodes the distribution of the radiance fields into a single probabilistic model.

Uncertainty Estimation in NeRF. Recently, some works [30,52] have attempted to incorporate uncertainty estimation into Neural Radiance Fields. NeRF-in-the-Wild (NeRF-W) [30] modelled uncertainty at pixel-level in order to detect potential transient objects such as cars or pedestrians in modelled scenes. For this purpose, NeRF-W employs a neural network to estimate an uncertainty value for each 3D spatial location. Subsequently, it computes a confidence score for each pixel in a rendered image by using an alpha-compositing strategy similar to the one used to estimate the pixel color in original NeRF. However, this approach is not theoretically grounded since there is no intuitive justification to apply the volume rendering process over uncertainty values. Additionally, NeRF-W is not able to evaluate the confidence associated with estimated depth. On the other hand, S-NeRF [52] has achieved state-of-the-art performance in quantifying the uncertainty of novel rendered views and depth-maps. Instead of learning a single radiance field as in original NeRF [32], S-NeRF models a distribution over all the possible radiance fields explaining the scene. During inference, this distribution is used to sample multiple color or depth predictions and compute a confidence score based on their associated variance. However, S-NeRF imposes strong constraints over the radiance field distribution and, as a consequence, this limits its ability to model scenes with complex appearance and geometry. In contrast, the proposed CF-NeRF combines a conditional normalizing flow and latent variable modelling to learn arbitrary complex radiance fields distributions without any prior assumption.

Complex Distribution Modelling with Normalizing Flows. Normalizing Flows (NF) have been extensively used to model complex distributions with unknown explicit forms. For this purpose, NF uses a sequence of invertible functions to transform samples from a simple known distribution to variables following an arbitrary probability density function. Additionally, the change-of-variables formula can be used to compute the likelihood of different samples according to the transformed distribution. Given its flexibility, Normalizing Flows have been used in several 3D modelling tasks. For instance, [44,63] introduced different flow-based generative models to model 3D point cloud distributions and sample from them. More recently, [36] used a normalizing flow in order to avoid color shifts at unseen viewpoints in the context of NeRF. To the best of our knowledge, our proposed CF-NeRF is the first approach employing Normalizing Flows in order to learn radiance fields distributions for 3D scene modelling.

3 Deterministic and Stochastic Neural Radiance Fields

Deterministic Neural Radiance Fields. Standard NeRF [32] represents a 3D volumetric scene as $\mathcal{F} = \{(\mathbf{r}(\mathbf{x}, \mathbf{d}), \alpha(\mathbf{x})) : \mathbf{x} \in \mathbb{R}^3, \mathbf{d} \in \mathbb{R}^2$, where $\mathcal{F}$ is a set containing the volume density $\alpha(\mathbf{x}) \in \mathbb{R}^+$ and RGB radiance $\mathbf{r}(\mathbf{x}, \mathbf{d}) \in \mathbb{R}^3$ from all the spatial locations $\mathbf{x}$ and view directions $\mathbf{d}$ in the scene.

In order to implicitly model the infinite set $\mathcal{F}$, NeRF employs a neural network $f_\theta(\mathbf{x}, \mathbf{d})$ with parameters θ which outputs the density α and radiance $\mathbf{r}$ for any given input location-view pair $\{\mathbf{x}, \mathbf{d}\}$. Using this network, NeRF is able to estimate the color $\mathbf{c}(\mathbf{x}_o, \mathbf{d})$ for any given pixel defined by a 3D camera position $\mathbf{x}_o$ and view direction $\mathbf{d}$ using the volumetric rendering function:

$$\mathbf{c}(\mathbf{x}_o, \mathbf{d}) = \int_{t_n}^{t_f} T(t)\alpha(\mathbf{x}_t)\mathbf{r}(\mathbf{x}_t, \mathbf{d})dt, \text{ where } T(t) = \exp(-\int_{t_n}^{t} \alpha(\mathbf{x}_s)ds), \quad (1)$$

and where $\mathbf{x}_t = \mathbf{x}_o + t\mathbf{d}$ corresponds to 3D locations along a ray with direction $\mathbf{d}$ originated at the camera origin and intersecting with the pixel at $\mathbf{x}_o$.

During training, NeRF optimizes the network parameters θ using Eq. (1) by leveraging Maximum Likelihood Estimation (MLE) over a training set $\mathcal{T}$ containing ground-truth images depicting views of the scene captured from different camera positions. More details about NeRF and its learning procedure can be found in the original paper [32].

Stochastic Neural Radiance Fields. Deterministic NeRF is not able to provide information about the underlying uncertainty associated with the rendered views or estimated depth maps. The reason is that the network $f_\theta(\mathbf{x}, \mathbf{d})$ is trained using Maximum Likelihood Estimation and thus, the learning process performs a single point estimate over all the plausible radiance fields $\mathcal{F}$ given the training set $\mathcal{T}$. As a consequence, model predictions are deterministic and it is not possible to sample multiple outputs to compute their associated variance.

To address this limitation, S-NeRF [52] employs Bayesian Learning to model the posterior distribution $p_\theta(\mathcal{F}|\mathcal{T})$ over all the plausible radiance fields explaining the scene given the training set. In this manner, uncertainty estimations can be obtained during inference by computing the variance over multiple predictions obtained from different radiance fields $\mathcal{F}$ sampled from this distribution.

In order to make this problem tractable, S-NeRF uses Variational Inference to approximate the posterior $p_\theta(\mathcal{F}|\mathcal{T})$ with a parametric distribution $q_\theta(\mathcal{F})$ implemented by a deep neural network. However, S-NeRF imposes two limiting constraints over $q_\theta(\mathcal{F})$. Firstly, it models the radiance $\mathbf{r}$ and density α for each location-view pair in the scene as independent variables. In particular, the probability of a radiance field given $\mathcal{T}$ is modelled with a fully-factorized distribution:

$$q_\theta(\mathcal{F}) = \prod_{\mathbf{x} \in \mathbb{R}^3} \prod_{\mathbf{d} \in \mathbb{R}^2} q_\theta(\mathbf{r}|\mathbf{x}, \mathbf{d}) q_\theta(\alpha|\mathbf{x}). \quad (2)$$

Whereas this conditional-independence assumption simplifies the optimization process, it ignores the fact that radiance and density values in adjacent spatial locations are usually correlated. As a consequence, S-NeRF tends to render noisy and low-quality images and depth maps (see Fig. 2).

4   Conditional Flow-Based Neural Radiance Fields

Our proposed Conditional Flow-based Neural Radiance Fields incorporates uncertainty estimation by using a similar strategy than S-NeRF. In particular, CF-NeRF learns a parametric distribution $q_\theta(\mathcal{F})$ approximating the posterior distribution $p(\mathcal{F}|\mathcal{T})$ over all the possible radiance fields given the training views. Different from S-NeRF, however, our method does not assume a simple and fully-factorized distribution for $q_\theta(\mathcal{F})$, but it relies on Conditional Normalizing Flows and Latent Variable Modelling to preserve model expressivity. In the following, we discuss the technical details of our approach (Sect. 4.1), the optimizing process following S-NeRF (Sect. 4.2) and inference procedure used to compute the uncertainty associated with novel rendered views and depth maps (Sect. 4.3).

4.1   Modelling Flexible Radiance Field Distributions with CF-NeRF

Radiance Field distribution with Global Latent Variable. As discussed in Sect. 3, S-NeRF formulation assumes that radiance and density variables at each spatial location in the field follow a fully-factorized distribution (Eq. (2)). As a consequence, they are forced to be independent from each other. This simplification was motivated by the fact that modelling the joint distribution over the infinite set of radiance and density variables in the field $\mathcal{F}$ is not trivial. To address this problem, our proposed CF-NeRF leverages De Finetti's representation theorem [17]. In particular, the theorem states that any joint distribution over sets of exchangeable variables can be written as a fully-factorized distribution conditioned on a global latent variable. Based on this observation, we define the approximate posterior $q_\theta(\mathcal{F})$:

$$q_\theta(\mathcal{F}) = \int_\mathbf{z} q_\vartheta(\mathbf{z}) q_\theta(\mathcal{F}|\mathbf{z}) d\mathbf{z} = \int_\mathbf{z} q_\vartheta(\mathbf{z}) \prod_{\mathbf{x}\in\mathbb{R}^3} \prod_{\mathbf{d}\in\mathbb{R}^2} q_\theta(\mathbf{r}|\mathbf{x},\mathbf{d},\mathbf{z}) q_\theta(\alpha|\mathbf{x},\mathbf{z}) d\mathbf{z}, \quad (3)$$

where the latent variable $\mathbf{z}$ is sampled from a Gaussian prior $q_\vartheta(\mathbf{z}) = \{\mu_z, \sigma_z\}$ with learned mean and variance. In this manner, all the 3D spatial-locations $\mathbf{x}$ and viewing-directions $\mathbf{d}$ generated from the same shared latent variable $\mathbf{z}$ and thus, they are conditionally dependent between them. This approach allows CF-NeRF to efficiently model the distribution over the radiance-density variables in the radiance field without any independence assumption. It is also worth mentioning that De Fineti's theorem has been also used in previous works learning joint distributions over sets for 3D point cloud modelling [18].

Radiance-Density Conditional Flows. Given that the radiance-density distributions can be highly complicated for complex scenes, modelling them with variants of Gaussian distributions as in Stochastic NeRF can lead to sub-optimal results. For this reason, CF-NeRF models $q_\theta(\mathbf{r}|\mathbf{x},\mathbf{d},\mathbf{z})$ and $q_\theta(\alpha|\mathbf{x},\mathbf{z})$ using a Conditional Normalizing Flow (CNF) [4]. This allows to learn arbitrarily complex distributions in a fully data-driven manner without any prior assumption.

For any input location-direction pair $(\mathbf{x},\mathbf{d})$, we use a sequence of K CNFs that transform the global latent variable $\mathbf{z}$ into samples from the radiance $\mathbf{r}$ or density α distribution $q_\theta(\mathbf{r}|\mathbf{x},\mathbf{d},\mathbf{z})$ or $q_\theta(\alpha|\mathbf{x},\mathbf{z})$. More formally, each flow is defined as an invertible parametric function $\mathbf{z}_k = f_k(\mathbf{z}_{k-1},\mathbf{x},\mathbf{d})$, where f_k maps a random variable $\mathbf{z}_{k-1}$ into another one $\mathbf{z}_k$ with a more complex distribution. Note that the each flow f_k is conditioned on the location and view direction

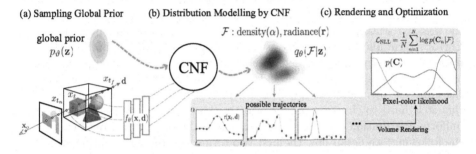

Fig. 3. (Left) We use two Conditional Normalizing Flow (CNF) to sample radiance and density values from distributions $q_\theta(\mathbf{r}|\mathbf{x}, \mathbf{d}, \mathbf{z})$ and $q_\theta(\alpha|\mathbf{x}, \mathbf{z})$, respectively. Each CNF computes a transformation of a sample from the latent distribution $q_\psi(\mathbf{z})$ conditioned to an embedding $\mathbf{h}$. This embedding which is computed by an MLP with the location-view pair $(\mathbf{x}, \mathbf{d})$ as input. (Right) Each CNF is composed by a sequence of invertible transformation functions $f_{1:K}$ conditioned on $\mathbf{h}$.

Fig. 4. Illustration of our pipeline for the inference and computation of the log-likelihood on the pixel color. (a) We sample a set of variables $\mathbf{z}$ from the global latent distribution. (b) Given each spatial location $\mathbf{x}$ along a camera ray with viewing direction $\mathbf{d}$, we can generate a set of density and radiance values by passing each $\mathbf{z}$ variable through our proposed CNF. (c) These values can be represented as a set of different density-radiance trajectories along the ray corresponding to each $\mathbf{z}$, followed by volume rendering techniques to composite each trajectory into a RGB value. Finally, these RGB values are used to compute the log-likelihood for the pixel color and also estimate the model prediction and its associated uncertainty using their mean and variance during inference.

$(\mathbf{x}, \mathbf{d})$. Finally, $\mathbf{z}_K$ is followed by a Sigmoid and Softplus activation functions for radiance and density samples, respectively. This process is detailed in Fig. 3.

Using the introduced CNF, radiance and density probabilities $q_\theta(\mathbf{r}|\mathbf{x}, \mathbf{d}, \mathbf{z})$ and $q_\theta(\alpha|\mathbf{x}, \mathbf{z})$ can be computed with the change-of-variables formula typically used in normalizing flows as:

$$q_\theta(\mathbf{r}|\mathbf{x}, \mathbf{d}, \mathbf{z}) = q_\vartheta(\mathbf{z}) \left| \det \frac{\partial \mathbf{z}}{\partial \mathbf{r}} \right| = q_\vartheta(\mathbf{z}) \left| \det \frac{\partial \mathbf{r}}{\partial \mathbf{z}_K} \right|^{-1} \prod_{k=1}^{K} \left| \det \frac{\partial \mathbf{z}_k}{\partial \mathbf{z}_{k-1}} \right|^{-1}, \quad (4)$$

where $|\det(\partial \mathbf{z}_k/\partial \mathbf{z}_{k-1})|$ measures the Jacobian determinant of the transformation function f_k. Note that $q_\theta(\alpha|\mathbf{x}, \mathbf{z})$ can be computed in a similar manner.

4.2   Optimizing Conditional-Flow NeRF

We adopt a Variational Bayesian approach to learn the parameters of the posterior distribution $q_\theta(\mathcal{F})$ defined in Eq. (3). Note that the optimized θ corresponds to the parameters of the CNFs defined in the previous section. More formally, we solve an optimization problem where we minimize the Kullback-Leibler (KL) divergence between $q_\theta(\mathcal{F})$ and the true posterior distribution $p(\mathcal{F}|\mathcal{T})$ of radiance fields given the training set:

$$\min_\theta \mathbb{KL}(q_\theta(\mathcal{F})||p(\mathcal{F}|\mathcal{T}))$$
$$= \min_\theta -\mathbb{E}_{q_\theta(\mathcal{F})} \log p(\mathcal{T}|\mathcal{F}) + \mathbb{E}_{q_\theta(\mathcal{F})} \log q_\theta(\mathcal{F}) - \mathbb{E}_{q_\theta(\mathcal{F})} \log p(\mathcal{F}). \quad (5)$$

The first term in Eq. (5) measures the expected log-likelihood of the training set $\mathcal{T}$ over the distribution of radiance fields $q_\theta(\mathcal{F})$. The second term indicates the negative Entropy of the approximated posterior. Intuitively, maximizing the Entropy term allows uncertainty estimation by preventing the optimized distribution to degenerate into a deterministic function where all the probability is assigned into a single radiance field $\mathcal{F}$. Finally, the third term corresponds to the cross-entropy between $q_\theta(\mathcal{F})$ and a prior over radiance fields $p(\mathcal{F})$. Given that it is hard to choose a proper prior in this case, we assume $p(\mathcal{F})$ to follow uniform distribution and thus, this term can be ignored during optimization. In the following, we detail how the first two terms are computed during training.

Computing the Log-Likelihood. Assuming that the training set $\mathcal{T}$ is composed by N triplets $\{\mathbf{C}_n, \mathbf{x}_n^o, \mathbf{d}_n\}$ representing the color, camera origin and view direction of a given pixel in a training image, the log-likelihood term in Eq. (5) is equivalent to: $\frac{1}{N} \sum_{n=1}^{N} \log p(\mathbf{C}_n|\mathcal{F})$. In order to compute an individual $p(\mathbf{C}_n|\mathcal{F})$ we use the following procedure.

Firstly, we sample a set of variables $\mathbf{z}^{1:K}$ from the global latent distribution $q_\vartheta(\mathbf{z})$. Secondly, given a training triplet $\{\mathbf{C}, \mathbf{x}, \mathbf{d}\}$ and a set of 3D spatial locations along a ray defined by $\mathbf{x}_t = \mathbf{x}_o + t\mathbf{d}$, we sample a set of density and radiance values $\{\alpha^{1:K}\}_{t_n:t_f}$ and $\{\mathbf{r}^{1:K}\}_{t_n:t_f}$ by using the Conditional Flow introduced in Sect. 4.1. In particular, we perform a forward pass over the flow with inputs $\mathbf{z}^k$ conditioned to $\mathbf{x}_t^*$ for all t. Subsequently, a set of K color estimates $\hat{\mathbf{C}}_{1:K}$ are obtained by using, for every k, the volume rendering formula in Eq. (1) over the sampled radiance and density values $\{\alpha^k\}_{t_n:t_f}$ and $\{\mathbf{r}^k\}_{t_n:t_f}$, respectively. Finally, with the set of obtained color estimations $\hat{\mathbf{C}}_{1:K}$, we use a non-parametric kernel density estimator as in [52] to approximate the log-likelihood $\log p(\mathbf{C}|\mathcal{F})$ of the pixel color. An illustration of this procedure is shown in Fig. 4.

Computing the Entropy Term. In order to compute the entropy term in Eq. (5), we use a Monte Carlo approximation with M samples as:

$$\mathbb{E}_{q_\theta(\mathcal{F})} \log q_\theta(\mathcal{F}) = \mathbb{E}_{q_\vartheta(\mathbf{z})} \prod_{\mathbf{x}\in\mathbb{R}^3} \prod_{\mathbf{d}\in\mathbb{R}^2} \log q_\theta(\mathbf{r}|\mathbf{x},\mathbf{d},\mathbf{z}) + \mathbb{E}_{q_\theta(\mathbf{z}^\alpha)} \prod_{\mathbf{x}\in\mathbb{R}^3} \prod_{\mathbf{d}\in\mathbb{R}^2} \log q_\theta(\alpha|\mathbf{x},\mathbf{z})$$
$$\sim \frac{1}{M} \sum_{m=1}^{M} \left(\log q_\theta(\mathbf{r}_m|\mathbf{x}_m,\mathbf{d}_m,\mathbf{z}_m) + \log q_\theta(\alpha_m|\mathbf{x}_m,\mathbf{z}_m) \right), \quad (6)$$

where $\mathbf{z}_m$ are obtained from the latent variable distribution $q_\vartheta(\mathbf{z})$ and $\{\mathbf{x}_m, \mathbf{d}_m\}$ are possible 3D locations and view directions in the scene which are randomly sampled. Finally, α_m and $\mathbf{r}_m$ are density and radiance values obtained by applying our conditional flow with inputs $(\mathbf{z}_m,\mathbf{x}_m,\mathbf{d}_m)$. Their probabilities $q_\theta(\alpha_m|\mathbf{x}_m, \mathbf{z}_m)$ and $q_\theta(\mathbf{r}_m|\mathbf{x}_m, \mathbf{d}_m, \mathbf{z}_m)$ can be computed by using Eq. (4).

4.3   Inference and Uncertainty Estimation

CF-NeRF allows us to quantify the uncertainty associated with rendered images and depth-maps. As described in Sect. 4.2, given any camera pose, we can obtain a set of color estimates $\hat{\mathbf{C}}_{1:K}$ for every pixel in a rendered image. These estimates are obtained by sampling a set of random variables $\mathbf{z}_{1:K}$ from latent distribution $q_\vartheta(\mathbf{z})$ and applying CF-NeRF. Finally, the mean and variance of the pixel colors over the K samples are treated as the predicted color and its associated uncertainty, respectively. For depth-map generation, we sample a sequence of density values $\{\alpha_k\}_{t_n:t_f}$ along a camera ray and we compute the expected termination depth of the ray as in [32]. In this way, we obtain a set of depth-values $d_{1:K}$ for each pixel in the depth-map for the rendered image. As in the case of the RGB color, its mean and variance correspond to the estimated depth and its associated uncertainty.

5   Experiments

Datasets. We conduct a set of exhaustive experiments over two benchmark databases typically used to evaluate NeRF-based approaches: the **LLFF** dataset from the original NeRF paper [32] and the Light Field **LF** dataset [66,67]. The first is composed of 8 relatively simple scenes with multiple-view forward-facing images. On the other hand, from the LF dataset we use 4 scenes: *Africa, Basket, Statue* and *Torch*. The evaluation over the LF scenes is motivated by the fact that they have a longer depth range compared to the ones in LLFF and, typically, they present more complicated geometries and appearance. As a consequence, the evaluation over LLFF gives more insights into the ability of NeRF-based methods to model complex 3D scenes. Same as [52], we use a sparse number of scene views (4∼5) for training and the last adjacent views for testing. As discussed in the cited paper, training in an extremely low-data regime is a challenging task and provides an ideal setup to evaluate the ability of the compared methods to quantify the uncertainty associated with the model predictions. While the ground truth of depth is not available in the original datasets, we compute pseudo ground truth by using the method in [60] trained on all the available views per scene.

Baselines. We compare our method with the state-of-the-art S-NeRF [52], NeRF-W [30] and two other methods, Deep-Ensembles (D.E.) [20] and MC-Dropout (Drop.) [11], which are generic approaches for uncertainty quantification in deep learning. For NeRF-W, we remove the latent embedding component

Table 1. Quality and uncertainty quantification metrics on rendered images over the LLFF dataset. Best results are shown in bold with second best underlined.

	Quality metrics			Uncertainty metrics		
	PSNR↑	SSIM↑	LPIPS↓	AUSE RMSE↓	AUSE MAE↓	NLL↓
D.E. [20]	**22.32**	<u>0.788</u>	0.236	0.0254	0.0122	1.98
Drop. [11]	21.90	0.758	0.248	0.0316	0.0162	1.69
NeRF-W [30]	20.19	0.706	0.291	0.0268	0.0113	2.31
S-NeRF [52]	20.27	0.738	<u>0.229</u>	<u>0.0248</u>	<u>0.0101</u>	<u>0.95</u>
CF-NeRF	<u>21.96</u>	**0.790**	**0.201**	**0.0177**	**0.0078**	**0.57**

of their approach and keep only the uncertainty estimation layers. For Deep-Ensembles, we train 3 different NeRF models in the ensemble in order to have a similar computational cost during training and testing compared to the rest of compared methods. In the case of MC-Dropout, we manually add one dropout layer after each odd layer in the network to sample multiple outputs using random dropout configurations. The described setup and hyper-parameters for the different baselines is the same previously employed in S-NeRF [52].

Implementations Details. In order to implement CF-NeRF and the different baselines, we inherit the same network architecture and hyper-parameters than the one employed in the original NeRF[1] implementation. In CF-NeRF, we use this architecture to compute the conditional part given $\mathbf{x}$ and $\mathbf{d}$. Since CF-NeRF uses an additional normalizing flow following this network, we add additional layers for the rest of baselines so that they have a similar computational complexity than our method. See the supplementary material for more details on hyper-parameters of our conditional normalizing flow.

Metrics. In our experiments, we address two different tasks using the compared methods: novel view synthesis and depth-map estimation. In particular, we evaluate the quality of generated images/depth-maps and the reliability of the quantified uncertainty using the following metrics:

Quality Metrics: We use standard metrics in the literature. Specifically, we report PSNR, SSIM [59], and LPIPS [68] for generated synthetic views. On the other hand, we compute RMSE, MAE and δ-threshold [9] to evaluate the quality of the generated depth-maps.

Uncertainty Quantification: To evaluate the reliability of the uncertainty estimated by each model we report two widely used metrics for this purpose. Firstly, we use the negative log likelihood (NLL) which is a proper scoring rule [20, 28] and has been previously used to evaluate the quality of model uncertainty [52]. Secondly, we evaluate the compared methods using sparsification curves [3, 42, 45]. Concretely, given an error metric (e.g. RMSE), we obtain two lists by sorting the values of all the pixels according to their uncertainty and the

---

[1] https://github.com/bmild/nerf.

computed error. By removing the top $t\%(t = 1 \sim 100)$ of the errors in each vector and repeatedly computing the average of the last subset, we can obtain the sparsification curve and the oracle curve respectively. The area between is the AUSE, which evaluates how much the uncertainty is correlated with the error.

5.1 Results over LLFF Dataset

Following a similar experimental setup than [52], we firstly evaluate the performance of the compared methods on the simple scenes in the LLFF dataset. All the views in each scene are captured in a restricted setting where all cameras are forward-facing towards a plane, which allows to use Normalized Device Coordinates (NDC) to bound all coordinates to a very small range (0–1). In Table 1, we report the performance of the different evaluated metrics averaged over all the scenes. As can be seen, S-NeRF achieves the second best performance in terms of uncertainty quantification with quality metrics comparable to the rest of baselines. These results are consistent with the results reported in their original paper and demonstrate that the expressivity of S-NeRF on these simple scenes is not severely limited by the imposed strong assumptions over the radiance field distribution. Nonetheless, our CF-NeRF still achieves a significant improvement over most of the metrics, showing the advantages of modelling the radiance field distribution using the proposed latent variable modelling and CNFs.

Table 2. Quality and uncertainty quantification metrics on rendered images over LF dataset. Best results are shown in bold with second best underlined.

Scene type	Methods	Quality metrics			Uncertainty metrics			Scene type	Quality metrics			Uncertainty metrics		
		PSNR↑	SSIM↑	LPIPS↓	AUSE RMSE↓	AUSE MAE↓	NLL↓		PSNR↑	SSIM↑	LPIPS↓	AUSE RMSE↓	AUSE MAE↓	NLL↓
Basket	D.E. [20]	25.93	0.87	0.17	0.206	0.161	1.26	Africa	23.14	0.78	0.32	0.385	0.304	2.19
	Drop. [11]	24.00	0.80	0.30	0.324	0.286	1.35		22.13	0.72	0.42	0.396	0.339	1.69
	NeRF-W [30]	19.81	0.73	0.31	0.333	0.161	2.23		21.14	0.71	0.42	0.121	0.089	1.41
	S-NeRF [52]	23.56	0.80	0.23	0.098	0.089	0.26		20.83	0.73	0.35	0.209	0.161	0.56
	CF-NeRF	26.39	0.89	0.11	0.039	0.018	−0.90		23.84	0.83	0.23	0.077	0.054	−0.25
Statue	D.E. [20]	24.57	0.85	0.21	0.307	0.214	1.53	Torch	21.49	0.73	0.43	0.153	0.101	1.80
	Drop. [11]	23.91	0.82	0.28	0.297	0.232	1.09		19.23	0.62	0.59	0.226	0.154	3.09
	NeRF-W [30]	19.89	0.73	0.41	0.099	0.071	3.03		15.59	0.56	0.69	0.132	0.131	1.52
	S-NeRF [52]	13.24	0.55	0.59	0.475	0.714	4.56		13.12	0.33	1.02	0.321	0.454	2.29
	CF-NeRF	24.54	0.87	0.16	0.040	0.019	−0.83		23.95	0.86	0.17	0.047	0.015	−0.86

Table 3. Quality and uncertainty quantification metrics on depth estimation over the LF dataset. All the results are computed from disparity values which are reciprocal to depth. Best results are shown in bold with second best underlined.

Scene type	Methods	Quality metrics			Uncertainty metrics			Scene type	Quality metrics			Uncertainty metrics		
		RMSE↓	MAE↓	δ_3↑	AUSE RMSE↓	AUSE MAE↓	NLL↓		RMSE↓	MAE↓	δ_3↑	AUSE RMSE↓	AUSE MAE↓	NLL↓
Basket	D.E. [20]	0.221	0.132	0.66	0.480	0.232	7.88	Africa	0.085	0.039	0.90	0.218	0.110	3.61
	Drop. [11]	0.241	0.153	0.43	0.297	0.157	10.96		0.216	0.141	0.31	0.544	0.503	10.36
	NeRF-W [30]	0.214	0.179	0.41	-	-	-		0.127	0.079	0.77	-	-	-
	S-NeRF [52]	0.417	0.401	0.23	0.305	0.312	8.75		0.239	0.155	0.36	0.234	0.252	6.55
	CF-NeRF	0.166	0.099	0.80	0.101	0.052	6.76		0.074	0.039	0.93	0.105	0.090	2.05
Statue	D.E. [20]	0.162	0.118	0.73	0.115	0.056	7.78	Torch	0.132	0.071	0.71	0.226	0.131	5.76
	Drop. [11]	0.197	0.128	0.59	0.164	0.109	10.89		0.263	0.173	0.06	0.982	0.809	10.84
	NeRF-W [30]	0.276	0.218	0.55	-	-	-		0.271	0.241	0.17	-	-	-
	S-NeRF [52]	0.751	0.709	0.26	0.353	0.386	11.51		0.274	0.236	0.14	0.770	1.013	8.75
	CF-NeRF	0.122	0.098	0.73	0.069	0.053	7.38		0.110	0.061	0.78	0.164	0.089	4.15

5.2   Results over LF Dataset

To further test the performance of different approaches on larger scenes with more complex appearances and geometries, we evaluate the different methods on the LF dataset. All images in these scenes have a large depth range and are randomly captured towards the target. As a consequence, coordinates cannot be normalized with NDC.

Quantitative Results. Results over rendered RGB images and estimated depth-maps for all the scenes and evaluated metrics are shown in Table 2 and Table 3, respectively. As can be seen, S-NeRF obtains poor performance in terms of quality and uncertainty estimation. This clearly shows that the imposed assumptions over the radiance fields distribution are sub-optimal in complex scenes and lead to inaccurate model predictions and unreliable uncertainty estimations. In contrast, our CF-NeRF outperforms all the previous approaches by

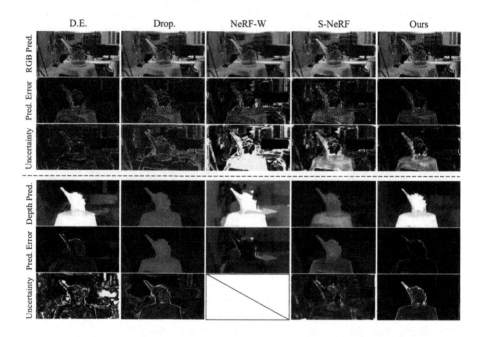

Fig. 5. Qualitative comparison between our CF-NeRF and other baselines over generated images (Top) and depth-maps (Bottom). The model prediction, its computed error with the Ground-Truth and its associated uncertainty estimation are shown respectively in each row. Larger values are shown in yellow while purple and black indicate smaller values of predicted error and uncertainty. NeRF-W is not able to generate multiple depth samples and hence cannot produce uncertainty for depth-maps. Among all these approaches, our CF-NeRF is the only approach that is able to generate both accurately rendered views and depth estimations and visually intuitive uncertainty maps which are highly correlated with the true prediction error. Refer to the supplementary materials for more visualized results. (Color figure online)

large margins across all the scenes and metrics both on image rendering and depth-maps estimation tasks. The better results obtained by our method can be explained because the use of latent variable modelling and conditional normalizing flows allows to learn arbitrarily complex radiance field distributions, which are necessary to model scenes with complicated appearance and geometry. This partly explains that our method achieves better performance, particularly an average 69% improvement compared to the second best method Deep-Ensembles on LPIPS, which measures the perceptual similarity at the image level. On the other hand, the performance of Deep-Ensembles and MC-Dropout is largely limited by the number of the trained models or dropout samples, which cannot be increased infinitely in practical cases. In contrast, the explicitly encoding of the radiance field distribution into a single probabilistic model with CF-NeRF allows to use a higher-number of samples in a more efficient manner.

Qualitative Results. In order to give more insights into the advantages of our proposed CF-NeRF, Fig. 5 shows qualitative results obtained by the compared methods on an example testing view of the LF dataset. By looking at the estimated uncertainty for RGB images, we can observe that NeRF-W obtains a higher prediction error which, additionally, is not correlated with the uncertainty estimates. On the other hand, Deep Ensembles and MC-Dropout render images with a lower predictive error compared to NeRF-W. As can be observed, however, their estimated uncertainties are noticeably not correlated with their errors. Interestingly, S-NeRF seems to obtain uncertainty estimates where the values are more correlated with the predictive error. However, the quality of the rendered image is poor, obviously shown in the background. In contrast, our CF-NeRF is the only method able to render both high-quality images and uncertainty estimates that better correlate with the prediction error.

By looking at the results for generated depth-maps, we can see that our method also obtains the most accurate depth estimates, followed by Deep Ensembles. Nonetheless, the latter generates depth maps with obvious errors in the background. Regarding the uncertainty estimation, we can observe a high correlation between the predicted error and the estimated uncertainty maps generated by our CF-NeRF. This contrasts with the rest methods which estimate low confidence values in the background of the scene inconsistent with their low prediction errors on this specific area. In conclusion, our results demonstrate the ability of our proposed method to provide both reliable uncertainty estimates and accurate model predictions.

6   Conclusion

We have presented CF-NeRF, a novel probabilistic model to address the problem of uncertainty quantification in 3D modelling using Neural Radiance Fields. In contrast to previous works employing models with limited expressivity, our method couples Latent Variable Modelling and Conditional Normalizing Flows in order to learn complex radiance fields distributions in a flexible and fully data-driven manner. In our experimental results, we show that this strategy allows

CF-NeRF to obtain significantly better results than state-of-the-art approaches, particularly on scenes with complicated appearance and geometry. Finally, it is also worth mentioning that our proposed framework can be easily combined with other NeRF-based architectures in order to provide them with uncertainty quantification capabilities.

Acknowledgements. This work is supported partly by the Chinese Scholarship Council (CSC) under grant (201906120031), by the Spanish government under project MoHuCo PID2020-120049RB-I00 and the Chistera project IPALM PCI2019-103386. We also thank Nvidia for hardware donation under the GPU grant program.

References

1. Aralikatti, R., Margam, D., Sharma, T., Thanda, A., Venkatesan, S.: Global SNR estimation of speech signals using entropy and uncertainty estimates from dropout networks. In: INTERSPEECH (2018)
2. Ashukha, A., Lyzhov, A., Molchanov, D., Vetrov, D.P.: Pitfalls of in-domain uncertainty estimation and ensembling in deep learning. In: ICLR (2020)
3. Bae, G., Budvytis, I., Cipolla, R.: Estimating and exploiting the aleatoric uncertainty in surface normal estimation. In: ICCV (2021)
4. van den Berg, R., Hasenclever, L., Tomczak, J., Welling, M.: Sylvester normalizing flows for variational inference. In: Proceedings of the Conference on Uncertainty in Artificial Intelligence (UAI) (2018)
5. Bi, S., et al.: Deep reflectance volumes: relightable reconstructions from multi-view photometric images. In: Vedaldi, A., Bischof, H., Brox, T., Frahm, J.-M. (eds.) ECCV 2020. LNCS, vol. 12348, pp. 294–311. Springer, Cham (2020). https://doi.org/10.1007/978-3-030-58580-8_18
6. Blundell, C., Cornebise, J., Kavukcuoglu, K., Wierstra, D.: Weight uncertainty in neural networks. In: ICML (2015)
7. Brachmann, E., Michel, F., Krull, A., Yang, M.Y., Gumhold, S., Rother, C.: Uncertainty-driven 6D pose estimation of objects and scenes from a single RGB image. In: CVPR (2016)
8. Djuric, N., et al.: Uncertainty-aware short-term motion prediction of traffic actors for autonomous driving. In: WACV (2020)
9. Eigen, D., Puhrsch, C., Fergus, R.: Depth map prediction from a single image using a multi-scale deep network. In: NIPS (2014)
10. Gafni, G., Thies, J., Zollhöfer, M., Nießner, M.: Dynamic neural radiance fields for monocular 4D facial avatar reconstruction. In: CVPR (2021)
11. Gal, Y., Ghahramani, Z.: Dropout as a Bayesian approximation: representing model uncertainty in deep learning. In: ICML (2016)
12. Geifman, Y., Uziel, G., El-Yaniv, R.: Bias-reduced uncertainty estimation for deep neural classifiers. In: ICLR (2019)
13. Hendrycks, D., Mazeika, M., Kadavath, S., Song, D.X.: Using self-supervised learning can improve model robustness and uncertainty. In: NeurIPS (2019)
14. Hernández, S., Vergara, D., Valdenegro-Toro, M., Jorquera, F.: Improving predictive uncertainty estimation using Dropout-Hamiltonian Monte Carlo. Soft. Comput. **24**, 4307–4322 (2020)
15. Jiakai, Z., et al.: Editable free-viewpoint video using a layered neural representation. In: ACM SIGGRAPH (2021)

16. Kajiya, J., von Herzen, B.: Ray tracing volume densities. ACM SIGGRAPH Comput. Graph. **18**, 165–174 (1984)
17. Kirsch, W.: An elementary proof of de Finetti's theorem. Stat. Probab. Lett. **151**(C), 84–88 (2019)
18. Klokov, R., Boyer, E., Verbeek, J.: Discrete point flow networks for efficient point cloud generation. In: Vedaldi, A., Bischof, H., Brox, T., Frahm, J.-M. (eds.) ECCV 2020. LNCS, vol. 12368, pp. 694–710. Springer, Cham (2020). https://doi.org/10.1007/978-3-030-58592-1_41
19. Kosiorek, A.R., et al.: NERF-VAE: a geometry aware 3D scene generative model. In: ICML (2021)
20. Lakshminarayanan, B., Pritzel, A., Blundell, C.: Simple and scalable predictive uncertainty estimation using deep ensembles. In: Advances in Neural Information Processing Systems (2017)
21. Li, Y., Li, S., Sitzmann, V., Agrawal, P., Torralba, A.: 3D neural scene representations for visuomotor control. In: CoRL (2021)
22. Li, Z., Niklaus, S., Snavely, N., Wang, O.: Neural scene flow fields for space-time view synthesis of dynamic scenes. In: CVPR (2021)
23. Liu, J., Paisley, J.W., Kioumourtzoglou, M.A., Coull, B.: Accurate uncertainty estimation and decomposition in ensemble learning. In: NeurIPS (2019)
24. Liu, L., Gu, J., Lin, K.Z., Chua, T.S., Theobalt, C.: Neural sparse voxel fields. In: NeurIPS (2020)
25. Liu, S., Zhang, X., Zhang, Z., Zhang, R., Zhu, J.Y., Russell, B.: Editing conditional radiance fields. In: ICCV (2021)
26. Lombardi, S., Simon, T., Saragih, J., Schwartz, G., Lehrmann, A., Sheikh, Y.: Neural volumes: learning dynamic renderable volumes from images. ACM Trans. Graph. **38**(4), 65:1–65:14 (2019)
27. Long, K., Qian, C., Cortes, J., Atanasov, N.: Learning barrier functions with memory for robust safe navigation. IEEE Robot. Autom. Lett. **6**(3), 1 (2021)
28. Loquercio, A., Segu, M., Scaramuzza, D.: A general framework for uncertainty estimation in deep learning. IEEE Robot. Autom. Lett. **5**(2), 3153–3160 (2020)
29. Malinin, A., Gales, M.J.F.: Predictive uncertainty estimation via prior networks. In: NeurIPS (2018)
30. Martin-Brualla, R., Radwan, N., Sajjadi, M.S.M., Barron, J.T., Dosovitskiy, A., Duckworth, D.: NeRF in the wild: neural radiance fields for unconstrained photo collections. In: CVPR (2021)
31. Mescheder, L., Oechsle, M., Niemeyer, M., Nowozin, S., Geiger, A.: Occupancy networks: learning 3D reconstruction in function space. In: CVPR (2019)
32. Mildenhall, B., Srinivasan, P.P., Tancik, M., Barron, J.T., Ramamoorthi, R., Ng, R.: NeRF: representing scenes as neural radiance fields for view synthesis. In: Vedaldi, A., Bischof, H., Brox, T., Frahm, J.-M. (eds.) ECCV 2020. LNCS, vol. 12346, pp. 405–421. Springer, Cham (2020). https://doi.org/10.1007/978-3-030-58452-8_24
33. Neal, R.M.: Bayesian Learning for Neural Networks. Springer, New York (1995)
34. Neapolitan, R.E.: Learning Bayesian networks. In: Proceedings of the 13th ACM SIGKDD International Conference on Knowledge Discovery and Data Mining (KDD) (2007)
35. Neff, T., et al.: DONeRF: towards real-time rendering of compact neural radiance fields using depth oracle networks. Comput. Graph. Forum **40**(4), 45–59 (2021)
36. Niemeyer, M., Barron, J.T., Mildenhall, B., Sajjadi, M.S.M., Geiger, A., Radwan, N.: RegNeRF: regularizing neural radiance fields for view synthesis from sparse inputs. arXiv abs/2112.00724 (2021)

37. Niemeyer, M., Mescheder, L., Oechsle, M., Geiger, A.: Occupancy flow: 4D reconstruction by learning particle dynamics. In: ICCV (2019)
38. Park, J.J., Florence, P., Straub, J., Newcombe, R.A., Lovegrove, S.: DeepSDF: learning continuous signed distance functions for shape representation. In: CVPR (2019)
39. Park, K., et al.: Nerfies: deformable neural radiance fields. In: ICCV (2021)
40. Peng, L.W., Shamsuddin, S.M.: 3D object reconstruction and representation using neural networks. In: Proceedings of the 2nd International Conference on Computer Graphics and Interactive Techniques in Australasia and South East Asia (2004)
41. Peng, S., et al.: Animatable neural radiance fields for human body modeling. In: CVPR (2021)
42. Poggi, M., Aleotti, F., Tosi, F., Mattoccia, S.: On the uncertainty of self-supervised monocular depth estimation. In: CVPR (2020)
43. Pumarola, A., Corona, E., Pons-Moll, G., Moreno-Noguer, F.: D-NeRF: neural radiance fields for dynamic scenes. In: CVPR (2021)
44. Pumarola, A., Popov, S., Moreno-Noguer, F., Ferrari, V.: C-flow: conditional generative flow models for images and 3D point clouds. In: CVPR (2020)
45. Qu, C., Liu, W., Taylor, C.J.: Bayesian deep basis fitting for depth completion with uncertainty. In: ICCV (2021)
46. Raj, A., et al.: PVA: pixel-aligned volumetric avatars. In: CVPR (2021)
47. Rebain, D., Jiang, W., Yazdani, S., Li, K., Yi, K.M., Tagliasacchi, A.: DeRF: decomposed radiance fields. In: CVPR (2020)
48. Ritter, H., Botev, A., Barber, D.: A scalable laplace approximation for neural networks. In: ICLR (2018)
49. Saito, S., Yang, J., Ma, Q., Black, M.J.: SCANimate: weakly supervised learning of skinned clothed avatar networks. In: CVPR (2021)
50. Schwarz, K., Liao, Y., Niemeyer, M., Geiger, A.: GRAF: generative radiance fields for 3D-aware image synthesis. In: NIPS (2020)
51. Shamsi, A., et al.: An uncertainty-aware transfer learning-based framework for Covid-19 diagnosis. IEEE Trans. Neural Netw. Learn. Syst. 32, 1408–1417 (2021)
52. Shen, J., Ruiz, A., Agudo, A., Moreno-Noguer, F.: Stochastic neural radiance fields: quantifying uncertainty in implicit 3D representations. In: 3DV (2021)
53. Sitzmann, V., Martel, J.N.P., Bergman, A.W., Lindell, D.B., Wetzstein, G.: Implicit neural representations with periodic activation functions. In: NIPS (2020)
54. Sitzmann, V., Zollhöfer, M., Wetzstein, G.: Scene representation networks: continuous 3D-structure-aware neural scene representations. In: NIPS (2019)
55. Su, S.Y., Yu, F., Zollhöfer, M., Rhodin, H.: A-NeRF: articulated neural radiance fields for learning human shape, appearance, and pose. In: NIPS (2021)
56. Tancik, M., et al.: Learned initializations for optimizing coordinate-based neural representations. In: CVPR (2021)
57. Tancik, M., et al.: Fourier features let networks learn high frequency functions in low dimensional domains. In: NIPS (2020)
58. Teye, M., Azizpour, H., Smith, K.: Bayesian uncertainty estimation for batch normalized deep networks. In: ICML (2018)
59. Wang, Z., Simoncelli, E., Bovik, A.: Multiscale structural similarity for image quality assessment. In: The Thirty-Seventh Asilomar Conference on Signals, Systems Computers, vol. 2, pp. 1398–1402 (2003)
60. Wei, Y., Liu, S., Rao, Y., Zhao, W., Lu, J., Zhou, J.: NerfingMVS: guided optimization of neural radiance fields for indoor multi-view stereo. In: ICCV (2021)
61. Xie, Y., et al.: Neural fields in visual computing and beyond (2021)

62. Xu, H., et al.: Digging into uncertainty in self-supervised multi-view stereo. In: ICCV (2021)
63. Yang, G., Huang, X., Hao, Z., Liu, M.Y., Belongie, S.J., Hariharan, B.: PointFlow: 3D point cloud generation with continuous normalizing flows. In: ICCV (2019)
64. Yen-Chen, L., Florence, P., Barron, J.T., Rodriguez, A., Isola, P., Lin, T.Y.: iNeRF: inverting neural radiance fields for pose estimation. In: IEEE/RSJ International Conference on Intelligent Robots and Systems (IROS) (2021)
65. Yu, A., Ye, V., Tancik, M., Kanazawa, A.: pixelNeRF: neural radiance fields from one or few images. In: CVPR (2021)
66. Yücer, K., Sorkine-Hornung, A., Wang, O., Sorkine-Hornung, O.: Efficient 3D object segmentation from densely sampled light fields with applications to 3D reconstruction. ACM Trans. Graph. **35**(3) (2016)
67. Zhang, K., Riegler, G., Snavely, N., Koltun, V.: NeRF++: analyzing and improving neural radiance fields. arXiv abs/2010.07492 (2020)
68. Zhang, R., Isola, P., Efros, A.A., Shechtman, E., Wang, O.: The unreasonable effectiveness of deep features as a perceptual metric. In: CVPR (2018)
69. Zhu, L., et al.: RGB-D local implicit function for depth completion of transparent objects. In: CVPR (2021)

Unsupervised Pose-aware Part Decomposition for Man-Made Articulated Objects

Yuki Kawana[1(✉)], Yusuke Mukuta[1,2], and Tatsuya Harada[1,2]

[1] The University of Tokyo, Tokyo, Japan
kawana@mi.t.u-tokyo.ac.jp
[2] RIKEN, Tokyo, Japan

Abstract. Man-made articulated objects exist widely in the real world. However, previous methods for unsupervised part decomposition are unsuitable for such objects because they assume a spatially fixed part location, resulting in inconsistent part parsing. In this paper, we propose PPD (unsupervised Pose-aware Part Decomposition) to address a novel setting that explicitly targets man-made articulated objects with mechanical joints, considering the part poses in part parsing. As an analysis-by-synthesis approach, We show that category-common prior learning for both part shapes and poses facilitates the unsupervised learning of (1) part parsing with abstracted part shapes, and (2) part poses as joint parameters under single-frame shape supervision. We evaluate our method on synthetic and real datasets, and we show that it outperforms previous works in consistent part parsing of the articulated objects based on comparable part pose estimation performance to the supervised baseline.

1 Introduction

Our daily life environments are populated with man-made articulated objects, ranging from furniture and household appliances such as drawers and ovens to tabletop objects such as eyeglasses and laptops. Humans are capable of recognizing such objects by decomposing them into simpler semantic parts based on part kinematics. Researchers have shown that even very young infants learn to group objects into semantic parts using the location, shape, and kinematics as a cue [37,38,42], even from a single image [18,34]. Although humans can naturally achieve such reasoning, it is challenging for machines, particularly in the absence of rich supervision.

3D part-level understanding of shapes and poses from a single frame observation has wide range of applications in computer vision and robotics. Learning to represent complex target shapes with simpler part components as a generative

---

Supplementary Information The online version contains supplementary material available at https://doi.org/10.1007/978-3-031-20062-5_32.

Fig. 1. (Left) Even through independent observations, infants can build a mental model of the articulated object for part parsing based on its kinematics. (Middle) Likewise, we propose an unsupervised generative method that learns to parse the single-frame, unstructured 3D data of articulated objects and predict the part-wise implicit fields as abstracted part shapes as well as their part poses as joint parameters. (Right) Our approach outperforms the previous works in consistent part parsing for man-made articulated objects.

approach enables applications such as structure modeling [25,33] and unsupervised 3D part parsing [7,28,29,39]. The previous unsupervised approaches have mainly focused on non-articulated objects. Because they exploit the consistent part location as a cue to group shapes into semantic parts, these approaches are unsuitable for decomposing articulated objects when considering the kinematics of *dynamic part locations*. For part pose, modeling kinematic structures as joint parameters has various applications, such as motion planning in robotic manipulation [1] and interaction with environment in augmented reality [4]. There exists a large body of works for discriminative approaches dedicated to man-made articulated objects for part pose estimation in addition to part segmentation. However, they require explicit supervision, such as segmentation labels and joint parameters [1,11,20,41,44]. Removing the need for such expensive supervision has been an important step toward more human-like representation learning [2].

In this study, as a novel problem setting, we investigate the unsupervised part decomposition task for man-made articulated objects with mechanical joints, considering part poses as *joint parameters*, in an *unsupervised fashion*. Specifically, we consider the revolute and prismatic parts with one degree-of-freedom joint state because they cover most of the kinematic types that common man-made articulated objects have [1,24,41]. This task aims to learn consistent part parsing as a generative shape abstraction approach for man-made articulated objects with various part poses from single-frame shape observation. An overview is shown in Fig. 1. Recent part decomposition studies have focused on novel part shape representations for *shape reconstruction*. In contrast, we focus on *part parsing* and *part pose modeling* as a first step to expand the current generative part decomposition's applications to man-made articulated objects in novel ways, such as part pose consistent segmentation and part pose estimation as joint parameter prediction. To realize the task, we identify the two challenges; (1) for pose-aware part decomposition, the model must consider the kinematics between possibly distant shapes to group them as a single part and (2) has to disentangle the part poses from shape supervision. A comparison with previous studies is presented in Table 1.

To address these challenges, we propose PPD (unsupervised Pose-aware Part Decomposition) that takes an unsegmented, single-frame point cloud with various underlying part poses as an input. PPD predicts abstracted part-wise shapes transformed using the estimated joint parameters as the part poses. We train PPD as an autoencoder using single-frame shape supervision. PPD employs category-common decoders to capture category-specific rest-posed part shapes and joint parameters. Learning to transform the rest-posed shapes properly disentangles shape and pose, and (2) constraining the position of the parts by the joint parameters forces shapes in distant space that share the same kinematics to be recovered as the same part. We also propose a series of losses to regularize the learning process. Furthermore, we employ non-primitive-based part shape representation and utilize deformation by part poses to induce part decomposition, in contrast to previous works that employ primitive shapes and rely on its limited expressive power as an inductive bias.

Our contributions are summarized as follows: (1) We propose a novel unsupervised generative part decomposition method for man-made articulated objects based on part kinematics. (2) We show that the proposed method learns disentangled part shape and pose: a non-primitive-based implicit field as part shape representation and the joint parameters as the part poses, using single-frame shape supervision. (3) We also demonstrate that the proposed method outperforms previous generative part decomposition methods in terms of semantic capability (parsimonious shape representation, consistent part parsing and interpretability of recovered parts) and show comparable part pose estimation performance to the supervised baseline.

Table 1. Overview of the previous works. We regard a method as unsupervised if the checked tasks can be learned only via shape supervision during training.

	Part segmentation	Joint parameter estimation	Generative	Unsupervised
ANSCH [20]	✓	✓		
A-SDF [26]	✓		✓	
Neural parts [28]	✓		✓	✓
Ours	✓	✓	✓	✓

2 Related Works

Unsupervised Part Decomposition. Existing unsupervised generative part decomposition studies mostly assume non-articulated objects in which the part shapes are in a fixed 3D location [7–9,15,27,39], or also targeting human body and hand shapes without considering part pose [28]. They induce part decomposition by limiting the expressive power of the shape decoders by employing learnable primitive shapes. Closest work of ours is BAE-Net [8], whose main focus is consistent part parsing by generative shape abstraction. It also employs a non-primitive-based implicit field as the part shape representation, similar to ours. However, it still limits the expressive power of the shape decoder using MLP with only three layers. In contrast, our approach assumes parts to be dynamic with the consistent kinematics and induces part decomposition through rigid transformation of the reconstructed part shapes with the estimated part poses to make the decomposition pose-aware.

Articulated Shape Representation. A growing number of studies have tackled the reconstruction of category-specific, articulated objects with a particular kinematic structure, such as the human body and animals. Representative works rely on the use of category-specific template models as the shape and pose prior [3,19,21,45,46]. Another body of works reconstruct target shapes without templates, such as by reconstructing a part-wise implicit field given a part pose as an input [10] or focusing on non-rigid tracking of the seen samples [5]. The recent work [26] targets man-made articulated objects and supervised part shape reconstruction. In contrast, our approach focuses on man-made articulated objects with various kinematic structures. Our approach learns the part shapes and poses during training, without any part label and pose information either as supervision or input, and is applicable to unseen samples.

Part Pose Estimation. In discriminative approaches, a number of studies have focused on the inference of part poses as joint parameters [1,20,41] targeting man-made articulated objects. These approaches require expensive annotations, such as part labels and ground-truth joint parameters. Moreover, they require category-specific prior knowledge of the kinematic structure. In contrast, our model is based on generative approach and is category agnostic. Moreover, it only requires shape supervision during training. A recent work [13] assumes an unsupervised setting where multi-frame, complete shape point clouds are available for both input and supervision signals during training and inference. Whereas our approach assumes a single-frame input and shape supervision, it also works with partial shape input during inference. Note that, in this study, the purpose of part pose estimation is, as an auxiliary task, to facilitate consistent part parsing. It is not our focus to outperform the state-of-the-art supervised approaches in part pose estimation.

3   Methods

In our approach, the goal is to represent an articulated object as a set of semantically consistent part shapes based on their underlying part kinematics. We represent the target object shape as an implicit field that can be evaluated at an arbitrary point $\mathbf{x} \in \mathbb{R}^3$ in 3D space as $O : \mathbb{R}^3 \to [0,1]$, where $\{\mathbf{x} \in \mathbb{R}^3 \mid O(\mathbf{x}) = 0\}$ defines the outside of the object, $\{\mathbf{x} \in \mathbb{R}^3 \mid O(\mathbf{x}) = 1\}$ the inside, and $\{\mathbf{x} \in \mathbb{R}^3 \mid O(\mathbf{x}) = 0.5\}$ the surface. Given a 3D point cloud $I \in \mathbb{R}^{P \times 3}$

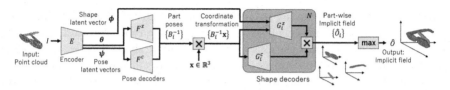

Fig. 2. Model overview. PPD infers implicit field $\hat{O}$ based on part poses $\{B_i\}$ and part-wise implicit fields $\{\hat{O}_i\}$ given input point cloud I. The category-common decoders F^c and $\{G_i^c\}$ capture part pose biases and part shape priors in constant latent vectors. Instance-dependent decoders F^z and $\{G_i^z\}$ model input specific components. Constraining the instance-dependent decoders by the category-common biases and the priors in the proposed approach realizes unsupervised part decomposition and joint parameter learning. Note we shorthand $\{*_i\}$ to denote an ordered set $\{*_i\}_{i=1}^N$ for brevity.

of P points as an input, we approximate the object shape using a composite implicit field $\hat{O}$ that is decomposed into a collection of N parts. The i-th part has an implicit field $\hat{O}_i(\mathbf{x} \mid I)$ as part shape and part pose $B_i \in \mathrm{SE}(3)$. We ensure that O is approximated as $O(\mathbf{x}) \approx \hat{O}(\mathbf{x} \mid I, \{B_i\}_{i=1}^N)$ through the losses.

An overview of PPD is shown in Fig. 2. PPD employs an autoencoder architecture, and is trained under single category setting. Given a point cloud I, the encoder derives the disentangled shape latent vector $\phi \in \mathbb{R}^m$ and the two pose latent vectors $\theta \in \mathbb{R}^n$ and $\psi \in \mathbb{R}^o$. Category-common pose decoder F^c captures joint parameter biases given ψ. Instance-dependent pose decoder F^z models residual joint parameters to the biases given θ. The part-wise category-common shape decoder G_i^c captures category-common shape prior. Given ϕ and conditioned by G_i^c, instance-dependent shape decoder G_i^z infers residual shape details of the target shape to decode a part-wise implicit field $\hat{O}_i$. We discuss the details about F^z and F^c in Sect. 3.1, and G_i^z and G_i^c in Sect. 3.2.

3.1   Part Pose Representation

We characterize part pose B_i by its part kinematic type and joint parameters. Each part kinematic type $y_i \in \{\text{fixed}, \text{prismatic}, \text{revolute}\}$ is manually set as a hyperparameter. The joint parameters consist of the joint direction $\mathbf{u}_i \in \mathbb{R}^3$ with the unit norm and joint state $s_i \in \mathbb{R}^+$. Additionally, the "revolute" part has the pivot point $\mathbf{q}_i \in \mathbb{R}^3$. We refer to the joint direction and pivot point as the joint configuration. For the "fixed" part, we set B_i as an identity matrix because no transformation is applied. For the "prismatic" part, we define $B_i = T(s_i\mathbf{u}_i)$, where $T(\cdot)$ represents a homogeneous translation matrix given the translation in $\mathbb{R}^3$, and s_i and $\mathbf{u}_i$ represent the translation amount and direction, respectively. For the "revolute" part, we set $B_i = T(\mathbf{q}_i)R(s_i, \mathbf{u}_i)$, where $R(\cdot)$ denotes a homogeneous rotation matrix given the rotation representation, and s_i and $\mathbf{u}_i$ represent the axis-angle rotation around the axis $\mathbf{u}_i$ by angle s_i. In human shape reconstruction methods using template shape, its pose is initialized to be close to the real distribution to avoid the local minima [14,19]. Inspired by these approaches, we parametrize the joint direction as $[\mathbf{u}_i; 1] = R(\mathbf{r}_i)[\mathbf{e}_i; 1]$, where $\mathbf{e}_i$ is a constant directional vector with the unit norm working as the initial joint direction as a hyperparameter and $\mathbf{r}_i \in \mathbb{R}^3$ represents the Euler-angle representation working as a residual from the initial joint direction $\mathbf{e}_i$. This allows us to manually initialize the joint direction in a realistic distribution through $\mathbf{e}_i$ by initializing $\mathbf{r}_i = \mathbf{0}$. Figure 4 illustrates the joint parameters.

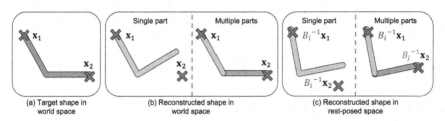

| (a) Target shape in world space | (b) Reconstructed shape in world space | (c) Reconstructed shape in rest-posed space |

Fig. 3. Illustration of part decomposition induction. "Single part" indicates that the model is degenerated to use only a single part to reconstruct the whole target shape. "Multiple parts" indicates that part decomposition is correctly induced. In (b), the "single part" model misclassifies query point $\mathbf{x}_2$ as outside, in contrast to $\mathbf{x}_1$. As shown in (c), a single part pose $\{B_i\}$ cannot correctly transform both query points inside the rest-posed shape. The "multiple parts" model successfully classifies both query points using different part poses per part. Minimizing the reconstruction loss incentivizes the model to use multiple parts and appropriate part types for $\{B_i\}$.

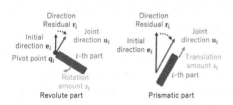

Fig. 4. Geometric relationship between the joint parameters.

Fig. 5. Visualization of the training process. The numbers in the figure show the training steps.

Based on our observations, we assume that the joint configuration has a category-common bias, while the joint state strongly depends on each instance. This is because the location of each part and the entire shape of an object can constrain the possible trajectory of the parts, which is defined by the joint configuration. To illustrate this idea, we propose to decompose the joint configuration into a category-common bias term and an instance-dependent residual term denoted as $\mathbf{r}_i = \mathbf{r}_i^c + \mathbf{r}_i^z$ and $\mathbf{q}_i = \mathbf{q}_i^c + \mathbf{q}_i^z$, respectively. We employ the category-common pose decoder $F^c(\mathrm{qt}(\boldsymbol{\psi}))$, which outputs $\{\mathbf{r}_i^c \mid i \in \mathbb{A}^p\}$ and $\{\mathbf{q}_i^c \mid i \in \mathbb{A}^r\}$, where $\mathbb{A}^p = \{i \in [N] \mid y_i \neq \text{fixed}\}$, $\mathbb{A}^r = \{i \in [N] \mid y_i = \text{revolute}\}$, $\boldsymbol{\psi}$ denotes a pose latent vector, and $\mathrm{qt}(\cdot)$ is a latent vector quantization operator following VQ-VAE [32]. The operator $\mathrm{qt}(\cdot)$ outputs the nearest constant vector to the input latent vector ψ among the N_{qt} candidates. Instead of using a single constant vector, the model selects a constant vector among multiple constant vectors to capture the discrete, multi-modal category-common biases. We also employ an instance-dependent pose decoder $F^z(\boldsymbol{\theta})$ that outputs $\{s_i \mid i \in \mathbb{A}^p\}$, $\{\mathbf{r}_i^z \mid i \in \mathbb{A}^p\}$, and $\{\mathbf{q}_i^z \mid i \in \mathbb{A}^r\}$. We constrain the possible distribution of the joint configuration around the category-common bias by the loss function explained in Sect. 3.3. This constraint incentivizes the model to reconstruct the instance-dependent shape variation by the joint state, which constrains the part location along the joint direction. This kinematic constraint biases the model to represent the shapes having the same kinematics with the same part. The previous works [9,15,29] do not impose such a constraint on the part localization, thus learned part decomposition is not necessarily consistent under different poses.

3.2   Part Shape Representation

We propose a non-primitive-based part shape representation that is decomposed into the category-common shape prior and instance-dependent shape details. We employ MLP-based decoders to model a part-wise implicit field. We capture the category-common shape prior using the category-common shape decoder $G_i^c(\mathbf{x})$. Because G_i^c does not take a latent vector from the encoder, it learns an input-independent, rest-posed part shape template as the category-common shape prior. We also employ an instance-dependent shape decoder $G_i^z(\mathbf{x} \mid \boldsymbol{\phi})$ to capture the additional instance-dependent shape details conditioned with the shape prior. We formulate a part-wise implicit field $\hat{O}_i$ as follows:

$$\hat{O}_i(\mathbf{x} \mid I) = \sigma(G_i^z(\mathbf{x}, \boldsymbol{\phi})\hat{O}_i^c(\mathbf{x})) \tag{1}$$

where $\sigma(\cdot)$ represents the sigmoid function and $\hat{O}_i^c(\mathbf{x}) = \sigma(G_i^c(\mathbf{x}))$. For brevity, we omit I in $\hat{O}_i$ and simply denote it as $\hat{O}_i(\mathbf{x})$. Given the part poses $\{B_i\}$ as part-wise locally rigid deformation, we formulate $\hat{O}$ as the composition of $\{\hat{O}_i\}$ defined as $\hat{O}(\mathbf{x} \mid I, \{B_i\}) = \max_i\{\hat{O}_i(B_i^{-1}\mathbf{x})\}$. As in the piecewise rigid model of [10], coordinate transformation $B_i^{-1}\mathbf{x}$ realizes locally rigid deformation by B_i of the part-wise implicit field by querying the rest-posed indicator. Note that, although we set the maximum number of parts N, the actual number of parts used for reconstruction can change; it is possible that some parts do not contribute to the reconstruction because of the max operation or simply because $\hat{O}_i < 0.5$ for all 3D locations.

In Eq. 1, we experimentally found that conditioning G_i^z by $\hat{O}_i^c$ through multiplication rather than addition effectively prevents G_i^z from deviating largely from G_i^c. This conditioning induces the unsupervised part decomposition. We illustrate the idea in Fig. 3. Considering reconstructing the target shape by single i-th part, since the multiplication makes it difficult to output shapes that deviating largely from the category-common prior shape, the large shape variations of target shapes are expressed by B_i regarded as the global pose of the reconstructed shape. However, the large shape variations in target shapes are due to the various local poses of multiple part shapes. Therefore, the large shape variations of target shapes cannot be expressed only by the single part and its part pose B_i. Thus, as an inductive bias of the unsupervised part decomposition, the model is incentivized to use a composition of multiple parts to express the shape variations due to various local part poses. We visualize the learning process in Fig. 5. First, the model learns high indicator values in spatial locations of static parts with high probabilities of space occupancy in any instance. Next, part decomposition is induced to accommodate various target shapes' part poses, generating multiple dynamic parts. Indicator values in the spatial locations with less displacement by different part poses (e.g., near pivot points of revolute parts) first exceed the iso-surface threshold. Then, the model simultaneously optimizes part pose estimation and shape reconstruction during training as an analysis-by-synthesis approach.

3.3 Training Losses

Shape Losses. To learn the shape decoders, we minimize the reconstruction loss using the standard binary cross-entropy loss (BCE) defined as:

$$\mathcal{L}_{\text{reconstruction}} = \lambda_{\text{reconstruction}} \text{BCE}(\hat{O}, O) + \lambda^c_{\text{reconstruction}} \text{BCE}(\hat{O}^c, O) \qquad (2)$$

where $\hat{O}^c(\mathbf{x} \mid B) = \max_i\{\hat{O}^c_i(B_i^{-1}\mathbf{x})\}$, and $\lambda_{\text{reconstruction}}$ and $\lambda^c_{\text{reconstruction}}$ are the loss weights. The second term in Eq. 2 is essential for stable training; it facilitates fast learning of $\{G^c_i\}$, so that $\{G^z_i\}$ can be correctly conditioned in the early stage of the training process. Moreover, because we consider the locally rigid deformation of the shape, the volumes of the shape before and after the deformation should not be changed by the intersection of parts; we formulate this constraint as follows:

$$\mathcal{L}_{\text{volume}} = \lambda_{\text{volume}} \bigg(\mathbb{E}_{\mathbf{x}}\Big[\text{ReLU}(\max_i\{G^z_i(B_i^{-1}\mathbf{x}, \phi)\}) \Big]$$
$$- \mathbb{E}_{\mathbf{x}}\Big[\text{ReLU}(\max_i\{G^z_i(\mathbf{x}, \phi)\}) \Big] \bigg)^2 \qquad (3)$$

Joint Parameter Losses. For the joint parameters $\mathbf{q}_i$ and $\mathbf{r}_i$, we prevent an instance-dependent term from deviating too much from the bias term, we regularize them by the loss:

$$\mathcal{L}_{\text{deviation}} = \lambda_{\text{deviation}} \bigg(\frac{1}{N^r} \sum_{i \in \mathbb{A}^r} \|\mathbf{q}^z_i\| + \frac{1}{N^p} \sum_{i \in \mathbb{A}^p} \|\mathbf{r}^z_i\| \bigg) \qquad (4)$$

where $N^r = |\mathbb{A}^r|$, $N^p = |\mathbb{A}^p|$, and $\lambda_{\text{deviation}}$ is the loss weight. Moreover, we propose a novel regularization loss that constrains the pivot point with the implicit fields. We assume that the line in 3D space, which consists of the pivot point and joint direction, passes through the reconstructed shape. The joint should connect at least two parts, which means that the joint direction anchored by the pivot point passes through at least two reconstructed parts. We realize this condition as follows:

$$\mathcal{L}_{\text{pivot}} = \frac{\lambda_{\text{pivot}}}{N^r} \sum_{i \in \mathbb{A}^r} \left(\min_{\mathbf{x} \in \mathbb{S}_{\text{GT}}} \|\mathbf{q}_i - \mathbf{x}\| + \frac{1}{2} \left(\min_{\mathbf{x} \in \mathbb{S}_i} \|\mathbf{q}_i - \mathbf{x}\| + \min_{\mathbf{x} \in \mathbb{S}_{i,j}} \|\mathbf{q}_i - \mathbf{x}\| \right) \right) \quad (5)$$

where $\mathbb{S}_{\text{GT}} = \{\mathbf{x} \in \mathbb{R}^3 \mid O(\mathbf{x}) = 1\}, \mathbb{S}_i = \{\mathbf{x} \in \mathbb{R}^3 \mid \hat{O}_i(B_i^{-1}\mathbf{x}) > 0.5\}, \mathbb{S}_{i,j} = \{\mathbf{x} \in \mathbb{R}^3 \mid \hat{O}_j(B_j^{-1}\mathbf{x}) > 0.5, j \in \mathbb{A}^r \setminus i\}$, and λ_{pivot} is the loss weight. Note that $\mathcal{L}_{\text{pivot}}$ is self-regularizing and not supervised by the ground-truth part segmentation. See supplementary material for an illustration of $\mathcal{L}_{\text{pivot}}$ and further details. To reflect the diverse part poses, we prevent the joint state s_i from degenerating into a static state. In addition, to prevent multiple decomposed parts from representing the same revolute part, we encourage the pivot points to be spatially spread. We realize these requirements by the loss defined as:

$$\mathcal{L}_{\text{variation}} = \frac{1}{N^p} \sum_{i \in \mathbb{A}^p} \left(\frac{\lambda_{\text{variation}^s}}{\text{std}(s_i)} + \lambda_{\text{variation}^q} \sum_{j \in \mathbb{A}^r \setminus i} \exp\left(-\frac{\|\mathbf{q}_i - \mathbf{q}_j\|}{v} \right) \right) \quad (6)$$

where $\text{std}(\cdot)$ denotes the batch statistics of the standard deviation, v is a constant that controls the distance between pivot points, and $\lambda_{\text{variation}^s}$ and $\lambda_{\text{variation}^q}$ are the loss weights. Lastly, following the loss proposed in [32], the pose latent vector ψ is optimized by the loss:

$$\mathcal{L}_{\text{quantization}} = \|\psi - \text{sg}(\text{qt}(\psi))\| \quad (7)$$

where sg denotes an operator stopping gradient on the backpropagation.

Adversarial Losses. Inspired by human shape reconstruction studies [6,30], we employ the adversarial losses from WGAN-GP [12] to regularize the shape and pose in the realistic distribution. The losses are defined as:

$$\mathcal{L}_{\text{discriminator}} = \lambda_{\text{discriminator}} \left(\mathbb{E}_{\tilde{\boldsymbol{x}} \sim \mathbb{P}_g}[D(\tilde{\boldsymbol{x}})] - \mathbb{E}_{\boldsymbol{x} \sim \mathbb{P}_r}[D(\boldsymbol{x})] \right)$$
$$+ \mathbb{E}_{\hat{\boldsymbol{x}} \sim \mathbb{P}_{\hat{x}}}[(\|\nabla_{\hat{\boldsymbol{x}}} D(\hat{\boldsymbol{x}})\| - 1)^2] \quad (8)$$

$$\mathcal{L}_{\text{generator}} = -\lambda_{\text{generator}} \mathbb{E}_{\tilde{\boldsymbol{x}} \sim \mathbb{P}_g}[D(\tilde{\boldsymbol{x}})] \quad (9)$$

where $D(\cdot)$ is a discriminator; $\tilde{\boldsymbol{x}}$ is a sample from the reconstructed shapes $\mathbb{P}_g$ transformed by the estimated joint configuration and randomly sampled joint state $\tilde{s}_i \sim \text{Uniform}(0, h_i)$, with the maximum motion amount h_i treated as a hyperparameter; $\boldsymbol{x}$ is a sample from the ground-truth shapes $\mathbb{P}_r$; $\hat{\boldsymbol{x}}$ is a sample from $\mathbb{P}_{\hat{x}}$, which is a set of randomly and linearly interpolated samples between $\hat{\boldsymbol{x}}$ and $\boldsymbol{x}$; and $\lambda_{\text{generator}}$ and $\lambda_{\text{discriminator}}$ are the loss weights. As an input to D, we concatenate the implicit field and corresponding 3D points to create a 4D point cloud, following [17].

3.4   Implementation Details

We use the Adam solvers [16] with a learning rate of 0.0001 with a batch size of 18 to optimize the sum of the losses: $\mathcal{L}_{\text{reconstruction}} + \mathcal{L}_{\text{volume}} + \mathcal{L}_{\text{quantization}} + \mathcal{L}_{\text{deviation}} + \mathcal{L}_{\text{pivot}} + \mathcal{L}_{\text{variation}} + \mathcal{L}_{\text{generator}}$ and the discriminator loss $\mathcal{L}_{\text{discriminator}}$, respectively. We use the complete shape point cloud with 4096 points sampled from the surface of the target shape as input, unless otherwise noted. We use 4096 coordinate points and their corresponding indicator values for the ground-truth implicit field. We set the loss weights as follows: $\lambda_{\text{reconstruction}} = 0.01$, $\lambda^c_{\text{reconstruction}} = 0.001$, $\lambda_{\text{deviation}} = 0.1$, $\lambda_{\text{pivot}} = 100$, $\lambda_{\text{variation}^s} = 0.1$, $\lambda_{\text{variation}^q} = 0.01$, $\lambda_{\text{volume}} = 1000$, $\lambda_{\text{generator}} = 0.65$, and $\lambda_{\text{discriminator}} = 0.35$. We set $v = 0.01$ in $\mathcal{L}_{\text{variation}}$ and $N_{qt} = 4$ for qt($\cdot$). For h_i in $\mathcal{L}_{\text{discriminator}}$, we set to $\frac{\pi}{2}$ and 0.4 the "revolute" and "prismatic" parts, respectively. Note that we experimentally found that it does not constrain the model to predict s_i larger than h_i to reconstruct the target shape. Because we do not impose any geometric constraints on the part shapes, we set the number of parts for each part kinematics y_i as its maximum number in the datasets plus an additional one part for over-parameterization. The detail of the datasets is explained in Sect. 4. We set $N = 8$, which consists of one "fixed" part, three "revolute" parts, and four "prismatic" parts. We use the same hyperparameter for all categories, without assuming the category-specific knowledge. During the training, the max operation is substituted with LogSumExp for gradient propagation to each shape decoder. See supplementary material for further training details.

Network Architecture. We use the PointNet [31]-based architecture from [23] as an encoder E and the one from [35] as a discriminator D. Our shape decoders $\{G^c_i\}$ and $\{G^z_i\}$ are MLP with sine activation [36] for a uniform activation magnitude suitable for propagating gradients to each shape decoder. For the category-common pose decoder F^c, we use separate networks of MLP for each kind of output variables. For the instance-dependent pose decoder F^z, we employ MLP with a single backbone having multiple output branches. The detailed network architecture can be found in supplementary material.

4   Experiments

Datasets. In our evaluation, we follow the recent part pose estimation studies targeting man-made articulated objects for the synthetic datasets and the object categories covering various part kinematics: oven, eyeglasses, laptop, and washing machine categories from Motion dataset [40], and the drawer category from SAPIEN dataset [41]. Each category has a fixed number of parts with the same kinematic structure. We generate 100 instances with different poses per sample, generating 24k instances in total. We divide the samples into the training and test sets with a ratio of approximately 8:2. We also normalize the side length of samples to 1, following [23]. Further details can be found in supplementary material. To verify the transferability of our approach trained on synthetic data to real data, we use the laptop category from RBO dataset [22] and Articulated Object Dataset [24], which is the intersecting category with the synthetic dataset.

Baselines. We compare our method with the state-of-the-art unsupervised generative part decomposition methods with various characteristics: BAE-Net [7] (non-primitive-based part shape representation), BSP-Net [7] (primitive-based part shape representation with part localization by 3D space partitioning), NSD [15] and Neural Parts [28] denoted as NP (primitive-based part shape representation with part localization in $\mathbb{R}^3$). For BSP-Net, we train up to 32^3 grids of the implicit field instead of 64^3 grids in the original implementation to match those used by other methods. For NSD and Neural Parts, we replace its image encoder with the same PointNet-based encoder in our approach. For the part pose estimation, we use NPCS [20] as the supervised baseline. NPCS performs part-based registration by iterative rigid-body transformation, which is a common practice in articulated pose estimation of rigid objects. See supplementary material for further training details of the baselines.

Metrics. For the quantitative evaluation of the consistent part parsing as a part segmentation task, we use the standard label IoU, following the previous studies [7–9,15]. As our method is unsupervised, we follow the standard initial part labeling procedure using a training set to assign each part a ground-truth label for evaluation purposes following [9,15]. A detailed step can be found in supplementary material. For the part pose evaluation, we evaluate the 3D motion flow of the deformation from the canonical pose to the predicted pose as the endpoint error (EPE) [43], which is a commonly used metric for pose estimation of articulated objects [5,40]. We scale it by 100 in experiment results.

Table 2. Part segmentation performance in label IoU. Higher is better. The starred numbers indicate the failure of part decomposition and that only one recovered part represents the entire shape. The average and the predefined maximum numbers of recovered parts or primitives are shown before and after the slash, in the last column.

	Drawer	Eye-glasses	Oven	Laptop	Washing machine	Mean	# of parts
BAE [8]	6.25*	11.11*	73.06	25.11*	80.30	39.17	1.42/8
BSP [7]	66.31	**70.69**	81.65	76.68	87.92	76.65	27.50/256
NSD [15]	38.39	42.11	74.67	74.44	89.11	63.75	10
NP [28]	60.57	64.69	**85.41**	86.23	74.65	74.31	5
Ours	**74.73**	66.18	82.07	**86.81**	**95.15**	**80.99**	4.16/8

4.1   Semantic Capability

We evaluate the semantic capability of our approach in part parsing. As part decomposition approaches aim to learn 3D structure reasoning with *as small a number of ground-truth labels as possible*, it is preferable to obtain the initial manual annotations with as *few numbers of shapes* as possible. This requirement is essential for articulated objects, which have diverse shape variations owing to the different articulations. As our approach is part pose consistent, we only need a minimal variety of instances for the initial manual labeling. To verify this, we evaluate the part segmentation performance using only the canonically posed (joint states were all zero) samples in the training set. See supplementary material for further studies on pose variation for the initial annotation.

The evaluation results are shown in Table 2. Our model uses a much smaller number of parts than BSP-Net [7]; however, it still performs the best. This shows that our model is more parsimonious, and each part has more semantic meaning in part parsing. The segmentation results are visualized in Fig. 6. To eliminate differences in the number of parts and primitives for each method, Table 3 shows the result when each method's maximum number of parts and primitives is aligned to $N = 8$. Our method outperforms the previous works by a large margin. For visualization procedure and additional results of our part segmentation result, see supplementary material.

We also visualize the generated part shapes in Fig. 7. We can see that a single part shape successfully reconstructs the complex target shape, such as disconnected shapes that a single primitive shape cannot express. Also, our part shapes are more semantic and interpretable than the previous works. This demonstrates the advantage of using non-primitive-based part shape representation. As we can see in the improved part segmentation performance, our approach realizes semantically more consistent part decomposition without a complicated mechanism such as grouping primitive shapes based on part kinematics.

Disentanglement Between the Part Shapes and Poses. Because our approach disentangles shape supervision into part shapes and poses, it realizes pose-aware part decomposition. To verify the learned disentanglement, we visualize the interpolation results of part shapes and joint states as part poses in Fig. 8. In the middle row, we show the shape interpolation between the source and the target while fixing the joint state s_i of the source to maintain the same part pose. The shape is smoothly deformed from the source to the target maintaining the original pose. In the bottom row, we interpolate the joint state s_i between the source and the target; the joint state changes from the source to the target maintaining the shape identity of the source shape. Our model successfully disentangles the part shapes and poses, unlike previous methods as shown in the top row.

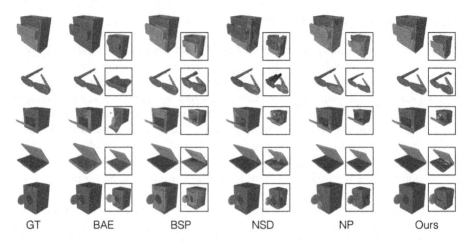

GT   BAE   BSP   NSD   NP   Ours

Fig. 6. Visualization of the part segmentation. Reconstructed shape in mesh is shown inside a box. The same color indicates the same segmentation part. (Color figure online)

Table 3. Label IoU with the aligned number of primitives and parts for all methods ($N = 8$).

	Label IoU ↑
BAE [8]	39.17
BSP [7]	66.79
NSD [15]	59.46
NP [28]	70.71
Ours	**80.99**

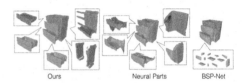

Ours   Neural Parts   BSP-Net

Fig. 7. Visualization of parts and primitives. The boxes represent the parts or primitives used to reconstruct the semantic parts.

4.2 Part Pose Estimation

To validate whether the predicted part decomposition is based on the reasonable part pose estimation, we quantitatively evaluate part pose estimation. Because we train our model without specifying a canonically posed shape, we use the part pose transformations between the target instance and the canonically posed instance of the same sample as the estimated part pose to align with the prediction of the supervised baseline, NPCS [20]. Note that NPCS assumes that part segmentation supervision and ground-truth of part-wise rigid-body transformations as part pose are available during training, and part kinematic type per part is known, which we do not assume. Therefore, NPCS offers an upper bound for our unsupervised approach. We present the evaluation results in Table 4. Our method is comparable with NPCS, with the same order of performance. Note again that we are not attempting to outperform supervised pose estimation methods; rather, we aim to show that our unsupervised approach can decom-

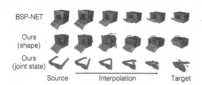

Source   Interpolation   Target

Fig. 8. Interpolation in terms of disentangled part shapes and joint states as part pose.

Table 4. Part pose estimation performance in EPE. Lower is better. NPCS is trained with ground-truth for both part labels and part-wise rigid-body transformations as part pose, offering an upper bound for our unsupervised approach.

	Drawer	Eye-glasses	Oven	Laptop	Washing machine	mean
NPCS [20] (supervised)	1.598	1.087	2.702	0.751	1.594	1.546
Ours (unsupervised)	3.452	2.631	3.360	2.546	2.529	2.903

Table 5. Ablation study of the losses and the proposed components: VQ, CP and CS indicates disabling the use of multiple constant vectors introduced in Sect. 3.1, the category-common pose decoder, and the category-common shape decoders, respectively. "Full" means using all the losses and the components.

	$\mathcal{L}_{\text{volume}}$	$\mathcal{L}_{\text{deviation}}$	$\mathcal{L}_{\text{pivot}}$	$\mathcal{L}_{\text{variation}}$	$\mathcal{L}_{\text{generator}}$	VQ	CS	CP	Full
Label IoU ↑	72.20	73.21	74.27	65.29	70.14	72.78	55.67	71.35	**80.99**
EPE ↓	4.362	6.628	9.250	6.676	7.276	10.772	8.827	7.219	**2.988**

pose parts based on reasonable part pose estimation. See supplementary material for further discussion on part pose estimation.

4.3 Ablation Studies

We evaluate the effect of the proposed losses, the multiple constant vectors for multi-modal category-common pose bias learning, and the category-common decoders on part segmentation and part pose estimation. We disable each loss and component one at a time. We only use the corresponding instance-dependent decoder(s) when disabling the category-common decoders for pose and shape. The results are shown in Table 5. Enabling all losses and the components performs the best. Particularly, disabling the category-common shape decoders significantly degrades both label IoU and EPE. This indicates that learning category-common shape prior is essential to perform proper part decomposition and to facilitate part pose learning, which is the core idea of this study.

Table 6. Comparison between the point cloud input types: complete shape and depth map.

	Label IoU ↑	EPE ↓
Complete	80.99	2.903
Depth	80.65	3.203

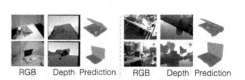

RGB   Depth Prediction   RGB   Depth Prediction

Fig. 9. Real depth map input. (Left) RBO dataset [22] and (Right) Articulated Object Dataset [24].

4.4   Depth Map Input and Real Data

Because PPD's decoders do not assume a complete shape as an input, it works with depth map input. Following BSP-Net [7], we train a new encoder that takes a depth map captured from various viewpoints as a partial point cloud and replace the original encoder. We minimize the mean squared error between the output latent vectors of the original and the new encoders so that their output are close for the same target shape. The results are shown in Table 6. The depth map input performs comparably to the complete point cloud input. We also verify that our model trained on synthetic depth maps reasonably generalizes to real data, as shown in Fig. 9.

5   Conclusion

We propose a novel unsupervised generative part decomposition method, PPD, for man-made articulated objects considering part kinematics. We show that the proposed method learns the disentangled representation of the part-wise implicit field as the decomposed part shapes and the joint parameters of each part as the part poses. We also show that our approach outperforms previous generative part decomposition methods in terms of semantic capability and show comparable part pose estimation performance with the supervised baseline.

As shown in qualitative results, our generative method achieves reasonable part shape reconstruction reflecting target shape variations sufficient to induce part decomposition and challenging joint parameter learning. As a limitation, our method currently fails to capture details of the target shapes up to the primitive-based previous works [7,15], focusing on the shape reconstruction performance rather than part pose consistency. Also, joint parameter learning requires manual initialization of joint direction and part types for each part. The future work will address the above limitation.

Acknowledgements. We would like to thank Atsuhiro Noguchi, Hao-Wei Yeh, Haruo Fujiwara, Qier Meng, Tomu Hirata, Yang Li, and Yusuke Kurose for their insightful feedback. We also appreciate the members of the Machine Intelligence Laboratory for constructive discussion during the research meetings. This work was partially supported by JST AIP Acceleration Research JPMJCR20U3, Moonshot R&D JPMJPS2011, CREST JPMJCR2015, JSPS KAKENHI JP19H01115, and Basic Research Grant (Super AI) of Institute for AI and Beyond of the University of Tokyo.

References

1. Abbatematteo, B., Tellex, S., Konidaris, G.: Learning to generalize kinematic models to novel objects. In: Proceedings of the Conference on Robot Learning (CoRL), pp. 1289–1299 (2020)
2. Becker, S., Hinton, G.E.: Self-organizing neural network that discovers surfaces in random-dot stereograms. Nature **355**(6356), 161–163 (1992)

3. Bogo, F., Kanazawa, A., Lassner, C., Gehler, P., Romero, J., Black, M.J.: Keep it SMPL: automatic estimation of 3D human pose and shape from a single image. In: Leibe, B., Matas, J., Sebe, N., Welling, M. (eds.) ECCV 2016. LNCS, vol. 9909, pp. 561–578. Springer, Cham (2016). https://doi.org/10.1007/978-3-319-46454-1_34
4. Bonanni, L., Lee, C.H., Selker, T.: Counterintelligence: augmented reality kitchen. In: Proceedings of the ACM Conference on Human Factors in Computing Systems (CHI), vol. 2239, p. 45 (2005)
5. Božič, A., Palafox, P., Zollhöfer, M., Thies, J., Dai, A., Nießner, M.: Neural deformation graphs for globally-consistent non-rigid reconstruction. In: Proceedings of the IEEE/CVF Conference on Computer Vision and Pattern Recognition (CVPR), pp. 1450–1459 (2021)
6. Chen, C.H., Tyagi, A., Agrawal, A., Drover, D., Stojanov, S., Rehg, J.M.: Unsupervised 3D pose estimation with geometric self-supervision. In: Proceedings of the IEEE/CVF Conference on Computer Vision and Pattern Recognition (CVPR), pp. 5714–5724 (2019)
7. Chen, Z., Tagliasacchi, A., Zhang, H.: BSP-Net: generating compact meshes via binary space partitioning. In: Proceedings of the IEEE/CVF Conference on Computer Vision and Pattern Recognition (CVPR), pp. 45–54 (2020)
8. Chen, Z., Yin, K., Fisher, M., Chaudhuri, S., Zhang, H.: BAE-Net: branched autoencoder for shape co-segmentation. In: Proceedings of the IEEE/CVF International Conference on Computer Vision (CVPR), pp. 8490–8499 (2019)
9. Deng, B., Genova, K., Yazdani, S., Bouaziz, S., Hinton, G., Tagliasacchi, A.: CvxNet: Learnable convex decomposition. In: Proceedings of the IEEE/CVF Conference on Computer Vision and Pattern Recognition (CVPR), pp. 31–44 (2020)
10. Deng, B., et al.: NASA neural articulated shape approximation. In: Vedaldi, A., Bischof, H., Brox, T., Frahm, J.-M. (eds.) ECCV 2020. LNCS, vol. 12352, pp. 612–628. Springer, Cham (2020). https://doi.org/10.1007/978-3-030-58571-6_36
11. Desingh, K., Lu, S., Opipari, A., Jenkins, O.C.: Factored pose estimation of articulated objects using efficient nonparametric belief propagation. In: 2019 International Conference on Robotics and Automation (ICRA), pp. 7221–7227 (2019). https://doi.org/10.1109/ICRA.2019.8793973
12. Gulrajani, I., Ahmed, F., Arjovsky, M., Dumoulin, V., Courville, A.C.: Improved training of Wasserstein GANs. In: Advances in Neural Information Processing Systems (NeurIPS), pp. 5769–5779 (2017)
13. Huang, J., et al.: MultiBodySync: multi-body segmentation and motion estimation via 3D scan synchronization. In: Proceedings of the IEEE/CVF Conference on Computer Vision and Pattern Recognition (CVPR), pp. 7108–7118 (2021)
14. Kanazawa, A., Black, M.J., Jacobs, D.W., Malik, J.: End-to-end recovery of human shape and pose. In: Proceedings of the IEEE Conference on Computer Vision and Pattern Recognition (CVPR), pp. 7122–7131 (2018)
15. Kawana, Y., Mukuta, Y., Harada, T.: Neural star domain as primitive representation. In: Advances in Neural Information Processing Systems (NeurIPS), pp. 7875–7886 (2020)
16. Kingma, D.P., Ba, J.: Adam: a method for stochastic optimization. arXiv preprint arXiv:1412.6980 (2014)
17. Kleineberg, M., Fey, M., Weichert, F.: Adversarial generation of continuous implicit shape representations. In: Eurographics, pp. 41–44 (2020)
18. Kourtzi, Z., Kanwisher, N.: Activation in human MT/MST by static images with implied motion. J. Cogn. Neurosci. **12**(1), 48–55 (2000)

19. Kulkarni, N., Gupta, A., Fouhey, D.F., Tulsiani, S.: Articulation-aware canonical surface mapping. In: Proceedings of the IEEE/CVF Conference on Computer Vision and Pattern Recognition (CVPR), pp. 452–461 (2020)
20. Li, X., Wang, H., Yi, L., Guibas, L.J., Abbott, A.L., Song, S.: Category-level articulated object pose estimation. In: Proceedings of the IEEE/CVF Conference on Computer Vision and Pattern Recognition (CVPR), pp. 3706–3715 (2020)
21. Loper, M., Mahmood, N., Romero, J., Pons-Moll, G., Black, M.J.: SMPL: a skinned multi-person linear model. ACM Trans. Graph. (TOG) 34(6), 1–16 (2015)
22. Martín-Martín, R., Eppner, C., Brock, O.: The RBO dataset of articulated objects and interactions. arXiv preprint arXiv:1806.06465 (2018)
23. Mescheder, L., Oechsle, M., Niemeyer, M., Nowozin, S., Geiger, A.: Occupancy networks: learning 3D reconstruction in function space. In: Proceedings of the IEEE/CVF Conference on Computer Vision and Pattern Recognition (CVPR), pp. 4460–4470 (2019)
24. Michel, F., Krull, A., Brachmann, E., Ying Yang, M., Gumhold, S., Rother, C.: Pose estimation of kinematic chain instances via object coordinate regression. In: Proceedings of the British Machine Vision Conference (BMVC), pp. 181.1–181.11 (2015)
25. Mo, K., et al.: StructEdit: learning structural shape variations. In: Proceedings of the IEEE/CVF Conference on Computer Vision and Pattern Recognition (CVPR), pp. 8859–8868 (2020)
26. Mu, J., Qiu, W., Kortylewski, A., Yuille, A., Vasconcelos, N., Wang, X.: A-SDF: learning disentangled signed distance functions for articulated shape representation. In: Proceedings of the IEEE/CVF International Conference on Computer Vision, pp. 13001–13011 (2021)
27. Paschalidou, D., van Gool, L., Geiger, A.: Learning unsupervised hierarchical part decomposition of 3D objects from a single RGB image. In: Proceedings IEEE/CVF Conference on Computer Vision and Pattern Recognition (CVPR) (2020)
28. Paschalidou, D., Katharopoulos, A., Geiger, A., Fidler, S.: Neural parts: learning expressive 3D shape abstractions with invertible neural networks. In: Proceedings of the IEEE/CVF Conference on Computer Vision and Pattern Recognition (CVPR), pp. 3204–3215 (2021)
29. Paschalidou, D., Ulusoy, A.O., Geiger, A.: Superquadrics revisited: learning 3D shape parsing beyond cuboids. In: Proceedings of the IEEE/CVF Conference on Computer Vision and Pattern Recognition (CVPR), pp. 10344–10353 (2019)
30. Pavllo, D., Feichtenhofer, C., Grangier, D., Auli, M.: 3D human pose estimation in video with temporal convolutions and semi-supervised training. In: Proceedings of the IEEE/CVF Conference on Computer Vision and Pattern Recognition (CVPR), pp. 7753–7762 (2019)
31. Qi, C.R., Su, H., Mo, K., Guibas, L.J.: PointNet: deep learning on point sets for 3D classification and segmentation. In: Proceedings of the IEEE Conference on Computer Vision and Pattern Recognition (CVPR), pp. 652–660 (2017)
32. Razavi, A., Oord, A.v.d., Vinyals, O.: Generating diverse high-fidelity images with VQ-VAE-2. arXiv preprint arXiv:1906.00446 (2019)
33. Roberts, D., Danielyan, A., Chu, H., Golparvar-Fard, M., Forsyth, D.: LSD-StructureNet: modeling levels of structural detail in 3D part hierarchies. In: Proceedings of the IEEE/CVF International Conference on Computer Vision, pp. 5836–5845 (2021)
34. Shirai, N., Imura, T.: Implied motion perception from a still image in infancy. Exp. Brain Res. 232(10), 3079–3087 (2014). https://doi.org/10.1007/s00221-014-3996-8

35. Shu, D.W., Park, S.W., Kwon, J.: 3D point cloud generative adversarial network based on tree structured graph convolutions. In: Proceedings of the IEEE/CVF International Conference on Computer Vision (ICCV) (2019)
36. Sitzmann, V., Martel, J., Bergman, A., Lindell, D., Wetzstein, G.: Implicit neural representations with periodic activation functions. In: Advances in Neural Information Processing Systems (NeurIPS), pp. 7462–7473 (2020)
37. Slater, A., Morison, V., Town, C., Rose, D.: Movement perception and identity constancy in the new-born baby. Br. J. Dev. Psychol. **3**(3), 211–220 (1985)
38. Spelke, E.S., Kestenbaum, R., Simons, D.J., Wein, D.: Spatiotemporal continuity, smoothness of motion and object identity in infancy. Br. J. Dev. Psychol. **13**(2), 113–142 (1995)
39. Tulsiani, S., Su, H., Guibas, L.J., Efros, A.A., Malik, J.: Learning shape abstractions by assembling volumetric primitives. In: Proceedings of the IEEE Conference on Computer Vision and Pattern Recognition (CVPR), pp. 2635–2643 (2017)
40. Wang, X., Zhou, B., Shi, Y., Chen, X., Zhao, Q., Xu, K.: Shape2Motion: joint analysis of motion parts and attributes from 3D shapes. In: Proceedings of the IEEE/CVF Conference on Computer Vision and Pattern Recognition (CVPR), pp. 8876–8884 (2019)
41. Xiang, F., et al.: SAPIEN: a simulated part-based interactive environment. In: Proceedings of the IEEE/CVF Conference on Computer Vision and Pattern Recognition (CVPR), pp. 11097–11107 (2020)
42. Xu, F., Carey, S.: Infants' metaphysics: the case of numerical identity. Cogn. Psychol. **30**(2), 111–153 (1996)
43. Yan, Z., Xiang, X.: Scene flow estimation: a survey. arXiv preprint arXiv:1612.02590 (2016)
44. Yi, L., Huang, H., Liu, D., Kalogerakis, E., Su, H., Guibas, L.: Deep part induction from articulated object pairs. ACM Trans. Graph. (TOG) **37**(6), 1–15 (2018)
45. Zuffi, S., Kanazawa, A., Berger-Wolf, T., Black, M.J.: Three-D Safari: learning to estimate zebra pose, shape, and texture from images "in the wild". In: Proceedings of the IEEE/CVF International Conference on Computer Vision (CVPR), pp. 5359–5368 (2019)
46. Zuffi, S., Kanazawa, A., Jacobs, D.W., Black, M.J.: 3D menagerie: modeling the 3D shape and pose of animals. In: Proceedings of the IEEE Conference on Computer Vision and Pattern Recognition (CVPR), pp. 6365–6373 (2017)

MeshUDF: Fast and Differentiable Meshing of Unsigned Distance Field Networks

Benoît Guillard$^{(\boxtimes)}$, Federico Stella, and Pascal Fua

CVLab, EPFL, Lausanne, Switzerland
{benoit.guillard,federico.stella,pascal.fua}@epfl.ch

Abstract. Unsigned Distance Fields (UDFs) can be used to represent non-watertight surfaces. However, current approaches to converting them into explicit meshes tend to either be expensive or to degrade the accuracy. Here, we extend the marching cube algorithm to handle UDFs, both fast and accurately. Moreover, our approach to surface extraction is differentiable, which is key to using pretrained UDF networks to fit sparse data.

1 Introduction

In recent years, deep implicit surfaces [8,27,29] have emerged as a powerful tool to represent and manipulate watertight surfaces. Furthermore, for applications that require an explicit 3D mesh, such as sophisticated rendering including complex physical properties [28] or optimizing physical performance [4], they can be used to parameterize explicit 3D meshes whose topology can change while preserving differentiability [1,16,31]. However, these approaches can only handle watertight surfaces. Because common 3D datasets such as ShapeNet [7] contain non-watertight meshes, one needs to preprocess them to create a watertight outer shell [29,34]. This is time consuming and ignores potentially useful inner components, such as seats in a car. An alternative is to rely on network initialization or regularization techniques to directly learn from raw data [2,3] but this significantly slows down the training procedure.

This therefore leaves open the problem of modeling non-watertight surfaces implicitly. It has been shown in [11,13,33,35] that occupancy fields and signed distance functions (SDFs) could be replaced by unsigned ones (UDFs) for this purpose. However, unlike for SDFs, there are no fast algorithms to directly mesh UDFs. Hence, these methods rely on a two-step process that first extracts a dense point cloud that can then be triangulated using slow standard techniques [5]. Alternatively, non-watertight surfaces can be represented as watertight thin ones surrounding them [13,16,33]. This amounts to meshing the ϵ iso-surface of an

Supplementary Information The online version contains supplementary material available at https://doi.org/10.1007/978-3-031-20062-5_33.

S. Avidan et al. (Eds.): ECCV 2022, LNCS 13663, pp. 576–592, 2022.
https://doi.org/10.1007/978-3-031-20062-5_33

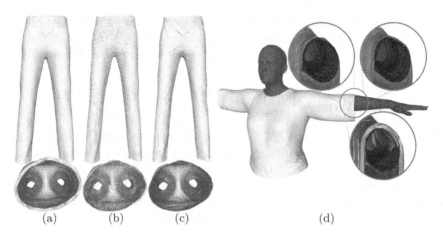

Fig. 1. Meshing the UDF of a garment. We present front and top views. **(a)** Inflating shapes to turn open surfaces into watertight ones [13,16,33] inherently reduces accuracy by making the surface thicker, as shown in top view. **(b)** Triangulating a cloud of 3D points collapsed on the 0-levelset [11] is time-consuming and tends to produce rough surfaces. **(c)** Directly meshing the UDF using our approach is more accurate and less likely to produce artifacts. In addition, it makes the iso-surface extraction process differentiable. **(d)** We mesh the UDF of a shirt and display it on a human body. The three insets represent the ground truth shirt, the reconstruction with our method, and the inflation approach, respectively. Our approach—in the upper right inset—produces fewer artifacts and no penetrations with the body.

UDF using marching cubes [26], for ϵ being a small strictly positive scalar. Unfortunately, that degrades reconstruction accuracy because the thin surfaces cannot be infinitely so, as ϵ cannot be arbitrarily small. Furthermore, some applications such as draping simulation [17,21,32] require surfaces to be single-faced and cannot be used in conjunction with this approach.

In this paper, we first show that marching cubes can be extended to UDFs by reasoning on their gradients. When neighboring gradients face in opposite directions, this is evidence that a surface element should be inserted between them. We rely on this to replace the sign flips on which the traditional marching cube algorithm depends and introduce a new approach that exploits the gradients instead. This yields vertices and facets. When the UDF is parameterized by latent vectors, we then show that the 3D position of these vertices can be differentiated with respect to the latent vectors. This enables us to fit the output of pre-trained networks to sparse observations, such as 3D points on the surface of a target object or silhouettes of that object.

In short, our contribution is a new approach to meshing UDFs and parameterizing 3D meshes to model non-watertight surfaces whose topology can change while preserving differentiability, which is something that had only been achieved for watertight surfaces before. We use it in conjunction with a learned shape prior to optimize fitting to partial observations via gradient descent. We demonstrate it achieves better reconstruction accuracy than current deep-learning based approaches to handling non-watertight surfaces, in a fraction of the computation time, as illustrated by Fig. 1. Our code is publicly available at https:// github.com/cvlab-epfl/MeshUDF/.

2   Related Work

Deep implicit surfaces [8,27,29] have proved extremely useful to model watertight surfaces using occupancy grids and SDFs, while non-watertight surfaces can be handled either using UDFs or inflating an SDF around them. As meshing almost always involves using a version of the classic marching cube algorithm [26], we discuss these first. We then review recent approaches to representing non-watertight surfaces using implicit surfaces.

Triangulating an Implicit Field. Marching cubes was originally proposed in [26] and refined in [10,22,25] to triangulate the 0-isosurface of a 3D scalar field. It marches sequentially across cubic grid cells and if field values at neighboring corners have opposing signs, triangular facets are created according to a manually defined lookup table. Vertices of these triangle facets are adjusted by linear interpolation over the field values. Since then, newer methods have been developed such as dual methods [19]. They are better at triangulating surfaces with sharp edges at the expense of increased complexity and requiring a richer input. Hence, due to its simplicity and flexibility, along with the availability of efficient implementations, the original algorithm of [22] remains in wide use [18,27,29,30,34]. More recently, [9] proposed a data driven approach at improving sharp features reconstructed by marching cubes. Even though marching cubes is not differentiable, it has been shown that gradients can be estimated for surface points, thus allowing backpropagation [1,31]. However, this approach requires surface normals whose orientation is unambiguous, which makes it impractical when dealing with non-watertight surfaces.

Triangulating Implicit Non-watertight Surfaces. Unfortunately, neither the original marching cubes algorithm nor any of its recent improvements are designed to handle non-watertight surfaces. One way around this is to surround the target surface with a thin watertight one [13,16,33], as shown in Fig. 1(a). One can think of the process as *inflating* a watertight surface around the original one. Marching cubes can then be used to triangulate the inflated surface, but the result will be some distance away from the target surface, resulting in a loss of accuracy. Another approach is to sample the minimum level set of an UDF field, as in NDF [11] and AnchorUDF [35]. This is done by projecting randomly initialized points on the surface using gradient descent. To ensure full coverage, points are re-sampled and perturbed during the process. This produces a cloud, but not a triangulated mesh with information about the connectivity of neighboring points. Then the ball-pivoting method [5], which connects neighboring points one triplet at a time, is used to mesh the cloud, as shown in Fig. 1(b). It is slow and inherently sequential.

3   Method

We now present our core contribution, a fast and differentiable approach to extracting triangulated isosurfaces from unsigned distance fields produced by a neural network. Let us consider a network that implements a function

$$\phi : \mathbb{R}^C \times \mathbb{R}^3 \rightarrow \mathbb{R}^+, \tag{1}$$
$$\mathbf{z}, \mathbf{x} \mapsto s,$$

where $\mathbf{z} \in \mathbb{R}^C$ is a parameter vector; $\mathbf{x}$ is a 3D point; s is the Euclidean distance to a surface. Depending on the application, $\mathbf{z}$ can either represent only a latent code that parameterizes the surface or be the concatenation of such a code and the network parameters. In Sect. 3.1, we propose an approach to creating a triangulated mesh $M = (V, F)$ with vertices V and facets F from the 0-levelset of the scalar field $\phi(\mathbf{z}, \cdot)$. Note that it could also apply to non-learned UDFs, as shown in the supplementary material. In Sect. 3.2, we show how to make the vertex coordinates differentiable with respect to $\mathbf{z}$. This allows refinement of shape codes or network parameters with losses directly defined on the mesh.

3.1   From UDF to Triangulated Mesh

Surface Detection Within Cells. As in standard marching cubes [26], we first sample a discrete regular grid G in the region of interest, typically $[-1, 1]^3$. At each location $\mathbf{x}_i \in G$ we compute

$$u_i = \phi(\mathbf{z}, \mathbf{x}_i), \qquad \mathbf{g}_i = \nabla_{\mathbf{x}} \phi(\mathbf{z}, \mathbf{x}_i),$$

where u_i is the unsigned distance to the implicit surface at location $\mathbf{x}_i$, and $\mathbf{g}_i \in \mathbb{R}^3$ is the gradient computed using backpropagation. Given a cubic cell and its 8 corners, let $(u_1, ..., u_8)$, $(\mathbf{x}_1, ..., \mathbf{x}_8)$, and $(\mathbf{g}_1, ..., \mathbf{g}_8)$ be the above values in each one. Since all u_i are positive, a surface traversing a cell does not produce a sign flip as it does when using an SDF. However, when corners $\mathbf{x}_i$ and $\mathbf{x}_j$ lie on opposite sides of the 0-levelset surface, their corresponding vectors $\mathbf{g}_i$ and $\mathbf{g}_j$ should have opposite orientations, provided the surface is sufficiently smooth within the cell. Hence, we define a *pseudo-signed distance*

$$s_i = \mathrm{sgn}(\mathbf{g}_1 \cdot \mathbf{g}_i) u_i, \tag{2}$$

where $\mathbf{x}_1$ is one of the cell corners that we refer to as the *anchor*. $\mathbf{x}_1$ is assigned a positive pseudo-signed distance and corners where the gradient direction is opposite to that at $\mathbf{x}_1$ a negative one. When there is at least one negative s_i, we use marching cubes' disjunction cases and vertex interpolation to reconstruct a triangulated surface in the cell. Computing pseudo-signs in this way is simple but has two shortcomings. First, it treats each cell independently, which may cause inconsistencies in the reconstructed facets orientations. Second, especially when using learned UDF fields that can be noisy [33], the above smoothness

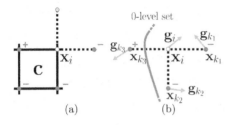

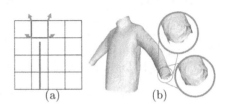

Fig. 2. Voting. (a) Corner $\mathbf{x}_i$ of cell **c** has 3 neighbors that already have a pseudo-sign and vote. (b) The projections of $\mathbf{g}_i$ and $\mathbf{g}_{k_1}$ on the edge connecting the two neighbors face each other. Thus $\mathbf{x}_{k_1}$ votes for $\mathbf{x}_i$ having the same sign as itself $(-)$. The other two neighbors vote for $-$ as well given the result of computing Eq. 3.

Fig. 3. Removing artifacts. (a) Given the blue 0-level surface, the red cell has gradients in opposing directions and yields an undesirable face. We prune these by evaluating the UDF on reconstructed faces. (b) Initially reconstructed borders are uneven (top). We smooth them during post-processing (bottom). (Color figure online)

assumption may not hold within the cells. This typically results in holes in the reconstructed meshes.

To mitigate the first problem, our algorithm starts by exploring the 3D grid until it finds a cell with at least one negative pseudo-sign. It then uses it as the starting point for a breadth-first exploration of the surface. Values computed at any cell corner are stored and never recomputed, which ensures that the normal directions and interpolated vertices are consistent in adjacent cells. The process is repeated to find other non-connected surfaces, if any. To mitigate the second problem we developed a more sophisticated method to assign a sign to each cell corner. We do so as described above for the root cell of our breadth-first search, but we use the voting scheme depicted by Fig. 2 for the subsequent ones. Voting is used to aggregate information from neighboring nodes to estimate pseudo-sign more robustly. Each corner $\mathbf{x}_i$ of a cell under consideration receives votes from all adjacent grid points $\mathbf{x}_k$ that have already been assigned a pseudo-sign, based on the relative directions of their gradients and the pseudo-sign of $\mathbf{x}_k$. Since gradients locally point towards the greatest ascent direction, if the projections of $\mathbf{g}_i$ and $\mathbf{g}_k$ along the edge connecting $\mathbf{x}_i$ and $\mathbf{x}_k$ face each other, there is no surface between them and the vote is in favor of them having the same sign: $v_{ik} = \mathrm{sgn}(s_k)$. Otherwise, the vote depends on gradient directions and we take it to be

$$v_{ik} = (\mathbf{g}_i \cdot \mathbf{g}_k)\mathrm{sgn}(s_k) \tag{3}$$

because the more the gradients are aligned, the more confident we are about the two points being on the same side of the surface or not, depending on the sign of the dot product. The sign of the sum of the votes is assigned to the corner.

If one of the $\mathbf{x}_k$ is zero-valued its vote does not contribute to the scheme, but it means that there is a clear surface crossing. This can happen when meshing learned UDF fields at higher resolutions, because their 0-level set can have a non-negligible volume. Thus, the first non-zero grid point along its direction takes its place in the voting scheme, provided that it has already been explored. To further increase the reliability of these estimates, grid points with many disagreeing votes are put into a lower priority queue to be considered later, when more nearby grid points have been evaluated and can help produce a more consistent sign estimate. In practice we only perform these computations within cells whose average UDF values of $(u_1, ..., u_8)$ are small. Others can be ignored, thus saving computation time and filtering bad cell candidates which have opposing gradients but lie far from the surface.

Global Surface Triangulation. The facets that the above approach yields are experimentally consistent almost everywhere, except for a small number of them, which we describe below and can easily remove in a post-processing stage. Note that the gradients we derive in Sect. 3.2 do not require backpropagation through the iso-surface extraction. Hence, this post-processing step does not compromise differentiability.

Removing Spurious Facets and Smoothing Borders. As shown in Fig. 3(a), facets that do not correspond to any part of the surfaces can be created in cells with gradients pointing in opposite directions without intersecting the 0-levelset. This typically happens near surface borders because our approach tends to slightly extend them, or around areas with poorly approximated gradients far from the surface in the case of learned UDF fields. Such facets can be detected by re-evaluating the distance field on all vertices. If the distance field for one vertex of a face is greater than half the side-length of a cubic cell, it is then eliminated. Moreover, since marching cubes was designed to reconstruct watertight surfaces, it cannot handle surface borders. As a result, they appear slightly jagged on initial reconstructions. To mitigate this, we apply Laplacian smoothing on the edges belonging to a single triangle. This smoothes borders and qualitatively improves reconstructions, as shown in Fig. 3(b).

3.2 Differentiating Through Iso-Surface Extraction

Let $\mathbf{v} \in \mathbb{R}^3$ be a point on a facet reconstructed using the method of Sect. 3.1. Even though differentiating $\mathbf{v}$ directly through marching cubes is not possible [23,31], it was shown that if ϕ were an SDF instead of an UDF, derivatives could be obtained by reasoning about surface inflation and deflation [1,31]. Unfortunately, for an UDF, there is no "in" or "out" and its derivative is undefined on the surface itself. Hence, this method does not directly apply. Here we extend it so that it does, first for points strictly within the surface, and then for points along its boundary.

Derivatives within the Surface. Let us assume that $\mathbf{v} \in \mathbb{R}^3$ lies within a facet where the surface normal $\mathbf{n}$ is unambiguously defined up to its orientation. Let us pick a small scalar value $\alpha > 0$ and consider

$$\mathbf{v}_+ = \mathbf{v} + \alpha\mathbf{n} \quad \text{and} \quad \mathbf{v}_- = \mathbf{v} - \alpha\mathbf{n},$$

the two closest points to $\mathbf{v}$ on the α-levelset on both sides of the 0-levelset. For α small enough, the outward oriented normals at these two points are close to being $\mathbf{n}$ and $-\mathbf{n}$. We can therefore use the formulation of [1,31] to write

$$\frac{\partial \mathbf{v}_+}{\partial \mathbf{z}} \approx -\mathbf{n}\frac{\partial \phi}{\partial \mathbf{z}}(\mathbf{z}, \mathbf{v}_+) \quad \text{and} \quad \frac{\partial \mathbf{v}_-}{\partial \mathbf{z}} \approx \mathbf{n}\frac{\partial \phi}{\partial \mathbf{z}}(\mathbf{z}, \mathbf{v}_-). \tag{4}$$

(a)   (b)

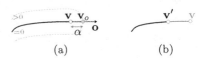

(a)   (b)

Fig. 5. Iso-surface shrinkage or extension: (a) with $\mathbf{v}$ on the border of the 0-levelset, we place $\mathbf{v}_o$ at a distance α in the direction of $\mathbf{o}$; (b) If the UDF increases at $\mathbf{v}_o$, $\mathbf{v}$ moves to $\mathbf{v}'$.

Fig. 4. Iso-surface deformation: (a) $\mathbf{v}$ on the 0-levelset, $\mathbf{v}_+$ and $\mathbf{v}_-$ at distance α; (b) $\mathbf{v}$ moves to $\mathbf{v}'$ if the UDF decreases at $\mathbf{v}_+$ and increases at $\mathbf{v}_-$.

Since $\mathbf{v} = \frac{1}{2}(\mathbf{v}_- + \mathbf{v}_+)$, Eq. 4, yields

$$\frac{\partial \mathbf{v}}{\partial \mathbf{z}} \approx \frac{\mathbf{n}}{2}\left[\frac{\partial \phi}{\partial \mathbf{z}}(\mathbf{z}, \mathbf{v} - \alpha\mathbf{n}) - \frac{\partial \phi}{\partial \mathbf{z}}(\mathbf{z}, \mathbf{v} + \alpha\mathbf{n})\right]. \tag{5}$$

We provide a more formal proof and discuss the validity of the approximation in appendix. Note that using $\mathbf{n}' = -\mathbf{n}$ instead of $\mathbf{n}$ yields the same result. Intuitively, this amounts to surrounding the 0-levelset with α-margins where UDF values can be increased on one side and decreased on the other, which allows local deformations perpendicular to the surface. Figure 4(a) depicts the arrangement of $\mathbf{v}$, $\mathbf{v}_+$ and $\mathbf{v}_-$ around the surface. The derivative of Eq. 5 implies that infinitesimally increasing the UDF value at $\mathbf{v}_-$ and decreasing it at $\mathbf{v}_+$ would push $\mathbf{v}$ in the direction of $\mathbf{n}$, as shown in Fig. 4(b), and conversely. In practice, we use $\alpha = 10^{-2}$ in all our experiments.

Derivatives at the Surface Boundaries. Let us now assume that $\mathbf{v}$ sits on the edge of a boundary facet. Mapping it to $\mathbf{v}_+$ and $\mathbf{v}_-$ and using the derivatives of Eq. 5 would mean that all deformations are perpendicular to that facet. Thus, it does not permit shrinking or expanding of the surface during shape optimization. In this setting, there is a whole family of closest points to $\mathbf{v}$ in the α-levelset;

they lay on a semicircle with radius α. To allow for shrinkage and expansion, we map $\mathbf{v}$ to the semicircle point along $\mathbf{o}$, a vector perpendicular to the edge, pointing outwards, and within the plane defined by the facet. Hence, we consider the point $\mathbf{v}_o$ which is the closest to $\mathbf{v}$ on the α-levelset in the direction of $\mathbf{o}$:

$$\mathbf{v}_o = \mathbf{v} + \alpha\mathbf{o} \tag{6}$$

For α small enough, the outward oriented normal at $\mathbf{v}_o$ is $\mathbf{o}$ and we again use the formulation of [1,31] and Eq. 6 to write

$$\frac{\partial \mathbf{v}_o}{\partial \mathbf{z}} = -\mathbf{o}\frac{\partial \phi}{\partial \mathbf{z}}(\mathbf{z}, \mathbf{v}_o) \text{ and } \frac{\partial \mathbf{v}}{\partial \mathbf{z}} = -\mathbf{o}\frac{\partial \phi}{\partial \mathbf{z}}(\mathbf{z}, \mathbf{v} + \alpha\mathbf{o}), \tag{7}$$

which we use for all points $\mathbf{v}$ on border edges. As shown in Fig. 5, this implies that increasing the UDF value at $\mathbf{v}_o$ would push $\mathbf{v}$ inwards and make the surface shrink. Conversely, decreasing it extends the surface in the direction of $\mathbf{o}$.

4 Experiments

We demonstrate our ability to mesh UDFs created by deep neural networks. To this end, we first train a deep network to map latent vectors to UDFs representing different garments, that is, complex open surfaces with many different topologies. We then show that, given this network, our approach can be used to effectively triangulate these garments and to model previously unseen ones. Next, we plug our triangulation scheme into existing UDF networks and show that it is a straightforward operation. Finally, the benefit of the border gradients of Sect. 3.2 is evaluated. The voting scheme proposed in Sect. 3.1 is ablated in appendix, where more qualitative results are also shown.

4.1 Network and Metrics

Our approach is designed to triangulate the output of networks that have been trained to produce UDF fields. To demonstrate this, we use an auto-encoding approach [29] with direct supervision on UDF samples on the MGN dataset [6] to train a network ϕ_θ that maps latent vectors of dimension 128 to UDFs that represent garments. These UDFs can in turn be triangulated using our algorithm to produce meshes such as those of Fig. 1. We provide details of this training procedure in the supplementary material. The MGN dataset comprises 328 meshes. We use 300 to train ϕ_θ and the remaining 28 for testing. For comparison purposes, we also use the publicly available pre-trained network of NDF [11] that regresses UDF from sparse input point clouds. It was trained on raw ShapeNet [7] meshes, without pre-processing to remove inner components make them watertight or consistently orient facets.

To compare the meshes we obtain to the ground-truth ones, we evaluate the following three metrics (details in the supplementary material):

- The **Chamfer distance** (CHD) measures the proximity of 3D points sampled from the surfaces, the lower the better.
- The **Image consistency** (IC) is the product of IoU and cosine similarity of 2D renderings of normal maps from 8 viewpoints, the higher the better.
- The **Normal consistency** (NC) quantifies the agreement of surface normals in 3D space, the higher the better.

4.2 Mesh Quality and Triangulation Speed

Figure 1 was created by triangulating a UDF produced by ϕ_θ using either our meshing procedure (*Ours*) or one of two baselines:

- *BP*. It applies the ball-pivoting method [5] implemented in [12] on a dense surface sampling of $900k$ points, as originally proposed in [11] and also used in [35]. Surface points are obtained by gradient descent on the UDF field.
- *Inflation* [13,16,33]. It uses standard marching cubes to mesh the ϵ-isolevel of the field, with $\epsilon > 0$.

Table 1. Comparing UDF meshing methods. Average Chamfer (CHD), image consistency (IC), normal consistency (NC) and processing time for 300 garments (left) and 300 ShapeNet cars (right). We use a single UDF network in each case and only change the meshing procedure. For BP, we decompose the time into sampling and meshing times.

	Garments, ϕ_θ network			Cars, NDF network [11]		
	BP	*Inflation*	*Ours*	*BP*	*Inflation*	*Ours*
CHD ($\downarrow$)	1.62	3.00	**1.51**	6.84	11.24	**6.63**
IC (%, $\uparrow$)	92.51	88.48	**92.80**	90.50	87.09	**90.87**
NC (%, $\uparrow$)	89.50	94.16	**95.50**	61.50	**73.19**	70.38
Time ($\downarrow$)	16.5 s + 3000 s	**1.0 s**	1.2 s	24.7 s + 8400 s	**4.8 s**	7.1 s

In Table 1 (left), we report metrics on the 300 UDF fields $\phi_\theta(\mathbf{z}_i, \cdot)$ for which we have latent codes resulting from the above-mentioned training. *Inflation* and *Ours* both use a grid size of 128^3 over the $[-1,1]^3$ bounding box, and we set *Inflation*'s ϵ to be 55% of marching cubes' step size. In Table 1 (right) we also report metrics for the pretrained NDF network [11] tested on 300 ShapeNet cars, in which case we increase *Inflation* and *Ours* resolution to 192^3 to account for more detailed shapes. An example is shown in Fig. 9 The experiments were run on a NVidia V100 GPU with an Intel Xeon 6240 CPU.

As shown on the left of Table 1, *Ours* is slightly more accurate than *NDF* in terms of all three metrics, while being orders of magnitude faster. *Inflation* is even faster—this reflects the overhead our modified marching cube algorithm imposes—but far less accurate. To show that this result is not specific to garments, we repeated the same experiment on 300 cars from the ShapeNet dataset and report the results on the right side of Table 1. The pattern is the same except for NC, which is slightly better for *Inflation*. We conjecture this to be a byproduct of the smoothing provided by *Inflation*, which is clearly visible in Fig. 1(a,c). To demonstrate that these results do not depend on the specific marching cube grid resolution we chose, we repeated the experiment for grid resolutions ranging from 64 to 512 and plot the average CHD as a function of resolution in Fig. 6. It remains stable over the whole range. For comparison purposes, we also repeated the experiment with *Inflation*. Each time we increase the resolution, we take the ϵ value that defines the iso-surface to be triangulated to be 10% greater than half the grid-size, as shown in Fig. 7. At very high resolution, the accuracy of *Inflation* approaches *Ours* but that also comes at a high-computational cost because operating on $512 \times 512 \times 512$ cubes instead of $128 \times 128 \times 128$ ones is much slower, even when using multi-resolution techniques.

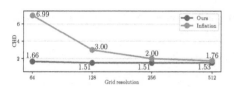

Fig. 6. CHD as a function of grid resolution. between reconstructed and ground truth meshes, averaged over the 300 training garments of MGN. *Ours* yields constantly accurate meshes, *Inflation* deforms the shapes at low resolutions.

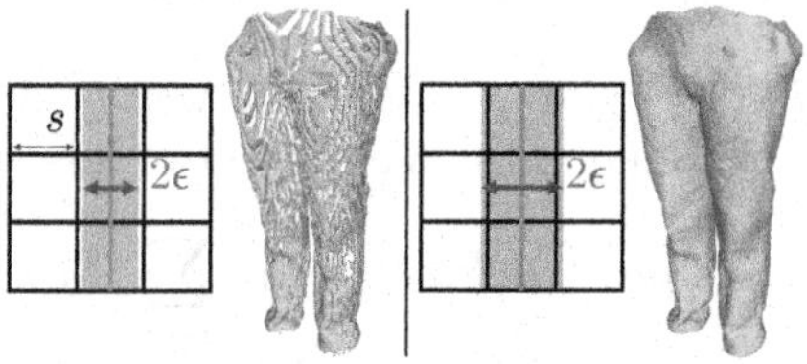

Fig. 7. Choosing ϵ for *Inflation*. When meshing a UDF's ϵ iso-level with standard marching cubes, the value of ϵ is lower bounded by half the step size s. **Left:** $2\epsilon < s$ yields many large holes. **Right:** $2\epsilon \geq s$ yields a watertight mesh.

4.3   Using Differentiability to Fit Sparse Data

Given the trained network ϕ_θ and latent codes for training shapes from Sect. 4.2, we now turn to recovering latent codes for the remaining 28 test garments. For each test garment G_j, given the UDF representing it, this would be a simple matter of minimizing the mean square error between it and the field $\phi_\theta(\mathbf{z}, \cdot)$ with respect to $\mathbf{z}$, which does not require triangulating. We therefore consider the more challenging and more realistic cases where we are only given either small set of 3D points P_j—in practice we use 200 points—or silhouettes and have to find a latent vector that generates the UDF that best approximates them.

Table 2. Fitting to sparse point clouds. The table shows average Chamfer (CHD), image consistency (IC), and normal consistency (NC) wrt. ground truth test garments. We report metrics for un-optimized latent codes (*Init.*), after optimizing ($\mathcal{L}_{PC,mesh}$) using our method, and optimizing either $\mathcal{L}_{PC,UDF}$ or $\widetilde{\mathcal{L}}_{PC,UDF}$ in the implicit domain. **(a)** A sparsely sampled ground truth mesh. **(b)** Mesh reconstructed by minimizing $\mathcal{L}_{PC,mesh}$, **(c)** $\mathcal{L}_{PC,UDF}$, **(d)** $\widetilde{\mathcal{L}}_{PC,UDF}$.

(a)   (b)   (c)   (d)

	Init.	$\mathcal{L}_{PC,mesh}$	$\mathcal{L}_{PC,UDF}$	$\widetilde{\mathcal{L}}_{PC,UDF}$
CHD ($\downarrow$)	20.45	**3.54**	4.54	4.69
IC (%,$\uparrow$)	69.54	**84.84**	82.80	82.31
NC (%,$\uparrow$)	74.54	**86.85**	80.68	86.35

Fitting to 3D Points. One way to do this is to remain in the implicit domain and to minimize one of the two loss functions

$$\mathcal{L}_{PC,UDF}(P_j, \mathbf{z}) = \tfrac{1}{|P_j|} \sum_{p \in P_j} |\phi_\theta(\mathbf{z}, p)|, \tag{8}$$

$$\widetilde{\mathcal{L}}_{PC,UDF}(P_j, \mathbf{z}) = \mathcal{L}_{PC,UDF}(P_j, \mathbf{z}) + \tfrac{1}{|A|} \sum_{a \in A} |\phi_\theta(\mathbf{z}, a) - \min_{p \in P_j} \|a - p\|_2 |,$$

where A is a set of randomly sampled points. Minimizing $\mathcal{L}_{PC,UDF}$ means that the given P_j points must be on the zero-level surface of the UDF. Minimizing $\widetilde{\mathcal{L}}_{PC,UDF}$ means that, in addition, the predicted UDF evaluated at points of A must match the approximated UDF computed from P_j. Since the latter is sparse, $\widetilde{\mathcal{L}}_{PC,UDF}$ only provides an approximate supervision.

An alternative is to use our approach to triangulate the UDFs and minimize the loss function

$$\mathcal{L}_{PC,mesh}(P_j, \mathbf{z}) = \tfrac{1}{|P_j|} \sum_{p \in P_j} \min_{a \in M_{\mathbf{z}}} \|a - p\|_2, \tag{9}$$

where $a \in M_{\mathbf{z}}$ means sampling 10k points a on the triangulate surface of $M_{\mathbf{z}}$. Minimizing $\mathcal{L}_{PC,mesh}$ means that the chamfer distance between the triangulated surfaces and the sample points should be small. Crucially, the results of Sect. 3.2 guarantee that $\mathcal{L}_{PC,mesh}$ is differentiable with respect to $\mathbf{z}$, which makes minimization practical. We tried minimizing the three loss functions defined above. In each case we started the minimization from a randomly chosen latent vector for a garment of the same type as the one we are trying to model, which corresponds to a realistic scenario if the initial estimate is provided by an upstream network. We report our results in Table 2. Minimizing $\mathcal{L}_{PC,mesh}$ clearly yields the best results, which highlights the usefulness of being able to triangulate and to differentiate the result.

Table 3. Fitting to silhouettes. Average Chamfer (CHD), image consistency (IC), and normal consistency (NC) wrt. ground truth test garments. We report metrics for un-optimized latent codes (*Init.*), using our method to minimize ($\mathcal{L}_{silh,mesh}$), and by minimizing ($\mathcal{L}_{silh,UDF}$) in the implicit domain. **(a)** Mesh reconstructed by minimizing $\mathcal{L}_{silh,mesh}$. **(b,c)** Superposition of a target silhouette (light gray) and of the reconstructions (dark gray) by minimizing $\mathcal{L}_{silh,UDF}$ or $\mathcal{L}_{silh,mesh}$. Black denotes perfect alignment and shows that the $\mathcal{L}_{silh,UDF}$ mesh is much better aligned.

	Init.	$\mathcal{L}_{silh,mesh}$	$\mathcal{L}_{silh,UDF}$
CHD	20.45	**9.68**	12.74
IC	69.54	**79.90**	74.46
NC	74.54	**81.37**	80.70

(a)   (b)   (c)

Fitting to Silhouettes. We now turn to the problem of fitting garments to rasterized binary silhouettes. Each test garment j is rendered into a front-facing binary silhouette $S_j \in \{0,1\}^{256 \times 256}$. Given S_j only, our goal is to find the latent code $\mathbf{z}_j$ that best encodes j. To this end, we minimize

$$\mathcal{L}_{silh,mesh}(S_j, \mathbf{z}) = L_1(rend(M_\mathbf{z}), S_j), \tag{10}$$

where *rend* is a differentiable renderer [20] that produces a binary image of the UDF triangulation $M_\mathbf{z}$ and $L_1(\cdot)$ is the L_1 distance. Once again, the differentiability of $M_\mathbf{z}$ with respect to $\mathbf{z}$ is key to making this minimization practical.

In theory, instead of rendering a triangulation, we could have used an UDF differential renderer. Unfortunately, we are not aware of any. Approaches such as that of [24] rely on finding sign changes and only work with SDFs. In contrast, CSP-Net [33] can render UDFs without meshing them but is not differentiable. To provide a baseline, we re-implemented SMPLicit's strategy [13] for fitting a binary silhouette by directly supervising UDF values. We sample a set of points $P \subset [-1,1]^3$, and project each $p \in P$ to S_j using the front-facing camera $\mathbf{c}$ to get its projected value s_p. If $s_p = 1$, point p falls within the target silhouette, otherwise it falls into the background. SMPLicit's authors advocate optimizing $\mathbf{z}$ by summing

$$\mathcal{L}_{silh,UDF}(S_j, \mathbf{z}) = \begin{cases} |\phi_\theta(\mathbf{z}, p) - d_{max}| & \text{if } s_p = 0 \\ \min_{\bar{p} \text{ s.t. } \mathbf{c}(\bar{p}) = \mathbf{c}(p)} |\phi_\theta(\mathbf{z}, \bar{p})| & \text{if } s_p = 1 \end{cases}. \tag{11}$$

on $p \in P$. That is, points projecting outside the silhouette ($s_p = 0$) should have a UDF value equal to the clamping value d_{max}. For points projecting inside the silhouette, along a camera ray we only consider $\bar{p}$, the closest point to the current garment surface estimate and its predicted UDF value should be close to 0. We report our results in Table 3. Minimizing $\mathcal{L}_{silh,mesh}$ yields the best results, which highlights the benefits of pairing our method with a differentiable mesh renderer.

Ablation Study. We re-ran the optimizations without the border derivative term of Eq. 7, that is, by computing the derivatives everywhere using the expression

Table 4. Ablation Study. Average Chamfer (CHD), image consistency (IC), and normal consistency (NC) for test garments using either our full approach to computing gradients (*normals + border*) vs. computing the gradients everywhere using only the formula of Eq. 5 (*normals*).

Fitting	Metric	Gradients: *normals*	Gradients: *normals + border*
Point cloud, $\mathcal{L}_{PC,mesh}$	CHD	3.75	**3.54**
	NC	84.28	**84.84**
	IC	86.71	**86.76**
Silhouette, $\mathcal{L}_{silh,mesh}$	CHD	10.45	**9.68**
	IC	78.84	**79.90**
	NC	80.86	**81.37**

of Eq. 5. As can be seen in Table 4, this reduces performance and confirms the importance of allowing for shrinkage and expansion of the garments.

4.4   Differentiable Topology Change

A key feature of all implicit surface representations is that they can represent surfaces whose topology can change. As shown in Fig. 8, our approach allows us to take advantage of this while simultaneously creating a mesh whose vertices have associated spatial derivatives. To create this example, we started from a latent code for a pair of pants and optimized with respect to it to create a new surface that approximates a sweater by minimizing the CHD loss of Eq. 9 over 10k 3D points on that sweater. The topology changes that occur on the mesh representing the deforming shape do not create any difficulties.

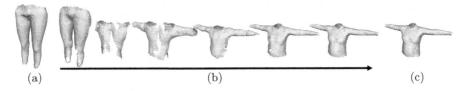

(a)   (b)   (c)

Fig. 8. Optimization with a change in topology: (a) Starting mesh associated to the initial latent code $\mathbf{z} = \mathbf{z}_{start}$; **(b)** Optimizing $\mathbf{z}$ with gradient descent by applying a 3D Chamfer loss between the reconstructed mesh and a target shape shown in **(c)**. During optimization, the latent code takes values that do not correspond to valid garments, hence the tears in our triangulations. Nevertheless, it eventually converges to the desired shape.

Fig. 9. Using our approach to triangulate the outputs of NDF [11] **(left) and AnchorUDF** [35] **(right).** In both cases, we display the input to the network, a point cloud in one case and a color image in the other, the dense cloud of points that is the final output of these methods, and a triangulation of the UDF they compute generated using our method. (Color figure online)

4.5   Generalization to Other UDF Networks

To show that our meshing procedure is applicable as-is to other UDF-based methods, we use it downstream of publicly available pre-trained networks. In Fig. 9 (bottom) we mesh the outputs of the garment reconstruction network of AnchorUDF [35]. In Fig. 9 (top) we apply it to the point cloud completion pipeline of NDF [11]. Both these methods output dense point clouds surface, which must then be meshed using the time-costly ball pivoting algorithm. Instead, our method can directly mesh the UDF and does so in a fraction of the time while preserving differentiability. That makes the whole algorithm suitable for inclusion into an end-to-end differentiable pipeline.

4.6   Limitations

Reliance on Learned UDF Fields. The proposed method can mesh the zero-surface of an unsigned distance field. In practice however, UDF fields are approximated with neural networks, and we find it difficult to learn a sharp 0-valued surface for networks with small capacities. It can for example happen that the approximate UDF field is not reaching zero, or that the zero surface thickens and becomes a volume, or that the gradients are not approximated well enough. In such cases, artifacts such as single-cell holes can appear when using our method at a high resolution. Note that applying our method to a real UDF would not exhibit such issues. By comparison however, applying marching cubes on an approximate and poorly learned SDF is more robust since it only requires the field to be continuous and to have a zero crossing to produce artifact-free surfaces. UDF networks could be made more accurate by using additional loss terms [15] or an adaptive training procedure [14], but this research direction is orthogonal to the method proposed in this paper. Moreover, similarly to [31] for SDFs, since the proposed gradients rely on the field being an UDF, they cannot be used to train a neural network from scratch. This would require network initialization or regularization strategies to ensure it regresses valid UDF fields, a topic we see as an interesting research direction.

Limitations of Marching Cubes. After locally detecting surface crossings via the pseudo-sign computation, we rely on standard marching cubes for meshing an open surface, which implies the need of a high resolution grid to detect high frequency details, and cubic scalability over grid resolution. Moreover, marching cubes was designed to handle watertight surfaces, and as a consequence some topological cases are missing, for example at surface borders or intersections. This could be remedied by detecting and handling such new cases with additional disjunctions. Finally, the breadth-first exploration of the surface makes the orientation of adjacent facets consistent with each other. However, non-orientable surfaces such as Möbius-strips would intrinsically produce juncture points with inconsistent orientations when two different branches of the exploration reach each other. In such points, our method can produce holes. Similarly, marching cubes has geometric guarantees on the topology of reconstructed meshes, but this is not true for the proposed method since there is no concept of *inside* and *outside* in UDFs.

5   Conclusion

We have shown that deep-implicit non-watertight surfaces expressed in terms of unsigned distance functions could be effectively and differentiably triangulated. This provides an explicit parameterization of such surfaces that can be integrated in end-to-end differentiable pipelines, while retaining all the strengths of implicit representations, mainly that a network can accurately represent shapes with different topologies (jeans, sweater...) from the same latent space. In future work, we will explore how it can be used to jointly optimize the pose and clothes of people wearing loose attire.

Acknowledgment. This project was supported in part by the Swiss National Science Foundation.

References

1. Atzmon, M., Haim, N., Yariv, L., Israelov, O., Maron, H., Lipman, Y.: Controlling neural level sets. In: Advances in Neural Information Processing Systems (2019)
2. Atzmon, M., Lipman, Y.: SAL: sign agnostic learning of shapes from raw data. In: Conference on Computer Vision and Pattern Recognition (2020)
3. Atzmon, M., Lipman, Y.: SALD: sign agnostic learning with derivatives. In: International Conference on Learning Representations (2020)
4. Baqué, P., Remelli, E., Fleuret, F., Fua, P.: Geodesic convolutional shape optimization. In: International Conference on Machine Learning (2018)
5. Bernardini, F., Mittleman, J., Rushmeier, H., Silva, C., Taubin, G.: The ball-pivoting algorithm for surface reconstruction. IEEE Trans. Visual Comput. Graphics 5(4), 349–359 (1999)
6. Bhatnagar, B.L., Tiwari, G., Theobalt, C., Pons-Moll, G.: Multi-garment net: learning to dress 3D people from images. In: International Conference on Computer Vision (2019)
7. Chang, A., et al.: ShapeNet: an information-rich 3D model repository. arXiv Preprint (2015)

8. Chen, Z., Zhang, H.: Learning implicit fields for generative shape modeling. In: Conference on Computer Vision and Pattern Recognition (2019)
9. Chen, Z., Zhang, H.: Neural marching cubes. ACM Trans. Graphics (Spec. Issue SIGGRAPH Asia) **40**(6), 1–15 (2021)
10. Chernyaev, E.V.: Marching cubes 33: construction of topologically correct isosurfaces. Institute for High Energy Physics, Moscow, Russia, Report CN/95-17 (1995)
11. Chibane, J., Mir, A., Pons-Moll, G.: Neural unsigned distance fields for implicit function learning. In: Advances in Neural Information Processing Systems (2020)
12. Cignoni, P., Callieri, M., Corsini, M., Dellepiane, M., Ganovelli, F., Ranzuglia, G.: MeshLab: an open-source mesh processing tool. In: Eurographics Italian Chapter Conference (2008)
13. Corona, E., Pumarola, A., Alenya, G., Pons-Moll, G., Moreno-Noguer, F.: SMPLicit: topology-aware generative model for clothed people. In: Conference on Computer Vision and Pattern Recognition (2021)
14. Duan, Y., Zhu, H., Wang, H., Yi, L., Nevatia, R., Guibas, L.J.: Curriculum DeepSDF. In: Vedaldi, A., Bischof, H., Brox, T., Frahm, J.-M. (eds.) ECCV 2020. LNCS, vol. 12353, pp. 51–67. Springer, Cham (2020). https://doi.org/10.1007/978-3-030-58598-3_4
15. Gropp, A., Yariv, L., Haim, N., Atzmon, M., Lipman, Y.: Implicit geometric regularization for learning shapes. In: International Conference on Machine Learning (2020)
16. Guillard, B., et al.: DeepMesh: differentiable iso-surface extraction. arXiv Preprint (2021)
17. Gundogdu, E., et al.: GarNet++: improving fast and accurate static 3D cloth draping by curvature loss. IEEE Trans. Pattern Anal. Mach. Intell. **22**(1), 181–195 (2022)
18. Hao, Z., Averbuch-Elor, H., Snavely, N., Belongie, S.: DualSDF: semantic shape manipulation using a two-level representation. In: Conference on Computer Vision and Pattern Recognition, pp. 7631–7641 (2020)
19. Ju, T., Losasso, F., Schaefer, S., Warren, J.: Dual contouring of hermite data. In: ACM SIGGRAPH (2002)
20. Kato, H., Ushiku, Y., Harada, T.: Neural 3D mesh renderer. In: Conference on Computer Vision and Pattern Recognition (2018)
21. Lähner, Z., Cremers, D., Tung, T.: DeepWrinkles: accurate and realistic clothing modeling. In: Ferrari, V., Hebert, M., Sminchisescu, C., Weiss, Y. (eds.) ECCV 2018. LNCS, vol. 11208, pp. 698–715. Springer, Cham (2018). https://doi.org/10.1007/978-3-030-01225-0_41
22. Lewiner, T., Lopes, H., Vieira, A.W., Tavares, G.: Efficient implementation of marching cubes' cases with topological guarantees. J. Graph. Tools **8**(2), 1–15 (2003)
23. Liao, Y., Donné, S., Geiger, A.: Deep marching cubes: learning explicit surface representations. In: Conference on Computer Vision and Pattern Recognition, pp. 2916–2925 (2018)
24. Liu, S., Zhang, Y., Peng, S., Shi, B., Pollefeys, M., Cui, Z.: DIST: rendering deep implicit signed distance function with differentiable sphere tracing. In: Conference on Computer Vision and Pattern Recognition, pp. 2019–2028 (2020)
25. Lopes, A., Brodlie, K.: Improving the robustness and accuracy of the marching cubes algorithm for isosurfacing. IEEE Trans. Visual Comput. Graphics **9**(1), 16–29 (2003)
26. Lorensen, W., Cline, H.: Marching cubes: a high resolution 3D surface construction algorithm. ACM SIGGRAPH **21**, 163–169 (1987)

592   B. Guillard et al.

27. Mescheder, L., Oechsle, M., Niemeyer, M., Nowozin, S., Geiger, A.: Occupancy networks: learning 3D reconstruction in function space. In: Conference on Computer Vision and Pattern Recognition, pp. 4460–4470 (2019)

28. Nimier-David, M., Vicini, D., Zeltner, T., Jakob, W.: Mitsuba 2: a retargetable forward and inverse renderer. ACM Trans. Graphics **38**(6), 1–17 (2019)

29. Park, J.J., Florence, P., Straub, J., Newcombe, R.A., Lovegrove, S.: DeepSDF: learning continuous signed distance functions for shape representation. In: Conference on Computer Vision and Pattern Recognition (2019)

30. Peng, S., Niemeyer, M., Mescheder, L., Pollefeys, M., Geiger, A.: Convolutional occupancy networks. In: Vedaldi, A., Bischof, H., Brox, T., Frahm, J.-M. (eds.) ECCV 2020. LNCS, vol. 12348, pp. 523–540. Springer, Cham (2020). https://doi.org/10.1007/978-3-030-58580-8_31

31. Remelli, E., et al.: MeshSDF: differentiable iso-surface extraction. In: Advances in Neural Information Processing Systems (2020)

32. Tang, M., Wang, T., Liu, Z., Tong, R., Manocha, D.: I-Cloth: incremental collision handling for GPU-based interactive cloth simulation. ACM Trans. Graphics **37**(6), 1–10 (2018)

33. Venkatesh, R., et al.: Deep implicit surface point prediction networks. In: International Conference on Computer Vision (2021)

34. Xu, Q., Wang, W., Ceylan, D., Mech, R., Neumann, U.: DISN: deep implicit surface network for high-quality single-view 3D reconstruction. In: Advances in Neural Information Processing Systems (2019)

35. Zhao, F., Wang, W., Liao, S., Shao, L.: Learning anchored unsigned distance functions with gradient direction alignment for single-view garment reconstruction. In: Conference on Computer Vision and Pattern Recognition (2021)

SPE-Net: Boosting Point Cloud Analysis via Rotation Robustness Enhancement

Zhaofan Qiu, Yehao Li, Yu Wang, Yingwei Pan, Ting Yao$^{(\boxtimes)}$, and Tao Mei

JD Explore Academy, Beijing, China
tingyao.ustc@gmail.com, tmei@jd.com

Abstract. In this paper, we propose a novel deep architecture tailored for 3D point cloud applications, named as SPE-Net. The embedded "Selective Position Encoding (SPE)" procedure relies on an attention mechanism that can effectively attend to the underlying rotation condition of the input. Such encoded rotation condition then determines which part of the network parameters to be focused on, and is shown to efficiently help reduce the degree of freedom of the optimization during training. This mechanism henceforth can better leverage the rotation augmentations through reduced training difficulties, making SPE-Net robust against rotated data both during training and testing. The new findings in our paper also urge us to rethink the relationship between the extracted rotation information and the actual test accuracy. Intriguingly, we reveal evidences that by locally encoding the rotation information through SPE-Net, the rotation-invariant features are still of critical importance in benefiting the test samples without any actual global rotation. We empirically demonstrate the merits of the SPE-Net and the associated hypothesis on four benchmarks, showing evident improvements on both rotated and unrotated test data over SOTA methods. Source code is available at https://github.com/ZhaofanQiu/SPE-Net.

1 Introduction

Pioneering efforts on 3D cloud point analysis have paid much attention on dealing with rotated data. The challenge here is that existing 3D training architecture usually lacks the ability to generalize well against rotated data. A natural solution could have been introducing rotation augmentations. However, observations show that existing architectures failed to benefit much from augmentations owing to the optimization difficulty and limited capacity of the network. Even worse, training with augmented data also introduces adversary effect that hurts the inference performance when test data is not rotated. Many works [3,9,10,13,25,29,49,50] attempted to address this issue through constructing rotation-invariant frameworks and features. Nevertheless, it is shown that rotation invariant features can still suffer evident performance drop when test data is inherently not rotated.

Z. Qiu and Y. Li contributed equally to this work.

© The Author(s), under exclusive license to Springer Nature Switzerland AG 2022
S. Avidan et al. (Eds.): ECCV 2022, LNCS 13663, pp. 593–609, 2022.
https://doi.org/10.1007/978-3-031-20062-5_34

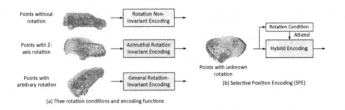

(a) Thee rotation conditions and encoding functions

Fig. 1. Illustration of three different rotation conditions that SPE-Net models.

It therefore forms our main motivation to seek a training strategy that can capture the rotation information and adaptively adjust the parameter optimization based on such rotation condition. We illustrate the different types of rotation conditions considered in this paper. Figure 1(a) top is an object without rotation; Fig. 1(a) middle illustrates an object that only exhibits Z-axis rotation; Fig. 1(a) bottom demonstrates the general scenario where an object is rotated arbitrarily along all X-Y-Z axes. Why knowing the rotation information can be critical? A loose analogy perhaps can be the modeling through some conditional distribution $p(\theta|r)$ versus the marginal distribution $p(\theta)$, where the uncertainty of variable θ always satisfies $\mathbb{E}[\text{Var}(\theta|r)] \leq \text{Var}(\theta)$ for any random variables θ and r. That being said, expected value of uncertainty on θ given observed evidence on r would be guaranteed to reduce in comparison to total variance. If we view θ as deep parameters, r as rotation condition, the optimization on θ can hopefully be restricted and eased given prior knowledge r.

The design of SPE-Net in this paper devotes to the motivation described above. SPE-Net aims to learn a compatibility function that can attend to the actual rotation condition of the input. The training then enjoys a reduced degree of freedom of the optimization based on such compatibility function, where the rotation condition serves as useful prior knowledge, such as the r variable. SPE-Net can henceforth flexibly benefit from stronger rotation training variations, without sacrificing much extra network capacity on encoding such global variations. In the meanwhile, SPE-Net effectively spares the learning to focus on finer local geometry structures, leading to better discriminative ability.

Essentially, the core SPE training unit consists of a critical attention mechanism and the special construction of "position encoding features". In order to abstract useful rotation conditions without exposure to rotation annotations, SPE-Net jointly incorporates those three types of features that are sensitive to different positions: rotation non-invariant features (CD), azimuthal rotation invariant features (Z-RI), and the general rotation-invariant features (A-RI). This logic is briefly illustrated in Fig. 1(b). As the training proceeds in fitting the ground truths, the attention block gradually learns to capture the compatibility response between a point and each of those three types of features, i.e., CD, Z-RI or A-RI. Such learned attention then translates into the desired rotation information that SPE-Net can later leverage on. SPE-MLP, i.e., the critical building component of SPE-Net, is then enabled to adaptively discriminate and to attend to the relevant rotation condition, using this prior knowledge to focus on finer local geometry structures learning. This would potentially relieve the overall optimization difficulties, as the training is effectively constrained with restricted parameterization. Figure 2 illustrates the overview of the SPE-Net architecture.

In brief summary, our contribution in this paper includes:

(1) We establish a new 3D point cloud training architecture, named SPE-Net. The proposed SPE-Net is a novel paradigm that can efficiently encode the rotation information of the input. This new architecture thus exhibits strong robustness against rotated input both during training and testing.
(2) Further inspection into the SPE-Net reveals intriguing insights: We found it beneficial to always incorporate the rotation-invariant features properly during training, i.e., even if the test data does not exhibit any inherent global rotation. We envision that rotation can take place in local regions. SPE-Net thus exclusively benefits from a finer abstraction of both local and global rotation information, leading to superior robustness against variations.
(3) We demonstrate the strong empirical advantage of SPE-Net over SOTA methods. On challenging benchmarks such as ShapeNet, PartNet and S3DIS, SPE-Net achieve more than 1% improvement, justifying the benefit through enhanced robustness against rotation.

2 Related Work

Deep Learning for Point Cloud Analysis. The research in this direction has proceeded along two different dimensions: projecting the point cloud or using the original point cloud. For the first dimension, the original point clouds are projected to intermedia voxels [22,32,54] or images [12,48], translating the challenging 3D analysis into the well-explored 2D problem. These works avoid the direct process of irregular and unordered point cloud data, and show great efficiency benefited from the highly optimized implementation of convolutions. Nevertheless, Yang *et al.* [47] highlight the drawback of the projection step that loses the detailed information in point cloud, which limits the performances of the subsequent deep models. To overcome this limitation, the works along the second dimension utilize deep neural network to process the original point cloud. The pioneering work PointNet [26] proposes to model unodered point data through shared MLPs, and then is extended to PointNet++ [27] by learning hierarchical representations through point cloud down-sampling and up-sampling. There are variants of approaches arisen from this methodology, which mainly focus on improving the capture of local geometry. For example, convolutions [8,11,14,34,37,41,45,46,51], graph models [16,19,31,39,52] and transformers [6,53] are utilized to model local relation between neighboring points.

Rotation-Robust Networks. To improve the robustness of the network for rotation, a series innovations have been proposed to build rotation-equivariant networks or rotation-invariant networks. The rotation-invariant networks [4,17, 29,30,40] are required to produces the output features that are rotated correspondingly with the input. For example, Spherical CNN [4] proposes to project the point cloud into spherical space and introduces a spherical convolution equivariant to input rotation. 3D steerable CNN [40] transfers the features into unit quaternions, which naturally satisfied the rotation-equivariant property. Another direction to enhance rotation-robustness is to learn rotation-invariant representations in networks. To achieve this, the rotation-invariant networks are derived by using kernelized convolutions [25,29], PCA normalization [9,10,49] and rotation-invariant position encoding [3,13,50].

Our work also falls into the category of rotation-robust architecture for point cloud analysis. Unlike the aforementioned methods that are required to guarantee the rotation-equivariant or rotation-invariant property, SPE-Net predicts the rotation condition based on the training data and adaptively chooses the optimal position encoding function. Therefore, this design, on one hand, improves the rotation robustness when the training data is manually rotated, and on the other, keeps the high learning capacity when rotation invariance is not required.

3   SPE-Net

We elaborate our core proposal: the Selective Position Encoding Networks (SPE-Net) in this section. The basic motivation is, if we have the knowledge of another random variable, i.e., the rotation condition r of the input, we can use this knowledge to potentially reduce the expected uncertainty of the parameterization. This is because $\mathrm{Var}(\theta) = \mathbb{E}(\mathrm{Var}(\theta|r)) + \mathrm{Var}(\mathbb{E}(\theta|r))$ for arbitrary θ and r. Note $\mathbb{E}[\theta|r]$ is a function of r by definition. If the three constructed features CD, Z-RI, and A-RI measurements can respond drastically different to the actual rotation condition r of the input, showing different prediction behaviors, then the value $\mathrm{Var}(\mathbb{E}(\theta|r))$ would likely to be non-zero in our 3D context. This then leads to reduced uncertainty on the parameter estimation θ, i.e., $\mathrm{Var}(\theta) \geq \mathbb{E}(\mathrm{Var}(\theta|r))$. That forms a principled incentive of our SPE-Net to ease the optimization and to improve the prediction given prior knowledge on rotation condition r.

3.1   Overall Architecture Flow

The upper part of Fig. 2 illustrates an overview of the SPE-Net. The basic architecture construction follows the philosophy of CNNs [7,33], where the channel dimension increases while the point number reduces and the layer goes deeper.

Points Embedding. The 3D point cloud input is of size $3 \times N$, where N denotes the number of input points. SPE-Net firstly takes the input and embeds each query point with the information from its K-nearest neighboring points. In detail, the 3-dimensional coordinate of each point is firstly mapped into a feature $\mathbf{f}_i$ of higher dimension $C_1 > 3$ by using a shared linear embedding layer. An SPE-MLP operation then applies on the input $\mathbf{f}_i$ feature to further encapsulate the context feature from its neighboring points. Such point embedding module finally outputs features with a shape of $C_1 \times N$.

Multi-stage Architecture. After the point embedding, several subsequent SPE-Blocks operate on the embedding out of the SPE-MLP layer. The overall structure can be grouped into five sequential stages, as illustrated in Fig. 2.

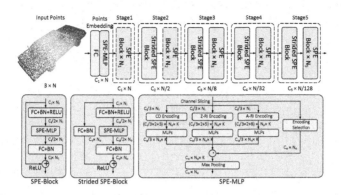

Fig. 2. An overview of our proposed Selective Position Encoding Networks (SPE-Net). It mainly consists of five stages of each stacks several SPE-Blocks. The first SPE-Block in each stage, called strided SPE-Block, increases the channel dimension while reduces the number of points. The size of output feature map is given as $num\_of\_channels \times num\_of\_points$ for each stage.

In each stage, the building block named Strided SPE-Block increases the number of channels and down-samples the points. The feature resolutions are preserved in the following SPE-Blocks within the same stage. The number of SPE-Blocks $\{N_{1\sim5}\}$ and channel dimensions $\{C_{1\sim5}\}$ are considered as predefined hyperparameters that can be tailored for different point cloud analysis of different scales.

Residual Block. Each residual block is composed of a shared fully-connected layer, an SPE-MLP operation and another shared fully-connected layer. The two fully-connected layers are utilized to respectively reduce and to recover the channel dimension, which behave similarly to the bottleneck structure in ResNet. Batch normalization is applied after each fully-connected layer.

3.2   SPE-MLP

Here we introduce the Selective Position Encoding MLP (SPE-MLP), our core learning unit. SPE-MLP builds upon traditional "point-wise MLP" structure while it provides further unique advantage in optimization from more restricted region of parameterisation. SPE-MLP can effectively predict the rotation condition r of the input, and using this knowledge to both ease the training and improve the test accuracy.

Position Feature Encoding. SPE-MLP operates by computing a compatibility function between each query and a couple of constructed position encoding functions applied on the query. The hypothesis here is that each constructed position feature encoding function can respond discriminatively towards different rotation conditions of training data, thus effectively revealing a point's dependency with certain types of rotation condition. While the training proceeds, the compatibility function gradually learns to attend to the relevant position encoding functions according to how well such attention r can reduce the total training

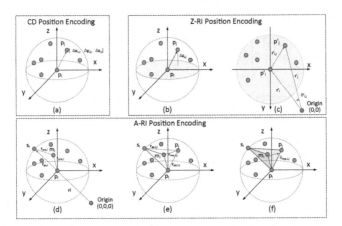

Fig. 3. An illustration of three position encoding functions including CD position encoding (a), Z-RI position encoding (b, c) and A-RI position encoding (d, e, f). The **blue,** orange and green points are the query, neighboring and support points, respectively. (Color figure online)

risks. The attention information would then efficiently convert to the potential rotation condition r of the input. We define three such position encoding functions that is practically suitable for our hypothesis, shown as in Fig. 3. These constructed position encoding functions are described as following.

(a) Coordinate difference (CD) encoding. In the PointNet-style networks, the function called "coordinate difference" is usually exploited as the position encoding function. Formally, given the coordinate of query point $\mathbf{p}_i$ and its neighborhood $\mathbf{p}_j$, the CD position encoding is calculated by

$$P_{\text{CD}}(\mathbf{p}_i, \mathbf{p}_j) = \mathbf{p}_j - \mathbf{p}_i = [\Delta x_{i,j}, \Delta y_{i,j}, \Delta z_{i,j}]. \tag{1}$$

CD position encoding is straightforward and shows promising performances in [20, 26, 27, 39]. However, such encoding strategy generalizes poorly against rotation variations, since the feature construction is non-invariant against rotation variations. The phenomenon is also reported in recent works [3, 10, 13, 44, 50]. Nevertheless, this phenomenon forms basic evidence that supports our hypothesis: the objects having actual rotations indeed would inherently show much weaker response on CD features during training.

(b) Z-axis rotation-invariant (Z-RI) encoding. The second feature encoding function must be complementary to the above CD feature function so that the desired attention mechanism is discriminative. We firstly adopt the most simple heuristic that 3D objects usually merely exhibit rotation around the Z-axis (azimuthal rotation). In Eq. (1), only the coordinate difference $\Delta z_{i,j}$ along Z-axis is Z-axis rotation-invariant. In order to better encode the relative position information along the other two axes, we further project the query point and its neighboring points to X-Y 2D plane, and utilize the distances between projected query p'_i, neighboring point $p'_{i,j}$ and origin point, along with the angle $\theta'_{i,j}$ as the encoded representation. Specifically, the Z-RI position encoding is formulated as

$$P_{\text{Z-RI}}(\mathbf{p}_i, \mathbf{p}_j) = [\Delta z_{i,j}, r'_{i,j}, r'_i, r'_j, \theta'_{i,j}]. \tag{2}$$

The construction of the Z-RI position feature encoding is intended to show best compatibility response with the training data having azimuthal rotation, while showing weaker response towards alternative rotation conditions.

(c) Arbitrary rotation-invariant (A-RI) encoding. The most general yet complex scenario is when arbitrary rotation takes place in 3D space. Compared to Z-axis rotation (azimuthal rotation), arbitrary rotation naturally incurs more complexity in parameterization using θ. It is also challenging to construct arbitrary rotation-invariant representation with only query point and its neighboring points. Therefore, by following [13], we additionally include two support points, i.e., the center point of neighborhoods m_i and the intersection s_i between the query ball and line extended from origin to query point. The center point is defined as the neighboring point having the minimum averaged distance from the other neighboring points. Eventually, A-RI position encoding consists of the distances among query, support and neighboring points, and the angle from $s_i - p_i - m_i$ plane to $s_i - p_i - p_{i,j}$ plane:

$$P_{\text{A-RI}}(\mathbf{p}_i, \mathbf{p}_j) = [r_i, r_{ms,i}, r_{ps,i}, r_{pm,i}, r_{sp,i,j}, r_{mp,i,j}, r_{pp,i,j}, \theta_{mp,i,j}]. \tag{3}$$

The construction of the arbitrary rotation-invariant (A-RI) encoding is expected to exhibit the strongest dependency on arbitrarily rotated training data.

Encoding Selection. SPE-Net can dynamically attend to the relevant position encoding functions for each point $\mathbf{p}_i$. This is realized through the construction of compatibility function as follows. For every stage of the SPE-Net, we firstly equally slice its input feature $\mathbf{f}_i$ into three partitions along channel dimension as $\mathbf{f}_i^{(1)}, \mathbf{f}_i^{(2)}, \mathbf{f}_i^{(3)} \in \mathbb{R}^{C/3}$. Three MLP mapping functions F_1, F_2 and F_3 are respectively applied to the features obtained via Eq. (1), (2), (3). Since the features Eq. (1), (2), (3) intrinsically appear to exhibit different responses to an object's rotation condition, related to how well each option can reduce the actual training risk, the three MLP mapping functions F_1, F_2 and F_3 are expected to learn to abstract such preference during the training. The output of encoded local feature by using different position encoding is defined as:

$$\begin{aligned}
\mathbf{g}_{i,j}^{(1)} &= F_1([\mathbf{f}_i^{(1)}, \Delta\mathbf{f}_{i,j}^{(1)}, P_{\text{CD}}(\mathbf{p}_i, \mathbf{p}_j)]), \\
\mathbf{g}_{i,j}^{(2)} &= F_2([\mathbf{f}_i^{(2)}, \Delta\mathbf{f}_{i,j}^{(2)}, P_{\text{Z-RI}}(\mathbf{p}_i, \mathbf{p}_j)]), \\
\mathbf{g}_{i,j}^{(3)} &= F_3([\mathbf{f}_i^{(3)}, \Delta\mathbf{f}_{i,j}^{(3)}, P_{\text{A-RI}}(\mathbf{p}_i, \mathbf{p}_j)]).
\end{aligned} \tag{4}$$

We calculate the weighted concatenation of the three encoded features followed by a max pooling layer:

$$[\alpha_i^{(1)}, \alpha_i^{(2)}, \alpha_i^{(3)}] = \text{Sigmoid}(\text{FC}(\mathbf{f}_i)), \tag{5}$$

$$\mathbf{g}_i = \underset{j}{\text{Max}}([\mathbf{g}_{i,j}^{(1)} \odot \alpha_i^{(1)}, \mathbf{g}_{i,j}^{(2)} \odot \alpha_i^{(2)}, \mathbf{g}_{i,j}^{(3)} \odot \alpha_i^{(3)}]). \tag{6}$$

Here, the Max operation serves as a maxing pooling. It outputs a vector that collects the entry-wise maximum value across all input vectors indexed by j. Symbol $\odot$ denotes element-wise product between two vectors that preserves the dimension of vectors. Weights $\alpha_i^{(1)}, \alpha_i^{(2)}, \alpha_i^{(3)} \in \mathbb{R}^{C/3}$ are learnable channel-wise attention vectors produced by an FC layer. These weights can learn to align with the respective F_1, F_2 and F_3 functions. Therefore, the training can be steered to focus on the relevant position encoding functions of each input, under the specific recognition task. All the weights are normalized to $0 \sim 1$ by the sigmoid function. The whole process is analogous to softly selecting rotation conditions r prior to the actual inference, so we call this procedure "Encoding Selection".

Equation (4) is inspired from the Point-wise MLP structure, which was originally proposed in PointNet/PointNet++ [26, 27]. A conventional Point-wise MLP applies several point-wise fully-connected (FC) layers on a concatenation of "relative position" and point feature to encode the context from neighboring points:

$$\underset{j}{\text{Max}}(F([\mathbf{f}_i, \Delta\mathbf{f}_{i,j}, P(\mathbf{p}_i, \mathbf{p}_j)])), \tag{7}$$

The max pooling operation across the K-nearest neighbors after the FC layer aggregates the feature of the query point, where $P(\cdot, \cdot)$ denotes the relatively position encoding between query point and neighboring point, $F(\cdot)$ is a point-wise mapping function (i.e., MLPs). The point-wise MLPs after concatenation operation can approximate any continuous function about the relative coordinates and context feature [27]. They also utilize the ball radius method [27] to achieve K neighboring points $\{\mathbf{p}_j, \mathbf{f}_j\}$, which is critical to achieve balanced sample density. Equation (4) borrow all of these merits from Point-wise MLP, while Eq. (4) exclusively incorporates the rotation information to achieve our goal.

Apart from the learnable weights, good initialization can help further improve the rotation robustness of SPE-Net. Particularly, we can mask out the CD and Z-RI position encoding in Eq. (4) during the first T epochs. In this way, the networks are forced to only use rotation-invariant features (A-RI) to represent the 3D object, at the earlier training stage. After T epochs, the network starts to incorporate the information from the other two position encodings (CD and Z-RI). The mask-out epochs T here is a trade-off hyperparameter. A much higher T will increase the rotation robustness of networks whereas it might hurt the performance due to the lack of training flexibility. We conduct ablation study against T in the experiments.

4   Experiments

4.1   Datasets

We empirically evaluate our SPE-Net on four challenging point cloud analysis datasets: ModelNet40 [42] for 3D classification, ShapeNet [2], PartNet [23] for part segmentation and S3DIS [1] for scene segmentation. The first three datasets are generated from 3D CAD models, and the last one is captured in real scenes.

Modelnet40 is one of the standard benchmarks for 3D classification. The dataset contains 12.3K meshed CAD models from 40 classes. The CAD models are officially divided into 9.8K and 2.5K for training and testing, respectively.

Shapenet is a standard part segmentation benchmark, covering 16 categories and 50 labeled parts. It consists of 12.1K training models, 1.9K validation models and 2.9K test models. We train our model on the union of training set and validation set, and report the performances on the test set.

Partnet is a more challenging benchmark for large-scale fine-grained part segmentation. It consists of pre-sampled point clouds of 26.7K 3D objects from 24 categories, annotated with 18 parts on average. We follow the official data splitting scheme, which partitions the objects into 70% training set, 10% validation set and 20% test set. We train our model on the training set and report the performances on validation set and test set, respectively.

S3DIS is an indoor scene segmentation dataset captured in 6 large-scale real indoor areas from 3 different buildings. There are 273M points in total labeled with 13 categories. Following [36], we use Area-5 as the test scene and the others as training scenes. Considering that each scene contains a large amount of points exceeding the processing capacity of GPU device, for each forward, we segment sub-clouds in spheres with radius of 2m. Such sub-clouds are randomly selected in scenes during training, and evenly sampled for testing.

4.2 Implementation Details

Backbone Network Architectures. As described in Sect. 3.1, the complexity of SPE-Net is determined by the settings of free parameters. We fix the repeat number as $N_t = 1|_{1 \leqslant t \leqslant 5}$, which means each stage contains one SPE-Blocks. The number of MLP layers in SPE-MLP block is set as 1. The number of output channels C_t is tuned to build a family of SPE-Net with various model complexities. For small-scale ModelNet40 and ShapeNet, we set $\{C_t\} = \{72, 144, 288, 576, 1152\}$, which are then expanded by 2× for large-scale PartNet and S3DIS.

Head Network Architectures. We attach a head network on top of SPE-Net to train for different tasks. For the classification head, the output features of SPE-Net are aggregated together by a max-pooling layer, followed by a three-layer MLP with output channels 576-288-c to perform c-class prediction. For the task of segmentation, we follow the architecture in [27] that progressively upsamples the output features from the backbone network and reuses the features from the earlier layers by the skip connections.

Training and Inference Strategy. Our proposal is implemented on PyTorch [24] framework, and SGD (for ModelNet40 and S3DIS) or AdamW (for ShapeNet and PartNet) algorithm is employed to optimize the model with random initialization. Considering that training deep models usually requires extensive data augmentation [15,20,21,28,38], we exploit dropout, drop path, label smoothing,

Table 1. Ablation study for each design in SPE-MLP on ModelNet40 dataset. The backbone network is SPE-Net-S.

Method	CD	Z-RI	A-RI	Sel	Param	N/N	Z/Z	Z/SO3	SO3/SO3
Single type	✓				1.6M	<u>93.6</u>	92.0	22.3	90.8
		✓			1.6M	92.9	<u>92.3</u>	19.9	91.0
			✓		1.6M	90.6	91.4	**91.4**	<u>91.3</u>
Multiple types	✓	✓	✓		1.3M	93.5	92.1	26.0	90.7
	✓	✓	✓	✓	1.5M	**93.9**	**92.6**	<u>88.4</u>	**91.5**

anisotropic random scaling and Gaussian noise to reduce the over-fitting effect. In the inference stage, we follow the common test-time augmentation of voting scheme [20, 27, 37] and augment each model 10 times using the same augmentation strategy in training stage.

4.3   Ablation Study on SPE-MLP

We firstly study how each particular design in SPE-MLP influences the overall performances. The basic strategy is to utilize only a single type of position encoding from either CD, Z-RI or A-RI encoding functions and compare with our attention based learning. To test these variants, we do not slice the input channels, and instead, we concatenate the full input channels with the certain single type of position encoding. For those relevant architecture variants that involve multiple types of position encoding, the three position encoding functions are either simply combined or fused by the proposed encoding selection (abbreviated as Sel). We compare the models under consideration on four different rotation conditions: (1) The original training and testing sets without any rotation: N/N. (2) Both training and testing sets are rotated around the Z-axis: Z/Z. (3) Training set is rotated around the Z-axis and testing set is randomly rotated: Z/SO3. (4) Both training and testing sets are randomly rotated: SO3/SO3. Table 1 evaluates the performances of different variants of SPE-MLP on ModelNet40 dataset. The ablation study aims to justify our basic hypotheses. For rapid comparisons, we exploit a lightweight version of SPE-Net, called SPE-Net-S, with output channels as $\{C_t\} = \{36, 72, 144, 288, 576\}$.

The first observation is intuitive and forms our basic motivation. When a single type of position encoding, i.e., one out of CD, Z-RI, or A-RI encoding is applied in the network, such selected encoding strategy would perform the best when the training data intrinsically exhibit such type of rotation. Take for instance, CD performs the best when both the training and test data shows no rotation. A-RI significantly outperforms other encoding schemes when the training data is rotated around the Z-axis while the test data is arbitrary rotated. In the meanwhile, it is also apparent that when the position encoding scheme does not model certain type of invariance assumption, the training fails drastically in learning that type of rotation condition, such as the CD and Z-RI features

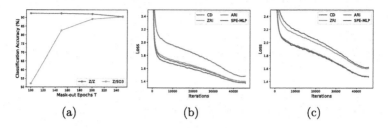

(a)   (b)   (c)

Fig. 4. (a) Effect of mask-out epochs. (b) Loss curves on ModelNet40 without rotation. (c) Loss curves on ModelNet40 with SO3 rotation.

against the arbitrary rotation observed in test data. However, it is also noted that even if we train the network with arbitrarily rotated invariance features (A-RI), such training can hardly outperform tailored feature encoding schemes, for example, the CD feature under N/N setup or Z-RI under the Z/Z setup.

One step further is to rigidly fuse all types of position condition with equal weights without attention based adaptation. In this way, the network are at least encouraged to make the predication based on all possible rotation conditions. We notice that such rigid combination of position encoding features indeed shows evident performance boost when training data and test data shows consistent rotation conditions. However, such encoding scheme performs poorly whenever the training and test data differs in their rotation type, owing to poor generalization of such encoding scheme.

In comparison, the proposed position encoding selection (the Sel. column in Table 1) based on the constructed attention scheme shows best robustness against rotation conditions both during training and testing. This is because SPE-net can adaptively learn to use the learned rotation condition as important prior information to make the prediction. Among all the compared counterparts when the training data and test data of the same rotation conditions, Sel. (implemented via SPE-MLP) performs consistently the best. The Sel. scheme also only incurs very limited performance drop when training and testing data are of different rotation types, justifying the advantage of the SPE attention operation and the good generalization ability. The only exception is that Sel. performs relatively worse than the A-RI scheme under Z/SO3 setup. However, recall that the A-RI can hardly outperform tailored feature encoding schemes whenever training data rotation matches the particularly encoding invariance assumption. A-RI feature also performs worse than Sel under all other training scenarios.

To clarify the effect of the mask-out epochs T (Sect. 3.2), we illustrate SPE-Net's performance curves under Z/Z and Z/SO3 setups on ModelNet40 against different mask-out epochs T in Fig. 4(a). As can be seen, with higher T, the accuracy of Z/Z setting slightly drops while the transferring setting Z/SO3 is improved. We choose a good trade-off and set $T = 200$ as the default choice. Figure 4(b) and 4(c) respectively shows the loss curves on ModelNet40 without rotation or with SO3 rotation, and compares SPE-MLP against three other single-type position encoding. The losses of SPE-MLP are much lower than

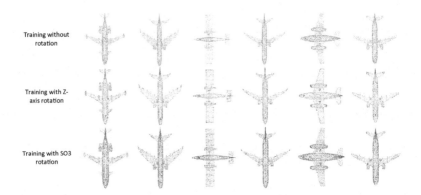

Fig. 5. The visualization of encoding selection on ModelNet40 dataset with different rotation condition. The red, green and **blue** points represent the points dominated with CD, Z-RI and A-RI encoding, respectively. (Color figure online)

Table 2. Performances on ModelNet40 for 3D classification with different rotation conditions. The last column records the differences between Z/SO3 and SO3/SO3.

Type	Method	Inputs	Z/Z	Z/SO3	SO3/SO3	Acc.drop
Rotation-sensitive	PointNet [26]	xyz	88.5	16.4	70.5	54.1
	PointNet++ [27]	xyz	89.3	28.6	85.0	56.4
	DGCNN [39]	xyz	<u>92.2</u>	20.6	81.1	60.5
	PointConv [41]	xyz	91.6	-	85.6	-
Rotation-robust	Spherical CNN [4]	Voxel	88.9	76.9	86.9	10.0
	α^3SCNN [17]	Voxel	89.6	87.9	88.7	0.8
	RIConv [50]	Feature	86.5	86.4	86.4	0.0
	SRI-Net [35]	Feature	87.0	87.0	87.0	0.0
	SPH-Net [25]	xyz	87.7	86.6	87.6	1.0
	SFCNN [29]	xyz	91.4	84.8	90.1	5.3
	PFE [49]	xyz+feature	89.2	89.2	89.2	0.0
	RI-GCN [9]	xyz	89.5	89.5	89.5	0.0
	REQNN [30]	xyz	83.0	83.0	83.0	0.0
	RotPredictor [5]	xyz	92.1	-	90.8	-
	Triangle-Net [43]	Feature	-	-	86.7	-
	RIF [13]	Feature	89.4	89.4	89.3	0.1
	DGCNN+PCA [10]	xyz	91.6	**91.6**	<u>91.6</u>	0.0
	SPE-Net (ours)	xyz	**92.7**	<u>89.7</u>	**91.8**	2.1

others across different iterations and different rotation conditions, and validate the robustness of SPE-MLP and the eased training optimization. Moreover, we also visualize the produced attention weights in Fig. 5. The attention weights of "encoding selection" in the first strided SPE-Block are visualized. Overall, the models trained without rotation and that with Z-axis rotation prefer to choose Z-RI encoding condition, while the model trained with SO3 rotation utilizes more A-RI encoding condition. An intriguing observation is that, the same parts of a

Table 3. Performances on ShapeNet for part segmentation with different rotation conditions. The last column records the differences between Z/SO3 and SO3/SO3.

Type	Method	Inputs	Z/SO3	SO3/SO3	mIoU.drop
Rotation-sensitive	PointNet [26]	xyz	37.8	74.4	36.6
	PointNet++ [27]	xyz	48.2	76.7	28.5
	PointCNN [14]	xyz	34.7	71.4	36.7
	DGCNN [39]	xyz	37.4	73.3	35.9
Rotation-robust	RIConv [50]	Feature	75.3	75.5	0.2
	SRI-Net [35]	Feature	80.0	80.0	0.0
	RI-GCN [9]	xyz	77.2	77.3	0.1
	Triangle-Net [43]	Feature	-	72.5	-
	RIF [13]	Feature	82.2	82.5	0.3
	DGCNN+PCA [10]	xyz	<u>83.1</u>	<u>83.1</u>	0.0
	SPE-Net (ours)	xyz	**87.1**	**87.8**	0.7

shape are very likely to attend to the same position encoding condition across different instances. It somewhat reveals that the proposed encoding selection achieves a unique fine-grained understanding in different parts of the 3D shape.

4.4   Evaluation on Point Cloud with Rotation

Next, we compare with several state-of-the-art techniques on ModelNet40 and ShapeNet with different rotation conditions to demonstrate the advantage of the proposed SPE-Net. The performance comparisons on ModelNet40 for 3D shape classification are summarized in Table 2. It is observed that rotation-sensitive methods such as PointNet and PointNet++ completely failed to generalize when test data shows different rotation than what it was trained on. The performance of these models also plummet under the SO3/SO3 setup owing to optimization difficulty raised by complex rotation augmentations. On the contrary, the SOTA rotation robust methods show certain robustness against rotations, particularly under the SO3/SO3 and Z/SO3 setting. But these methods perform generally worse than other paradigms, especially under the Z/Z setting. This is because the network parameterization had to trade-off the rotation robustness against the general prediction performance, under the limited network capacity. Our SPE-Net is also a kind of rotation robust 3D training scheme. Particularly, as SPE-Net further incorporates the rotation condition as prior, it can flexibly adapt to the most relevant position encoding schemes, showing both good robustness against rotations, as well as the eased optimization difficulties in terms of good generalization ability. To see this, SPE-Net reports the best 92.7% accuracy under the standard Z/Z setup, while it also simultaneously preserves good generalization ability against rotations changes. In comparison to DGCNN+PCA, SPE-Net still maintains a 0.2% superiority under the SO3/SO3 setup, proving the unique advantage of SPE-MLP encoding scheme.

Table 4. Performances on ModelNet40, PartNet and S3DIS without test-time rotation.

Method	ModelNet40		PartNet			S3DIS	
	Param	Acc	Param	Val	Test	Param	mIoU
DensePoint [18]	0.7M	93.2	-	-	-	-	-
KPConv [37]	15.2M	92.9	-	-	-	15.0M	65.7
PointCNN [14]	0.6M	92.5	4.4M	-	46.4	4.4M	65.4
Point-wise MLP [20]	26.5M	92.8	25.6M	48.1	51.5	25.5M	66.2
Pseudo grid [20]	19.5M	93.0	18.5M	50.8	53.0	18.5M	65.9
Adapt weights [20]	19.4M	93.0	18.5M	50.1	53.5	18.4M	66.5
PosPool [20]	19.4M	93.2	18.5M	50.6	53.8	18.4M	66.7
SPE-Net (ours)	7.2M	**94.0**	24.4M	**52.6**	**54.8**	24.3M	**67.8**

Table 3 summarizes the performance comparisons on ShapeNet for 3D part segmentation task. For evaluation on ShapeNet, we calculate the mean intersection of union (mIoU, %) for each shape and report the mean value over all instances. Generally speaking, we observe similar behaviors of various methods on ShapeNet as that in Table 2. Here rotation-sensitive methods still perform poorly under Z/SO3 and SO3/SO3 setups. We also observe a more significant performance gap between SPE-Net and DGCNN+PCA than that in Table 2. The reason might be that for segmentation tasks, different input points may need drastically different attention to each of the position encoding scheme, demonstrating a more local response towards the variation of the rotation conditions. SPE-Net can therefore benefit significantly from its more flexible and pointwise rotation condition adaptation to reach better segmentation results.

4.5   Evaluation on Point Cloud Without Rotation

Finally, we compare with several state-of-the-art techniques on the original training/testing sets of ModelNet40, PartNet and S3DIS for 3D shape classification, 3D part segmentation, 3D scene segmentation, respectively, to further validate the effectiveness of SPE-Net as a general backbone. The performances are summarized in Table 4. SPE-Net apparently has achieved the best performance among all comparisons. Note that the conventional point-wise MLP only takes into account the CD encoding, thus leading to a much worse performance than SPE-Net, even if both of the networks have adopted the residual learning structures. It is also intriguing to see that SPE-Net performs more than 1.1% better than its best competitor PosPool on the S3DIS dataset. Such phenomenon verifies that it is always beneficial to incorporate the rotation-invariant features properly during training, although the data does not exhibit any inherent global rotation. This is because rotation can take place in local regions. SPE-Net thus exclusively benefits from a finer abstraction of both local and global rotation information, showing consistent performance gain in comparison to others.

5 Conclusion

In this paper, we investigate the role of rotation conditions in 3D application's performance, and propose a novel deep 3D architecture named SPE-Net. SPE-Net can learn to infer and to encode various rotation condition present in the training data through an efficient attention mechanism. Such rotation condition then can effectively serve as useful prior information in improving the eventual prediction performance. Extensive empirical results validate our various assumptions and well verify the advantage of SPE-Net by leveraging on these priors.

Acknowledgments. This work was supported by the National Key R&D Program of China under Grant No. 2020AAA0108600.

References

1. Armeni, I., Sax, S., Zamir, A.R., Savarese, S.: Joint 2D–3D-semantic data for indoor scene understanding. arXiv preprint arXiv:1702.01105 (2017)
2. Chang, A.X., et al.: ShapeNet: an information-rich 3D model repository. arXiv preprint arXiv:1512.03012 (2015)
3. Chen, C., Li, G., Xu, R., Chen, T., Wang, M., Lin, L.: ClusterNet: deep hierarchical cluster network with rigorously rotation-invariant representation for point cloud analysis. In: CVPR (2019)
4. Esteves, C., Allen-Blanchette, C., Makadia, A., Daniilidis, K.: Learning SO(3) equivariant representations with spherical CNNs. In: Ferrari, V., Hebert, M., Sminchisescu, C., Weiss, Y. (eds.) ECCV 2018. LNCS, vol. 11217, pp. 54–70. Springer, Cham (2018). https://doi.org/10.1007/978-3-030-01261-8_4
5. Fang, J., Zhou, D., Song, X., Jin, S., Yang, R., Zhang, L.: Rotpredictor: unsupervised canonical viewpoint learning for point cloud classification. In: 3DV (2020)
6. Guo, M.H., Cai, J.X., Liu, Z.N., Mu, T.J., Martin, R.R., Hu, S.M.: PCT: point cloud transformer. Comput. Visual Media **7**(2), 187–199 (2021)
7. He, K., Zhang, X., Ren, S., Sun, J.: Deep residual learning for image recognition. In: CVPR (2016)
8. Hermosilla, P., Ritschel, T., Vázquez, P.P., Vinacua, À., Ropinski, T.: Monte Carlo convolution for learning on non-uniformly sampled point clouds. ACM Trans. Graphics **37**(6), 1–12 (2018)
9. Kim, S., Park, J., Han, B.: Rotation-invariant local-to-global representation learning for 3D point cloud. In: NeurIPS (2020)
10. Li, F., Fujiwara, K., Okura, F., Matsushita, Y.: A closer look at rotation-invariant deep point cloud analysis. In: ICCV (2021)
11. Li, J., Chen, B.M., Lee, G.H.: SO-Net: self-organizing network for point cloud analysis. In: CVPR (2018)
12. Li, L., Zhu, S., Fu, H., Tan, P., Tai, C.L.: End-to-end learning local multi-view descriptors for 3D point clouds. In: CVPR (2020)
13. Li, X., Li, R., Chen, G., Fu, C.W., Cohen-Or, D., Heng, P.A.: A rotation-invariant framework for deep point cloud analysis. IEEE Trans. Vis. Comput. Graphics (2021)
14. Li, Y., Bu, R., Sun, M., Wu, W., Di, X., Chen, B.: PointCNN: convolution on X-transformed points. In: NeurIPS (2018)

15. Li, Y., Yao, T., Pan, Y., Mei, T.: Contextual transformer networks for visual recognition. IEEE Trans. PAMI (2022)
16. Lin, Z.H., Huang, S.Y., Wang, Y.C.F.: Learning of 3D graph convolution networks for point cloud analysis. IEEE Trans. PAMI **44**(8), 4212–4224 (2021)
17. Liu, M., Yao, F., Choi, C., Sinha, A., Ramani, K.: Deep learning 3D shapes using Alt-AZ anisotropic 2-sphere convolution. In: ICLR (2018)
18. Liu, Y., Fan, B., Meng, G., Lu, J., Xiang, S., Pan, C.: DensePoint: learning densely contextual representation for efficient point cloud processing. In: ICCV (2019)
19. Liu, Y., Fan, B., Xiang, S., Pan, C.: Relation-shape convolutional neural network for point cloud analysis. In: CVPR (2019)
20. Liu, Z., Hu, H., Cao, Y., Zhang, Z., Tong, X.: A closer look at local aggregation operators in point cloud analysis. In: Vedaldi, A., Bischof, H., Brox, T., Frahm, J.-M. (eds.) ECCV 2020. LNCS, vol. 12368, pp. 326–342. Springer, Cham (2020). https://doi.org/10.1007/978-3-030-58592-1_20
21. Long, F., Qiu, Z., Pan, Y., Yao, T., Luo, J., Mei, T.: Stand-alone inter-frame attention in video models. In: CVPR (2022)
22. Maturana, D., Scherer, S.: VoxNet: a 3D convolutional neural network for real-time object recognition. In: IROS (2015)
23. Mo, K., et al.: PartNet: a large-scale benchmark for fine-grained and hierarchical part-level 3D object understanding. In: CVPR (2019)
24. Paszke, A., et al.: PyTorch: an imperative style, high-performance deep learning library. In: NeurIPS (2019)
25. Poulenard, A., Rakotosaona, M.J., Ponty, Y., Ovsjanikov, M.: Effective rotation-invariant point CNN with spherical harmonics kernels. In: 3DV (2019)
26. Qi, C.R., Su, H., Mo, K., Guibas, L.J.: PointNet: deep learning on point sets for 3D classification and segmentation. In: CVPR (2017)
27. Qi, C.R., Yi, L., Su, H., Guibas, L.J.: PointNet++: deep hierarchical feature learning on point sets in a metric space. In: NIPS (2017)
28. Qiu, Z., Yao, T., Ngo, C.W., Mei, T.: MLP-3D: a MLP-like 3D architecture with grouped time mixing. In: CVPR (2022)
29. Rao, Y., Lu, J., Zhou, J.: Spherical fractal convolutional neural networks for point cloud recognition. In: CVPR (2019)
30. Shen, W., Zhang, B., Huang, S., Wei, Z., Zhang, Q.: 3D-rotation-equivariant quaternion neural networks. In: Vedaldi, A., Bischof, H., Brox, T., Frahm, J.-M. (eds.) ECCV 2020. LNCS, vol. 12365, pp. 531–547. Springer, Cham (2020). https://doi.org/10.1007/978-3-030-58565-5_32
31. Shen, Y., Feng, C., Yang, Y., Tian, D.: Mining point cloud local structures by kernel correlation and graph pooling. In: CVPR (2018)
32. Shi, S., et al.: PV-RCNN: point-voxel feature set abstraction for 3D object detection. In: CVPR (2020)
33. Simonyan, K., Zisserman, A.: Very deep convolutional networks for large-scale image recognition. In: ICLR (2015)
34. Su, H., et al.: SPLATNet: sparse lattice networks for point cloud processing. In: CVPR (2018)
35. Sun, X., Lian, Z., Xiao, J.: SRINet: learning strictly rotation-invariant representations for point cloud classification and segmentation. In: ACM MM (2019)
36. Tchapmi, L., Choy, C., Armeni, I., Gwak, J., Savarese, S.: SEGCloud: semantic segmentation of 3D point clouds. In: 3DV (2017)
37. Thomas, H., Qi, C.R., Deschaud, J.E., Marcotegui, B., Goulette, F., Guibas, L.J.: KPConv: flexible and deformable convolution for point clouds. In: ICCV (2019)

38. Touvron, H., Cord, M., Douze, M., Massa, F., Sablayrolles, A., Jégou, H.: Training data-efficient image transformers & distillation through attention. In: ICML (2021)
39. Wang, Y., Sun, Y., Liu, Z., Sarma, S.E., Bronstein, M.M., Solomon, J.M.: Dynamic graph CNN for learning on point clouds. ACM Trans. Graphics **38**(5), 1–12 (2019)
40. Weiler, M., Geiger, M., Welling, M., Boomsma, W., Cohen, T.S.: 3D steerable CNNs: learning rotationally equivariant features in volumetric data. In: NeurIPS (2018)
41. Wu, W., Qi, Z., Fuxin, L.: PointConv: deep convolutional networks on 3D point clouds. In: CVPR (2019)
42. Wu, Z., et al.: 3D ShapeNets: a deep representation for volumetric shapes. In: CVPR (2015)
43. Xiao, C., Wachs, J.: Triangle-Net: towards robustness in point cloud learning. In: WACV (2021)
44. Xu, J., Tang, X., Zhu, Y., Sun, J., Pu, S.: SGMNet: learning rotation-invariant point cloud representations via sorted gram matrix. In: ICCV (2021)
45. Xu, M., Ding, R., Zhao, H., Qi, X.: PAConv: position adaptive convolution with dynamic kernel assembling on point clouds. In: CVPR (2021)
46. Xu, Y., Fan, T., Xu, M., Zeng, L., Qiao, Yu.: SpiderCNN: deep learning on point sets with parameterized convolutional filters. In: Ferrari, V., Hebert, M., Sminchisescu, C., Weiss, Y. (eds.) ECCV 2018. LNCS, vol. 11212, pp. 90–105. Springer, Cham (2018). https://doi.org/10.1007/978-3-030-01237-3_6
47. Yang, Z., Sun, Y., Liu, S., Shen, X., Jia, J.: STD: sparse-to-dense 3D object detector for point cloud. In: ICCV (2019)
48. You, H., Feng, Y., Ji, R., Gao, Y.: PVNet: a joint convolutional network of point cloud and multi-view for 3D shape recognition. In: ACM MM (2018)
49. Yu, R., Wei, X., Tombari, F., Sun, J.: Deep positional and relational feature learning for rotation-invariant point cloud analysis. In: Vedaldi, A., Bischof, H., Brox, T., Frahm, J.-M. (eds.) ECCV 2020. LNCS, vol. 12355, pp. 217–233. Springer, Cham (2020). https://doi.org/10.1007/978-3-030-58607-2_13
50. Zhang, Z., Hua, B.S., Rosen, D.W., Yeung, S.K.: Rotation invariant convolutions for 3D point clouds deep learning. In: 3DV (2019)
51. Zhang, Z., Hua, B.S., Yeung, S.K.: ShellNet: efficient point cloud convolutional neural networks using concentric shells statistics. In: ICCV (2019)
52. Zhao, H., Jiang, L., Fu, C.W., Jia, J.: PointWeb: enhancing local neighborhood features for point cloud processing. In: CVPR (2019)
53. Zhao, H., Jiang, L., Jia, J., Torr, P.H., Koltun, V.: Point transformer. In: ICCV (2021)
54. Zhou, Y., Tuzel, O.: VoxelNet: end-to-end learning for point cloud based 3D object detection. In: CVPR (2018)

The Shape Part Slot Machine: Contact-Based Reasoning for Generating 3D Shapes from Parts

Kai Wang[1][(✉)], Paul Guerrero[2], Vladimir G. Kim[2], Siddhartha Chaudhuri[2], Minhyuk Sung[2,3], and Daniel Ritchie[1]

[1] Brown University, Providence, USA
kai_wang@brown.edu
[2] Adobe Research, London, UK
[3] KAIST, Daejeon, South Korea

Abstract. We present the Shape Part Slot Machine, a new method for assembling novel 3D shapes from existing parts by performing contact-based reasoning. Our method represents each shape as a graph of "slots," where each slot is a region of contact between two shape parts. Based on this representation, we design a graph-neural-network-based model for generating new slot graphs and retrieving compatible parts, as well as a gradient-descent-based optimization scheme for assembling the retrieved parts into a complete shape that respects the generated slot graph. This approach does not require any semantic part labels; interestingly, it also does not require complete part geometries—reasoning about the slots proves sufficient to generate novel, high-quality 3D shapes. We demonstrate that our method generates shapes that outperform existing modeling-by-assembly approaches regarding quality, diversity, and structural complexity.

1 Introduction

There is increasing demand for high-quality 3D object models across multiple fields: gaming and virtual reality; advertising and e-commerce; synthetic training data for computer vision and robotics; and more. The traditional practice of manual 3D modeling is time-consuming and labor-intensive and is not well-suited to scaling to this demand. Thus, visual computing researchers have pursued data-driven methods which can augment human creative capabilities and accelerate the modeling process (Fig. 1).

One promising technology in this space are generative models of 3D shapes. Such generative models could suggest new, never-before seen shapes, freeing users from tedious and time-consuming low-level geometric manipulations to focus on high-level creative decisions. Recent work in this space has focused on

---

Supplementary Information The online version contains supplementary material available at https://doi.org/10.1007/978-3-031-20062-5_35.

S. Avidan et al. (Eds.): ECCV 2022, LNCS 13663, pp. 610–626, 2022.
https://doi.org/10.1007/978-3-031-20062-5_35

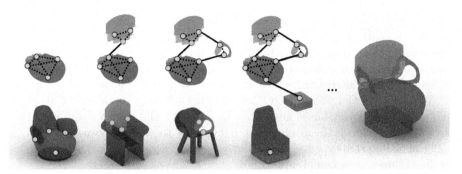

Fig. 1. Our system synthesizes novel 3D shapes by assembling them from parts. Internally, it represents shapes as a graph of the regions where parts connect to one another (which we call slots). It generates such a graph by retrieving part subgraphs from different shapes in a dataset. Once a full graph has been generated, the system then optimizes for affine part transformations to produce a final output shape.

deep generative models of shapes in the form of volumetric occupancy grids, point clouds, or implicit fields. While these methods demonstrate impressive abilities to synthesize the bulk shape of novel objects, the local geometry they produce often exhibits noticeable artifacts: oversmoothing, bumpiness, extraneous holes, etc. At present, none of these generative models has achieved geometric output quality resembling the shapes they are trained on. An alternative approach would be to avoid synthesizing novel geometry altogether and instead learn how to re-combine existing high-quality geometries created by skilled modeling artists. This paradigm is known in the computer graphics literature as *modeling by assembly*, where it once received considerable attention. Since the deep learning revolution, however, the focus of most shape generation research has shifted to novel geometry synthesis. The few post-deep-learning methods for modeling by assembly have shown promise but have not quite lived up to it: handling only coarse-grained assemblies of large parts, as well as placing parts by directly predicting their world-space poses (leading to 'floating part' artifacts).

In this paper, we present a new generative model for shape synthesis by part assembly which addresses these issues. Our key idea is to use a representation which focuses on the connectivity structure of parts. This choice is inspired by several recent models for novel geometry synthesis which achieve better structural coherence in their outputs by adopting a part-connectivity-based representation [10,15,25]. In our model, the first-class entities are the regions where one part connects to another. We call these regions *slots* and our model the *Shape Part Slot Machine*.

In our model, a shape is represented by a graph in which slots are nodes and edges denote connections between them. We define shape synthesis as iteratively constructing such a graph by retrieving parts and connecting their slots together. We propose an autoregressive generative framework for solving this problem, composed of several neural network modules tasked with retrieving compatible parts and determining their slot connections. Throughout the iterative assembly process, the partial shape is represented only by its slot graph: it is not necessary to assemble the retrieved parts together until the process is complete, at which point we use a gradient-descent-based optimization scheme to find poses and scales for the retrieved parts which are consistent with the generated slot graph.

We compare the Shape Part Slot Machine to other modeling-by-assembly and part-connectivity-based generative models. We find that our approach consistently outperforms the alternatives in its ability to generate visually and physically plausible shapes.

In summary, our contributions are:

- The *Slot graph* representation for reasoning about part structure of shapes.
- An autoregressive generative model for slot graphs by iterative part retrieval and assembly.
- A demonstration that local part connectivity structure is enough to synthesize globally-plausible shapes: neither full part geometries nor their poses are required.

2   Related Work

Modeling by Part Assembly: The Modeling By Example system pioneered the paradigm of modeling-by-assembly with interactive system for replacing parts of an object by searching in database [4]. The Shuffler system added semantic part labels, enabling automatic 'shuffling' of corresponding parts [13]. Later work handled more complex shapes by taking symmetry and hierarchy into account [9]. Other modes of user interaction include guiding exploration via sketches [23] or abstract shape templates [1], searching for parts by semantic attributes [2], or having the user play the role of fitness function in an evolutionary algorithm [24]. Probabilistic graphical models have been effective for suggesting parts [3] or synthesizing entire shapes automatically [12]. Part-based assembly has also been used for reconstructing shapes from images [18].

Our work is most closely related to ComplementMe, which trains deep networks to suggest and place unlabeled parts to extend a partial shape [19]. Our model is different in that we use a novel, part-contacts-only representation of shapes, which we show enables handling of more structurally complex shapes.

Deep Generative Models of Part-Based Shapes: Our work is also related to deep generative models which synthesize part-based shapes. One option is to make voxel-grid generative models part-aware [20,22]. Many models have been proposed which generate sets of cuboids representing shape parts [27]; some fill the cuboids with generated geometry in the form of voxel grids [14] or point clouds [10,11,15]. Other part-based generative models skip cuboid proxies and generate part geometries directly, as point clouds [17], implicit fields [21], or deformed genus zero meshes [5,25]. All of these models synthesize part geometry. In contrast, our model synthesizes shapes by retrieving and assembling existing high-quality part meshes.

Estimating Poses for 3D Parts: Many part-based shape generative models must pose the generated parts. Some prior work looks at this problem on its own: given a set of parts, how to assemble them together? One method predicts a 6DOF pose for each part such that they become assembled [8]; another predicts per-part translations and scales and also synthesizes geometry to make the transformed parts connect seamlessly [26]. Rather than predict part poses directly, we solve for per-part poses and scales that satisfies contact constraints encoded in a slot graph. This approach has its root in early work in modeling by assembly [12] but without the need for part labels and separate steps computing how parts should attach. It is also similar in spirit to that of ShapeAssembly [10], working with part meshes rather than cuboid abstractions.

3   Overview

Assembling novel shapes from parts requires solving two sub-problems: finding a set of compatible parts, and computing the proper transforms to assemble the parts. These tasks depend on each other, e.g. replacing a small chair seat with a large one will shift the chair legs further away from the center. Instead of solving these sub-problems separately, we propose a system for solving them jointly. Specifically, our system synthesizes shapes by iteratively constructing a representation of the contacts between parts. The assembly transformations for each part can then be computed directly from this representation.

In our system, a shape is represented as a *slot graph*: each node corresponds to a "slot" (part-to-part contact region) on a part; each edge is either a *part edge* connecting slots of the same part or a *contact edge* connecting slots on two touching parts. Section 4 defines this graph structure and describes how we extract them from available data.

This reduces the task of assembling novel shapes to a graph generation problem: retrieving sub-graphs representing parts from different shapes and combining them into new graphs. We solve this problem autoregressively, assembling part sub-graphs one-by-one into a complete slot graph. At each iteration, given a partial slot graph, our system inserts a new part using three neural network modules: the first determines *where* a part be should connect to the current partial graph, the second decides *what* part to connect, and third determines *how* to connect the part. We describe this generation process in Sect. 5.

Finally, given a complete contact graph, the system runs a gradient-based optimization process that assembles parts into shapes by solving for poses and scales of the individual parts such that the contacts implied by the generated slot graph are satisfied. We describe the process in Sect. 6.

4   Representing Shapes with Slot Graphs

In this section, we define slot graphs, describe how we extract them from segmented shapes, and how we encode them with neural networks.

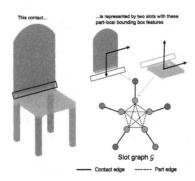

Fig. 2. A slot graph. Nodes are part-to-part contact regions called *slots* and describe the contact geometry with bounding boxes. *Contact edges* connect two slots on two adjacent parts, while *part edges* connect all slots of the same part.

4.1 Slot-Based Graph Representation of Shapes

A good shape representation that models how parts connect allows the generative model to reason independently about part connectivity and part geometry. Given a shape S and its part decomposition $\{P_1 \dots P_N\}$, we call regions where parts connect "slots", and use them as nodes in a graph $\mathcal{G} = (V, E_c, E_p)$, as illustrated in Fig. 2. Each pair of parts may be connected with multiple slots, and each slot $\mathbf{u}_{ij} \in V$ on part P_i that connects to P_j has a corresponding slot $\mathbf{u}_{ji}$ on part P_j that connects back to P_i. Each node $\mathbf{u}_{ij}$ stores the following properties:

- The axis-aligned bounding box (AABB) of the slot, in a coordinate frame centered on P_i.
- The same AABB, but normalized such that the bounding box of the entire part is a unit cube. This provides a scale-invariant view of how parts connect.

A slot graph $\mathcal{G}$ has two types of edges: *contact edges* $\mathbf{e}_{ij}^c \in E_c$ connect every pair of contacting slots $\mathbf{u}_{ij}, \mathbf{u}_{ji}$ and *part edges* $\mathbf{e}_{ijk}^p \in E_p$ connect every pair of slots $\mathbf{u}_{ij}, \mathbf{u}_{ik}$ in the same part P_i.

This representation encodes neither the geometry nor the pose of each part. Omitting this information encourages generalization: the choice of parts will be based only on the compatibility of their attachment regions and connectivity structure; it will not be biased by a part's world-space position in its original shape nor its complete geometry.

This representation also does not encode part symmetries; nevertheless, we demonstrate in Sect. 7 that our model often generates appropriately symmetrical shapes. We can also optionally include logic that enforces symmetries at test time (see Sect. 5).

4.2 Extracting Slot Graphs from Data

Given a set of part-segmented shapes, we follow StructureNet [15] to extract part adjacencies and symmetries. We use adjacencies to define slots, and define connecting regions as points within distance τ of the adjacent part. Additionally, we ensure that symmetrical parts have symmetrical slots and prune excess slots where multiple parts overlap at the same region. See supplemental for details.

4.3   Encoding Slots Graphs with Neural Networks

We encode a slot graph into a graph feature $h_{\mathcal{G}}$ and per-slot features $h_{\mathbf{u}}$ using messaging passing networks [6].

Initializing Node Embeddings: We initialize slot features $h_{\mathbf{u}}$ using a learned encoding of the slot properties $x_{\mathbf{u}}$ (two six-dimensional AABBs) with a three-layer MLP f_{init}: $h_{\mathbf{u}}^0 = f_{\text{init}}(x_{\mathbf{u}})$. As we discuss later, some of our generative model's modules also include an additional one-hot feature which is set to one for particular nodes that are relevant to their task (effectively 'highlighting' them for the network).

Graph Encoder: The node embeddings are then updated with our message passing network using an even number of message passing rounds. In each round, node embeddings are updated by gathering messages from adjacent nodes. We alternate the edge sets E during each round, using only part edges $E = E_p$ for odd rounds ($t = 1, 3, 5 \ldots$) and only contact edges $E = E_c$ for even rounds ($t = 2, 4, 6 \ldots$):

$$h_{\mathbf{t}} = f_{\text{update}}^t \left(h_{\mathbf{u}}^{t-1}, \sum_{\mathbf{uv} \in E} f_{\text{msg}}^t(h_{\mathbf{u}}^{t-1}, h_{\mathbf{v}}^{t-1}, h_{\mathbf{u}}^0, h_{\mathbf{v}}^0) \right)$$

where f_{msg} is a multi-layer perceptron (MLP) that computes a message for each pair of adjacent nodes, and f_{update} is a MLP that updates the node embedding from the summed messages. We also include skip connections to the initial node embeddings $h_{\mathbf{u}}^0$. All MLPs have separate weights for each round of message passing.

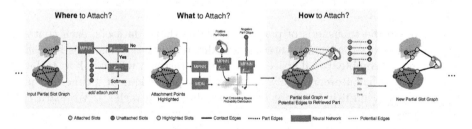

Fig. 3. Our slot graph generative model uses three neural network modules to build a graph step by step. *Where to Attach?*: Predicts which slots on the current partial shape the next-retrieved part should be attached to. *What to Attach?*: Learns an embedding space for part slot graphs and predicts a probability distribution over this space in which parts which are compatible with the highlighted slots have high probability. *How to attach?*: Determines which slots on the retrieved part should connect to which slots on the current partial shape. (Color figure online)

Gathering Information from the Graph: To obtain the final node features $h_{\mathbf{u}}$, we concatenate its initial embedding with as its embeddings after every even round of message passing (i.e. those using contact edges) and feed them into an MLP f_{node}:

$$h_{\mathbf{u}} = f_{\text{node}}(h_{\mathbf{u}}^0, h_{\mathbf{u}}^2 \dots h_{\mathbf{u}}^T)$$

To obtain the feature $h_{\mathcal{G}}$ of an entire graph, we first perform a graph readout over the embeddings at round t:

$$h_{\mathcal{G}}^t = \sum_{\mathbf{u} \in V} (f_{\text{project}}(h_{\mathbf{u}}^t) \cdot f_{\text{gate}}(h_{\mathbf{u}}^t))$$

where f_{project} projects node features into the latent space of graph features and f_{gate} assigns a weight for each of the mapped features. We then compute the final graph feature $h_{\mathcal{G}}$ similar to the way we compute the node features:

$$h_{\mathcal{G}} = f_{\text{graph}}(h_{\mathcal{G}}^0, h_{\mathcal{G}}^2 \dots h_{\mathcal{G}}^T)$$

In cases where we need a feature for a subset of nodes $V' \subset V$ in the graph, we simply perform the readout over V' instead of V.

5   Generating Slot Graphs

Our system casts shape synthesis by part assembly as a problem of generating novel slot graphs. To do so, we first extract a graph representation of each part: for every shape S in a dataset of shapes, and for every part $P_i \in S$ represented by a slot graph $\mathcal{G} = (V, E_c, E_p)$, we create a part clique $C_{P_i} \subseteq \mathcal{G}$ representing this part by taking all the slots $\mathbf{u}_{ij} \in V$ associated with this part, as well as all the part edges $\mathbf{e}_{ijk} \in E_p$. We remove the all contact edges $\mathbf{e}_{ij} \in E_c$ that connects P_i to other parts in the shape. Our goal, then, is find a set of part cliques $\mathbf{C}$ that can be connected together into a novel slot graph $\mathcal{G}' = (V', E_c', E_p')$, where $V' = \{\mathbf{u} \in \mathbf{C}\}$, $E_p' = \{\mathbf{e} \in \mathbf{C}\}$, and E_c' is the set of contact edges that need to be added to make all the slots attached i.e. connected to exactly one other slot via a contact edge.

There can be thousands of parts in available shape datasets, each containing multiple slots that can be attached in different ways. Thus, it is infeasible to search this combinatorial space exhaustively. Instead, we *learn* how to build novel slot graphs autoregressively, attaching one part clique at a time to a partial slot graph, until it is complete (i.e. all slots are attached). We learn this autoregressive process with teacher forcing: for every training sample, we take a random, connected partial slot graph $\mathcal{G}'$ consisting of one or more part cliques from a graph $\mathcal{G} = (V, E_c, E_P)$ extracted from a dataset shape S. We then select a random part clique $C_{P_j} | P_j \in S$ (referred to as C_{target} in the following sections) that is attached to $\mathcal{G}'$ on one or more slots $V_{\text{target}} = \{\mathbf{u}_{ij} \mid \mathbf{u}_{ij} \in \mathcal{G}', \mathbf{u}_{ji} \in C_{P_j}\}$ via set of contact edges $E_{\text{target}} = \{\mathbf{e}_{ij}^c \mid \mathbf{u}_{ij} \in V_{\text{target}}\}$. The goal of a single generation step, then, is to maximize

$$p(V_{\text{target}}, C_{\text{target}}, E_{\text{target}} \mid \mathcal{G}')$$

Rather than learn this complex joint distribution directly, we instead factor it into three steps using the chain rule:

- **Where** to attach: maximizing $p(V_{\text{target}} \mid \mathcal{G}')$
- **What** to attach: maximizing $p(C_{\text{target}} \mid \mathcal{G}', V_{\text{target}})$
- **How** to attach: maximizing $p(E_{\text{target}} \mid \mathcal{G}', V_{\text{target}}, C_{\text{target}})$

In the remainder of this section, we detail the formulation for the networks we use for each of the three steps, as well as how we use them during test time. Figure 3 visually illustrates these steps.

Where to Attach? Given a partial slot graph $\mathcal{G}'$, we first identify the slots V_{target} to which the next-retrieved part clique should attach. We predict each element of V_{target} autoregressively (in any order), where each step i takes as input $\mathcal{G}'$ and the already-sampled slots $V_{\text{target}}^i = \{V_{\text{target},0} \cdots V_{\text{target},i-1}\}$ (highlighted in $\mathcal{G}'$ with a one-hot node feature). We first use a MLP f_{continue} to predict the probability p_{continue} that another slot should be added ($p_{\text{continue}} = 0$ if $V_{\text{target}}^i = V_{\text{target}}$ and 1 otherwise). If more slots should be included, then we use an MLP f_{next} to predict a logit for each of the unattached slots $\tilde{V}$ in $\mathcal{G}'$ that are not already in V_{target}^i. These logits are then fed into a softmax to obtain a probability distribution over possible slots:

$$p(V_{\text{target}}|\mathcal{G}') = \prod_{i=1}^{|V_{\text{target}}|} p_{\text{cont}}^i \cdot p_{\text{next}}^i [V_{\text{target},i}]$$

$$p_{\text{cont}}^i = \begin{cases} p_{\text{continue}}(h_{\mathcal{G}'}|V_{\text{target}}^i) & i < |V_{\text{target}}| \\ 1 - p_{\text{continue}}(h_{\mathcal{G}'}|V_{\text{target}}^i) & i = |V_{\text{target}}| \end{cases}$$

$$p_{\text{next}}^i = \text{softmax}([f_{\text{next}}(h_{\mathbf{u}}|V_{\text{target}}^i)|\mathbf{u} \in \tilde{V}/V_{\text{target}}^i])$$

Input	Input + GT	GT	Best	2nd	5th	25th	50%

Fig. 4. Example outputs of the **What to Attach?** module. We visualize the input partial slot graph within the parts that contain them (grey) and the center of the selected slots (red), as well as the ground truth part (green, 2nd column). The parts and slots are in their ground truth world-space pose, which is *not* available to the neural network. We then visualize, individually, the ground truth part and the retrieved candidates ranked 1st, 2nd, 5th, 25th, and at the 50th percentile, respectively, along with all of their slots (red). (Color figure online)

What to Attach? Having selected the slots V_{target} to attach to, we then retrieve part cliques compatible with the partial graph $\mathcal{G}'$ and the selected slots. Similar to prior work [19], we take a contrastive learning approach to this problem: the probability of the ground truth part clique should be greater than that of randomly sampled other part cliques (i.e. negative examples) by some margin m:

$$p(C_{\text{target}} \mid \mathcal{G}', V_{\text{target}}) > p(C_{\text{negative}} \mid \mathcal{G}', V_{\text{target}}) + m$$

We use two neural networks to enforce this property. The first maps part cliques C into an embedding space $\mathbb{R}_{\text{emb}}$.

$$X_C = f_{\text{emb}}(h_C)$$

where f_{emb} is the embedding MLP and h_C is the graph feature computed from C alone. The second network is a mixture density network (MDN) that outputs a probability distribution over this embedding space:

$$P(X \mid \mathcal{G}', V_{\text{target}}, X \in \mathbb{R}_{\text{emb}}) = \text{MDN}(h'_{\mathcal{G}}, h_{\mathcal{G}'_{\text{target}}})$$

where V_{target} are highlighted in the input node features and $h_{\mathcal{G}'_{\text{target}}}$ is obtained by computing graph features using V_{target} only.

We visualize the behavior of this module trained on Chair in Fig. 4. When the input demands a very specific type of structure (first 2 rows), our module can retrieve the part cliques that match such structure. When the input has fewer constraints (3rd row), our module retrieves a wide variety of partial cliques that can be attached. In the 4th row, our module retrieves chair legs that are *structurally* compatible. The legs are not necessarily *geometrically* compatible, as geometry information is not available to the module.

How to Attach? The last module learns to connect the retrieved part clique C_{target} to the partial slot graph $\mathcal{G}'$. It predicts a probability for every pair of slots $\mathbf{u}_{ij} \in V_{\text{target}}, \mathbf{u}_{ji} \in C_{\text{target}}$ that could be connected via a contact edge:

$$p(\mathbf{e}_{ij}^c \mid \mathcal{G}, V_{\text{target}}, C_{\text{target}}) = f_{\text{edge}}(h_{\mathbf{u}_{ij}}, h'_{\mathbf{u}_{ji}})$$

Fig. 5. Typical structural outliers detected at test time. From left to right: redundant component (chair back), repetition of structures, inability to resolve local connections (chair base), not enough slots to finish structure.

where V_{target} are highlighted in input node features, f_{edge} is a MLP and $h_{\mathbf{u}_{ij}}$ and $h'_{\mathbf{u}_{ji}}$ are computed with two neural networks, one over $\mathcal{G}'$ and one over C_{target}. $p(\mathbf{e}_{ij}^c) = 1$ if $\mathbf{e}_{ij}^c \in E_{\text{target}}$ and 0 otherwise. If both V_{target} and C_{target} contain one slot, then these slots must be connected, and this module can be skipped. To encourage the networks to learn more general representations, we augment V_{target} with random unattached slots in $\mathcal{G}'$.

Generating New Slot Graphs at Test Time: At test time, we generate new slot graphs by iteratively querying the three modules defined above. Although the modules we learn are probabilistic and support random sampling, we find MAP inference sufficient to produce a diverse range of shapes. We terminate the generation process when the slot graph is complete i.e. when all slots in the graph are attached to exactly one slot from a different part.

This stopping criterion, while simple, is not robust to errors: a random set of part cliques can occasionally form a complete slot graph by chance. To combat these errors, we reject any partial shapes for which the "how" module assigns low probabilities to all candidate slot pairs. We also use one-class Support Vector Machines to reject other structural outliers (see Fig. 5 for examples).

Finally, we also include logic to enforce part symmetries. When retrieving a part to connect with slots that were part of a symmetry group in their original shape, we alter the rank order of parts returned by our "what" module to prioritize (a) parts that occurred in symmetry groups in the dataset, followed by (b) parts that are approximately symmetrical according to chamfer distance. See the supplemental for more details about these test-time sampling strategies.

6   Assembling Shapes from Slot Graphs

A generated slot graph defines connectivity between shape parts but does not explicitly give part poses. Thus, our system has an additional step to find world-space poses for all the retrieved parts. In this section, we describe a simple gradient-descent-based optimization procedure for doing so, which takes a generated slot graph $\mathcal{G} = (V, E_c, E_p)$ that describes N parts $P_1 \dots P_N$, and predicts an affine transformation matrix T_i for each part P_i.

Objective Function: To assemble a shape from its slot graph, we want each slot to be connected in the same way as it was in its original shape, which we approximate by enforcing that the distance from any point on a slot to the contacting slot should stay the same in the assembled shape. Formally, for each slot $\mathbf{u}_{ij} \in V$, we select the set of points S_{ij} that the slot contains (from the point sample of P_i from Sect. 4). For each point $p \in S_{ij}$, we compute its distance $d_o(p)$ to the closest point on the slot that was originally connected to $\mathbf{u}_{ij}$ in the dataset. We then optimize for $T_1 \dots T_N$ via the following objective: for every slot $\mathbf{u}_{ij} \in V$, every point sample $p \in S_{ij}$ should have the same distance to the connecting slot $\mathbf{u}_{ji}$ as the original distance $d_o(p)$:

$$f(T_1 \dots T_N) = \sum_{\mathbf{u}_{ij} \in V} \sum_{p \in S_{ij}} \left(\left(\min_{q \in S_{ji}} d(T_i p, T_j q) \right) - d_o(p) \right)^2$$

Optimization Process: We minimize this objective using gradient descent. Rather than full affine transformations, we optimize only translation and anisotropic scale. This prevents certain part re-uses from happening (e.g. re-using a horizontal crossbar as a vertical crossbar), but we find that the space of possible outputs is nonetheless expressive. To minimize unnecessary distortion, we prefer translation over scaling whenever possible: we optimize for translation only for the first 1000 iterations, and then alternate between translation and scaling every 50 iterations for the next 500 iterations. Optimizing for scales is essential in cases where translation alone cannot satisfy the slot graph. We show one such example in Fig. 6, where the shelf layers are scaled horizontally to match the V shape of the frame.

Translation Trans + scale

Fig. 6. Optimizing part affine transformations to satisfy a slot graph. We show the output of the initial translation-only phase of optimization & the final output with both translation and scale.

7   Results and Evaluation

In this section, we evaluate our method's ability to synthesize novel shapes. We use the PartNet [16] dataset, segmenting shapes with the finest-grained PartNet hierarchy level and filtering out shapes with inconsistent segmentations and/or disconnected parts. More implementation details are in the supplemental.

Novel Shape Synthesis: Figure 7 shows examples of shapes our method is capable of assembling. Our model learns to generate shapes with complex structures specific to each shape categories. Though it does not use global part position information during graph generation, the resulting slot graphs lead to consistent global positions for the individual parts once optimized. Although we choose not to encode full geometries, our model is still able to generate shapes with interesting variations both structurally and geometrically. We further quantitatively compare the results generated by our model against these alternatives:

- **ComplementMe** [19] is the previous state-of-art for modeling by part assembly. It retrieves compatible parts and places them together by predicting per-part translation vectors. ComplementMe also does not implement a stopping criteria for generation, so we train a network that takes a partial shape point cloud as input and predicts whether generation should stop. We also stop the generation early if the output of the part retrieval network does not change from one step to the next. Finally, ComplementMe relies on a part discovery process where most groups of symmetrical parts are treated as a single part

Fig. 7. Examples of range of shapes our method is able to generate. Each part has a different color that correlates with the order they are inserted. The blue part is used for initialization. See the supplementary material for more details about the color palette. (Color figure online)

(e.g. four chair legs). We notice that, when trained on our data, ComplementMe suffers from a significant performance decrease on Chair and Table, and struggles to generate more complex Storage, as is evident from the average number of parts (See Table 1). Therefore, for these categories, we also include results where parts are grouped by symmetry (w/sym) for reference. We stress that, under this condition, both retrieving and assembling parts are significantly easier, thus the results are not directly comparable.

- **StructureNet** [15] is an end-to-end generative model outputs a hierarchical shape structure, where each leaf node contains a latent code that can either be decoded into a cuboid or a point cloud. We modify it to output meshes by, for each leaf node, retrieving the part in the dataset whose StructureNet latent code is closest to the leaf node's latent code and then transforming the part to fit the cuboid for that leaf node.
- We also include an **Oracle** as an upper bound on retrieval-based shape generation. The oracle is an autoregressive model that takes as input at each step (a) the bounding boxes for all parts in a ground-truth shape and (b) point

Fig. 8. (a) Chairs in the first row of Fig. 7, where parts coming from the same source shape now have the same color. (b) Geometric nearest neighbor of the same chairs in the training set. (c) Chairs generated without enforcing part symmetries. (d) Chairs generated with the explicit rule that no parts coming from the same source shape can be attached together. Our method uses parts from different shapes to generate novel shapes. It can generate approximately symmetric shapes without explicit rules, and can connect parts from different shapes together plausibly. (Color figure online)

clouds for parts retrieved so far. Retrieved parts are scaled so that they fit exactly to the bounding box to which they are assigned.

See supplemental for more details about these baselines. We use an evaluation protocol similar to ShapeAssembly [10] which evaluates both the physical plausibility and quality of generated shapes:

- **Rootedness ↑ (Root)** measures the percentage of shapes for which there is a connected path between the ground to all parts;
- **Stability ↑ (Stable)** measures the percentage of shapes that remains upright under gravity and a small force in physical simulation, we do not report this for lamps because lamps such as chandeliers do not need to be stable;
- **Realism ↑ (Fool)** is the percentage of test set shapes classified as "generated" by a PointNet trained to distinguish between dataset and generated shapes;
- **Freschet Distance ↓ (FD)** [7] measures distributional similarity between generated and dataset shapes in the feature space of a pre-trained PointNet classifier.
- **Parts** is the mean number of parts in generated shapes.

Table 1 summarizes the results.

By using a contact-based representation, our model is able to generate shapes that are more physically plausible (rooted and stable) than the baselines. While being comparable in terms of the overall shape quality, measured by Frechet distance and classifier fool percentage. Our model performs particularly well for storage furniture; we hypothesize rich connectivity information of this shape category allows our model to pick parts that match particularly well. Our model

Table 1. Comparing our system to baselines and ablations on generating visually and physically plausible shapes.

Category	Method	Root↑	Stab↑	Fool↑	FD↓	Parts
Chair	Ours	98.1	70.1	6.4	61.1	7.8
	ComplementMe	90.2	41.1	6.6	83.0	5.7
	StructureNet	81.0	61.3	4.0	37.5	12.1
	Oracle	94.5	83.4	25.8	13.3	–
	ComplementMe (w/sym)	88.3	79.1	21.9	21.6	4.3
	Ground Truth	100.0	100.0	–	–	11.1
	Ours (no symmetry)	98.2	68.0	8.1	58.9	7.8
	Ours (no duplicate)	97.5	67.4	13.8	61.2	7.7
Table	Ours	98.2	82.8	10.6	61.6	6.8
	ComplementMe	90.2	62.0	7.7	93.5	4.7
	StructureNet	82.8	78.5	2.3	85.2	7.8
	ComplementMe (w/sym)	87.1	84.0	35.8	18.7	3.3
	Ground Truth	100.0	100.0	–	–	9.3
Storage	Ours	99.4	90.8	15.5	42.6	6.9
	ComplementMe	91.4	72.4	8.9	89.8	3.4
	StructureNet	89.6	82.2	6.8	105.5	8.3
	ComplementMe (w/sym)	85.3	70.6	11.5	71.4	3.3
	Ground Truth	100.0	99.4	–	–	13.6
Lamp	Ours	89.6	–	21.5	42.4	3.4
	ComplementMe	62.0	–	35.8	26.0	3.4
	Ground Truth	92.6	–	–	–	4.2

fares less well on lamps, where connectivity structure is simple and the geometric variability of parts (which out model does not encode) is highly variable. ComplementMe works well on lamps, thanks to its focus on part geometry. Its performance drops significantly on all other categories with more complicated shape structures. We provide more details, as well as random samples for all methods, in the supplementary material.

Generalization Capacity: It is important that a generative model that follows the modeling by assembly paradigm learns to recombine parts from different sources into novel shapes. We demonstrate our model's capacity for this in Fig. 8: it is able to assemble parts from multiple source shapes together into novel shapes different from those seen during training, with or without explicit restrictions whether parts from the same source shape can be connected to each other. We also see that while including symmetry reasoning improves geometric quality, our method is able to generate shapes that are roughly symmetrical without it. This is also reflected in Table 1: removing symmetry or prohibiting using multiple parts from the same source shape has minimal impact on our metrics. We provide more analysis of generalization in the supplemental.

Performance of Individual Modules: Finally, we evaluate each individual model module, using the following metrics:

- **Attach Acc**: How often the "where" module correctly selects the slots to attach, given the first slot.
- **Average Rank**: Average percentile rank of ground truth next part according to the "what" module.
- **Edge Acc**: How often the "how" module recovers the ground truth edge pairs.

Table 2 summarizes the results. Modules perform very well, with some lower numbers caused by inherent multimodality of the data.

Table 2. Evaluating our neural network modules in isolation.

	Attach Acc	Avg Rank	Edge Acc
Chair	96.70	99.05	94.79
Table	92.32	99.14	92.82
Storage	87.46	99.08	85.38
Lamp	98.87	91.36	91.89

Fig. 9. Typical failure cases of our method. From left to right: a chair with a tiny seat, two opposite-facing lamps attached together awkwardly, a chair with a implausible back, a chair that misses seat and legs completely.

Limitations: Even with outlier detection as mentioned in Sect. 5, poor-quality outputs can still occur. Figure 9 shows typical examples. Most are caused by our model's lack of focus on geometry: chairs with a tiny seat, lamps that face opposite directions, and chair backs that block the seat completely. Incorporating additional geometric features when appropriate could help.

8   Conclusion

We presented the Shape Part Slot machine, a new modeling-by-part-assembly generative model for 3D shapes. Our model synthesizes new shapes by generating slot graphs describing the contact structure between parts; it then assembles its retrieved parts by optimizing per-part affine transforms to be consistent with this structure. The slot graph encodes surprisingly little information, yet we demonstrated experimentally that our model outperforms multiple baselines and prior modeling-by-assembly systems on generating novel shapes from PartNet parts.

There are multiple directions for future work. Parts could be repurposed in more diverse ways if we had a method to transfer slot graphs between geometrically- and contextually-similar parts (so e.g. a chair seat that had armrests originally does not have to have them in all synthesized results). More variety could also be obtained by optimizing for part orientations (so e.g. a vertical slat could be used as a horizontal one).

Acknowledgements. This work was funded in part by NSF award #1907547 and a gift fund from Adobe. Daniel Ritchie is an advisor to Geopipe and owns equity in the company. Geopipe is a start-up that is developing 3D technology to build immersive virtual copies of the real world with applications in various fields, including games and architecture. Minhyuk Sung acknowledges the support of NRF grant (2022R1F1A1068681), NST grant (CRC 21011), and IITP grant (2022-0-00594) funded by the Korea government (MSIT), and grants from Adobe, KT, and Samsung Electronics corporations. Part of this work was done when Kai Wang interned at Adobe.

References

1. Averkiou, M., Kim, V., Zheng, Y., Mitra, N.J.: ShapeSynth: parameterizing model collections for coupled shape exploration and synthesis. In: Computer Graphics Forum (Special Issue of Eurographics 2014) (2014)
2. Chaudhuri, S., Kalogerakis, E., Giguere, S., Funkhouser, T.: ATTRIBIT: content creation with semantic attributes. In: ACM Symposium on User Interface Software and Technology (UIST) (2013)
3. Chaudhuri, S., Kalogerakis, E., Guibas, L., Koltun, V.: Probabilistic reasoning for assembly-based 3D modeling. ACM Trans. Graphics **30**(4), 1–10 (2011)
4. Funkhouser, T., et al.: Modeling by example. In: ACM SIGGRAPH 2004 Papers (2004)
5. Gao, L., et al.: SDM-Net: deep generative network for structured deformable mesh. In: SIGGRAPH Asia (2019)
6. Gilmer, J., Schoenholz, S.S., Riley, P.F., Vinyals, O., Dahl, G.E.: Neural message passing for quantum chemistry. CoRR arXiv:1704.01212 (2017)
7. Heusel, M., Ramsauer, H., Unterthiner, T., Nessler, B., Hochreiter, S.: GANs trained by a two time-scale update rule converge to a local nash equilibrium. In: NeurIPS (2017)
8. Huang, J., et al.: Generative 3D part assembly via dynamic graph learning. In: The IEEE Conference on Neural Information Processing Systems (NeurIPS) (2020)
9. Jain, A., Thormählen, T., Ritschel, T., Seidel, H.P.: Exploring shape variations by 3D-model decomposition and part-based recombination. Comput. Graph. Forum **31**(2pt3), 631–640 (2012). https://doi.org/10.1111/j.1467-8659.2012.03042.x
10. Jones, R.K., et al.: ShapeAssembly: learning to generate programs for 3D shape structure synthesis. ACM Trans. Graphics (TOG), SIGGRAPH Asia 2020 **39**(6), Article 234 (2020)

11. Jones, R.K., Charatan, D., Guerrero, P., Mitra, N.J., Ritchie, D.: ShapeMOD: macro operation discovery for 3D shape programs. ACM Trans. Graphics (TOG) **40**(4), 1–16 (2021)
12. Kalogerakis, E., Chaudhuri, S., Koller, D., Koltun, V.: A probabilistic model for component-based shape synthesis. ACM Trans. Graphics **31**(4), 1–11 (2012)
13. Kreavoy, V., Julius, D., Sheffer, A.: Model composition from interchangeable components. In: Proceedings of the 15th Pacific Conference on Computer Graphics and Applications, PG 2007, pp. 129–138. IEEE Computer Society, USA (2007). https://doi.org/10.1109/PG.2007.43
14. Li, J., Xu, K., Chaudhuri, S., Yumer, E., Zhang, H., Guibas, L.: GRASS: generative recursive autoencoders for shape structures. In: SIGGRAPH 2017 (2017)
15. Mo, K., et al.: StructureNet: hierarchical graph networks for 3D shape generation. In: SIGGRAPH Asia (2019)
16. Mo, K., et al.: PartNet: a large-scale benchmark for fine-grained and hierarchical part-level 3D object understanding. In: Proceedings of the IEEE/CVF Conference on Computer Vision and Pattern Recognition, pp. 909–918 (2019)
17. Schor, N., Katzir, O., Zhang, H., Cohen-Or, D.: CompoNet: learning to generate the unseen by part synthesis and composition. In: The IEEE International Conference on Computer Vision (ICCV) (2019)
18. Shen, C.H., Fu, H., Chen, K., Hu, S.M.: Structure recovery by part assembly. ACM Trans. Graphics **31**(6) (2012). https://doi.org/10.1145/2366145.2366199
19. Sung, M., Su, H., Kim, V.G., Chaudhuri, S., Guibas, L.: ComplementMe: weakly-supervised component suggestions for 3D modeling. ACM Trans. Graphics (TOG) **36**(6), 226 (2017)
20. Wang, H., Schor, N., Hu, R., Huang, H., Cohen-Or, D., Huang, H.: Global-to-local generative model for 3D shapes. ACM Trans. Graphics (Proc. SIGGRAPH ASIA) **37**(6), 214:1–214:10 (2018)
21. Wu, R., Zhuang, Y., Xu, K., Zhang, H., Chen, B.: PQ-Net: a generative part seq2seq network for 3D shapes. In: IEEE/CVF Conference on Computer Vision and Pattern Recognition (CVPR) (2020)
22. Wu, Z., Wang, X., Lin, D., Lischinski, D., Cohen-Or, D., Huang, H.: SAGNet: structure-aware generative network for 3D-shape modeling. ACM Trans. Graphics (Proc. SIGGRAPH 2019) **38**(4), 91:1–91:14 (2019)
23. Xie, X., et al.: Sketch-to-design: context-based part assembly. Comput. Graph. Forum **32**(8), 233–245 (2013)
24. Xu, K., Zhang, H., Cohen-Or, D., Chen, B.: Fit and diverse: set evolution for inspiring 3D shape galleries. ACM Trans. Graphics (Proc. of SIGGRAPH 2012) **31**(4), 57:1–57:10 (2012)
25. Yang, J., Mo, K., Lai, Y.K., Guibas, L.J., Gao, L.: DSM-Net: disentangled structured mesh net for controllable generation of fine geometry (2020)
26. Yin, K., Chen, Z., Chaudhuri, S., Fisher, M., Kim, V., Zhang, H.: COALESCE: component assembly by learning to synthesize connections. In: Proceedings of 3DV (2020)
27. Zou, C., Yumer, E., Yang, J., Ceylan, D., Hoiem, D.: 3D-PRNN: generating shape primitives with recurrent neural networks. In: ICCV 2017 (2017)

Spatiotemporal Self-attention Modeling with Temporal Patch Shift for Action Recognition

Wangmeng Xiang[1,2], Chao Li[2], Biao Wang[2], Xihan Wei[2], Xian-Sheng Hua[2], and Lei Zhang[1(✉)]

[1] The Hong Kong Polytechnic University, Hong Kong SAR, China
{cswxiang,cslzhang}@comp.polyu.edu.hk
[2] DAMO Academy, Alibaba, Hangzhou, China
{lllcho.lc,wb.wangbiao,xihan.wxh,xiansheng.hxs}@alibaba-inc.com

Abstract. Transformer-based methods have recently achieved great advancement on 2D image-based vision tasks. For 3D video-based tasks such as action recognition, however, directly applying spatiotemporal transformers on video data will bring heavy computation and memory burdens due to the largely increased number of patches and the quadratic complexity of self-attention computation. How to efficiently and effectively model the 3D self-attention of video data has been a great challenge for transformers. In this paper, we propose a Temporal Patch Shift (TPS) method for efficient 3D self-attention modeling in transformers for video-based action recognition. TPS shifts part of patches with a specific mosaic pattern in the temporal dimension, thus converting a vanilla spatial self-attention operation to a spatiotemporal one with little additional cost. As a result, we can compute 3D self-attention using nearly the same computation and memory cost as 2D self-attention. TPS is a plug-and-play module and can be inserted into existing 2D transformer models to enhance spatiotemporal feature learning. The proposed method achieves competitive performance with state-of-the-arts on Something-something V1 & V2, Diving-48, and Kinetics400 while being much more efficient on computation and memory cost. The source code of TPS can be found at https://github.com/MartinXM/TPS.

Keywords: Action recognition · Transformer · Temporal patch shift

1 Introduction

Significant progresses have been achieved for video based action recognition in recent years [4,13,22,31,38], largely driven by the development of 3D Convolutional Neural Networks (3D-CNN) and their factorized versions, including

---

W. Xiang—Work done during an internship at Alibaba.

Supplementary Information The online version contains supplementary material available at https://doi.org/10.1007/978-3-031-20062-5_36.

I3D [4], Slowfast [13], P3D [31], TSM [22]. With the recent success of transformer-based methods on image based tasks such as image classification, segmentation and detection [5,8,16,23,35,42], researchers have been trying to duplicate the success of transformers on image based tasks to video based tasks [1,2,24]. Specifically, videos are tokenized as 3D patches, then multi-head Self-Attention (SA) and Feed-Forward Networks (FFN) are utilized for spatiotemporal feature learning. However, the extra temporal dimension of video data largely increases the number of patches, which leads to an exponential explosion in computation and memory cost as the calculation of multi-head SA has a quadratic complexity.

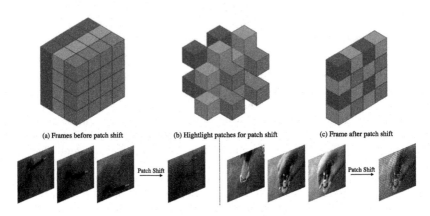

(a) Frames before patch shift   (b) Hightlight patches for patch shift   (c) Frame after patch shift

Fig. 1. An example of temporal patch shift for three adjacent frames.

Previous efforts to reduce the computational burden of spatiotemporal multi-head SA are mainly focused on how to factorize it into spatial and temporal domains and compute them separately [1,2]. For example, Timesformer [2] first applies spatial-only SA and then temporal-only SA in a transformer encoder. ViViT [1] adds a few temporal-only transformer encoders after spatial-only encoders. However, these factorization methods will introduce additional parameters and computation for temporal SA calculation comparing to a spatial-only transformer network.

With the above discussions, one interesting question is: Can we endow 2D transformers the capability of temporal SA modeling without additional parameters and computational cost? To answer this question, we propose a Temporal Patch Shift (TPS) method for efficient spatiotemporal SA feature learning. In TPS, specific mosaic patterns are designed for patch shifting along the temporal dimension. The TPS operation is placed before the SA layer. For each frame, part of its patches are replaced by patches from neighboring frames. Therefore, the current frame could contain information from patches in temporal domain, and the vanilla spatial SA module can be extended to a spatiotemporal one. It is worth noting that, although the spatiotemporal self-attention computed by TPS is sparse, the spatiotemporal receptive field can be naturally expanded as the TPS layers are stacked. A special case of TPS, where the patches from neighboring frames are shifted using a "Bayer filter", is shown in the first row of Fig. 1. We highlight the patches that are being shifted. It can be seen that, by replacing half of the patches in the current frame with patches from previous and next frames, the vanilla spatial SA is upgraded to spatiotemporal SA with a temporal receptive filed of 3. In the second row of Fig. 1, we show two examples of visualization for consecutive frames after patch shift, which indicate the motion of actions can be well presented within a single frame. The contributions of this work are summarized as follows:

- We propose a Temporal Patch Shift (TPS) operator for efficient spatiotemporal SA modeling. TPS is a plug-and-play module and can be easily embedded into many existing 2D transformers without additional parameters and computation costs.
- We present a Patch Shift Transformer (PST) for action recognition by placing TPS before the multi-head SA layer of transformers. The resulted PST is highly cost-effective in both computation and memory.

Extensive experiments on action recognition datasets show that TPS achieves 58.3%, 69.8%, 82.5% and 86.0% top-1 accuracy on Something-something V1 & V2, Kinetics400 and Diving48, which are comparable to or better than the best Transformer models but with less computation and memory cost.

2   Related Works

Action recognition is a challenging and cornerstone problem in vision. Many deep learning based methods have been proposed recently [4,6,13,14,20,22,28,30–33,36,38,41,44,45]. Based on the employed network architecture, they can be categorized into CNN-based ones and transformer-based ones.

CNN-Based Methods. CNN based methods typically use 3D convolution [4,13,36] or 2D-CNN with temporal modeling [22,31,38] to construct effective backbones for action recognition. For example, C3D [36] trains a VGG model with 3D-CNN to learn spatiotemporal features from a video sequence. I3D [4] inflates all the 2D convolution filters of an Inception V1 model [34] into 3D convolutions so that ImageNet pre-trained weights can be exploited for initialization. Slowfast [13] employs a two-stream 3D-CNN model to process frames at different sampling rates and resolutions. Due to the heavy computational burden of 3D-CNN, many works attempt to enhance 2D-CNN with temporal modules [20,22,26,31,37,38]. P3D [31] factorizes 3D convolution to 1D temporal convolution and 2D spatial convolution. TSM [22] presents an efficient shift module, which utilizes *left* and *right* shifts of sub-channels to substitute a group-wise weight-fixed 1D temporal convolution. TEA [20] employs motion excitation and multiple temporal aggregation to capture motion information and increase temporal receptive field. TEINet [26] uses motion enhanced module and depth-wise 1D convolution for efficient temporal modeling. However, CNN-based methods cannot effectively model long-range dependencies within or cross the frames, which limits their performances.

Transformer-Based Methods. Recently, with the advancement of transformers in 2D vision tasks [5,8,16,23,35,42], many works have been done to apply transformers on video action recognition [1,2,24,43]. Different from the temporal modeling for CNN, which is mainly implemented by 3D convolution or its factorized versions, in transformers the spatiotemporal SA is naturally introduced to explore the spatiotemporal video correlations. Intuitively, one can use all the spatiotemporal patches to directly compute the SA. However, this operation is very computation and memory expensive. Many works are then proposed to reduce the computation burdens of joint spatiotemporal SA modeling. Timesformer [2] adopts divided space-time SA, which adds temporal SA after each spatial SA. ViViT [1] increases the temporal modeling capability by adding several temporal transformer encoders on the top of spatial encoders. Video swin transformer [24] reduces both spatial and temporal dimension by using spatiotemporal local windows. Inspired by the temporal modeling methods in CNN, TokenShift [43] enhances ViT for temporal modeling by applying partial channel shifting on class tokens.

The success of temporal modules in 2D-CNN [20,22,26,31,37] motivates us to develop TPS to enhance a spatial transformer with spatiotemporal feature learning capability. Our work shares the spirits with TokenShift [43] in terms of enhancing the temporal modeling ability of transformers without extra parameters and computation cost. However, our TPS is essentially different from TokenShift. TPS models spatiotemporal SA, while TokenShift is a direct application of TSM in transformer framework, which is in the nature spatial SA with "temporal mixed token". In addition, TPS does not rely on class token (not exists in many recent transformer models [23]) and operates directly on patches, which makes it applicable to most recent transformer models.

3   Methodology

In this section, we present in detail the proposed Temporal Patch Shift (TPS) method, which aims to turn a spatial-only transformer model into a model with spatiotemporal modeling capability. TPS is a *plug-and-play* operation that can be inserted into transformer with no extra parameters and little computation cost. In the following, we first describe how to build a visual transformer for videos, and then introduce the design of TPS for action recognition.

3.1   Video-Based Vision Transformer

The video based transformer can be built by extending the image based ViT [8]. A video clip $X \in \mathbb{R}^{F \times H \times W \times C}$ can be divided into $s \times k \times k$ non-overlapped patches. The 3D patches are flattened into vectors $\mathbf{x}^{(t,p)} \in \mathbb{R}^{3sk^2}$ with $t = 1, \ldots, T$ denoting the temporal index with $T = F/s$, and $p = 1, \ldots, N$ denoting the spatial index with $N = HW/k^2$. The video patches are then mapped to visual tokens with a linear embedding layer

$$\mathbf{z}_0^{(t,p)} = E\mathbf{x}^{(t,p)} + \mathbf{e}_{pos}^{(t,p)} \tag{1}$$

where $E \in \mathbb{R}^{D \times 3sk^2}$ is the weight of a linear layer, $\mathbf{e}_{pos}^{(t,p)}$ is learnable spatiotemporal positional embedding, $\mathbf{z}_0^{(t,p)}$ represents an input spatiotemporal patch at location (t, p) for transformer. We represent the whole input sequence as $\mathbf{Z}_0$.

Suppose that a visual transformer contains L encoders, each consisting of multi-head SA, Layer-Norm (LN) and FFN. The transformer encoder could be represented as follows:

$$\begin{aligned}
\hat{\mathbf{Z}}_l &= \mathrm{SA}(\mathrm{LN}(\mathbf{Z}_{l-1})) + \mathbf{Z}_{l-1}, \\
\mathbf{Z}_l &= \mathrm{FFN}(\mathrm{LN}(\hat{\mathbf{Z}}_l)) + \hat{\mathbf{Z}}_l,
\end{aligned} \tag{2}$$

where $\hat{\mathbf{Z}}_l$ and $\mathbf{Z}_l$ denote the output features of the SA module and the FFN module for block l, respectively. The multi-head SA is computed as follows (LN is neglected for convenience):

$$\begin{aligned}
Q_l, K_l, V_l &= W_l^Q \mathbf{Z}_{l-1}, W_l^K \mathbf{Z}_{l-1}, W_l^V \mathbf{Z}_{l-1} \\
\hat{\mathbf{Z}}_l &= \mathrm{SoftMax}(Q_l K_l^T / \sqrt{d}) V_l,
\end{aligned} \tag{3}$$

where Q_l, K_l, V_l represent the *query*, *key* and *value* matrices for block l and W_l^Q, W_l^K, W_l^V are weights for linear mapping, respectively. d is the scaling factor that equals to *query/key* dimension.

Following transformer encoders, temporal and spatial averaging (or temporal averaging only if using class tokens) can be performed to obtain a single feature, which is then fed into a linear classifier. The major computation burden of transformers comes from the SA computation. Note that when full spatiotemporal SA is applied, the complexity of attention operation is $\mathcal{O}(N^2 T^2)$, while spatial-only attention costs $\mathcal{O}(N^2 T)$ in total. Next, we show how to turn a spatial-only SA operator to a spatiotemporal one with TPS.

3.2   Temporal Patch Shift

Generic Shift Operation. We first define a generic temporal shift operation in transformers as follows:

$$\begin{aligned}
\mathbf{Z}^t &= [\mathbf{z}_0, \mathbf{z}_1, \ldots, \mathbf{z}_N], \\
\mathbf{A} &= [\mathbf{a}_0, \mathbf{a}_1, \ldots, \mathbf{a}_N], \\
\hat{\mathbf{Z}}^t &= \mathbf{A} \odot \mathbf{Z}^{t'} + (1 - \mathbf{A}) \odot \mathbf{Z}^t,
\end{aligned} \tag{4}$$

where $\mathbf{Z}^t, \mathbf{Z}^{t'} \in \mathbb{R}^{D \times N}$ represent the patch features for current frame t and another frame t', respectively. N is the number of patches, and $\mathbf{A}$ represents the matrix of shift channels, with $\mathbf{a}_i \in \mathbb{R}^D$ represents the vector of channel shifts for patch i, each element of which is equal to 0 or 1. $\hat{\mathbf{Z}}^t$ is the output image patches after shift operation.

TSM [22] uses space-invariant channel shift for temporal redundancy modeling, which is a special case of our proposed patch shift operation by shifting α percent of channels (with α percent of elements in $\mathbf{a}_i$ equal to 1), where α is a constant for all patches. In our case, we mainly explore temporal spatial mixing and shift patches in a space-variant manner, where $\mathbf{a}_i = \mathbf{0}$ or $\mathbf{1}$. To reduce the mixing space, shift pattern $\mathbf{p}$ is introduced, which is applied repeatedly in a sliding window manner to cover all patches. For example, $\mathbf{p} = \{0, 1\}$ means shifting one patch for every two patches, therefore $\mathbf{A} = [\mathbf{0}, \mathbf{1}, \mathbf{0}, \mathbf{1}, \dots]$ in Eq. 4. In practice, 2D shift patterns are designed for video data, which will be discussed in detail in the section below.

0	0	0		0	1	0		-4	1	2
0	1	0		-1	0	-1		-1	0	3
0	0	0		0	1	0		-2	-3	4

(a)   (b)   (c)

Fig. 2. Examples of patch shift patterns when patch number is 3 × 3.

Table 1. Comparison of the complexities of different SA models.

Attention	SA-Complexity
Joint	$\mathcal{O}(N^2T^2)$
Divide	$\mathcal{O}(N^2T + T^2N)$
Sparse/Local	$\mathcal{O}(\alpha N^2T^2)$
PatchShift	$\mathcal{O}(N^2T)$

Patch Shift SA. By using the proposed patch shift operation, we can turn spatial-only SA into spatiotemporal SA. Given video patches $\mathbf{Z} \in \mathbb{R}^{D \times T \times N}$, the PatchShift function shifts the patches of each frame along the temporal dimension with pattern $\mathbf{p}$. As only part of patches are shifted in each frame, patches from different frames could be presented in the current frame, therefore, spatial-only SA naturally turns into a sparse spatiotemporal SA. After SA, patches from different frames are shifted back to their original locations. We follow [23] to add a relative position bias with an extension to 3D position. To keep the track of shifted patches, the 3D positions are shifted alongside. With PatchShift, the multi-head SA is computed as:

$$\{\mathbf{i}', \mathbf{Z}'_{l-1}\} = \text{PatchShift}(\mathbf{p}, \mathbf{i}, \mathbf{Z}_{l-1}),$$
$$Q_l, K_l, V_l = W_l^Q \mathbf{Z}'_{l-1}, W_l^K \mathbf{Z}'_{l-1}, W_l^V \mathbf{Z}'_{l-1}, \qquad (5)$$
$$\hat{\mathbf{Z}} = \text{ShiftBack}(\text{SoftMax}(Q_l K_l^T / \sqrt{d} + B(\mathbf{i}'))V_l),$$

where $\{\mathbf{i}, \mathbf{Z}_{l-1}\}$ and $\{\mathbf{i}', \mathbf{Z}'_{l-1}\}$ represent relative position bias indices and patches before and after PatchShift; B is the bias matrix.

Patch Shift Patterns. As mentioned before, in order to reduce the design space, our strategy is to employ repeated shift patterns, as it can scale up to different input sizes and is easy to implement. We adopt the following pattern design principles: a) Even spatial distribution. For each pattern, we uniformly sample the patches from the same frame to ensure they are evenly distributed. b) Reasonably large temporal receptive field. The temporal receptive field is set large enough to aggregate more temporal information. c) Adequate shift percentage. A higher percentage of shifted patches could encourage more inter-frame information communication. Various spatiotemporal SA models can be implemented with different patch shift patterns. We show several instantiations of **p** in Fig. 2. The numbers represent the indices of the frames that the patches are from, where "0", "−" and "+" indicate current, previous and next frames, respectively. Pattern (a) shifts a single patch from next frame to the center of current frame. Pattern (b) shifts patches with a "Bayer filter" like pattern from previous and next frames. Pattern (c) shifts patches with a temporal field of 9, with patch from current frame in the center and patches from previous and next 4 frames around it. For window size larger than the pattern size, we spatially repeat the pattern to cover all patches. We use cyclic padding in [23] for patches that exceed the temporal boundary. In the experiment section, we will discuss the design of shift patterns by extensive ablation studies.

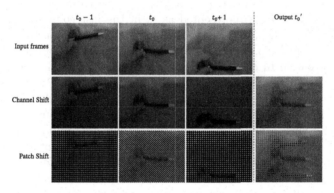

Fig. 3. An example of patch shift and channel shift for consecutive frames.

Patch shift is an efficient spatiotemporal SA modeling method for transformers as it only costs $\mathcal{O}(N^2 T)$ complexity in both computation and memory, which is much less than "Joint" space-temporal SA, where N and T are the spatial and temporal dimension of patches. Patch shift is also more efficient than other factorized attention methods such as "Divide" [1,2] (apply spatial-only and then temporal-only SA) and "Sparse/Local" [2,24] (subsample in space or temporal dimension). The complexity comparison of different SA models are in Table 1.

Discussions on Patch and Channel Shifts. Patch shift and channel shift are two zero parameter and low-cost temporal modeling methods. Patch shift is space-wise sparse and channel-wise dense, while channel shift is opposite. We show an example by applying patch shift and channel shift on three consecutive frames in Fig. 3. Here the shift operations are applied directly on RGB images

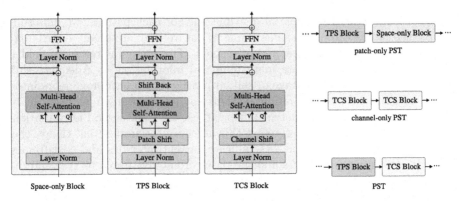

Fig. 4. An overview of building blocks and variants of PST.

for visualization, while in practice we apply shift operations on feature maps. In the output image of patch shifting, 1/4, 1/2 and 1/4 patches are from frames $t_0 - 1$, t_0 and $t_0 + 1$, respectively. For channel shift, the red, green and blue colors represent frames $t_0 - 1$, t_0 and $t_0 + 1$, respectively. The output of shift operation for frame t_0 is represented as t'_0 in the last column. As we can see from the figure, both patch shift and channel shift can capture the motion of action. Patch shift is spatially sparse while keeping the global channel information for each patch. In contrast, channel shift uses partial channel information in exchange for temporal information from other frames. Previous studies on vision transformer [5] have shown that feature channels encode activation of different patterns or objects. Therefore, replacing partial feature channels of the current frame with other frames could potentially lose important information of patterns/objects of interest. In comparison, patch shift contains full information of channels of patches. When patch shift is employed for SA modeling, it builds a sparse spatiotemporal SA with 3D relations among patches. In comparison, channel shift can be viewed as a "mix-patch" operation, by which temporal information is fused in each patch with shared 2D SA weights. Patch shift and channel shift perform shifting operations in orthogonal directions and they are complementary in nature.

3.3   Patch Shift Transformer

Based on the proposed TPS, we can build Patch Shift Transformers (PST) for efficient and effective spatiotemporal feature learning. A PST can be built by inserting TPS into the SA module of off-the-shelf 2D transformer blocks. Therefore, our model could directly benefit from the pre-trained models on 2D recognition tasks. The details of Temporal Patch Shift blocks (TPS block for short) can be seen in Fig. 4. TPS turns spatial-only SA to spatiotemporal SA by aggregating information of patches from other temporal frames. However, it gathers information in a sparse manner and sacrifices SA within frames. To alleviate this problem, we insert one TPS block for every two SA modules (*alternative shift* in short) so that spatial-only SA and spatiotemporal SA could work in turns to approximate full spatiotemporal SA.

We further improve the temporal modeling ability of spatial-only SA with channel shift. Specifically, partial channels of each patch are replaced with those from previous or next frames. We call this block a temporal channel shift (TCS) block. The final PST consists of both TPS and TCS blocks. We will also implement a channel-only PST for comparison to unveil the benefits of patch shift.

4   Experiments

4.1   Dataset

Something-Something V1 & V2. [15] are large collections of video clips, containing daily actions interacting with common objects. They focus on object motion without differentiating manipulated objects. V1 includes 108,499 video clips, while V2 includes 220,847 video clips. Both V1 and V2 have 174 classes. **Kinetics400** [17] is a large-scale dataset in action recognition, which contains 400 human action classes, with at least 400 video clips for each class. Each clip is collected from a YouTube video and then trimmed to around 10s. **Diving-48 V2** [21] is a fine-grained video dataset of competitive diving, consisting of 18k trimmed video clips of 48 unambiguous dive sequences. This dataset is a challenging task for modern action recognition systems as it reduces background bias and requires modeling of long-term temporal dynamics. We use the manually cleaned V2 annotations of this dataset, which contains 15,027 videos for training and 1,970 videos for testing.

4.2   Experiment Setup

Models. We choose swin transformer [23] as our backbone network and develop PST-T, PST-B with an increase in model size and FLOPs based on swin transformer Tiny and Base backbones, respectively. In ablation study, we use Swin-Tiny considering its good trade-off between performance and efficiency. We adopt 32 frames as input and the tubelet embedding strategy in ViViT [1] with patch size $2 \times 4 \times 4$ by default. As PST-T and PST-B are efficient models, when comparing with SOTA methods, we introduce PST-T† and PST-B†, which doubles the temporal attention window to 2 with slightly increased computation.

Training. For all the datasets, we first resize the short side of raw images to 256 and then apply center cropping of 224×224. During training, we follow [24] and use random flip, AutoAugment [7] for augmentation. We utilize AdamW [27] with the cosine learning rate schedule for network training. For PST-T, the base learning rate, warmup epoch, total epoch, stochastic depth rate, weight decay, batchsize are set to 10^{-3}, 2.5, 30, 0.1, 0.02, 64 respectively. For larger model PST-B, learning rate, drop path rate and weight decay are set to 3×10^{-4}, 0.2, 0.05, respectively.

Testing. For fair comparison, we follow the testing strategy in previous state-of-the-art methods. We report the results of two different sampling strategies. On Something-something V1 & V2 and Diving-48 V2, uniform sampling and center-crop (or three-crop) testing are adopted. On Kinetics400, we adopt the dense sampling strategy as in [1] with 4 view, three-crop testing.

4.3   Ablation Study

To investigate the design of patch shift patterns and the use of TPS blocks, we conduct a series of experiments in this section. All the experiments are conducted on Something-something V1 with Swin-Tiny as backbone (IN-1K pretrained). For experiments on design of patch shift we use patch-only PST for clarity.

The Number and Distribution of Shifted Patches. We start with a simple experiment by shifting only one center patch along temporal dimension within each window. It can be seen from Table 2(a) that this simple shift pattern (center-one) brings significant improvements (4.7% on top-1) over the model without shifting operation (none). We then increase the number of shifting patches to 1/2 of the total patches, however, in an uneven distribution (shift only the left half of patches). This uneven shift pattern does not improve over the simple "center-one" pattern. However, when the shifted patches are distributed evenly within the window (even-2), the performance increases by 0.9% on top-1. This indicates that, the shifted and non-shifted patches should be distributed evenly. It is also found that a large temporal field is helpful. When we increase the temporal field to 3 by shifting 1/4 patches to previous frame and 1/4 patches to next frame (even-3), the performance is improved by 2.4% on top-1 over shifting patches in one dimension.

Table 2. Ablation studies on TPS. All the experiments are conducted on Something-something V1 with Swin-Tiny as backbone.

(a) Patch distribution

Distribution	Top-1	Top-5
None	40.6	71.4
Center-one	45.3	75.1
Uneven	45.3	75.5
Even-2	46.2	76.1
Even-3	**48.6**	**77.8**

(b) Shift patterns

Pattern	Top-1	Top-5
A-3	48.6	77.8
B-4	50.7	79.3
C-9	**51.8**	**80.3**
D-16	50.0	79.5

(c) Number of stages with TPS

Stage 1	2	3	4	Top-1	Top-5
✓				47.3	77.0
✓	✓			48.4	77.6
✓	✓	✓		50.4	79.1
✓	✓	✓	✓	**51.8**	**80.3**

(d) Shift back, Alternative shift and shift RPE

Shift back	Alternative	Shift RPE	Top-1	Top-5
	✓	✓	47.3	77.0
✓		✓	46.4	76.6
✓	✓		46.1	76.0
✓	✓	✓	**51.8**	**80.3**

(e) Comparison of spatiotemporal attentions

	FLOPs	Memory	Top-1	Top-5
Avgpool	72G	3.7G	40.6	71.4
Joint	106G	20.2G	51.5	80.0
Local	88G	11G	49.9	79.2
Sparse	72G	4.0G	42.7	74.0
Channel-only	72G	3.7G	51.2	79.7
Patch-only	72G	3.7G	51.8	80.3
PST	**72G**	**3.7G**	**52.2**	**80.3**

Patch Shift Patterns. Based on the experiments in Table 2(a), we design a few different patch shift patterns with various temporal fields. The patches of different frames are distributed evenly within the window. Pattern A with temporal field 3 is shown in Fig. 2(b), which is "Bayer filter" like. Pattern B with temporal field 4 is implemented by replacing 1/4 of index "0" frame patches in pattern A as index "2" frame patches. Pattern C is shown in Fig. 2(c). Pattern D is designed by placing patches from 16 consecutive frames in a 4×4 pattern grid. More details can be found in the supplementary materials. We can see from the Table 2(b) that the performance of TPS gradually increases when the temporal field grows. The best performance is reached at temporal field 9, which achieves a good balance between spatial and temporal dimension. We use this pattern for the rest of our experiments.

The Number of Stages Using TPS Blocks. As can be seen in Table 2(c), by using TPS blocks in more stages of the network, the performance gradually increases. The model achieves the best performance when all the stages are equipped with TPS blocks.

Shift Back, Alternative Shift and Shift RPE. Shift back operation recovers the patches' locations and keeps the frame structure complete. Alternative shift is described in Sect. 3.3 for building connections between patches. Shift RPE represents whether relative positions are shifted alongside patches. As shown in Table 2(d), removing each of them would decrease performance by 4.5%, 5.4%, 5.7%, respectively. Therefore, we use all the operations in our model.

Comparison with Other Temporal Modeling Methods. In Table 2(e), we compare PST with other designs of spatiotemporal attention methods in FLOPs, peak training memory consumption and accuracy. "Avgpool" achieves only 40.6% Top-1 rate since it cannot distinguish temporal ordering. Joint spatiotemporal SA achieves a good performance at the price of high computation and memory cost. Local spatiotemporal attention [24] applies SA within a local window with 3D window size. It reduces the computation and memory cost but at the price of performance drop comparing to "Joint". We also implement a sparse spatiotemporal SA by subsampling spatial patches to half, while keeping the full temporal dimension. It performs poorly as only part of patches participate in SA computation in each layer. We implement channel-only PST with shift ratio equals 1/4, which is the same in the [22]. This channel-only PST also achieves strong performance.

Patch-only PST outperforms all other temporal modeling methods without additional parameters and FLOPs. The best performance comes from combining channel-only and patch-only PST, which indicates they are complementary in nature. Specifically, PST exceeds joint spatiotemporal SA with much less computation and only 1/5 of memory usage. It also outperforms other efficient spatiotemporal SA models with fewer computation and memory cost.

4.4   Comparison with SOTA

Something V1 & V2. The performance statistics on Something V1 & V2, including the pretrained dataset, classification results, inference protocols, the corresponding FLOPs and parameter numbers are shown in Table 3.

Table 3. Comparisons with the other methods on Something-something V1 & V2.

Model	Pretrain	Crops × Clips	FLOPs	Params	Sthv1		Sthv2	
					Top-1	Top-5	Top-1	Top-5
TSM [22]	K400	3 × 2	65G	24.3M	–	–	63.4	88.5
TEINet [26]	IN-1K	1 × 1	66G	30.4M	49.9	–	62.1	–
TEA [20]	IN-1K	1 × 1	70G	24.3M	51.9	80.3	–	–
TDN [37]	IN-1K	1 × 1	72G	24.8M	53.9	82.1	65.3	89.5
ACTION-Net [40]	IN-1K	1 × 1	70G	28.1M	–	–	64.0	89.3
SlowFast R101, 8x8 [13]	K400	3 × 1	106G	53.3M	–	–	63.1	87.6
MSNet [18]	IN-1K	1 × 1	101G	24.6M	52.1	82.3	64.7	89.4
blVNet [11]	IN-1K	1 × 1	129G	40.2M	–	–	65.2	90.3
Timesformer-HR [2]	IN-21K	3 × 1	1703G	121.4M	–	–	62.5	–
ViViT-L/16x2 [1]	IN-21K	3 × 1	903G	352.1M	–	–	65.9	89.9
MViT-B, 64×3 [9]	K400	3 × 1	455G	36.6M	–	–	67.7	90.9
Mformer-L [29]	K400	3 × 1	1185G	86M	–	–	68.1	91.2
X-ViT [3]	IN-21K	3 × 1	283G	92M	–	–	66.2	90.6
SIFAR-L [10]	K400	3 × 1	576G	196M	–	–	64.2	88.4
Video-Swin [25]	K400	3 × 1	321G	88.1M	–	–	69.6	92.7
PST-T	IN-1K	1 × 1	72G	28.5M	52.2	80.3	65.7	90.2
	IN-1K	3 × 1			52.8	80.5	66.4	90.2
	K400	1 × 1			53.2	82.2	66.7	90.6
	K400	3 × 1			53.6	82.2	67.3	90.5
PST-T†	K400	3 × 1	74G		54.0	82.3	67.9	90.8
PST-B	IN-21K	1 × 1	247G	88.8M	55.3	81.9	66.7	90.7
	IN-21K	3 × 1			55.6	82.2	67.4	90.9
	K400	1 × 1			57.4	83.2	68.7	91.3
	K400	3 × 1			57.7	83.4	69.2	91.9
PST-B†	K400	3 × 1	252G		**58.3**	**83.9**	**69.8**	**93.0**

The first compartment contains methods based on 3D CNNs or factorized (2+1)D CNNs. Using efficient inference protocol (16 views and center crop×1 clip), ImageNet1K pretrain, PST-T obtains 52.2% accuracy on V1 and 65.7% on V2, respectively, which outperforms all the CNN-based methods with similar FLOPs. Note that TDN [37] uses a different sampling strategy comparing to other methods, which requires 5 times more frames. Even though, PST-T still outperforms TDN on larger Something-something V2.

The second compartment contains transformer-based methods. Our small model PST-T pretrained on Kinetics400 offers competitive performance on

SomethingV2 comparing to these methods. PST-B is a larger model and pretrained on ImageNet21K/Kinetics400. PST-B achieves 57.7% and 69.2% on V1 & V2, outperforming Timesformer-HR [2], ViViT-L [1] and MViT-B [9] at a lower cost on computation or parameter. PST-B also outperforms Mformer-L [29] and X-ViT [3], which are recently proposed efficient temporal modeling methods. They apply trajectory self-attention and local spatiotemporal self-attention, respectively. Our PST-B† achieves 58.3% and 69.8% on V1 & V2, which outperforms other transformer-based methods. Note that, SIFAR-L [10] uses larger backbone network Swin-L, however, its performance is less satisfactory. PST-B† also outperforms Video-Swin [24], which uses full temporal window on this dataset. The performances of PST family on Something-something V1 & V2 confirms its remarkable ability for spatiotemporal modeling.

Kinetics400. We report our results on scene-focused Kinetics400 in Table 4 and compare them with previous state-of-the-arts. As we can see from Table 4, PST-T achieves 78.2% top-1 accuracy and outperforms majority of (2+1D) CNN-based methods such as TSM [22], TEINet [26], TEA [20], TDN [37] with less

Table 4. Comparisons with the state-of-the-art methods on Kinetics400.

Model	Pretrain	Crops × Clips	FLOPs	Params	Top-1	Top-5
I3D [4]	IN-1K	1 × 1	108G	28.0M	72.1	90.3
NL-I3D [39]	IN-1K	6 × 10	32G	35.3M	77.7	93.3
CoST [19]	IN-1K	3 × 10	33G	35.3M	77.5	93.2
SlowFast-R50 [13]	IN-1K	3 × 10	36G	32.4M	75.6	92.1
X3D-XL [12]	–	3 × 10	48G	11.0M	79.1	93.9
TSM [22]	IN-1K	3 × 10	65G	24.3M	74.7	91.4
TEINet [26]	IN-1K	3 × 10	66G	30.4M	76.2	92.5
TEA [20]	IN-1K	3 × 10	70G	24.3M	76.1	92.5
TDN [37]	IN-1K	3 × 10	72G	24.8M	77.5	93.2
Timesformer-L [2]	IN-21K	3 × 1	2380G	121.4M	80.7	94.7
ViViT-L/16x2 [1]	IN-21K	3 × 1	3980G	310.8M	81.7	93.8
X-ViT [3]	IN-21K	3 × 1	283G	92M	80.2	94.7
MViT-B, 32×3 [9]	IN-21K	1 × 5	170G	36.6M	80.2	94.4
MViT-B, 64×3 [9]	IN-21K	3 × 3	455G	36.6M	81.2	95.1
Mformer-HR [29]	K400	3 × 1	959G	86M	81.1	95.2
TokenShift-HR [43]	IN-21K	3 × 10	2096G	303.4M	80.4	94.5
SIFAR-L [10]	IN-21K	3 × 1	576G	196M	**82.2**	**95.1**
Video-Swin [24]	IN-21K	3 × 4	282G	88.1M	**82.7**	**95.5**
PST-T	IN-1K	3 × 4	72G	28.5M	78.2	92.2
PST-T†	IN-1K	3 × 4	74G	28.5M	78.6	93.5
PST-B	IN-21K	3 × 4	247G	88.8M	81.8	95.4
PST-B†	IN-21K	3 × 4	252G	88.8M	**82.5**	**95.6**

total FLOPs. Our larger model PST-B achieves 81.8% top-1 accuracy, which outperforms strong 3D-CNN counterparts such as SlowFast [13] and X3D [12].

Comparing to transformer-based methods such as Timesformer [2] and ViViT-L [1], our PST-B† achieves 82.5% with less computation overheads. Specifically, PST-B† outperforms SIFAR-L [10] which adopts larger size Swin-L as backbone network. PST-B† also achieves on par performance with recently developed Video-Swin [25] with less computation cost.

Diving-48 V2. In Table 5, we further evaluate our method on fine-grained action dataset Diving-48. As older version of diving-48 has labeling errors, we compare our methods with reproduced SlowFast [13] and Timesformer in [2] on V2. PST-T achieves competitive 79.2% top-1 performance with ImageNet-1K pretrain and costs much less computation resources than SlowFast, Timersformer and Timesformer-HR. When PST-T is pretrained on Kinetics400, it also outperforms Timersformer-L. Our larger model PST-B outperforms TimsFormer-L by a large margin of 2.6% when both are pretrained on ImageNet-21K with 9.7× less FLOPs. When model is pretrained on Kinetic400, PST-B achieves 85.0% top-1 accuracy. PST-T† and PST-B† further boost the performance to 82.1% and 86.0%, respectively.

Table 5. Comparisons with the other methods on Diving-48 V2.

Model	Pretrain	Crops × Clips	FLOPs	Params	Top-1	Top-5
SlowFast R101, 8x8 [13]	K400	3 × 1	106G	53.3M	77.6	–
Timesformer [2]	IN-21K	3 × 1	196G	121.4M	74.9	–
Timesformer-HR [2]	IN-21K	3 × 1	1703G	121.4M	78.0	–
Timesformer-L [2]	IN-21K	3 × 1	2380G	121.4M	81.0	–
PST-T	IN-1K	3 × 1	72G	28.5M	79.2	98.2
	K400	3 × 1	72G		81.2	98.7
PST-T†	K400	3 × 1	74G		82.1	98.6
PST-B	IN-21K	3 × 1	247G	88.1M	83.6	98.5
	K400	3 × 1	247G		85.0	98.6
PST-B†	K400	3 × 1	252G		**86.0**	**98.6**

Latency, Throughput and Memory. The inference latency, throughput (videos/second) and inference memory consumption are important for action recognition in practice. We performed measurement on a single NVIDIA Tesla V100 GPU. We use batch size of 1 for latency measurement and batch size of 4 for throughput measurement. The accuracy is tested on validation set of Something-something V1 & V2 dataset. The results are shown in Table 6. We make three observations: (1) Comparing to baseline "2D Swin-T" that uses 2D transformer with avgpooling for temporal modeling, PST-T has slightly higher latency, same memory consumption, but much better performance (11.6%, 9.0%

Table 6. Memory and latency comparison on Something-something V1 & V2 (Measured on NVIDIA Tesla V100 GPU)

Methods	FLOPs	Param	Memory	Latency	Throughput	Sthv1		Sthv2	
						Top-1	Top-5	Top-1	Top-5
2D Swin-T	72G	28.5M	1.7G	29 ms	35.5 v/s	40.6	71.4	56.7	84.1
Video-Swin-T [24]	106G($\uparrow$ 34G)		3.0G($\uparrow$ 1.3G)	62 ms($\uparrow$ 33ms)	17.7 v/s	51.5	80.0	65.7	90.1
PST-T	72G		1.7G	31 ms($\uparrow$ 2ms)	34.7 v/s	**52.2**	**80.3**	**65.7**	**90.2**
2D Swin-B	247G	88.8M	2.2G	71 ms	15.5 v/s	–	–	59.5	86.3
Video-Swin-B [24]	321G($\uparrow$ 74G)		3.6G($\uparrow$ 1.4G)	147 ms($\uparrow$ 76ms)	7.9 v/s	–	–	69.6	92.7
PST-B†	252G($\uparrow$ 5G)		2.4G($\uparrow$ 0.2G)	81ms($\uparrow$ 10ms)	13.8 v/s	–	–	**69.8**	**93.0**

top-1 improvements on Sthv1&v2, respectively). (2) Comparing to "Video-Swin-T" that utilizes full scale temporal information, PST-T uses 76% less memory and has 2 times faster inference speed, while achieves very competitive performance. (3) For larger model PST-B†, it achieves better performance than Video-Swin-B while using 50% less inference memory and 80% less time.

5   Conclusions

In this paper, we proposed a novel temporal patch shift method, which can be inserted into transformer blocks in a plug-and-play manner for efficient and effective spatiotemporal modeling. By comparing the patch shift and channel shift operations under transformer framework, we showed that they are two efficient temporal modeling methods and complementary in nature. PST achieved competitive performance comparing to previous methods on the datasets of Something-something V1 & V2 [15], Diving-48 [21] and Kinetics400 [17]. In addition, we presented in-depth ablation studies and visualization analysis on PST to investigate the design principles of patch shift patterns, and explained why it is effective for learning spatiotemporal relations. PST achieved a good balance between accuracy and computational cost for effective action recognition.

References

1. Arnab, A., Dehghani, M., Heigold, G., Sun, C., Lucic, M., Schmid, C.: ViViT: a video vision transformer. In: Computer Vision and Pattern Recognition (2021). arXiv
2. Bertasius, G., Wang, H., Torresani, L.: Is space-time attention all you need for video understanding?. In: Computer Vision and Pattern Recognition (2021). arXiv
3. Bulat, A., Perez-Rua, J.M., Sudhakaran, S., Martinez, B., Tzimiropoulos, G.: Space-time mixing attention for video transformer. In: NeurIPS (2021)
4. Carreira, J., Zisserman, A.: Quo Vadis, action recognition? A new model and the kinetics dataset. In: IEEE Conference on Computer Vision and Pattern Recognition, pp. 6299–6308 (2017)
5. Chen, C.F., Fan, Q., Panda, R.: CrossVit: cross-attention multi-scale vision transformer for image classification. arXiv preprint arXiv:2103.14899 (2021)

6. Christoph, R., Pinz, F.A.: Spatiotemporal residual networks for video action recognition. In: NIPS, pp. 3468–3476 (2016)
7. Cubuk, E.D., Zoph, B., Mane, D., Vasudevan, V., Le, Q.V.: AutoAugment: learning augmentation policies from data (2019). https://arxiv.org/pdf/1805.09501.pdf
8. Dosovitskiy, A., et al.: An image is worth 16x16 words: transformers for image recognition at scale. In: ICLR 2021: The Ninth International Conference on Learning Representations (2021)
9. Fan, H., et al.: Multiscale vision transformers. In: Proceedings of the IEEE/CVF International Conference on Computer Vision (ICCV), pp. 6824–6835 (2021)
10. Fan, Q., Chen, C., Panda, R.: An image classifier can suffice for video understanding. CoRR abs/2106.14104 (2021). https://arxiv.org/abs/2106.14104
11. Fan, Q., Chen, C.F.R., Kuehne, H., Pistoia, M., Cox, D.: More is less: learning efficient video representations by temporal aggregation modules. In: Advances in Neural Information Processing Systems 33 (2019)
12. Feichtenhofer, C.: X3D: expanding architectures for efficient video recognition. In: Proceedings of the IEEE/CVF Conference on Computer Vision and Pattern Recognition (CVPR) (2020)
13. Feichtenhofer, C., Fan, H., Malik, J., He, K.: SlowFast networks for video recognition. In: International Conference on Computer Vision, pp. 6202–6211 (2019)
14. Feichtenhofer, C., Pinz, A., Zisserman, A.: Convolutional two-stream network fusion for video action recognition. In: IEEE Conference on Computer Vision and Pattern Recognition, pp. 1933–1941 (2016). https://doi.org/10.1109/CVPR.2016.213
15. Goyal, R., et al.: The "something something" video database for learning and evaluating visual common sense. In: International Conference on Computer Vision, pp. 5842–5850 (2017)
16. Han, K., Xiao, A., Wu, E., Guo, J., Xu, C., Wang, Y.: Transformer in transformer. arXiv preprint arXiv:2103.00112 (2021)
17. Kay, W., et al.: The kinetics human action video dataset. arXiv preprint arXiv:1705.06950 (2017)
18. Kwon, H., Kim, M., Kwak, S., Cho, M.: MotionSqueeze: neural motion feature learning for video understanding. In: Vedaldi, A., Bischof, H., Brox, T., Frahm, J.-M. (eds.) ECCV 2020. LNCS, vol. 12361, pp. 345–362. Springer, Cham (2020). https://doi.org/10.1007/978-3-030-58517-4_21
19. Li, C., Zhong, Q., Xie, D., Pu, S.: Collaborative spatiotemporal feature learning for video action recognition. In: Proceedings of the IEEE/CVF Conference on Computer Vision and Pattern Recognition (CVPR) (2019)
20. Li, Y., Ji, B., Shi, X., Zhang, J., Kang, B., Wang, L.: TEA: temporal excitation and aggregation for action recognition. In: IEEE Conference on Computer Vision and Pattern Recognition, pp. 909–918 (2020)
21. Li, Y., Li, Y., Vasconcelos, N.: RESOUND: towards action recognition without representation bias. In: Ferrari, V., Hebert, M., Sminchisescu, C., Weiss, Y. (eds.) ECCV 2018. LNCS, vol. 11210, pp. 520–535. Springer, Cham (2018). https://doi.org/10.1007/978-3-030-01231-1_32
22. Lin, J., Gan, C., Han, S.: TSM: temporal shift module for efficient video understanding. In: International Conference on Computer Vision, pp. 7083–7093 (2019)
23. Liu, Z., et al.: Swin transformer: hierarchical vision transformer using shifted windows. arXiv preprint arXiv:2103.14030 (2021)
24. Liu, Z., et al.: Video swin transformer. In: Computer Vision and Pattern Recognition (2021). arXiv

25. Liu, Z., et al.: Video swin transformer. arXiv preprint arXiv:2106.13230 (2021)
26. Liu, Z.,et al.: TEINet: towards an efficient architecture for video recognition. In: AAAI (2020)
27. Loshchilov, I., Hutter, F.: Decoupled weight decay regularization. In: 7th International Conference on Learning Representations, ICLR 2019, New Orleans, LA, USA, 6–9 May 2019. OpenReview.net (2019). https://openreview.net/forum?id=Bkg6RiCqY7
28. Martinez, B., Modolo, D., Xiong, Y., Tighe, J.: Action recognition with spatial-temporal discriminative filter banks. In: International Conference on Computer Vision, pp. 5482–5491 (2019)
29. Patrick, M., et al.: Keeping your eye on the ball: trajectory attention in video transformers. In: Advances in Neural Information Processing Systems (NeurIPS) (2021)
30. Piergiovanni, A., Ryoo, M.S.: Representation flow for action recognition. In: IEEE Conference on Computer Vision and Pattern Recognition, pp. 9945–9953 (2019)
31. Qiu, Z., Yao, T., Mei, T.: Learning spatio-temporal representation with pseudo-3D residual networks. In: International Conference on Computer Vision, pp. 5533–5541 (2017)
32. Rohrbach, M., Rohrbach, A., Regneri, M., Amin, S., Andriluka, M., Pinkal, M., Schiele, B.: Recognizing fine-grained and composite activities using hand-centric features and script data. IJCV **119**(3), 346–373 (2016)
33. Simonyan, K., Zisserman, A.: Two-stream convolutional networks for action recognition in videos. In: NIPS, pp. 568–576 (2014). https://papers.nips.cc/paper/5353-two-stream-convolutional-networks-for-action-recognition-in-videos
34. Szegedy, C., et al.: Going deeper with convolutions. In: Computer Vision and Pattern Recognition (CVPR) (2015). https://arxiv.org/abs/1409.4842
35. Touvron, H., Cord, M., Matthijs, D., Massa, F., Sablayrolles, A., Jegou, H.: Training data-efficient image transformers & distillation through attention. In: ICML 2021: 38th International Conference on Machine Learning (2021)
36. Tran, D., Bourdev, L.D., Fergus, R., Torresani, L., Paluri, M.: Learning spatiotemporal features with 3D convolutional networks. In: International Conference on Computer Vision, pp. 4489–4497 (2015). https://doi.org/10.1109/ICCV.2015.510
37. Wang, L., Tong, Z., Ji, B., Wu, G.: TDN: temporal difference networks for efficient action recognition. In: IEEE Conference on Computer Vision and Pattern Recognition (2021)
38. Wang, L., et al.: Temporal segment networks: towards good practices for deep action recognition. In: Leibe, B., Matas, J., Sebe, N., Welling, M. (eds.) ECCV 2016. LNCS, vol. 9912, pp. 20–36. Springer, Cham (2016). https://doi.org/10.1007/978-3-319-46484-8_2
39. Wang, X., Girshick, R., Gupta, A., He, K.: Non-local neural networks. In: IEEE Conference on Computer Vision and Pattern Recognition (2018)
40. Wang, Z., She, Q., Smolic, A.: Action-Net: multipath excitation for action recognition. In: IEEE/CVF Conference on Computer Vision and Pattern Recognition (CVPR) (2021)
41. Yang, C., Xu, Y., Shi, J., Dai, B., Zhou, B.: Temporal pyramid network for action recognition. In: IEEE Conference on Computer Vision and Pattern Recognition, pp. 591–600 (2020)
42. Yuan, L., et al.: Tokens-to-token ViT: training vision transformers from scratch on imagenet. arXiv preprint arXiv:2101.11986 (2021)
43. Zhang, H., Hao, Y., Ngo, C.W.: Token shift transformer for video classification. In: Computer Vision and Pattern Recognition (2021). arXiv

44. Zhao, Y., Xiong, Y., Lin, D.: Recognize actions by disentangling components of dynamics. In: IEEE Conference on Computer Vision and Pattern Recognition, pp. 6566–6575 (2018)
45. Zheng, Y.D., Liu, Z., Lu, T., Wang, L.: Dynamic sampling networks for efficient action recognition in videos. TIP **29**, 7970–7983 (2020)

Proposal-Free Temporal Action Detection via Global Segmentation Mask Learning

Sauradip Nag[1,2(✉)], Xiatian Zhu[1,3], Yi-Zhe Song[1,2], and Tao Xiang[1,2]

[1] CVSSP, University of Surrey, Guildford, UK
{s.nag,xiatian.zhu,y.song,t.xiang}@surrey.ac.uk
[2] iFlyTek-Surrey Joint Research Centre on Artificial Intelligence, London, UK
[3] Surrey Institute for People-Centred Artificial Intelligence, University of Surrey, Guildford, UK

Abstract. Existing temporal action detection (TAD) methods rely on generating an overwhelmingly large number of proposals per video. This leads to complex model designs due to proposal generation and/or per-proposal action instance evaluation and the resultant high computational cost. In this work, for the first time, we propose a *proposal-free Temporal Action detection model via Global Segmentation mask* (TAGS). Our core idea is to learn a *global segmentation mask* of each action instance jointly at the full video length. The TAGS model differs significantly from the conventional proposal-based methods by focusing on global temporal representation learning to directly detect local start and end points of action instances without proposals. Further, by modeling TAD holistically rather than locally at the individual proposal level, TAGS needs a much simpler model architecture with lower computational cost. Extensive experiments show that despite its simpler design, TAGS outperforms existing TAD methods, achieving new state-of-the-art performance on two benchmarks. Importantly, it is $-20\times$ faster to train and $-1.6\times$ more efficient for inference. Our PyTorch implementation of TAGS is available at https://github.com/sauradip/TAGS.

1 Introduction

Temporal action detection (TAD) aims to identify the temporal interval (*i.e.*, the start and end points) and the class label of all action instances in an untrimmed video [5,16]. All existing TAD methods rely on *proposal generation* by either regressing predefined anchor boxes [8,15,22,42] (Fig. 1(a)) or directly predicting the start and end times of proposals [4,18,19,27,44–46] (Fig. 1(b)). Centered around proposals, existing TAD methods essentially take a local view of the video and focus on each individual proposal for action instance temporal refinement and classification. Such an approach thus suffers from several fundamental limitations: (1) An excessive (sometimes exhaustive) number of proposals are usually required for good performance. For example, BMN [18] generates

---

Supplementary Information The online version contains supplementary material available at https://doi.org/10.1007/978-3-031-20062-5_37.

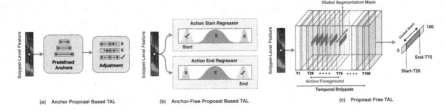

Fig. 1. All existing TAD methods, no matter whether (a) anchor-based or (b) anchor-free, all need to generate action proposals. Instead, (c) our *global segmentation mask model* (TAGS) is proposal-free.

−5000 proposals per video by exhaustively pairing start and end points predicted. Generating and evaluating such a large number of proposals means high computational costs for both training and inference. (2) Once the proposals are generated, the subsequent modeling is local to each individual proposal. Missing global context over the whole video can lead to sub-optimal detection.

In this work, for the first time, we address these limitations by proposing a proposal-free TAD model. Our model, termed TAGS, learns a *global segmentation mask* of action instances at the full video length (Fig. 1(c)). By modeling TAD globally rather than locally, TAGS not only removes the need for proposal generation, and the associated design and computational complexity, it is also more effective. Concretely, instead of predicting the start/end points of each action instance, TAGS learns to predict an action segmentation mask of an entire video. Such a mask represents the *global* temporal structure of all action instances in the video; TAGS is thus intrinsically global context-aware.

Taking a proposal-free approach to TAD, our TAGS has a simpler model architecture design than existing methods. Specifically, it takes each local snippet (*i.e.*, a short sequence of consecutive frames of a video) as a predictive unit. That is, taking as input a snippet feature representation for a given video, TAGS directly outputs the target action segmentation mask as well as class label concurrently. To facilitate global context modeling, we leverage self-attention [36] for capturing necessary video-level inter-snippet relationship. Once the mask is generated, simple foreground segment classification follows to produce the final TAD result. To facilitate global segmentation mask learning, we further introduce a novel boundary focused loss that pays more attention to temporal boundary regions, and leverage mask predictive redundancy and inter-branch consistency for prediction enhancement. During inference, once the masks and class labels are predicted, top-scoring segments with refined boundary can then be selected via non-maximal suppression (NMS) to produce the final TAD result.

We make the following **contributions**. (**I**) We present a novel proposal-free TAD model based on *global segmentation mask* (TAGS) learning. To the best of our knowledge, this is the first model that eliminates the need for proposal generation/evaluation. As a result, it has a much simpler model design with a lower computational cost than existing alternatives. (**II**) We improve TAD feature representation learning with global temporal context using self-attention leading to context-aware TAD. **(III)** To enhance the learning of temporal boundary, we propose a novel boundary focused loss function, along with mask predictive redundancy and inter-branch consistency. **(IV)** Extensive experiments show that the proposed TAGS method yields new state-of-the-art performance on two TAD datasets (ActivityNet-v1.3 and THUMOS'14). Importantly, our method is also significantly more efficient in both training/inference. For instance, it is 20/1.6× faster than G-TAD [46] in training and inference respectively.

2 Related Works

Although all existing TAD methods use proposals, they differ in how the proposals are generated.

Anchor-Based Proposal Learning Methods. These methods generate proposal based on a pre-determined set of anchors. Inspired by object detection in static images [30], R-C3D [42] proposes to use anchor boxes. It follows the structure of proposal generation and classification in design. With similar model design, TURN [15] aggregates local features to represent snippet-level features, which are then used for temporal boundary regression and classification. Later, GTAN [22] improves the proposal feature pooling procedure with a learnable Gaussian kernel for weighted averaging. PBR-Net [20] improves the detection performance using a pyramidal anchor based detection and fine-grained refinement using frame-level features. G-TAD [46] learns semantic and temporal context via graph convolutional networks for better proposal generation. MUSES [21] further improves the performance by handling intra-instance variations caused by shot change. VSGN [51] focuses on short-action detection in a cross-scale multi-level pyramidal architecture. Note that these anchor boxes are often exhaustively generated so are high in number.

Anchor-Free Proposal Learning Methods. Instead of using pre-designed and fixed anchor boxes, these methods directly learn to predict temporal proposals (*i.e.*, start and end times/points) [18,19,53]. For example, SSN [53] decomposes an action instance into three stages (starting, course, and ending) and employs structured temporal pyramid pooling to generate proposals. BSN [19] predicts the start, end and actionness at each temporal location and generates proposals using locations with high start and end probabilities. Later, BMN [18] additionally generates a boundary-matching confidence map to improve proposal generation. BSN++ [34] further extends BMN with a complementary boundary generator to capture rich context. CSA [33] enriches the proposal temporal context via attention transfer. Recently, ContextLoc [57] further pushes the boundaries by adapting global context at proposal-level and handling the context-aware inter-proposal relations. While no pre-defined anchor boxes are required, these methods often have to exhaustively pair all possible locations predicted with high scores. So both anchor-based and anchor-free TAD methods have a large quantity of temporal proposals to evaluate. This results in complex model design, high computational cost and lack of global context modeling. Our TAGS is designed to address all these limitations by being proposal-free.

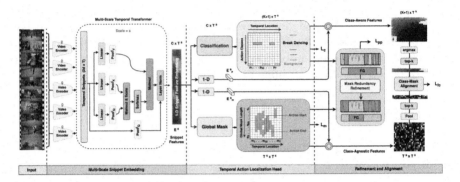

Fig. 2. Architecture of our proposal-free _Temporal Action detection model via Global Segmentation mask_(TAGS). Given an untrimmed video, TAGS first extracts a sequence of T snippet features with a pre-trained video encoder (*e.g.*, I3D [7]), and conducts self-attentive learning at multiple temporal scales s to obtain snippet embedding with global context. Subsequently, with each snippet embedding, TAGS classifies different actions (output $\boldsymbol{P}^s \in \mathbb{R}^{(K+1)\times T^s}$ with K the action class number) and predicts full-video-long foreground mask (output $\boldsymbol{M}^s \in \mathbb{R}^{T^s \times T^s}$) concurrently in a two-branch design. During training, TAGS minimizes the difference of class and mask predictions against the ground-truth. For more accurate localization, an efficient boundary refinement strategy is further introduced, along with mask predictive redundancy and classification-mask consistency regularization. During inference, TAGS selects top scoring snippets from the classification output $\boldsymbol{P}$, and then thresholds the corresponding foreground masks in $\boldsymbol{M}$ at each scale and then aggregates them to yield action instance candidates. Finally, softNMS is applied to remove redundant candidates.

Self-attention. Our snippet representation is learned based on self-attention, which has been firstly introduced in Transformers for natural language processing tasks [36]. In computer vision, non-local neural networks [41] apply the core self-attention block from transformers for context modeling and feature learning. State-of-the-art performance has been achieved in classification [13], self-supervised learning [9], semantic segmentation [50,54], object detection [6,48,56], few-shot action recognition [28,55], and object tracking [10] by using such an attention model. Several recent works [24–27,29,35,40] also use Transformers for TAD. They focus on either temporal proposal generation [35] or refinement [29]. In this paper, we demonstrate the effectiveness of self-attention in a novel proposal-free TAD architecture.

3   Proposal-Free Global Segmentation Mask

Our *global segmentation mask* (TAGS) model takes as input an untrimmed video V with a variable number of frames. Video frames are pre-processed by a feature encoder (*e.g.*, a Kinetics pre-trained I3D network [7]) into a sequence of localized snippets following the standard practice [18]. To train the model, we collect a set of labeled video training set $\mathcal{D}^{train} = \{V_i, \Psi_i\}$. Each video V_i is labeled with temporal segmentation $\Psi_i = \{(\psi_j, \xi_j, y_j)\}_{j=1}^{M_i}$ where ψ_j/ξ_j denote the start/end time, y_j is the action category, and M_i is the action instance number.

Architecture. As depicted in Fig. 2, a TAGS model has two key components: (1) a self-attentive snippet embedding module that learns feature representations with global temporal context (Sect. 3.1), and (2) a temporal action detection head with two branches for per-snippet multi-class action classification and binary-class global segmentation mask inference, respectively (Sect. 3.2).

3.1 Self-attentive Multi-scale Snippet Embedding

Given a varying length untrimmed video V, following the standard practice [18,46] we first sample T equidistantly distributed temporal snippets (points) over the entire length and use a Kinetics pre-trained video encoder (*e.g.*, a two-stream model [38]) to extract RGB $X_r \in \mathbb{R}^{d \times T}$ and optical flow features $X_o \in \mathbb{R}^{d \times T}$ at the snippet level, where d denotes the feature dimension. We then concatenate them as $F = [X_r; X_o] \in \mathbb{R}^{2d \times T}$. Each snippet is a short sequence of (*e.g.*, 16 in our case) consecutive frames. While F contains local spatio-temporal information, it lacks a global context critical for TAD. We hence leverage the self-attention mechanism [36] to learn the global context. Formally, we set the $Q/K/V$ of a Transformer encoder as the features $F/F/F$. To model finer action details efficiently, we consider multiple temporal scales in a hierarchy. We start with the finest temporal resolution (*e.g.*, sampling $T = 800$ snippets), which is progressively reduced via temporal pooling $P(\theta)$ with kernel size k, stride s and padding p. For efficiency, we first apply temporal pooling: $\hat{Q}^s = P(Q; \theta_Q), \hat{K}^s = P(K; \theta_K)$ and $\hat{V}^s = P(V; \theta_V)$ with the scale $s \in \{1, 2, 4\}$. The self-attention then follows as:

$$A_i^s = F + softmax(\frac{FW_{\hat{Q}^s}(FW_{\hat{K}^s})^\top}{\sqrt{d}})(FW_{\hat{V}^s}), \tag{1}$$

where $W_{\hat{Q}^s}, W_{\hat{K}^s}, W_{\hat{V}^s}$ are learnable parameters. In multi-head attention (MA) design, for each scale s we combine a set of n_h independent heads A_i to form a richer learning process. The snippet embedding E at scale s is obtained as:

$$E^s = MLP(\underbrace{[A_1^s \cdots A_{n_h}^s]}_{MA}) \in \mathbb{R}^{T^s \times C}. \tag{2}$$

The Multi-Layer Perceptron (MLP) block has one fully-connected layer with residual skip connection. Layer norm is applied before both the MA and MLP block. We use $n_h = 4$ heads by default.

3.2   Parallel Action Classification and Global Segmentation Masking

Our TAD head consists of two parallel branches: one for multi-class action classification and the other for binary-class global segmentation mask inference.

Multi-class Action Classification. Given the t-th snippet $E^s(t) \in \mathbb{R}^c$ (i.e., the t-th column of E^s), our classification branch predicts the probability $\boldsymbol{p}_t \in \mathbb{R}^{(K+1) \times 1}$ that it belongs to one of K target action classes or background. This is realized by a 1-D convolution layer H_c followed by a softmax normalization. Since a video has been encoded into T^s temporal snippets, the output of the classification branch can be expressed in column-wise as:

$$\boldsymbol{P}^s := softmax(H_c(E^s)) \in \mathbb{R}^{(K+1) \times T^s}. \tag{3}$$

Global Segmentation Mask Inference. In parallel to the classification branch, this branch aims to predict a global segmentation mask for each action instance of a video. Each global mask is action instance specific and class agnostic. For a training video, all temporal snippets of a single action instance are assigned with the same 1D global mask $\in \mathbb{R}^{T \times 1}$ for model optimization (refer to Fig. 3(a)). For each snippet $E^s(t)$, it outputs a mask prediction $\boldsymbol{m}_t = [q_1, \cdots, q_T] \in \mathbb{R}^{T^s \times 1}$ with the k-th element $q_k \in [0, 1]$ indicating the foreground probability of k-th snippet conditioned on t-th snippet. This process is implemented by a stack of three 1-D conv layers as:

$$\boldsymbol{M}^s := sigmoid(H_b(E^s)) \in \mathbb{R}^{T^s \times T^s}, \tag{4}$$

where the t-th column of $\boldsymbol{M}$ is the segmentation mask prediction at the t-th snippet. With the proposed mask signal as learning supervision, our TAGS model can facilitate context-aware representation learning, which brings clear benefit on TAD accuracy (see Table 4).

Remarks: Actionness [18,53] is a popular localization method which predicts a single mask in shape of $\in \mathbb{R}^{T \times 1}$. There are several key differences between actionness and TAGS: (1) Our per-snippet mask model TAGS focuses on a single action instance per snippet per mask so that all the foreground parts of a mask are intrinsically related; In contrast, actionness does not. (2) TAGS breaks the single multi-instance 1D actionness problem into a multiple 1D single-instance mask problem (refer to Fig. 3(a)). This takes a divide-and-conquer strategy. By explicitly segmenting foreground instances at different temporal positions, TAGS converts the regression based actionness problem into a position aware classification task. Each mask, associated with a specific time t, focuses on a single action instance. On the other hand, one action instance would be predicted by multiple successive masks. This predictive redundancy, simply removable by NMS, provides rich opportunities for accurate detection. (3) Whilst learning a 2D actionness map, BMN [18] relies on predicting 1D probability sequences which are highly noisy causing many false alarms. Further, its confidence evaluation cannot model the relations between candidates whilst our TAGS can (Eq. (7)). Lastly, our experiments in Table 8 validate the superiority of TAGS over actionness learning.

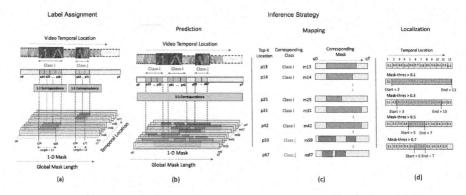

Fig. 3. Example of label assignment and model inference (see text for details).

3.3   Model Training

Ground-truth labels. To train TAGS, the ground-truth needs to be arranged into the designed format. Concretely, given a training video with temporal intervals and class labels (Fig. 3(a)), we label all the snippets (orange or blue squares) of a single action instance with the same action class. All the snippets off from action intervals are labeled as background. For an action snippet of a particular instance, its global mask is defined as the video-length binary mask of that action instance. Each mask is action instance specific. All snippets of a specific action instance share the same mask. For instance, all orange snippets (Fig. 3(a)) are assigned with a T-length mask (eg. m_{24} to m_{38}) with one in the interval of $[q24, q38]$.

Learning Objectives. The classification branch is trained by a combination of a cross-entropy based focal loss and a class-balanced logistic regression loss [12]. For a training snippet, we denote y the ground-truth class label, p the classification output, and r the per-class regression output obtained by applying sigmoid on top of H_c in Eq. (3) (discarded at inference time). The loss of the classification branch is then written as:

$$L_c = \lambda_1(1 - p(y))^\gamma \log(p_y) + (1 - \lambda_1)\big(\log(r_y) - \frac{\alpha}{|\mathcal{N}|}\sum_{k \in \mathcal{N}}(\log(1 - r(k)))\big), \quad (5)$$

where $\gamma = 2$ is a focal degree parameter, $\alpha = 10$ is a class-balancing weight, and $\mathcal{N}$ specifies a set of hard negative classes at size of $K/10$ where K is the totTAD action class number. We set the loss trade-off parameter $\lambda_1 = 0.4$.

For training the segmentation mask branch, we combine a novel boundary IOU (bIOU) loss and the dice loss in [23] to model two types of structured consistency respectively: mask boundary consistency and inter-mask consistency. Inspired by the boundary IOU metric [11], bIOU is designed particularly to penalize incorrect temporal boundary prediction w.r.t. the ground-truth segmentation mask. Formally, for a snippet location, we denote $m \in \mathbb{R}^{T \times 1}$ the predicted segmentation mask, and $g \in \mathbb{R}^{T \times 1}$ the ground-truth mask. The overall segmentation mask loss is formulated as:

$$L_m = 1 - \left(\frac{\cap(m, g)}{\cup(m, g)} + \frac{1}{\cap(m, g) + \epsilon} \frac{\|m - g\|_2}{c} \right) + \lambda_2 \left(1 - \frac{m^{\top} g}{\sum_{t=1}^{T} \left(m(t)^2 + g(t)^2 \right)} \right),$$
(6)

where $\cap(m, g) = \Phi(m) \cap \Phi(g)$ and $\cup(m, g) = \Phi(m) \cup \Phi(g)$, $\Phi(\cdot)$ represents a kernel of size k (7 in our default setting, see more analysis in Suppl.) used as a differentiable morphological erosion operation [31] on a mask and c specifies the ground-truth mask length. In case of no boundary overlap between the predicted and ground-truth masks, we use the normalized L_2 loss. The constant $\epsilon = e^{-8}$ is introduced for numerical stability. We set the weight $\lambda_2 = 0.4$.

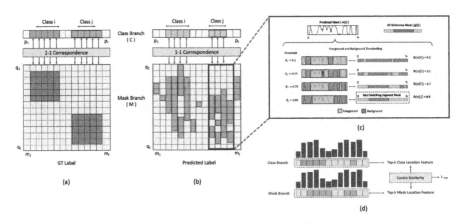

Fig. 4. An example of (a) ground-truth labels and (b) prediction along with an illustration of exploring (c) mask predictive redundancy (Eq. (7)) (d) classification-mask consistency ((Eq. (9)).

Mask predictive redundancy Although the mask loss Eq. (6) above treats the global mask as a 2D binary mask prediction problem, it cannot always regulate the behaviour of individual 1D mask within an action instance. Specifically, for a predicted mask m_t at time t, thresholding it at a specific threshold $\theta_j \in \Theta$ can result in binarized segments of foreground and background: $\pi[j] = \{(q_s^i, q_e^i, z_i)\}_{i=1}^{L}$ where q_s^i and q_e^i denotes the start and end of i-th segment, and $z_i \in \{0, 1\}$ indicates background or foreground. For a mask corresponding to an action snippet, ideally at least one of these $\{\pi[j]\}$ should be closer to the ground truth. To explore this redundancy, we define a prediction scoring criterion with the outer-inner-contrast [32] as follows:

$$\mathbb{R}(\pi[j]) = \frac{1}{L} \sum_{i=1}^{L} \left(\underbrace{\frac{1}{l_i} \sum_{r=q_s^i}^{q_e^i} u_i(r)}_{\text{inside}} - \underbrace{\frac{1}{\lceil \delta l_i \rceil + \lceil \delta l_i \rceil} \left(\sum_{r=q_s^i - \lceil \delta l_i \rceil}^{q_s^i - 1} u_i(r) + \sum_{r=q_e^i + 1}^{q_e^i + \lceil \delta l_i \rceil} u_i(r) \right)}_{\text{outside}} \right)$$

$$where \quad u_i(r) = \begin{cases} m_t[r], & \text{if } z_i = 1 \text{ (i.e., foreground)} \\ 1 - m_t[r], & \text{otherwise} \end{cases}$$

(7)

$l_i = q_e^i - q_s^i + 1$ is the temporal length of i-th segment, δ is a weight hyper-parameter which is set to 0.25. We obtain the best prediction with the maximal score as $j^* = argmax(\mathbb{R}(\pi[j]))$ (see Fig. 4(c)). Higher $\mathbb{R}(\pi[j^*])$ means a better prediction. To encourage this best prediction, we design a prediction promotion loss function:

$$L_{pp} = \left(1 - \mathbb{R}(\pi[j^*])\right)^{\beta} \|m_t - g_t\|_2,$$

(8)

where we set $\beta = 2$ for penalizing lower-quality prediction stronger. We average this loss across all snippets of each action instance per training video.

Classification-Mask Consistency. In TAGS, there is structural consistency in terms of foreground between class and mask labels by design (Fig. 4(a)). To leverage this consistency, we formulate a feature consistency loss as:

$$L_{fc} = 1 - \text{cosine}\left(\hat{F}_{clf}, \hat{F}_{mask}\right),$$

(9)

where $\hat{F}_{clf} = topk(argmax((P_{bin} * E_p)[: K, :]))$ is the features obtained from the top scoring foreground snippets obtained from the thresholded classification output $P_{bin} := \eta(P - \theta_c)$ with θ_c the threshold and E_p obtained by passing the embedding E into a 1D conv layer for matching the dimension of P. The top scoring features from the mask output M are obtained similarly as: $\hat{F}_{mask} = topk(\sigma(1DPool(E_m * M_{bin})))$ where $M_{bin} := \eta(M - \theta_m)$ is a binarization of mask-prediction M, E_m is obtained by passing the embedding E into a 1D conv layer for matching the dimension of M, $*$ is element-wise multiplication, $\eta(.)$ is the binarization function, and σ is sigmoid activation. Our intuition is that the foreground features should be closer and consistent after the classification and masking process (refer to Fig.. 4(d)).

Overall Objective. The overall objective loss function for training TAGS is defined as: $L = L_c + L_m + L_{pp} + L_{fc}$. This loss is calculated for each temporal scale s and finally aggregated over all the scales.

3.4 Model Inference

Our model inference is similar as existing TAD methods [18,46]. Given a test video, at each temporal scale s the action instance predictions are first generated separately based on the classification P^s and mask M^s predictions and combined for the following post-processing. Starting with the top scoring snippets from P (Fig. 3(b)), we obtain their segmentation mask predictions (Fig. 3(c)) by thresholding the corresponding columns of M (Fig. 3(d)). To generate sufficient candidates, we apply multiple thresholds $\Theta = \{\theta_i\}$ to yield action candidates with varying lengths and confidences. For each candidate, we compute its confidence score sc_{final} by multiplying the classification score (obtained from the corresponding top-scoring snippet in P) and the segmentation mask score (i.e., the *mean* predicted foreground segment in M). Finally, we apply SoftNMS [3] on top scoring candidates to obtain the final predictions.

4   Experiments

Datasets. We conduct extensive experiments on two popular TAD benchmarks. (1) *ActivityNet-v1.3* [5] has 19,994 videos from 200 action classes. We follow the standard setting to split all videos into training, validation and testing subsets in ratio of 2:1:1. (2) *THUMOS14* [16] has 200 validation videos and 213 testing videos from 20 categories with labeled temporal boundary and action class.

Table 1. Performance comparison with state-of-the-art methods on THUMOS14 and ActivityNet-v1.3. The results are measured by mAP at different IoU thresholds, and average mAP in [0.3 : 0.1 : 0.7] on THUMOS14 and [0.5 : 0.05 : 0.95] on ActivityNet-v1.3. Actn = Actioness; PF = Proposal Free; Bkb = Backbone.

Type	Model	Bkb	THUMOS14						ActivityNet-v1.3			
			0.3	0.4	0.5	0.6	0.7	Avg	0.5	0.75	0.95	Avg
Anchor	R-C3D [42]	C3D	44.8	35.6	28.9	–	–	–	26.8	–	–	–
	TAD [8]	I3D	53.2	48.5	42.8	33.8	20.8	39.8	38.2	18.3	1.3	20.2
	GTAN [22]	P3D	57.8	47.2	38.8	–	–	–	52.6	34.1	8.9	34.3
	PBR-Net [20]	I3D	58.5	54.6	51.3	41.8	29.5	–	53.9	34.9	8.9	35.0
	MUSES [21]	I3D	**68.9**	**64.0**	56.9	46.3	31.0	**53.4**	50.0	34.9	6.5	34.0
	VSGN [51]	I3D	66.7	60.4	52.4	41.0	30.4	50.1	52.3	36.0	8.3	35.0
Actn	BMN [18]	TS	56.0	47.4	38.8	29.7	20.5	38.5	50.1	34.8	8.3	33.9
	DBG [17]	TS	57.8	49.4	42.8	33.8	21.7	41.1	–	–	–	–
	G-TAD [46]	TS	54.5	47.6	40.2	30.8	23.4	39.3	50.4	34.6	9.0	34.1
	BU-TAL [52]	I3D	53.9	50.7	45.4	38.0	28.5	43.3	43.5	33.9	9.2	30.1
	BSN++ [34]	TS	59.9	49.5	41.3	31.9	22.8	–	51.2	35.7	8.3	34.8
	GTAD+CSA [33]	TS	58.4	52.8	44.0	33.6	24.2	42.6	51.8	**36.8**	8.7	35.7
	BC-GNN [2]	TS	57.1	49.1	40.4	31.2	23.1	40.2	50.6	34.8	9.4	34.3
	TCANet [29]	TS	60.6	53.2	44.6	36.8	26.7	–	52.2	36.7	6.8	35.5
	ContextLoc [57]	I3D	68.3	63.8	54.3	41.8	26.2	–	56.0	35.2	3.5	34.2
	RTD-Net [35]	I3D	68.3	62.3	51.9	38.8	23.7	–	47.2	30.7	8.6	30.8
Mixed	A2Net [47]	I3D	58.6	54.1	45.5	32.5	17.2	41.6	43.6	28.7	3.7	27.8
	GTAD+PGCN [49]	I3D	66.4	60.4	51.6	37.6	22.9	47.8	–	–	–	–
PF	**TAGS (Ours)**	I3D	68.6	63.8	**57.0**	46.3	31.8	52.8	**56.3**	36.8	9.6	**36.5**
	TAGS (Ours)	TS	**61.4**	**52.9**	**46.5**	**38.1**	**27.0**	**44.0**	53.7	36.1	**9.5**	**35.9**

Implementation Details. We use two pre-extracted encoders for feature extraction, for fair comparisons with previous methods. One is a fine-tuned two-stream model [18], with downsampling ratio 16 and stride 2. Each video's feature sequence F is rescaled to $T = 800/1024$ snippets for AcitivtyNet/THUMOS using linear interpolation. The other is Kinetics pre-trained I3D model [7] with a downsampling ratio of 5. Our model is trained for 15 epochs using Adam with learning rate of $10^{-4}/10^{-5}$ for AcitivityNet/THUMOS respectively. The batch size is set to 50 for ActivityNet and 25 for THUMOS. For classification-mask consistency, the threshold θ_m/θ_p is set to 0.5/0.3 and in $top-k$ to 40. In testing, we set the threshold set for mask $\Theta = \{0.1 - 0.9\}$ with step 0.05. We use the same set of threshold Θ for mask predictive redundancy during training.

4.1   Main Results

Results on ActivityNet. From Table 1, we can make the following observations: (1) TAGS with I3D feature achieves the best result in average mAP. Despite the fact that our model is much simpler in architecture design compared to the existing alternatives. This validates our assumption that with proper global context modeling, explicit proposal generation is not only redundant but also less effective. (2) When using the relatively weaker two-stream (TS) features, our model remains competitive and even surpasses I3D based BU-TAL [52], A2Net [47] and the very recent ContextLoc [57] and MUSES [21] by a significant margin. TAGS also surpasses a proposal refinement and strong G-TAD based approach CSA [33] on avg mAP. (3) Compared to RTD-Net which employs an architecture similar to object detection Transformers, our TAGS is significantly superior. This validates our model formulation in exploiting the Transformer for TAD.

Results on THUMOS14. Similar conclusions can be drawn in general on THUMOS from Table 1. When using TS features, TAGS achieves again the best results, beating strong competitors like TCANet [39], CSA [33] by a clear margin. There are some noticeable differences: (1) We find that I3D is now much more effective than two-stream (TS), e.g., 8.8% gain in average mAP over TS with TAGS, compared with 0.6% on ActivityNet. This is mostly likely caused by the distinctive characteristics of the two datasets in terms of action instance duration and video length. (2) Our method achieves the second best result with marginal edge behind MUSES [21]. This is partly due to that MUSES benefits from additionally tackling the scene-changes. (3) Our model achieves the best results in stricter IOU metrics (e.g., IOU@0.5/0.6/0.7) consistently using both TS and I3D features, verifying the effectiveness of solving mask redundancy.

Computational Cost Comparison. One of the key motivations to design a proposal-free TAD model is to reduce the model training and inference cost. For comparative evaluation, we evaluate TAGS against two representative and recent TAD methods (BMN [18] and G-TAD [46]) using their released codes. All the methods are tested on the same machine with one Nvidia 2080 Ti GPU. We measure the convergence time in training and average inference time per video in testing. The two-stream video features are used. It can be seen in Table 2 that our TAGS is drastically faster, *e.g.*, 20/25× for training and clearly quicker – 1.6/1.8× for testing in comparison to G-TAD/BMN, respectively. We also notice that our TAGS needs less epochs to converge. Table 3 also shows that our TAGS has the smallest FLOPs and the least parameter number.

4.2   Ablation Study and Further Analysis

Transformers vs. CNNs. We compare our multi-scale Transformer with CNN for snippet embedding. We consider two CNN designs: (1) a 1D CNN with 3 dilation rates (1, 3, 5) each with 2 layers, and (2) a multi-scale MS-TCN [14], and (3) a standard single-scale Transformer [36]. Table 4 shows that the Transformers are clearly superior to both 1D-CNN and a relatively stronger MS-TCN. This suggests that our global segmentation mask learning is more compatible with self-attention models due to stronger contextual learning capability. Besides, multi-scale learning with Transformer gives 0.4% gain in avg mAP validating the importance of larger snippets. As shown in Table 5, the gain almost saturates from 200 snippets, and finer scale only increases the computational cost.

Table 2. Analysis of model training and test cost.

Model	Epoch	Train	Test
BMN	13	6.45 h	0.21 s
G-TAD	11	4.91 h	0.19 s
TAGS	**9**	**0.26 h**	**0.12 s**

Table 3. Analysis of model parameters # and FLOPs.

Model	Params (in M)	FLOPs (in G)
BMN	5.0	91.2
GTAD	9.5	97.2
TAGS	**6.2**	**17.8**

Table 4. Ablation of transformer vs. CNN on ActivityNet.

Network	mAP	
	0.5	Avg
1D CNN	46.8	26.4
MS-TCN	53.1	33.8
Transformer	55.8	36.1
MS-Transformer	**56.3**	**36.5**

Table 5. Ablation on snippet embedding design and multiple temporal scales.

Scale	Snippet	Params (in M)	Infer (in sec)	mAP	
				0.5	Avg
{1}	100	2.9	0.09	55.8	36.1
{1,2}	**100,200**	**6.2**	**0.12**	56.3	**36.5**
{1,2,4}	100,200,400	9.8	0.16	**56.5**	36.4

Proposal-Based vs. Proposal-Free. We compare our proposal-free TAGS with conventional proposal-based TAD methods BMN [2] (anchor-free) and R-C3D [42] (anchor-based) via false positive analysis [1]. We sort the predictions by the scores and take the top-scoring predictions per video. Two major errors of TAD are considered: (1) *Localization error*, which is defined as when a proposal/mask is predicted as foreground, has a minimum tIoU of 0.1 but does not meet the tIoU threshold. (2) *Background error*, which happens when a proposal/mask is predicted as foreground but its tIoU with ground truth instance is smaller than 0.1. In this test, we use ActivityNet. We observe in Fig. 5 that TAGS has the most true positive samples at every amount of predictions. The proportion of localization error with TAGS is also notably smaller, which is the most critical metric for improving average mAP [1]. This explains the gain of TAGS over BMN and R-C3D.

Direction of Improvement Analysis. Two subtasks are involved in TAD – temporal localization and action classification, each of which would affect the final performance. Given the two-branch design in TAGS, the performance effect of one subtask can be individually examined by simply assigning ground-truth to the other subtask's output at test time. From Table 7, the following observations can be made: (1) There is still a big scope for improvement on both subtasks. (2) Regarding the benefit from the improvement from the other subtask, the classification subtask seems to have the most to gain at mAP@0.5, whilst the localization task can benefit more on the average mAP metric. Overall, this analysis suggests that further improving the efficacy on the classification subtask would be more influential to the final model performance.

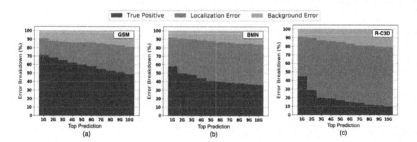

Fig. 5. False positive profile of TAGS, BMN and R-C3D on ActivityNet. We use top up-to $10G$ predictions per video, where G is the number of ground truth action instances.

Analysis of Components. We can see in Table 6 that without the proposed segmentation mask branch, the model will degrade significantly, *e.g.*, a drop of 7.6% in average mAP. This is due to its fundamental capability of modeling the global temporal structure of action instances and hence yielding better action temporal intervals. Further, for TAGS we use a pre-trained Untrimmed-Net (UNet) [37] as an external classifier instead of using the classification branch, resulted in a 2-stage method. This causes a performance drop of 4.7%, suggesting that both classification and mask branches are critical for model accuracy and efficiency.

Table 6. Analysis of TAGS's two branches on ActivityNet.

Model	mAP	
	0.5	Avg
TAGS(Full)	56.3	36.5
w/o Mask Branch	45.8	28.9
w/o Class Branch + UNet	49.7	31.8

Table 7. Improvement analysis of TAGS on ActivityNet.

Model	mAP	
	0.5	Avg
TAGS (full)	56.3	36.5
+ Ground-truth class	61.0	43.8 (↑ 7.3%)
+ Ground-truth mask	69.2	48.5 (↑ 12.0%)

Global Mask Design. We compare our global mask with previous 1D actionness mask [18,43]. We integrate actionness with TAGS by reformulating the mask branch to output 1D actionness. From the results in Table 8, we observe a significant performance drop of 11.5% in mAP@0.5 IOU. One reason is that the number of action candidates generated by actionness is drastically limited, leading to poor recall. Additionally, we visualize the cosine similarity scores of all snippet feature pairs on a random ActivityNet val video. As shown in Fig. 6, our single-instance mask (global mask) design learns more discriminating feature representation with larger separation between background and action, as compared to multi-instance actionness design. This validates the efficacy of our design in terms of jointly learning multiple per-snippet masks each with focus on a single action instance.

Table 8. Analysis of mask design of TAGS on ActivityNet dataset.

Mask Design	mAP		Avg masks/video
	0.5	Avg	
Actionness	44.8	27.1	30
Our Global Mask	**56.3**	**36.5**	**250**

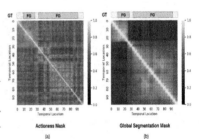

Fig. 6. Pairwise feature similarity

5   Limitations

In general, short foreground and background segments with the duration similar as or less than the snippet length would challenge snippet-based TAD methods. For instance, given short background between two foreground instances, our TAGS might wrongly predict it as part of the foreground. Besides, given a snippet with mixed background and foreground, TAGS tends to make a background prediction. In such cases, the ground-truth annotation involves uncertainty which however is less noted and investigated thus far.

6 Conclusion

In this work, we have presented the first proposal-free TAD model by Global Segmentation Mask (TAGS) learning. Instead of generating via predefined anchors, or predicting many start-end pairs (*i.e.*, temporal proposals), our model is designed to estimate the full-video-length segmentation mask of action instances directly. As a result, the TAD model design has been significantly simplified with more efficient training and inference. With our TAGS learning, we further show that learning global temporal context is beneficial for TAD. Extensive experiments validated that the proposed TAGS yields new state-of-the-art performance on two TAD benchmarks, and with clear efficiency advantages on both model training and inference.

References

1. Alwassel, H., Caba Heilbron, F., Escorcia, V., Ghanem, B.: Diagnosing error in temporal action detectors. In: Ferrari, V., Hebert, M., Sminchisescu, C., Weiss, Y. (eds.) ECCV 2018. LNCS, vol. 11207, pp. 264–280. Springer, Cham (2018). https://doi.org/10.1007/978-3-030-01219-9_16
2. Bai, Y., Wang, Y., Tong, Y., Yang, Y., Liu, Q., Liu, J.: Boundary content graph neural network for temporal action proposal generation. In: Vedaldi, A., Bischof, H., Brox, T., Frahm, J.-M. (eds.) ECCV 2020. LNCS, vol. 12373, pp. 121–137. Springer, Cham (2020). https://doi.org/10.1007/978-3-030-58604-1_8
3. Bodla, N., Singh, B., Chellappa, R., Davis, L.S.: Soft-nms-improving object detection with one line of code. In: Proceedings of the IEEE International Conference on Computer Vision, pp. 5561–5569 (2017)
4. Buch, S., Escorcia, V., Shen, C., Ghanem, B., Carlos Niebles, J.: Sst: single-stream temporal action proposals. In: CVPR (2017)
5. Caba Heilbron, F., Escorcia, V., Ghanem, B., Carlos Niebles, J.: Activitynet: a large-scale video benchmark for human activity understanding. In: CVPR, pp. 961–970 (2015)
6. Carion, N., Massa, F., Synnaeve, G., Usunier, N., Kirillov, A., Zagoruyko, S.: End-to-end object detection with transformers. In: Vedaldi, A., Bischof, H., Brox, T., Frahm, J.-M. (eds.) ECCV 2020. LNCS, vol. 12346, pp. 213–229. Springer, Cham (2020). https://doi.org/10.1007/978-3-030-58452-8_13
7. Carreira, J., Zisserman, A.: Quo vadis, action recognition? a new model and the kinetics dataset. In: proceedings of the IEEE Conference on Computer Vision and Pattern Recognition, pp. 6299–6308 (2017)
8. Chao, Y.W., Vijayanarasimhan, S., Seybold, B., Ross, D.A., Deng, J., Sukthankar, R.: Rethinking the faster r-cnn architecture for temporal action localization. In: CVPR (2018)
9. Chen, M., et al.: Generative pretraining from pixels. In: ICML (2020)
10. Chen, X., Yan, B., Zhu, J., Wang, D., Yang, X., Lu, H.: Transformer tracking. In: CVPR (2021)
11. Cheng, B., Girshick, R., Dollár, P., Berg, A.C., Kirillov, A.: Boundary iou: improving object-centric image segmentation evaluation. In: CVPR, pp. 15334–15342 (2021)
12. Dong, Q., Zhu, X., Gong, S.: Single-label multi-class image classification by deep logistic regression. In: AAAI, vol. 33, pp. 3486–3493 (2019)

13. Dosovitskiy, A., et al.: An image is worth 16x16 words: transformers for image recognition at scale. In: ICLR (2020)
14. Farha, Y.A., Gall, J.: Ms-tcn: multi-stage temporal convolutional network for action segmentation. In: CVPR, pp. 3575–3584 (2019)
15. Gao, J., Yang, Z., Chen, K., Sun, C., Nevatia, R.: Turn tap: temporal unit regression network for temporal action proposals. In: ICCV (2017)
16. Idrees, H., et al.: The thumos challenge on action recognition for videos "in the wild". Comput. Vis. Image Underst. **155**, 1–23 (2017)
17. Lin, C., et al.: Fast learning of temporal action proposal via dense boundary generator. In: AAAI, vol. 34, pp. 11499–11506 (2020)
18. Lin, T., Liu, X., Li, X., Ding, E., Wen, S.: Bmn: boundary-matching network for temporal action proposal generation. In: Proceedings of the IEEE/CVF International Conference on Computer Vision, pp. 3889–3898 (2019)
19. Lin, T., Zhao, X., Su, H., Wang, C., Yang, M.: BSN: boundary sensitive network for temporal action proposal generation. In: Ferrari, V., Hebert, M., Sminchisescu, C., Weiss, Y. (eds.) ECCV 2018. LNCS, vol. 11208, pp. 3–21. Springer, Cham (2018). https://doi.org/10.1007/978-3-030-01225-0_1
20. Liu, Q., Wang, Z.: Progressive boundary refinement network for temporal action detection. In: Proceedings of the AAAI Conference on Artificial Intelligence, vol. 34, pp. 11612–11619 (2020)
21. Liu, X., Hu, Y., Bai, S., Ding, F., Bai, X., Torr, P.H.: Multi-shot temporal event localization: a benchmark. In: Proceedings of the IEEE/CVF Conference on Computer Vision and Pattern Recognition, pp. 12596–12606 (2021)
22. Long, F., Yao, T., Qiu, Z., Tian, X., Luo, J., Mei, T.: Gaussian temporal awareness networks for action localization. In: CVPR (2019)
23. Milletari, F., Navab, N., Ahmadi, S.A.: V-net: fully convolutional neural networks for volumetric medical image segmentation. In: 2016 4th International Conference on 3D Vision (3DV), pp. 565–571. IEEE (2016)
24. Nag, S., Zhu, X., Song, Y.Z., Xiang, T.: Temporal action localization with global segmentation mask transformers (2021)
25. Nag, S., Zhu, X., Song, Y.z., Xiang, T.: Semi-supervised temporal action detection with proposal-free masking. In: ECCV (2022)
26. Nag, S., Zhu, X., Song, Y.z., Xiang, T.: Zero-shot temporal action detection via vision-language prompting. In: ECCV (2022)
27. Nag, S., Zhu, X., Xiang, T.: Few-shot temporal action localization with query adaptive transformer. arXiv preprint. arXiv:2110.10552 (2021)
28. Perrett, T., Masullo, A., Burghardt, T., Mirmehdi, M., Damen, D.: Temporal-relational crosstransformers for few-shot action recognition. In: CVPR (2021)
29. Qing, Z., et al.: Temporal context aggregation network for temporal action proposal refinement. In: CVPR, pp. 485–494 (2021)
30. Ren, S., He, K., Girshick, R., Sun, J.: Faster r-cnn: towards real-time object detection with region proposal networks. TPAMI **39**(6), 1137–1149 (2016)
31. Riba, E., Mishkin, D., Ponsa, D., Rublee, E., Bradski, G.: Kornia: an open source differentiable computer vision library for pytorch. In: WACV, pp. 3674–3683 (2020)
32. Shou, Z., Gao, H., Zhang, L., Miyazawa, K., Chang, S.-F.: AutoLoc: weakly-supervised temporal action localization in untrimmed videos. In: Ferrari, V., Hebert, M., Sminchisescu, C., Weiss, Y. (eds.) ECCV 2018. LNCS, vol. 11220, pp. 162–179. Springer, Cham (2018). https://doi.org/10.1007/978-3-030-01270-0_10
33. Sridhar, D., Quader, N., Muralidharan, S., Li, Y., Dai, P., Lu, J.: Class semantics-based attention for action detection. In: Proceedings of the IEEE/CVF International Conference on Computer Vision, pp. 13739–13748 (2021)

34. Su, H., Gan, W., Wu, W., Qiao, Y., Yan, J.: Bsn++: complementary boundary regressor with scale-balanced relation modeling for temporal action proposal generation. arXiv preprint. arXiv:2009.07641 (2020)
35. Tan, J., Tang, J., Wang, L., Wu, G.: Relaxed transformer decoders for direct action proposal generation. In: ICCV (2021)
36. Vaswani, A., et al.: Attention is all you need. arXiv preprint. arXiv:1706.03762 (2017)
37. Wang, L., Xiong, Y., Lin, D., Van Gool, L.: Untrimmednets for weakly supervised action recognition and detection. In: CVPR, pp. 4325–4334 (2017)
38. Wang, L., Xiong, Y., Wang, Z., Qiao, Yu., Lin, D., Tang, X., Van Gool, L.: Temporal segment networks: towards good practices for deep action recognition. In: Leibe, B., Matas, J., Sebe, N., Welling, M. (eds.) ECCV 2016. LNCS, vol. 9912, pp. 20–36. Springer, Cham (2016). https://doi.org/10.1007/978-3-319-46484-8_2
39. Wang, L., Yang, H., Wu, W., Yao, H., Huang, H.: Temporal action proposal generation with transformers. arXiv preprint. arXiv:2105.12043 (2021)
40. Wang, X., et al.: Oadtr: online action detection with transformers. In: ICCV (2021)
41. Wang, X., Girshick, R., Gupta, A., He, K.: Non-local neural networks. In: CVPR (2018)
42. Xu, H., Das, A., Saenko, K.: R-c3d: region convolutional 3d network for temporal activity detection. In: ICCV (2017)
43. Xu, M., et al.: Boundary-sensitive pre-training for temporal localization in videos. arXiv (2020)
44. Xu, M., et al.: Boundary-sensitive pre-training for temporal localization in videos. In: ICCV, pp. 7220–7230 (2021)
45. Xu, M., Perez-Rua, J.M., Zhu, X., Ghanem, B., Martinez, B.: Low-fidelity end-to-end video encoder pre-training for temporal action localization. In: NeurIPS (2021)
46. Xu, M., Zhao, C., Rojas, D.S., Thabet, A., Ghanem, B.: G-tad: sub-graph localization for temporal action detection. In: CVPR (2020)
47. Yang, L., Peng, H., Zhang, D., Fu, J., Han, J.: Revisiting anchor mechanisms for temporal action localization. IEEE Trans. Image Process. 29, 8535–8548 (2020)
48. Yin, M., et al.: Disentangled non-local neural networks. In: Vedaldi, A., Bischof, H., Brox, T., Frahm, J.-M. (eds.) ECCV 2020. LNCS, vol. 12360, pp. 191–207. Springer, Cham (2020). https://doi.org/10.1007/978-3-030-58555-6_12
49. Zeng, R., et al.: Graph convolutional networks for temporal action localization. In: ICCV (2019)
50. Zhang, L., Xu, D., Arnab, A., Torr, P.H.: Dynamic graph message passing networks. In: CVPR (2020)
51. Zhao, C., Thabet, A.K., Ghanem, B.: Video self-stitching graph network for temporal action localization. In: Proceedings of the IEEE/CVF International Conference on Computer Vision, pp. 13658–13667 (2021)
52. Zhao, P., Xie, L., Ju, C., Zhang, Y., Wang, Y., Tian, Q.: Bottom-up temporal action localization with mutual regularization. In: Vedaldi, A., Bischof, H., Brox, T., Frahm, J.-M. (eds.) ECCV 2020. LNCS, vol. 12353, pp. 539–555. Springer, Cham (2020). https://doi.org/10.1007/978-3-030-58598-3_32
53. Zhao, Y., Xiong, Y., Wang, L., Wu, Z., Tang, X., Lin, D.: Temporal action detection with structured segment networks. In: ICCV (2017)
54. Zheng, S., et al.: Rethinking semantic segmentation from a sequence-to-sequence perspective with transformers. In: CVPR (2021)

55. Zhu, X., Toisoul, A., Perez-Rua, J.M., Zhang, L., Martinez, B., Xiang, T.: Few-shot action recognition with prototype-centered attentive learning. arXiv preprint. arXiv:2101.08085 (2021)
56. Zhu, X., Su, W., Lu, L., Li, B., Wang, X., Dai, J.: Deformable detr: deformable transformers for end-to-end object detection. arXiv preprint (2020)
57. Zhu, Z., Tang, W., Wang, L., Zheng, N., Hua, G.: Enriching local and global contexts for temporal action localization. In: Proceedings of the IEEE/CVF International Conference on Computer Vision, pp. 13516–13525 (2021)

Semi-supervised Temporal Action Detection with Proposal-Free Masking

Sauradip Nag[1,2(✉)], Xiatian Zhu[1,3], Yi-Zhe Song[1,2], and Tao Xiang[1,2]

[1] CVSSP, University of Surrey, Guildford, UK
{s.nag,xiatian.zhu,y.song,t.xiang}@surrey.ac.uk
[2] iFlyTek-Surrey Joint Research Centre on Artificial Intelligence, London, UK
[3] Surrey Institute for People-Centred Artificial Intelligence,
University of Surrey, Guildford, UK

Abstract. Existing temporal action detection (TAD) methods rely on a large number of training data with segment-level annotations. Collecting and annotating such a training set is thus highly expensive and unscalable. Semi-supervised TAD (SS-TAD) alleviates this problem by leveraging unlabeled videos freely available at scale. However, SS-TAD is also a much more challenging problem than supervised TAD, and consequently much under-studied. Prior SS-TAD methods directly combine an existing proposal-based TAD method and a SSL method. Due to their *sequential* localization (*e.g.*, proposal generation) and classification design, they are prone to proposal error propagation. To overcome this limitation, in this work we propose a novel $\underline{Semi} - supervised\ \underline{T}emporal\ action\ detection\ model\ based\ on$ $\underline{Prop}\underline{O}sal - free\ \underline{T}emporal\ mask$ (SPOT) with a *parallel* localization (mask generation) and classification architecture. Such a novel design effectively eliminates the dependence between localization and classification by cutting off the route for error propagation in-between. We further introduce an interaction mechanism between classification and localization for prediction refinement, and a new pretext task for self-supervised model pre-training. Extensive experiments on two standard benchmarks show that our SPOT outperforms state-of-the-art alternatives, often by a large margin. The PyTorch implementation of SPOT is available at https://github.com/sauradip/SPOT

1 Introduction

Temporal action detection (TAD) aims to predict the temporal duration (*i.e.*, the start and end points) and the class label of each action instances in an untrimmed video [8,22]. Most state-of-the-art TAD methods [7,37,38,54,65,66,70] rely on training datasets containing a large number of videos (*e.g.*, hundreds) with exhaustive segment-level annotations. Obtaining such annotations is tedious and costly. This has severely limited the usability of existing TAD methods in low data setting [39,40].

Supplementary Information The online version contains supplementary material available at https://doi.org/10.1007/978-3-031-20062-5_38.

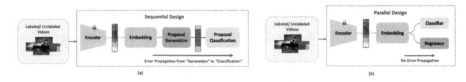

Fig. 1. Illustration of main design difference between existing and our SS-TAD methods. (a) Existing SS-TAD methods suffers from the intrinsic localization error propagation problem, due to the *sequential* localization (*e.g.*, proposal generation) and classification design. (b) We solve this problem by designing a Proposal Free Temporal Mask (SPOT) learning model with a *parallel* localization and classification architecture.

Semi-supervised learning (SSL) offers a solution to the annotation cost problem by exploiting a large amount of unlabeled data along with limited labeled data [47,51]. This has led to an emerging research interest [23,57] in semi-supervised TAD (SS-TAD). Existing methods adopt an intuitive strategy of combining an existing TAD models, dominated by proposal-based methods and a SSL method. However, this strategy is intrinsically sub-optimal and prone to an error propagation problem. As illustrated in Fig. 1(a), this is because existing TAD models adopt a *sequential* localization (*e.g.*, proposal generation) and classification design. When extended to SSL setting, the localization errors, inevitable when trained with unlabeled data, can be easily propagated to the classification module leading to accumulated errors in class prediction.

To overcome the above limitation, in this work we propose a novel Semi-supervised PropOsal-free Temporal Masking (SPOT) model with a *parallel* localization (mask generation) and classification architecture (see Fig. 1(b)). Concretely, SPOT consists of a classification stream and a mask based localization stream, established in parallel on a shared feature embedding module. This architecture design has no sequential dependence between localization and classification as in conventional TAD models, therefore eliminating the localization error propagation problem. We further introduce a boundary refinement algorithm and a novel pretext task for self-supervised model pre-training. We integrate the SPOT with pseudo labeling for SS-TAD with new classification and mask loss functions formulated specifically for our parallel design. Moreover, by virtue of being proposal free, our model is $30\times/2\times$ faster in training/inference than existing alternatives.

Contributions.. (1) To solve the localization error propagation problem suffered by existing SS-TAD methods, we propose a *Proposal-Free Temporal Masking* (SPOT) model with a new parallel classification and localization architecture[1]. (2) We further design a novel pretext task for model pre-training and a boundary refinement algorithm. (3) Extensive experiments on two standard benchmarks (ActivityNet-V1.3 and THUMOS14) show that the proposed SPOT outperforms significantly alternative state-of-the-art SSL methods.

---

[1] Note, instead of contributing a novel generic SSL algorithm, we propose a new TAD architecture designed particularly for facilitating the usage of prior SSL methods (*e.g.*, pseudo labeling) in the sense of minimizing localization error propagation.

2   Related Works

Temporal Action Detection . While all existing TAD methods use action proposals, they differ in how the proposals are produced.

Anchor-Based Proposal Learning Methods generate proposal with a predetermined set of anchors. Inspired by object detection in static images [44], R-C3D [62] proposes to use anchor boxes. It follows the structure of proposal generation and classification in design. With a similar model design, TURN [17] aggregates local features to represent snippet-level features, which are then used for temporal boundary regression and classification. Later, GTAN [30] improves the proposal feature pooling procedure with a learnable Gaussian kernel for weighted averaging. G-TAD [66] learns semantic and temporal context via graph convolutional networks for better proposal generation. Recently, VSGN [68] improves short-action localization with a cross-scale multi-level pyramidal architecture. Note that these anchor boxes are often exhaustively generated so are high in number.

Anchor-Free Proposal Learning Methods directly learn to predict temporal proposals (*i.e.*, start and end times) [27,28,70]. For example, SSN [70] decomposes an action instance into three stages (starting, course, and ending) and employs structured temporal pyramid pooling to generate proposals. BSN [28] predicts the start, end and actionness at each temporal location and generates proposals with high start and end probabilities. Later, BMN [27] additionally generates a boundary-matching confidence map to improve proposal generation. BSN++ [49] further extends BMN with a complementary boundary generator to capture rich context. CSA [48] enriches the proposal temporal context via attention transfer. While no pre-defined anchor boxes are required, these methods often have to exhaustively pair all possible locations predicted with high scores. So both anchor-based and anchor-free TAD methods have a large quantity of temporal proposals to evaluate. Critically, both groups of TAD models in essence adopt a *sequential* localization (mask generation) and classification architecture. This will cause the localization error propagation problem for SS-TAD. Our SPOT is designed to address this limitation by removing the dependence between localization and classification thus cutting off the path for error propagation.

Semi-supervised Learning (SSL). [10,71] has been widely adopted in computer vision for image classification [5,13,47], object detection [50,69], semantic segmentation [21,41], and pose estimation [15,35]. Two dominant learning paradigms in SSL are pseudo-labeling [24,26,47,67] and consistency regularization [25,36,51,60]. Key to pseudo-labeling is to reliably estimate the labels of unlabeled data which in turn are used to further train the model. Instead, consistency regularization enforces the output of a model to be consistent at the presence of variations in the input space and/or the model space. The variations can be implemented by adding noises, perturbations or forming multiple variants of the same data sample or the model. In this work, we focus on designing a TAD model particularly suitable for SSL, while following the pseudo-labelling paradigm for exploiting unlabeled data for training.

Semi-supervised Temporal Action Detection (SS-TAD). SSL has only been studied very recently in the context of TAD. Existing SS-TAD works [23,46,57] naively combine existing semi-supervised learning and TAD methods. They are thus particularly prone to the aforementioned localization error propagation problem when trained with unlabeled data. We solve this problem for the first time by introducing a novel proposal-free temporal mask learning model.

Self-supervised Learning aims to learn generic feature representations from a large amount of unlabeled data [11,18,19]. It is typically designed to provide a pre-trained model for a downstream task to further fine-tune with a specific labeled training data. We have seen a recent surge of self-supervised learning studies with a focus on both object recognition in images [11,12,18,19,33,53,59] and action classification in videos [1,4,31,34,58]. The most related works to our self-supervised learning based pre-training are very recently introduced in [64,65]. They aim to improve the video encoder for the fully supervised TAD problem. In contrast, we focus on pre-training a superior TAD head in the context of semi-supervised learning.

3 Proposal-Free Temporal Mask Learning

Approach Overview. In semi-supervised temporal action detection (SS-TAD), we have access to a small set of N_l labeled videos $\mathcal{D}^l = \{V_i, \Psi_i\}_{i=1}^{N_l}$ and a large set of N_u unlabeled videos $\mathcal{D}^u = \{U_i\}_{i=1}^{N_u}$. Each labeled video's annotation $\Psi_i = \{(\psi_j, \xi_j, y_j)\}_{j=1}^{M_i}$ contains the start time ψ_j, the end time ξ_j, and the class label $y_j \in \mathcal{Y}$ for each of M_i action instances. We denote the label space as $\mathcal{Y} = [1, \cdots, K+1]$ with K action and one background classes. For more effective SS-TAD, we propose a *Proposal-Free Temporal Mask* (SPOT) learning method (see Fig. 2). It has two components: video snippet embedding (Sect. 3.1), and TAD head (Sect. 3.2). The latter is our core contribution.

3.1 Video Snippet Embedding

Given a varying length untrimmed video V, following the standard practice [27,66] we first sample T equidistantly distributed temporal snippets (points) over the entire length and use a fine-tuned two-stream video encoder similar to [27] to extract RGB $X_r \in \mathbb{R}^{d \times T}$ and optical flow features $X_o \in \mathbb{R}^{d \times T}$ at the snippet level, where d denotes the feature dimension. We then concatenate them as $F = [X_r; X_o] \in \mathbb{R}^{2d \times T}$. Each snippet is a short sequence of (16 in this work) consecutive frames. While F contains local spatio-temporal information, it lacks a global context critical for TAD. We hence leverage the self-attention mechanism [52] to learn the global context. Formally, we set the input $\{query, key, value\}$ of a multi-head Transformer encoder $\mathcal{T}()$ as the features $\{F, F, F\}$ (Fig. 2(a)).

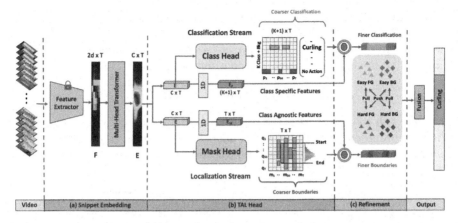

Fig. 2. Overview of the proposed *Semi-supervised Temporal action detection model based on* ***Prop**O**sal-free **T**emporal mask* (**SPOT**). Given an untrimmed video V, (a) we first extract a sequence of T snippet features with a pre-trained video encoder and conduct self-attention learning to obtain the snippet embedding E with a global context. (b) For each snippet embedding, we then predict a classification score P with the classification stream and a foreground mask M with the mask stream in parallel, (c) both of which are further used for boundary refinement. It is based on mining hard&easy foreground (FG) and background (BG) snippets. For SS-TAD, we alternately predict and leverage pseudo class and mask labels of unlabeled training videos, along with labeled videos.

Positional encoding is not applied as it is found to be detrimental (see Appendix B in Supplementary) The final snippet embedding is then obtained as $E = \mathcal{T}(F) \in \mathbb{R}^{C \times T}$ with C being the embedding dimension.

3.2 Temporal Action Detection Head

To realize a proposal-free design, we introduce a temporal mask learning based TAD head. It consists of two parallel streams (Fig. 2(b)): one for snippet classification and the other for temporal mask inference. This design breaks the sequential dependence between localization and classification which causes unwanted error propagation in the existing TAD models.

Snippet Classification Stream. Given the t-th snippet $E(t) \in \mathbb{R}^c$ (*i.e.*, the t-th column of E), our classification branch predicts a probability distribution $p_t \in \mathbb{R}^{(K+1) \times 1}$ over $\mathcal{Y}$. This is realized by a 1-D convolution layer H_c followed by a softmax normalization. For a video with T snippets, the output of the classification branch can be expressed as:

$$P := softmax\Big(H_c(E) \Big) \in \mathbb{R}^{(K+1) \times T}. \tag{1}$$

Temporal Mask Stream. In parallel to the classification stream, this stream predicts temporal masks of action instances across the whole temporal span of the video. Given the t-th snippet $E(t)$, it outputs a mask vector $\boldsymbol{m}_t = [q_1, \cdots, q_T] \in \mathbb{R}^{T \times 1}$ with each element $q_i \in [0,1]$ ($i \in [1,T]$) indicating the foreground probability of the i-th snippet (see Fig. 2(b) for illustration). This is implemented by a stack of three 1-D convolution layers H_m as:

$$\boldsymbol{M} := sigmoid\Big(H_m(E)\Big) \in \mathbb{R}^{T \times T}, \tag{2}$$

where the t-th column of $\boldsymbol{M}$ is the temporal mask prediction by the t-th snippet. With the proposed mask signal as the model output supervision, proposals are no longer required for facilitating SS-TAD learning.

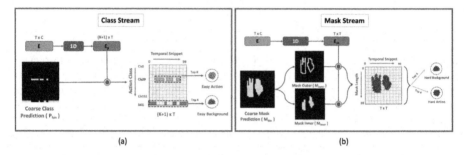

(a)   (b)

Fig. 3. Snippet selection for inter-stream interaction.

Boundary Refinement. TAD methods typically struggle at estimating accurately the boundary between foreground and background segments. This problem is more pronounced for a SS-TAD model by learning from unlabeled data. To mitigate this problem, we design an inter-stream interaction mechanism for TAD refinement at the end of the TAD head (Fig. 2(c)). More specifically, we focus on ambiguous snippets in the transition between foreground and background (*i.e.*, temporal boundary). They are considered as *hard* snippets, in contrast to those easy ones located inside mask or background intervals far away from temporal borders with more trustworthy interference. We detect hard snippets by examining the structure of temporal mask $\boldsymbol{M}$. First, we threshold the M to obtain a binary mask as $M_{bin} := \eta(M - \theta_m)$, where $\eta(.)$ is the Heavyside step function and θ_m is the threshold. As shown in Fig. 3(b), we consider the snippets spanned by the eroded mask boundary as *hard background* whereas those by the non-boundary mask as *hard foreground*. We use a differentiable morphological erosion [45] to obtain the eroded mask M_{outer}. We denote the complement of M_{outer} as M_{inner}. They are formally defined as:

$$M_{outer} = \mathbb{E}(M_{bin}, e), \quad M_{inner} = M_{bin} - M_{outer},$$

where $\mathbb{E}(.)$ is the differentiable erosion operation and e is the erosion kernel size. We represent the top k scoring hard snippets by multiplying the downsampled embedding E_m (obtained after applying 1-D convolution on the embedding E). They are obtained as:

$$X^{fg} = topk(M_{inner} * E_m), \quad X^{bg} = topk(M_{outer} * E_m),$$

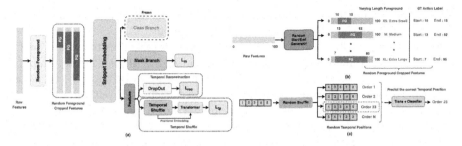

Fig. 4. Illustration of our self-supervised pre-training.

As the snippets from the same instance often predict different length 1-D masks, applying a binarization process on top generates masks of arbitrary shapes, as illustrated in Fig. 3(a). We calculate the boundary features for all of these mask clusters and select the top snippets from all of the clusters jointly. For inter-stream interaction, we further use high-confidence foreground and background snippets from the classification stream. We thus consider them as *easy foreground* and *easy background* due to their *easy to predict* property. As seen in Fig. 3(a), we similarly select top scoring foreground and background snippets from the thresholded classification output $P_{bin} := \eta(P - \theta_c)$ as:

$$Y^{fg} = topk(argmax((P_{bin} * E_p)[: K, :])), \quad Y^{bg} = topk((P_{bin} * E_p)[K + 1, :]).$$

where E_p is obtained by passing the embedding E into a 1-D conv layer for matching the dimension of P. We adopt infoNCE loss [20] for TAD refinement:

$$L_{ref} = tri(x^{fg}, y^{fg}, y^{bg}) + tri(y^{bg}, x^{bg}, y^{fg}), \tag{3}$$

where $x^* \in X^*$ and $y^* \in Y^*$ and $tri(\cdot, \cdot, \cdot)$ defines the foreground and background triplet training samples. In this way, we maximize the correlation between easy and hard snippets of the same category (foreground or background), refining the inter-stream feature representation for better perceiving temporal boundaries.

3.3   Model Training

To better exploit unlabeled data, we formulate a two-staged training pipeline, including self-supervised pre-training and semi-supervised fine-tuning.

Stage I: Self-supervised Pre-training. We introduce a pretext task based on a novel notion of *random foreground* specially designed for TAD model pre-training. Given a video feature sequence $F \in \mathbb{R}^{T \times d}$, we sample a random token segment (s, e) of varying proportions as foreground and the remaining tokens as background (Fig. 4). Cropping out foreground at feature level has shown to be useful in learning discriminative representation [42]. Motivated by this, we zero out the background snippet features whilst keeping for the pseudo foreground.

This shares a similar spirit with masked region modeling [3,14] with a different objective of detecting the location of masked segment.

With such a masked feature sequence, our pretext task aims to predict jointly (1) the temporal mask with the start s and end e (Fig. 4(b)), (2) the temporal position of each snippet after temporal shuffling (Fig. 4(c)), and (3) the reconstruction of snippet feature (Fig. 4(a)). We treat each of T temporal positions as a specific positional class, and apply a small Transformer with learnable positional embedding on the shuffled snippet sequences. All zeroed snippet features will become *non-zero* after the transformer's processing, preventing the model from learning a trivial solution. We use the cross-entropy loss L_{tp} for temporal position prediction. This supervision aims to learn the intrinsic temporal structure information in videos. The feature reconstruction loss L_{rec} is measured by L_2 normalized mean squared error between the backbone feature F and the embedding E from the transformer. The motivation is to preserve the video encoder's discriminative information in learning global context. By dropping random snippets, the Transformer is forced to aggregate and utilize information from the context to predict the dropped snippets. As a result, the model can learn temporal semantic relations and discriminative features useful for TAD. The pretext task loss for pre-training is formulated as:

$$L_{pre} = L_m + \lambda_1 L_{rec} + \lambda_2 L_{tp}, \tag{4}$$

where L_m is the mask learning loss as defined in Eq. (11) and λ_1 and λ_2 are two hyper-parameters set as 0.8 and 0.4 respectively. We use both labeled and unlabeled data for SPOT pre-training without using any ground-truth labels.

Stage II: Semi-supervised Fine-Tuning. We implement temporal mask semi-supervised learning following the pseudo label paradigm [47]. Concretely, we alternate between predicting and applying pseudo labels, starting by using the labeled samples alone.

Pseudo Label Prediction. Given an unlabeled video embedding E, the pseudo class label is obtained by:

$$\hat{y} = max\Big(softmax(H_c(E)/\tau_c)\Big), \tag{5}$$

where the sharpening operator $\tau_c = \tau - (\tau - 1)\hat{y}'_{max}$ with $\hat{y}'_{max}$ the maximum probability over the K classes, and τ a hyper-parameter controlling the largest sharpening strength. Similarly, we obtain the pseudo mask label $\hat{g}$ as:

$$\hat{g} = sig\Big(H_m(E)/\tau_m\Big), \tag{6}$$

where τ_m is the mask sharpening operator, and $sig()$ is the sigmoid function [29]. Then, we threshold the pseudo class and mask labels at θ_c/θ_m to be binary.

Loss Functions. For SS-TAD, we use both pseudo and ground-truth labels to minimize the objective loss function as formulated below. For the ***classification***

stream, we devise a class-balanced loss to tackle the intrinsic class imbalance challenge with TAD. Inspired by [16,56], we adopt the sigmoid regression based binary cross-entropy loss function. Given a snippet $E(t)$ with class label y, the classification loss function is designed as:

$$L_{bce} = -\log(p_y) - \sum_{k \neq y, k \in \mathcal{Y}} \Big(\log(1 - p_k) \Big), \tag{7}$$

where p_y denotes the logits from class stream P. Critically, this binary cross-entropy loss gives us the flexibility to regulate each class individually per training sample. This is useful because untrimmed videos often encompass a dominant proportion of background content, which would overwhelm the underrepresented tail action classes $\mathcal{Y}_t$ with small training data. To mitigate this problem, we further improve this loss by encouraging the activation of tail action classes. Concretely, given a *background* snippet, we still allow tail action classes to be activated under a certain degree ε (set as θ_c). This is realized by introducing a weighting mechanism as:

$$L_{wbce} = -\log(p_y) - \sum_{k \neq y, k \in \mathcal{Y}} \Big(w_k \log(1 - p_k) \Big) \tag{8}$$

$$\text{where } \omega_k = \begin{cases} 0 \; if \; k \in \mathcal{Y}_t \text{ and } p(k) < \varepsilon \\ 1 \qquad otherwise \end{cases} \tag{9}$$

Given a video with the background T_{bg} and foreground T_{fg} snippets, our final classification loss is expressed as:

$$L_c = \frac{1}{T} \Big(\sum_{t \in T_{fg}} L_{bce}(t) + \sum_{t \in T_{bg}} L_{wbce}(t) \Big). \tag{10}$$

For the **mask** stream, we exploit a weighted binary cross-entropy loss L_{mce} for balancing foreground and background classes, along with a binary dice loss L_{dice} [32]. For a snippet location t, we denote $\boldsymbol{m}(t) \in \mathbb{R}^{T \times 1}$ and $\boldsymbol{g}(t) \in \mathbb{R}^{T \times 1}$ as the predicted and ground-truth mask. The mask learning loss is designed as:

$$\begin{aligned} L_m = \beta_{fg} \sum_{t=1}^{T} \boldsymbol{g}(t) \log(\boldsymbol{m}(t)) + \beta_{bg} \sum_{t=1}^{T} (1 - \boldsymbol{g}(t)) \log(1 - \boldsymbol{m}(t)) \\ + \lambda_d \Big(1 - \frac{\boldsymbol{m}^\top \boldsymbol{g}}{\sum_{t=1}^{T} \big(\boldsymbol{m}(t)^2 + \boldsymbol{g}(t)^2 \big)} \Big), \end{aligned} \tag{11}$$

where β_{fg} and β_{bg} are the inverse proportion of foreground and background used for class balance, and λ_d is the dice loss weight which is empirically set as 0.6.

Overall Learning Objective. The overall objective loss is designed as $L = L_c + L_m + L_{ref} + L_{rec}$ where L_{ref} is the refinement loss (Eq. (3)) and L_{rec} is the feature reconstruction loss as described in the pre-training stage. This loss is applied on both ground-truth and pseudo labels for fine-tuning SPOT. Note that the temporal ordering loss term L_{tp} is not used during fine-tuning as it gives performance drop (see Appendix B in Supplementary). A plausible cause is its incompatibility with the fine-tuning loss L_c.

Table 1. SS-TAD results on the validation set of ActivityNet v1.3 and the test set of THUMOS14. Note: *All methods except SPOT* use the UNet [54] trained with *100% class labels* for proposal classification; These methods hence benefit from *extra classification supervision* in comparison to SPOT. *: Using only labeled training set.

Labels	Methods	ActivityNet				THUMOS					
		0.5	0.75	0.95	Avg	0.3	0.4	0.5	0.6	0.7	Avg
60%	BMN* [27]	47.6	31.7	7.5	31.5	50.8	45.9	34.8	23.7	16.3	34.3
	Mean Teacher [51]+BMN	48.0	32.1	7.4	31.9	53.5	45.0	36.9	27.4	19.0	35.8
	FixMatch [47]+BMN	48.7	32.9	7.7	32.8	53.8	46.2	37.8	28.7	19.5	36.9
	SSP [23]	49.8	34.5	7.0	33.5	53.2	46.8	39.3	29.7	19.8	37.8
	SSTAP [57]	50.1	34.9	7.4	34.0	56.4	49.5	41.0	30.9	21.6	39.9
	SPOT (Ours)	**52.8**	**35.0**	**8.1**	**35.2**	**58.9**	**50.1**	**42.3**	**33.5**	**22.9**	**41.5**
10%	BMN* [27]	35.4	26.4	8.0	25.8	38.3	28.3	18.8	11.4	5.6	20.5
	Mean Teacher [51]+BMN	36.0	27.2	7.4	26.6	41.2	32.1	23.1	15.0	7.0	23.7
	FixMatch [47]+BMN	36.8	27.9	8.0	26.9	42.0	32.8	23.0	15.9	8.5	24.3
	SSP [23]	38.9	28.7	8.4	27.6	44.2	34.1	24.6	16.9	9.3	25.8
	SSTAP [57]	40.7	29.6	**9.0**	28.2	45.6	35.2	26.3	17.5	10.7	27.0
	SPOT (Ours)	**49.9**	**31.1**	8.3	**32.1**	**49.4**	**40.4**	**31.5**	**22.9**	**12.4**	**31.3**

3.4 Model Inference

At test time, we generate action instance predictions for each test video by the classification P and mask M predictions. For P, we only consider the snippets whose class probabilities are greater than θ_c and select top scoring snippets. For each such top scoring action snippet, we then obtain the temporal mask by thresholding the t_i-th column of M using the localization threshold Θ. To produce sufficient candidates, we use a set of thresholds $\Theta = \{\theta_i\}$. For each candidate, we compute a confidence score s by multiplying the classification and max-mask scores. SoftNMS [6] is finally applied to obtain top scoring results.

4   Experiments

Datasets. We use two standard TAD datasets in our evaluation. (1) *ActivityNet v1.3* is a large-scale benchmark containing 19,994 untrimmed videos with 200 classes. We adopt the standard 2:1:1 training/validation/testing video data split. (2) *THUMOS14* provides 200 validation videos and 213 testing videos labeled with temporal annotations for action understanding. We train our model on the validation set and evaluate on the test set.

Implementation Details. For fair comparisons, we use both TSN [55] and I3D [9] features in our evaluations. For ActivityNet, we use fine-tuned TSN features for fair comparison with [27,57]. For THUMOS, we use TSN and I3D features both pre-trained on Kinetics [61]. The temporal dimension T is fixed at

100/256 for ActivityNet/THUMOS respectively (see the suppl. for more analysis). For AcitivityNet/THUMOS, we first pre-train SPOT (except the classification stream) on the training set including the unlabeled samples for 12 epochs and then we fine-tune SPOT for 15 epochs with a learning rate of $10^{-4}/10^{-5}$, a weight decay of $10^{-3}/10^{-5}$. For boundary refinement, we set top-$k = 40$ snippets, θ_c/θ_m is set as 0.3/0.7 and e is set as 7. In semi-supervised setting, the label sharpening operator τ is set as 1.1 and τ_m is set as 0.7. In testing, we set the threshold set for mask $\theta = \{0.1 \sim 0.9\}$ with a step 0.1. The SoftNMS is performed on ActivityNet/Thumos with a threshold of 0.6/0.4.

4.1   Comparative Results

Setting. We introduce two SS-TAD settings with different label sizes. For each dataset, we randomly select 10% or 60% training videos as the labeled set and the remaining as the unlabeled set. Both labeled and unlabeled sets are accessible for SS-TAD model training.

Competitors. We compared with the following methods. (**1**) Two state-of-the-art supervised TAD methods: BMN [27]+UNet [54] and GTAD [63]+UNet [54] (**2**) Two SSL+TAD methods: As SS-TAD is a new problem, we need to implement the competitors by extending existing SSL methods to TAD by ourselves. We select two top SSL methods (Mean Teacher [51] and FixMatch [47]), and a state-of-the-art TAD model based on a popular proposal generation method BMN [27] (using TSN features) and GTAD [63] (using I3D features). Both of these models use a common untrimmed video classification model UNet [54]. For FixMatch [47], we use temporal flip (*i.e.*, playing the video backwards) as strong augmentation and temporal feature shift as weak augmentation. For UNet, due to the lack of Caffe based training environment, we can only apply the official weights trained with 100% supervision (**3**) Two recent semi-supervised temporal proposal generation methods [23,57]. Note that the concurrent SS-TAD work [46] does not give reproducible experiment settings and prevents an exact comparison. Besides, [46] achieves only 12.27% avg mAP on ActivityNet v1.2 *vs.* 32.1% by SPOT on v1.3 (v1.2 has only half classes of v1.3 hence simpler), thus significantly inferior to the two compared methods [23,57].

Results. The SS-TAD results are reported in Table 1 and Table 5. We make the following observations: (**1**) Without leveraging unlabeled video data, the state-of-the-art fully supervised TAD method BMN [27] (with UNet [54]) achieves the poorest result among all the methods. This clearly suggests the usefulness of unlabeled data and the consistent benefits of adopting semi-supervised learning for TAD – a largely ignored research topic. (**2**) Combining existing TAD methods (*e.g.*, BMN [27]) with previous SSL methods (*e.g.*, Mean Teacher [51] and FixMatch [47]) is indeed effective in improving model generalization. Similar observations can be made on SSP [23] and SS-TAD [57], our two main competitors. Despite such performance improvements, these methods still suffer from the proposal error propagation problem that would limit their ability in exploiting unlabeled videos. (**3**) By solving this problem with a new parallel design, our

Table 2. Analysis of localization error propagation on ActivityNet with 10% supervision. GT: Ground-Truth.

Metric	mAP	
	0.5	Avg
BMN [27] + MLP		
GT proposals	55.7	45.3
Pseudo proposals	32.4	23.6
SPOT		
GT masks	59.2	47.0
Pseudo masks	49.9	32.1

Table 3. Analysis of SPOT model pre-training on ActivityNet with 10% label supervision.

Pre-training loss			mAP	
L_m	L_{rec}	L_{tp}	0.5	Avg
Random initialization				
✗	✗	✗	46.2	30.5
With our pre-training				
✓	✗	✗	47.6	31.4
✓	✓	✗	48.5	31.7
✓	✗	✓	47.9	31.5
✓	✓	✓	49.9	32.1

SPOT achieves the new state of the art on both datasets. It is worth pointing out the larger margin achieved by SPOT over all the competitors at the lower supervision case (10% label). For instance, with 10% label, SPOT surpasses the second best SSTAP by 3.9%/4.3% on ActivityNet/THUMOS. A plausible reason is that the proposal error propagation will become more severe when the labeled set is smaller, causing more harm to existing proposal based TAD methods. This validates the overall efficacy and capability of our model formulation in leveraging unlabeled video data for SS-TAD. (4) From Table 5 we observe similar findings as that of BMN [27] using TSN features (Table 1). Our SPOT outperforms the existing baselines and SS-TAD models by almost similar margin, confirming that the superiority of our method is feature agnostic.

4.2 Further Analysis

Localization Error Propagation Analysis. To examine the effect of localization error propagation with previous TAD models, we design a proof-of-concept experiment by measuring the performance drop between ground-truth proposals and pseudo proposals. Due to the lack of access to the now obsolete training environment for UNet [54], we adopt a MLP classifier with BMN [27] as the baseline TAD model. For our SPOT, we contrast ground-truth and pseudo masks. This experiment is tested on ActivityNet with 10% supervision. Table 2 shows that the proposal based TAD baseline suffers almost double performance degradation from localization (*i.e.*, proposal) error due to its sequential localization and classification design. This verifies the advantage of SPOT's parallel design.

Effectiveness of Model pre-training. We propose a two-staged training method characterized by model pre-training based on a novel pretext task (Sect. 4.2). We now examine how pre-training helps for model accuracy. Here, we take the 10% label supervision case on ActivityNet, with a comparison to the random

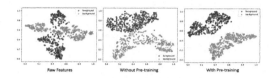

Fig. 5. Effect of our model pre-training on a random ActivityNet video.

Table 4. Effect of pre-training on ActivityNet with 10% labels.

Method	mAP	
	0.5	Avg
BMN + [54]	35.4	25.8
$BMN^\dagger$ + [54]	**36.2**	**26.3**

Table 5. SS-TAD results on THUMOS14 test-set using I3D features; All method except **SPOT** uses UNet [54]; *:Using only labeled set.

Labels	Method	mAP		
		0.3	0.5	0.7
60%	$GTAD^*$ [63]	50.9	35.4	16.5
	FixMatch [47]+GTAD	53.4	38.9	19.1
	SSP [23]	53.5	39.7	20.4
	SSTAP [57]+GTAD	55.9	41.6	22.0
	SPOT (Ours)	**58.7**	**42.4**	**23.1**
10%	$GTAD^*$ [63]	36.9	20.1	6.6
	FixMatch [47]+GTAD	42.1	23.8	9.7
	SSP [23]	43.1	25.5	9.6
	SSTAP [57]+GTAD	45.3	27.5	11.0
	SPOT (Ours)	**49.1**	**31.7**	**12.6**

Table 6. Performance of our SPOT model w/ and w/o unlabeled data on ActivityNet.

Labels	SSL modules		mAP	
	Pre-train	L_c	0.5	Avg
10%	✓	✓	**49.9**	**32.1**
	✓	✗	45.3	29.8
	✗	✓	46.2	30.5
	✗	✗	44.5	28.3
60%	✓	✓	**52.8**	**35.2**
	✓	✗	51.7	34.4
	✗	✓	52.1	34.9
	✗	✗	51.2	34.0

initialization baseline. Concretely, we examine three loss terms: the mask prediction loss (L_m), the feature reconstruction loss (L_{rec}), and the temporal position loss (L_{tp}). The results in Table 3 reveal that: **(1)** Compared to random initialization, our pre-training boosts the overall mAP by 1.6%. This gain is also supported by the more distinct separation of foreground and background features as shown in Fig. 5 This validates the importance of TAD model initialization and the efficacy of our pretext task. **(2)** All the loss terms are effective either in isolation or in the cohorts, suggesting they are complementary with good compatibility. Additionally, we evaluate the generic impact of our pre-training on BMN [27]. We observe from Table 4 that it again gives a good increase of 0.7% in Avg mAP, justifying its generic usefulness.

Effectiveness of Using Unlabeled Data. We evaluate the impact of using unlabeled data imposed by the pre-training and the loss term L_c (in Eq. (10)). Table 6 shows that without these components, the model will degrade in performance particularly in case of less labels, as expected. In particular, both SSL components (pretraining and L_c) are clearly effective in model performance. This

Table 7. Ablating SPOT objective loss terms on ActivityNet with 10% label. L_c: classification loss; L_{mce}: cross-entropy mask loss; L_{dice}: dice mask loss; L_{ref}: refinement loss; L_{rec}: feature reconstruction loss.

Loss	mAP	
	0.5	Avg
All	**49.9**	**32.1**
W/O L_c	45.3	29.8
W/O L_{mce}	47.8	31.5
W/O L_{dice}	47.0	31.2
W/O L_{rec}	45.9	30.2
W/O L_{ref}	46.8	30.7

Table 8. Fully supervised TAD results on the validation set of ActivityNet. All the compared methods use TSN features used in [57]

Method	mAP			
	0.5	0.75	0.95	Avg
BSN [28]	46.4	29.9	8.0	30.0
GTAD [66]	50.3	34.6	9.0	34.0
BC-GNN [2]	50.6	34.8	**9.4**	34.3
BMN [27]	50.0	34.8	8.3	33.8
BSN++ [49]	51.2	35.7	8.3	34.8
TCANet [43]	52.2	36.7	6.8	35.5
GTAD+CSA [48]	51.8	**36.8**	8.7	35.6
SPOT	**53.9**	35.9	**9.4**	**35.8**

verifies their designs. Besides, even without the SSL modules our model is better than SSTAP [57] in 10% label case and comparable in 60% label case, further indicating the advantage of our model design.

Contributions of Different Losses. We ablate the effect of SPOT's training loss functions for classification and mask (Sect. 3.3). We test the benefit of the classification loss (L_c), the weighted binary cross-entropy mask loss (L_{mce}), the dice mask loss (L_{dice}), the refinement loss (L_{ref}), and the feature reconstruction loss (L_{rec}). When testing L_c, we replace it with the standard cross-entropy loss. Table 7 shows that each loss term is beneficial for improving model accuracy, verifying their individual and collective efficacy.

Comparisons to Fully Supervised TAD Methods. Besides SS-TAD, our SPOT can be also applied for fully supervised TAD with the pseudo-labels replaced by ground-truth labels while keeping the remaining the same. This test is conducted on ActivityNet. Table 8 shows that when trained with fully-labeled data, our SPOT can also outperform state-of-the-art TAD methods in the overall result albeit by a smaller margin as compared to the semi-supervised case. This is as expected because in fully supervised setting there would be less proposal error and hence less harm by its propagation.

5 Conclusions

In this work, we have proposed a novel *Proposal-Free Temporal Mask* (SPOT) learning model for the under-studied yet practically useful semi-supervised temporal action detection (SS-TAD). It is characterized by a *parallel* localization (mask generation) and classification architecture designed to solve the localization error propagation problem with conventional TAD models. For superior optimization, we further introduced a novel pretext task for pre-training and a boundary refinement algorithm. Extensive experiments on ActivityNet and THUMOS demonstrate that our SPOT yields state-of-the-art performance under both semi-supervised and supervised learning settings.

References

1. Alwassel, H., Mahajan, D., Torresani, L., Ghanem, B., Tran, D.: Self-supervised learning by cross-modal audio-video clustering. In: NeurIPS (2020)
2. Bai, Y., Wang, Y., Tong, Y., Yang, Y., Liu, Q., Liu, J.: Boundary content graph neural network for temporal action proposal generation. In: Vedaldi, A., Bischof, H., Brox, T., Frahm, J.-M. (eds.) ECCV 2020. LNCS, vol. 12373, pp. 121–137. Springer, Cham (2020). https://doi.org/10.1007/978-3-030-58604-1_8
3. Bao, H., Dong, L., Wei, F.: Beit: bert pre-training of image transformers. arXiv preprint. arXiv:2106.08254 (2021)
4. Benaim, S., et al.: SpeedNet: learning the speediness in videos. In: CVPR (2020)
5. Berthelot, D., Carlini, N., Goodfellow, I., Papernot, N., Oliver, A., Raffel, C.: Mixmatch: a holistic approach to semi-supervised learning. In: NeurIPS (2019)
6. Bodla, N., Singh, B., Chellappa, R., Davis, L.S.: Soft-nms-improving object detection with one line of code. In: Proceedings of the IEEE International Conference on Computer Vision, pp. 5561–5569 (2017)
7. Buch, S., Escorcia, V., Shen, C., Ghanem, B., Carlos Niebles, J.: Sst: single-stream temporal action proposals. In: CVPR (2017)
8. Caba Heilbron, F., Escorcia, V., Ghanem, B., Carlos Niebles, J.: Activitynet: a large-scale video benchmark for human activity understanding. In: CVPR, pp. 961–970 (2015)
9. Carreira, J., Zisserman, A.: Quo vadis, action recognition? a new model and the kinetics dataset. In: proceedings of the IEEE Conference on Computer Vision and Pattern Recognition, pp. 6299–6308 (2017)
10. Chapelle, O., Scholkopf, B., Zien, A.: Semi-supervised learning. In: TNNLS (2009)
11. Chen, T., Kornblith, S., Norouzi, M., Hinton, G.: A simple framework for contrastive learning of visual representations. In: ICML (2020)
12. Chen, X., He, K.: Exploring simple siamese representation learning. In: CVPR (2021)
13. Chen, Y., Zhu, X., Gong, S.: Semi-supervised deep learning with memory. In: Ferrari, V., Hebert, M., Sminchisescu, C., Weiss, Y. (eds.) ECCV 2018. LNCS, vol. 11205, pp. 275–291. Springer, Cham (2018). https://doi.org/10.1007/978-3-030-01246-5_17
14. Chen, Y.C., et al.: UNITER: universal image-TExt representation learning. In: Vedaldi, A., Bischof, H., Brox, T., Frahm, J.-M. (eds.) ECCV 2020. LNCS, vol. 12375, pp. 104–120. Springer, Cham (2020). https://doi.org/10.1007/978-3-030-58577-8_7
15. Chen, Y., Tu, Z., Ge, L., Zhang, D., Chen, R., Yuan, J.: So-handnet: self-organizing network for 3d hand pose estimation with semi-supervised learning. In: ICCV (2019)
16. Dong, Q., Zhu, X., Gong, S.: Single-label multi-class image classification by deep logistic regression. In: AAAI, vol. 33, pp. 3486–3493 (2019)
17. Gao, J., Yang, Z., Chen, K., Sun, C., Nevatia, R.: Turn tap: temporal unit regression network for temporal action proposals. In: ICCV (2017)

18. Grill, J.B., et al.: Bootstrap your own latent: a new approach to self-supervised learning. In: NeurIPS (2020)
19. He, K., Fan, H., Wu, Y., Xie, S., Girshick, R.: Momentum contrast for unsupervised visual representation learning. In: CVPR (2020)
20. He, K., Fan, H., Wu, Y., Xie, S., Girshick, R.: Momentum contrast for unsupervised visual representation learning. In: Proceedings of the IEEE/CVF Conference on Computer Vision and Pattern Recognition, pp. 9729–9738 (2020)
21. Ibrahim, M.S., Vahdat, A., Ranjbar, M., Macready, W.G.: Semi-supervised semantic image segmentation with self-correcting networks. In: CVPR (2020)
22. Idrees, H., et al.: The thumos challenge on action recognition for videos "in the wild". Comput. Vis. Image Underst. **155**, 1–23 (2017)
23. Ji, J., Cao, K., Niebles, J.C.: Learning temporal action proposals with fewer labels. In: Proceedings of the IEEE/CVF International Conference on Computer Vision, pp. 7073–7082 (2019)
24. Kim, J., Hur, Y., Park, S., Yang, E., Hwang, S.J., Shin, J.: Distribution aligning refinery of pseudo-label for imbalanced semi-supervised learning. In: NeurIPS (2020)
25. Laine, S., Aila, T.: Temporal ensembling for semi-supervised learning. In: ICLR (2017)
26. Lee, D.H.: Pseudo-label: the simple and efficient semi-supervised learning method for deep neural networks. In: ICML Workshop (2013)
27. Lin, T., Liu, X., Li, X., Ding, E., Wen, S.: Bmn: boundary-matching network for temporal action proposal generation. In: Proceedings of the IEEE/CVF International Conference on Computer Vision, pp. 3889–3898 (2019)
28. Lin, T., Zhao, X., Su, H., Wang, C., Yang, M.: BSN: boundary sensitive network for temporal action proposal generation. In: Ferrari, V., Hebert, M., Sminchisescu, C., Weiss, Y. (eds.) ECCV 2018. LNCS, vol. 11208, pp. 3–21. Springer, Cham (2018). https://doi.org/10.1007/978-3-030-01225-0_1
29. Little, W.A.: The existence of persistent states in the brain. In: From High-Temperature Superconductivity to Microminiature Refrigeration (1974)
30. Long, F., Yao, T., Qiu, Z., Tian, X., Luo, J., Mei, T.: Gaussian temporal awareness networks for action localization. In: CVPR (2019)
31. Miech, A., Alayrac, J.B., Smaira, L., Laptev, I., Sivic, J., Zisserman, A.: End-to-end learning of visual representations from uncurated instructional videos. In: CVPR (2020)
32. Milletari, F., Navab, N., Ahmadi, S.A.: V-net: Fully convolutional neural networks for volumetric medical image segmentation. In: 2016 4th International Conference on 3D Vision (3DV), pp. 565–571. IEEE (2016)
33. Misra, I., Maaten, L.V.D.: Self-supervised learning of pretext-invariant representations. In: CVPR (2020)
34. Misra, I., Zitnick, C.L., Hebert, M.: Shuffle and learn: unsupervised learning using temporal order verification. In: Leibe, B., Matas, J., Sebe, N., Welling, M. (eds.) ECCV 2016. LNCS, vol. 9905, pp. 527–544. Springer, Cham (2016). https://doi.org/10.1007/978-3-319-46448-0_32
35. Mitra, R., Gundavarapu, N.B., Sharma, A., Jain, A.: Multiview-consistent semi-supervised learning for 3d human pose estimation. In: CVPR (2020)
36. Miyato, T., Maeda, S.I., Koyama, M., Ishii, S.: Virtual adversarial training: a regularization method for supervised and semi-supervised learning. IEEE TPAMI **41**(8), 1979–1993 (2018)
37. Nag, S., Zhu, X., Song, Y.Z., Xiang, T.: Temporal action localization with global segmentation mask transformers (2021)

38. Nag, S., Zhu, X., Song, Y.z., Xiang, T.: Proposal-free temporal action detection via global segmentation mask learning. In: ECCV (2022)
39. Nag, S., Zhu, X., Song, Y.z., Xiang, T.: Zero-shot temporal action detection via vision-language prompting. In: ECCV (2022)
40. Nag, S., Zhu, X., Xiang, T.: Few-shot temporal action localization with query adaptive transformer. arXiv preprint. arXiv:2110.10552 (2021)
41. Ouali, Y., Hudelot, C., Tami, M.: Semi-supervised semantic segmentation with cross-consistency training. In: CVPR (2020)
42. Patrick, M., et al.: Space-time crop & attend: Improving cross-modal video representation learning. arXiv preprint. arXiv:2103.10211 (2021)
43. Qing, Z., et al.: Temporal context aggregation network for temporal action proposal refinement. In: Proceedings of the IEEE/CVF Conference on Computer Vision and Pattern Recognition (CVPR), pp. 485–494 (2021)
44. Ren, S., He, K., Girshick, R., Sun, J.: Faster r-cnn: towards real-time object detection with region proposal networks. In: TPAMI, vol. 39, no. 6, pp. 1137–1149 (2016)
45. Riba, E., Mishkin, D., Ponsa, D., Rublee, E., Bradski, G.: Kornia: an open source differentiable computer vision library for pytorch. In: WACV, pp. 3674–3683 (2020)
46. Shi, B., Dai, Q., Hoffman, J., Saenko, K., Darrell, T., Xu, H.: Temporal action detection with multi-level supervision. In: CVPR, pp. 8022–8032 (2021)
47. Sohn, K., et al.: Fixmatch: simplifying semi-supervised learning with consistency and confidence. arXiv preprint. arXiv:2001.07685 (2020)
48. Sridhar, D., Quader, N., Muralidharan, S., Li, Y., Dai, P., Lu, J.: Class semantics-based attention for action detection. In: Proceedings of the IEEE/CVF International Conference on Computer Vision, pp. 13739–13748 (2021)
49. Su, H., Gan, W., Wu, W., Qiao, Y., Yan, J.: Bsn++: complementary boundary regressor with scale-balanced relation modeling for temporal action proposal generation. arXiv preprint. arXiv:2009.07641 (2020)
50. Tang, Y.S., Lee, G.H.: Transferable semi-supervised 3d object detection from rgb-d data. In: ICCV (2019)
51. Tarvainen, A., Valpola, H.: Mean teachers are better role models: weight-averaged consistency targets improve semi-supervised deep learning results. arXiv preprint. arXiv:1703.01780 (2017)
52. Vaswani, A., et al.: Attention is all you need. arXiv preprint. arXiv:1706.03762 (2017)
53. Vondrick, C., Shrivastava, A., Fathi, A., Guadarrama, S., Murphy, K.: Tracking emerges by colorizing videos. In: Ferrari, V., Hebert, M., Sminchisescu, C., Weiss, Y. (eds.) ECCV 2018. LNCS, vol. 11217, pp. 402–419. Springer, Cham (2018). https://doi.org/10.1007/978-3-030-01261-8_24
54. Wang, L., Xiong, Y., Lin, D., Van Gool, L.: Untrimmednets for weakly supervised action recognition and detection. In: CVPR, pp. 4325–4334 (2017)
55. Wang, L., et al.: Temporal segment networks: towards good practices for deep action recognition. In: Leibe, B., Matas, J., Sebe, N., Welling, M. (eds.) ECCV 2016. LNCS, vol. 9912, pp. 20–36. Springer, Cham (2016). https://doi.org/10.1007/978-3-319-46484-8_2
56. Wang, T., Zhu, Y., Zhao, C., Zeng, W., Wang, J., Tang, M.: Adaptive class suppression loss for long-tail object detection. In: Proceedings of the IEEE/CVF Conference on Computer Vision and Pattern Recognition, pp. 3103–3112 (2021)
57. Wang, X., Zhang, S., Qing, Z., Shao, Y., Gao, C., Sang, N.: Self-supervised learning for semi-supervised temporal action proposal. In: CVPR, pp. 1905–1914 (2021)

58. Wei, D., Lim, J., Zisserman, A., Freeman, W.T.: Learning and using the arrow of time. In: CVPR (2018)
59. Wu, Z., Xiong, Y., Yu, S.X., Lin, D.: Unsupervised feature learning via non-parametric instance discrimination. In: CVPR (2018)
60. Xie, Q., Dai, Z., Hovy, E., Luong, T., Le, Q.: Unsupervised data augmentation for consistency training. In: NeurIPS (2020)
61. Xiong, Y., et al.: Cuhk & ethz & siat submission to activitynet challenge 2016. arXiv preprint. arXiv:1608.00797 (2016)
62. Xu, H., Das, A., Saenko, K.: R-c3d: region convolutional 3d network for temporal activity detection. In: ICCV (2017)
63. Xu, M., et al.: Boundary-sensitive pre-training for temporal localization in videos (2020)
64. Xu, M., et al.: Boundary-sensitive pre-training for temporal localization in videos. In: ICCV, pp. 7220–7230 (2021)
65. Xu, M., Perez-Rua, J.M., Zhu, X., Ghanem, B., Martinez, B.: Low-fidelity end-to-end video encoder pre-training for temporal action localization. In: NeurIPS (2021)
66. Xu, M., Zhao, C., Rojas, D.S., Thabet, A., Ghanem, B.: G-tad: sub-graph localization for temporal action detection. In: CVPR (2020)
67. Yan, P., Li, G., Xie, Y., Li, Z., Wang, C., Chen, T., Lin, L.: Semi-supervised video salient object detection using pseudo-labels. In: ICCV (2019)
68. Zhao, C., Thabet, A.K., Ghanem, B.: Video self-stitching graph network for temporal action localization. In: Proceedings of the IEEE/CVF International Conference on Computer Vision, pp. 13658–13667 (2021)
69. Zhao, N., Chua, T.S., Lee, G.H.: Sess: Self-ensembling semi-supervised 3d object detection. In: CVPR (2020)
70. Zhao, Y., Xiong, Y., Wang, L., Wu, Z., Tang, X., Lin, D.: Temporal action detection with structured segment networks. In: ICCV (2017)
71. Zhu, X.J.: Semi-supervised learning literature survey. University of Wisconsin-Madison Department of Computer Sciences, Technical reports (2005)

Zero-Shot Temporal Action Detection via Vision-Language Prompting

Sauradip Nag[1,2(✉)], Xiatian Zhu[1,3], Yi-Zhe Song[1,2], and Tao Xiang[1,2]

[1] CVSSP, University of Surrey, Guildford, UK
{s.nag,xiatian.zhu,y.song,t.xiang}@surrey.ac.uk
[2] iFlyTek-Surrey Joint Research Centre on Artificial Intelligence, London, UK
[3] Surrey Institute for People-Centred Artificial Intelligence,
University of Surrey, Guildford, UK

Abstract. Existing temporal action detection (TAD) methods rely on large training data including segment-level annotations, limited to recognizing previously seen classes alone during inference. Collecting and annotating a large training set for each class of interest is costly and hence unscalable. Zero-shot TAD (ZS-TAD) resolves this obstacle by enabling a pre-trained model to recognize any unseen action classes. Meanwhile, ZS-TAD is also much more challenging with significantly less investigation. Inspired by the success of zero-shot image classification aided by vision-language (ViL) models such as CLIP, we aim to tackle the more complex TAD task. An intuitive method is to integrate an off-the-shelf proposal detector with CLIP style classification. However, due to the *sequential* localization (*e.g.*, proposal generation) and classification design, it is prone to localization error propagation. To overcome this problem, in this paper we propose a novel *zero-Shot Temporal Action detection model via Vision-LanguagE prompting* (STALE). Such a novel design effectively eliminates the dependence between localization and classification by breaking the route for error propagation in-between. We further introduce an interaction mechanism between classification and localization for improved optimization. Extensive experiments on standard ZS-TAD video benchmarks show that our STALE significantly outperforms state-of-the-art alternatives. Besides, our model also yields superior results on supervised TAD over recent strong competitors. The PyTorch implementation of STALE is available on https://github.com/sauradip/STALE.

Keywords: Zero-shot transfer · Temporal action localization · Language supervision · Task adaptation · Detection · Dense prediction

1 Introduction

The introduction of large pretrained Visual-Language (ViL) models (*e.g.*, CLIP [36] and ALIGN [16]) has surged recently the research attempts on *zero-shot transfer* to diverse downstream tasks via *prompting*. Central in this research

---

Supplementary Information The online version contains supplementary material available at https://doi.org/10.1007/978-3-031-20062-5_39.

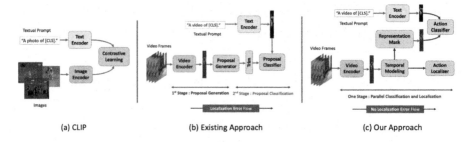

(a) CLIP   (b) Existing Approach   (c) Our Approach

Fig. 1. Illustration of the (a) standard vision-language model CLIP [36]. (b) Existing ZS-TAD method [17] suffers from the intrinsic localization error propagation problem, due to the *sequential* localization (*e.g.*, proposal generation) and classification design. (c) We solve this problem by designing a STALE model with a *parallel* localization and classification architecture.

line is a favourable ability of *synthesizing the classification weights* from natural language which can describe almost all the classes of interest, along with a strong image encoder trained with an objective of aligning a massive number of potentially noisy image-text pairs in a common feature space.

Whilst existing works mostly focus on image recognition tasks [12,54], how to capitalize the knowledge of such ViL models for natural video understanding tasks (*e.g.*, temporal action detection [4,20,26–29,47]) remains unsolved largely. There are several challenges to be solved. ***First***, as those *public accessible* large ViL models are often pretrained with big image data, temporal structured information is absent which is limited for video representation. ***Second***, ViL models favor classification type of tasks *without built-in detection capability* in formulation. That is, their optimization assumes implicitly limited background *w.r.t* the foreground content with the training data. In contrast, natural videos often come with a large, variable proportion of background, and detecting the content of interest (*e.g.*, human actions) is critical [1]. It is non-trivial to overcome these obstacles. On using ViL models for temporal action detection (TAD), indeed a recent attempt [17] is made. Specifically, [17] presents a two-stage video model: generating many action proposals with an off-the-shelf pre-trained proposal detector (*e.g.*, BMN [20]), followed by proposal classification. This method has obvious limitations: (1) It is unable to adapt the localization module (*i.e.*, proposal detection) which is pretrained and frozen throughout. (2) As a result, the compatibility between the localization and classification is limited, further leading to a localization error propagation problem due to the sequential localization and classification pipeline.

In this paper, to overcome the aforementioned limitations, we formulate a novel one-stage zero-shot temporal action localization architecture characterized with *parallel* classification and localization. This parallel head design naturally eliminates error propagation. Importantly, we introduce a learnable localization module based on a notion of *representation masking* – which is class-agnostic and hence generalizable to unseen classes. It can be optimized end-to-end, together with the classification component powered by a ViL model for zero-shot transfer, consequently solving the component compatibility problem. For improving cross-modal (from image to video) task adaptation, we further design an inter-stream alignment regularization along with the self-attention mechanism. We term our method *Zero-**S**hot **T**emporal **A**ction Detection Model via Vision-**L**anguag**E** Prompting* (STALE).

Contributions. **(1)** We investigate the under-studied yet critical problem of how to capitalize large pretrained ViL models for zero-shot temporal action localization (ZS-TAD) in untrimmed videos. **(2)** We present a novel one-stage model, STALE, featured with a parallel classification and localization design interleaved by a learnable class-agnostic representation masking component for enabling zero-shot transfer to unseen classes. For enhancing cross-modal task adaptation, we introduce an inter-stream alignment regularization in the Transformer framework. **(3)** Extensive experiments on standard ZS-TAD video benchmarks show that our STALE outperforms state-of-the-art alternative methods, often by a large margin. Besides, our model can be also applied to the fully supervised TAD setting and achieve superior performance in comparison to recent supervised competitors.

2   Related Works

Vision-Language Models. There have been a series of works on the interaction of computer vision and natural language processing fields, *e.g.*, text-to-image retrieval [43], image caption [46], visual question answering [2], and so on. Among these works, vision language (ViL) pre-training has attracted growing attention during the past few years [19,23]. As a milestone, Radford et al. [36] devise a large-scale pretraining ViL model, named CLIP, trained with a contrastive learning strategy on 400 million image-text pairs. It shows impressive zero-shot transferable ability over 30 classification datasets. Since then, many follow-ups have been proposed, including improved training strategy (*e.g.*, CoOp [54], CLIP-Adapter [12], Tip-adapter [50]). In video domains, similar idea has also been explored for transferable representation learning [24], text based action localization [33]. CLIP has also been used very recently in action recognition (*e.g.*, ActionCLIP [42]) and TAD [17]. Conceptually, all these methods use CLIP in a classification perspective. Commonly a two-stage pipeline is applied, where the first stage needs to crop the foreground followed by aligning the foreground using CLIP in the second stage. However, this strategy often suffers from the error propagation problem, that is, the errors from first stage would flow into the second stage and potentially amplify. In this work, we tackle this challenge by designing a one-stage ZS-TAD architecture featured with parallel classification and localization.

Temporal Action Detection. Substantial progress has been made in TAD. Inspired by object detection in static images [38], R-C3D [45] uses anchor boxes by following the design of proposal generation and classification. With a similar model design, TURN [11] aggregates local features to represent snippet-level features for temporal boundary regression and classification. SSN [52] decomposes an action instance into three stages (starting, course, and ending) and employs structured temporal pyramid pooling to generate proposals. BSN [21] predicts the start, end and actionness at each temporal location and generates proposals with high start and end probabilities. The actionness was further improved in BMN [20] via additionally generating a boundary-matching confidence map for improved proposal generation. GTAN [22] improves the proposal feature pooling procedure with a learnable Gaussian kernel for weighted averaging. G-TAD [47] learns semantic and temporal context via graph convolutional networks for more accurate proposal generation. BSN++ [40] further extends BMN with a complementary boundary generator to capture rich context. CSA [39] enriches the proposal temporal context via attention transfer. Recently, VSGN [51] improves short-action localization using a cross-scale multi-level pyramidal architecture. Commonly, the existing TAD models mostly adopt a 2-stage *sequential* localization and classification architecture. This would cause the localization error propagation problem particularly in low-data setting such as ZS-TAD. Our STALE is designed to address this limitation by designing a single stage model, thereby removing the dependence between localization and classification and cutting off the error propagation path.

Zero-Shot Temporal Action Detection. Zero-shot learning (ZSL) is designed to recognize new classes that are not seen during training [44]. The idea is to learn shared knowledge from prior information and then transfer that knowledge from seen classes to unseen classes [30,35]. Visual attributes (*e.g.*, color, shape, and any properties) are the typical forms of prior information. For example, Lampert et al. [18] prelearned the attribute classifiers independently to accomplish ZSL on unseen classes, while Parikh et al. [32] learned relative attributes. Despite promising results on ZSL, attribute-based methods have poor scalability because the attributes need to be manually defined. Semantic embeddings of seen and unseen concepts, another type of prior information, can solve this scalability problem [48]. They are generally learned in an unsupervised manner such as Word2Vec [13] or GloVe [34]. Zhang et al. [49] firstly applied zero-shot learning on TAD using Word2Vec. Very recently, EffPrompt [17] used image-text pretraining from CLIP [36] for ZS-TAD. However, due to a two-stage design, this method also has the error propagation problem, in addition to its inability of learning the action localization module. We address all these limitations by introducing a new one-stage ZS-TAD architecture.

3   Methodology

We aim to efficiently steer an image-based ViL model (CLIP [36]) to tackle dense video downstream tasks such as Zero-Shot Temporal Action Detection (ZS-TAD) in untrimmed videos. This is essentially a model adaptation process with the aim to leverage the rich semantic knowledge from large language corpus.

3.1   Preliminaries: Visual-Language Pre-training

The key capability of CLIP is to align the embedding spaces of visual and language data [36]. It consists of two encoders, namely an image encoder (*e.g.*,

ResNet [14] or ViT [9]) and a text encoder (*e.g.*, Transformer [41]). To learn rich transferable semantic knowledge, CLIP leverages 400 million image-text pairs during training. To exploit CLIP's knowledge for downstream classification tasks, an effective approach is to construct a set of text prompts with a template such as *"a photo of [CLS]."*, where [CLS] can be replaced by any class name of interest. Given an image, one can then use CLIP to compute the similarity scores between this image and the text prompts in the embedding space and take the class with the highest score as the prediction. Recently, a couple of works [12,54] have demonstrated that CLIP can obtain strong classification performance with few or even zero training examples per class. We raise an interesting question: ***Whether the impressive ability of CLIP can be transferred to more complex vision tasks like dense prediction?***

This extended transfer could be intrinsically nontrivial. *Firstly*, how to leverage the visual-language pre-trained model in dense prediction tasks is a barely studied problem especially in zero-shot setup [37]. A simple method is to only use the image encoder of CLIP. However, we argue that the language priors with the pretrained text encoder are also of great importance and should be leveraged together. *Secondly*, transferring the knowledge from CLIP to dense prediction is more difficult than classification tasks, due to the substantial task discrepancy involved. The pretraining focuses on global representation learning of both images and texts, which is incompatible for local pixel-level outputs as required in downstream tasks. RegionCLIP [53] recently solves this problem in a 2-stage design including class-agnostic masking generalizable to unseen classes, followed by CLIP style classification. EffPrompt [17] similarly tackles a dense video understanding task TAD. Nonetheless, this approach suffers from the notorious localization error propagation challenge.

3.2   Language Guided Temporal Action Detection

To solve the aforementioned issues, we propose a language guided proposal-free framework. It can better leverage the language-priors of the pre-trained CLIP model. In the following sections, we start by describing the problem scenario and notations followed by introducing the idea for model adaptation through prompt learning. We then discuss how masking can help maintain the zero-shot transfer property in a one-stage design. Lastly, we discuss about the refinement of boundaries.

Problem Definition. We assume a dataset D with the training $D_{train} = \{V_i, \psi_i\}_{i=1}^{N}$ and validation D_{val} sets. Each untrimmed training video V_i is labeled with temporal segmentation $\Psi_i = \{(\psi_j, \xi_j, y_j)\}_{j=1}^{M_i}$ where ψ_j/ξ_j denote the start/end time, y_j is the action category, and M_i is the action instance number. Respectively, y_j refers to one of the training (D_{train}) action labels in the text format for recognition, *e.g.*, y_j replaces the [CLS] token in a sentence of "a photo of [CLS]". We consider both closed-set and open-set scenarios. In the closed-set scenario, the action categories for training and evaluation are identical, *i.e.*,

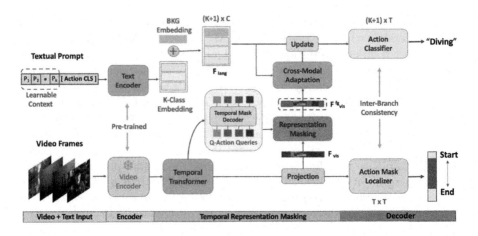

Fig. 2. Overview of the proposed *Zero-Shot Temporal Action Detection via Vision-Language Prompting* **(STALE) method.** Given an untrimmed video V, (a) we first extract a sequence of T snippet features with a pre-trained frozen video encoder and conduct self-attention learning using temporal embedding to obtain the snippet embedding E with a global context. (b) For each snippet embedding, we then predict a classification score P with the classification stream by masking the foreground feature and aligning with the text encoder embedding to obtain a classifier output P. The other branch of snippet embedding is used by action mask classifier to obtain a foreground mask M in parallel, (c) both of which are further used for consistency refinement at the feature level.

$D_{train} = D_{val}$. While in the open-set case, the action categories for training and evaluation are disjoint, *i.e.*, $D_{train} \cap D_{val} = \phi$.

Visual Language Embedding. Given a varying length untrimmed video V, following the standard practice [20,47] we first sample a very large T equidistantly distributed temporal snippets (points) over the entire length.

Visual Embedding: To extract features from the video snippets we use a frozen pre-trained video encoder (*e.g.*, a I3D [6], CLIP [36]) to extract RGB $X_r \in \mathbb{R}^{d \times T}$ and optical flow features $X_o \in \mathbb{R}^{d \times T}$ at the snippet level, where d denotes the feature dimension. We then concatenate them as $E = [X_r; X_o] \in \mathbb{R}^{2d \times T}$. Each snippet is a short sequence of (*e.g.*, 16 in our case) consecutive frames. While F contains local spatio-temporal information, it lacks a global context critical for TAD. We hence leverage the self-attention mechanism [41] to learn the global context. Formally, we set the input (`query`, `key`, `value`) of a multi-head Transformer encoder $\mathcal{T}()$ as the features (F,F,F) (Fig. 2)). Positional encoding is not applied as it is found to be detrimental (see the `supplementary material`). The final video snippet embedding is then obtained as

$$F_{vis} = \mathcal{T}(E) \in \mathbb{R}^{C \times T}, \tag{1}$$

with C being the embedding dimension.

Textual Encoding: For textual embedding, we use a standard CLIP pre-trained Transformer [36] with learnable prompt, similar to [54], and as opposed to hand-crafted prompt used in CLIP [36]. By making it learnable, textual contexts can now achieve better transferability in downstream classification tasks by directly optimizing the contexts using back-propagation. The input to the text encoder, formed as:

$$F_{lan} = [G_p; G_e^k] where G_p \in \mathbb{R}^{\hat{N} \times C'}, \tag{2}$$

are the learnable textual contexts, with $\hat{N}$ as the length of the contexts. The embedding $G_e^k \in \mathbb{R}^{C'}$ represents the textual embedding from CLIP vocabulary for each of the name of k-th class. The textual embedding for background class is not directly available from CLIP vocabulary, but necessary in TAD. To solve this issue, we learn a specific background embedding, denoted as $G_e^{bg} \in \mathbb{R}^{C'}$. We append this to the action class embedding G_e^k, making F_{lan} an embedding with $K + 1$ classes. The background embedding G_e^{bg} is initialized randomly.

Class Agnostic Representation Masking. We introduce a novel *class agnostic representation masking* concept for enabling the usage of a ViL model for ZS-TAD. This is conceptually inspired by mask-transformer [8] with focus on a totally different problem (image segmentation *without* the aid of ViL model). Specifically, given the snippet embedding F_{vis} per video and N_z mask queries particularly introduced in this work, we leverage a transformer decoder [5] to generate N_z latent embeddings. Then we pass each latent embedding through a masking projection layer to obtain a mask embedding for each segment as $B_q \in \mathbb{R}^{q \times C}$ where q indexes a query. A binary mask prediction $w.r.t$ each query can be then calculated as:

$$L_q = \sigma(B_q * F_{vis}) \in \mathbb{R}^{q \times T}, \tag{3}$$

where σ is sigmoid activation. As such, each snippet location is associated with q queries. To choose the optimal query per location, we deploy a tiny MLP to weigh these queries in a location specific manner. This is realized by learning a weight vector $W_q \in \mathbb{R}^{1 \times q}$ as:

$$\hat{L} = \sigma(W_q * L_q + b_q) \in \mathbb{R}^T. \tag{4}$$

We then binarize this mask at a threshold θ_{bin} and select the foreground mask, denoted by $\hat{L}_{bin}$. To obtain the foreground features F_{vis}^{fg}, we use $\hat{L}_{bin}$ to retrieve the snippet embedding F_{vis}. Given the binary nature of this foreground feature mask $\hat{L}_{bin}$, our representation masking can be first optimized on seen action classes and further generalize to unseen classes.

Vision-Language Cross-modal Adaption. Intuitively, integrating the descriptions of visual contexts is likely to enrich the text representation. For example, "a video of a man *playing kickball* in a big park" is richer than "a video of a man *playing kickball*". This motivates us to investigate how to use visual contexts to refine the text features. Specifically, we leverage the contextual-level visual feature to guide the text feature to adaptively explore informative regions of a video. For cross-attention, we adopt the standard architecture of the transformer [41]. Concretely, the cross attention module consists of a self-attention layer, a co-attention layer and a feed forward network formed as:

$$\hat{E}_c = \mathcal{T}_c(F_{lan}, F_{vis}^{fg}, F_{vis}^{fg}), \tag{5}$$

where $\mathcal{T}_c$ is a transformer layer, taking F_{lan} as the query, and F_{vis}^{fg} as the key and value. This module encourages the text features to find most related visual clues across the foreground snippets. We then update the text features through a residual connection:

$$\hat{F}_{lan} = F_{lan} + \alpha \hat{E}_c, \tag{6}$$

where $\alpha \in \mathbb{R}^C$ is a learnable parameter to control the scaling of the residual. α is initialized with very small values (*e.g.*, 10^{-3}) to maximally preserve the language priors of text features.

Parallel Classification and Mask Prediction. Our TAD head is featured with parallel classification and mask prediction as detailed below.

(I) Contextualized vision-language classifier: In the standard training process of CLIP [36], the global feature is normally used during contrastive alignment. In general, it estimates the snippet-text score pairs by taking the average pooling of snippet features and then uses it with the language features. However, this formulation is unsuitable for dense classification tasks like TAD where each temporal snippet needs to be assigned with a class label. Under this consideration, we instead use the updated textual features $\hat{F}_{lan} \in \mathbb{R}^{(K+1) \times C}$ and the masked foreground feature $F_{vis}^{fg} \in \mathbb{R}^{T \times C}$ as follows:

$$\mathcal{P} = \hat{F}_{lan} * (F_{vis}^{fg})^T, \tag{7}$$

where $\mathcal{P} \in \mathbb{R}^{(K+1) \times T}$ represents the classification output, where each snippet location $t \in T$ is assigned with a probability distribution $p_t \in \mathbb{R}^{(K+1) \times 1}$. Note, l_2 normalized along the channel dimension is applied prior to Eq. (7).

(II) Action mask localizer: In parallel to the classification stream, this stream predicts 1-D masks of action instances across the whole temporal span of the video. Since the 1-D masks are conditioned on the temporal location t, we exploit dynamic convolution [7]. This is because, in contrast to standard convolution, dynamic filters allow to leverage separate network branches to generate a filter at each snippet location. As a consequence, the dynamic filters can learn the context of the action (background) instances at each snippet location individually. More specifically, given the t-th snippet $F_{vis}(t)$, it outputs a 1-D mask vector $m_t = [q_1, ..., q_T] \in \mathbb{R}^{T \times 1}$ with each element $q_i \in [0, 1](i \in [1, T])$ indicating foreground probability of i-th snippet. This is implemented by a stack of three 1-D dynamic convolution layers H_m as follows:

$$\mathcal{M} = sigmoid(H_m(F_{vis})), \tag{8}$$

where t-th column of $\mathcal{M}$ is the temporal mask prediction by t-th snippet. More details on dynamic convolution formulation is given in supplementary material.

3.3 Model Training and Inference

Label Assignment. To train our one-stage STALE, the ground-truth needs to be arranged into the designed format. Concretely, given a training video with temporal intervals and class labels, we label all the snippets of a single action instance with the same action class. All the snippets off from action intervals are labeled as background. For an action snippet of a particular instance in the class stream, we assign the video-length binary instance mask at the same snippet location in the action mask stream. Each mask is action instance specific. All snippets of a specific action instance share the same mask. Refer to `supplementary material` for more details.

Learning Objective. The classification stream is composed of a simple cross-entropy loss. For a training snippet, we denote $y \in \mathbb{R}^{(K+1) \times T}$ the ground-truth class label, and $p \in \mathcal{P}$ the classification output. We compute the classification loss as:

$$L_c = CrossEntropy(p, y). \tag{9}$$

For the segmentation mask branch, we combine a weighted cross entropy and binary dice loss [25]. Formally, for a snippet location, we denote $\boldsymbol{m} \in \mathbb{R}^{T \times 1}$ the predicted segmentation mask, and $\boldsymbol{g} \in \mathbb{R}^{T \times 1}$ the ground-truth mask. The loss for the segmentation mask branch is formulated as:

$$L_m = \beta_{fg} \sum_{t=1}^{T} \boldsymbol{g}(t) \log(\boldsymbol{m}(t)) + \beta_{bg} \sum_{t=1}^{T} (1 - \boldsymbol{g}(t)) \log(1 - \boldsymbol{m}(t))$$
$$+ \lambda_2 \Big(1 - \frac{\boldsymbol{m}^\top \boldsymbol{g}}{\sum_{t=1}^{T} \left(\boldsymbol{m}(t)^2 + \boldsymbol{g}(t)^2 \right)} \Big), \tag{10}$$

where β_{fg}/β_{bg} is the inverse of foreground/background snippet's proportion. We set the loss trade-off coefficient $\lambda_2 = 0.4$.

We further impose a 1-D action completeness loss formed by binary cross entropy (BCE). It can penalize the foreground masking output $\hat{L} \in \mathbb{R}^{T \times 1}$. Given a ground truth one-hot foreground mask $\hat{g} \in \mathbb{R}^{T \times 1}$, we design the loss to model the completeness of foreground as follows:

$$L_{comp} = -\Big(\hat{g} * \log(\hat{L}) + \log(\hat{g}) * \hat{L} \Big). \tag{11}$$

Inter-Branch Consistency. In our STALE, there is structural consistency in terms of foreground between the class and mask labels by design. To leverage this consistency for improved optimization, we formulate the consistency loss as:

$$L_{const} = 1 - \text{cosine}\Big(\hat{F}_{clf}, \hat{F}_{mask} \Big), \tag{12}$$

where $\hat{F}_{clf} = topk(argmax((P_{bin} * E_p)[: K, :]))$ is the features obtained from the top scoring foreground snippets obtained from the thresholded classification output $P_{bin} := \eta(P - \theta_c)$ with θ_c the threshold and E_p obtained by passing the embedding E into a 1D conv layer for matching the dimension of P. The top scoring features from the mask output M are obtained similarly as: $\hat{F}_{mask} = topk(\sigma(1DPool(E_m * M_{bin})))$ where $M_{bin} := \eta(M - \theta_m)$ is a binarization of mask-prediction M, E_m is obtained by passing the embedding E into a 1D conv layer for matching the dimension of M, and σ is sigmoid activation.

Overall Objective. The overall objective loss function of our STALE is defined as: $L = L_c + L_m + L_{comp} + L_{const}$. This loss is used to train the model end-to-end, whilst leaving out the pre-trained video encoder frozen due to the GPU memory constraint.

Model Inference. At test time, we generate action instance predictions for each test video by the classification P and mask M predictions. For P, we only consider the snippets whose class probabilities are greater than θ_c and select top scoring snippets. For each such top scoring action snippet, we then obtain the temporal mask by thresholding the t_i-th column of M using the localization threshold Θ. To produce sufficient candidates, we use a set of thresholds $\Theta = \{\theta_i\}$. For each candidate, we compute a confidence score s by multiplying the classification and max-mask scores. SoftNMS [3] is finally applied to obtain top scoring results.

4   Experiments

Datasets. We conduct extensive experiments on two popular TAD benchmarks. (1) ActivityNet-v1.3 [4] has 19,994 videos from 200 action classes. We follow the standard setting to split all videos into training, validation and testing subsets in ratio of 2:1:1. (2) THUMOS14 [15] has 200 validation videos and 213 testing videos from 20 categories with labeled temporal boundary and action class

Implementation Details. For fair comparison with existing TAD works we use Kinetics pre-trained I3D [6] as the video encoder for both ActivityNet and THUMOS. We also use the two-stream features as used in [17] for fair-comparison. For comparing with CLIP based TAD baselines, we also adopt the image and text encoders from pre-trained CLIP (ViT-B/16+Transformer). For model-adaptation, the visual encoder is kept frozen, the trainable parts are textual prompt embeddings, text encoder, temporal embedding module, temporal masking modules and TAD decoder heads. For the CLIP encoders, the video frames are pre-processed to 224×224 spatial resolution, and the maximum number of textual tokens is 77 (following the original CLIP design). Each video's feature sequence F is rescaled to T = 100/256 snippets for AcitivtyNet/THUMOS using linear interpolation. Our model is trained for 15 epochs using Adam with learning rate of $10^{-4}/10^{-5}$ for ActivityNet/THUMOS respectively.

4.1   Comparative Results

Zero-Shot Action Detection Setting. In this section, we evaluate on the open-set scenario where $D_{train} \cap D_{val} = \phi$, *i.e.*, action categories for training

Table 1. Results of zero-shot action detection

Train split	Methods	THUMOS14						ActivityNet v1.3			
		0.3	0.4	0.5	0.6	0.7	Avg	0.5	0.75	0.95	Avg
75% Seen 25% Unseen	B-II	28.5	20.3	17.1	10.5	6.9	16.6	32.6	18.5	5.8	19.6
	B-I	33.0	25.5	18.3	11.6	5.7	18.8	35.6	20.4	2.1	20.2
	EffPrompt	39.7	31.6	23.0	14.9	7.5	23.3	37.6	22.9	3.8	23.1
	STALE	**40.5**	**32.3**	**23.5**	**15.3**	**7.6**	**23.8**	**38.2**	**25.2**	**6.0**	**24.9**
50% Seen 50% Unseen	B-II	21.0	16.4	11.2	6.3	3.2	11.6	25.3	13.0	3.7	12.9
	B-I	27.2	21.3	15.3	9.7	4.8	15.7	28.0	16.4	1.2	16.0
	EffPrompt	37.2	29.6	**21.6**	**14.0**	**7.2**	21.9	32.0	19.3	2.9	19.6
	STALE	**38.3**	**30.7**	21.2	13.8	7.0	**22.2**	**32.1**	**20.7**	**5.9**	**20.5**

and testing are disjoint. We follow the setting and dataset splits proposed by [17]. More specifically, we initiate two evaluation settings on THUMOS14 and ActivityNet1.3: (1) Training with 75% action categories and testing on the left 25% action categories; (2) Training with 50% categories and testing on the left 50% categories. To ensure statistical significance, we conduct 10 random samplings to split categories for each setting, following [17].

Competitors. As there is no open-source implementation for [17], we use their same reported baselines. More specifically, (1) One baseline using BMN [20] as proposal generator and CLIP [36] with hand crafted prompt. This is the same baseline as reported in [17]. This serves as a 2-stage TAD baseline using CLIP. We term it B-I. (2) One comparative CLIP based TAD EffPrompt [17]. (3) One CLIP + TAD model for one-stage baseline: As ZS-TAD is a relatively new problem, we need to implement the competitors by extending existing TAD methods using CLIP by ourselves. We select a variant of CLIP for dense prediction task [37] using the existing CLIP pre-trained weights. We term this baseline, DenseCLIP (w/ CLIP Pretrained Image Encoder) + TAD, as B-II. The text-encoders however are identical for both the baselines using CLIP pre-training weights. However, we could not compare with the earlier zero-shot TAD method ZS-TAD [49] due to unavailability of code and no common data-split between [49] and [17].

Performance. The ZS-TAD results are reported in Table 1. With 50% labeled data, our STALE surpasses both 1-stage and 2-stage baselines, as well as the CLIP based TAD method [17] by a good margin on ActivityNet. This suggests that our representation masking is able to perform the zero-shot transfer better than conventional 2-stage designs. This also indicates that the localization-error propagation hurts in low training data regime. Also noted that the one-stage baseline (B-II) performs worst among all other baselines. This suggests that a class-agnostic masking is necessary to achieve strong performance in ZS-TAD. The performance of our model however drops on THUMOS14 on stricter metrics, possibly due to the mask decoder suffering from foreground imbalance. We observe similar trend with 75% labeled data, our approach is again superior than all other competitors on both datasets. It is also interesting to note that

Table 2. Comparison with state-of-the-art on closed-set setting

Methods	Mode	Encoder backbone	THUMOS14						ActivityNet v1.3			
			0.3	0.4	0.5	0.6	0.7	Avg	0.5	0.75	0.95	Avg
TALNet	RGB+Flow	I3D	53.2	48.5	42.8	33.8	20.8	39.8	38.2	18.3	1.3	20.2
GTAN	RGB+Flow	P3D	57.8	47.2	38.8	–	–	–	52.6	34.1	8.9	34.3
MUSES	RGB+Flow	I3D	68.9	64.0	56.9	46.3	31.0	53.4	50.0	34.9	6.5	34.0
VSGN	RGB+Flow	I3D	66.7	60.4	52.4	41.0	30.4	50.1	52.3	36.0	8.3	35.0
Context-Loc	RGB+Flow	I3D	68.3	63.8	54.3	41.8	26.2	-	56.0	35.2	3.5	34.2
BU-TAL	RGB+Flow	I3D	53.9	50.7	45.4	38.0	28.5	43.3	43.5	33.9	9.2	30.1
B-III	RGB+Flow	I3D	68.3	62.3	51.9	38.8	23.7	-	47.2	30.7	8.6	30.8
STALE	RGB+Flow	I3D	**68.9**	**64.1**	**57.1**	**46.7**	**31.2**	**52.9**	**56.5**	**36.7**	**9.5**	**36.4**
TALNet	RGB	I3D	42.6	–	31.9	–	14.2	–	–	–	–	–
A2Net	RGB	I3D	45.0	40.5	31.3	19.9	10.0	29.3	39.6	25.7	2.8	24.8
B-I	RGB	CLIP	36.3	31.9	25.4	17.8	10.4	24.3	28.2	18.3	3.7	18.2
B-II	RGB	CLIP	57.1	49.1	40.4	31.2	23.1	40.2	51.5	33.3	6.6	32.7
EffPrompt	RGB	CLIP	50.8	44.1	35.8	25.7	15.7	34.5	44.0	27.0	5.1	27.3
STALE	RGB	CLIP	**60.6**	**53.2**	**44.6**	**36.8**	**26.7**	**44.4**	**54.3**	**34.0**	**7.7**	**34.3**

the one-stage baseline (B-II) has a larger performance gap with the two-stage baseline (B-I), around 3.1% avg mAP on ActivityNet. This however reduces to 0.6% when the number of labeled data increase, suggesting that the one-stage baseline has potential to improve with more data.

Closed-Set Action Detection Setting. Closed-set action detection refers to the common setting, where the model is trained and evaluated on videos of the same action categories, *i.e.*, $D_{train} = D_{val}$. For a fair comparison, we use the same dataset splits as in the literature.

Competitors. We considered the following methods for comparison. (1) Seven representative TAD methods with I3D encoder backbone; (2) One CLIP+TAD method EffPrompt [17]; (3) One two-stage CLIP based TAD baseline B-I; (4) One single-stage CLIP based TAD baseline B-II; (5) We also created another single-stage baseline by replacing CLIP-Pretrained encoder with Kinetics pretrained Video-Encoder (*e.g.*, I3D). We term it B-III.

Performance. From the results of Table 2, we observe that with more labeled data, our approach also surpasses existing TAD approaches often by a large margin. This is consistent over both the datasets. Thus the text-embedding is indeed helpful for our design. We also observe that our method performs better by almost similar margin when we use different feature backbone (*e.g.*, CLIP). Thus it proves our design is feature agnostic. Another key observation is that our single-stage baseline (B-II) performs significantly better than [17] by at least 5% in avg mAP for both the datasets. Thus justifies that our parallel design is better alternative for CLIP based approaches.

Table 3. Analysis of localization error propagation on ActivityNet with 75% split. GT: Ground-Truth.

Metric	mAP	
	0.5	Avg
Baseline-I(B-I)		
GT proposals	56.2	47.1
Predicted proposals	34.8	19.9
STALE		
GT masks	53.6	42.3
Predicted masks	38.2	24.9

Table 4. Analysis of representation-masking on 75% seen split on ActivityNet

Masking method	# Queries	mAP	
		0.5	Avg
No Mask	–	21.7	10.9
GT-Mask	–	54.3	35.8
1-D CNN	–	33.5	20.1
Maskformer [8]	5	37.5	24.4
	20	**38.2**	**24.9**
	100	39.0	25.1

4.2 Ablation

Localization Error Propagation Analysis. To examine the effect of localization error propagation with previous TAD models, we design a proof-of-concept experiment by measuring the performance drop between ground-truth proposals and pseudo proposals. Due to unavaiability of training code in [17], we carefully re-created B-I following the details in [17]. For our STALE model, we contrast ground-truth and output masks. This experiment is tested on ActivityNet with 75% label split. Table 3 shows that the proposal based TAD baseline suffers almost double performance degradation from localization (i.e., proposal) error due to its sequential localization and classification design. This verifies the advantage of STALE's parallel design.

Necessity of Representation Masking. To validate the role of *representation masking* in generalization of the classifier, we perform experiments in the 75% split setting. Firstly, we compare our approach by removing the Maskformer-Decoder [8] from the pipeline of STALE and passing the temporal feature F_{vis} directly into the cross-modal adaptation module for classification. As shown in Table 4, we observe a sharp drop of 14% in avg mAP, justifying that foreground features are indeed necessary to align the text embedding. This problem is also profound in DenseCLIP baseline (B-II) as illustrated in Table 1. We also tested another alternative to masking, e.g., vanilla 1-D CNN. It is evident that Maskformer-Decoder benefits from learning the query embedding over vanilla 1-D CNN. We also observe that increasing the number of queries improves the overall localization performance but comes with high memory footprint. Further, due to memory constraints of query-matching step of the decoder output during classification, we learn a MLP to reduce the cost. We verify that class-agnostic representation-masking has much stronger generalization in localizing unseen action categories. Interestingly, we observe that the maximum STALE can achieve avg mAP of 35.8% indicating a room for further improvement.

Importance of Text Encoder. We ablate the effect of text encoder fine-tuning. Note the video encoder is frozen due to memory constraint. We use CLIP

[36] pre-trained text transformer (denoted as CLIP-text) in this experiment. It can be observed from Table 5 that using a text-encoder is indeed important for the overall performance. Further, fine-tuning the text encoder is also effective due to the large domain gap between CLIP pre-training and TAD task.

Effect of Temporal Modeling. Recall that we use a multi-head Transformer (w/o positional encoding) for temporal modeling in STALE. We evaluate this design choice by comparing (I) a 1D CNN with 3 dilation rates (1, 3, 5) each with 2 layers, and (II) a multi-scale Temporal Convolutional Network MS-TCN [10]. Each CNN design substitutes the default Transformer while remaining all the others. Table 6 shows that the Transformer is clearly superior to both CNN alternatives. This suggests that our default design captures stronger contextual learning capability even in low-data setting like ZS-TAD.

Table 5. Importance of *text encoder* using CLIP vocabulary on 75% train split.

Text encoder	Fine-tune	mAP	
		0.5	Avg
No encoder	–	6.9	11.5
CLIP-text	✗	36.9	22.8
CLIP-text	✓	38.2	24.9

Table 6. Transformer vs. CNN on ActivityNet under 75% seen label setting.

Network	mAP	
	0.5	Avg
1D CNN	29.0	19.3
MS-TCN	33.5	21.4
Transformer	**38.2**	**24.9**

5   Limitation

Our proposed STALE is based upon a visual-language model pre-trained using large web image-text pair data. This could potentially incur few limitations. First, there may exist some unconstrained bias rooted with the training data. Second, there might be substantial domain gap against the target video data in fine-tuning (*e.g.*, no temporal knowledge) [31]. However, this could be naturally solved when video based visual-language models become available.

6   Conclusion

In this work, we have proposed a novel *Zero-Shot Temporal Action Detection via Vision-Language Prompting* (STALE) model for the under-studied yet practically useful zero-shot temporal action detection (ZS-TAD). It is characterized by a *parallel* localization (mask generation) and classification architecture designed to solve the localization error propagation problem with conventional ZS-TAD models. For improved optimization, we further introduced an inter-branch consistency regularization to exploit their structural relationships. Extensive experiments on ActivityNet and THUMOS have demonstrated that our STALE yields state-of-the-art performance under both zero-shot and supervised settings.

References

1. Alwassel, H., Caba Heilbron, F., Escorcia, V., Ghanem, B.: Diagnosing error in temporal action detectors. In: Ferrari, V., Hebert, M., Sminchisescu, C., Weiss, Y. (eds.) ECCV 2018. LNCS, vol. 11207, pp. 264–280. Springer, Cham (2018). https://doi.org/10.1007/978-3-030-01219-9_16
2. Antol, S., et al.: Vqa: visual question answering. In: Proceedings of the IEEE International Conference on Computer Vision, pp. 2425–2433 (2015)
3. Bodla, N., Singh, B., Chellappa, R., Davis, L.S.: Soft-nms-improving object detection with one line of code. In: Proceedings of the IEEE International Conference on Computer Vision, pp. 5561–5569 (2017)
4. Caba Heilbron, F., Escorcia, V., Ghanem, B., Carlos Niebles, J.: Activitynet: a large-scale video benchmark for human activity understanding. In: CVPR, pp. 961–970 (2015)
5. Carion, N., Massa, F., Synnaeve, G., Usunier, N., Kirillov, A., Zagoruyko, S.: End-to-end object detection with transformers. In: Vedaldi, A., Bischof, H., Brox, T., Frahm, J.-M. (eds.) ECCV 2020. LNCS, vol. 12346, pp. 213–229. Springer, Cham (2020). https://doi.org/10.1007/978-3-030-58452-8_13
6. Carreira, J., Zisserman, A.: Quo vadis, action recognition? a new model and the kinetics dataset. In: proceedings of the IEEE Conference on Computer Vision and Pattern Recognition, pp. 6299–6308 (2017)
7. Chen, Y., Dai, X., Liu, M., Chen, D., Yuan, L., Liu, Z.: Dynamic convolution: attention over convolution kernels. In: Proceedings of the IEEE/CVF Conference on Computer Vision and Pattern Recognition, pp. 11030–11039 (2020)
8. Cheng, B., Schwing, A., Kirillov, A.: Per-pixel classification is not all you need for semantic segmentation. In: Advances in Neural Information Processing Systems, vol. 34 (2021)
9. Dosovitskiy, A., et al.: An image is worth 16x16 words: transformers for image recognition at scale. In: ICLR (2020)
10. Farha, Y.A., Gall, J.: Ms-tcn: multi-stage temporal convolutional network for action segmentation. In: CVPR, pp. 3575–3584 (2019)
11. Gao, J., Yang, Z., Chen, K., Sun, C., Nevatia, R.: Turn tap: temporal unit regression network for temporal action proposals. In: ICCV (2017)
12. Gao, P., et al.: Clip-adapter: better vision-language models with feature adapters. arXiv preprint. arXiv:2110.04544 (2021)
13. Goldberg, Y., Levy, O.: word2vec explained: deriving mikolov et al'.s negative-sampling word-embedding method. arXiv preprint. arXiv:1402.3722 (2014)
14. He, K., Zhang, X., Ren, S., Sun, J.: Deep residual learning for image recognition. In: Proceedings of the IEEE Conference on Computer Vision and Pattern Recognition, pp. 770–778 (2016)
15. Idrees, H.: The thumos challenge on action recognition for videos "in the wild". Comput. Vis. Image Underst. **155**, 1–23 (2017)
16. Jia, C., et al.: Scaling up visual and vision-language representation learning with noisy text supervision. In: International Conference on Machine Learning, pp. 4904–4916. PMLR (2021)
17. Ju, C., Han, T., Zheng, K., Zhang, Y., Xie, W.: A simple baseline on prompt learning for efficient video understanding (2022)
18. Lampert, C.H., Nickisch, H., Harmeling, S.: Attribute-based classification for zero-shot visual object categorization. IEEE Trans. Pattern Anal. Mach. Intell. **36**(3), 453–465 (2013)

19. Lei, J., et al.: Less is more: clipbert for video-and-language learning via sparse sampling. In: Proceedings of the IEEE/CVF Conference on Computer Vision and Pattern Recognition, pp. 7331–7341 (2021)
20. Lin, T., Liu, X., Li, X., Ding, E., Wen, S.: Bmn: boundary-matching network for temporal action proposal generation. In: Proceedings of the IEEE/CVF International Conference on Computer Vision, pp. 3889–3898 (2019)
21. Lin, T., Zhao, X., Su, H., Wang, C., Yang, M.: BSN: boundary sensitive network for temporal action proposal generation. In: Ferrari, V., Hebert, M., Sminchisescu, C., Weiss, Y. (eds.) ECCV 2018. LNCS, vol. 11208, pp. 3–21. Springer, Cham (2018). https://doi.org/10.1007/978-3-030-01225-0_1
22. Long, F., Yao, T., Qiu, Z., Tian, X., Luo, J., Mei, T.: Gaussian temporal awareness networks for action localization. In: CVPR (2019)
23. Lu, J., Batra, D., Parikh, D., Lee, S.: Vilbert: pretraining task-agnostic visiolinguistic representations for vision-and-language tasks. In: Advances in Neural Information Processing Systems, vol. 32 (2019)
24. Miech, A., Alayrac, J.B., Smaira, L., Laptev, I., Sivic, J., Zisserman, A.: End-to-end learning of visual representations from uncurated instructional videos. In: Proceedings of the IEEE/CVF Conference on Computer Vision and Pattern Recognition, pp. 9879–9889 (2020)
25. Milletari, F., Navab, N., Ahmadi, S.A.: V-net: fully convolutional neural networks for volumetric medical image segmentation. In: 2016 4th International Conference on 3D Vision (3DV), pp. 565–571. IEEE (2016)
26. Nag, S., Zhu, X., Song, Y.Z., Xiang, T.: Temporal action localization with global segmentation mask transformers (2021)
27. Nag, S., Zhu, X., Song, Y.z., Xiang, T.: Proposal-free temporal action detection via global segmentation mask learning. In: ECCV (2022)
28. Nag, S., Zhu, X., Song, Y.z., Xiang, T.: Semi-supervised temporal action detection with proposal-free masking. In: ECCV (2022)
29. Nag, S., Zhu, X., Xiang, T.: Few-shot temporal action localization with query adaptive transformer. arXiv preprint. arXiv:2110.10552 (2021)
30. Niu, L., Cai, J., Veeraraghavan, A., Zhang, L.: Zero-shot learning via category-specific visual-semantic mapping and label refinement. IEEE Trans. Image Process. **28**(2), 965–979 (2018)
31. Pan, J., Lin, Z., Zhu, X., Shao, J., Li, H.: Parameter-efficient image-to-video transfer learning. arXiv preprint. arXiv:2206.13559 (2022)
32. Parikh, D., Grauman, K.: Relative attributes. In: 2011 International Conference on Computer Vision, pp. 503–510. IEEE (2011)
33. Paul, S., Mithun, N.C., Roy-Chowdhury, A.K.: Text-based localization of moments in a video corpus. IEEE Trans. Image Process. **30**, 8886–8899 (2021)
34. Pennington, J., Socher, R., Manning, C.D.: Glove: global vectors for word representation. In: Proceedings of the 2014 Conference on Empirical Methods in Natural Language Processing (EMNLP), pp. 1532–1543 (2014)
35. Qin, J., et al.: Zero-shot action recognition with error-correcting output codes. In: Proceedings of the IEEE Conference on Computer Vision and Pattern Recognition, pp. 2833–2842 (2017)
36. Radford, A., et al.: Learning transferable visual models from natural language supervision. In: International Conference on Machine Learning, pp. 8748–8763. PMLR (2021)
37. Rao, Y., et al.: Denseclip: language-guided dense prediction with context-aware prompting. arXiv preprint. arXiv:2112.01518 (2021)

38. Ren, S., He, K., Girshick, R., Sun, J.: Faster r-cnn: towards real-time object detection with region proposal networks. In: TPAMI, vol. 39, no. 6, pp. 1137–1149 (2016)
39. Sridhar, D., Quader, N., Muralidharan, S., Li, Y., Dai, P., Lu, J.: Class semantics-based attention for action detection. In: Proceedings of the IEEE/CVF International Conference on Computer Vision, pp. 13739–13748 (2021)
40. Su, H., Gan, W., Wu, W., Qiao, Y., Yan, J.: Bsn++: complementary boundary regressor with scale-balanced relation modeling for temporal action proposal generation. arXiv preprint. arXiv:2009.07641 (2020)
41. Vaswani, A., et al.: Attention is all you need. arXiv preprint. arXiv:1706.03762 (2017)
42. Wang, M., Xing, J., Liu, Y.: Actionclip: a new paradigm for video action recognition. arXiv preprint. arXiv:2109.08472 (2021)
43. Wang, Z., et al.: Camp: cross-modal adaptive message passing for text-image retrieval. In: Proceedings of the IEEE/CVF International Conference on Computer Vision, pp. 5764–5773 (2019)
44. Xian, Y., Lampert, C.H., Schiele, B., Akata, Z.: Zero-shot learning-a comprehensive evaluation of the good, the bad and the ugly. IEEE Trans. Pattern Anal. Mach. Intell. **41**(9), 2251–2265 (2018)
45. Xu, H., Das, A., Saenko, K.: R-c3d: region convolutional 3d network for temporal activity detection. In: ICCV (2017)
46. Xu, K., et al.: Show, attend and tell: neural image caption generation with visual attention. In: International Conference on Machine Learning, pp. 2048–2057. PMLR (2015)
47. Xu, M., Zhao, C., Rojas, D.S., Thabet, A., Ghanem, B.: G-tad: sub-graph localization for temporal action detection. In: CVPR (2020)
48. Xu, X., Hospedales, T., Gong, S.: Semantic embedding space for zero-shot action recognition. In: 2015 IEEE International Conference on Image Processing (ICIP), pp. 63–67. IEEE (2015)
49. Zhang, L., et al.: Zstad: zero-shot temporal activity detection. In: Proceedings of the IEEE/CVF Conference on Computer Vision and Pattern Recognition, pp. 879–888 (2020)
50. Zhang, R., et al.: Tip-adapter: training-free clip-adapter for better vision-language modeling. arXiv preprint. arXiv:2111.03930 (2021)
51. Zhao, C., Thabet, A.K., Ghanem, B.: Video self-stitching graph network for temporal action localization. In: Proceedings of the IEEE/CVF International Conference on Computer Vision, pp. 13658–13667 (2021)
52. Zhao, Y., Xiong, Y., Wang, L., Wu, Z., Tang, X., Lin, D.: Temporal action detection with structured segment networks. In: ICCV (2017)
53. Zhong, Y., et al.: Regionclip: Region-based language-image pretraining. arXiv preprint. arXiv:2112.09106 (2021)
54. Zhou, K., Yang, J., Loy, C.C., Liu, Z.: Learning to prompt for vision-language models. arXiv preprint. arXiv:2109.01134 (2021)

CycDA: Unsupervised Cycle Domain Adaptation to Learn from Image to Video

Wei Lin[1,5(✉)], Anna Kukleva[2], Kunyang Sun[1,3], Horst Possegger[1],
Hilde Kuehne[4], and Horst Bischof[1]

[1] Institute of Computer Graphics and Vision,
Graz University of Technology, Graz, Austria
{wei.lin,possegger,bischof}@icg.tugraz.at
[2] Max-Planck-Institute for Informatics, Saarbrücken, Germany
akukleva@mpi-inf.mpg.de
[3] Southeast University, Nanjing, China
sunky@seu.edu.cn
[4] Goethe University Frankfurt, Frankfurt, Germany
kuehne@uni-frankfurt.de
[5] Christian Doppler Laboratory for Semantic 3D Computer Vision,
Frankfurt, Germany

Abstract. Although action recognition has achieved impressive results over recent years, both collection and annotation of video training data are still time-consuming and cost intensive. Therefore, image-to-video adaptation has been proposed to exploit labeling-free web image source for adapting on unlabeled target videos. This poses two major challenges: (1) spatial domain shift between web images and video frames; (2) modality gap between image and video data. To address these challenges, we propose Cycle Domain Adaptation (CycDA), a cycle-based approach for unsupervised image-to-video domain adaptation. We leverage the joint spatial information in images and videos on the one hand and, on the other hand, train an independent spatio-temporal model to bridge the modality gap. We alternate between the spatial and spatio-temporal learning with knowledge transfer between the two in each cycle. We evaluate our approach on benchmark datasets for image-to-video as well as for mixed-source domain adaptation achieving state-of-the-art results and demonstrating the benefits of our cyclic adaptation.

Keywords: Image-to-video adaptation · Unsupervised domain adaptation · Action recognition

1 Introduction

The task of action recognition has seen tremendous success in recent years with top-performing approaches typically requiring large-scale labeled video datasets

Supplementary Information The online version contains supplementary material available at https://doi.org/10.1007/978-3-031-20062-5_40.

[10, 39, 40], which can be impractical in terms of both data collection and annotation effort. In the meanwhile, webly-supervised learning has been explored to leverage the large amount of easily accessible web data as a labeling-free data source for video recognition [12, 16, 24, 38, 41, 47].

In this work, we address the problem of image-to-video adaptation with webly-labeled images as the source domain and unlabeled videos as the target domain to allow for action classification without video annotation. This setting provides two major challenges: (1) the spatial domain shift between web images and video frames, based on difference in image styles, camera perspectives and semantic drifts; (2) the modality gap between spatial images and spatio-temporal videos. Specifically, this modality gap restrains that merely spatial knowledge can be transferred from source to target domain. Previous works on action recognition with web supervision either learn from web data directly [11, 13] or perform joint training by combining the web source with annotated target data [9, 29]. To specifically address the domain shift between web images and target videos, some approaches perform class-agnostic domain-invariant feature learning either within [19] or across modalities [27, 43, 44], in the absence of ensuring domain-invariance on the category-level.

In this context, we propose Cycle Domain Adaptation (CycDA), *i.e.* alternating knowledge transfer between a spatial model and a spatio-temporal model. Compared to other works, we address the two challenges at hand, domain-alignment and closing the modality gap in separate stages, cycling between both of them. An overview of the CycDA is given in Fig. 1. With the category knowledge from the spatio-temporal model, we achieve enhanced category-level domain invariance on the spatial model. With updated knowledge transferred from the spatial model, we attain better spatio-temporal learning. In this manner, we can better tackle each challenge for the corresponding model, with the updated knowledge transferred from the other.

More specifically, we propose a four stage framework to address the domain shift between images and videos on different levels. In stage 1, we enforce *class-agnostic* domain alignment on the spatial model between images and video frames. In stage 2, we use supervision from the spatial model to learn a spatio-temporal video model, bridging the gap between the two modalities. Stage 3 then focuses on *class-aware* domain alignment on the spatial model, given pseudo labels computed by the video model trained on stage 2. In stage 4, we update the video model with the improved pseudo labels from the spatial model of stage 3.

We first evaluate our approach on several challenging settings for web image based action recognition, where a single cycle already outperforms baselines and state-of-the-arts. Second, we show how CycDA can be flexibly applied for mixed-source image&video-to-video DA settings, leading to a performance competitive to the state-of-the-art requiring only 5% of the provided source videos.

We summarize our contributions as follows: (1) We propose to address web image-to-video domain adaptation by decoupling the domain-alignment and spatio-temporal learning to bridge the modality gap. (2) We propose cyclic alternation between spatial and spatio-temporal learning to improve spatial

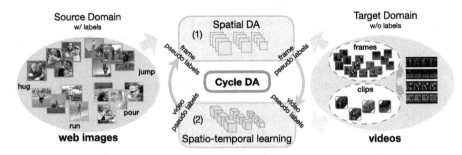

Fig. 1. Cycle Domain Adaptation (CycDA) pipeline: we address image-to-video adaption by training a spatial model and a spatio-temporal model alternately, passing pseudo labels to supervise each other in a cycle. The two alternating steps are: (1) domain alignment on the spatial model with pseudo labels from the spatio-temporal model, and (2) training the spatio-temporal model with updated pseudo labels from the spatial model.

and spatio-temporal models respectively. (3) We provide an extensive evaluation with different benchmark tasks that shows state-of-the-art results on unsupervised image-to-video domain adaptation and a competitive performance for the mixed-source image&video-to-video setting.

2   Related Work

Webly-Supervised Action Recognition. Various works have shown how web images and videos can be used as labeling-free data source to improve the performance of action recognition [9,11,13,29]. Gan *et al.* [11,13] train with web data only, without adaptation to the target domain. Ma *et al.* [29] combine web images and video frames to train a spatial model and achieve comparable performance by replacing parts of annotated videos with web images. Duan *et al.* [9] transform different types of web modalities to trimmed video clips and combine them with labeled target videos for joint training. In our work, we specifically address the domain shift on the spatial level and transfer the knowledge to the spatio-temporal level, without using any annotations on target data.

Image-to-Video DA. Compared to webly-supervised learning, image-to-video DA approaches actively address the domain shift between web images and target videos either by spatial alignment between web images and video frames [24,36, 45], or through class-agnostic domain-invariant feature learning for images and videos [27,43,44]. Li *et al.* [24] use a spatial attention map for cross-domain knowledge transfer from web images to videos. In this case, the DA is addressed on the spatial level without transfer to the temporal level. Liu *et al.* [27] perform domain-invariant representation learning for images, video keyframes and videos, and fuse features of different modalities. Furthermore, hierarchical GAN [44], symmetric GAN [43] and spatio-temporal causal graph [2] are proposed to learn

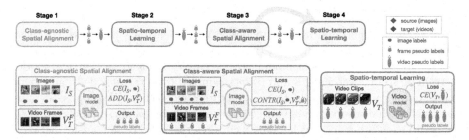

Fig. 2. Our CycDA framework alternates between spatial alignment (stage 1 and 3) and spatio-temporal learning (stage 2 and 4). See text for details.

the mapping between image features and video features. Closest to our work is probably the work of Kae *et al.* [19] which also employs a spatial and a spatio-temporal model for two stages of class-agnostic domain alignment, proposing to copy the weights from the spatial to the spatio-temporal model.

In contrast to these, we propose to transfer knowledge in the form of pseudo labels, without enforcing spatial information from the DA stage onto the spatio-temporal model. Moreover, we alternately conduct spatial alignment and spatio-temporal learning with knowledge transfer to each other. With category knowledge transferred to the spatial model, we perform class-aware domain alignment that induces domain-invariance within category-level.

Video-to-Video DA. Compared to image-to-video adaption, video-to-video adaptation methods adapt annotated source videos to unlabeled target videos [3,6,7,18,22,28,31–33], focusing mainly on the problem of domain alignment. Chen *et al.* [3] align the features spatially on the frame-level and temporally on the scale-level. Others propose feature alignment via self-attention [7], cross-domain co-attention [32], or across two-stream modalities of RGB and optical flow [22,31]. Sahoo *et al.* [33] propose temporal contrastive learning and background mixing for domain-invariance. In this work, we focus on image-to-video adaptation and use only single stream of RGB. We further show that we are able to extend the pipeline to the mixed-source case, where we achieve competitive performance compared to video-to-video adaptation methods while requiring only a small amount of source videos.

3   Cycle Domain Adaptation (CycDA)

We propose four stages to tackle image-to-video adaptation, which we summarize in Sect. 3.1. Afterwards, we detail each stage and motivate the cycling of stages in Sect. 3.2. Our CycDA can be flexibly extended (Sect. 3.3) for mixed-source video adaptation, where a limited amount of annotated source videos are available.

3.1 System Overview

The task of unsupervised image-to-video DA is to learn a video classifier given labeled source images and unlabeled target videos. In order to close the domain gap across these two different modalities, we employ (1) a spatial (image) model to train on source web images and frames sampled from target videos, and (2) a spatio-temporal (video) model to train on target video clips. We propose a training pipeline that alternately adapts the two models by passing pseudo labels to supervise each other in a cycle. This facilitates the knowledge transfer between both models, where pseudo labels efficiently guide the model through the corresponding task, *i.e.* semantic alignment (image model) or spatio-temporal learning (video model).

As shown in Fig. 2, our CycDA pipeline consists of four training stages. The initial pseudo labels from *class-agnostic* domain alignment (Stage 1) are improved via video spatio-temporal learning (Stage 2). In Stage 3, these pseudo labels on target data, together with ground truth labels on source, enable semantic alignment through the class-aware domain alignment. This again refines the pseudo labels, which further provide enhanced supervision for spatio-temporal learning in stage 4. In this manner, one iteration of CycDA facilitates the alternating knowledge transfer between the image and video models, whereby pseudo labels are improved on each stage and further provide strengthened supervision for better learning on the next stage.

Notations: First, we denote the feature extractor as $E(\cdot; \theta_E)$, the classifier as $C(\cdot; \theta_C)$, and the domain discriminator as $D(\cdot; \theta_D)$. Then, we have the image model $\phi^I = \{E^I(\cdot; \theta_E^I), C^I(\cdot; \theta_C^I), D^I(\cdot; \theta_D^I)\}$ and the video model $\phi^V = \{E^V(\cdot; \theta_E^V), C^V(\cdot; \theta_C^V)\}$. We use the superscripts I, V and F to denote modalities of image, video and video frame, correspondingly. S and T stand for *source* and *target* domains respectively. The labeled source image domain is denoted as $I_S = \{(i_j, l(i_j))|_{j=1}^{N_S^I}\}$, where $l(\cdot)$ is the ground truth label of the corresponding image. The unlabeled target video domain is $V_T = \{v_j|_{j=1}^{N_T^V}\}$ and each video v_j has M_j frames, the set of frames of unlabeled target videos $V_T^F = \{\{v_{j,m}^F|_{m=1}^{M_j}\}|_{j=1}^{N_T^V}\}$.

3.2 Stages

Stage 1 - Class-Agnostic Spatial Alignment. In the first stage, we learn the class-agnostic domain alignment between source web images and frames sampled from unlabeled target videos. Thus, we reduce the domain gap between the appearance of the web images and target videos even if the classes could be incorrectly aligned during this stage. We train the image model ϕ^I with a supervised cross entropy loss $\mathcal{L}_{CE}(I_S)$ and an adversarial domain discrimination loss $\mathcal{L}_{ADD}(I_S, V_T^F)$ on source images and target frames. With the classification loss on source images given as

$$\mathcal{L}_{CE}(I_S) = \sum_{(i_j, l(i_j)) \in I_S} -l(i_j) \cdot \log(C^I(E(i_j; \theta_E^I); \theta_C^I)) \tag{1}$$

and the binary cross entropy loss for domain discrimination given as

$$\mathcal{L}_{ADD}(I_S, V_T^F) = \sum_{i_j, v_{j',m}^F} \log D^I(E^I(i_j; \theta_E^I); \theta_D^I) + \log(1 - D^I(E^I(v_{j',m}^F; \theta_E^I); \theta_D^I)),$$

(2)

the overall objective is $\min_{\theta_E^I, \theta_C^I} \mathcal{L}_{CE}(I_S) + \beta \max_{\theta_E^I} \min_{\theta_D^I} \mathcal{L}_{ADD}(I_S, V_T^F)$, where β is the trade-off weight between the two losses. We train the domain discriminator D^I to distinguish between extracted features from different domains, while the feature extractor is trained adversely based on the domain discrimination task. In this case, the feature extractor learns to yield domain invariant features that the domain discriminator is unable to differentiate. The adversarial training is performed with a gradient reversal layer (GRL) [14,15] which reverses the sign of gradients of the domain discrimination loss on the feature extractor during back-propagation. The domain alignment on this stage is class-agnostic as there is not yet any pseudo label for category knowledge in the target domain. The alignment is performed globally at the domain level.

Stage 2 & Stage 4 - Spatio-Temporal Learning. In this stage, we use the trained image model ϕ^I from the previous stage to generate pseudo labels for the target videos. Then we perform supervised spatio-temporal learning with the pseudo labeled target data.

Specifically, we first use ϕ^I to predict the pseudo label $\hat{l}(\cdot)$ for each frame of the target videos. We employ a spatio-temporal model that trains on target videos capturing both spatial and temporal information in the target domain only. To select new pseudo label candidates, we temporally aggregate frame-level predictions into a video-level prediction. We discard predictions with confidence lower than a threshold δ_p and perform a majority voting among the remaining predictions to define the video label. From all videos, we only keep those that have at least one frame with a minimum confidence. We set the confidence threshold δ_p such that $p \times 100\%$ of videos remain after the thresholding.

We denote the target video set after thresholding as $\tilde{V}_T$. For stage 2, the supervised task on pseudo labeled target videos is to $\min_{\theta_E^V, \theta_C^V} \hat{\mathcal{L}}_{CE}(\tilde{V}_T)$, with

$$\hat{\mathcal{L}}_{CE}(\tilde{V}_T) = \sum_{v_j \in \tilde{V}_T} -\hat{l}(v_j) \cdot \log(C^V(E^V(V_j; \theta_E^V); \theta^V)).$$

(3)

In stage 4, we repeat the process as described above and re-train the video model on the target data with the updated pseudo labels from the third stage.

Stage 3 - Class-Aware Spatial Alignment. The adversarial learning for domain discrimination in the first stage aligns features from different domains globally, but not within each category (c.f. Fig. 3 (b) and (c)). In this case, target samples in a category A can be incorrectly aligned with source samples in a different category B. This would lead to inferior classification performance of the target classifier. To evade this misalignment, we perform class-aware domain alignment in the third stage between the source web images and the target video frames. Since the source data consists exclusively of images, we apply alignment on the spatial model between images and frames. Furthermore, as the target data is unlabeled, in order to align features across both domains within each category, we generate pseudo labels by the model ϕ^V from the second stage to provide category knowledge. Specifically, we use the video model to generate video-level labels that we disseminate into frame-level labels. To align images and video frames we use cross-domain contrastive learning by maximizing the similarity between samples across domains of the same class and minimizing the similarity between samples from different classes. We use $z = E^I(i; \theta_E^I)$ to denote the feature computed by the feature extractor on image i. The set of source image features is $Z_S^I = \{E^I(i; \theta_E^I) | i \in I_S\}$ and the set of target frame features is $Z_T^F = \{E^I(v^F; \theta_E^I) | v^F \in V_T^F\}$. During training, for each pseudo labeled target sample $z_j^F \in Z_T^F$, we randomly choose two samples from the source domain: a positive sample of the same label and a negative sample of a different label, $i.e.$ $z_{j\,+}^I, z_{j\,-}^I \in I_S$. The contrastive loss is formulated as

$$\mathcal{L}_{CONTR}(I_S, V_T^F) = -\sum_{z_j^F \in Z_T^F} \log \frac{h(z_j^F, z_{j\,+}^I)}{h(z_j^F, z_{j\,+}^I) + h(z_j^F, z_{j\,-}^I)}. \tag{4}$$

Following [5], we set $h(u, v) = \exp(\text{sim}(u, v)/\tau)$, where we use the cosine similarity $\text{sim}(u, v) = u^\mathsf{T} v / (\|u\| \|v\|)$ and τ is the temperature parameter. Thus, the objective of stage 3 on the image model is $\min_{\theta_E^I, \theta_C^I} \mathcal{L}_{CE}(I_S) + \mathcal{L}_{CONTR}(I_S, V_T^F)$.

In the third stage, an alternative of exploiting pseudo labels from the video model from the second stage is to self-train the video model on the target data, as self-training is a common practice in DA [26,46,48,49]. However, the category-level domain alignment with supervision from the source domain further regularizes the learning of class distribution in the target domain. This results in a significantly improved target classifier, as we show in Sect. 4.5.

Cycling of the Stages. The pseudo labels from the video model are exploited for class-aware domain alignment on the image model (stage 3) and the updated pseudo labels from the image model can supervise the training of the video model (stage 4). In this manner, stage 3 and stage 4 can be performed iteratively. We show in the evaluation (Table 1 and Fig. 5) the impact of this cyclic learning setup and how several iterations of CycDA can further improve the performance of the target classifier.

3.3   Mixed-Source Video Adaptation

Image-to-video DA applies to the case in which the source domain consists only of web images. However, other possible settings presume limited amount of annotated videos with the domain shift to the unlabeled target videos. We refer to this case as mixed-source video adaptation. CycDA can be adjusted for this setting as follows. We denote the labeled source video domain as $V_S = \{(v_j, l(v_j)) |_{j=1}^{N_S^V}\}$. For the class-agnostic (stage 1) and class-aware domain alignment (stage 3) stages we replace the source image domain $\{I_S\}$ by the mixed-source domain data $\{I_S, F_S\}$

which consists of web images and frames sampled from source videos. The supervised classification, adversarial domain discrimination and cross-domain contrastive learning are adapted accordingly. For the spatio-temporal learning of the video model ϕ^V (stage 2 and 4) we include additional supervised classification w.r.t. the ground truth labels for the source videos, therefore the overall loss is $\mathcal{L}_{CE}(V_S) + \hat{\mathcal{L}}_{CE}(\tilde{V}_T)$. In this case, the annotated source videos are utilized to regularize domain alignment on the image model, and provide further supervision for learning the classification task on the video model. In Sect. 4.4, we demonstrate that in the context of mixed-source video adaptation, even a limited amount of source videos is sufficient to achieve results competitive to video-to-video adaptation approaches that employ the entire source video dataset.

4 Experiments

4.1 Datasets

To evaluate our CycDA framework for image-to-video adaptation, we conduct experiments on 3 real-world image-video action recognition benchmark settings. Videos are from two large-scale action recognition datasets, UCF101 [35] and HMDB51 [23]. Web images are from the EADs (Extensive Action Dataset) [2], Stanford40 [42] and the BU101 dataset [29].

The three image-to-video adaptation tasks are: (1) Stanford40 → UCF101: the UCF101 action dataset contains 13320 videos collected from YouTube with 101 action classes. The Stanford40 dataset contains 9532 images collected from Google, Bing and Flickr, comprised of 40 action classes. Following [2,43,44], we select the 12 common action classes between the two datasets for image-to-video action recognition. (2) EADs→HMDB51: HMDB51 has 6766 videos with 51 action classes collected from online videos and movie clips. The EADs dataset consists of Stanford40 and the HII dataset [37]. It has 11504 images from 50 action classes. There are 13 shared action classes between the two datasets. (3) BU101→UCF101: BU101 consists of 23.8K web action images from 101 classes that completely correspond to classes on UCF101. We use data of all classes for evaluation on large-scale image-to-video adaptation.

UCF101 and HMDB51 both have three splits of training and test sets. Following [24,43,44], we report the average performance over all three splits.

The UCF-HMDB dataset [3] is a benchmark for video-to-video DA. It consists of the 12 common classes between UCF101 and HMDB51. On this dataset, we perform two types of evaluations: (1) *frame-to-video adaptation*: we use only a single frame from each source video to adapt to target videos; and (2) mixed-source video adaptation: we use source and target videos of UCF-HMDB, and extend the source domain with web images from BU101.

4.2 Implementation Details

For the image model, we use a ResNet-18 [17] pretrained on ImageNet [8]. We freeze the first 6 sequential blocks and train with a learning rate of 0.001 to

Table 1. Results on E→H (13 classes), S→U (12 classes) and B→U (101 classes), averaged over 3 splits. ResNet, C3D and I3D are pretrained on ImageNet [17], Sports-1M [20] and Kinetics400 [21]. * denotes our evaluation.

Method	Backbone	E→H	S→U	B→U
Source only	ResNet18	37.2	76.8	54.8
DANN [15]*	ResNet18	39.6	80.3	55.3
UnAtt [24]	ResNet101	–	–	66.4
HiGAN [44]	ResNet50, C3D	44.6	95.4	–
SymGAN [43]	ResNet50, C3D	55.0	97.7	–
CycDA (1 iteration)	ResNet50, C3D	56.6	98.0	–
DANN [15]+I3D*	ResNet18, I3D	53.8	97.9	68.3
HPDA [2]*	ResNet50, I3D	38.2	40.0	–
CycDA (1 iteration)	ResNet18, I3D	60.5	99.2	69.8
CycDA (2 iterations)	ResNet18, I3D	60.3	**99.3**	72.1
CycDA (3 iterations)	ResNet18, I3D	**62.0**	99.1	**72.6**
Supervised target	ResNet18, I3D	83.2	99.3	93.1

perform the domain alignment between web images and frames sampled from target videos. To avoid redundancy in the video frames, we uniformly divide a video into 5 segments. In each training epoch, we randomly sample one frame from each segment. As trade-off weight for domain discrimination, we follow the common practices in [4,14,15] to gradually increase β from 0 to 1. The temperature parameter τ is set to 0.05.

For the video model, we employ I3D Inception v1 [1] pretrained on the Kinetics dataset [21], which is common practice, e.g. [2,7,22,31,33]. We train the RGB stream only. To validate the efficacy of our CycDA pipeline, we use the I3D backbone with a shallow classifier of 2 FC layers, without any temporal aggregation module (e.g. GCN in [33] or self-attention module in [7]). We extract a clip of 64 frames from each video. Following [33], we use a learning rate of 0.001 for the backbone and 0.01 on other components. We keep $p = 70\%$ and 80% of videos in stage 2 and stage 4.

4.3   Image-to-Video DA

We compare the proposed approach to other image-to-video adaptation methods on the three described benchmark settings as shown in Table 1. As CycDA enables the iterative knowledge transfer between the image model and the video model, we can repeat stage 3 and stage 4 multiple times. We therefore report the performance for the first three iterations. We add the lower bound (source only) and the upper bound (ground truth supervised target) for reference.

We compare against several approaches: DANN [15] is classical adversarial domain discrimination on the image-level. UnAtt [24] applies a spatial attention

Table 2. Results of Cycle Adaption on UCF-HMDB in comparison to video-to-video adaptation (case A) approaches. For frame-to-video adaptation (case B), we use only one frame from each source video to adapt to target videos. For mixed-source video adaptation (case C), we combine BU101 web images and source videos as the source data. *We sample 50 web images per class from 12 classes in BU101.

DA setting	Method	Video backbone	Source data		U→H	H→U
			Web image	Videos (U or H) in %		
A: Video-to-video	AdaBN [25]	ResNet101	–	100%	75.5	77.4
	MCD [34]	ResNet101	–	100%	74.4	79.3
	TA^{3}N [3]	ResNet101	–	100%	78.3	81.8
	ABG [28]	ResNet101	–	100%	79.1	85.1
	TCoN [32]	ResNet101	–	100%	87.2	89.1
	DANN [15]	I3D	–	100%	80.7	88.0
	TA^{3}N [3]	I3D	–	100%	81.4	90.5
	SAVA [7]	I3D	–	100%	82.2	91.2
	MM-SADA [31]	I3D	–	100%	84.2	91.1
	CrossModal [22]	I3D	–	100%	84.7	92.8
	CoMix [33]	I3D	–	100%	86.7	93.9
B: Frame-to-video	CycDA	I3D	–	One frame	83.3	80.4
C: Mixed-source to video	CycDA	I3D	BU*	0%	77.8	88.6
			BU*	5%	82.2	93.1
			BU*	10%	82.5	93.5
			BU*	50%	84.2	95.2
			BU*	100%	88.1	98.0
Supervised target		I3D	–	–	94.4	97.0

map on video frames. HiGAN [44] and SymGAN [43] employ GANs for feature alignment (on backbone of ResNet50 and C3D) and define the current state-of-the-art on E→H and S→U. We also evaluate CycDA with the same backbones for fair comparison. DANN [15]+I3D is a strong baseline that trains the I3D model with pseudo labels from an adapted image model. HPDA [2] is a recent partial DA approach and for a fair comparison, we re-run its official implementation in a closed-set DA setting. Our CycDA outperforms all other approaches already after the first iteration. Except for the saturation on S→U, running CycDA for more iterations leads to a further performance boost on all evaluation settings.

We further explore the potential of CycDA on UCF-HMDB, which is a benchmark for video-to-video adaptation. For a strict comparison, we select data from the same source video dataset used in the video-to-video adaptation methods, without using any auxiliary web data for training. However, instead of directly using the source videos, we perform *frame-to-video* adaptation where we use only one frame from each source video to adapt to target videos. Here we sample the middle frame from each video and report the results in Table 2 (case B). We see that even when using only one frame per source video, on U→H, CycDA (83.3%) can already outperform TA^{3}N [3] (81.4%) and SAVA [7] (82.2%) which use all source videos for video-to-video adaptation. This demonstrates the strength of CycDA to exploit the large informativity in single images such that they could potentially replace videos as the source data. On H→U, our source domain contains only 840 frames from the 840 videos in the HMDB training set on UCF-HMDB, which leads to an inferior performance. We show that this can be easily addressed by adding auxiliary web data in Sect. 4.4.

4.4   Mixed-Source Image&Video-to-Video DA

For mixed-source adaptation, we assume to have both web images and some amount of source videos in the source domain. To evaluate this case, we use the source and target videos on UCF-HMDB, and extend the source domain with web images of the 12 corresponding action classes in BU101. We notice that using all web data from BU101 leads to performance saturation on the target video set of UCF-HMDB. Therefore, to validate the efficacy of CycDA, we only sample 50 web images per class as auxiliary training data. We vary the amount of source videos in the mixed-source domain and report the results in Table 2 (case C). First, by training with only sampled web images (without any source videos), we achieve baseline results of 77.8% (BU→H) and 88.6% (BU→U). By adding only 5% of videos to the mixed-source domain, we already achieve performance comparable to the video-to-video adaptation methods, *i.e.* 82.0% (BU+U→H) and 93.1% (BU+H→U). Furthermore, increasing the amount of source videos from 5% to 50% leads to another improvement of 2%. As web images are more informative than sampled video frames, using web images as auxiliary training data can thus significantly reduce the amount of videos required. Finally, with sampled web images and all source videos, we outperform all video-to-video adaptation methods, even exceeding the supervised target model for BU+H→U by 1%. Considering that we only use 50 web images per class, this further demonstrates that CycDA can exploit both, the information in web images and knowledge from the source data with domain shift, for a potentially improved learning.

4.5   Ablation Study

We perform several ablation studies to validate the proposed CycDA pipeline. We conduct these experiments on the setting of EADs → HMDB51 (split 1).

Stage-Wise Ablation Study. We first validate the efficacy of the CycDA pipeline by switching the stages with alternate counterparts. We report the quantitative results of six ablation settings in Table 3. Case A (source only), training the image model on web images only and predicting on target test set, demonstrates the lower bound of 39%. Case B (source only + video model), training with pseudo labeled target videos, is a vanilla baseline. It shows that training the video model with supervision from the image model already significantly improves performance by 11.5%. In case C, with class-agnostic domain alignment on the image model, the performance of B is improved by 1.8%. In case F, after completing the cycle with class-aware domain alignment in stage 3 and training the video model in stage 4 with the updated pseudo labels, we achieve the best performance with 60.8%.

Table 3. Stage-wise ablation study of the CycDA training pipeline on EADs → HMDB51 split 1. A: source only on image model. B: source only training on image model and video model training. C: class-agnostic DA (stage 1) and video model training (stage 2). D: case C + one stage of self-training the videos model. E: case C + two stages of self-training the video model. F: CycDA with stage 1∼4. Category-level pseudo labels of case C and F are compared in Fig. 4.

	Experiment	Stage 1	Stage 2	Stage 3	Stage 4	Acc
A:	Source only	$\mathcal{L}_{CE}(I_S)$	–	–	–	39.0
B:	Source only + video model	$\mathcal{L}_{CE}(I_S)$	$\hat{\mathcal{L}}_{CE}(V_T)$	–	–	50.5
C:	Class-agnostic DA + video model	$\mathcal{L}_{CE}(I_S)$, $\mathcal{L}_{ADD}(I_S, V_T^F)$	$\hat{\mathcal{L}}_{CE}(V_T)$	–	–	52.3
D:	Case C + vid. self-train×1	$\mathcal{L}_{CE}(I_S)$, $\mathcal{L}_{ADD}(I_S, V_T^F)$	$\hat{\mathcal{L}}_{CE}(V_T)$	$\hat{\mathcal{L}}_{CE}(V_T)$	–	55.4
E:	Case C + vid. self-train×2	$\mathcal{L}_{CE}(I_S)$, $\mathcal{L}_{ADD}(I_S, V_T^F)$	$\hat{\mathcal{L}}_{CE}(V_T)$	$\hat{\mathcal{L}}_{CE}(V_T)$	$\hat{\mathcal{L}}_{CE}(V_T)$	56.4
F:	CycDA	$\mathcal{L}_{CE}(I_S)$, $\mathcal{L}_{ADD}(I_S, V_T^F)$	$\hat{\mathcal{L}}_{CE}(V_T)$	$\mathcal{L}_{CE}(I_S)$, $\mathcal{L}_{CONTR}(I_S, V_T^F)$	$\hat{\mathcal{L}}_{CE}(V_T)$	**60.8**

Additionally, we conduct ablation experiments using pseudo labels from case C to self-train the video model. Although self-training the video model for 1 (case D) or 2 (case E) stages exhibits performance improvement compared to case C, it is still clearly outperformed by CycDA. This indicates that the elaborate step of knowledge transfer from the video model to the image model and class-aware domain alignment are critical for a good performance.

We further illustrate the t-SNE [30] feature visualizations of ablation cases in Fig. 3. By observing image features of the source only case (Fig. 3(a)), we see that web images (blue) gather in category clusters after supervised training, while target video frames (red) are far less discriminative and highly misaligned with source due to large domain shift. The class-agnostic domain alignment (Fig. 3(b)) in stage 1 results in a slightly better global alignment of source and target features. With category knowledge from the video model, the class-aware domain alignment (Fig. 3(c)) demonstrates distinctly better category-level association between source and target. By passing pseudo labels from the image model of Fig. 3(a)(b)(c) to supervise the spatio-temporal training, we get the corresponding video models whose features are plotted in Fig. 3(d)(e)(f). The vanilla baseline of source only + video model (Fig. 3(d)) leads to highly undiscriminative features on the difficult classes, which is slightly improved by class-agnostic

image features

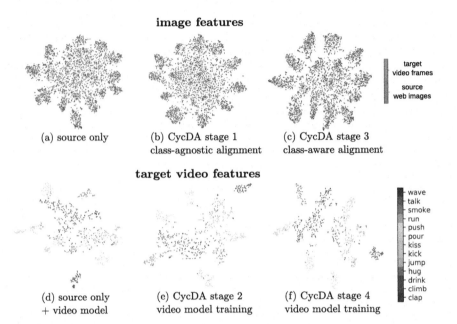

(a) source only

(b) CycDA stage 1
class-agnostic alignment

(c) CycDA stage 3
class-aware alignment

target
video frames

source
web images

target video features

(d) source only
+ video model

(e) CycDA stage 2
video model training

(f) CycDA stage 4
video model training

wave
talk
smoke
run
push
pour
kiss
kick
jump
hug
drink
climb
clap

Fig. 3. -SNE visualizations of image features (for both source and target) and target video features (colored w.r.t. ground truth). We plot the results of source only, source only and video model training, and results of each stage in CycDA.

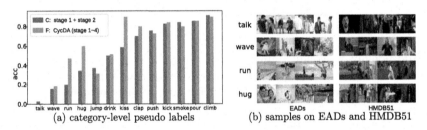

(a) category-level pseudo labels

(b) samples on EADs and HMDB51

Fig. 4. (a) Category-level pseudo label analysis on target. We compare the accuracy of category-level pseudo labels on target videos for the ablation case C and F from Table 3. Here we plot the accuracy of pseudo labels of the 13 common classes on EADs → HMDB51. (b) Samples of four categories on EADs and HMDB51.

alignment (Fig. 3(e)). Class-aware domain alignment (Fig. 3(f)) results in more pronounced category clusters with larger inter-class distances.

Category-Level Pseudo Label Analysis on Target. In Fig. 4(a), we plot the accuracy of category-wise pseudo labels on target videos for the ablation cases C and F from Table 3. On case C (blue) which consists of stage 1 (class-agnostic spatial domain alignment) and stage 2 (spatio-temporal learning), image-to-video action recognition has varying performance on different action classes. More specifically, it yields better results on appearance-based actions with dis-

Table 4. Comparison of DA strategies in stage 3 on EADs → HMDB51 split 1. A: supervised classification on pseudo labeled target frames. B: supervised classification on source and pseudo labeled target. C: B + adversarial domain discrimination. D: supervised classification on source + cross-domain contrastive learning.

Experiment		Stage 3	Stage 4	Acc
Stage 1–2		–	–	52.3
stage 1–4	A:	$\mathcal{L}_{CE}(V_T^F)$	$\hat{\mathcal{L}}_{CE}(V_T)$	55.6
	B:	$\mathcal{L}_{CE}(I_S, V_T^F)$		56.4
	C:	$\mathcal{L}_{CE}(I_S, V_T^F), \mathcal{L}_{ADD}(I_S, V_T^F)$		58.0
	D:	$\mathcal{L}_{CE}(I_S), \mathcal{L}_{CONTR}(I_S, V_T^F)$		**60.8**

tinct background (*e.g. climb*), or on actions with discriminative pose or gesture (*e.g. smoke, pour*). On the contrary, there is inferior performance on fine-grained actions with subtle movements (*e.g. talk*) or actions that are semantically highly generalized with large inter-class variation (*e.g. run, wave*), *c.f.* in Fig. 4(b).

By comparing the pseudo label accuracy of cases C and F, we see that the complete CycDA with stage 3 and stage 4 contributes to a significant performance boost on the difficult classes (*e.g. run, hug, kiss*) while keeping the performance on the easy classes. This can be attributed to the class-aware domain alignment that improves cross-domain association on the difficult classes while keeping the alignment on easy ones. Note that better class-aware domain alignment also leads to more support samples for difficult classes, which could result in slight performance drop on the easier classes.

Domain Adaptation Strategies in Stage 3. In stage 3, we transfer knowledge from the video model to the image model by passing pseudo labels from the video model to provide category information in domain alignment. We compare different DA strategies that use pseudo labels from the video model in Table 4. Intuitively, performing the supervised task on both source and target (case B) outperforms the case of pseudo labeled target only (case A). Adding the adversarial domain discrimination (case C) leads to a further boost. The cross-domain contrastive learning (case D) has the best performance among the 4 cases. In comparison to the case of only stage 1 and 2, a complete cycle with 4 stages leads to performance improvement of at least 3.3% for all cases. This indicates the benefits of transferring the knowledge from the video model onto the image model. The proposed CycDA generalizes well on different strategies using pseudo labels from the previous stage.

Temporal Aggregation of Frame-Level Pseudo Labels. Before video model training, we temporally aggregate frame-level pseudo labels. Here we compare three strategies of temporal aggregation in Table 5. Frame-level thresholding followed by temporal averaging (case C) outperforms the other two cases which perform temporal averaging before video-level thresholding. Frame-level thresh-

Table 5. Temporal aggregation of frame-level pseudo labels into video-level pseudo labels on EADs → HMDB51 split 1.

Aggregation		Acc
A:	Avg. + Class-balanced thresh.	50.3
B:	Avg. + Thresh.	55.9
C:	Thresh. + Avg.	**60.8**

Fig. 5. Performance of multiple iterations of CycDA (stage 3 and 4) on EADs → HMDB51. Average on 3 splits.

olding filters out frames of low confidence scores and effectively increases the accuracy of video pseudo labels.

Number of Iterations. Finally, we illustrate the performance after several iterations on EADs→HMDB51 in Fig. 5. It shows that within the first five iterations, performing CycDA iteratively results in a slight increase of performance. Further, within all the 9 iterations, CycDA delivers relatively stable performance, with the result fluctuating between 60.0% and 62.2% without dropping below the ablated alternatives shown in Table 3.

5   Conclusions

We presented CycDA to address the image-to-video adaptation problem. We proposed to alternately perform spatial domain alignment to address the domain shift between images and target frames, and spatio-temporal learning to bridge the modality gap. Our evaluations across several benchmarks and datasets demonstrate that CycDA exploits the large informativity in the source images for enhanced performance on the target video classifier.

Acknowledgements. This work was partially funded by the Austrian Research Promotion Agency (FFG) project 874065 and by the Christian Doppler Laboratory for Semantic 3D Computer Vision, funded in part by Qualcomm Inc.

References

1. Carreira, J., Zisserman, A.: Quo vadis, action recognition? a new model and the kinetics dataset. In: CVPR, pp. 6299–6308 (2017)
2. Chen, J., Wu, X., Hu, Y., Luo, J.: Spatial-temporal causal inference for partial image-to-video adaptation. In: AAAI, vol. 35, pp. 1027–1035 (2021)
3. Chen, M.H., Kira, Z., AlRegib, G., Yoo, J., Chen, R., Zheng, J.: Temporal attentive alignment for large-scale video domain adaptation. In: ICCV, pp. 6321–6330 (2019)
4. Chen, M.H., Li, B., Bao, Y., AlRegib, G., Kira, Z.: Action segmentation with joint self-supervised temporal domain adaptation. In: CVPR, pp. 9454–9463 (2020)
5. Chen, T., Kornblith, S., Norouzi, M., Hinton, G.: A simple framework for contrastive learning of visual representations. In: ICML, pp. 1597–1607. PMLR (2020)

6. Choi, J., Sharma, G., Chandraker, M., Huang, J.B.: Unsupervised and semi-supervised domain adaptation for action recognition from drones. In: WACV, pp. 1717–1726 (2020)
7. Choi, J., Sharma, G., Schulter, S., Huang, J.-B.: Shuffle and attend: video domain adaptation. In: Vedaldi, A., Bischof, H., Brox, T., Frahm, J.-M. (eds.) ECCV 2020. LNCS, vol. 12357, pp. 678–695. Springer, Cham (2020). https://doi.org/10.1007/978-3-030-58610-2_40
8. Deng, J., Dong, W., Socher, R., Li, L.J., Li, K., Fei-Fei, L.: Imagenet: a large-scale hierarchical image database. In: CVPR, pp. 248–255. IEEE (2009)
9. Duan, H., Zhao, Y., Xiong, Y., Liu, W., Lin, D.: Omni-sourced webly-supervised learning for video recognition. In: Vedaldi, A., Bischof, H., Brox, T., Frahm, J.-M. (eds.) ECCV 2020. LNCS, vol. 12360, pp. 670–688. Springer, Cham (2020). https://doi.org/10.1007/978-3-030-58555-6_40
10. Feichtenhofer, C.: X3d: expanding architectures for efficient video recognition. In: CVPR (2020)
11. Gan, C., Sun, C., Duan, L., Gong, B.: Webly-supervised video recognition by mutually voting for relevant web images and web video frames. In: Leibe, B., Matas, J., Sebe, N., Welling, M. (eds.) ECCV 2016. LNCS, vol. 9907, pp. 849–866. Springer, Cham (2016). https://doi.org/10.1007/978-3-319-46487-9_52
12. Gan, C., Sun, C., Nevatia, R.: Deck: discovering event composition knowledge from web images for zero-shot event detection and recounting in videos. In: AAAI, vol. 31 (2017)
13. Gan, C., Yao, T., Yang, K., Yang, Y., Mei, T.: You lead, we exceed: labor-free video concept learning by jointly exploiting web videos and images. In: CVPR, pp. 923–932 (2016)
14. Ganin, Y., Lempitsky, V.: Unsupervised domain adaptation by backpropagation. In: ICML, pp. 1180–1189. PMLR (2015)
15. Ganin, Y., et al.: Domain-adversarial training of neural networks. JMLR **17**(1), 2030–2096 (2016)
16. Guo, S., et al.: Curriculumnet: weakly supervised learning from large-scale web images. In: ECCV, pp. 135–150 (2018)
17. He, K., Zhang, X., Ren, S., Sun, J.: Deep residual learning for image recognition. In: CVPR, pp. 770–778 (2016)
18. Jamal, A., Namboodiri, V.P., Deodhare, D., Venkatesh, K.: Deep domain adaptation in action space. In: BMVC, vol. 2, p. 5 (2018)
19. Kae, A., Song, Y.: Image to video domain adaptation using web supervision. In: WACV, pp. 567–575 (2020)
20. Karpathy, A., Toderici, G., Shetty, S., Leung, T., Sukthankar, R., Fei-Fei, L.: Large-scale video classification with convolutional neural networks. In: CVPR, pp. 1725–1732 (2014)
21. Kay, W., et al.: The kinetics human action video dataset. arXiv preprint arXiv:1705.06950 (2017)
22. Kim, D., et al.: Learning cross-modal contrastive features for video domain adaptation. In: ICCV, pp. 13618–13627 (2021)
23. Kuehne, H., Jhuang, H., Garrote, E., Poggio, T., Serre, T.: Hmdb: a large video database for human motion recognition. In: ICCV, pp. 2556–2563. IEEE (2011)
24. Li, J., Wong, Y., Zhao, Q., Kankanhalli, M.S.: Attention transfer from web images for video recognition. In: ACM Multimedia, pp. 1–9 (2017)
25. Li, Y., Wang, N., Shi, J., Hou, X., Liu, J.: Adaptive batch normalization for practical domain adaptation. Pattern Recogn. **80**, 109–117 (2018)

26. Liu, H., Wang, J., Long, M.: Cycle self-training for domain adaptation. arXiv preprint arXiv:2103.03571 (2021)
27. Liu, Y., Lu, Z., Li, J., Yang, T., Yao, C.: Deep image-to-video adaptation and fusion networks for action recognition. TIP **29**, 3168–3182 (2019)
28. Luo, Y., Huang, Z., Wang, Z., Zhang, Z., Baktashmotlagh, M.: Adversarial bipartite graph learning for video domain adaptation. In: ACM Multimedia, pp. 19–27 (2020)
29. Ma, S., Bargal, S.A., Zhang, J., Sigal, L., Sclaroff, S.: Do less and achieve more: training cnns for action recognition utilizing action images from the web. Pattern Recogn. **68**, 334–345 (2017)
30. Van der Maaten, L., Hinton, G.: Visualizing data using t-sne. JMLR **9**(11) (2008)
31. Munro, J., Damen, D.: Multi-modal domain adaptation for fine-grained action recognition. In: CVPR, pp. 122–132 (2020)
32. Pan, B., Cao, Z., Adeli, E., Niebles, J.C.: Adversarial cross-domain action recognition with co-attention. In: AAAI, vol. 34, pp. 11815–11822 (2020)
33. Sahoo, A., Shah, R., Panda, R., Saenko, K., Das, A.: Contrast and mix: temporal contrastive video domain adaptation with background mixing. In: NeurIPS (2021)
34. Saito, K., Watanabe, K., Ushiku, Y., Harada, T.: Maximum classifier discrepancy for unsupervised domain adaptation. In: CVPR, pp. 3723–3732 (2018)
35. Soomro, K., Zamir, A.R., Shah, M.: Ucf101: a dataset of 101 human actions classes from videos in the wild. arXiv preprint arXiv:1212.0402 (2012)
36. Sun, C., Shetty, S., Sukthankar, R., Nevatia, R.: Temporal localization of fine-grained actions in videos by domain transfer from web images. In: ACM Multimedia, pp. 371–380 (2015)
37. Tanisik, G., Zalluhoglu, C., Ikizler-Cinbis, N.: Facial descriptors for human interaction recognition in still images. Pattern Recogn. Lett. **73**, 44–51 (2016)
38. Wang, L., Xiong, Y., Lin, D., Van Gool, L.: Untrimmednets for weakly supervised action recognition and detection. In: CVPR, pp. 4325–4334 (2017)
39. Wang, Z., She, Q., Smolic, A.: Action-net: multipath excitation for action recognition. In: CVPR (2021)
40. Yang, C., Xu, Y., Shi, J., Dai, B., Zhou, B.: Temporal pyramid network for action recognition. In: CVPR (2020)
41. Yang, J., Sun, X., Lai, Y.K., Zheng, L., Cheng, M.M.: Recognition from web data: a progressive filtering approach. TIP **27**(11), 5303–5315 (2018)
42. Yao, B., Jiang, X., Khosla, A., Lin, A.L., Guibas, L., Fei-Fei, L.: Human action recognition by learning bases of action attributes and parts. In: ICCV, pp. 1331–1338. IEEE (2011)
43. Yu, F., Wu, X., Chen, J., Duan, L.: Exploiting images for video recognition: heterogeneous feature augmentation via symmetric adversarial learning. TIP **28**(11), 5308–5321 (2019)
44. Yu, F., Wu, X., Sun, Y., Duan, L.: Exploiting images for video recognition with hierarchical generative adversarial networks. In: IJCAI (2018)
45. Zhang, J., Han, Y., Tang, J., Hu, Q., Jiang, J.: Semi-supervised image-to-video adaptation for video action recognition. IEEE Trans. Cybern. **47**(4), 960–973 (2016)
46. Zhang, Y., Deng, B., Jia, K., Zhang, L.: Label propagation with augmented anchors: a simple semi-supervised learning baseline for unsupervised domain adaptation. In: Vedaldi, A., Bischof, H., Brox, T., Frahm, J.-M. (eds.) ECCV 2020. LNCS, vol. 12349, pp. 781–797. Springer, Cham (2020). https://doi.org/10.1007/978-3-030-58548-8_45

47. Zhuang, B., Liu, L., Li, Y., Shen, C., Reid, I.: Attend in groups: a weakly-supervised deep learning framework for learning from web data. In: CVPR, pp. 1878–1887 (2017)
48. Zou, Y., Yu, Z., Kumar, B., Wang, J.: Unsupervised domain adaptation for semantic segmentation via class-balanced self-training. In: ECCV, pp. 289–305 (2018)
49. Zou, Y., Yu, Z., Liu, X., Kumar, B., Wang, J.: Confidence regularized self-training. In: ICCV, pp. 5982–5991 (2019)

S2N: Suppression-Strengthen Network for Event-Based Recognition Under Variant Illuminations

Zengyu Wan, Yang Wang, Ganchao Tan, Yang Cao, and Zheng-Jun Zha[✉]⬤

University of Science and Technology of China, Hefei, China
{wanzengy,tgc1997}@mail.ustc.edu.cn,
{ywang120,forrest,zhazj}@ustc.edu.cn

Abstract. The emerging event-based sensors have demonstrated outstanding potential in visual tasks thanks to their high speed and high dynamic range. However, the event degradation due to imaging under low illumination obscures the correlation between event signals and brings uncertainty into event representation. Targeting this issue, we present a novel suppression-strengthen network (S2N) to augment the event feature representation after suppressing the influence of degradation. Specifically, a suppression sub-network is devised to obtain intensity mapping between the degraded and denoised enhancement frames by unsupervised learning. To further restrain the degradation's influence, a strengthen sub-network is presented to generate robust event representation by adaptively perceiving the local variations between the center and surrounding regions. After being trained on a single illumination condition, our S2N can be directly generalized to other illuminations to boost the recognition performance. Experimental results on three challenging recognition tasks demonstrate the superiority of our method. The codes and datasets could refer to https://github.com/wanzengy/S2N-Suppression-Strengthen-Network.

Keywords: Event camera · Event degradation · Event-based recognition · Motion evolution

1 Introduction

Event cameras are neuromorphic vision sensors that continuously encode the brightness changes of scene and asynchronously output a sequence of events as

$$I(x,y,t) - I(x,y,t - \Delta t) \geq p \cdot C, \qquad (1)$$

Z. Wan and Y. Wang—Equal contribution.

Supplementary Information The online version contains supplementary material available at https://doi.org/10.1007/978-3-031-20062-5_41.

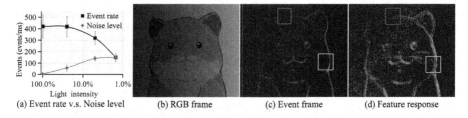

(a) Event rate v.s. Noise level   (b) RGB frame   (c) Event frame   (d) Feature response

Fig. 1. (a) Measured event rate and noise level versus illumination intensity. The noise level is calculated by counting the number of events in a still scene. (b) The captured scene with traditional frame camera. (c) With the decrease of illumination intensity, the noise level of the event camera gradually increases and the real activity events gradually reduce, which will attenuate the amplitude of feature response and destroy the completeness of structure as in (d). The red box and yellow box in (c) and (d) marks area under different illumination conditions. (Color figure online)

where $I(x, y, t)$ denotes the brightness on pixel location (x, y) at time t, Δt is the time interval between adjacent event at the same pixel, p indicates the direction of the brightness change and C is the contrast sensitivity. Benefited from the difference imaging mechanism, event camera has many advantages (*e.g.*, high dynamic range, low power consumption, and microsecond-scale temporal resolution [6,9,12,23,29,49]), and shows great application potential in many visual and robotics tasks [2,4,7,28,30,39,44,47,48].

Despite the numerous advances of event-based vision, current event sensor prototypes, *e.g.*, DAVIS240, still bear unconventional sensor degradation [14,19,36]. As shown in Fig. 1 (a, c), the output of the event camera is susceptible to noise (*e.g.*, background activity noise), and the noise level is inversely proportional to illumination. In addition, the lower illumination also weakens the signal photocurrent and pixel bandwidth [16,25,31], resulting in the number reduction of activity events. The event degradation will obscure the correlation between event signals, resulting in errors and uncertainties in the generated representations, as shown in Fig. 1 (d).

Recently, some event-based recognition methods have been proposed to capture the spatial-temporal correlation from event stream with orderless aggregating or graph [5,40,45]. However, these methods ignore the influence of event degradation, which is inevitable in low light or low reflection environments. And this will lead to noisy and incomplete feature representations and result in recognition performance drop significantly. To address this problem, we propose a novel Suppression-Strengthen Network (S2N), which consists of two subnetworks: Noise Suppression Network (NSN) and Feature Strengthen Network (FSN), accounting for noise reduction and feature enhancement, respectively.

Specifically, in the first stage, the NSN is devised to obtain intensity mapping between the degraded frames and the denoised enhancement frames by unsupervised learning. To distinguish the real activity event and random noise, three novel discriminant loss functions are introduced by exploiting the fact that, in a small neighborhood, the events are originated from the identical motion, while noises are not. In the second stage, a novel FSN is presented to guarantee the completeness of the feature by motion evolution perception and local variations encoding. The Evolution Aware Module(EAM) from FSN is firstly designed to perceive the motion evolution in each direction, resulting in a motion evolution map. Then through the Density-adaptive Central Differential Convolution(DCDC) process, the local center-surrounding variations of map are progressively encoded and adaptively aggregated into a complete event representation. Evaluations on three challenging event-based recognition tasks demonstrate the promising performance of our proposed method under variant illuminations. In summary, the main contributions of this paper are:

1. We propose the first S2N framework that considers event noise and real activity events reduction in event-based recognition to improve the inference accuracy and model robustness under various illumination conditions.
2. We devise a suppression sub-network to reduce random noise and enhance event frame contrast by learning an intensity mapping between the input and enhanced frames in an unsupervised manner. And subsequently, we propose a strengthen sub-network to generate robust event representation by perceiving the motion evolution with adaptive aggregation.
3. We collect two novel event-based datasets for gait and character recognition under variant illumination conditions, termed DAVIS346Gait and DAVIS346Character, respectively.
4. Our model can be well generalized to other illuminations after being trained in a single illumination scene, without fine-tuning. Extensive experiments on three challenging tasks show that our network outperforms the SOTA methods on various illumination conditions.

2   Related Work

In this section, we mainly review recent works, including event denoising and event-based recognition methods.

2.1   Event Denoising

One of the main challenges for event-based vision tasks is excessive noise. Considering the gap between events and RGB images [1,12,17,34,41], it is difficult to directly utilize the denoising method for RGB images in event-based work. Most existing event denoising methods work by exploiting the spatio-temporal correlation. Liu *et al.* [27] used the eight neighborhood pixels of an incoming event and considered it as noise if there lacks enough event support. Khodamoradi *et al.* [18] filtered BA (background activity) noise with compound memory cells, one for storing polarity and another for timestamp to improve the denoising process. Padala *et al.* [32] utilized the temporal correlation and spatial correlation and proposed filter with two layers to denoise. Wang *et al.* [42] tried to calculate

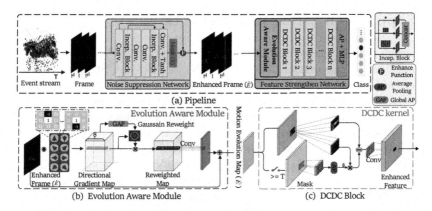

Fig. 2. The overall structure of S2N. The event stream will be firstly converted into the even frames as input and be send to the noise suppression network for noise reduction and contrast enhancement in an unsupervised manner. Next, the enhanced frames are transmitted to the Evolution Aware Module to extract the motion evolution map. Then, the evolution map is put into the density-adaptive central differential convolution process to extract the complete event representation.

the optical flow of events by local region fitting and remove the event above the threshold. Feng et al. [11] reduced the event noise based on the event density in the spatio-temporal neighborhood. The EDnCNN network [3] was developed for event denoising through labeling the probability of each event. These methods consider the noise effect but ignore the influence on activity event reduction, leading to an incomplete structure in the feature space.

2.2 Event-Based Recognition

Benefited from high-dynamic-range and high temporal resolution proprities, the event camera is widely applied to assist recognition tasks. Lagorce et al. [10,21,22,36] proposed event-based spatio-temporal features called time-surfaces and classified 36 characters by hand-crafted feature extractor. J.A.Pérez-Carrasco et al. [33] tried to accumulate the fixed-length event stream equally into an event frame and leveraged simple 4-layer CNN to learn to recognize the poker card symbol. Lee et al. [35,37] proposed to use SNN (Spiking Neuron Network) to extract event stream features. However SNN lacks an effective way to train the network and needs to work on specific hardware. Wang et al. [40,45] treated the event steam as point cloud and extracted the spatio-temporal structure with order-less aggregating through pointnet. Some recent works paid attention to graph convolution network [5,24,43] to extract spatio-temporal relations by building event graph. Also, a two-stage approach [42] was proposed to solve the noise interference by exploiting local motion consistency and desined a deep neural network to recognize gait from the denoised event stream. However, these recognition methods are susceptible to event degradation, while our work directs at enhancing the model's robustness to event noise and real-activity event reduction.

3   Suppression-Strengthen Network

Our proposed Suppression Strengthen Network (S2N) contains two sub-networks: Noise Suppression Network (NSN) and Feature Strengthen Network (FSN), which are responsible for noise reduction and feature enhancement, respectively as shown in Fig. 2. Given the event stream as input, we first accumulate the events within fixed time windows into two-channel frames according to the event polarity. The red and green colors of the event frames in Fig. 2 correspond to the event's positive and negative polarity, respectively. As we have emphasized above, the event degradation includes event noise and activity events reduction, which will lead to excessive noise, lower contrast ratio, and structure breakpoints in event frames. Thus, we firstly send the event frames to NSN for noise removal and contrast enhancement in an unsupervised manner (Sect. 3.1). Next, the enhanced frames are transmitted to FSN to reconstruct the complete structure under the guidance of gradient prior and generate a motion evolution map, which is utilized to guide the density-adaptive central differential convolution for robust recognition (Sect. 3.2).

3.1   Noise Suppression Network

To achieve event denoising and contrast enhancement, we propose a novel unsupervised Noise Suppression Network (NSN), as shown in Fig. 2 (a). The NSN contains six layers mixed with plain convolution and inception block [38], and we adopt the Tanh function as the activation function to output a confidence mask (denoted as S) of which the value belongs to -1 to 1, and the size is the same as input event frames. Under the constraints of the specifically designed loss functions, the weight of mask S will converge to -1 value at the noise position for suppression, while to 1 at the activity events area for enhancement. With the confidence mask, the enhanced event frame can be obtained as

$$\hat{E}(x,y) = E(x,y) + S(x,y)E(x,y)\left(1 - E(x,y)\right), \qquad (2)$$

where $\hat{E}(x,y)$, $E(x,y)$, $S(x,y)$ represents the intensity of enhanced event frame, input event frame and the mask at coordinate (x,y), respectively. Given $E(x,y) \in (0, 1)$ and $S(x,y) \in (-1, 1)$. The Eq. (2) satisfy three constraints: 1. Capable of non-linear stretching to enhance the contrast; 2. Ensure the output is between $[0,1]$ without overflow truncation; 3. Monotonous and derivable. We choose the second-order formula $E(1 - E)$ in Eq. (2) for easy implementation.

Loss Functions. To ensure that the confidence mask can effectively suppress noise and enhance activity events, we propose three loss functions: noise suppression loss, enhancement loss, and consistency loss. The design of the loss functions is based on the observation: in a small neighborhood, the events are originated from the identical motion while the noises are not. Consequently, we can distinguish noise from input event signals by local spatial correlation.

Noise Suppression Loss. Based on the above observation, we use a 3×3 kernel with the center weight of 0 and surrounding of 1 to filter the input event frame, and the output represents the strength of local correlation between the center pixel and surroundings. When the response amplitude exceeds a given threshold, the corresponding events are considered as real activity events; otherwise, as noise. In this paper, we set the threshold as the mean value of the whole image intensity as in Eq. (3). After obtaining the noise distribution, we directly constrain the enhancement result $\hat{E}(x)$ in the noise region to be 0:

$$\mathcal{L}_N = \sum_{p \in \mathcal{P}} \hat{E}(p),$$
$$\mathcal{P} = \{p \mid \sum_{i=1}^{3} \sum_{j=1}^{3} (\hat{E}_{i+p_x, j+p_y} W_{i,j}) \leq Mean(\hat{E})\}., \tag{3}$$

where $\mathcal{P}$ represents the set of noise location p, W is a 3×3 kernel with center weight as 0 and surrounding as 1.

Enhancement Loss. The event reduction under variant illumination conditions will result in low contrast of event frame. To this end, we propose enhancement loss to adaptively enhance the intensity of the event frame under different illumination conditions. The enhancement loss can be formulated as

$$\mathcal{L}_E = \sum_{p \notin \mathrm{P}} (A - \sqrt{A})^2,$$
$$A = \frac{1}{k^2} \sum_{i=1}^{k} \sum_{j=1}^{k} \hat{E}(i, j), \tag{4}$$

where k represents the size of the neighborhood and is set as 5 in this paper, and A represents the average intensity within the neighborhood. Based on Eq. (2), we can get that $A \in (0, 1)$ and $A < \sqrt{A}$. Thus, under the constraint of Eq. (4), the intensity of event frames can gradually increase. Note that we only perform Eq. (4) on valid event positions and the vale of $\sqrt{A}$ is truncated to greater than 0.5 (empirical threshold) to avoid gradient explosion.

Consistency Loss. To keep the consistent of the enhancement of two polarities in event frames, we propose a consistent loss function, defined as following:

$$\mathcal{L}_C = \sum (Y^p - Y^n)^2, \tag{5}$$

where Y^p is the average intensity value of the positive polarity channel of mask S, and Y^n denotes the average intensity value of the negative channel.

Total Loss. The total loss function can be expressed as

$$\mathcal{L} = \mathcal{L}_N + \lambda_1 \mathcal{L}_E + \lambda_2 \mathcal{L}_C, \tag{6}$$

where λ_1 and λ_2 are trade-off weights. We will represent the effect of each loss item in the supplementary material.

3.2   Feature Strengthen Network

In this section, we propose the Feature Strengthen Network (FSN) as shown in Fig. 2. Particularly, an evolution guided density-adaptive central difference convolution scheme is proposed to progressively encode the local center-surrounding variation and adaptively aggregate the features into a complete event representation under the guidance of the motion evolution map.

Motion Evolution Map. Due to the influence of event degradation, the input event frames inevitably exist breakpoints, leading to incomplete feature representation. To repair the corrupted information, we exploit the global motion evolution feature to guide the feature enhancement. Specifically, we first calculate the 8 directional gradient projections of an event frame, as follows:

$$\nabla \hat{E}_i = W_i \cdot \hat{E}, \quad i = 1, 2, \ldots, 8, \tag{7}$$

where W_i represents the i_{th} 3×3 directional kernel as shown in Fig. 2 (b). Then we perform Global Average Pooling (GAP) [26] on each gradient map to get the global evolution information as

$$Z_i = GAP(\nabla \hat{E}_i). \tag{8}$$

A larger pooling value corresponds to the direction of the main evolution pattern, while a smaller value corresponds to a direction that is the non-edge or broken edge region features which should be repaired. So to obtain the complete evolution pattern, we re-weight the directional gradient map by the Gaussian function and the normalized global information. The re-weighted map is then applied to the event frame to obtain the motion evolution map $\tilde{E}$:

$$\sigma_i = softmax(Z_i) = \frac{e^{Z_i}}{\sum_{j=1}^{8} e^{Z_j}}, \quad i = 1, \ldots, 8,$$
$$\nabla \tilde{E}_i = \nabla \hat{E}_i \exp(-(\left\| \nabla \hat{E}_i \right\| \Big/ \sigma_i)^2), \tag{9}$$
$$\tilde{E} = \hat{E} + W_i \cdot \nabla \tilde{E}_i,$$

where $\sigma_i = softmax(Z_i)$ represents the normalized global information, W_i represents a 1×1 convolution kernel and the Gaussian function helps to enhance the major evolution direction and suppress the weak evolution direction to diffuse the evolution tendency.

To guide subsequent operations, we need the evolution trend which is irrelevant of specific value. There, we perform a binary operation on the motion evolution map to obtain the trend mask M:

$$M(x, y) = \begin{cases} 1, & \tilde{E}(x, y) > T \\ 0, & \tilde{E}(x, y) \leq T, \end{cases} \tag{10}$$

where T represents the threshold and is set to 0 in this paper. Taking the motion evolution map $\tilde{E}$ and mask M as input, we perform density-adaptive central difference convolution to extract the feature.

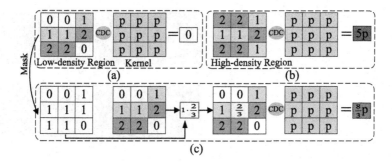

Fig. 3. (a) and (b) depict examples of CDC convolution acting in low-density regions and high-density regions, where density refers to the local proportion of valid values(> 0), i.e., the average value of the evolution mask (also known as the motion evolution map binarization). The differential effect of CDC leads to excessive attenuation of low-density areas. (c) This problem can be suppressed by multiply the mean value of the mask with the central value to reduce the weight of the central difference term. To facilitate understanding, we adopt the simplest convolution core of the same p-value.

Density-Adaptive CDC Kernel. Inspired by LBP (Local Binary Patterns), CDC [46] is devised to extract fine grained features by aggregating the center-oriented gradient of sampled values, which can ben formulated as:

$$y_{ec}(p_0) = \sum_{p_n \in R} w(p_n) \cdot (x(p_n + p_0) - x(p_0)). \tag{11}$$

However, the difference term of CDC will lead to excessive reduction of the low-density region, as shown in Fig. 3. To solve this problem, we propose a density-adaptive central difference convolution. Specifically, we perform local average pooling on the evolution mask M, and get the local valid density θ.

$$\theta(p_0) = \frac{1}{|R|} \sum_{p_n \in R} M(p_n + p_0), \tag{12}$$

where p_0 is the central pixel, R is $k \times k$ neighborhood of p_0 and k is set to 3 there, $|R|$ represents the area of R, the stride of the pooling is set 1 to keep the size unchanging. It is clear that pixels on structured regions tend to have larger density values, while the opposite is true for pixels on smooth regions. In each convolution process, we multiply θ by the central pixel on the difference term, by adjusting the differential intensity to suppress the attenuation:

$$y_{ec}(p_0) = \sum_{p_n \in R} w(p_n) \cdot (x(p_n + p_0)) - \theta(p_0) \cdot x(p_0)). \tag{13}$$

Besides, to maintain the feature response on smooth regions, we also introduce vanilla convolution and use the hyperparameter $C \in [0, 1]$ to tradeoff the contribution between vanilla convolution and DCDC as

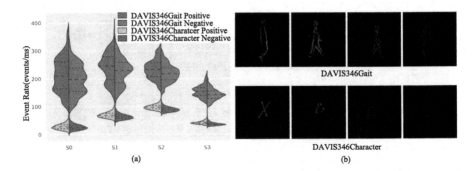

Fig. 4. (a) The event rate of each instance in DAVIS346Gait and DAVIS346Character datasets. With the illumination intensity decrease, the output of activity events gradually decreases and noise level gradually increases. The inner lines of the violins represent the quarterlies. (b) The examples of DAVIS346Gait and DAVIS346Character datasets under four illumination conditions.

$$y(p_0) = (1 - C) \cdot \sum_{p_n \in R} w(p_n) \cdot x(p_0 + p_n)$$

$$+ C \cdot \sum_{p_n \in R} w(p_n) \cdot (x(p_0 + p_n) - \theta(p_0)x(p_0))$$

$$= \sum_{p_n \in R} w(p_n) \cdot x(p_0 + p_n) - C \cdot \theta(p_0) \cdot x(p_0) \sum_{p_n \in R} w(p_n). \quad (14)$$

4   Experiment

In this section, we verify the effectiveness of each module in our network, evaluate the whole structure on three challenging event-based recognition tasks and analyze the performance.

4.1   Dataset

We adopt three datasets on three tasks to show the effectiveness of our method, which are all captured in the real scenes.

DVS128Gesture. The DVS128Gesture [2] is a gesture recognition benchmark captured by the DVS128 event camera, which contains 1,342 instances with 11 kinds of hand and arm gestures from 122 volunteers. DVS128Gesture is captured under five different illumination conditions, including fluorescent led, fluorescent, natural, led, and lab, and the illumination intensity is significantly different. For enough comparison, we segment the raw event stream through a 500 ms sliding window and we get 13034 samples for training and 3546 for testing without the last class which corresponds to random gestures.

Table 1. Ablation study resutlts on DVSGesture dataset. S0: fluorescent led, S1: fluorescent, S2: natural, S3: led, S4: lab. We train each model on single illumination condition and test it on other four conditions. We report the mean accuracy on each condition. 'w/o' means without, 'w/' means with. (Acc %)

| | Model | Train | Test | | | |
		S4	S0	S1	S2	S3
Loss Functions	NSN(w/o Le) + FSN	91.9	85.8(-11.4)	84.6(-11.5)	67.0(-25.1)	70.3(-21.2)
	NSN(w/o Ln) + FSN	96.0	95.9(-1.3)	93.3(-2.8)	86.6(-5.5)	88.0(-3.5)
	NSN(w/o Lc) + FSN	96.2	95.9(-1.3)	93.2(-2.9)	88.2(-3.9)	89.4(-2.1)
Modules	NSN + I3D	96.2	92.6(-4.6)	90.3(-5.8)	75.5(-16.6)	82.0(-9.5)
	FSN(w/ CDC)	96.4	90.6(-6.6)	89.9(-6.2)	74.5(-17.6)	78.9(-12.6)
	FSN(w/ DCDC)	96.9	91.2(-6.0)	91.6(-4.5)	77.4(-14.7)	79.6(-11.9)
	FSN(w/ EAM)	97.3	95.3(-1.9)	94.0(-2.1)	82.2(-9.9)	85.9(-5.6)
	FSN(w/ EAM & DCDC)	96.9	95.3(-1.9)	95.0(-1.1)	84.1(-8.0)	87.6(-3.9)
	NSN + FSN	**97.3**	**97.2**	**96.1**	**92.1**	**91.5**

DAVIS346Gait and DAVIS346Character. To further evaluate the performance of our method on other recognition tasks, we perform experiments on gait recognition and character recognition tasks. However, the existing datasets for the two tasks are not captured under variant illuminations, thus not applicable for the evaluation. For example, the instances of DVS128Gait [43] are captured from different volunteers under two illumination conditions. To complement this, we present new gait (DAVIS346Gait) and character (DAVIS346-Character) datasets captured under four kinds of illumination conditions, of which the light intensity is 300lux, 120lux, 15lux, and 6lux. Specifically, DAVIS-346Gait contains 4,320 instances captured from 36 volunteers. And each volunteer is captured 30 times for each illumination condition. DAVIS346Character dataset is also captured under the same illumination condition, which contains 34,560 instances with 36 kinds of characters from 0–9 and A-Z. Due to space limitations, please refer to the supplemental material for more details about our data collecting process.

4.2 Implementation Details

The S2N is implemented in PyTorch and trained on an NVIDIA 3090 GPU. We use Adam [20] optimizer with learning rate periodically decaying from 1e-4 to 1e-6 and train each model for 25 epochs with a batch size of 16. The NSN will be pretrained firstly on the same training data and then the weight fixed. The λ_1 and λ_2 in Eq. (2) are set to 1 and 10 respectively to keep loss balance, and the C is 0.3. Note that FSN is adapted from different backbones in different tasks, specifically, I3D in gesture recognition, EV-Gait-IMG in gait recognition and ResNet34 in character recognition.

4.3 Ablation Study

We use the instances of *lab scene* in DVSGesture as training set and the other four scenes as test sets. Table 1 shows the results from different combinations of

Table 2. The results comparsion on DVS128Gesture dataset. We train each model on single illumination condition and test it on all five conditions. We report the mean accuracy and variance after four conditions test. (Acc %)

Methods	S0 → all	S1 → all	S2 → all	S3 → all	S4 → all
I3D	**94.1 ± 2.9**	92.7 ± 5.2	91.4 ± 2.3	93.0 ± 2.3	84.5 ± 9.1
ResNet34	82.6 ± 7.8	83.9 ± 8.1	85.7 ± 5.5	85.3 ± 2.6	72.2 ± 13.1
PointNet++	86.7 ± 2.3	87.6 ± 3.4	85.0 ± 2.7	87.2 ± 2.5	83.3 ± 5.8
EST	93.8 ± 2.2	94.0 ± 2.6	88.1 ± 3.9	**93.3 ± 5.1**	**85.3 ± 8.0**
VN + I3D	93.9 ± 1.5	**93.6 ± 2.0**	**92.1 ± 2.6**	92.1 ± 1.9	83.0 ± 8.3
IN + I3D	92.3 ± 4.6	93.7 ± 3.3	91.9 ± 1.8	92.6 ± 2.0	81.9 ± 9.8
VN + EST	91.3 ± 3.1	87.1 ± 5.2	87.6 ± 3.6	88.5 ± 2.9	79.1 ± 8.8
YN + EST	89.7 ± 4.6	90.8 ± 5.7	86.6 ± 2.5	90.0 ± 2.2	78.3 ± 14.3
S2N	97.2 ± 0.8	94.6 ± 1.4	95.3 ± 2.2	94.6 ± 1.4	94.7 ± 2.8

Table 3. The results on DAVIS346Gait dataset. L0, L1, L2 and L3 represent the illumination condition of 300lux, 120lux, 15lux and 6lux respectively. (Acc %)

Methods	L0 → all	L1 → all	L2 → all	L3 → all
EST	29.7	48.6	47.5	29.8
EV-Gait-3DGraph	25.9	29.2	21.7	19.6
VN + EV-Gait-IMG	68.6	56.8	**84.6**	51.6
YN + EV-Gait-IMG	**75.0**	**82.3**	75.0	**55.6**
VN + EST	51.8	49.1	47.3	26.5
YN + EST	39.5	63.6	58.2	26.2
S2N	88.4	94.3	96.3	90.3

loss functions in NSN training and modules in our network. The result shows that each loss term contributes to better recognition results, with the exposure loss being the most important. And the EAM(Evolution-aware Module) and DCDC(Density-adaptive CDC) can strengthen feature effectively and consistently improve performance. Combining with the NSN(Noise Suppression Network), our whole network performs best, which again validates the effectiveness of each proposed module under variant illumination scenes.

4.4   Comparisons Against SOTA Methods

We compare our S2N against SOTA methods on three challenging event-based recognition tasks.

Performance on DVSGesture. We compare our method with four SOTA recognition methods: I3D [8], ResNet34 [15], PointNet++ [40], and EST [13].

Table 4. The results on DAVIS346Character dataset. L0, L1, L2 and L3 represent the illumination condition of 300lux, 120lux, 15lux and 6lux respectively. (Acc %)

Methods	L0 → all	L1 → all	L2 → all	L3 → all
ResNet34	27.0	70.0	**90.5**	78.5
EST	29.4	**90.7**	90.0	**88.7**
VN + ResNet34	34.8	75.3	76.4	68.6
YN + ResNet34	30.9	66.7	63.3	52.1
VN + EST	**47.7**	83.2	86.0	77.2
YN + EST	34.7	51.4	58.9	44.1
S2N	78.9	91.4	95.7	92.1

Besides, to demonstrate the effectiveness of our NSN, we also compare our S2N with SOTA denoising methods: VN [42], and YN [11] and report the results of the denoising methods combined with recognition models, including I3D and EST. We train each model on a single illumination condition and examine the performance on the other four illuminations, respectively. The results are shown in Table 2. Our method is 1.9% higher than the SOTA method I3D in recognition accuracy. It demonstrates that our proposed S2N can effectively suppress the influence of noise and strengthen the robustness of feature representation. Besides, compared with the combination of event denoising and recognition methods, our improvement is at least 1.3 % which is also significant. Furthermore, the overall variance of our results is smaller than other methods, which demonstrates the stability of our method.

Performance on DAVIS346Gait. We compare our method with SOTA gait recognition methods: EV-Gait-3DGraph and EST, as well as EV-Gait-IMG and EST combined with VN and YN. We randomly sample 50% data in each class and use it as the training set and the rest data as the test set. We train our model on one illumination condition and test it on other illuminations. The results are shown in Table 3. As can be seen, our method achieves the best performance under all illumination conditions.

Performance on DAVIS346Character. We compare our method with two character recognition methods: ResNet34 [15] and EST [13], as well as ResNet34 and EST combined with VN and YN. Like in DVSGesture and DAVIS-346Gait, We train each model on one illumination condition and examine the performance on the other four illuminations, respectively. The results shown in Table 4 validate the excellent performance of our method.

The above results demonstrate that our proposed method can be generalized to various recognition tasks. Furthermore, our method can be directly used to improve the performance under variant illumination conditions without fine-tuning. While the performance of point-distribution-dependent methods, like

Table 5. Denoising methods comparison. To be fair, we uniformly use I3D as the feature extractor to compare the impact of the denoising algorithm on feature extraction. We train each model on a single illumination condition and test it on the other four illuminations. S0: fluorescent led, S1: fluorescent, S2: natural, S3: led, S4: lab. (Acc %)

Methods	Train	Test			
	S4	S0	S1	S2	S3
I3D	97.5	90.3	87.0	75.0	78.4
VN + I3D	94.2	86.5(−3.8)	86.8(−0.2)	74.1(−0.9)	76.2(−2.2)
YN + I3D	97.3	83.7(−6.6)	84.1(−2.9)	70.5(−4.5)	77.9(−0.5)
NSN + I3D	96.2	92.6(+2.3)	90.3(+3.3)	75.5(+0.5)	82.0(+3.6)

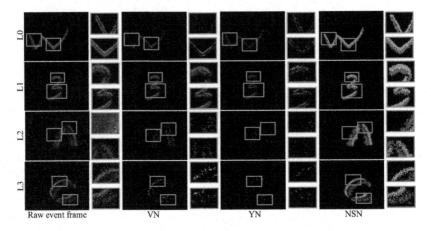

Fig. 5. Denoising comparison of different methods on four illumination conditions. L0, L1, L2 and L3 represent the illumination condition of 300lux, 120lux, 15lux and 6lux respectively. Compared with VN and YN, our NSN effectively removes the noise while preserving the original activity events.

EV-gait-3DGraph and Pointnet++, drop significantly because of the event distribution difference between variant illuminations.

4.5   Performance Analysis

Noise Suppression Results. To demonstrate the effectiveness of our proposed NSN, we compare our NSN with VN and YN qualitatively and quantitatively. From Fig. 5, we can observe that although VN can remove the noise to a certain extent, the enhanced results still have noise residual. While the YN algorithm can efficiently remove the unfavorable noise, the activity events are also obscured. Different from VN and YN, our NSN effectively removes the noise while keeping the original activity events unchanged. Furthermore, our NSN can also enhance

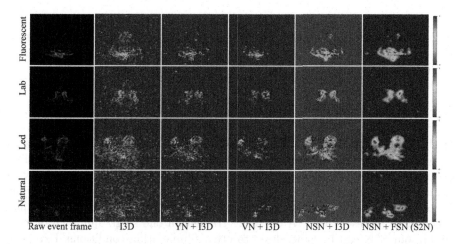

Fig. 6. The feature map visualization of different methods including I3D, YN + I3D, VN + I3D, NSN + I3D and our model S2N. The feature maps are from the output of the first layer of models. We select the features of the same channel, normalize, and then display them in pseudo color for visualization.

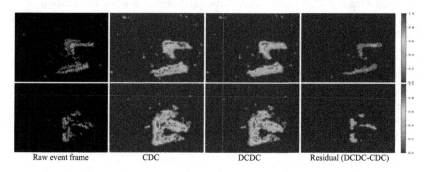

Fig. 7. The guiding role of motion evolution map.

the intensity, which boosts feature response and improve the recognition accuracy, as shown in Table 5. As the illumination scene changes, our NSN can stably remove the noise and enhance frame intensity to help to extract features, which shows our method's generalization ability under variant illuminations.

Feature Strengthen Results. We show the degraded feature and the feature enhancement results of different methods on four illumination conditions of DVS-Gesture in Fig. 6. Due to the influence of noise, the amplitude of feature response on discriminative regions is weakened and full of noise. The event denoising algorithm can suppress the influence of noise. However, these algorithms cannot significantly improve the amplitude of feature response. Compared with them, our method significantly improves the feature response amplitude on discriminative regions while suppressing the noise interference. Furthermore, we compare the feature representation between DCDC and CDC as in Fig. 7, which shows that the structural information will be well restored under the guidance of the motion evolution map.

5   Conclusion

In this paper, we propose a novel suppression-strengthen network for event-based recognition under variant illumination conditions. The NSN sub-network is first proposed to effectively reduce random noise and enhance the contrast of the event frame in an unsupervised manner. And then, the FSN sub-network progressively encodes the motion evolution information and aggregates the information into a complete representation. After being trained on one single illumination condition, our S2N can be generalized to other illumination conditions. Extensive experiments on different illumination conditions and three recognition tasks validate the effectiveness of our proposed method.

Acknowledgments. This work was supported by the National Key R&D Program of China under Grant 2020AAA0105702, National Natural Science Foundation of China (NSFC) under Grants U19B2038 and 61872327, the University Synergy Innovation Program of Anhui Province under Grants GXXT-2019–025.

References

1. Afshar, S., Ralph, N., Xu, Y., Tapson, J., van Schaik, A., Cohen, G.: Event-based feature extraction using adaptive selection thresholds. Sensors **20**(6), 1600 (2020)
2. Amir, A., et al.: A low power, fully event-based gesture recognition system. In: 2017 IEEE Conference on Computer Vision and Pattern Recognition (CVPR). IEEE, Honolulu, HI (2017)
3. Baldwin, R., Almatrafi, M., Asari, V., Hirakawa, K.: Event probability mask (epm) and event denoising convolutional neural network (edncnn) for neuromorphic cameras. In: Proceedings of the IEEE/CVF Conference on Computer Vision and Pattern Recognition, pp. 1701–1710 (2020)
4. Bardow, P., Davison, A.J., Leutenegger, S.: Simultaneous optical flow and intensity estimation from an event camera. In: 2016 IEEE Conference on Computer Vision and Pattern Recognition (CVPR) (2016)
5. Bi, Y., Chadha, A., Abbas, A., Bourtsoulatze, E., Andreopoulos, Y.: Graph-based object classification for neuromorphic vision sensing. In: 2019 IEEE/CVF International Conference on Computer Vision (ICCV). IEEE, Seoul, Korea (South) (2019)
6. Brandli, C., Berner, R., Yang, M., Liu, S.C., Delbruck, T.: A 240× 180 130 db 3 μs latency global shutter spatiotemporal vision sensor. IEEE J. Solid-State Circ. **49**(10), 2333–2341 (2014)
7. Calabrese, E., et al.: DHP19: dynamic Vision Sensor 3D Human Pose Dataset. In: 2019 IEEE/CVF Conference on Computer Vision and Pattern Recognition Workshops (CVPRW). IEEE, Long Beach, CA, USA (2019)

8. Carreira, J., Zisserman, A.: Quo vadis, action recognition? a new model and the kinetics dataset. In: proceedings of the IEEE Conference on Computer Vision and Pattern Recognition, pp. 6299–6308 (2017)

9. Chen, J., Wang, Y., Cao, Y., Wu, F., Zha, Z.J.: Progressivemotionseg: mutually reinforced framework for event-based motion segmentation. arXiv preprint arXiv:2203.11732 (2022)

10. Clady, X., Maro, J.M., Barré, S., Benosman, R.B.: A motion-based feature for event-based pattern recognition. Front. Neurosci. 10, 594 (2017)

11. Feng, Y., Lv, H., Liu, H., Zhang, Y., Xiao, Y., Han, C.: Event density based denoising method for dynamic vision sensor. Appl. Sci. 10(6), 2024 (2020)

12. Gallego, G., et al.: Event-based vision: a survey. IEEE Trans. Pattern Anal. Mach. Intell. 44(1), 154–180 (2020)

13. Gehrig, D., Loquercio, A., Derpanis, K., Scaramuzza, D.: End-to-end learning of representations for asynchronous event-based data. In: 2019 IEEE/CVF International Conference on Computer Vision (ICCV). IEEE, Seoul, Korea (South) (2019)

14. Guo, S., et al.: A noise filter for dynamic vision sensors using self-adjusting threshold. arXiv preprint arXiv:2004.04079 (2020)

15. He, K., Zhang, X., Ren, S., Sun, J.: Deep Residual Learning for Image Recognition. arXiv preprint arXiv:1512.03385 (2015)

16. Hu, Y., Liu, S.C., Delbruck, T.: v2e: from video frames to realistic DVS events. In: Proceedings of the IEEE/CVF Conference on Computer Vision and Pattern Recognition, pp. 1312–1321 (2021)

17. Huang, Y., Zha, Z.J., Fu, X., Zhang, W.: Illumination-invariant person re-identification. In: Proceedings of the 27th ACM International Conference on Multimedia, pp. 365–373 (2019)

18. Khodamoradi, A., Kastner, R.: O(N)-Space spatiotemporal filter for reducing noise in neuromorphic vision sensors. IEEE Trans. Emerg. Top. Comput. 9, 15–23 (2021)

19. Kim, J., Bae, J., Park, G., Zhang, D., Kim, Y.M.: N-imagenet: Towards robust, fine-grained object recognition with event cameras. In: Proceedings of the IEEE/CVF International Conference on Computer Vision (ICCV), pp. 2146–2156 (2021)

20. Kingma, D.P., Ba, J.: Adam: a method for stochastic optimization. arXiv preprint arXiv:1412.6980 (2014)

21. Lagorce, X., Orchard, G., Galluppi, F., Shi, B.E., Benosman, R.B.: HOTS: a hierarchy of event-based time-surfaces for pattern recognition. IEEE Trans. Pattern Anal. Mach. Intell. 39(7), 1346–1359 (2017)

22. Lee, J.H., et al.: Real-time gesture interface based on event-driven processing from stereo silicon retinas. IEEE Trans. Neural Netw. Learn. Syst. 25(12), 2250–2263 (2014)

23. Li, C., et al.: Design of an RGBW color VGA rolling and global shutter dynamic and active-pixel vision sensor. In: 2015 IEEE International Symposium on Circuits and Systems (ISCAS). IEEE, Lisbon, Portugal (2015)

24. Li, Y., et al.: Graph-based asynchronous event processing for rapid object recognition. In: Proceedings of the IEEE/CVF International Conference on Computer Vision (ICCV), pp. 934–943 (2021)

25. Lichtsteiner, P., Posch, C., Delbruck, T.: A 128× 128 120 dB 15 μs latency asynchronous temporal contrast vision sensor. IEEE J. Solid-state Cir. 43(2), 566-576 (2008)

26. Lin, M., Chen, Q., Yan, S.: Network in network. arXiv preprint arXiv:1312.4400 (2013)

27. Liu, H., Brandli, C., Li, C., Liu, S.C., Delbruck, T.: Design of a spatiotemporal correlation filter for event-based sensors. In: 2015 IEEE International Symposium on Circuits and Systems (ISCAS). IEEE (2015)
28. Maqueda, A.I., Loquercio, A., Gallego, G., Garcia, N., Scaramuzza, D.: Event-Based Vision Meets Deep Learning on Steering Prediction for Self-Driving Cars. In: 2018 IEEE/CVF Conference on Computer Vision and Pattern Recognition. IEEE, Salt Lake City, UT (2018)
29. Mitrokhin, A., Fermüller, C., Parameshwara, C., Aloimonos, Y.: Event-based moving object detection and tracking. In: 2018 IEEE/RSJ International Conference on Intelligent Robots and Systems (IROS), pp. 1–9. IEEE (2018)
30. Moeys, D.P., et al.: Steering a predator robot using a mixed frame/event-driven convolutional neural network. 2016 Second International Conference on Event-based Control, Communication, and Signal Processing (EBCCSP) (2016)
31. Nozaki, Y., Delbruck, T.: Temperature and parasitic photocurrent effects in dynamic vision sensors. IEEE Trans. Electr. Devices 64(8), 3239–3245 (2017)
32. Padala, V., Basu, A., Orchard, G.: A noise filtering algorithm for event-based asynchronous change detection image sensors on TrueNorth and its implementation on TrueNorth. Front. Neurosci. 12, 118 (2018)
33. Perez-Carrasco, J.A., et al.: Mapping from frame-driven to frame-free event-driven vision systems by low-rate rate coding and coincidence processing-application to feedforward convNets. IEEE Trans. Pattern Anal. Mach. Intell. 35(11), 2706–2719 (2013)
34. Ramesh, B., Yang, H., Orchard, G., Le Thi, N.A., Zhang, S., Xiang, C.: DART: distribution aware retinal transform for event-based cameras. IEEE Trans. Pattern Anal. Mach. Intell. 42(11), 2767–2780 (2020)
35. Shrestha, S.B., Orchard, G.: SLAYER: spike layer error reassignment in time. In: Advances in Neural Information Processing Systems, vol. 31. Curran Associates, Inc. (2018)
36. Sironi, A., Brambilla, M., Bourdis, N., Lagorce, X., Benosman, R.: Hats: histograms of averaged time surfaces for robust event-based object classification. In: Proceedings of the IEEE Conference on Computer Vision and Pattern Recognition, pp. 1731–1740 (2018)
37. Stromatias, E., Neil, D., Galluppi, F., Pfeiffer, M., Liu, S.C., Furber, S.: Scalable energy-efficient, low-latency implementations of trained spiking Deep Belief Networks on SpiNNaker. In: 2015 International Joint Conference on Neural Networks (IJCNN) (2015)
38. Szegedy, C., Vanhoucke, V., Ioffe, S., Shlens, J., Wojna, Z.: Rethinking the inception architecture for computer vision. In: Proceedings of the IEEE conference on computer vision and pattern recognition, pp. 2818–2826 (2016)
39. Tan, G., Wang, Y., Han, H., Cao, Y., Wu, F., Zha, Z.J.: Multi-grained spatio-temporal features perceived network for event-based lip-reading. In: Proceedings of the IEEE/CVF Conference on Computer Vision and Pattern Recognition (CVPR), pp. 20094–20103 (2022)
40. Wang, Q., Zhang, Y., Yuan, J., Lu, Y.: Space-time event clouds for gesture recognition: from rgb cameras to event cameras. In: 2019 IEEE Winter Conference on Applications of Computer Vision (WACV). IEEE, Waikoloa Village, HI, USA (2019)
41. Wang, Y., et al.: Progressive retinex: mutually reinforced illumination-noise perception network for low-light image enhancement. In: Proceedings of the 27th ACM International Conference on Multimedia, pp. 2015–2023 (2019)

42. Wang, Y., et al.: EV-Gait: event-based robust gait recognition using dynamic vision sensors. In: 2019 IEEE/CVF Conference on Computer Vision and Pattern Recognition (CVPR). IEEE, Long Beach, CA, USA (2019)
43. Wang, Y., et al.: Event-stream representation for human gaits identification using deep neural networks. IEEE Trans. Pattern Anal. Mach. Intell. **44**(7), 3436–3449 (2021)
44. Weng, W., Zhang, Y., Xiong, Z.: Event-based video reconstruction using transformer. In: Proceedings of the IEEE/CVF International Conference on Computer Vision (ICCV), pp. 2563–2572 (2021)
45. Yang, J., et al.: Modeling point clouds with self-attention and gumbel subset sampling. In: Proceedings of the IEEE/CVF Conference on Computer Vision and Pattern Recognition, pp. 3323–3332 (2019)
46. Yu, Z., et al.: Searching central difference convolutional networks for face antispoofing. In: Proceedings of the IEEE/CVF Conference on Computer Vision and Pattern Recognition, pp. 5295–5305 (2020)
47. Zhang, J., Yang, X., Fu, Y., Wei, X., Yin, B., Dong, B.: Object tracking by jointly exploiting frame and event domain. In: Proceedings of the IEEE/CVF International Conference on Computer Vision, pp. 13043–13052 (2021)
48. Zhu, A.Z., Yuan, L., Chaney, K., Daniilidis, K.: Unsupervised event-based learning of optical flow, depth, and egomotion. In: 2019 IEEE/CVF Conference on Computer Vision and Pattern Recognition (CVPR). IEEE, Long Beach, CA, USA (2019)
49. Zou, S., et al.: EventHPE: event-based 3D human pose and shape estimation. In: Proceedings of the IEEE/CVF International Conference on Computer Vision (ICCV), pp. 10996–11005 (2021)

CMD: Self-supervised 3D Action Representation Learning with Cross-Modal Mutual Distillation

Yunyao Mao[1], Wengang Zhou[1,2]([✉]), Zhenbo Lu[2], Jiajun Deng[1], and Houqiang Li[1,2]([✉])

[1] CAS Key Laboratory of Technology in GIPAS, EEIS Department, University of Science and Technology of China, Hefei, China
myy2016@mail.ustc.edu.cn, {zhwg,dengjj,lihq}@ustc.edu.cn
[2] Institute of Artificial Intelligence, Hefei Comprehensive National Science Center, Hefei, China
luzhenbo@iai.ustc.edu.cn

Abstract. In 3D action recognition, there exists rich complementary information between skeleton modalities. Nevertheless, how to model and utilize this information remains a challenging problem for self-supervised 3D action representation learning. In this work, we formulate the cross-modal interaction as a bidirectional knowledge distillation problem. Different from classic distillation solutions that transfer the knowledge of a fixed and pre-trained teacher to the student, in this work, the knowledge is continuously updated and bidirectionally distilled between modalities. To this end, we propose a new **Cross-modal Mutual Distillation (CMD)** framework with the following designs. On the one hand, the neighboring similarity distribution is introduced to model the knowledge learned in each modality, where the relational information is naturally suitable for the contrastive frameworks. On the other hand, asymmetrical configurations are used for teacher and student to stabilize the distillation process and to transfer high-confidence information between modalities. By derivation, we find that the cross-modal positive mining in previous works can be regarded as a degenerated version of our CMD. We perform extensive experiments on NTU RGB+D 60, NTU RGB+D 120, and PKU-MMD II datasets. Our approach outperforms existing self-supervised methods and sets a series of new records. The code is available at: https://github.com/maoyunyao/CMD.

Keywords: Self-supervised 3D action recognition · Contrastive learning

1 Introduction

Human action recognition, one of the fundamental problems in computer vision, has a wide range of applications in many downstream tasks, such as behavior

---

Supplementary Information The online version contains supplementary material available at https://doi.org/10.1007/978-3-031-20062-5_42.

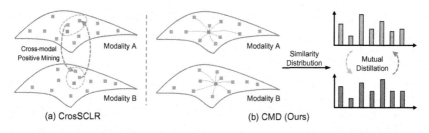

Fig. 1. CrosSCLR [23] vs. CMD (Ours). Given handful negative samples, CrosSCLR performs cross-modal positive mining according to the cosine similarity between embeddings. The nearest neighbor of the positive query in modality A will serve as an additional positive sample in modality B, and vice versa. In our approach, we reformulate cross-modal interaction as a bidirectional knowledge distillation problem, with similarity distribution that models the modality-specific knowledge.

analysis, human-machine interaction, virtual reality, *etc.*. Recently, with the advancement of human pose estimation algorithms [3,14,59], skeleton-based 3D human action recognition has attracted increasing attention for its light-weight and background-robust characteristics. However, fully-supervised 3D action recognition [7,13,20,24,25,30,44,46,47,62–64] requires large amounts of well-annotated skeleton data for training, which is rather labor-intensive to acquire. In this paper, we focus on the self-supervised settings, aiming to avoid the laborious workload of manual annotation for 3D action representation learning.

To learn robust and discriminative representation, many celebrated pretexts like motion prediction, jigsaw puzzle recognition, and masked reconstruction have been extensively studied in early works [27,32–34,50,65]. Recently, the contrastive learning frameworks [4,17,35] have been introduced to the self-supervised 3D action recognition community [27,41]. It achieves great success thanks to the capability of learning discriminative high-level semantic features. However, there still exist unsolved problems when applying contrastive learning on skeletons. On the one hand, the success of contrastive learning heavily relies on performing data augmentation [4], but the skeletons from different videos are unanimously considered as negative samples. Given the limited action categories, it would be unreasonable to just ignore potential similar instances, since they may belong to the same category as the positive one. On the other hand, cross-modal interactive learning is largely overlooked in early contrastive learning-based attempts [27,41], yet integrating multimodal information [8,11,12,26,45,56] is the key to improving the performance of 3D action recognition.

To tackle these problems, CrosSCLR [23] turns to cross-modal positive mining (see Fig. 1 (a)) and sample reweighting. Though effective, it suffers the following limitations. Firstly, the positive sample mining requires reliable preliminary knowledge, thus the representation in each modality needs to be optimized independently in advance, leading to a sophisticated two-stage training process. Secondly, the contrastive context, defined as the similarity between the positive query and negative embeddings, is treated as individual weights of samples in complementary modalities to participate in the optimization process. Such implicit knowledge exchange lacks a holistic grasp of the rich contextual information. Besides, the cross-modal consistency is also not explicitly guaranteed.

In this work, we go beyond heuristic positive sample mining and reformulate cross-modal interaction as a general bidirectional knowledge distillation [18] problem. As shown in Fig. 1 (b), in the proposed Cross-modal Mutual Distillation (CMD) framework, the neighboring similarity distribution is first extracted in each modality. It describes the relationship of the sample embedding with respect to its nearest neighbors in the customized feature space. Compared with individual features [18] or logits [42], such relational information is naturally suitable for modeling the knowledge learned with contrastive frameworks. Based on the relational information, bidirectional knowledge distillation between each two modalities is performed via explicit cross-modal consistency constraints. Since the representation in each skeleton modality is trained from scratch and there is no intuitive teacher-student relationship between modalities, embeddings from the momentum updated key encoder along with a smaller temperature are used for knowledge modeling on the teacher side, so as to stabilize the distillation process and highlight the high-confidence information in each modality.

Compared to previous works, the advantages of our approach are three-fold: i) Instead of heuristically reweighting training samples, the contextual information in contrastive learning is treated as a whole to model the modality-specific knowledge, explicitly ensuring the cross-modal consistency during distillation. ii) Unlike cross-modal positive sample mining, our approach does not heavily rely on the initial representation, thus is free of the sophisticated two-stage training. This largely benefits from the probabilistic knowledge modeling strategy. Moreover, the positive mining is also mathematically proved to be a special case of the proposed cross-modal distillation mechanism under extreme settings. iii) The proposed CMD is carefully designed to be well integrated into the existing contrastive framework with almost no extra computational overhead introduced.

We perform extensive experiments on three prevalent benchmark datasets: NTU RGB+D 60 [43], NTU RGB+D 120 [28], and PKU-MMD II [9]. Our approach achieves state-of-the-art results on all of them under all evaluation protocols. It's worth noting that the proposed cross-modal mutual distillation is easily implemented in a few lines of code. We hope this simple yet effective approach will serve as a strong baseline for future research.

2   Related Work

Self-supervised Representation Learning: Self-supervised learning methods can be roughly divided into two categories: generative and contrastive [29]. Generative methods [2,16,36] try to reconstruct the original input to learn meaningful latent representation. Contrastive learning [4,17,35] aims to learn feature representation via instance discrimination. It pulls positive pairs closer and pushes negative pairs away. Since no labels are available during self-supervised contrastive learning, two different augmented versions of the same sample are treated as a positive pair, and samples from different instances are considered to be negative. In MoCo [17] and MoCo v2 [5], the negative samples are taken from previous batches and stored in a queue-based memory bank. In contrast, SimCLR [4] and MoCo v3 [6] rely on a larger batch size to provide sufficient negative samples. Similar to the contrastive context in [23], the neighboring similarity in this paper is defined as the normalized product between positive embedding and its neighboring anchors. Our goal is to transfer such modality-specific information between skeleton modalities to facilitate better contrastive 3D action representation learning.

Self-supervised 3D Action Recognition: Many previous works have been proposed to perform self-supervised 3D action representation learning. In LongT GAN [65], an autoencoder-based model along with an additional adversarial training strategy are proposed. Following the generative paradigm, it learns latent representation via sequential reconstruction. Similarly, P&C [50] trains an encoder-decoder network to both predict and cluster skeleton sequences. To learn features that are more robust and separable, the authors also propose strategies to weaken the decoder, laying more burdens on the encoder. Different from previously mentioned methods that merely adopt a single reconstruction task, MS^{2}L [27] integrates multiple pretext tasks to learn better representation. In recent attempts [23,41,53,54], momentum encoder-based contrastive learning is introduced and better performance is achieved. Among them, CrosSCLR [23] is the first to perform cross-modal knowledge mining. It finds potential positives and re-weights training samples with the contrastive contexts from different skeleton modalities. However, the positive mining performed in CrosSCLR requires reliable initial representation, two-stage training is indispensable. Differently, in this paper, a more general knowledge distillation mechanism is introduced to perform cross-modal information interaction. Besides, the positive mining performed in CrosSCLR can be regarded as a special case of our approach.

Similarity-based Knowledge Distillation: Pairwise similarity has been shown to be useful information in relational knowledge distillation [38,40,55]. In PKT [39], CompRess [1], and SEED [15], similarities of each sample with respect to a set of anchors are converted into a probability distribution, which models the structural information of the data. After that, knowledge distillation is performed by training the student to mimic the probability distribution of the teacher. Recently, contextual similarity information has also shown great potential in image retrieval [37,58] and representation learning [22,51]. Our approach is partially inspired by these works. Differently, the cross-modal mutual distillation in our approach is designed to answer the question of *how to transfer the biased knowledge between complementary modalities during 3D action pre-training.*

3   Method

3.1   Framework Overview

By consolidating the idea of leveraging complementary information from cross-modal inputs to improve 3D action representation learning, we design the Cross-modal Mutual Distillation (CMD) framework. As shown in Fig. 2, the proposed CMD consists of two key components: Single-modal Contrastive Learning (SCL) and Cross-modal Mutual Distillation (CMD). Given multiple skeleton modalities (*e.g.* joint, motion, and bone) as input, SCL is applied to each of them to learn customized 3D action representation. Meanwhile, in CMD, the knowledge learned by SCL is modeled by the neighboring similarity distributions, which describe the relationship between the sample embedding and its nearest neighbors. Cross-modal knowledge distillation is then performed by bidirectionally minimizing the KL divergence between the distributions corresponding to each modality. SCL and CMD run synchronously and cooperatively so that each modality learns more comprehensive representation.

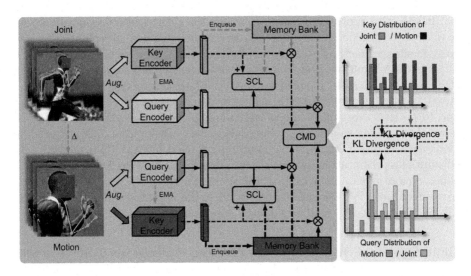

Fig. 2. The overall pipeline of the proposed framework. It contains two modules, Single-modal Contrastive Learning (SCL) and Cross-modal Mutual Distillation (CMD). Given multiple skeleton modalities (*e.g.* joint and motion) as input, the SCL module performs self-supervised contrastive learning in each modality and the CMD module simultaneously transfers the learned knowledge between modalities. SCL and CMD work collaboratively so that each modality learns more comprehensive representation.

3.2   Single-modal Contrastive Learning

In this section, we revisit the single-modal contrastive learning as the preliminary of our approach, which has been widely adopted in many tasks like image/video recognition [10,21,49] and correspondence learning [57]. In self-supervised 3D action recognition, previous works like AS-CAL [41], CrosSCLR [23], ISC [53], and AimCLR [54] also take the contrastive method MoCo v2 [5] as their baseline.

Given a single-modal skeleton sequence x, we first perform data augmentation to obtain two different views x_q and x_k (query and key). Then, two encoders are adopted to map the positive pair x_q and x_k into feature embeddings $z_q = E_q(x_q, \theta_q)$ and $z_k = E_k(x_k, \theta_k)$, where E_q and E_k denote query encoder and key encoder, respectively. θ_q and θ_k are the learnable parameters of the two encoders. Note that in MoCo v2, the key encoder is not trained by gradient descent but the momentum updated version of the query encoder: $\theta_k \leftarrow \alpha\theta_k + (1 - \alpha)\theta_q$, where α is a momentum coefficient that controls the updating speed. During self-supervised pre-training, the noise contrastive estimation loss InfoNCE [35] is used to perform instance discrimination, which is computed as follows:

$$\mathcal{L}_{\mathrm{SCL}} = -\log \frac{\exp(z_q^\top z_k/\tau_c)}{\exp(z_q^\top z_k/\tau_c) + \sum_{i=1}^{N} \exp\left(z_q^\top m_i/\tau_c\right)}, \tag{1}$$

where τ_c is a temperature hyper-parameter [18] that scales the distribution of instances and m_i is the key embedding of negative sample. N is the size of a queue-based memory bank $\mathbf{M}$ where all the negative key embeddings are stored. After the training of the current mini-batch, z_k is enqueued as a new negative key embedding and the oldest embeddings in the memory bank are dequeued.

Under the supervision of the InfoNCE loss, the encoder is forced to learn representation that is invariant to data augmentations, thereby focusing on semantic information shared between positive pairs. Nevertheless, the learned representation is often modally biased, making it difficult to account for all data characteristics. Though it can be alleviated by test-time ensembling, several times the running overhead will be introduced. Moreover, the inherent limitations of the learned representation in each modality still exist. Therefore, during self-supervised pre-training, cross-modal interaction is essential.

3.3 Cross-modal Mutual Distillation

While SCL is performed within each skeleton modality, the proposed CMD models the learned knowledge and transfers it between modalities. This enables each modality to receive knowledge from other perspectives, thereby alleviating the modal bias of the learned representation. Based on MoCo v2, CMD can be easily implemented in a few lines of code, as shown in Algorithm 1.

Knowledge Modeling: To perform knowledge distillation between modalities, we first need to model the knowledge learned in each modality in a proper way. It needs to take advantage of the existing contrastive learning framework to avoid introducing excessive computational overhead. Moreover, since the distillation is performed cross-modally for self-supervised learned knowledge, conventional methods that rely on individual features/logits are no longer applicable.

Inspired by recent relational knowledge distillation works [38,40,55], we utilize the pairwise relationship between samples for modality-specific knowledge modeling. Given an embedding z and a set of anchors $\{n_i\}_{i=1,2,\cdots,K}$, we compute the similarities between them as $\text{sim}(z, n_i) = z^\top n_i, i = 1, 2, \cdots, K$.

In the MoCo v2 [5] framework, there are a handful of negative embeddings stored in the memory bank. We can easily obtain the required anchors without additional model inference. Note that if all the negative embeddings are used as anchors, the set $\{z^\top m_i\}_{i=1,2,\cdots,N}$ is exactly the contrastive context defined in [23]. In our approach, we select the top K nearest neighbors of z as the anchors. The resulting pairwise similarities are further converted into probability distributions with a temperature hyper-parameter τ :

$$p_i(z, \tau) = \frac{\exp(z^\top n_i/\tau)}{\sum_{j=1}^{K} \exp(z^\top n_j/\tau)}, i = 1, 2, \cdots, K. \tag{2}$$

The obtained $\boldsymbol{p}(z, \tau) = \{p_i(z, \tau)\}_{i=1,2,\cdots,K}$ describes the distribution characteristic around the embedding z in the customized feature space of each modality.

Knowledge Distillation: Based on the aforementioned probability distributions, an intuitive way to perform knowledge distillation would be to directly establish consistency constraints between skeleton modalities. Different from previous knowledge distillation approaches that transfer the knowledge of a fixed and well-trained teacher model to the student, in our approach, the knowledge is continuously updated during self-supervised pre-training and each modality acts as both student and teacher.

To this end, based on the contrastive framework, we make two customized designs in the proposed approach: i) Different embeddings are used for teacher and student. As shown in Fig. 2, in MoCo v2 [5], two augmented views of the same sample are encoded into query z_q and key z_k, respectively. In our approach, the key distribution obtained in one modality is used to guide the learning of query distribution in other modalities, so that knowledge is transferred accordingly. Specifically, for the key embedding z_k^a from modality A and the query embedding z_q^b from modality B, we select the top K nearest neighbors of z_k^a as anchors and compute the similarity distributions as $\boldsymbol{p}(z_q^b, \tau)$ and $\boldsymbol{p}(z_k^a, \tau)$ according to Eq. 2. Knowledge distillation from modality A to modality B is performed by minimizing the following KL divergence:

$$\text{KL}\big(\boldsymbol{p}(z_k^a, \tau) \| \boldsymbol{p}(z_q^b, \tau)\big) = \sum_{i=1}^{K} p_i(z_k^a, \tau) \cdot \log \frac{p_i(z_k^a, \tau)}{p_i(z_q^b, \tau)}. \tag{3}$$

Since the key encoder is not trained with gradient, the teacher is not affected during unidirectional knowledge distillation. Moreover, the momentum updated key encoder provides more stable knowledge for the student to learn. ii) Asymmetric temperatures τ_t and τ_s are employed for teacher and student, respectively. Considering that there is no intuitive teacher-student relationship between modalities, a smaller temperature is applied for the teacher in CMD to emphasize the high-confidence information, as discussed in [52].

Algorithm 1. Pseudocode of the CMD module in a PyTorch-like style.

```
1   # z_q_a, z_q_b, z_k_a, z_k_b: query/key embeddings in modality A/B (BxC)
2   # queue_a, queue_b: queue of N keys in modality A/B (CxN)
3   # tau_s, tau_t: temperatures for student/teacher (scalars)
4
5   l_a, lk_a = torch.mm(z_q_a, queue_a), torch.mm(z_k_a, queue_a) # compute similarities
6   l_b, lk_b = torch.mm(z_q_b, queue_b), torch.mm(z_k_b, queue_b)
7
8   lk_a_topk, idx_a = torch.topk(lk_a, K, dim=-1) # select top K nearest neighbors
9   lk_b_topk, idx_b = torch.topk(lk_b, K, dim=-1)
10
11  loss_cmd = loss_kld(torch.gather(l_b, -1, idx_a) / tau_s, lk_a_topk / tau_t) # A to B
12           + loss_kld(torch.gather(l_a, -1, idx_b) / tau_s, lk_b_topk / tau_t) # B to A
13
14  def loss_kld(inputs, targets):
15      inputs, targets = F.log_softmax(inputs, dim=1), F.softmax(targets, dim=1)
16      return F.kl_div(inputs, targets, reduction='batchmean')
```

Since the knowledge distillation works bidirectionally, given two modalities A and B, the loss function for CMD is formulated as follows:

$$\mathcal{L}_{\mathrm{CMD}} = \mathrm{KL}\big(p(z_k^a, \tau_t) \| p(z_q^b, \tau_s)\big) + \mathrm{KL}\big(p(z_k^b, \tau_t) \| p(z_q^a, \tau_s)\big). \tag{4}$$

Note that Eq. 4 can be easily extended if more modalities are involved. The final loss function in our approach is the combination of $\mathcal{L}_{\mathrm{SCL}}$ and $\mathcal{L}_{\mathrm{CMD}}$:

$$\mathcal{L} = \mathcal{L}_{\mathrm{SCL}}^a + \mathcal{L}_{\mathrm{SCL}}^b + \mathcal{L}_{\mathrm{CMD}}, \tag{5}$$

where the superscripts a and b denote modality A and B, respectively.

3.4 Relationship with Positive Mining

Cross-modal Positive Mining: Cross-modal positive mining is the most important component in CrosSCLR [23], where the most similar negative sample is selected to boost the positive sets for contrastive learning in complementary modalities. The contrastive loss for modality B is reformulated as:

$$
\begin{aligned}
\mathcal{L}_{\mathrm{CPM}}^b &= -\log \frac{\exp(z_q^{b\top} z_k^b/\tau_c) + \exp(z_q^{b\top} m_u^b/\tau_c)}{\exp(z_q^{b\top} z_k^b/\tau_c) + \sum_{i=1}^N \exp(z_q^{b\top} m_i^b/\tau_c)} \\
&= \mathcal{L}_{\mathrm{SCL}}^b - \log \frac{\exp(z_q^{b\top} m_u^b/\tau_c)}{\exp(z_q^{b\top} z_k^b/\tau_c) + \sum_{i=1}^N \exp(z_q^{b\top} m_i^b/\tau_c)},
\end{aligned} \tag{6}
$$

where u is the index of most similar negative sample in modality A.
CMD with $\tau_t = 0$ and $K = N$: Setting temperature $\tau_t = 0$ and $K = N$, the key distribution $p(z_k^a, \tau_t)$ in Eq. 4 will be an one-hot vector with the only 1 at index u, and thus the loss works on modality B will be like:

$$
\begin{aligned}
\mathcal{L}^b &= \mathcal{L}_{\mathrm{SCL}}^b + \mathcal{L}_{\mathrm{CMD}}^b \\
&= \mathcal{L}_{\mathrm{SCL}}^b + \sum_{i=1}^N p_i(z_k^a, 0) \cdot \log \frac{p_i(z_k^a, 0)}{p_i(z_q^b, \tau_s)}
\end{aligned} \tag{7}
$$

$$= \mathcal{L}_{\text{SCL}}^b + 1 \cdot \log \frac{1}{p_u(z_q^b, \tau_s)}$$

$$= \mathcal{L}_{\text{SCL}}^b - \log \frac{\exp(z_q^{b^\top} m_u^b / \tau_s)}{\sum_{j=1}^N \exp(z_q^{b^\top} m_j^b / \tau_s)}.$$

We can find that the loss $\mathcal{L}_{\text{CMD}}^b$ is essentially doing contrastive learning in modality B with the positive sample mined by modality A. Compared with Eq. 6, the only difference is that when the mined m_u^b is taken as the positive sample, the key embedding z_k^b is excluded from the denominator. The same result holds for modality A. Thus we draw a conclusion that the cross-modal positive mining performed in CrosSCLR [23] can be regarded as a special case of our approach with the temperature of teacher $\tau_t = 0$ and the number of neighbors $K = N$.

4   Experiments

4.1   Implementation Details

Network Architecture: In our approach, we adopt a 3-layer Bidirectional GRU (BiGRU) as the base-encoder, which has a hidden dimension of 1024. Before the encoder, we additionally add a Batch Normalization [19] layer to stabilize the training process. Each skeleton sequence is represented in a two-actor manner, where the second actor is set to zeros if only one actor exists. The sequences are further resized to a temporal length of 64 frames.

Self-supervised Pre-training: During pre-training, we adopt MoCo v2 [5] to perform single-modal contrastive learning. The temperature hyper-parameter in the InfoNCE [35] loss is 0.07. In cross-modal mutual distillation, the temperatures for teacher and student are set to 0.05 and 0.1, respectively. The number of neighbors K is set to 8192. The SGD optimizer is employed with a momentum of 0.9 and a weight decay of 0.0001. The batch size is set to 64 and the initial learning rate is 0.01. For NTU RGB+D 60 [43] and NTU RGB+D 120 [28] datasets, the model is trained for 450 epochs, the learning rate is reduced to 0.001 after 350 epochs, and the size of the memory bank N is 16384. For PKU-MMD II [9] dataset, the total epochs are increased to 1000, and the learning rate drops at epoch 800. We adopt the same skeleton augmentations as ISC [53].

4.2   Datasets and Metrics

NTU RGB+D 60 [43]: NTU-RGB+D 60 (NTU-60) is a large-scale multi-modality action recognition dataset which is captured by three Kinect v2 cameras. It contains 60 action categories and 56,880 sequences. The actions are performed by 40 different subjects (actors). In this paper, we adopt its 3D skeleton data for experiments. Specifically, each human skeleton contains 25 body joints, and each joint is represented as 3D coordinates. Two evaluation protocols

Table 1. Performance comparison on NTU-60, NTU-120, and PKU-II in terms of the linear evaluation protocol. Our approach achieves state-of-the-art performance on all of them, both when taking single skeleton modality as input and when ensembling multiple modalities during evaluation. The prefix "3s-" denotes multi-modal ensembling.

Method	Modality	NTU-60		NTU-120		PKU-II
		x-sub	x-view	x-sub	x-set	x-sub
LongT GAN [65]	Joint only	39.1	48.1	–	–	26.0
MS^{2}L [27]	Joint only	52.6	–	–	–	27.6
P&C [50]	Joint only	50.7	76.3	42.7	41.7	25.5
AS-CAL [41]	Joint only	58.5	64.8	48.6	49.2	–
SeBiReNet [33]	Joint only	–	79.7	–	–	–
AimCLR [54]	Joint only	74.3	79.7	–	–	–
ISC [53]	Joint only	76.3	85.2	67.1	67.9	36.0
CrosSCLR-B	Joint only	77.3	85.1	67.1	68.6	41.9
CMD (Ours)	Joint only	**79.8**	**86.9**	**70.3**	**71.5**	**43.0**
3s-CrosSCLR [23]	Joint+Motion+Bone	77.8	83.4	67.9	66.7	21.2
3s-AimCLR [54]	Joint+Motion+Bone	78.9	83.8	68.2	68.8	39.5
3s-CrosSCLR-B	Joint+Motion+Bone	82.1	89.2	71.6	73.4	51.0
3s-CMD (Ours)	Joint+Motion+Bone	**84.1**	**90.9**	**74.7**	**76.1**	**52.6**

are recommended by the authors: cross-subject (x-sub) and cross-view (x-view). For x-sub, action sequences performed by half of the 40 subjects are used as training samples and the rest as test samples. For x-view, the training samples are captured by camera 2 and 3 and the test samples are from camera 1.

NTU RGB+D 120 [28]: Compared with NTU-60, NTU-RGB+D 120 (NTU-120) extends the action categories from 60 to 120, with 114,480 skeleton sequences in total. The number of subjects is also increased from 40 to 106. Moreover, a new evaluation protocol named cross-setup (x-set) is proposed as a substitute for x-view. Specifically, the sequences are divided into 32 different setups according to the camera distances and background, with half of the 32 setups (even-numbered) used for training and the rest for testing.

PKU-MMD [9]: PKU-MMD is a new benchmark for multi-modality 3D human action detection. It can also be used for action recognition tasks [27]. PKU-MMD has two phases, where Phase II is extremely challenging since more noise is introduced by large view variation. In this work, we evaluate the proposed method on Phase II (PKU-II) under the widely used cross-subject evaluation protocol, with 5,332 skeleton sequences for training and 1,613 for testing.

Evaluation Metrics: We report the top-1 accuracy for all datasets.

Table 2. Performance comparison on NTU-60 and NTU-120 in terms of the KNN evaluation protocol. The learned representation exhibits the best performance on both datasets. Surpassing previous state-of-the-art methods by a considerable margin.

Method	NTU-60		NTU-120	
	x-sub	x-view	x-sub	x-set
LongT GAN [65]	39.1	48.1	31.5	35.5
P&C [50]	50.7	76.3	39.5	41.8
ISC [53]	62.5	82.6	50.6	52.3
CrosSCLR-B	66.1	81.3	52.5	54.9
CMD (Ours)	**70.6**	**85.4**	**58.3**	**60.9**

Table 3. Performance comparison on PKU-II in terms of the transfer learning evaluation protocol. The source datasets are NTU-60 and NTU-120. The representation learned by our approach shows the best transferability.

Method	To PKU-II	
	NTU-60	NTU-120
LongT GAN [65]	44.8	–
MS^{2}L [27]	45.8	–
ISC [53]	51.1	52.3
CrosSCLR-B	54.0	52.8
CMD (Ours)	**56.0**	**57.0**

4.3 Comparison with State-of-the-Art Methods

In the section, the learned representation is utilized for 3D action classification under a variety of evaluation protocols. We compare the results with previous state-of-the-art methods. Note that during evaluation, we only take single skeleton modality (joint) as input by default, which is consistent with previous arts [27,50,53]. Integrating multiple skeleton modalities for evaluation can significantly improve the performance, but it will also incur more time overhead.

Linear Evaluation Protocol: For linear evaluation protocol, we freeze the pre-trained encoder and add a learnable linear classifier after it. The classifier is trained on the corresponding training set for 80 epochs with a learning rate of 0.1 (reduced to 0.01 and 0.001 at epoch 50 and 70, respectively). We evaluate the proposed method on the NTU-60, NTU-120, and PKU-II datasets. As shown in Table 1, we include the recently proposed CrosSCLR [23], ISC [53], and AimCLR [54] for comparison. Our approach outperforms previous state-of-the-art methods by a considerable margin on all the three benchmarks. Note that ISC and the proposed CMD share the same BiGRU encoder, which is different from the ST-GCN [60] encoder in CrosSCLR. For a fair comparison, we additionally train a variation of CrosSCLR with BiGRU as its base-encoder (denoted as CrosSCLR-B). We can find that our method still outperforms it on all the three datasets, which shows the superiority of the proposed cross-modal mutual distillation.

KNN Evaluation Protocol: An alternative way to use the pre-trained encoder for action classification is to directly apply a K-Nearest Neighbor (KNN) classifier to the learned features of the training samples. Following [50], we assign each test sample to the most similar class where its nearest neighbor is in (*i.e.* KNN

Table 4. Performance comparison on NTU-60 in terms of the semi-supervised evaluation protocol. We randomly select a portion of the labeled data to fine-tune the pre-trained encoder, and the average of five runs is reported as the final performance. Our approach exhibits the state-of-the-art results compared with previous methods.

Method	NTU-60							
	x-view				x-sub			
	(1%)	(5%)	(10%)	(20%)	(1%)	(5%)	(10%)	(20%)
LongT GAN [65]	–	–	–	–	35.2	–	62.0	–
MS^{2}L [27]	–	–	–	–	33.1	–	65.1	–
ASSL [48]	–	63.6	69.8	74.7	–	57.3	64.3	68.0
ISC [53]	38.1	65.7	72.5	78.2	35.7	59.6	65.9	70.8
CrosSCLR-B [23]	49.8	70.6	77.0	81.9	48.6	67.7	72.4	76.1
CMD (Ours)	**53.0**	**75.3**	**80.2**	**84.3**	**50.6**	**71.0**	**75.4**	**78.7**
3s-CrosSCLR [23]	50.0	–	77.8	–	51.1	–	74.4	–
3s-Colorization [61]	52.5	–	78.9	–	48.3	–	71.7	–
3s-AimCLR [54]	54.3	–	81.6	–	54.8	–	78.2	–
3s-CMD (Ours)	**55.5**	**77.2**	**82.4**	**86.6**	**55.6**	**74.3**	**79.0**	**81.8**

with k=1). As shown in Table 2, we perform experiments on the NTU-60 and NTU-120 benchmarks and compare the results with previous works. For both datasets, our approach exhibits the best performance, surpassing CrosSCLR-B [23] by 4.5%~6% in the more challenging cross-subject and cross-setup protocols.

Transfer Learning Evaluation Protocol: In transfer learning evaluation protocol, we examine the transferability of the learned representation. Specifically, we first utilize the proposed framework to pre-train the encoder on the source dataset. Then the pre-trained encoder along with a linear classifier are finetuned on the target dataset for 80 epochs with a learning rate of 0.01 (reduced to 0.001 at epoch 50). We select NTU-60 and NTU-120 as source datasets, and PKU-II as the target dataset. We compare the proposed approach with previous methods LongT GAN [65], MS^{2}L [27], and ISC [53] under the cross-subject protocol. As shown in Table 3, our approach exhibits superior performance on the PKU-II dataset after large-scale pre-training, outperforming previous methods by a considerable margin. This indicates that the representation learned by our approach is more transferable.

Semi-supervised Evaluation Protocol: In semi-supervised classification, both labeled and unlabeled data are included during training. Its goal is to train a classifier with better performance than the one trained with only labeled samples. For a fair comparison, we adopt the same strategy as ISC [53]. The pre-trained encoder is fine-tuned together with the post-attached linear classifier on a portion of the corresponding training set. We conduct experiments on the NTU-60 dataset. As shown in Table 4, we report the evaluation results when the proportion of supervised data is set to 1%, 5%, 10%, and 20%, respectively. Compared with previous methods LongT GAN [65], MS²L [27], ASSL [48], and ISC [53], our algorithm exhibits superior performance. For example, with the same baseline, the proposed approach outperforms ISC and CrosSCLR-B by a large margin. We also take 3s-CrosSCLR [23], 3s-Colorization [61], and recently proposed 3s-AimCLR [54] into comparison. In these methods, test-time multimodal ensembling is performed and the results of using 1% and 10% labeled data are reported. We can find that our 3s-CMD still outperforms all of these methods after ensembling multiple skeleton modalities.

4.4 Ablation Study

To justify the effectiveness of the proposed cross-modal mutual distillation framework, we conduct several ablative experiments on the NTU-60 dataset according to the cross-subject protocol. More results can be found in the supplementary.

Number of Neighbors: The number of nearest neighbors controls the abundance of contextual information used in the proposed cross-modal mutual distillation module. We test the performance of the learned representation with respect to different numbers of nearest neighbors K under the linear evaluation protocol. As shown in Fig. 3, on the downstream classification task, the performance of the pre-trained encoder improves as K increases. When K is large enough ($K \geq 8192$), continuing to increase its value hardly contributes to the performance. This is because the newly added neighbors are far away and contain little reference value for describing the distribution around the query sample. In addition, we can also find that when the value of K varies from 64 to 16384, the performance of our approach is consistently higher than that of CrosSCLR-B [23] and our baseline. This demonstrates the superiority and robustness of the proposed approach.

Modality Selection: In our approach, we consider three kinds of skeleton modalities for self-supervised pre-training as in [23]. They are joint, motion, and bone, respectively. Our approach is capable of performing knowledge distillation between any two of the above modalities. As shown in Table 5, we report the performance of the representation obtained by pre-training with different combinations of skeleton modalities. Note that the joint modality is always preserved since it is used for evaluation. There are several observations as follows: **i)** Cross-modal knowledge distillation helps to improve the performance of the representation in student

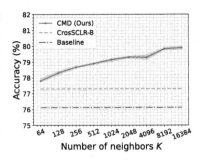

Fig. 3. Ablative study of the number of neighbors K in the cross-modal mutual distillation module. The performance is evaluated on the cross-subject protocol of the NTU-60 dataset.

Table 5. Ablative experiments of modality selection and bidirectional distillation. The performance is evaluated on the NTU-60 dataset according to the cross-subject protocol. J, M, and B denote joint, motion, and bone modality respectively. The horizontal arrows indicate the direction of distillation.

Modality and Direction	Linear evaluation				KNN evaluation			
	Bone	Motion	Joint	Δ	Bone	Motion	Joint	Δ
Baseline	74.4	73.1	76.1		62.0	56.8	63.4	
J ← B	74.4	–	76.5		62.0	–	64.3	
J ⇌ B	76.6	–	77.7	↑ 1.2	65.9	–	66.5	↑ 2.2
J ← M	–	73.1	78.9		–	56.8	64.8	
J ⇌ M	–	**77.5**	**79.8**	↑ 0.9	–	67.0	68.7	↑ 3.9
J ← M, J ← B	74.4	73.1	78.8		62.0	56.8	66.5	
J ⇌ M, J ⇌ B, M ⇌ B	**77.8**	77.1	79.4	↑ 0.6	**69.5**	**68.7**	**70.6**	↑ 4.1

modalities. **ii)** Under the linear evaluation protocol, knowledge distillation between joint and motion achieves the optimal performance, exceeding the baseline by 3.7%. **iii)** Under the KNN evaluation protocol, the learned representation shows the best results when all the three modalities are involved in knowledge distillation, which outperforms the baseline with an absolute improvement of 7.2%.

Bidirectional Distillation: In addition to modality selection, we also verify the effectiveness of bidirectional distillation. It enables the modalities involved in the distillation to interact with each other and progress together, forming a virtuous circle. In Table 5, the last column of each evaluation protocol reports the performance gain of bidirectional mutual distillation over unidirectional distillation in the joint modality. Results show that regardless of which skeleton modalities are used during pre-training, bidirectional mutual distillation further boosts the performance, especially under the KNN evaluation protocol.

Qualitative Results: We visualize the learned representation of the proposed approach and compare it with that of the baseline. The t-SNE [31] algorithm is adopted to reduce the dimensionality of the representation. To obtain clearer results, we select only 1/4 of the categories in the NTU-60 dataset for visualization. The final results are illustrated in Fig. 4. For both joint and motion modalities, the representation learned by our approach is more compactly clustered than those learned by the baseline in the feature space. This brings a stronger discrimination capability to the representation, explaining the stunning performance of our approach in Table 2.

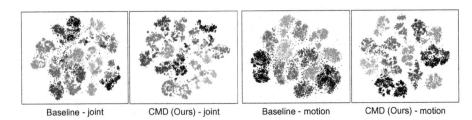

| Baseline - joint | CMD (Ours) - joint | Baseline - motion | CMD (Ours) - motion |

Fig. 4. t-SNE [31] visualization of feature embeddings. We sample 15 action classes from the NTU-60 dataset and visualize the features extracted by the proposed CMD and its baseline respectively. Compared with the baseline, CMD learns more compact and more discriminative representation in both joint and motion modalities.

5 Conclusion

In this work, we presented a novel approach for self-supervised 3D action representation learning. It reformulates cross-modal reinforcement as a bidirectional knowledge distillation problem, where the pairwise similarities between embeddings are utilized to model the modality-specific knowledge. The carefully designed cross-modal mutual distillation module can be well integrated into the existing contrastive learning framework, thus avoiding additional computational overhead. We evaluate the learned representation on three 3D action recognition benchmarks with four widely adopted evaluation protocols. The proposed approach sets a series of new state-of-the-art records on all of them, demonstrating the effectiveness of the cross-modal mutual distillation.

Acknowledgment. This work was supported by the National Natural Science Foundation of China under Contract U20A20183, 61836011, and 62021001. It was also supported by the GPU cluster built by MCC Lab of Information Science and Technology Institution, USTC.

References

1. Koohpayegani, S.A., Tejankar, A., Pirsiavash, H.: Compress: self-supervised learning by compressing representations. In: Proceedings of the Advances in Neural Information Processing Systems (NeurIPS), vol. 33, pp. 12980–12992 (2020)
2. Ballard, D.H.: Modular learning in neural networks. In: Proceedings of the AAAI Conference on Artificial Intelligence (AAAI), vol. 647, pp. 279–284 (1987)
3. Cao, Z., Hidalgo, G., Simon, T., Wei, S., Sheikh, Y.: Openpose: realtime multi-person 2D pose estimation using part affinity fields. IEEE Trans. Pattern Anal. Mach. Intell. (TPAMI) **43**(01), 172–186 (2021)
4. Chen, T., Kornblith, S., Norouzi, M., Hinton, G.: A simple framework for contrastive learning of visual representations. In: Proceedings of the International Conference on Machine Learning (ICML), pp. 1597–1607 (2020)
5. Chen, X., Fan, H., Girshick, R., He, K.: Improved baselines with momentum contrastive learning. arXiv preprint arXiv:2003.04297 (2020)

6. Chen, X., Xie, S., He, K.: An empirical study of training self-supervised vision transformers. In: Proceedings of the IEEE International Conference on Computer Vision (ICCV), pp. 9640–9649 (2021)
7. Chen, Y., Zhang, Z., Yuan, C., Li, B., Deng, Y., Hu, W.: Channel-wise topology refinement graph convolution for skeleton-based action recognition. In: Proceedings of the IEEE International Conference on Computer Vision (ICCV), pp. 13359–13368 (2021)
8. Cheng, K., Zhang, Y., He, X., Chen, W., Cheng, J., Lu, H.: Skeleton-based action recognition with shift graph convolutional network. In: Proceedings of the IEEE Conference on Computer Vision and Pattern Recognition (CVPR), pp. 183–192 (2020)
9. Chunhui, L., Yueyu, H., Yanghao, L., Sijie, S., Jiaying, L.: PKU-MMD: a large scale benchmark for continuous multi-modal human action understanding. arXiv preprint arXiv:1703.07475 (2017)
10. Deng, J., Dong, W., Socher, R., Li, L.J., Li, K., Fei-Fei, L.: ImageNet: a large-scale hierarchical image database. In: Proceedings of the IEEE Conference on Computer Vision and Pattern Recognition (CVPR), pp. 248–255 (2009)
11. Deng, J., Pan, Y., Yao, T., Zhou, W., Li, H., Mei, T.: Single shot video object detector. IEEE Trans. Multimedia 23, 846–858 (2021)
12. Deng, J., et al.: TransVG++: end-to-end visual grounding with language conditioned vision transformer. arXiv preprint arXiv:2206.06619 (2022)
13. Du, Y., Wang, W., Wang, L.: Hierarchical recurrent neural network for skeleton based action recognition. In: Proceedings of the IEEE Conference on Computer Vision and Pattern Recognition (CVPR), pp. 1110–1118 (2015)
14. Fang, H.S., Xie, S., Tai, Y.W., Lu, C.: RMPE: regional multi-person pose estimation. In: Proceedings of the IEEE International Conference on Computer Vision (ICCV), pp. 2334–2343 (2017)
15. Fang, Z., Wang, J., Wang, L., Zhang, L., Yang, Y., Liu, Z.: Seed: self-supervised distillation for visual representation. In: Proceedings of the International Conference on Learning Representations (ICLR) (2021)
16. He, K., Chen, X., Xie, S., Li, Y., Dollár, P., Girshick, R.: Masked autoencoders are scalable vision learners. In: Proceedings of the IEEE Conference on Computer Vision and Pattern Recognition (CVPR), pp. 16000–16009 (2022)
17. He, K., Fan, H., Wu, Y., Xie, S., Girshick, R.: Momentum contrast for unsupervised visual representation learning. In: Proceedings of the IEEE Conference on Computer Vision and Pattern Recognition (CVPR), pp. 9729–9738 (2020)
18. Hinton, G., et al.: Distilling the knowledge in a neural network. arXiv preprint arXiv:1503.02531 (2015)
19. Ioffe, S., Szegedy, C.: Batch normalization: accelerating deep network training by reducing internal covariate shift. In: Proceedings of the International Conference on Machine Learning (ICML), pp. 448–456 (2015)
20. Ke, Q., Bennamoun, M., An, S., Sohel, F., Boussaid, F.: A new representation of skeleton sequences for 3d action recognition. In: Proceedings of the IEEE Conference on Computer Vision and Pattern Recognition (CVPR), pp. 3288–3297 (2017)
21. Kuehne, H., Jhuang, H., Garrote, E., Poggio, T., Serre, T.: HMDB: a large video database for human motion recognition. In: Proceedings of the IEEE International Conference on Computer Vision (ICCV), pp. 2556–2563 (2011)
22. Li, J., Selvaraju, R.R., Gotmare, A.D., Joty, S., Xiong, C., Hoi, S.: Align before fuse: vision and language representation learning with momentum distillation. In: Proceedings of the Advances in Neural Information Processing Systems (NeurIPS) (2021)

23. Li, L., Wang, M., Ni, B., Wang, H., Yang, J., Zhang, W.: 3D human action representation learning via cross-view consistency pursuit. In: Proceedings of the IEEE Conference on Computer Vision and Pattern Recognition (CVPR), pp. 4741–4750 (2021)

24. Li, M., Chen, S., Chen, X., Zhang, Y., Wang, Y., Tian, Q.: Actional-structural graph convolutional networks for skeleton-based action recognition. In: Proceedings of the IEEE Conference on Computer Vision and Pattern Recognition (CVPR), pp. 3595–3603 (2019)

25. Li, T., Ke, Q., Rahmani, H., Ho, R.E., Ding, H., Liu, J.: Else-net: elastic semantic network for continual action recognition from skeleton data. In: Proceedings of the IEEE International Conference on Computer Vision (ICCV), pp. 13434–13443 (2021)

26. Liang, D., Fan, G., Lin, G., Chen, W., Pan, X., Zhu, H.: Three-stream convolutional neural network with multi-task and ensemble learning for 3d action recognition. In: Proceedings of the IEEE Conference on Computer Vision and Pattern Recognition Workshops (CVPRW), pp. 934–940 (2019)

27. Lin, L., Song, S., Yang, W., Liu, J.: MS2L: multi-task self-supervised learning for skeleton based action recognition. In: Proceedings of the 28th ACM International Conference on Multimedia (ACM MM), pp. 2490–2498 (2020)

28. Liu, J., Shahroudy, A., Perez, M., Wang, G., Duan, L.Y., Kot, A.C.: NTU RGB+D 120: a large-scale benchmark for 3d human activity understanding. IEEE Trans. Pattern Anal. Mach. Intell. (TPAMI) 42(10), 2684–2701 (2020)

29. Liu, X., et al.: Self-supervised learning: generative or contrastive. IEEE Transactions on Knowledge and Data Engineering (TKDE) (2021)

30. Liu, Z., Zhang, H., Chen, Z., Wang, Z., Ouyang, W.: Disentangling and unifying graph convolutions for skeleton-based action recognition. In: Proceedings of the IEEE Conference on Computer Vision and Pattern Recognition (CVPR), pp. 143–152 (2020)

31. Van der Maaten, L., Hinton, G.: Visualizing data using t-SNE. J. Mach. Learn. Res. (JMLR) 9(11), 2579–2605 (2008)

32. Misra, I., Zitnick, C.L., Hebert, M.: Shuffle and learn: unsupervised learning using temporal order verification. In: Leibe, B., Matas, J., Sebe, N., Welling, M. (eds.) ECCV 2016. LNCS, vol. 9905, pp. 527–544. Springer, Cham (2016). https://doi.org/10.1007/978-3-319-46448-0_32

33. Nie, Q., Liu, Z., Liu, Y.: Unsupervised 3D human pose representation with viewpoint and pose disentanglement. In: Vedaldi, A., Bischof, H., Brox, T., Frahm, J.-M. (eds.) ECCV 2020. LNCS, vol. 12364, pp. 102–118. Springer, Cham (2020). https://doi.org/10.1007/978-3-030-58529-7_7

34. Noroozi, M., Favaro, P.: Unsupervised learning of visual representations by solving jigsaw puzzles. In: Leibe, B., Matas, J., Sebe, N., Welling, M. (eds.) ECCV 2016. LNCS, vol. 9910, pp. 69–84. Springer, Cham (2016). https://doi.org/10.1007/978-3-319-46466-4_5

35. Van den Oord, A., Li, Y., Vinyals, O.: Representation learning with contrastive predictive coding. arXiv preprint arXiv:1809.03327 (2018)

36. van den Oord, A., Vinyals, O., kavukcuoglu, k.: Neural discrete representation learning. In: Proceedings of the Advances in Neural Information Processing Systems (NeurIPS) (2017)

37. Ouyang, J., Wu, H., Wang, M., Zhou, W., Li, H.: Contextual similarity aggregation with self-attention for visual re-ranking. In: Proceedings of the Advances in Neural Information Processing Systems (NeurIPS) (2021)

38. Park, W., Kim, D., Lu, Y., Cho, M.: Relational knowledge distillation. In: Proceedings of the IEEE Conference on Computer Vision and Pattern Recognition (CVPR), pp. 3967–3976 (2019)
39. Passalis, N., Tefas, A.: Learning deep representations with probabilistic knowledge transfer. In: Ferrari, V., Hebert, M., Sminchisescu, C., Weiss, Y. (eds.) ECCV 2018. LNCS, vol. 11215, pp. 283–299. Springer, Cham (2018). https://doi.org/10.1007/978-3-030-01252-6_17
40. Peng, B., et al.: Correlation congruence for knowledge distillation. In: Proceedings of the IEEE International Conference on Computer Vision (ICCV), pp. 5007–5016 (2019)
41. Rao, H., Xu, S., Hu, X., Cheng, J., Hu, B.: Augmented skeleton based contrastive action learning with momentum LSTM for unsupervised action recognition. Inf. Sci. **569**, 90–109 (2021)
42. Romero, A., Ballas, N., Kahou, S.E., Chassang, A., Gatta, C., Bengio, Y.: Fitnets: hints for thin deep nets. In: Proceedings of the International Conference on Learning Representations (ICLR) (2015)
43. Shahroudy, A., Liu, J., Ng, T.T., Wang, G.: NTU RGB + D: a large scale dataset for 3D human activity analysis. In: Proceedings of the IEEE Conference on Computer Vision and Pattern Recognition (CVPR), pp. 1010–1019 (2016)
44. Shi, L., Zhang, Y., Cheng, J., Lu, H.: Skeleton-based action recognition with directed graph neural networks. In: Proceedings of the IEEE Conference on Computer Vision and Pattern Recognition (CVPR), pp. 7912–7921 (2019)
45. Shi, L., Zhang, Y., Cheng, J., Lu, H.: Two-stream adaptive graph convolutional networks for skeleton-based action recognition. In: Proceedings of the IEEE Conference on Computer Vision and Pattern Recognition (CVPR), pp. 12026–12035 (2019)
46. Shi, L., Zhang, Y., Cheng, J., Lu, H.: AdaSGN: adapting joint number and model size for efficient skeleton-based action recognition. In: Proceedings of the IEEE International Conference on Computer Vision (ICCV), pp. 13413–13422 (2021)
47. Si, C., Chen, W., Wang, W., Wang, L., Tan, T.: An attention enhanced graph convolutional lstm network for skeleton-based action recognition. In: Proceedings of the IEEE Conference on Computer Vision and Pattern Recognition (CVPR), pp. 1227–1236 (2019)
48. Si, C., Nie, X., Wang, W., Wang, L., Tan, T., Feng, J.: Adversarial self-supervised learning for semi-supervised 3D action recognition. In: Vedaldi, A., Bischof, H., Brox, T., Frahm, J.-M. (eds.) ECCV 2020. LNCS, vol. 12352, pp. 35–51. Springer, Cham (2020). https://doi.org/10.1007/978-3-030-58571-6_3
49. Soomro, K., Zamir, A.R., Shah, M.: UCF101: a dataset of 101 human actions classes from videos in the wild. arXiv preprint arXiv:1212.0402 (2012)
50. Su, K., Liu, X., Shlizerman, E.: Predict & cluster: unsupervised skeleton based action recognition. In: Proceedings of the IEEE Conference on Computer Vision and Pattern Recognition (CVPR), pp. 9631–9640 (2020)
51. Tejankar, A., Koohpayegani, S.A., Pillai, V., Favaro, P., Pirsiavash, H.: ISD: self-supervised learning by iterative similarity distillation. In: Proceedings of the IEEE International Conference on Computer Vision (ICCV), pp. 9609–9618 (2021)
52. Tejankar, A., Koohpayegani, S.A., Pillai, V., Favaro, P., Pirsiavash, H.: ISD: self-supervised learning by iterative similarity distillation. In: Proceedings of the IEEE International Conference on Computer Vision (ICCV), pp. 9609–9618 (2021)
53. Thoker, F.M., Doughty, H., Snoek, C.G.: Skeleton-contrastive 3D action representation learning. In: Proceedings of the 29th ACM International Conference on Multimedia (ACM MM), pp. 1655–1663 (2021)

54. Tianyu, G., Hong, L., Zhan, C., Mengyuan, L., Tao, W., Runwei, D.: Contrastive learning from extremely augmented skeleton sequences for self-supervised action recognition. In: Proceedings of the AAAI Conference on Artificial Intelligence (AAAI) (2022)
55. Tung, F., Mori, G.: Similarity-preserving knowledge distillation. In: Proceedings of the IEEE International Conference on Computer Vision (ICCV), pp. 1365–1374 (2019)
56. Wang, M., Ni, B., Yang, X.: Learning multi-view interactional skeleton graph for action recognition. IEEE Transactions on Pattern Analysis and Machine Intelligence (TPAMI) (2020)
57. Wang, N., Zhou, W., Li, H.: Contrastive transformation for self-supervised correspondence learning. In: Proceedings of the AAAI Conference on Artificial Intelligence (AAAI), pp. 10174–10182 (2021)
58. Wu, H., Wang, M., Zhou, W., Li, H., Tian, Q.: Contextual similarity distillation for asymmetric image retrieval. In: Proceedings of the IEEE Conference on Computer Vision and Pattern Recognition (CVPR), pp. 9489–9498 (2022)
59. Xu, J., Yu, Z., Ni, B., Yang, J., Yang, X., Zhang, W.: Deep kinematics analysis for monocular 3d human pose estimation. In: Proceedings of the IEEE Conference on Computer Vision and Pattern Recognition (CVPR), pp. 899–908 (2020)
60. Yan, S., Xiong, Y., Lin, D.: Spatial temporal graph convolutional networks for skeleton-based action recognition. In: Proceedings of the AAAI Conference on Artificial Intelligence (AAAI), pp. 7444–7452 (2018)
61. Yang, S., Liu, J., Lu, S., Er, M.H., Kot, A.C.: Skeleton cloud colorization for unsupervised 3d action representation learning. In: Proceedings of the IEEE International Conference on Computer Vision (ICCV), pp. 13423–13433 (2021)
62. Zhang, P., Lan, C., Xing, J., Zeng, W., Xue, J., Zheng, N.: View adaptive neural networks for high performance skeleton-based human action recognition. IEEE Trans. Pattern Anal. Mach. Intell. (TPAMI) $41(8)$, 1963–1978 (2019)
63. Zhang, P., Lan, C., Zeng, W., Xing, J., Xue, J., Zheng, N.: Semantics-guided neural networks for efficient skeleton-based human action recognition. In: Proceedings of the IEEE Conference on Computer Vision and Pattern Recognition (CVPR), pp. 1112–1121 (2020)
64. Zhang, X., Xu, C., Tao, D.: Context aware graph convolution for skeleton-based action recognition. In: Proceedings of the IEEE Conference on Computer Vision and Pattern Recognition (CVPR), pp. 14333–14342 (2020)
65. Zheng, N., Wen, J., Liu, R., Long, L., Dai, J., Gong, Z.: Unsupervised representation learning with long-term dynamics for skeleton based action recognition. In: Proceedings of the AAAI Conference on Artificial Intelligence (AAAI), pp. 2644–2651 (2018)

Author Index

Printed in the United States
by Baker & Taylor Publisher Services